Digital Principles and Design

Related Titles

Brown, Vranesic: *Fundamentals of Digital Logic with VHDL Design*
Ham, Kostanic: *Principles of Neurocomputing for Science and Engineering*
Hamacher, Vranesic, and Zaky: *Computer Organization*
Hayes: *Computer Architecture and Organization*
Hwang: *Advanced Computer Architecture: Parallelism, Scalability, Programmability*
Hwang: *Scalable Parallel Computing: Technology, Architecture, Programming*
Leon-Garcia/Widjaja: *Communication Networks*
Marcovitz: *Introduction to Logic Design*
Navabi: *VHDL: Analysis and Modeling of Digital Systems*
Patt, Patel: *Introduction to Computing Systems: From Bits & Gates to C & Beyond*
Schalkoff: *Artificial Neural Networks*
Shen/Lipasti: *Modern Processor Design*

Digital Principles and Design

Donald D. Givone
University at Buffalo
The State University of New York

McGraw Hill

Boston Burr Ridge, IL Dubuque, IA Madison, WI New York San Francisco St. Louis
Bangkok Bogotá Caracas Kuala Lumpur Lisbon London Madrid Mexico City
Milan Montreal New Delhi Santiago Seoul Singapore Sydney Taipei Toronto

McGraw-Hill Higher Education

A Division of The **McGraw-Hill** *Companies*

DIGITAL PRINCIPLES AND DESIGN

Published by McGraw-Hill, a business unit of The McGraw-Hill Companies, Inc., 1221 Avenue of the Americas, New York, NY 10020.

This book is printed on acid-free paper.

International 1 2 3 4 5 6 7 8 9 0 QPF/QPF 0 9 8 7 6 5 4 3 2
Domestic 3 4 5 6 7 8 9 0 QPF/QPF 0 9 8 7 6 5

ISBN 0–07–252503–7
ISBN 0–07–119520–3 (ISE)

Publisher: *Elizabeth A. Jones*
Developmental editor: *Michelle L. Flomenhoft*
Executive marketing manager: *John Wannemacher*
Senior project manager: *Susan J. Brusch*
Senior production supervisor: *Sandy Ludovissy*
Lead media project manager: *Audrey A. Reiter*
Senior media technology producer: *Phillip Meek*
Coordinator of freelance design: *David W. Hash*
Cover designer: *Rokusek Design*
Cover image: *©Eyewire, Inc./Don Bishop*
Compositor: *UG / GGS Information Services, Inc.*
Typeface: *10/12 Times Roman*
Printer: *Quebecor World Fairfield, PA*

Library of Congress Cataloging-in-Publication Data

Givone, Donald D.
Digital principles and design / Donald D. Givone. — 1st ed.
p. cm.
ISBN 0–07–252503–7—ISBN 0–07–119520–3 (ISE)
1. Digital electronics. I. Title.

TK7868.D5 G57 2003
621.381—dc21 2002022661
CIP

INTERNATIONAL EDITION ISBN 0–07–119520–3

www.mhhe.com

To my children Donna and David and my brother Billy

BRIEF CONTENTS

CONTENTS

Appendix A
Digital Circuits 589

Appendix B
Tutorials 665

Bibliography 684

Index 687

Additional Resources

1. CD-ROM with Altera MAX+plus II and Multisim 2001 (included with book)
2. Website at http://www.mhhe.com/givone that includes labs for both Altera MAX+plus II and LogicWorks™4

PREFACE

With the strong impact of digital technology on our everyday lives, it is not surprising that a course in digital concepts and design is a standard requirement for majors in computer engineering, computer science, and electrical engineering. An introductory course is frequently encountered in the first or second year of their undergraduate programs. Additional courses are then provided to refine and extend the basic concepts of the introductory course.

This book is suitable for an introductory course in digital principles with emphasis on logic design as well as for a more advanced course. With the exception of the appendix, it assumes no background on the part of the reader. The intent of the author is not to just present a set of procedures commonly encountered in digital design but, rather, to provide justifications underlying such procedures. Since no background is assumed, the book can be used by students in computer engineering, computer science, and electrical engineering.

The approach taken in this book is a traditional one. That is, emphasis is on the presentation of basic principles of logic design and the illustration of each of these principles. The philosophy of the author is that a first course in logic design should establish a strong foundation of basic principles as provided by a more traditional approach before engaging in the use of computer-aided design tools. Once basic concepts are mastered, the utilization of design software becomes more meaningful and allows the student to use the software more effectively. Thus, it is the understanding of basic principles on which this book focuses and the application of these principles to the analysis and design of combinational and sequential logic networks. Each topic is approached by first introducing the basic theory and then illustrating how it applies to design. For those people who want to use CAD tools, we have included a CD-ROM containing Altera MAX+plus II 10.1 Student Edition, as well as software tutorials in an Appendix.

SCOPE OF THE BOOK

Chapter 1 discusses the differences between continuous, i.e., analog, and discrete, i.e., digital, networks and devices. Then, the basic operation of the digital computer is introduced as an example of a system that utilizes most of the concepts presented in the remaining chapters. The chapter concludes with an overview of the topics that will be introduced.

In Chapter 2 the general concepts of positional number systems, arithmetic, and conversion techniques are introduced. This material is developed for arbitrary positive integer bases rather than simply for the binary number system to emphasize the similarity of all positional number systems and their manipulations. Then, various codes and their properties are discussed with emphasis on error detection and correction.

The two-valued Boolean algebra is introduced in Chapter 3. How Boolean expressions are written, manipulated, and simplified is presented. Since there is a one-to-one correspondence between the two-valued Boolean algebra and logic networks, it is then shown how the algebra can serve as a mathematical model for the behavior and structure of combinational logic networks. The chapter concludes with a discussion of the gate properties that are relevant to logic networks, i.e., noise margin, fan-out, propagation delays, and power dissipation.

An important application of the Boolean algebra is to obtain those expressions which can best be associated with optimal networks. Under the assumption that the reduction in the delay time of a network is of paramount importance, it is possible to obtain efficient networks by systematic procedures. Two methods for obtaining minimal expressions are presented in Chapter 4. The first method, Karnaugh maps, is a graphical procedure that permits minimal expressions to be obtained very rapidly. However, since the procedure relies upon the recognition of patterns, there is a limit to the complexity of a problem for which the procedure is effective. This limit seems to be problems of six variables. A second method for obtaining minimal expressions is the Quine-McCluskey method. This method involves just simple mathematical manipulations. For problems with many variables, the Quine-McCluskey method can be carried out on a digital computer. The concepts of both approaches are then extended to a set of Boolean expressions describing multiple-output networks. The chapter concludes with a variation of the Karnaugh map concept, called variable-entered Karnaugh maps, in which Boolean functions can appear as map entries.

Chapter 5 is concerned with several MSI and LSI components. The intent of this chapter is to investigate combinational networks that are commonly encountered in digital systems. Several types of adders and subtracters are discussed. These include binary and decimal adders as well as high-speed adders using the carry lookahead concept. Also included in this chapter are discussions on comparators, decoders, encoders, and multiplexers. In the case of decoders and multiplexers, attention is given to their use as generic logic design devices. The final part of the chapter involves the three basic structures of programmable logic devices: programmable read-only memories, programmable logic arrays, and programmable array logic devices. Emphasis is placed on their utilization for the realization of logic networks, with special attention given to their strengths and weaknesses and the constraints placed on a logic design utilizing them.

Chapter 6 begins the presentation on sequential logic networks. In this chapter, various types of flip-flops, i.e., *JK, D, T,* and *SR* flip-flops, are introduced. The operational behavior of the three categories of flip-flops, i.e., latches, edge-triggered, and master-slave flip-flops, is discussed in detail. The remainder of the chapter is concerned with some simple flip-flop applications, in particular, registers and counters. Ripple and synchronous counters are presented and compared. The chapter concludes with a general design procedure for synchronous counters. This procedure serves as a basis for synchronous sequential logic design, which is elaborated upon in the next two chapters.

Chapters 7 and 8 involve clocked synchronous sequential networks. In Chapter 7 the classic Mealy and Moore models of a synchronous sequential network are presented. First, these networks are analyzed to establish various tabular representations of network behavior. Then, the process is reversed and synthesis is discussed. Chapter 8 also involves the design of clocked synchronous sequential networks; however, this time using the algorithmic state machine model. The relationship between the classic Mealy/Moore models and the algorithmic state machine model is discussed as well as the capability of the algorithmic state machine model to handle the controlling of an architecture of devices.

In Chapter 9 asynchronous sequential networks are studied. Paralleling the approach taken for synchronous sequential networks, the analysis of asynchronous sequential networks is first undertaken and then, by reversing the analysis procedure, the synthesis of these networks is presented. Included in this chapter is also a discussion on static and dynamic hazards. Although these hazards occur in combinational networks, their study is deferred to this chapter, since these hazards can have a major effect on asynchronous network behavior. A great deal of attention is given to the many design constraints that must be satisfied to achieve a functional design of an asynchronous network. In addition to the static and dynamic hazards, the concepts of races, the importance of the state assignment, and the effects of essential hazards are addressed.

An appendix on digital electronics is included for completeness. It is not intended to provide an in-depth study on digital electronics, since such a study should be reserved for a course in itself. Rather, its inclusion is to provide the interested reader an introduction to actual circuits that can occur in digital systems and the source of constraints placed upon a logic designer. For this reason, the appendix does not delve into circuit design but, rather, only into the analysis of electronic digital circuits. Emphasis is placed on the principles of operation of TTL, ECL, and MOS logic circuits. Since circuits are analyzed, the appendix does assume the reader has an elementary knowledge of linear circuit analysis. In particular, the reader should be familiar with Ohm's law along with Kirchhoff's current and voltage laws.

Another appendix with software tutorials is also included. These tutorials, provided by two contributors, include one on Altera MAX+plus II 10.1 Student Edition and one on LogicWorks™4. The tutorials are meant to provide basic introductions to these tools for those people who are using them in their course.

HOMEWORK PROBLEMS

With the exception of Chapter 1, each chapter includes a set of problems. Some of these problems provide for reinforcement of the reader's understanding of the material, some extend the concepts presented in the chapter, and, finally, some are applications-oriented.

ADDITIONAL RESOURCES

The expanded book website at *http://www.mhhe.com/givone* includes a downloadable version of the *Solutions Manual* for instructors only and PowerPoint slides. There are also a variety of labs using both the Altera Software and LogicWorks. A

CD-ROM containing Altera's MAX+plus II CAD software and Multisim 2001 is included free with every copy of the book.

WHAT CAN BE COVERED IN A COURSE

More material is included in this book than can be covered in a one-semester course. This allows the instructor to tailor the book to the background of the students and the time available. Different ways the book can be used include:

- A possible one-semester course based on this book would include Chapters 1 to 3, Sections 4.1 to 4.7, and Chapters 5 to 7. Sections 4.1 to 4.7 involve the simplification of Boolean functions using Karnaugh maps.
- Sections 4.8 to 4.11, involving the Quine-McCluskey method, might also be included in a slightly more quickly paced course.
- The material of Sections 4.12 to 4.14 and Chapters 8 and 9, along with a introduction to CAD tools, (including Appendix B) can serve as the basis for a second semester course.
- Appendix B, the CD-ROM and Labs at the website are optional material that can be worked in as needed.

A few formal proofs have been included for the interested reader. However, these proofs are clearly delineated and can be skipped without loss of continuity.

ACKNOWLEDGMENTS

I would like to thank the reviewers of the manuscript for their comments and suggestions. These include:

- Kenneth J. Breeding, The Ohio State University
- Kirk W. Cameron, University of South Carolina
- Mehmet Celenk, Ohio University
- Travis E. Doom, Wright State University
- Richard W. Freeman, Iowa State University
- Bruce A. Harvey, Florida State University
- Raj Katti, North Dakota State University
- Larry Kinney, University of Minnesota
- Wagdy H. Mahmoud, Tennessee Technological University
- Jeffery P. Mills, Illinois Institute of Technology
- Debashis Mohanty, Texas A&M University
- Richard G. Molyet, The University of Toledo
- Jane Moorhead, Mississippi State University
- Suku Nair, Southern Methodist University
- Emil C. Neu, Stevens Institute of Technology
- Tatyana D. Roziner, Boston University

- Salam Salloum, California State Polytechnic University, Pomona
- Susan Schneider, Marquette University
- Charles B. Silio, Jr., University of Maryland
- Dan Stanzione, Clemson University
- A. J. Thomas, Jr., Tennessee State University
- Massood Towhidnejad, Embry-Riddle Aeronautical University
- Murali Varanasi, University of South Florida
- Donald C. Wunsch II, University of Missouri-Rolla

Also, I would like to acknowledge the efforts of the staff at McGraw-Hill, particularly Betsy Jones, Michelle Flomenhoft, and Susan Brusch. In addition, I want to express my appreciation to Donna and David, who helped with the typing and artwork in the early drafts of the manuscript. I would also like to thank David for his work that led to the image on the cover of this book. Finally, I am grateful to my wife Louise for her support and patience during this project.

Donald D. Givone

ABOUT THE AUTHOR

Donald D. Givone received his B.S.E.E. degree from Rensselaer Polytechnic Institute and the M.S. and Ph.D. degrees in Electrical Engineering from Cornell University. In 1963, he joined the faculty at the University at Buffalo, where he is currently a Professor in the Department of Electrical Engineering.

He has received several awards for excellence in teaching. He is also the author of the textbook *Introduction to Switching Circuit Theory* and the coauthor of the textbook *Microprocessors/Microcomputers: An Introduction,* both of which were published by McGraw-Hill Book Company.

CHAPTER 1

Introduction

A way to measure human progress is through inventions that ease mental and physical burdens. The digital computer is one such great invention. The applications of this device seem to have no bounds, and, consequently, new vistas have opened up for humans to challenge.

The digital computer, however, is only one of many systems whose design and operation is based on digital concepts. The idea of representing information in a discrete form and the manipulation of such information is fundamental to all digital systems. In the ensuing chapters of this book we study number and algebraic concepts, logic design, digital networks, and digital circuits. These are the digital principles that serve as the foundation for the understanding and design of digital computers and, in general, digital systems. ■

1.1 THE DIGITAL AGE

Digital systems are not really something recent. The first mechanical digital calculator, developed by the French mathematician Blaise Pascal, dates back to 1642. Even the concept of a general-purpose digital computer dates to 1833. This innovation was the work of the English mathematician and scientist Charles Babbage. However, it was not until the 1930s that there appeared a fully realized practical digital system—the telephone switching system. This system utilized the electromechanical relay as its basic digital element.

The electromechanical relay was also used in early design attempts of the digital computer during the late 1930s and early 1940s. However, in order to achieve a higher speed of operation, it was necessary to utilize electronic devices. Thus, during the late 1940s and early 1950s a great deal of effort went into the development of general-purpose electronic digital computers with vacuum tubes as their basic digital element. These early electronic computers were only one of a kind. The commercial digital computer became a reality in 1951 with the UNIVAC (UNIVersal Automatic Computer). A total of 48 of these computers were constructed.

Vacuum tubes consumed a great amount of electrical power, dissipated a great deal of heat, and had short life spans. It is no wonder that with the development of the transistor a new and more rapid expansion in digital techniques emerged. More recently, advancements in solid-state electronics have enabled the fabrication of complete digital circuits as a single entity called integrated circuits. As the density of components in an integrated circuit increased, the concept of a programmable digital device, the microprocessor, became possible. With more and more supportive circuitry integrated with the microprocessor being achieved, a computer-on-a-chip has become a reality.

The combination of microelectronics and digital concepts has provided highly-reliable, cost-effective devices. As a consequence, there has been a rapid growth in the development of new digital systems. The applications of digital devices will have far-reaching effects upon the technology of tomorrow.

1.2 ANALOG AND DIGITAL REPRESENTATIONS OF INFORMATION

There are two general ways in which information is represented—*analog form* or *digital form.* In a digital representation, the information is denoted by a finite sequence of digits. Such a form is also said to be *discrete.* On the other hand, in an analog representation, a continuum is used to denote the information. Examples of such a continuum are the range of voltages between certain limits and an angular displacement.

To illustrate the idea of information representation, consider time as the information. A digital watch which expresses time in a numerical form, i.e., a sequence of digits, is a digital representation. A conventional watch expresses time in an analog form as the angular position of the watch hands.

Since analog information involves a continuum, the reading of the information becomes a measurement within the continuum, the precision of the measurement being the number of digits that are obtained from the measurement. Normally there is a limitation as to the precision that can be achieved when handling analog information. In the case of digital information, any degree of precision becomes possible simply by using more digits in the representation.

Systems that manipulate or process information, e.g., computers, have been designed for both analog and digital information. However, with today's technology, digital systems have a lower component cost, higher reliability, and greater versatility than analog systems.

1.3 THE DIGITAL COMPUTER

This book is not directly concerned with the digital computer. However, it is perhaps the most fascinating of all digital systems. Furthermore, because of its generality, it encompasses many digital concepts. For this reason, a brief and simplistic discussion on a basic organization of a digital computer and its operation is appropriate.

Basically, a digital computer receives numbers, called *data,* performs operations upon these numbers, and forms new numbers. The desired operations to be performed by the computer are also given to the computer in the form of numbers which are called *instructions.* Since numbers are stored and manipulated in the computer, a number system which lends itself to easy electronic representation is necessary. As a consequence, the binary number system or a coded binary number system is most frequently used, since highly reliable electronic devices with two stable states are easily fabricated.

A digital computer can solve very complex problems. However, it can perform only very simple operations. The solution of a problem thus becomes a matter of reducing the problem to a long sequence of very elementary mathematical and logical operations called a *program.* Even though these operations are performed one at a time, the computer has the capability to perform them at a very high speed. Two features of the computer permit it to perform a great number of operations in a short time. First, it has the capability to store the data and the sequence of instructions to solve a problem. Second, it has the capability to sequence through the given instructions without human intervention. Thus the computer has the necessary data at its disposal to solve a problem and is capable of performing the sequence of operations to solve a problem without slowing down or stopping between operations. Without these two features, it would be necessary to stop the computer many times in order to insert data, copy results, and determine the next operation.

1.3.1 The Organization of a Digital Computer

A simple way of viewing a digital computer is to subdivide it into five basic units: *arithmetic, control, memory, input,* and *output.* A computer organization involving the basic units and the flow lines showing the routing of information required for carrying out the elementary operations is shown in Fig. 1.1. These units are comprised of logic networks that provide for the manipulation and modification of binary information, i.e., the data and instructions. Provision is also made for holding binary information within these networks. This storage is achieved with devices

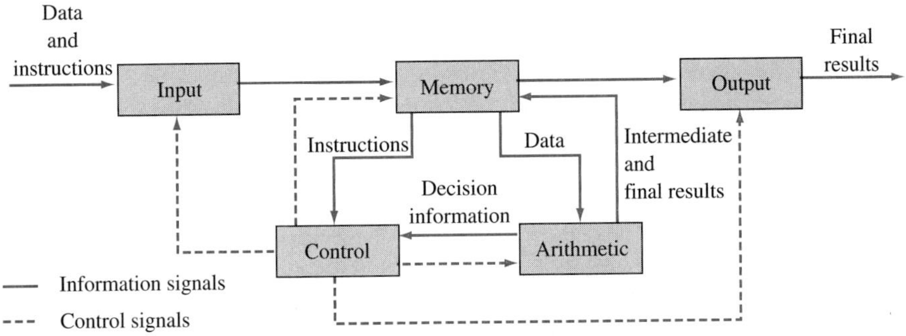

Figure 1.1 A basic organization of a digital computer.

called *registers.* In short, the operation of a digital computer and, in general, a digital system involves a series of data and instruction transfers from register to register with modifications and manipulations occurring during these transfers. To achieve this, many registers occur within a digital system.

Most mathematical and logical operations on data are performed in the arithmetic unit. The simple mathematical operations of a computer are addition, subtraction, multiplication, and division. The more complex mathematical operations, such as integration, taking of square roots, and formulation of trigonometric functions, can be reduced to the basic operations possible in the computer and are performed by a program. One of the more important of the logical operations a digital computer can perform is that of sensing the sign of a number. Depending upon whether the computer senses a positive or negative sign on a number, it can determine whether to perform one set of computations or an alternate set.

Referring to Fig. 1.1, it is seen that there is a two-way communication between the arithmetic unit and the memory unit. The arithmetic unit receives from the memory unit numbers on which operations are to be performed and sends intermediate and final results to the memory unit. All necessary data for the solution to the problem being run on the computer are stored in the memory unit. The memory unit is divided into substorage units (i.e., registers), each referenced by an *address,* which is simply an integral numerical designator. Only one number is stored at a particular address. Also stored in the memory unit, each at a separate address, are the instructions. Each of these consists of a *command,* which identifies the type of operation to be performed, plus one or more *addresses,* which indicate where the numerical data used in the operation are located. The instructions and the numerical data are placed in the memory unit before the start of the program run.

The control unit receives instructions, one at a time, from the memory unit for interpretation. Normally, the program instructions are in sequential order within the memory unit. By means of a *program counter* located in the control unit, indicating the next instruction's address, the correct instruction is transferred into the control unit, where it is held in the *instruction register* for decoding. After the decoding process, the control unit causes connections to be made in the various units so that each individual instruction is properly carried out. With the connections properly made, the arithmetic unit is caused to act as, say, an adder, subtracter, multiplier, or divider, as the particular instruction demands. The control unit also causes connections to be made in the memory unit so that the correct data for the instruction are obtained by the arithmetic unit. As shown in Fig. 1.1, the control unit is capable of receiving information from the arithmetic unit. It is along this path that, say, the sign of a number is sent. Such information gives the computer its decision-making capability mentioned previously. In addition, the control unit sends signals to the input and output units in order to have these units work at the proper time.

The input and output units are the contacts between the computer and the outside world. They act as buffers, translating data between the different speeds and languages with which computers and humans, or other systems, operate. The input unit receives data and instructions from the outside world and sends them to the memory unit. The output unit receives numerical results and communicates them to the user or to another system. Input and output units may be of a very simple nature or highly complicated, depending on the application the computer is expected to handle.

1.3.2 The Operation of a Digital Computer

Having explained the function of each of the various computer units, let us now consider the sequence of events that occur during a program run. The control unit oversees the operation by cycling through three phases: fetch, decode, and execute. As stated previously, the instructions are initially placed in the memory unit in sequential order as well as the necessary data. When the program is ready to be run, the program counter is set to indicate the address of the first instruction and the control unit is set to its fetch phase.

During the fetch phase, the content of the program counter, which is an address, is sent to the memory unit. The address is decoded by digital logic in the memory unit and a copy of the instruction located at that address in memory is sent to the control unit, where it is placed in the instruction register. At this time the program counter is incremented so that the address of the next instruction is available on the next fetch phase of the control unit.

Having completed the fetch phase, the control unit proceeds to the decode phase of its cycle. During this phase, the command portion of the instruction is deciphered and the appropriate connections made in accordance with the indicated operation.

Finally, the control unit enters its execute phase. During this time, the control unit generates the appropriate signals needed to carry out the instruction. If the instruction involves a stored operand, then the address portion of the instruction, which indicates the operand location, is sent to the memory unit so that the operand is retrieved and sent to the appropriate computer unit. After completing the execute phase, the control unit returns to its fetch phase and the fetch-decode-execute sequence is repeated for the next instruction. This process continues until a halt-type instruction is encountered.

In the above discussion, it was assumed that the program instructions are stored and executed sequentially. In general, however, it is frequently necessary to deviate from the sequential order, for example, as a consequence of the decision information from the arithmetic unit. To achieve this, special jump-type instructions are provided in the instruction set of the computer. The address portion of a jump-type instruction indicates the location of the next instruction to be fetched. Thus, when a jump-type instruction is encountered and the conditions for a jump are satisfied, the address portion of the instruction is placed into the program counter. In this way, when the control unit enters its next fetch phase, the appropriate next instruction is obtained.

1.4 AN OVERVIEW

As indicated in the previous section, this book is not about digital computers per se but rather about the fundamentals behind the logic design and behavior of digital systems. The digital computer was introduced simply as an excellent example of a digital system incorporating networks whose design and operation are the subject of this book. In general, digital systems involve the manipulation of numbers. Thus, in Chap. 2, the concept of numbers as a representation of discrete information is studied, along with how they are manipulated to achieve arithmetic operations.

It is the function of digital networks to provide for the manipulation of discrete information. In Chap. 3 an algebra, called a Boolean algebra, is introduced that is capable of describing the behavior and structure of logic networks, i.e., networks that make up a digital system. In this way, digital network design is accomplished via the manipulation of expressions in the algebra. The study of digital network design from this point of view is referred to as logic design. Chapter 4 then continues with the study of Boolean algebra to achieve expressions describing optimal logic networks.

Having developed mathematical tools for the logic design of digital networks, Chap. 5 studies several basic logic networks commonly encountered in digital systems, e.g., adders, subtracters, and decoders. These are all networks found in the digital computer. In addition, generic, complex logic networks have also been developed, referred to as programmable logic devices. In the second part of Chap. 5, these devices are studied for the purpose of showing how they are used for the design of specialized logic networks.

It was seen in the discussion on the digital computer that there is a need for the storage of digital information. The basic digital storage device in a digital system is the flip-flop. Chapter 6 deals with the operation of several flip-flop structures. Finally, the application of flip-flops to the logic design of registers and counters is presented.

The remaining three chapters continue with the logic design of those networks that involve the storage of information. These logic networks are referred to as sequential networks. There are two general classes of sequential networks—synchronous and asynchronous. Chapters 7 and 8 deal with the logic design of synchronous sequential networks, and Chap. 9 deals with the logic design of asynchronous sequential networks.

For completeness, an appendix is included which discusses the electronics of digital circuits. In the previous chapters, all designs are achieved on a logic level, i.e., without regard to the actual electronic circuits used. Several types of electronic digital circuits have been developed to realize the logic elements used in the networks of the previous chapters. It is the analysis of these electronic circuits, along with a comparison of their advantages and disadvantages, upon which the appendix focuses.

CHAPTER 2

Number Systems, Arithmetic, and Codes

As was mentioned in the previous chapter, the study of digital principles deals with discrete information, that is, information that is represented by a finite set of symbols. Certainly, numerical quantities are examples of discrete information. However, symbols can also be associated with information other than numerical quantities, as, for example, the letters of the alphabet. Nonnumeric symbols can always be encoded using a set of numeric symbols with the net result that discrete information appears as numbers.

At this time various number systems and how they denote numerical quantities are studied. One number system in particular, the binary number system, is very useful since it needs only two digit symbols. This is important, since many two-state circuits exist which can then be used for the processing of these symbols. This chapter is also concerned with how arithmetic is performed with these different number systems. Finally, it is shown how the numerical symbols are used to encode information. The encoding process can result in encoded information having desirable properties that provide for reliability and ease of interpretation. ■

2.1 POSITIONAL NUMBER SYSTEMS

The decimal number system is commonly accepted in our everyday lives. A typical decimal number is 872.64. This is really a contraction of the polynomial

$$\begin{aligned}872.64 &= 800 + 70 + 2 + 0.6 + 0.04\\ &= 8 \times 100 + 7 \times 10 + 2 \times 1 + 6 \times 0.1 + 4 \times 0.01\\ &= 8 \times 10^2 + 7 \times 10^1 + 2 \times 10^0 + 6 \times 10^{-1} + 4 \times 10^{-2}\end{aligned}$$

Each of the symbols in this number, i.e., 8, 7, 2, 6, and 4, by itself denotes an integer quantity. Furthermore, it is seen that the 8 in this case is weighted by the quantity 100 (or, 10^2), while the 7 is weighted by only 10 (or, 10^1). If the 8 and 7 were interchanged, then the 7 would be weighted by 100 and the 8 by 10. In general, the weighting factor is totally determined by the location of the symbol within the number. Thus, the quantity being denoted by a symbol (say, 8) is a function of both the symbol itself and its position.

The decimal number system is an example of a *radix-weighted positional number system* or, simply, *positional number system.** In a positional number system there is a finite set of symbols called *digits*. Each digit represents a nonnegative integer quantity. The number of distinct digits in the number system defines the *base* or *radix* of the number system. Formally, a *positional number system* is a method for representing quantities by means of the juxtaposition of digits, called *numbers,* such that the value contributed by each digit depends upon the digit symbol itself and its position within the number relative to a *radix point*. The radix point is a delimiter used to separate the integer and fraction parts of a number. Within this positioning arrangement each succeeding digit is weighted by a consecutive power of the base. Considering again the decimal number system, there are 10 distinct digits, 0, 1, 2, . . . , 9, and hence numbers in this system are said to be to the base 10.

From the above definitions it now follows that a general number N in a positional number system is represented by

$$\begin{aligned} N &= d_{n-1}d_{n-2}\cdots d_1d_0.d_{-1}\cdots d_{-m} \\ &= d_{n-1}\times r^{n-1} + d_{n-2}\times r^{n-2} + \cdots + d_0\times r^0 + d_{-1}\times r^{-1} + \cdots + d_{-m}\times r^{-m} \end{aligned}$$

where d_i denotes a digit in the number system such that $0 \le d_i \le (r-1)$, r is the base of the number system, n is the number of digits in the integer part of N, and m is the number of digits in the fraction part of N.† When referring to a particular digit in a number, it is frequently referenced by its *order;* that is, the power of the base that weights the digit. Thus, for integer quantities, the least significant digit is called the 0th-order digit, followed by the 1st-order digit, the 2nd-order digit, etc. Table 2.1 lists some of the more common positional number systems and their set of digit symbols.

Consider now the binary number system. In this system there are only two digit symbols, 0 and 1. A digit in the binary number system is usually referred to as a *bit,* an acronym for <u>bi</u>nary digi<u>t</u>. Thus, 1101.101 is a binary number consisting of seven binary digits or bits. To avoid possible confusion when writing a number, frequently a decimal subscript is appended to the number to indicate its base. In this case, the binary number 1101.101 is written as $1101.101_{(2)}$. This convention will be adhered to when the base is not apparent from the context or when attention is to be called to the base of the number system.

---

*The Roman number system is an example of a nonpositional number system. In this case many different symbols are used, each having a fixed definite quantity associated with it. The relative location of a symbol in the number plays a minimal role in determining the total quantity being represented. The only situation in which position becomes significant is in the special case where the symbol has a subtractive property as, for example, the I in IV indicates that one should be subtracted from five.

†The powers of the base are written, by convention, as decimal numbers since they are being used as an index to indicate the number of repeated multiplications of r; e.g., r^3 denotes $r \times r \times r$. This is the only circumstance in which digits not belonging to the number system itself appear in a number representation.

Table 2.1 Positional number systems and their digit symbols

Base	Number system	Digit symbols
2	Binary	0,1
3	Ternary	0,1,2
4	Quaternary	0,1,2,3
5	Quinary	0,1,2,3,4
8	Octal	0,1,2,3,4,5,6,7
10	Decimal	0,1,2,3,4,5,6,7,8,9
12	Duodecimal	0,1,2,3,4,5,6,7,8,9,A,B
16	Hexadecimal	0,1,2,3,4,5,6,7,8,9,A,B,C,D,E,F

From Table 2.1 it is seen that for those number systems whose base is less than 10, a subset of the digit symbols of the decimal number system is used. Thus, $732.16_{(8)}$ is an example of an octal number. In the case of the duodecimal and hexadecimal number systems, however, new digit symbols are introduced to denote integer quantities greater than nine. Typically, the first letters of the alphabet are used for this purpose. In the duodecimal number system, the quantity 10 is denoted by A and the quantity 11 is denoted by B. For the hexadecimal number system, the symbols A, B, . . . , F denote the decimal quantities 10, 11, . . . , 15, respectively. Hence, $1A6.B2_{(12)}$ is an example of a number in the duodecimal number system, while $8AC3F.1D4_{(16)}$ is a number in the hexadecimal number system.

The binary number system is the most important number system in digital technology. This is attributed to the fact that components and circuits which are binary in nature (i.e., have two distinct states associated with them) are easily constructed and are highly reliable. Even in those situations where the binary number system is not used as such, binary codes are employed to represent information. In computer technology, the octal and hexadecimal number systems also play a significant role. This is due to the simplicity of the conversion between the numbers in these systems and the binary number system, as is shown in Sec. 2.6.

2.2 COUNTING IN A POSITIONAL NUMBER SYSTEM

Perhaps the most fundamental operation that is performed with numbers is that of counting. In a positional number system this is a very simple process. First the distinct digits in the system are listed according to the integer quantities they represent. In the case of the decimal number system this becomes 0, 1, . . . , 9, while in the binary number system it is merely 0, 1. In order to continue the counting process, the digit 1 is introduced in the 1st-order digit position and the digit symbols in the 0th-order digit position are recycled, thus giving 10, 11, . . . , 19 for the decimal number system and 10, 11 for the binary number system. After each cycle of the digits in the 0th-order digit position, the digit in the 1st-order digit position is incremented by 1 until this is no longer possible; that is, a cycle has been completed in this position, at which time the digit 1 is introduced into the 2nd-order digit position. The above cycling procedure is then repeated in the 0th-order and 1st-order digit positions, etc. As is seen from the counting process, all quantities are represented in a positional number system by means of only a finite number of digit symbols merely by introducing more digit positions.

The concept of counting is illustrated in Table 2.2, where the first 32 integers in the binary, ternary, octal, and hexadecimal number systems are given, along with their decimal equivalents.

Table 2.2 The first 32 integers in the binary, ternary, octal, and hexadecimal number systems, along with their decimal equivalents

Decimal	Binary	Ternary	Octal	Hexadecimal
0	0	0	0	0
1	1	1	1	1
2	10	2	2	2
3	11	10	3	3
4	100	11	4	4
5	101	12	5	5
6	110	20	6	6
7	111	21	7	7
8	1000	22	10	8
9	1001	100	11	9
10	1010	101	12	A
11	1011	102	13	B
12	1100	110	14	C
13	1101	111	15	D
14	1110	112	16	E
15	1111	120	17	F
16	10000	121	20	10
17	10001	122	21	11
18	10010	200	22	12
19	10011	201	23	13
20	10100	202	24	14
21	10101	210	25	15
22	10110	211	26	16
23	10111	212	27	17
24	11000	220	30	18
25	11001	221	31	19
26	11010	222	32	1A
27	11011	1000	33	1B
28	11100	1001	34	1C
29	11101	1002	35	1D
30	11110	1010	36	1E
31	11111	1011	37	1F

2.3 BASIC ARITHMETIC OPERATIONS

The four basic arithmetic operations are addition, subtraction, multiplication, and division. How each of these operations is performed in various positional number systems is now studied. In each case the reader should note the similarity with the decimal number system. To further emphasize the similarities of arithmetic in any positional number system, examples of both binary and ternary arithmetic are given.

2.3.1 Addition

First, consider two-digit addition. This operation is easily stated in tabular form. Table 2.3 summarizes two-digit binary addition and two-digit ternary addition. The entry in each cell corresponds to the sum digit of $a + b$ and a carry if appropriate. As in the decimal number system, when the sum of the two digits equals or exceeds the base, a carry is generated to the next-higher-order digit position. Thus, in the lower right cell of Table 2.3*a*, corresponding to the binary sum $1_{(2)} + 1_{(2)} = 10_{(2)} = 2_{(10)}$, the sum digit is 0 and a carry of 1 is produced. The entries in these tables are easily checked by counting or using Table 2.2.

When the two numbers being added no longer are each single digits, the addition tables are still used by forming the sum in a serial manner. That is, after aligning the radix points of the two numbers, corresponding digits of the same order are added along with the carry, if generated, from the previous-order digit addition. The following examples illustrate the addition process.

EXAMPLE 2.1

$$\begin{array}{rl} 11 & = \text{carries} \\ 11010_{(2)} & = \text{augend} \\ +\ \ 11001_{(2)} & = \text{addend} \\ \hline 110011_{(2)} & = \text{sum} \end{array} \qquad \begin{array}{rl} 1\ \ 1 & = \text{carries} \\ 11.01_{(2)} & = \text{augend} \\ +\ \ 10.01_{(2)} & = \text{addend} \\ \hline 101.10_{(2)} & = \text{sum} \end{array}$$

EXAMPLE 2.2

$$\begin{array}{rl} 11 & = \text{carries} \\ 1102_{(3)} & = \text{augend} \\ +1022_{(3)} & = \text{addend} \\ \hline 2201_{(3)} & = \text{sum} \end{array} \qquad \begin{array}{rl} 11\ \ 1 & = \text{carries} \\ 1201.2_{(3)} & = \text{augend} \\ +\ \ 1200.1_{(3)} & = \text{addend} \\ \hline 10102.0_{(3)} & = \text{sum} \end{array}$$

2.3.2 Subtraction

The inverse operation of addition is subtraction. Two-digit subtraction in the binary and ternary number systems is given in Table 2.4. The entry in each cell denotes the resulting difference digit and if a borrow is needed to obtain the difference digit. As in decimal subtraction, when a larger digit is subtracted from a smaller digit, it is

Table 2.3 Two-digit addition tables. (*a*) Binary. (*b*) Ternary

$a + b$		b = 0	b = 1
a	0	0	1
	1	1	0 and carry 1

(*a*)

$a + b$		b = 0	b = 1	b = 2
a	0	0	1	2
	1	1	2	0 and carry 1
	2	2	0 and carry 1	1 and carry 1

(*b*)

necessary to perform borrowing. Borrowing is the process of bringing back to the next-lower-order digit position a quantity equal to the base of the number system. For example, in Table 2.4*a*, the upper right cell denotes the difference $0_{(2)} - 1_{(2)}$. In order to subtract the larger digit from the smaller digit, borrowing is necessary. Since this is binary subtraction, a borrow corresponds to bringing back the quantity 2, i.e., the base of the number system, from which 1 is subtracted. Thus, in the upper right cell of Table 2.4*a*,

Table 2.4 Two-digit subtraction tables. (*a*) Binary. (*b*) Ternary

$a - b$	$b = 0$	$b = 1$
$a = 0$	0	1 and borrow 1
$a = 1$	1	0

(*a*)

$a - b$	$b = 0$	$b = 1$	$b = 2$
$a = 0$	0	2 and borrow 1	1 and borrow 1
$a = 1$	1	0	2 and borrow 1
$a = 2$	2	1	0

(*b*)

the entry "1 and borrow 1" denotes that under the assumption that a borrow from the next-higher-order minuend digit is performed, the difference digit of 1 results.

As in the case of addition, subtraction tables can be used to form the difference between two numbers when they each involve more than a single digit. Again, after the radix points are aligned, subtraction is performed in a serial fashion starting with the least significant pair of digits. When borrowing is necessary, the next-higher-order minuend digit is decremented by 1. If this minuend digit is 0, then borrowing is performed on the first higher-order nonzero digit and the intervening 0's are changed to $r - 1$ where r is the base of the number system. It should be noted this is precisely the process one performs in decimal subtraction.

EXAMPLE 2.3

$$
\begin{array}{rl}
011 & \\
\not{1}\not{0}\not{0}01_{(2)} & = \text{minuend} \\
-\quad 1011_{(2)} & = \text{subtrahend} \\
\hline
110_{(2)} & = \text{difference}
\end{array}
\qquad
\begin{array}{rl}
00\ 0 & \\
\not{1}\not{1}0\not{1}.011_{(2)} & = \text{minuend} \\
-\quad 110.110_{(2)} & = \text{subtrahend} \\
\hline
110.101_{(2)} & = \text{difference}
\end{array}
$$

EXAMPLE 2.4

$$
\begin{array}{rl}
0 & \\
2\not{1}02_{(3)} & = \text{minuend} \\
-1021_{(3)} & = \text{subtrahend} \\
\hline
1011_{(3)} & = \text{difference}
\end{array}
\qquad
\begin{array}{rl}
020 & \\
\not{1}\not{0}\not{1}0.22_{(3)} & = \text{minuend} \\
-\quad 21.02_{(3)} & = \text{subtrahend} \\
\hline
212.20_{(3)} & = \text{difference}
\end{array}
$$

2.3.3 Multiplication

The third basic arithmetic operation is multiplication. Table 2.5 summarizes two-digit multiplication in the binary and ternary number systems. When the multiplier consists of more than a single digit, a tabular array of partial products is constructed and then added according to the rules of addition for the base of the numbers involved. The entries in this tabular array must be shifted such that the least significant digit of the partial product aligns with its respective multiplier digit. Multiplication is illustrated by the following examples.

EXAMPLE 2.5

$$
\begin{array}{rl}
10.11_{(2)} & = \text{multiplicand} \\
\times \quad 101_{(2)} & = \text{multiplier} \\
\hline
10\ 11 & \\
000\ 0 & \text{array of partial products} \\
1011 & \\
\hline
1101.11_{(2)} & = \text{product}
\end{array}
$$

EXAMPLE 2.6

$$
\begin{array}{rl}
2102_{(3)} & = \text{multiplicand} \\
\times \quad 102_{(3)} & = \text{multiplier} \\
\hline
11211 & \\
0000 & \text{array of partial products} \\
2102 & \\
\hline
222111_{(3)} & = \text{product}
\end{array}
$$

Table 2.5 Two-digit multiplication tables. (*a*) Binary. (*b*) Ternary

$a \times b$	$b = 0$	$b = 1$
$a = 0$	0	0
$a = 1$	0	1

(*a*)

$a \times b$	$b = 0$	$b = 1$	$b = 2$
$a = 0$	0	0	0
$a = 1$	0	1	2
$a = 2$	0	2	1 and carry 1

(*b*)

The simplicity of binary multiplication should be noted. If the multiplier bit is a 1, then the multiplicand is simply copied into the array of partial products; while if the multiplier bit is 0, then all 0's are written into the array.

2.3.4 Division

The final arithmetic operation to be considered is division. This process consists of multiplications and subtractions. The only difference in doing division in a base-r number system and in decimal is that base-r multiplication and subtractions are performed. The following two examples illustrate binary and ternary division.

EXAMPLE 2.7

```
                     110.1(2)   = quotient
divisor = 11(2) ) 10100.1(2)   = dividend
                 -11
                  100
                  -11
                   10
                  -00
                   10 1
                   -1 1
                    1 0(2)     = remainder
```

EXAMPLE 2.8

```
                     102(3)   = quotient
divisor = 12(3) )  2010(3)   = dividend
                  -12
                   11
                  -00
                   110
                  -101
                     2(3)    = remainder
```

The four basic arithmetic operations have been illustrated for only the binary and ternary number systems. However, the above concepts are readily extendable to handle any base-r positional number system by constructing the appropriate addition, subtraction, and multiplication tables.

2.4 POLYNOMIAL METHOD OF NUMBER CONVERSION

A number is a symbolic representation for a quantity. Therefore, it is only natural to expect that any quantity that can be represented in one number system can also be represented in another number system. In positional number systems with positive integer bases greater than 1, integers in one number system become integers in another number system; while fractions in one number system become fractions in another number system. There are two basic procedures for converting numbers in one number system into another number system: the *polynomial method* and the *iterative method.* Both methods involve arithmetic computations. The difference between the two methods lies in whether the computations are performed in the source or target number system. In this section the polynomial method is presented; the iterative method is discussed in the next section.

A number expressed in a base-r_1 number system has the form

$$\begin{aligned} N_{(r1)} &= d_{n-1_{(r1)}} d_{n-2_{(r1)}} \cdots d_{1_{(r1)}} d_{0_{(r1)}} . d_{-1_{(r1)}} \cdots d_{-m_{(r1)}} \\ &= d_{n-1_{(r1)}} \times r_{1_{(r1)}}^{n-1} + \cdots + d_{0_{(r1)}} \times r_{1_{(r1)}}^{0} + d_{-1_{(r1)}} \times r_{1_{(r1)}}^{-1} \\ &\quad + \cdots + d_{-m_{(r1)}} \times r_{1_{(r1)}}^{-m} \end{aligned} \tag{2.1}$$

The second subscript, $(r1)$, associated with each digit symbol d_i and base symbol r_1 in these equations is used to emphasize the fact that these are base-r_1 quantities. Furthermore, the base of a number system expressed in its own number system, i.e., $r_{1_{(r1)}}$, is always $10_{(r1)}$. This is readily seen in Table 2.2, where the quantity 2 in binary is $10_{(2)}$, the quantity 3 in ternary is $10_{(3)}$, the quantity 8 in octal is $10_{(8)}$, etc. This implies that Eq. (2.1) can be written as

$$\begin{aligned} N_{(r1)} &= d_{n-1_{(r1)}} \times 10_{(r1)}^{n-1} + \cdots + d_{0_{(r1)}} \times 10_{(r1)}^{0} + d_{-1_{(r1)}} \times 10_{(r1)}^{-1} \\ &\quad + \cdots + d_{-m_{(r1)}} \times 10_{(r1)}^{-m} \end{aligned} \tag{2.2}$$

Equation (2.2) is the general form of any number in a positional number system expressed in its own number system. Since this number denotes a quantity, the equivalent quantity is obtained by simply replacing each of the quantities in the right side of Eq. (2.2) by its equivalent quantity in the base-r_2 number system. That is, by replacing each of the digit symbols and the weighting factors as governed by the position of each digit in Eq. (2.2) by its equivalent quantity in base r_2, Eq. (2.2) becomes

$$\begin{aligned} N_{(r2)} &= d_{n-1_{(r2)}} \times r_{1_{(r2)}}^{n-1} + \cdots + d_{0_{(r2)}} \times r_{1_{(r2)}}^{0} + d_{-1_{(r2)}} \times r_{1_{(r2)}}^{-1} \\ &\quad + \cdots + d_{-m_{(r2)}} \times r_{1_{(r2)}}^{-m} \end{aligned} \tag{2.3}$$

where $d_{i_{(r2)}}$ is the quantity $d_{i_{(r1)}}$ expressed in base r_2 and $r_{1_{(r2)}}$ is the quantity r_1 expressed in base r_2. Since all quantities in Eq. (2.3) are now in base r_2, the evaluation of Eq. (2.3) must be the quantity $N_{(r1)}$ expressed as the base-r_2 number $N_{(r2)}$.

In summary, the above conversion procedure consists of the following steps: (1) Express the number $N_{(r1)}$ as a polynomial in its own number system, i.e., in base r_1 as indicated by Eq. (2.2). (2) Replace each digit symbol and $10_{(r1)}$ by their equivalent representations in base r_2. (3) Evaluate the polynomial using base-r_2 arithmetic.

To illustrate the above algorithm, consider the conversion of the binary number 1101 into its equivalent decimal number:*

$$\begin{aligned} 1101_{(2)} &= 1_{(2)} \times 10^3_{(2)} + 1_{(2)} \times 10^2_{(2)} + 0_{(2)} \times 10^1_{(2)} + 1_{(2)} \times 10^0_{(2)} \\ & \quad\downarrow \quad\downarrow \quad\downarrow \quad\downarrow \quad\downarrow \quad\downarrow \quad\downarrow \quad\downarrow \\ &\equiv 1_{(10)} \times 2^3_{(10)} + 1_{(10)} \times 2^2_{(10)} + 0_{(10)} \times 2^1_{(10)} + 1_{(10)} \times 2^0_{(10)} \\ &= 8 + 4 + 0 + 1 \\ &= 13_{(10)} \end{aligned}$$

The polynomial method of number conversion is especially useful for humans when converting a number in base r_1 into the decimal number system, since decimal arithmetic is always used when evaluating the polynomial.

The following five examples further illustrate the polynomial method of number conversion. In these examples attention should be paid to the manner in which each digit in base r_1 (as well as r_1 itself), denoting an integer quantity, becomes the corresponding integer quantity in base r_2 and that the arithmetic operations are performed using base-r_2 arithmetic.

EXAMPLE 2.9

Convert the binary number 101.011 into decimal.

$$\begin{aligned} 101.011_{(2)} &= 1_{(2)} \times 10^2_{(2)} + 0_{(2)} \times 10^1_{(2)} + 1_{(2)} \times 10^0_{(2)} \\ &\quad + 0_{(2)} \times 10^{-1}_{(2)} + 1_{(2)} \times 10^{-2}_{(2)} + 1_{(2)} \times 10^{-3}_{(2)} \\ &\equiv 1_{(10)} \times 2^2_{(10)} + 0_{(10)} \times 2^1_{(10)} + 1_{(10)} \times 2^0_{(10)} \\ &\quad + 0_{(10)} \times 2^{-1}_{(10)} + 1_{(10)} \times 2^{-2}_{(10)} + 1_{(10)} \times 2^{-3}_{(10)} \\ &= 4 + 0 + 1 + 0 + 0.25 + 0.125 \\ &= 5.375_{(10)} \end{aligned}$$

EXAMPLE 2.10

Convert the ternary number 201.1 into decimal.

$$\begin{aligned} 201.1_{(3)} &= 2_{(3)} \times 10^2_{(3)} + 0_{(3)} \times 10^1_{(3)} + 1_{(3)} \times 10^0_{(3)} + 1_{(3)} \times 10^{-1}_{(3)} \\ &\equiv 2_{(10)} \times 3^2_{(10)} + 0_{(10)} \times 3^1_{(10)} + 1_{(10)} \times 3^0_{(10)} + 1_{(10)} \times 3^{-1}_{(10)} \\ &= 18 + 0 + 1 + 0.3333\cdots \\ &= 19.3333\cdots_{(10)} \end{aligned}$$

It should be noted in Example 2.10 that the fraction part of the number having a finite number of digits in one number system converts into a fraction part with an

*In replacing the digits of base r_1 by those of base r_2, Table 2.2 is used to determine the necessary equivalences. The equivalence symbol (≡) is used in these equations to emphasize the fact that the same quantity is being denoted even though it is expressed in a different number system.

infinite number of digits in another number system. In such situations, a sufficient number of digits are used to have the desired precision.

EXAMPLE 2.11

Convert the decimal number 113.5 into binary.

$$\begin{aligned}113.5_{(10)} &= 1_{(10)} \times 10^{2}_{(10)} + 1_{(10)} \times 10^{1}_{(10)} + 3_{(10)} \times 10^{0}_{(10)} + 5_{(10)} \times 10^{-1}_{(10)}\\ &\equiv 1_{(2)} \times 1010^{2}_{(2)} + 1_{(2)} \times 1010^{1}_{(2)} + 11_{(2)} \times 1010^{0}_{(2)} + 101_{(2)} \times 1010^{-1}_{(2)}\\ &= 1100100 + 1010 + 11 + 0.1\\ &= 1110001.1_{(2)}\end{aligned}$$

EXAMPLE 2.12

Convert the binary number 11010 into ternary.

$$\begin{aligned}11010_{(2)} &= 1_{(2)} \times 10^{4}_{(2)} + 1_{(2)} \times 10^{3}_{(2)} + 0_{(2)} \times 10^{2}_{(2)} + 1_{(2)} \times 10^{1}_{(2)} + 0_{(2)} \times 10^{0}_{(2)}\\ &\equiv 1_{(3)} \times 2^{4}_{(3)} + 1_{(3)} \times 2^{3}_{(3)} + 0_{(3)} \times 2^{2}_{(3)} + 1_{(3)} \times 2^{1}_{(3)} + 0_{(3)} \times 2^{0}_{(3)}\\ &= 121 + 22 + 0 + 2 + 0\\ &= 222_{(3)}\end{aligned}$$

EXAMPLE 2.13

Convert the ternary number 2102 into binary.

$$\begin{aligned}2102_{(3)} &= 2_{(3)} \times 10^{3}_{(3)} + 1_{(3)} \times 10^{2}_{(3)} + 0_{(3)} \times 10^{1}_{(3)} + 2_{(3)} \times 10^{0}_{(3)}\\ &\equiv 10_{(2)} \times 11^{3}_{(2)} + 1_{(2)} \times 11^{2}_{(2)} + 0_{(2)} \times 11^{1}_{(2)} + 10_{(2)} \times 11^{0}_{(2)}\\ &= 110110 + 1001 + 0 + 10\\ &= 1000001_{(2)}\end{aligned}$$

2.5 ITERATIVE METHOD OF NUMBER CONVERSION

Inasmuch as the polynomial method of converting a number in base r_1 into base r_2 is characterized by the fact that base-r_2 arithmetic is performed, the iterative method is characterized by the fact that base-r_1 arithmetic is used. Thus, this method of number conversion is especially of interest to humans when converting a decimal number into its equivalent representation in some other positional number system. However, unlike the polynomial method, when a mixed number is converted by the iterative method, the integer and fraction parts of the number must be handled separately—the integer part converting into an integer part and the fraction part converting into a fraction part. Then, the two parts are combined to yield the equivalent mixed number in the new number system.

2.5.1 Iterative Method for Converting Integers

To convert an integer in base r_1 into its equivalent integer in base r_2, divide the number by $r_{2_{(r1)}}$, which is r_2 expressed in base r_1, using base-r_1 arithmetic. The resulting remainder is then converted into a single digit in base r_2 and is the 0th-order digit of the base-r_2 number. The process is then repeated on the resulting integer quotient to obtain the 1st-order digit of the base-r_2 number. The division procedure is continued until the resulting integer quotient in base r_1 becomes zero.

The above algorithm sounds more complicated than it really is. For example, to convert a decimal integer into binary, repeated division by 2 is performed using decimal arithmetic. The remainders as they are formed, being 0's and 1's, become the digits of the binary number starting with the least significant digit.

EXAMPLE 2.14

Conversion of $43_{(10)}$ into its binary equivalent proceeds as follows:

$$
\begin{aligned}
43_{(10)} \div 2_{(10)} &= 21_{(10)} + \text{remainder of } 1_{(10)};\ 1_{(10)} \equiv 1_{(2)} = \text{0th-order digit} \\
21_{(10)} \div 2_{(10)} &= 10_{(10)} + \text{remainder of } 1_{(10)};\ 1_{(10)} \equiv 1_{(2)} = \text{1st-order digit} \\
10_{(10)} \div 2_{(10)} &= 5_{(10)} + \text{remainder of } 0_{(10)};\ 0_{(10)} \equiv 0_{(2)} = \text{2nd-order digit} \\
5_{(10)} \div 2_{(10)} &= 2_{(10)} + \text{remainder of } 1_{(10)};\ 1_{(10)} \equiv 1_{(2)} = \text{3rd-order digit} \\
2_{(10)} \div 2_{(10)} &= 1_{(10)} + \text{remainder of } 0_{(10)};\ 0_{(10)} \equiv 0_{(2)} = \text{4th-order digit} \\
1_{(10)} \div 2_{(10)} &= 0_{(10)} + \text{remainder of } 1_{(10)};\ 1_{(10)} \equiv 1_{(2)} = \text{5th-order digit}
\end{aligned}
$$

Therefore, $43_{(10)} \equiv 101011_{(2)}$

EXAMPLE 2.15

Conversion of $213_{(10)}$ into its equivalent in hexadecimal simply involves repeated division by $16_{(10)}$. The procedure is as follows:

$$
\begin{aligned}
213_{(10)} \div 16_{(10)} &= 13_{(10)} + \text{remainder of } 5_{(10)};\ 5_{(10)} \equiv 5_{(16)} = \text{0th-order digit} \\
13_{(10)} \div 16_{(10)} &= 0_{(10)} + \text{remainder of } 13_{(10)};\ 13_{(10)} \equiv D_{(16)} = \text{1st-order digit}
\end{aligned}
$$

Therefore, $213_{(10)} \equiv D5_{(16)}$

EXAMPLE 2.16

Conversion of $1001011_{(2)}$ into its decimal equivalent by the iterative method requires repeated base-2 division by the quantity 10 expressed in binary, which is $1010_{(2)}$. The steps of the conversion are:

$$
\begin{aligned}
1001011_{(2)} \div 1010_{(2)} &= 111_{(2)} + \text{remainder of } 101_{(2)};\ 101_{(2)} \equiv 5_{(10)} = \text{0th-order digit} \\
111_{(2)} \div 1010_{(2)} &= 0_{(2)} + \text{remainder of } 111_{(2)};\ 111_{(2)} \equiv 7_{(10)} = \text{1st-order digit}
\end{aligned}
$$

Therefore, $1001011_{(2)} \equiv 75_{(10)}$

2.5.2 Verification of the Iterative Method for Integers*

For the interested reader, let us verify the above algorithmic procedure. Consider an integer in base r_1, i.e., $N_{(r1)}$. After this number is converted into base r_2, it has the form

$$d_{n-1_{(r2)}} \times 10^{n-1}_{(r2)} + d_{n-2_{(r2)}} \times 10^{n-2}_{(r2)} + \cdots + d_{1_{(r2)}} \times 10^{1}_{(r2)} + d_{0_{(r2)}} \times 10^{0}_{(r2)}$$

which is the general form of a number in its own system where $d_{i_{(r2)}}$ denotes a digit in the base-r_2 number system. Thus, the following equivalence is established:

$$N_{(r1)} \equiv d_{n-1_{(r2)}} \times 10^{n-1}_{(r2)} + d_{n-2_{(r2)}} \times 10^{n-2}_{(r2)} + \cdots + d_{1_{(r2)}} \times 10^{1}_{(r2)} + d_{0_{(r2)}} \times 10^{0}_{(r2)} \quad (2.4)$$

The digits $d_{i_{(r2)}}$ must now be determined from a knowledge of $N_{(r1)}$.

Proceeding as in the polynomial method, if each $d_{i_{(r2)}}$ coefficient and $10_{(r2)}$ are converted into their equivalents in base r_1, then the right side of Eq. (2.4) becomes a base-r_1 arithmetic expression. Performing the necessary substitutions gives

$$\begin{aligned} N_{(r1)} &= d_{n-1_{(r1)}} \times r^{n-1}_{2_{(r1)}} + d_{n-2_{(r1)}} \times r^{n-2}_{2_{(r1)}} + \cdots + d_{1_{(r1)}} \times r^{1}_{2_{(r1)}} + d_{0_{(r1)}} \times r^{0}_{2_{(r1)}} \\ &= [d_{n-1_{(r1)}} \times r^{n-2}_{2_{(r1)}} + \cdots + d_{1_{(r1)}} \times r^{0}_{2_{(r1)}}] \times r^{1}_{2_{(r1)}} + d_{0_{(r1)}} \times r^{0}_{2_{(r1)}} \end{aligned} \quad (2.5)$$

where $d_{i_{(r1)}}$ is the equivalent of $d_{i_{(r2)}}$ expressed in base r_1 and $r_{2_{(r1)}}$ is the equivalent of $10_{(r2)}$ expressed in base r_1. It should be noted that the last form of Eq. (2.5) was obtained by factoring $r^{1}_{2_{(r1)}}$ from the first $n - 1$ terms. If both sides of Eq. (2.5) are now divided by $r_{2_{(r1)}}$ using base-r_1 arithmetic, then the integer quotient corresponds to

$$d_{n-1_{(r1)}} \times r^{n-2}_{2_{(r1)}} + \cdots + d_{1_{(r1)}} \times r^{0}_{2_{(r1)}}$$

while the remainder corresponds to $d_{0_{(r1)}}$, i.e.,

$$\text{Remainder}\left[\frac{N_{(r1)}}{r_{2_{(r1)}}}\right] = d_{0_{(r1)}}$$

Recall that $d_{0_{(r1)}}$ is the base-r_1 representation of $d_{0_{(r2)}}$. It now follows that if this remainder, $d_{0_{(r1)}}$, is converted into its equivalent digit in base r_2 by Table 2.2, then the 0th-order digit of the base-r_2 number is obtained.

The above argument can now be applied to the resulting integer quotient,

$$\begin{aligned} &d_{n-1_{(r1)}} \times r^{n-2}_{2_{(r1)}} + \cdots + d_{1_{(r1)}} \times r^{0}_{2_{(r1)}} \\ &= [d_{n-1_{(r1)}} \times r^{n-3}_{2_{(r1)}} + \cdots + d_{2_{(r1)}} \times r^{0}_{2_{(r1)}}] \times r^{1}_{2_{(r1)}} + d_{1_{(r1)}} \times r^{0}_{2_{(r1)}} \end{aligned}$$

If the integer quotient is divided by $r_{2_{(r1)}}$, upon converting the remainder, $d_{1_{(r1)}}$, into a base-r_2 digit, then the 1st-order digit of the base-r_2 number is obtained. By repeating this process until the resulting quotient is zero, the coefficients of Eq. (2.4) are generated.

*This subsection may be skipped without loss of continuity.

2.5.3 Iterative Method for Converting Fractions

A slightly different algorithm is needed to convert a fraction expressed in base r_1 into its base-r_2 equivalent by the iterative method. Algorithmically, to convert a fraction in base r_1 into its equivalent fraction in base r_2, multiply the base-r_1 fraction by $r_{2_{(r1)}}$, which is r_2 expressed in base r_1, using base-r_1 arithmetic. The integer part of the product is then converted into a single digit in base r_2 and is the most significant digit of the base-r_2 fraction. The multiplication and converting process is then repeated on the resulting fraction part of the product to obtain the next-most-significant digit of the base-r_2 fraction. This procedure is continued until the resulting fraction part of the product becomes zero. It should be pointed out, however, that it is possible that an infinite number of digits may be needed to represent a base-r_2 fraction even though the base-r_1 fraction has a finite number of digits. In this case, the process is terminated when the desired precision is obtained.

For the special case of converting a decimal fraction into binary, repeated multiplication by 2 is performed. The integer parts of the products, being 0's and 1's, become the digits of the binary fraction starting with the bit closest to the binary point.

EXAMPLE 2.17

Conversion of $0.8125_{(10)}$ into its equivalent binary fraction proceeds as follows:

$0.8125_{(10)} \times 2_{(10)} = 1.6250_{(10)}$; $1_{(10)} \equiv 1_{(2)}$ = Most significant fraction digit
$0.6250_{(10)} \times 2_{(10)} = 1.2500_{(10)}$; $1_{(10)} \equiv 1_{(2)}$
$0.2500_{(10)} \times 2_{(10)} = 0.5000_{(10)}$; $0_{(10)} \equiv 0_{(2)}$
$0.5000_{(10)} \times 2_{(10)} = 1.0000_{(10)}$; $1_{(10)} \equiv 1_{(2)}$ = Least significant fraction digit
Therefore, $0.8125_{(10)} \equiv 0.1101_{(2)}$

EXAMPLE 2.18

Conversion of $0.1011_{(2)}$ into decimal proceeds as follows:

$0.1011_{(2)} \times 1010_{(2)} = 110.1110_{(2)}$; $110_{(2)} \equiv 6_{(10)}$ = Most significant fraction digit

$0.1110_{(2)} \times 1010_{(2)} = 1000.1100_{(2)}$; $1000_{(2)} \equiv 8_{(10)}$

$0.1100_{(2)} \times 1010_{(2)} = 111.1000_{(2)}$; $111_{(2)} \equiv 7_{(10)}$

$0.1000_{(2)} \times 1010_{(2)} = 101.0000_{(2)}$; $101_{(2)} \equiv 5_{(10)}$ = Least significant fraction digit

Therefore, $0.1011_{(2)} \equiv 0.6875_{(10)}$

2.5.4 Verification of the Iterative Method for Fractions*

In general, the equivalence between a fraction in base r_1, $N_{(r1)}$, and its representation in base r_2 is given by

$$N_{(r1)} \equiv d_{-1_{(r2)}} \times 10_{(r2)}^{-1} + d_{-2_{(r2)}} \times 10_{(r2)}^{-2} + \cdots + d_{-m_{(r2)}} \times 10_{(r2)}^{-m} \qquad (2.6)$$

where $d_{i_{(r2)}}$ denotes a digit in the base-r_2 number system. Converting each $d_{i_{(r2)}}$ coefficient and $10_{(r2)}$ into their equivalent representations in base r_1, Eq. (2.6) becomes

$$N_{(r1)} = d_{-1_{(r1)}} \times r_{2_{(r1)}}^{-1} + d_{-2_{(r1)}} \times r_{2_{(r1)}}^{-2} + \cdots + d_{-m_{(r1)}} \times r_{2_{(r1)}}^{-m}$$

where $d_{i_{(r1)}}$ is the equivalent of $d_{i_{(r2)}}$ expressed in base r_1 and $r_{2_{(r1)}}$ is the equivalent of $10_{(r2)}$ expressed in base r_1. Multiplying each side of this equation by $r_{2_{(r1)}}$ gives

$$r_{2_{(r1)}} \times N_{(r1)} = d_{-1_{(r1)}} \times r_{2_{(r1)}}^{0} + d_{-2_{(r1)}} \times r_{2_{(r1)}}^{-1} + \cdots + d_{-m_{(r1)}} \times r_{2_{(r1)}}^{-m+1}$$

If the integer part of this product, $d_{-1_{(r1)}}$, is converted into its equivalent digit in base r_2, then the most significant digit of the base-r_2 fraction is established. Repeating this process of multiplying the fraction part of the above product by $r_{2_{(r1)}}$ and converting the resulting integer part, the next-most-significant digit of the base-r_2 fraction is generated. By continuing this multiplication and converting process, the remaining digits of the base-r_2 fraction are obtained one at a time starting with the most significant digit of the fraction.

2.5.5 A Final Example

The following example illustrates the handling of a mixed number in which the integer and fraction parts are converted separately and then connected with a radix point. It should be noted that base 3 arithmetic is being used.

EXAMPLE 2.19

Conversion of $201.12_{(3)}$ into its binary equivalent proceeds as follows:

Integer part:

$201_{(3)} \div 2_{(3)} = 100_{(3)} +$ remainder of $1_{(3)}$; $1_{(3)} \equiv 1_{(2)} =$ Least significant integer digit

$100_{(3)} \div 2_{(3)} = 11_{(3)} +$ remainder of $1_{(3)}$; $1_{(3)} \equiv 1_{(2)}$

$11_{(3)} \div 2_{(3)} = 2_{(3)} +$ remainder of $0_{(3)}$; $0_{(3)} \equiv 0_{(2)}$

$2_{(3)} \div 2_{(3)} = 1_{(3)} +$ remainder of $0_{(3)}$; $0_{(3)} \equiv 0_{(2)}$

$1_{(3)} \div 2_{(3)} = 0_{(3)} +$ remainder of $1_{(3)}$; $1_{(3)} \equiv 1_{(2)} =$ Most significant integer digit

Therefore, $201_{(3)} \equiv 10011_{(2)}$

*This subsection may be skipped without loss of continuity.

Fraction part:

$$0.12_{(3)} \times 2_{(3)} = 1.01_{(3)};\ 1_{(3)} \equiv 1_{(2)} = \text{Most significant fraction digit}$$
$$0.01_{(3)} \times 2_{(3)} = 0.02_{(3)};\ 0_{(3)} \equiv 0_{(2)}$$
$$0.02_{(3)} \times 2_{(3)} = 0.11_{(3)};\ 0_{(3)} \equiv 0_{(2)}$$
$$0.11_{(3)} \times 2_{(3)} = 0.22_{(3)};\ 0_{(3)} \equiv 0_{(2)}$$
$$0.22_{(3)} \times 2_{(3)} = 1.21_{(3)};\ 1_{(3)} \equiv 1_{(2)}$$
$$0.21_{(3)} \times 2_{(3)} = 1.12_{(3)};\ 1_{(3)} \equiv 1_{(2)}$$

Up to this point the first six fraction digits are obtained. However, it is noted that the resulting fraction part of the above computation is $0.12_{(3)}$, which is also the fraction we began with. As a result, the next six fraction digits are the same as the first six fraction digits and the resulting fraction part of the computation is again $0.12_{(3)}$. Thus, the fraction conversion results in the nonterminating sequence $0.12_{(3)} \equiv 0.100011100011\cdots_{(2)}$. Furthermore, since this conversion results in a repeating sequence of fraction digits, we can write the conversion as

$$0.12_{(3)} \equiv 0.\overbrace{100011}^{\text{Repeating}}{}_{(2)}$$

Combining the integer and fraction parts:

$$201.12_{(3)} \equiv 10011.\overbrace{100011}^{\text{Repeating}}{}_{(2)}$$

2.6 SPECIAL CONVERSION PROCEDURES

When performing a number conversion between two bases in which one base is an integer power of the other, there is a simplified conversion process. Examples of such conversions are between numbers in base 2 (binary) and base 8 (octal) since $8 = 2^3$, and between numbers in base 2 (binary) and base 16 (hexadecimal) since $16 = 2^4$. One reason that the octal and hexadecimal number systems are of interest to computer people is because of these simple conversions.

Consider first conversions between binary and octal numbers. If a number is given in binary, then starting at the binary point and working both left and right, the bits are grouped by threes where leading and trailing 0's are added if necessary. For example, the bits of the binary number $11111101.0011_{(2)}$ are grouped as

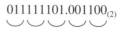

$$\underbrace{011}\,\underbrace{111}\,\underbrace{101}.\underbrace{001}\,\underbrace{100}{}_{(2)}$$

Then, each group of three bits is converted into its equivalent octal digit. For the above number, we have

$$
\begin{array}{ccccccc}
011 & 111 & 101 & . & 001 & 100_{(2)} \\
\downarrow & \downarrow & \downarrow & & \downarrow & \downarrow \\
3 & 7 & 5 & . & 1 & 4_{(8)}
\end{array}
$$

Thus, the octal equivalent of $11111101.0011_{(2)}$ is $375.14_{(8)}$.

By reversing the above procedure, octal numbers are readily converted into their equivalent binary numbers. In particular, to convert an octal number into its equivalent binary number, each octal digit is replaced by its equivalent three binary digits. For example, the octal number $173.24_{(8)}$ is converted into binary as follows:

$$
\begin{array}{ccccccc}
1 & 7 & 3 & . & 2 & 4_{(8)} \\
\downarrow & \downarrow & \downarrow & & \downarrow & \downarrow \\
001 & 111 & 011 & . & 010 & 100_{(2)}
\end{array}
$$

It is relatively simple to justify this algorithm for number conversions between base 2 and base 8. Consider the binary number $N_{(2)} = \cdots d_8 d_7 \cdots d_1 d_0 . d_{-1} d_{-2} d_{-3} \cdots$. Then, its decimal equivalent is given by

$$
\begin{aligned}
&\cdots + d_8 \times 2^8 + d_7 \times 2^7 + d_6 \times 2^6 + d_5 \times 2^5 + d_4 \times 2^4 + d_3 \times 2^3 + d_2 \times 2^2 \\
&\quad + d_1 \times 2^1 + d_0 \times 2^0 + d_{-1} \times 2^{-1} + d_{-2} \times 2^{-2} + d_{-3} \times 2^{-3} + \cdots \\
&= \cdots + (d_8 \times 2^2 + d_7 \times 2^1 + d_6 \times 2^0) \times 2^6 + (d_5 \times 2^2 + d_4 \times 2^1 + d_3 \times 2^0) \times 2^3 + \\
&\quad (d_2 \times 2^2 + d_1 \times 2^1 + d_0 \times 2^0) \times 2^0 + (d_{-1} \times 2^2 + d_{-1} \times 2^1 + d_{-3} \times 2^0) \times 2^{-3} \\
&\quad + \cdots \\
&= \cdots + (d_8 \times 2^2 + d_7 \times 2^1 + d_6 \times 2^0) \times 8^2 + (d_5 \times 2^2 + d_4 \times 2^1 + d_3 \times 2^0) \times 8^1 + \\
&\quad (d_2 \times 2^2 + d_1 \times 2^1 + d_0 \times 2^0) \times 8^0 + (d_{-1} \times 2^2 + d_{-1} \times 2^1 + d_{-3} \times 2^0) \times 8^{-1} \\
&\quad + \cdots
\end{aligned}
$$

The right side of this last equation has the form of an octal number with its coefficients, lying in the range 0 to 7, given in the form of binary numbers (where both the binary and octal forms are expressed in the decimal number system). Hence, by replacing each group of three bits by its equivalent octal digit, the conversion from binary to octal is achieved. By reversing this argument, the procedure for converting octal numbers into binary follows.

A similar procedure exists for conversions between binary and hexadecimal numbers since $2^4 = 16$. In this case, however, four binary digits are associated with a single hexadecimal digit. Thus, in converting a binary number into a hexadecimal number, the bits of the binary number are blocked off (working left and right from the hexadecimal point) in groups of four (adding leading and trailing 0's to complete a block if necessary), and each group of four bits is replaced by its equivalent hexadecimal digit. Conversely, when converting a hexadecimal number into a binary number, each hexadecimal digit is simply replaced by its equivalent four binary digits. For example, the binary number $1010110110.111_{(2)}$ is converted into its hexadecimal equivalent as follows:

$$\begin{array}{cccccc} \underbrace{0010} & \underbrace{1011} & \underbrace{0110} & . & \underbrace{1110}_{(2)} \\ \downarrow & \downarrow & \downarrow & & \downarrow \\ 2 & B & 6 & . & E_{(16)} \end{array}$$

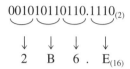

while the hexadecimal number $3AB.2_{(16)}$ is converted into its binary equivalent as follows:

$$\begin{array}{ccccc} 3 & A & B & . & 2_{(16)} \\ \downarrow & \downarrow & \downarrow & & \downarrow \\ \overbrace{0011} & \overbrace{1010} & \overbrace{1011} & . & \overbrace{0010}_{(2)} \end{array}$$

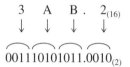

The binary number system is the most frequently used number system in digital systems. Hence the numbers in the memory and the various registers are strings of 0's and 1's. In these systems, it is often more convenient to regard these numbers as being either octal or hexadecimal rather than binary when referring to them since fewer digits are involved.

2.7 SIGNED NUMBERS AND COMPLEMENTS

In the above discussion of numbers, emphasis was placed on simply denoting the magnitude of a quantity. No attention was given to whether this magnitude is positive or negative. Certainly, one approach to represent signed quantities is to precede a number with a symbol, say, a plus sign (+) if it is positive and a minus sign (−) if it is negative. This form of signed numbers is known as the *sign-magnitude representation.* In actuality, digital systems utilizing the sign-magnitude representation use the binary digit 0 to denote the plus sign and the binary digit 1 to denote the minus sign.

It is possible to give a graphical interpretation to numbers in a sign-magnitude representation by assuming the real numbers appear as points along a line. In this case, the point denoting the zero quantity is called the *origin* of the line; positive quantities are considered as points lying to the right of the origin and negative quantities as points lying to the left of the origin. Figure 2.1 illustrates this concept. Thus, the sign serves the purpose of indicating which side of the origin the magnitude lies on and the magnitude itself as a measurement with respect to the origin.

Consider the possibility of defining a second origin, called the *offset origin,* at some point to the left of the origin associated with the zero quantity, called the *true origin.* This is illustrated in Fig. 2.2, where the offset origin is 10 units to the left of the true origin. Referring to this figure, the negative quantity 3 is a leftward measurement relative to the true origin, denoted by −3, or, equivalently, as a rightward measurement relative to the offset origin, denoted by *7. Both measurements can denote the same quantity without ambiguity as long as

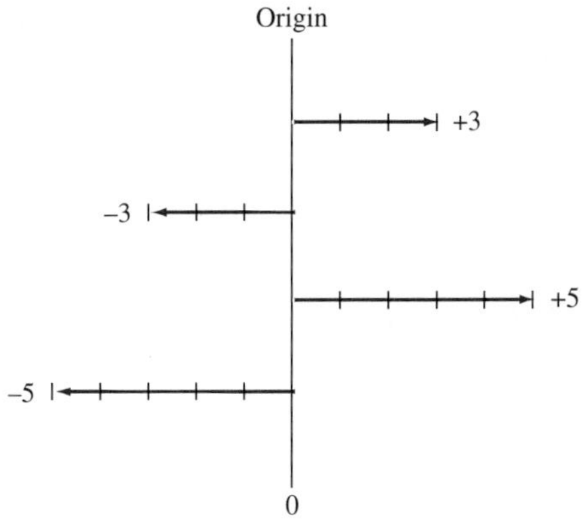

Figure 2.1 Graphical interpretation of sign-magnitude numbers.

the reference for the measurement is known. The asterisk was used in writing the number simply to indicate that the measurement is relative to the offset origin rather than the true origin. Furthermore, if the largest negative quantity to be represented is known, then it is always possible to place the offset origin sufficiently far to the left of the true origin so that all negative quantities are measured rightward of the offset origin. Since in digital systems the number of digits allocated to a quantity is fixed, the largest negative number that can be represented is always known.

Again consider a point to the left of the true origin which is denoted as an (unsigned) number N_1 representing a measurement relative to the true origin. When this same point is denoted as an (unsigned) number N_2 representing a measurement relative to the offset origin, N_2 is called the *complement* of N_1. Thus, in Fig. 2.2, it is

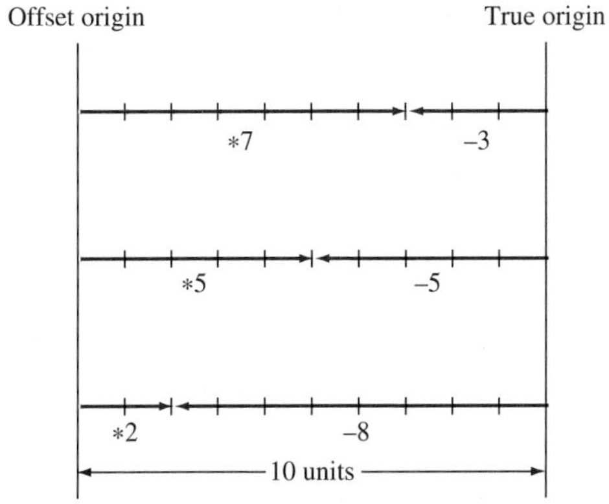

Figure 2.2 Graphical interpretation of complements.

said that 7 is the complement of 3. Formally, the complement of a number N_1 is defined as another number N_2 such that the sum $N_1 + N_2$ produces a specified result; in particular, this specified result is the displacement of the offset origin relative to the true origin.

There are two well-known types of complements: the *r's-complement* (also called the *radix complement* or the *true complement*) in which the offset origin is displaced r^n units to the left of the true origin and the *(r − 1)'s-complement* (also called the *diminished-radix complement* or the *radix-minus-one complement*) in which the offset origin is displaced by $r^n - r^{-m}$ units. In both cases, n is the number of integer digits of the largest quantity that must be represented, m is the number of fraction digits, and r is the base of the number expressed in its own number system, i.e., $r = 10$. Thus, given some sequence of digits denoting a number N in base r, the two types of complements are obtained by performing the following computations using base-r arithmetic:

$$r\text{'s-complement of } N = r^n - N = 10^n - N \tag{2.7}$$

$$(r-1)\text{'s-complement of } N = r^n - r^{-m} - N = 10^n - 10^{-m} - N \tag{2.8}$$

For the special case of decimal numbers, the r's-complement is called the *10's-complement* (or *tens-complement*) and the $(r - 1)$'s-complement is called the *9's-complement* (or *nines-complement*); while for binary numbers, the r's-complement is called the *2's-complement* (or *twos-complement*) and the $(r - 1)$'s-complement is called the *1's-complement* (or *ones-complement*).

The purpose of introducing the complements of numbers is to provide another means for denoting signed quantities. These are known as *complement representations*. Depending upon the offset used, signed numbers are expressed in either the *r's-complement representation* or *(r − 1)'s-complement representation*. In both cases the true origin is used for dealing with positive quantities, and an offset origin for dealing with negative quantities. In addition, a "sign digit" is appended to a number. The sign digit serves to indicate which origin is being used for a measurement. The binary digit 0 is appended to denote a positive number, i.e., a measurement relative to the true origin, and the digit 1 to denote

Table 2.6 Representations of signed numbers

Positive numbers:

All representations: $0_s N$

Negative numbers:

Sign-magnitude representation: $1_s N$

Signed r's-complement representation:*

$$1_s(r^n - N) = 1_s(10^n - N)$$

Signed $(r - 1)$'s-complement representation:*

$$1_s(r^n - r^{-m} - N) = 1_s(10^n - 10^{-m} - N)$$

*Recall the base of a number expressed in its own number system is 10.

a complement or negative number, i.e., a measurement relative to an offset origin.

The three representations of signed numbers are summarized in Table 2.6. In this table, the subscript s is regarded only as a delimiter to separate the sign digit from the measurement digits for ease of reading. Furthermore, it should be noted that in all three representations of signed numbers, the positive form of a number is the same since the true origin is used as the reference for the measurement.

The following examples illustrate the forming of complements and the writing of signed numbers. In all cases the same number of digits are used when writing the complement of a number as the number itself. This will be important in the following two sections when arithmetic is performed with complement numbers.

EXAMPLE 2.20

Given the unsigned decimal number 123.45, its 10's-complement is given by

$$\begin{aligned} 10^3 - 123.45 &= 1000 - 123.45 \\ &= 876.55 \end{aligned}$$

As a signed number in the 10's-complement representation, the positive representation of 123.45 is $0_s123.45$ and the negative representation is $1_s876.55$.

EXAMPLE 2.21

Given the unsigned decimal number 123.45, its 9's-complement is given by

$$\begin{aligned} 10^3 - 10^{-2} - 123.45 &= 1000 - 0.01 - 123.45 \\ &= 999.99 - 123.45 \\ &= 876.54 \end{aligned}$$

As a signed number in the 9's-complement representation, the positive representation of 123.45 is $0_s123.45$ and the negative representation is $1_s876.54$.

EXAMPLE 2.22

Given the unsigned binary number 1101.011, its 2's-complement is given by

$$\begin{aligned} 10^4_{(2)} - 1101.011_{(2)} &= 10000 - 1101.011 \\ &= 0010.101 \end{aligned}$$

As a signed number in the 2's-complement representation, the positive representation of 1101.011 is $0_s1101.011$ and the negative representation is $1_s0010.101$.

EXAMPLE 2.23

Given the unsigned binary number 1101.011, its 1's-complement is given by

$$10^4_{(2)} - 10^{-3}_{(2)} - 1101.011_{(2)} = 10000 - 0.001 - 1101.011$$
$$= 1111.111 - 1101.011$$
$$= 0010.100$$

As a signed number in the 1's-complement representation, the positive representation of 1101.011 is $0_s1101.011$ and the negative representation is $1_s0010.100$.

When the complements of an (unsigned) number are formed, it can always be done by using the mathematical definitions as given in Eqs. (2.7) and (2.8). However, there are also some simple procedures for forming complements. To form the r's-complement of N, working from right to left, keep all least significant zero digits of N unchanged, subtract the first least significant nonzero digit from r, the base of the number system, and subtract each of the remaining digits from $r - 1$. To form the $(r - 1)$'s-complement of N, simply subtract each digit of N from $r - 1$.

For the case of signed numbers in the r's-complement or $(r - 1)$'s-complement representations, the above procedures are applied to the measurement portion of the number, i.e., those digits to the right of the sign bit, when the complements are formed. In addition, for both cases, it is necessary to reverse the sign bit. That is, if the sign bit is 0, then it is replaced by a 1. Similarly, if the sign bit is a 1, then it is replaced by a 0. In general, taking the complement of a signed number is equivalent to taking the negative of the number.

It should be noted that the r's-complement of N can also be obtained by simply adding 1 to the least significant digit of the $(r - 1)$'s-complement of N.* Furthermore, for binary numbers, the 1's-complement is formed by merely replacing each 1 by a 0 and each 0 by a 1 in the original number. Finally, it should be observed that the complement of the complement of N is once again N. That is, the double complement of a number is the number itself. Readers are encouraged to test their understanding of these algorithms by applying them to Examples 2.20 to 2.23.

In closing this discussion on signed numbers and complements, one final comment is in order. Because of the relative simplicity of forming the $(r - 1)$'s-complements, it might appear that this representation is advantageous over the r's-complement representation. However, one objection that can be given against the $(r - 1)$'s-complement representation, as well as the sign-magnitude representation, is that there exists a minus zero. That is, for the case of binary numbers in the 1's-complement representation, a plus zero appears as $0_s00 \cdots 0$ and a minus zero appears as $1_s11 \cdots 1$. In the sign-magnitude representation a plus zero appears as $0_s00 \cdots 0$ and a minus zero as $1_s00 \cdots 0$. This situation does not occur in the 2's-complement representation since zero only appears as $0_s00 \cdots 0$.

---

*The single exception to this rule is $1_s00 \cdots 0$, representing the quantity $-10^n_{(r)}$ in the r's-complement representation, which cannot be complemented.

2.8 ADDITION AND SUBTRACTION WITH *r*'S-COMPLEMENTS

One reason for the interest in the complement form of numbers is that it is possible to subtract two numbers by doing addition if the subtrahend is first complemented. However, the subtraction procedure differs slightly depending upon whether the r's-complement or the $(r - 1)$'s-complement of a number is being used.

First a general procedure for the subtraction of two numbers by the addition of the r's-complement of the subtrahend is stated. The validity of the procedure is later established. Assume the difference $N_1 - N_2$ is to be obtained, and, for initial simplicity, assume that N_1 and N_2 are unsigned numbers in base r (thereby effectively implying that they are both positive). To perform subtraction, N_1 and N_2 are first expressed so that each has the same number of integer digits (i.e., n) and the same number of fraction digits (i.e., m). This can always be done by adding leading and trailing 0's to the numbers. The unsigned r's-complement of N_2, denoted by $\overline{\overline{N}}_2$, is then formed as was discussed in the previous section. Upon aligning the radix points of N_1 and $\overline{\overline{N}}_2$, the sum $N_1 + \overline{\overline{N}}_2$ is obtained using base-r addition. If a carry, called the *end carry,* is generated from the most-significant-digit position, i.e., if the sum has one more digit than the original numbers, then the carry digit is ignored when writing the sum. The resulting sum is the representation for the quantity $N_1 - N_2$. If $N_1 \geq N_2$, then the difference has the form of a positive number; while if $N_1 < N_2$, then the difference, being negative, appears in r's-complement form.* The occurrence of the end carry indicates that a positive difference has resulted, while the nonoccurrence of the end carry indicates that the difference is in r's-complement form.

The following examples illustrate subtraction by the addition of the r's-complement.

EXAMPLE 2.24

Consider the two decimal numbers $N_1 = 532$ and $N_2 = 146$. The 10's-complement of 146 is $\overline{\overline{N}}_2, = 854$. The difference $N_1 - N_2$ is now obtained by forming the sum $N_1 + \overline{\overline{N}}_2$.

Conventional subtraction	Subtraction by addition of the 10's-complement
$N_1 = 532$	$N_1 = 532$
$-N_2 = -146$	$+\overline{\overline{N}}_2 = +\ 854$
$N_1 - N_2 = 386$	$N_1 + \overline{\overline{N}}_2 = 1\vert 386$

↑ The end carry is ignored

Since an end carry has occurred, it is known that the result is positive.

*It should be carefully noted that a negative answer always appears in complement form.

EXAMPLE 2.25

To illustrate the effect of a negative difference, again consider the decimal numbers $N_1 = 532$ and $N_2 = 146$ where the 10's-complement of 532 is 468.

Conventional subtraction	Subtraction by addition of the 10's-complement
$N_2 = 146$	$N_2 = 146$
$-N_1 = -532$	$+\overline{\overline{N}}_1 = +468$
$N_2 - N_1 = -386$	$N_2 + \overline{\overline{N}}_1 = 614$

The fact that the end carry did not occur indicates that the result is in 10's-complement form. Since the 10's-complement of 386 is 614, the result $N_2 + \overline{\overline{N}}_1$ is the 10's-complement of the negative difference.

EXAMPLE 2.26

Consider the binary numbers $N_1 = 11101.11$ and $N_2 = 01011.10$.* The 2's-complement of N_2 is $\overline{\overline{N}}_2 = 10100.10$.

Conventional subtraction	Subtraction by addition of the 2's-complement
$N_1 = 11101.11$	$N_1 = 11101.11$
$-N_2 = -01011.10$	$+\overline{\overline{N}}_2 = +10100.10$
$N_1 - N_2 = 10010.01$	$N_1 + \overline{\overline{N}}_2 = 1\|10010.01$

The end carry is ignored

EXAMPLE 2.27

Using the same numbers as the above example, the difference $N_2 - N_1 = N_2 + \overline{\overline{N}}_1$ is obtained as follows where $\overline{\overline{N}}_1 = 00010.01$:

Conventional subtraction	Subtraction by addition of the 2's-complement
$N_2 = 01011.10$	$N_2 = 01011.10$
$-N_1 = -11101.11$	$+\overline{\overline{N}}_1 = +00010.01$
$N_2 - N_1 = -10010.01$	$N_2 + \overline{\overline{N}}_1 = 01101.11$

Since the 2's-complement of 10010.01 is 01101.11, the result $N_2 + \overline{\overline{N}}_1$ is the 2's-complement of the negative difference.

*Note that leading and trailing 0's are used in N_2 so that both N_1 and N_2 have the same number of digits.

It is a simple matter to justify the above addition procedure to achieve subtraction. Assume $N_1 - N_2$ is to be obtained and that the r's-complement of N_2 is denoted by $\overline{\overline{N}}_2$. Adding the r's-complement of the subtrahend to the minuend gives

$$N_1 + \overline{\overline{N}}_2 = N_1 + 10^n - N_2 = 10^n + (N_1 - N_2) \tag{2.9}$$

where base-r arithmetic is performed. If $N_1 - N_2 \geq 0$ in Eq. (2.9), then a 1 occurs in the nth-order digit position of $N_1 + \overline{\overline{N}}_2$ due to the 10^n term.* The digit 1 in this position indicates the existence of an end carry, and ignoring it when writing the sum results in the true difference $N_1 - N_2$ being expressed. On the other hand, if $N_1 - N_2 < 0$ in Eq. (2.9), then $N_1 + \overline{\overline{N}}_2 = (10^n - |N_1 - N_2|)$, which is precisely the r's-complement of $N_1 - N_2$. Furthermore, the nonoccurrence of the end carry indicates that the result is in r's-complement form. Thus, the validity of the subtraction procedure is established.

2.8.1 Signed Addition and Subtraction

It can also be proved that the subtraction of two signed numbers is achieved by adding the signed r's-complement of the subtrahend to the signed minuend. In this case, the sign digits are regarded as simply another digit of a number and are also "added." The measurement digits of the two signed numbers are added using base-r addition. However, in view of the fact that only 0's and 1's appear in the sign-digit position, binary addition is performed in the column associated with the sign digits independent of the arithmetic being used on the measurement digits. If a carry is generated from the addition of the most significant measurement digits, then it is carried over into the sign-digit column and is added along with the sign digits according to the rules of binary addition. This is illustrated shortly in Example 2.28. On the other hand, an end carry generated from the addition of the sign digits is ignored.† When the subtraction of signed numbers by the addition of a signed r's-complement is performed, the result of the operation has the correct sign digit. Hence, if the sign digit of the result is 1, then the measurement digits of the answer are in r's-complement form.

---

*Note that under the assumption of n integer digits in the operands, the highest-order digit position is the n-1st-order. Thus, 10^n corresponds to a 1 in the nth-order digit position.

†Although this approach for handling the sign digits appears rather awkward, when dealing with signed binary numbers no inconvenience is encountered since this simply implies that it is not necessary to distinguish the sign digit from the rest of the measurement digits. Alternatively, for nonbinary signed numbers, frequently the digit $r - 1$ is used as the sign digit of a negative quantity. For example, in the case of decimal numbers, the digit 9 is used to denote a negative quantity rather than 1. If this is done, then regular base-r addition can be performed on the sign digits instead of binary addition.

EXAMPLE 2.28

Consider the signed decimal numbers $N_1 = 0_s856.7$ and $N_2 = 0_s275.3$. The signed 10's-complement of $0_s275.3$ is $1_s724.7$. The difference $N_1 - N_2$ is obtained by forming the sum $N_1 + \overline{\overline{N}}_2$.

Conventional subtraction	Subtraction by addition of the 10's-complement
$N_1 = 856.7$	$N_1 = 0_s856.7$
$-N_2 = -275.3$	$+\overline{\overline{N}}_2 = +\ 1_s724.7$
$N_1 - N_2 = 581.4$	$N_1 + \overline{\overline{N}}_2 = 1\,\vert\,0_s581.4$

Binary addition is performed in this column

The end carry is ignored

EXAMPLE 2.29

Using the numbers N_1 and N_2 of the previous example, $N_2 - N_1$ is formed as follows where the signed 10's-complement of $0_s856.7$ is $1_s143.3$:

Conventional subtraction	Subtraction by addition of the 10's-complement
$N_2 = 275.3$	$N_2 = 0_s275.3$
$-N_1 = -856.7$	$+\overline{\overline{N}}_1 = +1_s143.3$
$N_2 - N_1 = -581.4$	$N_2 + \overline{\overline{N}}_1 = 1_s418.6$

The 1 in the sign digit position indicates that the answer is negative and the measurement digits are in the 10's-complement form.

EXAMPLE 2.30

Consider the signed binary numbers $N_1 = 0_s11011.01$ and $N_2 = 0_s10110.10$. Since the signed 2's-complement of N_2 is $1_s01001.10$, the difference $N_1 - N_2$ is obtained by using the signed 2's-complement of N_2 as follows:

Conventional subtraction	Subtraction by addition of the 2's-complement
$N_1 = 11011.01$	$N_1 = 0_s11011.01$
$-N_2 = -10110.10$	$+\overline{\overline{N}}_2 = +\ 1_s01001.10$
$N_1 - N_2 = 00100.11$	$N_1 + \overline{\overline{N}}_2 = 1\,\vert\,0_s00100.11$

The end carry is ignored

EXAMPLE 2.31

Using N_1 and N_2 of Example 2.30, $N_2 - N_1$ is achieved as follows:

Conventional subtraction	Subtraction by addition of the 2's-complement
$N_2 = 10110.10$	$N_2 = 0_s10110.10$
$-N_1 = -11011.01$	$+\overline{\overline{N}}_1 = +1_s00100.11$
$N_2 - N_1 = -00100.11$	$N_2 + \overline{\overline{N}}_1 = 1_s11011.01$

The 1 in the sign digit position indicates that the answer is negative and the measurement digits are in 2's-complement form.

Although the above discussion was based on the subtraction of two signed positive numbers, the concept presented applies to the algebraic addition and subtraction of any two signed numbers in r's-complement representation. As long as the measurement portions of the numbers are added, possibly after forming the signed r's-complement of the subtrahend when subtraction is specified, digit position by digit position using base-r arithmetic and the signs are added using binary addition, then the result is algebraically correct.* For example, if one of the operands is negative, and hence in its r's-complement form, then under the specification of addition the sum of the two operands results in the difference being obtained. On the other hand, if the difference between two operands is to be calculated, then the signed r's-complement of the subtrahend is simply added to the minuend. If the subtrahend is initially a negative quantity (and thereby expressed in r's-complement form), then taking its signed r's-complement results in a positive representation since the negative of a negative quantity is a positive quantity.

There is, however, one complication that can arise when dealing with algebraic addition and subtraction of signed numbers. Depending upon the signs of the operands, when the two signed numbers are added, possibly after the signed r's-complement of the subtrahend is formed when a subtraction operation is specified, it is possible that the operands are both positive or both negative. In such a case, if p digits are allocated to the measurement portion of the operands, then their sum could require $p + 1$ digits to properly indicate the measurement portion. However, it has been assumed in this discussion that a fixed number of digits are available for the measurement representation. When the resulting sum requires more digits than are available, an *overflow* condition† is said to occur. If an overflow occurs, then the

*It is seen shortly that there is a constraint that the algebraic result must be expressible with the number of digits allocated for the measurement portion.

†The reader should carefully note that an overflow condition is not the same as the end carry discussed previously.

algebraic sum is incorrect. One method of detecting an overflow condition is to detect when the signs of the two operands are the same, but the sign of the resulting sum is opposite to that of the operands. Another way of detecting an overflow condition involves detecting the carries into and from the sign digit position when the addition is performed. In this case, an overflow condition exists under two possibilities: (1) there is a carry into the sign digit position and no carry from the sign digit position or (2) there is no carry into the sign digit position and a carry from the sign digit position.

EXAMPLE 2.32

Consider the signed binary numbers $N_1 = 0_s11011.01$ and $N_2 = 0_s10110.10$. When the numbers are added to form $N_1 + N_2$, the following results:

$$\begin{aligned} N_1 &= 0_s11011.01 \\ +N_2 &= +0_s10110.10 \\ \hline N_1 + N_2 &= 1_s10001.11 \end{aligned}$$

In this case an overflow condition has occurred since the addition of two positive numbers results in a negative sum. The overflow condition is a consequence of an insufficient number of measurement digits to properly represent the sum. Alternatively, in the above addition, an overflow is detected since there is a carry into the sign digit position while no carry results from the addition of the sign digits.

2.9 ADDITION AND SUBTRACTION WITH (r – 1)'S-COMPLEMENTS

Just as subtraction is achievable by doing addition with r's-complements, it is also possible to do subtraction by doing addition using the $(r - 1)$'s-complements. The difference between the two procedures lies in the handling of the end carry.

Initially, assume the minuend and subtrahend are unsigned base-r numbers. To obtain the difference $N_1 - N_2$, the numbers N_1 and N_2 are first expressed so that they both have the same number of integer digits (i.e., n) and the same number of fraction digits (i.e., m). Upon rewriting N_2 in its $(r - 1)$'s-complement form as was discussed in Sec. 2.7, denoted by $\overline{N_2}$, the radix points of N_1 and $\overline{N_2}$ are aligned and their sum is obtained using base-r addition, i.e., $N_1 + \overline{N_2}$. If an end carry is generated, then it is carried around to the least-significant-digit position of the sum and added to it. This carry is known as the *end-around carry*. The resulting sum corresponds to $N_1 - N_2$. If $N_1 > N_2$, then the difference has the form of a positive number; while if $N_1 \leq N_2$, then the difference, being negative, appears in $(r - 1)$'s-complement form.* The occurrence of an end-around carry indicates that a positive difference has resulted, while the nonoccurrence of the end-around carry indicates that the difference is in $(r - 1)$'s-complement form and, thereby, denotes a negative result. The validity of this procedure is given shortly.

The following examples illustrate subtraction by the addition of the $(r - 1)$'s-complement.

EXAMPLE 2.33

Let $N_1 = 85.2_{(10)}$ and $N_2 = 32.5_{(10)}$. The 9's-complement of N_2 is $\overline{N}_2 = 67.4$. To obtain the difference $N_1 - N_2$ the sum $N_1 + \overline{N}_2$ is formed:

Conventional subtraction	Subtraction by addition of the 9's-complement
$N_1 = 85.2$	$N_1 = 85.2$
$-N_2 = -32.5$	$+\overline{N}_2 = +67.4$
$N_1 - N_2 = 52.7$	$N_1 + \overline{N}_2 = 1\,\vert 52.6$
	$+ \; 1$ = End-around carry
	52.7 = Difference

It should be noted that the end carry resulting upon forming the sum $N_1 + \overline{N}_2$ is added to the least-significant-digit position to obtain the final result.

EXAMPLE 2.34

Again let $N_1 = 85.2_{(10)}$ and $N_2 = 32.5_{(10)}$. The 9's-complement of N_1 is $\overline{N}_1 = 14.7$. To obtain the difference $N_2 - N_1$:

Conventional subtraction	Subtraction by addition of the 9's-complement
$N_2 = 32.5$	$N_2 = 32.5$
$-N_1 = -85.2$	$+\overline{N}_1 = +14.7$
$N_2 - N_1 = -52.7$	$N_2 + \overline{N}_1 = 47.2$ = Difference in 9's-complement form

In this case, no end carry occurred when adding. Thus, the result is in 9's-complement form.

*It should be noted that a zero difference appears in $(r - 1)$'s-complement form and hence as a negative quantity. The single exception is when a negative zero is subtracted from a positive zero. In this case, a positive zero is obtained since after the negative zero is complemented, a positive zero is added to a positive zero.

EXAMPLE 2.35

Let $N_1 = 110.1_{(2)}$ and $N_2 = 011.0_{(2)}$. The 1's-complement of N_2 is $\overline{N}_2 = 100.1$. To obtain the difference $N_1 - N_2$:

Conventional subtraction	Subtraction by addition of the 1's-complement
$N_1 = 110.1$	$N_1 = 110.1$
$-N_2 = -011.0$	$+\overline{N}_2 = +\ 100.1$
$N_1 - N_2 = 011.1$	$N_1 + \overline{N}_2 = 1\,\vert\,011.0$
	$+ \ 1$ = End-around carry
	011.1 = Difference

EXAMPLE 2.36

Again let $N_1 = 110.1_{(2)}$ and $N_2 = 011.0_{(2)}$. The 1's-complement of N_1 is $\overline{N}_1 = 001.0$. To obtain the difference $N_2 - N_1$:

Conventional subtraction	Subtraction by addition of the 1's-complement
$N_2 = 011.0$	$N_2 = 011.0$
$-N_1 = -110.1$	$+\overline{N}_1 = +001.0$
$N_2 - N_1 = -011.1$	$N_2 + \overline{N}_1 = 100.0$ = Difference in 1's-complement form

To establish the validity of achieving subtraction by the addition of the $(r - 1)$'s-complement of the subtrahend to the minuend, assume $N_1 - N_2$ is to be obtained and that the $(r - 1)$'s-complement of N_2 is denoted by $\overline{N}_2$. Adding the $(r - 1)$'s-complement of the subtrahend to the minuend results in

$$N_1 + \overline{N}_2 = N_1 + 10^n - 10^{-m} - N_2 = 10^n - 10^{-m} + (N_1 - N_2) \qquad (2.10)$$

where base-r arithmetic is performed in the above expression. If $N_1 - N_2 > 0$ in Eq. (2.10), then a 1 occurs in the nth-order digit position of $N_1 + \overline{N}_2$ due to the 10^n term. The digit 1 in this position indicates the existence of an end carry. By adding it to the least-significant-digit position of $N_1 + \overline{N}_2$, it cancels the effect of the -10^{-m} term and the difference $N_1 - N_2$ results. On the other hand, if $N_1 - N_2 \leq 0$ in Eq. (2.10), then $N_1 + \overline{N}_2 = (10^n - 10^{-m} - |N_1 - N_2|)$, which is precisely the $(r - 1)$'s-complement representation of $N_1 - N_2$. It should be noted in this case, the nonoccurrence of an end carry indicates the result is in $(r - 1)$'s-complement form.

2.9.1 Signed Addition and Subtraction

If the minuend and subtrahend are signed numbers, then the above procedure can still be applied by considering the sign digit as simply another digit of the number as was done in the previous section. Thus, when performing the base-r addition, the sign digits are also "added." However, in view of the fact that only 0's and 1's can appear in the sign-digit position, binary addition is performed in the column associated with the sign digits independent of the arithmetic being used on the measurement digits. If a carry is generated from the addition of the most significant measurement digits, then it is carried into the sign-digit column and is added along with the sign digits according to the rules of binary addition (see Example 2.37). On the other hand, an end carry generated from the addition of the sign digits serves as the end-around carry and must be added, using base-r addition, to the least significant digit of the previously generated sum.* After the addition involving the end-around carry, when necessary, the sign digit of the difference is always correct assuming there are a sufficient number of measurement digits to express the result.† That is, a 0 sign digit indicates a positive difference, while a 1 sign digit indicates a negative difference with the measurement digits in $(r - 1)$'s-complement form.

EXAMPLE 2.37

Let $N_1 = 0_s54.2_{(10)}$ and $N_2 = 0_s32.8_{(10)}$. The signed 9's-complement of N_2 is $\overline{N}_2 = 1_s67.1$. To obtain $N_1 - N_2$:

Conventional subtraction		Subtraction by addition of the 9's-complement		
$N_1 =$	54.2	$N_1 =$	$0_s54.2$	Binary addition is performed in this column
$-N_2 =$	-32.8	$+\overline{N}_2 =$	$+\ 1_s67.1$	
$N_1 - N_2 =$	21.4	$N_1 + \overline{N}_2 =$	$1\,|\,0_s21.3$	
		$+$	1	= End-around carry
			$0_s21.4$	= Positive difference

*Although this approach for handling the sign digits appears rather awkward, when dealing with signed binary numbers no inconvenience is encountered since this simply implies that it is not necessary to distinguish the sign digit from the rest of the measurement digits. Alternatively, for nonbinary signed numbers, frequently the digit $r - 1$ is used as the sign digit of a negative quantity. For example, in the case of decimal numbers, the digit 9 is used to denote a negative quantity rather than 1. If this is done, then regular base-r addition can be performed on the sign digits instead of binary addition.

†As is discussed shortly, adding two signed numbers that are both positive or both negative can cause an overflow condition, in which case the algebraic result is incorrect.

EXAMPLE 2.38

Again let $N_1 = 0_s54.2_{(10)}$ and $N_2 = 0_s32.8_{(10)}$. The signed 9's-complement of N_1 is $\overline{N}_1 = 1_s45.7$. To obtain $N_2 - N_1$:

Conventional subtraction	Subtraction by addition of the 9's-complement
$\begin{array}{rr} N_2 = & 32.8 \\ -N_1 = & \underline{-54.2} \\ N_2 - N_1 = & -21.4 \end{array}$	$\begin{array}{rrl} N_2 = & 0_s32.8 & \\ +\overline{N}_1 = & \underline{+1_s45.7} & \\ N_2 + \overline{N}_1 = & 1_s78.5 & = \text{Negative difference in} \\ & & \quad \text{9's-complement form} \end{array}$

EXAMPLE 2.39

Let $N_1 = 0_s110.101_{(2)}$ and $N_2 = 0_s010.110_{(2)}$. The signed 1's-complement of N_2 is $\overline{N}_2 = 1_s101.001$. To obtain $N_1 - N_2$:

Conventional subtraction	Subtraction by addition of the 1's-complement
$\begin{array}{rr} N_1 = & 110.101 \\ -N_2 = & \underline{-010.110} \\ N_1 - N_2 = & 011.111 \end{array}$	$\begin{array}{rrl} N_1 = & 0_s110.101 & \\ +\overline{N}_2 = & \underline{+\ 1_s101.001} & \\ N_1 + \overline{N}_2 = & 1 \mid 0_s011.110 & \\ & \underline{+ \hookrightarrow \quad 1} & = \text{End-around carry} \\ & 0_s011.111 & = \text{Positive difference} \end{array}$

EXAMPLE 2.40

Again let $N_1 = 0_s110.101_{(2)}$ and $N_2 = 0_s010.110_{(2)}$. The signed 1's-complement of N_1 is $\overline{N}_1 = 1_s001.010$. To obtain $N_2 - N_1$:

Conventional subtraction	Subtraction by addition of the 1's-complement
$\begin{array}{rr} N_2 = & 010.110 \\ -N_1 = & \underline{-110.101} \\ N_2 - N_1 = & -011.111 \end{array}$	$\begin{array}{rrl} N_2 = & 0_s010.110 & \\ +\overline{N}_1 = & \underline{+1_s001.010} & \\ N_2 + \overline{N}_1 = & 1_s100.000 & = \text{Negative difference in} \\ & & \quad \text{1's-complement form} \end{array}$

In the above discussion, N_1 and N_2 were assumed to be two signed positive numbers. The remarks at the end of Sec. 2.8 regarding the algebraic addition and subtraction of signed numbers and the concept of overflow are equally applicable for numbers in the $(r - 1)$'s-complement representation. That is, when the operands are in signed form, their base-r addition, with the possible need to handle the end-around carry, of the measurement digits and binary addition of the sign digits gives the correct algebraic result subject to the constraint of an overflow condition. Recall that an overflow condition is the lack of sufficient measurement digits to represent a quantity. When an overflow condition occurs, the result is not algebraically correct. The reader should carefully note that overflow is not the end-around carry needed to achieve the valid algebraic result. The detection of an overflow when using the signed $(r - 1)$'s-complement representation of numbers is exactly the same as when using the signed r's-complement representation.

2.10 CODES

Because of the availability and reliability of circuits that have two physical states associated with them, the binary number system is a natural choice for data handling and manipulation in digital systems. To one of these physical states of the circuit is associated the binary digit 0, while the binary digit 1 is associated with the other physical state. On the other hand, humans prefer the decimal number system. In addition, it is often desirable to have a digital system handle information other than numerical quantities, such as letters of the alphabet. A solution to this problem is to encode each of the decimal symbols, letters of the alphabet, and other special symbols by a unique string of binary digits, called a *code group*. In this way the digital system considers each code group as a single entity and can process and manipulate the elements comprising these code groups as binary digits.

2.10.1 Decimal Codes

Consider first the 10 symbols occurring in the decimal number system. There are many codes that can be conceived for just these symbols. Coded representations for the 10 decimal symbols are known as *binary-coded decimal* (or *BCD*) *schemes* or, simply, *decimal codes*. With 3 bits, there are 8 combinations ($2^3 = 8$) of 0's and 1's available to form a code group; while 4 bits allow 16 such combinations ($2^4 = 16$). Since there are 10 distinct digits in the decimal number system which must be coded, a minimum of 4 bits are necessary in each code group for a decimal digit. If the code group consists of 4 bits, then there are six combinations that are not used. It is interesting to note that there are approximately 30 billion coding schemes for the decimal digits in which the code groups consist of just 4 bits.*

Of the many 4-bit BCD coding schemes, the most common is the *8421 code*.† In this coding scheme, the 10 decimal digits are represented by their 4-bit binary equivalents as shown in Table 2.7. This is known as a *weighted code* since the corresponding decimal digit is easily determined by adding the weights associated with the 1's in the code group. The weights are given by the code name. In the case of

---

*In actuality, there are 16!/6! 4-bit codes for the 10 decimal digits.

†Because of its popularity, this coding scheme is often simply referred to as *BCD*.

Table 2.7 Weighted decimal codes

Decimal digit	8421 code	2421 code	5421 code	$753\bar{6}$ code	Biquinary code 5043210
0	0000	0000	0000	0000	0100001
1	0001	0001	0001	1001	0100010
2	0010	0010	0010	0111	0100100
3	0011	0011	0011	0010	0101000
4	0100	0100	0100	1011	0110000
5	0101	1011	1000	0100	1000001
6	0110	1100	1001	1101	1000010
7	0111	1101	1010	1000	1000100
8	1000	1110	1011	0110	1001000
9	1001	1111	1100	1111	1010000

the 8421 code, the 0th-order bit in the code group has the weight 1, the 1st-order bit has the weight 2, the 2nd-order bit has the weight 4, and the 3rd-order bit has the weight 8. In general, if the 4 bits of a code group are written as $b_3b_2b_1b_0$ and the weights for the corresponding bits are w_3, w_2, w_1, and w_0, then the decimal digit N is given by

$$N = b_3 \times w_3 + b_2 \times w_2 + b_1 \times w_1 + b_0 \times w_0$$

using base-10 arithmetic. To form the 8421 BCD representation of a decimal number, each decimal digit is simply replaced by its 4-bit code group. For example, the 8421 BCD representation of the decimal number 392 is 001110010010. It is important to note that the number of bits within each code group must be fixed to avoid any ambiguity in interpreting a coded number. Furthermore, it should be understood that a coded decimal number is not the binary equivalent of the decimal number as was discussed earlier in this chapter.

There are numerous other weighted codes. Among these are the *2421 code* and the *5421 code,* both of which are shown in Table 2.7. Again the code group for each decimal digit consists of 4 bits, and the weights associated with the bits in each code group are given by the name of the code.

Although the 8421 code is the most common BCD scheme, the 2421 code does have an important property not possessed by the 8421 code. In some codes, the 9's-complement of each decimal digit is obtained by forming the 1's-complement of its respective code group. That is, if each 0 is replaced by a 1 and each 1 is replaced by a 0 in the code group for the decimal digit X, then the code group for the decimal digit $9–X$ results. Codes having this property are said to be *self-complementing.* As indicated in Table 2.7, the 2421 code does have this property. For example, the 9's-complement of 7 is 2, and the 1's-complement of 1101 is 0010. As a consequence, the 9's-complement of an entire decimal number is obtained by forming the 1's-complement of its coded representation. As an illustration, the decimal number 328 appears as 001100101110 in 2421 code. Forming the 1's-complement of this coded representation results in 110011010001. This is the coded form for 671, which is the 9's-complement of 328. A self-complementing coding scheme is convenient in a digital system where subtraction is performed by the addition of the 9's-complement.

It is even possible to have codes with negative weights. An example of such a code is the *$753\bar{6}$ code,* where the bar over the 6 indicates that the weight associated with the 0th-order bit in the code group is −6. The code group for each decimal digit in the $753\bar{6}$ code is enumerated in Table 2.7. It should be noted that this is also a self-complementing code.

Although all the codes mentioned thus far have 4 bits, there are also weighted codes having more than 4 bits. The best known of these is the *biquinary code*. As indicated in Table 2.7, the weights for the biquinary code are 5043210. The name of the biquinary code is derived from the fact that for each decimal digit, two 1's appear in the code group—one of these among the first 2 bits of the code group (hence the prefix *bi*) and the other among the remaining 5 bits of the code group (hence the suffix *quinary*).

A well-known 4-bit nonweighted BCD scheme is the *excess-three code* (or *XS-3 code*) shown in Table 2.8. This code is derived by adding the binary equivalent of the decimal 3, that is, $0011_{(2)}$, to each of the code groups of the 8421 code. Thus, in this coding scheme, the decimal number 961 appears as 110010010100. As is evident from Table 2.8, this code is self-complementing.

The final decimal code to be introduced is the *2-out-of-5 code,* also shown in Table 2.8. This is a nonweighted code* in which exactly 2 of the 5 bits in each code group are 1's, the remaining 3 bits being 0's. An advantage of this code, as well as the biquinary code, is that it has error-detecting properties. Error detection is discussed in the next section.

Table 2.8 Nonweighted decimal codes

Decimal digit	Excess-3 code	2-out-of-5 code
0	0011	11000
1	0100	00011
2	0101	00101
3	0110	00110
4	0111	01001
5	1000	01010
6	1001	01100
7	1010	10001
8	1011	10010
9	1100	10100

*Except for the coding of the numeral 0, it is a weighted code having the weights 74210.

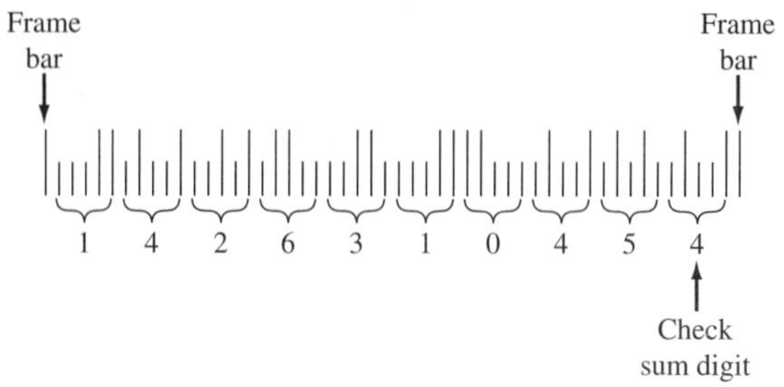

Figure 2.3 U.S. Postal Service bar code corresponding to the ZIP code 14263-1045.

An interesting application of the 2-out-of-5 code is the U.S. Postal Service bar code. Figure 2.3 shows the bar code that would appear on a piece of mail having the ZIP code 14263-1045. Each digit is coded using the 2-out-of-5 code where the binary digit 0 of a code group occurs as a short bar and the binary digit 1 of a code group occurs as a tall bar. The ZIP code appears between two tall bars, called frame bars, which serve to define the beginning and ending of the bar code. The frame bars are used for aligning the scanner which reads the bar code. A final check sum digit is also included in the bar code, e.g., the digit 4 in Fig. 2.3. The check sum digit is used for error correction and is discussed in Sec. 2.12.

2.10.2 Unit-Distance Codes

There is a class of codes, referred to as *unit-distance codes,* that are particularly important when an analog quantity must be converted into a digital representation. The basic property of a unit-distance code is that only one bit changes between two successive integers which are being coded. An example of a unit-distance code is the *Gray code,* which is given in Table 2.9 for the decimal numbers 0 to 15.

To illustrate the usefulness of a unit-distance code, assume the position of a shaft, an analog quantity, is to be digitally represented. To do this, a positional encoder wheel is attached to the shaft. For simplicity of this discussion, assume that it is sufficient to express the angular position of the shaft with only four binary digits.* Two possible angular position encoder wheels are shown in Fig. 2.4. In one case, the coding is done with conventional binary and the other utilizes the Gray code. To determine the angular position, i.e., sector, fixed photosensing devices arranged in a line can be used to detect the light and shaded cells across a sector of the encoder wheel. In this example, it is assumed that a light cell on the wheel is read by a photosensing device as the binary digit 1 and a dark cell as the binary digit 0.

*Thus, the angular position is given as increments of $360/16 = 22.5°$. Greater refinement is easily achieved by using more digits and an encoder with more sectors.

Table 2.9 Gray code

Decimal number	Gray code
0	0000
1	0001
2	0011
3	0010
4	0110
5	0111
6	0101
7	0100
8	1100
9	1101
10	1111
11	1110
12	1010
13	1011
14	1001
15	1000

If the conventional binary encoder wheel is used, then when moving from sector 3 to 4, the code word must change from 0011 to 0100. This requires 3 bits to change value. On the other hand, in the case of the Gray code encoder, the code word must change from 0010 to 0110, which involves only a change of 1 bit. Now assume that the photosensing devices are out of alignment such that the photosensing

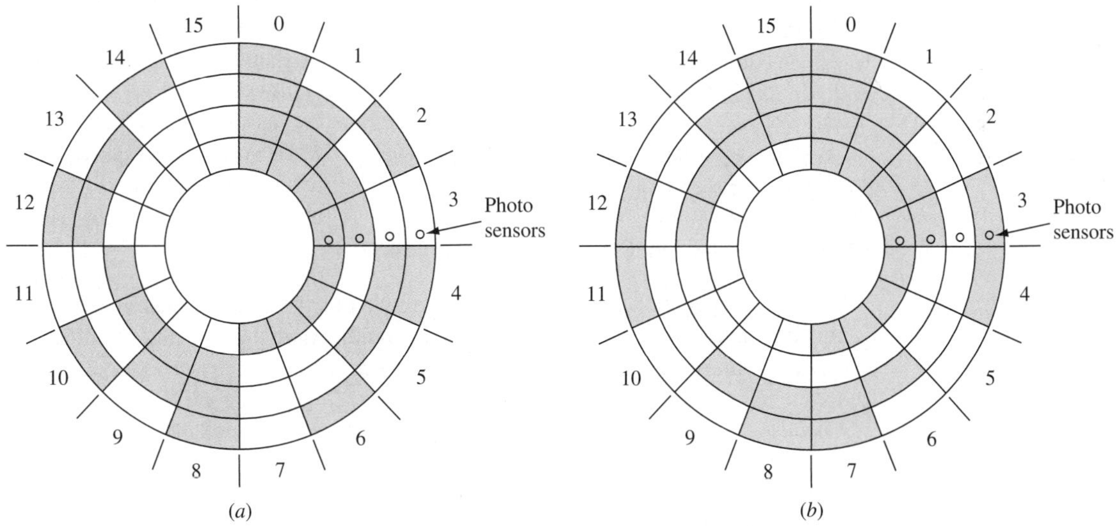

Figure 2.4 Angular position encoders. (*a*) Conventional binary encoder. (*b*) Gray code encoder.

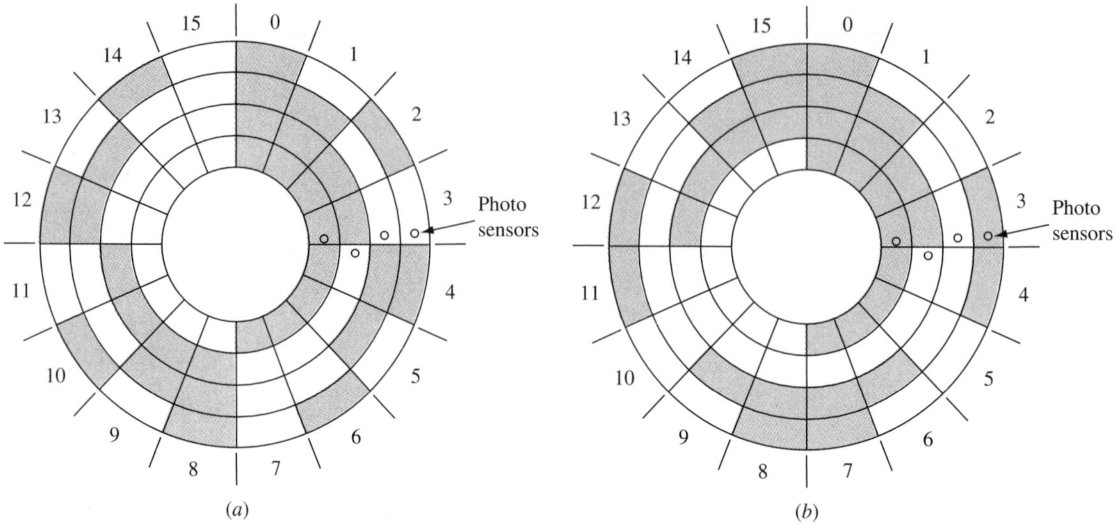

Figure 2.5 Angular position encoders with misaligned photosensing devices. (*a*) Conventional binary encoder. (*b*) Gray code encoder.

device reading the second most significant bit in the code word is slightly advanced, causing it to read ahead of the others. This is shown in Fig. 2.5*a*. When the angular position of the encoder is near the transition between sectors 3 and 4, it is possible that a reading of 0111 might result since the photosensing device for the second most significant digit is already reading sector 4 while the other photosensing devices are reading sector 3. A significant error has now occurred since a reading of 0111 indicates sector 7, which is several sectors away. On the other hand, if a unit-distance code is used, such as the Gray code, then the effect of the misalignment results in the code for the next sector being obtained prematurely as illustrated in Fig. 2.5*b*. With such a coding scheme, however, the error encountered in a digital representation can never exceed that of one sector since only 1 bit must change value between any two adjacent sectors.

2.10.3 Alphanumeric Codes

Thus far only coding schemes for decimal numbers have been considered. However, frequently alphabetic information must be handled by a digital system. In addition to alphabetic and numeric information, it has been found desirable to code special symbols such as punctuation marks, $, #, @, =, +, (,), etc., and control operations such as Backspace, Form Feed, Carriage Return, etc. In general, alphabetic symbols, numeric symbols, special symbols, and certain control operations are referred to as *characters*. Codes that are used to represent characters are called *alphanumeric codes*.

To code the 26 letters of the alphabet in both upper- and lowercase along with the 10 numeric symbols, at least 6 bits are necessary. Although many alphanumeric codes

Table 2.10 The 7-bit American Standard Code for Information Interchange (ASCII)

	$b_6 b_5 b_4$							
$b_3\ b_2\ b_1\ b_0$	000	001	010	011	100	101	110	111
0 0 0 0	NUL	DLE	SP	0	@	P	`	p
0 0 0 1	SOH	DC1	!	1	A	Q	a	q
0 0 1 0	STX	DC2	"	2	B	R	b	r
0 0 1 1	ETX	DC3	#	3	C	S	c	s
0 1 0 0	EOT	DC4	$	4	D	T	d	t
0 1 0 1	ENQ	NAK	%	5	E	U	e	u
0 1 1 0	ACK	SYN	&	6	F	V	f	v
0 1 1 1	BEL	ETB	'	7	G	W	g	w
1 0 0 0	BS	CAN	(	8	H	X	h	x
1 0 0 1	HT	EM	)	9	I	Y	i	y
1 0 1 0	LF	SUB	*	:	J	Z	j	z
1 0 1 1	VT	ESC	+	;	K	[	k	{
1 1 0 0	FF	FS	,	<	L	\	l	|
1 1 0 1	CR	GS	–	=	M	]	m	}
1 1 1 0	SO	RS	.	>	N	^	n	~
1 1 1 1	SI	US	/	?	O	—	o	DEL

Control Characters

NUL	Null	DC1	Device Control 1
SOH	Start of Heading	DC2	Device Control 2
STX	Start of Text	DC3	Device Control 3
ETX	End of Text	DC4	Device Control 4
EOT	End of Transmission	NAK	Negative Acknowledge
ENQ	Enquiry	SYN	Synchronous Idle
ACK	Acknowledge	ETB	End of Transmission Block
BEL	Bell	CAN	Cancel
BS	Backspace	EM	End of Medium
HT	Horizontal Tab	SUB	Substitute
LF	Line Feed	ESC	Escape
VT	Vertical Tab	FS	File Separator
FF	Form Feed	GS	Group Separator
CR	Carriage Return	RS	Record Separator
SO	Shift Out	US	Unit Separator
SI	Shift In	SP	Space
DLE	Data Link Escape	DEL	Delete

have been developed, the best known alphanumeric code is the 7-bit *American Standard Code for Information Interchange,* or *ASCII code.* Table 2.10 gives a listing of this code. As with the numeric codes using code groups, alphanumeric information is coded by the juxtaposition of the appropriate code groups for the characters.

More recently, the *Unicode Standard* has been developed. This 16-bit character coding system provides for the encoding of not only the English characters but also those of foreign languages including those of the Middle East and Asia. In addition, the Unicode Standard includes punctuation marks, mathematical symbols, technical symbols, geometric shapes, and dingbats.

2.11 ERROR DETECTION

In the process of transferring information between two points, it is possible for errors to be introduced. Since digital information consists of strings of 0's and 1's, an error is said to occur when at least one 0 inadvertently becomes a 1 or when at least one 1 becomes a 0. In such a situation it is desirable to detect the occurrence of the error. The ability to detect errors is inherent in some codes; while in other cases, additional bits are added to the information for this purpose.

In Sec. 2.10, the biquinary and 2-out-of-5 codes were discussed. In both of these cases, there are exactly two 1's in each code group for a decimal digit. Thus, if a single error should occur to any code group, that is, one 1 becomes a 0 or one 0 becomes a 1 (but not both), then there no longer are exactly two 1's appearing in the code group for the digit. For example, in the 2-out-of-5 code, if the code group 00110 is transmitted and 01110 is received, then the three 1's indicate that an error has occurred. By means of an appropriate logic network, the condition of other than exactly two 1's in a code group can be detected. Hence, it is said that codes of this type are *error-detecting codes*.

When error-detecting codes are not used to represent coded information or when information appears as conventional binary numbers, error detection is achieved by the addition of a *parity bit*. In this approach an additional bit is appended to the information so that the number of 1's in the code group or binary number, in the case of noncoded information, is even or odd, depending upon the parity rule being employed. When the odd parity scheme is employed, the parity bit is selected so that the number of 1's in the code group or binary number, including the parity bit, is odd. In the even parity scheme, the parity bit is selected so there are an even number of 1's in the code group or binary number, including the parity bit. The odd parity bit scheme as applied to the 8421 code is illustrated in Table 2.11*a*. If any single bit representing a character should erroneously change, including the parity bit, then there no longer is an odd number of 1's in the overall code group for that character. In Table 2.11*b*, the even parity bit scheme is applied to the 8421 code. In this case, each code group with the parity bit consists of an even number of 1's.

Testing for an even or odd number of 1's within a string of binary digits is readily done by a logic network. When an error is detected, the digital system can be designed to request the retransmission of the string of bits or emit a signal indicating a malfunction.

Inasmuch as single errors are detected by the parity-bit scheme, double errors are not detected since double errors do not cause the overall parity to change. However, triple errors also are detected, and, in general, it is possible to detect any odd number of errors by this method.

For the purpose of classification, the error-detecting capability of a coding scheme is defined as 1 less than the minimum number of errors it can *not always* detect. Thus, the parity-bit scheme is regarded as a single-error-detecting scheme even though triple errors are also detected.

Table 2.11 8421 code with a parity bit. (*a*) Odd-parity scheme. (*b*) Even-parity scheme

Decimal digit	8421*p*	Decimal digit	8421*p*
0	00001	0	00000
1	00010	1	00011
2	00100	2	00101
3	00111	3	00110
4	01000	4	01001
5	01011	5	01010
6	01101	6	01100
7	01110	7	01111
8	10000	8	10001
9	10011	9	10010
(*a*)		(*b*)	

Given the code groups for two characters in some coding scheme, the number of bits that must be changed in the first code group so that the second code group results is defined as the *distance* between the two code groups. Thus, referring to the 2-out-of-5 code, the distance between the code groups for the decimal digits 2, i.e., 00101, and 5, i.e., 01010, is four. Furthermore, the *minimum distance* of a code is the smallest distance between any two valid code groups appearing in the coding scheme. Again referring to the 2-out-of-5 code and considering all pairs of code groups, the minimum distance is two. Similarly, the minimum distance for the biquinary code is also two.

The significance of the minimum distance is that it is related to the error-detecting capability of a coding scheme, i.e., the maximum number of bits in error that is always detectable. In particular,

$$D = M - 1 \tag{2.11}$$

where D is the error-detecting capability of the code and M is its minimum distance. To see the validity of Eq. (2.11), consider a code whose minimum distance is two. This means that at least 2 bits must change before any valid code group becomes another valid code group in the same coding scheme. If only 1 bit should erroneously change, then the resulting code group consists of a combination of 0's and 1's that do not appear in the definition of the code. Hence, when such a code group is detected it can be concluded that an error has occurred in transmission. Since, in general, at least M bits must change in a code with minimum distance M before one code group can become another valid code group in the same coding scheme, any $M - 1$, or fewer, bit changes always results in an invalid code group. Thus, the existence of any of these code groups indicates the presence of detectable errors.

2.12 ERROR CORRECTION

In the previous section, error detection was studied. At that time no consideration was given to the exact nature of the error so that it could be corrected. It is also possible to construct codes where error correction can be performed on received information in which bits erroneously have been changed during transmission. The generalized form of Eq. (2.11), which gives the relationship between the minimum distance of a code and its error-detecting and error-correcting capabilities, is

$$C + D = M - 1 \qquad \text{where } C \leq D \tag{2.12}$$

In this equation C is the number of erroneous bits that always can be corrected, D is the number of erroneous bits that always can be detected, and M is the minimum distance of the code. The restriction $C \leq D$ is necessary since no error can be corrected without its first being detected. An implication of Eq. (2.12) is that for a given minimum distance, it is possible to perform a trade-off between the amount of the error-correcting and error-detecting capabilities of a code.

From Eq. (2.12), it is seen that single-error correction is achievable when a code has a minimum distance of three, i.e., when $C = 1$ and $D = 1$. In such a code at least 3 bits must change before a valid code group can convert into another valid code group. If a single error should occur, then the resulting code group is within 1 bit of matching the intended code group and within at least 2 bits of matching any other valid code group. By noting which single bit must be changed to obtain a valid code group it is possible to achieve the correction. However, if two errors occur, then erroneous correction might result since the invalid code group can now be within 1 bit of matching a nonintended code group. Thus, in a code having a minimum distance of three, only single-error correction is possible.

On the other hand, a code having a minimum distance of three can be used for double error-detection rather than single-error correction, i.e., when $C = 0$ and $D = 2$ in Eq. (2.12). If the code is being used in this manner, then it is only necessary to observe that an invalid code group is received. Since the minimum distance is three, the occurrence of one or two errors always results in an invalid code group.

By having codes with a minimum distance greater than three, it is possible to provide for additional error-detecting and error-correcting capabilities. This is shown in Table 2.12, which is obtained by evaluating Eq. (2.12).

Table 2.12 Amount of error detection D and error correction C possible with a code having a minimum distance M

M	1	2	3		4		5			6		
D	0	1	2	1	3	2	4	3	2	5	4	3
C	0	0	0	1	0	1	0	1	2	0	1	2

2.12.1 Hamming Code

Perhaps the best-known coding scheme that enables single-error correction was devised by R. W. Hamming and is known as the *Hamming code*. In a Hamming code several parity bits are included in a code group. The values of the parity bits are determined by an even-parity scheme over certain selected bits. When a code group is received, the parity bits are recalculated; that is, a check is made to see if the correct parity still exists over their selected bits. By comparing the recalculated parity bits against those received in the code group, it is possible to determine if the received code group is free from a single error or, if a single error has occurred, then exactly which bit has erroneously changed. If more than one bit is changed during transmission, then this coding scheme no longer is capable of determining the location of the errors.

For the case of 4 information bits, 3 parity bits are included along with the 4 information bits to form a 7-bit code group. The general organization of a code group in this case is as follows:

7	6	5	4	3	2	1	Position
b_4	b_3	b_2	p_3	b_1	p_2	p_1	Code group format

where the 7 bits of the code group are numbered from right to left, the three p's denote the parity bits, and the four b's denote the information bits being encoded. The values of the parity bits are determined by the following rules:

p_1 is selected so as to establish even parity over positions 1, 3, 5, and 7

p_2 is selected so as to establish even parity over positions 2, 3, 6, and 7

p_3 is selected so as to establish even parity over positions 4, 5, 6, and 7

That is, p_1 is a 0 when there are an even number of 1's in positions 3, 5, and 7; otherwise, p_1 is a 1. In this way, there are an even number of 1's in the four positions 1, 3, 5, and 7. In a similar manner, the values of p_2 and p_3 are determined so as to have an even number of 1's over their selected positions of the code group.

To illustrate the above rules for constructing a Hamming code group, assume the four information bits are $b_4b_3b_2b_1 = 0110$. These bits appear in positions 3, 5, 6, and 7 of the Hamming code group; that is,

7	6	5	4	3	2	1	Position
b_4	b_3	b_2	p_3	b_1	p_2	p_1	Code group format
0	1	1		0			Hamming code group with information bits placed

The next step is to determine the values of the parity bits in the code group. Parity bit p_1 is used to establish even parity over positions 1, 3, 5, and 7. Since position 5 has a 1 and positions 3 and 7 have 0's, parity bit p_1 must be a 1. In a similar manner, parity bit p_2 is a 1 so that even parity is established over positions 2, 3, 6, and 7.

Finally, parity bit p_3 is a 0 in order to have an even number of 1's in positions 4, 5, 6, and 7. This results in the following Hamming code group:

7	6	5	4	3	2	1	Position
b_4	b_3	b_2	p_3	b_1	p_2	p_1	Code group format
0	1	1	0	0	1	1	Hamming code group

The information bits in a Hamming code group may themselves be a code for a character. For example, Table 2.13 gives the complete Hamming code for the 10 decimal digits when they are coded by the 8421 BCD scheme.

Now consider how a 7-bit Hamming code group, upon being received, is checked for an error during transmission and, if necessary, how the location of a single error is determined. Upon the receipt of a Hamming code group, the parity bits are recalculated using the same even-parity scheme over the selected bit positions as was done for encoding. From the recalculation, a *binary check number,* $c_3^*c_2^*c_1^*$, is constructed. In particular, if the recalculation of parity bit p_i is the same as the p_i bit in the received Hamming code group, then c_i^* is set equal to 0. If, on the other hand, the recalculated value of p_i is not the same as the p_i bit in the received Hamming code group, then c_i^* is set equal to 1. In other words, if there are an even number of 1's in positions 1, 3, 5, and 7, then c_1^* is set equal to 0; while if there are an odd number of 1's in these positions, then c_1^* is set equal to 1. In a similar manner, c_2^* is set equal to 0 if and only if there are an even number of 1's in positions 2, 3, 6, and 7; while c_3^* is set equal to 0 if and only if there are an even number of 1's in positions 4, 5, 6, and 7. Otherwise, c_2^* and c_3^* are set equal to 1. The binary check number $c_3^*c_2^*c_1^*$ indicates the position of the error if one has occurred. If $c_3^*c_2^*c_1^* = 000$, then no position is in need of correction, i.e., no single error has occurred in the Hamming code group.

As an example, assume the previously constructed Hamming code group with the information bits $b_4b_3b_2b_1 = 0110$ is transmitted, i.e., 0110011, but the code group 0110111 is received. Thus, the bit in position 3 erroneously changed from 0 to 1 during transmission. Referring to bit positions 1, 3, 5, and 7 of the received code group,

Table 2.13 The Hamming code for the 10 decimal digits weighted by the 8421 BCD scheme

Decimal digit	7 8	6 4	5 2	4 p_3	3 1	2 p_2	1 p_1	Position 8421 BCD and parity bits
0	0	0	0	0	0	0	0	
1	0	0	0	0	1	1	1	
2	0	0	1	1	0	0	1	
3	0	0	1	1	1	1	0	
4	0	1	0	1	0	1	0	
5	0	1	0	1	1	0	1	
6	0	1	1	0	0	1	1	
7	0	1	1	0	1	0	0	
8	1	0	0	1	0	1	1	
9	1	0	0	1	1	0	0	

it is seen that there are an odd number of 1's. As stated above, this requires c_1^* to be set to 1 in the binary check number. In a similar manner, since there are an odd number of 1's in positions 2, 3, 6, and 7, it follows that $c_2^* = 1$. Finally, it is seen that there are an even number of 1's in positions 4, 5, 6, and 7. Thus, $c_3^* = 0$. The binary check number is therefore $c_3^*c_2^*c_1^* = 011$ which, in turn, is the binary equivalent of the decimal number 3. This indicates that the bit in position 3 is incorrect. Now that the location of the error is established, it is a simple matter to complement the bit in position 3 of the received Hamming code group to obtain the transmitted code group. In this example, it is concluded that the correctly transmitted Hamming code group was 0110011 and that the actual information bits were $b_4b_3b_2b_1 = 0110$. Although this example involved an error in one of the information bits, a change in a parity bit can equally well occur and be located upon constructing the binary check number.

The above procedure for constructing a Hamming code group that enables single-error correction is extendable to handle any number of information bits. If m information bits are to be encoded, then k parity bits are needed in each Hamming code group where

$$m \leq 2^k - k - 1$$

Table 2.14 gives a listing of the minimum number of parity bits k needed for various ranges of m information bits, resulting in a Hamming code group with $m + k$ bits. For example, when encoding information consisting of from 5 to 11 bits, four parity bits must appear in each code group. If the bit positions in a Hamming code group are numbered right to left from 1 to $m + k$, then those positions corresponding to 2 raised to a nonnegative integer power, i.e., positions 1, 2, 4, 8, etc., are allocated to the parity bits. The remaining bit positions are used for the information bits. Table 2.15 indicates which bit positions are associated with each parity bit for the purpose of establishing even parity over selected bit positions. For example, the parity bit in position 1, i.e., p_1, checks the bit in every other position beginning with the bit in position 1. The parity bit in position 2, i.e., p_2, considers every other group of 2 bits beginning with the parity bit in position 2. The third parity bit, p_3, considers every other group of 4 bits beginning with the parity bit in position 4. In general, the parity bit in position 2^i, i.e., p_i, considers every other group of 2^i bits beginning with the parity bit in position 2^i. To determine the location of a single error in a received Hamming code group, the binary check number $c_k^* \cdots c_2^*c_1^*$ is formed. This is done by recalculating the parity bits or, equivalently, checking the parity over the selected bits

Table 2.14 The number of parity bits k needed to construct a Hamming code with m information bits

Range of m information bits	Number of parity bits k
2–4	3
5–11	4
12–26	5
27–57	6
58–120	7

Table 2.15 Bit positions checked by each parity bit in a Hamming code

Parity bit position	Positions checked
1	1, 3, 5, 7, 9, 11, 13, 15, 17, . . .
2	2, 3, 6, 7, 10, 11, 14, 15, 18, . . .
4	4, 5, 6, 7, 12, 13, 14, 15, 20, . . .
8	8, 9, 10, 11, 12, 13, 14, 15, 24, . . .
⋮	⋮

indicated in Table 2.15. If the recalculated value of p_i is the same as the p_i bit received in the code group, then c_i^* is set equal to 0; otherwise, it is set equal to 1. The binary check number $c_k^* \cdots c_2^* c_1^*$ indicates the position of the error if one has occurred. If $c_k^* \cdots c_2^* c_1^* = 0 \cdots 00$, then a valid Hamming code group was received.

2.12.2 Single-Error Correction Plus Double-Error Detection

A Hamming code as constructed above provides for the detection and correction of only a single error. With a slight modification, it is possible to construct Hamming code groups in which single-error correction plus double-error detection is possible. To a Hamming code group constructed by the above procedure, an overall parity bit is appended and assigned a value such that the complete code group, including its overall parity bit, contains an even number of 1's. The overall parity bit position is not used in determining the values of the other parity bits p_1, p_2, etc. The resulting code group enables single-error correction plus double-error detection.

To interpret a received code group, three cases must be considered. As before, the binary check number $c_k^* \cdots c_2^* c_1^*$ is calculated as well as the overall parity of the received code group. Again, the overall parity bit position is not used in determining the values of the other parity bits p_i. If $c_k^* \cdots c_2^* c_1^* = 0 \cdots 00$ and the recalculation of the overall parity is correct, then no single or double errors have occurred in the transmission of the code group. If the recalculation of the overall parity is incorrect, then a single error has occurred and the bit position of the error is indicated by the binary check number $c_k^* \cdots c_2^* c_1^*$ where a binary check number of $c_k^* \cdots c_2^* c_1^* = 0 \cdots 00$ indicates that it is the overall parity bit that is in error. Hence, single-error correction is achieved. Finally, if $c_k^* \cdots c_2^* c_1^*$ is other than $0 \cdots 00$ and the recalculation of the overall parity is correct, then two errors have occurred. In this case, double-error detection is achieved. However, no correction is possible.

2.12.3 Check Sum Digits for Error Correction

Another approach to achieving error correction is through the use of check sum digits. An example of this approach is used in the U.S. Postal Service bar code. It was noted in Sec. 2.10 that an additional digit was appended to the encoded ZIP code in Fig. 2.3. This additional digit provides for single-error correction. In this case, the check sum digit is a single digit which when added to the sum of the digits in the ZIP code results in a total sum that is a multiple of 10. Mathematically, this is written as

$$(\text{ZIP digit sum} + \text{check sum digit})_{\text{mod } 10} = 0 \qquad (2.13)$$

For the example in Fig. 2.3, the sum of the seven ZIP digits is 26. Therefore, the check sum digit that is appended to the bar code is 4 since this digit increases the sum to the next multiple of 10. The reason mod 10 is used in this calculation is that there are 10 code groups in the bar code (or, equivalently, the 2-out-of-5 code).

To understand how single-error correction is obtained, again consider Fig. 2.3. Upon scanning the bar code, if the condition of three short bars and two tall bars is not satisfied for any block of five bars starting after the frame bar, then it is known that a particular digit is in error, i.e., single-error detection. The value of the erroneous digit is determined by summing the correct digits and applying Eq. (2.13). For example, assume the fifth digit read, i.e., digit 3, in the bar code of Fig. 2.3 is detected as being erroneous. Then, it is seen that the sum of the digits in the bar code is

$$1 + 4 + 2 + 6 + e + 1 + 0 + 4 + 5 + 4 = 27 + e$$

where e denotes the erroneous digit. Since Eq. (2.13) must be satisfied, i.e.,

$$(27 + e)_{\text{mod } 10} = 0$$

it immediately follows that the erroneous digit $e = 3$. Although the 2-out-of-5 code allows the detection of more than one error digit in the bar code, correction is possible only if a single digit in the bar code is in error.

CHAPTER 2 PROBLEMS

2.1 Continue Table 2.2 by listing the next 19 integers in each of the stated number systems.

2.2 Construct a table for the first 32 integers in the quaternary, quinary, and duodecimal number systems, along with their decimal equivalents.

2.3 Perform the following additions in the binary number system.

a. 1101 + 1001 b. 1001 + 111
c. 1100.01 + 101.11 d. 11.011 + 10.111
e. 111.01 + 11.1 f. 0.111 + 0.1011

2.4 Perform the following subtractions in the binary number system.

a. 1101 − 110 b. 11001.1 − 1011
c. 1001 − 11.01 d. 101.01 − 10.1
e. 100.1101 − 11.101 f. 1011 − 10.11

2.5 Perform the following multiplications in the binary number system.

a. 10111 × 110 b. 11011 × 1011
c. 1010 × 1.01 d. 101.1 × 11.01

2.6 Perform the following divisions in the binary number system.

a. $11001 \div 1010$ b. $10000101111 \div 10101$

c. $100111.11 \div 110$ d. $111101.111 \div 101.1$

2.7 Perform the following arithmetic operations in the ternary number system.

a. $2012 + 1102.1$ b. $220.12 + 121.2$

c. $20102 - 12121$ d. $12002.12 - 2121.2$

e. 120.21×122 f. 12202×21.2

g. $221200.1 \div 1012$ h. $11111.212 \div 212.1$

2.8 Construct addition, subtraction, and multiplication tables for the following number systems.

a. Quaternary b. Octal c. Hexadecimal

2.9 Perform the following additions and subtractions in the indicated number systems.

a. $31213_{(4)} + 23102_{(4)}$ b. $130012_{(4)} - 33321_{(4)}$

c. $466735_{(8)} + 375627_{(8)}$ d. $700605_{(8)} - 356742_{(8)}$

e. $8C9F65_{(16)} + 374B27_{(16)}$ f. $D62B053_{(16)} - 47E3C89_{(16)}$

2.10 Using the polynomial method of number conversion, determine the equivalent decimal number for each of the following:

a. $101101.1_{(2)}$ b. $110111.101_{(2)}$

c. $2110_{(3)}$ d. $12021.1_{(3)}$

e. $362_{(8)}$ f. $1475.2_{(8)}$

g. $2C3_{(16)}$ h. $AD.E_{(16)}$

2.11 Using the polynomial method of number conversion, determine the equivalent binary number for each of the following:

a. $42_{(10)}$ b. $78.5_{(10)}$

c. $201_{(3)}$ d. $21.2_{(3)}$

e. $204_{(8)}$ f. $56.3_{(8)}$

2.12 Using the polynomial method of number conversion, determine the equivalent ternary number for each of the following:

a. $11010_{(2)}$ b. $73.2_{(8)}$

c. $75_{(10)}$ d. $3D_{(16)}$

2.13 Determine the base r of a number system such that $225_{(r)} \equiv 89_{(10)}$.

2.14 Using the iterative method of number conversion, convert the decimal numbers 163.75 and 202.9 into

a. Binary b. Ternary

c. Octal d. Hexadecimal

(Note: For the fraction part, form a sufficient number of digits so that an exact equivalence or a repeating sequence is obtained.)

2.15 Using the iterative method of number conversion, convert the binary number 11100010.1101 into

a. Ternary
b. Octal
c. Decimal
d. Hexadecimal

(Note: For the fraction part, form a sufficient number of digits so that an exact equivalence or a repeating sequence is obtained.)

2.16 Using the iterative method of number conversion, convert the ternary number 10112.1 into

a. Binary
b. Octal
c. Decimal
d. Hexadecimal

(Note: For the fraction part, form a sufficient number of digits so that an exact equivalence or a repeating sequence is obtained.)

2.17 Convert each of the following binary numbers into its equivalent in the octal and hexadecimal number systems.

a. 111111001.00111101
b. 1010001011.1
c. 10111100010.01001011
d. 11100100110.101

2.18 Convert each of the following octal numbers into its equivalent in the binary number system.

a. 37.5
b. 45.1
c. 61.3
d. 724.06

2.19 Convert each of the following hexadecimal numbers into its equivalent in the binary number system.

a. 1C.3
b. F2.C
c. 450.B
d. 8EA.59

2.20 Using the ideas of Sec. 2.6, determine an algorithm to convert numbers between base 3 and base 9. Illustrate your algorithm by converting $21021.112_{(3)}$ into base 9.

2.21 a. Show that the r's-complement of the r's-complement of a number is the number itself.

b. Repeat for the $(r - 1)$'s-complement.

2.22 Form the 1's-complement and 2's-complement for each of the following binary numbers. In each case express the complement with the same number of integer and fraction digits as the original number.

a. 10111011
b. 101110100
c. 101100
d. 0110101
e. 010.11
f. 11011.100
g. 100101.101
h. 1010110.110

2.23 Form the 9's-complement and 10's-complement for each of the following decimal numbers. In each case express the complement with the same number of integer and fraction digits as the original number.

a. 285302 b. 39040
c. 059637 d. 610500
e. 7142.89 f. 5263.4580
g. 0283.609 h. 134.5620

2.24 Form the r's-complement and $(r - 1)$'s-complement for each of the following numbers. In each case express the complement with the same number of integer and fraction digits as the original number.

a. $0120.21_{(3)}$ b. $101.120_{(3)}$
c. $241.03_{(5)}$ d. $031.240_{(5)}$
e. $407.270_{(8)}$ f. $0156.0037_{(8)}$
g. $83D.9F_{(16)}$ h. $0070C.B6E_{(16)}$

2.25 Perform the following unsigned binary subtractions by the addition of the 1's-complement representation of the subtrahend. Repeat using the 2's-complement representation of the subtrahend. (Note: Recall that when dealing with complement representations, the two operands must have the same number of digits.)

a. 1101101 − 110110 b. 10100 − 110000
c. 10010.00111 − 101.11 d. 10110.01 − 1011.1101
e. 1101.1011 − 10110.11 f. 101.1001 − 11010.010011

2.26 Perform the following binary subtractions by expressing the quantities involved as signed numbers and using the 1's-complement representation of the subtrahend. Repeat using the 2's-complement representation of the subtrahend. (Note: Recall that when dealing with complement representations, the two operands must have the same number of digits.)

a. 10110 − 1101 b. 10111 − 110100
c. 110.1001 − 11.01 d. 10101.1 − 10101.1
e. 101.11 − 10.01011 f. 10111.10101 − 111010.11

2.27 Perform the following unsigned decimal subtractions by the addition of the 9's-complement representation of the subtrahend. Repeat using the 10's-complement representation of the subtrahend. (Note: Recall that when dealing with complement representations, the two operands must have the same number of digits.)

a. 7842 − 3791 b. 265 − 894
c. 508.3 − 94.7 d. 73.68 − 538.9
e. 427.08 − 89.3 f. 804.2 − 3621.47

2.28 Perform the following decimal subtractions by expressing the quantities involved as signed numbers and using the 9's-complement representation of the subtrahend. Repeat using the 10's-complement representation of the subtrahend. (Note: Recall that when dealing with complement representations, the two operands must have the same number of digits.)

a. 546 − 232 b. 384 − 726

c. 326.4 − 87.2 d. 76.23 − 209.4

e. 406.9 − 406.9 f. 63.4 − 240.36

2.29 Consider the signed binary numbers $A = 0_s1000110$ and $B = 1_s1010011$ where B is in 2's-complement form. Perform the operations

a. $A + B$ b. $A - B$

c. $B - A$ d. $-A - B$

by taking the signed 2's-complement of a signed operand when necessary and doing signed addition.

2.30 Consider the signed decimal numbers $A = 0_s601.7$ and $B = 1_s754.2$ where B is in 10's-complement form. Perform the operations

a. $A + B$ b. $A - B$

c. $B - A$ d. $-A - B$

by taking the signed 10's-complement of a signed operand when necessary and doing signed addition.

2.31 Consider the signed binary numbers $A = 0_s1010110$ and $B = 1_s1101100$ where B is in 1's-complement form. Perform the operations

a. $A + B$ b. $A - B$

c. $B - A$ d. $-A - B$

by taking the signed 1's-complement of a signed operand when necessary and doing signed addition.

2.32 Consider the signed decimal numbers $A = 0_s418.5$ and $B = 1_s693.0$ where B is in 9's-complement form. Perform the operations

a. $A + B$ b. $A - B$

c. $B - A$ d. $-A - B$

by taking the signed 9's-complement of a signed operand when necessary and doing signed addition.

2.33 Give the coded representation of the decimal number 853 in each of the following BCD coding schemes.

a. 8421 code b. $753\bar{6}$ code c. Excess-3 code

d. Biquinary code e. 2-out-of-5 code

2.34 Consider the sequence of digits 10001001010110000011. Determine the number being represented assuming each of the following BCD coding schemes.

a. 8421 code b. Excess-3 code c. 2-out-of-5 code

2.35 Encode each of the decimal digits 0 to 9 with 4 bits using the following weighted BCD codes. State which of these codes are self-complementing.

a. $763\bar{5}$ code b. $832\bar{4}$ code
c. $83\bar{4}\bar{2}$ code d. $86\bar{4}\bar{1}$ code

2.36 Prove that for a weighted BCD code having all positive weights, one of the weights must be 1, another must be either 1 or 2, and the sum of the weights must be greater than or equal to 9.

2.37 Prove that in a 4-bit weighted BCD code with all positive weights, at most one weight can exceed 4.

2.38 Prove that in a self-complementing BCD code, which can have both positive and negative weights, the algebraic sum of all the weights must be 9.

2.39 Prove that in a 4-bit weighted BCD code, at most two of the weights can be negative.

2.40 Give the coded representation for each of the following character strings using the 7-bit ASCII code.

a. 960 b. X + Y c. Code

2.41 Assume an 8th bit, b_7, serving as an even-parity bit is added to the 7-bit ASCII code. Give the coded representation for each of the following character strings as hexadecimal numbers.

a. 283 b. Z = 1 c. Bits

2.42 Construct a Hamming code to be used in conjunction with the following BCD codes.

a. 2421 code b. 2-out-of-5 code

2.43 Write the Hamming code groups for each of the following 8 bits of information.

a. 11100011 b. 01011000 c. 10010101

2.44 Assume the following 7-bit Hamming code groups, consisting of 4 information bits and 3 parity bits, are received in which at most a single error has occurred. Determine the transmitted 7-bit Hamming code groups.

a. 0011000 b. 1111000 c. 1101100

2.45 a. Construct a Hamming code group for the information bits 100101 that enables single-error correction plus double-error detection where the most significant bit position of the code group is for the overall even-parity bit.

b. Assume that errors occur in bit positions 2 and 9 of the above code group. Show how the double error is detected.

2.46 A certain code consists only of the following code groups:

00110, 01011, 10001, 11100

What error-detecting and error-correcting properties does this code have?

CHAPTER 3

Boolean Algebra and Combinational Networks

In 1854, George Boole (1815–1864), an English mathematician, wrote his now classic book *An Investigation of the Laws of Thought* in which he proposed an algebra for symbolically representing problems in logic so that they may be analyzed mathematically. It was Boole's intention to provide a means for systematically establishing the validity of complex logic statements involving propositions which are only true or false. The foundation laid by Boole has resulted in the calculus of propositions and the algebra of classes. Today, the mathematical systems founded upon the work of Boole are called *Boolean algebras* in his honor.

The application of a Boolean algebra to certain engineering problems was introduced in 1938 by Claude E. Shannon, then at the Massachusetts Institute of Technology. Shannon showed how a Boolean algebra could be applied to the design of relay networks in telephone systems. Upon the advent of digital computers, it was immediately recognized that this algebra had application to the design of any logic-type system consisting of elements with two-valued characteristics. The study of Boolean algebra as applied to logic design is also known as *switching circuit theory.*

Boolean algebra serves as a convenient way for describing the terminal properties of networks that appear in digital systems. There is a one-to-one correspondence between the algebraic expressions and their network realizations. Since Boolean algebraic expressions are subject to manipulations and simplification, it follows that the various ways of writing the expressions provide descriptions for different networks that can be constructed to achieve the same terminal behavior. By defining measures of equation complexity, it is possible to obtain economical and reliable networks using an algebraic approach. Thus, Boolean algebra becomes an effective tool for the logic design of digital systems.

The logic networks described by a Boolean algebra are divided into two general categories: *combinational networks* and *sequential networks.* Combinational networks are characterized by the fact that the outputs at any instant are only a function of the inputs at that instant. On the other hand, the outputs at any instant from sequential networks are not only a function of the current inputs but, in addition, depend upon the past history of inputs. Thus, sequential networks have a memory property, and the order in which the inputs are applied is significant. Both types of logic networks are found in digital systems.

The principles of Boolean algebra are presented in this chapter. It is shown how expressions written in this algebra are manipulated and simplified. In addition, it is shown how the algebra is applied to the analysis and design of combinational logic networks. The analysis and design of sequential logic networks is studied in later chapters. ■

3.1 DEFINITION OF A BOOLEAN ALGEBRA

A mathematical system is formulated by defining a set of elements, a set of operations, and a set of postulates. Of course the postulates are not arbitrarily defined but must be consistent so that noncontradictory conclusions, called *theorems*, are obtained. At this time a particular mathematical system known as a Boolean algebra is introduced. The postulates in the following definition are based on the work of E. V. Huntington and are only one of several sets of consistent postulates that are used to describe a Boolean algebra.

Definition: A mathematical system consisting of a set of elements B, two binary operations $(+)$ and $(\cdot)$, an equality sign $(=)$ to indicate equivalence of expressions (i.e., the expression on one side of the equality sign can be substituted for the expression on the other side), and parentheses to indicate the ordering of the operations is called a *Boolean algebra* if and only if the following postulates hold:

P1. The operations $(+)$ and $(\cdot)$ are closed; i.e., for all $x, y \in B$
   (a) $x + y \in B$
   (b) $x \cdot y \in B$

P2. There exist identity elements in B, denoted by 0 and 1, relative to the operations $(+)$ and $(\cdot)$, respectively; i.e., for every $x \in B$
   (a) $0 + x = x + 0 = x$
   (b) $1 \cdot x = x \cdot 1 = x$

P3. The operations $(+)$ and $(\cdot)$ are commutative; i.e., for all $x, y \in B$
   (a) $x + y = y + x$
   (b) $x \cdot y = y \cdot x$

P4. Each operation $(+)$ and $(\cdot)$ is distributive over the other; i.e., for all $x, y, z \in B$
   (a) $x + (y \cdot z) = (x + y) \cdot (x + z)$
   (b) $x \cdot (y + z) = (x \cdot y) + (x \cdot z)$

P5. For every element x in B there exists an element $\overline{x}$ in B, called the *complement* of x, such that
   (a) $x + \overline{x} = 1$
   (b) $x \cdot \overline{x} = 0$

P6. There exist at least two elements $x, y \in B$ such that $x \neq y$.

Some important observations should be made about the above definition. The actual elements in the set B (other than 0 and 1) are not specified and the operations $(+)$ and $(\cdot)$ are not defined. Thus, any mathematical system over a set B having two operations is a Boolean algebra if these six postulates are satisfied. Hence, in actuality, an entire class of algebras is being defined.

The elements of an algebra are called its *constants*. For a Boolean algebra the constants are the elements in the set B of which only two are required: 0 and 1. It is important that the reader realizes that these two symbols, in general, are nonnumerical and should not be confused with the binary symbols 0 and 1 studied in the previous chapter.

A symbol which represents an arbitrary element of an algebra is called a *variable*. Since the postulates of a Boolean algebra make reference to arbitrary elements in the set B, the symbols x, y, and z in the above definition are considered variables of the algebra. Furthermore, the variables in the above postulates and the theorems to follow can represent an entire expression as well as a single element. This follows from the fact that the operations of a Boolean algebra are defined to be closed by Postulate P1 and hence an expression, when evaluated, always represents an element of the algebra.

The symbols $(+)$ and $(\cdot)$ in the definition of a Boolean algebra are used to denote two arbitrary operations with properties satisfying the postulates. These symbols are commonly used in equations describing logic networks and should not be confused with the corresponding symbols in conventional arithmetic.

3.1.1 Principle of Duality

Having defined a Boolean algebra, additional properties of the mathematical system are developed from its postulates. These properties are stated as theorems in the next section. However, to reduce the amount of work in proving these theorems, advantage is taken of the symmetry incorporated in the postulates.

With the exception of Postulate P6, each postulate consists of two expressions such that one expression is transformed into the other by interchanging the operations $(+)$ and $(\cdot)$ as well as the identity elements 0 and 1. The expressions appearing in each of these postulates are called the *dual* of each other. A theorem or algebraic identity in a Boolean algebra is proved by applying a sequence of Boolean algebra postulates. If the dual postulates are applied in exactly the same sequence of steps, then a parallel argument is established that leads to the dual of the original theorem or algebraic identity. Consequently, every theorem or algebraic identity deducible from the postulates of a Boolean algebra is transformed into a second valid theorem or algebraic identity if the operations $(+)$ and $(\cdot)$ and the identity elements 0 and 1 are interchanged throughout. This is known as the *principle of duality*.

3.2 BOOLEAN ALGEBRA THEOREMS

From the definition of a Boolean algebra, a number of theorems can be proved. In this section the most important theorems are presented. The proofs of these theorems are included not only to establish their validity but also to illustrate how Boolean identities are manipulated.

Before proceeding with the basic Boolean algebra theorems, however, let us introduce two notational conveniences. This will simplify the writing of expressions in the algebra. First, the product $x \cdot y$ usually is written as the juxtaposition of x and y, that is, simply xy. This creates no ambiguities as long as variables are designated as single symbols, possibly with subscripts. Second, a hierarchy between the operations $(+)$ and $(\cdot)$ is assumed such that the operation $(\cdot)$ always takes precedence over the operation $(+)$. This allows less frequent use of parentheses since $xy + xz$ is understood to mean $(x \cdot y) + (x \cdot z)$. The reader should note that these same two notational conveniences are used in the case of conventional algebra and should offer no difficulty in understanding the expressions to which they are applied.

Theorem 3.1

The element $\bar{x}$ in Postulate P5 of a Boolean algebra is uniquely determined by x.

Proof

Suppose that for a given element x there are two elements $\bar{x}_1$ and $\bar{x}_2$ satisfying Postulate P5. Then $x + \bar{x}_1 = 1$, $x \cdot \bar{x}_1 = 0$, $x + \bar{x}_2 = 1$, and $x \cdot \bar{x}_2 = 0$.

$$
\begin{aligned}
\bar{x}_1 &= \bar{x}_1 \cdot 1 && \text{by P2}(b)\\
&= \bar{x}_1\,(x + \bar{x}_2) && \text{by substitution}\\
&= \bar{x}_1 x + \bar{x}_1\bar{x}_2 && \text{by P4}(b)\\
&= x\bar{x}_1 + \bar{x}_1\bar{x}_2 && \text{by P3}(b)\\
&= 0 + \bar{x}_1\bar{x}_2 && \text{by substitution}\\
&= x\bar{x}_2 + \bar{x}_1\bar{x}_2 && \text{by substitution}\\
&= \bar{x}_2 x + \bar{x}_2\bar{x}_1 && \text{by P3}(b)\\
&= \bar{x}_2\,(x + \bar{x}_1) && \text{by P4}(b)\\
&= \bar{x}_2 \cdot 1 && \text{by substitution}\\
&= \bar{x}_2 && \text{by P2}(b)
\end{aligned}
$$

Thus, any two elements that are the complement of the element x are equal. This implies that $\bar{x}$ is uniquely determined by x. ■*

---

*The symbol ■ is used to denote the end of a proof.

Since $\bar{x}$ is uniquely determined by x, the overbar symbol ($\bar{\ }$) is regarded as a *unary operation* that assigns to an element x in the set B the element $\bar{x}$ also in the set B.

Theorem 3.2

For each element x in a Boolean algebra

$$(a)\ \ x + 1 = 1$$

$$(b)\ \ x \cdot 0 = 0$$

Proof
First consider part (*a*) of the theorem.

$$\begin{aligned} x + 1 &= 1 \cdot (x + 1) && \text{by P2}(b) \\ &= (x + \overline{x})(x + 1) && \text{by P5}(a) \\ &= x + (\overline{x} \cdot 1) && \text{by P4}(a) \\ &= x + \overline{x} && \text{by P2}(b) \\ &= 1 && \text{by P5}(a) \end{aligned}$$

Part (*b*) of the theorem follows directly from the principle of duality. That is, if in the expression of part (*a*) (+) is replaced by (·) and 1 by 0, then the expression of part (*b*) results. However, let us prove part (*b*) in order that the steps of the proof can be compared with those of the first part.

$$\begin{aligned} x \cdot 0 &= 0 + (x \cdot 0) && \text{by P2}(a) \\ &= (x \cdot \overline{x}) + (x \cdot 0) && \text{by P5}(b) \\ &= x \cdot (\overline{x} + 0) && \text{by P4}(b) \\ &= x \cdot \overline{x} && \text{by P2}(a) \\ &= 0 && \text{by P5}(b) \end{aligned}$$

It should be noted that at each step in the above proof, the dual of the postulate in the proof of part (*a*) is applied. ■

As indicated in Sec. 3.1, the letter symbols in the Boolean algebra postulates and theorems can denote entire expressions as well as single elements. Thus, the first part of Theorem 3.2 implies that if the constant 1 is summed with any Boolean element or expression, then the result is equally well described by simply the constant 1. A dual statement applies as a consequence of the second part of this theorem.

Theorem 3.3
Each of the identity elements in a Boolean algebra is the complement of the other; i.e.,

$$(a)\ \overline{0} = 1$$
$$(b)\ \overline{1} = 0$$

Proof
By Theorem 3.1 there exists for the identity element 0 a unique element $\overline{0}$ in a Boolean algebra. In Postulate P2(*a*) let the element x be $\overline{0}$. Then $0 + \overline{0} = \overline{0}$. On the other hand, if x is 0 in Postulate P5(*a*), and hence $\overline{x} = \overline{0}$, then $0 + \overline{0} = 1$. Since it is always possible to equate something to itself, in particular, $0 + \overline{0} = 0 + \overline{0}$, upon substitution it follows that $\overline{0} = 1$. By duality it follows that $\overline{1} = 0$. ■

Theorem 3.4

The idempotent law. For each element x in a Boolean algebra

$$(a)\ \ x + x = x$$
$$(b)\ \ xx = x$$

Proof

$$\begin{aligned} x + x &= (x + x) \cdot 1 && \text{by P2}(b) \\ &= (x + x)(x + \bar{x}) && \text{by P5}(a) \\ &= x + x\bar{x} && \text{by P4}(a) \\ &= x + 0 && \text{by P5}(b) \\ &= x && \text{by P2}(a) \end{aligned}$$

The proof that $xx = x$ is carried out in a manner similar to the above by using the dual of each postulate at every step in the proof as was done for Theorem. 3.2. However, it also follows by the duality principle. ■

Theorem 3.5

The involution law. For every x in a Boolean algebra

$$\overline{(\bar{x})} = x$$

Proof

Let $\bar{x}$ be the complement of x and $\overline{(\bar{x})}$ be the complement of $\bar{x}$. Then, by Postulate P5, $x + \bar{x} = 1$, $x\bar{x} = 0$, $\bar{x} + \overline{(\bar{x})} = 1$, and $\bar{x}\overline{(\bar{x})} = 0$.

$$\begin{aligned} \overline{(\bar{x})} &= \overline{(\bar{x})} + 0 && \text{by P2}(a) \\ &= \overline{(\bar{x})} + x\bar{x} && \text{by substitution} \\ &= [\overline{(\bar{x})} + x]\,[\overline{(\bar{x})} + \bar{x}] && \text{by P4}(a) \\ &= [x + \overline{(\bar{x})}]\,[\bar{x} + \overline{(\bar{x})}] && \text{by P3}(a) \\ &= [x + \overline{(\bar{x})}] \cdot 1 && \text{by substitution} \\ &= [x + \overline{(\bar{x})}](x + \bar{x}) && \text{by substitution} \\ &= x + \overline{(\bar{x})}\bar{x} && \text{by P4}(a) \\ &= x + \bar{x}\overline{(\bar{x})} && \text{by P3}(b) \\ &= x + 0 && \text{by substitution} \\ &= x && \text{by P2}(a)\ ■ \end{aligned}$$

Theorem 3.6

The absorption law. For each pair of elements x and y in a Boolean algebra

$$(a)\ \ x + xy = x$$
$$(b)\ \ x(x + y) = x$$

Proof

$$
\begin{aligned}
x + xy &= x \cdot 1 + xy && \text{by P2}(b)\\
&= x(1 + y) && \text{by P4}(b)\\
&= x(y + 1) && \text{by P3}(a)\\
&= x \cdot 1 && \text{by Theorem 3.2}(a)\\
&= x && \text{by P2}(b)
\end{aligned}
$$

Part *(b)* follows from the duality principle. ■

Theorem 3.7

For each pair of elements x and y in a Boolean algebra

$$(a)\quad x + \bar{x}y = x + y$$

$$(b)\quad x(\bar{x} + y) = xy$$

Proof

$$
\begin{aligned}
x + \bar{x}y &= (x + \bar{x})(x + y) && \text{by P4}(a)\\
&= 1 \cdot (x + y) && \text{by P5}(a)\\
&= x + y && \text{by P2}(b)
\end{aligned}
$$

Part *(b)* follows from the duality principle. ■

Theorem 3.8

In every Boolean algebra, each of the operations $(+)$ and $(\cdot)$ is associative. That is, for every x, y, and z in a Boolean algebra

$$(a)\quad x + (y + z) = (x + y) + z$$

$$(b)\quad x(yz) = (xy)z$$

Proof

Let $A = x + (y + z)$ and $B = (x + y) + z$. It must now be shown that $A = B$. To begin with,

$$
\begin{aligned}
xA &= xA\\
&= x[x + (y + z)] && \text{by substitution}\\
&= x && \text{by Theorem 3.6}(b)
\end{aligned}
$$

and

$$
\begin{aligned}
xB &= xB\\
&= x[(x + y) + z] && \text{by substitution}\\
&= x(x + y) + xz && \text{by P4}(b)\\
&= x + xz && \text{by Theorem 3.6}(b)\\
&= x && \text{by Theorem 3.6}(a)
\end{aligned}
$$

Therefore, $xA = xB = x$. On the other hand,

$$
\begin{aligned}
\bar{x}A &= \bar{x}A \\
&= \bar{x}[x + (y + z)] && \text{by substitution} \\
&= \bar{x}x + \bar{x}(y + z) && \text{by P4}(b) \\
&= x\bar{x} + \bar{x}(y + z) && \text{by P3}(b) \\
&= 0 + \bar{x}(y + z) && \text{by P5}(b) \\
&= \bar{x}(y + z) && \text{by P2}(a)
\end{aligned}
$$

and

$$
\begin{aligned}
\bar{x}B &= \bar{x}B \\
&= \bar{x}[(x + y) + z] && \text{by substitution} \\
&= \bar{x}(x + y) + \bar{x}z && \text{by P4}(b) \\
&= (\bar{x}x + \bar{x}y) + \bar{x}z && \text{by P4}(b) \\
&= (x\bar{x} + \bar{x}y) + \bar{x}z && \text{by P3}(b) \\
&= (0 + \bar{x}y) + \bar{x}z && \text{by P5}(b) \\
&= \bar{x}y + \bar{x}z && \text{by P2}(a) \\
&= \bar{x}(y + z) && \text{by P4}(b)
\end{aligned}
$$

Therefore, $\bar{x}A = \bar{x}B = \bar{x}(y + z)$.

To complete the proof,

$$
\begin{aligned}
xA + \bar{x}A &= xA + \bar{x}A \\
xA + \bar{x}A &= xB + \bar{x}B && \text{by substituting for } xA \text{ and } \bar{x}A \\
Ax + A\bar{x} &= Bx + B\bar{x} && \text{by P3}(b) \\
A(x + \bar{x}) &= B(x + \bar{x}) && \text{by P4}(b) \\
A \cdot 1 &= B \cdot 1 && \text{by P5}(a) \\
A &= B && \text{by P2}(b)
\end{aligned}
$$

In other words, $x + (y + z) = (x + y) + z$.

Part (b) of the theorem follows from the principle of duality. ■

As a result of Theorem 3.8, it is not necessary to write $x(yz)$ and $(xy)z$; rather, xyz is sufficient. The same is true for $x + (y + z)$ and $(x + y) + z$, which simply can be written as $x + y + z$. It is also possible to generalize the above theorem to handle any number of elements. That is, for any n elements of a Boolean algebra, the sum and product of the n elements is independent of the order in which they are taken.

Theorem 3.9

DeMorgan's law. For each pair of elements x and y in a Boolean algebra

$$(a)\quad \overline{(x + y)} = \bar{x}\,\bar{y}$$
$$(b)\quad \overline{(xy)} = \bar{x} + \bar{y}$$

Proof

By Theorem 3.1 and Postulate P5, for every x in a Boolean algebra there is a unique $\overline{x}$ such that $x + \overline{x} = 1$ and $x\overline{x} = 0$. Thus, to prove part *(a)* of the theorem, it is sufficient to show that $\overline{x}\,\overline{y}$ is the complement of $x + y$. This is achieved by showing that $(x + y) + (\overline{x}\,\overline{y}) = 1$ and $(x + y)(\overline{x}\,\overline{y}) = 0$.

$$\begin{aligned}
(x + y) + \overline{x}\,\overline{y} &= [(x + y) + \overline{x}]\,[(x + y) + \overline{y}] && \text{by P4}(a)\\
&= [(y + x) + \overline{x}]\,[(x + y) + \overline{y}] && \text{by P3}(a)\\
&= [y + (x + \overline{x})]\,[x + (y + \overline{y})] && \text{by Theorem 3.8}(a)\\
&= (y + 1)(x + 1) && \text{by P5}(a)\\
&= 1 \cdot 1 && \text{by Theorem 3.2}(a)\\
&= 1 && \text{by Theorem 3.4}(b)
\end{aligned}$$

Also,

$$\begin{aligned}
(x + y)(\overline{x}\,\overline{y}) &= (\overline{x}\,\overline{y})(x + y) && \text{by P3}(b)\\
&= (\overline{x}\,\overline{y})x + (\overline{x}\,\overline{y})y && \text{by P4}(b)\\
&= (\overline{y}\,\overline{x})x + (\overline{x}\,\overline{y})y && \text{by P3}(b)\\
&= \overline{y}(\overline{x}x) + \overline{x}(\overline{y}y) && \text{by Theorem 3.8}(b)\\
&= \overline{y}(x\overline{x}) + \overline{x}(y\overline{y}) && \text{by P3}(b)\\
&= \overline{y} \cdot 0 + \overline{x} \cdot 0 && \text{by P5}(b)\\
&= 0 + 0 && \text{by Theorem 3.2}(b)\\
&= 0 && \text{by Theorem 3.4}(a)
\end{aligned}$$

Part *(b)* of the theorem follows from the principle of duality. ■

The generalization of DeMorgan's law is stated as: For the set of elements $\{w, x, \ldots, y, z\}$ in a Boolean algebra,

$$(a)\quad \overline{(w + x + \cdots + y + z)} = \overline{w}\,\overline{x} \cdots \overline{y}\,\overline{z}$$

$$(b)\quad \overline{(wx \cdots yz)} = \overline{w} + \overline{x} + \cdots + \overline{y} + \overline{z}$$

Generalized statements were made regarding the associative and DeMorgan's laws. It is also possible to make generalized statements about the commutative and distributive laws which appear as Postulates P3 and P4. In particular, in a Boolean algebra, the sum or product of n elements can be rearranged in any order. The generalized form of the distributive law is written as

$$(a)\quad w + xy \cdots z = (w + x)(w + y) \cdots (w + z)$$

$$(b)\quad w(x + y + \cdots + z) = wx + wy + \cdots + wz$$

As in the case of the postulates, the symbols $x, y, z, \cdots$ appearing in the theorems of this section are considered variables. Consequently, the systematic substitution of complemented variables or algebraic expressions for these variables does not change the meaning of the theorems. For example, if the complemented variable $\overline{x}$

Table 3.1. Summary of the basic Boolean identities

(a)	(b)	Theorem or postulate
$\overline{0} = 1$	$\overline{1} = 0$	T3
$X + 0 = X$	$X \cdot 1 = X$	P2
$X + 1 = 1$	$X \cdot 0 = 0$	T2
$X + X = X$	$XX = X$	T4, idempotent law
$X + \overline{X} = 1$	$X\overline{X} = 0$	P5
$\overline{(\overline{X})} = X$		T5, involution law
$X + Y = Y + X$	$XY = YX$	P3, commutative law
$X + XY = X$	$X(X + Y) = X$	T6, absorption law
$X + \overline{X}Y = X + Y$	$X(\overline{X} + Y) = XY$	T7
$\overline{(X + Y)} = \overline{X}\,\overline{Y}$	$\overline{(XY)} = \overline{X} + \overline{Y}$	T9, DeMorgan's law
$X + YZ = (X + Y)(X + Z)$	$X(Y + Z) = XY + XZ$	P4, distributive law
$X + (Y + Z) = (X + Y) + Z$	$X(YZ) = (XY)Z$	T8, associative law
$= X + Y + Z$	$= XYZ$	

is substituted for the variable x, then Theorem 3.6(a) becomes $\overline{x} + \overline{x}y = \overline{x}$, Theorem 3.7($a$) becomes $\overline{x} + xy = \overline{x} + y$, and Theorem 3.9($a$) becomes $\overline{(\overline{x} + y)} = x\overline{y}$. In the last two examples, use was made of the involution law (Theorem 3.5).

The postulates and basic theorems of a Boolean algebra are very useful in the study of digital principles. Hence, they are summarized in Table 3.1 for easy reference. Uppercase letters are used in this table to emphasize the fact that these variables can represent expressions as well as single variables.

In proving the theorems of this section, every step was shown, and the justification for that step was given. Whenever manipulations are performed on expressions of a Boolean algebra in the remainder of this book, many of the obvious steps are omitted. Also, the postulate or theorem applied at each step of the manipulation no longer is stated unless special attention is to be drawn to which postulate or theorem is being used.

3.3 A TWO-VALUED BOOLEAN ALGEBRA

Up to this point a Boolean algebra has been considered as a general mathematical system. Two operations were postulated for this mathematical system. However, even though the actual operations were not defined, identities were established in the previous section which are true for any Boolean algebra. These identities are a result of the properties of the operations as stated in the postulates. Certainly, this general approach can be continued and additional theorems for any Boolean algebra developed. However, the objective in this chapter is to establish a relationship between a Boolean algebra and logic networks and to show how a Boolean algebra is a useful tool in logic network analysis and design.

The definition of a Boolean algebra actually encompasses an entire class of algebras. Two well-known algebras in this class are the algebra of sets and the propositional calculus. At this time a special two-valued Boolean algebra is established by specifying all the elements in the set B and defining the two operations.

Theorem 3.10

The set $B = \{0,1\}$ where $\overline{0} = 1$ and $\overline{1} = 0$ along with the operations $(+)$, called the *or-operation,* and $(\cdot)$, called the *and-operation,* defined by

$x + y$	$y = 0$	$y = 1$
$x = 0$	0	1
$x = 1$	1	1

$x \cdot y$	$y = 0$	$y = 1$
$x = 0$	0	0
$x = 1$	0	1

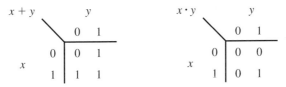

is a Boolean algebra.

Let us now show that the postulates of a Boolean algebra are indeed satisfied under the conditions stated in the theorem. First it is noted that the set B only consists of two elements. The operations $(+)$ and $(\cdot)$ work on pairs of elements in the set B. In general, an operation is said to be closed if for every pair of elements in the set the result of the operation is also in the set. Postulate P1, which requires closure, is satisfied since the entries in the tabular definitions of the operations are all specified and are elements of the set $B = \{0, 1\}$.

Postulate P2 requires the existence of identity elements relative to the two operations. These identity elements are detected by searching for a column and a row in each of the tables defining an operation such that the entries for that column and row are the same as the row and column designators, respectively. In the first table, it is seen that for the 0 column, $x + 0 = x$ for all $x \in B$; and for the 0 row, $0 + x = x$. Similarly, in the second table, it is seen that for the 1 column, $x \cdot 1 = x$ for all $x \in B$; and for the 1 row, $1 \cdot x = x$. Thus, 0 is the identity element relative to the or-operation, and 1 is the identity element relative to the and-operation.

The operations $(+)$ and $(\cdot)$ are commutative since the tables which define these operations are symmetrical about the diagonal from the upper left to lower right corners. Hence, Postulate P3 is satisfied.

To show that Postulate P4 is satisfied, perfect induction is used. Perfect induction is proof by exhaustion in which all possibilities are considered. In this case, by substituting all possible combinations of the elements 0 and 1 into Postulate P4 and applying the definitions of the operations, it becomes a simple matter to determine whether both sides of the equality sign yield identical results for each combination. In Postulate P4 the symbols x, y, and z can each represent the elements 0 and 1. Under this condition there are eight possible combinations of 0 and 1 for x, y, and z. Table 3.2 has one row for each of these eight combinations. In the fourth column of the table, $x + yz$ is evaluated for each combination; while in the fifth column, $(x + y)(x + z)$ is evaluated. For example, in the $x = y = z = 0$ row, $x + yz$ becomes $0 + 0 \cdot 0 = 0 + 0 = 0$ and $(x + y)(x + z)$ becomes $(0 + 0) \cdot (0 + 0) = 0 \cdot 0 = 0$. In a like manner, the entries

Table 3.2 Verifying Postulate P4 by perfect induction for a two-valued Boolean algebra

x	y	z	$x + yz$	$(x + y)(x + z)$	$x(y + z)$	$xy + xz$
0	0	0	0	0	0	0
0	0	1	0	0	0	0
0	1	0	0	0	0	0
0	1	1	1	1	0	0
1	0	0	1	1	0	0
1	0	1	1	1	1	1
1	1	0	1	1	1	1
1	1	1	1	1	1	1

in the fourth and fifth columns of the remaining seven rows are determined. Since these two columns are identical row by row, the identity of Postulate P4(a) is established. Similarly, the sixth and seventh columns of Table 3.2 establish the identity of Postulate P4(b). Thus, each operation is distributive over the other.

The fifth postulate requires there be an $\overline{x}$ for every x such that $x + \overline{x} = 1$ and $x \cdot \overline{x} = 0$. Table 3.3 is constructed using perfect induction, where $\overline{0} = 1$ and $\overline{1} = 0$ as stated in the theorem. Since the $x + \overline{x}$ column has all 1 entries and the $x \cdot \overline{x}$ column has all 0 entries, Postulate P5 is satisfied.

Finally, to satisfy Postulate P6 it is necessary to establish that 0 and 1 are distinct, i.e., $0 \neq 1$. It is immediately seen that in the tables defining the two operations, only 0 is the identity element for the or-operation and only 1 is the identity element for the and-operation. This implies $0 \neq 1$. Since the six postulates of a Boolean algebra are satisfied, the special two-valued algebra specified in Theorem 3.10 is indeed a Boolean algebra.

The two-valued Boolean algebra just developed is also known as the *switching algebra.* In the literature involving the analysis and design of logic networks, it is common to refer to the two-valued Boolean algebra simply as a Boolean algebra without any additional qualification. This convention is adhered to in this text. It should be kept in mind that all the theorems previously established in Sec. 3.2 remain valid for this two-valued Boolean algebra. Frequently, the two constants, 0 and 1, are referred to as *logic-0* and *logic-1.* In this book, the two constants are usually referred to as simply 0 and 1. The more specific references of logic-0 and logic-1 are used for emphasis or when it is necessary to avoid confusion with the binary arithmetic symbols 0 and 1.

Table 3.3 Verifying Postulate P5 by perfect induction for a two-valued Boolean algebra

x	$\overline{x}$	$x + \overline{x}$	$x \cdot \overline{x}$
0	1	1	0
1	0	1	0

In the literature, other symbols are occasionally used for the two operations of a Boolean algebra. In particular, the symbols $\cup$ and $\vee$ are used to designate the or-operation and $\cap$ and $\wedge$ for the and-operation. Finally, the overbar ($\bar{\ }$) is considered a unary operation since it uniquely determines the value of $\bar{x}$ for any x. This operation is called the *not-operation.* As previously mentioned, $\bar{x}$ is the complement of x. It is also referred to as the *negation* of x. The not-operation is also designated in the literature by a prime ($'$), in which case the complement of x is written as x'.

Again it should be mentioned that the words "product" and "sum" are commonly used when referring to the operations of "and" and "or," respectively, owing to the symbols used. However, it should be kept in mind that these operations have been defined for a Boolean algebra and must always be interpreted in this context. Even though conventional addition and multiplication occur occasionally in future discussions, there should be no difficulty in determining from context at that time the correct interpretation of the operation.

3.4 BOOLEAN FORMULAS AND FUNCTIONS

Boolean expressions or *formulas* are constructed by connecting the Boolean constants and variables with the Boolean operations. Boolean expressions, in turn, are used to describe *Boolean functions.* For example, if the Boolean expression $(\bar{x} + y)z$ is used to describe the function f, then this is written as

$$f(x,y,z) = (\bar{x} + y)z \qquad \text{or} \qquad f = (\bar{x} + y)z$$

The value of the function f is easily determined for any set of values of x, y, and z by applying the definitions of the and-, or-, and not-operations. For the above, the value of not-x is first or-ed with the value of y to form the value of $\bar{x} + y$. This, in turn, is and-ed with the value of z. Because of the closure property of the Boolean operations, the value of f always is either 0 or 1 for a given set of values of x, y, and z. Hence, f is considered a dependent Boolean variable, while the variables x, y, and z are the independent Boolean variables.

In general, an n-variable (complete*) Boolean function $f(x_1, x_2, \ldots, x_n)$ is a mapping that assigns a unique value, called the value of the function, for each combination of values of the n independent variables in which all values are limited to the set $\{0,1\}$. This definition of an n-variable Boolean function suggests that it can be represented by a table with $n + 1$ columns in which the first n columns provide for a complete listing of all the combinations of values of the n independent variables and the last column represents the value of the function for each combination. Since each variable can assume two possible values, it immediately follows that if there are n independent variables in the function, then there are 2^n combinations of values of the variables. Thus, the table has 2^n rows. Such a table denoting a Boolean function is called a *truth table* or *table of combinations.* A simple way of writing all

*In Sec. 3.8 the concept of an incomplete Boolean function is discussed. Unless otherwise indicated, Boolean functions are assumed to be complete.

Table 3.4 A Boolean function of n variables

x_1	x_2	$\cdots$	x_{n-1}	x_n	f
0	0	$\cdots$	0	0	$f(0, 0, \ldots, 0, 0)$
0	0	$\cdots$	0	1	$f(0, 0, \ldots, 0, 1)$
0	0	$\cdots$	1	0	$f(0, 0, \ldots, 1, 0)$
0	0	$\cdots$	1	1	$f(0, 0, \ldots, 1, 1)$
.	.	$\cdots$	.	.	.
.	.	$\cdots$	.	.	.
.	.	$\cdots$	.	.	.
1	1	$\cdots$	1	1	$f(1, 1, \ldots, 1, 1)$

the combinations of values is to count in the binary number system from the decimal equivalent of 0 to $2^n - 1$.* Once all the combinations of values are established, the value of the function for each combination is entered. This is achieved by evaluating the expression describing the function for each combination of values. Letting $f(x_1, x_2, \ldots, x_n) = f(0, 0, \ldots, 0)$ denote the value of the function when $x_1 = 0$, $x_2 = 0, \ldots, x_n = 0$, $f(x_1, x_2, \ldots, x_n) = f(0, 0, \ldots, 1)$ denote the value of the function when $x_1 = 0$, $x_2 = 0, \ldots, x_n = 1$, etc., the general form of the truth table for an n-variable function is shown in Table 3.4.

In line with common usage, the formula describing a function is referred to as the function itself. For example, it hereafter is said "the function $f(x,y,z) = (\bar{x} + y)z$" or "the function $f = (\bar{x} + y)z$" rather than "the three-variable function whose formula is $(\bar{x} + y)z$."

To illustrate the construction of a truth table, consider the function $f = (\bar{x} + y)z$. Since f is a function of three variables, there are $2^3 = 8$ different combinations of values that are assigned to the variables. In Table 3.5 the eight combinations are listed in the first three columns. It should be noted that these eight rows correspond to the binary numbers 000 to 111 which, in turn, correspond to the decimal numbers 0 to $2^3 - 1 = 7$.

To complete the construction of the truth table, the expression $(\bar{x} + y)z$ is evaluated for each of the eight combinations on a row-by-row basis. This results in the last column of Table 3.5. However, an alternate approach to completing the truth table is to carry out the Boolean operations on the columns of the table according to the expression being evaluated. For example, since $\bar{x}$ appears in the equation, a fourth column is added to the table such that the values in this column are the complements of those in the first column. Next, the or-ing of the values of $\bar{x}$ given in the fourth column is performed with the values of y given in the second column. This results in the fifth column, which shows the evaluation of the expression $\bar{x} + y$. Finally, the entries in the fifth column are and-ed with those in the third column. Thus,

*This rule for determining the rows of the truth table is a convenience that is possible by allowing a one-to-one correspondence to exist between the Boolean constants and the binary digits. However, the elements in the resulting table are the Boolean constants logic-0 and logic-1.

Table 3.5 Truth table for the function $f = (\overline{x} + y)z$

x	y	z	$\overline{x}$	$\overline{x} + y$	$f = (\overline{x} + y)z$
0	0	0	1	1	0
0	0	1	1	1	1
0	1	0	1	1	0
0	1	1	1	1	1
1	0	0	0	0	0
1	0	1	0	0	0
1	1	0	0	1	0
1	1	1	0	1	1

the final column shows the value of $(\overline{x} + y)z$ for each combination of values of the variables x, y, and z. For the special case when $x = 0$, $y = 1$, and $z = 0$, it is seen from the third row of the truth table that the value of the expression is 0.

As indicated above, a (complete) Boolean function of n variables is represented by a truth table with 2^n rows. It is now a simple matter to determine the number of distinct Boolean functions of n variables. For each of the rows of the truth table, there are two possible values that can be assigned as the value of the function. Consequently, with 2^n rows to the truth table, there are $2^{(2^n)}$ different ways in which the last column of the truth table can be written, each representing a different Boolean function.

Because of the closure property of the Boolean operations, every n-variable Boolean formula describes a unique n-variable Boolean function. However, in general, many appearingly different Boolean formulas describe the same Boolean function. Thus, two Boolean formulas A and B are said to be *equivalent,* written $A = B$, if and only if they describe the same Boolean function. The equality sign occurring in the postulates and theorems of a Boolean algebra relates expressions that yield identical results for any assignment to the variables. Thus, these theorems and postulates can be applied to a Boolean formula in order to determine an equivalent expression.

3.4.1 Normal Formulas

It is useful at times to categorize Boolean expressions based on their structure. One such categorization are the *normal formulas.* Consider the four-variable Boolean function

$$f(w,x,y,z) = \overline{x} + w\overline{y} + \overline{w}\,\overline{y}z \tag{3.1}$$

A *literal* is defined as each occurrence of either a complemented or an uncomplemented variable in a describing formula. Therefore, Eq. (3.1) consists of six literals. A *product term* is defined as either a literal or a product (also called conjunction) of literals. Equation (3.1) contains three product terms, namely, $\overline{x}$, $w\overline{y}$, and $\overline{w}\,\overline{y}z$. A Boolean formula that is written as a single product term or as a sum (also called disjunction) of product terms is said to be in *sum-of-products form* or *disjunctive normal form* and is called a *disjunctive normal formula.* Thus, Eq. (3.1) is a disjunctive normal formula.

Consider another four-variable Boolean function

$$f(w,x,y,z) = z(x + \bar{y})(w + \bar{x} + \bar{y}) \tag{3.2}$$

The expression consists of six literals since a total of six complemented and uncomplemented variables appear in the formula. A *sum term* is defined as either a literal or a sum (also called disjunction) of literals. In the case of Eq. (3.2), it consists of three sum terms, namely, z, $(x + \bar{y})$, and $(w + \bar{x} + \bar{y})$. A Boolean formula which is written as a single sum term or as a product (also called conjunction) of sum terms is said to be in *product-of-sums form* or *conjunctive normal form* and is called a *conjunctive normal formula.* The Boolean expression of Eq. (3.2) is an example of a conjunctive normal formula.

3.5 CANONICAL FORMULAS

In the previous section, Boolean formulas and functions were introduced. Boolean formulas are used to describe Boolean functions, i.e., truth tables; hence, there is a relationship between truth tables and Boolean expressions. As discussed previously, to construct a truth table from an expression, it is only necessary to evaluate the formula under all possible assignments of the independent variables. At this time, the process is reversed and it is shown how Boolean formulas are written from a truth table. Two types of expressions are obtained directly from a truth table: the *minterm canonical formula* and the *maxterm canonical formula.* These two canonical formula types are special cases of the disjunctive normal formula and conjunctive normal formula, respectively.

3.5.1 Minterm Canonical Formulas

Table 3.6 gives the truth table for some function f of three variables x, y, and z. Consider the first occurrence in the table in which the value of the function is 1. This corresponds to the second row in which $x = 0$, $y = 0$, and $z = 1$. Now consider the

Table 3.6 The truth table for a function $f(x,y,z)$

x	y	z	f
0	0	0	0
0	0	1	1
0	1	0	0
0	1	1	1
1	0	0	1
1	0	1	0
1	1	0	0
1	1	1	0

product term $\bar{x}\bar{y}z$. If the values $x = 0$, $y = 0$, and $z = 1$ are substituted into this product term, the term then evaluates to 1, i.e., $\bar{0} \cdot \bar{0} \cdot 1 = 1 \cdot 1 \cdot 1 = 1$. In addition, for all of the remaining possible seven combinations of values of x, y, and z, the term $\bar{x}\bar{y}z$ has the value 0, since at least one of the literals in the term has the value of 0. It is therefore seen that the single product term $\bar{x}\bar{y}z$ has a functional value of 1 if and only if $x = 0$, $y = 0$, and $z = 1$ and, consequently, can be used to algebraically describe the conditions in which the second row of the truth table has a functional value of 1.

Again considering Table 3.6, the next row in which the function has the value of 1 occurs in the fourth row. This row corresponds to the assignment $x = 0$, $y = 1$, and $z = 1$. If this assignment of values is substituted into the product term $\bar{x}yz$, then the value of the term is 1. Furthermore, as can easily be checked, this is the only assignment of values to the variables that causes the term $\bar{x}yz$ to have the value of 1. Thus, the conditions in which the fourth row of Table 3.6 has a functional value of 1 are algebraically described by the product term $\bar{x}yz$.

The only remaining row of Table 3.6 in which the function has the value of 1 is the fifth row. The assignment associated with this row is $x = 1$, $y = 0$, and $z = 0$. If this assignment is substituted into the product term $x\bar{y}\bar{z}$, the term then has the value of 1. In addition, this product term has the property that it has the value of 1 only for this assignment.

Combining the above results, the Boolean expression

$$f(x,y,z) = \bar{x}\bar{y}z + \bar{x}yz + x\bar{y}\bar{z} \tag{3.3}$$

precisely describes the function $f(x,y,z)$ given in Table 3.6 since each product term in the expression corresponds to exactly one row in which the function has the value of 1, and the logical sum corresponds to the collection of all such rows. Furthermore, for all those rows in which the function has the value of 0, the above expression also has the value of 0. Expressions of this type are called *minterm canonical formulas, standard sum-of-products*, or *disjunctive canonical formulas.*

In general, a minterm canonical formula describing an n-variable function is an expression consisting of a sum of product terms in which each of the n variables of the function appears exactly once, either complemented or uncomplemented, in each product term. Product terms that have this property of all variables appearing exactly once (and, consequently, having the value of 1 for only one combination of values of the function variables) are called *minterms** or *standard products.*

Generalizing from the above example, a procedure can be stated for writing a minterm canonical formula for any truth table. Each row of a truth table for which an n-variable function has the value of 1 is represented by a single product term, i.e., a minterm, in which the n variables appear exactly once. Within each minterm, a variable appears complemented if for that row the value of the variable is 0 and

---

*The word minterm is derived from the fact that the term describes a minimum number of rows of a truth table, short of none at all, that have a functional value of 1.

uncomplemented if for that row the value of the variable is 1. If the minterms describing precisely those rows of the truth table having a functional value of 1 are connected by or-operations, then the resulting expression is the minterm canonical formula describing the function.

3.5.2 *m*-Notation

Each row of a truth table corresponds to an assignment of values to the independent variables of the function. If this assignment is read as a binary number, then a row is readily referenced by its decimal number equivalent. Using the letter m to symbolize a minterm, the notation m_i is used to denote the minterm that is constructed from the row whose decimal equivalent of the independent variable assignment is i. Table 3.7 illustrates this notation for the case of three-variable truth tables. For example, the minterm $xy\bar{z}$ is associated with the row in which $x = 1$, $y = 1$, and $z = 0$. If 110 is read as a binary number, and thereby has the decimal equivalent of 6, then the corresponding minterm is denoted by m_6. This notation is readily extendable to handle any number of truth table variables.

In an effort to simplify the writing of a minterm canonical formula for a function, the symbol m_i, with the appropriate decimal subscript i, can replace each minterm in the expression. In this way, the minterm canonical formula given by Eq. (3.3) is written simply as

$$f(x,y,z) = m_1 + m_3 + m_4 \tag{3.4}$$

In addition, since a minterm canonical formula always consists of a sum of minterms, the writing of the expression is simplified further by denoting the summation of minterms by Σm and just listing within parentheses the decimal designators of those minterms being summed. Thus, Eq. (3.4) becomes

$$f(x,y,z) = \Sigma m(1,3,4)$$

It should be realized that no ambiguity results from this notation if the actual variables of the Boolean function are listed in the function symbol $f(x,y,z)$ and are assumed to be in the same order within a minterm.

Table 3.7 *m*-notation for the three-variable minterms

Rows of truth table $x\ y\ z$	Decimal designator of row	Minterm	m-notation
0 0 0	0	$\bar{x}\bar{y}\bar{z}$	m_0
0 0 1	1	$\bar{x}\bar{y}z$	m_1
0 1 0	2	$\bar{x}y\bar{z}$	m_2
0 1 1	3	$\bar{x}yz$	m_3
1 0 0	4	$x\bar{y}\bar{z}$	m_4
1 0 1	5	$x\bar{y}z$	m_5
1 1 0	6	$xy\bar{z}$	m_6
1 1 1	7	xyz	m_7

EXAMPLE 3.1

Consider the four-variable Boolean function given in Table 3.8. The corresponding minterm canonical formula is

$$f(w,x,y,z) = \overline{w}\overline{x}yz + \overline{w}x\overline{y}z + w\overline{x}\overline{y}\overline{z} + w\overline{x}y\overline{z} + w\overline{x}yz$$

and is written in m-notation as

$$f(w,x,y,z) = m_3 + m_5 + m_8 + m_{10} + m_{11} = \Sigma m(3,5,8,10,11)$$

Table 3.8 A four-variable Boolean function

w	x	y	z	f
0	0	0	0	0
0	0	0	1	0
0	0	1	0	0
0	0	1	1	1
0	1	0	0	0
0	1	0	1	1
0	1	1	0	0
0	1	1	1	0
1	0	0	0	1
1	0	0	1	0
1	0	1	0	1
1	0	1	1	1
1	1	0	0	0
1	1	0	1	0
1	1	1	0	0
1	1	1	1	0

EXAMPLE 3.2

A three-variable Boolean expression in m-notation is

$$f(x,y,z) = \Sigma m(0,4,7) = m_0 + m_4 + m_7$$

To obtain its algebraic form, it is only necessary to convert each of the decimal subscripts into a three-digit binary number and then replace each 0-bit by a complemented variable and each 1-bit by an uncomplemented variable. Under the assumption that the three variables x, y, and z of the function occur in the same order within the minterms, then the algebraic form

$$f(x,y,z) = \overline{x}\overline{y}\overline{z} + x\overline{y}\overline{z} + xyz$$

immediately follows.

3.5.3 Maxterm Canonical Formulas

There is a second type of canonical formula describing a function that is written directly from a truth table. This is known as the *maxterm canonical formula, standard product-of-sums*, or *conjunctive canonical formula.*

To see how the maxterm canonical formula is obtained, again consider the function $f(x,y,z)$ given in Table 3.6. Rather than algebraically describing those rows of the truth table having functional values of 1, those rows having functional values of 0 are algebraically described instead. For Table 3.6, the first row of the truth table has a functional value of 0 and corresponds to the condition $x = 0$, $y = 0$, and $z = 0$. Consider the sum term $x + y + z$. If the assignment $x = 0$, $y = 0$, and $z = 0$ is substituted into this sum term, then the term evaluates to 0, i.e., $0 + 0 + 0 = 0$. Furthermore, for all of the remaining possible seven combinations of values of x, y, and z, the term $x + y + z$ has the value of 1. It is therefore seen that this sum term has a functional value of 0 only when $x = 0$, $y = 0$, and $z = 0$. Thus, it can be used to algebraically describe the conditions in which the first row of the truth table has a functional value of 0.

The next row corresponding to a 0 functional value is the third row. In this case, $x = 0$, $y = 1$, and $z = 0$. Now consider the sum term $x + \bar{y} + z$. If the assignment of values corresponding to the third row is substituted into this sum term, then the value of the term is 0, i.e., $0 + \bar{1} + 0 = 0 + 0 + 0 = 0$. In addition, this is the only assignment of values to the variables x, y, and z that causes this sum term to be 0. Thus, it is concluded that the conditions in which the third row of Table 3.6 has a functional value of 0 is algebraically described by the sum term $x + \bar{y} + z$.

The analysis of Table 3.6 can be continued for the remaining rows in which the value of $f(x,y,z)$ is 0. In particular, the sixth row, corresponding to $x = 1$, $y = 0$, $z = 1$, is described by the sum term $\bar{x} + y + \bar{z}$; the seventh row, corresponding to $x = 1$, $y = 1$, $z = 0$, is described by the sum term $\bar{x} + \bar{y} + z$; and, finally, the last row, corresponding to $x = 1$, $y = 1$, $z = 1$, is described by the sum term $\bar{x} + \bar{y} + \bar{z}$.

Taking the Boolean product of the five sum terms results in

$$f(x,y,z) = (x + y + z)(x + \bar{y} + z)(\bar{x} + y + \bar{z})(\bar{x} + \bar{y} + z)(\bar{x} + \bar{y} + \bar{z}) \quad (3.5)$$

This expression has the value 0 if and only if any single sum term has the value 0. Hence, it has the value 0 for the five conditions in which the function $f(x,y,z)$ is 0 and has the value 1 for the remaining three conditions. Equation (3.5) is the maxterm canonical formula describing the function given in Table 3.6.

In general, a maxterm canonical formula describing an n-variable function is an expression consisting of a product of sum terms in which each of the n variables of the function appears exactly once, either complemented or uncomplemented, in each sum term. Sum terms that have this property of all variables appearing exactly once (and, consequently, having the value of 0 for only one combination of values of the function variables) are called *maxterms** or *standard sums.*

---

*A single maxterm has the value 0 for only one combination of values and has the value of 1 for all other combinations of values. Hence, its name depicts the fact that it is a term that assigns a functional value of 1 to a maximum number of rows of a truth table, short of all of them.

Generalizing from the above discussion, a procedure can be stated for writing a maxterm canonical formula for any truth table. Each row of a truth table for which an n-variable function has the value of 0 is represented by a single sum term, i.e., a maxterm, in which the n variables appear exactly once. Within each maxterm, a variable appears complemented if for that row the value of the variable is 1 and uncomplemented if for that row the value of the variable is 0. If the maxterms describing precisely those rows of the truth table having a functional value of 0 are connected by and-operations, then the resulting expression is the maxterm canonical formula describing the function.

3.5.4 *M*-Notation

As was the case with minterms, a decimal notation is used for maxterms. Again, if the variable assignment associated with a row of a truth table is read as a binary number, then the row is readily referenced by its decimal number equivalent. A maxterm constructed for the row with decimal equivalent i is then denoted by M_i. This notation is illustrated in Table 3.9 for the case of three-variable truth tables. For example, the maxterm $\bar{x} + \bar{y} + z$ is associated with the row in which $x = 1$, $y = 1$, and $z = 0$. Regarding 110 as a binary number, the decimal equivalent is 6. Hence, the maxterm is represented by M_6. Although Table 3.9 gives the M-notation for three-variable maxterms, this notation is extendable to handle any number of truth table variables.

Replacing each maxterm in a maxterm canonical formula by its corresponding M_i, the formula is written in a more compact form. For example, the maxterm canonical formula given by Eq. (3.5) becomes

$$f(x,y,z) = M_0M_2M_5M_6M_7 \tag{3.6}$$

A further simplification in writing maxterm canonical formulas is achieved by using ΠM to denote a product of maxterms and listing the decimal designator of each maxterm for the function within parentheses. Thus, a simplified form of writing Eq. (3.6) is

$$f(x,y,z) = \Pi M(0,2,5,6,7)$$

Table 3.9 *M*-notation for the three-variable maxterms

Rows of truth table $x\ y\ z$	Decimal designator of row	Maxterm	M-notation
0 0 0	0	$x + y + z$	M_0
0 0 1	1	$x + y + \bar{z}$	M_1
0 1 0	2	$x + \bar{y} + z$	M_2
0 1 1	3	$x + \bar{y} + \bar{z}$	M_3
1 0 0	4	$\bar{x} + y + z$	M_4
1 0 1	5	$\bar{x} + y + \bar{z}$	M_5
1 1 0	6	$\bar{x} + \bar{y} + z$	M_6
1 1 1	7	$\bar{x} + \bar{y} + \bar{z}$	M_7

Under the assumption that the variables of the maxterms are always arranged in the same order as they appear in the function notation $f(x,y,z)$, no ambiguity results from this decimal notation.

EXAMPLE 3.3

Consider the four-variable Boolean function given in Table 3.8. The corresponding maxterm canonical formula is

$$\begin{aligned} f(w,x,y,z) = & (w + x + y + z)(w + x + y + \bar{z})(w + x + \bar{y} + z) \\ & \cdot (w + \bar{x} + y + z)(w + \bar{x} + \bar{y} + z)(w + \bar{x} + \bar{y} + \bar{z}) \\ & \cdot (\bar{w} + x + y + \bar{z})(\bar{w} + \bar{x} + y + z)(\bar{w} + \bar{x} + y + \bar{z}) \\ & \cdot (\bar{w} + \bar{x} + \bar{y} + z)(\bar{w} + \bar{x} + \bar{y} + \bar{z}) \end{aligned}$$

and is written in M-notation as

$$\begin{aligned} f(w,x,y,z) &= M_0M_1M_2M_4M_6M_7M_9M_{12}M_{13}M_{14}M_{15} \\ &= \Pi M(0,1,2,4,6,7,9,12,13,14,15) \end{aligned}$$

EXAMPLE 3.4

A three-variable Boolean expression in M-notation is

$$f(x,y,z) = \Pi M(0,2,3,6) = M_0M_2M_3M_6$$

To obtain its algebraic form, it is only necessary to convert each of the decimal subscripts into a three-digit binary number and then write the corresponding sum term in which a 0-bit becomes an uncomplemented variable and a 1-bit becomes a complemented variable. Under the assumption that the variables within the maxterms appear in the same order as in the function notation, the algebraic form becomes

$$f(x,y,z) = (x + y + z)(x + \bar{y} + z)(x + \bar{y} + \bar{z})(\bar{x} + \bar{y} + z)$$

In closing this section, a comment on the importance of canonical formulas is in order. For complete Boolean functions, the minterm and maxterm canonical formulas are unique. That is, for any complete Boolean function, there is only one minterm canonical formula and only one maxterm canonical formula. Thus, if two dissimilar-looking Boolean equations are manipulated into the same minterm or maxterm canonical formulas, then it can be concluded that the two formulas are describing the same Boolean function.

Another application of the canonical formulas is that they serve as the starting point for formal techniques to determine simple formulas that describe a function. Simplification procedures are studied in the next chapter.

3.6 MANIPULATIONS OF BOOLEAN FORMULAS

A Boolean function is describable by many different formulas. By applying the postulates and theorems of a Boolean algebra, it is possible to manipulate a Boolean expression into another form describing the same Boolean function. The type of manipulation that must be performed depends upon some objective that is to be achieved. For example, it may be desirable to obtain an expression having the fewest literals that describes a function, or the objective might be to obtain a canonical formula when the given formula is not in canonical form. In this section several examples of Boolean equation manipulations with various objectives are given.

3.6.1 Equation Complementation

A Boolean equation is a description of a Boolean function. This description is a rule expressed in algebraic form that assigns functional values for all combinations of values of the independent variables of the function. For every Boolean function f there is associated a *complementary function* $\overline{f}$ in which $\overline{f}(x_1, x_2, \ldots, x_n) = 1$ if $f(x_1, x_2, \ldots, x_n) = 0$ and $\overline{f}(x_1, x_2, \ldots, x_n) = 0$ if $f(x_1, x_2, \ldots. x_n) = 1$ for all combinations of values of $x_1, x_2, \ldots, x_n$. That is, the functional value column appearing in the truth table for $\overline{f}$ has the opposite values from those in the functional value column in the truth table for f. A Boolean formula for $\overline{f}$ is obtained by complementing the Boolean expression for f. For example, if the function f is described by

$$f = \overline{w}x\overline{z} + w(x + \overline{y}z)$$

then the function $\overline{f}$ is described by

$$\overline{f} = \overline{[\overline{w}x\overline{z} + w(x + \overline{y}z)]}$$

By repeated use of DeMorgan's law, i.e., Theorem 3.9, the not-operation over the entire formula is brought inside the parentheses so that not-operations only appear with the individual variables.

EXAMPLE 3.5

The complementation of the Boolean expression

$$f = \overline{w}x\overline{z} + w(x + \overline{y}z)$$

proceeds as follows using DeMorgan's law (Theorem 3.9) and the involution law (Theorem 3.5):

$$\begin{aligned}\overline{f} = \overline{[\overline{w}x\overline{z} + w(x + \overline{y}z)]} &= \overline{(\overline{w}x\overline{z})}\;\overline{[w(x + \overline{y}z)]}\\ &= [\overline{(\overline{w})} + \overline{x} + \overline{(\overline{z})}]\,[\overline{w} + \overline{(x + \overline{y}z)}]\\ &= (w + \overline{x} + z)\,[\overline{w} + \overline{x}\overline{(\overline{y}z)}]\\ &= (w + \overline{x} + z)\,\{\overline{w} + \overline{x}[\overline{(\overline{y})} + \overline{z}]\}\\ &= (w + \overline{x} + z)\,[\overline{w} + \overline{x}(y + \overline{z})]\end{aligned}$$

3.6.2 Expansion about a Variable

There are occasions when it is desirable to single out a variable and rewrite a Boolean formula $f(x_1, \ldots, x_i, \ldots, x_n)$ so that it has the general structure

$$x_i g_1 + \bar{x}_i g_2$$

or

$$(x_i + h_1)(\bar{x}_i + h_2)$$

where g_1, g_2, h_1, and h_2 are expressions *not* containing the variable x_i. These special forms of a Boolean formula $f(x_1, \ldots, x_i, \ldots, x_n)$ are said to be expansions about the variable x_i. The expansions about a single variable are achieved by the following theorem, known as *Shannon's expansion theorem.*

Theorem 3.11

(a) $f(x_1, x_2, \ldots, x_i, \ldots, x_n)$
$= x_i \cdot f(x_1, x_2, \ldots, 1, \ldots, x_n) + \bar{x}_i \cdot f(x_1, x_2, \ldots, 0, \ldots, x_n)$

(b) $f(x_1, x_2, \ldots, x_i, \ldots, x_n)$
$= [x_i + f(x_1, x_2, \ldots, 0, \ldots, x_n)] \cdot [\bar{x}_i + f(x_1, x_2, \ldots, 1, \ldots, x_n)]$

where $f(x_1, x_2, \ldots, k, \ldots, x_n)$, for $k = 0, 1$, denotes the formula $f(x_1, x_2, \ldots, x_i, \ldots, x_n)$ upon the substitution of the constant k for all occurrences of the variable x_i.

EXAMPLE 3.6

Consider the Boolean expression

$$f(w,x,y,z) = \overline{w}\overline{x} + (wx + y)z$$

Assume that an equivalent expression is desired having the general form

$$x \cdot g_1(w,y,z) + \bar{x} \cdot g_2(w,y,z)$$

This is achieved by expanding the expression $f(w,x,y,z)$ about the x variable as follows

$$\begin{aligned} f(w,x,y,z) &= \overline{w}\overline{x} + (wx + y)z \\ &= x[\overline{w} \cdot \overline{1} + (w \cdot 1 + y)z] + \bar{x}[\overline{w} \cdot \overline{0} + (w \cdot 0 + y)z] \qquad \text{by Theorem 3.11}(a) \\ &= x[\overline{w} \cdot 0 + (w + y)z] + \bar{x}[\overline{w} \cdot 1 + yz] \\ &= x(w + y)z + \bar{x}(\overline{w} + yz) \end{aligned}$$

3.6.3 Equation Simplification

As is seen in Sec. 3.7, there is a direct correspondence between the structure of logic networks and Boolean formulas. Since the postulates and theorems of a Boolean algebra enable the manipulations of a formula into equivalent forms, for a particular Boolean function one formula might be more desirable than another. This is particularly true if the formula is manipulated so as to correspond to the "best" network. Of course, a criterion is needed that can be applied to a formula to measure the desirability of the corresponding network. This has led to defining "simple" or "minimal" expressions with the intent that they correspond to the least-cost network.

One possible way of measuring the simplicity of a Boolean expression is to observe the number of literals contained within the formula. For the purpose of this chapter, the simplest form of an expression is defined as the normal formula having the fewest number of literals.*

EXAMPLE 3.7

Consider the expression

$$(x + xy)(\bar{x} + y) + yz$$

consisting of seven literals. It is simplified as follows:

$$\begin{aligned}(x + xy)(\bar{x} + y) + yz &= x(\bar{x} + y) + yz && \text{by Theorem 6}(a)\\ &= xy + yz && \text{by Theorem 7}(b)\\ &= y(x + z) && \text{by P2}(b)\end{aligned}$$

The resulting expression is a conjunctive normal formula, i.e., a formula in product-of-sums form, consisting of three literals.

EXAMPLE 3.8

Consider the expression

$$\bar{w}\bar{y}\bar{z} + wz + \bar{y}z + xyz$$

consisting of 10 literals. It is simplified as follows:

$$\begin{aligned}\bar{w}\bar{y}\bar{z} + wz + \bar{y}z + xyz &= \bar{w}\bar{y}\bar{z} + wz + z(\bar{y} + xy)\\ &= \bar{w}\bar{y}\bar{z} + wz + z(\bar{y} + x)\\ &= \bar{w}\bar{y}\bar{z} + wz + \bar{y}z + xz\\ &= \bar{w}\bar{y}\bar{z} + wz + 1 \cdot \bar{y}z + xz\\ &= \bar{w}\bar{y}\bar{z} + wz + (w + \bar{w})\bar{y}z + xz\\ &= \bar{w}\bar{y}\bar{z} + wz + w\bar{y}z + \bar{w}\bar{y}z + xz\\ &= \bar{w}\bar{y}\bar{z} + \bar{w}\bar{y}z + wz + w\bar{y}z + xz\\ &= \bar{w}\bar{y}(\bar{z} + z) + wz(1 + \bar{y}) + xz\\ &= \bar{w}\bar{y} + wz + xz\end{aligned}$$

The resulting expression is a disjunctive normal formula, i.e., a formula in sum-of-products form, consisting of six literals.

Certainly it is not obvious that the final expression in Example 3.8 is the simplest disjunctive normal formula. Nor was it obvious which theorems or postulates were

*The subject of measuring the simplicity of an expression is further explored in Chapter 4.

the most appropriate to apply in order to achieve the reduction. Clearly, there is a need for systematic reduction techniques that guarantee minimal resulting expressions. In the next chapter algorithmic procedures for obtaining expressions under different measures of minimality are studied.

3.6.4 The Reduction Theorems

For the purpose of obtaining simple Boolean formulas, two additional theorems are particularly useful. These are known as *Shannon's reduction theorems.*

Theorem 3.12

(*a*) $x_i \cdot f(x_1, x_2, \ldots, x_i, \ldots, x_n) = x_i \cdot f(x_1, x_2, \ldots, 1, \ldots, x_n)$

(*b*) $x_i + f(x_1, x_2, \ldots, x_i, \ldots, x_n) = x_i + f(x_1, x_2, \ldots, 0, \ldots, x_n)$

where $f(x_1, x_2, \ldots, k, \ldots, x_n)$, for $k = 0, 1$, denotes the formula $f(x_1, x_2, \ldots, x_i, \ldots, x_n)$ upon the substitution of the constant k for all occurrences of the variable x_i.

Theorem 3.13

(*a*) $\bar{x}_i \cdot f(x_1, x_2, \ldots, x_i, \ldots, x_n) = \bar{x}_i \cdot f(x_1, x_2, \ldots, 0, \ldots, x_n)$

(*b*) $\bar{x}_i + f(x_1, x_2, \ldots, x_i, \ldots, x_n) = \bar{x}_i + f(x_1, x_2, \ldots, 1, \ldots, x_n)$

where $f(x_1, x_2, \ldots, k, \ldots, x_n)$, for $k = 0, 1$, denotes the formula $f(x_1, x_2, \ldots, x_i, \ldots, x_n)$ upon the substitution of the constant k for all occurrences of the variable x_i.

EXAMPLE 3.9

Consider a function described by the following Boolean expression:

$$f(w,x,y,z) = x + \bar{x}\bar{y} + \bar{w}\bar{x}(w + z)(y + \bar{w}z)$$

Denoting $\bar{x}\bar{y} + \bar{w}\bar{x}(w + z)(y + \bar{w}z)$ by $g(w,x,y,z)$, the above expression has the form

$$f(w,x,y,z) = x + g(w,x,y,z)$$

By Theorem 3.12(*b*), all occurrences of the x variable in $g(w,x,y,z)$ can now be replaced by the Boolean constant 0. Therefore,

$$\begin{aligned} f(w,x,y,z) &= x + \bar{0} \cdot \bar{y} + \bar{w} \cdot \bar{0} \cdot (w + z)(y + \bar{w}z) \\ &= x + \bar{y} + \bar{w}(w + z)(y + \bar{w}z) \end{aligned}$$

It is next noted that by letting $(w + z)(y + \bar{w}z)$ be denoted by $h(w,y,z)$, then

$$\bar{w}(w + z)(y + \bar{w}z) = \bar{w} \cdot h(w,y,z)$$

By Theorem 3.13(*a*) all occurrences of the w variable in $h(w,y,z)$ can be replaced by the constant 0. Thus,

$$\begin{aligned} \bar{w}(w + z)(y + \bar{w}z) &= \bar{w}(0 + z)(y + \bar{0} \cdot z) \\ &= \bar{w}z(y + z) \end{aligned}$$

At this point the original Boolean expression reduces to

$$f(w,x,y,z) = x + \bar{y} + \bar{w}z(y + z)$$

Finally, by letting $x + \bar{w}z(y + z)$ be denoted by $k(w,x,y,z)$, then

$$f(w,x,y,z) = \bar{y} + k(w,x,y,z)$$

By Theorem 3.13(*b*) the y variable in $k(w,x,y,z)$ can be replaced by the constant 1. Thus,

$$\begin{aligned} f(w,x,y,z) &= \bar{y} + x + \bar{w}z(1 + z) \\ &= \bar{y} + x + \bar{w}z \end{aligned}$$

which is the simplest disjunctive normal formula describing the given function.

3.6.5 Minterm Canonical Formulas

Section 3.5 introduced the minterm canonical formula and its construction from a truth table. The significance of the minterm canonical formula is that it is a unique description of a complete Boolean function. Thus, a method of determining if two Boolean formulas are equivalent is to express them in their minterm canonical forms and compare them minterm by minterm.

By the use of the postulates and theorems of a Boolean algebra, it is a simple matter to manipulate any formula into its minterm canonical form. This is achieved by first applying DeMorgan's law, i.e., Theorem 3.9, a sufficient number of times until all not-operations only appear with the variables. Next the distributive law of (·) over (+), i.e., Postulate P4(*b*), is applied in order to manipulate the formula into its disjunctive normal form, i.e., a sum of product terms. Duplicate literals and terms are removed by the idempotent law, i.e., Theorem 3.4, as well as any terms that are identically 0 by Postulate P5(*b*). If any product term in the resulting disjunctive normal formula does not have all the variables of the function, then these missing variables are introduced by and-ing the term with logic-1 in the form of $x_i + \bar{x}_i$ where x_i is the missing variable being introduced. This process is continued for each missing variable in each of the product terms of the disjunctive normal formula. After applying the distributive law of (·) over (+) again, each variable appears exactly once in each term. Upon removing any duplicate terms, the resulting expression is the minterm canonical formula.

EXAMPLE 3.10

Consider the Boolean formula consisting of the variables $x,y,$ and z

$$f(x,y,z) = \overline{(x + y)} + (y + xz)(x + \bar{y})$$

Applying DeMorgan's law, the expression is rewritten so that the not-operations only appear with the variables. Thus,

$$f(x,y,z) = \bar{x}\bar{y} + (y + xz)(x + \bar{y})$$

Next the distributive law of (·) over (+) is applied to remove all parentheses. This results in

$$f(x,y,z) = \bar{x}\bar{y} + xy + xxz + y\bar{y} + x\bar{y}z$$

The duplication of the x literal in the third term and the identically 0 term $y\bar{y}$ are removed. At this point a disjunctive normal formula is obtained, i.e.,

$$f(x,y,z) = \bar{x}\bar{y} + xy + xz + x\bar{y}z$$

The first term in this expression is lacking the z variable. The variable is introduced by and-ing the term with logic-1 in the form of $z + \bar{z}$. In a similar manner, the missing variables in the second and third terms are introduced. Thus,

$$\begin{aligned} f(x,y,z) &= \bar{x}\bar{y} \cdot 1 + xy \cdot 1 + x \cdot 1 \cdot z + x\bar{y}z \\ &= \bar{x}\bar{y}(z + \bar{z}) + xy(z + \bar{z}) + x(y + \bar{y})z + x\bar{y}z \end{aligned}$$

Application of the distributive law of (·) over (+) results in

$$f(x,y,z) = \bar{x}\bar{y}z + \bar{x}\bar{y}\bar{z} + xyz + xy\bar{z} + xyz + x\bar{y}z + x\bar{y}z$$

Finally, the duplicate occurrences of the xyz and $x\bar{y}z$ terms are deleted, resulting in the minterm canonical formula

$$f(x,y,z) = \bar{x}\bar{y}z + \bar{x}\bar{y}\bar{z} + xyz + xy\bar{z} + x\bar{y}z$$

3.6.6 Maxterm Canonical Formulas

Just as any Boolean expression can be manipulated into its unique minterm canonical form, it is also possible to manipulate it into its unique maxterm canonical form. The procedure is the dual to that described previously for obtaining the minterm canonical formula. In this case the distributive law of (+) over (·) is used, i.e., Postulate P4(a), to bring the expression into its conjunctive normal form, i.e., product-of-sums form, after DeMorgan's law is applied so that all not-operations appear only with the variables in the function. Then the missing variables are introduced into the sum terms by or-ing logic-0's in the form of $x_i\bar{x}_i$ where x_i is the missing variable, and the distributive law of (+) over (·) is again applied. Duplicate terms and literals are deleted as well as terms identically 1 if they occur during the course of formula manipulation.

EXAMPLE 3.11

Again consider the formula of Example 3.10

$$f(x,y,z) = \overline{(x + y)} + (y + xz)(x + \bar{y})$$

First DeMorgan's law is applied so that the expression has all the not-operations occurring only with the variables. Thus,

$$f(x,y,z) = \bar{x}\bar{y} + (y + xz)(x + \bar{y})$$

Next the distributive law of (+) over (·) is applied a sufficient number of times to manipulate the expression into conjunctive normal form. In particular,

$$\begin{aligned} f(x,y,z) &= \bar{x}\bar{y} + (y + x)(y + z)(x + \bar{y}) \\ &= (\bar{x}\bar{y} + y + x)(\bar{x}\bar{y} + y + z)(\bar{x}\bar{y} + x + \bar{y}) \\ &= (\bar{x} + y + x)(\bar{y} + y + x)(\bar{x} + y + z)(\bar{y} + y + z)(\bar{x} + x + \bar{y})(\bar{y} + x + \bar{y}) \end{aligned}$$

The first, second, fourth, and fifth terms are identically 1, by Postulate P5(*a*) and Theorem T2(*a*), and, hence, are now dropped as well as the duplicate literal in the last term. The resulting expression is

$$f(x,y,z) = (\bar{x} + y + z)(x + \bar{y})$$

The first term is already a maxterm since all three variables appear. However, the second term is not a maxterm since it lacks the z variable. The z variable is next introduced into this term in the form $z\bar{z}$, i.e.,

$$\begin{aligned} f(x,y,z) &= (\bar{x} + y + z)(x + \bar{y} + 0) \\ &= (\bar{x} + y + z)(x + \bar{y} + z\bar{z}) \end{aligned}$$

Finally, the distributive law of (+) over (·) is again applied to yield the maxterm canonical formula

$$f(x,y,z) = (\bar{x} + y + z)(x + \bar{y} + z)(x + \bar{y} + \bar{z})$$

3.6.7 Complements of Canonical Formulas

In terms of the truth table, the complement of a complete Boolean function involves a functional value column having values just opposite to those of the original function. Recall that the minterm canonical formula of a function is written directly from a truth table by summing the minterms for precisely those rows in which the function has the value 1. It therefore immediately follows that the minterm canonical formula for the complement of a complete Boolean function is obtained by summing those minterms not contained in the minterm canonical formula of the original function.

A similar observation can be made with regard to the maxterm canonical formulas for a function and its complement since it is the 0 functional-value rows of the truth table that determine which maxterms are to appear in the canonical formula. That is, the maxterm canonical formula of a complementary function consists of the product of precisely those maxterms that do not appear in the maxterm canonical formula of the original function.

For a complete Boolean function of n variables, the truth table consists of 2^n rows. It was stated in Sec. 3.5 that each of these rows is referenced by a decimal integer in the range from 0 to 2^n–1. Hence, in terms of the decimal notation, the decimal description of a complementary function consists of the set of integers in the range from 0 to 2^n–1 not appearing in the set for the original function. This is illustrated by the next two examples.

EXAMPLE 3.12

The complement of the minterm canonical formula

$$f(w,x,y,z) = \Sigma m(0,1,3,8,9,12,15)$$

is given by

$$\bar{f}(w,x,y,z) = \Sigma m(2,4,5,6,7,10,11,13,14)$$

EXAMPLE 3.13

The complement of the maxterm canonical formula

$$f(w,x,y,z) = \Pi M(1,2,6,10,12,13,14)$$

is given by

$$\bar{f}(w,x,y,z) = \Pi M(0,3,4,5,7,8,9,11,15)$$

Now consider a single minterm of n variables. Since the minterm is written as the product of n variables, if the minterm is complemented by applying DeMorgan's law, then the result is a sum term in which each of the n variables still remains. For example, $\overline{(w\bar{x}yz)} = \bar{w} + x + \bar{y} + \bar{z}$. Thus it is readily seen that the complement of an n-variable minterm is an n-variable maxterm. Similarly, applying DeMorgan's law to an n-variable maxterm results in an n-variable minterm.

Assuming that a canonical term is given by its decimal representation, the decimal subscript is not affected by the complementation process even though each literal is complemented as a result of DeMorgan's law. This follows from the way in which the decimal notation was developed in Sec. 3.5. In particular, in the case of minterms, the decimal representation is derived from the binary number in which 0's are associated with complemented variables and 1's with uncomplemented variables. However, for maxterms, the decimal representation is derived from the binary number in which 0's are associated with uncomplemented variables and 1's are associated with complemented variables. For the above example, it is seen the complement of minterm m_{11}, i.e., $\overline{(w\bar{x}yz)}$, becomes $\bar{w} + x + \bar{y} + \bar{z}$, which is maxterm M_{11}. In general, $\overline{m}_i = M_i$ and $\overline{M}_i = m_i$ where i is a decimal subscript.

The above discussion suggests a second way of forming the complement of a canonical expression and still having a canonical expression result. If a function is expressed as a minterm canonical formula in decimal notation, then its complement in decimal notation is a maxterm canonical formula with the same decimal subscripts. Similarly, if a function is expressed as a maxterm canonical formula in decimal notation, then its complement in decimal notation is a minterm canonical formula with the same decimal subscripts.

EXAMPLE 3.14

Consider the minterm canonical formula

$$f(w,x,y,z) = m_1 + m_3 + m_7 + m_{12} + m_{13}$$

Applying DeMorgan's law directly to this expression results in

$$\bar{f}(w,x,y,z) = \overline{m}_1\overline{m}_3\overline{m}_7\overline{m}_{12}\overline{m}_{13}$$

Finally, since $\overline{m}_i = M_i$ the complementary function is written in maxterm canonical form as

$$\bar{f}(w,x,y,z) = M_1M_3M_7M_{12}M_{13}$$

Two methods have been introduced for complementing a canonical expression when given in decimal notation. From the way the complement of a Boolean function is defined, if the complement of an expression describing a function is taken twice, then the resulting expression again describes the original function. In other words, $\overline{\overline{f}}(x_1, x_2, \ldots, x_n) = f(x_1, x_2, \ldots, x_n)$. Using the above results, it is a simple matter to transform a minterm or maxterm canonical expression in decimal form into its equivalent canonical expression in decimal form of the opposite type. First, the expression is complemented by replacing the set of decimal describers by the set consisting of decimal integers in the range from 0 to 2^n–1 not appearing in the original set. Second, the double complement is achieved by applying DeMorgan's law to the newly formed complemented expression and using the result $\overline{m}_i = M_i$ or $\overline{M}_i = m_i$. Certainly, the two steps of the above transformation process can be taken in either order.

EXAMPLE 3.15

Consider the minterm canonical formula

$$f(w,x,y,z) = m_0 + m_1 + m_4 + m_5 + m_7 + m_8 + m_{12} + m_{13} + m_{14}$$

Forming the complement by listing the minterms not included in the original expression results in

$$\overline{f}(w,x,y,z) = m_2 + m_3 + m_6 + m_9 + m_{10} + m_{11} + m_{15}$$

Finally, taking the second complement by DeMorgan's law results in the maxterm canonical formula of the original function:

$$\begin{aligned}\overline{\overline{f}}(w,x,y,z) &= \overline{m}_2\overline{m}_3\overline{m}_6\overline{m}_9\overline{m}_{10}\overline{m}_{11}\overline{m}_{15}\\ &= M_2M_3M_6M_9M_{10}M_{11}M_{15}\\ &= f(w,x,y,z)\end{aligned}$$

3.7 GATES AND COMBINATIONAL NETWORKS

Thus far in this chapter, attention has been directed to the development of a Boolean algebra. The purpose for introducing this algebra is its application to the analysis and design (also called synthesis) of logic systems. Logic systems consist of logic elements called *gates* and *flip-flops.* Gates are electronic circuits whose terminal characteristics correspond to the various Boolean operations; while flip-flops are memory devices that are capable of storing the logic constants. The interconnections of gates and flip-flops result in *logic networks.* A drawing that depicts the interconnections of the logic elements is called a *logic diagram.* These networks are related to the Boolean algebra in that a Boolean function is used to *represent* or *describe* a logic network and, alternatively, a logic network is a *realization* or *implementation* of a Boolean function.

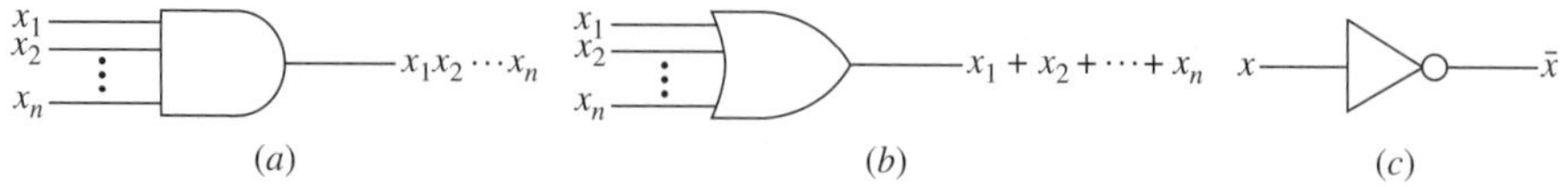

Figure 3.1 Gate symbols. (*a*) And-gate. (*b*) Or-gate. (*c*) Not-gate.

3.7.1 Gates

Electronic circuits can be designed in which only two possible steady-state voltage signal values appear at the terminals of the circuits at any time.* Such two-state circuits receive two-valued input signals and are capable of producing two-valued output signals in the steady state. Rather than dealing with the actual voltage signal values at the circuit terminals, it is possible to assign two arbitrary symbols to the two steady-state voltage signal values. Let these symbols be logic-0 and logic-1.

An electronic circuit in which the output signal is a logic-1 if and only if all its input signals are logic-1 is called an *and-gate.* This circuit is a physical realization of the Boolean and-operation. Similarly, an electronic circuit in which the output signal is a logic-1 if and only if at least one of its input signals is a logic-1 is called an *or-gate.* The or-gate is a physical realization of the Boolean or-operation. Finally, an electronic circuit in which the output signal is always opposite to that of the input signal is called a *not-gate* or *inverter* and is the physical realization of the Boolean not-operation. Since the input and output lines, or terminals, of a gate have different values, i.e., logic-0 and logic-1, at different times, each of these lines is assigned a two-valued variable. Hence, the terminal characteristics of each of these gates are describable with a two-valued Boolean algebra. Figure 3.1 illustrates a set of symbols for the above three gates and the corresponding algebraic expressions for their behavior at the output terminals.

3.7.2 Combinational Networks

The interconnections of gates result in a *gate network.* If the network has the property that its outputs at any time are determined strictly by the inputs at that time, then the network is said to be a *combinational network.* A combinational network is represented by the general diagram of Fig. 3.2. The set of signals applied to the n input terminals at any time is called the *input state* or *input vector* of the network; while the set of resulting signals appearing at the m output terminals is called the *output state* or *output vector.* In general, for a combinational network, the outputs $z_1, z_2, \ldots, z_m$ can be expressed as a Boolean function of its inputs $x_1, x_2, \ldots, x_n$. That is, $z_i = f_i(x_1, x_2, \ldots, x_n)$ for $i = 1, 2, \ldots, m$ where $f_i(x_1, x_2, \ldots, x_n)$ is a Boolean function.

Not all interconnections of gates satisfy the above requirement that the network outputs are a function of only its current inputs. However, a sufficient, but not nec-

*In actuality two *ranges* of voltage signal values are associated with each terminal. However, for simplicity in this discussion it is not necessary to regard the electrical signals as ranges, but rather two values suffice. Gate properties are further discussed in Sec. 3.10.

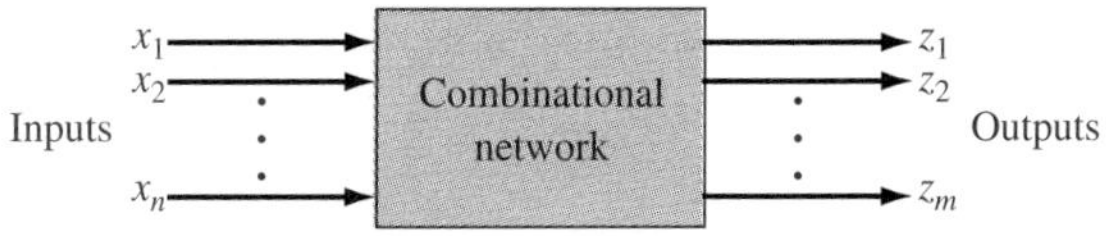

Figure 3.2 Block diagram of a combinational network.

essary, condition for a combinational network is that the network contains no closed loops or feedback paths. Networks that satisfy this constraint are said to be *acyclic*.

A second type of logic network is the *sequential network*. Sequential networks have a memory property so that the outputs from these networks are dependent not only upon the current inputs but upon previous inputs as well. Feedback paths form a necessary part of sequential networks. At this time, only acyclic gate networks are studied. This ensures that the networks being considered are indeed combinational.

There is a very important inherent assumption in the establishment of Boolean algebra as a mathematical model for a combinational gate network. A two-valued Boolean algebra has only two different symbols to assign to the physical signal values present at any time at the gate terminals. However, when a physical signal changes from one of its values to the other, a continuum of values appear at the input or output terminals. Furthermore, in the real world, changes cannot occur instantaneously, i.e., in zero time. To eliminate these transient-type problems, only the steady-state conditions occurring in a network are considered. Under this steady-state assumption, Boolean algebra can serve as a mathematical model for combinational gate networks. In Sec. 3.10, further remarks are made about the nature of the signals within a combinational network.

At this time, the analysis and synthesis of gate combinational networks is studied. Analysis involves obtaining a behavioral description of the network. This is achieved by writing a Boolean expression or, equivalently, by forming a truth table to describe the network's logic behavior. Synthesis, on the other hand, involves specifying the interconnections of the gates, i.e., topological structure, for a desired behavior. This, in turn, results in a logic diagram from which a physical realization is constructed.

3.7.3 Analysis Procedure

Given a gate network with no feedback paths, it is a simple matter to develop an analysis procedure. To begin with, each gate output that is only a function of the input variables is labeled. Algebraic expressions for the outputs of each of these gates are then written. Next, those gate outputs that are a function of just the input variables and previously labeled gate outputs are labeled. The equations for these gate outputs are written using the previously assigned labels as input variables. Then, each of the previously defined labels is replaced by the already written Boolean equations. This process is continued until the output of the network is labeled and the appropriate expression obtained. Finally, the expression can be used to construct a truth table to complete the analysis procedure.

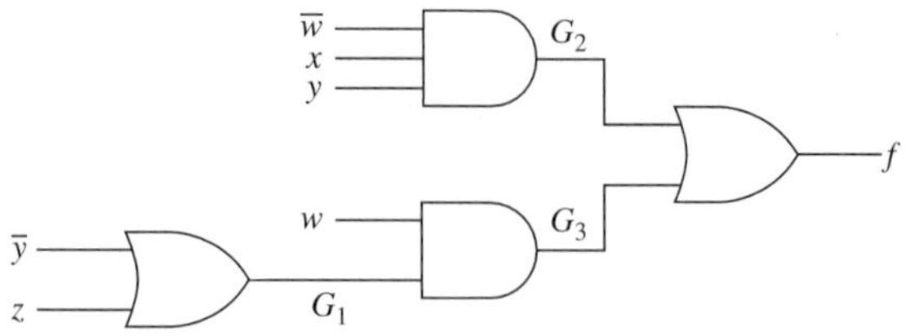

Figure 3.3 A gate combinational network.

The above analysis procedure is illustrated by the gate network of Fig. 3.3. The or-gate whose output is labeled G_1 is described by the formula $G_1 = \bar{y} + z$. Also, the and-gate whose output is labeled G_2 is described by the formula $G_2 = \bar{w}xy$. Next the and-gate whose output is labeled G_3 is described in terms of the input variable w and the previously labeled output G_1. Thus, the formula for the output of the and-gate labeled G_3 is $G_3 = w \cdot G_1 = w(\bar{y} + z)$. Finally, the output of the network is described in terms of the labels G_2 and G_3; that is, $f(w,x,y,z) = G_2 + G_3 = \bar{w}xy + w(\bar{y} + z)$. Once the expression is written, the corresponding truth table can be constructed, as previously explained in Sec. 3.4.

3.7.4 Synthesis Procedure

The synthesis procedure, or logic design, begins with the specifications of the desired terminal behavior of a gate network. The truth table is a very convenient form for describing the network specifications. Each line of the truth table corresponds to an input state of the network (i.e., a set of input signals represented by 0's and 1's) and an output state (i.e., a set of output signals represented by 0's and 1's corresponding to the values of the functions). Once this table is formed, Boolean formulas are written, one for each output function. Manipulations of a formula are achieved by the postulates and theorems of a Boolean algebra. Each time the formula is manipulated, a different, but equivalent, gate configuration is described. For example, a network implementation with a minimum number of gate input lines is obtained from the expression with a minimum number of literals. Once the desired form of the Boolean expression is obtained, it is a simple matter to draw a logic diagram for a gate network without feedback paths. By applying the analysis procedure in reverse, a direct topological drawing of the equation is constructed. That is, the order in which the operations occur within the equation is also the order in which the gates are connected to process the signals.

For simplicity, it is assumed that all variables and their complements are always available as inputs. This is known as *double-rail logic*. If the variables and their complements are not both available, then not-gates can always be used to obtain the complements. This case when complementary variables are not available is called *single-rail logic*.

In gate networks, the largest number of gates a signal must pass through from input to output is called the number of *levels of logic*. In Fig. 3.3 this path is through

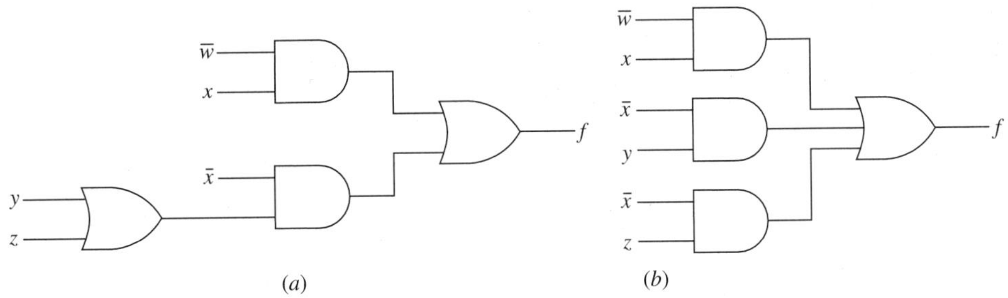

Figure 3.4 Synthesis of a gate combinational network. (*a*) $f(w,x,y,z) = \overline{w}x + \overline{x}(y+z)$. (*b*) $f(w,x,y,z) = \overline{w}x + \overline{x}y + \overline{x}z$.

the or-gate whose output is labeled G_1, the and-gate whose output is G_3, and finally the output or-gate. Thus, Fig. 3.3 shows a three-level gate network under the assumption of double-rail logic.

To illustrate the construction of a logic diagram from a Boolean expression, consider the Boolean function described by the formula

$$f(w,x,y,z) = \overline{w}x + \overline{x}(y + z)$$

The logic diagram of this equation is shown in Fig. 3.4*a* where the topological arrangement of the gates is in direct correspondence with the evaluation of the formula. That is, an or-gate producing $y + z$ is followed by an and-gate to obtain $\overline{x}(y + z)$. Concurrently, an and-gate is used to generate $\overline{w}x$. Finally, an output or-gate is used to combine the outputs of the subnetworks for $\overline{x}(y + z)$ and $\overline{w}x$. The resulting network consists of three levels.

When the above expression is rewritten in sum-of-products form, i.e., disjunctive normal form, it becomes

$$f(w,x,y,z) = \overline{w}x + \overline{x}y + \overline{x}z$$

This formula suggests the two-level network shown in Fig. 3.4*b*. Since the two expressions are equivalent, both of these networks have the same logical terminal behavior.

3.7.5 A Logic Design Example

The logic design process begins with a set of specifications. Although frequently it is possible to write a Boolean expression directly from the problem specifications, a more formal approach is to start with a truth table.

Consider the design of a gate combinational network which is to have the following characteristics: The inputs to the network are the binary numbers 0 to 15 and the output of the network is to produce the corresponding parity bit using an odd-parity-bit scheme. The concept of the parity bit was introduced in Sec. 2.11. Thus, the inputs to the network are 4-bit combinations of 0's and 1's ranging from 0000 to 1111. The proposed network must generate a 1 parity bit when there is an even

Table 3.10 Truth table for an odd-parity-bit generator for the first 16 binary numbers

w	x	y	z	p
0	0	0	0	1
0	0	0	1	0
0	0	1	0	0
0	0	1	1	1
0	1	0	0	0
0	1	0	1	1
0	1	1	0	1
0	1	1	1	0
1	0	0	0	0
1	0	0	1	1
1	0	1	0	1
1	0	1	1	0
1	1	0	0	1
1	1	0	1	0
1	1	1	0	0
1	1	1	1	1

number of 1's in the input state of the network and a 0 parity bit when there is an odd number of 1's. In this way, the total number of 1's in the input state and the parity bit collectively is odd.

The truth table for this odd-parity-bit generator is given in Table 3.10. The variables w, x, y, and z denote the 4 bits of the input state where w corresponds to the most significant bit and z corresponds to the least significant bit. The truth table has 16 rows corresponding to each of the possible input states. The functional values of the truth table are determined by the statement of the problem. In this case, the functional values, column p, are the desired parity bits the network produces and are assigned so that the number of 1's in each entire row of the table is odd.

Having obtained the truth table, a corresponding Boolean expression can be written. For example, the minterm canonical formula for Table 3.10 is

$$p(w,x,y,z) = \overline{w}\,\overline{x}\,\overline{y}\,\overline{z} + \overline{w}\,\overline{x}yz + \overline{w}x\overline{y}z + \overline{w}xy\overline{z} + w\overline{x}\,\overline{y}z + w\overline{x}y\overline{z} + wx\overline{y}\,\overline{z} + wxyz \quad (3.7)$$

Although it is not obvious at this time, Eq. (3.7) is also the simplest disjunctive normal formula, i.e., a formula consisting of a sum of product terms, describing the odd-parity-bit generator. The reader will be able to readily verify this fact after studying techniques for obtaining minimal expressions in the next chapter. Alternatively, the maxterm canonical formula for this example could be written, which is the simplest conjunctive normal formula, i.e., a formula consisting of a product of sum terms. Equation (3.7) is used to obtain the logic diagram shown in Fig. 3.5.

In general, a disjunctive normal formula always results in a network consisting of a set of and-gates followed by a single or-gate; while a conjunctive normal for-

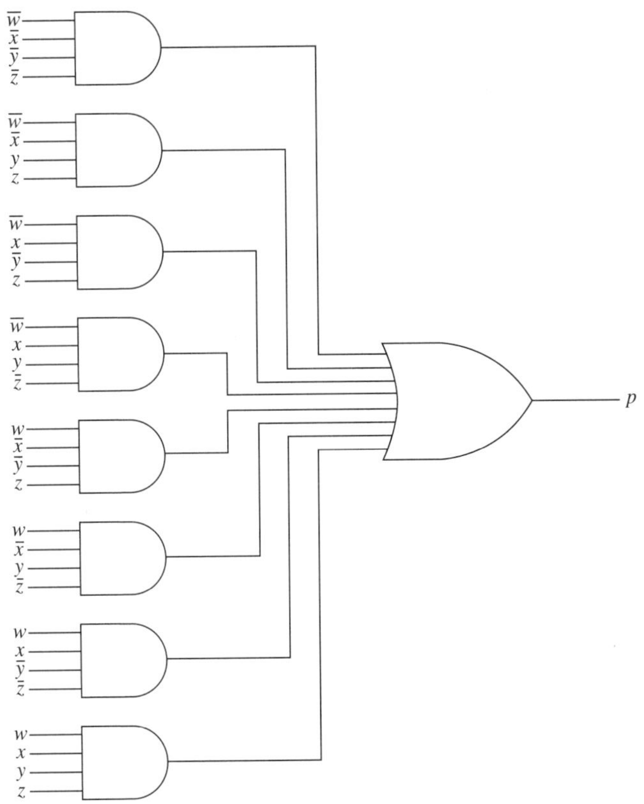

Figure 3.5 Two-level gate network for the odd-parity-bit generator.

mula always results in a network consisting of a set of or-gates followed by a single and-gate. Under the assumption of double-rail logic, every variable is available in both its complemented and uncomplemented form. Hence, not-gates are unnecessary and a realization based on either a disjunctive or conjunctive normal formula is a two-level network.

3.8 INCOMPLETE BOOLEAN FUNCTIONS AND DON'T-CARE CONDITIONS

In Sec. 3.4 a Boolean function was defined as a mapping that assigns a unique functional value to *each* combination of values of the n independent variables in which all values are limited to the set $\{0,1\}$. This type of Boolean function is said to be *completely specified.* An *incomplete Boolean function* differs from a complete Boolean function in that functional values are assigned to only a proper subset of the combinations of values of the n independent variables. Formally, an n-variable incomplete Boolean function $f(x_1, x_2, \ldots, x_n)$ is a mapping that assigns a unique value, called the value of the function, to a proper subset of the 2^n combinations of values of the n independent variables in which all specified values are limited to the set {0,1}. Incomplete Boolean functions are also called *incompletely specified functions.*

As in the case of a complete Boolean function, an n-variable incomplete Boolean function is represented by a truth table with $n + 1$ columns and 2^n rows. Again the first n columns provide for a complete listing of all the 0-1 combinations of values of the n variables and the last column gives the value of the function for each row. However, for those combinations of values in which a functional value is not to be specified, a symbol, say, $-$, is entered as the functional value in the last column of the table. Table 3.11*a* illustrates an incomplete Boolean function in which functional values are not specified for the combinations $(x,y,z) = (0,1,1)$ and $(1,0,1)$.

The complement, $\overline{f}(x_1, x_2, \ldots, x_n)$, of an incomplete Boolean function $f(x_1, x_2, \ldots, x_n)$ is also an incomplete Boolean function having the same unspecified rows in the truth table. The functional values in the remaining rows of the truth table for $\overline{f}$, however, are opposite to the functional values in the corresponding rows of the truth table for f. Table 3.11*b* shows the complement of the Boolean function given in Table 3.11*a*.

Table 3.11 An example of a three-variable incomplete Boolean function and its complement

x	y	z	f
0	0	0	1
0	0	1	1
0	1	0	0
0	1	1	—
1	0	0	0
1	0	1	—
1	1	0	0
1	1	1	1

(*a*)

x	y	z	$\overline{f}$
0	0	0	0
0	0	1	0
0	1	0	1
0	1	1	—
1	0	0	1
1	0	1	—
1	1	0	1
1	1	1	0

(*b*)

3.8.1 Describing Incomplete Boolean Functions

It was shown in Sec. 3.5 that a complete Boolean function can always be described by either a minterm canonical formula or a maxterm canonical formula in decimal notation. In order to obtain similar-type expressions for incomplete Boolean functions, a slight modification is needed.

Because of the way in which incomplete Boolean functions arise from logic-design problems, those rows of the truth table in which the functional values are *not* specified are called *don't-care conditions.* As was done previously, minterms and maxterms are still written for those rows having 1 and 0 functional values, respectively. However, it is also necessary to append information indicating the unspecified rows, i.e., the don't-care conditions. The most common approach is to simply add to the minterm or maxterm canonical formula a listing of the decimal equivalents of the rows associated with the don't-care conditions. For example, again consider Table 3.11*a*. Since the don't-care conditions correspond to rows 3 and 5, the term

$$dc(3,5)$$

is appended to the canonical formulas in decimal notation. In particular, the minterm canonical formula for Table 3.11*a* is given as

$$f(x,y,z) = \Sigma m(0,1,7) + dc(3,5)$$

and the maxterm canonical formula is written as

$$f(x,y,z) = \Pi M(2,4,6) + dc(3,5)$$

Manipulating Boolean equations, using the postulates and theorems of Boolean algebra, that are derived from incomplete Boolean functions is a very difficult task since one is free to use at will the various don't-care conditions in the manipulations. However, as is shown in the next chapter, for the purpose of obtaining minimal expressions there are procedures that can handle the don't-care conditions with no great amount of complexity.

3.8.2 Don't-Care Conditions in Logic Design

In the previous section, consideration was given to the logic design of gate networks that are described by complete Boolean functions. This involved constructing a truth table and specifying an output state for each row. Many logic-design problems, however, have a restricted set of input states. These problems are characterized by incomplete Boolean functions.

There are two ways in which a restricted set of input states can come about during the formulation of a mathematical model from the specifications of a problem. First, some input states may simply never occur. Consequently, the output states are irrelevant. Second, the input states may occur, but the corresponding output states need not be specified because of the environment in which the network is placed. In either case, these input states correspond to don't-care conditions.

These two types of don't-care conditions are equivalent for the purpose of formalizing the statement of a problem. If an input state never occurs, then the output state cannot be observed. For the case in which the output state is not specified for some input state that can occur, by convention it is agreed that the output state is of no consequence or, equivalently, is not to be observed. Thus, it is concluded that when a design problem involves don't-care conditions, a truth table may be formed without the need of specifying all the functional values. These truth tables are incomplete Boolean functions.

Once a gate network is synthesized, it is completely deterministic. That is, for every input state some output state must result. This is true even if a don't-care condition is applied to the network. Don't-care conditions provide the designer with flexibility. In particular, this allows the designer to judiciously choose the assignment of the output states to the don't-care conditions so that the realization is optimal. This procedure does not violate the mathematical concept of incomplete Boolean functions since incomplete Boolean functions describe a network's required behavior only for a selected set of input states. Thus, in designing such networks, the output states for the required behavior are determined by the problem specifications, and the output states for the don't-care conditions are determined by a criterion of an optimal realization.

To illustrate the formulation of an incomplete Boolean function as a mathematical model for a logic-design problem, assume it is desired to design a gate network that is an odd-parity-bit generator for the decimal digits 0 to 9 represented in 8421 BCD. Table 3.12 gives the truth table for the odd-parity-bit generator. The variable w denotes the bit in the 8421 code group whose weight is 8, the variable x denotes the bit whose

Table 3.12 Truth table of an odd-parity-bit generator when the decimal digits are represented in 8421 BCD

w	x	y	z	p
0	0	0	0	1
0	0	0	1	0
0	0	1	0	0
0	0	1	1	1
0	1	0	0	0
0	1	0	1	1
0	1	1	0	1
0	1	1	1	0
1	0	0	0	0
1	0	0	1	1
1	0	1	0	—
1	0	1	1	—
1	1	0	0	—
1	1	0	1	—
1	1	1	0	—
1	1	1	1	—

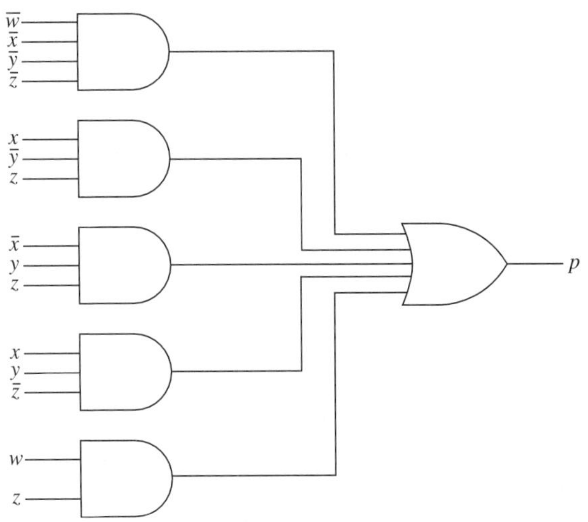

Figure 3.6 Logic diagram for the 8421 BCD odd-parity-bit generator.

weight is 4, the variable y denotes the bit whose weight is 2, and the variable z denotes the bit whose weight is 1. The parity bit that is to be produced by the gate network is shown in the p column. Functional values are only specified for the first 10 rows as determined by the statement of the problem. The last six rows are don't-care conditions since the binary combinations 1010 to 1111 cannot occur because they do not represent possible inputs to the logic network. That is, this network can only have as its inputs the 10 binary combinations associated with the 10 decimal digits expressed in 8421 BCD.

The minterm canonical formula describing Table 3.12 is

$$p(w,x,y,z) = \Sigma m(0,3,5,6,9) + dc(10,11,12,13,14,15)$$

Using the procedures of the next chapter, a simplified expression for this function is

$$p(w,x,y,z) = \bar{w}\bar{x}\bar{y}\bar{z} + x\bar{y}z + \bar{x}yz + xy\bar{z} + wz$$

The corresponding gate network is given in Fig. 3.6.

3.9 ADDITIONAL BOOLEAN OPERATIONS AND GATES

Up to this point, the development of a Boolean algebra and the correspondence between a Boolean algebra and gate realizations have been limited to three Boolean operations: and, or, and not. In actuality, these operations are really Boolean functions since they provide a mapping of a set of 0 and 1 symbol combinations onto the set of 0 and 1 symbols. These mappings are the tabular definitions previously stated as part of Theorem 3.10 in Sec. 3.3. Furthermore, a gate is an electronic circuit realization of a Boolean function. At this time, some additional specialized Boolean functions that are regarded as operations and having commercial gate realizations are studied.

Table 3.13 The nand-function

x	y	xy	**nand**$(x,y) = \overline{(xy)}$
0	0	0	1
0	1	0	1
1	0	0	1
1	1	1	0

3.9.1 The Nand-Function

Consider Table 3.13. The third column corresponds to the and-function of x and y and, hence, is described by the expression xy. The fourth column is the complement of the third column and is the definition of the *nand-function,* or simply *nand,* of x and y. Algebraically this is written as $\overline{(xy)}$. As is evident by the Boolean expression, the name nand is a contraction of not-and.

It is possible to generalize the definition of the nand-function when more than two variables are involved. In particular, the nand of n variables, $x_1, x_2, \ldots, x_n$, is defined algebraically as*

$$nand(x_1, x_2, \cdots, x_n) = \overline{(x_1 x_2 \cdots x_n)}$$

The nand-function is readily realizable with electronic circuit elements. A symbol for the nand-gate is shown in Fig. 3.7*a*. This symbol is a composite of the and-gate symbol and the inversion bubble associated with a not-gate. In general, a small circle on an input or output terminal of a gate symbol is regarded as the Boolean not-operation. Furthermore, as a consequence of DeMorgan's law, it immediately follows that

$$\overline{(x_1 x_2 \cdots x_n)} = \bar{x}_1 + \bar{x}_2 + \cdots + \bar{x}_n$$

This expression provides an alternate algebraic description of the nand-function and suggests the alternate gate symbol shown in Fig. 3.7*b*. Verbally, the output of a nand-gate is a logic-1 if and only if at least one of its inputs has the value of logic-0; otherwise, the output is logic-0.

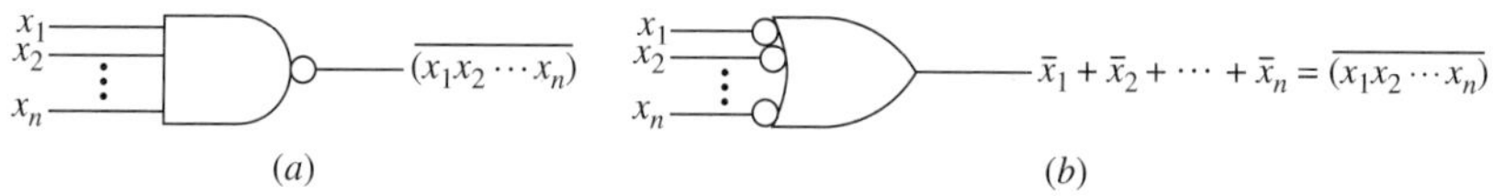

Figure 3.7 Nand-gate symbols. (*a*) Normal symbol. (*b*) Alternate symbol.

*Occasionally a special symbol is used to denote the nand-operation on a set of variables. One such symbol is $|$ and is referred to as a *stroke.* Thus, the stroke-operation on a set of n variables is defined by the expression $x_1 \mid x_2 \mid \cdots \mid x_n = \overline{(x_1 x_2 \cdots x_n)}$.

Table 3.14 The nor-function

x	y	$x + y$	$\text{nor}(x,y) = \overline{(x + y)}$
0	0	0	1
0	1	1	0
1	0	1	0
1	1	1	0

3.9.2 The Nor-Function

The dual concept to the nand-function is the *nor-function.* The third column of Table 3.14 corresponds to the or-function as applied to the variables x and y. The complement of this function is given as the fourth column and serves as the definition of the nor-function for two variables. The name nor is a contraction for not-or. Since the fourth column of Table 3.14 is the complement of the third, it immediately follows that an algebraic description of the nor-function is

$$\text{nor}(x,y) = \overline{(x + y)}$$

For the general case of n variables,*

$$\text{nor}(x_1, x_2, \ldots, x_n) = \overline{(x_1 + x_2 + \cdots + x_n)}$$

In an analogous manner to that for the nand-function, the definition of the nor-function suggests the gate symbol shown in Fig. 3.8*a*. An alternate gate symbol is given in Fig. 3.8*b* and follows by the use of DeMorgan's law, i.e.,

$$\overline{(x_1 + x_2 + \cdots + x_n)} = \bar{x}_1\bar{x}_2 \cdots \bar{x}_n$$

Again inversion bubbles are used in the gate symbols to indicate that algebraically a Boolean not-operation occurs at the terminal at which the inversion bubble appears. Verbally, the output of a nor-gate is logic-1 if and only if all of its inputs are at logic-0; otherwise, the output is logic-0.

3.9.3 Universal Gates

An important property of nand-gates and nor-gates is that it is possible to realize any combinational network with a collection of just one of these gate types. When

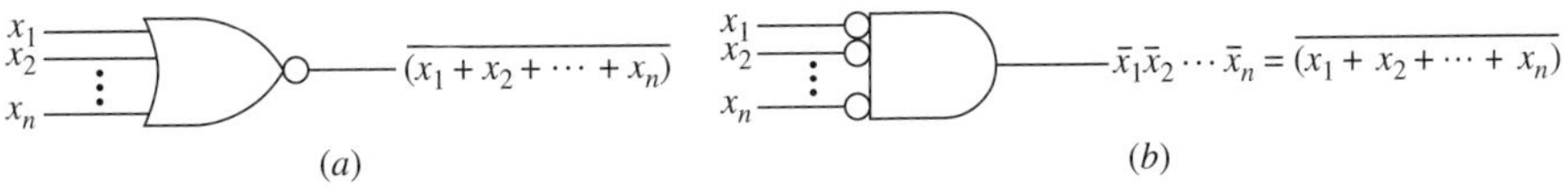

Figure 3.8 Nor-gate symbols. (*a*) Normal symbol. (*b*) Alternate symbol.

*Occasionally a special symbol is used to denote the nor-operation on a set of variables. One such symbol is $\downarrow$, referred to as a *dagger.* Thus, the dagger-operation on a set of n variables is defined by the expression $x_1 \downarrow x_2 \downarrow \cdots \downarrow x_n = \overline{(x_1 + x_2 + \cdots + x_n)}$.

network configurations utilizing only a single type of gate result in the realizations of the and-, or-, and not-functions, such a gate is called a *universal gate.* Both nand-gates and nor-gates are universal gates. Another important property of nand-gates and nor-gates is that their circuit realizations are more easily achieved.

The universal property of nand-gates is illustrated in Fig. 3.9. Since in Boolean algebra $xx = x$, by complementing both sides of the expression it immediately follows that $\overline{(xx)} = \bar{x}$. Hence, as shown in Fig. 3.9*a,* a two-input nand-gate with its inputs tied together is equivalent to a not-gate. Alternatively, since in Boolean algebra $x \cdot 1 = x$, then $\overline{(x \cdot 1)} = \bar{x}$ implies that a two-input nand-gate in which one input is x and the other is the constant logic-1 also serves as a not-gate. Figure 3.9*b* illustrates how the or-function is realized by the use of just nand-gates. In particular, since $\overline{(\bar{x}\bar{y})} = x + y$, using two nand-gates to form the complements of x and y and then using these as the inputs to a third nand-gate, the overall behavior of the network is that of the Boolean or-function. Finally, since $\overline{[\overline{(xy)}]} = xy$, the Boolean and-function is achieved by the network of Fig. 3.9*c* where the inputs x and y are applied to a single nand-gate to form $\overline{(xy)}$ and then the output of the gate is complemented, using a second nand-gate, to obtain the desired results.

Nor-gates are also universal gates. Thus, they can be used to form $\bar{x}$, $x + y$, and xy according to the relationships

$$\overline{(x + x)} = \bar{x} \qquad \text{or} \qquad \overline{(x + 0)} = \bar{x}$$

$$\overline{[\overline{(x + y)}]} = x + y$$

$$\overline{(\bar{x} + \bar{y})} = xy$$

These relationships are illustrated in Fig. 3.10.

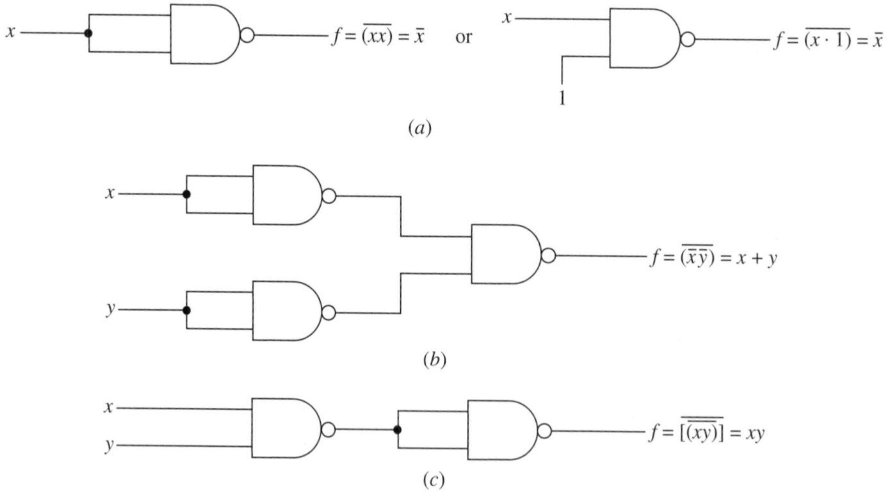

Figure 3.9 The universal property of nand-gates. (*a*) Not realization. (*b*) Or realization. (*c*) And realization.

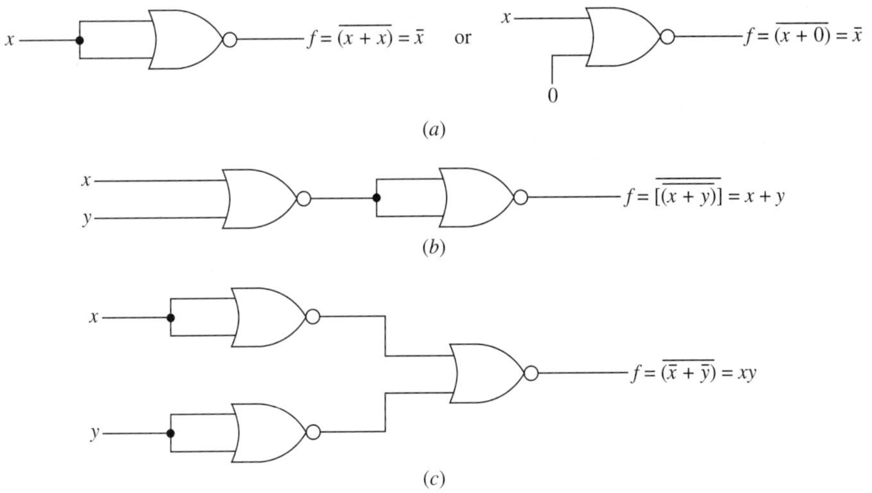

Figure 3.10 The universal property of nor-gates. (*a*) Not realization. (*b*) Or realization. (*c*) And realization.

As a result of the above discussion, any Boolean expression is realizable with a sufficient number of a single type of universal gate. For example, this can be done by simply replacing the and-, or-, and not-gates in a logic diagram by the networks shown in either Fig. 3.9 or Fig. 3.10. However, such an approach uses an excessive number of gates.

3.9.4 Nand-Gate Realizations

A better approach for obtaining a logic diagram of a combinational network utilizing only nand-gates involves manipulating its Boolean expression into the general form of the algebraic definition of the nand-function, i.e., nand$(A, B, \ldots, C) = \overline{(AB \cdots C)}$. To illustrate this procedure, consider the expression

$$f(w,x,y,z) = \bar{w}z + w\bar{z}(x + \bar{y})$$

Using DeMorgan's law, this expression is rewritten as

$$f(w,x,y,z) = \overline{\{\overline{(\bar{w}z)}\;\overline{[w\bar{z}(x + \bar{y})]}\}}$$

It is now noted that the general form of this expression is $\overline{(AB)}$ where $A = \overline{(\bar{w}z)}$ and $B = \overline{[w\bar{z}(x + \bar{y})]}$. Thus, a nand-gate having A and B as inputs results in the desired realization. This step is shown in Fig. 3.11*a*. The process is now repeated by manipulating the expressions for A and B so that they have the general form of the algebraic definition of the nand-function. Both of the expressions $A = \overline{(\bar{w}z)}$ and $B = \overline{[w\bar{z}(x + \bar{y})]}$ have the desired form. Thus, the expression for A is realized with a nand-gate having inputs $\bar{w}$ and z; while the expression for B is realized with a nand-gate having inputs w, $\bar{z}$, and $(x + \bar{y})$. This step is shown in Fig. 3.11*b*. Finally, it is

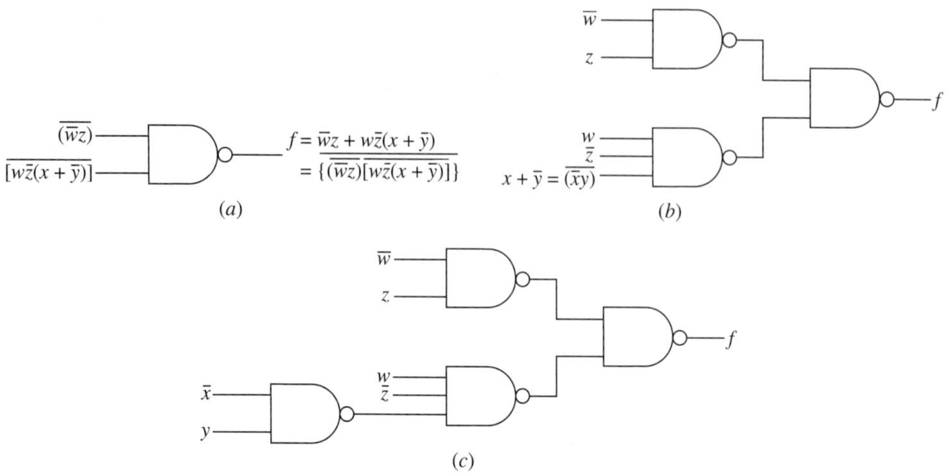

Figure 3.11 Steps involved to realize the Boolean expression $f(w,x,y,z) = \overline{w}z + w\overline{z}(x + \overline{y})$ using only nand-gates.

necessary to obtain the $x + \overline{y}$ input. Again, the general approach of manipulating an expression to conform to the definition of the nand-function is applied. In this case, $x + \overline{y} = \overline{(\overline{x}y)}$. This implies that the $x + \overline{y}$ input can be obtained as the output of a nand-gate whose inputs are $\overline{x}$ and y. Under the assumption of double-rail logic, the final realization is shown in Fig. 3.11*c*.

To apply the above procedure, it is necessary that the highest-order operation in the given Boolean expression be an or-operation. The highest-order operation of an expression is the last operation that is performed when the expression is evaluated. In the above example, the highest-order operation is the or-operation connecting the $\overline{w}z$ and $w\overline{z}(x + \overline{y})$ terms. If the highest-order operation of a Boolean expression is the and-operation, then the above procedure must be modified slightly. In particular, the expression is first complemented. This causes an overbar to occur over the entire expression, with the net result that the appropriate form for a nand-gate realization is obtained. The above realization procedure is then carried out on the complemented expression. Finally, a not-gate (or a nand-gate equivalent as previously shown in Fig. 3.9*a*) is placed at the output of the network for $\overline{f}$ to complete the realization.

As an illustration of this variation, consider the expression

$$f(x,y,z) = x(\overline{y} + z)$$

Since the highest-order operation is the and-operation connecting x with $\overline{y} + z$, it is necessary to first complement the expression to begin the nand-gate realization procedure; that is,

$$\overline{f}(x,y,z) = \overline{[x(\overline{y} + z)]}$$

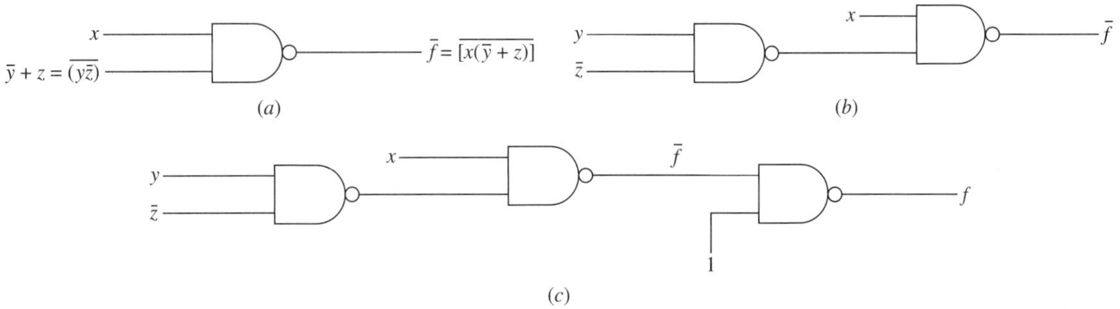

Figure 3.12 Steps involved to realize the Boolean expression $f(x,y,z) = x(\bar{y} + z)$ using only nand-gates.

Now that the desired form for a nand-gate realization is obtained, the procedure explained previously is carried out. This is illustrated in Fig. 3.12*a* and *b*. Finally, in order to obtain a realization of the original expression f, the output of the network is complemented as shown in Fig. 3.12*c*.

The above algebraic procedure to obtain a nand-gate realization can also be performed graphically. This procedure makes use of the two gate symbols shown in Fig. 3.7 for a nand-gate. By making use of both symbols within the same logic diagram, the application of DeMorgan's law, required in the above algebraic procedure, is readily achieved. The steps in the graphical procedure are as follows:

1. Apply DeMorgan's law to the expression so that all unary operations appear only with single variables. Draw the logic diagram using and-gates and or-gates.
2. Replace each and-gate symbol by the nand-gate symbol of Fig. 3.7*a* and each or-gate symbol by the nand-gate symbol of Fig. 3.7*b*.
3. Check the bubbles occurring on all lines *between* two gate symbols. For every bubble that is not compensated by another bubble along the same line, insert the appropriate not-gate symbol from Fig. 3.13 so that the not-gate bubble occurs on the same side as the gate bubble.
4. Whenever an input variable enters a gate symbol at a bubble, complement the variable. If the output line has a bubble, then insert an output not-gate symbol.
5. Replace all not-gates by a nand-gate equivalent if desired.

To illustrate this graphical procedure, again consider the expression

$$f(w,x,y,z) = \bar{w}z + w\bar{z}(x + \bar{y})$$

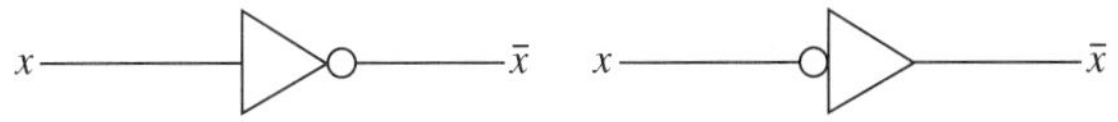

Figure 3.13 Two equivalent not-gate symbols.

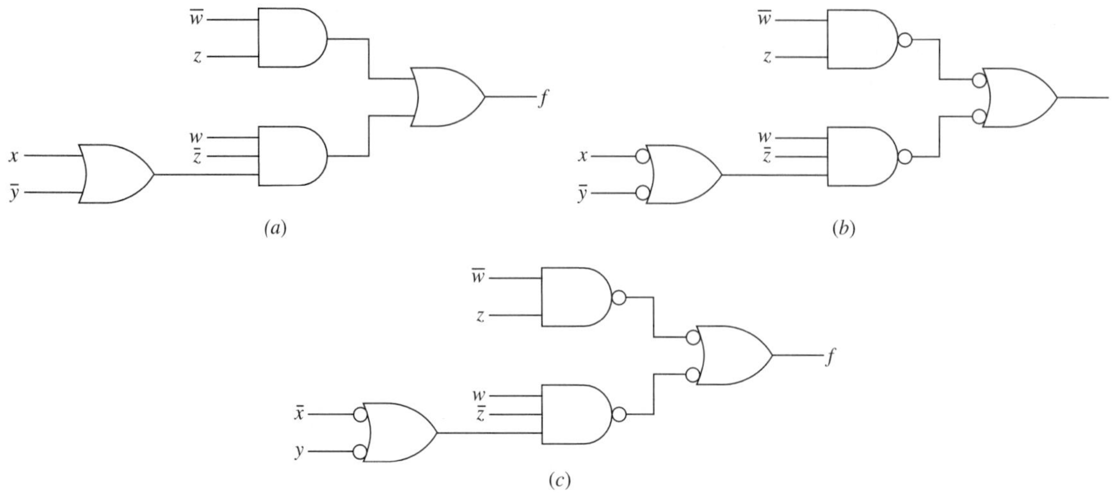

Figure 3.14 Steps illustrating the graphical procedure for obtaining a nand-gate realization of the expression $f(w,x,y,z) = \overline{w}z + w\overline{z}(x + \overline{y})$.

The corresponding logic diagram using and-gates and or-gates is shown in Fig. 3.14*a*. Next, according to Step 2, each and-gate symbol is replaced by the nand-gate symbol of Fig. 3.7*a* and each or-gate symbol is replaced by the nand-gate symbol of Fig. 3.7*b* as shown in Fig. 3.14*b*. Since each gate output bubble is connected directly to a gate input bubble, Step 3 is not needed. Finally, as indicated in Step 4, since the inputs x and $\overline{y}$ in Fig. 3.14*b* are entering at bubbles, they are complemented as shown in Fig. 3.14*c*. If the alternate nand-gate symbols are replaced by the conventional nand-gate symbols, then the network of Fig. 3.14*c* becomes that of Fig. 3.11*c*.

3.9.5 Nor-Gate Realizations

In much the same way that nand-gate realizations are obtained from Boolean expressions, nor-gate realizations can also be obtained. One such procedure is based on manipulating the Boolean expression describing the network behavior to conform to the general algebraic definition of the nor-function; that is, $\text{nor}(A,B,\ldots,C) = \overline{(A + B + \cdots + C)}$. If the highest-order operation of the original expression is the and-operation, then it is a simple matter to progress step by step, starting with the output nor-gate, to produce the desired logic diagram. On the other hand, if the highest-order operation is the or-operation, then the procedure must be modified slightly. The logic diagram for the complement of the original expression is first obtained and then a not-gate (or a not-gate equivalent as previously shown in Fig. 3.10*a*) is placed at the output.

Again consider the Boolean expression

$$f(w,x,y,z) = \overline{w}z + w\overline{z}(x + \overline{y})$$

To construct a nor-gate realization for it, first it is noted that the highest-order operation is the or-operation appearing between the $\overline{w}z$ and $w\overline{z}(x+\overline{y})$ terms. Thus, it is necessary to first complement the original expression, i.e.,

$$\overline{f}(w,x,y,z) = \overline{[\overline{w}z + w\overline{z}(x+\overline{y})]}$$

Since the general form of this expression is $\overline{(A+B)}$ where $A = \overline{w}z$ and $B = w\overline{z}(x+\overline{y})$, it immediately follows that $\overline{f}$ appears at the output of a nor-gate whose inputs are $\overline{w}z$ and $w\overline{z}(x+\overline{y})$. This is shown in Fig. 3.15*a*. The two terms $\overline{w}z$ and $w\overline{z}(x+\overline{y})$ are next rewritten so as to have the appropriate form according to the algebraic definition of the nor-function. In particular, $\overline{w}z = \overline{(w+\overline{z})}$ and $w\overline{z}(x+\overline{y}) = \overline{[\overline{w}+z+\overline{(x+\overline{y})}]}$. These two expressions are now realized using nor-gates as shown in Fig. 3.15*b*. It is immediately noted that the term $\overline{(x+\overline{y})}$ is simply realizable as the output from a nor-gate having x and $\overline{y}$ as inputs. At this point, the logic diagram appears as in Fig. 3.15*c*. Finally, an output nor-gate is used to complement the function $\overline{f}$ thus far realized in order to obtain the realization of the original Boolean expression f. The final logic diagram is given in Fig. 3.15*d*.

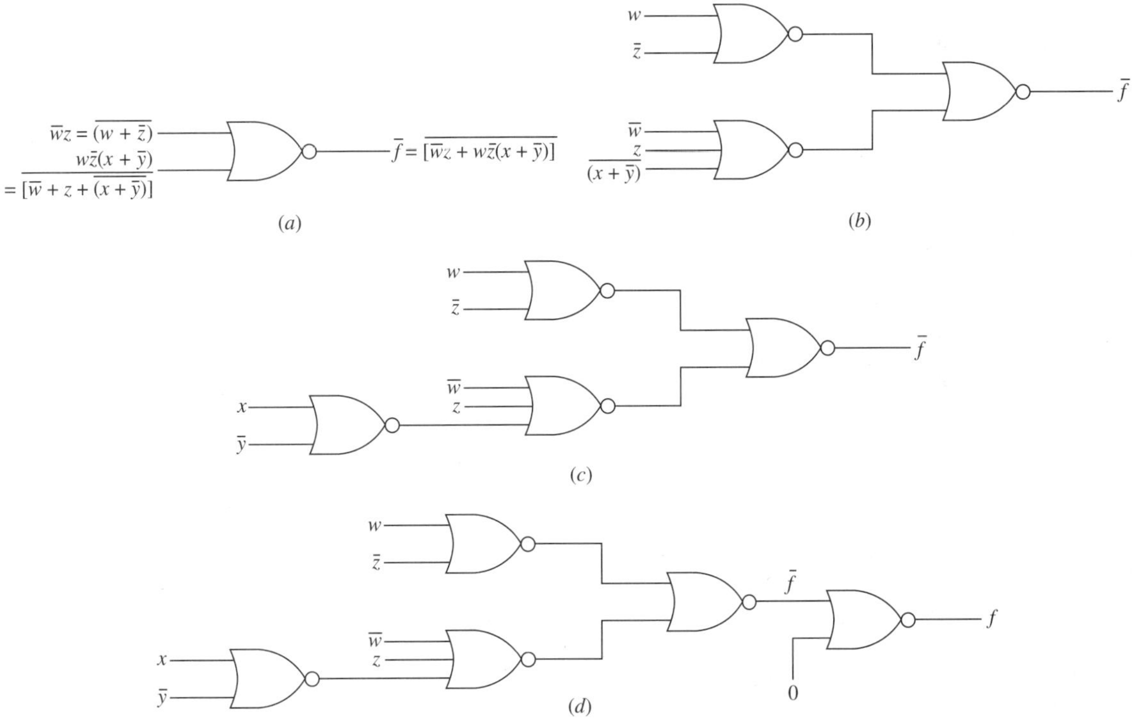

Figure 3.15 Steps involved to realize the Boolean expression $f(w,x,y,z) = \overline{w}z + w\overline{z}(x+\overline{y})$ using only nor-gates.

Analogously to that of nand-gate realizations, the above algebraic procedure can be performed graphically. In this case, use is made of the two gate symbols shown in Fig. 3.8 for nor-gates. The steps of this graphical procedure are as follows:

1. Apply DeMorgan's law to the expression so that all unary operations appear only with single variables. Draw the logic diagram using and-gates and or-gates.
2. Replace each or-gate symbol by the nor-gate symbol of Fig. 3.8*a* and each and-gate symbol by the nor-gate symbol of Fig. 3.8*b*.
3. Check the bubbles occurring on all lines *between* two gate symbols. For every bubble that is not compensated by another bubble along the same line, insert the appropriate not-gate symbol from Fig. 3.13 so that the not-gate bubble occurs on the same side as the gate bubble.
4. Whenever an input variable enters a gate symbol at a bubble, complement the variable. If the output line has a bubble, then insert an output not-gate symbol.
5. Replace all not-gates by a nor-gate equivalent if desired.

Figure 3.16 shows the steps of the graphical procedure again being applied to the Boolean expression

$$f(w,x,y,z) = \overline{w}z + w\overline{z}(x + \overline{y})$$

The logic diagram is first drawn using conventional and-gates and or-gates as shown in Fig. 3.16*a*. As specified in Step 2 of the above procedure, each or-gate symbol is replaced by the nor-gate symbol of Fig. 3.8*a* and each and-gate symbol is replaced by the nor-gate symbol of Fig. 3.8*b*. At this point, the diagram appears as

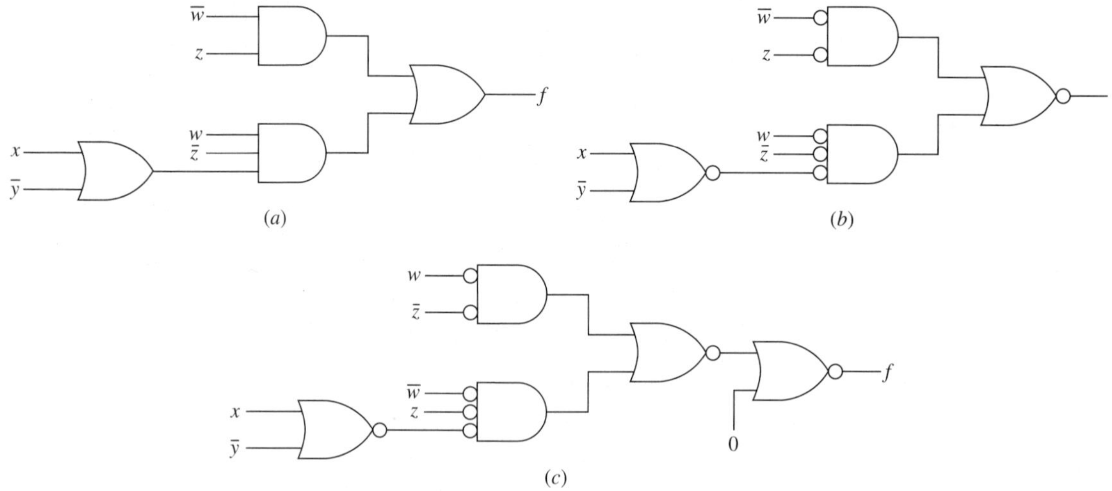

Figure 3.16 Steps illustrating the graphical procedure for obtaining a nor-gate realization of the expression $f(w,x,y,z) = \overline{w}z + w\overline{z}(x + \overline{y})$.

Table 3.15 The exclusive-or-function

x	y	$x \oplus y$
0	0	0
0	1	1
1	0	1
1	1	0

in Fig. 3.16*b*. Checking all lines between gates, each inversion bubble at one end has a matching inversion bubble at the other end. Hence, Step 3 does not have to be applied. Finally, as indicated by Step 4, the four inputs entering at bubbles are complemented and an output not-gate is appended since the output gate in Fig. 3.16*b* has a bubble. This gives the logic diagram shown in Fig. 3.16*c*. Comparing Fig. 3.16*c* to Fig. 3.15*d* and recalling that two symbols are possible for a nor-gate, it is seen that the same results are obtained.

3.9.6 The Exclusive-Or-Function

Another specialized Boolean function of interest is the *exclusive-or-function.* The exclusive-or of x and y is denoted by $x \oplus y$ and is defined by Table 3.15. As indicated by the definition, the exclusive-or of x and y is a logic-1 if and only if x or y, but not both x and y, has the value of logic-1; otherwise, the exclusive-or is logic-0. As is evident from the definition, it is possible to write the algebraic expression

$$x \oplus y = \bar{x}y + x\bar{y}$$

Comparing the definition of the exclusive-or-function with that of the Boolean or-function previously defined, it is seen that they differ only when both x and y have the value of logic-1. To emphasize this distinction, the conventional Boolean or-function is also referred to as the *inclusive-or-function.*

A special gate symbol has been defined for the exclusive-or-function. This symbol is shown in Fig. 3.17 and is frequently referred to as an xor-gate. Normally, xor-gates are available only as two-input gates.

The exclusive-or-function has many interesting properties. These are summarized in Table 3.16. Uppercase letters are used in this table to emphasize the fact that these variables can represent expressions as well as single variables. To reduce the number of occurrences of parentheses, by convention, it is assumed that the and-operation takes precedence over the exclusive-or-operation. No precedence between the inclusive-or- and exclusive-or-operations is assumed and, hence, parentheses

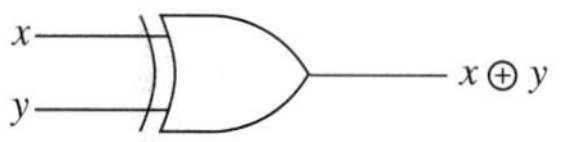

Figure 3.17 The xor-gate symbol.

Table 3.16 Properties of the exclusive-or-operation

	(a)	*(b)*
(i)	$X \oplus Y = \overline{X}Y + X\overline{Y} = (X + Y)(\overline{X} + \overline{Y})$	$\overline{(X \oplus Y)} = \overline{X}\,\overline{Y} + XY = (\overline{X} + Y)(X + \overline{Y})$
(ii)	$X \oplus 0 = X$	$X \oplus 1 = \overline{X}$
(iii)	$X \oplus X = 0$	$X \oplus \overline{X} = 1$
(iv)	$\overline{X} \oplus \overline{Y} = X \oplus Y$	$\overline{X} \oplus Y = X \oplus \overline{Y} = \overline{(X \oplus Y)}$
(v)	$X \oplus Y = Y \oplus X$	
(vi)	$X \oplus (Y \oplus Z) = (X \oplus Y) \oplus Z = X \oplus Y \oplus Z$	
(vii)	$X(Y \oplus Z) = XY \oplus XZ$	
(viii)	$X + Y = X \oplus Y \oplus XY$	
(ix)	$X \oplus Y = X + Y$ if and only if $XY \equiv 0$	
(x)	If $X \oplus Y = Z$, then $Y \oplus Z = X$ or $X \oplus Z = Y$	

are needed when these two operations appear within an expression. All of the properties given in Table 3.16 are easily proved by perfect induction.

To illustrate the use of the exclusive-or properties given in Table 3.16 and to show the usefulness of xor-gates in logic design, again consider the odd-parity-bit generator that was designed in Sec. 3.7. At that time the Boolean expression for the generator was obtained, i.e., Eq. (3.7). Starting from that point, the following Boolean manipulations can now be performed:

$$
\begin{aligned}
p(w,x,y,z) &= \overline{w}\,\overline{x}\,\overline{y}\,\overline{z} + \overline{w}\,\overline{x}yz + \overline{w}x\overline{y}z + \overline{w}xy\overline{z} + w\overline{x}\,\overline{y}z + w\overline{x}y\overline{z} + wx\overline{y}\,\overline{z} + wxyz \\
&= \overline{w}\,\overline{x}(\overline{y}\,\overline{z} + yz) + \overline{w}x(\overline{y}z + y\overline{z}) + w\overline{x}(\overline{y}z + y\overline{z}) + wx(\overline{y}\,\overline{z} + yz) \\
&= \overline{w}\,\overline{x}\overline{(y \oplus z)} + \overline{w}x(y \oplus z) + w\overline{x}(y \oplus z) + wx\overline{(y \oplus z)} && \text{by Prop. (i}a\text{-}b\text{)} \\
&= (\overline{w}\,\overline{x} + wx)\overline{(y \oplus z)} + (\overline{w}x + w\overline{x})(y \oplus z) \\
&= \overline{(w \oplus x)}\,\overline{(y \oplus z)} + (w \oplus x)(y \oplus z) && \text{by Prop. (i}a\text{-}b\text{)} \\
&= \overline{[(w \oplus x) \oplus (y \oplus z)]} && \text{by Prop. (i}b\text{)} \\
&= \overline{(w \oplus x)} \oplus (y \oplus z) && \text{by Prop. (iv}b\text{)} \\
&= (\overline{w} \oplus x) \oplus (y \oplus z) && \text{by Prop. (iv}b\text{)}
\end{aligned}
$$

A realization based on the final equation is shown in Fig. 3.18 in which it is assumed that only two-input exclusive-or-gates are available. It should be noted how much simpler this realization is than the one given in Fig. 3.5.

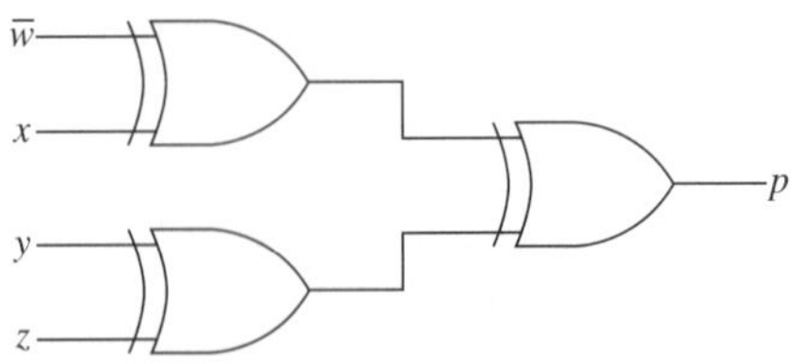

Figure 3.18 Another realization of the odd-parity-bit generator.

Table 3.17 The exclusive-nor-function

x	y	$x \odot y = \overline{(x \oplus y)}$
0	0	1
0	1	0
1	0	0
1	1	1

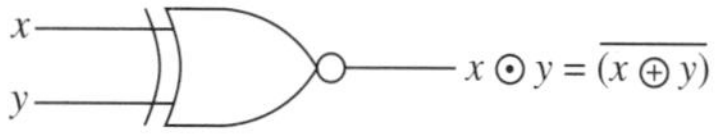

Figure 3.19 The xnor-gate symbol.

3.9.7 The Exclusive-Nor-Function

The last specialized Boolean function to be introduced is the *exclusive-nor-function,* which is simply the complement of the exclusive-or-function. Thus, the exclusive-nor of x and y, written $x \odot y$, is a logic-1 if and only if the logic values of both x and y are the same; otherwise, the value of $x \odot y$ is logic-0. Thus, the exclusive-nor-function is also called the *equivalence-function.* The definition of the exclusive-nor-function is tabulated in Table 3.17. The gate symbol for this function is shown in Fig. 3.19 and is frequently referred to as an xnor-gate. As in the case of the xor-gates, xnor-gates are normally only available with two inputs.

3.10 GATE PROPERTIES

Several types of logical gates were introduced in this chapter. It has been shown that there is a direct correspondence between Boolean equations and the topological structure of combinational gate networks. In establishing the two-valued Boolean algebra as a mathematical model for combinational logic networks, it was assumed that only two signal values occur at the gate terminals and that the transient behavior of the combinational networks was to be ignored.

Actual circuits of the logic gates are discussed in the Appendix. In general, there are many different circuit designs for a given gate type. These designs are dependent upon the components and circuit technology used. A class of digital circuits having a common circuit technology and general structure is called a *logic family.* Among these are *transistor-transistor logic* (TTL), *emitter-coupled logic* (ECL), and *complementary metal-oxide semiconductor logic* (CMOS logic). Furthermore, within each logic family there are usually more than one *logic series.* The circuits within the series have, in addition to a specific circuit technology and structure, some common distinctive characteristic. For example, within the TTL logic family some of the logic series are 54/74 standard TTL, Schottky TTL, advanced Schottky TTL, low-power Schottky TTL, and advanced low-power Schottky TTL. The appropriate logic family and series for a given digital system depend upon what operating requirements must be met.

Although the Appendix deals with the specifics of various logic families, it is appropriate at this time to consider some of the gate properties that are relevant to the logic design process. As was previously mentioned, the two signal values associated with logic-0 and logic-1 are not really single values but, rather, ranges of values. The assignment being used in this book is that if a signal value is in some low-level

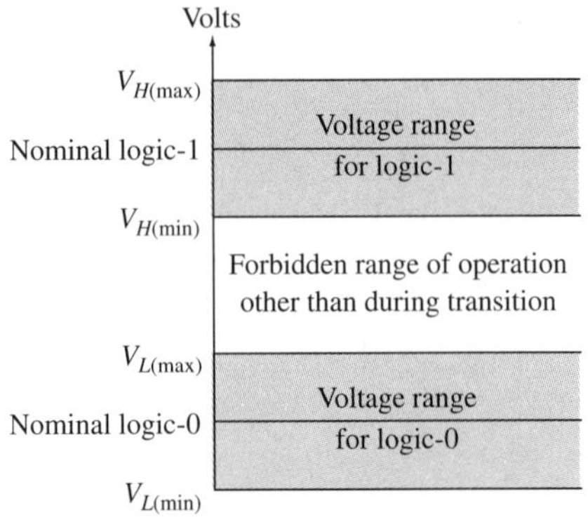

Figure 3.20 Voltage ranges of logic inputs for positive logic.

voltage range between $V_{L(\min)}$ and $V_{L(\max)}$, then it is assigned to logic-0. Similarly, when a signal value is in some high-level voltage range between $V_{H(\min)}$ and $V_{H(\max)}$, it is assigned to logic-1. This is illustrated in Fig. 3.20.* As long as the signal values stay within their assigned ranges, except during transit between ranges, the logic gates behave as intended. Steady-state signals within the forbidden range result in unreliable gate behavior. It is because a prespecified range of signal values is regarded as the same logic value that digital systems are highly reliable under such conditions as induced noise, temperature variations, component fabrication variations, and power supply variations. However, for simplicity in discussion, nominal values of the signals are frequently regarded as their true values.

In manufacturer's literature, the terminal behavior of the logic elements is stated in terms of the symbols L and H, denoting low and high voltage ranges, rather than logic-0 and logic-1. For example, Table 3.18 illustrates how a manufacturer might specify the terminal behavior of some type of gate circuit. Upon substituting 0 and 1 for L and H, respectively, the Boolean definition of the and-function results and, hence, such a circuit is a (positive) and-gate.†

There are several properties associated with logic gates that determine the environment in which a digital system can operate as well as introduce constraints on its topological structure. These include *noise margins, fan-out, propagation delays,* and *power dissipation.* Noise margins are a measure of the capability of a circuit to operate reliably in the presence of induced noise. The fan-out of a circuit is the

*This is the positive-logic concept. Alternatively, logic-0 can be assigned to the higher voltage range and logic-1 to the lower voltage range. Such as assignment is referred to as negative logic.

†It should be noted that if 0 and 1 are substituted for H and L, respectively, in Table 3.18, then the circuit behavior becomes that of an or-gate. Thus, under positive logic, a circuit that behaves as an and-gate becomes, under negative logic, an or-gate. To avoid any confusion, this book has adopted the positive-logic convention.

Table 3.18 Voltage table for a (positive) and-gate

Inputs		Output
x	y	z
L	L	L
L	H	L
H	L	L
H	H	H

number of gates or loads that can be connected to the output of the circuit and still maintain reliable operation. The propagation delays of a gate circuit are influencing factors that determine the overall operating speed of a digital system since they establish how fast the circuit can perform its intended function. Finally, power dissipation is the power consumed by the gate that, in turn, determines the size of the power supply needed for the digital system.

3.10.1 Noise Margins

For performance purposes, gate circuits are designed so that $V_{H(\text{min})}$ is different at the input and output terminals of a gate. That is, the minimal signal value that is acceptable as a logic-1 at the input to a gate is different from the minimal logic-1 signal value that a gate produces at its output. A similar situation also occurs for $V_{L(\text{max})}$. Thus, manufacturers normally state a $V_{IL(\text{max})}$, $V_{IH(\text{min})}$, $V_{OL(\text{max})}$, and $V_{OH(\text{min})}$ in the gate specifications. That is, the manufacturer guarantees that any input voltage less than $V_{IL(\text{max})}$ is recognized by the gate as corresponding to a low-range (logic-0) voltage input. On the other hand, any input voltage greater than $V_{IH(\text{min})}$ is recognized by the gate as corresponding to a high-range (logic-1) voltage input. Furthermore, the manufacturer guarantees that the low-range (logic-0) voltage output of the gate does not exceed $V_{OL(\text{max})}$ and that the high-range (logic-1) voltage output of the gate does exceed $V_{OH(\text{min})}$. Of course, this assumes that any manufacturer-specified loading, temperature, and power supply constraints are adhered to. In addition, gate circuit behavior is meaningful only if $V_{OL(\text{max})} < V_{IL(\text{max})} < V_{IH(\text{min})} < V_{OH(\text{min})}$.

To understand the significance of these gate specifications, consider the effect of connecting the output of a gate to another gate as shown in Fig. 3.21*a*, in which noise is induced between the two gates. In Fig. 3.21*b* the four values discussed above are drawn on a straight line so as to emphasize their relative values. Since the low-level output of gate 1, i.e., logic-0, is less than $V_{OL(\text{max})}$ and any signal less than $V_{IL(\text{max})}$ is regarded as a low-level input to gate 2, i.e., also a logic-0, it is seen that any additive noise induced between the gates less than $V_{IL(\text{max})} - V_{OL(\text{max})}$ does not affect the logic behavior of the two gates in cascade. This is called the *worst-case low-level noise margin.* In a similar manner, since the high-level output of gate 1, i.e., logic-1, is greater than $V_{OH(\text{min})}$ and any input signal greater than $V_{IH(\text{min})}$ is regarded as a high-level input to gate 2, i.e., also a logic-1, it is seen that any subtractive noise induced between the gates less than

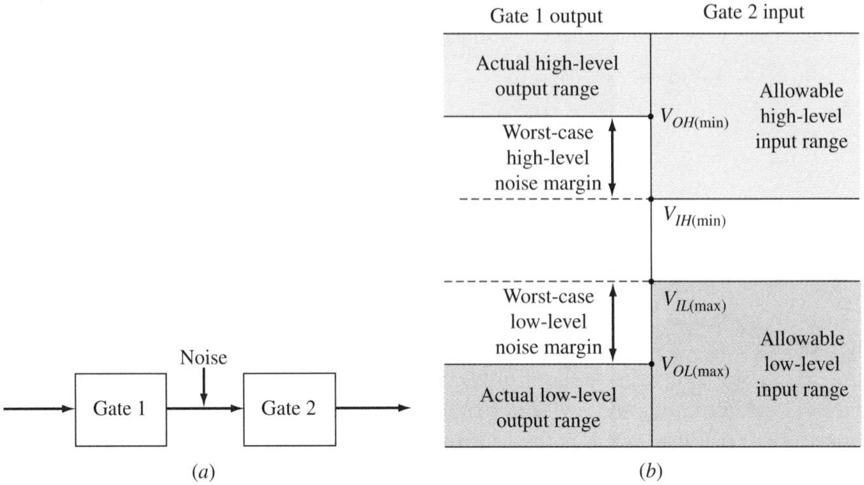

Figure 3.21 Noise effects. (*a*) Interconnection of two gates with induced noise. (*b*) Noise margins.

$V_{OH(\min)} - V_{IH(\min)}$ does not affect the logic behavior of the two gates in cascade. This is called the *worst-case high-level noise margin.* As seen from these definitions, noise margins are a measure of a digital circuit's immunity to the presence of induced electrical noise.

It should be noted that the above noise margins are worst-case values. If the actual low-level output voltage of gate 1 is V_{OL1}, where $V_{OL1} \le V_{OL(\max)}$, then the actual low-level noise margin, NM_L, is given by

$$NM_L = V_{IL(\max)} - V_{OL1}$$

Similarly, if the actual high-level output voltage of gate 1 is V_{OH1}, where $V_{OH1} \ge V_{OH(\min)}$, then the actual high-level noise margin, NM_H, is

$$NM_H = V_{OH1} - V_{IH(\min)}$$

3.10.2 Fan-Out

As discussed in the Appendix, the signal value at the output of a gate is dependent upon the number of gates to which the output terminal is connected. Since for proper operation the signal values must always remain within their allowable ranges, this implies that there is a limitation to the number of gates that can serve as loads to a given gate. This is known as the *fan-out capability* of the gate. Again, manufacturers specify this limitation. It is then the responsibility of the designer of a logic network to adhere to the limitation. To do this, circuits known as *buffers,* which have no logic properties but rather serve as amplifiers, are sometimes incorporated into a logic network.

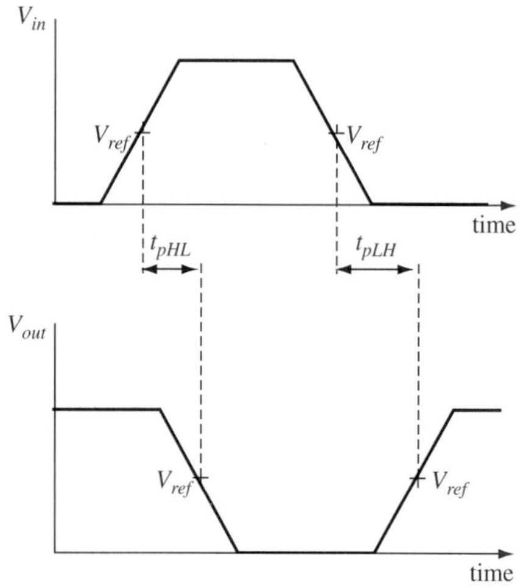

Figure 3.22 Propagation delay times.

3.10.3 Propagation Delays

Digital signals do not change nor do circuits respond instantaneously. For this reason there is a limitation to the overall speed of operation associated with a gate. Figure 3.22 shows waveforms at the input and output terminals of a not-gate.* Here finite rise and fall times are indicated as well as delays in response to the input changes. That is, the signals do not go between their logic-0 and logic-1 values in zero time. In addition, the effect of a change at the input terminal does not appear immediately as a change at the output terminal. Rather, owing to the physical behavior of the electronic components in the gate there is a time delay before the output changes. Using a specified reference point, say the 50 percent point, on the rise and fall of the signals, V_{ref}, two time delays are indicated in Fig. 3.22. These are referred to as *propagation delays.* The time required for the output signal to change from its high level to its low level as a consequence of an input signal change is t_{pHL}; while the time required for the output signal to change from its low level to its high level as a consequence of an input signal change is t_{pLH}. These two delay times, t_{pHL} and t_{pLH}, are, in general, not equal. Manufacturers normally give maximum values for these times in the gate specifications. As a general measure of the response speed of a gate, one frequently uses an average propagation delay time, t_{pd}, which is defined as

$$t_{pd} = \frac{t_{pHL} + t_{pLH}}{2}$$

*Similar waveforms can be drawn for other types of gates under the assumption that all but one of the gate inputs are held fixed and the remaining input is changed to cause the output to change, possibly, but not necessarily, with an inversion.

3.10.4 Power Dissipation

In the course of operation, a digital circuit consumes power as a result of the flow of currents. There are two components to this power dissipation. *Static power dissipation* occurs when the circuit is in its steady-state condition; while *dynamic power dissipation* occurs as the result of changes of the various signals. In both cases, the necessary currents must be provided by the power supply of the digital system.

Certainly it is desirable in a digital system to have gates with low power dissipation and high speed of operation (i.e., low propagation delay times). However, these two performance parameters are in conflict with each other. As a result, a common measure of gate performance is the product of the propagation delay and the power dissipation of the gate. This is known as the *delay-power product.*

CHAPTER 3 PROBLEMS

3.1 Using the basic Boolean identities given in Table 3.1, prove the following relationships by going from the expression on the left side of the equals sign to the expression on the right side. State which postulate or theorem is applied at each step.

a. $xy + x\bar{y} + \bar{x}\bar{y} = x + \bar{y}$

b. $\overline{(\bar{x}\bar{z} + \bar{x}y + \bar{x}z + xy)} = x\bar{y}$

c. $(x + y)(\bar{x}\bar{z} + z)\overline{(\bar{y} + xz)} = \bar{x}y$

d. $\overline{(xy + yz + xz)} = \bar{x}\bar{y} + \bar{y}\bar{z} + \bar{x}\bar{z}$

e. $xy + yz + \bar{x}z = xy + \bar{x}z$ (consensus theorem)

f. $(x + y)(\bar{x} + z) = xz + \bar{x}y$

g. $(x + y)(y + z)(x + z) = xy + yz + xz$

h. $x\bar{y} + y\bar{z} + \bar{x}z = \bar{x}y + \bar{y}z + x\bar{z}$

3.2 Prove that in a Boolean algebra the cancellation law does not hold; that is, show that, for every x, y, and z in a Boolean algebra, $xy = xz$ does not imply $y = z$. Does $x + y = x + z$ imply $y = z$?

3.3 Using the method of perfect induction, prove the following identities for a two-valued Boolean algebra.

a. $\bar{x}z + xy = (\bar{x} + y)(x + z)$

b. $\overline{(x + y + z)} = \bar{x}\bar{y}\bar{z}$

c. $xy + yz + \bar{x}z = xy + \bar{x}z$ (consensus theorem)

3.4 Prove that no Boolean algebra has exactly three distinct elements.

3.5 Construct the truth table for each of the following Boolean functions.

a. $f(x,y,z) = yz + (\bar{x} + y)(\bar{x} + \bar{z})$

b. $f(x,y,z) = \overline{(xy + \bar{x}z)} + yz$

c. $f(x,y,z) = (x + \overline{y})(y + z)(\overline{x} + z)$

d. $f(w,x,y,z) = wxy + \overline{w}(\overline{y} + z)$

3.6 For each of the truth tables in Table P3.6, write the corresponding minterm canonical formula in algebraic form and in m-notation.

3.7 Write each of the following minterm canonical formulas in algebraic form and construct their corresponding truth tables.

a. $f(x,y,z) = \Sigma m(0,2,4,5,7)$

b. $f(w,x,y,z) = \Sigma m(1,3,7,8,9,14,15)$

3.8 For each of the truth tables in Table P3.6, write the corresponding maxterm canonical formula in algebraic form and in M-notation.

Table P3.6

x	y	z	f
0	0	0	1
0	0	1	1
0	1	0	0
0	1	1	1
1	0	0	0
1	0	1	1
1	1	0	1
1	1	1	0

(a)

w	x	y	z	f
0	0	0	0	0
0	0	0	1	1
0	0	1	0	1
0	0	1	1	0
0	1	0	0	1
0	1	0	1	0
0	1	1	0	1
0	1	1	1	1
1	0	0	0	0
1	0	0	1	0
1	0	1	0	0
1	0	1	1	1
1	1	0	0	1
1	1	0	1	1
1	1	1	0	0
1	1	1	1	1

(b)

3.9 Write each of the following maxterm canonical formulas in algebraic form and construct their corresponding truth tables.

a. $f(x,y,z) = \Pi M(0,1,2,5,7)$

b. $f(w,x,y,z) = \Pi M(0,3,6,7,9,10,12,13,15)$

3.10 Complement each of the following Boolean expressions.

a. $(w + x + y)(\overline{w} + xz) + \overline{y}\,\overline{z}$

b. $\overline{x}(\overline{w}\,\overline{y} + xy\overline{z})$

c. $w\overline{y}[\overline{(w\overline{y})} + x\overline{z}]$

d. $wx + z[\overline{(w + \overline{x} + \overline{y})} + \overline{(x + y)}]$

3.11 Applying the expansion theorem to the Boolean expression

$$f(w,x,y,z) = \overline{w}xy\overline{z} + z(x\overline{y} + w\overline{x})$$

rewrite the expression in the following forms.

a. $f(w,x,y,z) = x \cdot g_1(w,y,z) + \overline{x} \cdot g_2(w,y,z)$

b. $f(w,x,y,z) = [z + h_1(w,x,y)][\overline{z} + h_2(w,x,y)]$

3.12 Using the Boolean algebra postulates and theorems, simplify each of the following expressions as disjunctive normal formulas with the least number of literals.

a. $yz + \overline{x}\,\overline{y}z + xy\overline{z}$

b. $\overline{x}\,\overline{y}\,\overline{z} + \overline{x}\,\overline{y}z + \overline{x}y\overline{z} + x\overline{y}\,\overline{z} + x\overline{y}z + xy\overline{z}$

c. $x\overline{y} + xz + \overline{x}\,\overline{z} + xy\overline{z} + \overline{x}\,\overline{y}z$

d. $\overline{(x + yz)} + \overline{y}z$

e. $\overline{w}\,\overline{x}\,\overline{y}z + w\overline{x}\,\overline{y}z + xz + xy\overline{z}$

f. $\overline{w}\,\overline{x}yz + wxy + \overline{w}\,\overline{y} + x\overline{y} + \overline{x}\,\overline{y}$

g. $(w + x + \overline{y} + z)(w + x + \overline{y} + \overline{z})(w + \overline{x} + \overline{y} + z)(w + \overline{x} + \overline{y} + \overline{z})$
$\cdot (\overline{w} + \overline{x} + \overline{y} + z)(\overline{w} + \overline{x} + \overline{y} + \overline{z})$

h. $(x + z)(w + x)(\overline{y} + z)(w + \overline{y})$

3.13 Prove Shannon's reduction Theorem 3.12 in Sec. 3.6.

3.14 Express each of the following functions by a minterm canonical formula without first constructing a truth table.

a. $f(x,y,z) = \overline{x}(\overline{y} + z) + \overline{z}$

b. $f(x,y,z) = (x + \overline{y})(x+z)$

3.15 Express each of the following functions by a maxterm canonical formula without first constructing a truth table.

a. $f(x,y,z) = (y + \overline{z})(x\overline{y} + z)$

b. $f(x,y,z) = x + \overline{x}\,\overline{z}(y + z)$

3.16 Express the complement of each of the following functions in disjunctive canonical form and conjunctive canonical form using decimal notation.

a. $f(x,y,z) = \Sigma m(0,2,5)$

b. $f(x,y,z) = \Pi M(1,2,5,7)$

c. $f(w,x,y,z) = \Sigma m(1,4,6,7,8,12,14)$
d. $f(w,x,y,z) = \Pi M(3,7,8,10,12,13)$

3.17 Transform each of the following canonical expressions into its other canonical form in decimal notation.

a. $f(x,y,z) = \Sigma m(1,3,5)$
b. $f(x,y,z) = \Pi M(3,4)$
c. $f(w,x,y,z) = \Sigma m(0,1,2,3,7,9,11,12,15)$
d. $f(w,x,y,z) = \Pi M(0,2,5,6,7,8,9,11,12)$

3.18 Write a Boolean expression for each of the logic diagrams in Fig. P3.18.

3.19 Draw the logic diagram using gates corresponding to the following Boolean expressions. Assume that the input variables are available in both complemented and uncomplemented forms.

a. $f(w,x,y,z) = \bar{w}(x + y)(\bar{x} + z) + x\bar{z}$
b. $f(v,w,x,y,z) = (x + y)\{\bar{v} + (\bar{w} + y)[v + (\bar{w} + z)(\bar{v} + x + z)]\}$
c. $f(v,w,x,y,z) = v[\overline{w(xy + \bar{z}) + \bar{x}z}] + \bar{v}\bar{w}$

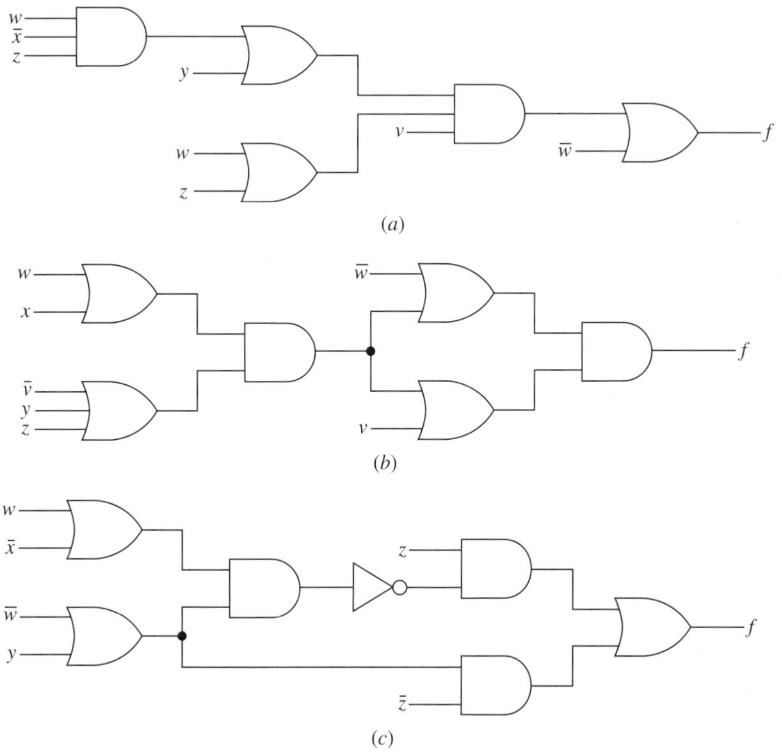

Figure P3.18

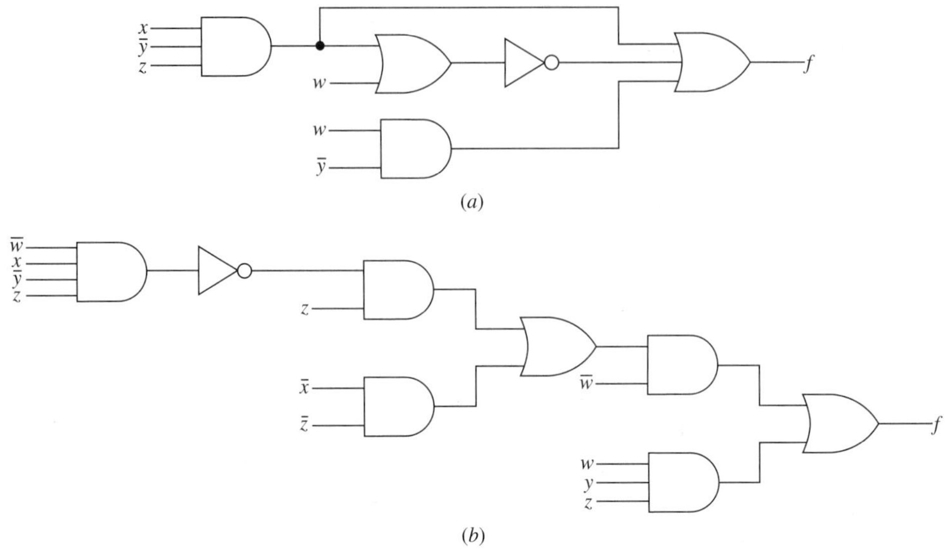

Figure P3.20

3.20 For each of the gate networks shown in Fig. P3.20, determine an equivalent gate network with as few gate inputs as possible.

3.21 Besides gate networks, networks consisting of other two-state devices are also related to a Boolean algebra. For example, a Boolean expression for a configuration of switches can be written to describe whether there is an open or closed path between the network terminals. The Boolean constant 1 is assigned to a closed switch and the existence of a closed path between the terminals of the configuration of switches; while the Boolean constant 0 is assigned to an open switch and the existence of an open path between the terminals of the configuration of switches. Algebraically, each switch is denoted by a Boolean variable in which the variable is uncomplemented if the switch is normally open and complemented if it is normally closed. Under this assignment, switches placed in series can be denoted by the and-

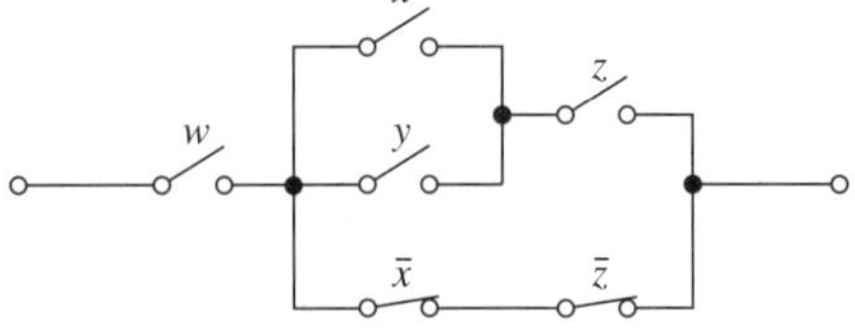

Figure P3.21

operation and those in parallel with the or-operation. Using this correspondence between Boolean algebra and a configuration of switches:

a. Determine a Boolean expression to describe the behavior of the configuration shown in Fig. P3.21.

b. Determine a series-parallel configuration of switches whose behavior is described by the Boolean expression

$$f(w,x,y,z) = (wx + \bar{z})(\bar{y} + z) + \bar{w}(x + \bar{y})$$

3.22 For the truth table of Table P3.22

a. Write both the minterm and maxterm canonical formulas in decimal notation for the function.

b. Construct the truth table of the complement function.

c. Write both the minterm and maxterm canonical formulas in decimal notation for the complement function.

3.23 Show that the nand-operation is not associative, i.e., nand[x, nand(y, z)] $\neq$ nand[nand(x, y), z]. Is the nor-operation associative?

3.24 Write a Boolean expression for each of the logic diagrams in Fig. P3.24.

3.25 Using algebraic manipulations, obtain a logic diagram consisting of only nand-gates for each of the following Boolean expressions. Do not alter the given form of the expressions. Assume the independent

Table P3.22

w	x	y	z	f
0	0	0	0	—
0	0	0	1	—
0	0	1	0	1
0	0	1	1	1
0	1	0	0	0
0	1	0	1	—
0	1	1	0	1
0	1	1	1	0
1	0	0	0	0
1	0	0	1	—
1	0	1	0	1
1	0	1	1	—
1	1	0	0	0
1	1	0	1	—
1	1	1	0	—
1	1	1	1	1

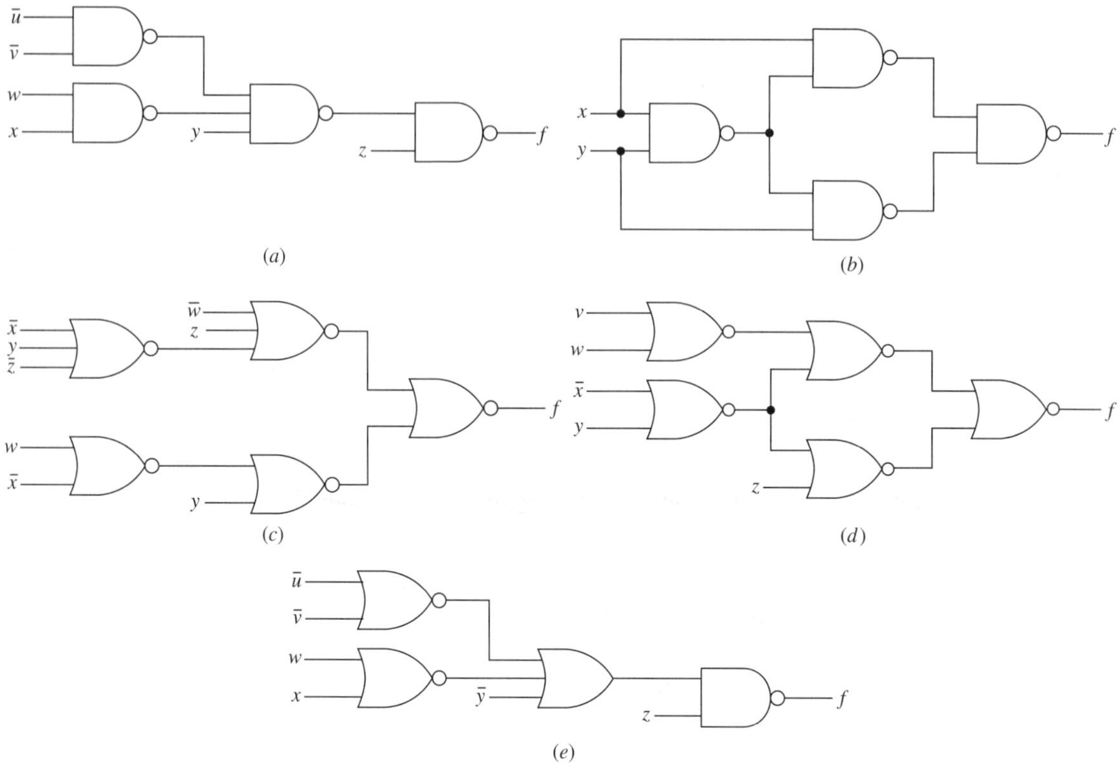

Figure P3.24

variables are available in both complemented and uncomplemented form.

a. $f(w,x,y,z) = \bar{y} + w\bar{x} + \bar{w}x\bar{z}$

b. $f(w,x,y,z) = (w + y)(\bar{x} + \bar{z})(\bar{w} + \bar{x} + \bar{y})$

c. $f(w,x,y,z) = \bar{w}(x\bar{y} + \bar{x}y) + z(x + y)$

d. $f(w,x,y,z) = (\bar{x} + y\bar{z})[w + (y + z)(\bar{y} + \bar{z})]$

3.26 Repeat Problem 3.25 using the graphical procedure.

3.27 Using algebraic manipulations, obtain a logic diagram consisting of only nor-gates for each of the Boolean expressions in Problem 3.25. Do not alter the given form of the expressions. Assume the independent variables are available in both complemented and uncomplemented form.

3.28 Repeat Problem 3.27 using the graphical procedure.

3.29 Using the graphical procedures, convert the logic diagram of Fig. P3.29 into a logic diagram consisting of only nand-gates and a logic diagram consisting

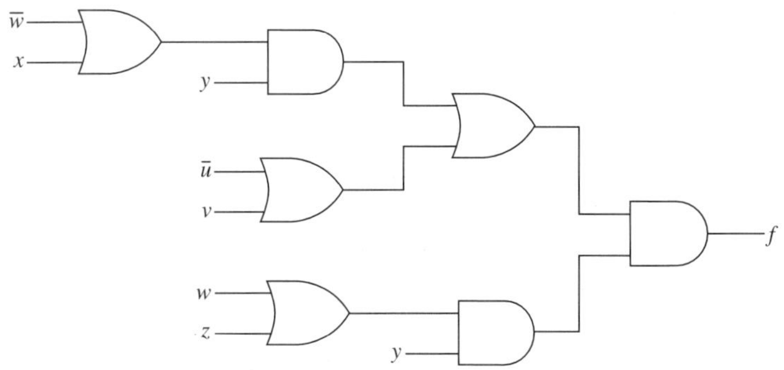

Figure P3.29

of only nor-gates.* Verify your results by obtaining the Boolean expression for each network.

3.30 Prove that $(x + y) \oplus (x + z) = \bar{x}(y \oplus z)$.

3.31 Show that the exclusive-or-operation is not distributive over the and-operation, i.e., $x \oplus yz \neq (x \oplus y)(x \oplus z)$.

3.32 Algebraically verify the following identities.

a. $x \odot 1 = x$ b. $x \odot 0 = \bar{x}$

c. $x \odot x = 1$ d. $x \odot \bar{x} = 0$

e. $\bar{x} \odot \bar{y} = x \odot y$ f. $\bar{x} \odot y = \overline{x \odot y}$

g. $(x + y) \odot (x + z) = x + (y \odot z)$ h. $x \odot y \odot (x + y) = xy$

3.33 The dual $f_d(x_1, x_2, \ldots, x_n)$ of a function $f(x_1, x_2, \ldots, x_n)$ is defined as

$$f_d(x_1, x_2, \ldots, x_n) = \bar{f}(\bar{x}_1, \bar{x}_2, \ldots, \bar{x}_n)$$

Using this, show that the dual of the exclusive-or-function is the exclusive-nor-function.

3.34 In Sec. 2.10 the Gray code was discussed. The following rule converts an n-bit Gray code group $g_{n-1}g_{n-2} \cdots g_1g_0$ into its equivalent n-bit binary number $b_{n-1}b_{n-2} \cdots b_1b_0$:

1. The most significant bits are equal, i.e.,

$$b_{n-1} = g_{n-1}$$

*Networks involving identical gate types following each other can evolve when using gates with a limited number of inputs. In this network it is assumed that only two-input and-gates and or-gates are available.

2. Each of the remaining bits is obtained as follows:

$$b_{k-1} = \begin{cases} g_{k-1} \text{ if } b_k = 0 \\ \overline{g}_{k-1} \text{ if } b_k = 1 \end{cases} \qquad \text{for } n - 1 \geq k \geq 1$$

a. Design an n-bit Gray-to-binary converter.

b. Using the above algorithm as a starting point, devise an algorithm to convert an n-bit binary number into an n-bit Gray code group. Design the corresponding n-bit binary-to-Gray converter.

3.35 For the Hamming code discussed in Sec. 2.12, design a logic network which accepts the 7-bit code groups, where at most a single error has occurred, and generates the corresponding corrected 7-bit code groups. To do this, first design networks for c_1^*, c_2^*, and c_3^*. Then, design a network for correcting the appropriate bit. Use exclusive-or-gates whenever possible. However, assume that all available exclusive-or-gates have only two input terminals. (Hint: The network for c_i^* can be constructed with just two-input exclusive-or-gates.)

CHAPTER 4

Simplification of Boolean Expressions

In Sec. 3.6 it was shown that by use of the theorems and postulates of a Boolean algebra, it is possible to obtain "simple" expressions. Although the concept of simplicity was not formally defined, it was observed that neither the approach to equation simplification nor the capability of concluding when an equation is simple is obvious.

At this time the simplification problem is studied in detail and formal techniques for achieving simplification are developed. In particular, two general approaches are presented. First, a graphical method is introduced that can handle Boolean expressions up to six variables. Then, a tabular procedure is developed that is not bounded by six variables and that is capable of being programmed on a computer since it is algorithmic. These approaches are applied to both a single Boolean expression that describes single-output network behavior, and a collection of Boolean expressions describing multiple-output networks. ■

4.1 FORMULATION OF THE SIMPLIFICATION PROBLEM

In the design of logic networks, many factors should be considered when evaluating the merit of a network. One such factor is its cost. The cost of a network is a function of the cost of its components, the cost of the design and construction of the network, and the cost of maintaining the network. In addition, the reliability of the network should also be considered in its overall merit evaluation. Reliability is achieved by using highly reliable components or by redundancy techniques in which a greater number of less reliable components are used. A third factor that should be considered in the merit evaluation of a logic network is the time it takes the network to respond to changes at its inputs. These three factors do not form an exhaustive list of items that should be considered in the network evaluation, nor are they independent.

Even though all of the above factors are important, a single simple design procedure encompassing them all does not exist. However, if certain aspects of these factors are considered of prominent importance, then a formal approach to the design of optimal logic networks can be developed.

4.1.1 Criteria of Minimality

Let us assume that the overall response time of a network should be minimal for a given circuit technology. This is achieved by minimizing the number of levels of logic that a signal must pass through since all gates introduce propagation delays. Recalling that every combinational network is describable by a canonical formula, it follows that it is possible to construct any logic network with at most two levels of logic under the double-rail logic assumption. Throughout this chapter, it is assumed that a variable and its complement are always available as inputs in a realization. By applying the theorems of a Boolean algebra to this canonical expression, various two-level networks are represented in algebraic form. In general, any normal formula, i.e., those in sum-of-products form or product-of-sums form, corresponds to a logic network with two levels or less. It can now be concluded, therefore, in order to keep the propagation delay time of a network to a minimum, attention should be restricted to networks with normal formula representations.

Furthermore, let us assume that the component cost is the only other factor influencing the merit evaluation of a logic network. In general, for any Boolean function there are many two-level realizations, each represented by a normal formula. Thus, it is desirable to determine the normal formula with the minimal component cost in its realization. One simple measurement of component cost is the number of gates in the realization. In terms of algebraic expressions in normal form, the number of gates is one greater than the number of terms with more than one literal in the expression. (However, if there is only one term, then the number of gates is simply one.) A second measurement of component cost is a count of the total number of gate inputs within the network. Again this can be related to algebraic expressions in normal form. The number of gate inputs is equal to the number of literals in the expression plus the number of terms containing more than one literal. (However, if there is only one term, then the number of gate inputs is simply equal to the number of literals.)

By applying either of the above two criteria to a Boolean expression, it is possible to obtain a measure of its complexity. This numerical quantity is called the *cost* of the expression.

Inherent in the above discussion is that only single-output combinational networks are being realized. A multiple-output combinational network is described by a set of Boolean expressions. In such a case, it is necessary to modify the cost criteria. For now, attention is restricted to single-output combinational networks. In Secs. 4.12 and 4.13, the concepts of cost and minimality are extended to the more general case.

4.1.2 The Simplification Problem

The determination of Boolean expressions that satisfy some criterion of minimality is called the *simplification* or *minimization problem.* Unless otherwise specified, the second cost criterion presented above is assumed. That is, for single-output networks, a minimal Boolean expression is that normal expression representing a two-level network with a minimum total number of gate inputs.

Before beginning the development of formal simplification procedures, one final point must be considered. Product and sum terms were previously defined as a product and sum of literals, respectively. This definition permits repetition of variables to appear in these terms. However, repetition of variables in a term makes little sense in a realization and only adds to the cost of the expression. A *fundamental term* is defined as a product or sum of literals in which no variable appears more than once. A fundamental term is obtained from any term by the application of Postulate P5 of a Boolean algebra, i.e., $x + \bar{x} = 1$ and $x \cdot \bar{x} = 0$, and the idempotent law, i.e., $x + x = x$ and $x \cdot x = x$. It is hereafter assumed that all terms are fundamental terms and are referred to as simply terms.

4.2 PRIME IMPLICANTS AND IRREDUNDANT DISJUNCTIVE EXPRESSIONS

As the first step toward the development of techniques leading to minimal Boolean expressions, it is necessary to establish some basic concepts. These concepts are studied in this and the next sections. Once that is done, the techniques to simplify Boolean expressions readily follow.

In an effort to keep the presentation as simple as possible, it is initially assumed that the Boolean functions are completely specified. After mastering this special case, the reader should have no trouble in extending the concepts to incomplete Boolean functions. This generalization is discussed in Sec. 4.6.

4.2.1 Implies

Consider two complete Boolean functions of n variables, f_1 and f_2. The function f_1 *implies* the function f_2 if there is no assignment of values to the n variables that makes f_1 equal to 1 and f_2 equal to 0. Hence, for the complete Boolean functions f_1 and f_2, whenever f_1 equals 1, then f_2 must also equal 1; and, alternatively, whenever f_2 equals 0, then f_1 must equal 0. Since terms and formulas (or, expressions) describe functions, the concept of implies may also be applied to terms and formulas, e.g., whether or not a particular term implies a function. To illustrate the concept of implies, consider the functions $f_1(x,y,z) = xy + yz$ and $f_2(x,y,z) = xy + yz + \bar{x}z$ tabulated in Table 4.1*a*. By applying the above definition to the truth table, it is readily seen that f_1 implies f_2. As a second example, consider the functions $f_3(x,y,z) = (x + y)(y + z)(\bar{x} + z)$ and $f_4(x,y,z) = (x + y)(y + z)$ shown in Table 4.1*b*. In this case f_3 implies f_4.

Now consider a single term that appears in the normal formula for a function. In the case of a disjunctive normal formula, i.e., one in sum-of-products form, each

Table 4.1 Illustration of function implication. (*a*) f_1 implies f_2. (*b*) f_3 implies f_4

x	y	z	f_1	f_2
0	0	0	0	0
0	0	1	0	1
0	1	0	0	0
0	1	1	1	1
1	0	0	0	0
1	0	1	0	0
1	1	0	1	1
1	1	1	1	1

(*a*)

x	y	z	f_3	f_4
0	0	0	0	0
0	0	1	0	0
0	1	0	1	1
0	1	1	1	1
1	0	0	0	0
1	0	1	1	1
1	1	0	0	1
1	1	1	1	1

(*b*)

of its product terms implies the function being described by the formula. This follows from the fact that whenever the product term has the value 1, the function must also have the value 1. On the other hand, for a conjunctive normal formula, i.e., one in product-of-sums form, each sum term is implied by the function, i.e., the function implies the sum term. In this case, whenever the sum term has the value 0, the function must also have the value 0.

4.2.2 Subsumes

A comparison between two product terms or two sum terms is also possible. A term t_1 is said to *subsume* a term t_2 if and only if all the literals of the term t_2 are also literals of the term t_1. As an example, consider the product terms $x\overline{y}\overline{z}$ and $x\overline{z}$. From the definition of subsumes, the product term $x\overline{y}\overline{z}$ subsumes the product term $x\overline{z}$. In a similar manner, for the two sum terms $x + \overline{y} + \overline{z}$ and $x + \overline{z}$, the sum term $x + \overline{y} + \overline{z}$ subsumes the sum term $x + \overline{z}$.

From the above discussion it is seen that if a product term t_1 subsumes a product term t_2, then t_1 implies t_2 since whenever t_1 has the value 1, t_2 also has the value 1. On the other hand, if a sum term t_3 subsumes a sum term t_4, then t_4 implies t_3

since whenever t_3 has the value 0, t_4 also has the value 0. By the absorption law, i.e., Theorem 3.6, if one term subsumes another in an expression, then the subsuming term can always be deleted from the expression without changing the function being described.

4.2.3 Implicants and Prime Implicants

A product term is said to be an *implicant* of a complete function if the product term implies the function. As a result, each of the product terms in a disjunctive normal formula describing a complete Boolean function is an implicant of the function since these product terms contribute to describing the functional values of 1. Thus, the minterms of a function are examples of its implicants. As a further illustration, consider the truth table shown in Table 4.2. The term $\bar{x}$ is equal to 1 for the four 3-tuples (x,y,z) = (0,0,0), (0,0,1), (0,1,0), and (0,1,1) and is equal to 0 for all other 3-tuples. It is now noted that for those 3-tuples in which the term $\bar{x}$ equals 1, so does the function given in Table 4.2. It therefore follows that $\bar{x}$ is an implicant of that function. Similarly, another implicant of the function given in Table 4.2 is $\bar{y}z$ since the term has the value 1 when (y,z) = (0,1) and the function has the value 1 for the two 3-tuples (x,y,z) = (0,0,1) and (1,0,1).

An implicant of a function is said to be a *prime implicant* if the implicant does not subsume any other implicant with fewer literals of the same function. Thus, a prime implicant of a function is a product term that implies the function with the additional property that if any literal is removed from the term, then the resulting product term no longer implies the function. For example, again consider the function of Table 4.2. The product term $x\bar{y}z$ is an implicant of the function since it is the minterm that describes the sixth row of the truth table. The three product terms having one less literal that $x\bar{y}z$ subsumes are $\bar{y}z$, xz, and $x\bar{y}$. If at least one of these three terms is an implicant of the function, then $x\bar{y}z$ is not a prime implicant. As indicated previously, the product term $\bar{y}z$ is an implicant of the function. Consequently, the term $x\bar{y}z$ is not a prime implicant of the function. On the other hand, although the product term xz is also subsumed by $x\bar{y}z$, it does not imply the function since xz has

Table 4.2 A 3-variable Boolean function

x	y	z	f
0	0	0	1
0	0	1	1
0	1	0	1
0	1	1	1
1	0	0	0
1	0	1	1
1	1	0	0
1	1	1	0

the value 1 and the function has the value 0 when $(x,y,z) = (1,1,1)$. Consequently, xz is not an implicant of the function. Similarly, the product term $x\overline{y}$ is not an implicant since it has the value 1 when $(x,y,z) = (1,0,0)$ but the function has the value 0. Now that it has been established that $\overline{y}z$ is an implicant of the function given in Table 4.2, we can ask if $\overline{y}z$ is a prime implicant of the function. To answer this, consider the possible product terms having one less literal that are subsumed by $\overline{y}z$, namely, the term $\overline{y}$ and the term z. It is easily checked with the aid of Table 4.2 that neither the term x nor the term $\overline{y}$ implies the function. Hence, $\overline{y}z$ is an implicant of the function that subsumes no other implicant of the same function. By definition, $\overline{y}z$ is a prime implicant. By a similar analysis, $\overline{x}$ is also a prime implicant of the function given in Table 4.2.

The significance of prime implicants is given by the following theorem:

Theorem 4.1

When the cost, assigned by some criterion, for a minimal Boolean formula is such that decreasing the number of literals in the disjunctive normal formula does not increase the cost of the formula, there is at least one minimal disjunctive normal formula that corresponds to a sum of prime implicants.

Proof

To justify the above theorem, assume that there is a minimal disjunctive normal formula of a given Boolean function that is not the sum of only prime implicants. In particular, let t_1 be one such term. t_1 must still be an implicant of the function since, being a term describing the function, it must imply the function. By definition of a prime implicant, there must be some term t_2 that is a prime implicant such that t_1 subsumes t_2. By definition of subsumes, t_2 must have fewer literals. Since t_2 also implies the function, it may be added to the original formula without changing the function being described. But t_1 subsumes t_2. By the absorption law, t_1 can be removed, leaving an expression with the same number of terms but with fewer literals. Since it is assumed that the cost of a formula does not increase by decreasing the number of literals, the cost of the new expression is no greater than the cost of the original expression. If this argument is applied to every term that was not originally a prime implicant, then an expression of only prime implicants and of minimal cost results. ■

As a consequence of the above theorem, the prime implicants are of interest for establishing a minimal disjunctive Boolean formula. This formula, in turn, suggests a minimal two-level realization with and-gates followed by a single or-gate. The set of prime implicants of a function can be obtained by forming all possible product terms involving the variables of the function, testing to see which terms imply the function, and then, for those that do, checking to see if they do not subsume some other product terms that also imply the function. Efficient algorithmic procedures can be developed to carry out this seemingly complex process.

4.2.4 Irredundant Disjunctive Normal Formulas

An *irredundant disjunctive normal formula* describing a complete function is defined as an expression in sum-of-products form such that (1) every product term in the expression is a prime implicant and (2) no product term may be eliminated from the expression without changing the function described by the expression.

Theorem 4.2

For any cost criterion such that the cost of a formula does not increase when a literal is removed, at least one minimal disjunctive normal formula describing a function is an irredundant disjunctive normal formula.

Proof

If a minimal disjunctive normal formula is not an irredundant expression, then it must fail at least one of the two properties of an irredundant expression. If any of the terms is not a prime implicant, then the term can be replaced by a product term that is a prime implicant. In this way the expression is written with fewer literals. If any term can be eliminated from the expression, then the new expression without this term also has fewer literals. In both cases the number of literals is decreased. Since it is assumed that the cost of the expression does not increase by decreasing the number of literals, the resulting expression is still minimal. Furthermore, by definition, it is an irredundant disjunctive normal formula. ■

The reader should carefully observe that an expression being an irredundant disjunctive normal formula is not sufficient to guarantee the expression is minimal. Part of the algorithmic procedures for determining minimal Boolean expressions involves the judicious selection of some (but not necessarily all) of the prime implicants.

4.3 PRIME IMPLICATES AND IRREDUNDANT CONJUNCTIVE EXPRESSIONS

In the previous section it was shown that minimal two-level gate realizations having and-gates on the first level and a single or-gate on the second level are related to disjunctive normal formulas, i.e., those consisting of a sum of product terms, whose terms are prime implicants. A second form of two-level gate networks involves or-gates feeding into a single and-gate. These networks are described by conjunctive normal formulas, i.e., those consisting of a product of sum terms. Using the definitions of minimality introduced in Sec. 4.1, it is now desired to establish the properties for minimal expressions of this type. Most of the material in this section is simply the dual concept to that of the previous section.

A sum term is said to be an *implicate* of a complete Boolean function if the function implies the sum term. A *prime implicate* of a complete Boolean function is an implicate of the function that subsumes no other implicate of the function with fewer literals. Thus, a prime implicate is a sum term that is implied by the function with the additional property that if any literal is removed from the term, then the resulting sum term no longer is implied by the function.

The maxterms of a function are examples of its implicates. This follows from the fact that any time a maxterm of a function has the value 0, the function must also have the value 0. Therefore, by the definition of implies, the function must imply its maxterms. Referring again to Table 4.2, it is readily observed that one of the implicates of the function is the maxterm $\bar{x} + y + z$. In addition, the sum term $\bar{x} + z$ has the value 0 for the two 3-tuples $(x,y,z) = (1,0,0)$ and $(1,1,0)$. Since the function given in Table 4.2 has the value 0 for these two 3-tuples, it immediately follows that the sum term $\bar{x} + z$ also is implied by the function and is therefore an implicate of the function. Since $\bar{x} + y + z$ subsumes $\bar{x} + z$, $\bar{x} + y + z$ is not a prime implicate. Finally, neither the term $\bar{x}$ nor the term z is implied by the function. Thus, $\bar{x} + z$ must be a prime implicate of the function.

Using an argument similar to that in the previous section, prime implicates can be used to obtain minimal conjunctive normal formulas. Formally,

Theorem 4.3

When the cost, assigned by some criterion, for a minimal Boolean formula is such that decreasing the number of literals in the conjunctive normal formula does not increase the cost of the formula, there is at least one minimal conjunctive normal formula that corresponds to a product of prime implicates.

An *irredundant conjunctive normal formula* describing a complete Boolean function is defined as an expression in product-of-sums form such that (1) every sum term in the expression is a prime implicate and (2) no sum term can be eliminated from the expression without changing the function described by the expression. The dual of Theorem 4.2 can now be stated.

Theorem 4.4

For any cost criterion such that the cost of a formula does not increase when a literal is removed, at least one minimal conjunctive normal formula describing a function is an irredundant conjunctive normal formula.

It should be noted that prime implicates are the dual concept to that of prime implicants and irredundant conjunctive normal formulas are the dual concept to irredundant disjunctive normal formulas. Future discussions revolve around both minimal disjunctive normal formulas and minimal conjunctive normal formulas. Although it is beyond the scope of this book to prove formally, it can be shown that the prime implicates of a complete Boolean function f are precisely the complements of the prime implicants of the function $\bar{f}$. In addition, the irredundant conjunctive normal formulas of the complete Boolean function f are exactly the complements of the irredundant disjunctive normal formulas of $\bar{f}$. Finally, the minimal conjunctive normal formulas of f are the complements of the minimal disjunctive normal formulas of $\bar{f}$.

Reviewing, two criteria for minimal normal expressions have been defined. Furthermore, it has been established that algebraically the terms that comprise the minimal expressions can be prime implicants in the case of disjunctive normal formulas and prime implicates in the case of conjunctive normal formulas. At this point, systematic procedures to determine minimal Boolean expressions can be developed.

4.4 KARNAUGH MAPS

A method for graphically determining implicants and implicates of a Boolean function was developed by Veitch and modified by Karnaugh. The method involves a diagrammatic representation of a Boolean function. This representation is called a *map*. The variation on the construction of these maps that was proposed by Karnaugh is used in this text.

In Sec. 3.4, it was shown that an n-variable complete Boolean function is represented by a truth table. Since each variable has the value of 0 or 1, the truth table has 2^n rows. Each row of the truth table consists of two parts: (1) an n-tuple which corresponds to an assignment to the n-variables and (2) a functional value.

A Karnaugh map is a geometrical configuration of 2^n cells such that each of the n-tuples corresponding to a row of a truth table uniquely locates a cell on the map. The functional values assigned to the n-tuples are placed as entries in the cells. Thus, for any n-tuple in which the functional value is 0, a 0 is placed in the associated cell; while 1's are placed as cell entries for those n-tuples that have functional values of 1. In this way, the Karnaugh map becomes a diagrammatic representation of a truth table and, correspondingly, a diagrammatic representation of a Boolean function.

Significant about the construction of a Karnaugh map is the arrangement of the cells. Two cells are physically adjacent within the configuration if and only if their respective n-tuples differ in exactly one element. For example, the cells for the two 3-tuples (0,1,1) and (0,1,0) are physically adjacent on the map since these 3-tuples differ only in their third element. On the other hand, the cells for the two 3-tuples (1,0,1) and (1,1,0) are not physically adjacent since these two 3-tuples differ in two elements; namely, their second and third elements. As a consequence of this adjacency property of the cells, each cell on the map must be adjacent to exactly n cells since for any n-tuple there are n other n-tuples which differ from it by just one element.

4.4.1 One-Variable and Two-Variable Maps

The Karnaugh maps for one-variable and two-variable Boolean functions are shown in Figs. 4.1 and 4.2. These maps consist of $2^1 = 2$ and $2^2 = 4$ cells, respectively. Referring to these figures, the n-tuple associated with each cell is determined using

x	$f(x)$
0	$f(0)$
1	$f(1)$

(*a*)

x: 0	1
$f(0)$	$f(1)$

(*b*)

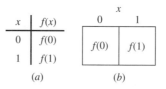

Figure 4.1 A one-variable Boolean function. (*a*) Truth table. (*b*) Karnaugh map.

a coordinate system according to the axes labeling. Thus, the 2-tuple $(x,y) = (0,1)$ uniquely locates the cell in the first row, second column of Fig. 4.2*b*. The corresponding functional values appear as entries in the cells. Note that two cells are physically adjacent on the map if and only if their corresponding n-tuples differ in exactly one element.

4.4.2 Three-Variable and Four-Variable Maps

A three-variable Karnaugh map has $2^3 = 8$ cells. To satisfy the adjacency property of cells, each cell of a three-variable map must be adjacent to exactly three other cells. To achieve this, a three-variable map is constructed on the surface of a cylinder as shown in Fig. 4.3*b*. In view of the fact that three-dimensional maps are hard to draw, it is desirable to represent these maps in two dimensions. If the cylinder is cut along its vertical axis and unrolled, then the two-dimensional map of Fig. 4.3*c* results. Although no longer appearing physically adjacent, it must be remembered that the left and right edges of the map of Fig. 4.3*c* are really connected, and hence the cells on the left and right sides are, from an interpretive point of view, still adjacent. Particular attention should be given to the labels along the top of the map. In order to achieve the requirement that two cells are physically adjacent if and only if

x	y	$f(x,y)$
0	0	$f(0,0)$
0	1	$f(0,1)$
1	0	$f(1,0)$
1	1	$f(1,1)$

(*a*)

$x \backslash y$	0	1
0	$f(0,0)$	$f(0,1)$
1	$f(1,0)$	$f(1,1)$

(*b*)

Figure 4.2 A two-variable Boolean function. (*a*) Truth table. (*b*) Karnaugh map.

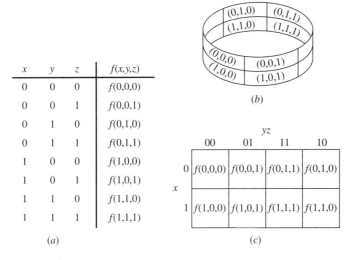

x	y	z	$f(x,y,z)$
0	0	0	$f(0,0,0)$
0	0	1	$f(0,0,1)$
0	1	0	$f(0,1,0)$
0	1	1	$f(0,1,1)$
1	0	0	$f(1,0,0)$
1	0	1	$f(1,0,1)$
1	1	0	$f(1,1,0)$
1	1	1	$f(1,1,1)$

(*a*)

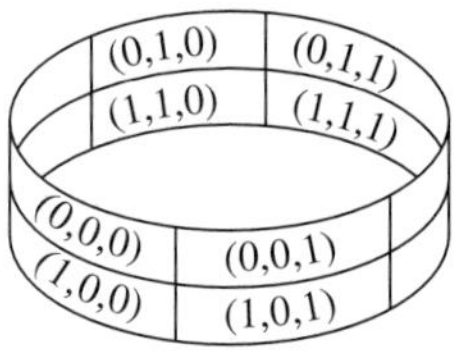

(*b*)

x \ yz	00	01	11	10
0	$f(0,0,0)$	$f(0,0,1)$	$f(0,1,1)$	$f(0,1,0)$
1	$f(1,0,0)$	$f(1,0,1)$	$f(1,1,1)$	$f(1,1,0)$

(*c*)

Figure 4.3 A three-variable Boolean function. (*a*) Truth table. (*b*) Karnaugh map. (*c*) Two-dimensional representation of the Karnaugh map.

their respective 3-tuples differ in exactly one element, the labels along the top of the map are 00, 01, 11, and 10.

To illustrate the mapping of a specific Boolean function, consider the truth table of Fig. 4.4*a*. Since this is a three-variable function, the general map structure of Fig. 4.3*c* is used. The completed Karnaugh map is shown in Fig. 4.4*b*.

A four-variable Karnaugh map has $2^4 = 16$ cells in which each cell is adjacent to exactly four other cells. This is achieved by having the map appear on the surface of a torus. By making two cuts on the torus and then unrolling it, a two-dimensional

x	y	z	f
0	0	0	1
0	0	1	0
0	1	0	1
0	1	1	0
1	0	0	1
1	0	1	1
1	1	0	0
1	1	1	0

(*a*)

x \ yz	00	01	11	10
0	1	0	0	1
1	1	1	0	0

(*b*)

Figure 4.4 An illustrative three-variable Boolean function. (*a*) Truth table. (*b*) Karnaugh map.

w	x	y	z	$f(w,x,y,z)$
0	0	0	0	$f(0,0,0,0)$
0	0	0	1	$f(0,0,0,1)$
0	0	1	0	$f(0,0,1,0)$
0	0	1	1	$f(0,0,1,1)$
0	1	0	0	$f(0,1,0,0)$
0	1	0	1	$f(0,1,0,1)$
0	1	1	0	$f(0,1,1,0)$
0	1	1	1	$f(0,1,1,1)$
1	0	0	0	$f(1,0,0,0)$
1	0	0	1	$f(1,0,0,1)$
1	0	1	0	$f(1,0,1,0)$
1	0	1	1	$f(1,0,1,1)$
1	1	0	0	$f(1,1,0,0)$
1	1	0	1	$f(1,1,0,1)$
1	1	1	0	$f(1,1,1,0)$
1	1	1	1	$f(1,1,1,1)$

(*a*)

wx \ yz	00	01	11	10
00	$f(0,0,0,0)$	$f(0,0,0,1)$	$f(0,0,1,1)$	$f(0,0,1,0)$
01	$f(0,1,0,0)$	$f(0,1,0,1)$	$f(0,1,1,1)$	$f(0,1,1,0)$
11	$f(1,1,0,0)$	$f(1,1,0,1)$	$f(1,1,1,1)$	$f(1,1,1,0)$
10	$f(1,0,0,0)$	$f(1,0,0,1)$	$f(1,0,1,1)$	$f(1,0,1,0)$

(*b*)

Figure 4.5 A four-variable Boolean function. (*a*) Truth table. (*b*) Karnaugh map.

representation of the map is obtained. This map is shown in Fig. 4.5*b*. In this case it is necessary to keep in mind that, from an interpretive point of view, the left and right edges are connected and the top and bottom edges are connected. Under these restrictions it should be noticed that each cell is adjacent to exactly four other cells and that two cells are physically adjacent if and only if their respective 4-tuples differ in exactly one element.

A variation on Karnaugh map construction that is occasionally seen is shown in Fig. 4.6. In this case, the axes are not labeled with the 0 and 1 elements, but rather a bracket is used to indicate those rows and columns associated with a variable having an assignment of 1. Thus, the map in Fig. 4.6*a* is analogous to the map in Fig. 4.3*c* and the map in Fig. 4.6*b* is analogous to the map in Fig. 4.5*b*.

4.4.3 Karnaugh Maps and Canonical Formulas

In Chapter 3 it was established that each row of a truth table is described algebraically by a minterm if complemented variables are associated with the 0 elements of the n-tuple and uncomplemented variables are associated with the 1 elements. Consequently, each cell of a Karnaugh map can also be associated with a minterm. For example, the cell for the first row, fourth column of Fig. 4.4*b* is associated with the minterm $\bar{x}y\bar{z}$, as is easily determined by referring to the axes labels. Since the minterm canonical expression for a function is the sum of those minterms for which the function has the value of 1, the minterm canonical expression is easily

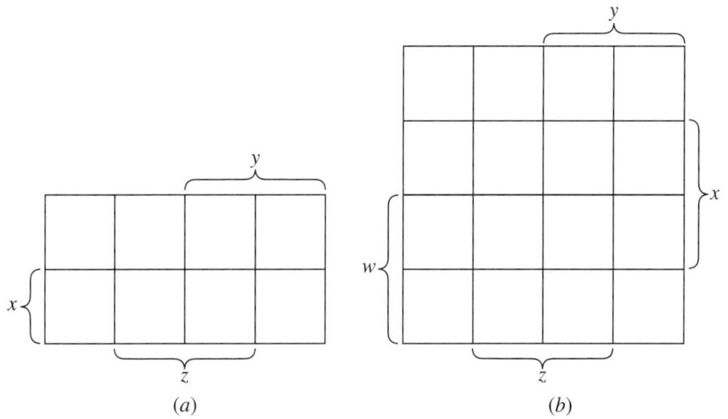

Figure 4.6 Karnaugh map variations. (*a*) Three-variable map. (*b*) Four-variable map.

read from a map. For the map of Fig. 4.4*b,* each cell containing a 1 represents a minterm of the function. Thus, directly from the map we can write

$$f(x,y,z) = \overline{x}\,\overline{y}\,\overline{z} + \overline{x}y\overline{z} + x\overline{y}\,\overline{z} + x\overline{y}z$$

The reverse of this process gives a procedure for obtaining a map directly from a Boolean function expressed in minterm canonical form. For example, the expression

$$f(w,x,y,z) = \overline{w}\,\overline{x}\,\overline{y}\,\overline{z} + \overline{w}\,\overline{x}\,\overline{y}z + \overline{w}\,\overline{x}y\overline{z} + \overline{w}x\overline{y}\,\overline{z} + \overline{w}x\overline{y}z + w\overline{x}\,\overline{y}\,\overline{z} + w\overline{x}y\overline{z} \quad (4.1)$$

is represented on a map by replacing, in each minterm, complemented variables by 0, uncomplemented variables by 1, and then placing a 1 on the map for each 4-tuple describing a minterm. In the remaining cells, 0 entries are placed. Applying this process to Eq. (4.1) results in the map of Fig. 4.7.

wx \ *yz*	00	01	11	10
00	1	1	0	1
01	1	1	0	0
11	0	0	0	0
10	1	0	0	1

Figure 4.7 Karnaugh map for a four-variable function.

It was also established in Chapter 3 that each row of a truth table is described by a maxterm if 0's of the n-tuples are used to denote uncomplemented variables and 1's of the n-tuples are used to denote complemented variables. Correspondingly, each cell of a Karnaugh map can also be associated with a maxterm. The maxterm canonical expression for a function is obtained by forming the product of maxterms for those n-tuples in which the function has the value of 0. Thus, for each cell of a Karnaugh map with a 0 entry, a maxterm can be written. For example, the map of Fig. 4.4*b* corresponds to the maxterm canonical expression

$$f(x,y,z) = (x + y + \bar{z})(x + \bar{y} + \bar{z})(\bar{x} + \bar{y} + \bar{z})(\bar{x} + \bar{y} + z)$$

The reverse of this process permits a Karnaugh map to be formed from a maxterm canonical expression. If the expression is

$$\begin{aligned} f(w,x,y,z) = {} & (w + x + \bar{y} + \bar{z})(w + \bar{x} + \bar{y} + \bar{z})(wx + \bar{x} + \bar{y} + z) \\ & \cdot (\overline{w} + \bar{x} + y + z)(\overline{w} + \bar{x} + y + \bar{z})(\overline{w} + \bar{x} + \bar{y} + \bar{z}) \\ & \cdot (\overline{w} + \bar{x} + \bar{y} + z)(\overline{w} + x + y + \bar{z})(\overline{w} + x + \bar{y} + \bar{z}) \end{aligned}$$

then by using 0's for uncomplemented variables and 1's for complemented variables in the maxterms and by entering a 0 on the map for each n-tuple describing a maxterm and a 1 otherwise, the map of Fig. 4.7 results.

Finally, recall that a decimal representation for minterms and maxterms was introduced in Chapter 3. In particular, the decimal equivalent of the n-tuple for each row of a truth table is used to designate the minterm or maxterm associated with that row. Thus, each cell of a map can be referenced by a decimal number. Figure 4.8 shows the decimal numbers which define each cell of a Karnaugh map. In this way, for the Karnaugh map of Fig. 4.4*b,* the decimal representation of the canonical expression is written directly as

$$f(x,y,z) = \Sigma m(0,2,4,5)$$

or

$$f(x,y,z) = \Pi M(1,3,6,7)$$

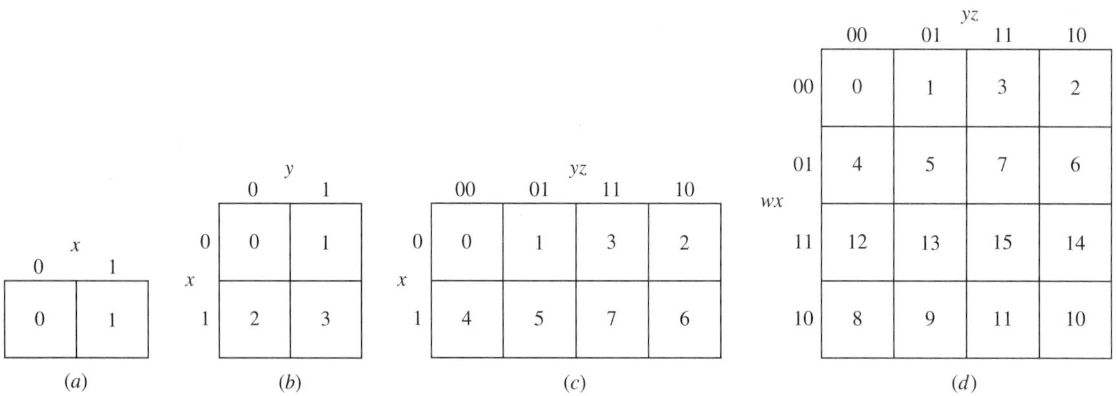

Figure 4.8 Karnaugh maps with cells designated by decimal numbers. (*a*) One-variable map. (*b*) Two-variable map. (*c*) Three-variable map. (*d*) Four-variable map.

In a similar manner, given the canonical expression in decimal form

$$f(w,x,y,z) = \Sigma m(0,1,2,4,5,8,10)$$

or

$$f(w,x,y,z) = \Pi M(3,6,7,9,11,12,13,14,15)$$

the map of Fig. 4.7 is constructed.

4.4.4 Product and Sum Term Representations on Karnaugh Maps

The importance of Karnaugh maps lies in the fact that it is possible to determine the implicants and implicates of a function from the patterns of 0's and 1's appearing on the maps. A cell of a Karnaugh map with a 1 entry is referred to as a *1-cell* and a cell with a 0 entry as a *0-cell*. The construction of an n-variable map is such that any set of 1-cells which form a $2^a \times 2^b$ rectangular grouping describes a product term with $n - a - b$ variables where a and b are nonnegative integers. Rectangular groupings of these dimensions are referred to as *subcubes*. Since the dimensions of a subcube are $2^a \times 2^b$, it immediately follows that the total number of cells in a subcube must be a power-of-two, i.e., 2^{a+b}. Thus, for appropriate values of a and b, $2^a \times 2^b = 2^{a+b}$ equals 1, 2, 4, 8, etc. It must be remembered that the three-variable and four-variable Karnaugh maps have certain edges which are considered connected, and hence subcubes may be split when viewed on the two-dimensional representations of the maps. Figures 4.9 to 4.11 illustrate some typical subcubes which represent product terms. Particular attention should be paid to the subcubes of Fig. 4.10*d* and *e*. On the surface of a torus, the four 1-cells of these subcubes form $2^1 \times 2^1$ rectangles. Similarly, the subcube of Fig. 4.9*c* illustrates a $2^0 \times 2^1$ rectangle, the subcube of Fig. 4.9*d* illustrates a $2^1 \times 2^0$ rectangle, the subcube of Fig. 4.11*c* illustrates a $2^1 \times 2^2$ rectangle, and the subcube of Fig. 4.11*d* illustrates a $2^2 \times 2^1$ rectangle.

Again consider the map of Fig. 4.9*a*. Each 1-cell represents a minterm, i.e., $\overline{w}x\overline{y}z$ and $\overline{w}xyz$. Thus, the two 1-cells represent the sum of the two minterms, i.e., $\overline{w}x\overline{y}z + \overline{w}xyz$. Notice that by factoring this expression as $\overline{w}xz(\overline{y} + y)$, it is equivalent to the single product term $\overline{w}xz$. The Karnaugh map is constructed such that two cells are adjacent if they differ in exactly one element of their associated n-tuples. Since each n-tuple describes a minterm, the minterms of any two adjacent 1-cells must only differ in exactly one literal. The relation $AB + \overline{A}B = B$ can always be applied in this case, where A represents a single variable and B represents a product of $n - 1$ variables. Thus, any pair of adjacent 1-cells represents a product term with one variable eliminated. Pairs of adjacent 1-cells are always subcubes of dimensions $2^0 \times 2^1$ or $2^1 \times 2^0$.

Given an n-variable map with a pair of adjacent 1-cells, the product term of $n - 1$ variables can be read directly from the map. This is done by referring to the labels along its axes. The $n - 1$ variables of the product term are precisely those $n - 1$ variables whose values are the same for each cell in the subcube. Then, as was done for minterms, the variable in the product term is complemented if its value is always 0 in the subcube and is uncomplemented if its value is always 1.

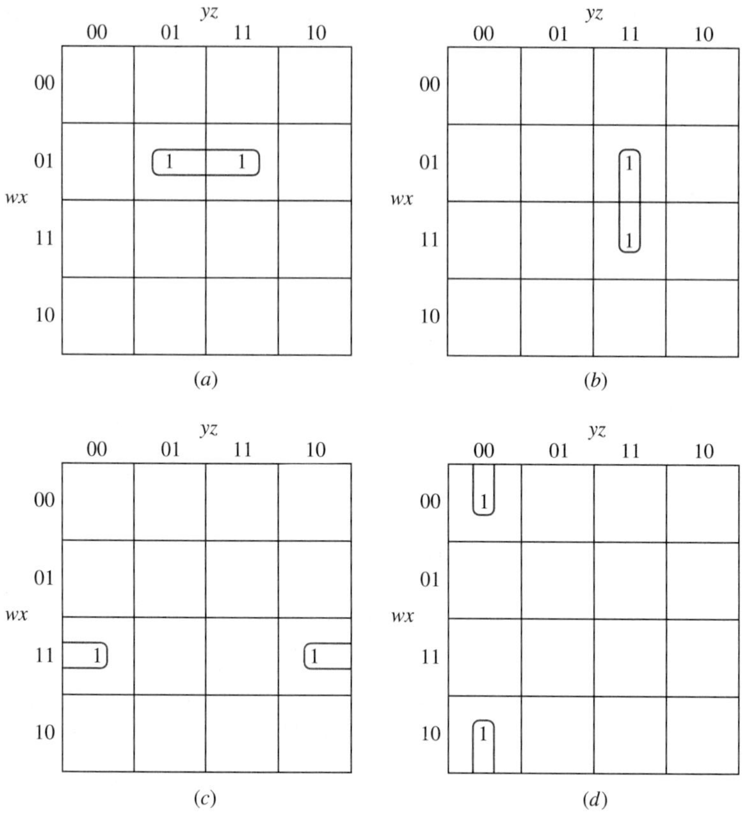

Figure 4.9 Typical map subcubes for the elimination of one variable in a product term. (*a*) $\overline{w}xz$. (*b*) xyz. (*c*) $wx\overline{z}$. (*d*) $\overline{x}\,\overline{y}\,\overline{z}$.

With reference to Fig. 4.9*a* and the labels on the map's axes, the variable w has the value of 0 for both 1-cells and the variable x has the value of 1 for both 1-cells. Since these variables keep the same value for all cells in the subcube, they must appear in the product term as $\overline{w}x$. In addition, the subcube occurs in the two center columns of the map. As indicated by the map labels in these two columns, the y variable changes value while for both 1-cells the z variable has the value of 1. Thus, the y variable is the one that is eliminated as a consequence of the cell adjacencies, and the product term has the literal z as a consequence of the z variable having the same value for both 1-cells. Combining the results, the subcube of Fig. 4.9*a* corresponds to the product term $\overline{w}xz$. In a similar manner, the product terms corresponding to the other subcubes in Fig. 4.9 are written.

Just as a subcube consisting of two 1-cells corresponds to a product term with $n - 1$ variables, any subcube of four 1-cells represents a product term with two variables less than the number of variables associated with the map. To illustrate this, consider the four 1-cells of Fig. 4.10*a*. Algebraically these four cells corre-

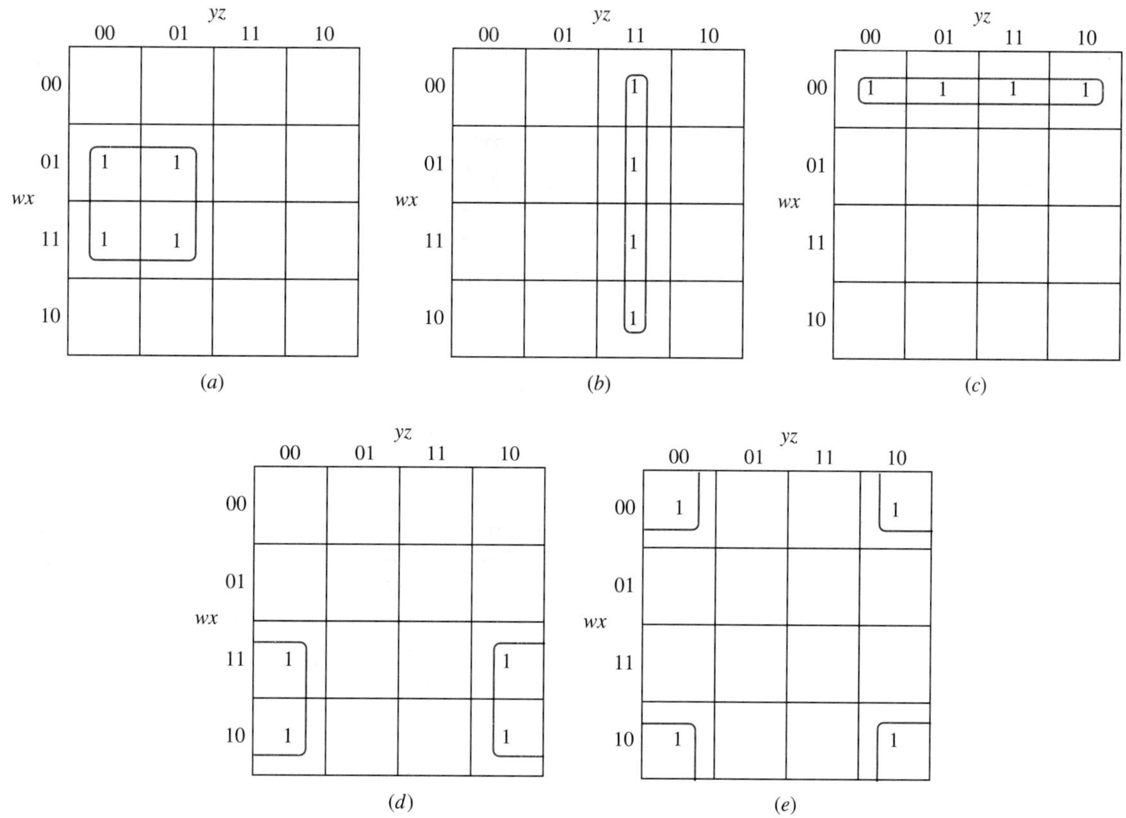

Figure 4.10 Typical map subcubes for the elimination of two variables in a product term. (*a*) $x\overline{y}$. (*b*) yz. (*c*) $\overline{w}\,\overline{x}$. (*d*) $w\overline{z}$. (*e*) $\overline{x}\,\overline{z}$.

spond to the expression $\overline{w}x\overline{y}\,\overline{z} + \overline{w}x\overline{y}z + wx\overline{y}\,\overline{z} + wx\overline{y}z$. The following algebraic manipulations can now be performed:

$$\begin{aligned}\overline{w}x\overline{y}\,\overline{z} + \overline{w}x\overline{y}z + wx\overline{y}\,\overline{z} + wx\overline{y}z &= \overline{w}x\overline{y}(\overline{z} + z) + wx\overline{y}(\overline{z} + z)\\ &= \overline{w}x\overline{y} + wx\overline{y}\\ &= (\overline{w} + w)x\overline{y}\\ &= x\overline{y}\end{aligned}$$

By inspecting the axes labels for these four cells, the product term is written directly. The subcube appears in the two center rows of the map, from which it is seen that the variable w changes value (and hence is eliminated) while the variable x has the value of 1. Thus, the literal x appears in the product term. Furthermore, the subcube appears in the first two columns of this map, from which it is seen that y has the value of 0 while z changes value (and hence is eliminated). This implies the

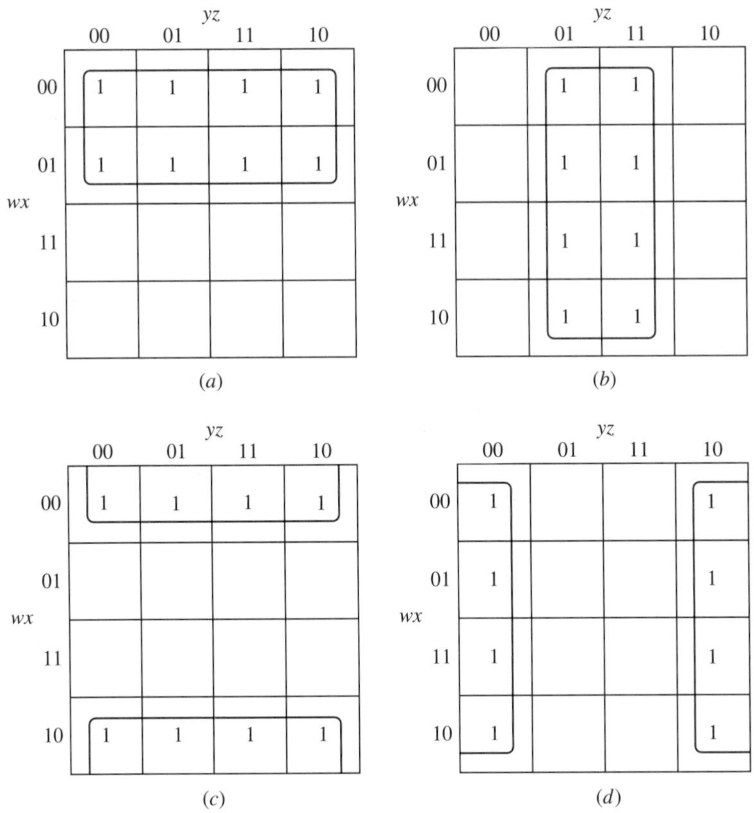

Figure 4.11 Typical map subcubes for the elimination of three variables in a product term. (*a*) $\overline{w}$. (*b*) z. (*c*) $\overline{x}$. (*d*) $\overline{z}$.

product term has the literal $\overline{y}$. Combining the results, it is concluded that this subcube is associated with the product term $x\overline{y}$.

As a final illustration, consider Fig. 4.10*b*. It is first noted that no row variables have the same value for every 1-cell of the columnar subcube. Thus, neither the w nor the x variable appears in the product term. Furthermore, since both the y and z variables have the value of 1 for all 1-cells of the subcube, the resulting product term is yz.

Summarizing, any rectangular grouping of 1-cells on an n-variable map having dimensions $2^a \times 2^b$ consists of 2^{a+b} 1-cells and represents a product term with $n - a - b$ variables where a and b are nonnegative integers. The corresponding product term has an uncomplemented variable if the variable has the value of 1 for every 1-cell associated with the subcube and a complemented variable if the variable has the value of 0. The variables that are eliminated correspond to those that change values.

The above discussion was concerned with the recognition of product terms on a Karnaugh map and how they are read directly. A similar discussion applies to

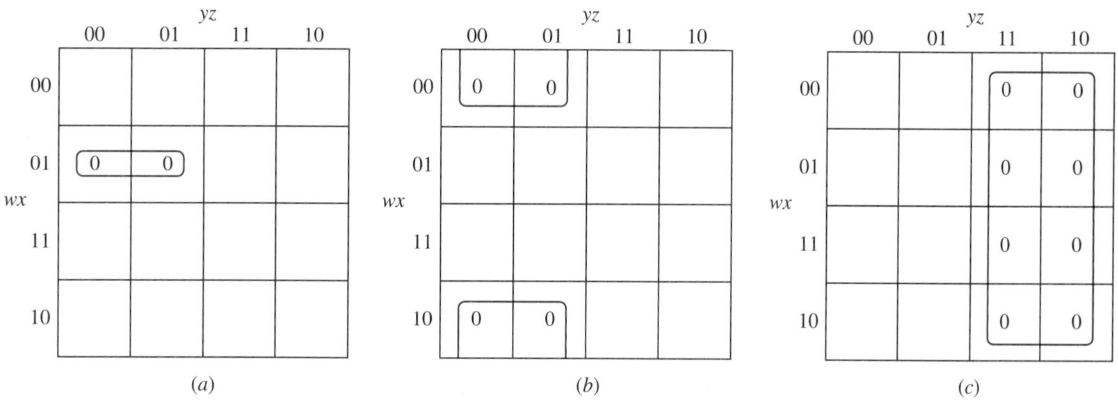

Figure 4.12 Typical map subcubes describing sum terms. (*a*) $w + \overline{x} + y$. (*b*) $x + y$. (*c*) $\overline{y}$.

0-cells. Any $2^a \times 2^b$ rectangular grouping, i.e., subcube, of 0-cells on an *n*-variable map represents a sum term with $n - a - b$ variables, where *a* and *b* are nonnegative integers. The sum term is read directly from the map by noting which variables do not change values for the 0-cells of the subcube. As was the case for single 0-cells representing maxterms, a 0 along the axis denotes an uncomplemented variable, and a 1 along the axis denotes a complemented variable. Figure 4.12 shows the subcubes for some typical sum terms. That two adjacent 0-cells describe a sum term with one variable eliminated follows from the relation $(A + B)(\overline{A} + B) = B$ where *A* represents a single variable and *B* represents a sum of $n - 1$ variables.

In closing, one final point should be emphasized. By definition of a subcube, it must have dimensions $2^a \times 2^b$, which in turn implies that it must consist of a power-of-two number of cells. Thus, at no time is a non-power-of-two grouping of cells, e.g., 3 cells, ever considered a subcube.

4.5 USING KARNAUGH MAPS TO OBTAIN MINIMAL EXPRESSIONS FOR COMPLETE BOOLEAN FUNCTIONS

In the previous section it was shown that certain rectangular configurations of 1-cells on a Karnaugh map represent a single product term. Similarly, it was shown that certain rectangular configurations of 0-cells represent a single sum term. At this time, the simplification problem is attacked.

4.5.1 Prime Implicants and Karnaugh Maps

Consider a Karnaugh map for a Boolean function. Every $2^a \times 2^b$ rectangular grouping, i.e., subcube, of 1-cells represents a product term. Since each term equals 1 for those *n*-tuples included in the subcube, each product term implies the function and, hence, is an implicant of the function. Now assume a set of subcubes is selected

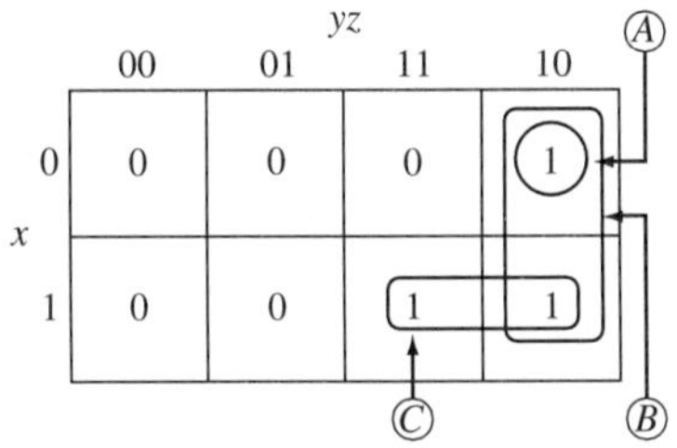

Figure 4.13 Illustrating the concept of prime implicants on a Karnaugh map.

such that every 1-cell, and no 0-cells, is included in at least one of these subcubes. The corresponding product terms are all implicants of the function. Furthermore, by summing the product terms associated with this set of subcubes, an algebraic expression is obtained that describes the function. One obvious case is if the individual 1-cells themselves are selected as $2^0 \times 2^0$ subcubes. Then, the resulting expression is the minterm canonical formula.

Although all the implicants of a function can be determined using a Karnaugh map, it is the prime implicants that are of particular interest as evident by Theorems 4.1 and 4.2 in Sec. 4.2. Recalling from Sec. 4.2, a prime implicant is an implicant of a function that subsumes no smaller implicant that implies the same function. The question can now be asked: How is this related to the subcubes on the Karnaugh map?

To answer this question, consider the map shown in Fig. 4.13. The $2^0 \times 2^0$ subcube labeled Ⓐ corresponds to an implicant of the function; namely, the minterm $\bar{x}y\bar{z}$. However, the cell associated with subcube Ⓐ can also be grouped with the cell below it to form the $2^1 \times 2^0$ subcube Ⓑ. The corresponding product term for this subcube is $y\bar{z}$ and is also an implicant of the function. Note that subcube Ⓐ is totally contained within subcube Ⓑ. Furthermore, the term $\bar{x}y\bar{z}$ subsumes the term $y\bar{z}$ and, hence, $\bar{x}y\bar{z}$ is not a prime implicant. As is seen by this illustration, as a subcube gets larger, the corresponding product term gets smaller, i.e., has fewer literals. In addition, if one subcube is totally contained within another subcube, then the literals associated with the product term of the larger subcube are always a subset of the literals associated with the product term of the smaller subcube. Again consider the map of Fig. 4.13. It can now be concluded that a smaller term than $y\bar{z}$, which is subsumed by $y\bar{z}$, requires a subcube of 1-cells that totally contains subcube Ⓑ. However, since the next allowable larger size subcube of 1-cells must consist of four 1-cells,* it is seen that no such subcube is possible in Fig. 4.13. Hence, this leads to

*Recall that a $2^a \times 2^b$ rectangular grouping must always consist of a power-of-two number of cells. Furthermore, all references to subcubes on a Karnaugh map imply that they have the dimensions $2^a \times 2^b$.

the conclusion that $y\bar{z}$ is a prime implicant of the function. By a similar argument, subcube Ⓒ corresponds to another prime implicant of the function; namely, xy. It should be noted that a 1-cell can be used for more than one subcube. In general, any subcube of 1-cells that cannot be totally contained within another subcube of 1-cells corresponds to a prime implicant.

Continuing the analysis of Fig. 4.13, a disjunctive normal formula of the function is given by $f(x,y,z) = y\bar{z} + xy$ since all the 1-cells appear in at least one subcube. The two product terms in this expression are the only prime implicants of this function. Knowing there is at least one minimal disjunctive normal formula that is the sum of prime implicants (by Theorem 4.1) and observing that neither term may be dropped from the expression without changing the function being described, i.e., having all 1-cells appear in at least one subcube, the expression $f(x,y,z) = y\bar{z} + xy$ must be a minimal disjunctive normal formula. Hence, it is seen that a minimal expression is obtained by use of Karnaugh maps. It might be noticed that this expression may be factored to yield $f(x,y,z) = y\bar{z} + xy = y(x + \bar{z})$. Using the count of total number of gate inputs in a two-level realization as the criterion of minimality,* the first expression has a cost of 6, while the factored expression has a cost of 4. However, it should also be realized that the first expression is a disjunctive normal formula, i.e., consists of a sum of product terms, while the factored expression is a conjunctive normal formula, i.e., consists of a product of sum terms. For now, only minimal disjunctive normal formulas are of interest. Minimal conjunctive normal formulas are discussed later in this section.

A general procedure can now be stated for determining the set of all prime implicants of a Boolean function from a Karnaugh map. For an n-variable map, if all 2^n entries are 1's, then the function is identically equal to 1. This 1 is the only prime implicant of the function. If all 2^n entries are not 1's, then a search is made for all subcubes of 1-cells with dimensions $2^a \times 2^b = 2^{n-1}$. Each of these subcubes represents a 1-variable term. Since no two different subcubes can represent the same term, and since all cells in the subcube are 1-cells, they must describe prime implicants. Next, a search is made for all subcubes of 1-cells with dimensions $2^a \times 2^b = 2^{n-i}$, for $i = 2$, such that no subcube is totally contained within a single previously obtained subcube. Each of these subcubes represents an i-variable product term which implies the function. Since no subcube is totally contained within a single previously obtained subcube, its associated product term does not subsume any previously determined product term and hence is a prime implicant. This process is repeated for $i = 3, 4, \ldots, n$. The product terms established are the prime implicants. Furthermore, these are all the prime implicants since any other subcube of 1-cells must be totally contained within at least one of the subcubes already obtained. A flowchart for this algorithm is shown in Fig. 4.14.

---

*As indicated in Sec. 4.1, the number of gate inputs in a two-level realization of a normal formula is given by the sum of the number of literals and the number of terms having more than 1 literal in the expression and then subtracting 1 if the expression consists of only a single term.

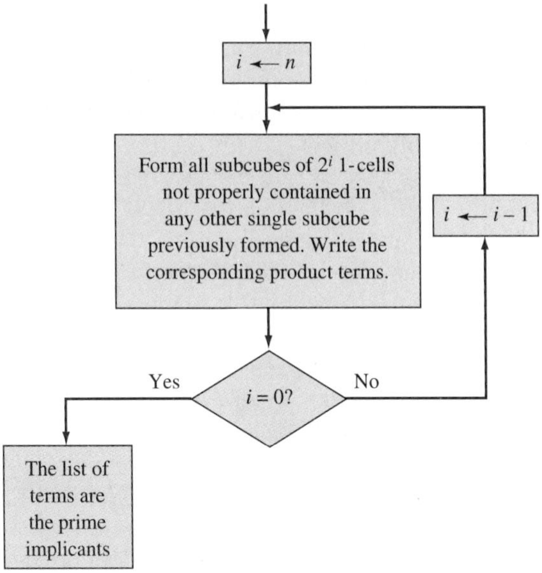

Figure 4.14 Algorithm to find all prime implicants.

To illustrate the above procedure, consider the 3-variable function $f(x,y,z) = \Sigma m(0,1,5,7)$. The map for this function is shown in Fig. 4.15. To determine the prime implicants, note first that there is no subcube of 1-cells consisting of $2^3 = 8$ cells. That is, this function is not identically equal to 1. The next step is to find all subcubes of 1-cells consisting of $2^2 = 4$ cells. Again there are no such subcubes. A search is next conducted for subcubes of 1-cells consisting of $2^1 = 2$ cells. There are three such subcubes on the map. Subcube Ⓐ represents the term $\bar{x}\bar{y}$, subcube Ⓑ the term xz, and subcube Ⓒ the term $\bar{y}z$. All three subcubes represent prime implicants. It should be noted, in particular, that subcube Ⓒ represents a prime implicant. It is true that subcube Ⓒ is partially contained in both subcube Ⓐ and sub-

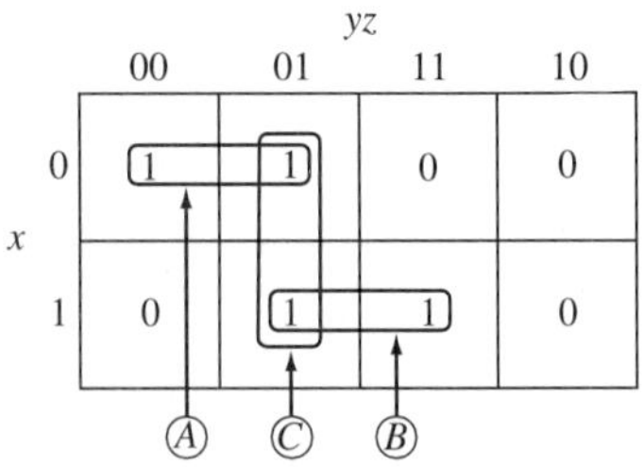

Figure 4.15 Karnaugh map for $f(x,y,z) = \Sigma m(0,1,5,7)$.

cube Ⓑ; however, it is not totally contained in either of these subcubes. Hence, the product term associated with subcube Ⓒ does not subsume either of the other two product terms. Finally, there are no subcubes of 1-cells that consist of $2^0 = 1$ cell and that are not contained in one of the previous three subcubes. Thus, there are three prime implicants of this function. It should be noted that all the 1-cells are contained in some subcube if just the subcubes Ⓐ and Ⓑ are considered. Consequently, the function is describable by the expression $f(x,y,z) = \overline{x}\,\overline{y} + xz$. It can be concluded from this example that not all the prime implicants are needed, in general, to obtain a minimal disjunctive normal formula.

As another example of determining the prime implicants of a function from a Karnaugh map, consider the function shown in Fig. 4.16. The largest subcubes of 1-cells forming a $2^a \times 2^b = 2^{a+b}$ rectangle are subcubes Ⓐ and Ⓑ, each of which consists of $2^2 = 4$ 1-cells. These subcubes represent the terms $\overline{w}z$ and $\overline{w}y$, respectively. Next it is necessary to find all subcubes of 1-cells that consist of $2^1 = 2$ cells and that are not entirely contained in any other single subcube already found. Only subcube Ⓒ, which represents the term $x\overline{y}z$, satisfies this condition. Finally, all remaining 1-cells (subcubes of $2^0 = 1$ cell) not contained in some already found subcube correspond to prime implicants. In this case, subcube Ⓓ establishes that the term $w\overline{x}\,\overline{y}\,\overline{z}$ is a prime implicant. For this function there are four prime implicants, all of which are necessary for the minimal disjunctive normal formula.

With practice it becomes relatively easy to recognize the prime implicants on a Karnaugh map. More important still, however, is the fact that an optimum set of prime implicants is fairly evident by inspection.

Before continuing with the discussion of minimal expressions, a simple observation can be made. If a function is described by a Boolean formula not in canonical form, then it is possible to draw the Karnaugh map without having to first obtain the

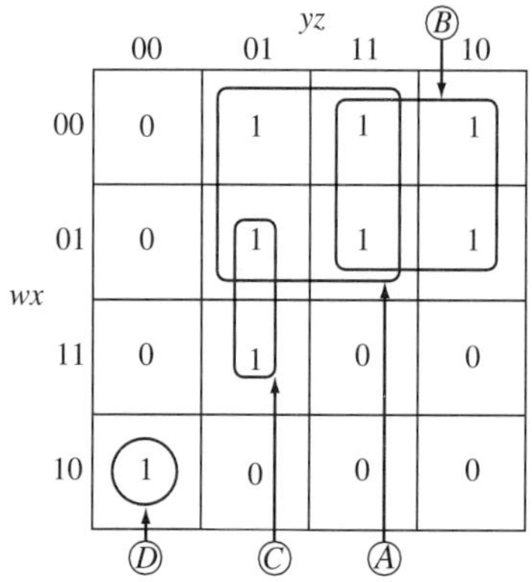

Figure 4.16 Karnaugh map for $f(w,x,y,z) = \Sigma m(1,2,3,5,6,7,8,13)$.

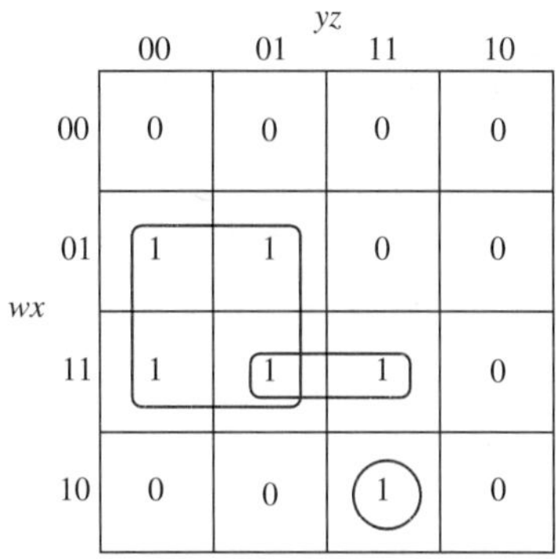

Figure 4.17 Using the Karnaugh map in reverse.

canonical formula or constructing its truth table. The map is obtained by first manipulating the expression into sum-of-products form and then placing 1's in the appropriate cells for each product term. For example, consider the function

$$f(w,x,y,z) = x\bar{y} + wxz + w\bar{x}yz$$

and its representation on a four-variable map. If the term $x\bar{y}$ were to be read from the map, then the subcube would have to encompass those 1-cells in which the variable x is 1 and the variable y is 0. It is the second and third rows of a four-variable map in which the variable x has the value 1; while the variable y has the value 0 in the first and second columns. The intersection of these rows and columns corresponds to the 1-cells for this term and appears as the subcube of four 1-cells in Fig. 4.17. In a similar manner, the other two subcubes in the figure represent the terms wxz and $w\bar{x}yz$. Since these terms also imply the function, the corresponding subcubes locate 1-cells. All the remaining cells are then filled in with 0's.

4.5.2 Essential Prime Implicants

A minimal disjunctive normal formula describing a function consisting of prime implicants is referred to as a *minimal sum.* Similarly, a *minimal product* is a minimal conjunctive normal formula describing a function consisting of prime implicates. As indicated by the statement of the simplification problem, our objective is to determine minimal sums and minimal products.

Using the decimal notation of Fig. 4.8 to refer to cells of a Karnaugh map, again consider Fig. 4.15 in which all the prime implicants are shown. It is observed that some 1-cells may appear in only one prime implicant subcube, e.g., cells 0 and 7; while other 1-cells may appear in more than one prime implicant subcube, e.g., cells 1 and 5. A 1-cell that can be in only one prime implicant subcube is called an *essential 1-cell* and the corresponding prime implicant is called an *essential prime implicant.* A test for an essential 1-cell is that all possible subcubes containing that 1-cell are subsets of the single largest subcube (which corresponds to a prime implicant) in the collection. Thus, in Fig. 4.15, cells 0 and 7 are essential 1-cells and $\bar{x}\bar{y}$ and xz are essential prime implicants. Similarly, in Fig. 4.16, cells 1, 2, 6, 8, and 13 are essential 1-cells. All the prime implicants of Fig. 4.16 are essential prime implicants. It should be noted in Fig. 4.16 that essential 1-cells 2 and 6 are both associated with the same prime implicant.

What is significant about essential prime implicants is that every essential prime implicant of a function must appear in all the irredundant disjunctive normal formulas of the function and, hence, in a minimal sum. That this is true follows from the fact that each essential prime implicant has at least one 1-cell that is associated with no other prime implicant. Certainly that particular 1-cell represents an n-tuple for which the function is 1; and the corresponding essential prime implicant is the only prime implicant that equals 1 for this n-tuple. Since an irredundant disjunctive normal formula consists of a sum of prime implicants and the expression must equal 1 for all n-tuples in which the function is 1, the essential prime implicants are necessary in forming the irredundant expressions.

4.5.3 Minimal Sums

A general approach for determining a minimal sum can now be stated. First, a map of the function is drawn. The essential prime implicants are next determined by detecting essential 1-cells. This can be done either by using the test for essential 1-cells described above or by first determining all the prime implicants on the map and then noting which ones contain essential 1-cells. If all the subcubes established at this point encompass all the 1-cells of the map, then the minimal sum is simply the sum of the essential prime implicants. However, if there remain 1-cells that are not included in some subcube, then additional subcubes (representing prime implicants) must be selected to include the remaining 1-cells. As guiding rules, these additional subcubes should be as large as possible (i.e., contain as many 1-cells as possible and still satisfy the constraint that there be a power-of-two cells), and the number of additional subcubes should be as few as possible. The sum of the terms associated with all the subcubes selected is the minimal sum.

Several examples are now presented to illustrate the determination of minimal sums from Karnaugh maps.

EXAMPLE 4.1

Consider the function

$$f(w,x,y,z) = \bar{w}\bar{x} + \bar{w}xz + yz$$

Using the Karnaugh map in reverse, each term is placed on the map as explained previously. The resulting map is shown in Fig. 4.18*a*, where the indicated subcubes correspond to the three product terms of the given function.* To obtain a minimal sum, it is necessary to determine the essential prime implicants by first

*These subcubes are not necessarily the subcubes associated with a minimal sum.

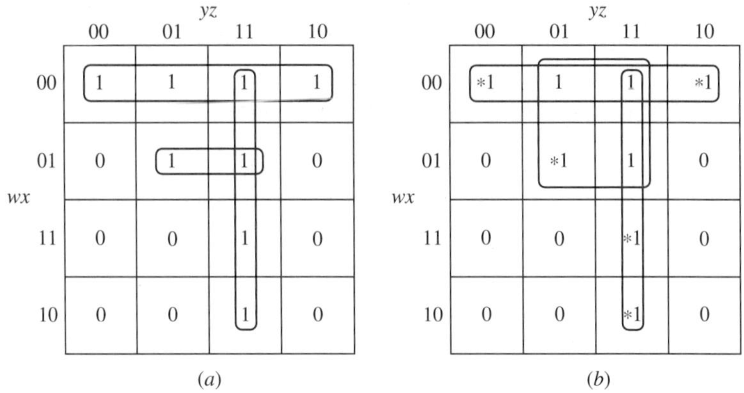

Figure 4.18 Example 4.1.

detecting essential 1-cells. Consider cell 0. It is observed that all subcubes incorporating cell 0 are a subset of the single $2^0 \times 2^2$ subcube consisting of the first row of cells. Thus, cell 0 is an essential 1-cell, indicated by an asterisk in Fig. 4.18*b,* and is associated with the prime implicant $\overline{w}\,\overline{x}$. Alternatively, it should be noted that cell 2 is also an essential 1-cell for the same term. Next, it is noted that cell 5 is an essential 1-cell and is associated with the prime implicant $\overline{w}z$. Finally, it is observed that cell 11 is an essential 1-cell (as well as cell 15) and is associated with the prime implicant yz. It is now seen in Fig. 4.18*b* that all the 1-cells are included in some subcube. Thus, the minimal sum consists of the three essential prime implicants; i.e.,

$$f(w,x,y,z) = \overline{w}\,\overline{x} + \overline{w}z + yz$$

EXAMPLE 4.2

Consider the function

$$f(w,x,y,z) = \Sigma m(0,1,2,4,5,7,9,12)$$

shown in Fig. 4.19. The essential 1-cells are indicated by asterisks, and the subcubes associated with the essential prime implicants are also shown. Since all 1-cells are covered, the minimal sum is

$$f(w,x,y,z) = \overline{w}\,\overline{x}\,\overline{z} + \overline{w}xz + x\overline{y}\,\overline{z} + \overline{x}\,\overline{y}z$$

Note that if the essential 1-cells are not grouped first, then it would be tempting to group the four 1-cells in the upper left corner of the map. If this is done, then it might erroneously be believed that the term $\overline{w}\,\overline{y}$, which is a prime implicant, should be in the minimal sum.

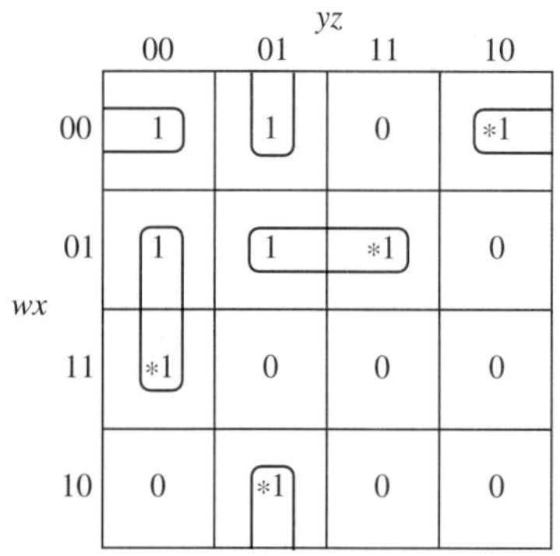

Figure 4.19 Example 4.2.

EXAMPLE 4.3

Consider the map in Fig. 4.20. There are four prime implicants of this function. These are indicated by the four subcubes in the figure. Two of the prime implicants are essential since they include the essential 1-cells indicated by asterisks. The essential prime implicants are $\bar{y}\bar{z}$ and yz. After these two subcubes are formed, there is only one 1-cell that must still be grouped (cell 6). This cell can be placed in either the subcube representing the term xy or the subcube representing the term $x\bar{z}$, both of which are indicated as dashed subcubes. Since only one of the two dashed subcubes is needed to complete the covering of all the 1-cells, there are two minimal sums for this function

$$f(x,y,z) = \bar{y}\bar{z} + yz + xy$$

and

$$f(x,y,z) = \bar{y}\bar{z} + yz + x\bar{z}$$

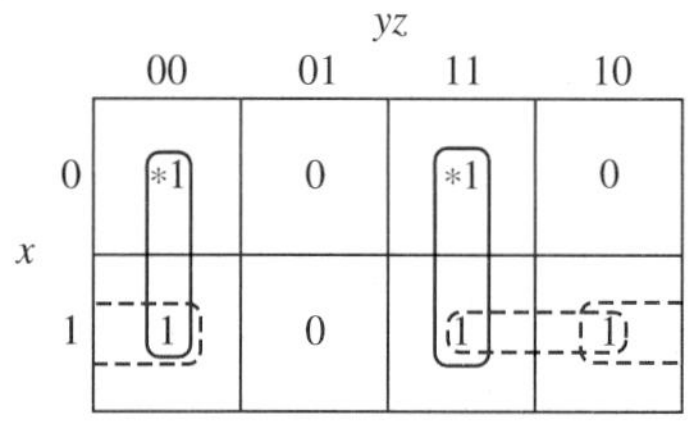

Figure 4.20 Example 4.3.

EXAMPLE 4.4

Consider the map in Fig. 4.21. First the essential prime implicants are determined. Cells 0, 2, and 9 are the only essential 1-cells. Cells 0 and 2 belong to the essential prime implicant $\bar{w}\bar{z}$; while cell 9 belongs to the essential prime implicant $w\bar{y}z$. At

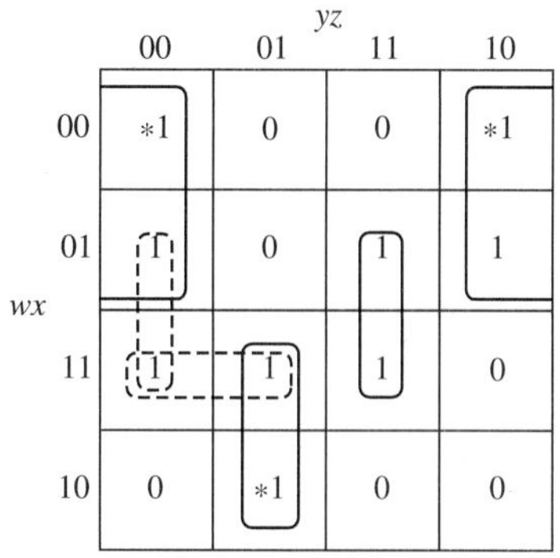

Figure 4.21 Example 4.4.

this point, three 1-cells still need to be grouped, namely, cells 7, 12, and 15. Since none of these cells are essential 1-cells, the constraint of using as few subcubes as possible and keeping the subcubes as large as possible is applied. This suggests that cells 7 and 15 should be grouped together, which corresponds to the prime implicant *xyz*. The remaining 1-cell (cell 12) can be grouped with either the cell above it or the cell next to it as indicated by the dashed subcubes in the figure. Only one of these subcubes is needed to complete the covering of all the 1-cells. Thus, there are two minimal sums

$$f(w,x,y,z) = \overline{w}\,\overline{z} + w\overline{y}z + xyz + x\overline{y}\,\overline{z}$$

and

$$f(w,x,y,z) = \overline{w}\,\overline{z} + w\overline{y}z + xyz + wx\overline{y}$$

EXAMPLE 4.5

Consider the map in Fig. 4.22. None of the 1-cells are essential 1-cells and hence there are no essential prime implicants. Careful analysis reveals that there are six prime implicants for this function. These correspond to the six subcubes shown collectively in Fig. 4.22*a* and *b*. However, with the interest of using a minimum num-

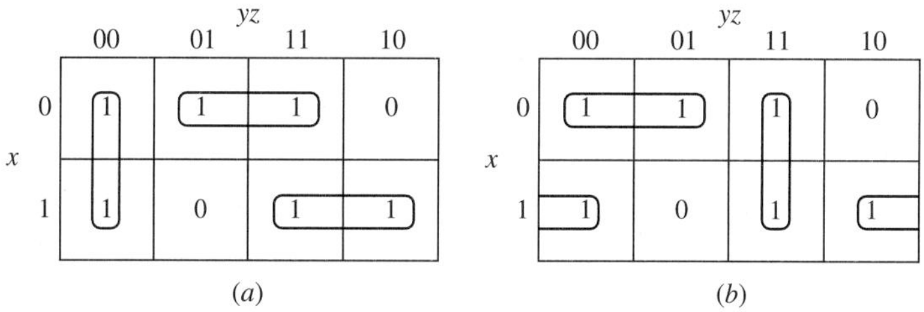

Figure 4.22 Example 4.5.

ber of prime implicants, either of the groupings shown in Fig. 4.22*a* or *b* suggests a minimal sum. Thus, both

$$f(x,y,z) = \bar{y}\bar{z} + \bar{x}z + xy$$

and

$$f(x,y,z) = \bar{x}\bar{y} + yz + x\bar{z}$$

are minimal sums.

4.5.4 Minimal Products

To determine a minimal product, i.e., a conjunctive normal formula describing a function that is minimal according to some cost criterion, a procedure similar to the above is applied to the 0-cells. In the previous section it was stated that a $2^a \times 2^b$ rectangular grouping of 0-cells corresponds to a sum term. Applying the principle of duality to the above discussion in this section, it follows that each of these sum terms is an implicate of a function. Thus, by applying the techniques that have been presented to the 0-cells, prime implicates and minimal products are determined. In particular, all the 0-cells, and no 1-cells, must be grouped at least once while satisfying the constraints of using the largest possible and the fewest number of groupings, i.e., subcubes. To read the sum terms corresponding to the subcubes directly from the map, again it is necessary to observe which labels do not change value. In this case, a 0 along the axis of the map denotes an uncomplemented variable and a 1 along the axis denotes a complemented variable.

The map of Fig. 4.23 represents the function

$$f(w,x,y,z) = \Sigma m(1,3,4,5,6,7,11,14,15)$$

The minimal sum, from Fig. 4.23*a*, is

$$f(w,x,y,z) = \bar{w}x + \bar{w}z + xy + yz$$

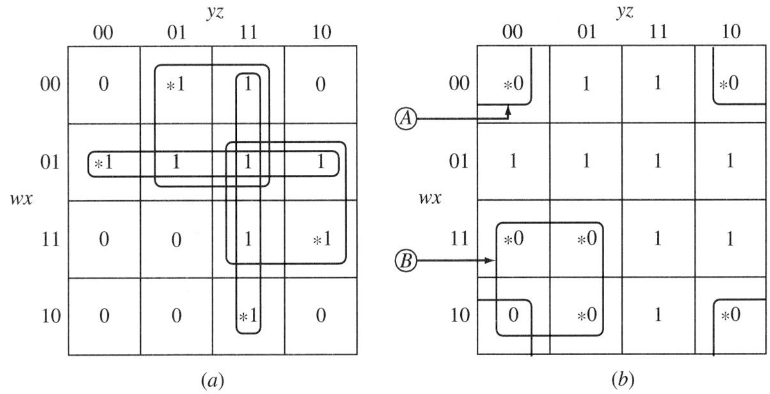

Figure 4.23 Map for the function $f(w,x,y,z) = \Sigma m(1,3,4,5,6,7,11,14,15)$.

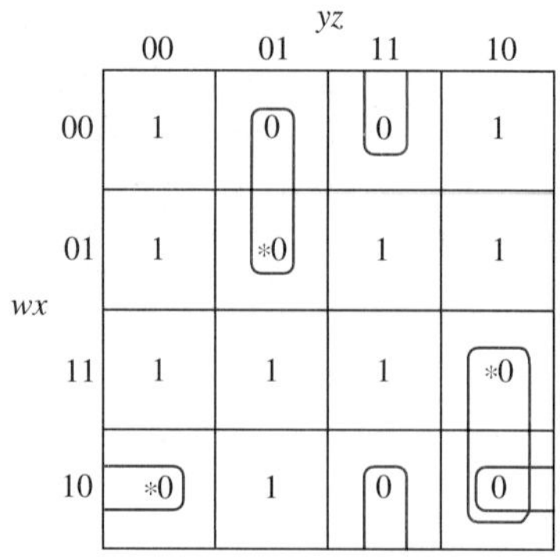

Figure 4.24 Example 4.4.

Using the cost criterion of number of gate input terminals, the minimal sum has a cost of 12. Now consider the 0-cells of this function and Fig. 4.23*b*. Cell 0, as well as cells 2 and 10, is an *essential 0-cell* since all subcubes involving this cell are contained within the $2^1 \times 2^1$ subcube labeled Ⓐ.* The corresponding essential prime implicate is $(x + z)$. Similarly, cell 13, as well as cells 9 and 12, is an essential 0-cell. Thus, the subcube labeled Ⓑ corresponds to the essential prime implicate $(\overline{w} + y)$. Since all the 0-cells are now included in at least one subcube, the minimal product for this function is

$$f(w,x,y,z) = (x + z)(\overline{w} + y)$$

The cost of this expression is 6 using the cost criterion of number of gate input terminals.

When a minimal two-level gate network is to be realized, it is necessary to determine both the minimal sum and the minimal product of the function. Although both expressions are equivalent, in general one form has a lower cost than the other. There is no way to determine which form has the lower cost until both the minimal sum and minimal product are obtained. However, since the minimal sum and minimal product can both be determined from the same Karnaugh map, it is not difficult to obtain both expressions. For the function of Fig. 4.23, a minimal two-level gate network would be realized from the minimal product because of its lower cost.

As a second example, consider again the map of Fig. 4.21. This map is redrawn in Fig. 4.24. All of the essential 0-cells are indicated with asterisks. These three cells are used to determine the three essential prime implicates. At this point there remain two 0-cells still ungrouped, i.e., cells 3 and 11. In an effort to use as few subcubes as possible, they are grouped together. Thus, for this function the minimal product is

$$f(w,x,y,z) = (w + y + \overline{z})(\overline{w} + \overline{y} + z)(\overline{w} + x + z)(x + \overline{y} + \overline{z})$$

---

*Recall that for a 4-variable map, the top and bottom edges as well as the left and right edges are connected to form a torus.

In this case the minimal sum, having a cost of 15, has a lower cost than the minimal product, having a cost of 16. It is interesting to note that for this example, there are two minimal sums but there is only one minimal product.

There is a slight variation to the above procedure for obtaining minimal products that can be used instead. Recall that the complement of a function is obtained by replacing all 0 functional values by 1's and all 1 functional values by 0's. Thus, if the 0-cells of a Karnaugh map are grouped and product terms are written for the groupings (where, since product terms are being written, uncomplemented variables correspond to 1 labels on the axes of the map and complemented variables correspond to 0 labels on the axes), then a minimal sum for the complement function is obtained. By applying DeMorgan's law to the expression, and thereby complementing it, the resulting product of sum terms corresponds to the minimal product of the original function. Thus, for the map in Fig. 4.24 the minimal sum for the complement function, found by grouping the 0's and writing product terms, is

$$\bar{f}(w,x,y,z) = \bar{w}\bar{y}z + wy\bar{z} + w\bar{x}\bar{z} + \bar{x}yz$$

Applying DeMorgan's law, the minimal product for the original function results, i.e.,

$$\bar{\bar{f}}(w,x,y,z) = f(w,x,y,z) = (w + y + \bar{z})(\bar{w} + \bar{y} + z)(\bar{w} + x + z)(x + \bar{y} + \bar{z})$$

which is the minimal product obtained previously.

One final point should be mentioned before closing this section. It was stated earlier that when a Boolean function is described by a disjunctive normal formula, the Karnaugh map is easily constructed by reversing the reading process, i.e., entering 1's in those cells corresponding to the various product terms. A similar process can be applied if a function is initially described by a conjunctive normal formula. That is, for each sum term the corresponding 0's are entered into the map. Once the map is constructed, the minimal sum and minimal product are determined.

4.6 MINIMAL EXPRESSIONS OF INCOMPLETE BOOLEAN FUNCTIONS

It was shown in Sec. 3.8 that incomplete Boolean functions can arise in logic design. Truth tables in such cases contain dashed functional entries indicating don't-care conditions. Since a Karnaugh map is a diagrammatic representation of a truth table, incomplete Boolean functions result in Karnaugh maps containing three possible entries—0's, 1's, and –'s.* For the purpose of obtaining minimal sums and minimal products, it is necessary to slightly modify the procedures introduced so as to handle the occurrences of dashed entries. Cells containing dashed entries on a Karnaugh map are referred to as *don't-care cells.*

---

*In this text, dashes are used in a map to signify don't-care functional values to be consistent with the entries in the truth table. Frequently, however, *d*'s, ×'s, or ϕ's are used in a Karnaugh map to denote don't-care conditions.

The prime implicants of an incomplete Boolean function are the prime implicants of the complete Boolean function obtained by regarding all the don't-care conditions as having functional values of 1. Similarly, the prime implicates of an incomplete Boolean function are the prime implicates of the complete Boolean function in which all the don't-care conditions are regarded as having 0 functional values. Accepting these conclusions, it is a simple matter to obtain minimal sums and minimal products for incomplete Boolean functions from a Karnaugh map.

4.6.1 Minimal Sums

To obtain a minimal sum, the prime implicants of the incomplete Boolean function are determined. To do this, attention is paid to both the 1-cells and the don't-care cells. For the purpose of forming large $2^a \times 2^b$ rectangular groupings, i.e., subcubes, the don't-care cells are considered as 1-cells. However, only those conditions for which the function actually has the value of 1 need to be described by the Boolean expression. Thus, it is only necessary to have a sufficient number of subcubes such that each actual 1-cell is included in at least one subcube. Note that it is *not* necessary to include all the don't-care cells. In this way, don't-care cells are used optionally in order to establish the best possible groupings. As in the case of

w	x	y	z	f
0	0	0	0	1
0	0	0	1	1
0	0	1	0	0
0	0	1	1	1
0	1	0	0	0
0	1	0	1	–
0	1	1	0	0
0	1	1	1	1
1	0	0	0	1
1	0	0	1	0
1	0	1	0	–
1	0	1	1	0
1	1	0	0	1
1	1	0	1	–
1	1	1	0	–
1	1	1	1	0

(*a*)

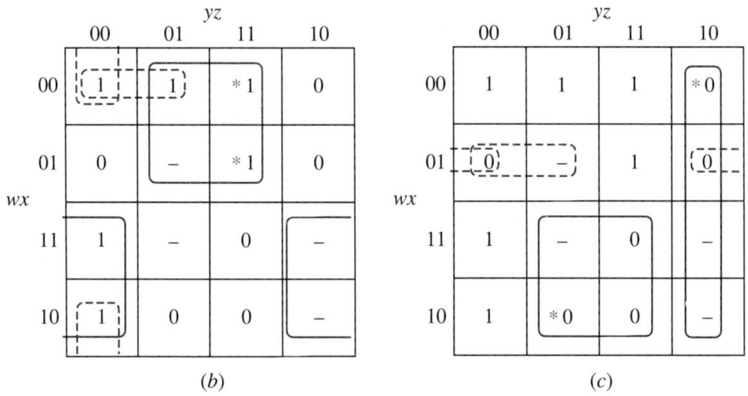

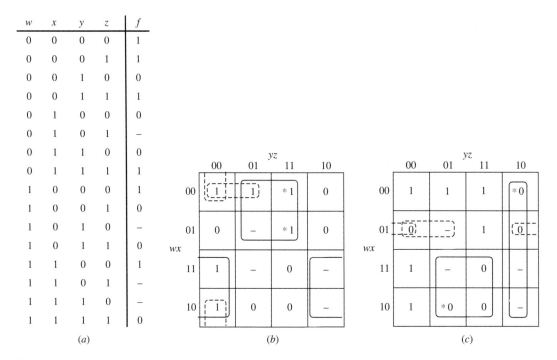

Figure 4.25 Incomplete Boolean function $f(w,x,y,z) = \Sigma m(0,1,3,7,8,12) + dc(5,10,13,14)$. (*a*) Truth table. (*b*) Karnaugh map for obtaining minimal sums. (*b*) Karnaugh map for obtaining minimal products.

complete Boolean functions, the essential prime implicants should first be obtained. In the case of incomplete functions, however, only the *actual* 1-cells in the map are candidates for essential 1-cells. The don't-care cells are not candidates since the don't-care cells do not have to be included in at least one subcube.

As an example of obtaining a minimal sum for an incomplete Boolean function, consider the truth table in Fig. 4.25*a*. The corresponding Karnaugh map is shown in Fig. 4.25*b*. Cell 3 (as well as cell 7) is an essential 1-cell. The subcube with this essential 1-cell corresponds to the only essential prime implicant of this function. It should be noted that the subcube for the essential prime implicant includes a don't-care cell since don't-care cells are regarded as containing 1's for the purpose of maximizing the size of the subcubes. It is next observed that cell 12 can be placed in a subcube of four cells by including two don't-care cells. Cell 12 is not an essential 1-cell since grouping it with don't-care cell 13 forms another prime implicant for this function. At this point only cell 0 still needs to be grouped. Two prime-implicant subcubes, shown dashed, are possible, each containing two cells. Hence, there are two minimal sums

$$f(w,x,y,z) = \overline{w}z + w\overline{z} + \overline{x}\,\overline{y}\,\overline{z}$$

and

$$f(w,x,y,z) = \overline{w}z + w\overline{z} + \overline{w}\,\overline{x}\,\overline{y}$$

Notice that don't-care cell 13 is never grouped since only the 1-cells must be covered.

4.6.2 Minimal Products

When a minimal product is to be obtained, the don't-care cells are regarded as 0-cells for the purpose of establishing the prime implicates. However, only the actual 0-cells must be included in at least one subcube. In all other respects, the procedure for obtaining the minimal product is the same as that for complete Boolean functions.

Because of the way don't-care conditions are interpreted, some don't-care cells may appear in both the groupings of the 1-cells and the 0-cells. Also, since don't-care cells do not necessarily have to be grouped, it is possible that some don't-care cells may appear in no groupings. As a consequence of the fact that don't-care cells are regarded as both, or neither, 0-cells and 1-cells, minimal sum and minimal product expressions, in general, are not algebraically equivalent. However, for all conditions in which the functional values are specified, the minimal sum and minimal product expressions do yield the same values.

Again consider the function of Fig. 4.25*a*. The minimal product for this function is determined from the map of Fig. 4.25*c*. In this case, cells 2 and 9 are essential 0-cells. The remaining ungrouped 0-cell, cell 4, can be grouped in either of two equal-sized subcubes. Thus, two minimal products are found, i.e.,

$$f(w,x,y,z) = (\overline{y} + z)(\overline{w} + \overline{z})(w + \overline{x} + y)$$

and

$$f(w,x,y,z) = (\overline{y} + z)(\overline{w} + \overline{z})(w + \overline{x} + z)$$

It should be noted that don't-care cells 10 and 14 appear in both a subcube of 1-cells and a subcube of 0-cells. That is, their use when grouping the 1's did not preclude their later use when grouping the 0's. Using the gate input terminal count as the cost criterion, all four of the minimal expressions for this function have the same cost.

4.7 FIVE-VARIABLE AND SIX-VARIABLE KARNAUGH MAPS

It is possible to extend the basic concept of the Karnaugh map to handle more than four variables. As is seen in this section, the maps get more difficult to interpret since the $2^a \times 2^b$ rectangular groupings can become split when viewed on their 2-dimensional representations. However, the use of maps for obtaining simple expressions for five-variable and six-variable functions is still manageable with effort. In keeping with the principle behind the Karnaugh map, each cell in a five-variable map must be adjacent to five other cells, while each cell in a six-variable map must be adjacent to six other cells. This is achieved by using 2 or 4 four-variable maps, respectively.

4.7.1 Five-Variable Maps

Figure 4.26*a* shows one variation of a five-variable Karnaugh map. Each cell is marked with the decimal equivalent of the n-tuple for the corresponding row of the truth table. This five-variable map consists of 2 four-variable maps which are the mirror image of each other about the double center line. It is the mirror image of each cell that provides its fifth adjacency. For example, cells 9 and 13 are considered adjacent since they are mirror images of each other about the double center line.

Within each half, any $2^a \times 2^b$ rectangular grouping, i.e., subcube, that is permissible on a four-variable map is also permissible on the five-variable map. In addition, subcubes are also possible about the mirror-image line. In particular, if there are two rectangular groupings of the same $2^a \times 2^b$ dimensions on both halves of the map, and, in addition, the two groupings are the mirror image of each other, then the two groupings collectively form a single subcube. Notice that the number of cells in all such single subcubes is a power of 2; namely, 2^{a+b+1}. The number of literals in the term represented by the subcube is $n - a - b - 1$. As in the case of all other maps, the literals of a term are determined by noting which variables have the same values for all cells that comprise the subcube.

A common variation of the five-variable map is shown in Fig. 4.26*b*. In this case, the 2 four-variable maps are envisioned as being on top of each other, rather than being mirror images of each other. Here the upper map corresponds to those n-tuples in which $v = 0$ and the lower map corresponds to those n-tuples in which $v = 1$. In Fig. 4.26*b* each cell is again marked with the decimal equivalent of the n-tuple for the corresponding row of the truth table. With such a structure, the fifth adjacency occurs between the two layers. For example, cell 0 is adjacent to cell 16, cell 1 is adjacent to cell 17, etc. Subcubes that are permissible on a four-variable map

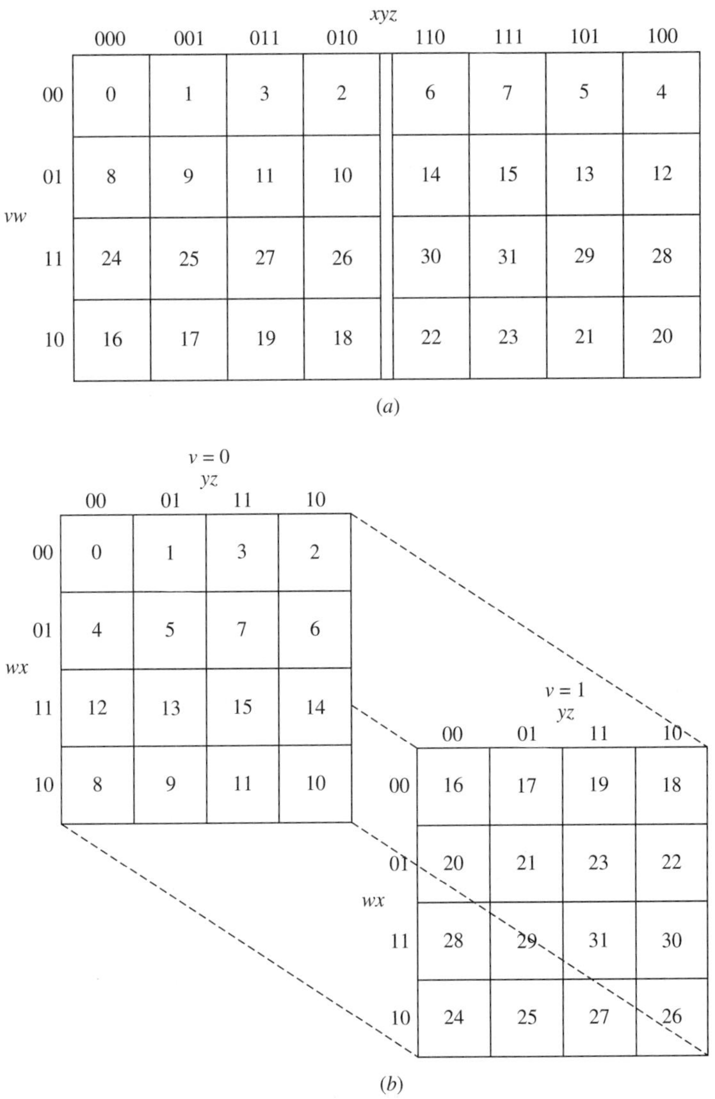

Figure 4.26 Five-variable Karnaugh maps. (*a*) Reflective structure. (*b*) Layer structure.

are also permissible on each layer of the five-variable map. In addition, if each layer contains a $2^a \times 2^b$ subcube such that they can be viewed as being directly above and below each other, then the two subcubes collectively form a single subcube consisting of 2^{a+b+1} cells. As was done previously, the literals of the corresponding term are determined by noting which variables have the same values for all cells that comprise the subcube.

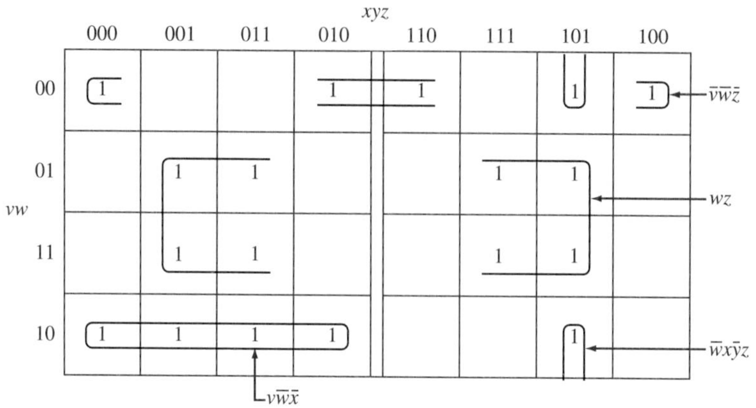

Figure 4.27 Typical subcubes on a five-variable map.

Figure 4.27 shows various ways of forming subcubes on a reflective five-variable map and their associated product terms. No attempt has been made to perform any type of minimization on this map. The subcube consisting of cells 5 and 21, on the right half of the map, is associated with the product term $\bar{w}x\bar{y}z$ since each half of the five-variable map is a four-variable map and, correspondingly, the top and bottom edges of the map are assumed connected. Similarly, the subcube consisting of cells 16, 17, 18, and 19, on the left half of the map, corresponds to the product term $v\bar{w}\bar{x}$. Cells 0 and 2 can be grouped on the left side of the map and cells 4 and 6 can be grouped on the right side. Since the mirror images of cells 0 and 2 are cells 4 and 6, all four cells form a single subcube as explained above. This subcube represents the term $\bar{v}\bar{w}\bar{z}$ because the variables v, w, and z do not change values for these four cells. Finally, the $2^1 \times 2^1$ grouping consisting of cells 9, 11, 25, and 27, on the left half of the map, and the $2^1 \times 2^1$ grouping consisting of cells 13, 15, 29, and 31, on the right half of the map, correspond to the single product term wz since the two groupings are mirror images of each other and collectively form a single subcube.

As an example of using a reflective five-variable map for minimization, consider Fig. 4.28. Again essential cells, indicated by asterisks, should first be detected. In this example, all terms appearing in the minimal expressions are essential terms. The minimal sum is

$$f(v,w,x,y,z) = \bar{w}\bar{x}\bar{y} + yz + \bar{v}\bar{w}y$$

and the minimal product is

$$f(v,w,x,y,z) = (\bar{w} + y)(\bar{w} + z)(\bar{v} + \bar{y} + z)(\bar{x} + y)$$

In the minimal product, the sum term $(\bar{w} + y)$ is the result of grouping cells 8, 9, 12, 13, 24, 25, 28, and 29; while the sum term $(\bar{w} + z)$ is the result of grouping cells 8, 10, 12, 14, 24, 26, 28, and 30.

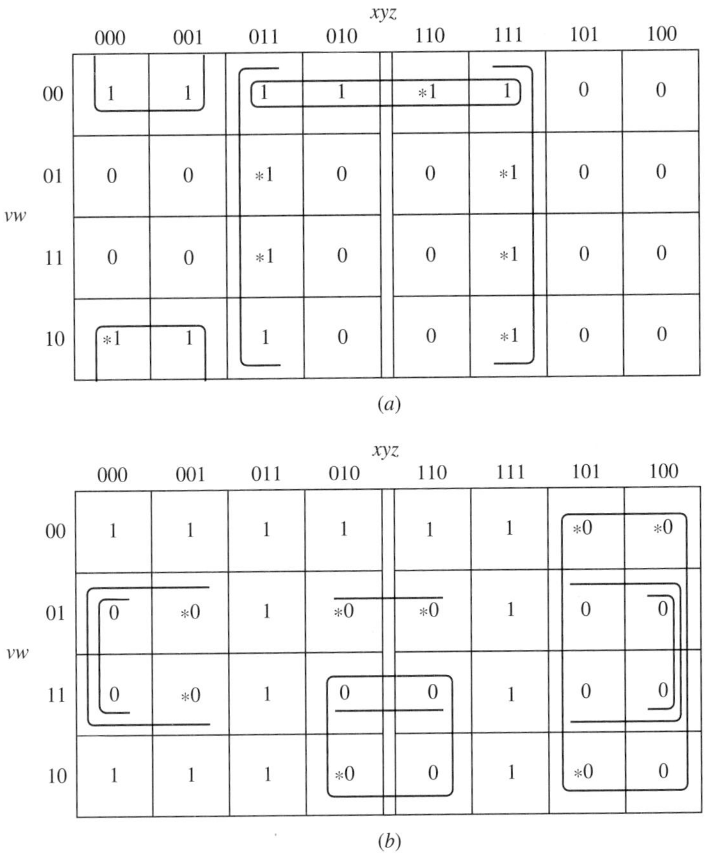

Figure 4.28 Map for $f(v,w,x,y,z) = \Sigma m(0,1,2,3,6,7,11,15,16,17,19,23,27,31)$. (*a*) Subcubes for the minimal sum. (*b*) Subcubes for the minimal product.

4.7.2 Six-Variable Maps

The six-variable Karnaugh map consists of 4 four-variable maps. One possible structure of a six-variable map is shown in Fig. 4.29*a*. In this case, every cell has an adjacent cell about the horizontal and vertical mirror-image lines. For example, cells 13 and 41 are both adjacent to cell 9. As in the case of the four-variable map, any rectangular grouping of dimensions $2^a \times 2^b$, i.e., subcube, in a single quadrant represents a single term. Also, two groupings having the same $2^a \times 2^b$ dimensions that are the mirror image of each other about either the vertical or horizontal mirror-image lines are a single subcube. These situations are similar to those of five-variable maps. A third possible way in which subcubes may be formed on six-variable maps is if each quadrant has a rectangular grouping of dimensions $2^a \times 2^b$ and each

uvw \ *xyz*	000	001	011	010	110	111	101	100
000	0	1	3	2	6	7	5	4
001	8	9	11	10	14	15	13	12
011	24	25	27	26	30	31	29	28
010	16	17	19	18	22	23	21	20
110	48	49	51	50	54	55	53	52
111	56	57	59	58	62	63	61	60
101	40	41	43	42	46	47	45	44
100	32	33	35	34	38	39	37	36

(*a*)

Figure 4.29 Six-variable Karnaugh maps. (*a*) Reflective structure.

grouping is a mirror image of the other about *both* the horizontal and vertical mirror-image lines. Then, the four groupings collectively form a single subcube and correspond to a single term.

As in the case of the five-variable map, an alternate structure is also possible. In this case, 4 four-variable maps are assumed to be layered one upon the other as shown in Fig. 4.29*b*. For each layer, the values of the variables *v* and *w* are assumed to be fixed. In Fig. 4.29*b*, $uv = 00$ in the top layer, $uv = 01$ in the second layer, $uv = 11$ in the third layer, and $uv = 10$ in the bottom layer. Since each cell must be adjacent to six cells in a six-variable map, in addition to the four adjacencies within each layer, the fifth and sixth adjacencies occur between adjacent layers where it is assumed that the top layer, i.e., the $uv = 00$ layer, and the bottom layer, i.e., the $uv = 10$ layer, of the overall structure are adjacent. For example, cell 21 on the second layer is adjacent to cells 17, 20, 23, and 29 on that layer as well as cell 5 on the first layer and cell 53 on the third layer. Similarly, cell 4 on the first layer is adjacent to cells 0, 1, 5, and 6 on that layer as well as cell 20 on the second layer and cell 36 on the fourth layer. Subcubes occurring in corresponding positions on two adjacent layers collectively form a single subcube. In addition, subcubes occurring in corresponding positions on all four layers collectively form a single subcube.

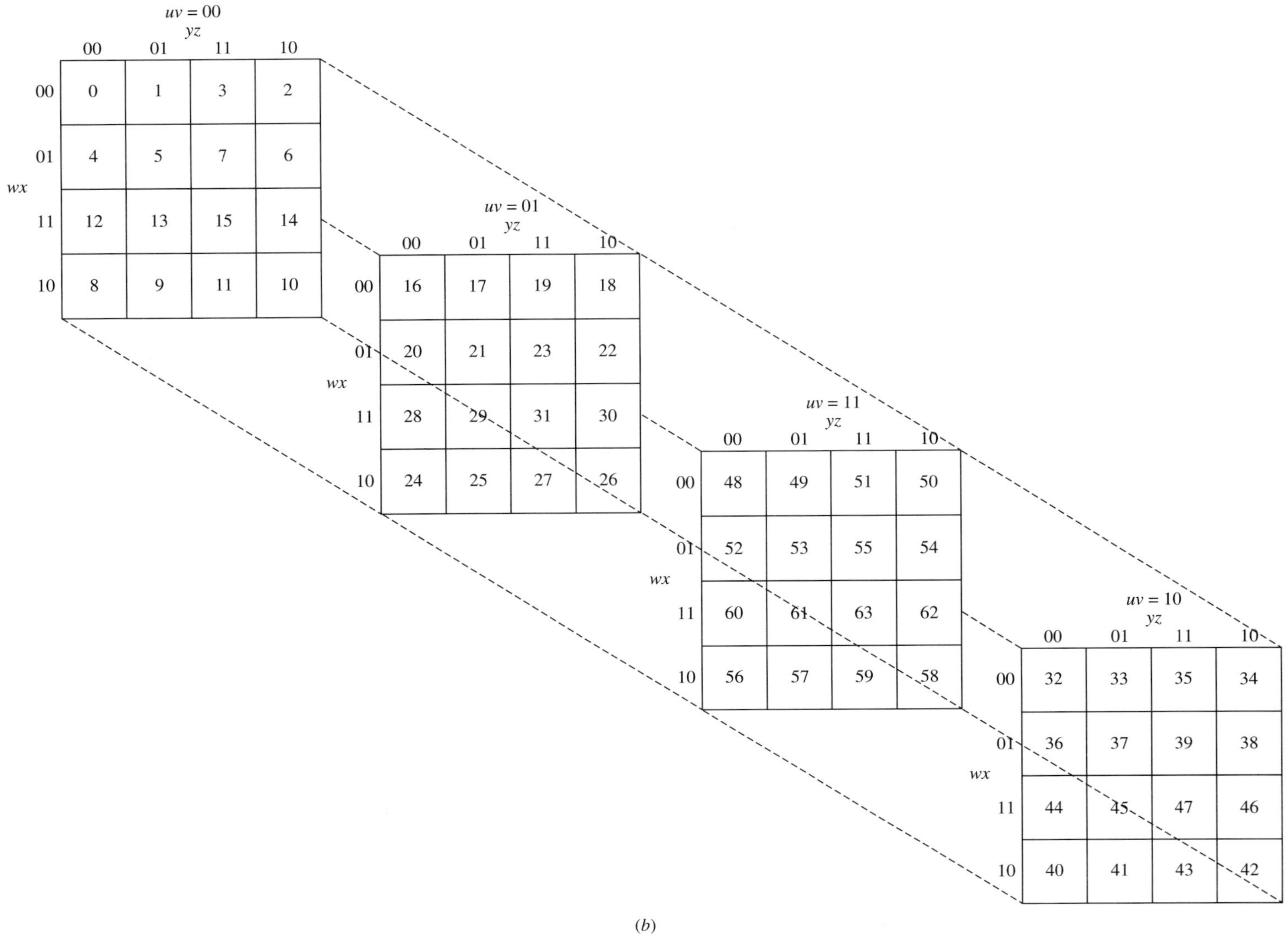

Figure 4.29 (*Cont.*) (*b*) Layer structure.

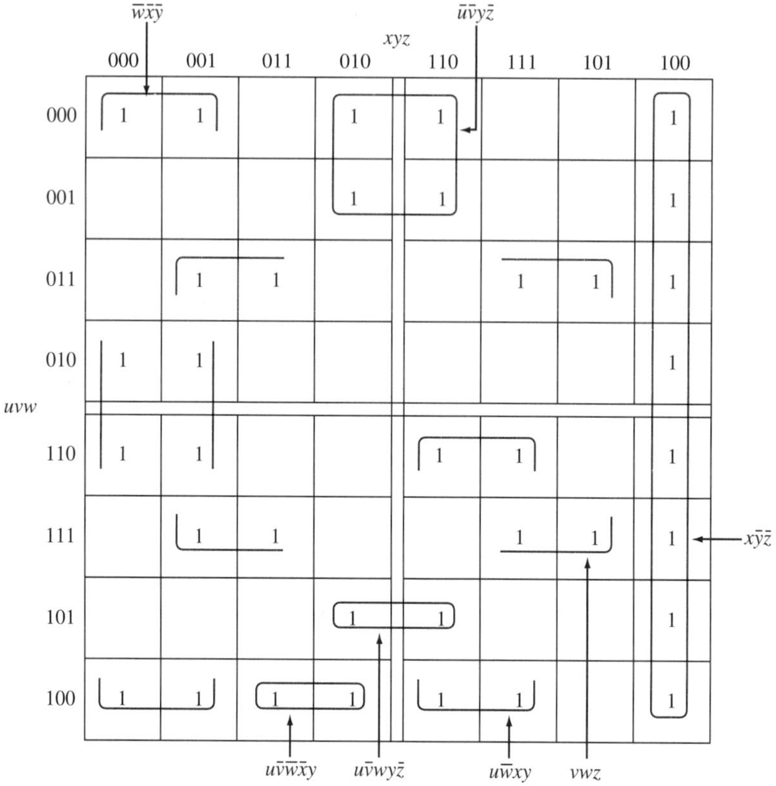

Figure 4.30 Typical subcubes on a six-variable map.

Figure 4.30 shows various subcubes on a reflective six-variable map and their associated product terms. No attempt has been made to perform any type of minimization on this map. The reader should pay particular attention to the subcube for the *vwz* product term. This subcube corresponds to the situation in which part of the grouping appears in each of the four quadrants. In particular, this subcube consists of cells 25, 27, 29, 31, 57, 59, 61, and 63.

Interpreting five-variable and six-variable maps can be a challenge. Although the map concept is extendable to more than six variables, it is evident that another procedure is needed when dealing with functions having a large number of variables.

4.8 THE QUINE-McCLUSKEY METHOD OF GENERATING PRIME IMPLICANTS AND PRIME IMPLICATES

The Karnaugh map method for obtaining simplified Boolean expressions is a very effective method for functions with no more than six variables. However, a general procedure which is applicable to functions of any number of variables is desirable.

Such a procedure should be algorithmic so that it can be programmed for a digital computer. One such procedure was originally suggested by Quine and later modified by McCluskey.

The Quine-McCluskey method consists of two phases. In the first phase, the set of all prime implicants (or prime implicates) of the function is systematically obtained. In the second phase, the set of all irredundant expressions for the function is determined. From the set of irredundant expressions the minimal expressions are selected.

4.8.1 Prime Implicants and the Quine-McCluskey Method

All the implicants of a complete Boolean function can be generated from its set of minterms by repeatedly applying the relationship $AB + \overline{A}B = B$. This relationship provides for combining two product terms to form a new single product term when A denotes a single variable and B denotes a product of variables. In essence, the application of this relationship involves repeated comparisons. To do this, the minterms are initially placed in a list. Two minterms that differ in precisely one literal are related by AB and $\overline{A}B$ and hence combine to form a single term B. This new term B is then placed in a second list. Furthermore, although the two minterms AB and $\overline{A}B$ are implicants of the function, it can be concluded that neither of these minterms is a prime implicant of the function since they each subsume the generated term B. This is indicated by placing a check mark next to the two generating minterms. The comparison process is carried out on all pairs of minterms that comprise the initial list. However, the existence of a check mark does not disqualify a minterm from further comparisons with other minterms in order to generate additional terms.

The new list of terms consisting of one less variable is then subjected to the above comparison process. That is, if two terms have the forms AB and $\overline{A}B$ where A is a single variable and B is a product of variables, then the two terms are combined to form a new single term B that is entered in a third list. Again the two generating terms are checked to indicate that they are not prime implicants. Duplicate terms are not entered in the new list. Once all pairs of terms in the second list of terms are compared, the comparison process is applied to the third list to form a fourth list. The comparison process is continued on each new list until no new list is generated. At that time, all terms contained in the set of lists are all the implicants of the function and those that are *not* checked are the prime implicants.

To illustrate the basic concept of repeated application of the relationship $AB + \overline{A}B = B$ in order to generate implicants, consider the function

$$f(w,x,y,z) = \Sigma m(1,3,4,5,7,8,15)$$

The minterms are listed in the first column of Table 4.3 along with their decimal designators. It is now necessary to consider every pair of minterms in the first column to determine if the relationship $AB + \overline{A}B = B$ is applicable. First consider minterms 1 and 3. Both of these minterms are identical except in the y variable. Thus, these two minterms are combined using the relationship $AB + \overline{A}B = B$ to

Table 4.3 Obtaining the prime implicants of the function $f(w,x,y,z) = \Sigma m(1,3,4,5,7,8,15)$

1: $\overline{w}\,\overline{x}\,\overline{y}z$ √	$\overline{w}\,\overline{x}z$ √	$\overline{w}z$
3: $\overline{w}\,\overline{x}yz$ √	$\overline{w}\,\overline{y}z$ √	
4: $\overline{w}x\overline{y}\,\overline{z}$ √	$\overline{w}yz$ √	
5: $\overline{w}x\overline{y}z$ √	$\overline{w}x\overline{y}$	
7: $\overline{w}xyz$ √	$\overline{w}xz$ √	
8: $w\overline{x}\,\overline{y}\,\overline{z}$	xyz	
15: $wxyz$ √		

form the product term $\overline{w}\,\overline{x}z$, which is entered in the second column. Furthermore, since $\overline{w}\,\overline{x}\,\overline{y}z$ and $\overline{w}\,\overline{x}yz$ subsume the term $\overline{w}\,\overline{x}z$, the two minterms are checked to indicate that they are not prime implicants. The comparison process is continued by next considering minterms 1 and 4. Notice that even though minterm 1 has a check mark, it is still used for further comparisons. However, minterms 1 and 4 do not combine since they differ in more than one literal.* Next minterms 1 and 5 are compared. They are combined to form a single term in accordance with the relationship $AB + \overline{A}B = B$. This results in the term $\overline{w}\,\overline{y}z$ being entered in the second column and a check mark being placed next to minterm 5. Since minterm 1 already has a check mark, it is not necessary to place a second check mark next to it. The reader can easily verify that upon comparing minterm 1 with the remaining minterms in the first column, no additional terms are formed. Next, minterm 3 is compared with all the minterms in the first column. However, it is only necessary to apply the comparison process to the remaining minterms below the one currently being studied, in this case minterm 3, due to the commutative property of a Boolean algebra. As a result, minterms 3 and 4 are compared and then minterms 3 and 5. In both cases they differ in more than a single literal and the relationship $AB + \overline{A}B = B$ is not applicable. Next, minterms 3 and 7 are used to generate the term $\overline{w}yz$ shown in the second column. Furthermore, minterm 7 is checked off, since it subsumes the new term. Continuing as above, after all comparisons of the minterms in the first column are completed, the terms of the second column result and the minterms successfully used in the comparison process are those with check marks.

The above comparison process is now carried out on the second column of Table 4.3. Starting with the first term in the second column, terms $\overline{w}\,\overline{x}z$ and $\overline{w}xz$ are the first pair of terms that satisfy the relationship $AB + \overline{A}B = B$ where A corresponds to x and B corresponds to $\overline{w}z$. As a consequence, these two terms are used to form the term $\overline{w}z$ shown in the third column. The two terms $\overline{w}\,\overline{x}z$ and $\overline{w}xz$ are checked to indicate that they are not prime implicants, since they both subsume the generated term $\overline{w}z$. Continuing the comparison process on all of the remaining pairs of terms in the second column, the only other successful application of the relation-

*The check mark next to minterm 4 in Table 4.3 is the result of a future comparison.

ship $AB + \overline{A}B = B$ involves terms $w\overline{y}z$ and $\overline{w}yz$. These two terms again generate the term $\overline{w}z$, and hence the duplicate is not entered in the third column. However, the two terms $w\overline{y}z$ and $\overline{w}yz$ are checked in the second column to again indicate they are not prime implicants.

The process is now continued by comparing all pairs of terms in the third column. Since only one term appears, no new terms are generated. Since a fourth column is not formed, the comparison process terminates. All the terms appearing in Table 4.3 are implicants of the original function, while those that are *not* checked correspond to its prime implicants.

Before stating the above process formally as an algorithm, some general observations are appropriate that reduce and simplify the mechanics of the procedure. Any product term of an n-variable function can be represented without ambiguity by 0's, 1's, and dashes if the ordering of the variables is specified, where 0 is used to represent a complemented variable, 1 is used to represent an uncomplemented variable, and a dash (–) is used to represent the absence of a variable. For example, if $\overline{w}y$ is a term of the function $f(v,w,x,y,z)$, then it is represented as –0–1– where the ordering of the variables in the term is given by the arrangement of the variables in the function notation. The first dash signifies that variable v does not appear in the term, while the second and third dashes represent the absence of the x and z variables. The 0 represents the literal $\overline{w}$, and the 1 represents the literal y. When representing minterms with this notation, there are no dashes, and this procedure simply yields the binary representation of the minterm, as was discussed in the previous chapter.

Now let the *index* of a term be defined as the number of 1's appearing in the 0-1-dash representation of the term. Any two minterms which satisfy the relationship $AB + \overline{A}B = B$ where A is a single variable must have the same binary representation except for the one position corresponding to A. In this position one binary representation has a 0 and the other a 1. Thus, the indices of the two terms differ by exactly 1. Furthermore, when one term is formed from combining two minterms, the literals that are the same in both minterms are the literals appearing in the resulting term. A representation for this combined term has the same 0's and 1's as the original minterms except for that position in which the minterms differed. This position has a dash.

In the comparison technique introduced above for generating prime implicants, all pairs of minterms are inspected to see if they combine by the relationship $AB + \overline{A}B = B$. If the minterms of the function are divided into sets such that the minterms in each set have the same index, then it is only necessary to compare the minterms in those sets whose indices differ by exactly 1. Two terms whose indices are the same or differ by more than 1 can never result in their combining into a single term. This enables a reduction in the number of comparisons that must be made.

It has been seen that two product terms of a function can combine into a single term if they have the same variables and differ in exactly one literal. In terms of the 0-1-dash notation, this implies that the dashes in the representations for both terms must appear in the same relative positions, and that in all but one of the remaining positions the two representations must have the same 0's and 1's. For example, the terms $v\overline{w}\,\overline{y}$ and $vw\overline{y}$ of a function $f(v,w,x,y,z)$ can combine to form the term $v\overline{y}$. The first term is represented by 10–0– and the second term by 11–0–. Since the two 0-1-dash representations have their dashes in the same relative positions and the representations differ only in the second position, they can combine to form 1––0–, which represents the term $v\overline{y}$. The dash now appearing in the second position denotes the elimination of the x variable as the result of the two terms being combined.

4.8.2 Algorithm for Generating Prime Implicants

The Quine-McCluskey algorithm for determining the prime implicants of a function can now be stated.

1. Express each minterm of the function in its binary representation.
2. List the minterms by increasing index.
3. Separate the sets of minterms of equal index with lines.
4. Let $i = 0$.
5. Compare each term of index i with each term of index $i + 1$. For each pair of terms that can combine, i.e., differ in exactly one bit position, place the newly formed term (also in 0-1-dash notation) in the section of index i of a new list, unless it is already present. In either event, place a check mark next to the two terms that combined (if not already checked). In the comparison process, a checked term does not disqualify it from further comparisons. After all pairs of terms with indices i and $i + 1$ are inspected in the original list, a line is drawn under the last term in the new list.
6. Increase i by 1 and repeat Step 5. The increase of i is continued until all terms are compared. The new list contains all those implicants of the function that have one less variable than those implicants in the generating list.
7. Each section of the new list formed has terms of equal index. Steps 4, 5, and 6 are repeated on this list to form another list. Recall that two terms combine only if they have their dashes in the same relative positions and if they differ in exactly one bit position.
8. The process terminates when no new list is formed.
9. All terms without check marks are prime implicants.

To illustrate the algorithm, consider the function

$$f(w,x,y,z) = \overline{w}\,\overline{x}\,\overline{y}\,\overline{z} + \overline{w}x\overline{y}z + \overline{w}xy\overline{z} + \overline{w}xyz + w\overline{x}\,\overline{y}z + w\overline{x}y\overline{z} + wx\overline{y}z + wxy\overline{z} + wxyz$$
$$= \Sigma m(0,5,6,7,9,10,13,14,15)$$

The process for obtaining the prime implicants using the above procedure is shown in Table 4.4. To begin, all minterms with index zero are placed in the first column. Only minterm 0 has index zero. This is indicated in Table 4.4 by the first entry in the first column where minterm 0 is represented in both its decimal and binary forms. (The decimal representation is included for easy reference and is not really

Table 4.4 Obtaining the prime implicants of the function $f(w,x,y,z) = \Sigma m(0,5,6,7,9,10,13,14,15)$

	wxyz		*wxyz*		*wxyz*
0	0000 *E*	5,7	01–1 √	5,7,13,15	–1–1 *A*
		5,13	–101 √	6,7,14,15	–11–*B*
5	0101 √	6,7	011– √		
6	0110 √	6,14	–110 √		
9	1001 √	9,13	1–01 *C*		
10	1010 √	10,14	1–10 *D*		
7	0111 √	7,15	–111 √		
13	1101 √	13,15	11–1 √		
14	1110 √	14,15	111– √		
15	1111 √				

necessary in the actual process.) A line is drawn after this minterm. Next all minterms of index one are listed. Since there are no minterms for this function having index one, no entries are made for it in the first column. Again a line is drawn. All minterms of index two are next listed. These are minterms 5, 6, 9, and 10. A line is drawn after the last minterm of this set. In a similar manner, minterms 7, 13, and 14, having index three, are added to the list. Finally, minterm 15, having index four, is added. This completes the first three steps of the algorithm. Next, the minterm of index zero is compared with all minterms of index one to see if they can combine by the rule $AB + \overline{A}B = B$. Since there are no minterms of index one, minterm 0 cannot be used in comparisons with another minterm. Similarly, no minterms of index one combine with minterms of index two since the set of minterms having index one is empty. Next the minterms of index two are compared with those of index three. Minterms 5, represented by 0101, and 7, represented by 0111, combine since they differ in exactly one bit position to form the term $\overline{w}xz$, which is represented by 01–1 in the second column. Check marks are then placed after minterms 5 and 7. For convenience, the 01–1 in the second column is labeled with the decimal numbers 5,7 to indicate that these are the minterms that combined to form the term represented by 01–1. Next minterms 5 and 13 are compared. Notice that a check mark does not disqualify a minterm from further comparisons. The minterms 5 and 13 form the term represented by –101 in the second column. Since minterm 5 already has a check mark, it is not checked again. However, a check mark is placed after minterm 13. Finally, minterms 5 and 14 are compared. Since they cannot be combined because they differ in three bit positions, no new entry is made in the second column as a result of this comparison and minterm 14 is not checked (at this time). Next minterms 6 and 7, 6 and 13, and 6 and 14 are compared. These comparisons account for the entries 011– and –110 in the second column and check marks being placed next to minterms 6 and 14 in the first column. The process is repeated until minterms 10 and 14 are compared. A line is then drawn under the partially completed list of the second column. Next the minterms in the first column of index three are compared with those of index four. These comparisons yield three terms in the second column. At this point all minterms, except minterm 0, in the first column have been checked off, and no additional comparisons are possible. This completes steps 4, 5, and 6 of the algorithm.

Using the second column as a new list, each term in a group is compared with each term in its adjacent group. First, term 01–1 is compared with –111. Since their dashes are in different positions, they cannot be combined. Next term 01–1 is compared with 11–1. This comparison forms a new term –1–1 in the third column since their 0-1-dash representations differ in exactly one bit position. The two terms which combined, i.e., 01–1 and 11–1 in the second column, are then checked. Term 01–1 is next compared with term 111–. These terms cannot be combined since their dashes do not align. Next terms –101 and –111 are compared. This comparison also yields the term –1–1 in the third column. Since this term already is written once, it is not entered again. However, terms –101 and –111 must be checked. After all comparisons are made, the newly formed list, column 3, has only two terms, both of which appear in the same group since they have the same index. Since no comparisons are possible with the terms of the third column, the process terminates. It is seen that five terms have no check marks. These terms, labeled *A* through *E,* are the prime implicants of the given function. Replacing the symbols 0 and 1 by their as-

Table 4.5 Obtaining the prime implicants of the incomplete Boolean function $f(v,w,x,y,z) = \Sigma m(4,5,9,11,12,14,15,27,30) + dc(1,17,25,26,31)$

	vwxyz		*vwxyz*		*vwxyz*
1	00001 √	1,5	00–01 *F*	1,9,17,25	––001 *A*
4	00100 √	1,9	0–001 √	9,11,25,27	–10–1 *B*
5	00101 √	1,17	–0001 √	11,15,27,31	–1–11 *C*
9	01001 √	4,5	0010– *G*	14,15,30,31	–111– *D*
12	01100 √	4,12	0–100 *H*	26,27,30,31	11–1– *E*
17	10001 √	9,11	010–1 √		
11	01011 √	9,25	–1001 √		
14	01110 √	12,14	011–0 *I*		
25	11001 √	17,25	1–001 √		
26	11010 √	11,15	01–11 √		
15	01111 √	11,27	–1011 √		
27	11011 √	14,15	0111– √		
30	11110 √	14,30	–1110 √		
31	11111 √	25,27	110–1 √		
		26,27	1101– √		
		26,30	11–10 √		
		15,31	–1111 √		
		27,31	11–11 √		
		30,31	1111– √		

sociated complemented and uncomplemented literals, respectively, the algebraic forms of the prime implicants are xz, xy, $w\bar{y}z$, $wy\bar{z}$, and $\bar{w}\bar{x}\bar{y}\bar{z}$.

As a second example, consider the incomplete Boolean function

$$f(v,w,x,y,z) = \Sigma m(4,5,9,11,12,14,15,27,30) + dc(1,17,25,26,31)$$

As was mentioned in the discussion of Karnaugh maps, the prime implicants of an incomplete Boolean function are the prime implicants of the complete Boolean function in which all the don't-care conditions are regarded as having functional values of 1. Thus, to determine the prime implicants of the above incomplete Boolean function, the Quine-McCluskey procedure is carried out on the complete Boolean function

$$f(v,w,x,y,z) = \Sigma m(1,4,5,9,11,12,14,15,17,25,26,27,30,31)$$

This is illustrated in Table 4.5. The nine prime implicants are labeled A through I, i.e., $\bar{x}\bar{y}z$, $w\bar{x}z$, wyz, wxy, vwy, $\bar{v}\bar{w}\bar{y}z$, $\bar{v}\bar{w}x\bar{y}$, $\bar{v}x\bar{y}\bar{z}$, and $\bar{v}wx\bar{z}$.

Although the procedure just presented is very tedious for hand computation, the intent of the Quine-McCluskey method is to provide an algorithmic procedure for obtaining prime implicants that can be programmed for a digital computer. This objective has been achieved.

4.8.3 Prime Implicates and the Quine-McCluskey Method

If it is desired to obtain the prime implicates of a function using the Quine-McCluskey method, then two approaches are possible. By the duality principle, the Quine-McCluskey method can be applied directly to the set of maxterms. In this case, the comparison procedure makes use of the relationship $(A + B)(\bar{A} + B) = B$ where A is a single variable and B is a sum of variables. Each sum term is represented in 0-1-dash notation where 0 is used to denote an uncomplemented variable, 1 is used to denote a complemented variable, and a dash is used to denote the absence of a variable.* For example, if $\bar{v} + w + z$ is a sum term of the function $f(v,w,x,y,z)$, then it is represented as 10−−0. If the function is incompletely specified, then the don't-care conditions are regarded as having 0 functional values.

The second approach for obtaining the prime implicates of a function is based on the fact that the complements of the prime implicants of the complement of a Boolean function are the prime implicates of the function. Thus, given a Boolean function, the prime implicants of the complement function are first determined by the Quine-McCluskey method. DeMorgan's law is then applied to each of the prime implicants to form the prime implicates of the original function. Since the Quine-McCluskey method is being applied to product terms in this case, 0 is used to represent a complemented variable and 1 is used to represent an uncomplemented variable in the 0-1-dash notation.

*It should be noted that this is consistent with the binary notation for maxterms introduced in the previous chapter.

4.9 PRIME-IMPLICANT/PRIME-IMPLICATE TABLES AND IRREDUNDANT EXPRESSIONS

Having obtained the set of prime implicants of a function, the next step is to determine the minimal sums. Since minimal sums consist of prime implicants, it now becomes a matter of determining which prime implicants should be used. To do this, a subset of the prime implicants is selected, subject to some cost criterion, such that each minterm of the function subsumes at least one prime implicant in the selected subset. This is analogous to the selection of a set of subcubes on a Karnaugh map such that each 1-cell is included in at least one subcube.

A convenient way to show the relationship between the minterms and prime implicants of a function is the *prime-implicant table.* The minterms are placed along the abscissa of the table and the prime implicants are placed along the ordinate. At the intersection of a row and column, an × is entered if the minterm of that column subsumes the prime implicant of that row. For an incompletely specified Boolean function, only those minterms which describe rows of the truth table where the function equals 1 are placed along the abscissa. That is, the minterms describing the don't-care conditions are not included along the abscissa. Ignoring the don't-care terms is valid since the minimal-cost selection of prime implicants does not require that don't-care terms subsume at least one prime implicant.

The prime implicant table for the example of Table 4.4 is given in Table 4.6; while that for the example of Table 4.5 is given in Table 4.7. In Tables 4.6 and 4.7 the single letter designating the prime implicant is also shown. For example, prime implicant xz in Table 4.6 is also referred to as prime implicant A. The decimal numbers appearing next to the prime implicants of Tables 4.4 and 4.5 are the minterms that subsume that prime implicant, since these were the minterms that combined to form the prime implicant. These numbers simplify the process of determining the entries in the prime-implicant table. For any particular prime implicant, these numbers indicate which columns of the prime-implicant table should contain an ×. For example, prime implicant A in Table 4.4 is the result of combining minterms 5, 7, 13, and 15. Thus, ×'s appear in precisely these columns of the first row of the prime-implicant table given in Table 4.6. In Table 4.7 it should be noted that those conditions associated with don't-cares do not appear along the abscissa. Corre-

Table 4.6 Prime-implicant table for the example of Table 4.4

		m_0	m_5	m_6	m_7	m_9	m_{10}	m_{13}	m_{14}	m_{15}
A:	xz		×		×			×		×
B:	xy			×	×				×	×
C:	$w\bar{y}z$					×		×		
D:	$wy\bar{z}$						×		×	
E:	$\bar{w}\bar{x}\bar{y}\bar{z}$	×								

Table 4.7 Prime-implicant table for the example of Table 4.5

		m_4	m_5	m_9	m_{11}	m_{12}	m_{14}	m_{15}	m_{27}	m_{30}
A:	$\bar{x}\bar{y}z$			×						
B:	$w\bar{x}z$			×	×				×	
C:	wyz				×			×	×	
D:	wxy						×	×		×
E:	vwy								×	×
F:	$\bar{v}\bar{w}\bar{y}z$		×							
G:	$\bar{v}\bar{w}x\bar{y}$	×	×							
H:	$\bar{v}x\bar{y}\bar{z}$	×				×				
I:	$\bar{v}wx\bar{z}$					×	×			

spondingly, even though prime implicant A in Table 4.5 results from combining minterms 1, 9, 17, and 25, an × only appears in the m_9 column of Table 4.7.

In Sec. 4.2 an irredundant disjunctive normal formula was defined as a sum of prime implicants such that no prime implicant from the sum can be removed without changing the function being described. In addition, it was shown that minimal sums are irredundant disjunctive normal formulas. In terms of the prime-implicant table, any set of rows such that each column of the table has an × in at least one row of the set and subject to the constraint that the removal of any row from the set results in at least one column no longer having an × in at least one row of the reduced set defines an irredundant expression. The irredundant expression is formed by summing those prime implicants that are in the set that satisfy the above requirement.

4.9.1 Petrick's Method of Determining Irredundant Expressions

At this time a general method is given that was suggested by Petrick to determine all the irredundant disjunctive normal formulas of a function. In this way, the minimal sums of the function are also determined since they are irredundant. In the next section it is shown that certain manipulations on the prime-implicant table can be performed to simplify the process of obtaining the irredundant expressions and minimal sums.

From the way the prime-implicant table is constructed, each × entry signifies that the minterm of its column subsumes the prime implicant of its row. Alternatively, it can be stated that an × entry signifies that the prime implicant of its row *covers* the minterm of its column. The entire prime-implicant table is said to be covered by a subset of the prime implicants if and only if each minterm of the table is covered at least once by the prime implicants of the subset. The problem of determining a subset of the prime implicants that covers the table is commonly referred to as the *covering problem.* An *irredundant cover* is a cover from which no prime implicant corresponding to a row can be deleted and still remain a cover. Each irredundant cover corresponds to an irredundant disjunctive normal formula of the function. A *minimal cover* of a prime-implicant table is an irredundant cover that corresponds to a minimal sum of the function.

For simplicity in future discussions, no distinction is made between a row of a prime-implicant table and the prime implicant associated with that row. Similarly, a column of a prime-implicant table is considered synonymous with the minterm associated with the column. Thus, occasionally a row is said to cover a column instead of the prime implicant corresponding to a row covers the minterm corresponding to a column.

Consider now the conditions under which Table 4.7 is covered. The first column of the table indicates that either prime implicants G or H must be selected to cover minterm 4. Similarly, prime implicants F or G must be selected to cover minterm 5. In a like manner, by noting the $\times$ entries in each column, it is a simple matter to determine which prime implicants must be selected to cover a given minterm. Furthermore, to determine a cover of the prime-implicant table, all of the covering conditions for its minterms must be satisfied.

If a variable is now associated with each row of the prime-implicant table such that the variable has the value of 1 if the corresponding prime implicant is selected and the value 0 if it is not selected, then an algebraic expression can be written, called a *p-expression,* that describes the conditions for covering a prime-implicant table. Let that variable be the single-letter designator of the prime implicant. Then, the p-expression is a product of sum terms in which each sum term corresponds to one column of the table and consists of the sum of the prime implicant designators in which the column has $\times$'s. Thus, for Table 4.7 we can write

$$p = (G + H)(F + G)(A + B)(B + C)(H + I)(D + I)(C + D) \cdot (B + C + E)(D + E) \tag{4.2}$$

The p-expression equals 1 only when a sufficient subset of the prime implicants is selected, by assigning the value 1 to a subset of the variables in the p-expression, to cover the prime-implicant table. When the p-expression has the value of 0, indicating the prime-implicant table is not covered, at least one sum term must be 0, which in turn implies that the corresponding column is not covered.

To illustrate the interpretation of a p-expression, let $B = D = G = H = 1$ and $A = C = E = F = I = 0$ in Eq. (4.2). In this case, it is seen that each sum term equals 1 and hence $p = 1$. This means that if rows B, D, G, and H of the prime-implicant table are selected, then each column has a least one $\times$. Furthermore, selecting only three of these four rows in the table results in some column not having an $\times$. This is easily verified using Eq. (4.2) by noting that if only three of the four variables B, D, G, and H are assigned the value 1 and all the other variables are assigned the value 0, then the p-expression has the value 0. Thus, prime implicants B, D, G, and H form an irredundant cover of Table 4.7, and the sum of these prime implicants corresponds to an irredundant disjunctive normal formula describing the Boolean function having the minterms listed along the abscissa of the prime-implicant table.

To determine all the irredundant disjunctive normal formulas of a Boolean function, it is necessary to determine all the irredundant covers of its prime-implicant table. This can be achieved by using the p-expression. The p-expression is in itself a

Boolean expression, and hence can be manipulated according to the rules of a Boolean algebra. If a p-expression is manipulated into its sum-of-products form using the distributive law, duplicate literals deleted in each resulting product term, and subsuming product terms deleted, then each remaining product term of the resulting expression represents an irredundant cover of the prime-implicant table. When any product term in the sum-of-products form of the p-expression has the value of 1, p also has the value of 1. Thus, by selecting those prime implicants represented by the variables in a single product term of the sum-of-products form of the p-expression, a cover of the prime-implicant table is obtained. Furthermore, since all subsuming product terms have been deleted, the resulting product terms must each describe an irredundant cover. Correspondingly, each product term in the sum-of-products form of the p-expression suggests an irredundant disjunctive normal formula. The formula is obtained by summing the prime implicants indicated by the variables in a product term.

Consider again the p-expression for Table 4.7, i.e., Eq. (4.2), then*

$$
\begin{aligned}
p &= (G+H)(F+G)(A+B)(B+C)(H+I)(D+I)(C+D)(\cancel{B+C+E})(D+E) \\
&= (G+H)(F+G)(A+B)(B+C)(H+I)(D+I)(C+D)(D+E) \\
&= (G+FH)(B+AC)(I+DH)(D+CE) \\
&= (BG+ACG+BFH+ACFH)(DI+CEI+DH+\cancel{CDEH}) \\
&= (BG+ACG+BFH+ACFH)(DI+CEI+DH) \\
&= BDGI+BCEGI+BDGH+ACDGI+ACEGI+ACDGH+\cancel{BDFHI} \\
&\quad +BCEFHI+BDFH+\cancel{ACDFHI}+ACEFHI+ACDFH \\
&= BDGI+BCEGI+BDGH+ACDGI+ACEGI+ACDGH+BCEFHI \\
&\quad +BDFH+ACEFHI+ACDFH
\end{aligned}
$$

This last expression, which was obtained from the expression above it by dropping the subsuming terms indicated by slashes, implies that there are 10 irredundant disjunctive normal formulas for the Boolean function. The first term suggests that one irredundant expression is the sum of prime implicants B, D, G, and I. Referring to Table 4.5 or Table 4.7, this expression is

$$f_1(v,w,x,y,z) = B + D + G + I = w\bar{x}z + wxy + \bar{v}\bar{w}x\bar{y} + \bar{v}wx\bar{z}$$

The second term of the p-expression describes the irredundant expression

$$
\begin{aligned}
f_2(v,w,x,y,z) &= B + C + E + G + I \\
&= w\bar{x}z + wyz + vwy + \bar{v}\bar{w}x\bar{y} + \bar{v}wx\bar{z}
\end{aligned}
$$

Notice that $f_2(v,w,x,y,z)$ is irredundant even though it has more terms than $f_1(v,w,x,y,z)$, since if any term from $f_2(v,w,x,y,z)$ is deleted, then it no longer describes the function of Table 4.5. Thus, not all irredundant disjunctive normal

*Slashed terms are deleted as a consequence of the absorption property of a Boolean algebra, i.e., Theorem 3.6.

expressions are minimal sums. If each of the 10 irredundant expressions is now evaluated by the cost criterion proposed in Sec. 4.1 involving the total number of gate inputs, then the minimal sums are obtained since a minimal expression is irredundant. For this particular example, there are three minimal sums. These correspond to the first, third, and eighth terms in the sum-of-products form of the *p*-expression. The minimal sums are

$$f_1(v,w,x,y,z) = w\bar{x}z + wxy + \bar{v}\bar{w}x\bar{y} + \bar{v}wx\bar{z}$$

$$f_3(v,w,x,y,z) = w\bar{x}z + wxy + \bar{v}\bar{w}x\bar{y} + \bar{v}x\bar{y}\bar{z}$$

$$f_8(v,w,x,y,z) = w\bar{x}z + wxy + \bar{v}\bar{w}\bar{y}z + \bar{v}x\bar{y}\bar{z}$$

4.9.2 Prime-Implicate Tables and Irredundant Conjunctive Normal Formulas

When dealing with prime implicates for the purpose of determining irredundant conjunctive normal formulas and minimal products, a *prime-implicate table* is formed in a completely analogous manner as a prime-implicant table. In such a case, the prime implicates are placed along the ordinate and the maxterms associated with functional values of 0 along the abscissa. Again a *p*-expression is written. Since a *p*-expression indicates how a table is covered, it can be used to determine the irredundant covers of a prime-implicate table. Thus, each product term in the sum-of-products form of the *p*-expression obtained by using the distributive law (in which subsuming terms are dropped) corresponds to an irredundant cover that, in turn, suggests an irredundant conjunctive normal formula. The formula is obtained by forming the product of the prime implicates indicated by the variables in a product term of the sum-of-products form of the *p*-expression. From the set of irredundant conjunctive normal formulas, the minimal products are determined by applying an appropriate cost criterion.

As an alternative for determining irredundant conjunctive normal formulas and minimal products, the prime implicants of the complement of a given Boolean function are obtained as indicated at the end of the previous section. In this case, the prime-implicant table is formed and the *p*-expression written. The *p*-expression is then manipulated into its sum-of-products form using the distributive law and subsuming terms are dropped. From the product terms in the resulting *p*-expression the irredundant disjunctive normal formulas for the complement of the original Boolean function are determined. If DeMorgan's law is applied to each of these expressions, then the irredundant conjunctive normal formulas for the originally given Boolean function are obtained. Upon applying a cost criterion to each irredundant expression, the minimal products are established.

4.10 PRIME-IMPLICANT/PRIME-IMPLICATE TABLE REDUCTIONS

As was seen in the previous section, once a prime-implicant table for a Boolean function is obtained, the irredundant disjunctive normal formulas and, in particular, the minimal sums are readily determined. However, the amount of work necessary to do this is dependent upon the size of the prime-implicant table. It is frequently possible to reduce the number of columns and rows of a prime-implicant table, thus allowing irredundant disjunctive normal formulas and minimal sums to be more quickly obtained.

4.10.1 Essential Prime Implicants

In Sec. 4.5 it was established that every essential prime implicant of a function must appear in all its minimal sums. In actuality, from the definition of essential prime implicants, they must also appear in all the irredundant disjunctive normal formulas of the function. Essential prime implicants are easily detectable in the prime-implicant table.

An essential prime implicant was defined, relative to the Karnaugh map of a function, as a product term corresponding to a prime-implicant subcube that contains a 1-cell that cannot be a member of any other prime-implicant subcube. Realizing that a 1-cell on a Karnaugh map corresponds to a minterm of a function, an essential prime implicant can then be redefined as a prime implicant that is subsumed by a minterm of the function that subsumes no other prime implicant of the function. From the construction of the prime-implicant table, if a column has only a single $\times$, then the minterm associated with that column subsumes only the prime implicant of the row in which the $\times$ appears. Thus, by definition, the prime implicant is essential. The row in which the $\times$ appears is called an *essential row*. All essential rows must be selected when forming an irredundant cover of a prime-implicant table.

Once it is known that a given prime implicant must be selected for a cover, it is possible to reduce the size of the prime-implicant table in order to establish which additional prime implicants should be selected in order to obtain an irredundant or minimal cover of the table. To determine the additional prime implicants, a reduced table is formed in which (1) all columns corresponding to the minterms that subsume the selected prime implicant are deleted and (2) the row corresponding to the selected prime implicant is deleted. All the irredundant covers of this reduced prime-implicant table, along with the selected prime implicant, are the irredundant covers of the original table. The validity of this procedure follows from the fact that in order to obtain a cover of a prime-implicant table, each minterm corresponding to a column of the table must subsume at least one prime implicant in the selected set of rows that forms the cover. However, once the minterm of a column is covered, it is not necessary to cover it again. Thus, the reduced table indicates only those minterms that remain to be covered.

To illustrate the usefulness of the above results, again consider Table 4.6. In this table, five columns have single $\times$'s, and the rows of these $\times$'s correspond to the essential prime implicants of the function. Upon the selection of these prime implicants, all the columns of the table are covered. Thus, the sum of just the essential prime implicants represents the only irredundant expression for this example. Consequently, this expression is also a minimal sum. In general, whenever the set of essential rows forms a cover of a prime-implicant table, there is only one minimal sum for the function. This minimal sum is given by the sum of the prime implicants associated with the essential rows. Although in this particular example all the prime implicants are essential, in general, this is not the case, even when the minimal sum is unique.*

4.10.2 Column and Row Reductions

Besides the table reduction due to essential prime implicants, additional reductions of a prime-implicant table are frequently possible. However, before considering these reductions, it is necessary to review the two criteria of minimality introduced in Sec. 4.1. The first criterion defined a minimal sum as a disjunctive normal formula having the minimal number of terms with more than one literal. Since only terms having more than one literal can contribute to the cost of an expression, for the purpose of cost evaluation, a cost of 1 is assigned to each prime implicant having more than one literal and a cost of 0 to each prime implicant having exactly one literal.

In the second criterion of minimality, the cost of an expression is related to the total number of gate inputs in a two-level realization. In this case, for terms having more than one literal, the cost associated with each prime implicant is one greater than the number of literals in the term since the number of literals corresponds to the number of input terminals of the first-level and-gate and the additional one corresponds to the input terminal of the second-level or-gate. If the term has only a single literal, then the cost is simply one that corresponds to the direct input to the second-level or-gate. Once a cost criterion is established, the appropriate cost for a prime implicant can be appended to each row of a prime-implicant table. This is illustrated in Table 4.8, where a cost column is added to the prime-implicant table for the function $f(v,w,x,y,z) = \Sigma m(1,9,10,11) + dc(0,3,14,25,27)$ under the assumption of the second criterion of minimality.

Two columns of a prime-implicant table having their ×'s in exactly the same rows are said to be *equal.* Furthermore, a column c_i of a prime-implicant table is said to *dominate* column c_j of the same table if column c_i has ×'s in all the rows in which column c_j has ×'s and if, in addition, column c_i has at least one × in a row in which column c_j does not have an ×. For the prime-implicant table shown in Table 4.8, the column for minterm m_{11} dominates the column for minterm m_9.

In a prime-implicant table, a column c_i can be removed without affecting the irredundant covers being sought if (1) there is another column c_j in the same table that is equal to column c_i or (2) there is another column c_k in the same table that is dominated by column c_i. The reason a dominating column can be removed from the prime-implicant table follows from the fact that any set of rows that covers the dominated column must also cover the dominating column. Hence, it is only necessary to ensure the covering of the dominated column. Similarly, when two columns are equal, the cover of one column is sufficient to guarantee the cover of the other column. Therefore, only one of the two columns is needed in the prime-implicant

*Example 4.2 in Sec. 4.5 illustrates a function having a unique minimal sum in which not all its prime implicants are essential.

Table 4.8 Prime-implicant table for the function $f(v,w,x,y,z) = \Sigma m(1,9,10,11) + dc(0,3,14,25,27)$

	m_1	m_9	m_{10}	m_{11}	Cost
A: $\bar{v}\bar{x}z$	×	×		×	4
B: $w\bar{x}z$		×		×	4
C: $\bar{v}\bar{w}\bar{x}\bar{y}$	×				5
D: $\bar{v}w\bar{x}y$			×	×	5
E: $\bar{v}wy\bar{z}$			×		5

table. Applying this result, the reduced prime-implicant table of Table 4.9 can be used to determine the irredundant covers of Table 4.8.

The concepts of dominance and equality can also be applied to rows of a prime-implicant table. Two rows of a prime-implicant table are said to be *equal* if they have ×'s in exactly the same columns. A row r_i of a prime-implicant table is said to *dominate* another row r_j of the same table if row r_i has ×'s in all the columns in which row r_j has ×'s and if, in addition, row r_i has at least one × in a column in which row r_j does not have an ×. Referring again to Table 4.8, it is seen that row A dominates both rows B and C, while row D dominates row E.

The row dominance and equality concepts can also be used for prime-implicant table reductions. Assume that there is some irredundant cover of a prime-implicant table and that this cover contains a row r_j that is dominated by or that is equal to a row r_i. Those columns covered by row r_j are also covered by row r_i, by definition of a dominating or equal row. Hence, an irredundant cover still results if row r_i is used instead of r_j. Furthermore, if the cost of row r_i is not greater than the cost of row r_j, then the expression obtained by summing the prime implicants associated with the cover having row r_i does not have a higher cost than the disjunctive normal formula obtained if the prime implicant associated with r_j is used instead. Since a minimal cover is an irredundant cover, a row r_j of a prime-implicant table can be removed and at least one minimal cover of the original table, from which a minimal sum is written, is obtainable from the reduced table if (1) there is another row r_i of the same table that is equal to row r_j and does not have a higher cost than r_j or (2) there is another row r_k of the same table which dominates row r_j and that does not have a higher cost than row r_j.

Table 4.9 Table 4.8 after deleting the dominating column

	m_1	m_9	m_{10}	Cost
A	×	×		4
B		×		4
C	×			5
D			×	5
E			×	5

It is important to note that the removal of an equal or dominated row is only applicable if it is not necessary to obtain all irredundant disjunctive normal formulas or all minimal sums of a function. This is usually not a serious restriction, since in most cases only one minimal sum is needed. In addition, the column and row reduction procedures can be applied any number of times to a prime-implicant table and in any order.

To illustrate the application of the above column and row reduction concepts to obtain minimal sums, again consider Table 4.7. The table is redrawn in Table 4.10*a* with a cost column according to the second criterion for minimality. In particular, since each prime implicant has more than a single literal, the cost assigned to each row is the number of literals in its prime implicant plus one. Next, it is noted that the column for m_{27} dominates the column for m_{11}. Since dominating columns can be removed, Table 4.10*b* results. In the reduced table, row *B* dominates row *A,* row *D* dominates row *E,* and row *G* dominates row *F.* Since in each case the dominated row has a cost equal to its dominating row, the dominated rows are deleted. This results in Table 4.10*c*. Even though column and row reductions have been used, a minimal sum can still be obtained by finding a minimal cover of Table 4.10*c*. It is now noted that three columns of Table 4.10*c* have a single ×. These ×'s are circled. The rows in which the ×'s appear must be selected for the minimal cover to guarantee that the corresponding columns are covered. Rows *B, D,* and *G* have double asterisks placed next to them to indicate that they are selected. The selection of rows *B, D,* and *G* results in minterms m_4, m_5, m_9, m_{11}, m_{14}, m_{15}, and m_{30} being covered. Hence, these rows and columns are deleted from the table for the purpose of determining which additional rows must be selected to obtain a minimal cover. The resulting table is shown in Table 4.10*d*. Notice that row *C* does not appear in the table since it does not cover any of the remaining minterms. Upon selection of either row *H* or row *I,* a minimal cover is obtained. Therefore, one minimal cover consists of rows *B, D, G,* and *H,* and another minimal cover consists of rows *B, D, G,* and *I.* These two covers were also obtained in the previous section when Petrick's method was applied to Table 4.7. However, as was mentioned previously, not all minimal covers are necessarily obtained when row reduction is applied, but at least one minimal cover is guaranteed. For this example, Petrick's method did yield a third minimal cover. Finally, once a minimal cover is established, the minimal sum expression can be written.

In general, it is not possible to obtain a minimal cover solely by applying the table reduction procedures. A prime-implicant table in which each column contains at least two ×'s and in which no column or row can be deleted as a result of dominance or equality is said to be a *cyclic table.* When this condition occurs, one can revert to Petrick's method for completing the determination of a minimal cover of the table. In this way, columns and rows are deleted until a cyclic table results. Once the reduced prime-implicant table becomes cyclic, Petrick's method is applied. The rows selected by Petrick's method plus any rows selected previously during the prime-implicant table reduction procedures form a minimal cover of the original table.

Table 4.10 Prime-implicant table reduction applied to Table 4.7. (*a*) Table 4.7 with a cost column. (*b*) After deleting dominating column. (*c*) After deleting dominated rows. (*d*) After selecting rows *B*, *D*, and *G*

	m_4	m_5	m_9	m_{11}	m_{12}	m_{14}	m_{15}	m_{27}	m_{30}	Cost
A			×							4
B			×	×				×		4
C				×			×	×		4
D						×	×		×	4
E								×	×	4
F		×								5
G	×	×								5
H	×				×					5
I					×	×				5

(*a*)

	m_4	m_5	m_9	m_{11}	m_{12}	m_{14}	m_{15}	m_{30}	Cost
A			×						4
B			×	×					4
C				×			×		4
D						×	×	×	4
E								×	4
F		×							5
G	×	×							5
H	×				×				5
I					×	×			5

(*b*)

	m_4	m_5	m_9	m_{11}	m_{12}	m_{14}	m_{15}	m_{30}	Cost
***B*			⊗	×					4
C				×			×		4
***D*						×	×	⊗	4
***G*	×	⊗							5
H	×				×				5
I					×	×			5

(*c*)

	m_{12}	Cost
H	×	5
I	×	5

(*d*)

4.10.3 A Prime-Implicant Selection Procedure

When a single minimal sum is to be obtained, the following procedure can be applied to a prime-implicant table:

1. Find all the essential prime implicants by checking the table for columns with a single ×. Place an asterisk next to each essential prime implicant. Rule a line through the essential rows and all columns which have an × in an essential row. If all columns are ruled out, then the minimal sum is the sum of the essential prime implicants.
2. Rule a line though all dominating columns and dominated rows, keeping in mind the cost restriction for deleting rows, until no further reductions are possible.
3. Check to see if any unruled column has a single ×. If there are no such columns, then the table is cyclic. If there are some columns with a single ×, then place a double asterisk next to the rows in which these ×'s appear. These are called *secondary essential rows.* Rule a line through each secondary essential row and each column in which an × appears in a secondary essential row.
4. If all columns are ruled out, then the minimal sum is given by the sum of all the prime implicants which are associated with rows that have asterisks next to them. If all columns are not ruled out, then repeat Steps 2 and 3 until either there are no columns to be ruled or a cyclic table results.
5. If a cyclic table results, then Petrick's method is applied to the cyclic table, and a minimal cover is obtained for it. The sum of all prime implicants that are marked with asterisks plus the prime implicants for the minimal cover of the cyclic table as determined by Petrick's method is a minimal sum.

Although the discussion in this section involved prime-implicant tables, the procedures introduced can equally well be applied to prime-implicate tables for obtaining minimal products.

4.11 DECIMAL METHOD FOR OBTAINING PRIME IMPLICANTS

In Sec. 4.8 the prime implicants of a function were obtained by comparing the 0-1-dash representations of the minterms and generated product terms. This process can also be carried out using the decimal representations of the minterms. So that the reader can compare the decimal procedure with that of Sec. 4.8, the process is applied to the function $f(w,x,y,z) = \Sigma m(0,5,6,7,9,10,13,14,15)$, which was previously studied in Table 4.4. The generation of the prime implicants using the decimal method is given in Table 4.11.

In the first column of Table 4.11, the decimal numbers are arranged in groups such that their associated minterms have equal index within each group, and the groups are ordered by increasing index. This part of the decimal procedure is identical to that of Sec. 4.8.

Table 4.11 Obtaining prime implicants using decimal numbers

0 *E*	5,7 (2) √	5,7,13,15 (2,8) *A*
——	5,13 (8) √	6,7,14,15 (1,8) *B*
	6,7 (1) √	
——	6,14 (8) √	
5 √	9,13 (4) *C*	
6 √	10,14 (4) *D*	
9 √	——	
10 √	7,15 (8) √	
——	13,15(2) √	
7 √	14,15 (1) √	
13 √		
14 √		
——		
15 √		

The next step is to compare the minterms in adjacent groups. In general, two minterms represented by decimal numbers can combine to form a single product term if and only if their decimal difference is a power of 2 and the smaller decimal number represents the minterm with index i and the larger decimal number represents a minterm with index $i + 1$ where $i = 0,1,2, \ldots$. Thus, two minterms m_a and m_b of index i and $i + 1$, respectively, can combine if $b - a$ is positive and a power of 2. The combined term is written as $a,b(c)$, where c is the power-of-2 difference.

Again referring to Table 4.11, since the second group of minterms, i.e., those having index 1, is an empty set, no comparisons are possible between the first and second groups and the second and third groups. However, applying the above rule to the third and fourth groups of the first column generates the first group in the second column. For example, minterms 5 and 7 combine, since $7 - 5 = 2$, to form the second-column entry 5,7(2). On the other hand, minterms 6 and 13 cannot combine since the difference $13 - 6 = 7$ is not a power of 2; whereas minterms m_9 and m_7 cannot combine since the difference $7 - 9$ is negative. Similarly, the fourth and fifth groups of the first column yield the second group in the second column. As in Sec. 4.8, terms that combine are checked. It should be noted that the power of 2 appearing in parentheses is the weight of the variable, under a binary representation, which is eliminated.

To continue the comparison process, special attention must be given to the numbers in parentheses since the combining of terms is only possible when they have the same variables. Let $a_1,a_2,\cdots,a_{2^k}(c_1,c_2,\cdots,c_k)$ denote a term, referred to as term a, which is the result of combining minterms $m_{a_1}, m_{a_2}, \ldots, m_{a_{2^k}}$. That is, $a_1, a_2, \cdots, a_{2^k}$ are the decimal numbers of the minterms that combined, and $c_1, c_2, \cdots, c_k$ are the power-of-2 differences that represent the variables eliminated. Furthermore, let the decimal numbers $a_1, a_2, \cdots, a_{2^k}$ be in increasing numerical order; similarly for the decimal numbers $c_1, c_2, \cdots, c_k$. In an analogous manner, let

$b_1,b_2,\cdots,b_{2^k}(d_1,d_2,\cdots,d_k)$ denote another term, referred to as term *b*. Term *a* and term *b* can combine to form a single term if and only if the numbers in parentheses for the two terms are the same (i.e., $c_1 = d_1$, $c_2 = d_2, \ldots, c_k = d_k$), the difference $b_1 - a_1$ is positive and a power of 2, and term *a* has index *i* while term *b* has index $i + 1$. It should be noted that only the leading (i.e., smallest) decimal designators of terms *a* and *b* are subtracted. The newly combined term consists of all the minterm decimal designators of terms *a* and *b*. The numbers in parentheses for the new term are the same as terms *a* and *b* along with the new difference $b_1 - a_1$. Again, the terms which enter into combination, i.e., term *a* and term *b*, are checked.

Returning to Table 4.11, the third column is obtained from the second column. Term 5,7(2) combines with term 13,15(2) in its adjacent group to form the term 5,7,13,15(2,8) since the two terms have the same numbers in parentheses and the difference between each term's smallest designator (i.e., $13 - 5 = 8$) is a power of 2. Terms 5,7(2) and 13,15(2) are both checked. The difference $13 - 5 = 8$ is included in the parentheses of the combined term since this number indicates which new variable is eliminated as a result of the combination. Next it is noted that term 5,13(8) combines with term 7,15(8). The result of this combination is the term 5,7,13,15(2,8), which was obtained previously and hence is not written a second time. However, any time two terms combine, they must be checked to indicate that they are not prime implicants. As a result, terms 5,13(8) and 7,15(8) in the second column are checked. After all comparisons between the two groups of the second column in Table 4.11 are completed, the resulting third column consists of only a single group having two terms. With only a single group in the third column, no comparisons are possible, and the prime-implicant generation process is completed. The five unchecked terms are the prime implicants.

In order to write the prime implicants in algebraic form, it is necessary to transform the decimal representation of a term into its 0-1-dash representation. Consider prime implicant *C* in the second column of Table 4.11, i.e., term 9,13(4). The steps for the transformation are shown in Table 4.12*a*. First, the variables of the function are listed along with the weights of these variables when a binary representation is used. In the decimal representation of a term, the numbers in parentheses indicate the weights of the eliminated variables. Thus, since the weight of the eliminated variable in the term 9,13(4) is $2^2 = 4$, a dash is placed under the *x* variable in Table 4.12*a*. Next, the 1's of the 0-1-dash representation are determined. The weights which sum to the smallest minterm number in the term determine the positions where 1's appear in the 0-1-dash representation. Since 9 is the smallest minterm number in the term 9,13(4), 1's are entered in the columns of weights $2^0 = 1$ and $2^3 = 8$ in Table 4.12*a*. Finally, all the remaining positions that do not have dashes or 1's must have 0's in the 0-1-dash representation. Thus, the 0-1-dash representation of term 9,13(4) is 1–01, which corresponds to the algebraic form $w\bar{y}z$.

As a second example, consider prime implicant *A*, i.e., term 5,7,13,15(2,8). Table 4.12*b* shows the steps leading to its 0-1-dash representation. In this particular case, after the positions for the dashes and 1's are determined, no positions are

Table 4.12 Transforming decimal representation of terms into 0-1-dash representation. (*a*) 9,13(4). (*b*) 5,7,13,15(2,8)

w	*x*	*y*	*z*	⟵	variables
2^3	2^2	2^1	2^0	⟵	weights of the binary representation
	–			⟵	dash for position of weight 4
1			1	⟵	1's for the positions that sum to the smallest minterm number (i.e., 9)
		0		⟵	0's for all remaining positions
1	–	0	1	⟵	0-1-dash representation

(*a*)

w	*x*	*y*	*z*	⟵	variables
2^3	2^2	2^1	2^0	⟵	weights of the binary representation
–		–		⟵	dashes for positions of weights 2 and 8
	1		1	⟵	1's for the positions that sum to the smallest minterm number (i.e., 5)
–	1	–	1	⟵	0-1-dash representation

(*b*)

available for 0's. Hence, no 0's appear in the 0-1-dash representation. Since –1–1 is the 0-1-dash representation of the prime implicant, its algebraic form is xz. The reader can easily verify that if all the entries of Table 4.11 are transformed into 0-1-dash representation (including the checked terms), then Table 4.4 results.

The decimal process introduced in this section yields all the prime implicants of a Boolean function. Once the prime implicants are obtained, the prime-implicant table is drawn, and a minimal sum is found by the techniques of Secs. 4.9 and 4.10.

Although the above discussion pertained to a decimal method for obtaining prime implicants, by starting with a set of decimal maxterms the procedure produces the prime implicates of a function.

4.12 THE MULTIPLE-OUTPUT SIMPLIFICATION PROBLEM

Up to this point, the simplification problem has been directed to combinational networks having a single output. However, general combinational networks can have several output terminals as illustrated in Fig. 4.31. In such a case, the output behavior of the network is described by a set of functions, $f_1, f_2, \ldots, f_m$, one for each output terminal, each involving the same input variables, $x_1, x_2, \ldots, x_n$. This set of functions is represented by a truth table with $m + n$ columns. The first n columns denote all the combinations of values of the n input variables, and the last m columns represent the values at the m output terminals for each input combination.

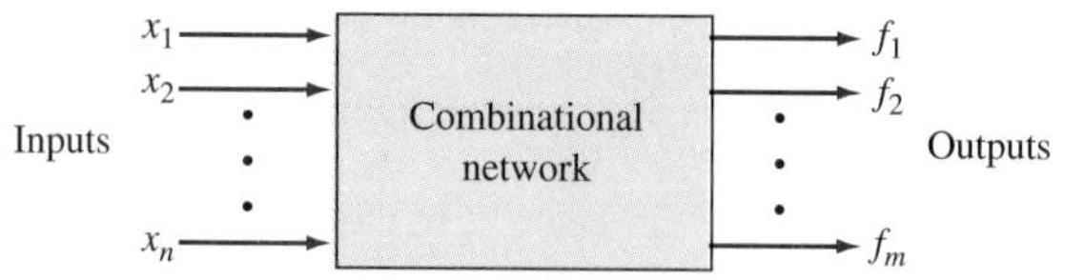

Figure 4.31 A multiple-output combinational network.

With the objective of designing a multiple-output network of minimal cost, one might approach the design by simply constructing a realization based on the minimal expressions for each output function independently of the others. For example, Table 4.13 gives a truth table for a combinational network having two outputs. Using the Karnaugh maps in Fig. 4.32*a,* the minimal sum for each function is

$$f_1(x,y,z) = \bar{x}\bar{y} + yz$$

$$f_2(x,y,z) = yz + xy$$

The corresponding realization is shown in Fig. 4.32*b,* which has a total of 6 gates and 12 gate inputs. However, since the two expressions share a common term, i.e., yz, a more economical realization is shown in Fig. 4.32*c* having only 5 gates and 10 gate inputs.

Unfortunately, the multiple-output simplification problem is normally more difficult than simply sharing common terms in the independently obtained minimal expressions. For example, consider the pair of functions

$$f_1(x,y,z) = \Sigma m(1,3,5)$$

$$f_2(x,y,z) = \Sigma m(3,6,7)$$

Table 4.13 Truth table for a multiple-output combinational network described by the pair of functions $f_1(x,y,z) = \Sigma m(0,1,3,7)$ and $f_2(x,y,z) = \Sigma m(3,6,7)$

x	y	z	f_1	f_2
0	0	0	1	0
0	0	1	1	0
0	1	0	0	0
0	1	1	1	1
1	0	0	0	0
1	0	1	0	0
1	1	0	0	1
1	1	1	1	1

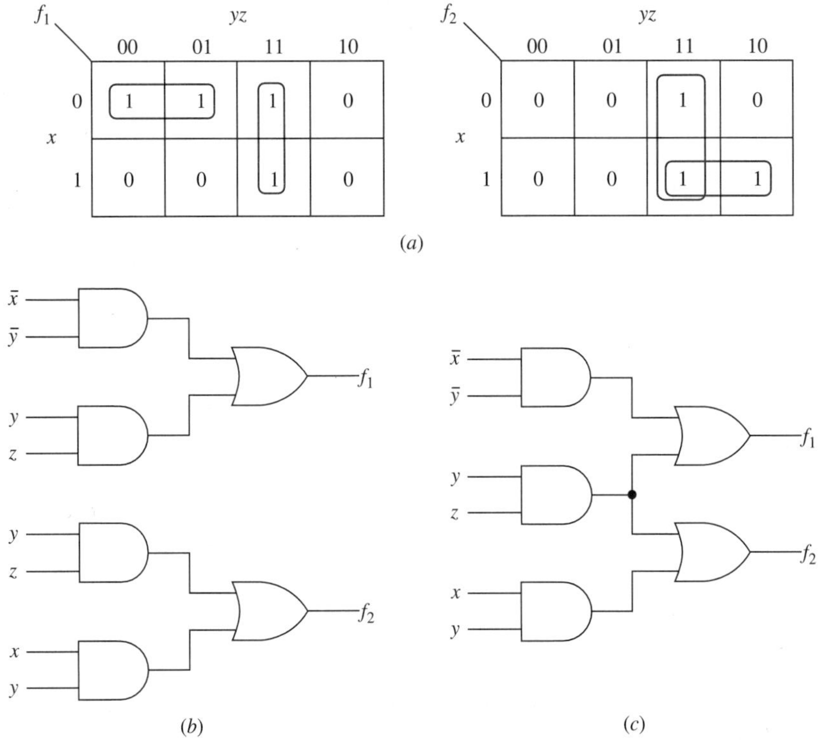

Figure 4.32 Realization of Table 4.13. (*a*) Karnaugh maps for minimal sums. (*b*) Realization of individual minimal sums. (*c*) Realization based on shared term.

Figure 4.33*a* shows the Karnaugh maps for the independently obtained minimal sums that suggest the realization of Fig. 4.33*b*. This realization uses 6 gates with 12 gate inputs. On the other hand, if the 1-cells of the maps are grouped as shown in Fig. 4.33*c* to obtain the expressions

$$f_1(x,y,z) = \bar{y}z + \bar{x}yz$$
$$f_2(x,y,z) = \bar{x}yz + xy$$

then the corresponding realization of Fig. 4.33*d* results, which uses 5 gates and 11 gate inputs. Certainly, this is a lower-cost realization if cost is measured by either the number of gates or the number of gate input terminals. Furthermore, it was achieved without every term in the expressions being prime implicants of the individual functions. In particular, the term $\bar{x}yz$ is a prime implicant of neither f_1 nor f_2. However, since the two functions have a term in common, it should be suspected that a relationship exists between the common term and the product function $f_1 \cdot f_2$, that is, the function obtained when the two functions are and'ed together. In this particular case, the product function has the single prime implicant $\bar{x}yz$.

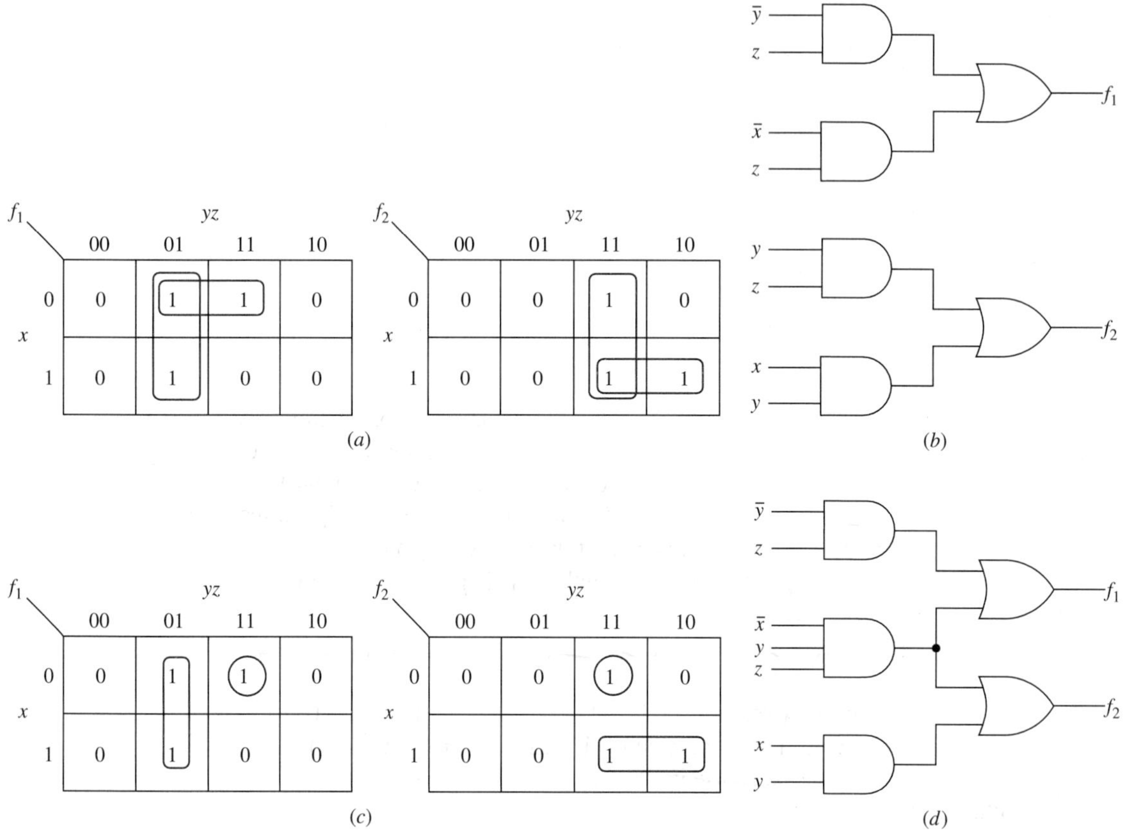

Figure 4.33 Realization of the pair of functions $f_1(x,y,z) = \Sigma m(1,3,5)$ and $f_2(x,y,z) = \Sigma m(3,6,7)$. (*a*) Karnaugh maps for minimal sums of individual functions. (*b*) Realization of independently obtained minimal sums. (*c*) Karnaugh maps for alternate groupings. (*d*) Realization based on alternate map groupings.

From an algebraic standpoint, a *minimal representation* of a multiple-output logic network is defined as a set of normal expressions that has associated with it a minimal cost as given by some cost criterion. As in the case of single-output networks, the cost measure can be based on either the number of gates in the realization* or the number of gate input terminals in the realization. If the minimal representation consists of all disjunctive normal expressions, then the representation is called a *multiple-output minimal sum.* On the other hand, if the minimal representation consists of all conjunctive normal formulas, then the representation is called a *multiple-output minimal product.*

*In the case of multiple-output networks, the number of gates is closely related to the number of *distinct* terms appearing in the set of output expressions.

4.12.1 Multiple-Output Prime Implicants

A prime implicant was defined previously for a single Boolean function as a product term which implies the function and subsumes no shorter product term that also implies the function. However, when dealing with a set of functions in which product terms can be shared, it is necessary to extend this definition. A *multiple-output prime implicant* for a set of Boolean functions $f_1, f_2, \ldots, f_m$, involving the same set of variables, is a product term that is either (1) a prime implicant of one of the individual functions f_i, for $i = 1, 2, \ldots, m$, or (2) a prime implicant of one of the product functions

$$f_i \cdot f_j \cdot \cdots \cdot f_k \qquad i, j, k = 1, 2, \ldots, m$$
$$i \neq j \neq \cdots \neq k$$

Thus, a multiple-output prime implicant is a prime implicant of any of the m single functions $f_1, f_2, \ldots, f_m$, as well as a prime implicant of any of the possible product functions, i.e., a prime implicant of any two of the functions $f_i \cdot f_j$, any three of the functions $f_i \cdot f_j \cdot f_k$, up to and including a prime implicant of all m functions $f_1 \cdot f_2 \cdots f_m$. For the special case of a single function, only the first part of the definition applies.

The significance of multiple-output prime implicants is given by the following generalization to Theorem 4.1.

Theorem 4.5

Let the cost, assigned by some criterion, for a multiple-output minimal sum be such that decreasing the number of literals in the set of disjunctive normal formulas does not increase its cost. Then there is at least one set of formulas for the multiple-output minimal sum that consists only of sums of multiple-output prime implicants such that all the terms in the expression for f_i are prime implicants of f_i or of a product function involving f_i.

Although the above discussion involved multiple-output prime implicants and multiple-output minimal sums, in an analogous manner multiple-output prime implicates are defined for multiple-output minimal products. In the next section, the Quine-McCluskey method is generalized to accommodate the multiple-output simplification problem.

4.13 OBTAINING MULTIPLE-OUTPUT MINIMAL SUMS AND PRODUCTS

To obtain a multiple-output minimal sum with Karnaugh maps is, in general, a difficult process since it is necessary to work with several maps simultaneously. For example, for a set of three functions f_1, f_2, and f_3, it is necessary to consider the prime implicants on seven different maps, i.e., the maps for f_1, f_2, f_3, $f_1 \cdot f_2$, $f_1 \cdot f_3$, $f_2 \cdot f_3$, and $f_1 \cdot f_2 \cdot f_3$, and determine an optimal collection of these prime implicants for the minimal sum. As a variation, one might first obtain all the multiple-output prime implicants from the seven maps and then use the multiple-output prime-implicant table, which is described later in this section, to perform the selection process. The approach that is taken here is to extend the more formal Quine-McCluskey procedure since it is intended for computer-aided logic design.

When considering a set of Boolean functions, it is possible that one or more functions in the set are incomplete. For the purpose of determining the multiple-output prime implicants, all don't-cares are assigned a functional value of 1, as was done with single functions earlier in this chapter. In this way, the incomplete functions are transformed into complete functions. The prime implicants of these newly obtained complete functions are also the prime implicants of the incomplete functions.

4.13.1 Tagged Product Terms

In order to describe product terms that are shared in the expressions for more than one function, the concept of *tagged product terms* is introduced. These terms consist of two parts, a *kernel* and a *tag*. The kernel is a product term involving the variables of the function and corresponds to an implicant. The tag is an appended entity used for "bookkeeping" purposes and denotes which functions are implied by its kernel. For example, given a truth table involving a set of functions, a tagged product term is constructed for each row in which at least one of the functional values in the row is not 0. In this case, the kernel is the minterm corresponding to the row of the table, and the tag denotes which complete functions include this minterm. However, for convenience in applying the comparison process of the Quine-McCluskey method, it is common to use the binary representation of the kernel or its decimal equivalent, as was done for single functions, rather than the algebraic form. Furthermore, to facilitate readability, the tags in this discussion consist of the same number of symbols as there are functions in the set. Thus, for the jth row of the truth table, the ith symbol of the tag is f_i if the minterm for the jth row implies the function f_i (that is, if the functional value in the f_i column is 1 or dash); otherwise, the ith symbol of the tag is a dash.

Table 4.14 gives the truth table for a two-output combinational network. The minterm associated with the fourth row is $\bar{x}yz$, its binary representation is 011, and its decimal equivalent is 3. The tag is written as $-f_2$ to indicate that this minterm im-

Table 4.14 A truth table for a multiple-output combinational network

x	y	z	f_1	f_2
0	0	0	1	0
0	0	1	1	1
0	1	0	1	1
0	1	1	0	1
1	0	0	0	0
1	0	1	1	-
1	1	0	0	0
1	1	1	1	1

Table 4.15 The tagged product terms for Table 4.14. (*a*) Kernels in algebraic form. (*b*) Kernels in binary form. (*c*) Kernels in decimal form

$\bar{x}\bar{y}\bar{z}f_1-$	$000f_1-$	$0f_1-$
$\bar{x}\bar{y}zf_1f_2$	$001f_1f_2$	$1f_1f_2$
$\bar{x}y\bar{z}f_1f_2$	$010f_1f_2$	$2f_1f_2$
$\bar{x}yz{-}f_2$	$011{-}f_2$	$3{-}f_2$
$x\bar{y}zf_1f_2$	$101f_1f_2$	$5f_1f_2$
$xyzf_1f_2$	$111f_1f_2$	$7f_1f_2$
(*a*)	(*b*)	(*c*)

plies the f_2 function but not the f_1 function. The entire tagged product term is therefore written as $\bar{x}yz{-}f_2$, $011{-}f_2$, or $3{-}f_2$. In a similar manner, the sixth row of Table 4.14 is written as $x\bar{y}zf_1f_2$, $101f_1f_2$, or $5f_1f_2$. Even though the functional value of f_2 for the 3-tuple $(x,y,z) = (1,0,1)$ is unspecified, a 1 is assigned to the functional value for the purpose of determining the multiple-output prime implicants. The complete list of tagged product terms for Table 4.14 is shown in Table 4.15 in all three forms. It should be noted that no tagged product terms are written for those rows in which both functional values are 0 since the kernels for these rows imply no functions.

4.13.2 Generating the Multiple-Output Prime Implicants

Through the use of tagged product terms, the Quine-McCluskey method is easily modified for the determination of the tagged multiple-output prime implicants. Formally, a *tagged multiple-output prime implicant* is a tagged product term in which the kernel implies each of the functions indicated by the tag with the provisions there is no other tagged product term simultaneously having a shorter kernel that is subsumed and a tag with at least the same function symbols. To obtain the multiple-output prime implicants, the comparison process of the Quine-McCluskey method is applied to the kernels of the tagged product terms and a simple and-type operation is applied to the tags. To do this, the tagged product terms are first written from the truth table for a given set of Boolean functions. From these terms, additional tagged product terms are generated. Two tagged product terms generate a new tagged product term by the following rules: (1) The kernel of the generated term is the result of the relationship $AB + \bar{A}B = B$ if it can be successfully applied to the kernels of the two generating terms as prescribed by the Quine-McCluskey method and (2) the tag of the generated term has an f_i if and only if f_i appears in *both* the tags of the generating terms; otherwise, the ith position of the tag is a dash. During this process, a generating term is checked, as in the Quine-McCluskey method, if and only if the kernel of the generating term subsumes the kernel of the generated term *and* the tag of the generating term is the *same* as the tag of the generated term. If the tag of a generated term has no f_i symbols, then the term is not added to the list of newly generated terms. The comparison process is then repeated on all the generated tagged product terms until all comparisons have been made and no new tagged product terms are generated, at which time the unchecked terms are the tagged multiple-output prime implicants.

It should be noted in the above procedure that there are only two modifications to the Quine-McCluskey method when dealing with tagged product terms. First, there is a tag which must be considered. When combining terms, the tag of the new term consists of only those f_i's that are common to the two terms being combined. Second, when two terms are combined, the two generating terms are not necessarily checked. A generating term is checked only if its tag is identical to the tag of the generated term.

To illustrate the above procedure, consider the binary representations of the tagged product terms shown in Table 4.15*b*. These terms are grouped according to the index of the kernels. This results in the first column of Table 4.16*a*. Terms whose index differs by one are now compared. For example, consider the terms $000f_1-$ and $001f_1f_2$. By the Quine-McCluskey method, the kernels are combined since they differ in exactly 1 bit position. Furthermore, since f_1 appears in both tags, these two terms generate the term $00\text{–}f_1-$ shown in the second column of Table 4.16*a*. At this time, however, only the term $000f_1-$ is checked since its kernel sub-

Table 4.16 Obtaining the tagged multiple-output prime implicants for the functions of Table 4.14. (*a*) Using 0-1-dash notation. (*b*) Using decimal notation

xyz	*xyz*	*xyz*
000 f_1- √	00– f_1- *B*	––1 $-f_2$ *A*
	0–0 f_1- *C*	
001 f_1f_2 √		
010 f_1f_2 *G*	0–1 $-f_2$ √	
	–01 f_1f_2 *D*	
011 $-f_2$ √	01– $-f_2$ *E*	
101 f_1f_2 √		
	–11 $-f_2$ √	
111 f_1f_2 √	1–1 f_1f_2 *F*	

(*a*)

0 f_1- √	0,1 (1) f_1- *B*	1,3,5,7 (2,4) $-f_2$ *A*
	0,2 (2) f_1- *C*	
1 f_1f_2 √		
2 f_1f_2 *G*	1,3 (2) $-f_2$ √	
	1,5 (4) f_1f_2 *D*	
3 $-f_2$ √	2,3 (1) $-f_2$ *E*	
5 f_1f_2 √		
	3,7 (4) $-f_2$ √	
7 f_1f_2 √	5,7 (2) f_1f_2 *F*	

(*b*)

sumes the kernel of the generated term and its tag is the same as the tag of the generated term. The term $001f_1f_2$ is checked at a later time when it and the term $101f_1f_2$ are used to generate the term $-01f_1f_2$. After all comparisons of terms whose index differs by one in the first column of Table 4.16*a* are completed, the comparison process is applied to the second column to construct the third column. It should be noticed in the second column that the two terms $0{-}0f_1{-}$ and $0{-}1{-}f_2$ do not generate a new term, even though the kernels can be combined by the Quine-McCluskey method, since there is no f_i symbol common to both of these terms. The seven tagged product terms in Table 4.16*a* with a letter after them are the tagged multiple-output prime implicants, and their kernels are simply the multiple-output prime implicants. A tagged multiple-output prime implicant having more than one function symbol in its tag corresponds to a multiple-output prime implicant for the product function indicated by the tag.

The above procedure can also be carried out using the decimal representation of the tagged product terms. In this case, the decimal Quine-McCluskey method, as explained in Sec. 4.11, is applied to the kernels, while the tags are determined as with the 0-1-dash notation. The procedure is illustrated in Table 4.16*b*.

4.13.3 Multiple-Output Prime-Implicant Tables

Having established the multiple-output prime implicants, it is next necessary to select a subset of them for the purpose of obtaining a multiple-output minimal sum. This can be done by extending the concept of the prime-implicant table to handle a set of Boolean functions.

The multiple-output prime-implicant table is a direct extension of the prime-implicant table introduced in Sec. 4.9. However, since the multiple-output prime implicants are associated with the set of Boolean functions $f_1, f_2, \ldots, f_m$, provision is made for each of the Boolean functions in the set. This is done by constructing a table whose abscissa is partitioned into m sections, one section for each function f_i. Within each section, the abscissa is labeled with the minterms associated with the function of that section; that is, those minterms of f_i which have a functional value of 1. Don't-care terms are not included. Along the ordinate of the table, the multiple-output prime implicants are listed. For convenience, the ordinate can also be partitioned in accordance with the tags associated with the multiple-output prime implicants. A $\times$ is placed at the intersection of a row and column in the multiple-output prime-implicant table if the minterm of the column for the function f_i subsumes the multiple-output prime implicant of the row *and* the multiple-output prime implicant implies the function f_i. Thus, those multiple-output prime implicants whose tags consist of a single function symbol provide $\times$'s only for that section of the multiple-output prime-implicant table associated with the function. On the other hand, the multiple-output prime implicants having more than a single function symbol in their tags provide $\times$'s for each of the sections of their associated functions.

For the multiple-output prime implicants obtained in Table 4.16, the multiple-output prime-implicant table shown in Table 4.17 is constructed. This table has two

Table 4.17 Prime-implicant table for the functions of Table 4.14

			f_1					f_2			
			m_0	m_1	m_2	m_5	m_7	m_1	m_2	m_3	m_7
f_1	B:	$\bar{x}\bar{y}$	×	×							
	C:	$\bar{x}\bar{z}$	×		×						
f_2	A:	z						×		×	×
	E:	$\bar{x}y$							×	×	
	D:	$\bar{y}z$		×		×		×			
$f_1 \cdot f_2$	F:	xz				×	×				×
	G:	$\bar{x}y\bar{z}$			×				×		

sections, one for f_1 and the other for f_2. The minterms associated with each function are listed along the abscissa. As in Sec. 4.9, any minterms associated with don't-care conditions are not listed. Also in Table 4.17, the ordinate is partitioned according to whether the multiple-output prime implicant implies f_1, f_2, or $f_1 \cdot f_2$. Those multiple-output prime implicants associated only with f_1 or f_2 have ×'s just in their respective sections of the table; the multiple-output prime implicants associated with $f_1 \cdot f_2$ have ×'s in both sections.

4.13.4. Minimal Sums Using Petrick's Method

Once the multiple-output prime-implicant table is constructed, an extension of Petrick's method can be applied to determine the irredundant covers from which the multiple-output minimal sums are obtained. To do this, again the p-expression is written as a product-of-sum terms in which each sum term corresponds to a single column of the multiple-output prime implicant table. However, since the various prime implicants are associated with different functions, this information must also be included. This is achieved by subscripting the variables that denote the multiple-output prime implicants to indicate which function utilizes it. That is, each variable in a sum term written for a column in the f_i section of the multiple-output prime-implicant table has the subscript i. For example, referring to the first column of Table 4.17, prime implicant B or C must be used to cover minterm m_0 of function f_1. Algebraically this is written as $(B_1 + C_1)$.

Once the p-expression is written, it is then manipulated into its sum-of-products form using the distributive law and the subsuming terms are dropped in the resulting expression. However, it should be realized that a variable with different subscripts must be regarded as corresponding to different prime implicants. For example, if a term in the sum-of-products form of the p-expression has both an R_i and an R_j, then they are considered to be distinct since in one case the multiple-output prime implicant R is related to function f_i and in the other case it is related to function f_j. Finally, by evaluating each product term in the sum-of-products form of the p-expression according to some cost criterion, a multiple-output minimal sum is obtained.

As an illustration of this procedure, again consider Table 4.17. The p-expression for this table is written as

$$p(A_2, B_1, \ldots, G_1, G_2) = (B_1 + C_1)(B_1 + D_1)(C_1 + G_1)(D_1 + F_1) \cdot F_1(A_2 + D_2)(E_2 + G_2)(A_2 + E_2)(A_2 + F_2)$$

Upon manipulating it into its sum-of-products form using the distributive law and dropping subsuming terms, the p-expression becomes

$$\begin{aligned} p(A_2, B_1, \ldots, G_1, G_2) = {} & A_2B_1C_1E_2F_1 + A_2B_1C_1F_1G_2 + B_1C_1D_2E_2F_1F_2 \\ & + A_2B_1E_2F_1G_1 + A_2B_1F_1G_1G_2 + B_1D_2E_2F_1F_2G_1 \\ & + A_2C_1D_1E_2F_1 + A_2C_1D_1F_1G_2 + C_1D_1D_2E_2F_1F_2 \end{aligned} \tag{4.3}$$

Each product term in Eq. (4.3) corresponds to an irredundant cover of the two functions. Depending upon the cost criterion being used, each of these covers is evaluated for minimality. Two cost criteria were introduced in the previous section. In the first criterion, the cost of the realization is associated with the number of distinct terms in the set of disjunctive normal formulas. With respect to Eq. (4.3), this implies the multiple-output minimal sums correspond to the product terms in the p-expression having the fewest number of distinct letters, i.e., without regard to the subscripts. The reason for this is that no additional cost is associated with using a prime implicant (which is denoted by the letter) more than once. For Eq. (4.3), two terms satisfy this criterion, namely, $A_2B_1F_1G_1G_2$ and $C_1D_1D_2E_2F_1F_2$. In each case, the minimal sum consists of four distinct terms. Using the multiple-output prime implicants with the subscript 1 in the expression for f_1 and those with the subscript 2 in the expression for f_2, the term $A_2B_1F_1G_1G_2$ in the p-expression suggests the expressions for the multiple-output minimal sum

$$f_1(x,y,z) = \bar{x}\bar{y} + xz + \bar{x}y\bar{z}$$

$$f_2(x,y,z) = z + \bar{x}y\bar{z}$$

while the term $C_1D_1D_2E_2F_1F_2$ suggests the expressions

$$f_1(x,y,z) = \bar{x}\bar{z} + \bar{y}z + xz$$

$$f_2(x,y,z) = \bar{y}z + \bar{x}y + xz$$

If a multiple-output minimal sum is to be based on the fewest number of gate input terminals as suggested by the second cost criterion introduced in the previous section, then it is necessary to evaluate each of the product terms in Eq. (4.3) using this criterion. The number of gate input terminals is calculated as follows: Let $f_1, f_2, \ldots, f_m$ be the set of normal Boolean expressions describing a multiple-output combinational network and let $t_1, t_2, \ldots, t_p$ be the set of all distinct terms appearing in the m output expressions. Now let α_i equal the number of terms in f_i unless there is only a single term, in which case let α_i equal 0. Also, let β_j equal the number of literals in the term t_j unless the term consists of a single literal, in which case let β_j equal 0. The number of gate input terminals in the realization of the multiple-output combinational network is given by the numerical quantity $\sum_{i=1}^{m}\alpha_i + \sum_{j=1}^{p}\beta_j$. Under the assumption of the second cost criterion, only one multiple-output minimal sum is indicated by Eq. (4.3). This corresponds to the fifth term, $A_2B_1F_1G_1G_2$, which has an associated cost of 12. The set of expressions for this multiple-output minimal sum is

$$f_1(x,y,z) = \bar{x}\,\bar{y} + xz + \bar{x}y\bar{z}$$
$$f_2(x,y,z) = z + \bar{x}y\bar{z}$$

4.13.5 Minimal Sums Using Table Reduction Techniques

The prime-implicant table reduction techniques given in Sec. 4.10 can also be applied to multiple-output prime-implicant tables. To begin with, in the f_i section of the multiple-output prime-implicant table there may be a column with a single $\times$. In such a case, the row in which the $\times$ appears corresponds to an essential multiple-output prime implicant for the function f_i, since only this prime implicant covers the particular minterm associated with the column having the single $\times$. It should be noted that if the multiple-output prime implicant implies more than one function, then it is not necessarily essential for all the functions that it implies, but rather for only those functions in which the prime implicant is an only cover for a minterm of a function. Certainly, an essential multiple-output prime implicant for the function f_i must appear in the expression describing the function. When a multiple-output prime implicant is essential for a function f_i, all columns in the f_i section of the multiple-output prime-implicant table are deleted which have $\times$'s in the row corresponding to the prime implicant. The row itself is deleted only if the prime implicant is essential for each function it implies.

As for single-function prime-implicant tables, a dominated or equal row is deleted when its associated cost is not less than the cost associated with a dominating or equal row. A column associated with a function f_i is removed if it dominates or equals another column associated with the same function f_i. By deleting columns and rows and selecting multiple-output prime implicants that must cover minterms of a function, the size of a multiple-output prime-implicant table is reduced until either it becomes cyclic, that is, cannot be reduced any further, or a multiple-output minimal sum is determined.

To illustrate the prime-implicant table reduction techniques, let us now obtain a multiple-output minimal sum for Table 4.17 under the input terminals count criterion. The table is redrawn in Table 4.18*a*, where a column is added to indicate the cost associated with the multiple-output prime implicants. For example, prime implicant $\bar{x}\,\bar{y}$ consists of two literals and hence requires an and-gate with two input terminals in any realization. If this term is used in a realization for f_1, then the output of the and-gate must go to a terminal of the output or-gate for f_1. Thus, a total of three input terminals is associated with the realization of the term $\bar{x}\,\bar{y}$, and hence a cost of 3 is assigned to this prime implicant. The cost associated with prime implicant z is simply 1. If it appears in a realization for f_2, then no and-gate is necessary to generate the term and only the single terminal on the output or-gate for f_2 must be

Table 4.18 Obtaining a multiple-output minimal sum by prime-implicant table reduction using the minimal input terminals count criterion

		f_1					f_2				
		m_0	m_1	m_2	m_5	m_7	m_1	m_2	m_3	m_7	**Cost**
B:	$\bar{x}\bar{y}$	×	×								3
C:	$\bar{x}\bar{z}$	×		×							3
A:	z						×		×	×	1
E:	$\bar{x}y$							×	×		3
D:	$\bar{y}z$		×		×		×				3,4
F:	xz				×	⊗				×	3,4
G:	$\bar{x}y\bar{z}$			×				×			4,5

(*a*)

			f_1			f_2				
			m_0	m_1	m_2	m_1	m_2	m_3	m_7	**Cost**
	B:	$\bar{x}\bar{y}$	×	×						3
	C:	$\bar{x}\bar{z}$	×		×					3
	A:	z				×		×	×	1
	E:	$\bar{x}y$					×	×		3
	D:	$\bar{y}z$		×		×				3,4
*1	F:	xz							×	1
	G:	$\bar{x}y\bar{z}$			×		×			4,5

$f_1(x,y,z) = xz + \cdots$

$f_2(x,y,z) = \cdots$

(*b*)

			f_1			f_2				
			m_0	m_1	m_2	m_1	m_2	m_3	m_7	**Cost**
	B:	$\bar{x}\bar{y}$	×	×						3
	C:	$\bar{x}\bar{z}$	×		×					3
*2	A:	z				×		×	⊗	1
	E:	$\bar{x}y$					×	×		3
	D:	$\bar{y}z$		×		×				3,4
	G:	$\bar{x}y\bar{z}$			×		×			4,5

$f_1(x,y,z) = xz + \cdots$

$f_2(x,y,z) = z + \cdots$

(*c*)

(Cont.)

Table 4.18 *(Cont.)*

		f_1 m_0	m_1	m_2	f_2 m_2	Cost
B:	$\bar{x}\bar{y}$	×	×			3
C:	$\bar{x}\bar{z}$	×		×		3
E:	$\bar{x}y$				×	3
D:	$\bar{y}z$		×			3
G:	$\bar{x}y\bar{z}$			×	×	4,5

$f_1(x,y,z) = xz + \cdots$
$f_2(x,y,z) = z + \cdots$

(*d*)

		f_1 m_0	m_1	m_2	f_2 m_2	Cost
*1 B:	$\bar{x}\bar{y}$	×	⊗			3
C:	$\bar{x}\bar{z}$	×		×		3
E:	$\bar{x}y$				×	3
G:	$\bar{x}y\bar{z}$			×	×	4,5

$f_1(x,y,z) = xz + \bar{x}\bar{y} + \cdots$
$f_2(x,y,z) = z + \cdots$

(*e*)

		f_1 m_2	f_2 m_2	Cost
C:	$\bar{x}\bar{z}$	×		3
E:	$\bar{x}y$		×	3
G:	$\bar{x}y\bar{z}$	×	×	4,5

$f_1(x,y,z) = xz + \bar{x}\bar{y} + \cdots$
$f_2(x,y,z) = z + \cdots$

(*f*)

counted. Two costs are associated with prime implicant $\bar{y}z$. The first cost corresponds to the situation in which the term is used for f_1 or f_2 but not both; the second cost pertains to the situation in which it is used in the realization for both functions.

It is now noted in Table 4.18*a* that the fifth column has a single ×. Thus, the multiple-output prime implicant xz is essential for the function f_1. The fourth and fifth columns can be then removed since the selected prime implicant xz covers minterms m_5 and m_7 of f_1. However, the m_7 column in the f_2 section of the table cannot be removed since xz is not essential for f_2. At this point, the reduced version of Table 4.18*a* appears as shown in Table 4.18*b*. The symbol *1 next to row F indicates that prime implicant xz is used in the expression for f_1. The partial multiple-output minimal sum thus far established is given beneath the table. Furthermore, the cost for prime implicant xz is changed to 1 to indicate that if the term is also to be used for f_2, then only the additional single input terminal of the output or-gate for f_2 is needed.

Table 4.18*b* is now searched for dominated rows and dominating columns. It is seen that row *A* dominates row *F*. Furthermore, since the cost associated with row *A* is not greater than the cost associated with row *F*, it follows that row *F* can be deleted. Once this is done, Table 4.18*c* results. It is now observed that the multiple-output prime implicant z must appear in the expression for f_2 since this is the only term that covers m_7 of f_2. Again the partial expressions for the multiple-output minimal sum are given beneath the table. Upon selecting prime implicant z, those columns in which ×'s appear in row *A* are deleted. This results in Table 4.18*d*.

The cost associated with each multiple-output prime implicant is recalculated and included in Table 4.18*d*. The only change from Table 4.18*c* is that prime implicant $\bar{y}z$ now can be used only for f_1; hence, its cost is simply 3. At this time row *D* can be deleted since it is dominated by row *B* and since the cost associated with row *B* is not greater than the cost associated with row *D*. However, row *E* cannot be deleted even though it is dominated by row *G* since the cost associated with row *G* is greater than the cost associated with row *E*. The reduced table appears as Table 4.18*e*.

It is now seen that the multiple-output prime implicant $\bar{x}\bar{y}$ is needed in the expression for f_1. This results in the partial expressions given beneath the table. After the columns with ×'s in row *B* are deleted, Table 4.18*f* is obtained. In this table it is not permissible to delete the dominated rows *C* and *E* since their associated costs are lower than the cost associated with their dominating row *G*. Thus, this table is cyclic since no further reductions are possible. Formally, Petrick's method can be applied at this point to determine the remaining covers. However, by observation it is seen that cost is minimized by letting the multiple-output prime implicant $\bar{x}y\bar{z}$ appear in the expressions for both f_1 and f_2, with a cost of 5, rather than having $\bar{x}\bar{z}$ in the expression for f_1 and $\bar{x}y$ in the expression for f_2, with a total cost of 6. This results in the multiple-output minimal sum

$$f_1(x,y,z) = xz + \bar{x}\bar{y} + \bar{x}y\bar{z}$$

$$f_2(x,y,z) = z + \bar{x}y\bar{z}$$

which was obtained previously by Petrick's method.

Although table reduction was illustrated using the input terminals count criterion, the distinct terms criterion could have been used instead, the difference being how the cost column is calculated. In this case, the cost of each prime implicant is initially 1. If a prime implicant is used for additional functions after being selected the first time, then its future cost is 0.

4.13.6 Multiple-Output Minimal Products

The discussion thus far in this section was concerned with determining multiple-output minimal sums for a set of Boolean functions. However, it is possible that a lower-cost two-level multiple-output realization exists based on a multiple-output minimal product.

Multiple-output minimal products can be obtained by determining the multiple-output minimal sums for the complementary functions and applying DeMorgan's law. In this approach, tagged product terms are again written from the truth table. The kernel of a tagged product term is the minterm corresponding to a row, and its tag indicates the functions *not* implied by the minterm; that is, the tag contains an $\bar{f}_i$ if the functional value for f_i is 0 in the row. In this case, don't-care conditions are considered to have 0 functional values. Once the initial list of tagged product terms is formed, the multiple-output prime implicants are obtained by the procedure given earlier in this section. A multiple-output prime-implicant table is then constructed, and Petrick's method or prime-implicant table reduction techniques are applied to the multiple-output prime-implicant table. This results in a multiple-output minimal sum for the complementary functions. If DeMorgan's law is applied to each expression obtained, then the multiple-output minimal product results.

As an alternate approach, tagged sum terms are written from the truth table. The kernel denotes the maxterm corresponding to a row in which at least one function has the value of 0, and the tag contains an f_i for each function in that row having a 0 functional value. Again, don't-care conditions are assumed to have 0 functional values. Once the initial list of tagged sum terms is formed, the comparison process previously explained is carried out to generate the multiple-output prime implicates. Upon constructing a multiple-output prime-implicate table, a multiple-output minimal product is obtained by using either Petrick's method or table reduction techniques.

In closing, it should be emphasized that the Quine-McCluskey method for single functions and sets of functions along with Petrick's method and table reduction techniques are not intended for hand computation. Rather, these are algorithmic procedures that are applicable to computer-aided design. Their inclusion in this chapter has been to present concepts that are computer programmable and provide a solution to the simplification problem.

4.14 VARIABLE-ENTERED KARNAUGH MAPS

In the study of Karnaugh maps, the entries within the cells were limited to 0's, 1's, and don't-cares. An interesting and useful extension of the map concept allows functions of one or more Boolean variables as map entries. Such Karnaugh maps are referred to as *variable-entered maps.* The variables associated with the entries in these maps are called the *map-entered variables.*

The significance of variable-entered maps is that they provide for map compression. Let the *order* of a Karnaugh map be defined as the total number of variables associated with its column and row labels. Up to this point, an n-variable function was associated with a Karnaugh map of order n. However, by letting functions of one variable appear as entries within the map, a map of order $n - 1$ is used to represent an n-variable Boolean function. In general, by permitting entries corresponding to m-variable functions, a map representation of an n-variable function is possible with a Karnaugh map of order $n - m$ where $m < n$.

A useful application for variable-entered maps arises in problems that have infrequently appearing variables. In such a situation, it is convenient to have the functions of the infrequently appearing variables be the entries within a map, allowing a high-order Boolean function to be represented by a low-order map.

4.14.1 Constructing Variable-Entered Maps

To understand the construction of variable-entered Karnaugh maps, consider the generic truth table shown in Fig. 4.34*a,* where the functional value for row i is denoted by f_i.* From the truth table, the Karnaugh map given in Fig. 4.34*b* is constructed. The entries within the cells are the f_i's which, in turn, correspond to the 0's, 1's, and don't-cares that normally appear in the last column of the truth table.

Alternately, a generic minterm canonical formula for the truth table of Fig. 4.34*a* is written as

$$\begin{aligned} f(x,y,z) = {} & f_0 \cdot \bar{x}\bar{y}\bar{z} + f_1 \cdot \bar{x}\bar{y}z + f_2 \cdot \bar{x}y\bar{z} + f_3 \cdot \bar{x}yz \\ & + f_4 \cdot x\bar{y}\bar{z} + f_5 \cdot x\bar{y}z + f_6 \cdot xy\bar{z} + f_7 \cdot xyz \end{aligned} \tag{4.4}$$

If this expression is manipulated according to the rules of Boolean algebra, then a possible factored form of Eq. (4.4) is

$$f(x,y,z) = \bar{x}\bar{y}(f_0 \cdot \bar{z} + f_1 \cdot z) + \bar{x}y(f_2 \cdot \bar{z} + f_3 \cdot z) + x\bar{y}(f_4 \cdot \bar{z} + f_5 \cdot z) + xy(f_6 \cdot \bar{z} + f_7 \cdot z)$$

Since this equation consists of the four combinations of the x and y variables in their complemented and uncomplemented form, a map is constructed from the equation by having the x and y variables appear as the row and column labels and the expressions within parentheses as cell entries. This is illustrated in Fig. 4.34*c.* It is seen, therefore, that a Karnaugh map of order 2 is now being used to represent a three-variable function. Hence, map compression is achieved. In this case, x and y are called the map variables. The cell entries are functions of the single variable z. Thus, z is referred to as the map-entered variable.

The above factored form of Eq. (4.4) is only one of three possibilities. Another factored form of Eq. (4.4) is

$$f(x,y,z) = \bar{x}\bar{z}(f_0 \cdot \bar{y} + f_2 \cdot y) + \bar{x}z(f_1 \cdot \bar{y} + f_3 \cdot y) + x\bar{z}(f_4 \cdot \bar{y} + f_6 \cdot y) + xz(f_5 \cdot \bar{y} + f_7 \cdot y)$$

This expression suggests the compressed Karnaugh map shown in Fig. 4.34*d.* In this case, x and z are the map variables and y is the map-entered variable. The third possible factored form of Eq. (4.4) is

$$f(x,y,z) = \bar{y}\bar{z}(f_0 \cdot \bar{x} + f_4 \cdot x) + \bar{y}z(f_1 \cdot \bar{x} + f_5 \cdot x) + y\bar{z}(f_2 \cdot \bar{x} + f_6 \cdot x) + yz(f_3 \cdot \bar{x} + f_7 \cdot x)$$

and the corresponding compressed Karnaugh map is given in Fig. 4.34*e.* Here, y and z are the map variables and x is the map-entered variable.

---

*Note the different use of f_i from the previous section.

x	y	z	f
0	0	0	f_0
0	0	1	f_1
0	1	0	f_2
0	1	1	f_3
1	0	0	f_4
1	0	1	f_5
1	1	0	f_6
1	1	1	f_7

(a)

x \ yz	00	01	11	10
0	f_0	f_1	f_3	f_2
1	f_4	f_5	f_7	f_6

(b)

x \ y	0	1
0	$f_0 \cdot \bar{z} + f_1 \cdot z$	$f_2 \cdot \bar{z} + f_3 \cdot z$
1	$f_4 \cdot \bar{z} + f_5 \cdot z$	$f_6 \cdot \bar{z} + f_7 \cdot z$

(c)

x \ z	0	1
0	$f_0 \cdot \bar{y} + f_2 \cdot y$	$f_1 \cdot \bar{y} + f_3 \cdot y$
1	$f_4 \cdot \bar{y} + f_6 \cdot y$	$f_5 \cdot \bar{y} + f_7 \cdot y$

(d)

y \ z	0	1
0	$f_0 \cdot \bar{x} + f_4 \cdot x$	$f_1 \cdot \bar{x} + f_5 \cdot x$
1	$f_2 \cdot \bar{x} + f_6 \cdot x$	$f_3 \cdot \bar{x} + f_7 \cdot x$

(e)

x = 0	x = 1
$f_0 \cdot \bar{y}\bar{z} + f_1 \cdot \bar{y}z + f_2 \cdot y\bar{z} + f_3 \cdot yz$	$f_4 \cdot \bar{y}\bar{z} + f_5 \cdot \bar{y}z + f_6 \cdot y\bar{z} + f_7 \cdot yz$

(f)

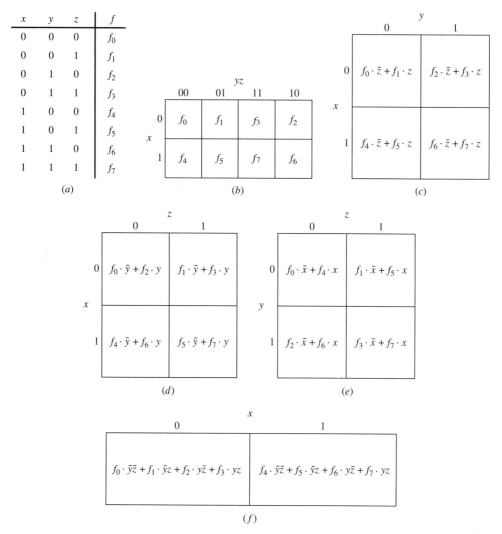

Figure 4.34 Map compressions of a three-variable function. (a) A generic three-variable truth table. (b) Conventional three-variable Karnaugh map. (c) Compressed Karnaugh map of order 2 with x and y as the map variables and z as the map-entered variable. (d) Compressed Karnaugh map of order 2 with x and z as the map variables and y as the map-entered variable. (e) Compressed Karnaugh map of order 2 with y and z as the map variables and x as the map-entered variable. (f) Compressed Karnaugh map of order 1 with x as the map variable and y and z as the map-entered variables.

In the three cases illustrated above, a three-variable Boolean function is represented by a Karnaugh map of order 2. Conceptually, further compression is possible by having the cell entries of the variable-entered map be functions of two variables. For example, if Eq. (4.4) is factored as

$$f(x,y,z) = \overline{x}(f_0 \cdot \overline{y}\,\overline{z} + f_1 \cdot \overline{y}z + f_2 \cdot y\overline{z} + f_3 \cdot yz) + x(f_4 \cdot \overline{y}\,\overline{z} + f_5 \cdot \overline{y}z + f_6 \cdot y\overline{z} + f_7 \cdot yz)$$

then the variable-entered map of Fig. 4.34*f* is constructed. Now, only x is the map variable and y and z are the map-entered variables associated with the two-variable functions that appear as cell entries. Thus, the three-variable function is represented by a Karnaugh map of order 1. As is discussed shortly, the degree of difficulty in interpreting compressed maps lies in the complexity of the entered functions.

In the above discussion, the concept of variable-entered maps was developed from the factorization of a Boolean expression describing a truth table. An alternate way of arriving at variable-entered maps is via a partitioning of the truth table itself. For example, Table 4.19 shows a generic three-variable truth table. The rows are paired such that they correspond to equal values of the x and y variables. The two possible values of the z variable appear within each pair. This pairing of the z variable corresponds to the single-variable functions of z given in the last column of Table 4.19. Since within each partition the x and y variables have fixed values, this partitioned truth table can now be used to form the variable-entered map of Fig. 4.34*c*. That is, for each of the four combinations of values of the x and y variables, the cell entries become the single-variable functions of z. In a similar way, partitioning a truth table around the y and x variables, respectively, leads to the corresponding maps of Fig. 4.34*d* and *e*.

At this time, let us turn our attention to the entries of a variable-entered map when they correspond to single-variable functions. As seen in Fig. 4.34*c–e,* these entries always have the form $f_i \cdot \overline{v} + f_j \cdot v$, where f_i and f_j correspond to the functional values in the ith and jth rows of the truth table and v is the map-entered variable. Assuming the Boolean function is completely specified, the values of f_i and f_j are

Table 4.19 A generic three-variable truth table partitioned around the *z* variable

x	y	z	f	f
0	0	0	f_0	$f_0 \cdot \overline{z} + f_1 \cdot z$
0	0	1	f_1	
0	1	0	f_2	$f_2 \cdot \overline{z} + f_3 \cdot z$
0	1	1	f_3	
1	0	0	f_4	$f_4 \cdot \overline{z} + f_5 \cdot z$
1	0	1	f_5	
1	1	0	f_6	$f_6 \cdot \overline{z} + f_7 \cdot z$
1	1	1	f_7	

Table 4.20 Single-variable map entries for complete Boolean functions

f_i	f_j	$f_i \cdot \overline{v} + f_j \cdot v$	**Map entry**
0	0	$0 + 0 = 0$	0
0	1	$0 + v = v$	v
1	0	$\overline{v} + 0 = \overline{v}$	$\overline{v}$
1	1	$\overline{v} + v = 1$	1

restricted to only 0's and 1's. Table 4.20 tabulates the four possible value assignments to f_i and f_j, the evaluation of $f_i \cdot \overline{v} + f_j \cdot v$, and the corresponding entries for a variable-entered map. Later in this section the effects of don't-cares are considered.

Figure 4.35 illustrates a three-variable truth table and the corresponding variable-entered map. From the truth table we can write

$$\begin{aligned} f(x,y,z) &= \overline{x}\,\overline{y}\,\overline{z} + \overline{x}\,\overline{y}z + \overline{x}y\overline{z} + x\overline{y}z \\ &= \overline{x}\,\overline{y}(\overline{z} + z) + \overline{x}y(\overline{z}) + x\overline{y}(z) \\ &= \overline{x}\,\overline{y}(1) + \overline{x}y(\overline{z}) + x\overline{y}(z) \end{aligned}$$

The expressions within parentheses correspond to the single-variable functions that serve as the map entries. Furthermore, since the functional value is 0 for rows $(x,y,z) = (1,1,0)$ and $(x,y,z) = (1,1,1)$, no term appears in the equation for these two cases, i.e., the term xy does not appear. This is equivalent to the term $xy(0)$. Thus, the entry in the cell for $x = 1$ and $y = 1$ is 0. Equivalently, the map of Fig. 4.35*b* could have been obtained by comparing Table 4.19 and Fig. 4.35*a*.

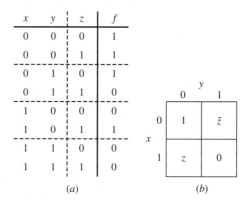

x	y	z	f
0	0	0	1
0	0	1	1
0	1	0	1
0	1	1	0
1	0	0	0
1	0	1	1
1	1	0	0
1	1	1	0

(*a*)

$x \backslash y$	0	1
0	1	$\overline{z}$
1	z	0

(*b*)

Figure 4.35 A three-variable function. (*a*) Truth table. (*b*) Variable-entered map.

x \ yz	00	01	11	10
0	A	1	1	0
1	0	0	1	B

Figure 4.36 An example of a variable-entered map with infrequently appearing variables.

As a second example, consider the Boolean expression

$$f(A,B,x,y,z) = A\bar{x}\bar{y}\bar{z} + \bar{x}\bar{y}z + \bar{x}yz + Bxy\bar{z} + xyz$$

In this expression, the variables A and B appear infrequently; while the variables x, y, and z appear in each term. By using x, y, and z as map variables and A and B as map-entered variables, the variable-entered map of Fig. 4.36 is easily constructed. The entries are simply the coefficients of the terms $\overset{*}{x}\overset{*}{y}\overset{*}{z}$ where the asterisks indicate various combinations of the complemented and uncomplemented form of the variables x, y, and z. In this case, a five-variable function is represented by a map of order 3.

4.14.2 Reading Variable-Entered Maps for Minimal Sums

Just as minimal sums and minimal products are obtained by proper interpretation of regular Karnaugh maps, these types of minimal expressions can also be obtained from variable-entered maps. Again rectangular groupings having dimensions $2^a \times 2^b$, i.e., subcubes, are formed. However, when obtaining a minimal sum, it is necessary to form subcubes involving the map-entered variables in addition to the 1's. Similarly, when obtaining a minimal product, the map-entered variables are grouped as well as the 0's.

Consider first the problem of getting a minimal sum of a completely specified Boolean function from a variable-entered map. To understand how subcubes are formed on these maps, three cases must be considered. The map of Fig. 4.37*a* shows two adjacent cells having a z literal. These cells correspond to the two terms $\bar{x}\bar{y}z$ and $x\bar{y}z$. Furthermore, the sum of these two terms describes the Boolean function associated with this map, i.e., $f(x,y,z) = \bar{x}\bar{y}z + x\bar{y}z$. Factoring the $\bar{y}z$ from each term gives $\bar{x}\bar{y}z + x\bar{y}z = \bar{y}z(\bar{x} + x) = \bar{y}z$. This same result is obtained by grouping the two corresponding cells on the map. The resulting product term is formed by noting which variables along the map's axes do not change value. In this case, the product term contains the $\bar{y}$ literal since $y = 0$ for the cells within the subcube. This

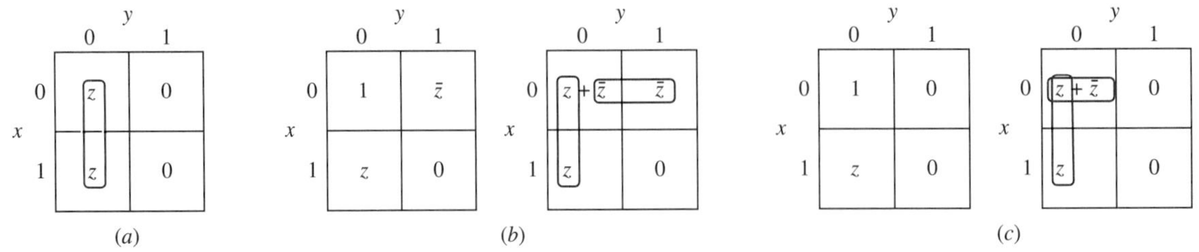

Figure 4.37 Variable-entered maps grouping techniques. (*a*) Grouping cells with the same literal. (*b*) Grouping a 1-cell with both the z literal and the $\bar{z}$ literal. (*c*) Grouping a 1-cell with the z literal.

literal is then and-ed with the z literal occurring within the subcube, i.e., the map entry. In general, normal Karnaugh map techniques are applied to form subcubes of cells that contain the same literal. The described product term is obtained by and-ing the map variables that do not change values with the literal used to form the subcube.

As indicated in Table 4.20, four entries are possible in variable-entered maps for complete Boolean functions, i.e., a literal, its complement, 0, and 1. Literals and their complements are grouped separately as just described. Furthermore, 0's are never grouped when forming minimal sums. Now consider how 1-cells are handled. The first map in Fig. 4.37*b* shows a situation in which z, $\bar{z}$, and 1 appear as cell entries. The cells containing the literals z and $\bar{z}$ correspond to the product terms $x\bar{y}z$ and $\bar{x}y\bar{z}$. Now consider the 1-cell. From the laws of Boolean algebra, the constant 1 can be written as $z + \bar{z}$. This equivalent form of 1 is shown as an entry in the second map of Fig. 4.37*b*. In this case, the 1-cell is regarded as the expression $\bar{x}\bar{y}z + \bar{x}\bar{y}\bar{z}$. Combining these results, the maps of Fig. 4.37*b* correspond to the expression $x\bar{y}z + \bar{x}\bar{y}z + \bar{x}\bar{y}\bar{z} + \bar{x}y\bar{z}$. This expression can be factored as $\bar{y}z(x + \bar{x}) + \bar{x}\bar{z}(\bar{y} + y) = \bar{y}z + \bar{x}\bar{z}$, which is a minimal sum. As indicated in Fig. 4.37*b*, the same result is achieved by grouping the z-cell with the z portion of the $(z + \bar{z})$-cell to form the term $\bar{y}z$ and the $\bar{z}$-cell with the $\bar{z}$ portion of the $(z + \bar{z})$-cell to form the term $\bar{x}\bar{z}$. With both the z and $\bar{z}$ portions being used, the 1-cell is said to be *completely covered.* In general, 1-cells can be used when forming subcubes involving literals. Furthermore, if a 1-cell appears in a subcube for a literal and in another subcube for the complement of the same literal, then no further consideration of the 1-cell is needed when obtaining a minimal sum.

The final case that needs to be discussed is shown in the first map of Fig. 4.37*c*. Here there is a 1-cell and a z-cell, but there are no $\bar{z}$-cells. Again the 1-cell is regarded as a $(z + \bar{z})$-cell in the second map of Fig. 4.37*c*. This map corresponds to the expression $x\bar{y}z + \bar{x}\bar{y}z + \bar{x}\bar{y}\bar{z}$. The first two terms in the expression can be combined to form the term $\bar{y}z$. This is analogous to forming the vertical subcube shown in the second map of Fig. 4.37*c*. But what about the $\bar{x}\bar{y}\bar{z}$ term in the above expression? It is noted that the $(z + \bar{z})$-cell in the second map of Fig. 4.37*c* is not completely covered since the $\bar{z}$ portion is not used. To complete the covering, the $\bar{x}\bar{y}\bar{z}$ portion of the $(z + \bar{z})$-cell is grouped with the $\bar{x}\bar{y}z$ portion of the same cell. This results in the term $\bar{x}\,\bar{y}$, which is equivalent to simply regarding the $(z + \bar{z})$-cell as a 1-cell and grouping it as on a regular Karnaugh map. The two subcubes yield the expression $\bar{y}z + \bar{x}\,\bar{y}$, which is the minimal sum of $x\bar{y}z + \bar{x}\,\bar{y}z + \bar{x}\,\bar{y}\,\bar{z}$.

It is important to note in the last two cases that 1-cells must also be considered when forming subcubes on a variable-entered map. In particular, they must be grouped with a map-entered literal and its complement or they must be used as basic 1-cells. Although the above discussion was restricted to subcubes of two cells, any rectangular grouping of dimensions $2^a \times 2^b$ involving a common literal denotes a single product term.

As a result of the above discussion, a two-step procedure for obtaining minimal sums for completely specified Boolean functions from a variable-entered map with a single map-entered variable can now be stated:

Step 1. Consider each map entry having the literals v and $\bar{v}$. Form an optimal collection of subcubes involving the literal v using the cells containing 1's as don't-care cells and the cells containing the literal $\bar{v}$ as 0-cells. Next form an optimal collection of subcubes involving the literal $\bar{v}$ using the cells containing 1's as don't-care cells and the cells containing the literal v as 0-cells. As in the case of regular Karnaugh maps, by an optimal collection it is meant that the size of the subcubes should be maximized and the number of subcubes should be minimized.

Step 2. Having grouped the cells containing the literals v and $\bar{v}$, an optimal collection of subcubes involving the 1-cells not completely covered in Step 1, i.e., 1-cells that were not used for both a subcube involving the v literal and a subcube involving the $\bar{v}$ literal in Step 1, is next determined. One approach for doing this is to let all cells containing the literals v and $\bar{v}$ become 0-cells and all 1-cells that were completely covered in Step 1 become don't-care cells. Another way of handling the not completely covered 1-cells is to use v-cells or $\bar{v}$-cells from Step 1 that ensure that the 1-cells now become completely covered.*

Figure 4.38 illustrates how the above procedure is applied to obtain a minimal sum from a variable-entered map. The compressed map is shown in Fig. 4.38*a*. The first step is to consider each of the distinct literals z and $\bar{z}$, in turn, and form optimal subcube collections for each case. This step is shown in Fig. 4.38*b*. In the first map, in which the $\bar{z}$-cell is replaced by 0 since it cannot be used in z-subcubes, the z-cell is grouped with the 1-cell to its right since all 1-cells are regarded as don't-cares in this step. The resulting term is $\bar{w}\bar{x}z$. At this point all cells containing z entries appear in at least one subcube. Next, the cells containing $\bar{z}$ entries are considered. This is shown in the second map of Fig. 4.38*b*, where the z-cell is replaced by 0. Again 1-cells are used as don't-cares for the purpose of maximizing the size of the subcubes. The indicated subcube corresponds to the term $y\bar{z}$. This completes Step 1 of

*This second case is illustrated shortly when Fig. 4.40 is discussed.

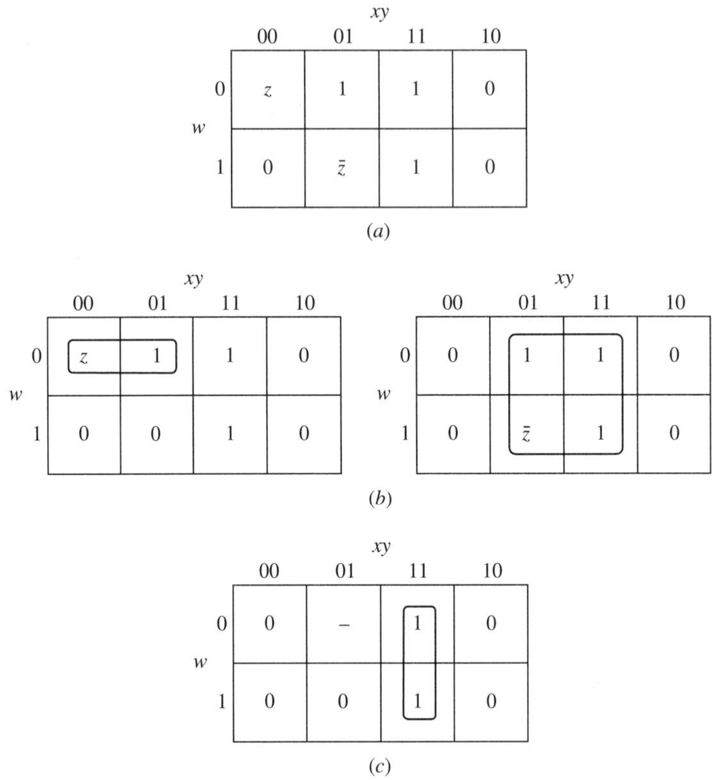

Figure 4.38 Obtaining a minimal sum from a map having single-variable map entries. (*a*) Variable-entered map. (*b*) Step 1. (*c*) Step 2.

the map-reading procedure. Step 2 involves those 1-cells that were not completely covered in Step 1. Note that the 1-cell at location $(w,x,y) = (0,0,1)$ in Fig. 4.38*b* was used for the grouping of both the z literal and the $\bar{z}$ literal. Hence, this 1-cell is regarded as a don't-care cell in Step 2. All the remaining 1-cells must next be grouped optimally since they were not completely covered. This is shown in Fig. 4.38*c*. Here the 1-cells are placed into a single subcube, yielding the term xy. Collecting the three terms corresponding to the three subcubes that were formed, the resulting minimal sum is

$$f(w,x,y,z) = \bar{w}\bar{x}z + y\bar{z} + xy$$

For illustrative purposes, the above example was done using three separate maps. However, the entire process can readily be carried out on the variable-entered map.

Some care must be taken in applying the above two-step process if a minimal sum is to be obtained. To see this, consider the variable-entered map shown in Fig. 4.39, where all the subcubes are shown on a single map. Starting with the $\bar{z}$ entry, the only possible subcube is with the 1-cell to its right, since z-cells are

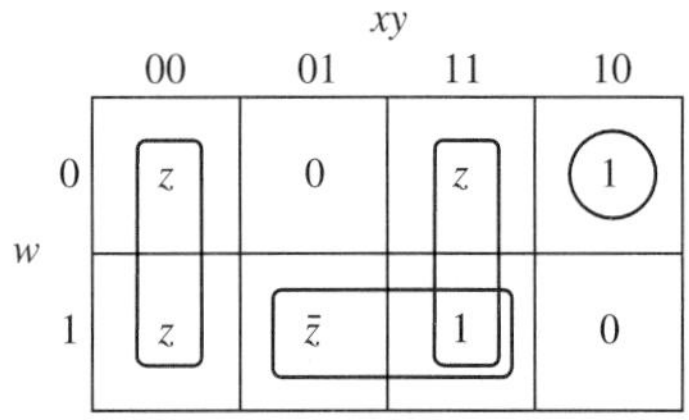

Figure 4.39 Illustrating optimal groupings on a variable-entered map.

regarded as 0-cells, to form the term $wy\bar{z}$. Now consider the z entries. Since the z-cell in the lower left corner can only be grouped with the cell above it, the two cells that comprise the first column of the map yield the term $\bar{x}\bar{y}z$. With a z entry remaining ungrouped, another subcube is necessary. Two equal-sized subcubes are possible in this case: the subcube shown that corresponds to the term xyz and the subcube consisting of the z entry with the 1-cell to its right that corresponds to the term $\bar{w}xz$. Although both subcubes appear to be equally good since they consist of the same number of cells, it should be noted that the first possibility uses a 1-cell that was previously grouped with the $\bar{z}$ entry. Anticipating Step 2 of the process, if the xyz subcube is selected rather than the $\bar{w}xz$ subcube, then the 1-cell corresponding to $(w,x,y) = (1,1,1)$ becomes a don't-care cell in Step 2, since it is completely covered, and only the one remaining 1-cell needs to be grouped at that time. If the alternate possibility is elected, then two 1-cells must be grouped in Step 2. This results in an extra term at that time. Thus, the xyz subcube must be selected. Finally, according to Step 2, the not completely covered 1-cell is grouped. This results in the term $\bar{w}x\bar{y}$. The minimal sum is

$$f(w,x,y,z) = wy\bar{z} + \bar{x}\,\bar{y}z + xyz + \bar{w}x\bar{y}$$

As a final example, consider the variable-entered map in Fig. 4.40*a*. Step 1 requires the three subcubes shown in Fig. 4.40*b*. As required by Step 2, it is still

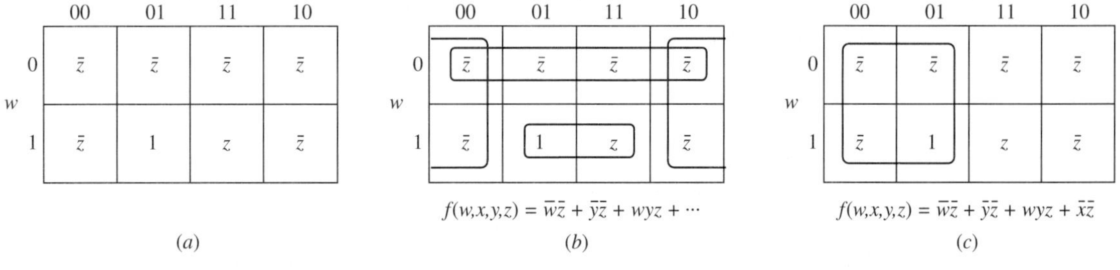

Figure 4.40 Obtaining a minimal sum from a map having single-variable map entries. (*a*) Variable-entered map. (*b*) Step 1. (*c*) Step 2.

necessary to either form a subcube for the not completely covered 1-cell or ensure that the 1-cell becomes completely covered by using it with some of the $\bar{z}$-cells. In the first case, the 1-cell must be grouped alone, resulting in the term $w\bar{x}y$. However, as illustrated in Fig. 4.40*c*, the 1-cell can be grouped with a collection of $\bar{z}$-cells. This results in the term $\bar{x}\bar{z}$. If this is done, then the 1-cell becomes completely covered since it was previously grouped when forming the wyz term. Because the term $\bar{x}\bar{z}$ has one less literal than the term $w\bar{x}y$, the $\bar{x}\bar{z}$ subcube should be selected. The minimal sum is

$$f(w,x,y,z) = \bar{w}\bar{z} + \bar{y}\bar{z} + wyz + \bar{x}\bar{z}$$

4.14.3 Minimal Products

By duality, it is a simple matter to modify the above two-step process to obtain a minimal product from a variable-entered map for a completely specified function with a single map-entered variable. In this case, the 0-cells are regarded as don't-care cells when grouping the v and $\bar{v}$ literals in Step 1. Step 2 requires the grouping of all not completely covered 0-cells. Completely covered 0-cells are used as don't-cares in Step 2. The subcubes formed denote sum terms. When writing the sum terms in Step 1, the literals appearing in the subcubes are or-ed with the literals normally read from the axes of the map.* A formal statement of the procedure is obtained by replacing every occurrence of "1" by "0" and every occurrence of "0" by "1" in the above algorithm for obtaining minimal sums.

An example of obtaining a minimal product from a variable-entered map is shown in Fig. 4.41. Two subcubes are necessary to optimally cover the z literals entered in the map. These correspond to the sum terms $x + y + z$ and $w + \bar{y} + z$. It

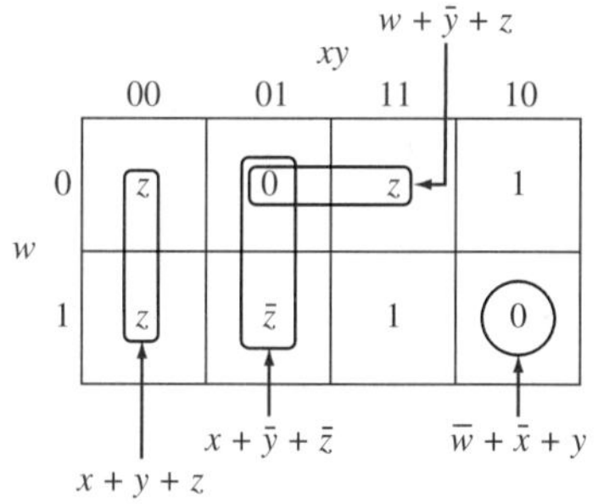

Figure 4.41 Obtaining a minimal product from a map having single-variable map entries.

*Recall that when reading sum terms from a Karnaugh map, 0's on the map axes denote uncomplemented variables and 1's denote complemented variables.

should be noted that a 0-cell was used in one of the subcubes as a don't-care cell. The $\bar{z}$ literal is covered by a single subcube that again uses the 0-cell as a don't-care cell. This results in the sum term $x + \bar{y} + \bar{z}$. Finally, only one 0-cell is not completely covered. Hence, an additional subcube is needed, corresponding to the sum term $\bar{w} + \bar{x} + y$. The resulting minimal product is

$$f(w,x,y,z) = (x + y + z)(w + \bar{y} + z)(x + \bar{y} + \bar{z})(\bar{w} + \bar{x} + y)$$

4.14.4 Incompletely Specified Functions

Up to this point it has been assumed that the Boolean function represented by a variable-entered map was completely specified. However, incompletely specified Boolean functions, i.e., those having don't-cares, commonly occur in logic-design problems. It is possible to generalize the construction and reading of variable-entered maps to handle don't-care conditions.

Again assume that the map entries in a variable-entered map correspond to single-variable functions. It was previously shown that these entries correspond to the evaluation of the expression $f_i \cdot \bar{v} + f_j \cdot v$ where f_i and f_j are the functional values in the ith and jth rows of the truth table and v is the map-entered variable. Since the Boolean function is now assumed to be incompletely specified, the values of f_i and f_j are 0, 1, or don't-care. Table 4.21 lists the nine possible assignments to f_i and f_j, the evaluation of $f_i \cdot \bar{v} + f_j \cdot v$ in each case, and the corresponding entries for a variable-entered map. For the purpose of this table, the don't-care dash (–) is assumed to be a legitimate symbol in a Boolean expression.

It is seen from the table that double entries may appear in a map. For example, consider the case when $f_i = 0$ and $f_j = -$. The reduced form of $f_i \cdot \bar{v} + f_j \cdot v$ is $- \cdot v$. Since the dash represents either a 0 or a 1, the expression $- \cdot v$ evaluates to 0 when the dash is a 0 and evaluates to v when the dash is a 1. Hence, the map entry v,0 signifies that the map cell can be regarded either as a v-cell, i.e., a cell having the entry v, or as a 0-cell. Similarly, when $f_i = -$ and $f_j = 1$, the reduced form of $f_i \cdot \bar{v} + f_j \cdot v$ is $- \cdot \bar{v} + v$. Under the assumption that the dash denotes a 0, $0 \cdot \bar{v} + v = 0 + v = v$; while when the dash denotes a 1, $1 \cdot \bar{v} + v = \bar{v} + v = 1$. In this case, the double

Table 4.21 Single-variable map entries for incompletely specified Boolean functions

f_i	f_j	$f_i \cdot \bar{v} + f_j \cdot v$	Map entry
0	0	$0 \cdot \bar{v} + 0 \cdot v = 0 + 0 = 0$	0
0	1	$0 \cdot \bar{v} + 1 \cdot v = 0 + v = v$	v
0	–	$0 \cdot \bar{v} + - \cdot v = 0 + - \cdot v = - \cdot v$	v,0
1	0	$1 \cdot \bar{v} + 0 \cdot v = \bar{v} + 0 = \bar{v}$	$\bar{v}$
1	1	$1 \cdot \bar{v} + 1 \cdot v = \bar{v} + v = 1$	1
1	–	$1 \cdot \bar{v} + - \cdot v = \bar{v} + - \cdot v$	$\bar{v}$,1
–	0	$- \cdot \bar{v} + 0 \cdot v = - \cdot \bar{v} + 0 = - \cdot \bar{v}$	$\bar{v}$,0
–	1	$- \cdot \bar{v} + 1 \cdot v = - \cdot \bar{v} + v$	v,1
–	–	$- \cdot \bar{v} + - \cdot v$	–

entry v,1 is used to signify that the map cell can be a v-cell, i.e., a cell having the entry v, or a 1-cell. In the following discussion, the first part of a double entry is referred to as the literal part and the second part of a double entry is referred to as the constant part.

The process of reading a variable-entered map for incompletely specified Boolean functions is more complex since the double-entry cells in the map provide flexibility. Again, reading the map is done as a two-step process. For obtaining minimal sums, all cells containing the v and $\bar{v}$ literals alone are grouped separately in the first step, as was done previously. Cells containing 1's and –'s alone are used as don't-cares. In addition, the cells with double entries must also be considered. A double-entry cell having a 0 constant part can be used as a don't-care for subcubes involving its literal part during Step 1. These cells, regardless of how used in Step 1, become 0-cells in Step 2. On the other hand, any double-entry cell having a 1 constant part can be used as a don't-care in Step 1 regardless of the literal part. However, how it is used in Step 1 determines how it must be used in Step 2. To illustrate this, consider a cell with the double entry v,1. This cell can be used optionally for subcubes involving the v literal in Step 1, in which case it becomes a don't-care in Step 2. Alternately, it can be used as a 1-cell in Step 1. Since 1-cells are normally regarded as don't-care cells in Step 1, the v,1-cell can then also be used to group $\bar{v}$ literals in Step 1. If this option is used, it must be either completely covered in Step 1, in which case it becomes a don't-care in Step 2, or, if not completely covered, it must be considered a 1-cell in Step 2, as was done previously when reading variable-entered maps of completely specified functions.

The two-step process for obtaining minimal sums for incompletely specified Boolean functions from a variable-entered map with a single map-entered variable is summarized as follows:

Step 1. Form an optimal collection of subcubes for all entries that consist of only a single literal, i.e., v and $\bar{v}$, using the –'s, 1's, and double entries having a 1 constant part as don't-cares. In addition, double entries having a 0 constant part can be used as don't-cares for subcubes that agree with the literal part of the double entry. The subcubes must be rectangular and have dimensions $2^a \times 2^b$ and should be minimized in number and maximized in size.

Step 2. Form a Step 2 map as follows:

a. Replace the single literal entries, i.e., v and $\bar{v}$, by 0.
b. Retain the single 0 and – entries.
c. Replace each single 1 entry by a – if it was completely covered in Step 1; otherwise, retain the single 1 entry.
d. Replace the double entries having a 0 constant part, i.e., v,0 and $\bar{v}$,0, by 0.
e. Replace each double entry having a 1 constant part by a – if the cell was used in Step 1 to form at least one subcube agreeing with the literal part; otherwise, replace the double entry having a 1 constant part by a 1. (It should be noted that the second case corresponds to

the cell not being covered at all or only used in subcubes involving the complement of the literal part of the double entry.)

The resulting Step 2 map only has 0, 1, and – entries. An optimal collection of subcubes for the 1-cells should be determined using the cells containing –'s as don't-care cells.

To illustrate the above process, consider the Boolean function $f(w,x,y,z) = \Sigma m(3,5,6,7,8,9,10) + dc(4,11,12,14,15)$. The corresponding truth table is given in Fig. 4.42*a*. Arbitrarily selecting *w, x,* and *y* as the map variables and *z* as the map-entered variable, the truth table is partitioned as indicated by the dashed lines. For corresponding pairs of rows within a partition, the expression $f_i \cdot \bar{z} + f_j \cdot z$ is evaluated and the map entries are determined. The variable-entered map is then constructed as shown in Fig. 4.42*b*. Figure 4.42*c* shows how the map entries are grouped in Step 1. It is observed that there is only one *z*-cell. Since both 1-cells and

w	x	y	z	f	$f_i \cdot \bar{z} + f_j \cdot z$	Map entry
0	0	0	0	0	$0 + 0$	0
0	0	0	1	0		
0	0	1	0	0	$0 + z$	z
0	0	1	1	1		
0	1	0	0	–	$- \cdot \bar{z} + z$	z,1
0	1	0	1	1		
0	1	1	0	1	$\bar{z} + z$	1
0	1	1	1	1		
1	0	0	0	1	$\bar{z} + z$	1
1	0	0	1	1		
1	0	1	0	1	$\bar{z} + - \cdot z$	$\bar{z}$,1
1	0	1	1	–		
1	1	0	0	–	$- \cdot \bar{z} + 0$	$\bar{z}$,0
1	1	0	1	0		
1	1	1	0	–	$- \cdot \bar{z} + - \cdot z$	–
1	1	1	1	–		

(*a*)

w \ xy	00	01	11	10
0	0	z	1	z,1
1	1	$\bar{z}$,1	–	$\bar{z}$,0

(*b*)

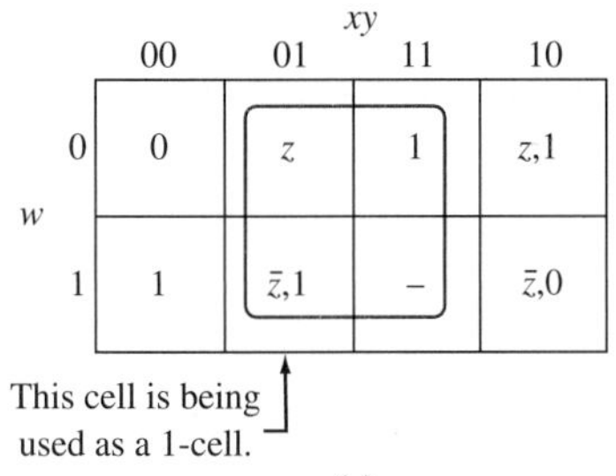

(*c*)

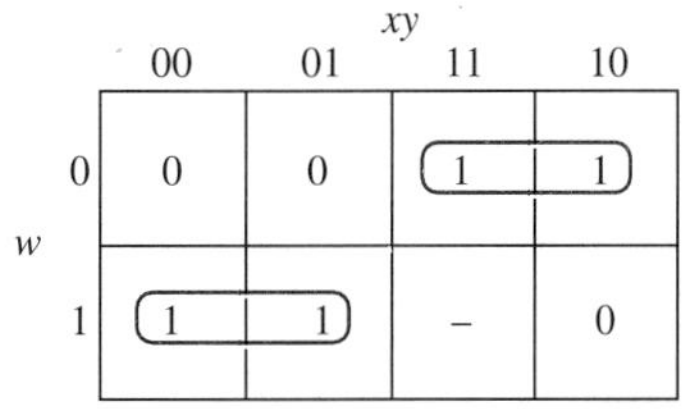

(*d*)

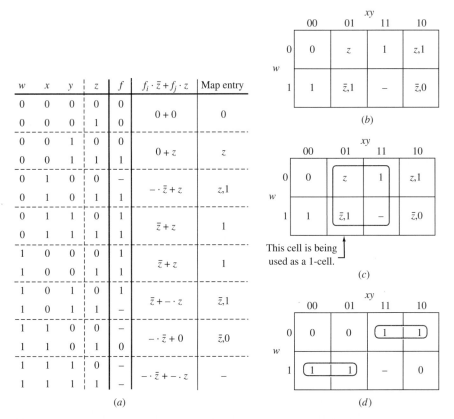

Figure 4.42 Obtaining a minimal sum for the incompletely specified Boolean function $f(w,x,y,z) = \Sigma m(3,5,6,7,8,9,10) + dc(4,11,12,14,15)$ using a variable-entered map. (*a*) Truth table. (*b*) Variable-entered map. (*c*) Step 1 map and subcubes. (*d*) Step 2 map and subcubes.

$\bar{z}$,1-cells can be used as don't-cares when grouping z-cells, the single subcube shown in the figure is formed. This results in the term yz. With no other cells having single-literal entries remaining ungrouped, Step 1 is completed. The Step 2 map is shown in Fig. 4.42*d*. It should be noted that Step 2*e* requires the $\bar{z}$,1-cell to be replaced by a 1 rather than by a – since this cell was previously used only in a z-subcube and not also in a $\bar{z}$-subcube, and the z,1-cell to be replaced by a 1 since it was not used as a z-cell. The 1-cells are now grouped on the Step 2 map, resulting in the terms $\overline{w}x$ and $w\overline{x}$. The minimal sum is thus given as

$$f(w,x,y,z) = yz + \overline{w}x + w\overline{x}$$

As a second example, consider the incomplete function $f(w,x,y,z) = \Sigma m(0,4,5,6,13,14,15) + dc(2,7,8,9)$. The partitioned truth table under the assumption that z is the map-entered variable is shown in Fig. 4.43*a*, and the corresponding variable-entered map is shown in Fig. 4.43*b*. The $\bar{z}$-cell is covered by grouping the first row of the map. This is permissible since the $\bar{z}$,0-cell, the $\bar{z}$,1-cell, and the 1-cell can all be regarded as don't-cares when grouping a $\bar{z}$-cell. This gives the term $\overline{w}\,\overline{z}$. The z-cell is next put into a 2 × 2 subcube. Here the 1-cells and $\bar{z}$,1-cell are

w	x	y	z	f	$f_i \cdot \bar{z} + f_j \cdot z$	Map entry
0	0	0	0	1	$\bar{z} + 0$	$\bar{z}$
0	0	0	1	0		
0	0	1	0	–	$- \cdot \bar{z} + 0$	$\bar{z}$,0
0	0	1	1	0		
0	1	0	0	1	$\bar{z} + z$	1
0	1	0	1	1		
0	1	1	0	1	$\bar{z} + - \cdot z$	$\bar{z}$,1
0	1	1	1	–		
1	0	0	0	–	$- \cdot \bar{z} + - \cdot z$	–
1	0	0	1	–		
1	0	1	0	0	$0 + 0$	0
1	0	1	1	0		
1	1	0	0	0	$0 + z$	z
1	1	0	1	1		
1	1	1	0	1	$\bar{z} + z$	1
1	1	1	1	1		

(*a*)

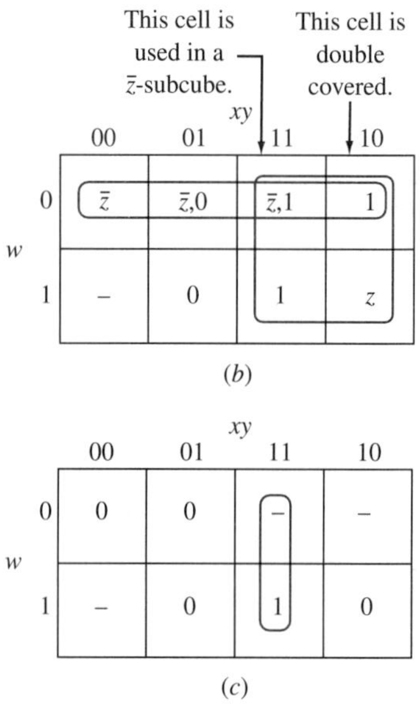

Figure 4.43 Obtaining a minimal sum for the incompletely specified Boolean function $f(w,x,y,z) = \Sigma m(0,4,5,6,13,14,15) + dc(2,7,8,9)$ using a variable-entered map. (*a*) Truth table. (*b*) Step 1 map and subcubes. (*c*) Step 2 map and subcubes.

used as don't-cares. The term associated with this subcube is xz. At this point the Step 2 map is formed as shown in Fig. 4.43*c*. Since the $\bar{z}$,1-cell in Fig. 4.43*b* was used in a $\bar{z}$-subcube, the corresponding cell is a don't-care in Fig. 4.43*c*. In addition, the 1-cell in the upper right corner of Fig. 4.43*b* was completely covered during Step 1. Hence, it also becomes a don't-care cell in the Step 2 map. However, since the other 1-cell in Fig. 4.43*b* was not completely covered, it remains a 1-cell in Fig. 4.43*c*. The single 1-cell in Fig. 4.43*c* is now grouped with a don't-care cell, resulting in the term xy. The minimal sum is

$$f(w,x,y,z) = \bar{w}\bar{z} + xz + xy$$

By duality, the above two-step procedure for obtaining minimal sums of incompletely specified Boolean functions can be restated for minimal products. To restate the procedure, all occurrences of "1" should be replaced by "0" and all occurrences of "0" replaced by "1" in the algorithm for determining minimal sums.

As an illustration of obtaining a minimal product, again consider the partitioned truth table given in Fig. 4.43*a* from which the variable-entered map of Fig. 4.44*a* is constructed. Step 1 requires grouping the $\bar{z}$-cell and the z-cell individually using –'s, 0's, double entries containing 0's, and double entries having a 1 constant part with an agreeing literal part as don't-cares. This results in the two subcubes shown in Fig. 4.44*a* and the corresponding sum terms $x + \bar{z}$ and $\bar{w} + y + z$. The Step 2 map is then constructed as shown in Fig. 4.44*b* using the dual construction procedure (to the one) previously stated for Step 2 minimal-sum maps, i.e., upon interchanging all occurrences of 1's and 0's. On the Step 2 map, the 0's are optimally grouped using dashes as don't-cares. In this case, there is only one 0 entry. Since it can be grouped in two ways, one minimal product is

$$f(w,x,y,z) = (x + \bar{z})(\bar{w} + y + z)(x + \bar{y})$$

and another is

$$f(w,x,y,z) = (x + \bar{z})(\bar{w} + y + z)(\bar{w} + x)$$

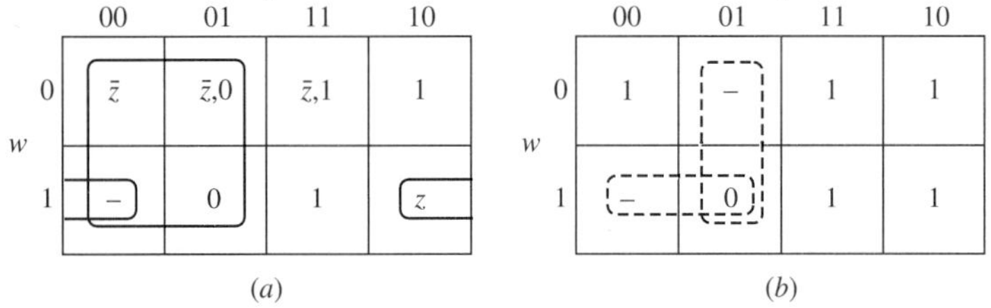

Figure 4.44 Obtaining a minimal product for the incompletely specified Boolean function $f(w,x,y,z) = \Sigma m(0,4,5,6,13,14,15) + dc(2,7,8,9)$ using a variable-entered map. (*a*) Step 1 map and subcubes. (*b*) Step 2 map and subcubes.

4.14.5 Maps Whose Entries Are Not Single-Variable Functions

In the discussion on constructing variable-entered maps, it was shown that conceptually the cell entries can be functions of more than a single variable. This was illustrated in Figs. 4.34*f* and 4.36. In general, the analysis of variable-entered maps is rather difficult when complex expressions appear as cell entries. However, for the case of infrequently appearing variables, as in Fig. 4.36, the cell entries are normally simple enough expressions so that map analysis is manageable. Three cases are particularly common on variable-entered maps having infrequently appearing variables: the expressions within the cells are single literals, the sum of single literals, and the product of single literals. These cases are now considered in detail for obtaining only minimal sums of completely specified Boolean functions. The reader should be able to extend these concepts to incompletely specified functions. Obtaining minimal products from the same map is a rather difficult problem when the entries are more complex than simply single literals, and is not discussed.

Figure 4.45*a* shows a variable-entered map in which the map entries involve two variables. However, the variable entries themselves are simply single literals. In such cases, Step 1 of the two-step process discussed previously is carried out on each literal individually. That is, by setting all the literals to 0 except one, optimal subcubes for each literal, in turn, are obtained. Again, all 1-cells are regarded as don't-cares in Step 1. In actuality, however, a 1-cell is a $(v + \bar{v})$-cell. If a 1-cell does not become completely covered in Step 1, i.e., functionally equal to 1, then it must be grouped in a Step 2 map. For the map of Fig. 4.45*a,* the $\bar{z}$ literal is set to 0 and the y-cell is grouped with the 1-cell, which is regarded as a $(y + \bar{y})$-cell. This is shown in Fig. 4.45*b*. The resulting term is wy. Next, the y literal is set to 0 and the appropriate subcube for the $\bar{z}$-cell is formed as shown in Fig. 4.45*c*, where the 1-cell is now considered a $(z + \bar{z})$-cell. This subcube corresponds to the term $x\bar{z}$. Since each of the individual literals is grouped, it is next necessary to consider all the 1-cells that were not completely covered. A 1-cell is completely covered if the covered part is functionally equal to 1. In this example, since the first subcube covered a y and the second subcube covered a $\bar{z}$, the covered part of the cell is algebraically

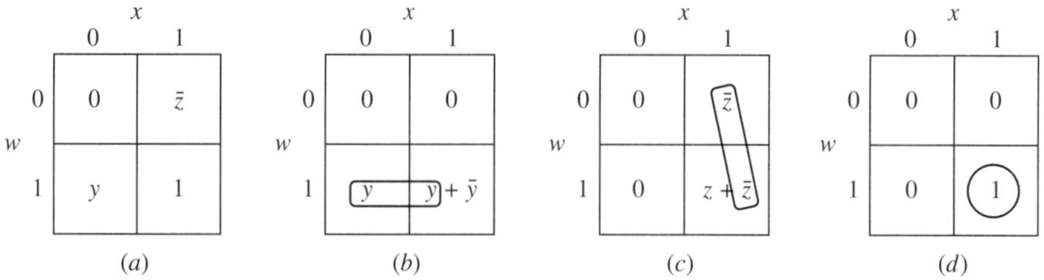

Figure 4.45 Maps having entries involving more than one variable. (*a*) Variable-entered map. (*b*) Grouping the *y* literal. (*c*) Grouping the $\bar{z}$ literal. (*d*) Grouping the not completely covered 1-cell.

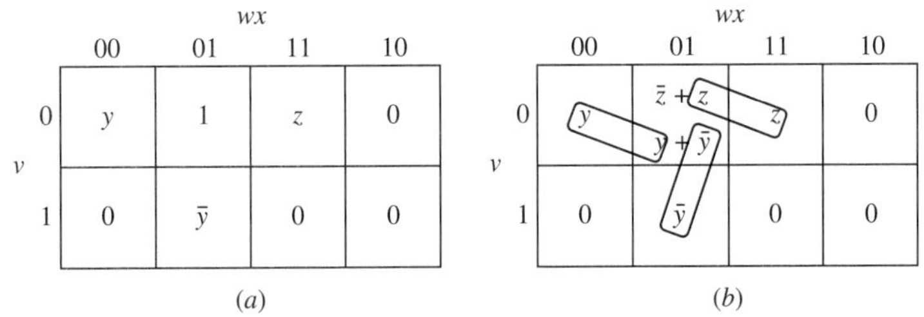

Figure 4.46 Obtaining a minimal sum from a variable-entered map having several single-literal map entries. (*a*) Variable-entered map. (*b*) Optimal collection of subcubes.

described by $y + \bar{z}$, which is not functionally equal to 1. Any 1-cells that are not completely covered in Step 1 become 1-cells in a Step 2 map. Thus, the Step 2 map of Fig. 4.45*d* must be constructed for this example and a minimal covering obtained, which is wx. This results in the minimal sum

$$f(w,x,y,z) = wy + x\bar{z} + wx$$

Although separate maps were drawn in this example to illustrate the various subcubes, the procedure can be carried out on a single map.

Another example of a variable-entered map with two-variable map entries is shown in Fig. 4.46*a*. In Fig. 4.46*b* the Step 1 subcubes, i.e., subcubes for each literal, are shown. The 1-cell is viewed as a $(y + \bar{y})$-cell when grouping the y and $\bar{y}$ literals, and as a $(z + \bar{z})$-cell when grouping the z literal. The covered portion of this 1-cell can be written as $y + \bar{y} + z$. Since $y + \bar{y} + z$ is functionally equal to 1, i.e., $y + \bar{y} + z = 1 + z = 1$, this cell is completely covered and no Step 2 map is required. The minimal sum is

$$f(v,w,x,y,z) = \bar{v}\,\bar{w}y + \bar{w}x\bar{y} + \bar{v}xz$$

The situation when cells consist of sum terms, i.e., the or-ing of single literals, is illustrated in Fig. 4.47*a*. This case is handled in essentially the same manner as the

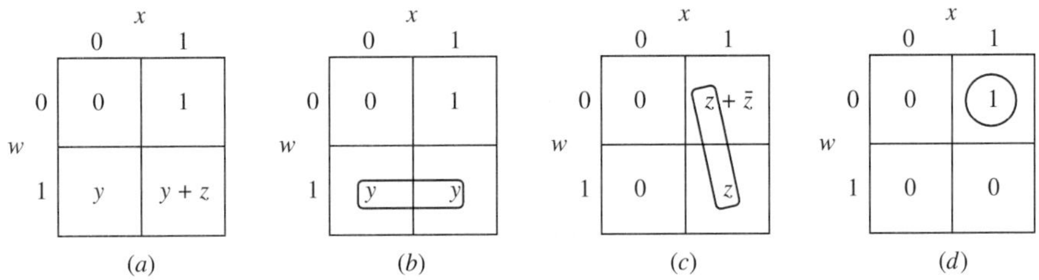

Figure 4.47 Maps having sum terms as entries. (*a*) Variable-entered map. (*b*) Grouping the *y* literal. (*c*) Grouping the *z* literal. (*d*) Grouping the not completely covered 1-cell.

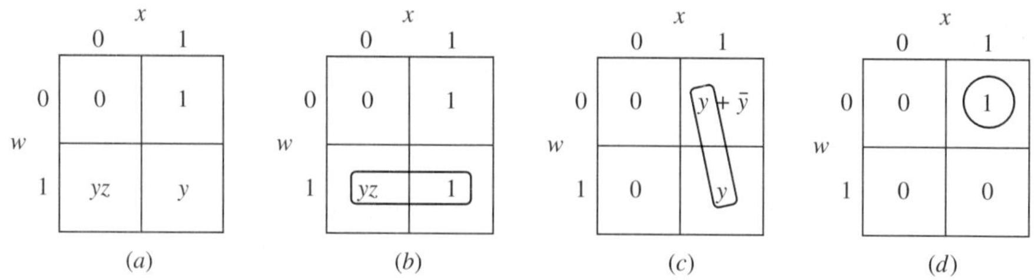

Figure 4.48 Maps having product terms as entries. (*a*) Variable-entered map. (*b*) Grouping the *yz* term. (*c*) Grouping the *y* literal. (*d*) Grouping the not completely covered 1-cell.

previous case. In Step 1 each literal in the map is considered, in turn, by setting all the other literals to 0. The optimal subcubes are formed using 1-cells as don't-cares. Again Step 2 is used to group all 1-cells that are not completely covered in Step 1. In Fig. 4.47*a* it is noted that two distinct literals appear within the cells, i.e., y and z. Setting the z literal to 0 yields the map of Fig. 4.47*b*. The subcube involving the y literal results in the term wy. Next the y literal in the map of Fig. 4.47*a* is set to 0. Figure 4.47*c* illustrates the resulting map where the 1-cell is rewritten as a $(z + \bar{z})$-cell for emphasis. A subcube involving the z literal is then formed that results in the term xz. Since all the literals of the original map are grouped, it is next necessary to group all 1-cells that are not completely covered. The Step 2 map is formed by replacing all literals by 0's, completely covered 1-cells by –'s, and not completely covered 1-cells by 1's. For this example, the map shown in Fig. 4.47*d* results. The grouping of the 1-cell corresponds to the term $\bar{w}x$. Thus, the minimal sum is given by

$$f(w,x,y,z) = wy + xz + \bar{w}x$$

Again individual maps were drawn to illustrate the process. However, normally all subcubes can be formed on a single map.

The third case to be considered involves cells containing product terms, i.e., the and-ing of single literals. An example of this is shown in Fig. 4.48*a*. Each distinct product term, in turn, is grouped as an entity while setting the literals that comprise the product term to 1 and those not contained within the product term to 0 in all the remaining cells that contain a different product term.* For Fig. 4.48*a* the product term is yz. Thus, all cells having the y and z literals alone are replaced by 1's. This results in the map shown in Fig. 4.48*b*. Using 1-cells as don't-cares, a yz-subcube is formed, resulting in the term wyz. Since the map of Fig. 4.48*a* also has a cell with a single-literal product term, this cell must also be grouped. This is done by setting all literals, except y, equal to 0. As a consequence, the cell containing the yz term is replaced by 0. The resulting map is shown in Fig. 4.48*c*, where the 1-cell is rewritten as a $(y + \bar{y})$-cell for emphasis. Grouping the y literal results in the term xy. Finally, Step 2 is performed to cover all 1-cells in the original map that are not completely covered in Step 1. All map entries involving product terms are replaced by 0's and

*Recall that a product term can consist of a single literal.

completely covered 1-cells by don't-cares. In this example, Fig. 4.48*d* is the Step 2 map and the cover is given by $\overline{w}x$. The minimal sum is

$$f(w,x,y,z) = wyz + xy + \overline{w}x$$

When both sum and product terms appear within the same map, the analysis needed to obtain a minimal sum becomes more difficult since greater attention must be given to the functional covering of cells. In all the previous examples, the concept of functional covering only involved the 1-cells. In general, a cell is functionally covered if the sum of the coverings from the subcubes involving the cell is equal to the function specified within the cell. To illustrate this point, consider the map of Fig. 4.49*a*. To obtain a minimal sum, the yz-cell is first considered. As was done previously, the occurrences of the y and z literals in the remaining cells are replaced by 1's and the necessary subcubes established. This results in the map shown in Fig. 4.49*b*, from which the product term $\overline{x}yz$ is obtained. Since the original $(\overline{y} + z)$-cell was included in the subcube, it now has become partially covered. The expression in the $(\overline{y} + z)$-cell of Fig. 4.49*a* can be written as $\overline{y} + z = \overline{y} + (y + \overline{y})z = \overline{y} + yz + \overline{y}z$. It is noted that the second term of this expression is covered by the yz-subcube. The remaining two terms simplify to $\overline{y} + \overline{y}z = \overline{y}$. Thus, this cell may now be regarded as simply a $\overline{y}$-cell for the purpose of determining the remaining subcubes for the map. That is, the simplification problem is now reduced to the map shown in Fig. 4.49*c*. From this map, the $\overline{y}$-subcube results in the term $\overline{w}\,\overline{y}$. Finally, since no 1-cells appeared in the original map, the Step 2 part of the process is not needed and the resulting minimal sum is

$$f(w,x,y,z) = \overline{x}yz + \overline{w}\,\overline{y}$$

Although obtaining minimal expressions from variable-entered maps is rather difficult at times, these maps provide a convenient solution to obtaining "good" expressions for functions having a large number of variables. This is particularly true when dealing with problems having infrequently occurring variables that would normally require the use of high-order maps. Such situations commonly occur when designing controller-oriented synchronous sequential systems. The application of variable-entered maps to these design problems is further discussed in Chapter 8.

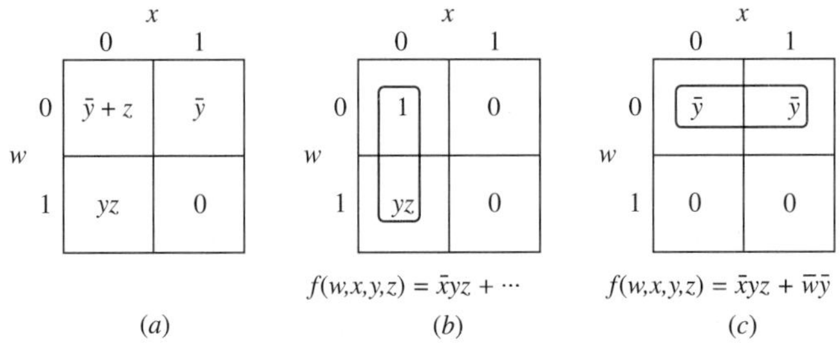

Figure 4.49 Maps having product and sum terms as entries. (*a*) Variable-entered map. (*b*) Grouping the *yz* term. (*c*) Grouping the $\overline{y}$ literal.

CHAPTER 4 PROBLEMS

4.1 Relative to the Boolean function

$$f(w,x,y,z) = \Sigma m(5,8,9,10,11,12,14)$$

classify each of the following terms as to whether it is (1) a prime implicant, (2) an implicant but not prime, (3) a prime implicate, (4) an implicate but not prime, (5) both an implicant and an implicate, or (6) neither an implicant nor an implicate.

a. $w\bar{z}$ b. $y + z$ c. $w + x$

d. $w\bar{x}z$ e. $xy\bar{z}$ f. $w + \bar{y} + \bar{z}$

g. $\bar{w} + \bar{x} + \bar{z}$ h. $\bar{w}x\bar{y}z$

4.2 Represent each of the following Boolean functions on a Karnaugh map.

a. $f(w,x,y,z) = \bar{w}\bar{x}y\bar{z} + \bar{w}\bar{x}yz + \bar{w}x\bar{y}\bar{z} + \bar{w}x\bar{y}z + w\bar{x}y\bar{z} + wx\bar{y}z$

b. $f(w,x,y,z) = (w + x + \bar{y} + z)(w + \bar{x} + y + \bar{z})(\bar{w} + x + \bar{y} + \bar{z})$
$\cdot(\bar{w} + \bar{x} + y + z)(\bar{w} + \bar{x} + y + \bar{z})(\bar{w} + \bar{x} + \bar{y} + \bar{z})$

c. $f(w,x,y,z) = \Sigma m(1,6,7,8,10,12,14)$

d. $f(w,x,y,z) = \Pi M(0,3,4,7,9,13,14)$

e. $f(x,y,z) = x\bar{y} + \bar{x}y + \bar{y}z$

f. $f(x,y,z) = (x + z)(y + z)(\bar{y} + \bar{z})$

4.3 Using a Karnaugh map, determine all the implicants of the function $f(w,x,y,z) = \Sigma m(0,1,2,5,10,11,14,15)$. Which of these are prime implicants?

4.4 Using Karnaugh maps, determine all the prime implicants of each of the following functions. In each case, indicate the essential prime implicants.

a. $f(w,x,y,z) = \Sigma m(0,1,2,5,6,7,8,9,10,13,14,15)$

b. $f(w,x,y,z) = \Pi M(0,2,3,8,9,10,12,14)$

c. $f(w,x,y,z) = \bar{w}\bar{y}z + \bar{w}yz + \bar{x}\bar{y}\bar{z} + w\bar{x}y + \bar{w}\bar{x}y\bar{z}$

d. $f(w,x,y,z) = (w + x + \bar{z})(\bar{w} + x + \bar{z})(w + \bar{x} + \bar{y} + z)(\bar{w} + \bar{x} + \bar{y} + \bar{z})$
$\cdot(\bar{w} + \bar{x} + \bar{y} + z)$

4.5 The flowchart shown in Fig. 4.14 for determining prime implicants on a Karnaugh map can equally well be used to determine the prime implicates. In this case the 0-cells are inspected and sum terms are written. For each of the functions in Problem 4.4, determine all the prime implicates and indicate which are essential prime implicates.

4.6 Using Karnaugh maps, determine all the minimal sums and minimal products for each of the following Boolean functions.

a. $f(x,y,z) = \Sigma m(1,3,4,5,6,7)$

b. $f(x,y,z) = \Sigma m(2,3,4,5,7)$

c. $f(x,y,z) = \Pi M(2,4,7)$

d. $f(x,y,z) = \Pi M(1,2,5,6,7)$

4.7 Using Karnaugh maps, determine all the minimal sums and minimal products for each of the following Boolean functions.

a. $f(x,y,z) = \Sigma m(2,4,5,6,7)$

b. $f(x,y,z) = \Sigma m(0,1,2,3,4,6,7)$

c. $f(x,y,z) = \Pi M(1,4,5,6)$

d. $f(x,y,z) = \Pi M(1,4,5)$

4.8 Using Karnaugh maps, determine all the minimal sums and minimal products for each of the following Boolean functions.

a. $f(w,x,y,z) = \Sigma m(0,1,6,7,8,14,15)$

b. $f(w,x,y,z) = \Sigma m(3,4,6,9,11,12,13,14,15)$

c. $f(w,x,y,z) = \Sigma m(1,3,4,6,7,9,11,13,15)$

d. $f(w,x,y,z) = \Pi M(1,3,4,5,10,11,12,14)$

e. $f(w,x,y,z) = \Pi M(1,4,5,6,14)$

f. $f(w,x,y,z) = \Pi M(4,6,7,8,12,14)$

g. $f(w,x,y,z) = \overline{w}\,\overline{x}z + xyz + w\overline{x}z + x\overline{y}\,\overline{z}$

h. $f(w,x,y,z) = xz + x\overline{y}\,\overline{z} + \overline{w}\,\overline{x}y + wy\overline{z}$

i. $f(w,x,y,z) = (w + \overline{x} + \overline{z})(w + \overline{x} + \overline{y})(\overline{x} + \overline{y} + \overline{z})(\overline{w} + \overline{x} + z)$
$\cdot (w + x + \overline{y} + \overline{z})$

j. $f(w,x,y,z) = (w + y + \overline{z})(\overline{x} + y + \overline{z})(\overline{w} + \overline{x} + y)(w + x + y + z)$
$\cdot (w + \overline{x} + \overline{y} + \overline{z})(\overline{w} + \overline{x} + \overline{y} + z)$

4.9 Using Karnaugh maps, determine all the minimal sums and minimal products for each of the following Boolean functions.

a. $f(w,x,y,z) = \Sigma m(0,2,6,7,9,10,15)$

b. $f(w,x,y,z) = \Sigma m(0,1,2,4,5,6,7,8,9)$

c. $f(w,x,y,z) = \Sigma m(0,1,5,6,7,8,15)$

d. $f(w,x,y,z) = \Pi M(0,2,6,8,10,12,14,15)$

e. $f(w,x,y,z) = \Pi M(0,2,3,5,6,9,10,11,13)$

f. $f(w,x,y,z) = \Pi M(1,5,10,14)$

g. $f(w,x,y,z) = wx + \overline{y}z + w\overline{x}\,\overline{y} + \overline{w}xyz$

h. $f(w,x,y,z) = xy + y\overline{z} + \overline{x}\,\overline{y}\,\overline{z} + x\overline{y}z + wx\overline{y} + w\overline{y}z$

i. $f(w,x,y,z) = (w + \overline{x})(w + y + z)(\overline{w} + \overline{x} + \overline{z})(w + \overline{y} + z)$

j. $f(w,x,y,z) = (w + \overline{y} + \overline{z})(\overline{w} + x + \overline{y})(w + x + \overline{y} + z)$
$\cdot (\overline{w} + \overline{x} + y + z)$

4.10 Using Karnaugh maps, determine all the prime implicants and prime implicates for each of the following incomplete Boolean functions. In each case, indicate which are essential.

a. $f(w,x,y,z) = \Sigma m(0,2,5,7,8,10,13,15) + dc(1,4,11,14)$

b. $f(w,x,y,z) = \Sigma m(1,3,5,7,8,10,12,13,14) + dc(4,6,15)$

c. $f(w,x,y,z) = \Pi M(0,1,4,5,8,9,11) + dc(2,10)$

4.11 Using Karnaugh maps, determine all the minimal sums and minimal products for each of the following incomplete Boolean functions.

a. $f(w,x,y,z) = \Sigma m(0,1,2,5,8,15) + dc(6,7,10)$
b. $f(w,x,y,z) = \Sigma m(2,8,9,10,12,13) + dc(7,11)$
c. $f(w,x,y,z) = \Sigma m(1,7,9,10,12,13,14,15) + dc(4,5,8)$
d. $f(w,x,y,z) = \Sigma m(7,9,11,12,13,14) + dc(3,5,6,15)$
e. $f(w,x,y,z) = \Sigma m(0,2,6,8,10) + dc(1,4,7,11,13,14)$
f. $f(w,x,y,z) = \Sigma m(1,4,6,8,9,10,11,12,13) + dc(3,15)$
g. $f(w,x,y,z) = \Sigma m(2,6,7,8,9,10,12,13) + dc(0,1,4)$
h. $f(w,x,y,z) = \Pi M(0,8,10,11,14) + dc(6)$
i. $f(w,x,y,z) = \Pi M(2,8,11,15) + dc(3,12,14)$
j. $f(w,x,y,z) = \Pi M(0,2,6,11,13,15) + dc(1,9,10,14)$

4.12 Using Karnaugh maps, determine all the minimal sums and minimal products for each of the following incomplete Boolean functions.

a $f(w,x,y,z) = \Sigma m(6,7,9,10,13) + dc(1,4,5,11,15)$
b. $f(w,x,y,z) = \Sigma m(1,5,8,14) + dc(4,6,9,11,15)$
c. $f(w,x,y,z) = \Sigma m(0,2,4,5,8,13,15) + dc(1,10,14)$
d. $f(w,x,y,z) = \Sigma m(1,3,4,6,12) + dc(0,9,13)$
e. $f(w,x,y,z) = \Sigma m(0,1,2,3,4,9,13) + dc(5,10,11,14)$
f. $f(w,x,y,z) = \Sigma m(1,2,3,4,6,9,12,14) + dc(5,7,15)$
g. $f(w,x,y,z) = \Sigma m(2,3,6,8,13,14,15) + dc(4,5,12)$
h. $f(w,x,y,z) = \Pi M(1,4,9,11,13) + dc(0,14,15)$
i. $f(w,x,y,z) = \Pi M(1,2,3,4,9,10) + dc(0,14,15)$
j. $f(w,x,y,z) = \Pi M(0,3,4,11,13) + dc(2,6,8,9,10)$

4.13 Let $g(w,x,y,z) = \Sigma m(1,3,4,12,13)$ and $f_1(w,x,y,z) = \Sigma m(0,1,3,4,6,8,10,11,12,13)$. Determine a minimal sum and a minimal product for function $f_2(w,x,y,z)$ such that $g(w,x,y,z) = f_1(w,x,y,z) \cdot f_2(w,x,y,z)$.

4.14 Using a Karnaugh map, determine a minimal sum and a minimal product for each of the following functions.

a. $f(v,w,x,y,z) = \Sigma m(1,5,9,11,13,20,21,26,27,28,29,30,31)$
b. $f(v,w,x,y,z) = \Sigma m(3,7,8,9,11,12,13,15,16,19,20,23,27,30,31)$
c. $f(v,w,x,y,z) = \Sigma m(1,3,4,5,11,14,15,16,17,19,20,24,26,28,30)$
d. $f(v,w,x,y,z) = \Pi M(0,2,4,6,8,12,14,15,16,18,20,22,30,31)$

4.15 Using a Karnaugh map, determine a minimal sum and a minimal product for the function

$$f(u,v,w,x,y,z) = \Sigma m(4,5,6,7,8,10,12,14,36,37,38,39,40,42,44,46,48,49,50,51,52,53,54,55,56,58,60,62)$$

4.16 Design a three-input, one-output minimal two-level gate combinational network that has a logic-1 output when the majority of its inputs are logic-1 and has a logic-0 output when the majority of its inputs are logic-0.

4.17 In Sec. 3.8 the truth table for generating the odd-parity bit for decimal digits in 8421 code was developed. Verify that the minimal sum stated in that section is correct. What is the minimal product? Can a simpler network be obtained if exclusive-or-gates are used?

4.18. A network appearing in many digital systems is the binary full adder. This network has as its inputs 1 bit from the addend (x_i), 1 bit from the augend (y_i), and 1 bit corresponding to the carry (c_i) from the previous order addition. The outputs from the adder are a sum bit (s_i) and a carry bit (c_{i+1}) to be used in adding the next pair of addend and augend bits. By letting a one-to-one correspondence exist between a binary symbol and a logic symbol, a truth table can be constructed for a binary full adder. Design a three-input, two-output minimal two-level gate combinational network to generate the sum and carry bits of the adder. Treat each output independently.

4.19 A network appearing in many digital systems is the binary full subtracter. This network has as its inputs 1 bit from the minuend (x_i), 1 bit from the subtrahend (y_i), and 1 bit corresponding to the borrow (b_i) from the previous order subtraction. The outputs from the subtracter are a difference bit (d_i) and a borrow bit (b_{i+1}) to be used in subtracting the next pair of minuend and subtrahend bits. By letting a one-to-one correspondence exist between a binary symbol and a logic symbol, a truth table can be constructed for a binary full subtracter. Design a three-input, two-output minimal two-level gate combinational network to generate the difference and borrow bits of the subtracter. Treat each output independently.

4.20 Design a minimal two-level gate combinational network that detects the presence of any of the six illegal code groups in the 8421 code by providing a logic-1 output.

4.21 A panel light in the control room at the launching of a satellite is to go on if and only if the pressure in both the fuel and oxidizer tanks is equal to or above a required minimum and there are 10 min or less to liftoff, or if the pressure in the oxidizer tank is equal to or above a required minimum and the pressure in the fuel tank is below a required minimum but there are more than 10 min to liftoff, or if the pressure in the oxidizer tank is below a required minimum but there are more than 10 min to liftoff. Design a minimal two-level gate combinational network to control the panel light.

4.22 Design a four-input, four-output gate combinational network that converts the decimal digits in 2421 code (as previously given in Table 2.7) into their equivalent forms in 8421 code. Treat each output independently.

4.23 Design a four-input, one-output gate combinational network that has the $753\bar{6}$ code groups as inputs (as previously given in Table 2.7) and has an output of logic-1 if the input digit D is in the range $0 \leq D \leq 3$.

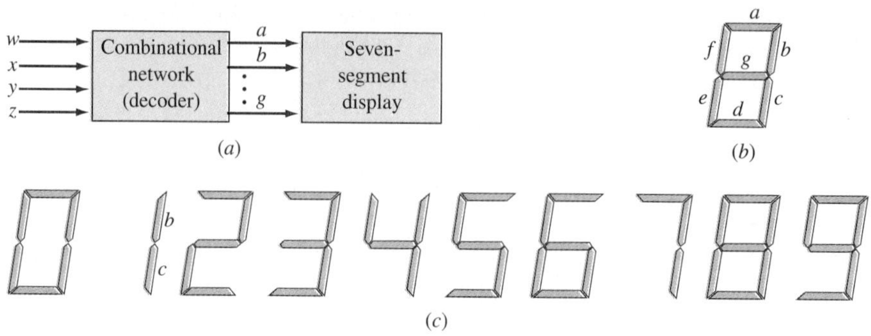

Figure P4.24

4.24 A BCD-to-seven-segment decoder is a combinational network that accepts a decimal digit expressed in the 8421 code and generates outputs for controlling the segments of a seven-segment display that shows the corresponding decimal digit. The decoder has the structure shown in Fig. P4.24*a* where the four input variables *w, x, y,* and *z* correspond to the four bits of the 8421 code. The general form of the seven-segment display and the relationship between the segments and the outputs of the decoder are shown in Fig. P4.24*b*. When a logic-1 appears as a network output, the corresponding segment is lit. Since only the decimal digits (in binary form) can appear as inputs to the decoder, the patterns shown in Fig. P4.24*c* are chosen to represent the decimal digits. Note that segments *b* and *c* are used to indicate the decimal digit 1. Design a logic network based on minimal sum expressions for controlling each of the seven segments. Treat each output of the network independently.

4.25 Using the Quine-McCluskey method, obtain all the prime implicants for each of the following Boolean functions.

a. $f(w,x,y,z) = \Sigma m(0,2,3,4,8,10,12,13,14)$

b. $f(v,w,x,y,z) = \Sigma m(4,5,6,7,9,10,14,19,26,30,31)$

c. $f(w,x,y,z) = \Sigma m(7,9,12,13,14,15) + dc(4,11)$

d. $f(w,x,y,z) = \Sigma m(0,1,2,6,7,9,10,12) + dc(3,5)$

4.26 Using the Quine-McCluskey method, obtain all the prime implicates for each of the following Boolean functions.

a. $f(v,w,x,y,z) = \Pi M(1,3,6,10,11,12,14,15,17,19,20,22,24,29,30)$

b. $f(w,x,y,z) = \Pi M(0,2,3,4,5,12,13) + dc(8,10)$

4.27 Using the Quine-McCluskey and Petrick methods, determine all the irredundant disjunctive normal formulas for the following Boolean functions. Indicate which expressions are minimal sums.

a. $f(w,x,y,z) = \Sigma m(4,5,7,12,14,15)$

b. $f(w,x,y,z) = \Sigma m(4,5,8,9,12,13) + dc(0,3,7,10,11)$

4.28 Using the Quine-McCluskey and Petrick methods, determine all the irredundant conjunctive normal formulas for the following Boolean functions. Indicate which expressions are minimal products.

a. $f(w,x,y,z) = \Pi M(3,4,5,8,9,11,13,14,15)$

b. $f(w,x,y,z) = \Pi M(0,6,7,8,9,13) + dc(5,15)$

4.29 For each of the prime-implicant tables shown in Table P4.29, determine a minimal cover. The cost column indicates the cost associated with each row. State your reasons for deleting any rows or columns.

Table P4.29

	c_1	c_2	c_3	c_4	c_5	c_6	c_7	Cost
r_1			×		×		×	3
r_2				×		×		4
r_3		×	×			×		4
r_4	×	×				×		4
r_5			×		×		×	4
r_6	×	×			×	×		6
r_7			×	×	×			6

(*a*)

	c_1	c_2	c_3	c_4	c_5	c_6	c_7	c_8	c_9	c_{10}	c_{11}	Cost
r_1		×		×	×		×					3
r_2						×				×		3
r_3											×	4
r_4	×	×						×	×			4
r_5	×			×			×					4
r_6				×					×	×		5
r_7	×						×	×				6
r_8			×			×			×	×		7
r_9		×	×		×				×			7

(*b*)

	c_1	c_2	c_3	c_4	c_5	c_6	c_7	Cost
r_1	×				×			3
r_2			×	×			×	4
r_3		×		×		×		4
r_4		×	×			×	×	5
r_5			×		×		×	5
r_6	×	×			×	×		6
r_7			×	×	×			7

(*c*)

4.30 Using the Quine-McCluskey method and prime-implicant table reductions, determine a minimal sum for the incomplete Boolean function

$$f(w,x,y,z) = \Sigma m(3,4,5,7,10,12,14,15) + dc(2)$$

4.31 Using the decimal Quine-McCluskey method and prime-implicant table reductions, determine a minimal sum for the incomplete Boolean function

$$f(w,x,y,z) = \Sigma m(1,3,6,8,9,10,12,14) + dc(7,13)$$

4.32 For the following set of Boolean functions, apply Petrick's method to determine all the multiple-output minimal sums based on the number of distinct terms and on the number of gate input terminals in the realization.

$$f_1(x,y,z) = \Sigma m(1,2,4,6)$$
$$f_2(x,y,z) = \Sigma m(0,1,3,4,7)$$
$$f_3(x,y,z) = \Sigma m(1,4,5,7)$$

4.33 For each of the following sets of Boolean functions, determine a multiple-output minimal sum based on the number of gate input terminals in the realization.

a. $f_1(x,y,z) = \Sigma m(0,2,3,4,6)$
$f_2(x,y,z) = \Sigma m(0,2,5)$
$f_3(x,y,z) = \Sigma m(3,4,5,6)$

b. $f_1(x,y,z) = \Sigma m(1,2,5) + dc(6,7)$
$f_2(x,y,z) = \Sigma m(3,5,6,7) + dc(1,4)$
$f_3(x,y,z) = \Sigma m(1,4,6) + dc(0)$

4.34 For each of the following Boolean functions, determine a minimal sum and a minimal product using variable-entered maps where *w*, *x*, and *y* are the map variables.

a. $f(w,x,y,z) = \Sigma m(2,3,4,5,10,12,13)$
b. $f(w,x,y,z) = \Sigma m(0,3,4,5,8,9,11,12,13)$
c. $f(w,x,y,z) = \Sigma m(1,3,8,9,10,11,12,14,15)$
d. $f(w,x,y,z) = \Sigma m(4,7,8,12,13,15)$
e. $f(w,x,y,z) = \Sigma m(3,4,5,7,8,11,12,13,15)$
f. $f(w,x,y,z) = \Sigma m(0,2,5,8,9,10,11,13,15)$

4.35 For each of the following Boolean functions, determine a minimal sum and a minimal product using variable-entered maps where *w*, *x*, and *y* are the map variables.

a. $f(w,x,y,z) = \Sigma m(2,3,5,12,14) + dc(0,4,8,10,11)$
b. $f(w,x,y,z) = \Sigma m(1,5,6,7,9,11,12,13) + dc(0,3,4)$
c. $f(w,x,y,z) = \Sigma m(1,5,7,10,11) + dc(2,3,6,13)$
d. $f(w,x,y,z) = \Sigma m(5,6,7,12,13,14) + dc(3,8,9)$
e. $f(w,x,y,z) = \Sigma m(2,3,4,10,13,14,15) + dc(7,9,11)$

$w \backslash x$	0	1
0	0	$y + \bar{z}$
1	$y\bar{z}$	1

(*a*)

$v \backslash wx$	00	01	11	10
0	0	$\bar{y} + z$	1	$\bar{y}\bar{z}$
1	0	$y + z$	$y\bar{z}$	0

(*b*)

$v \backslash wx$	00	01	11	10
0	yz	–	$\bar{y}z$	–
1	$y + \bar{z}$	–	$\bar{y} + \bar{z}$	1

(*c*)

Figure P4.37

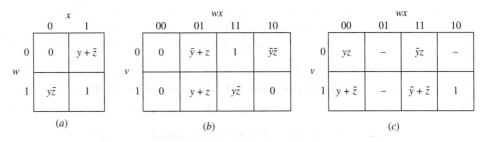

4.36 For each of the following Boolean functions, determine a minimal sum using variable-entered maps where x, y, and z are the map variables.

a. $f(A,B,x,y,z) = A\bar{x}\bar{y}z + Bx\bar{y}\bar{z} + Bxy\bar{z} + \bar{x}yz$

b. $f(A,B,x,y,z) = A\bar{x}\bar{y}\bar{z} + A\bar{x}\bar{y}z + Ax\bar{y}z + \bar{B}\bar{x}\bar{y}z + B\bar{x}y\bar{z} + \bar{x}yz + x\bar{y}\bar{z}$

c. $f(A,B,x,y,z) = \bar{A}\bar{x}y\bar{z} + Axyz + AB\bar{x}\bar{y}z + ABx\bar{y}z + \bar{x}yz$

4.37 For each of the variable-entered maps in Fig. P4.37, determine a minimal sum.

5 CHAPTER

Logic Design with MSI Components and Programmable Logic Devices

It is possible to obtain fabricated circuit chips, or packages, that have from a small set of individual gates to a highly complex interconnection of gates corresponding to an entire logic network. The complexity of a single chip is known as the *scale of integration.* As a rough rule of thumb, circuit chips containing from 1 to 10 gates are said to be *small-scale integrated (SSI) circuits*, those having from 10 to 100 gates as *medium-scale integrated (MSI) circuits*, those having 100 to 1,000 gates as *large-scale integrated (LSI) circuits*, and those having more than 1,000 gates as *very-large-scale integrated (VLSI) circuits.*

Chapter 4 was concerned with obtaining optimal logic networks. At that time, emphasis was placed on minimizing the number of gates and the number of gate input terminals. Thus, the realization cost was based on chips having single gates. However, if more than one gate is included on a chip, then the cost more realistically should be associated with the entire package rather than the individual gates. In such a case, a good realization from a cost point of view does not necessarily require the use of a minimal expression according to the previous criteria but rather requires one that does not exceed the capacity of the circuit package.

Another occurring situation in logic design is that certain gate configurations have become so common and useful that manufacturers fabricate these networks on a single chip using medium-scale and large-scale integration. These configurations normally provide a high degree of flexibility, allowing them to be used as logic-design components. Again, good realizations of logic networks are achieved by proper use of these generalized circuits without having to form minimal expressions.

This chapter first introduces some specialized MSI components that have extensive use in digital systems. These include adders, comparators, decoders, encoders, and multiplexers. Their principle of operation and, in some cases, how they can be used as logic-design components are presented.

Unlike the MSI circuits which are designed to perform specific functions, LSI technology introduced highly generalized circuit structures known as *programmable logic devices* (PLDs). In their simplest form, programmable logic devices consist of an array of and-gates and an array of or-gates. However, they must be modified for a specific application. Modification involves specifying the connections within these arrays using a hardware procedure. This procedure is known as *programming.* As a result of programming the arrays, it is possible to achieve realizations of specific functions using generalized components.

In the second part of this chapter, three programmable logic device structures are studied. In particular, the programmable read-only memory (PROM), the programmable logic array (PLA), and the programmable array logic (PAL)* are discussed. ■

5.1 BINARY ADDERS AND SUBTRACTERS

The most fundamental computational process encountered in digital systems is that of binary addition. In Sec. 2.3 the concept of binary addition was introduced. As was seen at that time, when two binary numbers are added, in general, it is necessary to consider at each bit position an augend bit, x_i, an addend bit, y_i, and a carry-in from the previous bit position, c_i. The result of the addition at each bit position is a sum bit, s_i, and a carry-out bit, c_{i+1}, which is used when adding at the next higher-order bit position. Table 5.1 summarizes the addition process for each bit position, i.e., the values of s_i and c_{i+1} for all the possible assignment of values to x_i, y_i, and c_i.

Although Table 5.1 was constructed as an addition table, it can also be regarded as the truth table for a logic network that performs addition at a single bit position. Such a network is referred to as a *binary full adder.*

Table 5.1 Truth table for a binary full adder

x_i	y_i	c_i	c_{i+1}	s_i
0	0	0	0	0
0	0	1	0	1
0	1	0	0	1
0	1	1	1	0
1	0	0	0	1
1	0	1	1	0
1	1	0	1	0
1	1	1	1	1

*PAL is a registered trademark of Advanced Micro Devices, Inc.

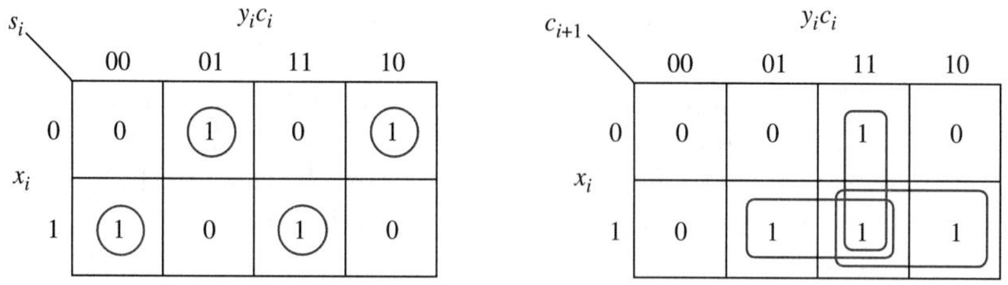

Figure 5.1 Karnaugh maps for the binary full adder.

Having obtained a truth table, let us determine a logic network realization. Karnaugh maps for the sum and carry-out outputs of the binary full adder are shown in Fig. 5.1. The corresponding minimal sums are

$$\begin{aligned} s_i &= \bar{x}_i\bar{y}_ic_i + \bar{x}_iy_i\bar{c}_i + x_i\bar{y}_i\bar{c}_i + x_iy_ic_i \\ c_{i+1} &= x_iy_i + x_ic_i + y_ic_i \end{aligned} \tag{5.1}$$

Although the minimal sum for the sum output is just its minterm canonical formula, a possible simplification of the sum equation is achieved by making use of the exclusive-or operation. In particular,

$$\begin{aligned} s_i &= \bar{x}_i\bar{y}_ic_i + \bar{x}_iy_i\bar{c}_i + x_i\bar{y}_i\bar{c}_i + x_iy_ic_i \\ &= c_i(\bar{x}_i\bar{y}_i + x_iy_i) + \bar{c}_i(\bar{x}_iy_i + x_i\bar{y}_i) \\ &= c_i\overline{(x_i \oplus y_i)} + \bar{c}_i(x_i \oplus y_i) \\ &= c_i \oplus (x_i \oplus y_i) \end{aligned} \tag{5.2}$$

In arriving at Eq. (5.2), it should be noted that the form of the expression on the line above it is $A\bar{B} + \bar{A}B$, where $A = c_i$ and $B = (x_i \oplus y_i)$, which corresponds to $A \oplus B$. The logic diagram for the binary full adder based on Eqs. (5.1) and (5.2) is shown in Fig. 5.2.

The binary full adder is only capable of handling one bit each of an augend and addend along with a carry-in generated as a carry-out from the addition of the previ-

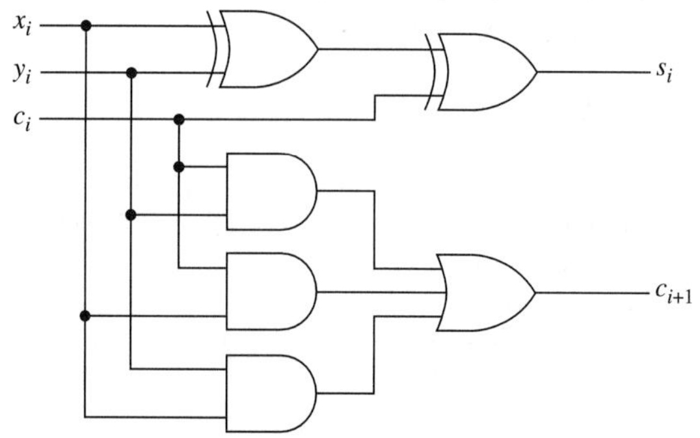

Figure 5.2 A realization of the binary full adder.

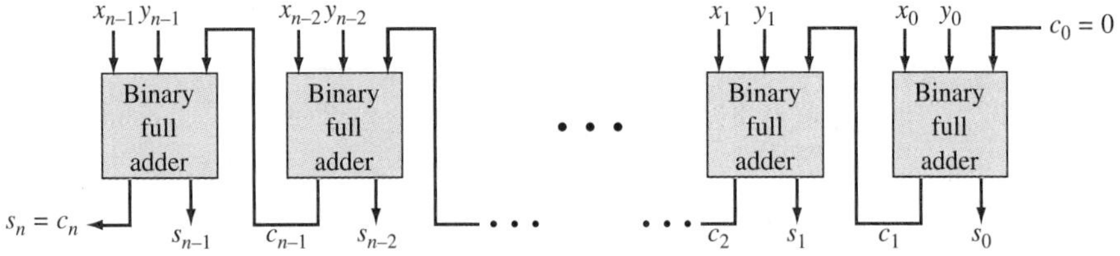

Figure 5.3. Parallel (ripple) binary adder.

ous lower-order bit position. Consider now the addition of two binary numbers each consisting of n bits, i.e., $x_{n-1}x_{n-2} \cdots x_1x_0$ and $y_{n-1}y_{n-2} \cdots y_1y_0$. This, in general, results in an $(n + 1)$-bit sum $s_ns_{n-1} \cdots s_1s_0$. A direct approach for designing a binary adder in this case is to write a truth table with 2^{2n} rows corresponding to all the combinations of values assignable to the $2n$ operand bits, and specifying the values for the $n + 1$ sum bits. Clearly, this is a formidable task.

As an alternate approach, n binary full adders, e.g., of the type shown in Fig. 5.2, can be cascaded as illustrated in Fig. 5.3, where c_n, the carry-out from the highest-order bit position, becomes the highest-order sum bit, s_n.* Since for the least-significant-bit position there is no carry-in, a 0 is entered on the corresponding input line. When inputs are applied simultaneously to a logic network, as in Fig. 5.3, it is commonly referred to as a *parallel* input. Thus, the adder network shown in Fig. 5.3 is called a *parallel binary adder.* Although the inputs to this adder are applied simultaneously, the output sum bits do not necessarily occur simultaneously due to the propagation delays associated with the gates. In particular, the network of Fig. 5.3 is prone to a ripple effect in that a carry-out generated at the ith-bit position can affect the sum bits at higher-order bit positions. Hence, the value for a higher-order sum bit is not produced until the carry at its previous order bit position is established. Consequently, this logic network is also referred to as a *ripple binary adder.*

As was discussed in Chapter 2, binary numbers can be signed or unsigned, in which case the output of the adder must be interpreted accordingly as a signed or unsigned result. Another factor affecting the interpretation of the output of the adder is if a final carry-out occurs, i.e., s_n, since it may correspond to an overflow. The reader is referred back to Chapter 2 for the details of binary arithmetic with signed and unsigned numbers and the concept of overflow.

5.1.1 Binary Subtracters

Binary subtraction was also discussed in Sec. 2.3. A binary subtracter can be designed using the same approach as that for a binary adder. The binary subtraction process is summarized in Table 5.2. Again, in general, three bits are involved at each bit order, a minuend bit, x_i, a subtrahend bit, y_i, and a borrow-in bit from the previous bit-order position, b_i. The result of the subtraction is a difference bit, d_i, and a

*Networks consisting of a cascade connection of identical subnetworks are frequently referred to as *iterative networks.*

Table 5.2 Truth table for a binary full subtracter

x_i	y_i	b_i	b_{i+1}	d_i
0	0	0	0	0
0	0	1	1	1
0	1	0	1	1
0	1	1	1	0
1	0	0	0	1
1	0	1	0	0
1	1	0	0	0
1	1	1	1	1

borrow-out bit, b_{i+1}. The difference bit at each order is obtained by subtracting both the subtrahend and borrow-in bits from the minuend bit. To achieve this result, however, a borrow-out from the next higher-order bit position may be necessary.

For the purpose of obtaining a realization, Table 5.2 can also be viewed as a truth table for a *binary full subtracter.* Since the d_i column of Table 5.2 is identical to the s_i column of Table 5.1, it is immediately concluded that the difference equation for a binary full subtracter is

$$d_i = b_i \oplus (x_i \oplus y_i)$$

By using a Karnaugh map, the minimal-sum expression for the borrow-out is readily determined as

$$b_{i+1} = \bar{x}_i y_i + \bar{x}_i b_i + y_i b_i$$

These results can be used to construct a logic diagram for a binary full subtracter.

As was done for addition, by cascading n binary full subtracters, a *ripple binary subtracter* is realized for handling two n-bit operands. The structure of such a realization is shown in Fig. 5.4, where $x_{n-1}x_{n-2} \cdots x_1x_0$ is the n-bit minuend and $y_{n-1}y_{n-2} \cdots y_1y_0$ is the n-bit subtrahend.

Recalling from Secs. 2.8 and 2.9, subtraction can be replaced by addition through the use of complements. For example, adding the 2's-complement of the subtrahend to the minuend results in the difference between the two numbers.

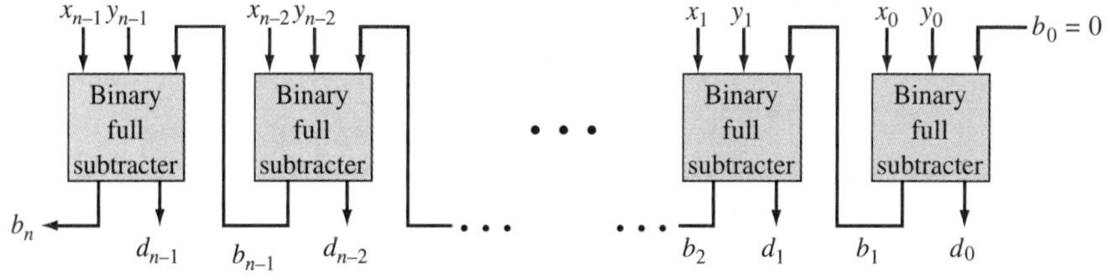

Figure 5.4. Parallel (ripple) binary subtracter.

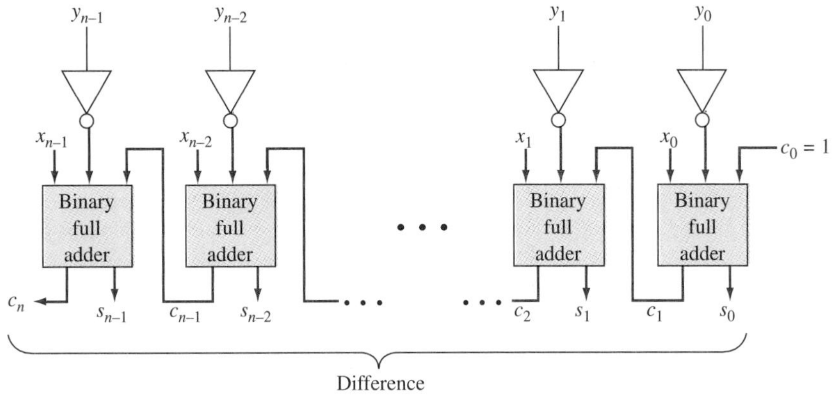

Figure 5.5. Parallel binary subtracter constructed using a parallel binary adder.

Furthermore, the 2's-complement of a binary number is readily obtained by adding one to its 1's-complement. Figure 5.5 shows the design of a subtracter using this approach. The 1's-complement of the subtrahend is formed by inverting each of its bits, and a carry-in of 1 in the least-significant-bit position provides for the addition of 1 to the 1's-complement.

By making use of the fact that $y_i \oplus 1 = \overline{y}_i$, Fig. 5.6 gives a realization of a parallel adder/subtracter. The behavior of this network is determined by the control signal Add/Sub. The subtraction operation is obtained by letting Add/Sub $= 1$, in which case 1's are appropriately entered into the exclusive-or-gates to provide the 1's-complement of the subtrahend and the initial carry-in of 1. The parallel binary adder then produces the difference. On the other hand, when the two operands are to be added, Add/Sub $= 0$. The bits of the addend are not modified

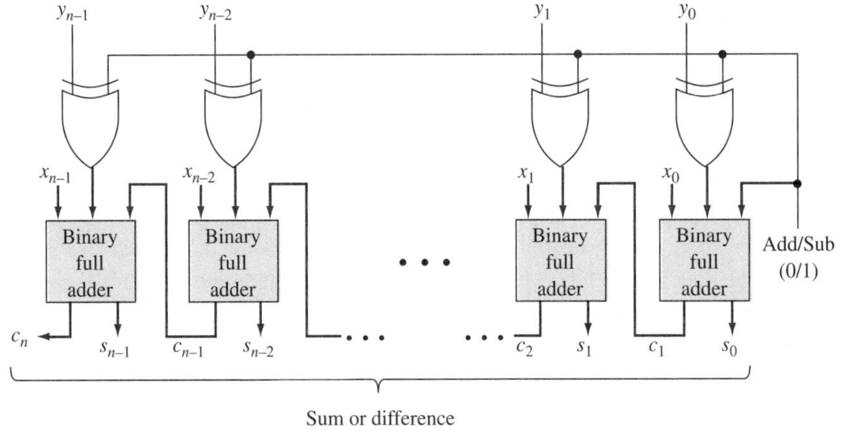

Figure 5.6. Parallel binary adder/subtracter.

by the exclusive-or-gates prior to entering the parallel binary adder and the necessary initial carry-in of 0 is provided.

Since the operands in subtraction can be either signed or unsigned, the output of a binary subtracter must be interpreted appropriately. For example, for unsigned operands, the output from the binary subtracter of Fig. 5.4 is the true difference if the minuend is greater than or equal to the subtrahend. However, the output from the subtracter is the 2's-complement representation of the difference if the minuend is less than the subtrahend. Again the reader is referred back to Chapter 2 for the details of binary arithmetic with signed and unsigned numbers.

5.1.2 Carry Lookahead Adder

In view of the fact that subtraction is readily achievable through the addition of complements, further discussion of the addition/subtraction process is restricted only to the realization of binary adders.

Although the operands are applied in parallel, all the networks illustrated thus far in this section are subject to a ripple effect. The ripple effect dictates the overall speed at which the network operates. To see this, consider the ripple binary adder of Fig. 5.3. It is possible that a carry is generated in the least-significant-bit-position stage, and, owing to the operands, this carry must propagate through all the remaining stages to the highest-order-bit-position stage. For example, such a situation occurs when the two n-bit operands are $01 \cdots 11$ and $00 \cdots 01$ so that the n-bit sum $10 \cdots 00$ is produced. Assuming the binary full adder of Fig. 5.2, two levels of logic are needed to generate the carry at the least-significant-bit-position stage, two levels of logic are needed to propagate the carry through each of the next n–2 higher-order stages, and two levels of logic are needed to form the sum or carry at the highest-order-bit-position stage. If each gate is assumed to introduce a unit time of propagation delay, then the maximum propagation delay for the ripple adder becomes $2n$ units of time. Of course, this is a worst-case condition. However, since normally all signals must complete their propagations through a network before new inputs are applied, this worst-case condition becomes a limiting factor in the network's overall speed of operation. To decrease the time required to perform addition, an effort must be made to speed up the propagation of the carries. One approach for doing this is to reduce the number of logic levels in the path of the propagated carries. Adders designed with this consideration in mind are called *high-speed adders.*

Equations (5.1) and (5.2) are the sum and carry equations for the outputs at the ith stage of a binary adder. As seen by these equations, the sum and carry outputs at a given stage are a function of the output carry from the previous stage, which, in turn, is a function of the output carry from still another previous stage, etc. This corresponds to the undesirable ripple effect. If the input carry at a given stage is expressed in terms of the operand variables themselves, i.e., $x_0, x_1, \ldots, x_{n-1}$ and $y_0, y_1, \ldots, y_{n-1}$, then the ripple effect is eliminated and the overall speed of the adder increased.

To see how this is done, again consider Eq. (5.1) for the output carry at the ith stage, i.e.,

$$\begin{aligned} c_{i+1} &= x_i y_i + x_i c_i + y_i c_i \\ &= x_i y_i + (x_i + y_i) c_i \end{aligned}$$

The first term in the last equation, x_iy_i, is called the *carry-generate function* since it corresponds to the formation of a carry at the ith stage. The second term, $(x_i + y_i)c_i$, corresponds to a previously generated carry c_i that must propagate past the ith stage to the next stage. The $x_i + y_i$ part of this term is called the *carry-propagate function.* Letting the carry-generate function be denoted by the Boolean variable g_i and the carry-propagate function by p_i, i.e.,

$$g_i = x_iy_i \tag{5.3}$$

$$p_i = x_i + y_i \tag{5.4}$$

the output carry equation for the ith stage is given by

$$c_{i+1} = g_i + p_ic_i$$

Using this general result, the output carry at each of the stages can be written in terms of just the carry-generate functions, the carry-propagate functions, and the initial input carry c_0 as follows:

$$c_1 = g_0 + p_0c_0 \tag{5.5}$$

$$\begin{aligned} c_2 &= g_1 + p_1c_1 \\ &= g_1 + p_1(g_0 + p_0c_0) \\ &= g_1 + p_1g_0 + p_1p_0c_0 \end{aligned} \tag{5.6}$$

$$\begin{aligned} c_3 &= g_2 + p_2c_2 \\ &= g_2 + p_2(g_1 + p_1g_0 + p_1p_0c_0) \\ &= g_2 + p_2g_1 + p_2p_1g_0 + p_2p_1p_0c_0 \end{aligned} \tag{5.7}$$

$$\begin{aligned} c_4 &= g_3 + p_3c_3 \\ &= g_3 + p_3(g_2 + p_2g_1 + p_2p_1g_0 + p_2p_1p_0c_0) \\ &= g_3 + p_3g_2 + p_3p_2g_1 + p_3p_2p_1g_0 + p_3p_2p_1p_0c_0 \end{aligned} \tag{5.8}$$

$$\vdots$$

$$c_{i+1} = g_i + p_ig_{i-1} + p_ip_{i-1}g_{i-2} + \cdots + p_ip_{i-1}\cdots p_1g_0 + p_ip_{i-1}\cdots p_0c_0 \tag{5.9}$$

Since each carry-generate function and carry-propagate function is itself only a function of the operand variables as indicated by Eqs. (5.3) and (5.4), the output carry and, correspondingly, the input carry, at each stage can be expressed as a function of the operand variables and the initial input carry c_0. In addition, since the output sum bit at any stage is also a function of the previous stage output carry as indicated by Eq. (5.2), it also can be expressed in terms of just the operand variables and c_0 by the substitution of an appropriate carry equation having the form of Eq. (5.9). Parallel adders whose realizations are based on the above equations are called *carry lookahead adders.* The general organization of a carry lookahead adder is shown in Fig. 5.7*a* where the carry lookahead network corresponds to a logic network based on Eqs. (5.5) to (5.9). The sigma blocks correspond to the logic needed to form the sum bit, the carry-generate function, and the

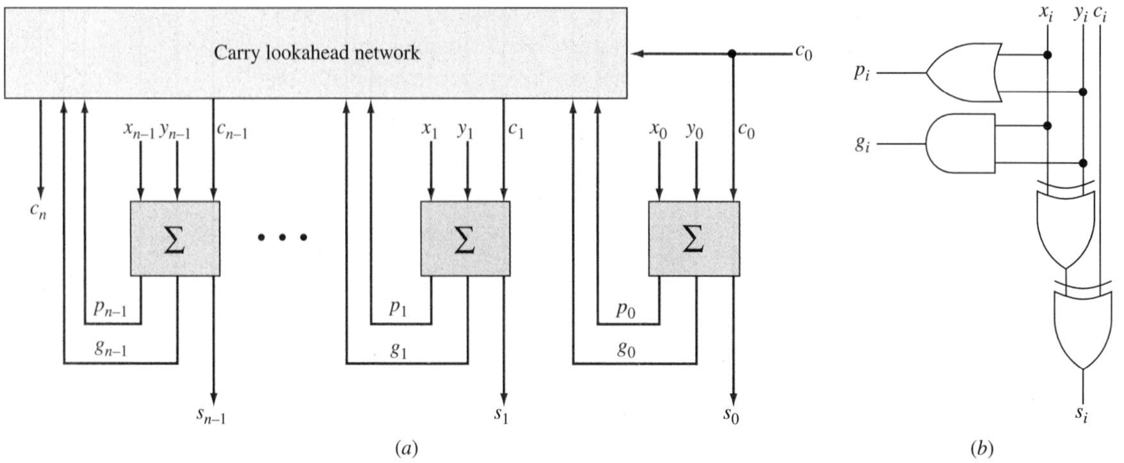

Figure 5.7 A carry lookahead adder. (*a*) General organization. (*b*) Sigma block.

carry-propagate function at each stage. A sigma block based on Eqs. (5.2) to (5.4) is shown in Fig. 5.7*b*.

From the above discussion, the logic diagram of a carry lookahead adder which handles two 4-bit operands is shown in Fig. 5.8. Generalizing from this figure, the path length from the generation of a carry to its appearance as an input at any higher-order stage, i.e., the path length through any stage of the carry lookahead network, is two levels of logic. Thus, with one level of logic to form g_i, two levels of logic for the carry to propagate between any two stages, and one level of logic to have the carry effect a sum output, the maximum propagation delay for a carry lookahead adder is 4 units of time under the assumption that each gate introduces a unit time of propagation delay.

5.1.3 Large High-Speed Adders Using the Carry Lookahead Principle

The basic carry lookahead principle involves minimizing the propagation delay time between the generation of a carry and its utilization at any higher-order stage of an adder. Essentially this is done by having the carry input to each stage be a direct function of the operand bits. Thus, the idea of having sum and carry outputs of the *i*th stage be a function of x_i, y_i, and c_i is replaced by having these outputs be a function of $x_0, x_1, \ldots, x_i, y_0, y_1, \ldots, y_i$, and c_0. In this way, the rippling effect of generated carries to higher-order stages is alleviated.

Although the carry lookahead adder of Fig. 5.8 performs high-speed addition based on the carry lookahead principle, it presents a limitation in the realization of large high-speed adders. The carry lookahead network can get quite large in terms of gates and gate inputs as the number of bits in the operands increases. One approach to circumvent this problem is to divide the bits of the operands into blocks.

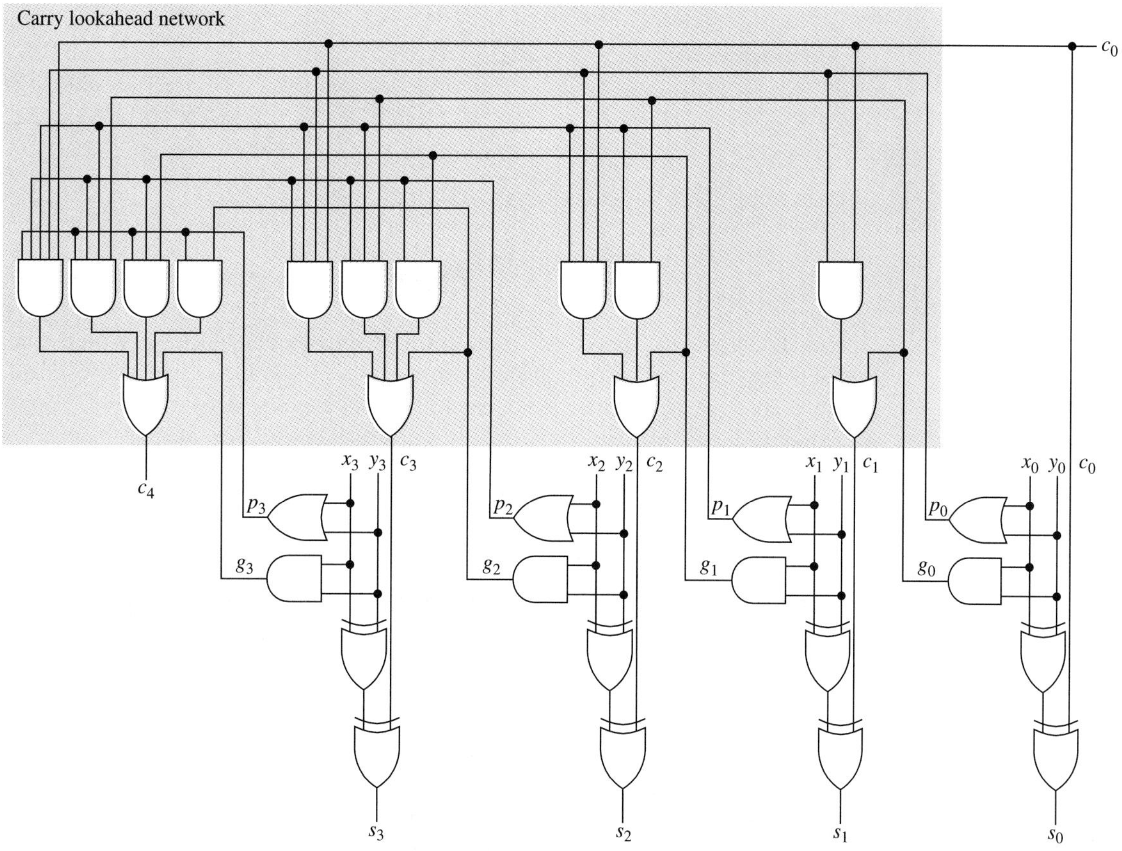

Figure 5.8 A 4-bit carry lookahead adder.

Then, by using carry lookahead adders for each block, their cascade connection results in a large adder. Figure 5.9 illustrates this approach by cascading 4-bit carry lookahead adders. In this case, ripple carries occur between the cascaded 4-bit carry lookahead adders.

Another approach to realizing large high-speed adders again relies on the partitioning of the operands into blocks. However, use is made of generic carry lookahead networks called *carry lookahead generators.* Figure 5.10*a* shows a possible 4-bit carry lookahead generator. It is the same as the first three stages of the carry lookahead network of Fig. 5.8 with two additional outputs G and P, described by the expressions

$$G = g_3 + p_3g_2 + p_3p_2g_1 + p_3p_2p_1g_0$$

and

$$P = p_3p_2p_1p_0$$

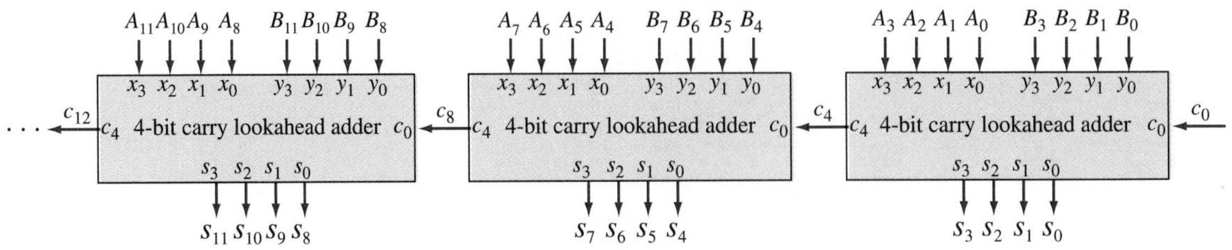

Figure 5.9 Cascade connection of 4-bit carry lookahead adders.

These outputs provide for a block carry-generate signal and a block carry-propagate signal. Using this 4-bit carry lookahead generator, the 16-bit high-speed adder shown in Fig. 5.10*b* is realized where the Σ-blocks correspond to the network of Fig. 5.7*b*.

Both of the above two compromises, i.e., cascading carry lookahead adders or utilizing block carry lookahead generators, result in a large parallel adder much faster than that of the ripple parallel adder.

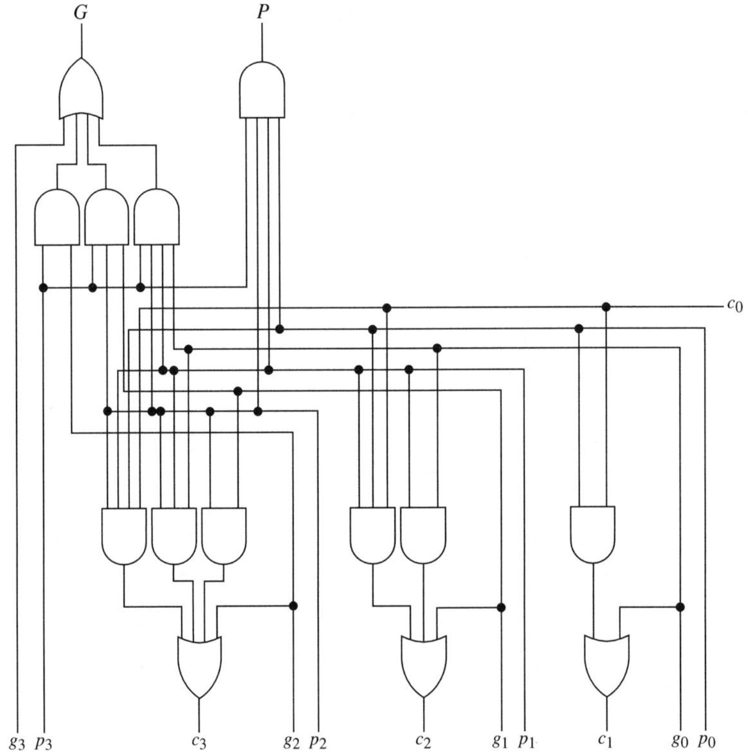

(*a*)

Figure 5.10 (*a*) A carry lookahead generator.

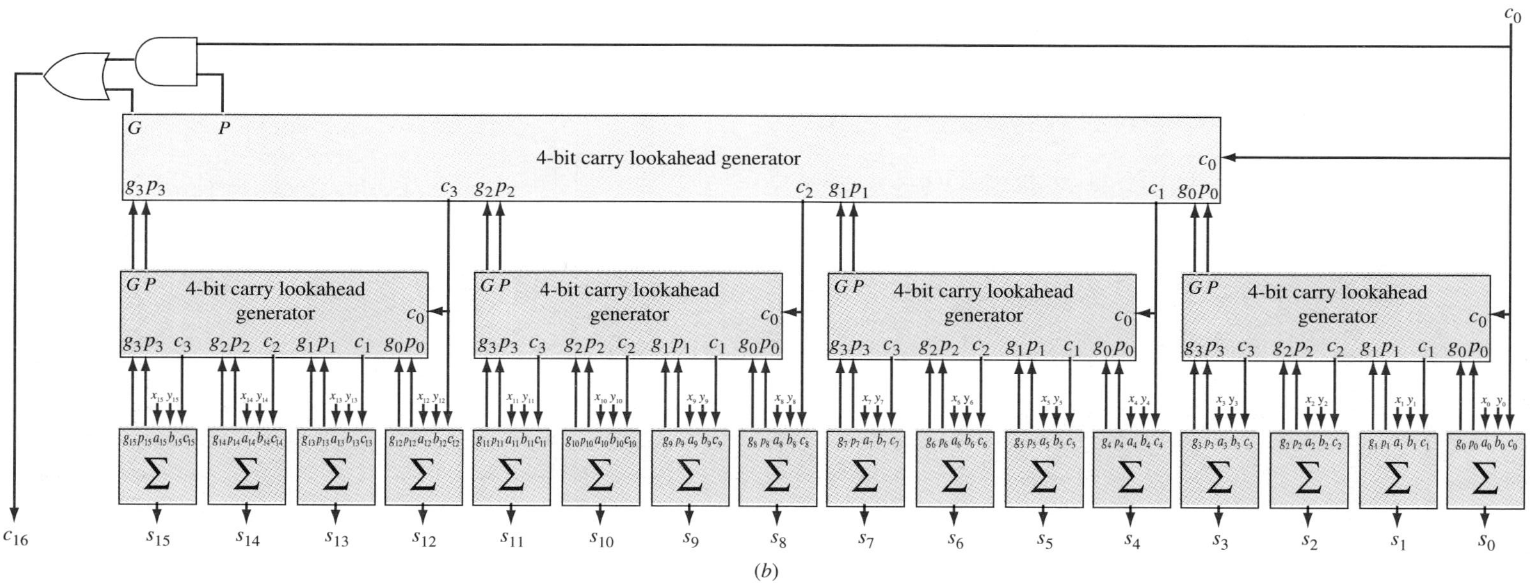

Figure 5.10 (*b*) a 16-bit high-speed adder.

5.2 DECIMAL ADDERS

At times, digital systems are required to handle decimal numbers. As was mentioned in Chapter 2, owing to the availability and reliability of two-valued circuits, the decimal digits are represented by groups of binary digits. Numerous codes for this purpose were given in Sec. 2.10. When performing arithmetic in these digital systems, the system must be capable of accepting the operands in some binary-coded form and producing results also in the same coding scheme.

Again only addition is considered in this section since subtraction can be achieved by means of complements. The use of complements with decimal numbers was also discussed in Chapter 2.

The general form of a single-decade decimal adder, i.e., an adder corresponding to a single-order digit position, is given in Fig. 5.11. In this figure it is assumed that a 4-bit code is used for each decimal digit. Here the two decimal digits serving as operands are denoted by $A_3A_2A_1A_0$ and $B_3B_2B_1B_0$. A carry, denoted by C_{in}, also appears as an input from the addition of the previous decade. The outputs from the adder are a single sum digit, $Z_3Z_2Z_1Z_0$, and a carry, C_{out}. Although the signal values denoting the decimal digits depend upon the code being used, the carries, C_{in} and C_{out}, are only 0 or 1. Thus, only a single line is shown in the figure for each of them.

From Fig. 5.11 it is seen that the five output variables Z_3, Z_2, Z_1, Z_0, and C_{out} are Boolean functions of the nine input variables A_3, A_2, A_1, A_0, B_3, B_2, B_1, B_0, and C_{in}. To design the single-decade adder, a truth table for the output functions can be constructed in which the desired sum digit and output carry are given for each possible pair of input digits and input carry. This truth table has $2^9 = 512$ rows. However, since each of the decimal digits has only 10 code groups and since the carry from the previous decade is only 0 or 1, it follows that the output variables have specified values for only 200 of the 512 rows. Even so, this is an extremely large table with which to work, so an alternate approach should be considered.

The 8421 weighted coding scheme is the most commonly occurring in digital systems and is frequently referred to as simply BCD for binary-coded decimal. When using BCD, a single-decade decimal adder can be constructed by first per-

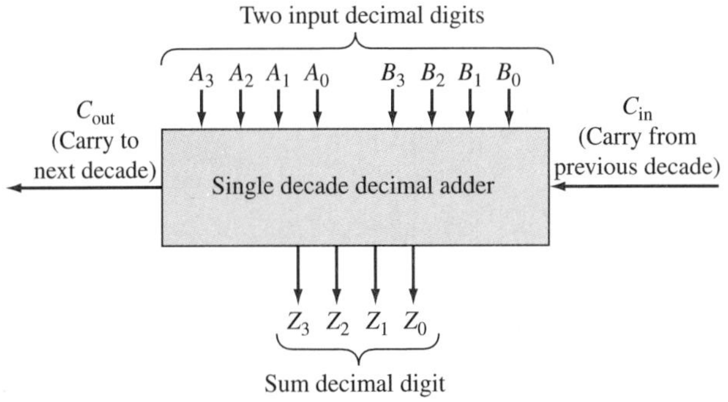

Figure 5.11 Organization of a single-decade decimal adder.

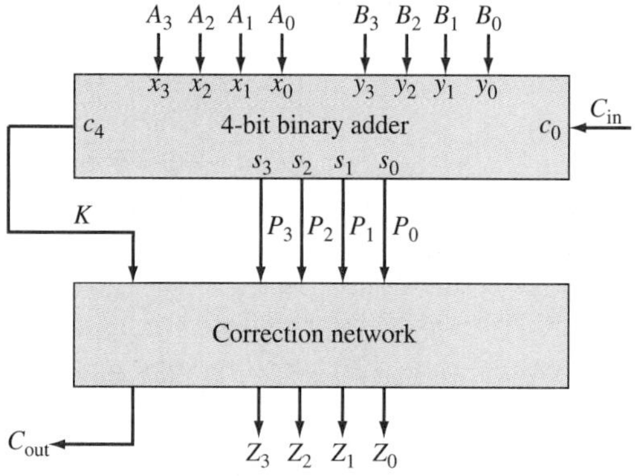

Figure 5.12 Organization of a single-decade BCD adder.

forming conventional binary addition on the two binary-coded operands and then applying a corrective procedure. This approach is illustrated in Fig. 5.12. The code groups for the two decimal digits are added using a 4-bit binary adder as discussed in the previous section to produce intermediate results $KP_3P_2P_1P_0$. These results are then modified so as to obtain the appropriate output carry and code group for the sum digit, i.e., $C_{out}Z_3Z_2Z_1Z_0$. Since each operand digit has a decimal value from 0 to 9 along with the fact that a carry from a previous digit position is at most 1, the decimal sum at each digit position must be in the range from 0 to 19. Table 5.3 summarizes the various outputs from the 4-bit binary adder and the required outputs from the single-decade decimal adder. As shown in the table, if the sum of the two decimal digits and input carry is less than 10, then the code group for the required BCD sum and output carry digits appear at the outputs of the 4-bit binary adder. In this case no corrective procedure is necessary since $KP_3P_2P_1P_0 = C_{out}Z_3Z_2Z_1Z_0$. On the other hand, when the two decimal-digit operands and carry from the previous decade produce an output from the 4-bit binary adder of $KP_3P_2P_1P_0 = 01010$, 01011, . . . , 10011, which corresponds to the decimal sums of 10 through 19, corrective action must be taken to get the appropriate values for $C_{out}Z_3Z_2Z_1Z_0$.

The need for a correction is divided into two cases as indicated by the dashed lines in Table 5.3. Consider first the situation when the decimal sums are in the range from 16 to 19. Here, the outputs from the 4-bit binary adder appear as $KP_3P_2P_1P_0 = 10000$, 10001, 10010, or 10011; while the required outputs from the single-decade decimal adder should be $C_{out}Z_3Z_2Z_1Z_0 = 10110$, 10111, 11000, or 11001, respectively. In each of these cases, it is immediately recognized that the occurrence of the carry K indicates that a carry C_{out} also is necessary. Furthermore, if the binary quantity 0110 is added to the output $P_3P_2P_1P_0$, then the correct sum digit, $Z_3Z_2Z_1Z_0$, is obtained. That is, the addition of a decimal 6, i.e., binary 0110, to the output from the 4-bit binary adder is the necessary correction whenever the carry bit K is 1.

Table 5.3 Comparing binary and BCD sums

Decimal sum	Binary sum					Required BCD sum				
	K	P_3	P_2	P_1	P_0	C_{out}	Z_3	Z_2	Z_1	Z_0
0	0	0	0	0	0	0	0	0	0	0
1	0	0	0	0	1	0	0	0	0	1
2	0	0	0	1	0	0	0	0	1	0
3	0	0	0	1	1	0	0	0	1	1
4	0	0	1	0	0	0	0	1	0	0
5	0	0	1	0	1	0	0	1	0	1
6	0	0	1	1	0	0	0	1	1	0
7	0	0	1	1	1	0	0	1	1	1
8	0	1	0	0	0	0	1	0	0	0
9	0	1	0	0	1	0	1	0	0	1
10	0	1	0	1	0	1	0	0	0	0
11	0	1	0	1	1	1	0	0	0	1
12	0	1	1	0	0	1	0	0	1	0
13	0	1	1	0	1	1	0	0	1	1
14	0	1	1	1	0	1	0	1	0	0
15	0	1	1	1	1	1	0	1	0	1
16	1	0	0	0	0	1	0	1	1	0
17	1	0	0	0	1	1	0	1	1	1
18	1	0	0	1	0	1	1	0	0	0
19	1	0	0	1	1	1	1	0	0	1

Now consider the situation when the output from the 4-bit binary adder corresponds to the decimal sums 10 to 15. These outputs appear as $KP_3P_2P_1P_0 = 01010$, $01011, \ldots, 01111$ and the required outputs are $C_{out}Z_3Z_2Z_1Z_0 = 10000, 10001, \ldots,$ 10101, respectively. In each of these cases, it is necessary to have $C_{out} = 1$ even though $K = 0$. Again it is immediately recognized that the addition of decimal 6, i.e., binary 0110, to the output from the 4-bit binary adder, $P_3P_2P_1P_0$, results in the correct sum digit. That is, whenever the six binary combinations $P_3P_2P_1P_0 = 1010$, $1011, \ldots, 1111$ occur, the corrective procedure is to add the decimal quantity 6. These six binary combinations correspond to the invalid code groups in the 8421 code. To obtain a Boolean expression to detect these six binary combinations, a Karnaugh map is constructed as shown in Fig. 5.13. Obtaining the minimal sum from the map, it is seen that a correction is needed to the binary sum whenever the Boolean expression $P_3P_2 + P_3P_1$ has the value of 1.

In summary, to design a single-decade BCD adder having the organization of Fig. 5.12, the two decimal digits are added as binary numbers. No correction to the binary sum is necessary when $KP_3P_2P_1P_0 \leq 01001$, but the binary equivalent of the decimal 6 must be added to $P_3P_2P_1P_0$ when $KP_3P_2P_1P_0 > 01001$. The Boolean expression describing the need for a correction is

$$\text{Add } 6 = K + P_3P_2 + P_3P_1 \tag{5.10}$$

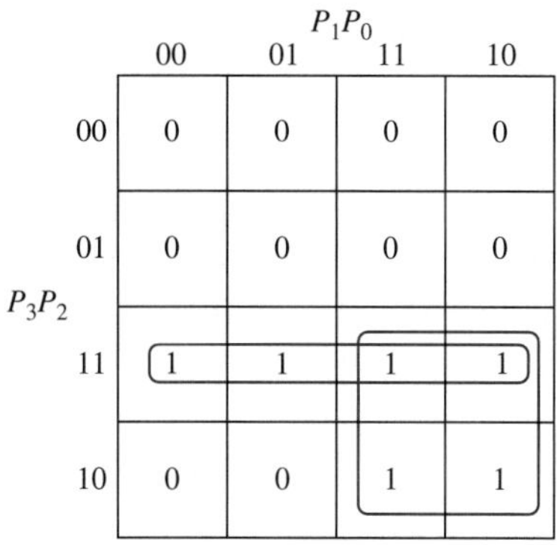

P_1P_0
00
01
11
10
P_3P_2
00
01
11
10
0 0 0 0
0 0 0 0
1 1 1 1
0 0 1 1

Figure 5.13 Karnaugh map to detect the combinations $P_3P_2P_1P_0 = 1010$, 1011, . . . , 1111.

The first term corresponds to the situation when $10000 \leq KP_3P_2P_1P_0 \leq 10011$, i.e., whenever the carry bit K is 1, and the remaining two terms correspond to the situation when $01010 \leq KP_3P_2P_1P_0 \leq 01111$, i.e., whenever the code group for the sum digit is invalid. It is also noted from Table 5.3 that whenever a corrective action is necessary, a carry C_{out} should be sent to the next decade. Thus, Eq. (5.10) also describes the conditions for the generation of a carry. Figure 5.14 shows the logic diagram of

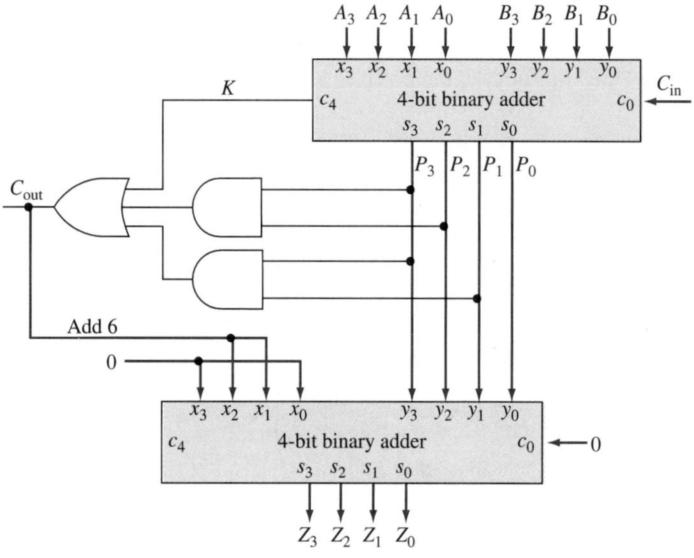

Figure 5.14 A single-decade BCD adder.

a single-decade BCD adder. In this diagram whenever $C_{out} = 0$, the outputs from the upper 4-bit binary adder are sent to the lower 4-bit binary adder and the decimal quantity of zero is added to it, which results in no corrective action. However, whenever $C_{out} = 1$, decimal 6, i.e., binary 0110, is added to the outputs from the upper 4-bit binary adder so that the correct sum digit is obtained.

The above discussion was concerned with the design of a single-decade BCD adder. A decimal adder for two n-digit BCD numbers can be constructed by cascading the network of Fig. 5.14 in much the same way as was done for the ripple binary adder.

5.3 COMPARATORS

A commonly encountered situation in logic design is the need for a network to compare the magnitudes of two binary numbers for the purpose of establishing whether one is greater than, equal to, or less than the other. A conceptually simple approach to the design of such a network, called a *comparator*, makes use of a cascade connection of identical subnetworks in much the same way as was done in the design of the parallel adder.*

To see how such a subnetwork is designed, consider two n-bit binary numbers $A = A_{n-1} \cdots A_iA_{i-1} \cdots A_1A_0$ and $B = B_{n-1} \cdots B_iB_{i-1} \cdots B_1B_0$. For the purpose of this design, assume that only one bit of corresponding order from each number is entering the subnetwork, say, A_i and B_i, and that the two binary numbers are to be analyzed from right to left. This subnetwork is called a *1-bit comparator*. The function of the 1-bit comparator is to establish whether $A_iA_{i-1} \cdots A_1A_0$ is greater than, equal to, or less than $B_iB_{i-1} \cdots B_1B_0$ given the values of A_i, B_i, and whether $A_{i-1} \cdots A_1A_0$ is greater than, equal to, or less than $B_{i-1} \cdots B_1B_0$. The three conditions describing the relative magnitudes of $A_{i-1} \cdots A_1A_0$ and $B_{i-1} \cdots B_1B_0$ are assigned to three variables G_i, E_i, and L_i where $G_i = 1$ denotes $A_{i-1} \cdots A_1A_0 > B_{i-1} \cdots B_1B_0$, $E_i = 1$ denotes $A_{i-1} \cdots A_1A_0 = B_{i-1} \cdots B_1B_0$, and $L_i = 1$ denotes $A_{i-1} \cdots A_1A_0 < B_{i-1} \cdots B_1B_0$. Thus, the 1-bit comparator is a 5-input, 3-output network as shown in Fig. 5.15.

Having obtained the organization of the 1-bit comparator, it is now necessary to develop a rule for specifying the values of G_{i+1}, E_{i+1}, and L_{i+1} given the values of A_i, B_i, G_i, E_i, and L_i. Upon a little thought it should become clear that, regardless of

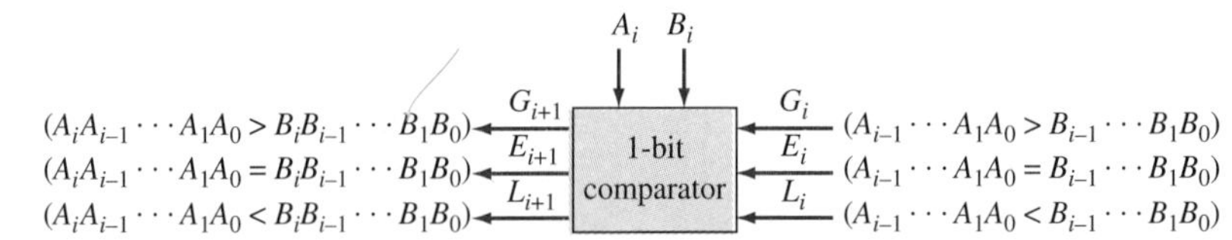

Figure 5.15 Organization of a 1-bit comparator.

*This design of a comparator is another example of an iterative network.

Table 5.4 Truth table for a 1-bit comparator

A_i	B_i	G_i	E_i	L_i	G_{i+1}	E_{i+1}	L_{i+1}	A_i	B_i	G_i	E_i	L_i	G_{i+1}	E_{i+1}	L_{i+1}
0	0	0	0	0	–	–	–	1	0	0	0	0	–	–	–
0	0	0	0	1	0	0	1	1	0	0	0	1	1	0	0
0	0	0	1	0	0	1	0	1	0	0	1	0	1	0	0
0	0	0	1	1	–	–	–	1	0	0	1	1	–	–	–
0	0	1	0	0	1	0	0	1	0	1	0	0	1	0	0
0	0	1	0	1	–	–	–	1	0	1	0	1	–	–	–
0	0	1	1	0	–	–	–	1	0	1	1	0	–	–	–
0	0	1	1	1	–	–	–	1	0	1	1	1	–	–	–
0	1	0	0	0	–	–	–	1	1	0	0	0	–	–	–
0	1	0	0	1	0	0	1	1	1	0	0	1	0	0	1
0	1	0	1	0	0	0	1	1	1	0	1	0	0	1	0
0	1	0	1	1	–	–	–	1	1	0	1	1	–	–	–
0	1	1	0	0	0	0	1	1	1	1	0	0	1	0	0
0	1	1	0	1	–	–	–	1	1	1	0	1	–	–	–
0	1	1	1	0	–	–	–	1	1	1	1	0	–	–	–
0	1	1	1	1	–	–	–	1	1	1	1	1	–	–	–

the relative magnitudes of $A_{i-1} \cdots A_1A_0$ and $B_{i-1} \cdots B_1B_0$, if $A_i = 1$ and $B_i = 0$ then $A_i \cdots A_1A_0 > B_i \cdots B_1B_0$; while if $A_i = 0$ and $B_i = 1$ then $A_i \cdots A_1A_0 < B_i \cdots B_1B_0$. However, if A_i and B_i are the same, then the relative magnitudes of $A_i \cdots A_1A_0$ and $B_i \cdots B_1B_0$ are the same as the relative magnitudes of $A_{i-1} \cdots A_1A_0$ and $B_{i-1} \cdots B_1B_0$. From this analysis, the truth table shown in Table 5.4 is constructed. The large number of don't-care conditions should be noted. This is a consequence of the fact that one and only one of the three variables G_i, E_i, and L_i has the value of logic-1 at any time. The minimal sum Boolean expressions for Table 5.4 are

$$G_{i+1} = A_i\overline{B}_i + A_iG_i + \overline{B}_iG_i$$
$$E_{i+1} = \overline{A}_i\overline{B}_iE_i + A_iB_iE_i$$
$$L_{i+1} = \overline{A}_iB_i + B_iL_i + \overline{A}_iL_i$$

and the corresponding logic network is shown in Fig. 5.16*a*. Cascading n 1-bit comparators, as shown in Fig. 5.16*b*, results in a network capable of determining the relative magnitudes of two n-bit binary numbers A and B. Particular attention should be given to the 1-bit comparator having the bit-pair A_0 and B_0 as inputs. In order to commence the comparison process, it is necessary to indicate that no previous digits exist. This is achieved by assigning the values $E_0 = 1$ and $G_0 = L_0 = 0$ to the first 1-bit comparator.

For the purpose of illustrating the concept of binary comparison, the above discussion was based on the design of a 1-bit comparator. Several MSI comparators are commercially available. A typical commercial comparator provides for 4 bits of each number to be compared within each subnetwork. This allows for a more efficient

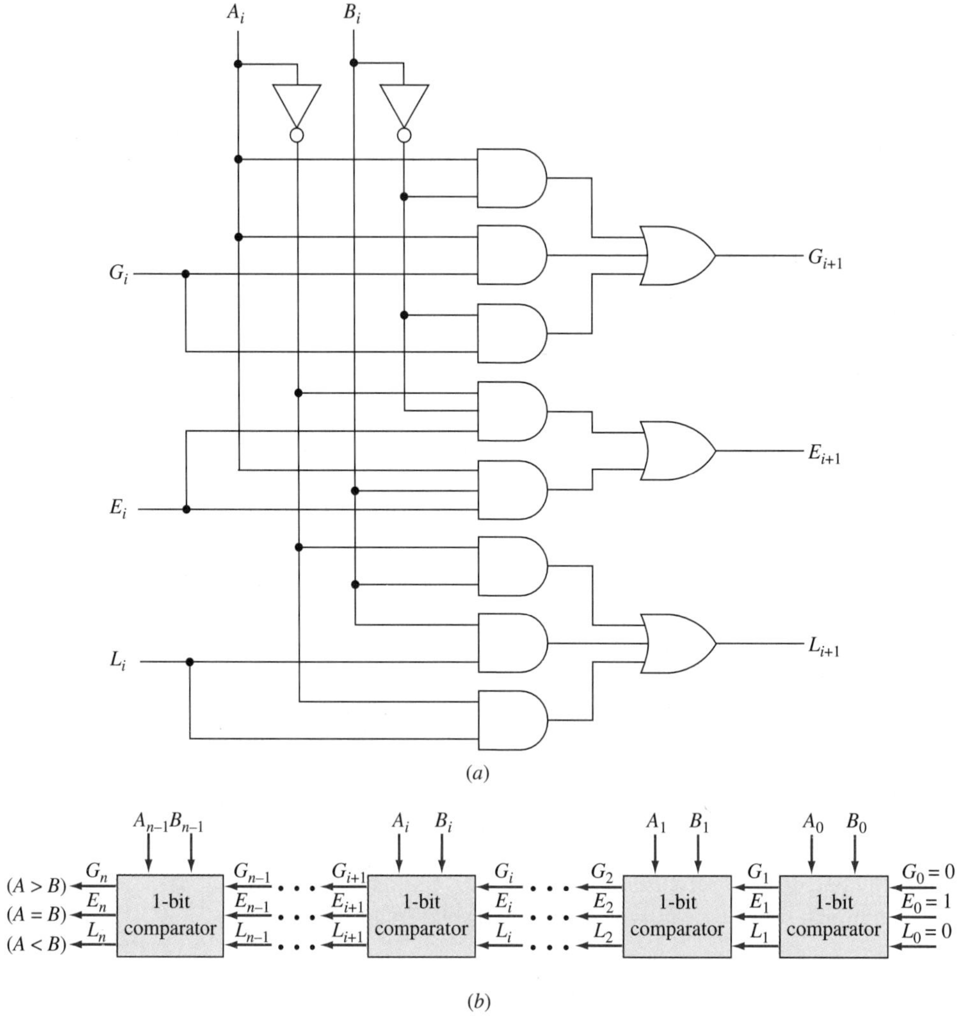

Figure 5.16 Comparing two binary numbers *A* and *B*. (*a*) 1-bit comparator network. (*b*) Cascade connection of 1-bit comparators.

design of the subnetwork. Numbers consisting of more than 4 bits are then compared by cascading these 4-bit comparator subnetworks in the same manner as was illustrated above for the 1-bit comparators.

5.4 DECODERS

Frequently, digital information represented in some binary form must be converted into some alternate binary form. This is achieved by a multiple-input, multiple-output logic network referred to as a *decoder*. The most commonly used decoder is the

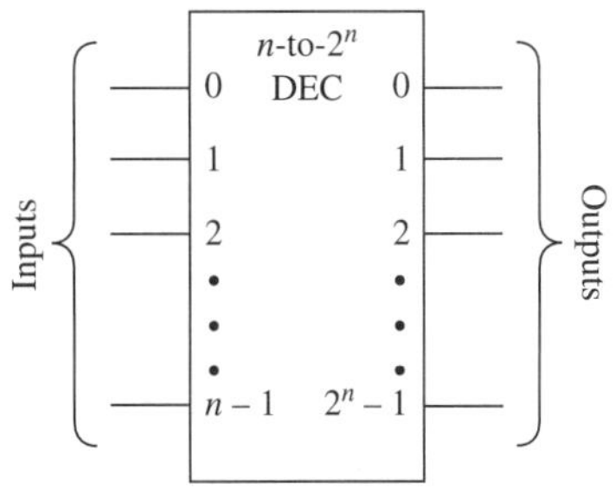

Figure 5.17 An n-to-2^n-line decoder symbol.

n-to-2^n-line decoder. This digital network has n-input lines and 2^n-output lines with the property that only one of the 2^n-output lines responds, say with a logic-1, to a given input combination of values on its n-input lines. A symbol for such a device is shown in Fig. 5.17.

The realization of the n-to-2^n-line decoder is straightforward. Figure 5.18 shows the logic diagram, truth table, and symbol of a 3-to-8-line decoder. In this figure the three input lines are assigned the variables x_0, x_1, and x_2; while the eight output lines are assigned the variables $z_0, z_1, \ldots, z_7$. As shown in the truth table, only one output line responds, i.e., is at logic-1, for each of the input combinations.

To further understand the labels in the symbol of Fig. 5.18*c*, let a binary 0 be associated with a logic-0 and a binary 1 be associated with a logic-1. In addition, let the ith-input line be weighted by 2^i, for $i = 0,1,2$. In this way, the input combinations can be regarded as binary numbers with the consequence that the jth-output line is at logic-1, for $j = 0, 1, \ldots, 7$, only when input combination j is applied.

The n-to-2^n-line decoder is only one of several types of decoders. *Function-specific decoders* exist having fewer than 2^n outputs. For example, a decoder having 4 inputs and 10 outputs in which a single responding output line corresponds to a combination of the 8421 code is referred to as a BCD-to-decimal decoder. There are also function-specific decoders in which more than one output line responds to a given input combination. For example, there is a four-input-line, seven-output-line decoder that accepts the 4 bits of the 8421 code and is used to drive a seven-segment display. However, the n-to-2^n-line decoders are more flexible than the function-specific decoders. It is now shown that they can be used as a general component for logic design.

5.4.1 Logic Design Using Decoders

In Fig. 5.18, the Boolean expressions describing the outputs of the decoder are also written. Each of these output expressions corresponds to a single minterm.

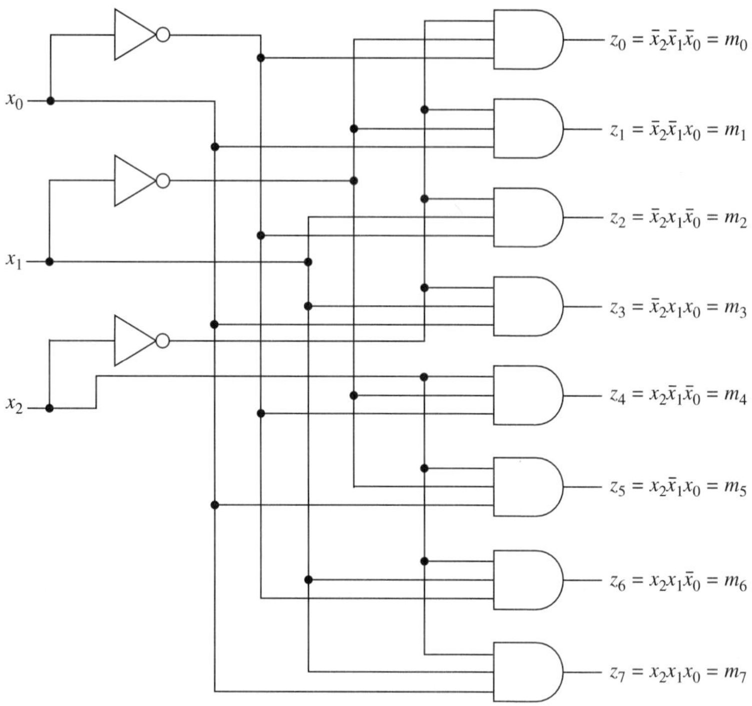

(a)

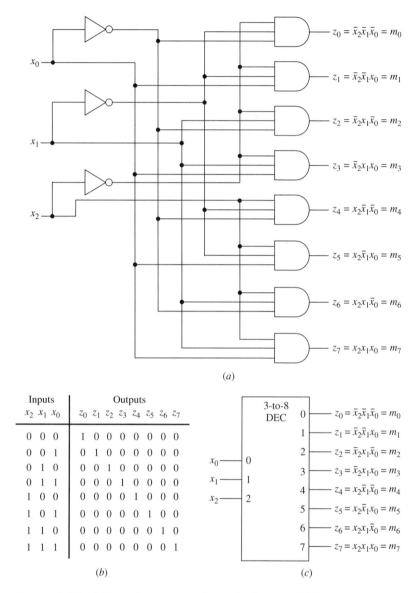

Inputs			Outputs							
x_2	x_1	x_0	z_0	z_1	z_2	z_3	z_4	z_5	z_6	z_7
0	0	0	1	0	0	0	0	0	0	0
0	0	1	0	1	0	0	0	0	0	0
0	1	0	0	0	1	0	0	0	0	0
0	1	1	0	0	0	1	0	0	0	0
1	0	0	0	0	0	0	1	0	0	0
1	0	1	0	0	0	0	0	1	0	0
1	1	0	0	0	0	0	0	0	1	0
1	1	1	0	0	0	0	0	0	0	1

(b)

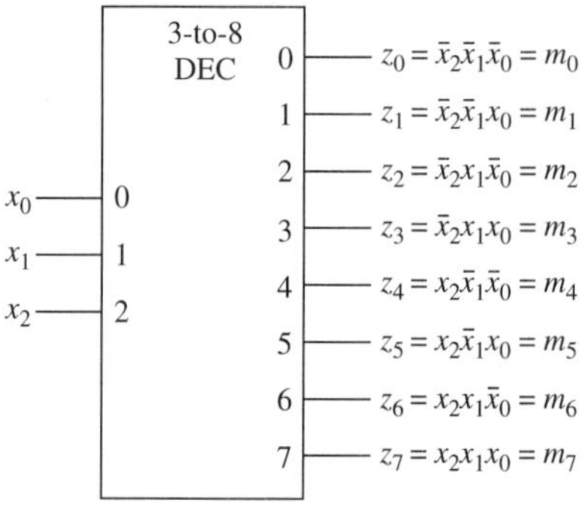

(c)

Figure 5.18 A 3-to-8-line decoder. (*a*) Logic diagram. (*b*) Truth table. (*c*) Symbol.

Hence, an n-to-2^n-line decoder is a *minterm generator*. Recall that any Boolean function is describable by a sum of minterms. Thus, by using or-gates in conjunction with an n-to-2^n-line decoder, realizations of Boolean functions are possible. Although these realizations do not correspond to minimal sum-of-products expressions, the realizations are simple to produce due to the nature of the n-to-2^n-line decoder. This is particularly convenient when several functions of the same variables have to be realized. To illustrate this, consider the pair of expressions

$$f_1(x_2,x_1,x_0) = \Sigma m(1,2,4,5)$$
$$f_2(x_2,x_1,x_0) = \Sigma m(1,5,7)$$

Using a single 3-to-8-line decoder and two or-gates, the realization shown in Fig. 5.19 is immediately obtained.

In the realization of Fig. 5.19, the number of input terminals required of each or-gate is equal to the number of minterms that must be summed by the gate. When more than one-half the total number of minterms must be or-ed, it is usually more convenient to use nor-gates rather than or-gates to perform the summing. This results in a net reduction in the total number of input terminals required of the summing gates. For example, consider the pair of expressions

$$f_1(x_2,x_1,x_0) = \Sigma m(0,1,3,4,5,6)$$
$$f_2(x_2,x_1,x_0) = \Sigma m(1,2,3,4,6)$$

It is possible to realize these expressions with a 3-to-8-line decoder and two or-gates having a total of 11 input terminals between them. However, recalling that the complement of a minterm canonical formula is the sum of those minterms not appearing in the original formula, the complementary expressions are written as

$$\bar{f}_1(x_2,x_1,x_0) = \Sigma m(2,7)$$
$$\bar{f}_2(x_2,x_1,x_0) = \Sigma m(0,5,7)$$

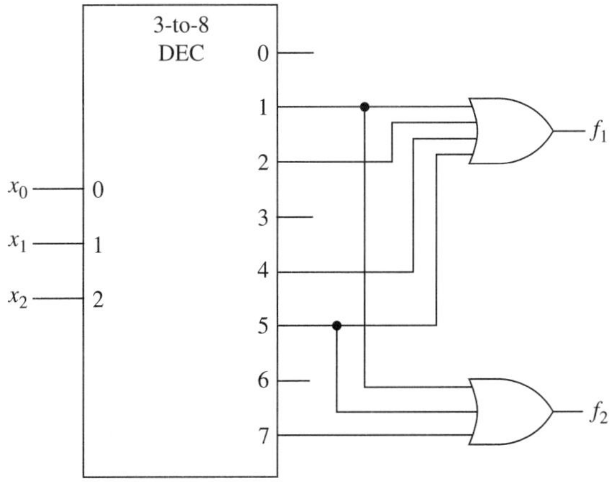

Figure 5.19 Realization of the Boolean expressions $f_1(x_2,x_1,x_0) = \Sigma m(1,2,4,5)$ and $f_2(x_2,x_1,x_0) = \Sigma m(1,5,7)$ with a 3-to-8-line decoder and two or-gates.

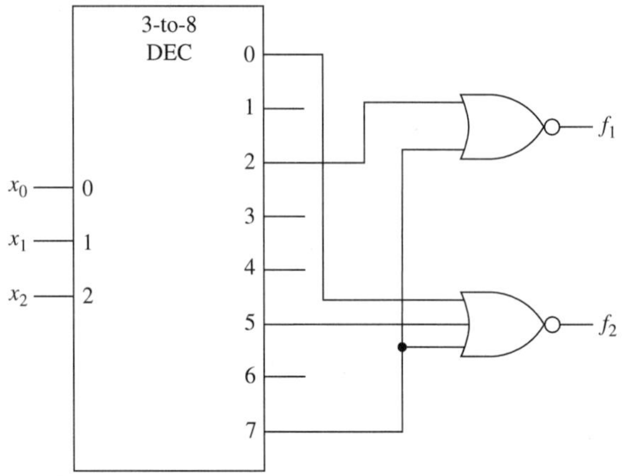

Figure 5.20 Realization of the Boolean expressions $f_1(x_2,x_1,x_0) = \Sigma m(0,1,3,4,5,6) = \overline{\Sigma m(2,7)}$ and $f_2(x_2,x_1,x_0) = \Sigma m(1,2,3,4,6) = \overline{\Sigma m(0,5,7)}$ with a 3-to-8-line decoder and two nor-gates.

Finally, complementing these expressions by DeMorgan's law gives

$$\overline{\overline{f}}_1(x_2,x_1,x_0) = f_1(x_2,x_1,x_0) = \overline{\Sigma m(2,7)}$$
$$\overline{\overline{f}}_2(x_2,x_1,x_0) = f_2(x_2,x_1,x_0) = \overline{\Sigma m(0,5,7)}$$

This final pair of expressions corresponds to the realization shown in Fig. 5.20. Here, a total of only five gate-input terminals are required.

It is also possible to obtain realizations of maxterm canonical formulas using n-to-2^n-line decoders. In Chapter 3 it was shown that any maxterm canonical formula can be converted into an equivalent minterm canonical formula. For example, consider the pair of expressions

$$f_1(x_2,x_1,x_0) = \Pi M(0,1,3,5)$$
$$f_2(x_2,x_1,x_0) = \Pi M(1,3,6,7)$$

Using the transformation technique introduced in Sec. 3.6, these expressions are rewritten as

$$f_1(x_2,x_1,x_0) = \Pi M(0,1,3,5) = \Sigma m(2,4,6,7)$$
$$f_2(x_2,x_1,x_0) = \Pi M(1,3,6,7) = \Sigma m(0,2,4,5)$$

These expressions lead to the realization shown in Fig. 5.21*a*. Alternately, from the above discussion on using nor-gates as summing devices, the expressions can also be written as

$$f_1(x_2,x_1,x_0) = \Pi M(0,1,3,5) = \overline{\Sigma m(0,1,3,5)}$$
$$f_2(x_2,x_1,x_0) = \Pi M(1,3,6,7) = \overline{\Sigma m(1,3,6,7)}$$

which suggests the realization of Fig. 5.21*b*.

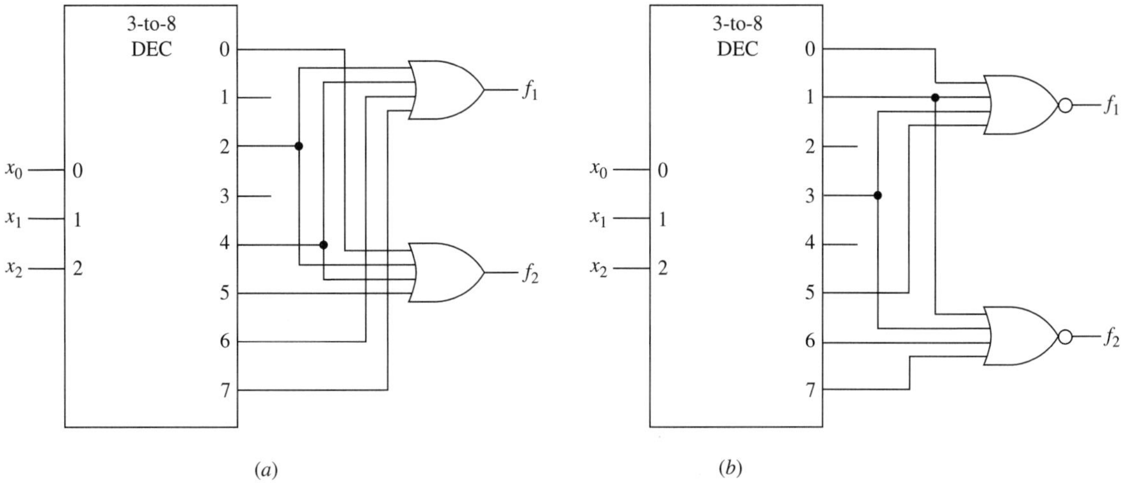

Figure 5.21 A decoder realization of $f_1(x_2,x_1,x_0) = \Pi M(0,1,3,5)$ and $f_2(x_2,x_1,x_0) = \Pi M(1,3,6,7)$. (*a*) Using output or-gates. (*b*) Using output nor-gates.

Frequently, n-to-2^n-line decoders are constructed from nand-gates. An example of a 3-to-8-line decoder using nand-gates, along with its truth table and symbol, is shown in Fig. 5.22. The Boolean expressions of the outputs are also given in the figure. In this case, for each input combination the single responding output line is associated with a logic-0, as is readily seen by the truth table. Since each output is logic-0 for only one input combination, it follows that each output is describable by a single maxterm. Thus, a nand-gate realization of a decoder is a *maxterm generator.* Particular attention should be given to the output terminals in the symbol of the decoder where bubble notation is used to indicate complementation is occurring. It should also be recalled from Sec. 3.6 that $\overline{m_i} = M_i$.

Since any Boolean function is describable by a product of maxterms, a nand-gate decoder, along with an and-gate, can serve as the basis of a maxterm canonical formula realization. For example, the realization of the pair of maxterm canonical expressions

$$f_1(x_2,x_1,x_0) = \Pi M(0,3,5)$$
$$f_2(x_2,x_1,x_0) = \Pi M(2,3,4)$$

is shown in Fig. 5.23.

When more than one-half of the total possible maxterms occur in a Boolean expression, the output and-gate can be replaced by a nand-gate so as to reduce the number of inputs needed to the output gate. To illustrate this, consider the pair of expressions

$$f_1(x_2,x_1,x_0) = \Pi M(0,1,3,4,7)$$
$$f_2(x_2,x_1,x_0) = \Pi M(1,2,3,4,5,6)$$

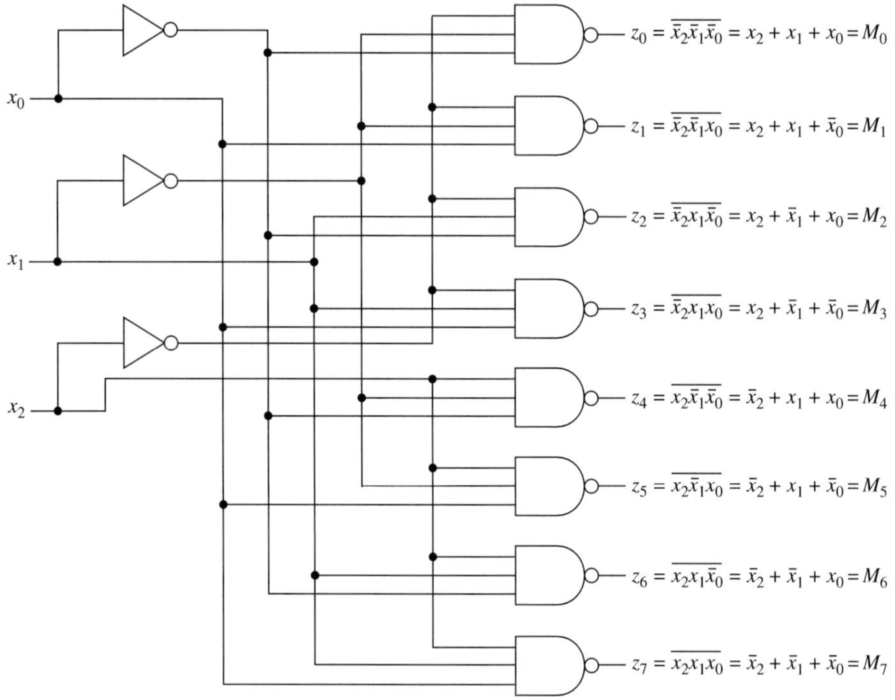

(a)

Inputs			Outputs							
x_2	x_1	x_0	z_0	z_1	z_2	z_3	z_4	z_5	z_6	z_7
0	0	0	0	1	1	1	1	1	1	1
0	0	1	1	0	1	1	1	1	1	1
0	1	0	1	1	0	1	1	1	1	1
0	1	1	1	1	1	0	1	1	1	1
1	0	0	1	1	1	1	0	1	1	1
1	0	1	1	1	1	1	1	0	1	1
1	1	0	1	1	1	1	1	1	0	1
1	1	1	1	1	1	1	1	1	1	0

(b)

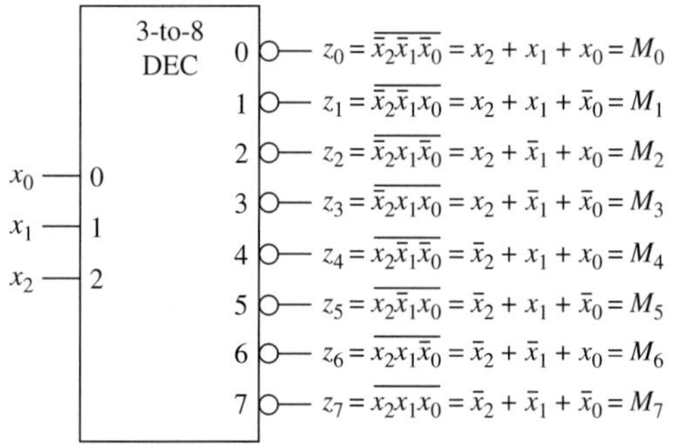

(c)

Figure 5.22 A 3-to-8-line decoder using nand-gates. (*a*) Logic diagram. (*b*) Truth table. (*c*) Symbol.

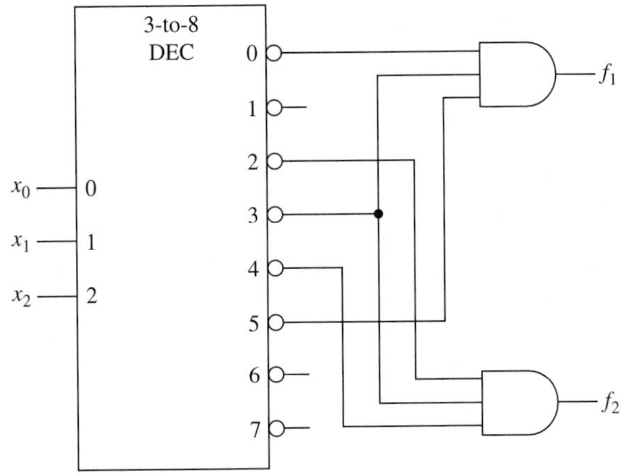

Figure 5.23 Realization of the pair of maxterm canonical expressions $f_1(x_2,x_1,x_0) = \Pi M(0,3,5)$ and $f_2(x_2,x_1,x_0) = \Pi M(2,3,4)$ with a 3-to-8-line decoder and two and-gates.

Using the fact that the complement of a maxterm canonical formula is the product of those maxterms not appearing in the original formula, the complementary formulas are

$$\overline{f}_1(x_2,x_1,x_0) = \Pi M(2,5,6)$$
$$\overline{f}_2(x_2,x_1,x_0) = \Pi M(0,7)$$

Complementing both sides of each equation results in

$$\overline{\overline{f}}_1(x_2,x_1,x_0) = f_1(x_2,x_1,x_0) = \overline{\Pi M(2,5,6)}$$
$$\overline{\overline{f}}_2(x_2,x_1,x_0) = f_2(x_2,x_1,x_0) = \overline{\Pi M(0,7)}$$

These expressions suggest the realization of Fig. 5.24.

Although the nand-gate version of an n-to-2^n-line decoder is a maxterm generator, it can also be used to realize expressions in minterm canonical form. This is done by simply transforming the minterm canonical formula into its equivalent maxterm canonical formula, as was discussed in Sec. 3.6. Again, either and-gates or nand-gates are used to collect the maxterms. For example, the pair of minterm canonical formulas

$$f_1(x_2,x_1,x_0) = \Sigma m(0,2,6,7)$$
$$f_2(x_2,x_1,x_0) = \Sigma m(3,5,6,7)$$

can be written as

$$f_1(x_2,x_1,x_0) = \Sigma m(0,2,6,7) = \Pi M(1,3,4,5)$$
$$f_2(x_2,x_1,x_0) = \Sigma m(3,5,6,7) = \Pi M(0,1,2,4)$$

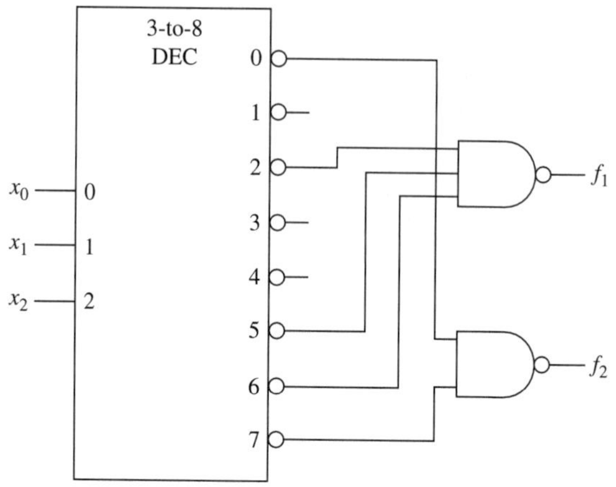

Figure 5.24 Realization of the Boolean expressions $f_1(x_2,x_1,x_0) = \Pi M(0,1,3,4,7) = \overline{\Pi M(2,5,6)}$ and $f_2(x_2,x_1,x_0) = \Pi M(1,2,3,4,5,6) = \overline{\Pi M(0,7)}$ with a 3-to-8-line decoder and two nand-gates.

which has the realization shown in Fig. 5.25*a*, or written as

$$f_1(x_2,x_1,x_0) = \Sigma m(0,2,6,7) = \overline{\Pi M(0,2,6,7)}$$
$$f_2(x_2,x_1,x_0) = \Sigma m(3,5,6,7) = \overline{\Pi M(3,5,6,7)}$$

which has the realization shown in Fig. 5.25*b*.

5.4.2 Decoders with an Enable Input

Normally decoders have one or more additional input lines that are referred to as *enable inputs.* This is illustrated in Fig. 5.26, where a single enable input, E, is used in an and-gate realization of a 2-to-4-line decoder and in Fig. 5.27, where a single enable input, $\overline{E}$, is used in a nand-gate realization of a 2-to-4-line decoder. In each figure, a truth table and symbol are included. These truth tables are said to be *compressed* since not all input combinations explicitly appear. In compressed truth tables the ×'s indicate don't-care conditions. In this way, several rows of a normal truth table are replaced by a single row in a compressed truth table.

To function as the previously explained decoders, a logic-1 is applied to the enable input E of the decoder in Fig. 5.26; while in Fig. 5.27 a logic-0 is applied to the enable input $\overline{E}$. In such cases, the decoders are said to be *enabled.* On the other hand, when the enable inputs are such as to prevent the decoding process, the decoders are said to be *disabled.* In the case of Fig. 5.26, all outputs of the decoder are at logic-0 when it is disabled; while in the case of Fig. 5.27, all outputs of the decoder are at logic-1 when it is disabled. Particular attention should be given to the symbol of Fig. 5.27*c*, where the bubble on the enable input line indicates that the decoder is enabled when the input on this line is at logic-0.

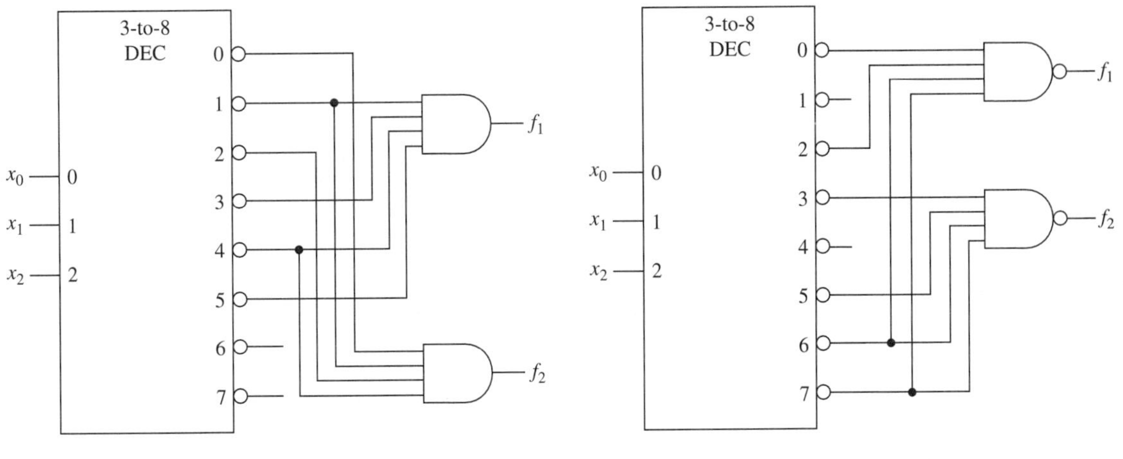

(*a*) (*b*)

Figure 5.25 A decoder realization of $f_1(x_2,x_1,x_0) = \Sigma m(0,2,6,7)$ and $f_2(x_2,x_1,x_0) = \Sigma m(3,5,6,7)$. (*a*) Using output and-gates. (*b*) Using output nand-gates.

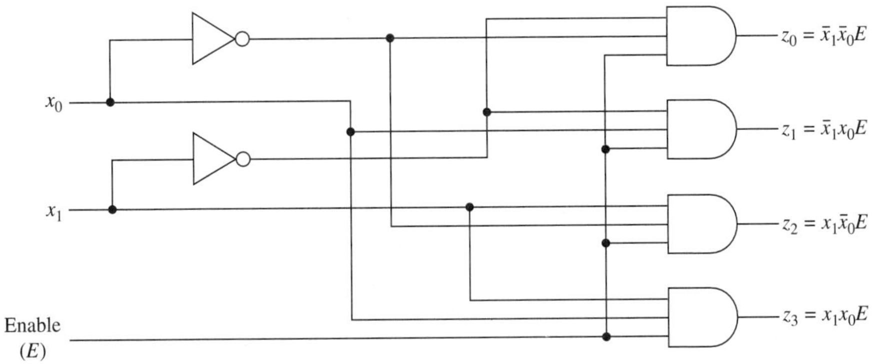

(*a*)

Inputs E	x_1	x_0	Outputs z_0	z_1	z_2	z_3
0	×	×	0	0	0	0
1	0	0	1	0	0	0
1	0	1	0	1	0	0
1	1	0	0	0	1	0
1	1	1	0	0	0	1

(*b*)

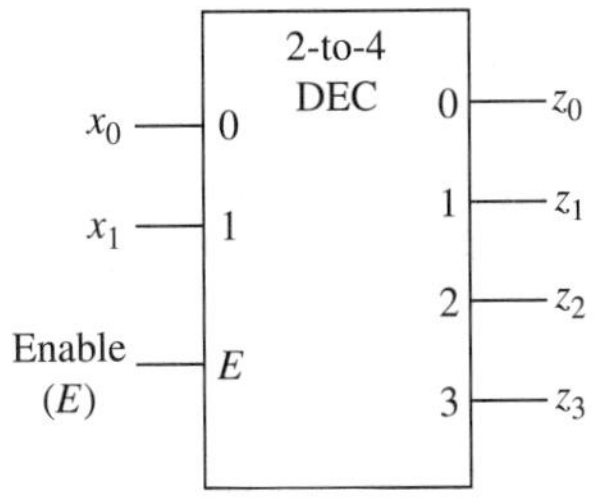

(*c*)

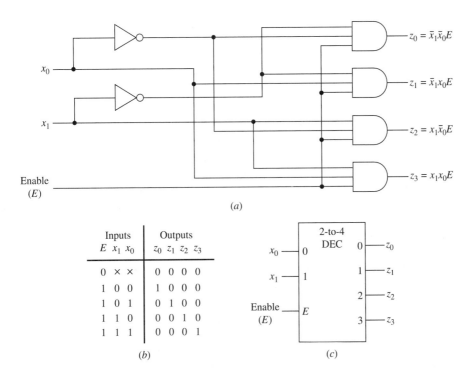

Figure 5.26 And-gate 2-to-4-line decoder with an enable input. (*a*) Logic diagram. (*b*) Compressed truth table. (*c*) Symbol.

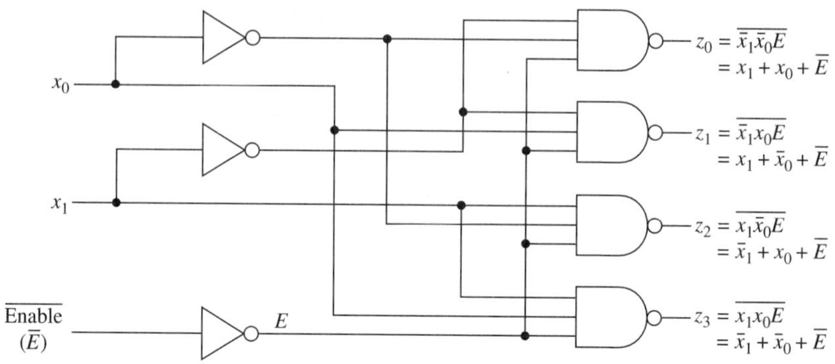

(*a*)

Inputs $\bar{E}$	x_1	x_0	Outputs z_0	z_1	z_2	z_3
0	0	0	0	1	1	1
0	0	1	1	0	1	1
0	1	0	1	1	0	1
0	1	1	1	1	1	0
1	×	×	1	1	1	1

(*b*)

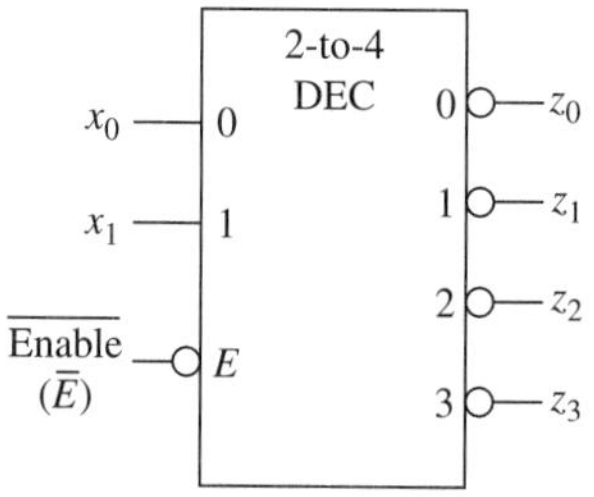

(*c*)

Figure 5.27 Nand-gate 2-to-4-line decoder with an enable input. (*a*) Logic diagram. (*b*) Compressed truth table. (*c*) Symbol.

The enable input provides the decoder with additional flexibility. For example, suppose a digital network is to be designed which accepts data information and must channel it to one of four outputs. This is achieved using a decoder in the configuration shown in Fig. 5.28. Here, the data are applied to the enable input. By entering a binary combination on the other two input lines, labeled as *select lines* in the figure, precisely one output line is selected to receive the information appearing on the data input line. In particular, if $x_1 = 0$ and $x_0 = 1$, then the output line labeled

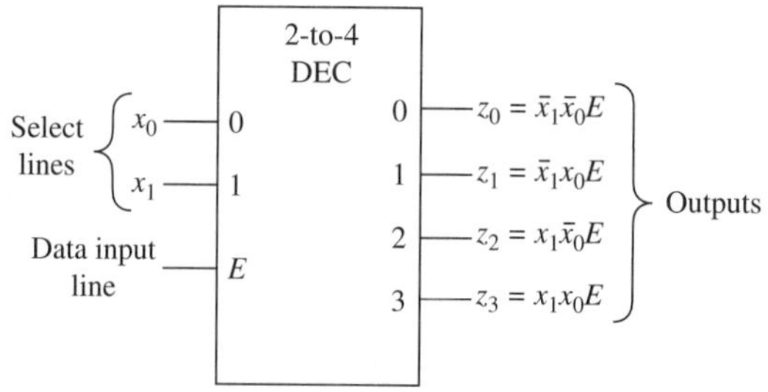

Figure 5.28 Demultiplexer.

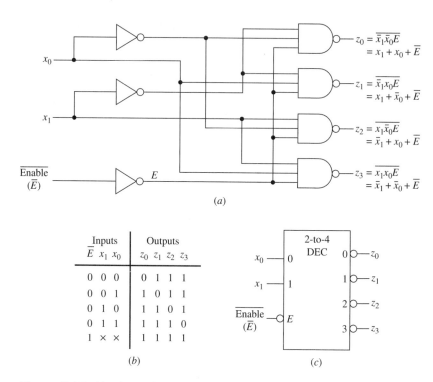

1, which is described by the Boolean expression $\bar{x}_1 x_0 E$, corresponds to $\bar{0} \cdot 1 \cdot E = E$ and hence follows the data on the input line E; i.e., the output line z_1 has the same bit value as on the data input line E. All the other output lines are at logic-0 during this time. This process is known as *demultiplexing*. For this reason, decoders with enable inputs are also referred to as *decoders/demultiplexers.*

Decoders with enable inputs are also used to construct larger decoders from smaller decoders. An example of this is shown in Fig. 5.29, where all the decoder

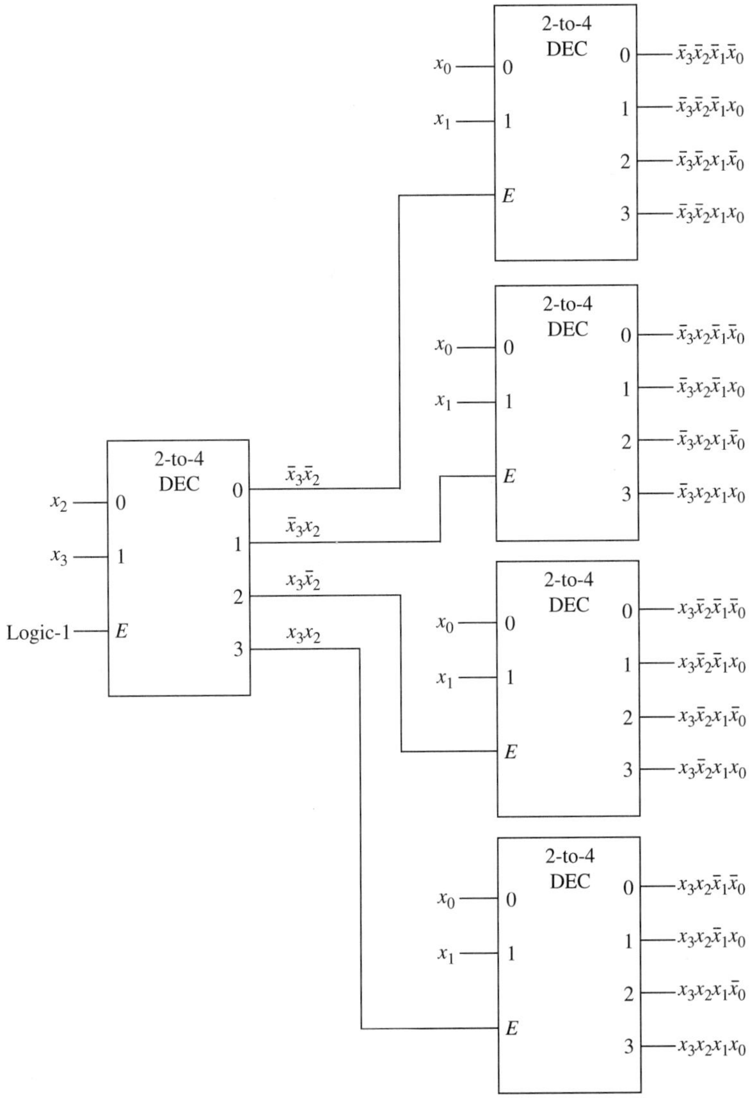

Figure 5.29 A 4-to-16-line decoder constructed from 2-to-4-line decoders.

output lines are labeled with their corresponding Boolean expressions. Here the first-level decoder is used to generate the four combinations of the x_2 and x_3 variables since $E = 1$. Each of these combinations is applied to the enable input at a second-level decoder that introduces the four combinations of the x_0 and x_1 variables. The net result is a network that generates the 16 minterms of four variables or, equivalently, serves as a 4-to-16-line decoder.

5.5 ENCODERS

Like decoders, *encoders* also provide for the conversion of binary information from one form to another. Encoders are essentially the inverse of decoders. Normally decoders have more output lines than input lines. On the other hand, decoders that have more input lines than output lines are usually called encoders.

Perhaps the simplest encoder is the *2^n-to-n-line encoder* in which an assertive logic value*, say, logic-1, on one of its 2^n input lines causes the corresponding binary code to appear at the output lines. If it is assumed that at most one input line is asserted at any time, then the 2^n-to-n-line encoder is simply a collection of or-gates. Figure 5.30 shows a 2^n-to-n-line encoder symbol and Fig. 5.31 shows the logic diagram for an 8-to-3-line encoder. The equations for the three outputs of Fig. 5.31 are

$$z_0 = x_1 + x_3 + x_5 + x_7$$
$$z_1 = x_2 + x_3 + x_6 + x_7$$
$$z_2 = x_4 + x_5 + x_6 + x_7$$

In general, the Boolean expression for the output z_i is the sum of each input x_j in which the binary representation of j has a 1 in the 2^i-bit position.

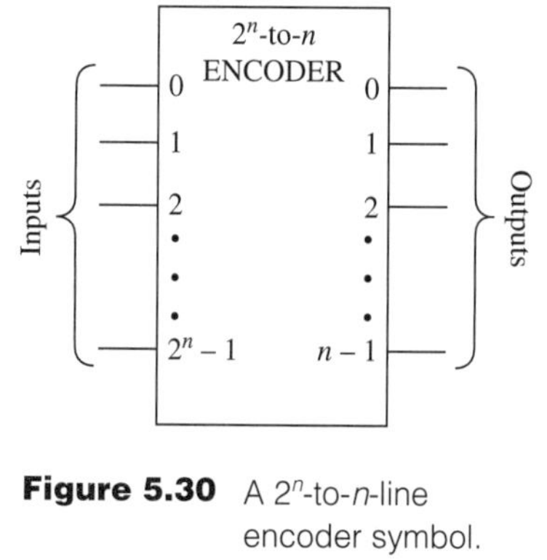

Figure 5.30 A 2^n-to-n-line encoder symbol.

*When a named input signal to a logic network is to cause an action when at logic-1, the signal is said to be *active high.* Similarly, when a named input signal to a logic network is to cause an action when at logic-0, the signal is said to be *active low.* When a signal is at its active level, it is said to be *asserted.*

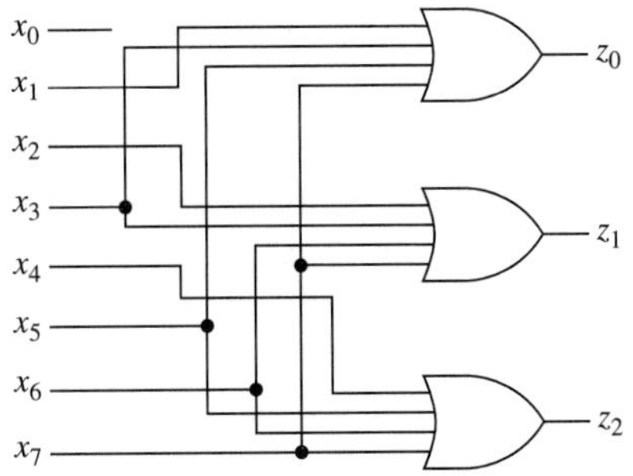

Figure 5.31 An 8-to-3-line encoder.

The assumption that at most a single input to the 2^n-to-n-line encoder is asserted at any time is significant in its operation. For example, in the encoder of Fig. 5.31, assume that both x_3 and x_5 are simultaneously logic-1. Logic-1's then appear at all three output terminals, implying that x_7 must have been logic-1. For this reason, *priority encoders* have been developed. In a priority encoder, a priority scheme is assigned to the input lines so that whenever more than one input line is asserted at any time, the output is determined by the input line having the highest priority. For example, Table 5.5 is a compressed truth table specifying the behavior of a priority encoder where the output is determined by the asserted input having the highest index, i.e., x_i has higher priority than x_j if $i > j$. Thus, referring to Table 5.5, if $x_4 = x_5 = x_6 = x_7 = 0$ and $x_3 = 1$, then $z_2z_1z_0 = 011$ regardless of the values of the x_0, x_1, and x_2 inputs.

An output is also included in Table 5.5, labeled *valid*, to indicate that at least one input line is asserted. This is done so as to distinguish the situation that no input line is asserted from when the x_0 input line is asserted, since in both cases $z_2z_1z_0 = 000$.

Table 5.5 Compressed truth table for an 8-to-3 line priority encoder

Inputs								Outputs			
x_0	x_1	x_2	x_3	x_4	x_5	x_6	x_7	z_2	z_1	z_0	Valid
0	0	0	0	0	0	0	0	0	0	0	0
1	0	0	0	0	0	0	0	0	0	0	1
×	1	0	0	0	0	0	0	0	0	1	1
×	×	1	0	0	0	0	0	0	1	0	1
×	×	×	1	0	0	0	0	0	1	1	1
×	×	×	×	1	0	0	0	1	0	0	1
×	×	×	×	×	1	0	0	1	0	1	1
×	×	×	×	×	×	1	0	1	1	0	1
×	×	×	×	×	×	×	1	1	1	1	1

5.6 MULTIPLEXERS

Another very useful MSI device is the *multiplexer.* Multiplexers are also called *data selectors.* The basic function of this device is to select one of its 2^n *data input lines* and place the corresponding information appearing on this line onto a single output line. Since there are 2^n data input lines, n bits are needed to specify which input line is to be selected. This is achieved by placing the binary code for a desired data input line onto its n *select input lines.* A symbol for a 2^n-to-1-line multiplexer is shown in Fig. 5.32. Typically an *enable*, or *strobe*, *line* is also included to provide greater flexibility as in the case of decoders. The multiplexer shown in Fig. 5.32 is enabled by applying a logic-1 to the E input terminal. Some commercial multiplexers require a logic-0 for enabling. In such a case an inversion bubble appears in the symbol at the E input terminal.

A realization of a 4-to-1-line multiplexer is given in Fig. 5.33 along with its compressed truth table and symbol. The $\times$'s in the compressed truth table denote irrelevant, i.e., don't-care, conditions. As shown in the figure, each data input line I_i goes to its own and-gate. The select lines are used to uniquely select one of the and-gates. Thus, if the multiplexer is enabled, then the output corresponds to the value on the data input line of the selected and-gate. As in the case of decoders, the 0-1 combinations on the select lines are regarded as binary numbers. The decimal equivalents of these numbers determine which data input lines are selected and serve to identify the corresponding input terminals in the symbol.

Table 5.6 provides an alternate description of the behavior of the 4-to-1-line multiplexer. This description is frequently referred to as a *function table.* Here, rather than listing the functional values on the output lines, the input that appears at the output is listed for each combination of values on the select lines. Again a $\times$ in the table indicates an irrelevant condition. From either the logic diagram or function table, an algebraic description of the multiplexer can immediately be written as

$$f = (I_0\bar{S}_1\bar{S}_0 + I_1\bar{S}_1S_0 + I_2S_1\bar{S}_0 + I_3S_1S_0)E \tag{5.11}$$

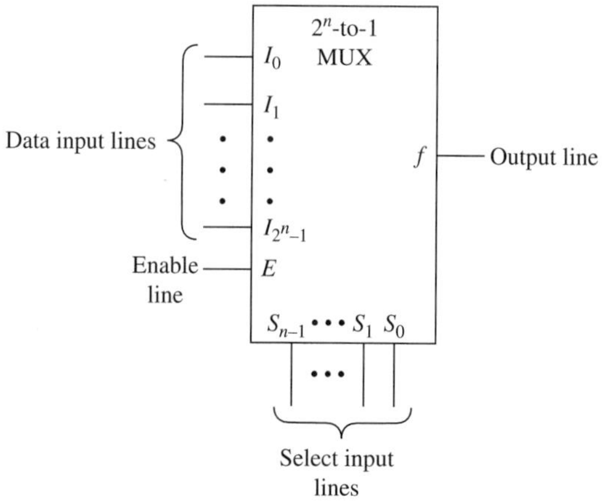

Figure 5.32 A 2^n-to-1-line multiplexer symbol.

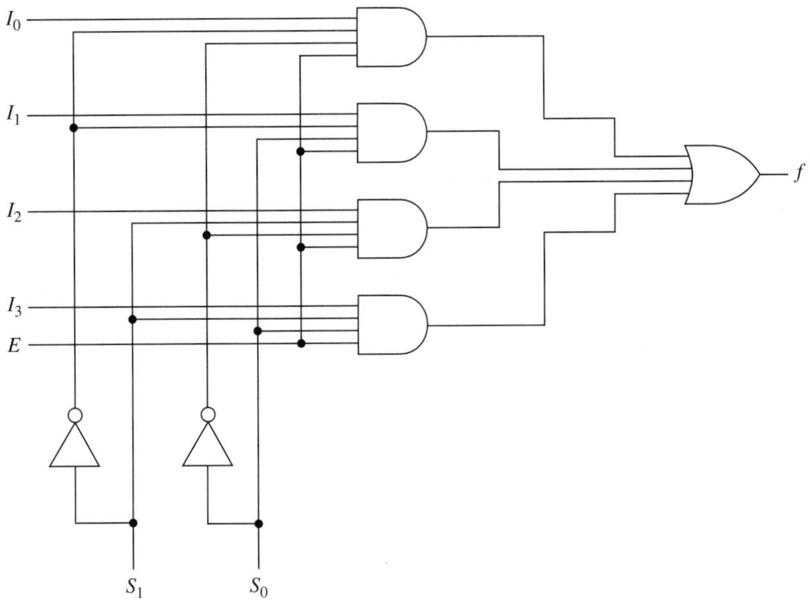

(*a*)

E	S_1	S_0	I_0	I_1	I_2	I_3	f
0	×	×	×	×	×	×	0
1	0	0	0	×	×	×	0
1	0	0	1	×	×	×	1
1	0	1	×	0	×	×	0
1	0	1	×	1	×	×	1
1	1	0	×	×	0	×	0
1	1	0	×	×	1	×	1
1	1	1	×	×	×	0	0
1	1	1	×	×	×	1	1

(*b*)

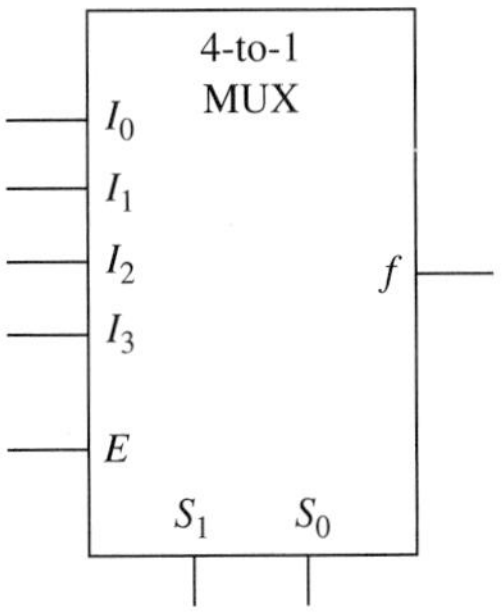

(*c*)

Figure 5.33 A 4-to-1-line multiplexer. (*a*) Logic diagram. (*b*) Compressed truth table. (*c*) Symbol.

Table 5.6 Function table for a 4-to-1-line multiplexer

E	S_1	S_0	f
0	×	×	0
1	0	0	I_0
1	0	1	I_1
1	1	0	I_2
1	1	1	I_3

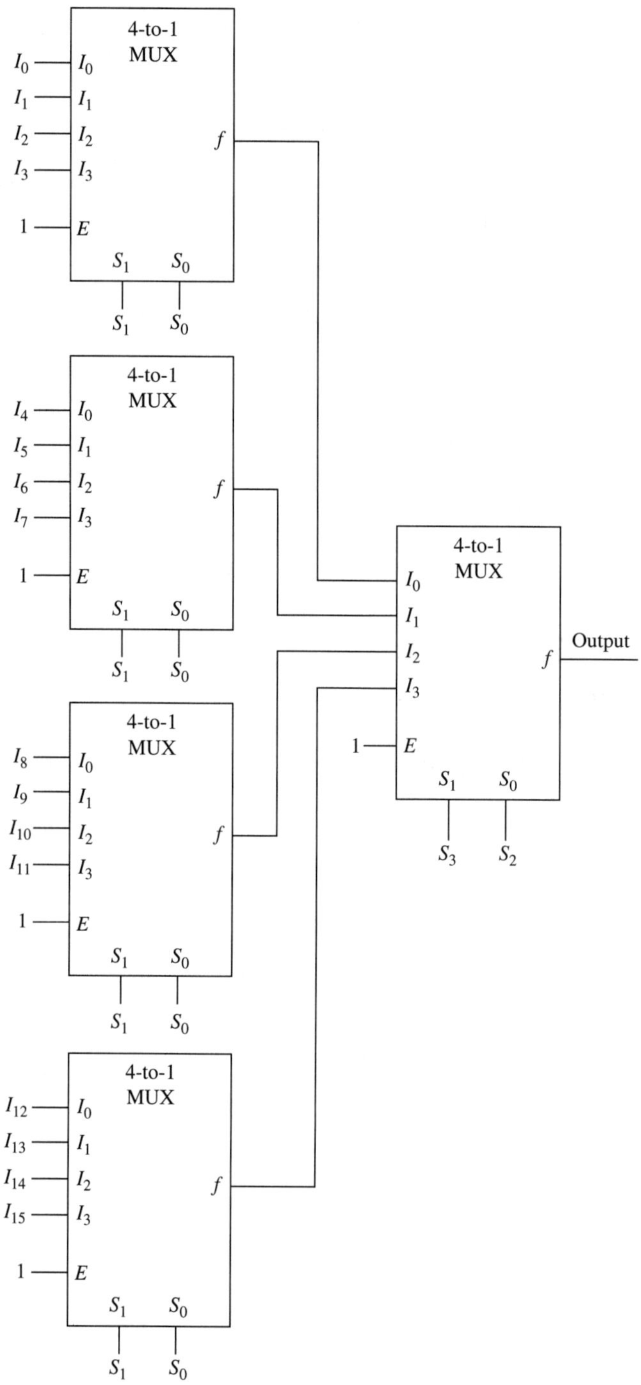

Figure 5.34 A multiplexer tree to form a 16-to-1-line multiplexer.

In addition to the 4-to-1-line multiplexer shown in Fig. 5.33, 2-to-1-line, 8-to-1-line, and 16-to-1-line multiplexers are also commercially available. By interconnecting several multiplexers in a treelike structure, it is possible to produce a larger multiplexer. For example, Fig. 5.34 illustrates how five 4-to-1-line multiplexers are used to construct a 16-to-1-line multiplexer. Particular attention should be given to the select lines. As a 16-to-1-line multiplexer, there are four select inputs S_3, S_2, S_1, and S_0. It should be noted that S_3 is the most significant select line in that its input is most heavily weighted when viewed as a binary digit; while S_0 is the least significant select line. In this way, if i is the binary combination on the $S_3S_2S_1S_0$-lines, then data line I_i is selected to appear at the output. In actuality, the S_1S_0-inputs select one data input from each of the first-level multiplexers. The second-level multiplexer, via its S_3S_2-lines, then selects which data input reaches the output of the multiplexer tree.

One of the primary applications of multiplexers is to provide for the transmission of information from several sources over a single path. This process is known as *multiplexing*. When a multiplexer is used in conjunction with a demultiplexer, i.e., a decoder with an enable input, an effective means is provided for connecting information from several source locations to several destination locations. This basic application of multiplexers and demultiplexers is illustrated in Fig. 5.35.* In this figure, one bit of information from any of four sources is selected according to the source address lines. This information is then placed on a wire, known as a *bus*, that connects to a demultiplexer similar to the one described in Sec. 5.4. The bit-combination on the destination address lines then determines on which of the four output lines of the demultiplexer the data information is placed. By using n of the

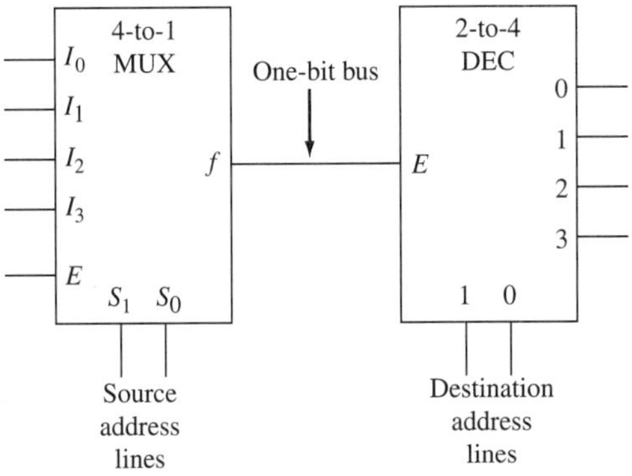

Figure 5.35 A multiplexer/demultiplexer arrangement for information transmission.

*In Fig. 5.35 the demultiplexer symbol was modified from Fig. 5.28 to emphasize the multiplexer/demultiplexer arrangement.

structures shown in Fig. 5.35 in parallel, an n-bit word from any of four source locations is transferred to any of four destination locations.

5.6.1 Logic Design with Multiplexers

Multiplexers are also used as general logic-design devices for realizing Boolean functions. Let us begin this discussion by considering the most direct way this is done. Consider a three-variable Boolean function and its truth table as shown in Fig. 5.36*a*. The Boolean expression corresponding to this truth table can be written as

$$f(x,y,z) = f_0 \cdot \bar{x}\bar{y}\bar{z} + f_1 \cdot \bar{x}\bar{y}z + f_2 \cdot \bar{x}y\bar{z} + f_3 \cdot \bar{x}yz + f_4 \cdot x\bar{y}\bar{z} + f_5 \cdot x\bar{y}z + f_6 \cdot xy\bar{z} + f_7 \cdot xyz \quad (5.12)$$

where f_i denotes functional values 0 and 1.* The Boolean expression for a 4-to-1-line multiplexer was previously written as Eq. (5.11). In an analogous manner to Eq. (5.11), an 8-to-1-line multiplexer is described by the Boolean expression

$$f = (I_0\bar{S}_2\bar{S}_1\bar{S}_0 + I_1\bar{S}_2\bar{S}_1S_0 + I_2\bar{S}_2S_1\bar{S}_0 + I_3\bar{S}_2S_1S_0 + I_4S_2\bar{S}_1\bar{S}_0 + I_5S_2\bar{S}_1S_0 + I_6S_2S_1\bar{S}_0 + I_7S_2S_1S_0)E \quad (5.13)$$

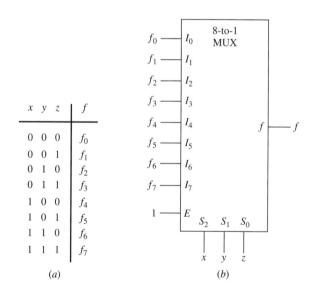

x	y	z	f
0	0	0	f_0
0	0	1	f_1
0	1	0	f_2
0	1	1	f_3
1	0	0	f_4
1	0	1	f_5
1	1	0	f_6
1	1	1	f_7

(*a*)

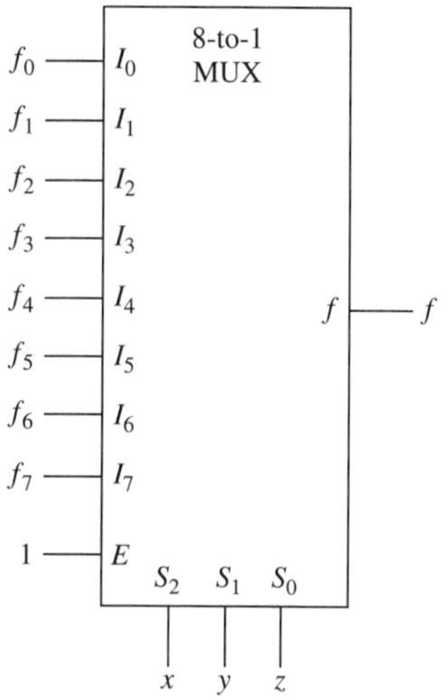

(*b*)

Figure 5.36 Realization of a three-variable function using an 8-to-1-line multiplexer. (*a*) Three-variable truth table. (*b*) General realization.

*Note that f_i denotes a functional value in this presentation and not an entire function as in other sections of this book.

If E is assumed to be logic-1, then Eq. (5.13) is transformed into Eq. (5.12) by replacing I_i with f_i, S_2 with x, S_1 with y, and S_0 with z. In other words, by placing x, y, and z on select lines S_2, S_1, and S_0, respectively, and placing the functional values f_i on data input lines I_i, an enabled 8-to-1-line multiplexer realizes a general three-variable truth table. This realization is shown in Fig. 5.36*b*.

As a specific example, consider the truth table of Fig. 5.37*a*. By placing a logic-1 on the enable input line, the eight functional values on the eight data input lines of an 8-to-1-line multiplexer, and connecting the select lines S_2,S_1,S_0 to x,y,z, respectively, the configuration of Fig. 5.37*b* becomes a realization of the given truth table.

Rather than working from a truth table, one could start with a minterm canonical formula to obtain a realization with a multiplexer. Since each minterm in an expression algebraically describes a row of a truth table having a functional value of 1, the realization is obtained by simply applying a 1 input to the I_i line if minterm m_i appears in the expression and applying a 0 input to the I_j line if m_j does not appear in the expression. For example, consider the minterm canonical formula

$$f(x,y,z) = \Sigma m(0,2,3,5)$$

The realization is obtained by placing x, y, and z on the S_2, S_1, and S_0 lines, respectively, logic-1 on data input lines I_0, I_2, I_3, and I_5, and logic-0 on the remaining data input lines, i.e., I_1, I_4, I_6, and I_7. In addition, the multiplexer must be enabled by setting $E = 1$. This again is the realization shown in Fig. 5.37*b*.

If at least one input variable of a Boolean function is assumed to be available in both its complemented and uncomplemented form, or, equivalently, a not-gate

x	y	z	f
0	0	0	1
0	0	1	0
0	1	0	1
0	1	1	1
1	0	0	0
1	0	1	1
1	1	0	0
1	1	1	0

(*a*)

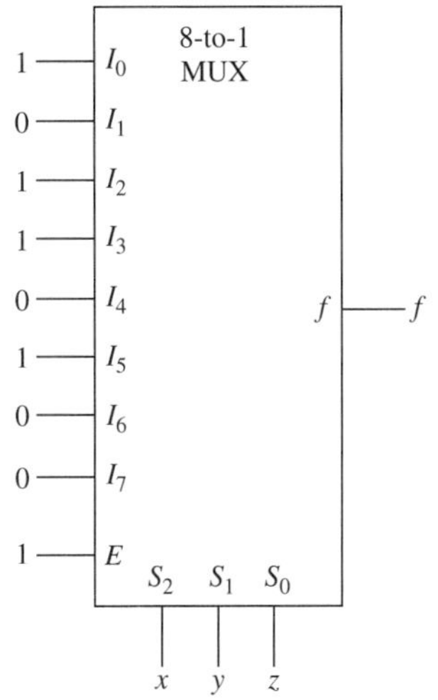

(*b*)

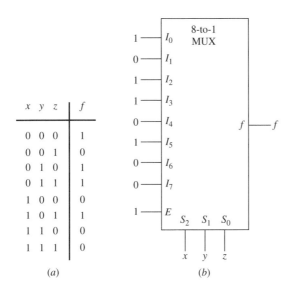

Figure 5.37 Realization of $f(x,y,z) = \Sigma m(0,2,3,5)$. (*a*) Truth table. (*b*) 8-to-1-line multiplexer realization.

is used to generate the complement of a variable, then any n-variable function is realizable with a 2^{n-1}-to-1-line multiplexer. For example, in the case of a three-variable function, this implies that only a 4-to-1-line multiplexer is needed for a realization. To see this, again consider Eq. (5.12). Doing some simple factoring, Eq. (5.12) becomes

$$f(x,y,z) = (f_0 \cdot \bar{z} + f_1 \cdot z)\bar{x}\bar{y} + (f_2 \cdot \bar{z} + f_3 \cdot z)\bar{x}y + (f_4 \cdot \bar{z} + f_5 \cdot z)x\bar{y} + (f_6 \cdot \bar{z} + f_7 \cdot z)xy$$

Furthermore, when $E = 1$ Eq. (5.11) has the form

$$f = I_0\bar{S}_1\bar{S}_0 + I_1\bar{S}_1S_0 + I_2S_1\bar{S}_0 + I_3S_1S_0$$

Comparing these last two equations, it immediately follows that a realization of any three-variable Boolean function is obtained by placing the x and y variables on the S_1 and S_0 select lines of a 4-to-1-line multiplexer, the single-variable functions $f_i \cdot \bar{z} + f_j \cdot z$ on the data input lines, and letting $E = 1$ as shown in Fig. 5.38. In any particular situation, the single-variable functions $f_i \cdot \bar{z} + f_j \cdot z$ reduce to 0, 1, z, or $\bar{z}$ depending upon the values of f_i and f_j.

As an illustration, again consider the truth table in Fig. 5.37*a*. Since $f_0 = 1$ and $f_1 = 0$, $f_0 \cdot \bar{z} + f_1 \cdot z$ evaluates to $\bar{z}$. Similarly, with $f_2 = 1$ and $f_3 = 1$, then $f_2 \cdot \bar{z} + f_3 \cdot z = 1$; with $f_4 = 0$ and $f_5 = 1$, then $f_4 \cdot \bar{z} + f_5 \cdot z = z$; and with $f_6 = 0$ and $f_7 = 0$, then $f_6 \cdot \bar{z} + f_7 \cdot z = 0$. Thus, the realization is obtained by placing x and y on the S_1 and S_0 select lines, respectively, $\bar{z}$ on the I_0 line, logic-1 on the I_1 line, z on the I_2 line, and logic-0 on the I_3 line. In addition, the multiplexer must be enabled. The resulting realization is shown in Fig. 5.39.

Alternatively, the minterm canonical formula for the truth table in Fig. 5.37*a* is

$$f(x,y,z) = \bar{x}\bar{y}\bar{z} + \bar{x}y\bar{z} + \bar{x}yz + x\bar{y}z$$

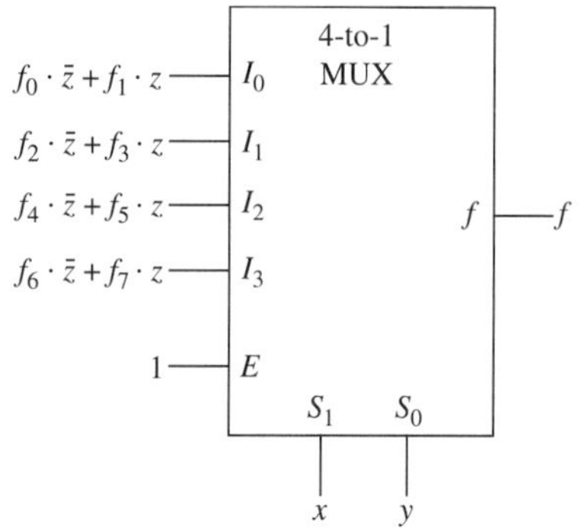

Figure 5.38 A general realization of a 3-variable Boolean function using a 4-to-1-line multiplexer.

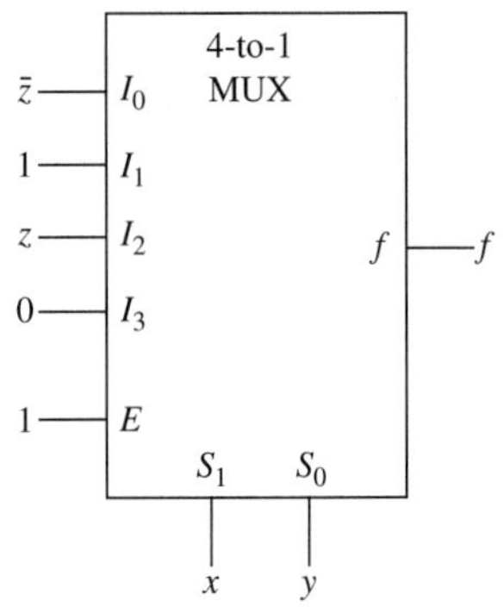

Figure 5.39 Realization of $f(x,y,z) = \Sigma m(0,2,3,5)$ using a 4-to-1-line multiplexer.

When the expression is factored into the following form

$$f(x,y,z) = \bar{x}\bar{y}(\bar{z}) + \bar{x}y(\bar{z} + z) + x\bar{y}(z)$$
$$= \bar{x}\bar{y}(\bar{z}) + \bar{x}y(1) + x\bar{y}(z) + xy(0)$$

the realization of Fig. 5.39 again results, where the entities in parentheses appear on the data input lines. The last term, $xy(0)$, was included to indicate what input must appear on the I_3 line to provide for the appropriate output when selected with $x = y = 1$.

Although in the above discussion the x and y variables appear on the select lines and functions of z appear on the data lines, by appropriate factoring of Eq. (5.12) realizations are possible where other variables appear on the select and data lines. In this way, if only one variable is available in its complemented and uncomplemented form, then it should be used for the data lines; while the remaining variables are used for the select lines. Furthermore, it should be noted that the order in which variables are assigned to the select lines affects the order in which the single-variable functions appear as inputs to the data input lines.

Karnaugh maps provide a convenient tool for obtaining multiplexer realizations. First it is necessary to establish which variables to assign to the select lines. Once this is done, the inputs for the I_i data lines are read directly from the map. To illustrate this, again consider a three-variable Boolean function of x, y, and z. Assume x is placed on the S_1 line and y is placed on the S_0 line. Figure 5.40*a* shows a three-variable Karnaugh map along with this assignment indicated by double arrows. Applying this assignment to Eq. (5.11) and letting $E = 1$, Eq. (5.11) becomes

$$f = I_0\bar{x}\bar{y} + I_1\bar{x}y + I_2x\bar{y} + I_3xy$$

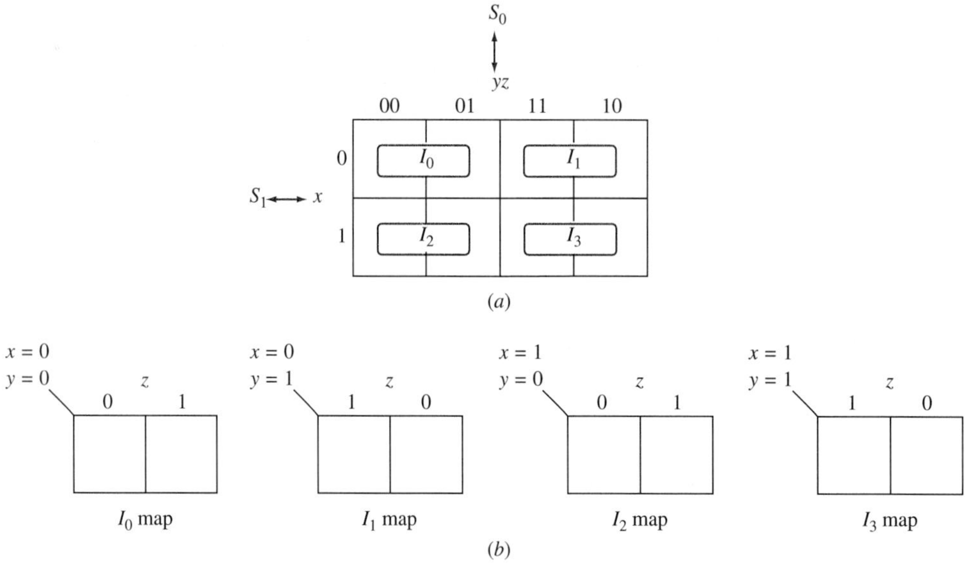

Figure 5.40 Obtaining multiplexer realizations using Karnaugh maps. (*a*) Cell groupings corresponding to the data line functions. (*b*) Karnaugh maps for the I_i subfunctions.

Now consider each term in this expression. The first term, $I_0\bar{x}\bar{y}$, corresponds to those cells in which $x = 0$ and $y = 0$. These are the two upper left cells of the Karnaugh map in Fig. 5.40 labeled as I_0. These two cells can be regarded as a submap for the z variable as indicated in Fig. 5.40*b*. Thus, depending upon the 0-1 entries within this submap, the expression for I_0 is readily obtained. In a similar manner, the second term, $I_1\bar{x}y$, corresponds to those cells in which $x = 0$ and $y = 1$. These are the two upper right cells of the map. The entries within these cells correspond to the I_1 input. The cells associated with I_2 and I_3 are obtained in a like manner and are also shown in Fig. 5.40*a*.

As an example, again consider the truth table of Fig. 5.37*a*. The Karnaugh map is drawn in Fig. 5.41*a*. For emphasis, the four pairs of cells corresponding to the data inputs are redrawn as single-variable submaps in Fig. 5.41*b*. It should be noted that the axis labels for the I_1 and I_3 submaps are shown in reverse order to be consistent with the Karnaugh map of Fig. 5.41*a*. Grouping the 1-cells, the expressions for the subfunctions are now written. In particular, $I_0 = \bar{z}$, $I_1 = 1$, $I_2 = z$, and $I_3 = 0$. This again leads to the realization shown in Fig. 5.39. Although submaps were drawn in Fig. 5.41*b*, the expressions for the subfunctions are obtained from the original map by noting the patterns within the appropriate pair of cells. When both cells contain 0's or 1's, then the subfunctions are 0 or 1, respectively. When one cell contains a 0 and the other a 1, $I_i = z$ if the 1 occurs in the cell in which $z = 1$; while $I_i = \bar{z}$ if the 1 occurs in the cell in which $z = 0$.

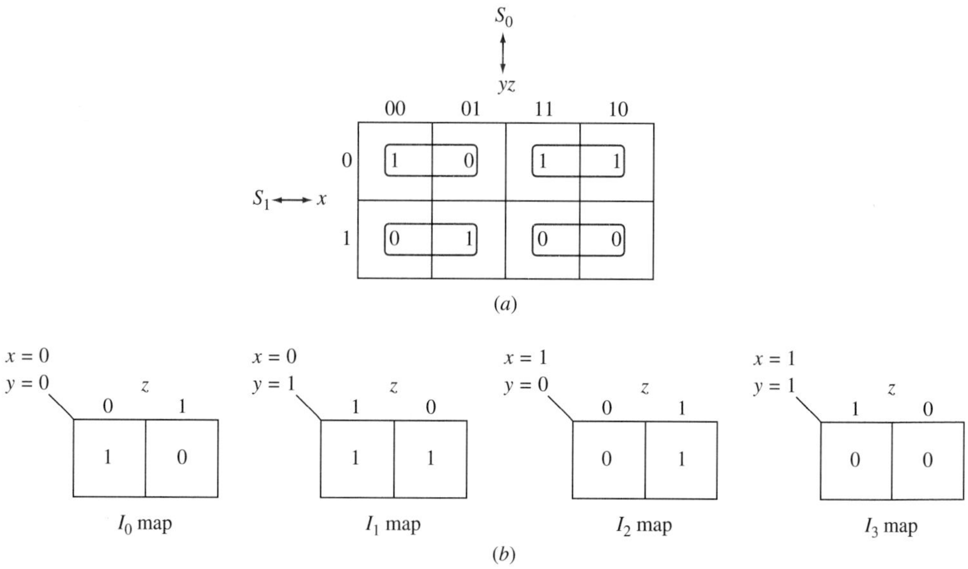

Figure 5.41 Realization of $f(x,y,z) = \Sigma m(0,2,3,5)$. (*a*) Karnaugh map. (*b*) I_0, I_1, I_2, and I_3 submaps.

Karnaugh maps can readily handle other assignments of the input variables to the select lines. For example, Fig. 5.42 illustrates the I_i submaps under two additional assignments. In Fig. 5.42*a*, input variable y is applied to select line S_1 and input variable z is applied to select line S_0. In Fig. 5.42*b*, input variable x is applied to select line S_0 and input variable y is applied to select line S_1. Depending upon the assignment, the submaps for functions of the third variable are located differently.

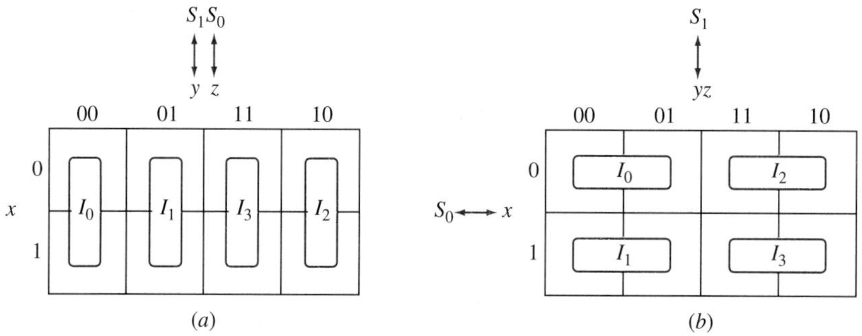

Figure 5.42 Using Karnaugh maps to obtain multiplexer realizations under various assignments to the select inputs. (*a*) Applying input variables y and z to the S_1 and S_0 select lines. (*b*) Applying input variables x and y to the S_0 and S_1 select lines.

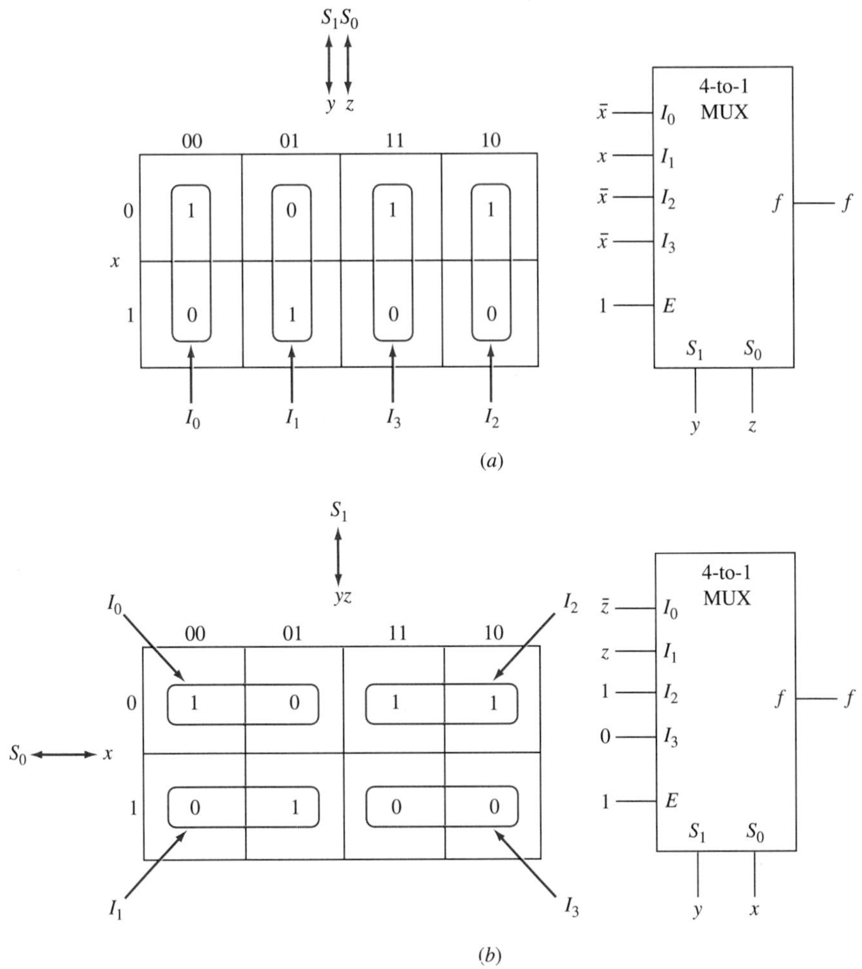

Figure 5.43 Alternative realizations of $f(x,y,z) = \Sigma m(0,2,3,5)$. (*a*) Applying input variables *y* and *z* to the S_1 and S_0 select lines. (*b*) Applying input variables *x* and *y* to the S_0 and S_1 select lines.

However, in each case, the submaps correspond to the four combinations of values to the variables on the select lines. Realizations of the truth table of Fig. 5.37*a* using the two assignments of Fig. 5.42 are shown in Fig. 5.43.

An 8-to-1-line multiplexer can be used to realize any four-variable Boolean function. Three of the variables are placed on the select lines. The inputs to the data lines are then the possible single-variable functions of the fourth variable, namely, 0, 1, the variable, and its complement. Figure 5.44 shows the relationships between the map cells and the data-line inputs under the assumption that the input variables

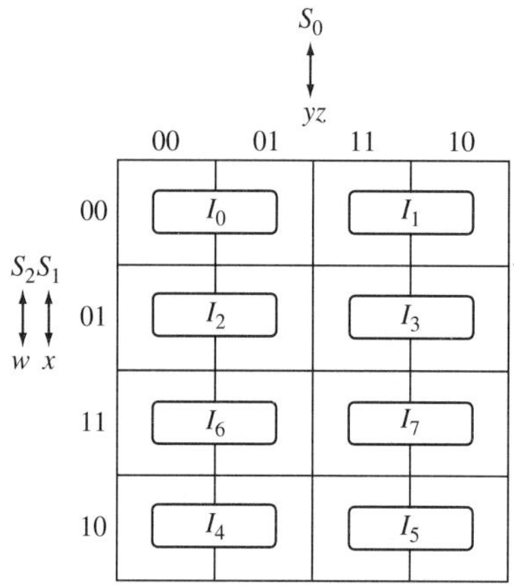

Figure 5.44 A select line assignment and corresponding data line functions for a multiplexer realization of a four-variable function.

w, x, and y are applied to select lines S_2, S_1, and S_0, respectively. In this case, the eight I_i inputs are determined by pairs of cells associated with the eight combination of values to the x, y, and z variables. An example of a four-variable function on a Karnaugh map, along with the multiplexer realization, is given in Fig. 5.45. Particular attention should be given to I_7 since $z = 0$ corresponds to the right cell and $z = 1$ corresponds to the left cell of the I_7 submap. As in the case of the three-variable Karnaugh map, it is a simple matter to reinterpret a four-variable map for different assignments of the input variables to the select lines.

In the above discussion, 2^n-to-1-line multiplexers were used to realize functions of $n + 1$ variables. This was achieved by applying functions of a single variable to the data input lines. By allowing realizations of m variable functions as inputs to the data input lines, 2^n-to-1-line multiplexers can be used in the realization of $(n + m)$-variable functions. To illustrate this, Fig. 5.46 shows a four-variable Karnaugh map in which it is assumed that the input variables w and x are applied to the S_1 and S_0 select inputs, respectively, of a 4-to-1-line multiplexer. This implies that functions of the y and z variables must appear at the data input lines in the overall realization. To determine these functions, it is necessary to consider the four cases corresponding to the four assignments of 0's and 1's to the variables on the select lines. As indicated in Fig. 5.46, there are four cells corresponding to $wx = 00$. These four cells form the submap for the function at the I_0 terminal. Similarly, the input to the I_1 terminal is described by the four cells in which $wx = 01$, the input to the I_2 terminal is

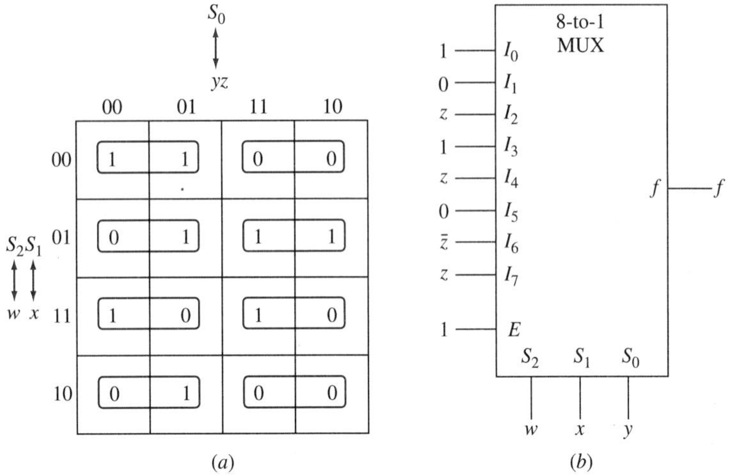

Figure 5.45 Realization of $f(w,x,y,z) = \Sigma m(0,1,5,6,7,9,12,15)$. (*a*) Karnaugh map. (*b*) Multiplexer realization.

described by the four cells in which $wx = 10$, and the input to the I_3 terminal is described by the four cells in which $wx = 11$. By analyzing these submaps, appropriate logic is readily determined for these input terminals.

As an example, consider the Karnaugh map of Fig. 5.47*a*. Although the four submaps can be interpreted directly on the Karnaugh map itself, they are redrawn in Fig. 5.47*b* to *e* for clarity. These are two-variable Karnaugh maps where it is as-

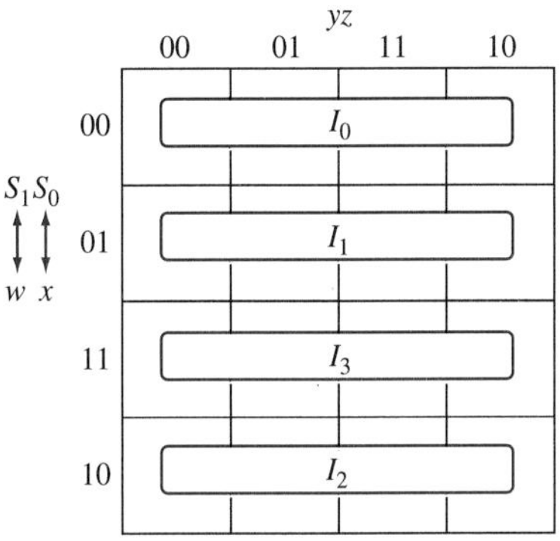

Figure 5.46 Using a four-variable Karnaugh map to obtain a Boolean function realization with a 4-to-1-line multiplexer.

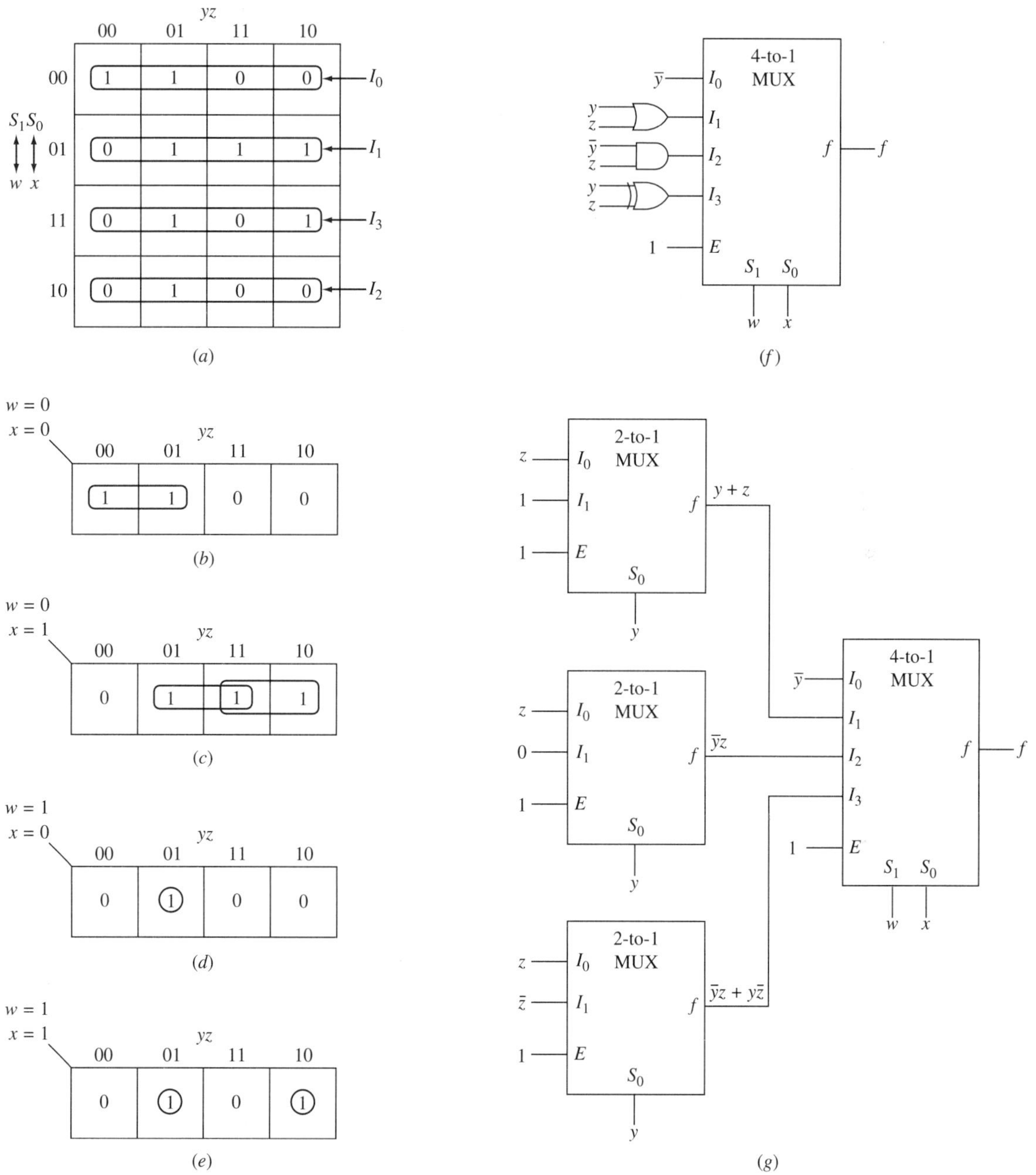

Figure 5.47 Realization of the Boolean function $f(w,x,y,z) = \Sigma m(0,1,5,6,7,9,13,14)$. (*a*) Karnaugh map. (*b*) I_0 submap. (*c*) I_1 submap. (*d*) I_2 submap. (*e*) I_3 submap. (*f*) Realization using a 4-to-1-line multiplexer. (*g*) Realization using a multiplexer tree.

sumed that the left and right edges are connected. From the four submaps, it immediately follows that

$$I_0 = \bar{y}$$
$$I_1 = y + z$$
$$I_2 = \bar{y}z$$
$$I_3 = \bar{y}z + y\bar{z} = y \oplus z$$

The realization of the Boolean function is given in Fig. 5.47*f*.

As a further variation in using multiplexers to realize functions of $n + m$ variables, each of the functions involving the m variables can itself be realized with multiplexers creating a treelike structure of multiplexers. For example, each two-variable function at the data input lines in Fig. 5.47*f* can be realized with 2-to-1-line multiplexers. This results in the realization shown in Fig. 5.47*g*.

5.7 PROGRAMMABLE LOGIC DEVICES (PLDs)

With the advent of large-scale integration technology, it has become feasible to fabricate large circuits within a single chip. One such consequence of this technology are the *programmable logic devices* (PLDs). Three such devices are studied in the remainder of this chapter: the *programmable read-only memory* (PROM), the *programmable logic array* (PLA), and the *programmable array logic** (PAL) device.

The general structure of programmable logic devices is illustrated in Fig. 5.48. The inputs to the PLD are applied to a set of buffer/inverters. The logic equivalent of the buffer/inverter is shown in Fig. 5.49. These devices have both the true value of the input as well as the complemented value of the input as its outputs. In addi-

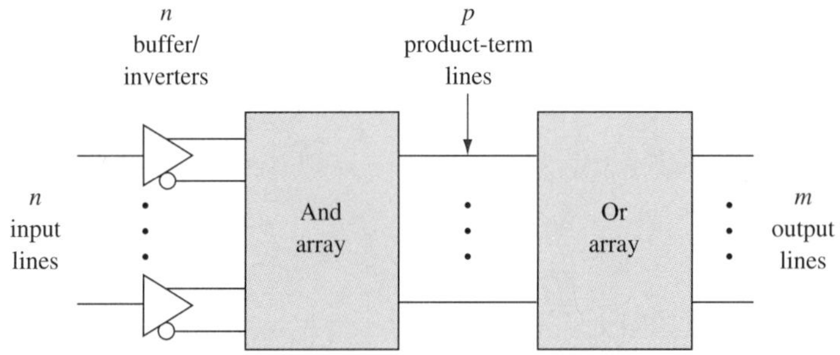

Figure 5.48 General structure of PLDs.

*Programmable array logic is a registered trademark of Monolithic Memories, Inc., a division of Advanced Micro Devices, Inc.

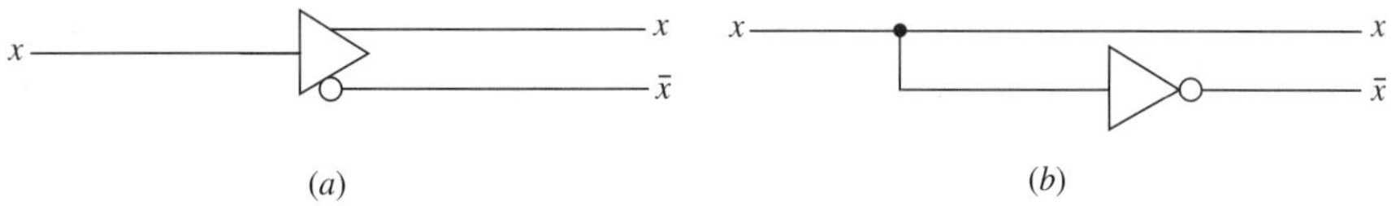

Figure 5.49 Buffer/inverter. (*a*) Symbol. (*b*) Logic equivalent.

tion, these devices produce the necessary drive for the and-array which follows since, in general, the outputs from these devices serve as inputs to a very large number of gates. The array of and-gates accepts the n input variables and their complements and is used to generate a set of p product terms. These product terms, in turn, serve as inputs to an array of or-gates to realize a set of m sum-of-product expressions.

In PLDs, one or both of the gate arrays are programmable in the sense that the logic designer can specify the connections within an array. In this way, PLDs serve as general circuits for the realization of a set of Boolean functions. Table 5.7 summarizes which arrays are programmable for the various PLDs. In the case of the programmable read-only memory (PROM) and the programmable array logic (PAL) devices, only one array is programmable; while both arrays are programmable in the case of the programmable logic array (PLA).

In a programmable array, the connections to each gate can be modified. One simple approach to fabricating a programmable gate is to have each of its inputs connected to a fuse as illustrated in Fig. 5.50*a*. In this figure, the gate realizes the product term *abcd*. Assume, however, that the product term *bc* is to be generated. To do this, the gate is programmed by removing the *a* and *d* connections. This is done by blowing the corresponding fuses. The net result is to have a gate with the desired connections as illustrated in Fig. 5.50*b*. It is assumed in this discussion that an open input to an and-gate is equivalent to a constant logic-1 input and that an

Table 5.7 Types of PLDs

Device	And-array	Or-array
PROM	Fixed	Programmable
PLA	Programmable	Programmable
PAL	Programmable	Fixed

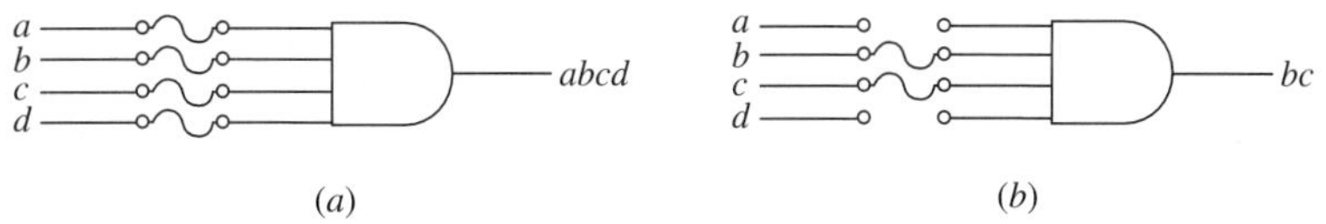

Figure 5.50 Programming by blowing fuses. (*a*) Before programming. (*b*) After programming.

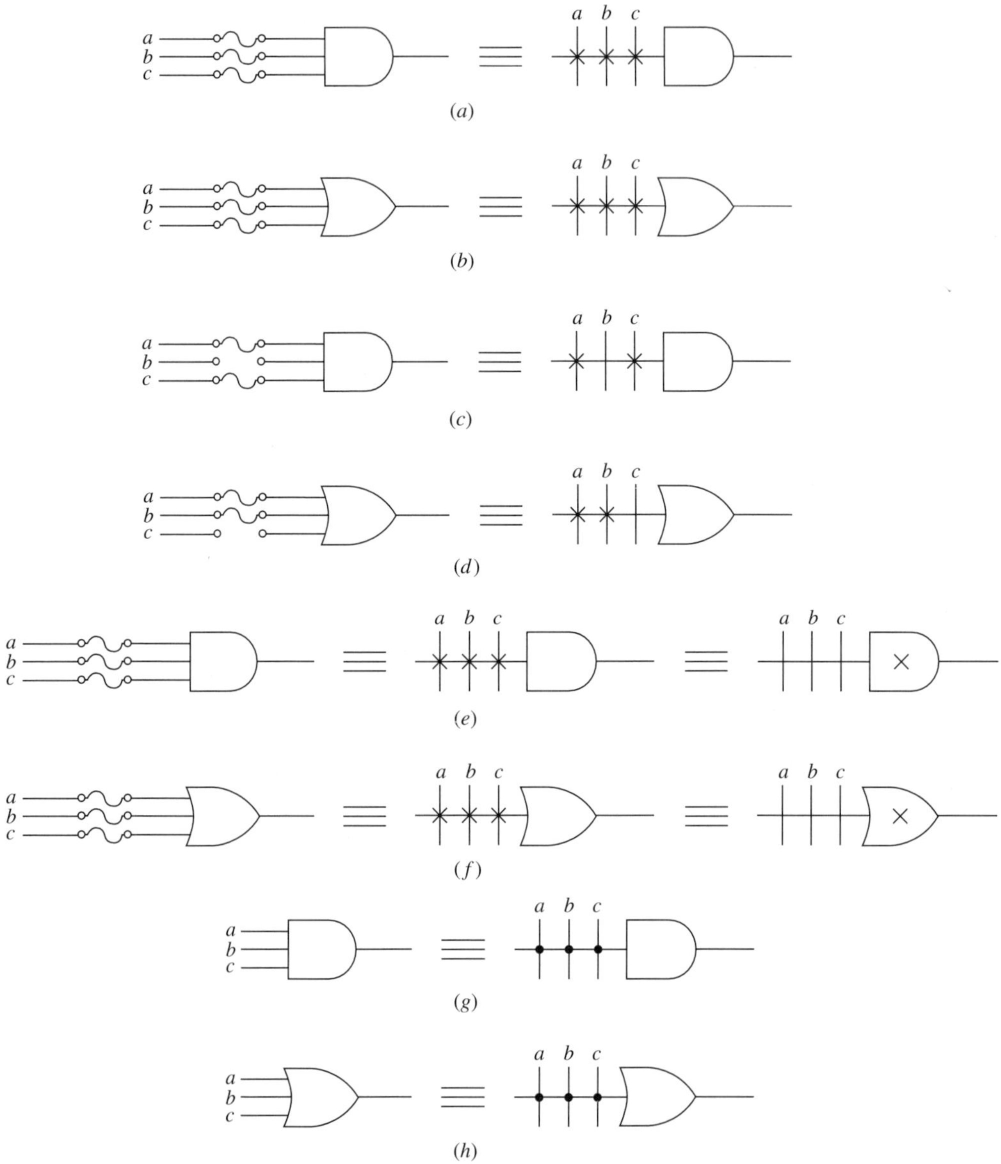

Figure 5.51 PLD notation. (*a*) Unprogrammed and-gate. (*b*) Unprogrammed or-gate. (*c*) Programmed and-gate realizing the term *ac*. (*d*) Programmed or-gate realizing the term $a + b$. (*e*) Special notation for an and-gate having all its input fuses intact. (*f*) Special notation for an or-gate having all its input fuses intact. (*g*) And-gate with nonfusible inputs. (*h*) Or-gate with nonfusible inputs.

open input to an or-gate is equivalent to a constant logic-0 input. Although other schemes are used in addition to simple fuse inputs, for the purpose of this presentation, this simple approach is assumed.

It should be noted that programming is really a hardware procedure. Specialized equipment, called *programmers*, is needed to carry out the programming of a PLD by an end-user. Clearly, fused-programmable devices are programmed only once. However, manufacturers offer devices that are reprogrammable, called *erasable PLDs*. In this case, the connections can be reset to their original conditions and then reprogrammed. Depending upon the type of device, erasing is achieved by exposing the PLD to ultraviolet light or using electrical signals.

In the above discussion it was stated that the PLD is programmed by the user. These PLDs are said to be *field programmable*. Alternatively, the user can specify the desired connections and supply the information to the manufacturer. The manufacturer then prepares an overlay that is used to complete the connections as the last step in the fabrication process. Such PLDs are referred to as *mask programmable*.

5.7.1 PLD Notation

To indicate the connections in the and-array and or-array of a PLD, a simplified notation is frequently used. This notation is illustrated in Fig. 5.51. Rather than drawing all the inputs to the and-gates and or-gates, the gates are drawn with a single input line. The inputs themselves are indicated by lines at right angles to the single gate line. The intersections between the input lines and the single gate line correspond to the types of connections. A cross at the intersection denotes a fusible link that is intact; while the lack of a cross indicates the fuse is blown or no connection exists. The occurrence of a hard-wired connection, i.e., one that is not fusible, is indicated by a junction dot. Figure 5.51*a* and *b* illustrates the notation for an and-gate and an or-gate prior to being programmed; while Fig. 5.51*c* and *d* shows examples of the notation for these gates after programming. For the special case when all the input fuses to a gate are kept intact, instead of showing a cross at the intersection between each input line and the single gate line, a cross is simply placed inside the gate symbol as indicated in Fig. 5.51*e* and *f*. Finally, an and-gate and or-gate with nonfusible inputs, but, rather, having hard-wire connections, are illustrated in Fig. 5.51*g* and *h*.

5.8 PROGRAMMABLE READ-ONLY MEMORIES (PROMs)

The basic structure of a programmable read-only memory (PROM) is shown in Fig. 5.52 and its equivalent logic diagram in Fig. 5.53*a*. As a PLD, it consists of an and-array with a set of buffer/inverters and an or-array. The and-array with buffer/inverters is really an n-to-2^n-line decoder and the or-array is simply a collection of programmable or-gates. The or-array is also called the *memory array*. The decoder serves as a minterm generator. The n-variable minterms appear on the 2^n lines at the

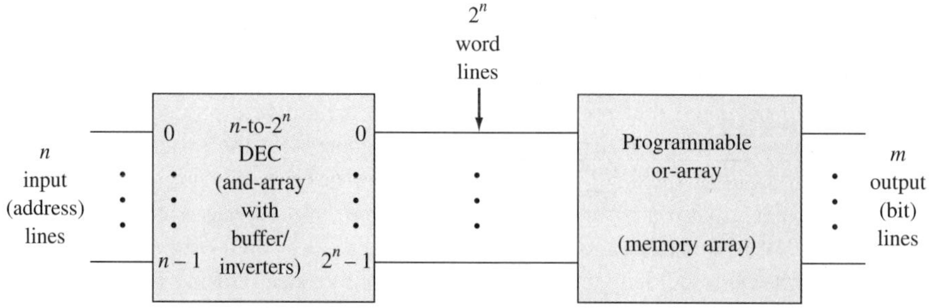

Figure 5.52 Structure of a PROM.

decoder output. These are known as *word lines.* As is seen in Fig. 5.53*a*, all 2^n outputs of the decoder are connected to each of the m gates in the or-array via programmable fusible links. The n input lines are called the *address lines* and the m output lines the *bit lines.* A PROM is characterized by the number of output lines of the decoder and the number of output lines from the or-array. Hence, the PROM of Fig. 5.53*a* is referred to as a $2^n \times m$ PROM.

The logic diagram of Fig. 5.53*a* is redrawn in Fig. 5.53*b* using the PLD notation introduced in the previous section. Since the and-array is fixed, i.e., not programmable, connections are shown by junction dots. The fusible connections in the or-array, however, are shown by crosses since this array is programmable.

The realization of a set of Boolean expressions using a decoder and or-gates was discussed in Sec. 5.4. The very same approach is applicable in using a PROM since a PROM is a device that includes both the decoder and or-gates within the same network. Given a set of Boolean expressions in minterm canonical form or a set of Boolean functions in truth table form, it is only necessary to determine which programmable links of a PROM to retain and which to open. The programming of the PROM is then carried out by blowing the appropriate fuses. PROMs are typically used for code conversions, generating bit patterns for characters, and as lookup tables for arithmetic functions.

As a simple example of using a PROM for combinational logic design, consider the Boolean expressions

$$f_1(x_2,x_1,x_0) = \Sigma m(0,1,2,5,7)$$
$$f_2(x_2,x_1,x_0) = \Sigma m(1,2,4,6)$$

The corresponding truth table is given in Fig. 5.54*a*. Since these are functions of three input variables, a PROM having a 3-to-8-line decoder is needed. In addition, since there are two functions being realized, the or-array must consist of two gates. Hence, an 8×2 PROM is needed for the realization. The realization is shown in Fig. 5.54*b* using the PLD notation. A blown fusible link on the input of an or-gate is equivalent to a logic-0 input. It should be emphasized that this example is for illustrative purposes only. From a practical point of view, PROMs are intended for combinational networks having a large number of inputs and outputs.

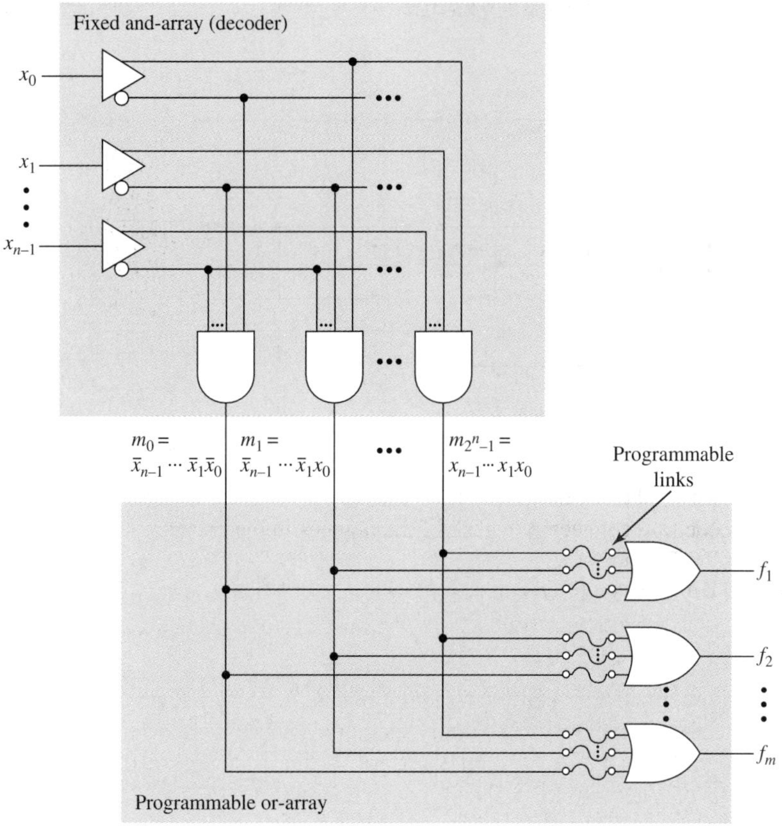

(*a*)

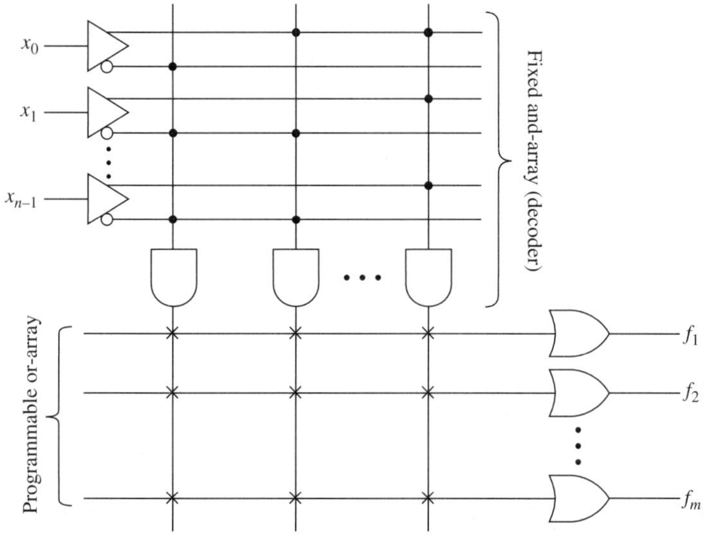

(*b*)

Figure 5.53 A $2^n \times m$ PROM. (*a*) Logic diagram. (*b*) Representation in PLD notation.

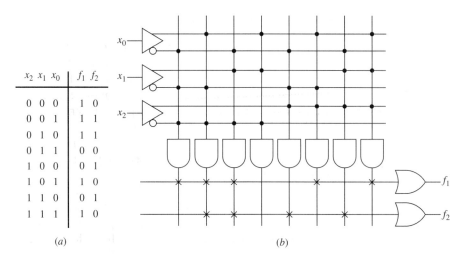

x_2	x_1	x_0	f_1	f_2
0	0	0	1	0
0	0	1	1	1
0	1	0	1	1
0	1	1	0	0
1	0	0	0	1
1	0	1	1	0
1	1	0	0	1
1	1	1	1	0

(*a*)

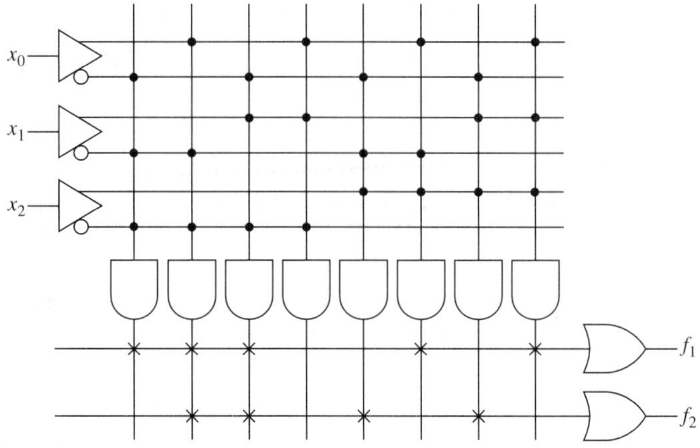

(*b*)

Figure 5.54 Using a PROM for logic design. (*a*) Truth table. (*b*) PROM realization.

It may seem strange that the structure of Fig. 5.52, as a logic-design device, is called a read-only memory. Read-only memory devices were originally developed to store permanent data in a digital system. In these devices each piece of data, called a *word*, is accessible by specifying an address.

To see how the structure of Fig. 5.52 is viewed as a memory device, again consider Fig. 5.54. By applying a 3-bit combination to the x_0, x_1, and x_2 lines, precisely one and-gate in the decoder is selected in the sense that its output line, i.e., word line, is logic-1. Thus, each input combination is regarded as an *address* of one of the word lines. As a consequence of selecting a given word line, a pattern of 0's and 1's, i.e., a word, as determined by the fusible connections to the selected word line appears at the output terminals, i.e., the bit lines, of the device. This 0-1 pattern is considered the word *stored* at the address associated with the selected word line. For example, the word stored at address $x_2x_1x_0 = 100$ in Fig. 5.54 is $f_1f_2 = 01$. Finally, the fact that the connections associated with the fusible links normally cannot be altered once they are formed makes the term *read-only* appropriate for this device. Hence, the realization shown in Fig. 5.54 is a read-only memory storing eight words each consisting of 2 bits.

For each additional input line to a PROM, the number of gates in the decoder and the number of inputs to each gate in the or-array double. This is because all possible minterms are generated by the decoder and all the minterms appear as inputs to the gates in the or-array. However, in many applications, not all the minterms are necessary. In such cases, the and-array is not utilized efficiently. Also, as was seen in the discussion on minimization, collections of minterms can frequently be replaced by a single product term. If the and-array is made programmable so that only necessary product terms are generated, then its size can be controlled. As is seen in the next two sections, programmable and-arrays occur in the PLA and PAL devices.

5.9 PROGRAMMABLE LOGIC ARRAYS (PLAs)

Another type of programmable logic device is the programmable logic array (PLA). The PLA has the general structure of Fig. 5.48 where both the and-array and the or-array are programmable. A logic diagram for a general PLA is given in Fig. 5.55. For proper operation it is assumed that open input terminals to an and-gate, i.e., terminals connected to blown fuses, behave as logic-1's; while open input terminals to an or-gate behave as logic-0's. PLAs are characterized by three numbers: the number of input lines n, the number of product terms that can be generated p, i.e., the number of and-gates, and the number of output lines m. Consequently, they are designated as $n \times p \times m$ PLAs. A typical PLA is $16 \times 48 \times 8$.

As was mentioned in the previous section, in many logic design situations, not all the minterms are needed for a realization. This is particularly true in problems involving a large number of don't-care conditions, since minterms denoting these conditions do not have to appear in the implementation. For n input variables, there are 2^n minterms. This is also the number of gates in the and-array of a PROM. However, in a PLA the number of gates in the and-array is significantly less than 2^n. To see the extent of the reduction in the size of the and-array, consider functions of 16 input variables.

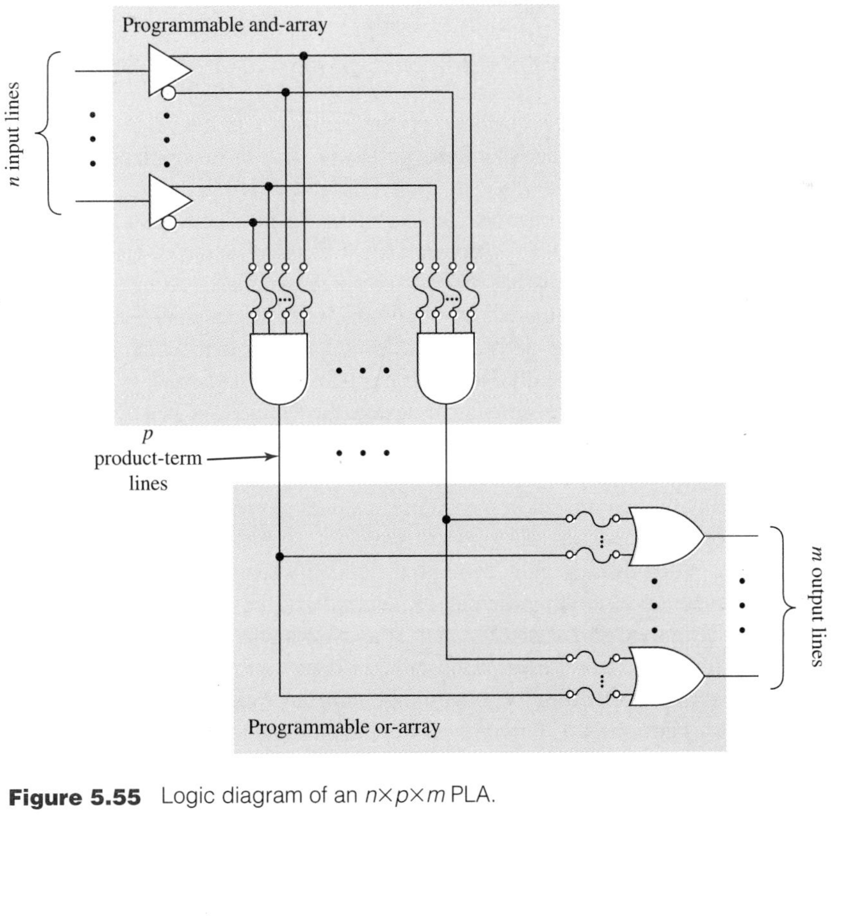

Figure 5.55 Logic diagram of an $n \times p \times m$ PLA.

In this case there are $2^{16} = 65{,}536$ minterms. However, in a $16\times48\times8$ PLA, provision is made to realize only 48 product terms. Referring to Fig. 5.55, it should be noted that both complemented and uncomplemented inputs, for a total of $2n$ inputs, appear at each and-gate to provide maximum flexibility in product-term generation.

Since all minterms are generated in a PROM, the realization of a set of Boolean functions is based on minterm canonical expressions. It is never necessary to minimize these expressions prior to obtaining a realization with a PROM. On the other hand, in the case of PLAs, depending upon how the fuses are programmed, the and-gates are capable of generating product terms that are not necessarily minterms. As a consequence, a realization using a PLA is based on sum-of-product expressions that may not be canonical. However, what is significant is that the logic designer is bounded by the number of product terms that are realizable by the and-array. This implies that it is necessary to obtain a set of expressions in which the total number of distinct product terms does not exceed the number of gates in the and-array. Thus, some degree of equation simplification generally is appropriate. Techniques for minimizing a set of Boolean expressions using the criterion of minimal number of distinct terms were previously discussed in Chapter 4.

To illustrate the use of a PLA for combinational logic design, consider the expressions

$$f_1(x,y,z) = \Sigma m(0,1,3,4)$$
$$f_2(x,y,z) = \Sigma m(1,2,3,4,5)$$

Assume that a $3\times4\times2$ PLA is available for the realization of the expressions. Before continuing, however, the reader should be well aware that this is not a practical application of the use of PLAs due to its simplicity, but it does serve the purpose of showing the concept of PLA combinational logic design. It is now noted that the size of the or-array in the available PLA is sufficient since it has two output or-gates. However, there are six distinct minterms between the two expressions. A realization based on the canonical expressions is therefore not possible with the assumed PLA since only four and-gates appear in the and-array. A formal approach to obtaining a pair of equivalent expressions, hopefully having at most four distinct terms, is to first establish the multiple-output prime implicants using the Quine-McCluskey method and then, using a multiple-output prime-implicant table, to find a multiple-output minimal sum having the fewest terms as discussed in Secs. 4.12 and 4.13. Of course, for real-world problems the minimization mechanics is done by specialized software written for this purpose. However, at this time let us attempt to obtain a solution using simple observations. When dealing with two output functions, it is known from Chapter 4 that the complete set of multiple-output prime implicants consists of all the prime implicants of the individual functions f_1 and f_2 as well as the prime implicants of the product function $f_1 \cdot f_2$. It was also established in Chapter 4 that there exists a multiple-output minimal sum consisting of just multiple-output prime implicants. A subset of the prime implicants of f_1 and $f_1 \cdot f_2$ are used in the multiple-output minimal sum for f_1; while a subset of the prime implicants of f_2 and $f_1 \cdot f_2$ are used in the multiple-output minimal sum for f_2. Figure 5.56a shows the prime implicants of f_1, f_2, and $f_1 \cdot f_2$ as they

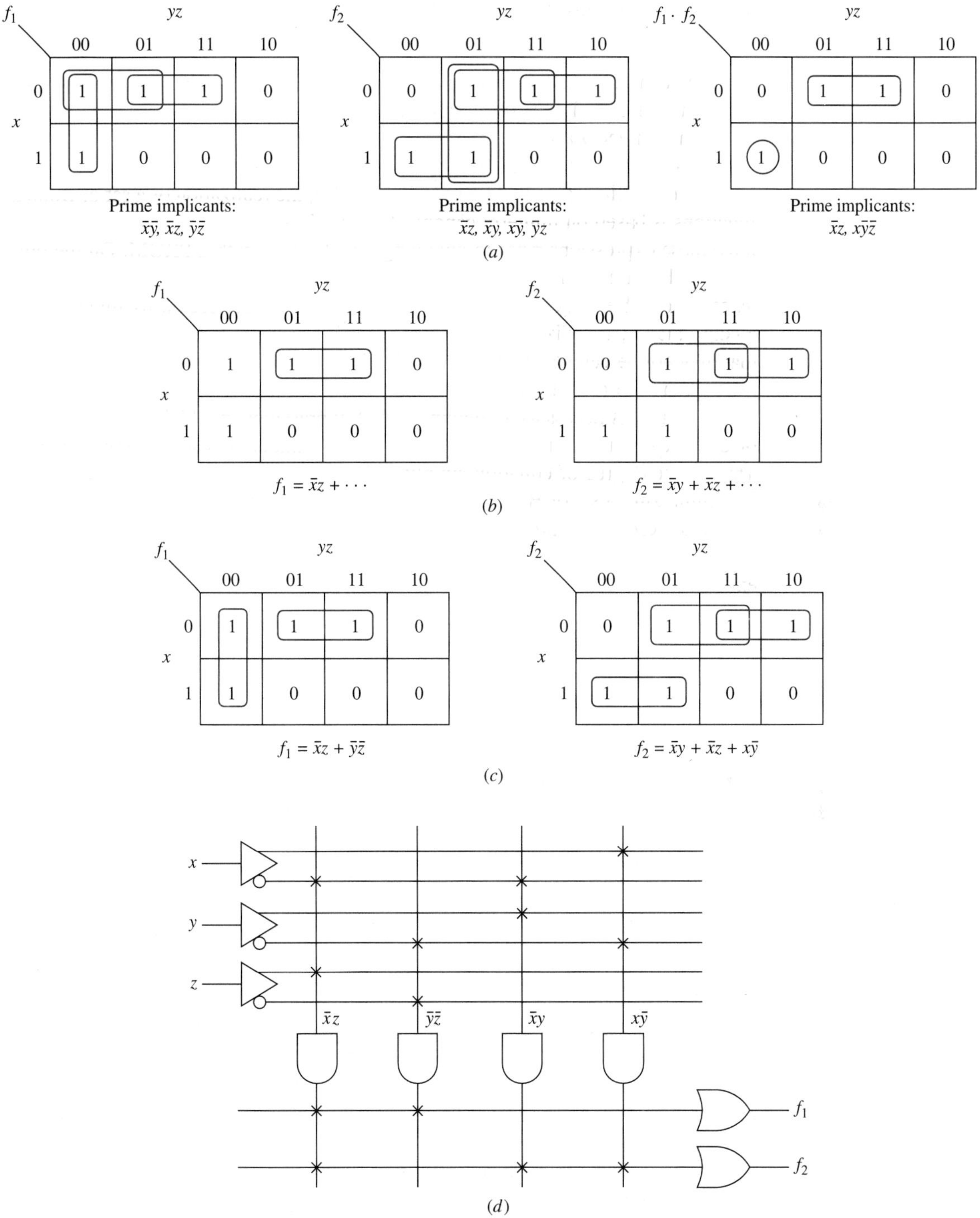

Figure 5.56 Example of combinational logic design using a PLA. (*a*) Maps showing the multiple-output prime implicants. (*b*) Partial covering of the f_1 and f_2 maps. (*c*) Maps for the multiple-output minimal sum. (*d*) Realization using a 3×4×2 PLA.

appear on Karnaugh maps.* There are a total of seven *distinct* prime implicants. Referring to the f_1 and $f_1 \cdot f_2$ maps to determine the terms for the minimized f_1 expression, it is now noted that of the four distinct prime implicants in these maps only prime implicant $\bar{x}z$ covers the $xyz = 011$ 1-cell of f_1. Similarly, referring to the f_2 and $f_1 \cdot f_2$ maps to determine the terms for the minimized f_2 expression, $\bar{x}y$ is the only prime implicant of the five distinct prime implicants in these maps that covers the $xyz = 010$ 1-cell of f_2. Hence, these two prime implicants must occur in the multiple-output minimal sum. Furthermore, it is next noted that prime implicant $\bar{x}z$, which is being used for f_1, can also be used for f_2 to cover the $xyz = 001$ 1-cell. Figure 5.56*b* shows the covering of the f_1 and f_2 maps at this point, along with the incomplete multiple-output minimal sum having two distinct product terms. From these maps it is immediately seen that using one additional prime implicant subcube for each of the functions, as shown in Fig. 5.56*c*, results in a multiple-output minimal sum having four distinct terms, i.e.,

$$f_1(x,y,z) = \bar{x}z + \bar{y}\,\bar{z}$$

$$f_2(x,y,z) = \bar{x}y + \bar{x}z + x\bar{y}$$

The corresponding 3×4×2 PLA realization is shown in Fig. 5.56*d*.

Although, in the above example, the final expressions for f_1 and f_2 could have been obtained using the prime implicants of the individual functions and ignoring the product function $f_1 \cdot f_2$, it should not be concluded that simply minimizing the individual expressions always results in a multiple-output minimal sum. A second example illustrates this point. Consider the expressions

$$f_1(x,y,z) = \Sigma m(0,1,3,5)$$

$$f_2(x,y,z) = \Sigma m(3,5,7)$$

Again a realization with a 3×4×2 PLA is attempted. The Karnaugh maps displaying the multiple-output prime implicants are shown in Fig. 5.57*a*. Using an analysis similar to the previous example, Fig. 5.57*b* shows the covering for the multiple-output minimal sum

$$f_1(x,y,z) = \bar{x}\,\bar{y} + \bar{x}z + x\bar{y}z$$

$$f_2(x,y,z) = yz + x\bar{y}z$$

which consists of only four distinct product terms. Hence, a realization using a 3×4×2 PLA is possible. An alternative covering, shown in Fig. 5.57*c*, corresponds to the multiple-output minimal sum

$$f_1(x,y,z) = \bar{x}\,\bar{y} + \bar{y}z + \bar{x}yz$$

$$f_2(x,y,z) = xz + \bar{x}yz$$

The realization based on the expressions obtained from Fig. 5.57*b* is shown in Fig. 5.57*d* using the PLD notation. It should be noted that a realization would not be possible with the assumed 3×4×2 PLA if the expressions were individually minimized.

*Recall that the minterms of the product function $f_1 \cdot f_2$ are the minterms common to both f_1 and f_2.

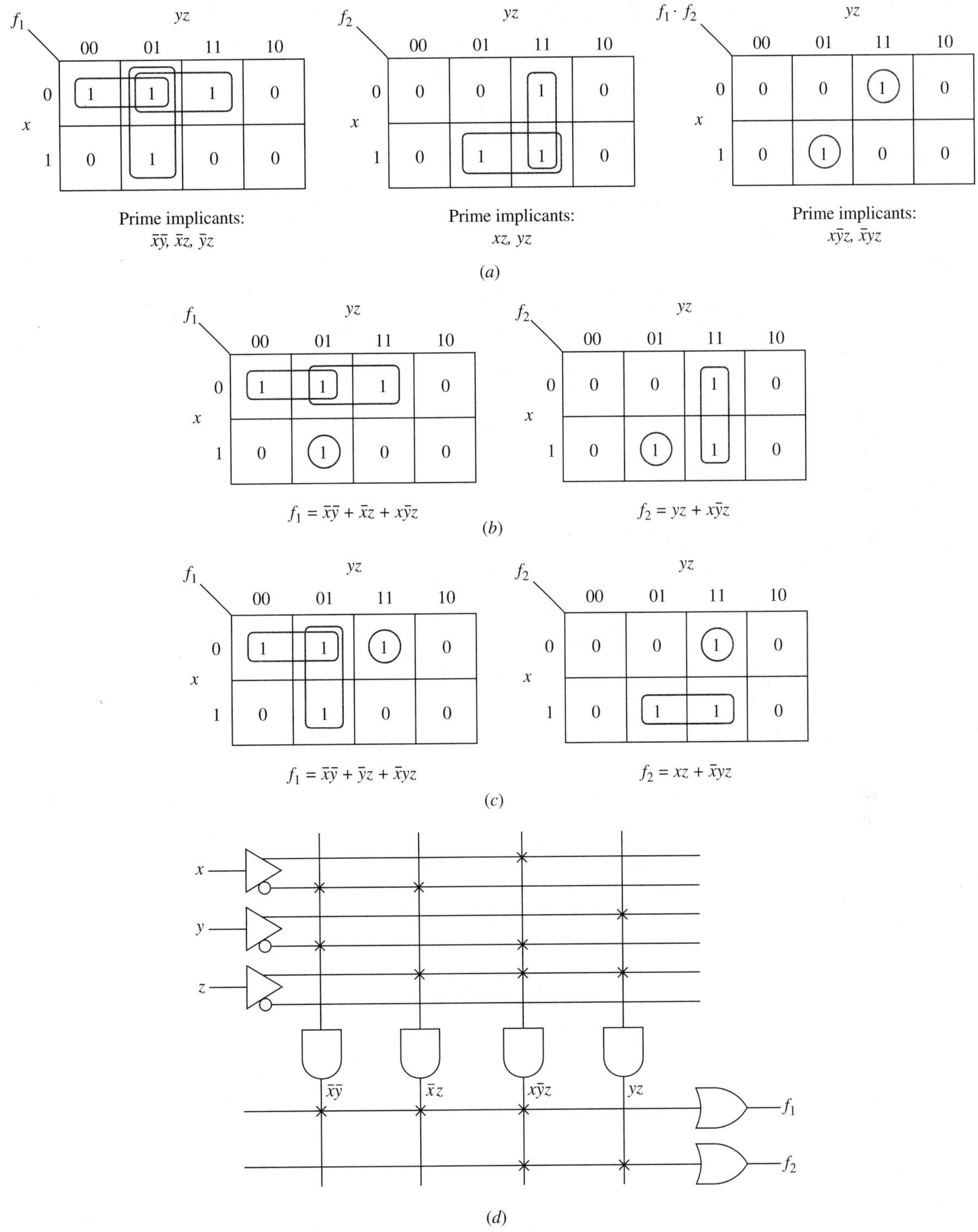

Figure 5.57 Example of combinational logic design using a PLA. (*a*) Maps showing the multiple-output prime implicants. (*b*) A multiple-output minimal sum covering. (*c*) Alternative multiple-output minimal sum covering. (*d*) realization using a 3×4×2 PLA.

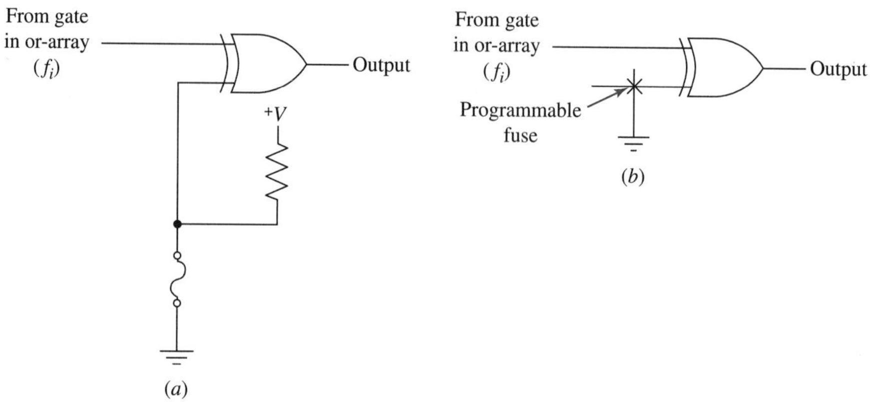

Figure 5.58 Exclusive-or-gate with a programmable fuse. (*a*) Circuit diagram. (*b*) Symbolic representation.

For greater flexibility, PLAs normally make provision for either a true output or a complemented output. One way in which this is achieved is illustrated in Fig. 5.58*a*. The output from each gate in the or-array, f_i, feeds into one input of an exclusive-or-gate. The other input to the exclusive-or-gate, having a programable fuse to ground, is connected to a pull-up resistor as shown in the figure. Assuming positive logic, when the fuse is left intact, the lower input to the exclusive-or-gate is at ground which is equivalent to a logic-0. Since $f_i \oplus 0 = f_i$, it follows that the output of the exclusive-or-gate is the same as the upper input. That is, the output corresponds to the true realization of f_i. On the other hand, when the fuse is blown, a positive voltage, i.e., logic-1, is applied to the lower input of the exclusive-or-gate. Since $f_i \oplus 1 = \overline{f}_i$, the net result is that the output of the exclusive-or-gate corresponds to the complemented realization of f_i. The symbolic representation of the programmable exclusive-or-gate is given in Fig. 5.58*b*. The general structure of a PLA with true or complemented output capability is shown in Fig. 5.59.

Now consider the Boolean functions

$$f_1(x,y,z) = \Sigma m(1,2,3,7)$$

$$f_2(x,y,z) = \Sigma m(0,1,2,6)$$

The Karnaugh maps of these functions are given in Fig. 5.60. The upper two maps are used to obtain a multiple-output minimal sum for f_1 and f_2; while the lower two maps are used to obtain the multiple-output minimal sum for $\overline{f}_1$ and $\overline{f}_2$. Again assume a realization of these functions using a 3×4×2 PLA is to be attempted. As in the previous examples, realizations of functions of this simplicity are not justified using PLAs. However, the interest here is to illustrate the use of complemented functions. If a 3×4×2 PLA is to be used, then only four product terms can be generated. Thus, a realization is not possible using the subcubes of 1-cells as indicated in the upper two maps of Fig. 5.60. On the other hand, the indicated

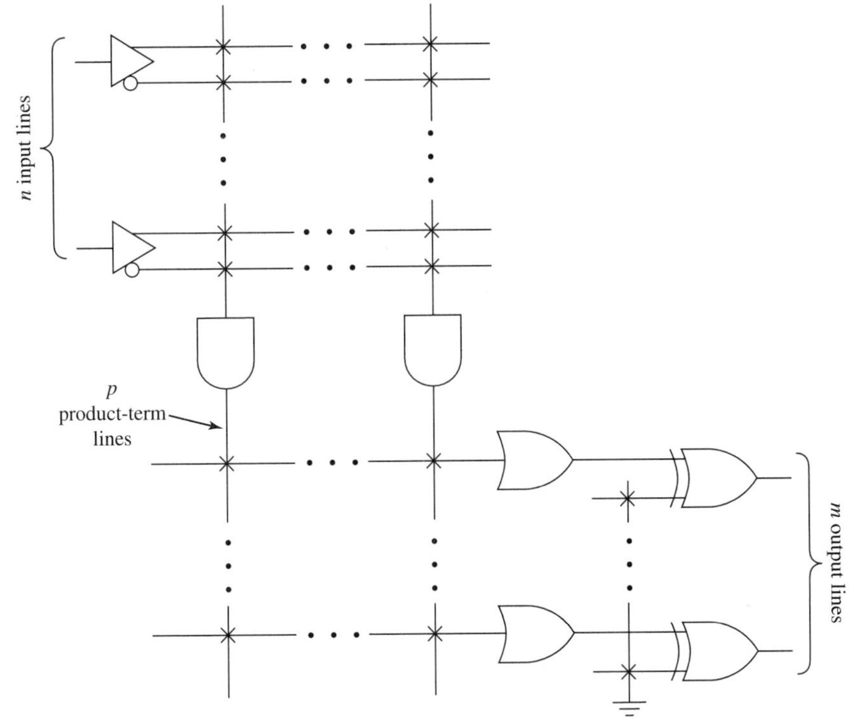

Figure 5.59 General structure of a PLA having true and complemented output capability.

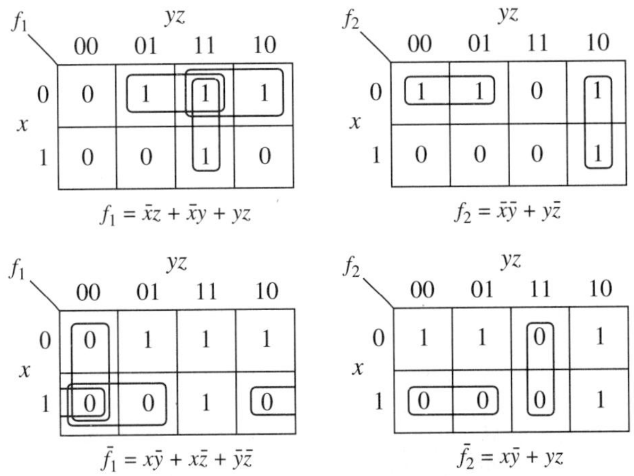

Figure 5.60 Karnaugh maps for the functions $f_1(x,y,z) = \Sigma m(1,2,3,7)$ and $f_2(x,y,z) = \Sigma m(0,1,2,6)$.

subcubes of the 1-cells for f_1 and the subcubes of the 0-cells for f_2 in Fig. 5.60 result in the expressions

$$f_1(x,y,z) = \bar{x}z + \bar{x}y + yz$$
$$\bar{f}_2(x,y,z) = x\bar{y} + yz$$

For these two expressions there are only four distinct product terms: $\bar{x}z$, $\bar{x}y$, yz, and $x\bar{y}$. Thus, the fuses in the and-array and or-array can be programmed for the f_1 and $\bar{f}_2$ expressions. If the 3×4×2 PLA has provisions for complementing its outputs as was illustrated in Fig. 5.58, then by leaving the fuse for the f_1 output exclusive-or-gate intact and blowing the fuse for the f_2 output, the desired realization is possi-

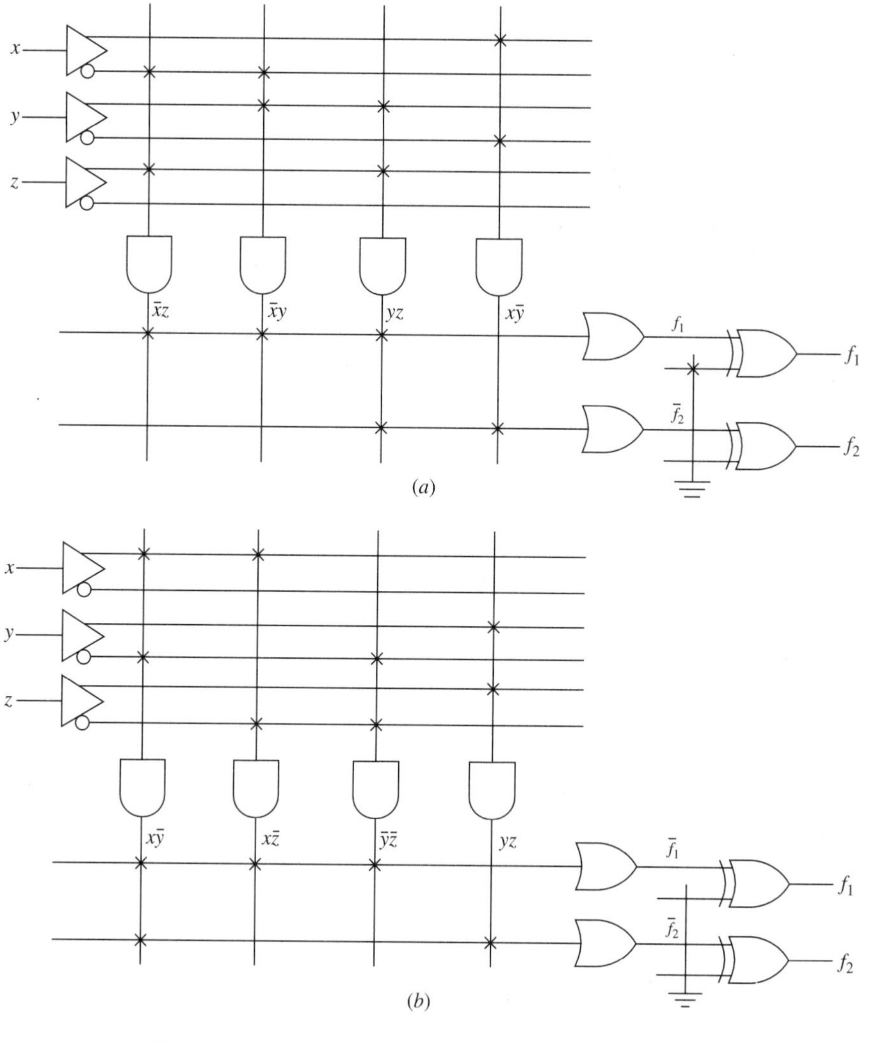

Figure 5.61 Two realizations of $f_1(x,y,z) = \Sigma m(1,2,3,7)$ and $f_2(x,y,z) = \Sigma m(0,1,2,6)$. (*a*) Realization based on f_1 and $\bar{f}_2$ (*b*) Realization based on $\bar{f}_1$ and $\bar{f}_2$.

ble. This is shown in Fig. 5.61*a*. It should be noted that $\bar{f}_2$ really occurs at one of the outputs of the or-array. By programming the corresponding exclusive-or-gate fuse, $\bar{\bar{f}}_2 = f_2$ appears at the output of the PLA.

In Fig. 5.60, it is also observed that there are only four distinct product terms in the expressions for $\bar{f}_1$ and $\bar{f}_2$. Hence, an alternative realization using a 3×4×2 PLA with output complementation capability can be based on these expressions. In this case, both output exclusive-or-gate fuses must be blown. This results in complementing the expressions so that the original functions are realized. The corresponding realization is shown in Fig. 5.61*b*.

A common way of specifying the connections in a PLA is via the *PLA table*. PLA tables for the two realizations of Fig. 5.61 are given in Table 5.8. In general, the PLA table has three sections for indicating connections: an input section, an output section, and a *T/C* section. Each product term is assigned a row in the table. The input section is used to specify the connections between the inputs and the gates in the and-array, thereby describing the connections needed to generate the product terms. The input variables are listed across the top of the input section. A 1 entry in this section indicates that a connection is to exist between the uncomplemented form of the input variable listed in the column heading and the and-gate associated with the row. On the other hand, a 0 entry in the input section indicates that a connection is to exist between the complemented form of the input variable listed in the column heading and the and-gate associated with the row. Finally, a dash indicates that there are no connections for the associated variable and the corresponding and-gate.

Table 5.8 PLA tables for the realizations of the functions given by the Karnaugh maps of Fig. 5.60. (*a*) PLA table for Fig. 5.61*a*. (*b*) PLA table for Fig. 5.61*b*

Product term	**Inputs** x	y	z	**Outputs** f_1	f_2
$\bar{x}z$	0	–	1	1	–
$\bar{x}y$	0	1	–	1	–
yz	–	1	1	1	1
$x\bar{y}$	1	0	–	–	1
			T/C	*T*	*C*

(*a*)

Product term	**Inputs** x	y	z	**Outputs** f_1	f_2
$x\bar{y}$	1	0	–	1	1
$x\bar{z}$	1	–	0	1	–
$\bar{y}\bar{z}$	–	0	0	1	–
yz	–	1	1	–	1
			T/C	*C*	*C*

(*b*)

The output section of the PLA table is used to specify the connections between the outputs of the and-gates and the inputs to the or-gates. The column headings correspond to the functions being realized. Here a 1 entry indicates that a connection is to exist between the and-gate associated with the row and the or-gate associated with the column. A dash entry in the output section indicates that the and-gate associated with the row is not connected to the or-gate associated with the column.

The *T/C* section indicates how the exclusive-or-gate fuses are programmed. A *T* entry means that the true output is used, thereby implying the fuse should be kept intact; while a *C* entry means that the output should be complemented, implying the fuse should be blown.

The above examples were contrived so that multiple-output minimal expressions were required to obtain the desired PLA realizations. However, PLAs are available in a variety of sizes. Nothing is gained by performing minimization if the minimized and nonminimized expressions result in using the same size PLA. PLAs are intended to provide for convenient realizations. For this reason, complete minimization becomes a secondary consideration when obtaining a PLA realization, since no simplification or only slight simplification of expressions may be sufficient for a realization using a PLA of a specified size. For example, simply minimizing the individual expressions and making use of any common terms might be sufficient to obtain an efficient realization without the need for determining the multiple-output minimal sum that involves the prime implicants of the product functions. In Chapter 8, PLAs are used without regard to determining multiple-output minimal sums. It will be seen that the networks being designed at that time are modeled in a form that immediately suggests a PLA realization.

5.10 PROGRAMMABLE ARRAY LOGIC (PAL) DEVICES

The final PLD to be discussed is the programmable array logic (PAL) device. In this type of device, only the and-array is programmable. The or-array is fixed by the manufacturer of the device. This makes the PAL device easier to program and less expensive than the PLA. On the other hand, since the or-array is fixed, it is less flexible than the PLA.

To illustrate the structure of a PAL device, a simple four-input, three-output PAL device is shown in Fig. 5.62. The reader should be aware that this PAL device is for illustrative purposes only and does not represent one that is commercially available. Commercial PAL devices can handle 10 or more inputs and may provide complemented outputs. In the figure, particular attention should be given to the fixed or-array. Here, two of the or-gates have three inputs each, while the third or-gate has only two inputs. All the input variables and their complements appear at the inputs to each of the and-gates. This allows each and-gate to generate any product term up to four variables. However, the output of each and-gate serves as an input to only one or-gate. For this simple, illustrative PAL device, three Boolean expressions can be realized in which two expressions can have at most three product terms and one expression can have at most two product terms.

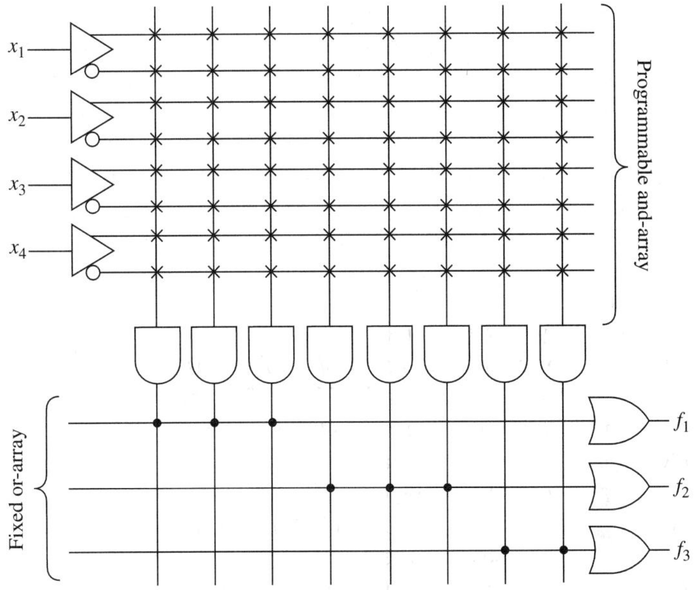

Figure 5.62 A simple four-input, three-output PAL device.

As an illustration of using a PAL device to realize combinational logic, consider the two functions

$$f_1(x,y,z) = \Sigma m(1,2,4,5,7)$$
$$f_2(x,y,z) = \Sigma m(0,1,3,5,7)$$

The corresponding Karnaugh maps are drawn in Fig. 5.63*a* from which the minimal sums are found to be

$$f_1(x,y,z) = x\bar{y} + xz + \bar{y}z + \bar{x}y\bar{z}$$
$$f_2(x,y,z) = z + \bar{x}\,\bar{y}$$

To use the illustrative PAL device of Fig. 5.62, a problem occurs with the realization of f_1 since the minimal expression consists of four product terms, while no or-gate in this device has more than three inputs. However, a realization is achievable if the realization is based upon the three expressions

$$f_1 = f_3 + \bar{y}z + \bar{x}y\bar{z}$$
$$f_2 = z + \bar{x}\,\bar{y}$$
$$f_3 = x\bar{y} + xz$$

This realization is shown in Fig. 5.63*b*. Here the first two product terms of f_1 are generated as the subfunction f_3. The f_3 subfunction is then fed back into an input terminal and combined with the remaining product terms of f_1 to produce the desired realization of f_1. To realize f_2, only two terms need to be generated. Since a three-input or-gate is used, the third input must correspond to a logic-0 so as not

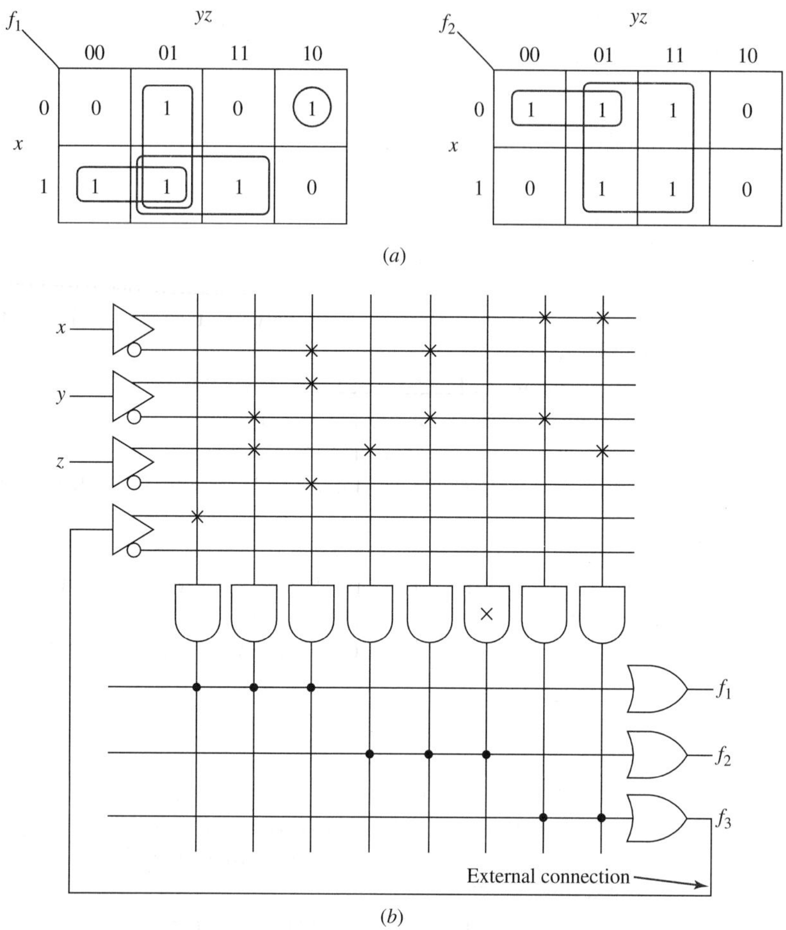

Figure 5.63 An example of using a PAL device to realize two Boolean functions. (*a*) Karnaugh maps. (*b*) Realization.

to affect the f_2 output. This is achieved by keeping all the fuses intact to the and-gate that serves as the third input to the f_2 or-gate. With a variable and its complement as inputs to an and-gate, the output of the gate is always at logic-0. As was mentioned in Sec. 5.7, the × in the gate symbol indicates that all its fuses are kept intact.

CHAPTER 5 PROBLEMS

5.1 Assume an adder/subtracter of the type shown in Fig. 5.6 is capable of handling two 5-bit operands. For each of the following set of unsigned operands, *X* and *Y*, and control input, Add/Sub, determine the output. Check your answers by converting the binary numbers into decimal.

a. $X = 10111$, $Y = 00110$, Add/Sub $= 0$

b. $X = 11010$, $Y = 01101$, Add/Sub $= 0$

c. $X = 11001$, $Y = 00101$, Add/Sub $= 1$

d. $X = 10011$, $Y = 11010$, Add/Sub $= 1$

5.2 Assume the binary adder/subtracter shown in Fig. 5.6 is to handle signed binary numbers in which x_{n-1} and y_{n-1} are the sign bits. Two methods were given in Sec. 2.8 for the detection of an overflow condition, one based on the sign bits of the operands and the other based on the carries into and from the sign digit position during addition.

a. Determine the additional logic needed if an overflow condition is to be detected based on the sign bits of the operands.

b. Determine the additional logic needed if an overflow condition is to be detected based on the carries into and from the sign digit position during addition.

5.3 Consider the cascade connection illustrated in Fig. 5.9 of 4-bit carry lookahead adders to obtain a large parallel adder. For this configuration, calculate the maximum propagation delay time, assuming each gate introduces a unit time of propagation delay, for a parallel adder handling

a. 8 bits.

b. 20 bits.

c. 40 bits.

d. n bits where n is divisible by 4.

5.4 Consider the 16-bit adder using carry lookahead generators shown in Fig. 5.10*b*. Calculate the maximum propagation delay time assuming each gate introduces a unit time of propagation delay.

5.5 a. Using a 4-bit binary adder, design a network to convert a decimal digit in 8421 code into a decimal digit in excess-3 code.

b. Using a 4-bit binary adder, design a network to convert a decimal digit in excess-3 code into a decimal digit in 8421 code.

5.6 Using an approach similar to that for the design of a single decade 8421 BCD adder, design a single decade 8421 BCD subtracter incorporating 4-bit binary subtracters.

5.7 Using an approach similar to that for the design of a single decade 8421 BCD adder, design a single decade adder in which the operand digits are in excess-3 code.

5.8 Design a specialized comparator for determining if two n-bit numbers are equal. To do this, design the necessary 1-bit comparator that can be cascaded to achieve this task.

5.9 In the design of the 1-bit comparator in Sec. 5.3, conditions $A > B$, $A = B$, and $A < B$ corresponded to $GEL = 100, 010$, and 001, respectively. Another approach to the design of a 1-bit comparator is to code the three conditions.

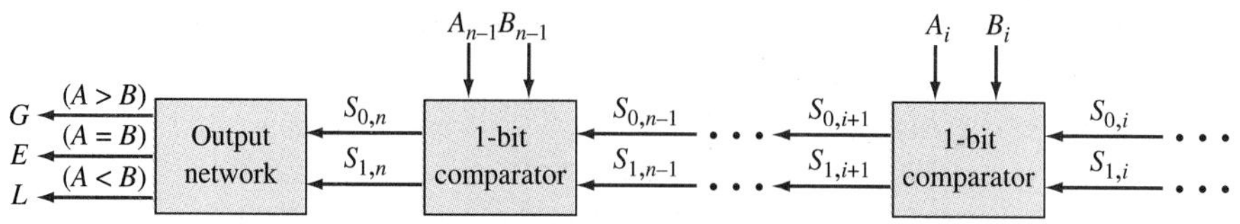

Figure P5.9

One possible code is $S_1S_0 = 10, 00,$ and 01 for $A > B$, $A = B$, and $A < B$, respectively. This implies that only two output lines occur from each 1-bit comparator. However, at the output of the last 1-bit comparator, an additional network must be designed to convert the end result into terms of G, E, and L. This approach is illustrated in Fig. P5.9. Design a 1-bit comparator and output network for this approach.

5.10 Using or-gates and/or nor-gates along with a 3-to-8-line decoder of the type shown in Fig. 5.18, realize the following pairs of expressions. In each case, the gates should be selected so as to minimize their total number of input terminals.

a. $f_1(x_2,x_1,x_0) = \Sigma m(1,3)$
$f_2(x_2,x_1,x_0) = \Sigma m(3,6,7)$

b. $f_1(x_2,x_1,x_0) = \Sigma m(0,1,5,6,7)$
$f_2(x_2,x_1,x_0) = \Sigma m(1,2,3,6,7)$

c. $f_1(x_2,x_1,x_0) = \Sigma m(0,2,4)$
$f_2(x_2,x_1,x_0) = \Sigma m(1,2,4,5,7)$

5.11 Using or-gates and/or nor-gates along with a 3-to-8-line decoder of the type shown in Fig. 5.18, realize the following pairs of expressions. In each case, the gates should be selected so as to minimize their total number of input terminals.

a. $f_1(x_2,x_1,x_0) = \Pi M(0,3,5,6,7)$
$f_2(x_2,x_1,x_0) = \Pi M(2,3,4,5,7)$

b. $f_1(x_2,x_1,x_0) = \Pi M(0,1,7)$
$f_2(x_2,x_1,x_0) = \Pi M(1,5,7)$

c. $f_1(x_2,x_1,x_0) = \Pi M(1,2,5)$
$f_2(x_2,x_1,x_0) = \Pi M(0,1,3,5,7)$

5.12 Using and-gates and/or nand-gates along with a 3-to-8-line decoder of the type shown in Fig. 5.22, realize the pairs of expressions of Problem 5.11. In each case, the gates should be selected so as to minimize their total number of input terminals.

5.13 Using and-gates and/or nand-gates along with a 3-to-8-line decoder of the type shown in Fig. 5.22, realize the pairs of expressions of Problem 5.10. In each case, the gates should be selected so as to minimize their total number of input terminals.

5.14 Using a 4-to-16-line decoder constructed from nand-gates and having an enable input $\overline{E}$, design an excess-3 to 8421 code converter. Select gates so as to minimize their total number of input terminals.

5.15 Using two 2-to-4-line decoders of the type shown in Fig. 5.26 along with any necessary gates, construct a 3-to-8-line decoder.

5.16 Write the condensed truth table for a 4-to-2-line priority encoder with a valid output where the highest priority is given to the input having the highest index. Determine the minimal sum equations for the three outputs.

5.17 Repeat Problem 5.16 where the highest priority is given to the input having the lowest index.

5.18 Figure 5.34 showed the structure of a 16-to-1-line multiplexer constructed from only 4-to-1-line multiplexers. Other structures are possible depending upon the type of multiplexers used. Construct a multiplexer tree for a 16-to-1-line multiplexer

a. Using only 2-to-1-line multiplexers.

b. Using 2-to-1-line and 4-to-1-line multiplexers. (Note: three different structures are possible.)

c. Using 2-to-1-line and 8-to-1-line multiplexers. (Note: two different structures are possible.)

5.19 Determine a Boolean expression in terms of the input variables that correspond to each of the multiplexer realizations shown in Fig. P5.19.

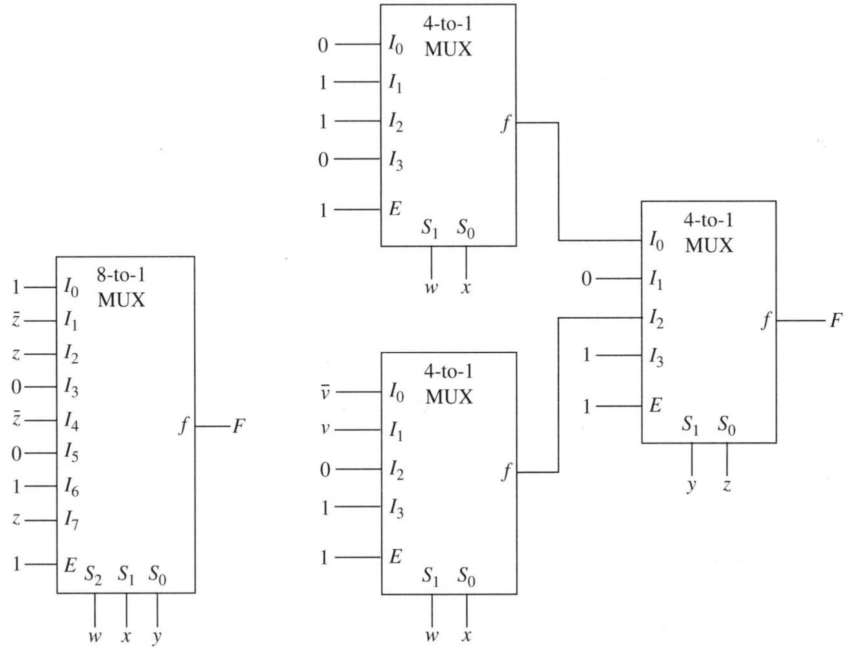

(a) (b)

Figure P5.19

5.20 For each of the following assignments to the select lines of an 8-to-1-line multiplexer, show the location of the I_i submaps, for $i = 0,1, \ldots, 7$, on a 4-variable Karnaugh map having the variables w, x, y, and z.

a. x, y, and z on select lines S_2, S_1, and S_0, respectively.

b. w, y, and z on select lines S_2, S_1, and S_0, respectively.

c. y, x, and w on select lines S_2, S_1, and S_0, respectively.

5.21 Realize each of the following Boolean expressions using an 8-to-1-line multiplexer where w, x, and y appear on select lines S_2, S_1, and S_0, respectively.

a. $f(w,x,y,z) = \Sigma m(1,2,6,7,9,11,12,14,15)$

b. $f(w,x,y,z) = \Sigma m(2,5,6,7,9,12,13,15)$

c. $f(w,x,y,z) = \Sigma m(1,2,4,5,8,10,11,15)$

d. $f(w,x,y,z) = \Sigma m(0,4,6,8,9,11,13,14)$

5.22 Repeat Problem 5.21 where x, y, and z appear on select lines S_2, S_1, and S_0, respectively.

5.23 For the function given by the Karnaugh map in Fig. 5.47*a,* determine a realization using a 4-to-1-line multiplexer and external gates if the w and x variables are applied to the S_0 and S_1 select lines, respectively.

5.24 Realize the Boolean expression

$$f(w,x,y,z) = \Sigma m(4,5,7,8,10,12,15)$$

using a 4-to-1-line multiplexer and external gates.

a. Let w and x appear on the select lines S_1 and S_0, respectively.

b. Let y and z appear on the select lines S_1 and S_0, respectively.

5.25 Realize the Boolean expression

$$f(w,x,y,z) = \Sigma m(0,2,4,5,7,9,10,14)$$

using a multiplexer tree structure. The first level should consist of two 4-to-1-line multiplexers with variables w and z on their select lines S_1 and S_0, respectively, and the second level should consist of a single 2-to-1-line multiplexer with the variable y on its select line.

5.26 A *shifter* is a combinational network capable of shifting a string of 0's and 1's to the left or right, leaving vacancies, by a fixed number of places as a result of a control signal. For example, assuming vacated positions are replaced by 0's, the string 0011 when shifted right by 1 bit position becomes 0001 and when shifted left by 1 bit position becomes 0110. A shifter to handle an n-bit string can be readily designed with n multiplexers. Bits from the string are applied to the data input lines. The control signals for the various actions are applied to the select input lines. The shifted string appears on the output lines. Design a shifter for handling a 4-bit string where Table P5.26 indicates the control signals and the desired actions. Vacated positions should be filled with 0's.

Table P5.26

S_1	S_0	Action
0	0	No change, i.e., pass input string to output
0	1	Shift right 1 bit position
1	0	Shift right 2 bit positions
1	1	Shift left 1 bit position

5.27 For the PROM realization shown in Fig. P5.27, determine the corresponding Boolean expressions for the outputs.

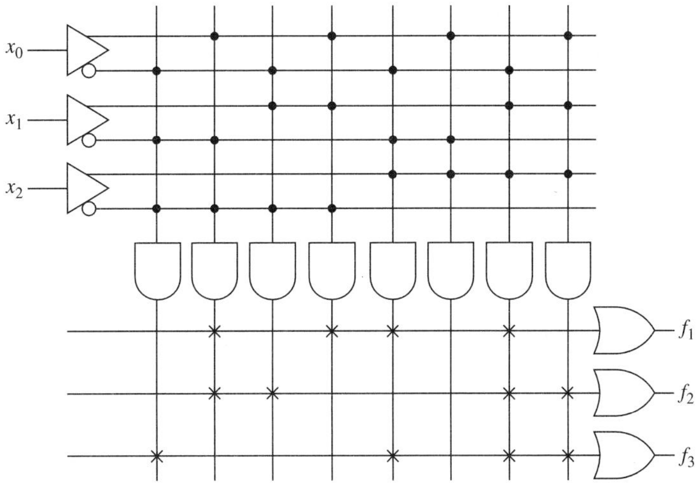

Figure P5.27

5.28 An application of PROMs is to perform code conversion. Using a PROM of an appropriate size, draw the logic diagram in PLD notation for a PROM realization to convert 4-bit binary numbers into Gray code. (Refer to Table 2.9 for the Gray code.)

5.29 An application of PROMs is to realize lookup tables for arithmetic functions. Using a PROM of the smallest appropriate size, draw the logic diagram in PLD notation for a PROM realization of the lookup table corresponding to the decimal arithmetic expression $F(X) = 3X + 2$ for $0 \leq X \leq 7$ where $F(X)$ and X are expressed in binary.

5.30 The pair of Boolean functions

$$f_1(w,x,y,z) = \Sigma m(2,4,5,10,12,13,14)$$

$$f_2(w,x,y,z) = \Sigma m(2,9,10,11,13,14,15)$$

are to be realized with a PLA having only true outputs. By considering just the prime implicants of each individual function and the product function, determine the minimal number of product terms needed for a realization. Draw the logic diagram of the realization in PLD notation and show the corresponding PLA table.

5.31 The following sets of Boolean functions are to be realized with PLAs having both true and complemented outputs. By considering just the prime implicants of the individual functions and their complements, determine the minimal number of product terms needed for each realization. In each case, draw the logic diagram of the realization in PLD notation and show the corresponding PLA table.

a. $f_1(x,y,z) = \Sigma m(3,6,7)$
$f_2(x,y,z) = \Sigma m(0,1,2,6,7)$
$f_3(x,y,z) = \Sigma m(0,1,3,4,5)$

b. $f_1(x,y,z) = \Sigma m(0,1,2,5,7)$
$f_2(x,y,z) = \Sigma m(3,4,5)$
$f_3(x,y,z) = \Sigma m(3,4,5,6)$

c. $f_1(x,y,z) = \Sigma m(1,3,4,6)$
$f_2(x,y,z) = \Sigma m(0,2,4,5,7)$
$f_3(x,y,z) = \Sigma m(1,3,5,6,7)$

5.32 Using the PAL device in Fig. 5.62, draw the logic diagram of a realization in PLD notation for the following set of Boolean functions.

$$f_1(x,y,z) = \Sigma m(1,2,4,6,7)$$

$$f_2(x,y,z) = \Sigma m(2,4,5,6)$$

$$f_3(x,y,z) = \Sigma m(1,4,6)$$

CHAPTER 6

Flip-Flops and Simple Flip-Flop Applications

The logic networks studied thus far are combinational networks. A combinational network is defined as a two-valued network in which the outputs at any instant are dependent only upon the inputs present at that instant. As a consequence of this definition, it is possible to describe each output of a combinational network by a single algebraic expression whose variables are the inputs to the network.

The above behavioral definition established only one class of logic networks. At this time, attention is turned to another class of logic networks. A *sequential network* is defined as a two-valued network in which the outputs at any instant are dependent not only upon the inputs present at that instant but also upon the past history (or sequence) of inputs. The past history of inputs must be preserved by the network. For this reason, sequential networks are said to have *memory*. The mechanism which is used to explain and represent the information preserved is referred to as the *internal state*, *secondary state*, or simply *state*, of the network. Physically, the internal state is a collection of signals at a set of points within the network. In this way, the inputs at any time to a sequential network, along with its present internal state, determine the outputs of the network.

There are two basic types of sequential networks. They are distinguished by the timing of the signals within the network. A *synchronous sequential network* is one in which its behavior is determined by the values of the signals at only discrete instants of time. These networks typically have a master-clock generator which produces a sequence of clock pulses. It is these clock pulses that effectively sample the input signals to determine the network behavior. This type of network is formally studied in Chapters 7 and 8. The second type of sequential network is the *asynchronous sequential network*. In this case the behavior of the network is immediately affected by the input signal changes. Asynchronous sequential networks are studied in Chapter 9.

The basic logic element that provides memory in many sequential networks is the *flip-flop*. Actually, the flip-flop itself is a simple sequential network. It can be shown that all sequential networks require the existence of feedback. In Sec. 6.1 it is seen that feedback is present in flip-flop circuits. A flip-flop has two stable conditions. To each of these stable conditions is associated a state, or, equivalently, the storage of a binary symbol. This chapter is concerned with the structure and operation of several types of flip-flops and some simple networks, e.g., registers and counters, that are constructed using them. ■

6.1 THE BASIC BISTABLE ELEMENT

Central to all flip-flop circuits is the *basic bistable element* which is shown in Fig. 6.1. This circuit has two outputs, Q and $\overline{Q}$. As seen from the figure, it consists of two cross-coupled not-gates, i.e., the output of the first not-gate serving as the input to the second and the output of the second not-gate serving as the input to the first. Clearly, this structure involves feedback.

As its name implies, the basic bistable element is a circuit having two stable conditions (or states). To see this, first assume $x = 0$ in Fig. 6.1. The output of the upper not-gate is then 1, i.e., $Q = \overline{x} = 1$. Since the output of the upper not-gate is the input to the lower not-gate, $\overline{x} = y = 1$. Consequently, the output of the lower not-gate, i.e., $\overline{y}$, is 0. However, since the output of the lower not-gate is connected to the input of the upper not-gate, $\overline{Q} = \overline{y} = x = 0$. This is precisely what was assumed to be the value of x. Thus, the circuit is stable with $\overline{Q} = x = \overline{y} = 0$ and $Q = \overline{x} = y = 1$.

Using a similar argument, it is easy to show that if it is assumed that $x = 1$, then the basic bistable element is stable with $\overline{Q} = x = \overline{y} = 1$ and $Q = \overline{x} = y = 0$. This is the second stable condition associated with the basic bistable element.

As a result of having two stable conditions, the basic bistable element is used to store binary symbols. In the case of positive logic, when the output line Q is 1, the element is said to be *storing a 1*; while when the output line Q is 0, the element is said to be *storing a 0.* It should be noted that the two outputs are complementary. That is, when $Q = 0$, $\overline{Q} = 1$; and when $Q = 1$, $\overline{Q} = 0$.

The binary symbol that is stored in the basic bistable element is referred to as the *content* or *state* of the element. The state of the basic bistable element is given by the signal value at the Q output terminal. Hence, the Q output termi-

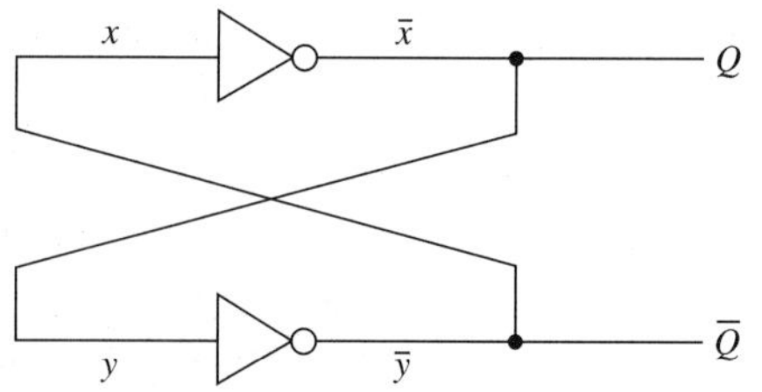

Figure 6.1 Basic bistable element.

nal is called the *normal output*; while the $\overline{Q}$ output is referred to as the *complementary output.* When the device is storing a 1, it is said to be in its *1-state* or *set.* On the other hand, when the device is storing a 0, it is said to be in its *0-state* or *reset.*

Although the bistable element is normally in one of its two stable conditions, there is one more equilibrium condition that can exist. This occurs when the two output signals are about halfway between those associated with logic-0 and logic-1. Thus, the output is not a valid logic signal. This is known as the *metastable state.* However, a small change in any of the internal signal values of the circuit, say, due to circuit noise, quickly causes the basic bistable element to leave the metastable state and enter one of its two stable states. Unfortunately, the amount of time a device can stay in its metastable state, if it should occur, is unpredictable. For this reason, the metastable state should be avoided. To avoid the metastable state, certain restrictions are placed on the operation of the basic bistable element. This is further discussed in Sec. 6.3.

The basic bistable element of Fig. 6.1 has no inputs. When power is applied, it becomes stable in one of its two stable states. It remains in this state until power is removed. For the circuit to be useful, provisions must be made to force the device into a particular state. A *flip-flop* is a bistable device, with inputs, that remains in a given state as long as power is applied and until input signals are applied to cause its output to change. It consists of a basic bistable element in which appropriate logic is added in order to control its state. The process of storing a 1 into a flip-flop is called *setting* or *presetting* the flip-flop; while the process of storing a 0 into a flip-flop is called *resetting* or *clearing* the flip-flop.

The inputs to a flip-flop are of two types. An *asynchronous* or *direct input* is one in which a signal change of sufficient magnitude and duration essentially produces an immediate change in the state of the flip-flop. In physical circuits, the response actually occurs after a very short time delay. This point is elaborated upon in Sec. 6.3 when the timing of signals is discussed in greater detail. On the other hand, a *synchronous input* does not immediately affect the state of the flip-flop, but rather affects the state of the flip-flop only when some control signal, usually called an *enable* or *clock* input, also occurs. In the next several sections, various input schemes to the basic bistable element are introduced that result in different types of flip-flops.

6.2 LATCHES

The storage devices called *latches* form one class of flip-flops. This class is characterized by the fact that the timing of the output changes is not controlled. That is, the output essentially responds immediately to changes on the input lines, although a special control signal, called the *enable* or *clock,* might also need to be present. Thus, the input lines are continuously being interrogated. In Secs. 6.4 and 6.5 flip-flops in which the timing of the output changes is controlled are studied. It this case, the inputs are normally sampled and not interrogated continuously.

6.2.1 The *SR* Latch

Figure 6.2*a* shows the *SR* (or *set-reset*) *latch* that consists of two cross-coupled nor-gates. It has two inputs, S and R, referred to as the *set* and *reset inputs*, and two outputs, Q and $\overline{Q}$. As is immediately evident from the second logic diagram in Fig. 6.2*a*, when $S = R = 0$, the logic diagram simplifies to the basic bistable element described in the previous section, i.e., the cross-coupling of two not-gates. Thus, the latch is in one of its two stable states when these inputs are applied. This condition corresponds to the first row of the function table given in Fig. 6.2*b*. In the table, Q denotes the *present state* of the latch. That is, Q is the state of the device at the time the input signals are applied. The response of the latch at the Q and $\overline{Q}$ output terminals as a consequence of applying the various inputs is denoted by Q^+ and $\overline{Q}^+$, respectively. Thus, Q^+ is called the *next state* of the latch. For $S = R = 0$, the entries Q and $\overline{Q}$ in the Q^+ and $\overline{Q}^+$ columns, respectively, are interpreted to mean that the next state of the device is the same as its present state. That is, the outputs do not change and the present state is retained.

Now assume a 1 is applied to the R input of the upper nor-gate in Fig. 6.2*a* and a 0 is applied to the S input of the lower nor-gate. Regardless of the second input to the upper nor-gate, the output Q must become 0 since $R = 1$. This signal, which is fed back to the lower nor-gate along with the 0 on the S input, causes the output of the lower nor-gate, $\overline{Q}$, to become 1. Thus it is seen that a 1 on the R input and 0 on the S input results in the latch being reset. This is given by the second row of the function table in Fig. 6.2*b*. If the input R is subsequently returned to 0, then the latch retains its present reset state as described by the first row of the function table

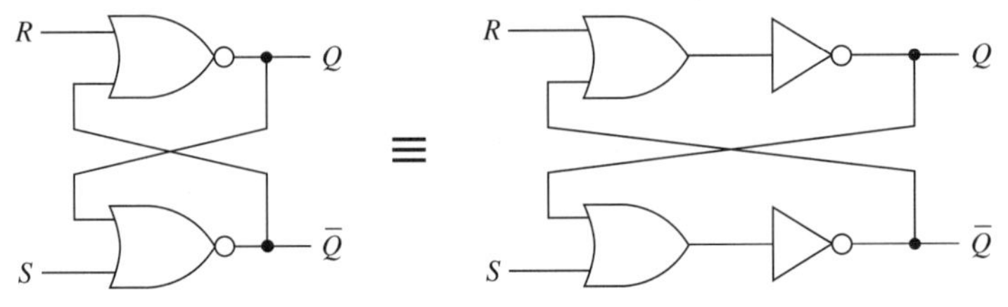

(*a*)

Inputs		Outputs	
S	R	Q^+	$\overline{Q}^+$
0	0	Q	$\overline{Q}$
0	1	0	1
1	0	1	0
1	1	0^*	0^*

*Unpredictable behavior will result if inputs return to 0 simultaneously

(*b*)

(*c*)

Figure 6.2 *SR* latch. (*a*) Logic diagrams. (*b*) Function table where Q^+ denotes the output Q in response to the inputs. (*c*) Two logic symbols.

since the $\overline{Q} = 1$ signal applied to the lower input of the upper nor-gate maintains the outputs $Q = 0$ and $\overline{Q} = 1$.

By a similar argument, if a 1 is applied to the S input and a 0 is applied to the R input, then the latch becomes set regardless of its present state. That is, the new outputs are $Q = 1$ and $\overline{Q} = 0$. This corresponds to the third row of the function table. Furthermore, the latch remains in the 1-state when the S input returns to 0.

For the three situations just discussed, the outputs Q and $\overline{Q}$ are complementary. Consider now the case when $S = R = 1$. This causes the outputs of both nor-gates to become 0 as indicated in the function table, and, consequently, they are not complementary outputs. Difficulty is encountered when the inputs return to 0. If one input should return to 0 before the other, then the final state of the latch is determined by the order in which the inputs are changed. In particular, the last input to stay at 1 determines the final state. In the event of both inputs returning to 0 simultaneously, the device may enter its metastable state. This is a condition that should be avoided as discussed previously. Eventually, the device becomes stable, but its final state is unpredictable since it is based on such things as construction differences and thermal noise. For this reason, along with the fact that the outputs are not complementary, the $S = R = 1$ input is frequently regarded as a forbidden input condition.

From the function table of the *SR* latch it should be noted that a 1 serves as the activation signal of the device. That is, a 1 on either the S or R input terminal causes the device to set or reset, respectively. Furthermore, since changes on the S and R inputs can immediately affect the outputs of the latch, the S and R inputs are regarded as asynchronous (or direct) inputs.

Two logic symbols for the *SR* latch are given in Fig. 6.2*c*. In the second symbol, the output bubble indicates the inversion of the normal state of the latch. Thus the output terminal with the bubble corresponds to $\overline{Q}$.

6.2.2 An Application of the *SR* Latch: A Switch Debouncer

A common problem involving switches is the occurrence of *contact bounce*. This is illustrated in Fig. 6.3*a*. As indicated by the waveforms, with the center contact of the switch in its lower position, the voltage at terminal B is $+V$ volts, while the voltage at terminal A is zero. Now if the center contact is moved from its lower position to its upper position, then it is noted that the voltage at terminal B first becomes zero, followed by the voltage at terminal A becoming $+V$ volts when the center contact reaches the upper terminal. However, as a result of contact bounce, the center contact of the switch leaves terminal A, causing the output voltage at that terminal to return to zero, and then upon returning to terminal A, causing the voltage at terminal A to become $+V$ volts again. This opening and closing effect, due to the springiness of the contacts, may occur several times before the center contact of the switch remains in its upper position. It is important to note that during contact bounce, the center contact does not return all the way to terminal B. Similarly, as indicated by the waveforms of Fig. 6.3*a*, contact bounce again occurs when the switch is moved from its upper position to its lower position. The effect of contact

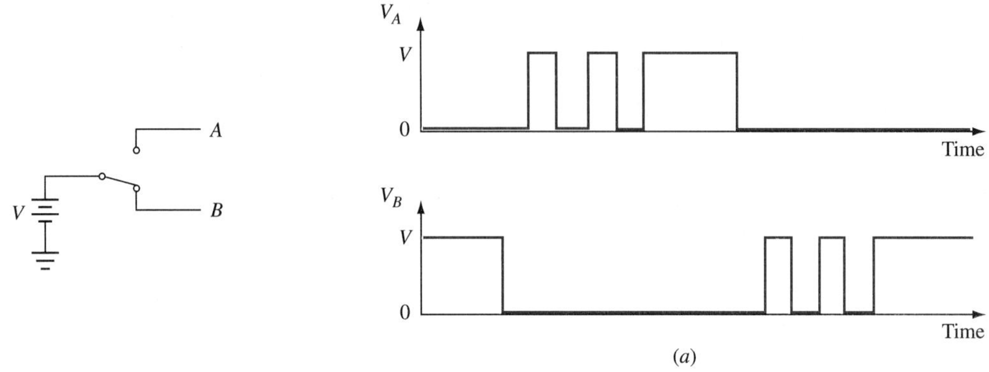

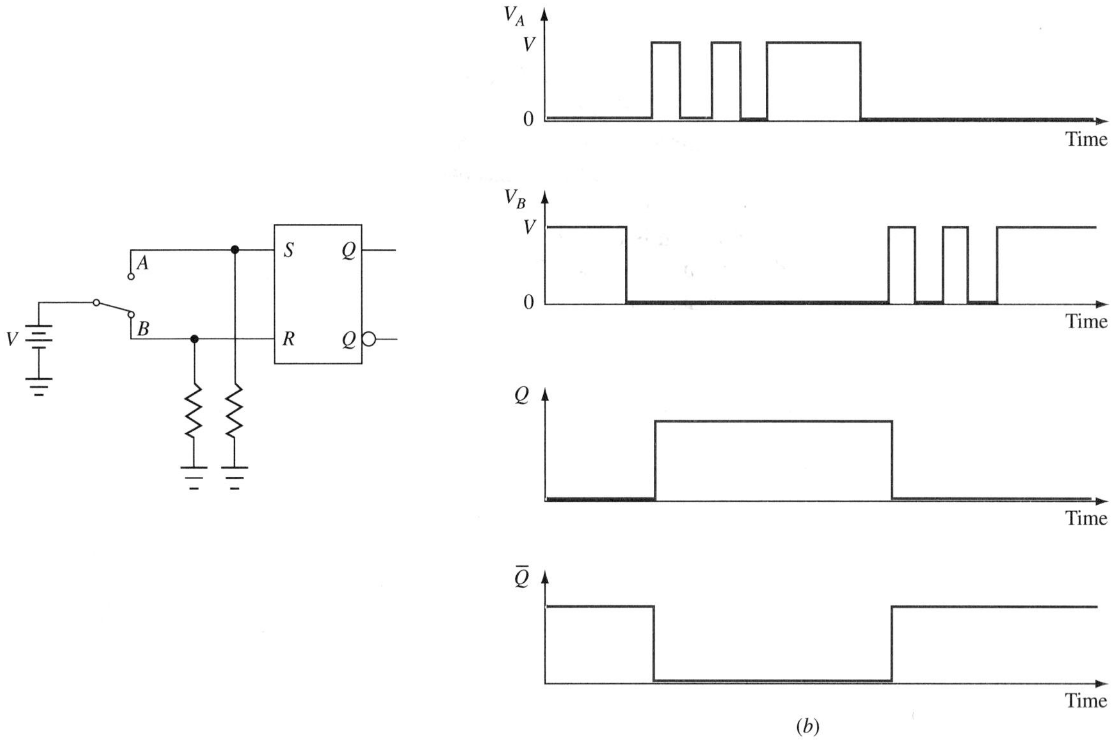

Figure 6.3 An application of the *SR* latch. (*a*) Effects of contact bounce. (*b*) A switch debouncer.

bounce is normally undesirable. For example, in the case of push-button keys on a keyboard, contact bounce may cause a system to respond as though a key was depressed several times in succession.

A very simple, but important, application of the *SR* latch is to eliminate the effect of contact bounce. A *switch debouncer* circuit and corresponding waveforms are shown in Fig. 6.3*b*. Assume positive logic so that $+V$ volts corresponds to logic-1 and ground to logic-0. By use of the two pull-down resistors, logic-0 values are ensured at the S and R terminals of the SR latch whenever the center contact of the switch is not connected to either terminals A or B, i.e., whenever the switch is open. Thus, when the center contact moves from its lower position to its upper position, the SR latch remains in its reset state until the center contact reaches terminal A, at which time the Q output of the SR latch becomes 1. If the switch now opens, as a result of contact bounce, then the 0 input to the S and R terminals of the latch causes the Q and $\overline{Q}$ outputs to remain unchanged. Hence, by use of the SR latch, the effect of contact bounce is eliminated. In a similar manner, the effect of contact bounce is also eliminated when the switch moves from its upper position to its lower position.

6.2.3 The $\overline{S}\,\overline{R}$ Latch

Another type of latch, the $\overline{S}\overline{R}$ *latch*, is constructed by cross-coupling two nand-gates. Such a latch is shown in Fig. 6.4*a* and its function table is given in Fig. 6.4*b*. From the second logic diagram of Fig. 6.4*a*, it is immediately seen that when $\overline{S} = \overline{R} = 1$ the logic diagram reverts to the basic bistable element of Sec. 6.1, i.e., the cross-coupling of two not-gates. Thus, the device has two stable states. This is indicated by the last row of the function table.

If just one of the inputs to the $\overline{S}\overline{R}$ latch is made 0 while the other is 1, then the output of the nand-gate having the 0 input becomes 1. This, in turn, is applied as an input to the second nand-gate that also has a 1 as its other input. Consequently, the

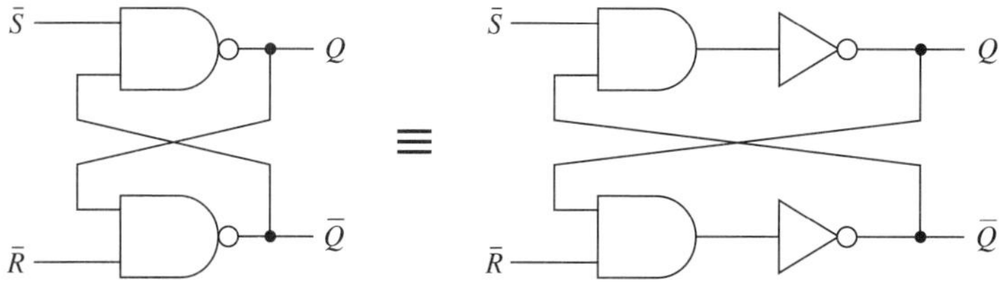

(*a*)

Inputs		Outputs	
$\overline{S}$	$\overline{R}$	Q^+	$\overline{Q}^+$
0	0	1*	1*
0	1	1	0
1	0	0	1
1	1	Q	$\overline{Q}$

*Unpredictable behavior will result if inputs return to 1 simultaneously

(*b*)

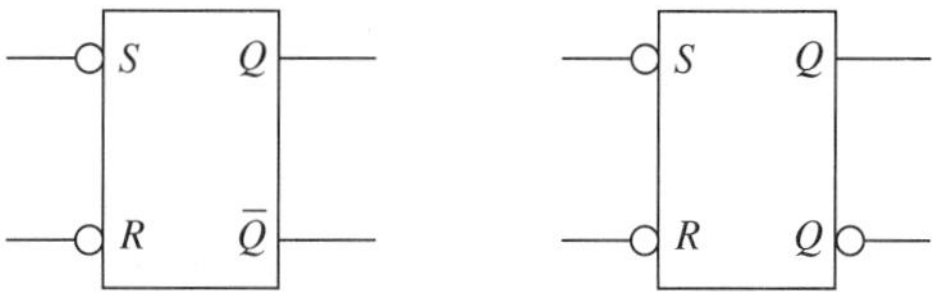

(*c*)

Figure 6.4 $\overline{S}\overline{R}$ latch. (*a*) Logic diagrams. (*b*) Function table where Q^+ denotes the output Q in response to the inputs. (*c*) Two logic symbols.

output of the second nand-gate becomes 0. Thus, if $\overline{R} = 0$ and $\overline{S} = 1$, then the latch resets; while if $\overline{R} = 1$ and $\overline{S} = 0$, then the latch sets. These conditions are described by the two middle rows of the function table. In either case, when the 0 input returns to 1, the $\overline{S}\overline{R}$ latch retains its present state.

Similar to the *SR* latch, the fourth possible input combination causes difficulty. In this case, if 0 is applied to both the $\overline{S}$ and $\overline{R}$ inputs, then both outputs become 1. Now if the inputs subsequently return to 1 simultaneously, then unpredictable behavior results in a similar way, as was discussed for the *SR* latch. Thus, the application of $\overline{S} = \overline{R} = 0$ is normally not recommended.

Referring to the function table of Fig. 6.4*b,* it is readily seen that 0 serves to initiate action in the $\overline{S}\overline{R}$ latch. That is, a 0 on the $\overline{S}$ terminal causes the latch to set; while a 0 on the $\overline{R}$ terminal causes it to reset.

Two symbols for the $\overline{S}\overline{R}$ latch are shown in Fig. 6.4*c*. It should be noted that inversion bubbles appear at the input terminals of the symbols since the latch responds to 0's on the inputs.

6.2.4 The Gated *SR* Latch

The inputs for both the *SR* latch and the $\overline{S}\overline{R}$ latch just described are asynchronous (or direct). That is, a change in value of these inputs causes an immediate change of the outputs. It is frequently desirable to prevent input activation signals from affecting the state of the latch immediately, but rather to have the effect occur at some desirable time or, alternatively, to allow the input changes to be effective only during a prescribed period of time. For these situations, a *gated SR latch* is used. The gated *SR* latch is also called an *SR latch with enable.*

A gated *SR* latch is shown in Fig. 6.5*a*. It consists of the $\overline{S}\overline{R}$ latch along with two additional nand-gates and a *control input, C,* referred to as the *enable, gate,* or *clock input.* The enable input, *C,* determines when the *S* and *R* inputs become effective. As long as the enable input is 0, the outputs of nand-gates *A* and *B* are 1, which, according to the $\overline{S}\overline{R}$-latch function table of Fig. 6.4*b,* keeps the $\overline{S}\overline{R}$ latch in its current stable state. In this case, any changes on the *S* and *R* lines are blocked and the output is said to be *latched* in its present state. Equivalently, the latch is said to be *disabled.* This is indicated by the last row of the function table in Fig. 6.5*b.* The crosses in the table under the *S* and *R* inputs are interpreted as "regardless of the value" or, simply, "irrelevant."

The remaining four rows of the function table correspond to those situations when the enable signal, *C,* is 1. In these cases the gated latch is said to be *enabled.* Here the latch behaves as a regular *SR* latch. The nand-gates *A* and *B* serve to invert the signals on the *S* and *R* input lines when the latch is enabled. Thus, a 1 on just one *S* or *R* input, in turn, becomes a 0 to the cross-coupled nand-gates and causes the latch to set or reset, respectively. Applying 1 simultaneously to both the *S* and *R* input terminals when $C = 1$ is not recommended in order to avoid the possibility of an unpredictable state if the activation signals are subsequently removed simultaneously or if *C* is changed to 0 while both the

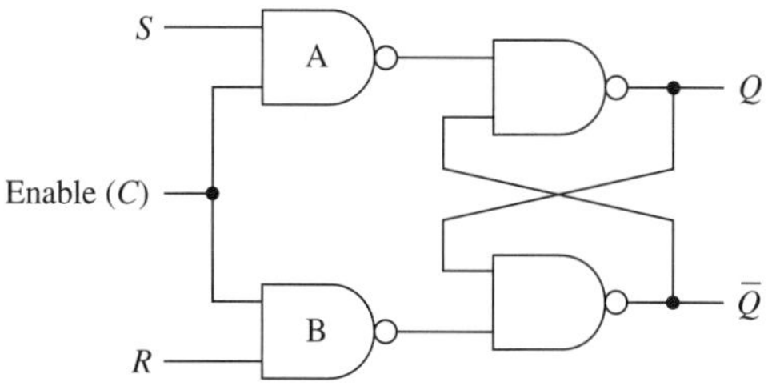

(a)

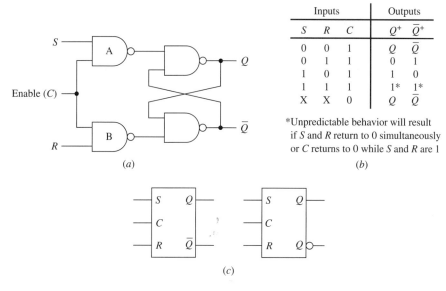

Inputs			Outputs	
S	R	C	Q^+	$\overline{Q}^+$
0	0	1	Q	$\overline{Q}$
0	1	1	0	1
1	0	1	1	0
1	1	1	1*	1*
X	X	0	Q	$\overline{Q}$

*Unpredictable behavior will result if S and R return to 0 simultaneously or C returns to 0 while S and R are 1

(b)

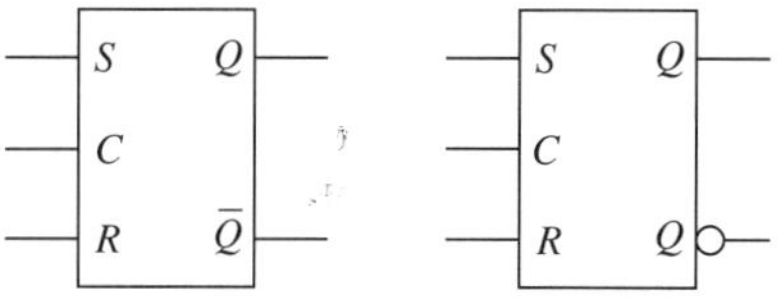

(c)

Figure 6.5 Gated *SR* latch. (*a*) Logic diagram. (*b*) Function table where Q^+ denotes the output Q in response to the inputs. (*c*) Two logic symbols.

activation signals are present. Since the effects of the S and R inputs are dependent upon the presence of an enable signal, these inputs are classified as synchronous inputs.

Two symbols for the gated *SR* latch are given in Fig. 6.5*c*. Again, the output terminal having the bubble corresponds to $\overline{Q}$.

6.2.5 The Gated *D* Latch

The three latches discussed thus far each has an input combination that is not recommended. In particular, the situation in which both of the noncontrol inputs, i.e., S and R or $\overline{S}$ and $\overline{R}$, are simultaneously active. The *gated D* (or *data*) *latch*, whose logic diagram and function table are shown in Fig. 6.6*a-b*, does not have this problem.

The gated D latch is a gated *SR* latch in which a not-gate is connected between the S and R terminals. Thus, the latch consists of a single input D that determines its next state and a control, i.e., enable, input C that determines when the D input is effective. As indicated in the function table, when the latch is enabled, i.e., $C = 1$, the output of the latch follows the values applied to the D input terminal. In particular, if $D = 0$, then the latch switches to or remains in the 0-state; while if $D = 1$, then the latch switches to or remains in the 1-state. However, when the latch is disabled, i.e., $C = 0$, the latch remains in the state prior to the enable signal going to 0. Two logic symbols for the gated D latch are given in Fig. 6.6*c*.

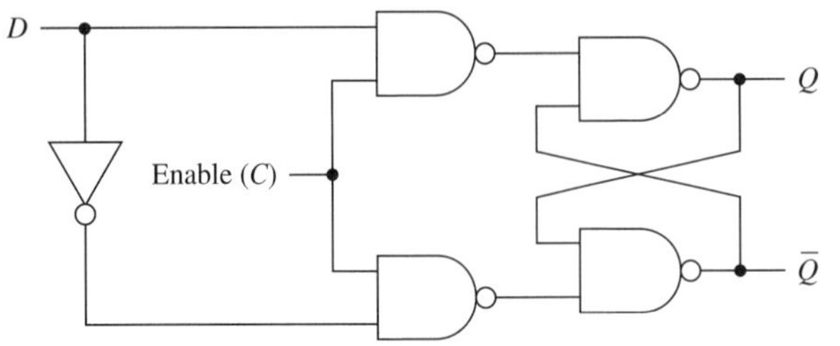

(a)

Inputs		Outputs	
D	C	Q^+	$\overline{Q}^+$
0	1	0	1
1	1	1	0
X	0	Q	$\overline{Q}$

(b)

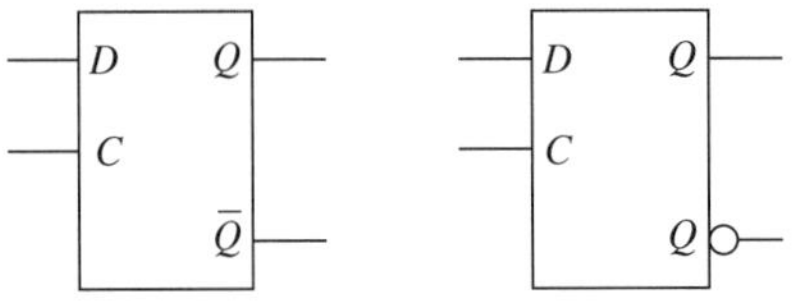

(c)

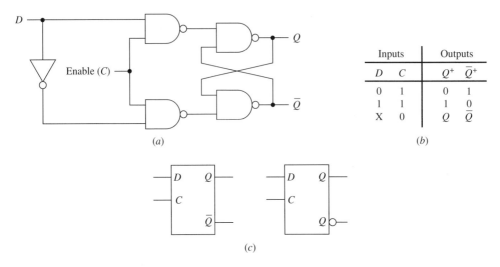

Figure 6.6 Gated *D* latch. (*a*) Logic diagram. (*b*) Function table where Q^+ denotes the output *Q* in response to the inputs. (*c*) Two logic symbols.

6.3 TIMING CONSIDERATIONS

The function tables for the various latches introduced specify the state outputs as a result of applying the input signals. However, the responses to the inputs are not really immediate, but rather occur after some appropriate time delay. This is due to the time delays associated with the gates themselves, as was discussed in Sec. 3.10. Furthermore, to achieve the desired responses, certain timing constraints must normally be satisfied. These timing constraints are presented in this section with reference to latches; however, they also pertain to the additional types of flip-flops that are discussed in the next two sections.

A convenient way of showing the terminal behavior of a flip-flop is the *timing diagram.* A timing diagram is a graph that depicts the input and output transitions of a flip-flop as a function of time.

6.3.1 Propagation Delays

The *propagation delay* is the time it takes a change in an input signal to produce a change in an output signal. In general, the propagation delay between each pair of input and output terminals is different, as well as whether the change causes the output to go from low to high, i.e., from 0 to 1 in positive logic, or from high to low, i.e., from 1 to 0 in positive logic. The various propagation delays of a flip-flop are specified by the manufacturer.

Propagation delays in an *SR* latch are illustrated in Fig. 6.7. Finite slopes of the rising and falling edges of the signals are shown since their midpoints are used in the specifications of the delay times. This figure shows the effect of first setting and then resetting an *SR* latch. It should be noted that the outputs do not change in-

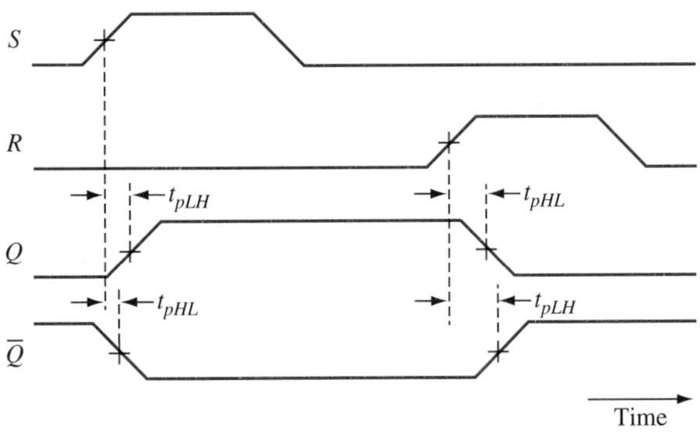

Figure 6.7 Propagation delays in an *SR* latch.

stantaneously to an input change nor do the outputs change simultaneously. Thus, the propagation delays from low to high, i.e., from 0 to 1 in positive logic, denoted by t_{pLH}, and from high to low, i.e., from 1 to 0 in positive logic, denoted by t_{pHL}, are, in general, different as well as whether the Q or $\overline{Q}$ output terminals are being viewed.

Figure 6.8 shows the outputs of an *SR* latch as various signal values are applied to the *S* and *R* inputs. This timing diagram is based on the function table of Fig. 6.2*b*. For simplicity, the finite slopes of the rising and falling edges of the signals are not shown and the propagation delays are assumed to be all equal. It should be noted in the figure that when $S = R = 1$, both the Q and $\overline{Q}$ outputs become 0. In addition, special attention should be given to the response of the latch at time t_{15}. Here it is assumed that the signals on the S and R input terminals are simultaneously changed from 1 to 0. As a consequence, the response of the latch is unpredictable as indicated by the shaded area. The latch may be in its 0-state, 1-state, or metastable state. At

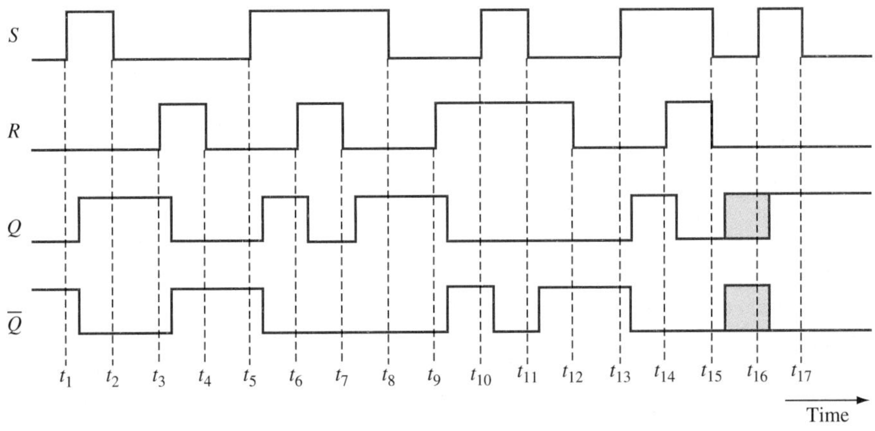

Figure 6.8 Timing diagram for an *SR* latch.

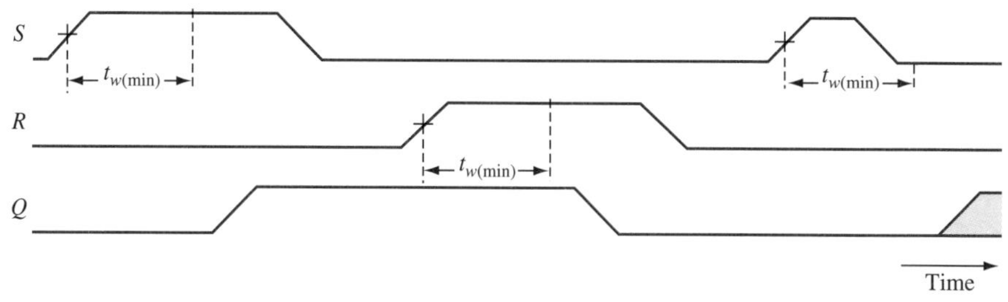

Figure 6.9 Minimum pulse width constraint.

time t_{16}, however, the application of the 1 on the set input terminal returns the latch to predictable behavior after a short propagation delay time.

6.3.2 Minimum Pulse Width

Another specification stated by the manufacturers of latches is that of a *minimum pulse width* $t_{w(min)}$. This is the minimum amount of time a signal must be applied in order to produce a desired result. Failure to satisfy this constraint may not cause the intended change or possibly have the latch enter its metastable state. In either event unintended behavior results. The minimum pulse width constraint is illustrated in Fig. 6.9. The shaded area of the output signal Q indicates that the state of the latch is unpredictable since the set signal did not satisfy the minimum pulse width constraint.

6.3.3 Setup and Hold Times

A timing diagram for a gated D latch whose function table was given in Fig. 6.6*b* is shown in Fig. 6.10. Again, for simplicity, the finite slopes of the rising and falling edges of the signals are not shown and all propagation delays are assumed to be equal. In accordance with the function table, and as illustrated in the figure, the Q-output of the latch follows the input signal at the D terminal whenever the enable signal, C, is 1. Whenever the enable signal is 0, changes at the D terminal are ig-

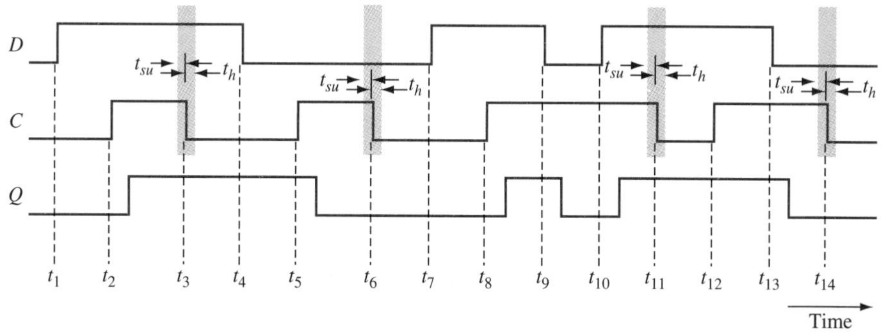

Figure 6.10 Timing diagram for a gated D latch.

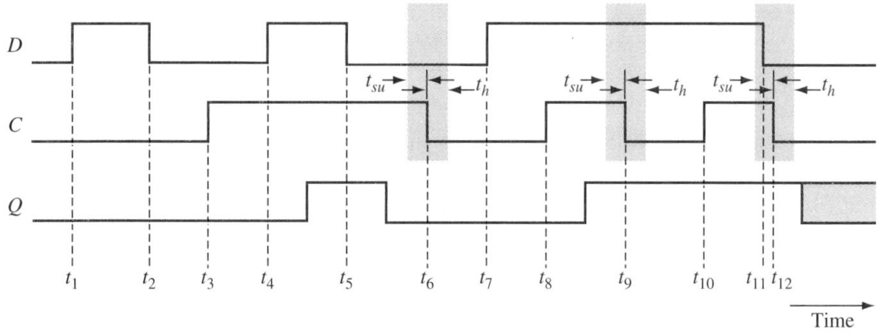

Figure 6.11 Illustration of an unpredictable response in a gated *D* latch.

nored and the *Q*-output retains the state of the latch just prior to the 1 to 0 change in the enable signal.

To achieve this operation of a gated latch, constraints are normally placed on the time intervals between input changes. Consider times t_3, t_6, t_{11}, and t_{14} in Fig. 6.10. At these times the enable signal *C* is returned to 0, causing the output to latch onto its current state. However, to guarantee this latching action, a constraint is placed upon the *D* signal for some minimum time before and after the enable signal goes from 1 to 0. This is shown as the shaded areas in Fig. 6.10. For proper operation, the *D* signal must not change during this period. The minimum time the *D* signal must be held fixed before the latching action, t_{su}, is called the *setup time*; while the minimum time the *D* signal must be held fixed after the latching action, t_h, is called the *hold time.*

Failure to satisfy the setup time and hold time constraints can result in unpredictable output behavior, including metastability. This is illustrated in Fig. 6.11, where unpredictable behavior occurs when latching is attempted at time t_{12} since the signal on the *D* line changed at time t_{11}, which is assumed to have occurred within the setup time of the gated *D* latch.

Setup and hold time constraints are very important properties when considering the behavior of all types of flip-flops. In the next two sections master-slave and edge-triggered flip-flops are discussed. The need to satisfy setup and hold times in these types of flip-flops relative to changes in their control signal must be adhered to for their proper operation.

6.4 MASTER-SLAVE FLIP-FLOPS (PULSE-TRIGGERED FLIP-FLOPS)

In addition to latches, there are two other general categories of flip-flops. These are the *master-slave flip-flops* (also called *pulse-triggered flip-flops*) and the *edge-triggered flip-flops.* The first of these two categories is considered in this section and the second is presented in the next section.

It was observed in Sec. 6.2 that latches have the common property of immediate output responses (to within the propagation delay times) while enabled caused by changes on the *information input lines,* i.e., the *S, R,* and *D* lines. This property is referred to as *transparency.* In certain applications this is an undesirable property. Rather, it is necessary that the output changes occur only coincident with changes on a *control input line.* This is particularly the case when it is necessary to sense the current state of a flip-flop while simultaneously allowing new state information to be entered as determined by the information lines. The property of having the timing of a flip-flop response being related to a control input signal is achieved with master-slave and edge-triggered flip-flops.

A master-slave flip-flop consists of two cascaded sections, each capable of storing a binary symbol. The first section is referred to as the *master* and the second section as the *slave.* Information is entered into the master on one edge or level of a control signal and is transferred to the slave on the next edge or level of the control signal. In its simplest form, each section is a latch.

6.4.1 The Master-Slave *SR* Flip-Flop

Figure 6.12*a* shows the master-slave *SR* flip-flop as constructed from two gated *SR* latches and an inverter. The information input lines *S* and R are used to set and reset the flip-flop. A clock signal, *C*, is applied to the control input line. The timing behavior of the master-slave flip-flop is referenced to the control signal. This behavior is illustrated in Fig. 6.12*b.* The transition of the control signal from its low to high value, i.e., 0 to 1 in positive logic, is called the *rising*, *leading*, or *positive* edge of the control signal; while the transition of the control signal from its high to low value, i.e., 1 to 0 in positive logic, is called the *falling*, *trailing*, or *negative* edge of the control signal.

Referring to Fig. 6.12, as long as $C = 0$ the master, being a gated *SR* latch, is disabled and any changes on the *S* and *R* input lines are ignored. At the same time, the slave is enabled due to the presence of the inverter. Hence, the slave is in the same state as that of the master since the Q_M and $\overline{Q}_M$ outputs of the master are connected to the *S* and *R* inputs, respectively, of the slave. As the control signal starts to rise, the slave is disabled, by design, at time t_1; while the master remains disabled. Thus, the slave becomes disconnected from the master but retains the state of the master. The control signal continues to rise, and it is at time t_2 that the master is enabled. While $C = 1$, the master, being a gated *SR* latch, responds to the inputs on the *S* and *R* lines, as was discussed in Sec. 6.2. Meanwhile, since the slave is disabled due to the presence of the inverter, any changes to the state of the master are not reflected to the slave. The control signal is subsequently returned to its low level at time t_3. At this time, the master is disabled, causing it to latch onto its new state. However, it is not until time t_4 that the slave is enabled. This results in the slave taking on the state of the master as the connection is made. It is important to note that for very short periods during the rising and falling edges of the control signal both the master and slave latches are disabled. This is critical to the operation of a master-slave flip-flop.

It should be observed that although the master can change its state (and, correspondingly, its output) at any time while the control signal is 1, it is only as the control signal goes from 1 to 0 that the slave changes its state. Thus, the output change of the master-slave flip-flop is synchronized to the falling edge of the control signal.

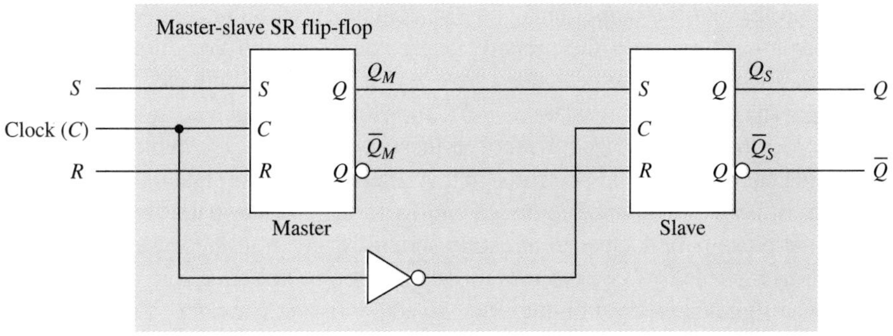

(*a*)

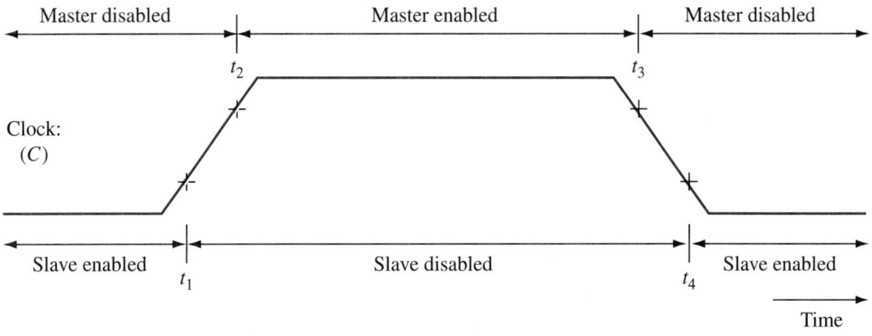

(*b*)

Inputs			Outputs	
S	R	C	Q^+	$\overline{Q}^+$
0	0	⎍	Q	$\overline{Q}$
0	1	⎍	0	1
1	0	⎍	1	0
1	1	⎍	Undefined	Undefined
X	X	0	Q	$\overline{Q}$

(*c*)

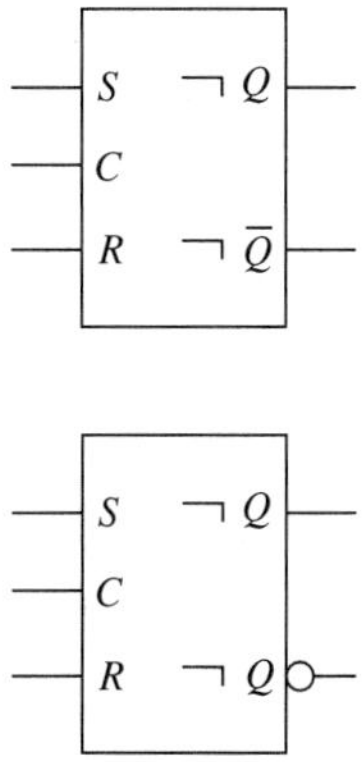

(*d*)

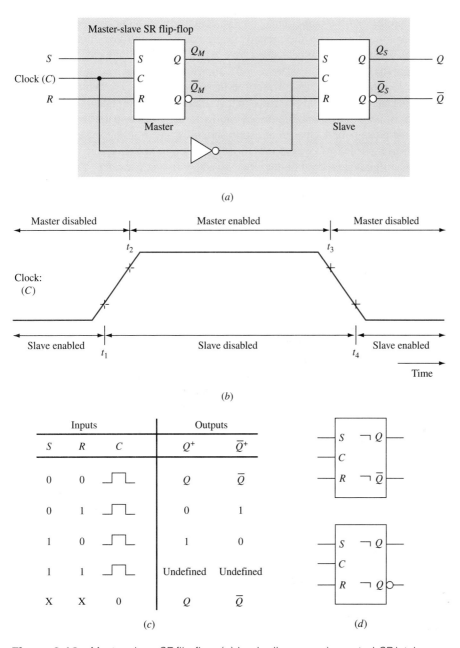

Figure 6.12 Master-slave *SR* flip-flop. (*a*) Logic diagram using gated *SR* latches. (*b*) Flip-flop action during the control signal. (*c*) Function table where Q^+ denotes the output Q in response to the inputs. (*d*) Two logic symbols.

This controlling of the output change to be coincident with the change on the control input line is precisely the property being sought by flip-flops not in the latch category. The master-slave principle is one way in which this property is achieved.

The behavior of the master-slave *SR* flip-flop is summarized by the function table in Fig. 6.12*c*. The pulse symbol in the *C* column, ⎍, indicates that the master is enabled while the control signal is high and that the state of the master is transferred to the slave, and, correspondingly, to the output of the flip-flop, at the end of the pulse period. Special attention should be given to the fourth row of the function table. This row corresponds to the situation of both *S* and *R* being 1 when the control signal goes from high to low. Since the master is a latch, it enters an unpredictable state, including the possibility of the metastable state. This state value is then subsequently transferred to the slave. Hence, the output of the master-slave *SR* flip-flop itself becomes unpredictable. Such a condition should be avoided. Since the behavior of master-slave flip-flops constructed from latches is dependent upon the rising and falling edges of the control signal as well as the period of time in which the control signal is high, they are also referred to as *pulse-triggered flip-flops*.

Two logic symbols for the master-slave *SR* flip-flop are given in Fig. 6.12*d*. The ⅂ symbol, called the *postponed-output indicator*, at the output terminals is used to imply that the output change is postponed until the end of the pulse period. For the master-slave flip-flop of Fig. 6.12*a*, this corresponds to the time when the control signal goes from high to low. Also, as in the case of latches, bubble notation is used to indicate the complementary output $\overline{Q}$ of the flip-flop in the second logic symbol shown.

Figure 6.13 shows a timing diagram for the input and output terminals of a master-slave *SR* flip-flop along with a timing diagram for the output terminals of the master section of the flip-flop. For simplicity, the finite slopes of the rising and

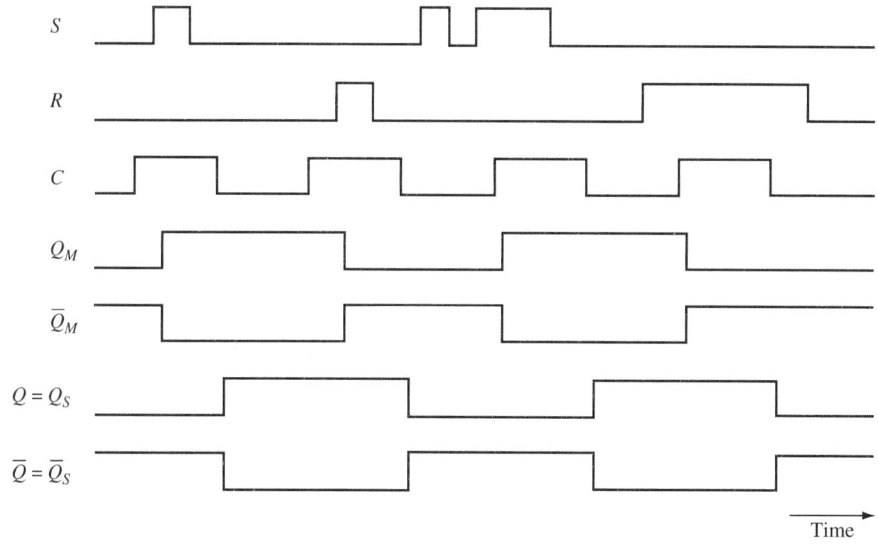

Figure 6.13 Timing diagram for a master-slave *SR* flip-flop.

falling edges of the signals are not shown and the propagation delays are assumed to be all equal. However, the sequence of events during the rise and fall times of the control signal as indicated in Fig. 6.12*b* is still occurring.

6.4.2 The Master-Slave *JK* Flip-Flop

Since the output state of a master-slave *SR* flip-flop is undefined upon returning the control input to 0 when $S = R = 1$, it is necessary to avoid this condition. The *master-slave JK flip-flop*, on the other hand, does allow its two information input lines to be simultaneously 1. This results in the toggling of the output of the flip-flop. That is, if the present state is 0, then the next state is 1; while if the present state is 1, then the next state is 0. The logic diagram of a master-slave *JK* flip-flop is shown in Fig. 6.14*a*. The *J* and *K* inputs have the effect of setting and resetting the flip-flop, respectively, and hence are analogous to the *S* and *R* inputs of the master-slave *SR* flip-flop. In addition, two and-gates are used to sense and steer the state of the slave.

To see how this flip-flop works, assume the master-slave *JK* flip-flop of Fig. 6.14*a* is in its 1-state, the control signal, i.e., the clock, is 0, and that $J = K = 1$. Thus, the master and slave latches are both in the 1-state with $Q = Q_S = 1$ and $\overline{Q} = \overline{Q}_S = 0$. As a result of the feedback lines, the output of the *J*-input and-gate is logic-0 and the output of the *K*-input and-gate is logic-1. The net effect is that $S = 0$ and $R = 1$ at the inputs to the master latch, although these inputs cannot affect the state of the master at this time since $C = 0$. If the clock is now changed from 0 to 1, then the master resets; while the slave, being disabled, remains in its 1-state. However, upon the clock returning to 0, the content of the master is transferred to the slave, causing the new state of the master-slave *JK* flip-flop to become the 0-state. Thus, the output of the master-slave *JK* flip-flop toggled when $J = K = 1$ as the result of the control signal.

Now assume the master-slave *JK* flip-flop is in its 0-state, again $J = K = 1$, and the control signal, i.e., the clock, is low. Thus, $Q = Q_S = 0$ and $\overline{Q} = \overline{Q}_S = 1$. In this case the output of the *J*-input and-gate is logic-1; while the output of the *K*-input and-gate is logic-0. At the master input terminals, $S = 1$ and $R = 0$. Hence, when the clock is changed from 0 to 1, the master enters its 1-state, which is subsequently transferred to the slave when the clock changes from 1 to 0. Again, the state of the master-slave *JK* flip-flop toggled. The toggling behavior of the flip-flop when $J = K = 1$ is indicated by the fourth row in the function table shown in Fig. 6.14*b*.

Consider now the third row of the function table that indicates that a 1 on just the *J* input line has the effect of setting the flip-flop. To see this, assume the master-slave *JK* flip-flop is in its 1-state when the clock is low. Thus, $Q = Q_S = 1$ and $\overline{Q} = \overline{Q}_S = 0$. Since the slave is enabled and in its 1-state, the master must also be in its 1-state, i.e., $Q_M = 1$ and $\overline{Q}_M = 0$. If $J = 1$ and $K = 0$, then the outputs of both and-gates are logic-0 since they each have a 0 on one of their inputs, i.e., the upper and-gate has $\overline{Q}_S = 0$ and the lower and-gate has $K = 0$. Consequently, at the input terminals of the master, $S = R = 0$. When the clock becomes 1, the state of the master does not change, i.e., it remains in its 1-state. Upon returning the clock to 0, the slave, which in turn takes on the value of the master, also remains in its 1-state.

On the other hand, if the master and slave latches are in their 0-states when $J = 1$, $K = 0$, and the clock is low, then $Q = Q_M = Q_S = 0$ and $\overline{Q} = \overline{Q}_M = \overline{Q}_S = 1$.

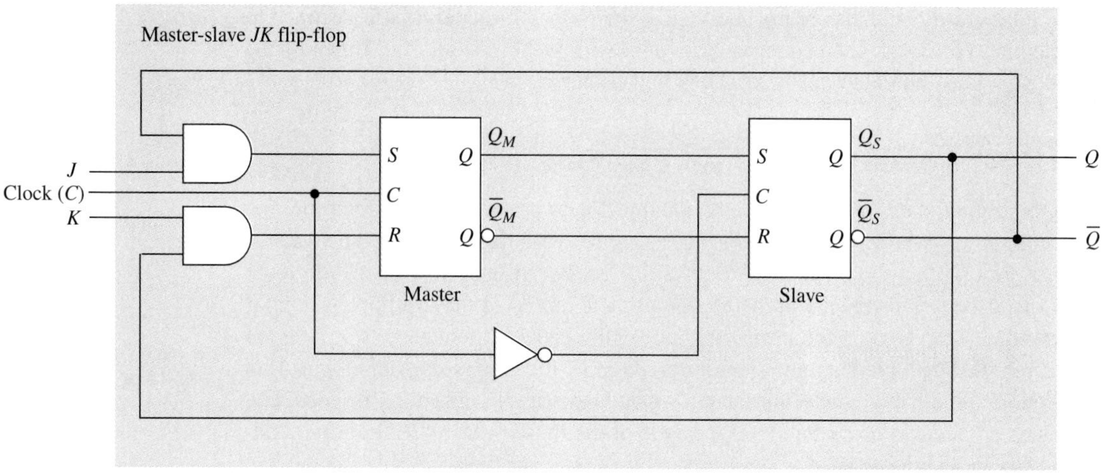

(a)

Inputs			Outputs	
J	K	C	Q^+	$\overline{Q}^+$
0	0	⎍	Q	$\overline{Q}$
0	1	⎍	0	1
1	0	⎍	1	0
1	1	⎍	$\overline{Q}$	Q
X	X	0	Q	$\overline{Q}$

(b)

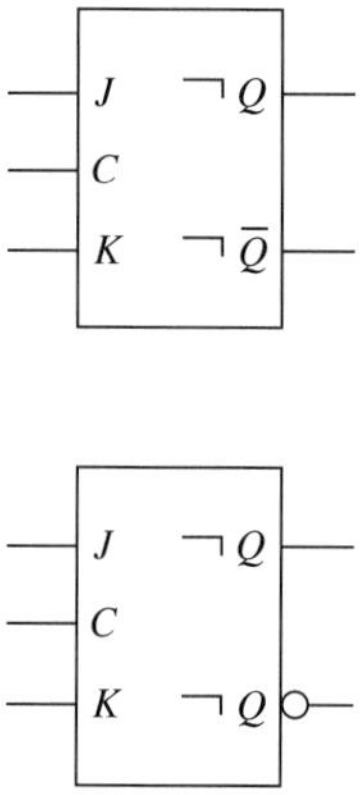

(c)

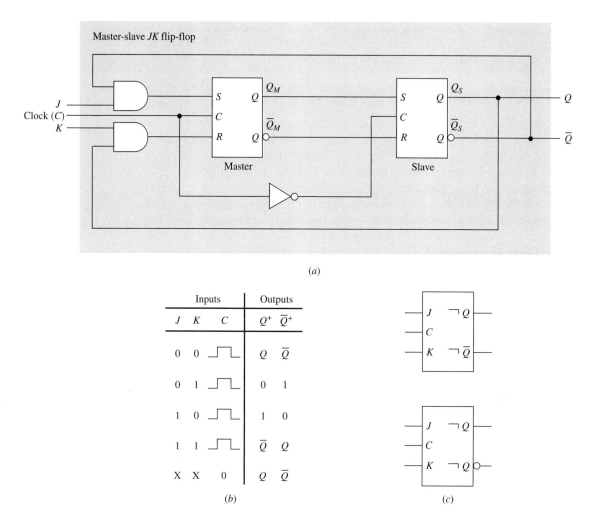

Figure 6.14 Master-slave *JK* flip-flop. (*a*) Logic diagram using gated *SR* latches. (*b*) Function table where Q^+ denotes the output Q in response to the inputs. (*c*) Two logic symbols.

The output of the J-input and-gate is logic-1 and the output of the K-input and-gate is logic-0. Thus, $S = 1$ and $R = 0$ at the inputs to the master latch. When the clock goes high, the master is set. The 1-state of the master is then subsequently transferred to the slave when the clock returns to 0. In summary, regardless of its present state when $J = 1$ and $K = 0$, the master-slave *JK* flip-flop enters or remains in its 1-state upon the occurrence of the pulse signal on the control line. This corresponds to the third row of the function table.

By a similar argument, if $J = 0$ and $K = 1$, then the master-slave *JK* flip-flop enters or remains in its 0-state after a clock pulse has occurred. This resetting effect is described by the second row of the function table.

Considering the remaining rows of the function table, the first row indicates that the master-slave *JK* flip-flop retains its current state when $J = K = 0$ during a clock pulse. Similarly, the last row indicates that whenever the clock is low, i.e., $C = 0$, the state of the flip-flop does not change.

In Fig. 6.14*c* two symbols are shown for the master-slave *JK* flip-flop. Again, the postponed-output indicator is used to symbolize that the output change occurs coincident with the falling edge of the control signal, i.e., when the control signal changes from 1 to 0.

For ease of the above analysis, the logic-1 values on the *J* and *K* lines were assumed to be applied prior to the application of the clock pulse. In actuality, these values can occur anytime while the control signal is 1 since the master, being a latch, is enabled during that time.

A timing diagram illustrating the behavior of a master-slave *JK* flip-flop is shown in Fig. 6.15. Again, for simplicity, propagation delays are assumed to be equal and the finite slopes of the rising and falling edges of the signals are not shown. In addition, manufacturer's constraints regarding minimum width of the signals, i.e., minimum time durations that signals are applied, and setup and hold times of the information signals relative to the control signal must be adhered to for proper operation of master-slave flip-flops. It is assumed these constraints are satisfied in the timing diagram of Fig. 6.15.

6.4.3 0's and 1's Catching

As was indicated above and illustrated in Fig. 6.15, the master of the master-slave *JK* flip-flop, being a latch, is enabled during the entire period the control signal is 1.

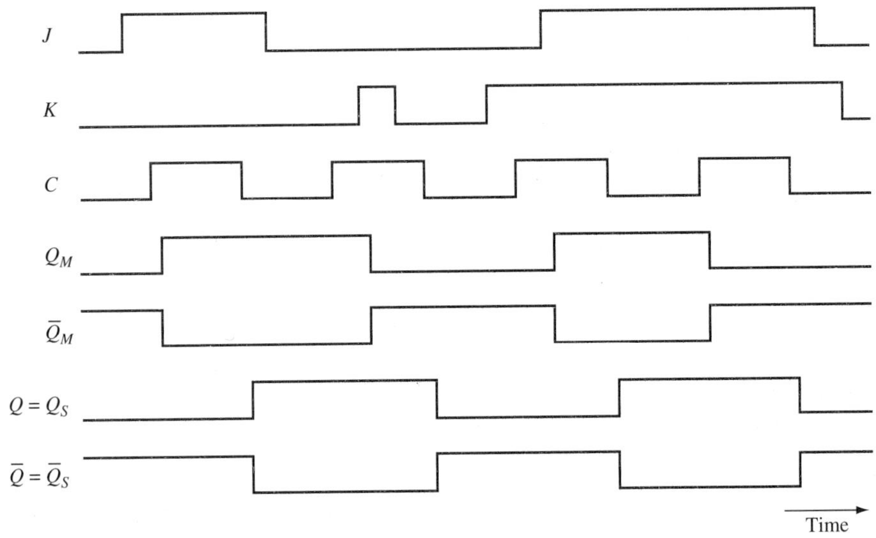

Figure 6.15 Timing diagram for a master-slave *JK* flip-flop.

Thus, if the slave latch is in its 1-state, then a logic-1 on the K input line while the control signal is 1 causes the master latch to reset. This subsequently results in the slave becoming reset when the control signal returns to 0. An example of this occurred during the second clock pulse in Fig. 6.15. This behavior is known as *0's catching*. It should be noted that once the master latch is reset by a logic-1 signal on the K input line, a subsequent logic-1 signal on the J input line during the same period in which $C = 1$ does not cause the master to again become set. This is due to the fact that since the slave does not change its state until C returns to 0, the feedback signal from the slave, i.e., $\overline{Q}_S = 0$, keeps the output of the J-input and-gate at logic-0.

In a similar manner, if the slave is storing a 0, then a logic-1 on the J input line while the control signal is 1 causes the master latch to be set, which subsequently results in the setting of the slave upon the occurrence of the falling edge of the control signal. This behavior occurred during the third clock pulse in Fig. 6.15 and is known as *1's catching*.

In many applications, the 0's and 1's catching behavior is undesirable. Hence, it is normally recommended that the J and K input values should be held fixed during the entire interval that the master is enabled. To satisfy this constraint, any changes in the J and K inputs must occur while the control signal is 0. This was done during the first and fourth clock pulses in Fig. 6.15. The function table of Fig. 6.14*b* does not account for 0's and 1's catching but, rather, assumes the J and K inputs are held fixed during the entire period the control signal is 1. The problem of 0's and 1's catching is also solved by the use of another class of flip-flops called *edge-triggered flip-flops*. This class of flip-flops is studied in Sec. 6.5. Alternatively, a variation of the master-slave flip-flop, called the *master-slave flip-flop with data lockout*, is available that is not subject to 0's and 1's catching. This variation also is discussed in the next section.

6.4.4 Additional Types of Master-Slave Flip-Flops

So far the master-slave SR and JK flip-flops have been discussed. From these, additional types of master-slave flip-flops can be constructed. For example, by placing an inverter between the S and R inputs of a master-slave SR flip-flop, as shown in Fig. 6.16, a *master-slave D flip-flop* is obtained.

Another type of master-slave flip-flop is shown in Fig. 6.17*a*, where the J and K input terminals are tied together so that $T = J = K$. In this case the flip-flop

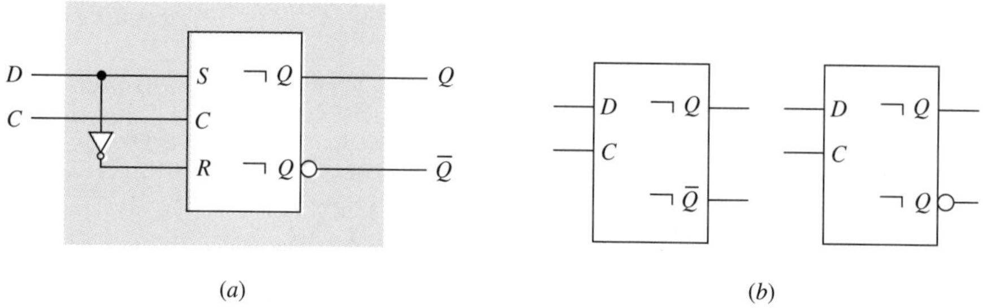

Figure 6.16 Master-slave D flip-flop. (a) Logic diagram using a master-slave SR flip-flop. (b) Two logic symbols.

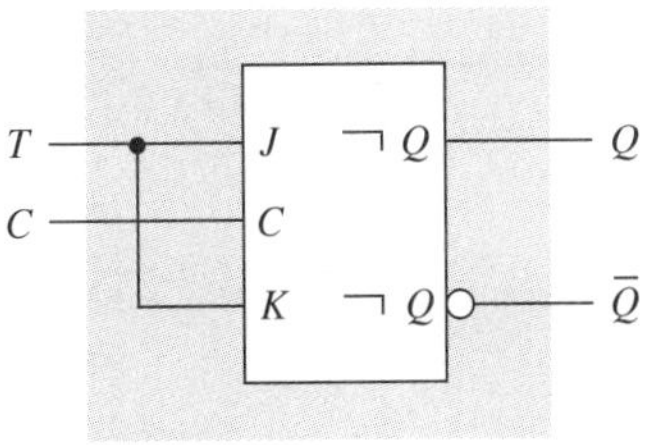

(*a*)

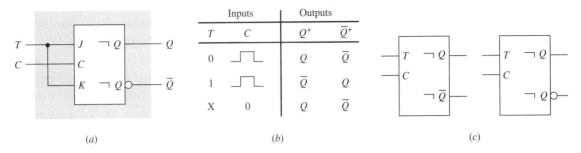

Inputs		Outputs	
T	C	Q^+	$\overline{Q}^+$
0	⊓	Q	$\overline{Q}$
1	⊓	$\overline{Q}$	Q
X	0	Q	$\overline{Q}$

(*b*)

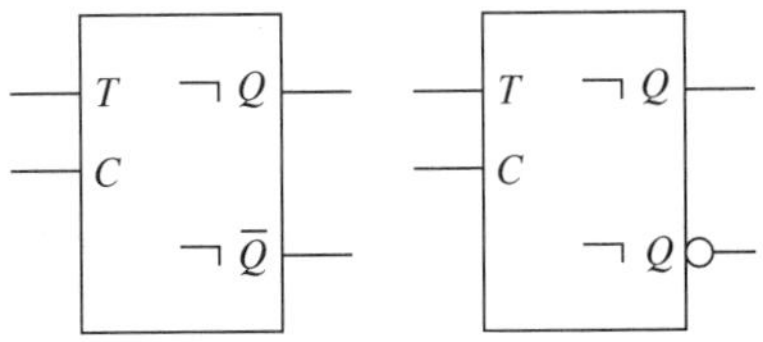

(*c*)

Figure 6.17 Master-slave *T* flip-flop. (*a*) Logic diagram using a master-slave *JK* flip-flop. (*b*) Function table where Q^+ denotes the output Q in response to the inputs. (*c*) Two logic symbols.

changes state, or toggles, with each control pulse if $T = 1$ and retains its current state with each control pulse if $T = 0$. This is called a *master-slave T flip-flop.* The function table of the master-slave *T* flip-flop and its logic symbols are given in Fig. 6.17*b-c*.

6.5 EDGE-TRIGGERED FLIP-FLOPS

In basic master-slave flip-flops, the master is enabled during the entire period the control input is 1. As was mentioned previously, this can result in 0's and 1's catching. To avoid the catching problem, the signals on the information lines are restricted from changing during the time the master is enabled. In this way the state of the master is established during the positive edge of the control signal and then transferred to the slave on the negative edge of the control signal. As a consequence of this process, the effect of the information signals appears delayed at the output of the master-slave flip-flop.

Edge-triggered flip-flops use just one of the edges of the control, i.e., clock, signal to affect the reading of the information input lines. This is referred to as the *triggering edge.* These flip-flops are designed to use either the positive or negative transition of the control signal for this purpose. The response to the triggering edge at the outputs of the flip-flop is almost immediate since it is dependent only on the propagation delay times of its components. Once the triggering edge occurs, the flip-flop remains unresponsive to information input changes until the next triggering edge of the control signal.

6.5.1 The Positive-Edge-Triggered *D* Flip-Flop

The logic diagram of a positive-edge-triggered *D* flip-flop is shown in Fig. 6.18*a*, where *D* is the information input and *C* is the control, or clock, input. By positive-edge-triggered it is meant that the setting or resetting of the flip-flop is established by the rising, or positive, edge of the control signal. The behavior of the positive-edge-triggered *D* flip-flop, given in Fig. 6.18*b*, is similar to that of the *D* latch, with the major difference being that the value of the *D* input is transferred to the output only as a consequence of the rising edge of the signal on the control line. Thus, the

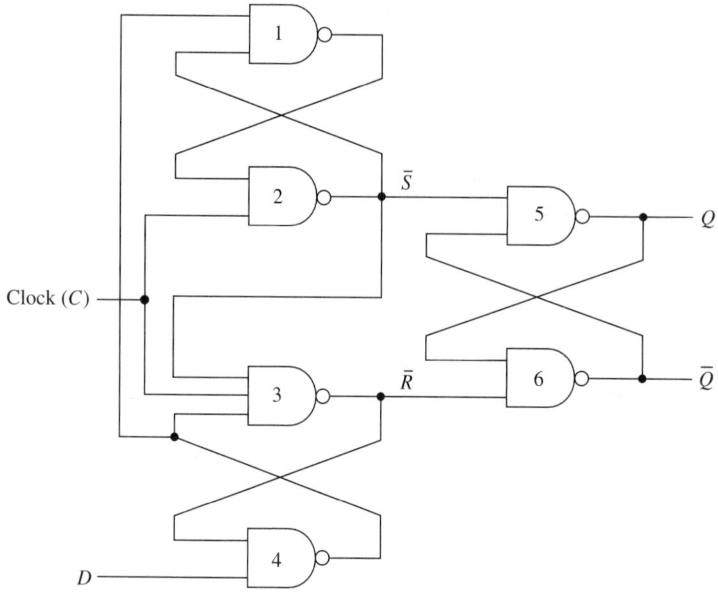

(a)

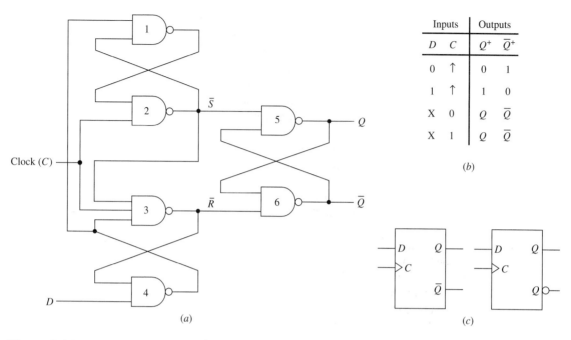

Inputs		Outputs	
D	C	Q^+	$\overline{Q}^+$
0	↑	0	1
1	↑	1	0
X	0	Q	$\overline{Q}$
X	1	Q	$\overline{Q}$

(b)

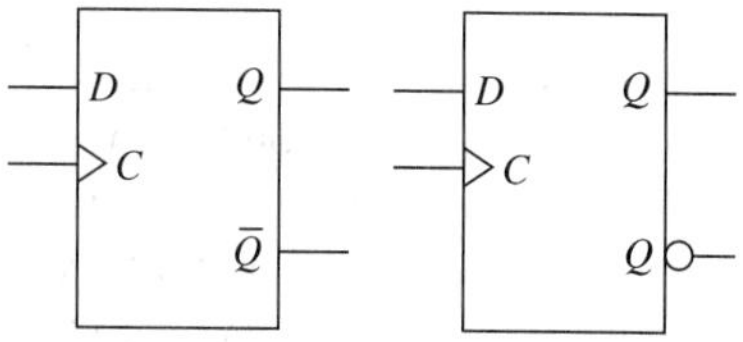

(c)

Figure 6.18 Positive-edge-triggered D flip-flop. (a) Logic diagram. (b) Function table where Q^+ denotes the output Q in response to the inputs. (c) Two logic symbols.

positive edge of the control input has the effect of sampling the D input line. This is indicated in the function table by the ↑ symbol. At all other times, including the time while the clock is at 1, the D input is inhibited and the state of the flip-flop cannot change.

To see how the positive-edge-triggered D flip-flop operates, consider the logic diagram in Fig. 6.18a. Nand-gates 5 and 6 serve as an $\overline{S}\overline{R}$ latch whose behavior was previously described by the function table in Fig. 6.4b. Thus, as long as $\overline{S} = \overline{R} = 1$, the state of the latch cannot change; while whenever either $\overline{S}$ or $\overline{R}$ is 0, but not both, the latch sets or resets, respectively.

Assume the control input, i.e., clock, C, is 0. Regardless of the input at D, the outputs of nand-gates 2 and 3 are 1. These signals are applied to the $\overline{S}\overline{R}$ output latch, causing it to hold its current state. Now assume that D is also 0. This holds the output of gate 4 at 1. In turn, the output of gate 1 is 0 since the outputs of gates 2 and 4 are 1's. When the clock goes from 0 to 1, i.e., the positive edge of the control signal, all three inputs to gate 3 become 1, causing the output of the gate to change to 0. Meanwhile, the output of gate 2, $\overline{S}$, remains at 1 since the output of gate 1 is still 0. The 0 on the $\overline{R}$ line and the 1 on the $\overline{S}$ line cause the $\overline{S}\overline{R}$ latch to enter or remain in its reset state, i.e., $Q = 0$ and $\overline{Q} = 1$. In addition, the output of gate 3, which is currently 0, is also fed back as an input to gate 4. This now keeps the output of gate 4 at 1, and any subsequent changes in the D input while C is 1 have no effect upon the output of gate 4 and, correspondingly, gate 1. Thus, after the occurrence of the positive edge of the clock signal when $D = 0$, the flip-flop is in its 0-state and any changes in the D input are inhibited even though the clock is 1.

Again assume $C = 0$, but now let $D = 1$. As before, the outputs of gates 2 and 3 are 1, causing the $\overline{S}\overline{R}$ latch to hold its current state. However, the $D = 1$ input causes the output of gate 4 to be 0, and this output, in turn, causes the output of gate 1 to be 1. Now when the clock changes to 1, both inputs to gate 2 are 1 and, consequently, its output, $\overline{S}$, becomes 0. Since the output of gate 4 is 0, the output of gate 3, $\overline{R}$, remains at 1. The $\overline{S} = 0$ and $\overline{R} = 1$ results in the setting of the $\overline{S}\overline{R}$ latch consisting of gates 5 and 6. The 0 output from gate 2 serves as an input to both gates 1 and 3 that, in turn, guarantees that their outputs remain at 1. Thus, if D should subsequently change from 1 to 0 while the clock is 1, causing the output of gate 4 to change, then the outputs of gates 1 and 3 do not change. Therefore, once the positive edge of the clock has occurred, changes in the D input while $C = 1$ have no effect upon the state of the flip-flop.

In summary, only upon the occurrence of the positive edge of the clock signal does the flip-flop respond to the value of the D input. Once the new output state is established, changes in the D input while $C = 1$ are ineffectual. When the clock signal returns to 0, both $\overline{S}$ and $\overline{R}$ become 1, and the $\overline{S}\overline{R}$ latch retains the state entered as a consequence of sampling the D input by the positive edge of the control signal.

Two logic symbols for the positive-edge-triggered D flip-flop are shown in Fig. 6.18*c*. Since the outputs of the flip-flop respond essentially immediately to the positive edge of the control signal, postponed-output indicators do not appear. To signify that the output change can only occur as a consequence of the transition of the control signal, a triangular symbol, called the *dynamic-input indicator*, is used at the control input of the logic symbol.

Figure 6.19 shows a timing diagram for the positive-edge-triggered D flip-flop. For simplicity, the finite slopes of the rising and falling edges of the signals are not shown and all propagation delays are assumed to be equal. Indicated in Fig. 6.19 are the setup, t_{su}, and hold, t_h, times with respect to the triggering edge of the control signal that need to be satisfied. During these times the D input must not change; otherwise, an unpredictable output, including the metastable state, is possible.

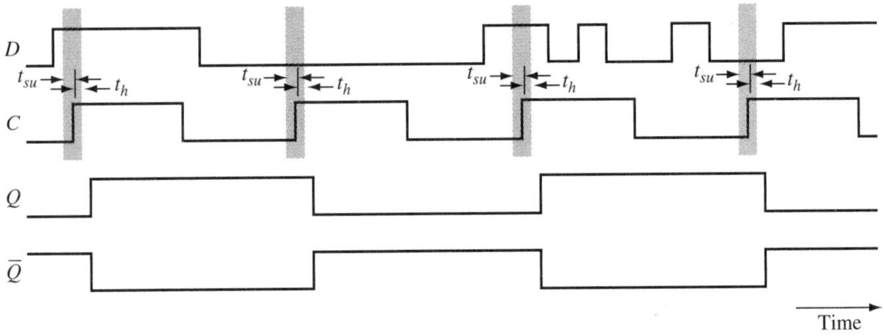

Figure 6.19 Timing diagram for a positive-edge-triggered D flip-flop.

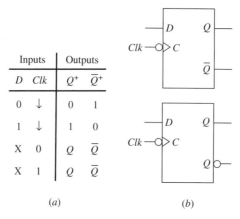

Inputs		Outputs	
D	Clk	Q^+	$\overline{Q}^+$
0	↓	0	1
1	↓	1	0
X	0	Q	$\overline{Q}$
X	1	Q	$\overline{Q}$

(*a*)

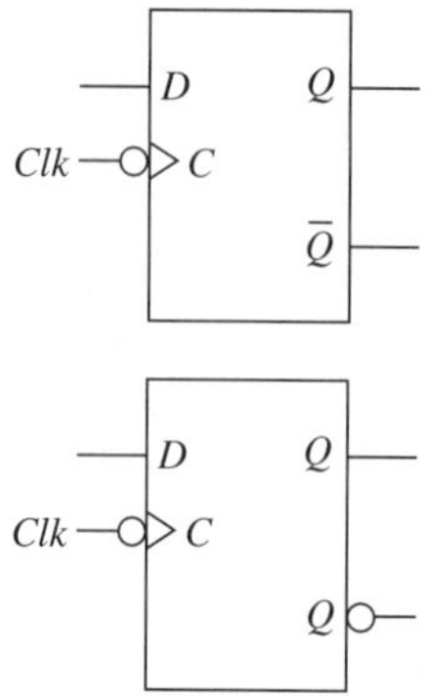

(*b*)

Figure 6.20 Negative-edge-triggered *D* flip-flop. (*a*) Function table where Q^+ denotes the output *Q* in response to the inputs. (*b*) Two logic symbols.

6.5.2 Negative-Edge-Triggered *D* Flip-Flops

A slight variation of the positive-edge-triggered *D* flip-flop is the *negative-edge-triggered D flip-flop*. In this case the falling edge, i.e., a high to low transition, of the control signal is used to sample the *D* input line rather than the rising edge. This can be achieved by simply placing an inverter at the control input of the flip-flop shown in Fig. 6.18*a*. The function table and logic symbols for this type of flip-flop are given in Fig. 6.20. It should be noted that an inversion bubble appears at the control input of the symbol in addition to the dynamic-input indicator. This inversion bubble and dynamic-input indicator combination denotes negative-edge triggering.

6.5.3 Asynchronous Inputs

Earlier in this chapter, the information inputs of flip-flops were categorized into two types: synchronous and asynchronous. These inputs are distinguished by whether or not they require the presence of a control signal to make them effective. All the information inputs of the edge-triggered and master-slave flip-flops that have been presented thus far are synchronous inputs. To provide greater flexibility, many flip-flops have both asynchronous and synchronous inputs within the same device. The asynchronous inputs, usually called *preset* (denoted by PR) and *clear* (denoted by CLR), are used to forcibly set and reset the flip-flop, respectively, independently of the control input. These inputs are particularly useful for bringing a flip-flop into a desired initial state prior to normal clocked operation.

A logic diagram for a positive-edge-triggered *D* flip-flop with asynchronous preset and clear inputs is shown in Fig. 6.21*a* and its corresponding function table is given in Fig. 6.21*b*. In this network, a logic-0 initiates action on the asynchronous lines. This logic-0 activation is indicated by the bubbles on the asynchronous inputs of the logic symbols shown in Fig. 6.21*c*. Hence, a logic-0 on the $\overline{PR}$ input line causes the flip-flop to enter its 1-state, i.e., to be set, while a logic-0 on the $\overline{CLR}$ input line causes the flip-flop to enter its 0-state, i.e., to be reset.

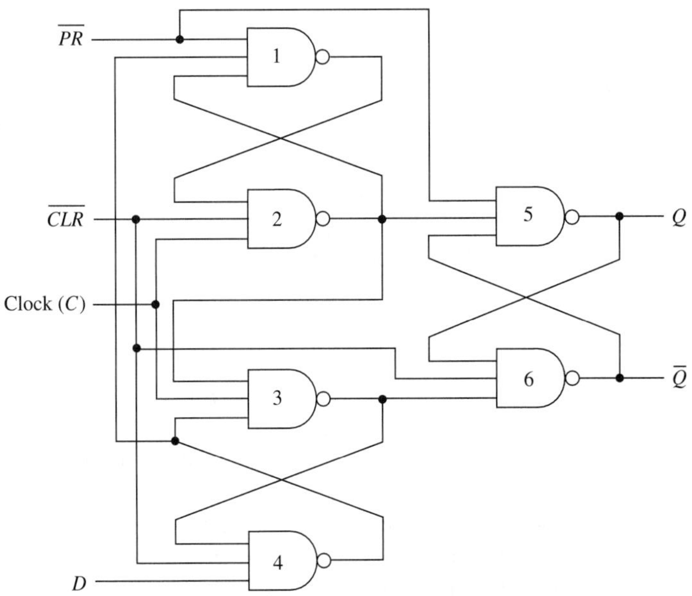

(*a*)

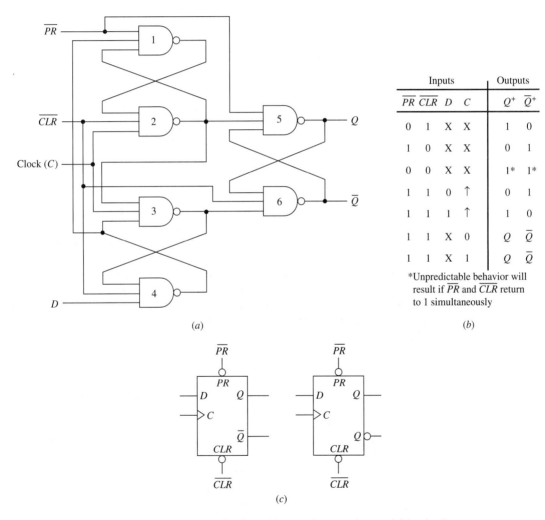

Inputs				Outputs	
$\overline{PR}$	$\overline{CLR}$	D	C	Q^+	$\overline{Q}^+$
0	1	X	X	1	0
1	0	X	X	0	1
0	0	X	X	1*	1*
1	1	0	↑	0	1
1	1	1	↑	1	0
1	1	X	0	Q	$\overline{Q}$
1	1	X	1	Q	$\overline{Q}$

*Unpredictable behavior will result if $\overline{PR}$ and $\overline{CLR}$ return to 1 simultaneously

(*b*)

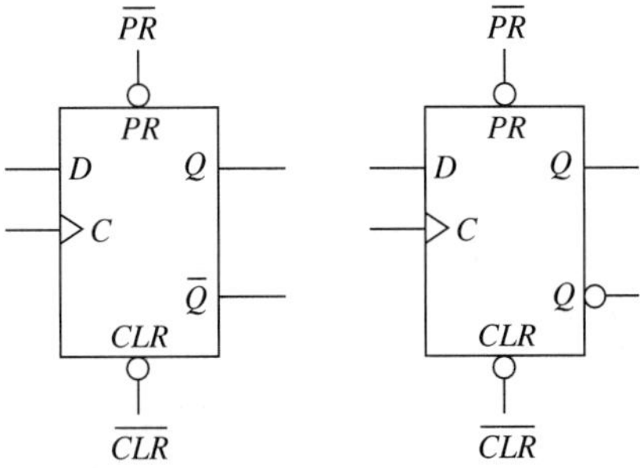

(*c*)

Figure 6.21 Positive-edge-triggered *D* flip-flop with asynchronous inputs. (*a*) Logic diagram. (*b*) Function table where Q^+ denotes the output *Q* in response to the inputs. (*c*) Two logic symbols.

Referring to the function table, the first two rows indicate the fact that a 0 on just the $\overline{PR}$ or $\overline{CLR}$ input lines causes the flip-flop to set or reset asynchronously, i.e., regardless of the values on the D and C lines as denoted by crosses in the D and C columns. The third row corresponds to the situation when both the $\overline{PR}$ and $\overline{CLR}$ inputs are simultaneously active. This condition is not recommended since unpredictable behavior results if both asynchronous inputs return to 1 simultaneously. Only when both asynchronous inputs are 1's does the flip-flop behave as a positive-edge-triggered D flip-flop. This corresponds to the last four rows of the function table.

Again consider the logic diagram of Fig. 6.21*a*. If the asynchronous lines are removed, then the logic diagram of Fig. 6.18*a* results. This is analogous to having 1's on both the $\overline{PR}$ and $\overline{CLR}$ input lines. In this case the operation of the device is as discussed previously for the positive-edge-triggered D flip-flop.

If $\overline{PR} = 0$ and $\overline{CLR} = 1$ while the control signal C is 0, then the output of nand-gate 5 becomes 1 and the output of nand-gate 6 becomes 0. Thus, the $\overline{S}\overline{R}$ latch portion of the flip-flop is forced into the 1-state, i.e., to be set. Similarly, if $\overline{PR} = 1$ and $\overline{CLR} = 0$ is applied, then the $\overline{S}\overline{R}$ latch portion of the flip-flop is forced into the 0-state, i.e., to be reset. The $\overline{PR}$ and $\overline{CLR}$ inputs are also applied to nand-gates 1, 2, and 4. This is done to ensure the effect of an asynchronous input on the flip-flop outputs while the control signal C is 1. That is, if either $\overline{PR}$ or $\overline{CLR}$ becomes 0 while the clock is 1, then the flip-flop accordingly responds immediately.

Although the above discussion was concerned with asynchronous inputs in a positive-edge-triggered D flip-flop, asynchronous inputs also may occur in negative-edge-triggered D flip-flops as well as in the other types of edge-triggered flip-flops that are discussed shortly. In addition, asynchronous inputs also occur in pulse-triggered flip-flops. Occasionally, however, only one asynchronous input appears in commercial flip-flops.

6.5.4 Additional Types of Edge-Triggered Flip-Flops

Thus far, only positive-edge-triggered and negative-edge-triggered D flip-flops have been considered. Other types of edge-triggered flip-flops are possible. Since the hold time of an edge-triggered D flip-flop is less than its propagation delay times, by using an edge-triggered D flip-flop, along with additional gates, other flip-flop types can be constructed. For example, Fig. 6.22 shows a logic diagram, function table, and logic symbols for a positive-edge-triggered JK flip-flop. Edge-triggered JK flip-flops are not subject to the 0's and 1's catching phenomenon since they respond to the values on the information input lines only at the time of the triggering edge.

Figure 6.23 shows two possible ways of constructing a positive-edge-triggered T flip-flop. One approach is to simply tie together the J and K inputs of a positive-edge-triggered JK flip-flop. The second approach involves the use of an exclusive-or-gate with a positive-edge-triggered D flip-flop.

As in the case of all previously discussed flip-flops, setup and hold time requirements on the J, K, and T inputs relative to the active triggering edge of the control signal must be satisfied to ensure proper operation.

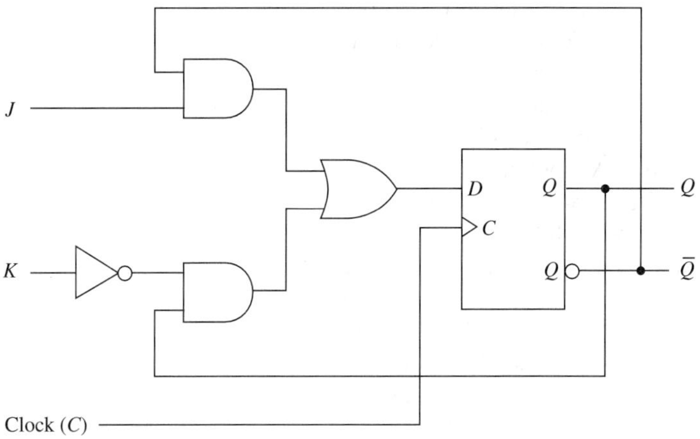

(*a*)

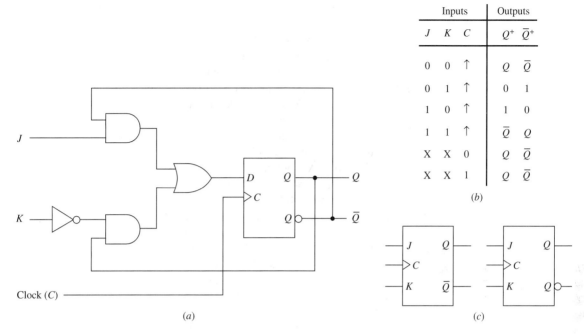

Inputs			Outputs	
J	K	C	Q^+	$\overline{Q}^+$
0	0	↑	Q	$\overline{Q}$
0	1	↑	0	1
1	0	↑	1	0
1	1	↑	$\overline{Q}$	Q
X	X	0	Q	$\overline{Q}$
X	X	1	Q	$\overline{Q}$

(*b*)

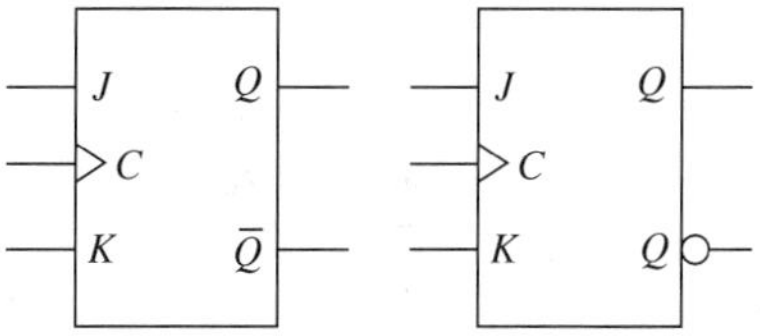

(*c*)

Figure 6.22 Positive-edge-triggered *JK* flip-flop. (*a*) Logic diagram. (*b*) Function table where Q^+ denotes the output Q in response to the inputs. (*c*) Two logic symbols.

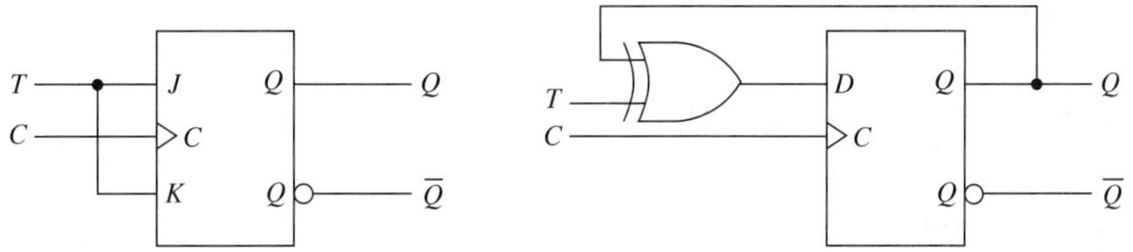

(*a*)

Inputs		Outputs	
T	C	Q^+	$\overline{Q}^+$
0	↑	Q	$\overline{Q}$
1	↑	$\overline{Q}$	Q
X	0	Q	$\overline{Q}$
X	1	Q	$\overline{Q}$

(*b*)

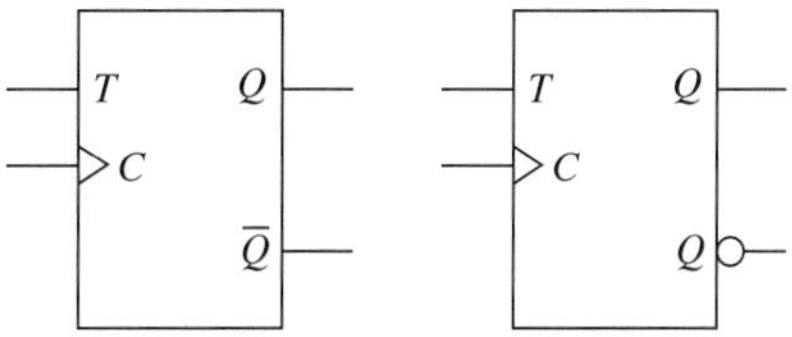

(*c*)

Figure 6.23 Positive-edge-triggered *T* flip-flop. (*a*) Logic diagrams. (*b*) Function table where Q^+ denotes the output Q in response to the inputs. (*c*) Two logic symbols.

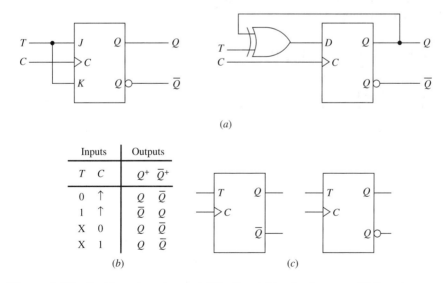

6.5.5 Master-Slave Flip-Flops with Data Lockout

There are situations in which delayed outputs from flip-flops are desirable. In such cases a master-slave configuration is appropriate. However, to avoid the 0's and 1's catching behavior, the master should respond to the information lines only on one edge of the control signal and then transfer its content to the slave on the next opposite edge of the control signal. Master-slave flip-flops having this property are said to have *data lockout.*

A possible construction for a *master-slave JK flip-flop with data lockout* is shown in Fig. 6.24*a*. Here a positive-edge-triggered *JK* flip-flop is used for the master and an *SR* latch is used for the slave. Because of the presence of the inverter between the two sections, information only enters the master on the positive edge of the control signal. Since the master is an edge-triggered flip-flop, any changes on the *J* or *K* information lines while the control signal is 1 are disregarded. The content of the master is subsequently transferred to the slave during the negative-edge transition of the control signal. Hence, the desired output delay is achieved. For proper operation, set and hold time requirements relative to the triggering edge of the control signal must be satisfied.

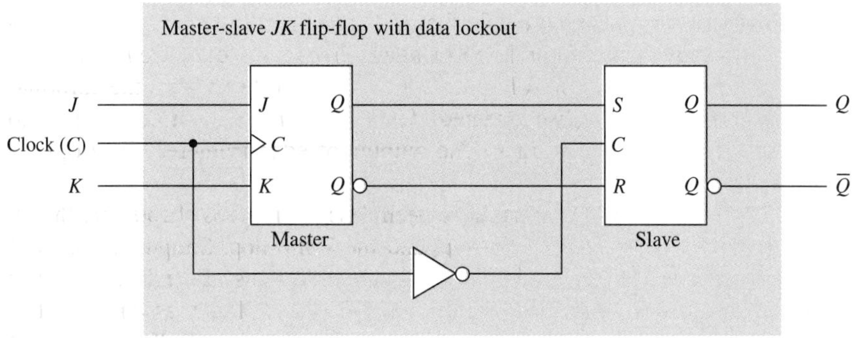

(*a*)

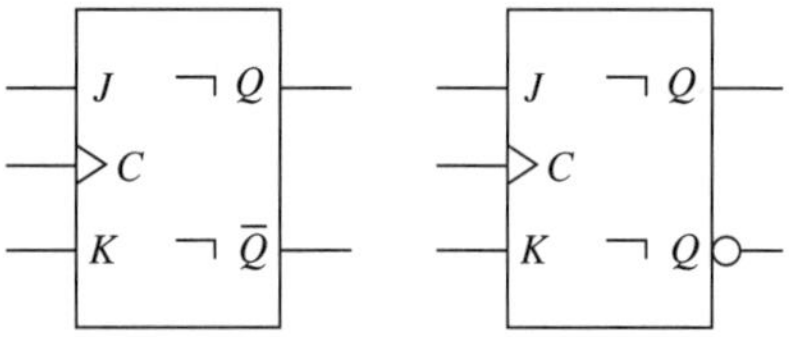

(*b*)

Figure 6.24 Master-slave *JK* flip-flop with data lockout. (*a*) Logic diagram. (*b*) Two logic symbols.

Symbols for the master-slave *JK* flip-flop with data lockout are given in Fig. 6.24*b*. The dynamic-input indicator is used since the information input lines are sampled on the positive edge of the control signal. Postponed-output indicators appear in the symbols since the output change is delayed as a consequence of the master-slave configuration.

6.6 CHARACTERISTIC EQUATIONS

Three classes of flip-flops have been presented in this chapter: latches, pulse-triggered flip-flops, and edge-triggered flip-flops. The timing scheme utilized by the flip-flops served as the basis for the classifications. Furthermore, within each class, several types of flip-flops were described. The types were associated with the information inputs of the flip-flops.

The first class of flip-flops consisted of the latches. This class is characterized by their outputs responding immediately at all times while enabled. The second class was the pulse-triggered flip-flops using the master-slave structure. In this class, information enters the master on the first edge of the control signal, in the case of those with data lockout, or during an entire pulse period, in the case of those without data lockout. In both cases, the content of the master is transferred to the slave at the time of the second edge of the triggering pulse. Thus, this class of flip-flops is characterized by the outputs being postponed until the end of the triggering pulse period. In the third class of flip-flops, i.e., the edge-triggered flip-flops, inputs from the information lines are accepted only upon the occurrence of one of the control input edges. At all other times, the information inputs are effectively disconnected. Thus, the control input edge serves to sample the information input lines. The outputs of edge-triggered flip-flops respond immediately.

The four types of flip-flops that have been described in this chapter are the *SR* flip-flop, the *JK* flip-flop, the *D* flip-flop, and the *T* flip-flop. Simplified forms of their function tables are given in Table 6.1. In these versions of the function tables the control signal is not explicitly shown, but rather is implicitly assumed. In this way, these tables serve to summarize the functional behavior of all four types of flip-flops regardless of the flip-flop class. Special attention should be given to the last row of the simplified *SR* flip-flop function table. The dash indicates that the input combination $S = R = 1$ is not permitted since the output is subject to unpredictable behavior if S and R should return to 0 simultaneously. Finally, only the next-state values of Q, i.e., Q^+, are shown in the tables. It is implied the next-state values of $\overline{Q}$ are the opposite to those of Q.

A variation of the simplified function tables, called the *next-state tables*, is given in Table 6.2 for the four types of flip-flops. The next-state tables show the value of the next state of the flip-flops for each combination of values to the present state of the flip-flops and their information input lines. Since Q can have two values, each row of the simplified function table becomes two rows in the next-state table. For each table, the appropriate interpretation is that for a given present state Q and

Table 6.1 Simplified flip-flop function tables. Q denotes the current state and Q^+ denotes the resulting state as a consequence of the information inputs and the control signal. (*a*) *SR* flip-flop. (*b*) *D* flip-flop. (*c*) *JK* flip-flop. (*d*) *T* flip-flop.

S	R	Q^+
0	0	Q
0	1	0
1	0	1
1	1	–

(*a*)

D	Q^+
0	0
1	1

(*b*)

J	K	Q^+
0	0	Q
0	1	0
1	0	1
1	1	$\overline{Q}$

(*c*)

T	Q^+
0	Q
1	$\overline{Q}$

(*d*)

inputs, the application of a control signal causes the flip-flop to change to the next-state Q^+.

The algebraic description of the next-state table of a flip-flop is called the *characteristic equation* of the flip-flop. This description is easily obtained by constructing the Karnaugh map for Q^+ in terms of the present state and information input variables. An example of such a Karnaugh map for an *SR* flip-flop is shown in Fig. 6.25*a*. For the purpose of this map, the inputs that cause an undefined output are regarded as don't-cares since these inputs are assumed to not occur. From the Karnaugh map of Fig. 6.25*a*, the characteristic equation

$$Q^+ = S + \overline{R}Q$$

immediately follows. In the case of *SR* flip-flops, a constraining equation, $SR = 0$, is included to signify that S and R should not be 1 simultaneously for proper operation. The characteristic equations for the four types of flip-flops presented in this chapter are given in Fig. 6.25*b*.

As in the case of the next-state tables, the characteristic equations only specify the functional behavior of the flip-flops. Thus, it is implied that the stated functional response is a consequence of an appropriate control signal, i.e., an enable signal in the case of latches, a pulse in the case of pulse-triggered flip-flops, and a specific edge in the case of edge-triggered flip-flops.

Table 6.2 Flip-flop next-state tables. Q denotes the current state and Q^+ denotes the resulting state as a consequence of the information inputs and the control signal. (*a*) *SR* flip-flop. (*b*) *D* flip-flop. (*c*) *JK* flip-flop. (*d*) *T* flip-flop.

S	R	Q	Q^+	
0	0	0	0	
0	0	1	1	
0	1	0	0	
0	1	1	0	
1	0	0	1	
1	0	1	1	
1	1	0	–	Inputs not allowed
1	1	1	–	

(*a*)

D	Q	Q^+
0	0	0
0	1	0
1	0	1
1	1	1

(*b*)

J	K	Q	Q^+
0	0	0	0
0	0	1	1
0	1	0	0
0	1	1	0
1	0	0	1
1	0	1	1
1	1	0	1
1	1	1	0

(*c*)

T	Q	Q^+
0	0	0
0	1	1
1	0	1
1	1	0

(*d*)

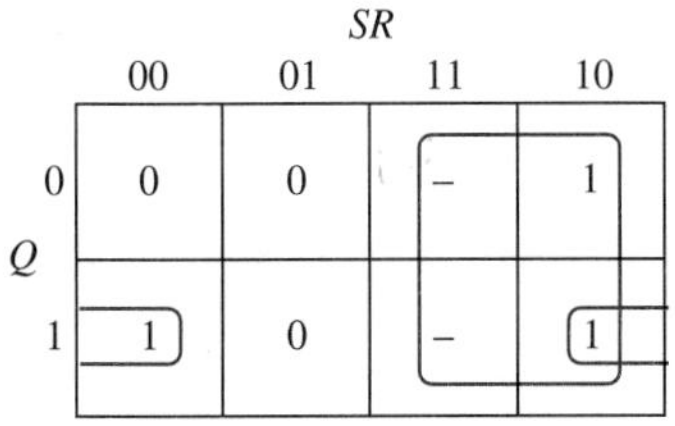

$Q^+ = S + \bar{R}Q \quad (SR = 0)$

(*a*)

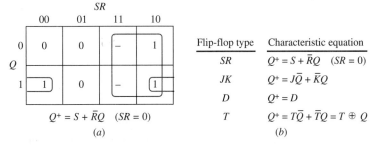

Flip-flop type	Characteristic equation
SR	$Q^+ = S + \bar{R}Q \quad (SR = 0)$
JK	$Q^+ = J\bar{Q} + \bar{K}Q$
D	$Q^+ = D$
T	$Q^+ = T\bar{Q} + \bar{T}Q = T \oplus Q$

(*b*)

Figure 6.25 Characteristic equations. (*a*) Derivation of characteristic equation for an *SR* flip-flop. (*b*) Summary of characteristic equations.

For many of the networks encountered in this book, it is necessary that the output changes occur coincident with the changes on the control input line. Either edge-triggered or pulse-triggered flip-flops can be used for this purpose. Thus, they are categorically referred to as simply *clocked flip-flops.*

6.7 REGISTERS

In the remaining sections of this chapter, attention is turned to some simple applications involving clocked flip-flops. These applications are examples of sequential networks. Sequential networks are formally discussed in the next three chapters of this book. However, the intention at this time is to illustrate the use of clocked flip-flops as network devices. Sequential networks, unlike combinational networks, possess a memory property. This can be achieved with flip-flops since they have the capability of storing the symbols 0 and 1, whether they correspond to the binary digits or the logic values.

A *register* is simply a collection of flip-flops taken as an entity. The basic function of a register is to hold information within a digital system so as to make it available to the logic elements during the computing process. However, a register may also have additional capabilities associated with it.

Since a register consists of a finite number of flip-flops and since each flip-flop is capable of storing a 0 or a 1 symbol, there are only a finite number of 0-1 combinations that can be stored in a register. Each of these combinations is known as the *state* or *content* of the register.

Registers that are capable of moving information positionwise upon the occurrence of a clock signal are called *shift registers.* These registers are normally classified by whether they can move the information in one or two directions, i.e., unidirectional or bidirectional.

The manner in which information is entered into and outputted from a register is another way in which they are categorized. There are two basic ways in which these transfers are done: serially or in parallel. When information is transferred in a parallel manner, all the 0-1 symbols that comprise the information are handled simultaneously as an entity in a single unit of time. Such information transfers require as many lines as symbols being transferred. On the other hand, the serial handling of information involves the symbol-by-symbol availability of the information in a time sequence. These information transfers only require a single line to perform the transfer. Thus, there are four possible ways registers can transfer information: serial-in/serial-out, serial-in/parallel-out, parallel-in/parallel-out, and parallel-in/serial-out.

Figure 6.26 illustrates the *serial-in, serial-out unidirectional shift register* constructed from positive-edge-triggered D flip-flops. The Q output of each flip-flop is connected to the D input of the flip-flop to its right. The control inputs of all the flip-flops are connected together to a common synchronizing signal called the clock. Thus, upon the occurrence of a positive edge of the clock signal, the content of each flip-flop is shifted one position to the right. The content of the leftmost flip-flop after the clock signal depends upon the signal value on the serial-data-in line, and the content of the rightmost flip-flop prior to the clock signal is lost. The output from the shift register occurs at the rightmost flip-flop on the serial-data-out line.

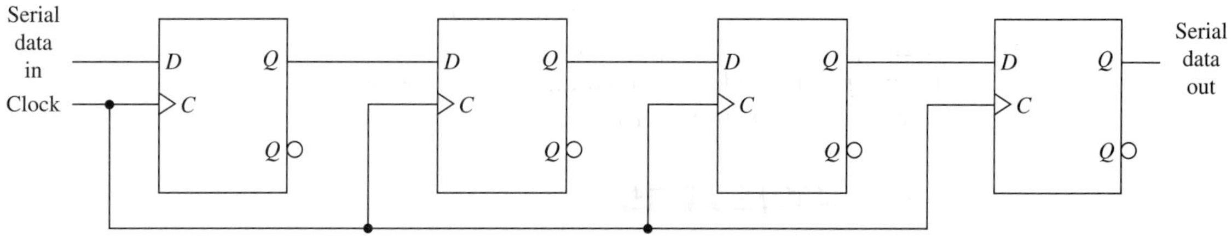

Figure 6.26 Serial-in, serial-out unidirectional shift register.

For the register of Fig. 6.26, if the initial content of the four flip-flops is 1011 and a logic-0 is applied to the serial-data-in line prior to the positive edge of the clock signal, then the content of the register becomes 0101 after the positive edge of the clock signal. The signal value that is shifted in, i.e., the logic-0, becomes available as an output on the serial-data-out line after four clock pulses.

In some applications, the information within a register must be preserved, but only a reorientation of the information is desired. To achieve this, the serial-data-out line of Fig. 6.26 is connected to the serial-data-in line. In this way the content of the register is again shifted one position to the right upon the occurrence of each clock signal, but the state of the leftmost flip-flop is replaced by the state of the rightmost flip-flop. For example, again assume the initial content of the register is 1011, but the output of the rightmost flip-flop is connected to the input of the leftmost flip-flop. Then after the occurrence of the positive edge of the clock signal, the register contains 1101. Shift registers having this type of connection are called *circular shift registers.*

It is important to note that the flip-flops of a register are subject to a change in state while they are being interrogated by the next flip-flop in the cascade connection. That is, a flip-flop is simultaneously being read into while being read by another flip-flop. Thus, edge-triggered or pulse-triggered, i.e., master-slave, flip-flops are used. Latches are not appropriate in such an application since their outputs are subject to changes during the entire period in which they are enabled.

The *serial-in, parallel-out unidirectional shift register* is illustrated in Fig. 6.27. In this case, outputs are provided from each flip-flop. Once information is shifted

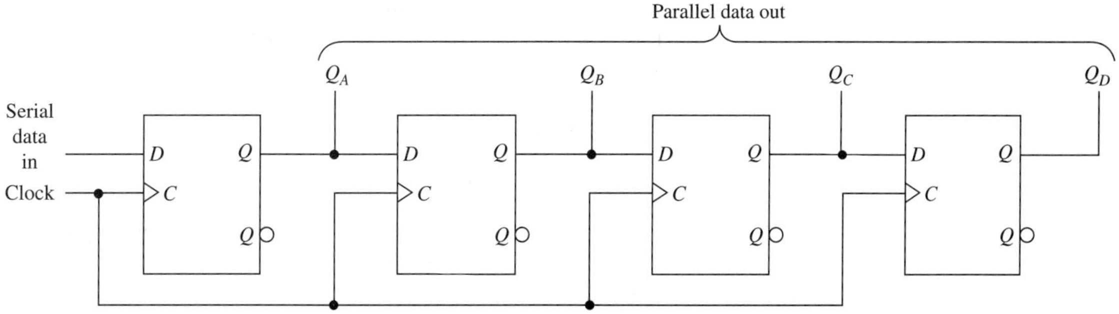

Figure 6.27 Serial-in, parallel-out unidirectional shift register.

into the register, i.e., serial in, the information is available as a single entity, i.e., parallel out, at the flip-flop output terminals. Since information is transferred into this register serially and, after an appropriate number of shifts, made available in parallel, this type of register provides for the *serial-to-parallel conversion* of information.

The register shown in Fig. 6.28 is used as a *parallel-in, serial-out unidirectional shift register.* The operation of the register is controlled by the $\overline{\text{Load}}$/Shift line. When a logic-0 signal appears on this line, the signals on the parallel-data-in lines $I_A I_B I_C I_D$ are transferred into the register upon the occurrence of a positive-edge clock signal. Then, when a logic-1 signal appears on the $\overline{\text{Load}}$/Shift line, the D flip-flops become a cascade connection that functions as a unidirectional shift register providing the serial output. In this way, the register of Fig. 6.28 provides for the *parallel-to-serial conversion* of information. By taking the outputs from the individual flip-flops, the register functions as a *parallel-in, parallel-out unidirectional shift register.* It should be noted that the register illustrated in Fig. 6.28 can also function as a serial-in, parallel-out unidirectional shift register and as a serial-in, serial-out unidirectional shift register.

The second general classification of shift registers consists of the *bidirectional shift registers.* These types of registers are capable of shifting their contents either left or right depending upon the signals present on appropriate control input lines.

An example of a bidirectional shift register is shown in Fig. 6.29. This register is also known as the *universal shift register.* Depending upon the signal values on the select lines of the multiplexers, i.e., the mode control lines, the register can retain its current state, shift right, shift left, or be loaded in parallel. Each of these operations is the result of the occurrence of a positive edge on the clock line. In addition, the register is cleared asynchronously if a logic-0 is applied to the line labeled $\overline{\text{CLEAR}}$.

As an illustration of the operation of the universal shift register, according to the table in Fig. 6.29*b* the register performs the shift-right operation when the logic values on the select lines $S_1 S_0$ of the multiplexers are 01. Under this condition the I_1 input of each multiplexer is connected to its f output. Thus, as seen in Fig. 6.29*a*, the input to the leftmost D flip-flop is the signal on the serial-input-for-shift-right line, the input to the second leftmost D flip-flop is the output of the leftmost D flip-flop, the input to the third leftmost D flip-flop is the output of the second leftmost D flip-flop, and the input to the fourth leftmost D flip-flop is the output of the third leftmost D flip-flop. Upon the occurrence of the positive-edge signal on the clock line, the register shifts its content one position to the right. The remaining three register operations listed in Fig. 6.29*b* are easily verified in a similar manner. A symbol for the universal shift register is given in Fig. 6.29*c*.

Registers are available commercially as MSI components. In these circuits, the control lines for the clock inputs of the flip-flops are connected together and appropriate logic is included to provide various capabilities, e.g., unidirectional or bidirectional shifting, and handling ability of the information input and output lines.

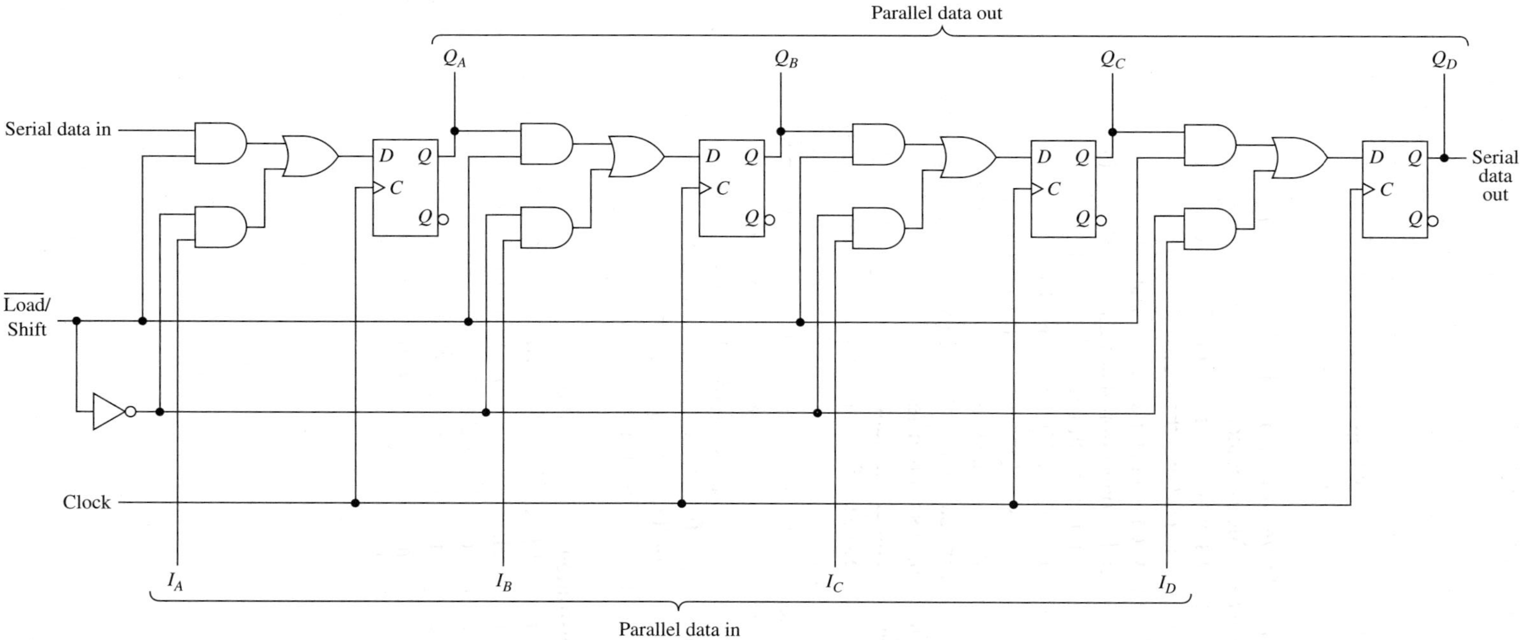

Figure 6.28 Parallel-in unidirectional shift register.

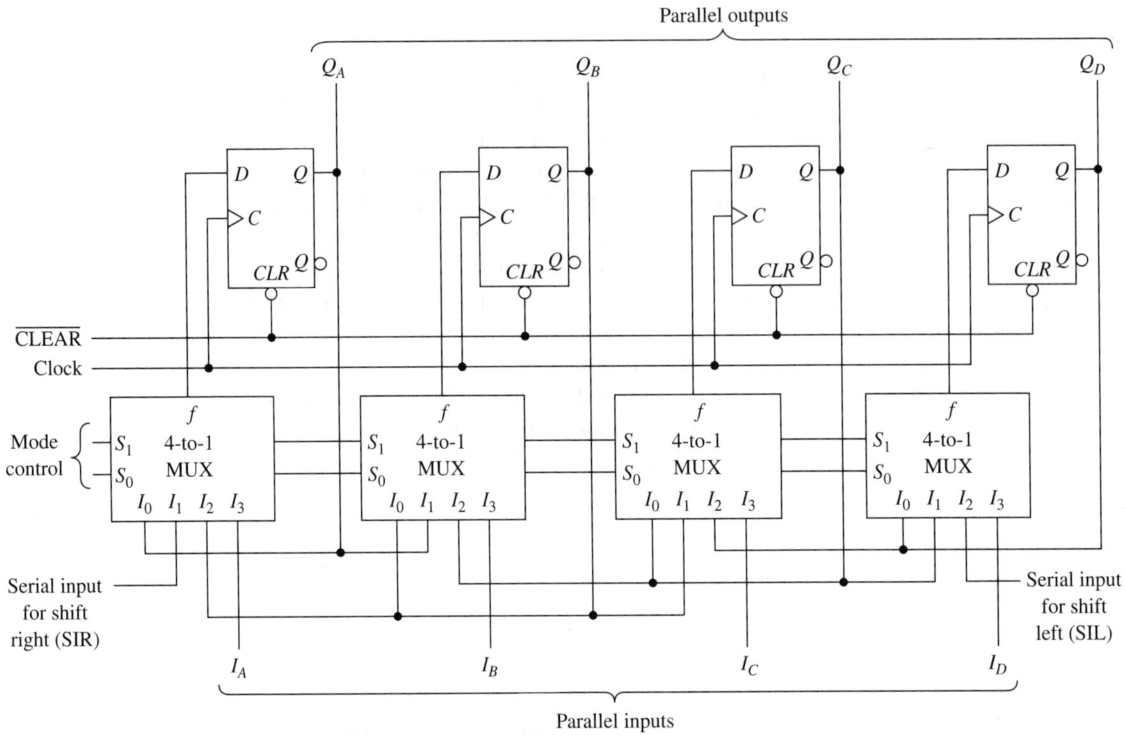

(a)

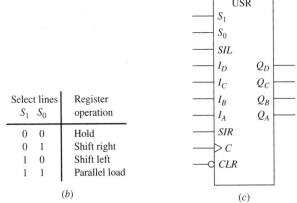

Select lines S_1 S_0	Register operation
0 0	Hold
0 1	Shift right
1 0	Shift left
1 1	Parallel load

(b)

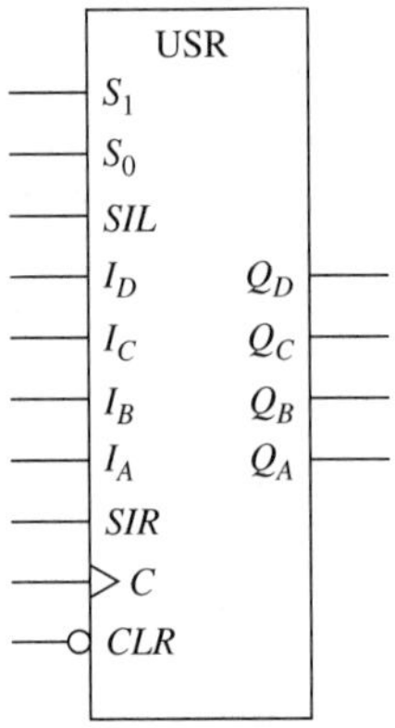

(c)

Figure 6.29 Universal shift register. (*a*) Logic diagram. (*b*) Mode control. (*c*) Symbol.

6.8 COUNTERS

A counter is another example of a register. Its primary function is to produce a specified output pattern sequence. For this reason, it is also a *pattern generator.* This pattern sequence might correspond to the number of occurrences of an event or it might be used to control various portions of a digital system. In this latter case, each pattern is associated with a distinct operation that the digital system must perform.

As in the case of a register, each of the 0-1 combinations that are stored in the collection of flip-flops that comprise the counter, i.e., the output pattern, is known as a *state* of the counter. The total number of states is called its *modulus.* Thus, if a counter has m distinct states, then it is called a *modulus-m counter* or *mod-m counter* for short. The order in which the states appear is referred to as its *counting sequence.*

The counting sequence is often depicted by a directed graph called a *state diagram.* Figure 6.30 shows a state diagram for a mod-m counter where each node, S_i, denotes one of the states of the counter and the arrows in the graph denote the order in which the states occur.

6.8.1 Binary Ripple Counters

Counters whose counting sequence corresponds to that of the binary numbers are called *binary counters.* The modulus of a binary counter is 2^n, where n is the number of flip-flops in the counter. This follows from the fact that there are 2^n combinations of 0's and 1's consisting of n bits. For the case of a binary up-counter, the counting sequence is from $00 \cdots 0_{(2)}$ to $11 \cdots 1_{(2)}$, which is equivalent to $0_{(10)}$ to $(2^n - 1)_{(10)}$. After reaching its maximum count, the counting sequence is then repeated. The counting sequence for a binary down-counter is in reverse order, i.e., $11 \cdots 1_{(2)}$ to $00 \cdots 0_{(2)}$.

Figure 6.31*a* shows a four-bit binary up-counter implemented with positive-edge triggered T flip-flops. Recall this type of flip-flop is readily constructed by connecting together the J and K terminals of a positive-edge triggered JK flip-flop and labeling this common terminal as T. In this way, each positive transition, i.e., from logic-0 to logic-1, on the C terminal causes the flip-flop to toggle.

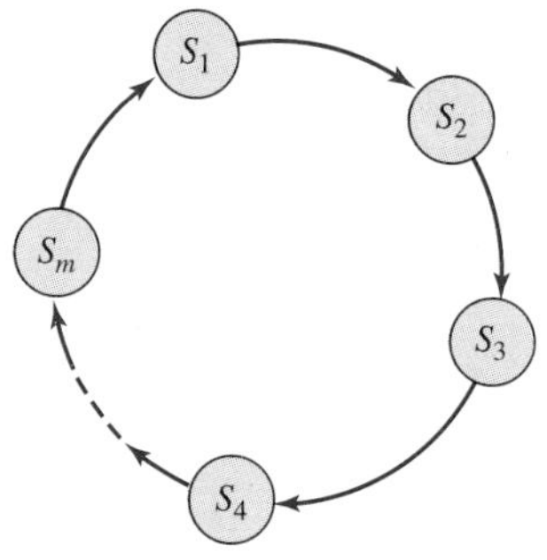

Figure 6.30 State diagram of a counter.

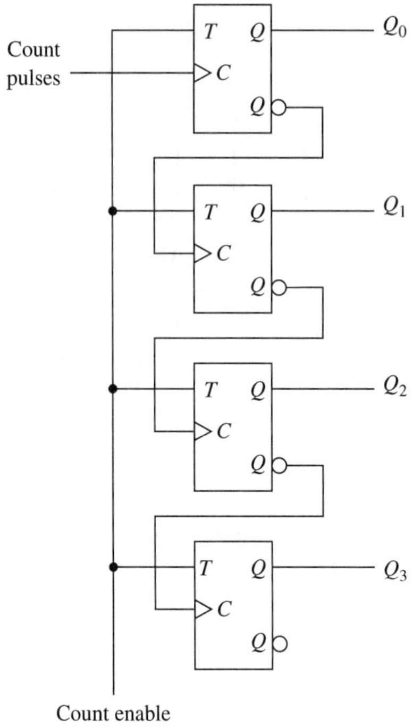

(a)

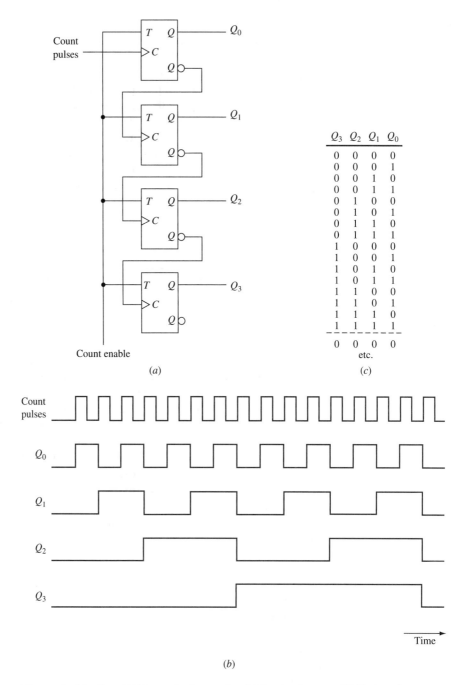

Q_3	Q_2	Q_1	Q_0
0	0	0	0
0	0	0	1
0	0	1	0
0	0	1	1
0	1	0	0
0	1	0	1
0	1	1	0
0	1	1	1
1	0	0	0
1	0	0	1
1	0	1	0
1	0	1	1
1	1	0	0
1	1	0	1
1	1	1	0
1	1	1	1
0	0	0	0

etc.

(c)

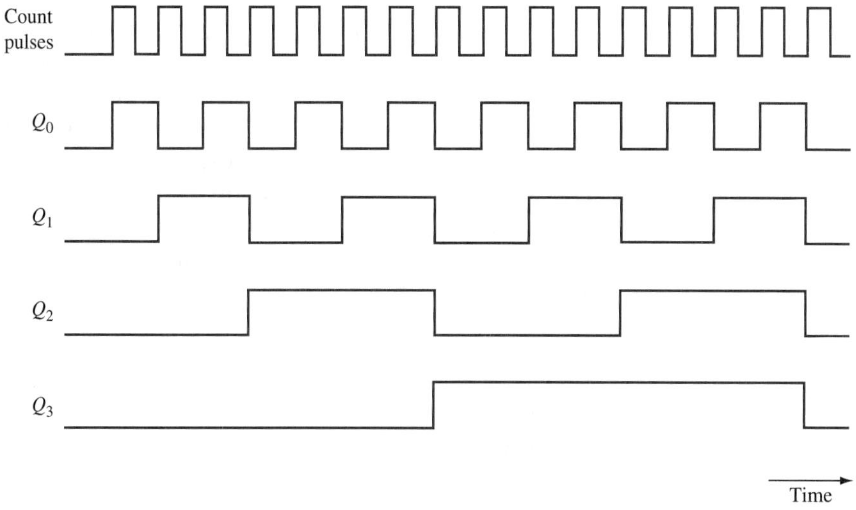

(b)

Figure 6.31 Four-bit binary ripple counter. (*a*) Logic diagram. (*b*) Timing diagram. (*c*) Counting sequence.

Since this is a 4-bit up-counter, its modulus is $2^4 = 16$ and its counting sequence is from $0000_{(2)}$ to $1111_{(2)}$. The output of the counter appears at the Q output terminals of the four flip-flops where the flip-flop output Q_i corresponds to the ith-order bit of the binary number. The input to the counter is a count enable signal and a series of count pulses applied to the flip-flop associated with the lowest-order binary digit. In this way, as long as the count enable signal is logic-1, the Q_0 flip-flop changes state on each positive edge of a count pulse. The control input, i.e., C, of the remaining flip-flops is connected to the $\overline{Q}$ output of its previous-order flip-flop. Thus, when the Q_{i-1} flip-flop changes, from its 1-state to its 0-state, thereby resulting in the $\overline{Q}_{i-1}$ output to change from logic-0 to logic-1, a positive triggering edge occurs at the control input of the Q_i flip-flop causing it to toggle.

Figures 6.31*b-c* illustrate the counter's behavior. Although propagation delays are associated with each flip-flop, i.e., the output changes occur *after* an input change, these delays are not included in the timing diagram for simplicity. The counter is assumed to be initially in its 0000 state and the count enable signal is logic-1. Upon the occurrence of the positive edge of the first count pulse, the Q_0 flip-flop changes to its 1-state. Since the $\overline{Q}_0$-output terminal goes from logic-1 to logic-0, flip-flop Q_1 is not affected by the input pulse. The state of the counter is now 0001. When the positive edge of the second count pulse arrives, the Q_0 flip-flop is again toggled. This time it returns to its 0-state. Furthermore, since the $\overline{Q}_0$ output goes from logic-0 to logic-1, a positive edge appears at the control input of the Q_1 flip-flop and causes it to toggle. The change in state of the Q_1 flip-flop does not affect the Q_2 flip-flop since a negative edge occurs at its control input. Hence, at the end of the second count pulse, the state of the counter is 0010. The third count pulse causes only the Q_0 flip-flop to change state, and the count to become 0011. When the positive edge of the fourth pulse occurs, the Q_0 flip-flop returns to its 0-state. This causes a positive edge to occur at the $\overline{Q}_0$ terminal. Thus, the Q_1 flip-flop is toggled, returning it to its 0-state. In addition, when the Q_1 flip-flop changes its state, the Q_2 flip-flop is toggled by the logic-0 to logic-1 transition appearing at the $\overline{Q}_1$-output terminal. The counter now stores the binary number 0100. The binary counting sequence continues until the count 1111 is reached. At that time, a count pulse causes the Q_0 flip-flop to return to its 0-state. This, in turn, causes the Q_1 flip-flop to return to its 0-state. A consequence of this change causes the Q_2 flip-flop to return to its 0-state and, finally, this change returns the Q_3 flip-flop to its 0-state. Thus, the state of the counter becomes 0000. If any further count pulses are applied to the counter, then it repeats its counting sequence.

The binary counter of Fig. 6.31*a* is known as a *ripple counter* since a change in state of the Q_{i-1} flip-flop is used to toggle the Q_i flip-flop. Thus, the effect of a count pulse must ripple through the counter. Ripple counters are also referred to as *asynchronous counters.* Recalling there is a propagation delay between the input and output of a flip-flop, this rippling behavior affects the overall time delay between the occurrence of a count pulse and when the stabilized count appears at the output terminals. The worst case occurs when the counter goes from its $11 \cdots 1$-state to its $00 \cdots 0$-state since toggle signals must propagate through the entire length of the counter. For an n-stage binary ripple counter, the worst-case settling time becomes $n \times t_{pd}$, where t_{pd} is the propagation delay time associated with each flip-flop.

6.8.2 Synchronous Binary Counters

The settling time problem associated with ripple counters is avoided in *synchronous counters.* For synchronous counters, the count pulses are applied directly to the control inputs, C, of all the clocked flip-flops. This causes all the flip-flops to change simultaneously after the appropriate propagation delay associated with a single flip-flop.

Referring to the binary counting sequence given in Fig. 6.31c, it is noted that for each count pulse, the lowest-order flip-flop, Q_0, must toggle. Furthermore, for each of the remaining flip-flops, a flip-flop Q_i must toggle upon the occurrence of a count pulse if all its lower-order flip-flops, i.e., Q_{i-p} for $p = 1, 2, \ldots, i$, are in their 1-states.

Figure 6.32 shows a synchronous binary up-counter based on this observation. As is characteristic of a synchronous counter, the count pulses are applied to the control input, C, of each clocked flip-flop. Furthermore, as long as the counter is enabled, i.e., the count-enable signal is logic-1, the counter follows the binary counting sequence. In particular, the lowest-order flip-flop, Q_0, toggles on the positive edge of each count pulse. The and-gate preceding each T input terminal of the remaining flip-flops detects if all the lower-order flip-flops are in their 1-states. If this condition is satisfied, then the flip-flop toggles upon the occurrence of the positive edge of the count pulse. Since the count pulses are applied directly to each flip-flop, the only delay incurred between the application of a count pulse and the availability of the new count output is the propagation delay time of a flip-flop.

The synchronous counter of Fig. 6.32 does have its drawbacks. In particular, there are p inputs to the and-gate connected to the pth flip-flop. Thus, if the counter consists of a large number of flip-flops, then and-gates having a large number of inputs are required. In addition, if there are n stages to the counter, then the output of the pth flip-flop must appear as inputs to n–p and-gates. Again, if the number of flip-flops is large, then the low-order flip-flops must drive a large number of gates, which may introduce loading complications.

It is observed in Fig. 6.32 that the output of the and-gate preceding the Q_i flip-flop consists of precisely the inputs to the and-gate preceding the Q_{i-1} flip-flop plus the output of the Q_{i-1} flip-flop. This observation leads to the variation of the synchronous binary counter shown in Fig. 6.33. Now each and-gate only requires two inputs, and the output of each flip-flop is only needed as an input to the next-stage and-gate. In this variation, propagation delays are incurred between the positive edges of the count pulses due to the serial connection of and-gates. This puts a constraint on the count pulse rate. However, as typical with synchronous counters, all the flip-flops change state simultaneously after the propagation delay time of a flip-flop.

It should be noted in the above discussion on asynchronous and synchronous binary counters, the counter speed was based on the availability of the next count at

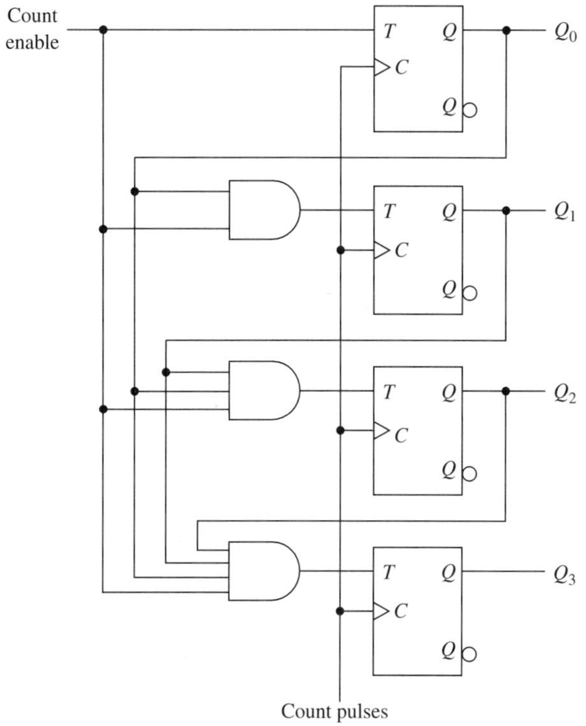

Figure 6.32 Four-bit synchronous binary counter.

the output terminals. In this sense, synchronous counters are faster than asynchronous counters. It is the gate delays and the flip-flop propagation delay in a synchronous counter that determine the rate at which count pulses can be applied. In an asynchronous counter, the allowable count pulse rate is determined by simply the first stage of the counter. This implies that an asynchronous counter is very fast relative to its input. That is, once the first flip-flop changes state it can accept the next count pulse even though the change has not propagated through the rest of the counter. However, it is not until the rippling effect is completed that the count is available for use.

If provisions are made to the synchronous counter structures of Figs. 6.32 or 6.33 so that they are loaded in parallel with an initial binary number prior to the counting operation, then the mod-2^n counter can be used as a mod-m counter where $m < 2^n$. The counter structure of Fig. 6.33 modified to provide for parallel loading is shown in Fig. 6.34*a*. *JK* flip-flops, rather than *T* flip-flops, are used in this network to facilitate the handling of the parallel load inputs. Two enable signals are utilized. One is to allow the parallel loading of the data inputs D_0, D_1, D_2, and D_3, and a second to provide for counting. Both of these operations are synchronized with the positive edges of the count pulses. The load function takes precedence over the count

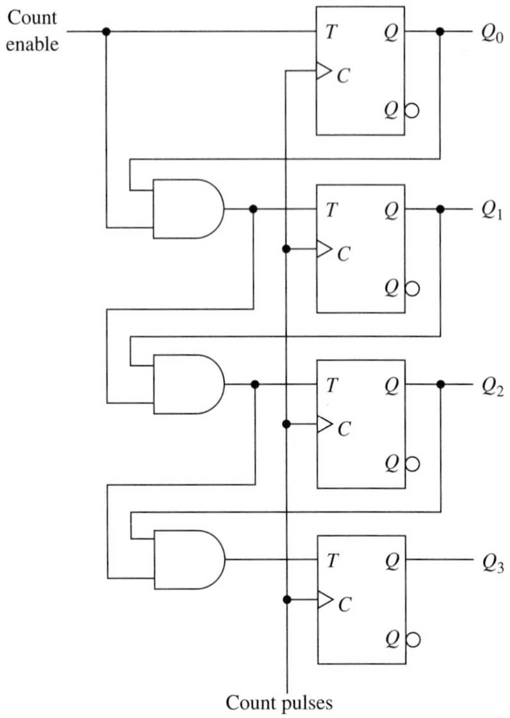

Figure 6.33 Four-bit synchronous binary counter variation.

function* so that if a logic-1 is placed on the load enable line, regardless of the signal value on the count enable line, then the signal values on the data input lines, i.e., D_0, D_1, D_2, and D_3, are entered into the four flip-flops of the counter upon the occurrence of the positive edge of the count pulse. If a logic-0 is applied to the load enable line and a logic-1 is applied to the count enable line, then the network of Fig. 6.34*a* behaves as a binary up-counter in the same way as the counter of Fig. 6.33. Finally, a logic-0 applied to both the load enable and count enable lines causes the count pulses to be ignored and the counter to retain its current state since logic-0's appear at the *J* and *K* terminals of each flip-flop. A symbol for the counter of Fig. 6.34*a* is given in Fig. 6.34*b*.

Figure 6.35*a* shows how the counter of Fig. 6.34*a* is converted to function as a mod-10, i.e., decimal, counter having the counting sequence given in Fig. 6.35*b*. The normal counting sequence for the counter of Fig. 6.34*a* is that of a 4-bit binary up-counter when enabled with a logic-1 on the count enable input. To limit the counting sequence to the first 10 binary numbers, an and-gate is used to detect the

---

*This is due to the not-gate connected to the load enable line.

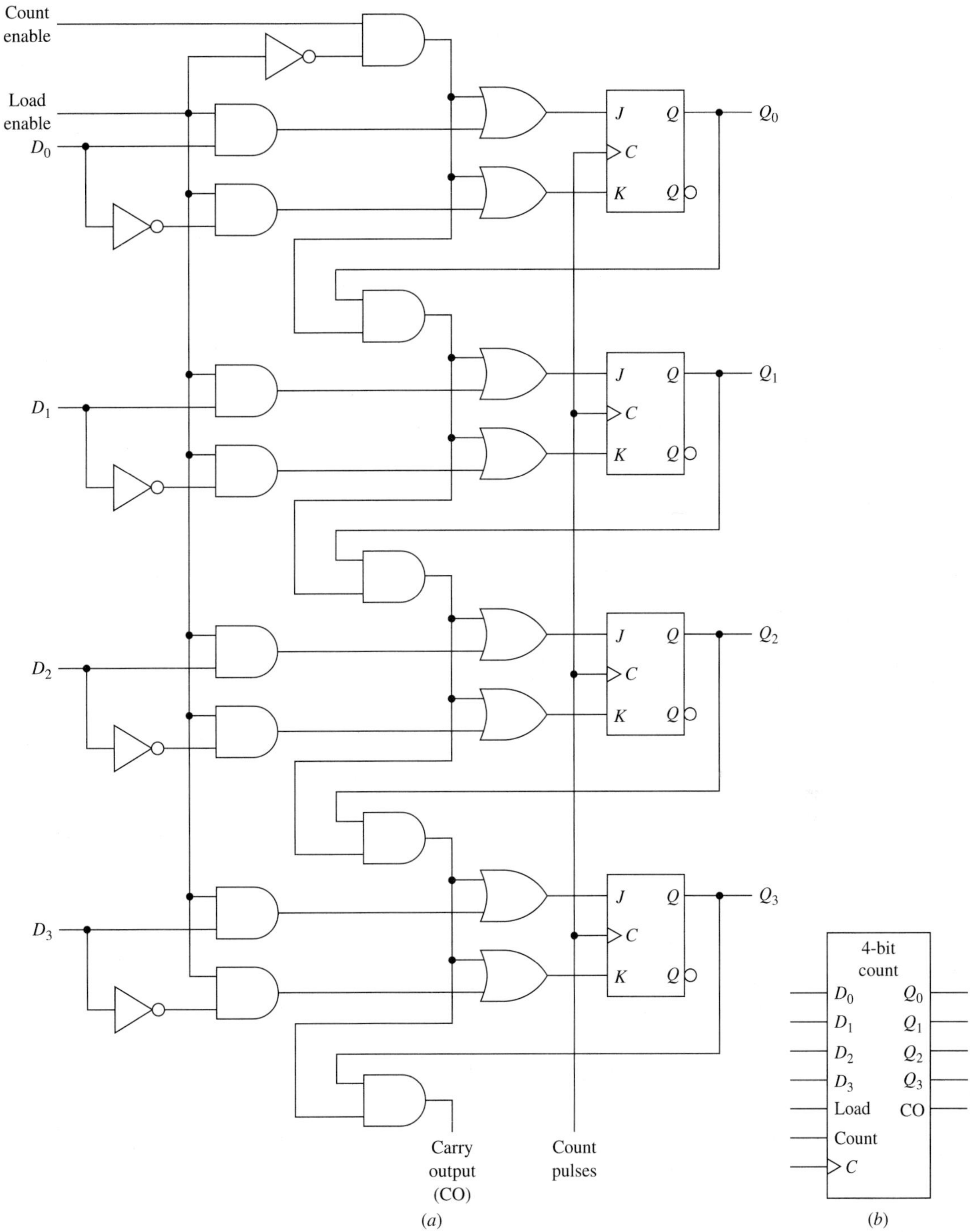

Figure 6.34 Four-bit synchronous binary counter with parallel load inputs. (*a*) Logic diagram. (*b*) Symbol.

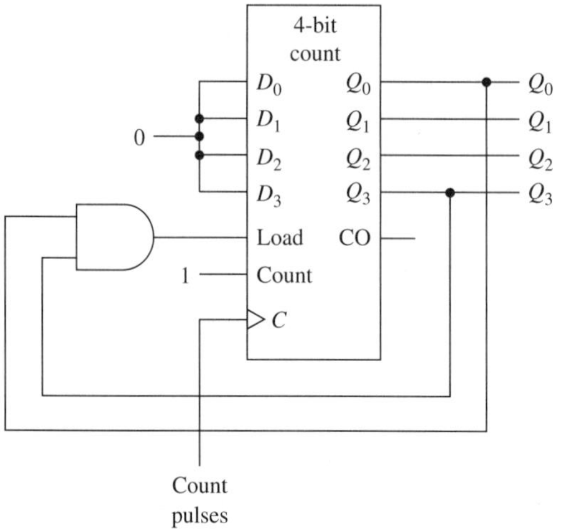

(*a*)

Q_3	Q_2	Q_1	Q_0
0	0	0	0
0	0	0	1
0	0	1	0
0	0	1	1
0	1	0	0
0	1	0	1
0	1	1	0
0	1	1	1
1	0	0	0
1	0	0	1
0	0	0	0

etc.

(*b*)

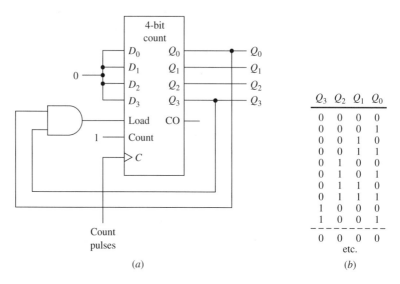

Figure 6.35 Synchronous mod-10 counter. (*a*) Connections. (*b*) Counting sequence.

count of 1001. Starting from the 0000 state, the first occurrence of $Q_0 = Q_3 = 1$ causes the output of the and-gate to be logic-1. Since the load function takes precedence over the count function, by connecting the and-gate output to the load enable input the counter is loaded with 0000, i.e., the values on the D_i inputs, upon the next occurrence of a positive edge of a count pulse. In this way, the counting sequence is 0000, 0001, . . . , 1001, 0000, etc.

Also incorporated into the counter of Fig. 6.34*a* is a carry output, *CO*, in which a logic-1 appears whenever the counter state is 1111 and the counter is in its count mode, i.e., when the count enable signal is logic-1 and the load enable signal is logic-0. This output is used for constructing larger binary counters by cascading two or more 4-bit binary counters. Figure 6.36 shows the connections necessary to construct an 8-bit binary counter. When the state of the upper 4-bit binary counter is 1111, which corresponds to the four least significant binary digits of the 8-bit binary counter, its carry output signal is logic-1. This signal is applied to the count enable input of the lower 4-bit counter that is used for the four most significant binary digits of the 8-bit binary counter. In this way, upon the occurrence of the positive edge of the next count pulse, the upper 4-bit binary counter of Fig. 6.36 returns to its 0000 state, while the lower 4-bit binary counter is incremented by 1.

Many different types of MSI counters are commercially available. These include counters of both the asynchronous and synchronous types. Commercial counters may provide for downward counting as well as upward counting.

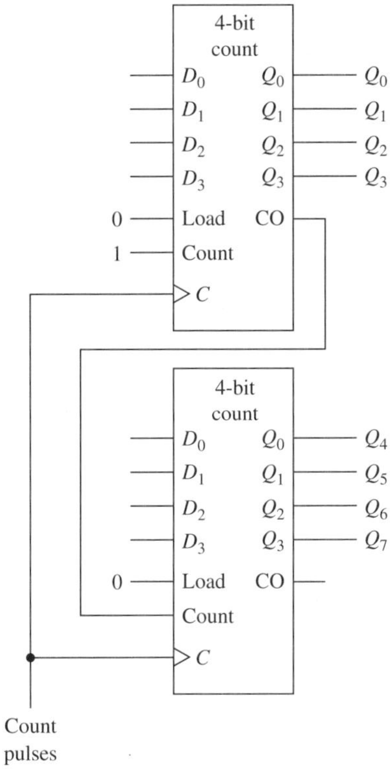

Figure 6.36 8-bit synchronous binary counter constructed from two 4-bit synchronous binary counters.

6.8.3 Counters Based on Shift Registers

As will become evident in the future chapters, the overall operation of a digital system is divided into a sequence of time periods. In order to determine the various time periods, one approach is to assign them to states of a binary counter. Then, by incorporating a decoder along with the counter, the various states, and, correspondingly, time periods, are identified. Rather than using a decoder, a nonbinary counter could be used whose counting sequence provides a series of patterns that simplify the detection of its states, possibly at the cost of increasing the number of flip-flops used. Examples of such nonbinary counters, based on the structure of the shift register, are the *ring counter* and the *switch-tail counter.*

A *ring counter* is a circular shift register which is initialized so that only one of its flip-flops is in the 1-state; while the others are in their 0-states. Then, upon the

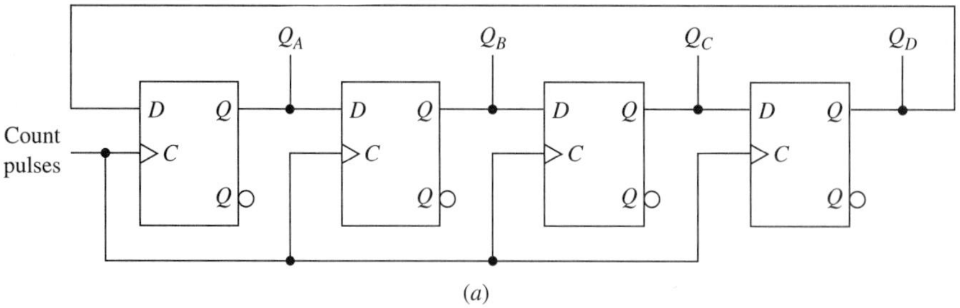

Q_A	Q_B	Q_C	Q_D
1	0	0	0
0	1	0	0
0	0	1	0
0	0	0	1
1	0	0	0

etc.

(b)

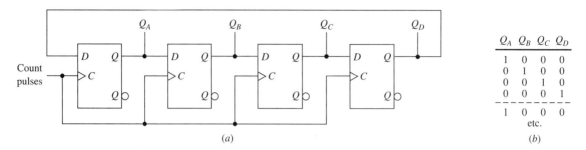

Figure 6.37 Mod-4 ring counter. (*a*) Logic diagram. (*b*) Counting sequence.

occurrence of each count pulse, the single 1 is shifted to its adjacent flip-flop. As a consequence, a ring counter consisting of *n* flip-flops has only *n* states in its counting sequence. Figure 6.37*a* shows a circular shift-right register. This configuration is capable of serving as a mod-4 ring counter. If it is assumed that the counter is initialized to its $Q_AQ_BQ_CQ_D = 1000$ state, then the counting sequence given in Fig. 6.37*b* results.

Although the ring counter is not efficient in the number of flip-flops used, it provides a *decoded output.* That is, to detect any particular state in the counting sequence, it is only necessary to interrogate the output of a single flip-flop. For example, the 0001 state is readily detected by observing the output terminal Q_D. Whenever a logic-1 value appears at this terminal, the state of the counter is known to be 0001. Similarly, the determination of any other state only requires observing the output of a single flip-flop.

A variation of the ring counter is the *switch-tail counter,* also known as the *twisted-ring counter* or *Johnson counter.* This counter is illustrated in Fig. 6.38*a* and its counting sequence is given in Fig. 6.38*b* assuming the counter starts in the $Q_AQ_BQ_CQ_D = 0000$ state. In this counter, the complement of the rightmost flip-flop serves as the input to the leftmost flip-flop in the shift-right register configuration.

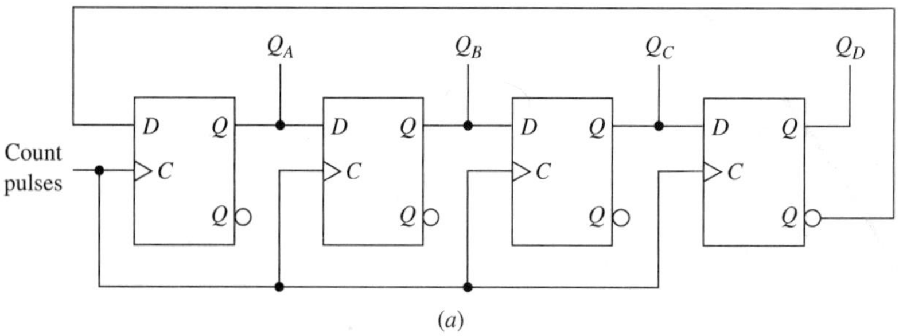

Q_A	Q_B	Q_C	Q_D	And-gate inputs
0	0	0	0	$\bar{Q}_A\bar{Q}_D$
1	0	0	0	$Q_A\bar{Q}_B$
1	1	0	0	$Q_B\bar{Q}_C$
1	1	1	0	$Q_C\bar{Q}_D$
1	1	1	1	Q_AQ_D
0	1	1	1	$\bar{Q}_AQ_B$
0	0	1	1	$\bar{Q}_BQ_C$
0	0	0	1	$\bar{Q}_CQ_D$
0	0	0	0	

etc.

(b)

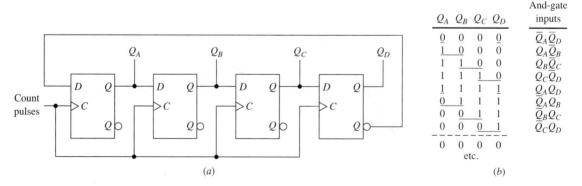

Figure 6.38 Mod-8 twisted-ring counter. (*a*) Logic diagram. (*b*) Counting sequence.

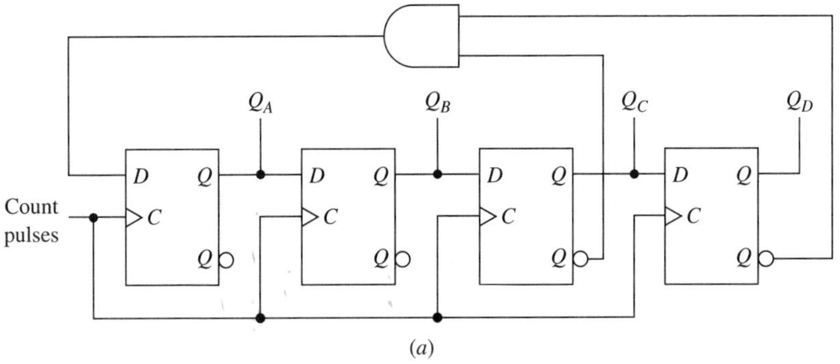

Q_A	Q_B	Q_C	Q_D	And-gate inputs
0	0	0	0	$\overline{Q}_A\overline{Q}_D$
1	0	0	0	$Q_A\overline{Q}_B$
1	1	0	0	$Q_B\overline{Q}_C$
1	1	1	0	$Q_C\overline{Q}_D$
0	1	1	1	$\overline{Q}_A Q_B$
0	0	1	1	$\overline{Q}_B Q_C$
0	0	0	1	$\overline{Q}_C Q_D$
0	0	0	0	
etc.				

(b)

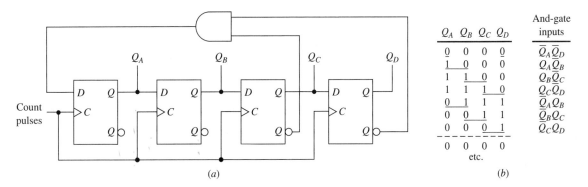

Figure 6.39 Mod-7 twisted-ring counter. (*a*) Logic diagram. (*b*) Counting sequence.

As a result of this connection, $2n$ states occur in the counting sequence of an n-stage counter.

Unlike the ring counter, to detect any particular state in the counting sequence of a twisted-ring counter it is necessary to incorporate some logic elements. Referring to the counting sequence of Fig. 6.38*b*, it is readily noted that the underlined pairs of bits uniquely determine a state. Thus, only a single two-input and-gate, whose logic expression is also given in Fig. 6.38*b*, is required to obtain a decoded output.

A twisted-ring counter having the above structure always has an even number of states in its counting sequence. A twisted-ring counter having an odd number of states is shown in Fig. 6.39*a* and its counting sequence is given in Fig. 6.39*b*. In this variation, the state consisting of all 1's is eliminated from the counting sequence. This is achieved by connecting $\overline{Q}_C\overline{Q}_D$ to the input of the leftmost D flip-flop. Again, each state is detectable by use of a single two-input and-gate as indicated in Fig. 6.39*b*.

6.9 DESIGN OF SYNCHRONOUS COUNTERS

The synchronous counter was introduced in the previous section. This type of counter is characterized by the count pulses being applied directly to the control inputs, C, of the clocked flip-flops that comprise the counter. As a result, all the flip-flops change simultaneously and the new state of the counter is observable in a minimum amount of time. At that time, emphasis was on the binary counter and counters based on shift registers. However, depending upon the application, other types of counters might be desirable, e.g., one that counts according to the Gray code.

It was also previously mentioned that a counter is a pattern generator in which the counting sequence serves as the order in which a series of various patterns is produced. These patterns can then be used to enable or disable various portions of a logic network so as to control its behavior. The use of counters as pattern generators

Table 6.3 Counting sequence for a mod-6 counter

Q_1	Q_2	Q_3
0	0	0
0	1	0
0	1	1
1	1	0
1	0	1
0	0	1
0	0	0
	etc.	

is further explored in the next two chapters. In any event, nonbinary counting sequences are often desirable.

At this time a general procedure is developed for designing synchronous counters having a prespecified output pattern sequence. For illustrative purposes, synchronous mod-6 counters having the counting sequence shown in Table 6.3 are designed using the four types of clocked flip-flops introduced in this chapter.

6.9.1 Design of a Synchronous Mod-6 Counter Using Clocked *JK* Flip-Flops

To begin the design of the synchronous mod-6 counter, consider its general structure assuming the use of clocked *JK* flip-flops. This is shown in Fig. 6.40. The three clocked *JK* flip-flops have the count pulses applied directly to their control inputs, *C*. The count pulses may be clock signals or they may originate

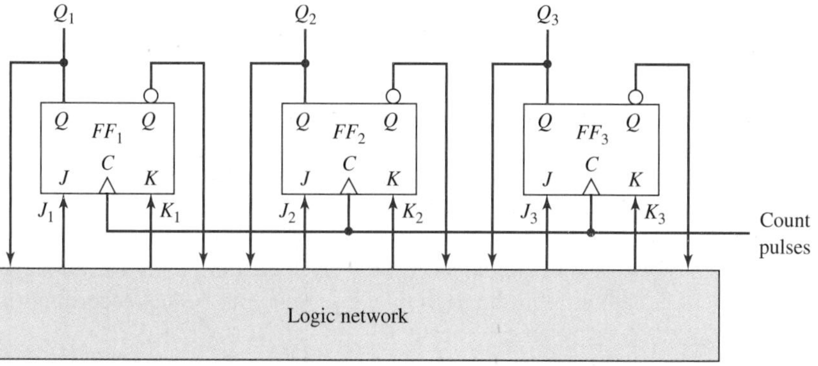

Figure 6.40 General structure of a synchronous mod-6 counter using positive-edge-triggered *JK* flip-flops.

from some other source. The current state of the counter is applied to a logic network. The function of the logic network is to generate the appropriate signals for the J and K terminals of the clocked flip-flops so that the specified next state in the counting sequence results upon the occurrence of the triggering edge of a count pulse. What needs to be designed is the appropriate logic network. In this case, the logic structure of this network can be described by six Boolean expressions, one for each of the six inputs to the three flip-flops, in terms of the Boolean variables Q_1, Q_2, and Q_3 that correspond to the present state of the counter. To obtain these expressions, a truth table for the logic network, called an *excitation table*, is first developed and then the simplified Boolean expressions are obtained.

Table 6.4 shows the excitation table for the synchronous mod-6 counter. It is divided into three sections labeled *present state*, *next state*, and *flip-flop inputs.* At this point, the first two sections can be completed. The counting sequence is listed in the present-state section and the desired next state for each present state is entered in the next-state section.

Before the third section can be filled-in, it is necessary to consider the terminal behavior of a clocked *JK* flip-flop. In general, there are four distinct actions that a flip-flop can undergo as a consequence of a triggering signal at its control input. In particular, a flip-flop should remain in its 0-state, a flip-flop should remain in its 1-state, a flip-flop should go from its 0-state to its 1-state, and, finally, a flip-flop should go from its 1-state to its 0-state. To see how these four actions are achieved, it is necessary to consider the flip-flop next-state tables previously established in Table 6.2. Using the table for the *JK* flip-flop, it is seen that the conditions for a *JK* flip-flop to remain in its 0-state are given by the first and third rows where $Q = 0$ and $Q^+ = 0$. In the first row $J = 0$, $K = 0$ and in the third row $J = 0$, $K = 1$. Thus, for a *JK* flip-flop to remain in its 0-state upon the occurrence of a triggering signal on its control input, a logic-0 must appear at its J input terminal but either a logic-0 or a logic-1 may appear at its K input terminal. This is summarized by the first row of the *JK* flip-flop *application table* given in Table 6.5, where the dash denotes a don't-care.

Table 6.4 Excitation table for a synchronous mod-6 counter using clocked *JK* flip-flops

Present state			Next state			Flip-flop inputs					
Q_1	Q_2	Q_3	Q_1^+	Q_2^+	Q_3^+	J_1	K_1	J_2	K_2	J_3	K_3
0	0	0	0	1	0	0	–	1	–	0	–
0	1	0	0	1	1	0	–	–	0	1	–
0	1	1	1	1	0	1	–	–	0	–	1
1	1	0	1	0	1	–	0	–	1	1	–
1	0	1	0	0	1	–	1	0	–	–	0
0	0	1	0	0	0	0	–	0	–	–	1

Table 6.5 Application table for a clocked *JK* flip-flop

Q	Q^+	J	K
0	0	0	–
0	1	1	–
1	0	–	1
1	1	–	0

Continuing this analysis, the fifth and seventh rows of the *JK* flip-flop next-state table shown in Table 6.2 indicate the necessary conditions at the J and K terminals when it is required to have it change from its present 0-state to its 1-state upon the occurrence of a triggering signal. From the fifth row it is seen that this occurs when $J = 1, K = 0$ and from the seventh row it is seen that this occurs when $J = 1, K = 1$. Thus, it immediately follows that to change a *JK* flip-flop from its 0-state to its 1-state, it is necessary that $J = 1$ and that K can be either logic-0 or logic-1. This condition is given by the second row of Table 6.5.

The remaining two rows of Table 6.5 are again obtained from Table 6.2. From the fourth and eighth rows of the *JK* flip-flop next-state table, it follows that the action of changing a *JK* flip-flop from its 1-state to its 0-state requires that $K = 1$ and that either a logic-0 or a logic-1 appear at the J input terminal. Finally, the second and sixth rows of the *JK* flip-flop next-state table lead to the last row of the *JK* application table shown in Table 6.5, denoting the conditions needed for a *JK* flip-flop to remain in its 1-state. In this case, $K = 0$ and J is either a logic-0 or a logic-1.

Returning to Table 6.4 for the synchronous mod-6 counter, it is now a simple matter to determine the logic signals that must be applied to the three *JK* flip-flops in order to produce the present-state to next-state transitions specified in each row. For example, when the present state of the counter is $Q_1Q_2Q_3 = 000$, its next state is to be $Q_1^+Q_2^+Q_3^+ = 010$. Flip-flop Q_1 must remain in its 0-state. As indicated in Table 6.5, this is achieved by having $J_1 = 0$ and $K_1 = –$. Thus, these become the first two entries in the first row of the flip-flop inputs section of Table 6.4. Similarly, since flip-flop Q_2 must go from its 0-state to its 1-state, this is achieved by having $J_2 = 1$ and $K_2 = –$ according to Table 6.5. Finally, the last pair of entries in the first row of the mod-6 counter excitation table, $J_3 = 0$ and $K_3 = –$, corresponds to the necessary conditions for flip-flop Q_3 to remain in its 0-state. The remaining entries in the flip-flop inputs section are determined row by row in a similar manner, thus completing Table 6.4.

Referring to Fig. 6.40 and Table 6.4, the inputs to the logic network correspond to the present-state section of the excitation table and the outputs from the logic network correspond to the flip-flop inputs section of the excitation table. Thus, the first and third sections of the counter's excitation table is really the truth table for the logic network. Using just these two sections, the six Karnaugh

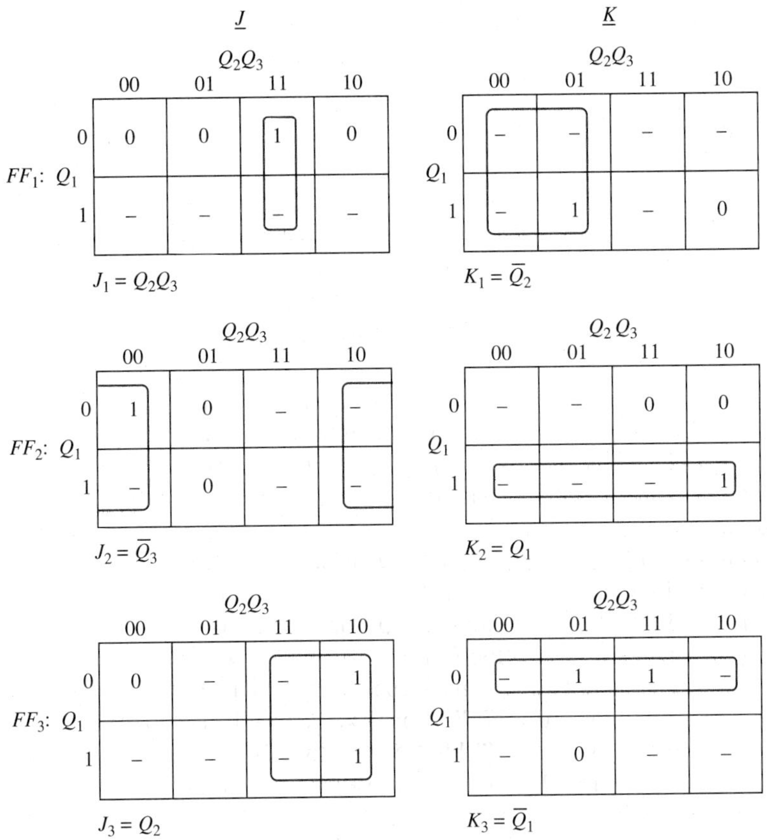

Figure 6.41 Determination of the minimal-sum expressions for a synchronous mod-6 counter using clocked *JK* flip-flops.

maps of Fig. 6.41 are drawn. The six maps correspond to the six flip-flop input functions and a cell of the map corresponds to a *present state* of the counter. Thus, for example, from the first row of Table 6.4, $Q_1Q_2Q_3 = 000$, entries are made into the upper left cell of each map for the appropriate values of J_1, K_1, J_2, K_2, J_3, and K_3. After considering the remaining five rows of Table 6.4, six of the eight cells of each map have entries. Finally, the two cells $Q_1Q_2Q_3 = 100$ and 111 correspond to the two states that do not occur in the counting sequence. Hence, dashes are placed in these two cells of each map since these present states should never occur. A minimal-sum expression for each map is also included in Fig. 6.41. These expressions lead to the logic diagram of Fig. 6.42 for the synchronous mod-6 counter. Although minimal-sum expressions were written, minimal-product expressions could have been obtained instead by grouping the 0's and the don't-cares.

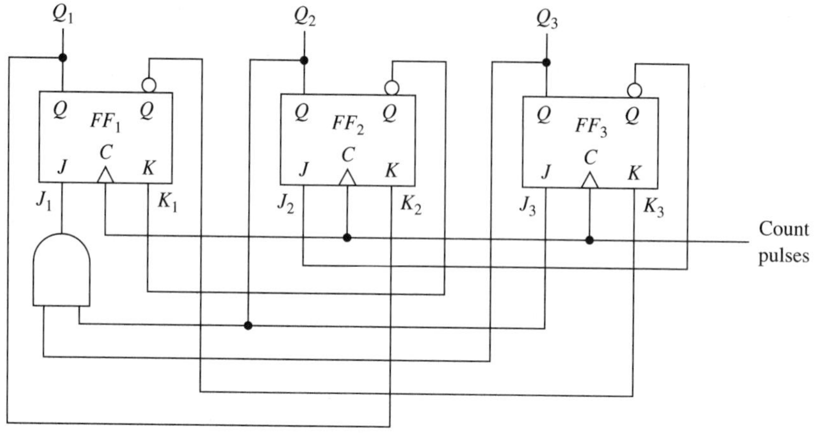

Figure 6.42 Logic diagram of a synchronous mod-6 counter.

6.9.2 Design of a Synchronous Mod-6 Counter Using Clocked *D*, *T*, or *SR* Flip-Flops

The mod-6 counter of Table 6.3 can equally well be designed using clocked *D*, *T*, or *SR* flip-flops. The structure of Fig. 6.40 is still applicable except the *JK* flip-flops are replaced by some other type of clocked flip-flops. To describe the logic network, an excitation table again is constructed. The first two sections, i.e., the present-state and next-state sections, are the same as those of Table 6.4. However, the third section, i.e., the flip-flop inputs section, must correspond to the type of flip-flop being used. To complete the third section, it is necessary to first determine how the four possible state transitions are achieved using the specified type of flip-flop. Once this is done, the third section is readily completed. The first and third sections again correspond to a truth table from which minimal excitation expressions for the flip-flop inputs can be obtained and the logic diagram drawn.

Assume that clocked *D* flip-flops are to be used to design the synchronous mod-6 counter of Table 6.3. Referring to the *D* flip-flop next-state table shown in Table 6.2, the *D* flip-flop application table given in Table 6.6 immediately follows.

Table 6.6 Application table for a clocked *D* flip-flop

Q	Q^+	D
0	0	0
0	1	1
1	0	0
1	1	1

Table 6.7 Excitation table for a synchronous mod-6 counter using clocked *D* flip-flops

Present state			Next state			Flip-flop inputs		
Q_1	Q_2	Q_3	Q_1^+	Q_2^+	Q_3^+	D_1	D_2	D_3
0	0	0	0	1	0	0	1	0
0	1	0	0	1	1	0	1	1
0	1	1	1	1	0	1	1	0
1	1	0	1	0	1	1	0	1
1	0	1	0	0	1	0	0	1
0	0	1	0	0	0	0	0	0

This table simply states that whatever next-state value is needed of a clocked *D* flip-flop, that logic value should appear at its *D* input terminal upon the occurrence of a triggering edge at its control input. Using the information of Table 6.6, the third section of the mod-6 counter excitation table is completed in a manner analogous to that done previously for *JK* flip-flops. This is shown in Table 6.7.* Finally, regarding the first and third sections of Table 6.7 as a truth table, the Karnaugh maps for the three output functions, D_1, D_2, and D_3, are constructed as shown in Fig. 6.43. Again don't-cares occur in the two cells of each map corresponding to the two unused states of the counting sequence, i.e., $Q_1Q_2Q_3 = 100$ and 111. From these maps, minimal expressions for the logic network are obtained. In this case, a minimal-sum expression describing the logic preceding each *D* flip-flop is written beneath its Karnaugh map. Once the expressions for the logic network are established, the logic diagram can be drawn.

The above procedure is readily modified when clocked *T* flip-flops are used for the counter. As was done previously, the application table for a clocked *T* flip-flop is first obtained and then the excitation table for the synchronous mod-6 counter is constructed. Table 6.8 gives the *T* flip-flop application table. This table again immediately follows from the *T* flip-flop next-state table given in Table 6.2 by noting what logic value should be applied to the *T* input terminal for each of the four present-state/next-state combinations. According to the clocked *T* flip-flop application table, a logic-1 is needed at the *T* input terminal if the flip-flop is to change state upon the occurrence of a triggering edge at its control input; otherwise, a logic-0 should occur at the *T* input terminal. Using Table 6.8, the third section of the synchronous mod-6 counter excitation table shown in Table 6.9 is completed. From the first and third sections of Table 6.9, the Karnaugh maps for the synchronous mod-6 counter with clocked *T* flip-flops, given in Fig. 6.44, are obtained. Using these maps, minimal sums are easily written.

*Since $D_i = Q_i^+$, it should be no surprise that the next-state and flip-flop inputs sections of Table 6.7 are identical.

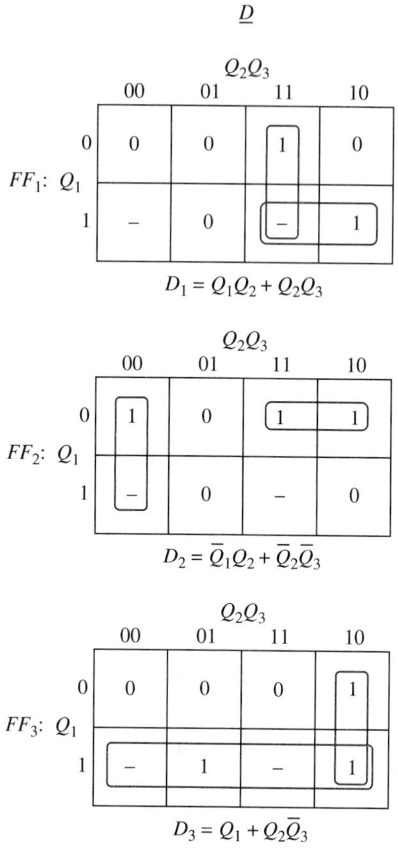

D
Q_2Q_3
00 01 11 10
FF_1: Q_1
0 0 0 1 0
1 – 0 – 1
$D_1 = Q_1Q_2 + Q_2Q_3$
Q_2Q_3
00 01 11 10
FF_2: Q_1
0 1 0 1 1
1 – 0 – 0
$D_2 = \overline{Q}_1Q_2 + \overline{Q}_2\overline{Q}_3$
Q_2Q_3
00 01 11 10
FF_3: Q_1
0 0 0 0 1
1 – 1 – 1
$D_3 = Q_1 + Q_2\overline{Q}_3$

Figure 6.43 Determination of the minimal-sum expressions for a synchronous mod-6 counter using clocked *D* flip-flops.

Table 6.8 Application table for a clocked *T* flip-flop

Q	Q^+	T
0	0	0
0	1	1
1	0	1
1	1	0

Table 6.9 Excitation table for a synchronous mod-6 counter using clocked *T* flip-flops

Present state			Next state			Flip-flop inputs		
Q_1	Q_2	Q_3	Q_1^+	Q_2^+	Q_3^+	T_1	T_2	T_3
0	0	0	0	1	0	0	1	0
0	1	0	0	1	1	0	0	1
0	1	1	1	1	0	1	0	1
1	1	0	1	0	1	0	1	1
1	0	1	0	0	1	1	0	0
0	0	1	0	0	0	0	0	1

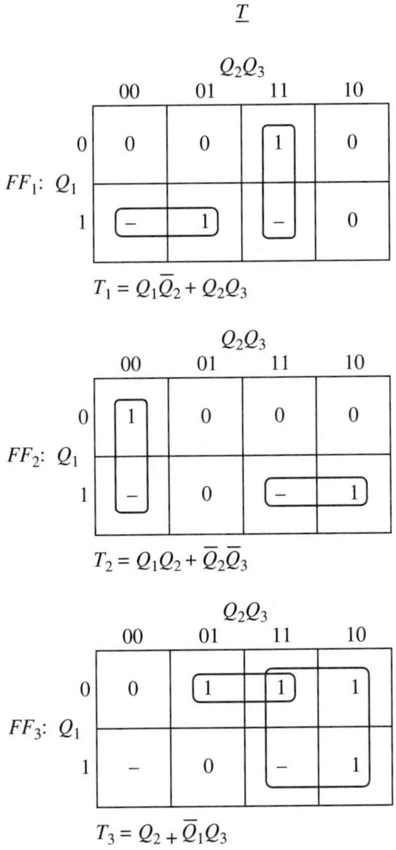

Figure 6.44 Determination of the minimal-sum expressions for a synchronous mod-6 counter using clocked *T* flip-flops.

Table 6.10 Application table for a clocked *SR* flip-flop

Q	Q^+	S	R
0	0	0	–
0	1	1	0
1	0	0	1
1	1	–	0

Finally, consider the design of the synchronous mod-6 counter, having the counting sequence given in Table 6.3, with clocked *SR* flip-flops. Table 6.10 gives the necessary *SR* flip-flop application table from which the flip-flop inputs section of the counter excitation table is completed. Table 6.2 is used to construct the *SR* flip-flop application table by using the same type of analysis previously used to obtain the *JK* flip-flop application table. However, since an *SR* flip-flop has nonallowable input combinations, these combinations must not be used in forming Table 6.10. Thus, when a clocked *SR* flip-flop is to change from its 0-state to its 1-state, according to Table 6.2 this is achieved only if $S = 1$ and $R = 0$. Table 6.11, the excitation table for the synchronous mod-6 counter using *SR* flip-flops, is next constructed. From this table the Karnaugh maps of Fig. 6.45 are formed and the minimal sums written.

6.9.3 Self-Correcting Counters

The counting sequence of the mod-6 counter given in Table 6.3 did not include states 100 and 111. Once the counter is designed, definite next states result if either of these states should occur.

When a system is initially started, i.e., when power is first applied to the network, the initial states of the flip-flops are unpredictable. Consequently, either of the two states 100 and 111 can occur. As a solution to this problem, the counter could be initialized prior to its use. One way in which this can be done is by applying appropriate signals to the asynchronous input terminals of the flip-flops to force them into the first state of the counting sequence. However, noise signals

Table 6.11 Excitation table for a synchronous mod-6 counter using clocked *SR* flip-flops

Present state			Next state			Flip-flop inputs					
Q_1	Q_2	Q_3	Q_1^+	Q_2^+	Q_3^+	S_1	R_1	S_2	R_2	S_3	R_3
0	0	0	0	1	0	0	–	1	0	0	–
0	1	0	0	1	1	0	–	–	0	1	0
0	1	1	1	1	0	1	0	–	0	0	1
1	1	0	1	0	1	–	0	0	1	1	0
1	0	1	0	0	1	0	1	0	–	–	0
0	0	1	0	0	0	0	–	0	–	0	1

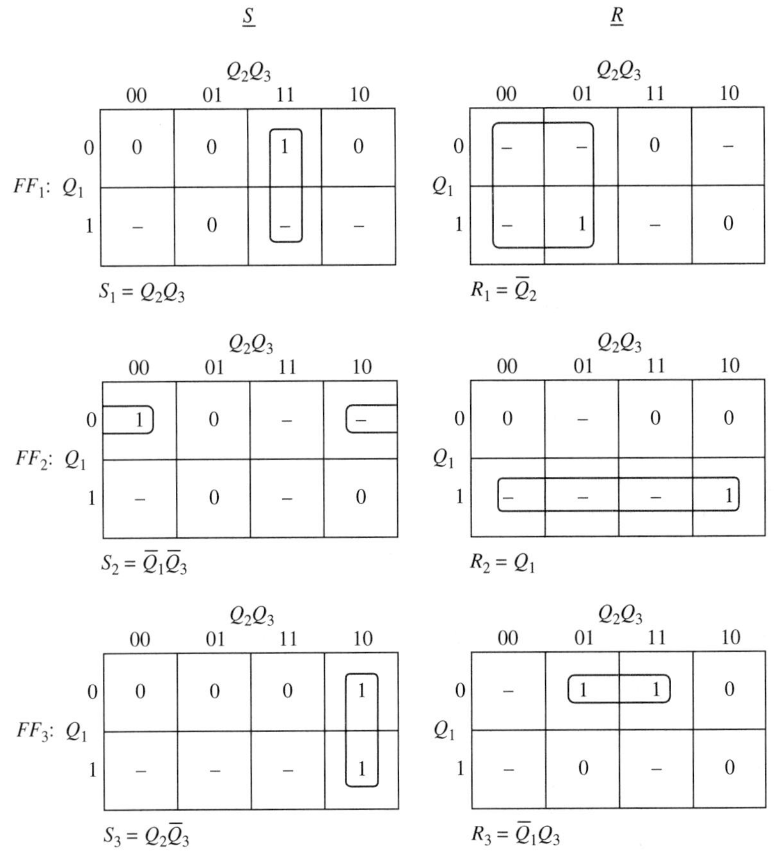

Figure 6.45 Determination of the minimal-sum expressions for a synchronous mod-6 counter using clocked *SR* flip-flops.

can also cause the counter to enter one of its initially unused states. Thus, it is of interest to consider the behavior of a counter under the assumption that the unused states of a counting sequence occur. A counter in which all the states not included in the original counting sequence eventually lead to the normal counting sequence after one or more count pulses are applied to the control inputs, *C*, is said to be *self-correcting*. To avoid having the counter "hang up," it should always be designed as self-correcting.

Again consider the synchronous mod-6 counter previously designed with *JK* flip-flops. State $Q_1Q_2Q_3 = 100$ was not included in the counting sequence. Substituting these values into the flip-flop input equations obtained in Fig. 6.41 for the realization, it is seen that $J_1 = 0$, $K_1 = 1$, $J_2 = 1$, $K_2 = 1$, $J_3 = 0$, and $K_3 = 0$. Consequently, upon the occurrence of the count pulse, flip-flop Q_1 resets, flip-flop Q_2 toggles, and flip-flop Q_3 remains unchanged, with the net result that the next state of the counter is $Q_1^+Q_2^+Q_3^+ = 010$. Hence, a valid state of the counting sequence is

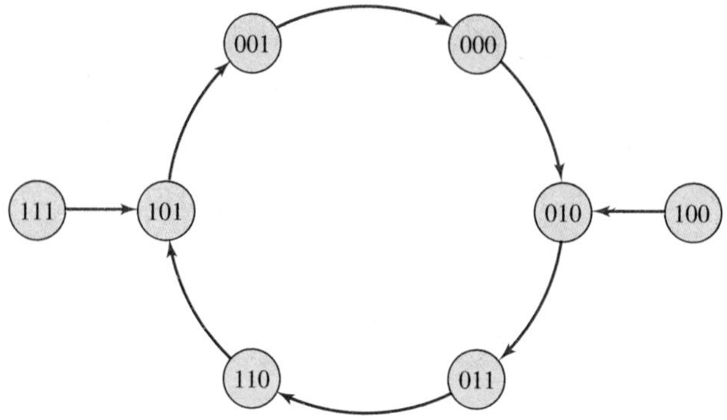

Figure 6.46 Complete state diagram for the synchronous mod-6 counter of Fig. 6.42.

reached if the initially unused state should occur. In a similar manner, it is easily checked that $Q_1Q_2Q_3 = 111$ leads to the valid next state $Q_1^+Q_2^+Q_3^+ = 101$ in the counting sequence. Figure 6.46 shows the complete state diagram for the synchronous mod-6 counter whose realization was given in Fig. 6.42. Included are the effects of the two initially unused states. Since these states lead to the normal counting sequence, the realization is that of a self-correcting counter. In an analogous manner, it can be shown that the other three realizations of the synchronous mod-6 counter are also self-correcting.

Counters having no unused states are always self-correcting. It is the assignment to the don't-cares associated with the unused states when the logic expressions are obtained that can cause a counter not to be self-correcting. By actually specifying the next states for each of the unused states in the counting sequence prior to constructing the Karnaugh maps, a self-correcting counter realization can be guaranteed.

CHAPTER 6 PROBLEMS

6.1 Design a switch debouncer using an $\overline{S}\,\overline{R}$ latch.

6.2 The input signals shown in Fig. P6.2 are applied to the *SR* latch of Fig. 6.2*a* when initially in its 0-state. Sketch the Q and $\overline{Q}$ output signals. Assume all timing constraints are satisfied.

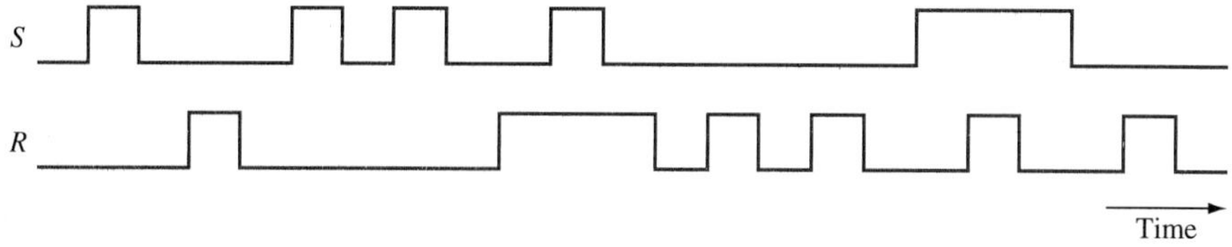

Figure P6.2

6.3 The input signals shown in Fig. P6.3 are applied to the $\overline{S}\,\overline{R}$ latch of Fig. 6.4*a* when initially in its 0-state. Sketch the Q and $\overline{Q}$ output signals. Assume all timing constraints are satisfied.

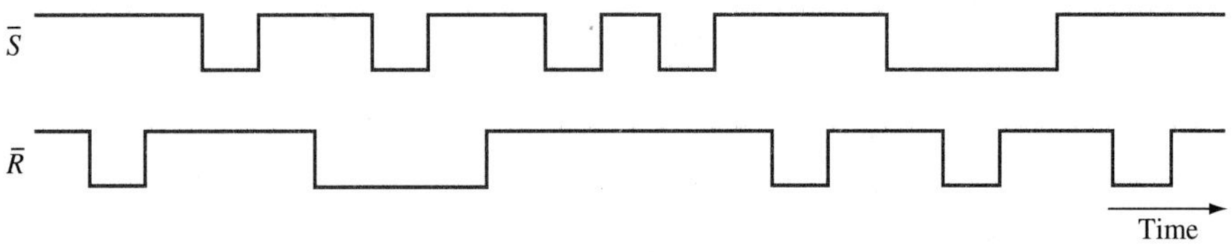

Figure P6.3

6.4 The input signals shown in Fig. P6.4 are applied to the gated *SR* latch of Fig. 6.5*a* when initially in its 0-state. Sketch the Q and $\overline{Q}$ output signals. Assume all timing constraints are satisfied.

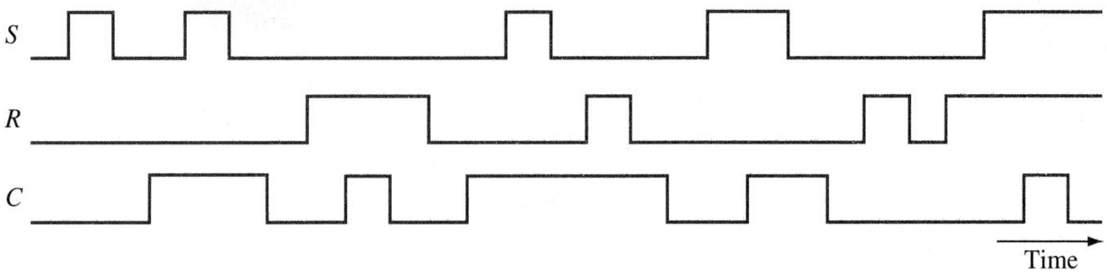

Figure P6.4

6.5 The input signals shown in Fig. P6.5 are applied to the gated *D* latch of Fig. 6.6*a* when initially in its 0-state. Sketch the Q and $\overline{Q}$ output signals. Assume all timing constraints are satisfied.

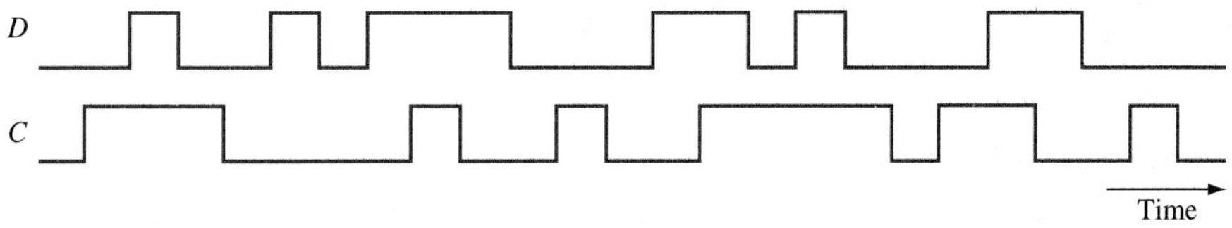

Figure P6.5

6.6 The input signals shown in Fig. P6.6 are applied to the master-slave *SR* flip-flop of Fig. 6.12*a* when initially in its 0-state. Sketch the Q_M, $\overline{Q}_M$, Q_S, and $\overline{Q}_S$ output signals. Assume all timing constraints are satisfied.

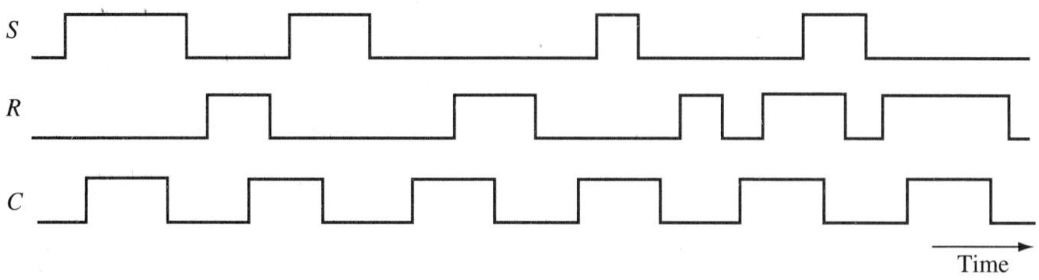

Figure P6.6

6.7 The input signals shown in Fig. P6.7 are applied to the master-slave *JK* flip-flop of Fig. 6.14*a* when initially in its 0-state. Sketch the Q_M and Q_S output signals. Assume all timing constraints are satisfied.

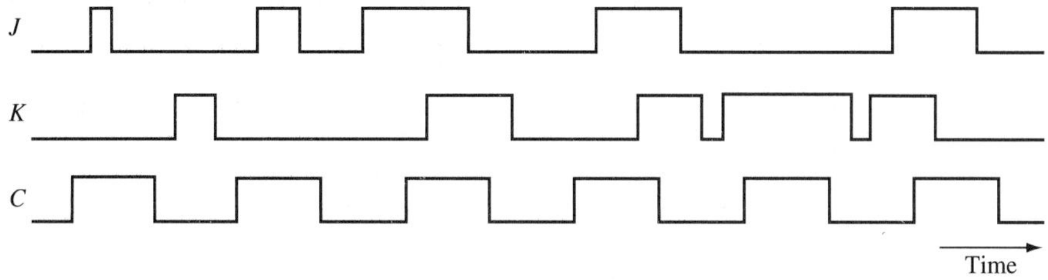

Figure P6.7

6.8 The input signals shown in Fig. P6.8 are applied to the master-slave *D* flip-flop of Fig. 6.16*a* when initially in its 0-state. Sketch the Q_M and Q_S output signals. Assume all timing constraints are satisfied.

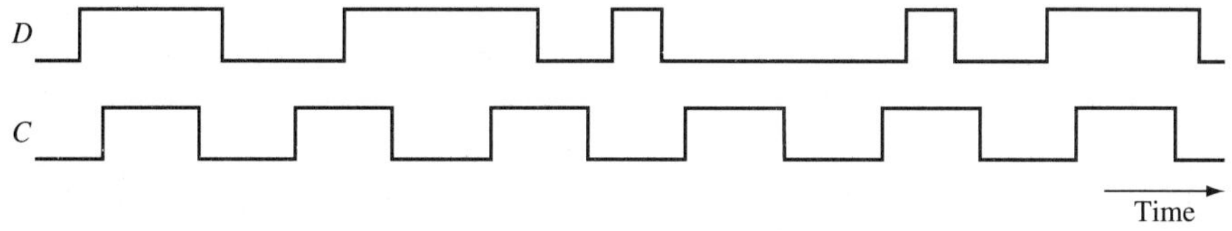

Figure P6.8

6.9 The input signals shown in Fig. P6.9 are applied to the master-slave T flip-flop of Fig. 6.17*a* when initially in its 0-state. Sketch the Q_M and Q_S output signals. Assume all timing constraints are satisfied.

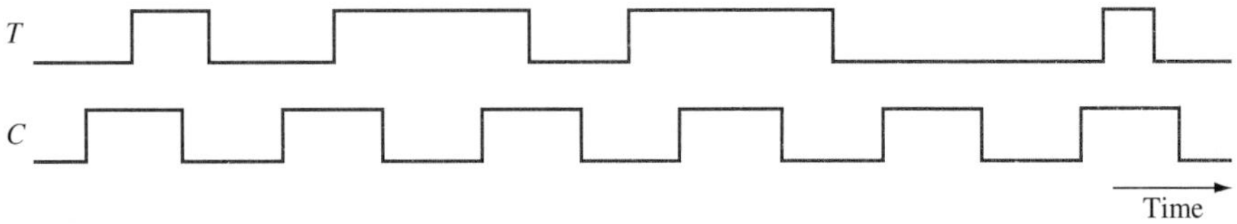

Figure P6.9

6.10 A logic diagram and function table for a proposed gated JK latch is shown in Fig. P6.10. Discuss the problems that can be encountered with this network and under what constraints proper JK flip-flop behavior is achieved.

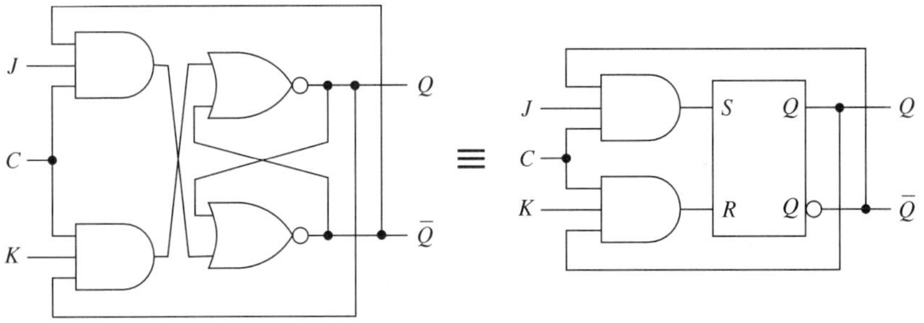

(*a*)

Inputs			Outputs	
J	K	C	Q^+	$\overline{Q}^+$
0	0	1	Q	$\overline{Q}$
0	1	1	0	1
1	0	1	1	0
1	1	1	$\overline{Q}$	Q
X	X	0	Q	$\overline{Q}$

(*b*)

Figure P6.10

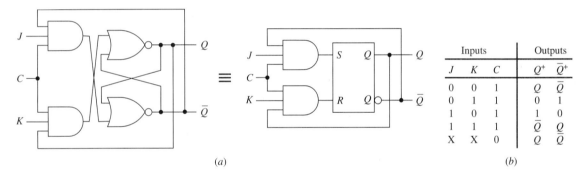

6.11 The input signals shown in Fig. P6.8 are applied to the positive-edge-triggered D flip-flop of Fig. 6.18*a* when initially in its 0-state. Sketch the Q output signal. Assume all timing constraints are satisfied.

6.12 The input signals shown in Fig. P6.7 are applied to the positive-edge-triggered JK flip-flop of Fig. 6.22*a* when initially in its 0-state. Sketch the Q output signal. Assume all timing constraints are satisfied.

6.13 The input signals shown in Fig. P6.9 are applied to the positive-edge-triggered T flip-flop of Fig. 6.23*a* when initially in its 0-state. Sketch the Q output signal. Assume all timing constraints are satisfied.

6.14 The input signals shown in Fig. P6.7 are applied to the master-slave JK flip-flop with data lockout of Fig. 6.24*a* when initially in its 0-state. Sketch the Q_M and Q_S output signals. Assume all timing constraints are satisfied.

6.15 The positive-edge-triggered D flip-flop shown in Fig. P6.15a has the signals of Fig. P6.15b applied when initially in its 0-state. Sketch the Q output signal. Assume all timing constraints are satisfied.

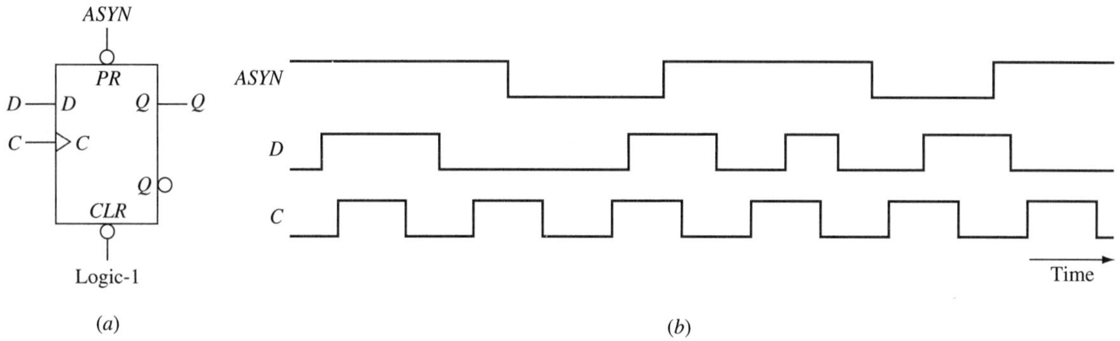

Figure P6.15

6.16 Show that for the positive-edge-triggered D flip-flop of Fig. 6.21a, it resets when $\overline{PR} = 1$ and $\overline{CLR} = 0$ and that the C and D inputs have no effect on its behavior. Show that the flip-flop sets when $\overline{PR} = 0$ and $\overline{CLR} = 1$.

6.17 Show that the master-slave configuration involving two gated D latches as given in Fig. P6.17 is best described by the positive-edge-triggered D flip-flop function table of Fig. 6.18b.

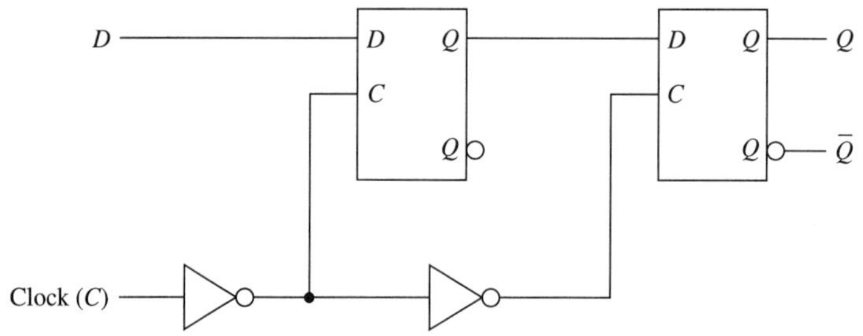

Figure P6.17

6.18 Verify the characteristic equations for the JK, D, and T flip-flops given in Fig. 6.25b by constructing the appropriate Karnaugh maps and obtaining the minimal sums.

6.19 Assume the shift register of Fig. 6.26 initially contains 1101. What is the content of the register after the positive edge of each clock signal if the values occurring on the serial-data-in line are 1, 1, 0, 1, 0, 1, and 0 in that order?

6.20 Modify the register of Fig. 6.26 so that it is synchronously cleared. That is, incorporate a clear/shift control input line in which, upon the occurrence of the clock signal, all the flip-flops enter their 0-state when the control signal is 0 and behaves as a shift-right register when the control signal is 1.

6.21 Design a register, incorporating four multiplexers and four positive-edge-triggered *D* flip-flops, having the behavior specified in Table P6.21.

Table P6.21

Select lines S_1	S_0	Register operation
0	0	Hold
0	1	Synchronous clear
1	0	Complement contents
1	1	Circular shift right

6.22 For a 3-bit binary ripple up-counter similar to the one in Fig. 6.31, draw the Count pulse, Q_0, Q_1, and Q_2 signals assuming a propagation delay of τ for each flip-flop.

6.23 Design a 4-bit binary ripple up-counter using negative-edge-triggered *JK* flip-flops.

6.24 Design a 4-bit binary ripple up-counter using positive-edge-triggered *D* flip-flops. Do not include a count-enable line.

6.25 Design a 4-bit binary ripple down-counter using positive-edge-triggered *T* flip-flops.

6.26 Using a structure similar to that of Fig. 6.33, design a 4-bit synchronous binary down-counter.

6.27 a. Using a structure similar to that of Fig. 6.33, design a 4-bit synchronous binary up/down-counter having a count enable input line and an up/down input line. When the signal value on the up/down input line is logic-1, the counter should behave as a binary up counter; when the signal value on the up/down input line is logic-0, the counter should behave as a binary down counter.

b. Repeat part (*a*) using a structure similar to that of Fig. 6.34. The CO output should be logic-1 when the counter is going down and the counter state is 0000 and when the counter is going up and the counter state is 1111.

6.28 Using the counter of Fig. 6.34, design a mod-5 counter

a. whose counting sequence consists of its first five states, i.e., 0000, 0001, . . . , 0100, 0000, etc.

b. whose counting sequence consists of its last five states, i.e., 1011, 1100, . . . , 1111, 1011, etc.

6.29 Modify the synchronous mod-256 binary counter shown in Fig. 6.36 to become a synchronous mod-77 binary counter.

6.30 Realize the 4-bit ring counter of Fig. 6.37 using the universal shift register of Fig. 6.29. Use the parallel load capability of the register to initialize the counter.

6.31 Realize the 4-bit twisted-ring counter of Fig. 6.38 using the universal shift register of Fig. 6.29. Use the asynchronous clear capability of the register to initialize the counter.

6.32 Using the general design procedure of Sec. 6.9, design a synchronous mod-16 binary counter by obtaining its minimal-sum equations. Use positive-edge-triggered *D* flip-flops.

6.33 Using the general design procedure of Sec. 6.9, design a synchronous mod-10 binary counter, i.e., one whose counting sequence corresponds to the first 10 binary numbers, by obtaining its minimal-sum equations.

a. Use positive-edge-triggered *JK* flip-flops.
b. Use positive-edge-triggered *D* flip-flops.
c. Use positive-edge-triggered *T* flip-flops.
d. Use positive-edge-triggered *SR* flip-flops.
e. For the design of part (*a*), determine if the counter is self-correcting by constructing the complete state diagram.

6.34 Design a synchronous mod-10 counter whose counting sequence corresponds to the 5421 code (see Table 2.7) by obtaining its minimal-sum equations.

a. Use positive-edge-triggered *JK* flip-flops.
b. Use positive-edge-triggered *D* flip-flops.
c. Use positive-edge-triggered *T* flip-flops.
d. Use positive-edge-triggered *SR* flip-flops.

6.35 Design a synchronous mod-10 counter whose counting sequence corresponds to the $753\overline{6}$ code (see Table 2.7) by obtaining its minimal-sum equations.

a. Use positive-edge-triggered *JK* flip-flops.
b. Use positive-edge-triggered *D* flip-flops.
c. Use positive-edge-triggered *T* flip-flops.

6.36 Design a synchronous mod-6 counter whose counting sequence is 000, 001, 100, 110, 111, 101, 000, etc., by obtaining its minimal-sum equations.

a. Use positive-edge-triggered *JK* flip-flops.
b. Use positive-edge-triggered *D* flip-flops.

c. Use positive-edge-triggered *T* flip-flops.
d. Use positive-edge-triggered *SR* flip-flops.
e. For each of the above designs, determine if the counter is self-correcting by drawing the complete state diagram.

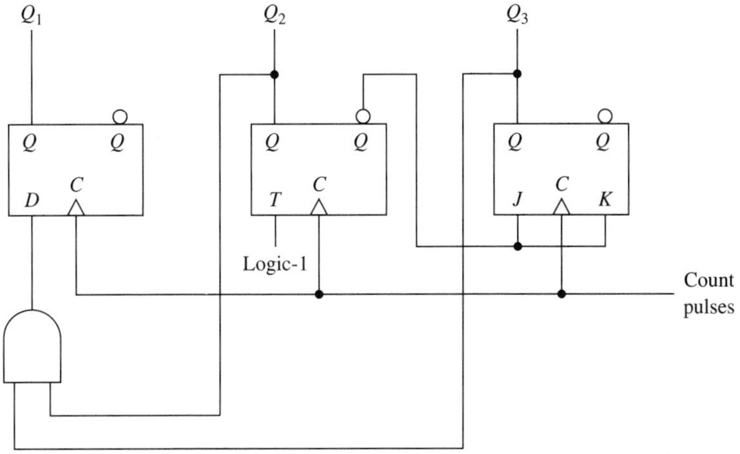

Figure P6.37

6.37 Consider the synchronous counter shown in Fig. P6.37 constructed with positive-edge-triggered flip-flops. Assuming it is initialized to 000 prior to the first count pulse, determine the counting sequence. Is this counter self-correcting?

6.38 From the Karnaugh maps of Fig. 6.43, it is seen that the synchronous mod-6 counter could also be realized from the equations

$$D_1 = Q_1\overline{Q}_3 + Q_2Q_3$$
$$D_2 = \overline{Q}_1\overline{Q}_3 + Q_2Q_3$$
$$D_3 = Q_1 + Q_2\overline{Q}_3$$

Determine the effect of the two unused states 100 and 111 based on such a realization.

6.39 It is a simple matter to formally convert any type of clocked flip-flop into another type using the same triggering scheme. For example, Fig. P6.39*a* shows the necessary structure to convert a positive-edge-triggered *JK* flip-flop into a positive-edge-triggered *AB* flip-flop whose simplified function table is given in Fig. P6.39*b*. To do this, the three-section table shown in Fig. P6.39*c* is completed. For each combination of the *AB* flip-flop inputs and present state, the Q^+ section indicates the required next-state of the *AB* flip-flop and the *JK* section indicates how the state transition is achieved using a *JK* flip-flop. The first and third sections of the completed table provide a truth table for the logic network. Using this approach, design a positive-edge-triggered *AB* flip-flop.

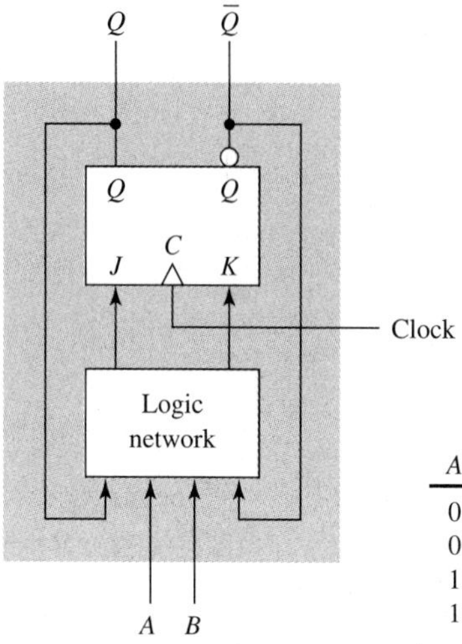

(*a*)

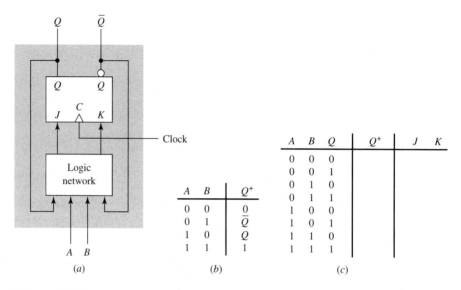

A	B	Q^+
0	0	0
0	1	$\overline{Q}$
1	0	Q
1	1	1

(*b*)

A	B	Q	Q^+	J	K
0	0	0			
0	0	1			
0	1	0			
0	1	1			
1	0	0			
1	0	1			
1	1	0			
1	1	1			

(*c*)

Figure P6.39

6.40 Using the approach suggested in Problem 6.39,

a. convert a positive-edge-triggered *D* flip-flop into a positive-edge-triggered *AB* flip-flop.

b. convert a positive-edge-triggered *T* flip-flop into a positive-edge-triggered *AB* flip-flop.

c. convert a positive-edge-triggered *D* flip-flop into a positive-edge-triggered *JK* flip-flop.

6.41 Using the positive-edge-triggered *AB* flip-flop described in Problem 6.39, design a synchronous mod-6 counter whose counting sequence is 000, 110, 101, 011, 010, 001, 000, etc., by obtaining its minimal-sum equations.

CHAPTER 7

Synchronous Sequential Networks

In the previous chapter, several examples of logic networks incorporating flip-flops were studied. Those networks are examples of *synchronous sequential networks*. Also at that time, a general design procedure was introduced for counters. In this chapter, a more detailed and formal study of synchronous sequential networks is undertaken.

What distinguishes sequential networks from combinational networks is the existence of *memory*. In a combinational network, the outputs at any instant of time are dependent only upon the inputs present at that instant. However, in the case of sequential networks, in addition to the outputs at any instant being dependent upon the inputs present at that instant, they are also dependent upon the past history, i.e., the sequence, of inputs. At any time, the entire past history of inputs is preserved by the network as internal information that is referred to as the *present state*, or, simply, *state*, of the network. In this way, the outputs of a sequential network are only a function of the present external inputs and its present state. Furthermore, upon the arrival of a new set of external input signals, the network must enter a new state since the past history of inputs must now include the last previous input signals. Thus, the external inputs and present state determine the *next state* of the network.

Figure 7.1 shows a general model of a sequential network corresponding to the above discussion. The box labeled "memory" provides for the preservation of information about the past history of inputs. In a physical system, flip-flops are frequently used for holding this information. The current outputs of the flip-flops denote the present state of the system. The inputs to the memory box are associated with the next state that, in turn, becomes available as a present state at some appropriate later time. Thus, it is observed that a delay time is associated with the memory.

As seen from the above discussion, the operation of a sequential network involves a time sequence of inputs, outputs, and states. The nature of the timing relationship

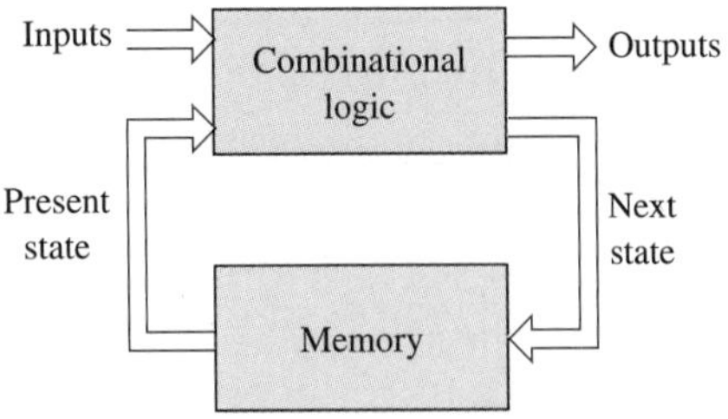

Figure 7.1 General model of a sequential network.

classifies sequential networks into two broad categories: *synchronous* and *asynchronous.* In the case of synchronous sequential networks it is assumed that the behavior of the system is totally determined by the values of the present state and external input signals at *discrete instants of time.* Special timing signals are used to define these time instants. In addition, it is only at these discrete instants of time that the memory of the system is allowed to undergo changes. In this way it is possible to describe the behavior of the system relative to the set of ordinal numbers that are assigned to the timing signals. The counters of the previous chapter are examples of synchronous sequential networks where the discrete instants of time are associated with the occurrences of the triggering edge of the count pulses.

The second category of sequential networks is the asynchronous sequential networks. In these networks, it is the order in which input signals change that affects the network behavior. Furthermore, these changes are allowed to occur at any instants of time. This class of sequential networks is studied in Chapter 9. ■

7.1 STRUCTURE AND OPERATION OF CLOCKED SYNCHRONOUS SEQUENTIAL NETWORKS

In synchronous sequential networks, the network behavior is defined at specific instants of time associated with special timing signals. The most common method of providing timing in a synchronous sequential network is by means of a single master clock that appears at the control inputs of all the flip-flops that make up the memory portion of the network. In this way, all the flip-flops receive the common clock signal simultaneously. Such sequential networks are referred to as *clocked synchronous sequential networks.* The structure of clocked synchronous sequential networks is shown in Fig. 7.2.*

*Although edge-triggered flip-flops are shown in the figure, master-slave flip-flops can also be used.

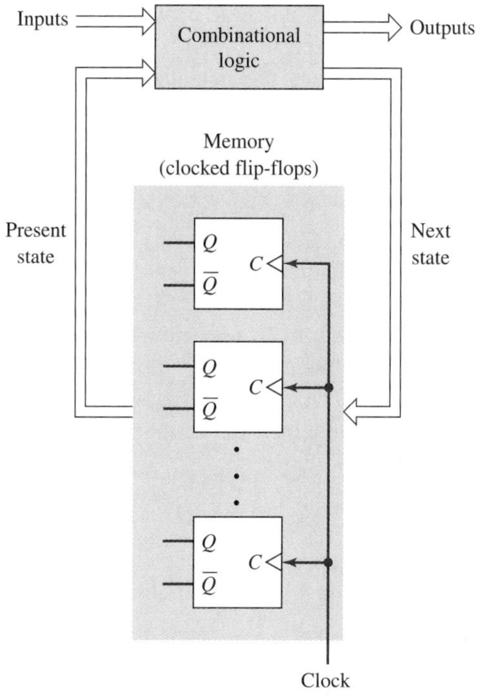

Figure 7.2 Structure of a clocked synchronous sequential network.

The clock signal is a periodic waveform having one positive edge and one negative edge during each period. Thus, during part of the period the clock signal has the value of logic-1 and during the other part of the period it has the value of logic-0. Since this control signal is applied to clocked flip-flops, one edge is used for triggering in the case of edge-triggered flip-flops. Alternatively, the time duration in which the clock signal is in one of its logic states, along with its associated edges, is used to achieve a pulse for pulse-triggered flip-flops. For simplicity, no distinction is made in this chapter between these edges or pulses, and their occurrence is hereafter referred to as the *triggering times* or *active times* of the clock signal.

The use of a single master clock provides for network synchronization and has the advantage of preventing many timing problems. The basic operation of clocked synchronous sequential networks proceeds as follows. After the input and new present state signals in Fig. 7.2 are applied to the combinational logic, the effects of the signals must propagate through the logic network since gates have finite propagation delay times. As a result, the final values at the flip-flop inputs occur at different times depending upon the number of gates involved in the signal paths and the actual propagation delays of each gate. In any event, it is only after the final values are reached that the active time of the clock signal is allowed to occur and cause any state changes. Since the clock signal is applied simultaneously to all the flip-flops in the memory portion of the network, all state changes of the flip-flops occur at the same time.* The process is then repeated. That is, new inputs are applied and then the synchronizing clock signal affects the state changes. It is important to note that the flip-flops are only allowed to undergo at most a single state change for each clock period. That is, any changes in the outputs of the flip-flops incurred as a result of the clock signal cannot cause another state change until the next clock period. As was seen in the previous chapter, edge-triggered and pulse-triggered, i.e., master-slave, flip-flops provide this type of behavior.

As shown in Fig. 7.2, combinational logic is used to generate the next-state and output signals. The present state of the network is the current content of the flip-flops that comprise the memory portion of the network. The next state corresponds to the updated information about the past history of inputs that must be preserved by the system. Thus, if X denotes the collective external input signals and Q the collective present states of the flip-flops, then the next state of the network, denoted by Q^+, is functionally given by

$$Q^+ = f(X,Q) \tag{7.1}$$

Similarly, if Z is regarded as the collective output signals of the network, then under the assumption that the outputs are a function of both the inputs and present state, it immediately follows that

$$Z = g(X,Q) \tag{7.2}$$

Equations (7.1) and (7.2) suggest the general structure of a clocked synchronous sequential network shown in Fig. 7.3. This model is frequently referred to as the *Mealy model* or *Mealy machine.*

A variation to the Mealy model occurs when the outputs are only a function of the present state and not of the external inputs. In this case

$$Z = g(Q) \tag{7.3}$$

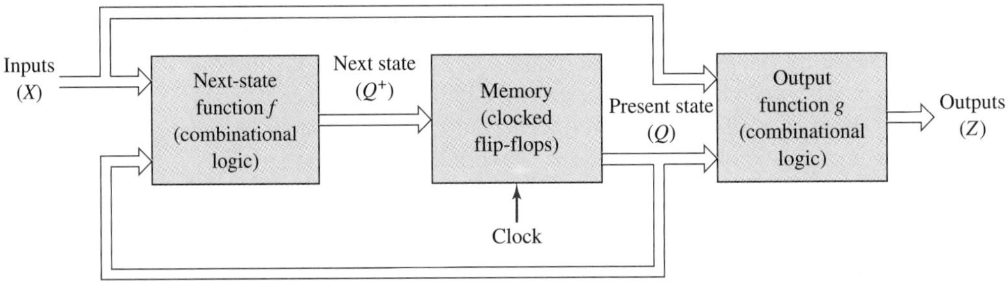

Figure 7.3 Mealy model of a clocked synchronous sequential network.

*As is seen in Chapter 9, this is in contrast to asynchronous sequential networks, which are allowed to respond to signal changes on the inputs as they occur.

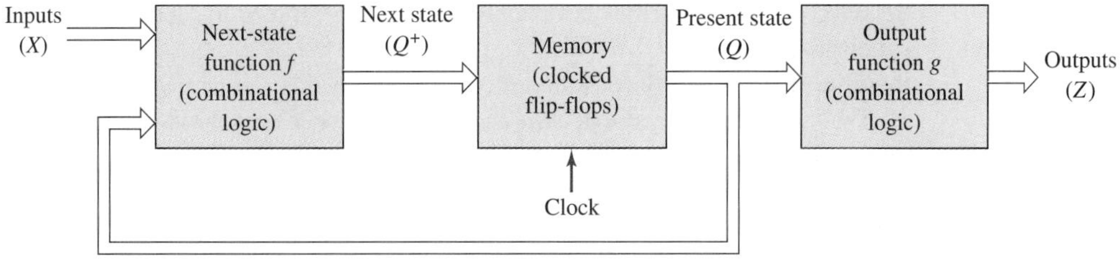

Figure 7.4 Moore model of a clocked synchronous sequential network.

Again the next state of the network, Q^+, is a function of the external inputs and the present state as given by Eq. (7.1). This variation of a clocked synchronous sequential network is referred to as the *Moore model* or *Moore machine.* The general structure suggested by Eqs. (7.1) and (7.3) is illustrated in Fig. 7.4.

Although the use of a master clock is the most common method of synchronizing sequential networks, there are other timing mechanisms. For example, pulses of controlled duration from one or more sources can be used to trigger the flip-flops. However, such pulse-type timing introduces complications in realizations that do not occur when a single master clock is used. The concepts of Mealy and Moore models are still applicable to such synchronous sequential networks if these pulses only can cause single state changes. In this chapter, however, the study of synchronous sequential networks is restricted to only those that are single master-clock controlled.

In the general models of Figs. 7.1 to 7.4, the inputs to the memory portion of the sequential network are labeled "next state." The interpretation here is that appropriate signals are applied to the clocked flip-flops so that after the triggering edge or pulse of the clock signal, the states of the flip-flops reflect the updated state information. In a realization, the actual signals that must be applied to the flip-flops are really *excitation signals* that achieve the appropriate next state. These signals are dependent upon the type of clocked flip-flops used for the memory. That is, the necessary excitation signals depend upon whether *JK*, *SR*, *D*, or *T* flip-flops are used. In the previous chapter, relationships were established between the present-state/next-state transitions of a flip-flop and the logic values needed at its input terminals to achieve these transitions.

7.2 ANALYSIS OF CLOCKED SYNCHRONOUS SEQUENTIAL NETWORKS

There are two main reasons for beginning the study of clocked synchronous sequential networks with analysis. First, analysis provides tabular descriptions of sequential networks. These are particularly useful when sequential networks are to be designed. The steps involved in the synthesis of clocked synchronous sequential networks are basically the reverse of those involved in the analysis procedure.

Second, analysis provides a means for studying the terminal behavior of clocked synchronous sequential networks. In particular, given a time sequence of inputs, the time sequence of outputs and next states is readily determined.

In the previous section, two models of clocked synchronous sequential networks were presented: the Mealy model as defined by Eqs. (7.1) and (7.2) and the Moore model as defined by Eqs. (7.1) and (7.3). For both models, the next states (and, correspondingly, excitation) of the flip-flops are a function of the external inputs and the present states of the flip-flops. However, the two models differed in the case of the network outputs. The outputs of Mealy sequential networks are also a function of both the external inputs and the present states of the flip-flops; while for Moore sequential networks the outputs are a function of just the present states of the flip-flops.

Two clocked synchronous sequential networks are analyzed in this section. They are shown in Figs. 7.5 and 7.6 and are referred to as Examples 7.1 and 7.2, respectively, during the course of this discussion. As required for clocked synchronous sequential networks, a clock signal is applied simultaneously to each of the flip-flops for synchronization. In both examples, positive-edge-triggered flip-flops are used for the memory portion of the network. Thus, the flip-flops change state only at the occurrence of a leading edge of the clock signal. In order to explain variations to the analysis procedure, however, one network utilizes *D* flip-flops and the other *JK* flip-flops.

The realization of Fig. 7.5 corresponds to a Mealy network. The diagram has been laid out so as to resemble Fig. 7.3. The present state of the sequential network corresponds to the signals at the output terminals of the flip-flops. These signals are

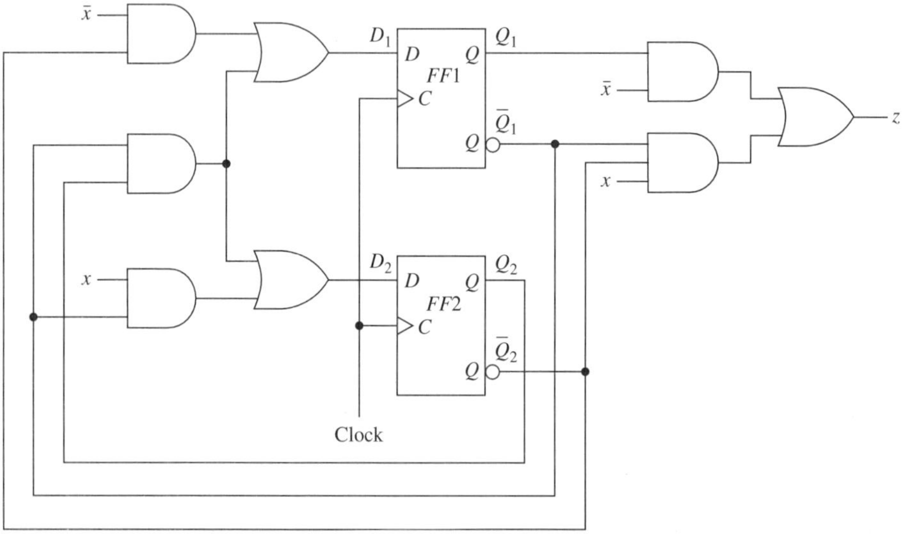

Figure 7.5 Logic diagram for Example 7.1.

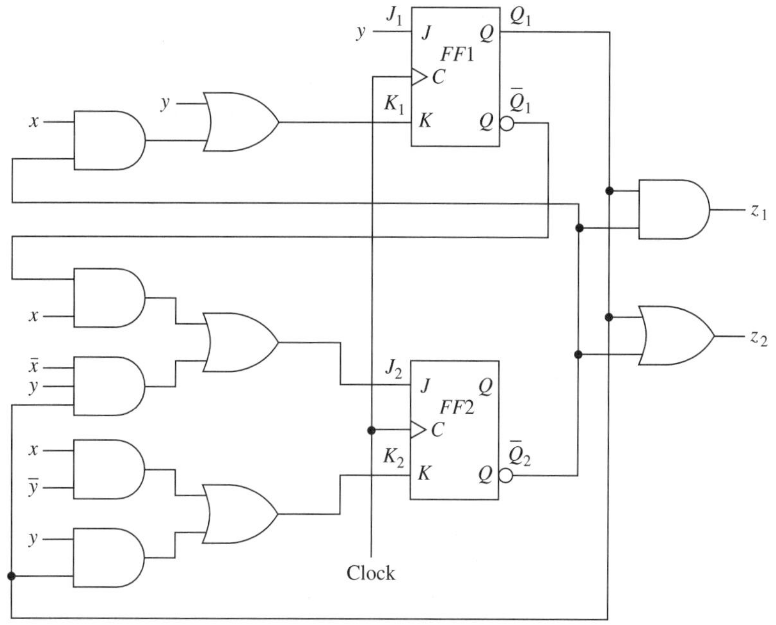

Figure 7.6 Logic diagram for Example 7.2.

fed back to the combinational logic that precedes the flip-flop input terminals. It is this present state along with the external input signal x that serves as the inputs to the combinational logic that provides the excitation signals to the D flip-flops. As easily seen in the figure, the output portion of the sequential network is also a function of the external input x and the present states of the flip-flops. Thus, the two combinational subnetworks satisfy the functional relationships given by Eqs. (7.1) and (7.2) for a Mealy network.

The logic diagram for Example 7.2, i.e., Fig. 7.6, is for a Moore network. The diagram has been laid out to correspond to the general structure shown in Fig. 7.4. As previously noted, the difference between Mealy and Moore models involves the output portion of the network. In the case of Fig. 7.6, it is seen that the two outputs, z_1 and z_2, are only a function of the present states of the flip-flops and not a function of the external inputs x and y. On the other hand, the excitations to the J and K terminals of the flip-flops are indeed a function of both the external inputs and the present states of the flip-flops.

7.2.1 Excitation and Output Expressions

Throughout the study of combinational networks, algebraic expressions served as mathematical representations of the networks. It is also possible to write algebraic expressions for sequential networks. To do this, it is first necessary to assign present-state variables to each of the output terminals of the flip-flops. For the two examples under discussion, the upper flip-flop outputs are assigned the variables Q_1 and $\overline{Q}_1$ for the true and complemented outputs, respectively; while the lower flip-flops have outputs Q_2 and $\overline{Q}_2$. In addition, it is necessary to assign excitation variables to the inputs of the flip-flops. This is done by defining the excitation variables to be the same as the input terminal designators of the flip-flops, subscripted according to the number assigned to the flip-flop. Thus D_1 is the excitation variable for the upper flip-flop of Example 7.1 and J_1 and K_1 are the excitation variables for the upper flip-flop of Example 7.2. In a similar manner, excitation variables are assigned to the lower flip-flops of the two examples. Since the clock signal is applied directly to the clock input terminal of all the flip-flops, it is not necessary to write expressions for the clock inputs. Once the state and excitation variables are defined, Boolean expressions for the flip-flop excitations are readily written in terms of the present-state variables and the external input variables.

The excitations to the flip-flops of Fig. 7.5 correspond to the logic values that appear at the D input terminals of flip-flops $FF1$ and $FF2$. Algebraically,

$$D_1 = \bar{x}\overline{Q}_2 + \overline{Q}_1 Q_2 \tag{7.4}$$

$$D_2 = x\overline{Q}_1 + \overline{Q}_1 Q_2 \tag{7.5}$$

To complete the algebraic description of a sequential network, it is also necessary to write algebraic expressions for the network outputs. For the case of Fig. 7.5, the output is given by

$$z = \bar{x}Q_1 + x\overline{Q}_1\overline{Q}_2 \tag{7.6}$$

The algebraic description for Example 7.2, i.e., Fig. 7.6, is done in a similar manner. In this case, the flip-flop excitations correspond to the logic values that appear at the J and K terminals of flip-flops $FF1$ and $FF2$. From Fig. 7.6, the excitation expressions are immediately written as

$$J_1 = y \tag{7.7}$$

$$K_1 = y + x\overline{Q}_2 \tag{7.8}$$

$$J_2 = x\overline{Q}_1 + \bar{x}yQ_1 \tag{7.9}$$

$$K_2 = x\bar{y} + yQ_1 \tag{7.10}$$

Finally, the outputs of the sequential network are given by

$$z_1 = Q_1\overline{Q}_2 \tag{7.11}$$

$$z_2 = Q_1 + \overline{Q}_2 \tag{7.12}$$

7.2.2 Transition Equations

The general structures for Mealy and Moore models given in Figs. 7.3 and 7.4 show the inputs to the memory portion of the sequential network as next states rather than excitation signals. Effectively, these structures are independent of the flip-flop types used in a realization. To convert excitation expressions into next-state expressions, it is necessary to use the characteristic equations of the flip-flops. Characteristic equations for the various types of flip-flops were previously developed in Chapter 6. As indicated in Fig. 6.25*b*, the characteristic equation for a *D* flip-flop is

$$Q^+ = D$$

and for a *JK* flip-flop it is

$$Q^+ = J\overline{Q} + \overline{K}Q$$

These equations indicate the next state of a flip-flop for given excitations at its input terminals. By substituting the excitation expressions for a flip-flop into its characteristic equation, an algebraic description of the next state of the flip-flop is obtained. These expressions are referred to as *transition equations.*

Since Example 7.1 consists of *D* flip-flops, the next states of the flip-flops are given by

$$Q_1^+ = D_1$$
$$Q_2^+ = D_2$$

Substituting Eqs. (7.4) and (7.5) into the above equations gives the transition equations

$$Q_1^+ = \overline{x}\overline{Q}_2 + \overline{Q}_1Q_2 \tag{7.13}$$
$$Q_2^+ = x\overline{Q}_1 + \overline{Q}_1Q_2 \tag{7.14}$$

For the case of Example 7.2, the characteristic equations for the two flip-flops are

$$Q_1^+ = J_1\overline{Q}_1 + \overline{K}_1Q_1$$
$$Q_2^+ = J_2\overline{Q}_2 + \overline{K}_2Q_2$$

The transition equations, obtained by substituting Eqs. (7.7) to (7.10), become

$$\begin{aligned} Q_1^+ &= y\overline{Q}_1 + \overline{(y + x\overline{Q}_2)}Q_1 \\ &= y\overline{Q}_1 + \overline{y}(\overline{x} + Q_2)Q_1 \\ &= y\overline{Q}_1 + \overline{x}\,\overline{y}Q_1 + \overline{y}Q_1Q_2 \end{aligned} \tag{7.15}$$

$$\begin{aligned} Q_2^+ &= (x\overline{Q}_1 + \overline{x}yQ_1)\overline{Q}_2 + \overline{(x\overline{y} + yQ_1)}Q_2 \\ &= (x\overline{Q}_1 + \overline{x}yQ_1)\overline{Q}_2 + (\overline{x} + y)(\overline{y} + \overline{Q}_1)Q_2 \\ &= x\overline{Q}_1\overline{Q}_2 + \overline{x}yQ_1\overline{Q}_2 + \overline{x}\,\overline{y}Q_2 + \overline{x}\overline{Q}_1Q_2 + y\overline{Q}_1Q_2 \end{aligned} \tag{7.16}$$

7.2.3 Transition Tables

Rather than using the algebraic descriptions for the next state and outputs of a sequential network, it is often more convenient and useful to express the information in tabular form. The *transition table* is the tabular representation of the transition and output equations. This table consists of three sections, one each for the present-state variables, the next-state variables, and the output variables.

The present-state section lists all the possible combinations of values for the state variables. Thus, if there are p state variables, then this section consists of 2^p rows. The length of the present-state section determines the length of the transition table.

The next-state section has one column for each combination of values of the external input variables. Hence, if there are n external input variables, then this section consists of 2^n columns. Each entry in this section is a p-tuple corresponding to the next state for each combination of present state (as indicated by its row) and external input (as indicated by its column).

The structure of the third section of the transition table depends upon whether the network is of the Mealy or Moore type. In the case of a Mealy sequential network, the outputs of the network are a function of both the present state and external inputs. Thus, as in the next-state section, there is one column for each combination of values of the input variables, and the entries within the section indicate the outputs for each present-state/input combination. On the other hand, since the outputs of Moore sequential networks are only a function of the present state, the output section of the transition table has only a single column. The entries within this column correspond to the outputs for the associated entries given in the present-state section of the table.

Table 7.1 shows the transition table for Example 7.1. In the present-state section, the four combinations of values of Q_1 and Q_2 are listed. Next, the next-state section is constructed. Since there is only one external input variable, x, there are $2^1 = 2$ columns in this section. One column is for $x = 0$ and the other is for $x = 1$. The entries within this section correspond to the pair of Q_1^+ and Q_2^+ values for the various values of x, Q_1, and Q_2 given by the column and row labels. These entries are obtained by evaluating Eqs. (7.13) and (7.14). Attention should be paid as to the order of the pair of elements for each entry in the table. To illustrate the determination of the first entry of each pair from Eq. (7.13), $Q_1^+ = 1$ when $\overline{x}\overline{Q}_2 = 1$, i.e., when $x = 0$ and $Q_2 = 0$. Thus, 1's occur as the first element in the first column, $x = 0$, and first and third rows, $Q_2 = 0$, of the next-state section. In addition, $Q_1^+ = 1$ when $\overline{Q}_1 Q_2 = 1$, i.e., when $Q_1 = 0$ and $Q_2 = 1$. This accounts for additional 1's as the first element in both columns of the second row of the next-state section. This completes all present-state/input combinations that causes $Q_1^+ = 1$. Thus, all the remaining first elements in the next-state section of the transition table are 0's. In a similar manner, Eq. (7.14) is used to determine the second element for each entry in the next-state section of the transition table.

Since Example 7.1 corresponds to a Mealy sequential network, the output section also has two columns to correspond to the two possible values of the input vari-

Table 7.1 Transition table for Example 7.1

Present state (Q_1Q_2)	Next state ($Q_1^+Q_2^+$)		Output (z)	
	Input (x)		Input (x)	
	0	**1**	**0**	**1**
00	10	01	0	1
01	11	11	0	0
10	10	00	1	0
11	00	00	1	0

Table 7.2 Transition table for Example 7.2

Present state (Q_1Q_2)	Next state ($Q_1^+Q_2^+$)				Output (z_1z_2)
	Inputs (xy)				
	00	01	10	11	
00	00	10	01	11	01
01	01	11	00	11	00
10	10	01	00	00	11
11	11	00	10	00	01

able x. The entries within this section of the table are obtained by evaluating Eq. (7.6) for the eight combinations of values of x, Q_1, and Q_2.

The transition table for Example 7.2 is given in Table 7.2. Again the present-state section consists of four rows that correspond to all the combinations of values to Q_1 and Q_2. The next-state section has four columns since there are $2^2 = 4$ combinations of values of the two external input variables x and y. The entries within this section consist of pairs of elements corresponding to Q_1^+ and Q_2^+. These entries are obtained by evaluating Eqs. (7.15) to (7.16). In this example, the output section of the transition table has only a single column since the logic diagram is of a Moore sequential network. The entries in this column correspond to the evaluation of Eqs. (7.11) to (7.12) for the four combinations of values of Q_1 and Q_2 given in the present-state section.

It should be noted that the transition table is really the truth table for the transition and output equations. The only difference lies in the fact it is represented as a two-dimensional array where the rows denote the values of the present-state variables and the columns denote the values of the external input variables.

7.2.4 Excitation Tables

The transition table was constructed as the result of substituting excitation expressions into the flip-flop characteristic equations. An alternate approach to the construction of the transition table is to first construct the *excitation table* directly from the excitation and output expressions. The excitation table consists of three sections: the present-state section, the excitation section, and the output section. The present-state and output sections of the excitation table are constructed the same way as the corresponding sections of the transition table. In particular, the present-state section lists all combinations of values of the state variables and the output section corresponds to the evaluation of the output expressions of the network. However, the excitation expressions are used to form the excitation section in an analogous way as the transition expressions were used to form the next-state section of the transition table. The excitation section consists of one column for each combination of values of the external input variables. The entries in this section are r-tuples corresponding to the evaluation of the r excitation equations.

The excitation table for Example 7.1 is shown in Table 7.3. For this example there are two excitation equations, given by Eqs. (7.4) and (7.5), for D_1 and D_2. The evaluation of this pair of equations for the eight combinations of values of the present-state and input variables leads to the excitation section shown in Table 7.3.

Table 7.3 Excitation table for Example 7.1

Present state (Q_1Q_2)	Excitation (D_1D_2)		Output (z)	
	Input (x)		Input (x)	
	0	**1**	**0**	**1**
00	10	01	0	1
01	11	11	0	0
10	10	00	1	0
11	00	00	1	0

However, in view of the fact that the characteristic equation for a D flip-flop is $Q^+ = D$, it is readily seen that the excitation section of Table 7.3 is the same as the next-state section of Table 7.1. Hence, for sequential networks using D flip-flops, the excitation table and the transition table are identical except for the label assignment to the entries in the second section.

Table 7.4 gives the excitation table for Example 7.2. Equations (7.7) to (7.10) are the excitation equations for this example. These four expressions are used to determine the 4-tuples appearing as entries in the excitation section by evaluating the expressions in the same manner as the transition equations were previously evaluated. The comma in each 4-tuple is used just to delineate the excitations of flip-flop $FF1$ from flip-flop $FF2$.

In order to obtain the transition table from the excitation table, it is necessary to analyze each entry of the excitation table to determine the effect of the indicated excitation values. The effects of excitation signals on the states of the various types of flip-flops were previously given in Table 6.2.

To illustrate the construction of the transition table from an excitation table, consider the entry in the fourth column, first row of the excitation section of Table 7.4, i.e., $J_1K_1,J_2K_2 = 11,10$. The present state associated with the first row of the table is $Q_1Q_2 = 00$. Thus, for flip-flop $FF1$, $J_1 = 1$, $K_1 = 1$, and $Q_1 = 0$. From Table 6.2 it is immediately seen that under this condition $Q_1^+ = 1$. That is, when a logic value of 1 appears at both the J and K terminals of a JK flip-flop at the triggering time of the clock signal, the state of the flip-flop is complemented. For flip-flop $FF2$, $J_2 = 1$, $K_2 = 0$, and $Q_2 = 0$. Again from Table 6.2 it is seen that $Q_2^+ = 1$. That

Table 7.4 Excitation table for Example 7.2

Present state (Q_1Q_2)	Excitation (J_1K_1,J_2K_2)				Output (z_1,z_2)
	Inputs (xy)				
	00	**01**	**10**	**11**	
00	00,00	11,00	01,11	11,10	01
01	00,00	11,00	00,11	11,10	00
10	00,00	11,11	01,01	11,01	11
11	00,00	11,11	00,01	11,01	01

is, a logic value of 1 on just the J terminal of a JK flip-flop at the triggering time of the clock signal causes it to set. Hence, the next state of the sequential network when $xy = 11$ and $Q_1Q_2 = 00$ is $Q_1^+Q_2^+ = 11$. This is precisely the entry in the fourth column, first row of the next-state section of Table 7.2. By repeating this procedure on each entry in the excitation section of Table 7.4, the next-state section of Table 7.2 is obtained. The present-state and output sections of both the excitation table and transition table are always the same.

7.2.5 State Tables

In studying the output terminal behavior of a sequential network, the actual binary codes used to represent the states are not important. Hence, alphanumeric symbols can be assigned to represent these states. When this relabeling is done to the transition table, the resulting table is called the *state table.*

The state table consists of three sections: the present-state section, the next-state section, and the output section. Each combination of values of the state variables, which, in turn, corresponds to a state of the memory portion of the sequential network, is assigned a unique alphanumeric symbol. Then, the present-state and next-state sections of the state table are obtained by simply replacing the binary code for each state in the transition table by the newly defined symbol. The output section of the state table is identical with the output section of the transition table.

Again consider Examples 7.1 and 7.2 and their corresponding transition tables given in Tables 7.1 and 7.2. In both of these examples, the sequential networks consist of four states. If the assignments $A = 00$, $B = 01$, $C = 10$, and $D = 11$ are made to the four states, then the state tables shown in Tables 7.5*a* and 7.6 result.

Table 7.5 State table for Example 7.1

Present state	Next state		Output (z)	
	Input (x)		Input (x)	
	0	1	0	1
$00 \rightarrow A$	C	B	0	1
$01 \rightarrow B$	D	D	0	0
$10 \rightarrow C$	C	A	1	0
$11 \rightarrow D$	A	A	1	0

(*a*)

Present state	Next state, Output (z)	
	Input (x)	
	0	1
A	$C, 0$	$B, 1$
B	$D, 0$	$D, 0$
C	$C, 1$	$A, 0$
D	$A, 1$	$A, 0$

(*b*)

Table 7.6 State table for Example 7.2

Present state	Next state				Output (z_1z_2)
	Inputs (xy)				
	00	01	10	11	
$00 \rightarrow A$	A	C	B	D	01
$01 \rightarrow B$	B	D	A	D	00
$10 \rightarrow C$	C	B	A	A	11
$11 \rightarrow D$	D	A	C	A	01

For Mealy sequential networks, frequently alternate, more compact forms of the transition tables, excitation tables, and state tables are used. This is illustrated in Table 7.5*b* for the state table of Example 7.1. In this variation, the next-state and output sections of Table 7.5*a* are superimposed since they have exactly the same column headings. Similarly, alternate forms of the excitation and transition tables are obtained by superimposing their second and third sections. Such alternate forms are not possible for Moore sequential networks.

7.2.6 State Diagrams

There is also a graphical representation of the state table. This is called the *state diagram.* Each state of the network is represented by a labeled node. Directed branches connect the nodes to indicate transitions between states. The directed branches are labeled according to the values of the external input variables that permit the transition to exist. The outputs of the sequential network are also entered on a state diagram. For Mealy sequential networks, the outputs appear on the directed branches along with the external inputs. In this case, the label for a branch leaving a node consists of a present-input/output combination for the state associated with the node. For Moore networks, the outputs are included within the nodes along with their associated states.

Consider first the construction of a state diagram for a Mealy sequential network. A node is drawn and labeled for each state. If a transition is possible between two, possibly the same, states, then a directed branch is drawn connecting the two corresponding nodes. The branch is labeled with the input values that causes the transition, a slash, and the outputs that are associated with the present-state/input combination. To illustrate this construction procedure, consider the state table for Example 7.1, i.e., Table 7.5. The corresponding state diagram is shown in Fig. 7.7. The four states are represented by four nodes. A branch is directed from node A to node C since, according to the next-state section of Table 7.5, the input $x = 0$ applied to the network when in present-state A results in the next-state C. In addition, the same present-state/input combination has a 0 output as shown in the output section of the state table. Hence, the branch is labeled as 0/0 to indicate an input of 0 produces an output of 0 while in state A. Similarly, a branch connects node A to node B since B is the next state for present-state A when $x = 1$. As indicated in the output section of Table 7.5, $z = 1$ for this present-state/input combination. Thus, the branch is labeled as 1/1. The remaining branches of Fig. 7.7 are obtained from

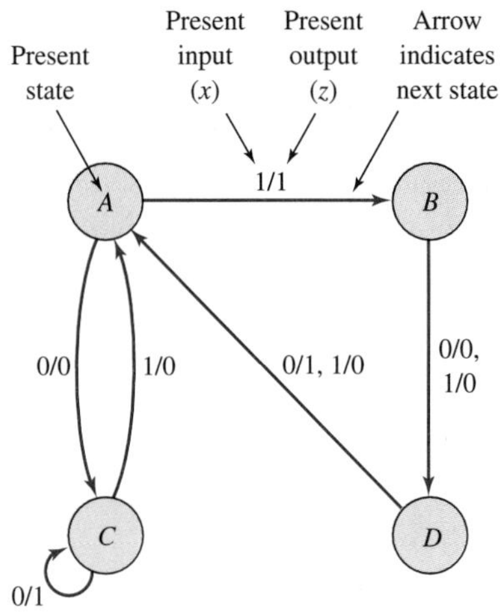

Figure 7.7 State diagram for Example 7.1.

Table 7.5 in exactly the same way. For simplicity, if more than one input causes a transition to occur between two states, then multiple labels are used on a single branch. This is seen in Fig. 7.7 for present-state B where D is the next state for $x = 0$ and $x = 1$. In both cases, the output is 0.

When state diagrams for Moore sequential networks are constructed, the outputs associated with each state are entered in the node along with the state designator. The branch labels in this case are just the input combinations that affect the state transitions. Figure 7.8 shows the state diagram for Table 7.6. Each

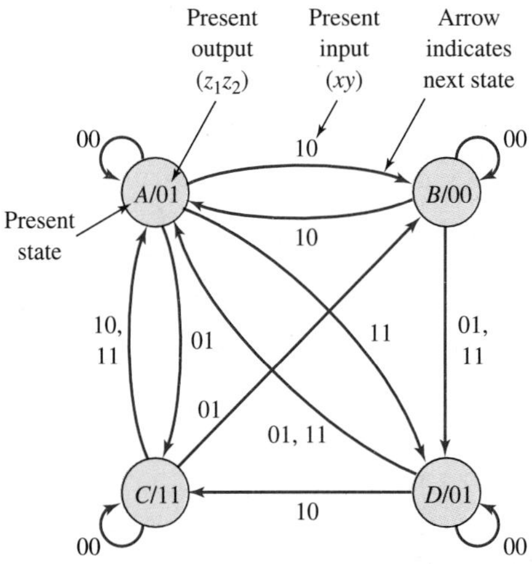

Figure 7.8 State diagram for Example 7.2.

node is labeled with a state and its associated outputs separated by a slash. The multiple label on the branch connecting nodes B and D corresponds to the situation in which two input combinations affect a transition between the same two states.

In Sec. 8.2 another diagrammatic form describing sequential network behavior is discussed. This form is a chart bearing some resemblance to a flowchart frequently encountered in computer programming. However, it is time-oriented rather than task-oriented.

7.2.7 Network Terminal Behavior

As was mentioned at the beginning of this section, one objective of sequential network analysis is to describe the time response of a network to a sequence of inputs. Although this can be done from the logic diagram by tracing signals, the state table or state diagram simplifies the process. For example, again consider Example 7.1. Assume the flip-flops are both in their 0-states, which corresponds to state A in Table 7.5 or Fig. 7.7, and the input sequence $x = 0011011101$ is applied to the network.* From the general discussion on the operation of clocked synchronous sequential networks, the inputs are assumed to be applied prior to the triggering time of the clock signal that can affect a state transition, and the effects of the inputs have propagated through the combinational logic so that final values appear at the network outputs and flip-flop inputs. Therefore, according to Table 7.5 or Fig. 7.7 it is seen that when the first $x = 0$ input is applied to the network when in state A, the network produces a $z = 0$ output. Furthermore, upon receipt of the positive edge of the clock signal, the memory portion of the network goes to state C. Next, another $x = 0$ is applied. Since the network is now in state C, a current output of 1 is produced and the network remains in state C upon receipt of the next positive edge of the clock signal. It can readily be checked that the input sequence $x = 0011011101$ applied to the network of Example 7.1 when initially in state A produces the following state and output sequences:

$$\begin{aligned} \text{Input sequence } x &= 0\ 0\ 1\ 1\ 0\ 1\ 1\ 1\ 0\ 1 \\ \text{State sequence } &= A\ C\ C\ A\ B\ D\ A\ B\ D\ A\ B \\ \text{Output sequence } z &= 0\ 1\ 0\ 1\ 0\ 0\ 1\ 0\ 1\ 1 \end{aligned}$$

The state diagram for a Mealy sequential network is a little misleading relative to the outputs. Although the outputs are shown on the directed branches of the state diagram, this does *not* mean that the outputs are produced during the transition between two states. Rather, the outputs appearing on the branches are continuously available while in a present state and the indicated inputs are applied.

*Whenever a time sequence of symbols is given, it is assumed to occur from left to right. In this case, the first input for x is 0, then another 0, then a 1, etc.

The fact that the outputs from a Mealy sequential network are a function of both the external inputs and the present state introduces the possibility of false outputs or glitches. When the state and output sequences are determined from a state table or state diagram, as was done above, the values of the external input variables only at the triggering time of the clock signal are considered. However, the external input variables may change values any time during the clock period. Although these input changes can continuously affect the network outputs, the consequences of these input changes do not appear in the listing of the output sequences.

To illustrate this problem of false outputs, a timing diagram for the input sequence $x = 0011011101$ applied to state A of Example 7.1 is shown in Fig. 7.9. For simplicity, propagation delays are assumed to be zero so that the effects of all signal changes occur immediately. Since positive-edge-triggered flip-flops are used in the realization, any state changes occur coincident with the positive edges of the clock signal. Previously it was seen that this input sequence produced the output sequence $z = 0101001011$. However, as can be seen in the figure, the actual output sequence is $z = 01010(1)0101(0)1$ where the two outputs in parentheses are false outputs. Consider the first of these false outputs. An input of $x = 0$ applied to the network when in present-state B causes the network to go to state D upon the occurrence of the positive edge of the clock signal.

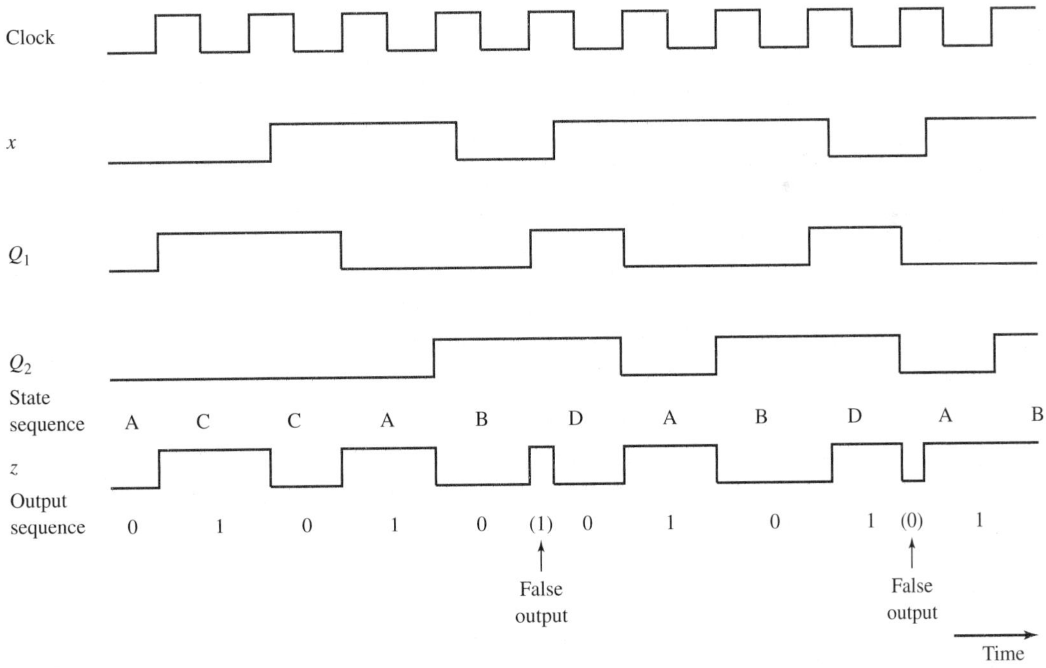

Figure 7.9 Timing diagram for Example 7.1.

However, immediately after the state transition, the input x is still 0. Referring to the state table or the state diagram for Example 7.1, it is seen that when in present-state D, the input $x = 0$ produces a 1 output. It is not until the input x changes to 1 that the output for present-state D becomes 0. Hence, for the period of time in which the network is in its new state and the old input is still being applied, there is a false logic-1 output. The second false output shown in Fig. 7.9 is the result of x still being 0 for a short time after the state transition from state D to state A.

The above discussion only considered one possible cause of false outputs. False outputs can also occur as a result of propagation delays. This topic is further investigated in Chapter 9.

Terminal behavior of a Moore sequential network is also readily determinable from its state table or state diagram. For the Moore sequential network of Example

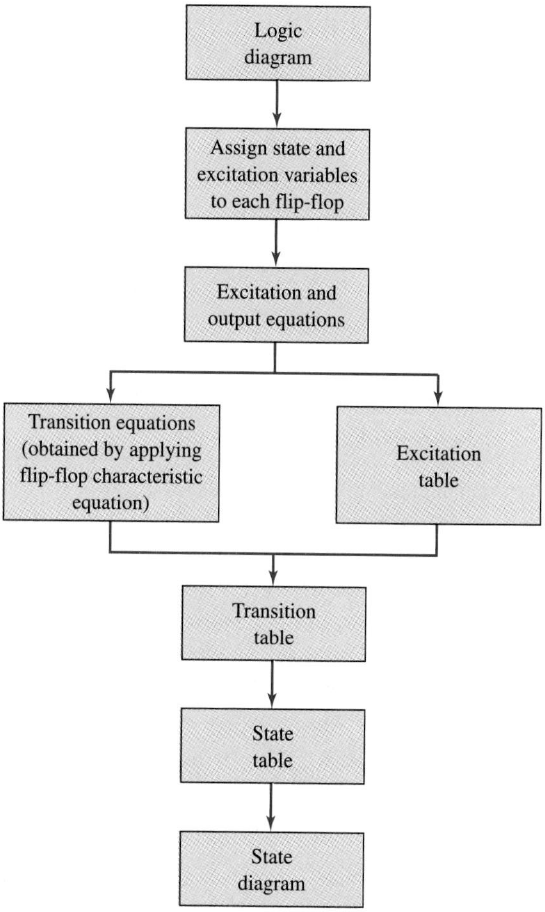

Figure 7.10 The analysis procedure.

7.2, the state table shown in Table 7.6 or the state diagram in Fig. 7.8 is used. If it is assumed the network begins operation in state A, then the following is an example of input, state, and output sequences:

$$\text{Input sequence}\begin{cases} x = 0\ 0\ 0\ 0\ 1\ 0\ 1 \\ y = 0\ 1\ 1\ 0\ 1\ 1\ 1 \end{cases}$$

$$\text{State sequence} = A\ A\ C\ B\ B\ D\ A\ D$$

$$\text{Output sequence}\begin{cases} z_1 = 0\ 0\ 1\ 0\ 0\ 0\ 0 \\ z_2 = 1\ 1\ 1\ 0\ 0\ 1\ 1 \end{cases}$$

The analysis procedure presented in this section is summarized in Fig. 7.10. Here the order in which the various steps of the analysis are performed is diagrammatically illustrated.

7.3 MODELING CLOCKED SYNCHRONOUS SEQUENTIAL NETWORK BEHAVIOR

In this and the remaining sections of this chapter, an approach to the synthesis of clocked synchronous sequential networks is undertaken. The synthesis procedure involves the establishment of a network realization that satisfies a set of input-output specifications.

Basically, the procedure leading to the network realization is the reverse of the analysis procedure introduced in the previous section. From the word specifications of a network, a state table or state diagram is constructed. However, in the course of constructing the state table, more states may be introduced than are really necessary. By means of a state reduction technique it is possible to obtain a state table with a minimum number of states. From this reduced state table a transition table is formed by coding the states of the state table with a sequence of binary symbols. Then, an excitation table is constructed based on the flip-flop types to be used in the realization. From the excitation table, the excitation and output expressions for the network are determined. Finally, the logic diagram is drawn.

The first step in the synthesis of clocked synchronous sequential networks is the establishment of a formal description of the network specifications. This is an abstract model of the network behavior that is obtained from the sometimes ambiguous natural language description. Such a model is the state table or state diagram. There is no standard technique for obtaining these models from the statements of the desired network behavior. Rather, by understanding the network specifications and knowing how to interpret a state table or state diagram, an appropriate model for the network to be designed is constructed. This modeling step of the synthesis procedure is presented in this section via a series of examples.

7.3.1 The Serial Binary Adder as a Mealy Network

One approach to the modeling of a set of input-output specifications is to define a priori a set of states needed by the network to preserve the information regarding the past history of inputs. One of these states should correspond to an *initial state* that signifies that no past inputs have been applied. This preliminary analysis of listing the states may not produce all the necessary states of the network. However, it does serve as a starting point for the construction of the model. As the state table or state diagram is formed, additional states are added to the proposed collection if none of the initially defined states adequately describes the information to be preserved at some point in time. It is also possible that too many states are proposed and used in the model. This problem is readily handled, as is seen in Sec. 7.4, by applying a systematic reduction technique to the state table. An important point to remember, however, is that the state table must be finite in length. Thus, although states can be continually added to the proposed listing, for a realization to exist, only a finite number of states are allowed.

The first network to be modeled is the serial binary adder. Let us assume that the realization is to be a Mealy network having the general structure shown in Fig. 7.11. Two binary sequences, corresponding to the two operands being added, are applied to the network inputs x and y, least significant bits first. The values on the x and y inputs are applied prior to the triggering time of the clock signal that is used for synchronization. The binary sum of the two numbers appears as a time sequence, also least significant bit first, on the single output line z.

At any time, there are four possible input combinations for the two external inputs x and y, i.e., 00, 01, 10, and 11. As was discussed previously, the state of a sequential network must preserve any necessary past history in order to determine a present output and a next state. From the discussion on binary addition in Sec. 2.3, it was seen that with the exception of the addition of the least significant pair of bits, the sum bit for any order position is determined by the two operand bits of that order as well as whether or not any carry was generated from the addition of the previous order of bits. Thus the existence or nonexistence of a carry must be the required internally preserved information needed to perform the addition process upon any pair of operand bits. Two states can now be defined for the network reflecting this fact. The first state, say, A, is associated with the past history "no carry was generated from the previous order addition," and a state, say, B, is associated with the past history "a carry was generated from the previous order addition." When the first pair of bits is added, i.e., the least significant pair of bits, the correct sum bit is obtained if it is assumed that the carry from the previous order addition

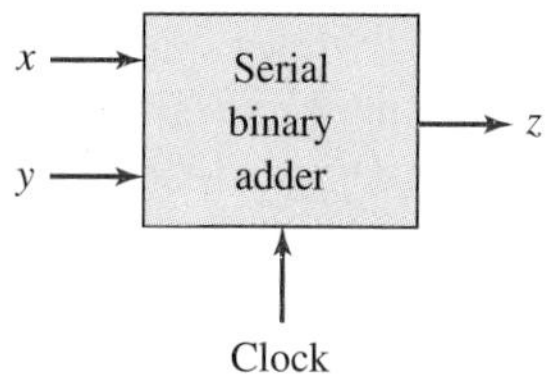

Figure 7.11 The serial binary adder.

was 0. It is now seen that knowledge of the state information and the current pair of operand bits is sufficient to determine a sum bit and an appropriate next state with state A serving as the initial state of the network.

Having defined a set of states describing the information that must be preserved about the past history, the construction of a state diagram is started by introducing a node for each state. Since there are two input bits present at any time, corresponding to the bit values on the x and y lines, four input-bit combinations must be considered for each node. Since state A denotes no carry was generated from the previous order addition, the appropriate sum bit to be produced while in state A is simply the binary sum of the two bits on the x and y lines. Furthermore, the next state must correspond to whether or not a carry results from the current two-bit addition. No carry occurs upon the bit-pair addition of the input combinations 00, 01, and 10. The first of these three input combinations results in a sum bit of 0, while the other two combinations result in a sum bit of 1. This behavior is illustrated in Fig. 7.12*a* as the loop on node A. The letters "I.S." next to node A indicate that it is the initial state. The fourth input combination, 11, also results in a sum bit of 0, but since a carry is generated, the network must go to state B so as to preserve this information about the past history. This appears in Fig. 7.12*a* as the directed branch from node A to node B.

Next it is necessary to describe the behavior of the network under the four input conditions while in state B. When the network is in state B, it is remembering that a carry was produced from the previous order addition. Thus, the appropriate sum bit for this state must be one greater than the binary sum of the two input bits. Hence, the xy inputs 01 and 10 must produce a zero sum bit plus a carry. Since state B corresponds to the remembering of a carry, an arc is directed from node B to node B for these two cases as shown in Fig. 7.12*b*. Similarly, the arc also is labeled with the input combination 11 since again the sum of these two bits and a "remembered" carry results in a carry. However, the output in this case is a 1. The final

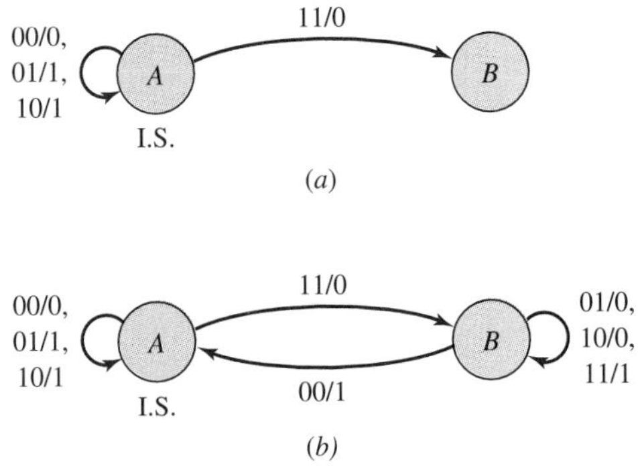

Figure 7.12 Obtaining the state diagram for a Mealy serial binary adder.
(*a*) Partial state diagram.
(*b*) Completed state diagram.

Table 7.7 State table for a Mealy serial binary adder

Present state	Next state				Output (z)			
	Inputs (xy)				Inputs (xy)			
	00	01	10	11	00	01	10	11
$*A$	A	A	A	B	0	1	1	0
B	A	B	B	B	1	0	0	1

input combination for the network while in state B corresponds to $xy = 00$. In this case, the appropriate sum bit is a 1 due to the remembered carry. The next state, however, must correspond to a state that preserves the information of "no carry was generated for the previous order addition." This is precisely the meaning of state A. Hence, a transition from state B to state A must occur for the input combination of 11 as shown in Fig. 7.12*b*.

Using two binary numbers, the reader can easily check that the state diagram of Fig. 7.12*b* models the behavior of a serial binary adder assuming the process is started in state A. Since state A is the initial state, provision must be made to start the network in this state when the realization is completed. The initialization process is discussed further in Sec. 7.6.

In many cases, such as the example just completed, the state diagram is a convenient way of formalizing the network behavior of a synchronous sequential network. However, for the remaining steps of the synthesis procedure, the state table is more useful. Since there is a one-to-one correspondence between a state diagram and a state table, it is a simple matter to construct a state table. As was explained in the previous section, for a Mealy sequential network, both the next-state and output sections of the state table have one column for each possible input combination. The rows of the state table, listed in the present-state section, correspond to the states of the network. The entries in the remaining two sections of the table are readily determined by noting the next state and output for each present-state/input combination appearing on the state diagram. The state table for the serial binary adder is shown in Table 7.7. An asterisk is placed next to state A in the present-state section to indicate that it is the initial state.

7.3.2 The Serial Binary Adder as a Moore Network

Let us now repeat the design of the serial binary adder under the assumption that the realization is to be a Moore sequential network. Unlike Mealy sequential networks, the outputs from a Moore sequential network are a function of only the present state. This makes the modeling process more difficult when the network specifications indicate that the outputs are also a function of the current external inputs. In this example, the correct sum bit from the adder cannot be established until the next state is reached or, equivalently, until the next clock period, since in a Moore sequential network the current external inputs do not affect the present output. In effect, this imposes a unit delay on the output of the network. Since an output is normally specified for the initial state, this first output must be ignored and only the subsequent outputs are relevant as the output sequence. Furthermore, in a Moore sequential network, each state must be associated with both an output and information regarding how the past history of inputs causes that output. For this reason two states are not sufficient for modeling the serial binary adder as a Moore sequential network since either a 0 or 1 sum bit is possible both with and without the existence of a carry from the previous order addition. A little reflection upon the problem leads to the conclusion that four states are necessary, one state for each combination of sum bit and carry bit from the previous order addition. Thus, the following four states are defined:

A: *The sum bit is 0 and no carry was generated from the previous order addition.*

B: *The sum bit is 0 and a carry was generated from the previous order addition.*

C: *The sum bit is 1 and no carry was generated from the previous order addition.*

D: *The sum bit is 1 and a carry was generated from the previous order addition.*

Having defined the states for the network, the construction of the state diagram for the serial binary adder under the Moore sequential network assumption proceeds in much the same way as was done previously. Appropriate next states are determined for each state under the four input combinations of values occurring on the x and y input lines of the network. The corresponding state diagram is shown in Fig. 7.13 and the state table is given in Table 7.8. It is important to realize that the first valid sum bit occurs immediately after entering the first state from the initial state. After that, the sum bits are produced in sequential order. Thus, either state A or state C can serve as the initial state since the first output must be ignored. In this example, state A is chosen as the initial state.

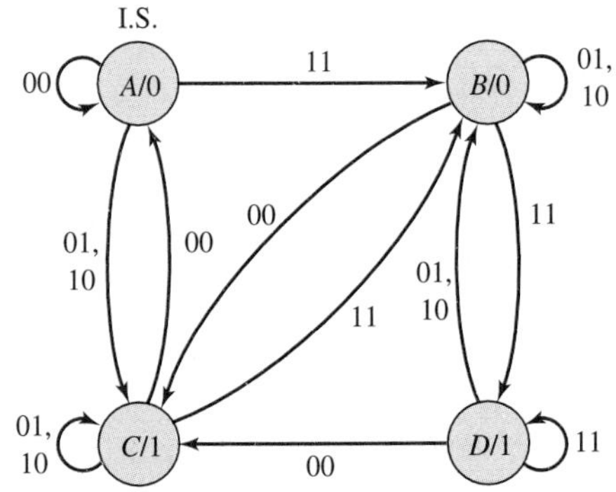

Figure 7.13 State diagram for a Moore serial binary adder.

Table 7.8 State table for a Moore serial binary adder

Present state	Next state				Output (z)
	Inputs (xy)				
	00	01	10	11	
$*A$	A	C	C	B	0
B	C	B	B	D	0
C	A	C	C	B	1
D	C	B	B	D	1

In summary, every Mealy sequential network has a corresponding Moore sequential network under the assumption that the output for the initial state from the Moore network is to be ignored. However, Moore sequential networks inherently require more states than a Mealy sequential network since outputs are associated with the states and not with the inputs. Finally, since the outputs of a Moore sequential network are not a function of the current inputs, the output sequence from a Moore sequential network has an inherent delay of one clock period.

As was illustrated by the above two examples, one can approach clocked synchronous sequential network modeling under the assumption of either a Mealy network or a Moore network. However, one model is normally more appropriate than the other since the two models are not really equivalent. It was seen in the above that it was necessary to make assumptions about the network behavior in order that the Moore model could be applied, i.e., the acceptance of a delayed output and the ignoring of the first output. Such assumptions may not always be appropriate. The required network behavior should be taken into consideration when determining a model. In general, if the outputs of a synchronous sequential network are also a function of the current external inputs, then the Mealy network model is the more appropriate; while if the outputs are only a function of the past history of inputs, then the Moore network model should be considered. In the ensuing examples, only one model is established in each case.

7.3.3 A Sequence Recognizer

Another approach to the modeling of a word description involves the step-by-step construction of a state table or state diagram under the assumption that inputs are being applied to the network when in its various states, rather than defining the states prior to the construction. To do this, a state is initially defined as the starting point. From this initial state, additional entries in the state table or nodes in the state diagram are introduced as needed to reflect the different past histories that must be retained by the network. The process is continued until no new entries in the state table or no new nodes in the state diagram are created. This approach is illustrated by the following two examples.

Consider the design of a clocked synchronous sequential network having a single input line x in which the symbols 0 and 1 are applied and a single output line z.

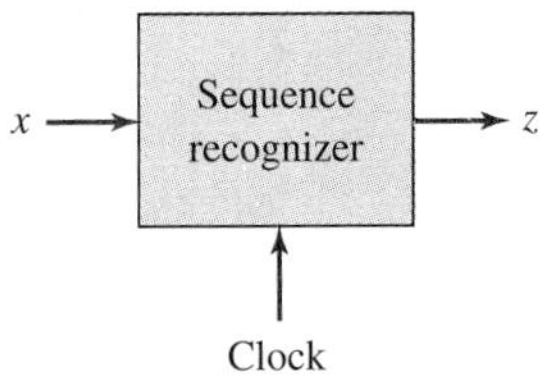

Figure 7.14 A sequence recognizer.

An output of 1 is to be produced if and only if the three input symbols following two consecutive input 0's include at least one 1. At all other times the output is to be 0. Once the consecutive pair of 0's is detected, the network must analyze the next three input symbols to determine if at least one of them is a 1. The output of 1, when appropriate, is to be coincident with the third input symbol of the three-input-symbol sequence. Upon completing the analysis of the three input symbols following the pair of 0 inputs, the network is to reset itself and wait for another pair of 0's and then at least one 1 in the following sequence of three input symbols. Since the output is to be coincident with the third input symbol of the three-input-symbol sequence, a Mealy network is implied. The general structure of the network is shown in Fig. 7.14. An example of an input sequence and the desired responding output sequence for the recognizer is

$$x = 0\ 1\ \overline{0\ 0\ 0\ 1\ 0}\ 0\ 1\ \overline{0\ 0\ 1\ 0\ 0}\ 1\ \overline{0\ 0\ 0\ 0\ 0}\ \overline{0\ 0\ 0\ 1\ 1}$$
$$z = 0\ 0\ 0\ 0\ 0\ 0\ 1\ 0\ 0\ 0\ 0\ 0\ 0\ 1\ 0\ 0\ 0\ 0\ 0\ 0\ 0\ 0\ 0\ 0\ 1$$

The sequences that must be analyzed are shown bracketed. It should be noted that one of these sequences does not satisfy the conditions for producing a 1 output.

Let A be the initial state of the network. It is first necessary to detect two consecutive 0 inputs. This phase is illustrated in Fig. 7.15*a*. The network remains in state A as long as 1's are applied. When the first 0 occurs, the network goes to state B. If a 1 should occur at this time, then the network must return to state A to again wait for a pair of consecutive 0 inputs. However, when the network is in state B, a second 0 input sends it to state C to indicate that the initial pair of 0 inputs has been detected. The outputs are 0's for all these inputs since all the conditions of the network specifications have not been satisfied. The definitions of the first three states, along with those states to be introduced later, are given in Fig. 7.15*d*.

Once the network is in state C, it must analyze the next three inputs. If at least one of these inputs is a 1, then an output of 1 is to be produced coincident with the third input and the network is to return to its initial state A. The state diagram is continued as shown in Fig. 7.15*b*. If the first input is 1 when the network is in state C, then the detection conditions of the network specifications are satisfied. However, the network goes to state D with an output of 0 since, also according to the network specifications, it must produce an output of 1 coincident with the third input after entering state C. Similarly, a state E is introduced after state D to

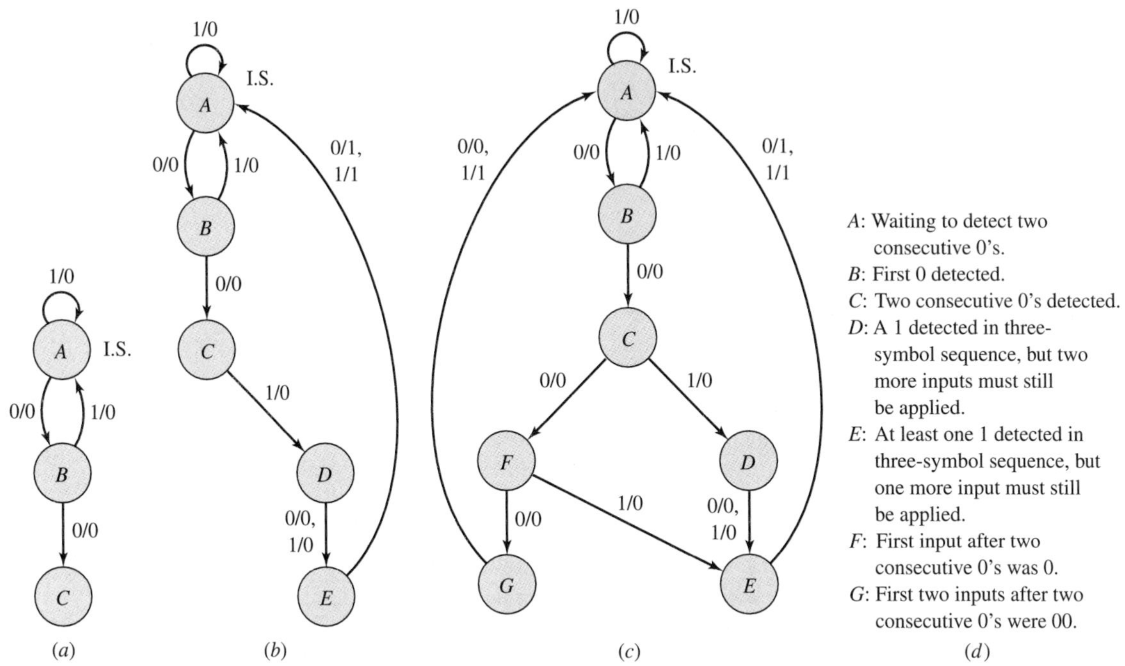

Figure 7.15 State diagram for a sequence recognizer. (*a*) Detection of two consecutive 0's. (*b*) Partial analysis of the three-symbol sequence. (*c*) Completed state diagram. (*d*) Definition of states.

continue the waiting time needed before producing the 1 output. When the network is in state *E*, the third input occurs. Since at least one 1 has occurred during the last three inputs, the output is 1, regardless of the current input, and the network returns to state *A* to repeat the recognition procedure.

The state diagram of Fig. 7.15*b* is still not complete since the situation of a 0 input occurring while in state *C* must be considered. As shown in Fig. 7.15*c*, the network in this case goes to state *F*, with a 0 output, to indicate that the first input after the initial pair of 0's was also a 0. When in state *F*, the occurrence of a 1 input implies that the conditions of the network specifications are satisfied, but the network must still wait one more time period before producing a 1 output. This is precisely the meaning of state *E*. Thus a directed branch, for the 1 input, is drawn from state *F* to state *E* with a 0 output. However, if the input is 0 while in state *F*, then two consecutive 0's have occurred in the sequence of three inputs that is being analyzed. The network enters state *G* to signify this fact and a 0 output is produced. One more input must be considered when the network is in state *G*. Regardless of this input, however, the network must return to the initial state *A*. If this third input is a 1, then a 1 output is produced according to the network specifications. On the other hand, a 0 input implies that the three inputs that followed the initial pair of 0 inputs were also 0's and, consequently, the output is 0.

Table 7.9 State table for a sequence recognizer

Present state	Next state		Output (z)	
	Input (x)		Input (x)	
	0	1	0	1
*A	B	A	0	0
B	C	A	0	0
C	F	D	0	0
D	E	E	0	0
E	A	A	1	1
F	G	E	0	0
G	A	A	0	1

The state table corresponding to Fig. 7.15*c* is shown in Table 7.9. An asterisk is placed next to state *A* to signify that this is the initial state of the network.

7.3.4 A 0110/1001 Sequence Recognizer

Now consider the design of another sequence recognizer having the block diagram of Fig. 7.14. In this case, it is desired that the network produce a 1 output if and only if the current input and the previous three inputs correspond to either of the sequences 0110 or 1001. The 1 output is to occur at the time of the fourth input of the recognized sequence. Outputs of 0 are to be produced at all other times. Again a Mealy network model is developed since the output is a function of the current input x. It should be noted in this example that the network is not required to reset upon the occurrence of the fourth input. Thus, the sequences are allowed to overlap. An example of an input sequence and the appropriate responding output sequence for this network is

$$x = 0\,0\,1\,1\,0\,1\,1\,1\,0\,0\,1\,0\,1\,0\,1\,1\,0\,0\,1\,1\,0\,0\,1\,0\,1$$
$$z = 0\,0\,0\,0\,1\,0\,0\,0\,0\,0\,1\,0\,0\,0\,0\,0\,1\,0\,1\,0\,1\,0\,1\,0\,0$$

The sequences to be detected according to the network specifications are indicated by brackets.

Figure 7.16*a* shows the first step in constructing the state diagram by just considering the two sequences that lead to a 1 output. State *A* is the initial state. States are added to record the past history of received inputs that eventually lead to an output of 1. Since the output is to be coincident with the fourth input of a detected sequence, states are needed to record the various input sequences up to 011 and 100. These two sequences lead to states *F* and *G*, respectively. From the network specifications it immediately follows that an input of 0 when in state *F* or an input of 1 when in state *G* should produce 1 outputs as indicated in the figure. Figure 7.16*b* gives the definitions of the various states that were introduced. A question that remains is what are the next-states for the branches leaving states *F* and *G* in Fig. 7.16*a*. The exit branch from state *F* corresponds to the input sequence 0110. Referring to Fig. 7.16*b*, it is seen that

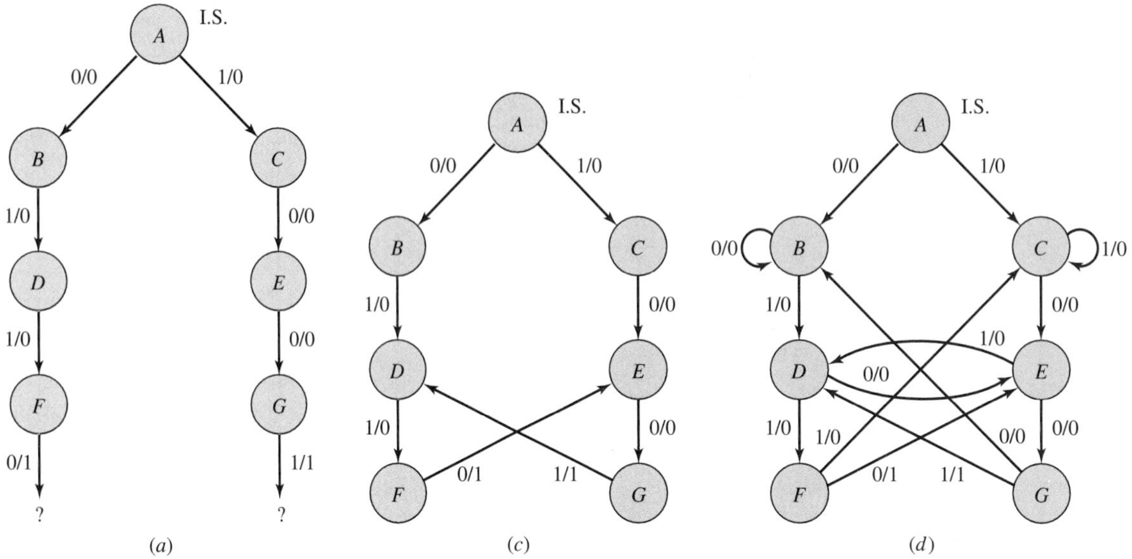

A: No inputs received (initial state).
B: Last input received was 0 but not 10 nor 100.
C: Last input received was 1 but not 01 nor 011.
D: Last two inputs received were 01.
E: Last two inputs received were 10.
F: Last three inputs received were 011.
G: Last three inputs received were 100.

(*b*)

Figure 7.16 A 0110/1001 sequence recognizer. (*a*) Beginning the detection of the sequences 0110 or 1001. (*b*) Definition of states. (*c*) Completing the detection of the two sequences 0110 or 1001. (*d*) Completed state diagram.

state *E* was initially introduced to record the occurrence of the input sequence 10. This 10 sequence can also be the first two inputs of a sequence that must produce a 1 output if it is followed by 01. Since the two sequences that must be recognized, i.e., 0110 and 1001, are allowed to overlap and 10 are the last two inputs of the 0110 sequence, the 0/1 branch from state *F* should be directed to state *E* as shown in Fig. 7.16*c* to record the fact that another potentially detectable sequence has started. Using a similar analysis, the next state for state *G* under a 1 input is state *D*.

The state diagram of Fig. 7.16*c* is still incomplete since each node must have exit branches for both 0 and 1 inputs. A 1 input when in state *F* corresponds to an input sequence of 0111. This last 1 input could be the first 1 of a 1001 sequence. From Fig. 7.16*b*, state *C* was defined to record such a situation. Hence, the next state from *F* should be *C* if the input is 1. This is shown in Fig. 7.16*d.* By a similar argument the next state from state *G* with a 0 input should be state *B.* Next the second input during states *D* and *E* is studied. State *D* records the fact that the last two inputs were 01 and a 0 input during state *D* implies the last three inputs are 010. The 10 portion of this sequence can be the beginning of the sequence 1001 that results in a 1

Table 7.10 State table for the 0110/1001 sequence recognizer

Present state	Next state		Output (z)	
	Input (x)		Input (x)	
	0	1	0	1
$*A$	B	C	0	0
B	B	D	0	0
C	E	C	0	0
D	E	F	0	0
E	G	D	0	0
F	E	C	1	0
G	B	D	0	1

output. This is precisely the meaning of state E. Thus, the next state from state D is state E upon the occurrence of a 0 input as shown in Fig. 7.16*d*. Similarly, the next state from state E is state D when the input is 1. Finally, loops are added to nodes B and C since any 0 input while in state B can be the first 0 in a 0110 sequence and any 1 input while in state C can be the first 1 in a 1001 sequence. This completes the state diagram of Fig. 7.16*d*. The corresponding state table is shown in Table 7.10.

Table 7.11 shows an alternate model for the 0110/1001 sequence recognizer, except it consists of 15 states. Lowercase letters are used to define the states in

Table 7.11 Alternate state table for the 0110/1001 sequence recognizer

	Present state	Next state		Output (z)	
		Input (x)		Input (x)	
State definition		0	1	0	1
No inputs received	$*a$	b	c	0	0
Input 0 received	b	d	e	0	0
Input 1 received	c	f	g	0	0
Inputs 00 received	d	h	i	0	0
Inputs 01 received	e	j	k	0	0
Inputs 10 received	f	l	m	0	0
Inputs 11 received	g	n	o	0	0
Last three inputs were 000	h	h	i	0	0
Last three inputs were 001	i	j	k	0	0
Last three inputs were 010	j	l	m	0	0
Last three inputs were 011	k	n	o	1	0
Last three inputs were 100	l	h	i	0	1
Last three inputs were 101	m	j	k	0	0
Last three inputs were 110	n	l	m	0	0
Last three inputs were 111	o	n	o	0	0

this table to distinguish them from the states of Table 7.10. In this case, the first seven states, i.e., states *a* to *g*, are defined to correspond to the occurrence of all possible sequences of less than three inputs. These states produce 0 outputs since at least three previous inputs must be applied before the network is to produce an output of 1. The remaining eight states, i.e., states *h* to *o*, correspond to the eight possible combinations of the last three inputs. Once the network gets in the range of states *h* to *o*, the state of the network remains within this range by retaining the history of the last three inputs. For example, when in state *m*, indicating the last three inputs were 101, the next state upon the occurrence of a 0 input is state *j* to reflect that the updated last three inputs, i.e., the last two inputs of 101 and the current input 1, were 010. When the network is in state *k*, representing the input sequence 011, an input of 0 causes a 1 output to be produced as required. Similarly, when the network is in state *l*, representing the input sequence 100, an input of 1 causes a 1 output to be produced. As was mentioned earlier, the modeling process can lead to more states than are really needed. Table 7.10 is the state table having the fewest number of states for the 0110/1001 sequence recognizer. In the next section, an algorithm for determining a state table having the fewest number of states is presented. At that time, it is shown how Table 7.11 is reduced to that of Table 7.10.

7.3.5 A Final Example

As a final example, consider the design of a clocked synchronous sequential network having a single input x and a single output z, each of which can have the values of 0 and 1. The output of the network, initially 0, is to change on the next input immediately following each even occurrence of $x = 1$.

From the network specifications, it is noted that the output is to change *after* the clock period in which $x = 1$ an even number of times. That is, the effect of the input is to be delayed by one clock period. In addition, the value of x during the next clock period does not affect the output of the network at that time. This implies that the network must have a unit time delay and that the current output is not a function of the current input. Thus, a Moore sequential network is to be realized. Sample input and output sequences for this network are

$$x = 0\,0\,1\,1\,0\,0\,0\,1\,0\,1\,0\,1\,1\,1\,0$$

a *b* *c*

$$z = 0\,0\,0\,0\,1\,1\,1\,1\,1\,1\,0\,0\,0\,1\,1$$

The initial outputs from the network are seen to be 0's as required by the network specifications. At time *a* in the above sequences, $x = 1$ for the second time. Hence, an output change to 1 becomes effective when the next input symbol occurs. Times *b* and *c* correspond to the fourth and sixth occurrences of $x = 1$, respectively. Immediately following these times, again the value of z changes.

A set of states can now be defined. To do this, it is first noted that a record must be maintained as to whether the current $x = 1$ input is even or odd. Second, for ei-

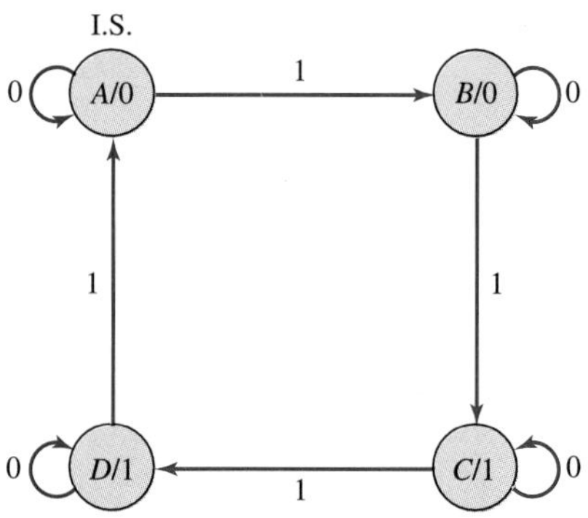

Figure 7.17 State diagram for the final example.

ther case, the output z can be 0 or 1. It is now concluded that four states are needed. They are

A: The output changes to 0 since the last occurrence of $x = 1$ *was even.*
B: The output remains at 0 since the last occurrence of $x = 1$ *was odd.*
C: The output changes to 1 since the last occurrence of $x = 1$ *was even.*
D: The output remains at 1 since the last occurrence of $x = 1$ *was odd.*

According to the network specifications, the output is to start with $z = 0$. State A serves as the initial state since it has the appropriate output value and no occurrences of $x = 1$ is an even number.

The state diagram for the network is shown in Fig. 7.17 and the state table is given in Table 7.12. A loop on each state for $x = 0$ is needed to indicate that a 0 input does not change the evenness or oddness of the number of 1's received. Furthermore, every other 1 input causes the output to change value as required by the network specifications.

Table 7.12 State table for Fig. 7.17

Present state	Next state		Output (z)
	Input (x) 0	1	
*A	A	B	0
B	B	C	0
C	C	D	1
D	D	A	1

7.4 STATE TABLE REDUCTION

The state table is a description for the terminal behavior of a clocked synchronous sequential network. When the table is formed, all the specifications of the network to be designed are incorporated into the table. To achieve this description, states are introduced to denote the past history of inputs. During this process more states may be defined then are really necessary. For example, in the previous section, either Table 7.10 or Table 7.11 adequately models the 0110/1001 sequence recognizer. However, one state table consists of 7 states while the other consists of 15 states. Thus, it is concluded that in some state tables it should be possible to replace two or more states by a single state without changing the description of the terminal behavior of the described network.

When the analysis of clock synchronous sequential networks in Sec. 7.2 was performed, it was seen that binary codes for the states were replaced by arbitrary symbols when going from the transition table to the state table. For synthesis, the opposite of this process is performed. In particular, the arbitrary state symbols are replaced by binary codes. The minimum number of binary digits needed to denote the states of a clocked synchronous sequential network is the smallest integer greater than or equal to the base-2 logarithm of the number of states. By reducing the number of states in a state table, hopefully fewer binary digits are needed to code the states. For example, if a state table has 9 states, then a minimum of four binary digits is needed to code these states. But, if the number of states is reduced to, say, 8 states, then only three binary digits are needed. On the other hand, a reduction from 7 states to 5 states does not result in a reduction in the number of binary digits needed to code the states. In both cases, a minimum of three bits is required. Since each binary digit of the state code is associated with a flip-flop in the clocked synchronous sequential network, a reduction in the number of binary digits in the code implies a reduction in the number of flip-flops in the realization.

Even if the number of flip-flops is not reduced, then by reducing the number of states in a state table there is a possibility that the combinational logic that precedes the inputs to the flip-flops might be simpler. As is seen in Sec. 7.6, for a fixed number of flip-flops, reducing the number of states permits more don't-cares to exist when designing the combinational logic. Normally, this should result in a simpler logic network.

Although there is justification for reducing the number of states in a state table, it should be understood that such a reduction does not guarantee that there will be a cost reduction in the realization. However, the potential savings serves as motivation to pursue the investigation on how state table reduction is performed.

In essence, the state table reduction problem is one of determining whether there exist any states in a network that need not be differentiable with regard to the network's terminal specifications. If two clocked synchronous sequential networks, possibly each with a different number of states, produce identical output sequences for every possible input sequence, then these two networks are considered as being equivalent. Our objective is to determine a state table having the fewest number of states that produces a realization equivalent to the realization produced by the state table initially modeled from the network specifications. Such a state table is referred to as a *minimal state table.*

In this section, a procedure is developed for obtaining the minimal state table. It is assumed that the state table produced from the network specifications is *completely specified.* That is, next states and outputs are specified for all locations in the corresponding sections of the state table. Special situations can arise when a next state and/or output need not be specified and, hence, denoted by a dash in the state table. Reduction of such incompletely specified state tables requires a generalization to the procedure of this section that is more complex and beyond the scope of this book.

The state table reduction procedure is a three-step process. First, equivalent pairs of states are determined. Second, from the knowledge of the equivalent pairs of states, sets of equivalent states are established. Finally, the reduced state table is constructed having one state for each of the sets of equivalent states. In this section, algorithms are presented for each of these steps.

7.4.1 Determining Equivalent Pairs of States

Let us now perform a simple experiment on two clocked synchronous sequential networks. In Sec. 7.2 it was shown that given a state table, an input sequence, and some starting state, the resulting output sequence is readily determined. For the sake of this experiment, assume the first clocked synchronous sequential network, described by some state table, is started in state p and the second clocked synchronous sequential network, possibly described by the same state table, is started in state q. Finally, assume the same arbitrary input sequence is applied to both networks. Figure 7.18 illustrates the layout of the experiment. Note that for the purpose of this experiment, use is not being made of what was previously introduced as the initial state required by the network specifications, but, rather, each network is assumed to be initially in some possibly different state that is being referred to as

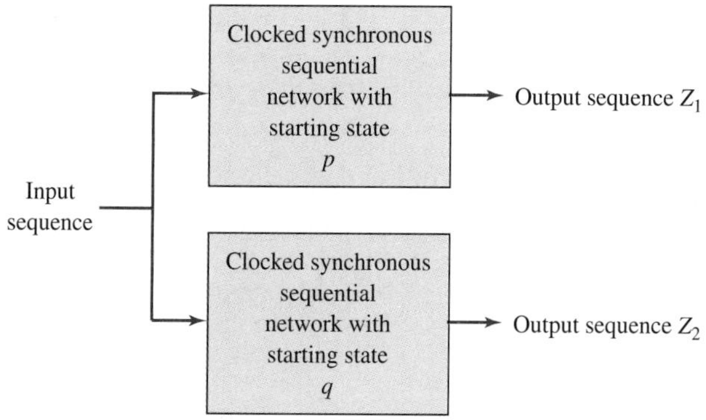

Figure 7.18 Experiment for determining equivalent pairs of states.

its starting state. States p and q are said to be *equivalent* or *indistinguishable*, written $p \equiv q$, if and only if for all input sequences applied to the two starting states, as shown in Fig. 7.18, identical output sequences from both networks result, i.e., $Z_1 = Z_2$. If states p and q are not equivalent, then they are said to be *distinguishable*, written $p \not\equiv q$. From this definition of equivalency, by simply observing the input/output terminals of the networks, it is not possible to distinguish state p from state q since the responses starting from these states, regardless of the input sequence, are the same.

The above experiment requires the use of all possible input sequences of all possible lengths to determine if two states are equivalent. The following theorem provides the basis of an algorithm for this determination.

Theorem 7.1

Two states p and q of a clocked synchronous sequential network are equivalent if and only if for each combination of values of the input variables (1) their outputs are identical and (2) their next states are equivalent.

Proof

* For ease in proving this theorem, it is first necessary to introduce some notation. Denote a single combination of values of the input variables by the input symbol x. For a single input symbol x and present state q, let $\omega(q,x)$ denote the output produced and $\delta(q,x)$ denote the next state. These are referred to as the output and next-state functions, respectively. If J is now used to denote any arbitrary input sequence, then $\omega(q,J)$ corresponds to the output sequence produced starting in state q when applying the input sequence J. From the definition of equivalency, $p \equiv q$ if and only if $\omega(p,J) = \omega(q,J)$ for all sequences including the input sequence consisting of the single input symbol x.

Consider the if part of this theorem, i.e., if the two conditions stated in the theorem are true, then $p \equiv q$. Assume the outputs produced by a network having starting states p and q are identical, i.e.,

$$\omega(p,x) = \omega(q,x) \tag{7.17}$$

Also, assume the next states for any single input symbol x are equivalent, i.e.,

$$\delta(p,x) \equiv \delta(q,x)$$

From the definition of equivalency, the pairwise equivalence of $\delta(p,x)$ and $\delta(q,x)$ implies

$$\omega[\delta(p,x),J] = \omega[\delta(q,x),J] \tag{7.18}$$

*The reader may skip the proof of this theorem without loss of continuity. Although Mealy sequential networks are assumed in this proof, with only slight modifications the proof can be restated for Moore sequential networks.

for all input sequences J. If the input sequence xJ, i.e., the single input symbol x followed by the sequence J, is applied to the starting state p, then

$$\omega(p,xJ) = \omega(p,x)\omega[\delta(p,x),J] \tag{7.19}$$

where $\omega(p,x)$ is the first symbol of the output sequence and $\omega[\delta(p,x),J]$ are the remaining output symbols. Similarly, applying the same input sequence xJ to starting state q results in

$$\omega(q,xJ) = \omega(q,x)\omega[\delta(q,x),J] \tag{7.20}$$

Substituting Eqs. (7.17) and (7.18) into Eq. (7.19) gives

$$\omega(p,xJ) = \omega(q,x)\omega[\delta(q,x),J]$$

Since the right side of this expression is the same as the right side of Eq. (7.20), the left sides of these expressions can be equated, i.e.,

$$\omega(p,xJ) = \omega(q,xJ)$$

This equation implies that regardless of the input sequence, since x and J were both arbitrarily chosen, the same output sequence is produced when a network is started in state p or in state q. Hence, by definition of equivalency of states, $p \equiv q$. This completes the proof of the if statement of the theorem.

To prove the only if part of the theorem, i.e., if $p \equiv q$, then the two conditions stated in the theorem are true, assume $p \equiv q$. If the input sequence xJ is applied to a clocked synchronous sequential network with starting states p and q, then

$$\omega(p,xJ) = \omega(q,xJ)$$

or

$$\omega(p,x)\omega[\delta(p,x),J] = \omega(q,x)[\delta(q,x),J] \tag{7.21}$$

Since Eq. (7.21) is describing two output sequences, it follows that

$$\omega(p,x) = \omega(q,x) \tag{7.22}$$

and

$$\omega[\delta(p,x),J] = \omega[\delta(q,x),J] \tag{7.23}$$

Equation (7.22) states that the outputs of a network with starting states p and q are identical for any single input symbol x. Furthermore, by Eq. (7.23), the starting states $\delta(p,x)$ and $\delta(q,x)$ also produce identical output sequences for any arbitrary input sequence J. Thus, from the definition of pairwise equivalence, $\delta(p,x) \equiv \delta(q,x)$. This completes the proof of the theorem. ■

To see how Theorem 7.1 is applied, consider the state table shown in Table 7.13. Condition (1) in Theorem 7.1 requires that for two states to be equivalent their present outputs must not be contradictory for any present-state/input combination. Now consider the pair of states (A,B). The states in this pair are not equivalent since

Table 7.13 Example of a state table in which state reduction can be performed

Present state	Next state		Output (z)	
	Input (x)		Input (x)	
	0	1	0	1
$*A$	A	B	0	0
B	D	C	0	1
C	F	E	0	0
D	D	F	0	0
E	B	G	0	0
F	G	C	0	1
G	A	F	0	0

the output for state A when $x = 1$ is $z = 0$, while the output for state B when $x = 1$ is $z = 1$. As another example, consider the pair of states (A,E). For this pair of states, condition (1) of Theorem 7.1 is satisfied since the outputs are not contradictory for either $x = 0$ or $x = 1$. However, condition (2) of the theorem requires that the pair of next states for each input be equivalent in order for a pair of present states to be equivalent. In this case, when $x = 0$, the pair of next states for (A,E) is (A,B). But it was previously established that states A and B are not equivalent. Hence, states A and E are not equivalent. As a final example of applying Theorem 7.1 to Table 7.13, consider the pair of states (A,D). Again condition (1) of Theorem 7.1 is satisfied. Condition (2), however, requires the pair of states (A,D) to be equivalent *as well as* the pair of states (B,F). Since we are trying to establish the equivalence of the (A,D) pair, the constraint that (A,D) be equivalent is redundant. Hence, it is only necessary to determine if the pair (B,F) is equivalent. To do this, it is necessary to check if this pair of states satisfies the conditions of Theorem 7.1. Condition (1) is satisfied for the (B,F) pair since they both have the same output when $x = 0$ and they both have the same output when $x = 1$, but condition (2) requires (D,G) and (C,C) to be equivalent pairs. Since every state is equivalent to itself, (C,C) is an equivalent pair of states. Thus, only the equivalence of the pair (D,G) needs to be established. Finally, the equivalence of the pair (D,G) is dependent upon the equivalence of (A,D) and (F,F). The equivalence of (F,F) is obviously satisfied. However, the equivalence requirement of (A,D) returns us to our starting point of determining if states A and D are equivalent. Actually, two states are equivalent unless it can be established otherwise. This follows from the fact that if two states are not equivalent, then they must be distinguishable, which implies that there is at least one input sequence that when applied to these two states produces different output sequences. That is, there must be a contradictory pair of outputs for some input in the sequence in order that two states be distinguishable. If such an input does not exist, then the two states are equivalent. Thus, it is now concluded that the initial pair of states (A,D) are equivalent.

Although the equivalency or distinguishability of pairs of states can always be determined by the above type of analysis, a formal procedure is desirable. One such procedure uses the *implication table.* Let us now give an algorithm for determining equivalent pairs of states based on Theorem 7.1 and then illustrate it.

1. Let $q_1, q_2, \ldots, q_n$ be the states of a state table. Construct an implication table, as shown in Fig. 7.19, so that there is one cell in the implication table for each pair of distinct states. [No cell is needed for the (q_k,q_k) pair since a state is always equivalent to itself. Also, since the pairs of states are not ordered, the pair (q_i,q_j) is the same as the pair (q_j,q_i)].
2. Call the cell that corresponds to the pair of present states q_i and q_j, as defined by the axis labels, the (q_i,q_j)-cell. Place a $\times$ in the (q_i,q_j)-cell if the outputs for these present states are contradictory for some input. (In the case of Moore-model state tables, the outputs only correspond to the states and, hence, the two output entries for the q_i and q_j states must not be contradictory.) If there are no contradictory outputs for the present states q_i and q_j of the state table, then enter in the (q_i,q_j)-cell the pair of next states for each input. Duplications are not entered. For convenience, any next-state pair for the (q_i,q_j)-cell, that is, (q_i,q_j), (q_j,q_i) or (q_k,q_k), need not be entered since they do not correspond to constraints that must be satisfied when the table is processed. Furthermore, the ordering of the states in each pair is not significant. Hence, in the remainder of the algorithm, the pairs (q_i,q_j) and (q_j,q_i) are not distinguished and simply referred to as the pair (q_i,q_j). Finally, if neither a $\times$ nor pairs of states are entered in the cell, then a check mark is inserted. A check mark denotes that the pair of states (q_i,q_j) are equivalent since their outputs are not contradictory and there are no next-state constraints.
3. All state pair entries in the implication table are now inspected by the following process: If the state pair (q_a,q_b) is an entry in the (q_i,q_j)-cell and if the

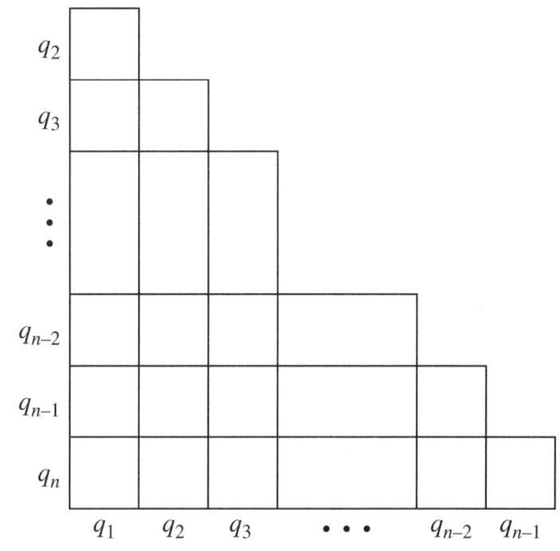

Figure 7.19 The structure of an implication table.

(q_a,q_b)-cell contains a ×, then a × is placed in the (q_i,q_j)-cell. If a × is placed in the (q_i,q_j)-cell, then any additional entries in the (q_i,q_j)-cell are ignored, and a state pair in another cell, not previously inspected, is selected. On the other hand, if the above procedure does not result in a × being placed in the (q_i,q_j)-cell and if additional state pairs appear in the (q_i,q_j)-cell that have not been inspected, then the process is repeated on one of these other state pairs.

4. Repeat Step 3 until it is possible to make an entire pass of the implication table using the above inspection procedure without any additional ×'s being entered. The process then terminates. If the (q_i,q_j)-cell has no × at this time, then the states q_i and q_j are equivalent.

To illustrate the above algorithm, again consider the state table shown in Table 7.13. Figure 7.20*a* shows the implication table that results as a consequence of the first two steps of the algorithm. A × is placed in the cell corresponding to the state pair (*A*,*B*) since the rows in the output section of the state table are distinct for these two states, i.e., there is a contradictory pair of outputs for at least one input. Hence, it is immediately concluded that states *A* and *B* are not equivalent. Next the pair of states (*A*,*C*) is considered. Since the rows in the output section of the state table of Table 7.13 are identical for the state pair (*A*,*C*), the next states for this state pair are entered in the (*A*,*C*)-cell of Fig. 7.20*a*. In particular, the next states for the state pair (*A*,*C*) are (*A*,*F*) when $x = 0$ and (*B*,*E*) when $x = 1$. This pair of entries signifies that for the state pair (*A*,*C*) to be equivalent, the pair of states (*A*,*F*) must be equivalent *and* the pair of states (*B*,*E*) must also be equivalent. Upon considering all pairs of rows of the state table of Table 7.13, the implication table of Fig. 7.20*a* is completed. It should be noted in completing the implication table that if the next states for some input are a pair of identical states, then these next states are not entered in the cells of the implication table. Thus, in the (*A*,*G*)-cell, the state pair (*A*,*A*) is not entered. Similarly, the next states of a state pair are not entered if they are the same as the state pair itself. For example, in the (*A*,*D*)-cell, only the next-state pair (*B*,*F*) is entered and not the next-

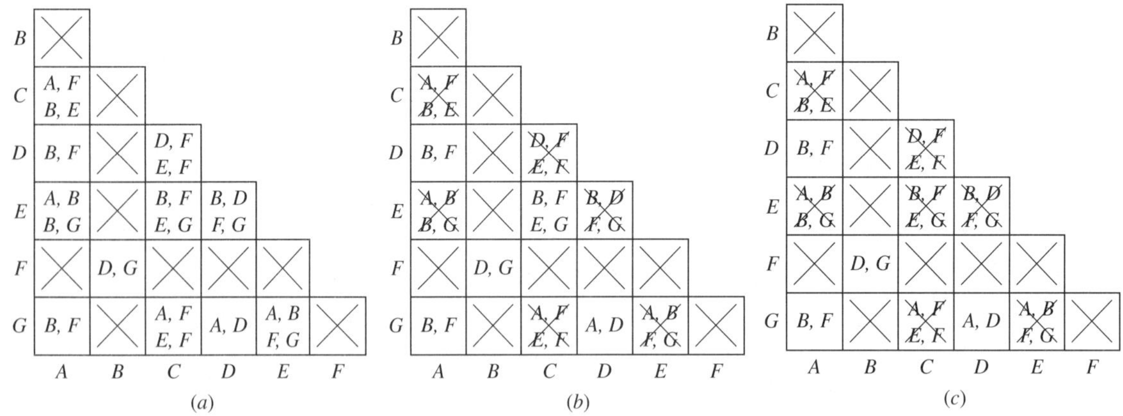

Figure 7.20 Implication table for determining the equivalent states of Table 7.13. (*a*) The initial table. (*b*) After the first pass. (*c*) After the second pass.

state pair (A,D). These two simplifications are for convenience only and are not necessary for the algorithmic procedure. Also for convenience, the state-pair entries appear in alphabetical order, since these are not ordered sets, and without parentheses.

Step 3 of the algorithm is now applied to the implication table of Fig. 7.20*a*. This is done by working through the table from top to bottom and left to right. In the (A,C)-cell there is the entry (A,F). Checking the (A,F)-cell, it is seen that there is a $\times$. Hence, a $\times$ is placed in the (A,C)-cell of the implication table since it is now concluded that the state pair (A,C) is not equivalent according to Theorem 7.1. Since this cell now contains a $\times$, the second entry in the cell, i.e., (B,E), is not relevant and, hence, ignored. Next the (A,D)-cell is inspected. It contains the entry (B,F). Since no $\times$ appears in the (B,F)-cell in the implication table, no $\times$ is entered in the (A,D)-cell. In this manner, every pair of entries in the implication table of Fig. 7.20*a* is inspected. Upon the completion of the first pass, the table appears as shown in Fig. 7.20*b*. A second pass through the implication table is now made to check if any pair of next-state entries might correspond to a cell that became $\times$'ed during the first pass. As a consequence of this pass, the (C,E)-cell becomes $\times$'ed due to the (E,G) entry. At the end of the second pass, the implication table appears as shown in Fig. 7.20*c*. Since a new cell has become $\times$'ed, another pass through the table is necessary. In general, as long as some pass through the table results in $\times$'s being entered, another pass is needed. For the example of Fig. 7.20*c*, however, the next pass through the implication table introduces no new $\times$'s. Thus, the inspection process terminates. The equivalent state pairs are now determined from the implication table. They correspond to the cells (not the cell entries) with non-$\times$ entries. In particular, from Fig. 7.20*c* it is seen that $A \equiv D$, $A \equiv G$, $B \equiv F$, and $D \equiv G$ since there are no crosses in the (A,D)-cell, (A,G)-cell, (B,F)-cell, and (D,G)-cell, respectively.

A slight variation to the above algorithm does the processing of the implication table by working with the cells containing $\times$'s. In this case, Steps 3 and 4 of the above algorithm are replaced by the following two steps:

3. The implication table is now processed. If the entry in the (q_i,q_j)-cell is a single $\times$, then a single $\times$ is placed in every cell that has (q_i,q_j) or (q_j,q_i) as an entry and a second $\times$ is placed in the (q_i,q_j)-cell. Once a $\times$ is placed in a cell, all other entries in that cell are ignored in all further steps.
4. Repeat Step 3 until all $\times$'ed cells have two $\times$'s. The process then terminates. If the (q_i,q_j)-cell has no $\times$'s at this time, then the states q_i and q_j are equivalent.

If this variation is used on the state table of Table 7.13, then the implication table of Fig. 7.20*c* again results except that two $\times$'s appear in each of the $\times$'ed cells.

7.4.2 Obtaining the Equivalence Classes of States

The second step in the state reduction procedure is to obtain the *equivalence classes of states*. This is the smallest collection of sets of states such that all members in each set are equivalent and in which every state appears in some set. To form a set of equivalent states, all pairs of states in the set must be equivalent.

Again consider Table 7.13. For this table, it was seen that $A \equiv D$, $A \equiv G$, $D \equiv G$, and $B \equiv F$. The first three pairs of equivalent states are used to form the set

(A,D,G) since each pair in this set is equivalent. The next set of equivalent states is simply (B,F), which corresponds to the fourth equivalent pair of states previously determined. Finally, the remaining states of Table 7.13 that do not appear in these two sets are C and E. Since these states are equivalent to no other states, they form sets by themselves. Hence, for Table 7.13, the equivalence classes of states is $\{(A,D,G),(B,F),(C),(E)\}$.

Although inspection of the equivalent pairs of states can be used to form the equivalence classes of states, the same result is obtained by the following algorithm applied to the implication table:

1. Starting with the rightmost column of the processed implication table and working toward the left, move to the first column that has a cell that does not contain a $\times$. Write down the pairs of equivalent states for this column as indicated by the axis labels of the cells not containing a $\times$. This forms the initial list of equivalence classes of states.
2. Move to the next column to the left, say column i, which contains one or more non-$\times$ cells. If state i is equivalent to all members of any set of states in the list, then add state i to the set. Otherwise, add to the list the pairwise equivalent states containing state i.
3. Repeat Step 2 until all columns are examined. Finally, add to the list, as sets consisting of single states, any states that do not appear in one of the other sets in the list.

To illustrate the above algorithm, consider the processed implication table for Table 7.13. The algorithmic procedure starts with column D of Fig. 7.20*c* since this is the first column, starting from the right, that has an equivalent pair of states. At this point the list of equivalence classes of states appears as $\{(D,G)\}$. The procedure continues by moving left to column B. In this column it is seen that $B \equiv F$ as indicated by the axis labels. Thus, the pair of states (B,F) is added to the list giving $\{(D,G),(B,F)\}$. Next column A is considered. Here it is seen that state A is equivalent to both states D and G. Hence, the (D,G) set is expanded to include state A. This results in the collection $\{(A,D,G),(B,F)\}$. Finally, as required by Step 3 of the algorithm, any states of the state table not already in the collection of equivalent states must be included as single sets. Thus, the final equivalence classes of states is $\{(A,D,G),(B,F),(C),(E)\}$.

7.4.3 Constructing the Minimal State Table

The third and final step of the state table reduction procedure is to construct the minimal state table. As defined previously, this is the state table having the minimum number of states that can serve as a model for a given word description of network behavior. Once the equivalence classes of states is obtained, the minimal state table is constructed as follows:

1. Let the original state table be called Q and the minimal state table be called P. Let the sets of states that make up the equivalence classes of states be denoted

by $C_1, C_2, \ldots, C_s$. Finally, let the input columns for state tables P and Q be the same and denoted by $I_1, I_2, \ldots, I_m$.

2. Assign a state p_i to each of the sets C_i, for $i = 1, 2, \ldots, s$. Then, the present state section of the minimal state table P consists of states $p_1, p_2, \ldots, p_s$.
3. To determine the next-state entry in the p_i-row, I_k-column of state table P proceed as follows: Select any state in the set C_i. Using state table Q, determine its next state for input I_k. Assume this next state is a member of C_j. Then, the next-state entry in the p_i-row, I_k-column of state table P is p_j.
4. If state tables P and Q are Mealy models, then the output entry for the p_i-row, I_k-column of state table P is determined as follows: Select any state in the set C_i. Assume in state table Q the output for this state and input I_k is z_t. Then the output entry in the p_i-row, I_k-column of state table P is z_t. If state tables P and Q are Moore models, then the output entry for the p_i-row of state table P is determined as follows: Select any state in the set C_i. Assume the output for this state in state table Q is z_t. Then, the output entry in the p_i-row of state table P is z_t.
5. If the initial state of state table Q is a member of C_r, then p_r is the initial state of state table P.

As seen in the above algorithm, the minimal state table has one state for each of the sets that comprises the equivalence classes of states. Thus, the information associated with a set of states is "lumped" into a single state.

The above algorithm for the final step of the state table reduction procedure can now be applied to Table 7.13 to construct its minimal form. This is shown in Table 7.14. In this table, state α is used to represent the equivalence class (A,D,G), state β the equivalence class (B,F), state γ the equivalence class (C), and state δ the equivalence class (E). Select state A as the representative element of the set (A,D,G). This state is used to determine the next states and outputs for the α row of the minimal state table since state α is assigned to the set (A,D,G). From Table 7.13 it is seen that for present state A and input $x = 0$, the next state is A and the output is 0. Since the next state, i.e., A, is a member of (A,D,G) and α is the state assigned to the set (A,D,G), the next-state entry when $x = 0$ in the α row of Table 7.14 is α and the output entry is 0. Similarly, for present state A and input $x = 1$, the next state and output in Table 7.13 is B and $z = 0$. Hence, since state B is a member of the set (B,F) that is assigned to state β, the next-state entry in Table 7.14 in the α row when

Table 7.14 Minimal state table for Table 7.13

Present state		Next state		Output (z)	
		Input (x)		Input (x)	
		0	1	0	1
(A,D,G):	$*\alpha$	α	β	0	0
(B,F):	β	α	γ	0	1
(C):	γ	β	δ	0	0
(E):	δ	β	α	0	0

$x = 1$ is β and the output entry is 0. Next the entries for the β row of the minimal state table are determined. To do this, an element from the set (B,F), say, B, is selected. Using Table 7.13, the next state and output for state B when $x = 0$ is D and $z = 0$. Thus, for row β when $x = 0$, the next state is α, since D is an element of (A,D,G) and α is assigned to this set, and the output is $z = 0$. Also, the next state and output for state B when $x = 1$ is C and $z = 1$. This results in the two entries of γ and $z = 1$ in the β row when the input is $x = 1$. All the remaining entries in Table 7.14 are obtained by a similar process. Finally, since state A is the initial state for the state table of Table 7.13 and since state A is an element of the equivalence class (A,D,G) that is represented by α, state α is the initial state for the minimal state table given in Table 7.14.

There is an alternate process for constructing the minimal state table. After a state is assigned to each equivalence class, each present state and next state in the original state table is replaced by the assigned state representing the equivalence class in which it is a member. Once this is done, the state table consists of duplicate rows whenever an equivalence class has more than one member. Deleting all but one occurrence of the duplicate rows results in the minimal state table. The row that corresponds to the initial state should be the row that is retained if there are duplicates of it.

To illustrate the above variation for constructing the minimal state table, again consider the state table shown in Table 7.13. Let the equivalence classes (A,D,G), (B,F), (C), and (E) be represented by states α, β, γ, and δ, respectively. Thus, in Table 7.13, all occurrences of states A, D, and G are replaced by α; all occurrences of states B and F are replaced by β; all occurrences of state C by γ; and all occurrences of state E by δ. The state table which results after these substitutions are made is shown in Table 7.15. Since the fourth and seventh rows of this table are identical with the first row, the fourth and seventh rows are deleted. Similarly, the sixth row is deleted since it is identical with the second row of the table. The resulting minimal state table is now that of Table 7.14.

Table 7.15 Alternate procedure for constructing a minimal state table

Present state	Next state		Output (z)	
	Input (x)		Input (x)	
	0	1	0	1
*~~A~~α	~~A~~α	~~B~~β	0	0
~~B~~β	~~D~~α	~~C~~γ	0	1
~~C~~γ	~~F~~β	~~E~~δ	0	0
~~D~~α	~~D~~α	~~F~~β	0	0
~~E~~δ	~~B~~β	~~G~~α	0	0
~~F~~β	~~G~~α	~~C~~γ	0	1
~~G~~α	~~A~~α	~~F~~β	0	0

The above algorithms showed how some state table P is constructed from a state table Q. Formally, it is still necessary to establish that the new state table P obtained in this manner can serve as a replacement for state table Q. Previously the equivalence of two states was defined. Let us now define the equivalence of two clocked synchronous sequential networks that are described by two different completely specified state tables P and Q. Two clocked synchronous sequential networks are *equivalent* if for each state p_i in the network described by state table P there is at least one state q_j in the network described by state table Q so that $p_i \equiv q_j$, and, conversely, for each state q_j in the network described by state table Q there is at least one state p_i in the network described by state table P so that $q_j \equiv p_i$. Thus, two clocked synchronous sequential networks are equivalent if there is no way to distinguish between them by observing the responses to any input sequence when started in equivalent states. Hence, they are both capable of performing the same job.

If it can be established that a clocked synchronous sequential network realization based on some state table from a word description of network behavior is equivalent to the realization based on the minimal state table obtained from the above construction procedures, then it can be concluded that the minimal state table is an appropriate model for the same word description of network behavior that generated the initial state table. That this is indeed the case is given by the following theorem.

Theorem 7.2

Let state table Q correspond to some word description of network behavior and state table P correspond to the minimal state table constructed from Q. Then, the two clocked synchronous sequential networks realized from state tables P and Q are equivalent.

Proof

*To prove this theorem, it is necessary to show that for every state in the network realized from state table Q there is at least one equivalent state in the network realized from state table P and vice versa. Then, by the definition of clocked synchronous sequential network equivalence, the theorem follows. Theorem 7.1 stated that if two states are equivalent then their outputs for a given input are identical and their next states are equivalent. As a direct consequence of this, if $\{C_1, C_2, \ldots, C_s\}$ is the equivalence classes of states for state table Q then the following two conclusions can be made. First, for all members of C_i, the outputs for a single input are identical. Second, for all members of C_i and a single input, the next states are always members of the same equivalence class C_j (where j can be the same as i).

*The reader may skip the proof of this theorem without loss of continuity.

Now let $q^{(i)}$ denote any arbitrary state in the equivalence class C_i and let $x_1x_2 \cdots x_h$ denote any arbitrary input sequence. Assume the sequence is applied to the network realized from state table Q when in state $q^{(i)}$. Let the resulting sequence of states be $q^{(i1)}, q^{(i2)}, \ldots, q^{(ih)}$ and the resulting output sequence be $z_1z_2 \cdots z_h$. Next let the same input sequence $x_1x_2 \cdots x_h$ be applied to the network realized from state table P when in state p_i where p_i is the representative state for the equivalence class C_i. From the way in which state table P is constructed from state table Q and the two properties of the equivalence classes of states concluded above, the resulting sequence of states is $p_{i1}, p_{i2}, \ldots, p_{ih}$, where p_{ik} is the representative state for the set that contains $q^{(ik)}$, and the resulting output sequence is the same output sequence $z_1z_2 \cdots z_h$. Since $x_1x_2 \cdots x_h$ and $q^{(i)}$ were arbitrarily selected, it follows that for every state in the network realization from state table Q that belongs to any equivalence class C_i there is an equivalent state p_i in the network realized from state table P. Using a similar argument, the sequence $x_1x_2 \cdots x_h$ can be applied first to the network realized from state table P and then to the network realized from state table Q to establish that for every state of the network realized from state table P there is an equivalent state in the network realized from state table Q. Thus, by definition of clocked synchronous sequential network equivalence, the networks realized from state tables P and Q are equivalent. ■

7.4.4 The 0110/1001 Sequence Recognizer

Before closing this section on state table reduction, let us return to the 0110/1001 sequence recognizer modeled in Sec. 7.3. Two state tables were developed for this example; the first, given as Table 7.10, consisted of 7 states and the other, given as Table 7.11, consisted of 15 states. At this time let us verify that Table 7.10 is the minimal state table version of Table 7.11.

Figure 7.21*a* gives the implication table for the state table of Table 7.11 before being processed. After the table is processed, it appears as shown in Fig. 7.21*b*. As seen in Fig. 7.21*b*, the equivalent pairs of states are $b \equiv d$, $b \equiv h$, $c \equiv g$, $c \equiv o$, $d \equiv h$, $e \equiv i$, $e \equiv m$, $f \equiv j$, $f \equiv n$, $g \equiv o$, $i \equiv m$, and $j \equiv n$. From the knowledge of the equivalent pairs of states, the equivalence classes of states is readily determined as $\{(a),(b,d,h),(c,g,o),(e,i,m),(f,j,n),(k),(l)\}$. If state A is used to represent the equivalence class (a), state B the equivalence class (b,d,h), state C the equivalence class (c,g,o), state D the equivalence class (e,i,m), state E the equivalence class (f,j,n), state F the equivalence class (k), and state G the equivalence class (l), then the state table of Table 7.11 reduces to that of Table 7.10.

The implication table provides a formal solution to the state reduction problem. However, as seen in the example of the 0110/1001 sequence recognizer, its use may involve a significant amount of labor. Frequently, preprocessing of a state table to reduce the number of states is possible before the more formal algorithm is applied. If the next-state and output entries for two rows in a state table are identical, column by column, then the conditions of Theorem 7.1 are satisfied. Hence, the states associated with these rows are equivalent. In such a case, one of the rows is eliminated and all occurrences of the eliminated state in the next-state section of the state table are replaced by its equivalent state.

To illustrate the preprocessing of a state table, again consider Table 7.11. It is seen that rows d and h are identical. Thus, $d \equiv h$. As shown in Table 7.16*a*, row h is ruled out in the table, denoting deletion, and all next-state h entries are replaced by d. Next it is noted that rows e, i, and m are identical in Table 7.16*a*. This implies $e \equiv i \equiv m$. Hence, rows i and m are deleted and all occurrences of both state i and state m are replaced by state e. At this point, the state table appears as shown in Table 7.16*b*. Continuing in this manner, it is noted that $f \equiv j \equiv n$

	a	b	c	d	e	f	g	h	i	j	k	l	m	n
b	b, d c, e													
c	b, f c, g	d, f e, g												
d	b, h c, i	d, h e, i	f, h g, i											
e	b, j c, k	d, j e, k	f, j g, k	h, j i, k										
f	b, l c, m	d, l e, m	f, l g, m	h, l i, m	j, l k, m									
g	b, n c, o	d, n e, o	f, n g, o	h, n i, o	j, n k, o	l, n m, o								
h	b, h c, i	d, h e, i	f, h g, i	✓	h, j i, k	h, l i, m	h, n i, o							
i	b, j c, k	d, j e, k	f, j g, k	h, j i, k	✓	j, l k, m	j, n k, o	h, j i, k						
j	b, l c, m	d, l e, m	f, l g, m	h, l i, m	j, l k, m	✓	l, n m, o	h, l i, m	j, l k, m					
k	X	X	X	X	X	X	X	X	X	X				
l	X	X	X	X	X	X	X	X	X	X	X			
m	b, j c, k	d, j e, k	f, j g, k	h, j i, k	✓	j, l k, m	j, n k, o	h, j i, k	✓	j, l k, m	X	X		
n	b, l c, m	d, l e, m	f, l g, m	h, l i, m	j, l k, m	✓	l, n m, o	h, l i, m	j, l k, m	✓	X	X	j, l k, m	
o	b, n c, o	d, n e, o	f, n g, o	h, n i, o	j, n k, o	l, n m, o	✓	h, n i, o	j, n k, o	l, n m, o	X	X	j, n k, o	l, n m, o

(*a*)

(*Cont.*)

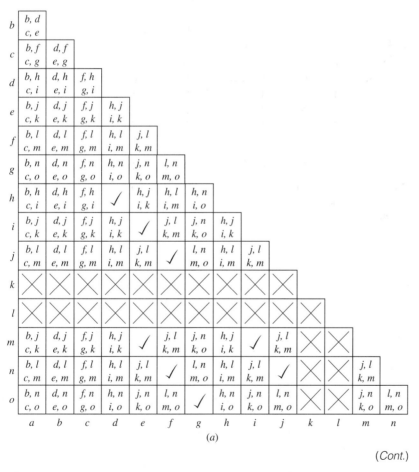

Figure 7.21 Implication table for determining equivalent states of the 0110/1001 sequence recognizer. (*a*) Initial table.

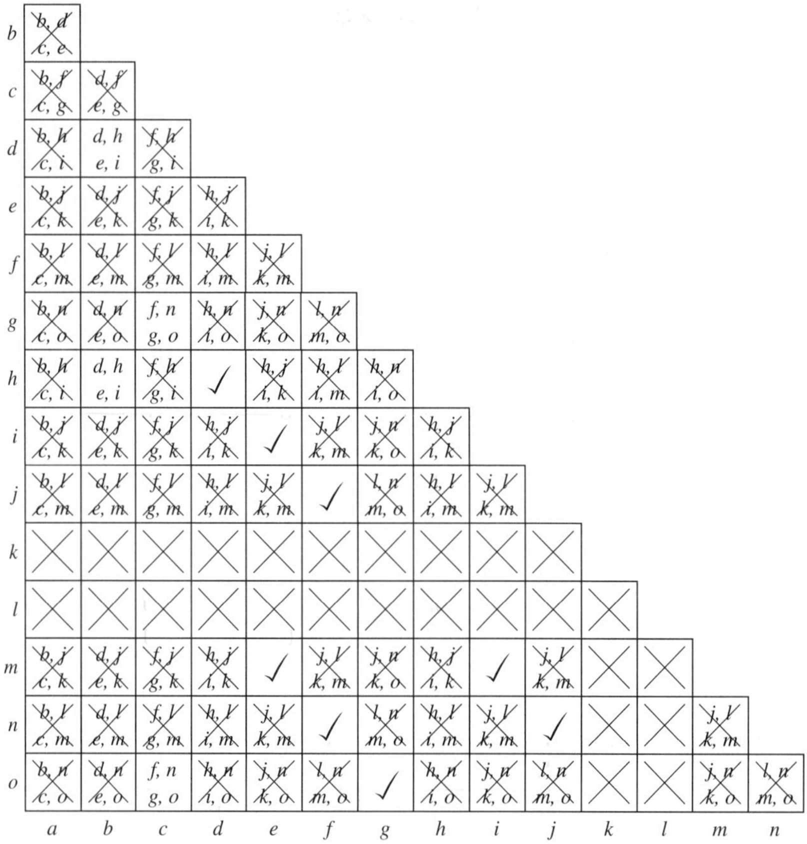

(b)

Figure 7.21 (*Cont.*) (*b*) Final table.

and $g \equiv o$ in Table 7.16*b*. After ruling out rows *j*, *n*, and *o* and replacing all next-state *j* and *n* entries by *f* and all next-state *o* entries by *g*, the preprocessed state table appears as shown in Table 7.16*c*. Finally, in Table 7.16*c*, it is seen that rows *b* and *d* are identical as well as rows *c* and *g*. Deleting rows *d* and *g* and replacing all next-state *d* entries by *b* and all next-state *g* entries by *c*, the resulting state table appears as shown in Table 7.16*d*. Table 7.16*e* gives the final version of the preprocessed table in which the ruled-out rows are deleted and only the final values of the state entries are shown. This state table, with only seven states, is the minimal state table for the 0110/1001 sequence recognizer, as the reader can easily verify by applying the state reduction algorithm. Although the elimination of identical rows in this case produced the minimal state table, this is not always the case. Hence, in general, the state reduction algorithm still must be applied.

Table 7.16 Preprocessing of the 0110/1001 sequence recognizer state table. (*a*) Results of $d \equiv h$. (*b*) Results of $e \equiv i \equiv m$.

Present state	Next state		Output (*z*)	
	Input (*x*)		Input (*x*)	
	0	**1**	**0**	**1**
**a*	*b*	*c*	0	0
b	*d*	*e*	0	0
c	*f*	*g*	0	0
d	~~*h*~~*d*	*i*	0	0
e	*j*	*k*	0	0
f	*l*	*m*	0	0
g	*n*	*o*	0	0
~~*h*~~	~~*h*~~	~~*i*~~	~~0~~	~~0~~
i	*j*	*k*	0	0
j	*l*	*m*	0	0
k	*n*	*o*	1	0
l	~~*h*~~*d*	*i*	0	1
m	*j*	*k*	0	0
n	*l*	*m*	0	0
o	*n*	*o*	0	0

(*a*)

Present state	Next state		Output (*z*)	
	Input (*x*)		Input (*x*)	
	0	**1**	**0**	**1**
* *a*	*b*	*c*	0	0
b	*d*	*e*	0	0
c	*f*	*g*	0	0
d	~~*h*~~*d*	~~*i*~~*e*	0	0
e	*j*	*k*	0	0
f	*l*	~~*m*~~*e*	0	0
g	*n*	*o*	0	0
~~*h*~~	~~*h*~~	~~*i*~~	~~0~~	~~0~~
~~*i*~~	~~*j*~~	~~*k*~~	~~0~~	~~0~~
j	*l*	~~*m*~~*e*	0	0
k	*n*	*o*	1	0
l	~~*h*~~*d*	~~*i*~~*e*	0	1
~~*m*~~	~~*j*~~	~~*k*~~	~~0~~	~~0~~
n	*l*	~~*m*~~*e*	0	0
o	*n*	*o*	0	0

(*b*)

(*Cont.*)

Table 7.16 (*Cont.*) (*c*) Results of $f \equiv j \equiv n$ and $g \equiv o$. (*d*) Results of $b \equiv d$ and $c \equiv g$.

Present state	Next state		Output (z)	
	Input (x)		Input (x)	
	0	1	0	1
*a	b	c	0	0
b	d	e	0	0
c	f	g	0	0
d	~~h~~d	~~i~~e	0	0
e	~~j~~f	k	0	0
f	l	~~m~~e	0	0
g	~~n~~f	~~o~~g	0	0
~~h~~	~~h~~	~~i~~	~~0~~	~~0~~
~~i~~	~~j~~	~~k~~	~~0~~	~~0~~
~~j~~	~~l~~	~~~~m~~e~~	~~0~~	~~0~~
k	~~n~~f	~~o~~g	1	0
l	~~h~~d	~~i~~e	0	1
~~m~~	~~j~~	~~k~~	~~0~~	~~0~~
~~n~~	~~l~~	~~~~m~~e~~	~~0~~	~~0~~
~~o~~	~~n~~	~~o~~	~~0~~	~~0~~

(*c*)

Present state	Next state		Output (z)	
	Input (x)		Input (x)	
	0	1	0	1
*a	b	c	0	0
b	~~d~~b	e	0	0
c	f	~~g~~c	0	0
~~d~~	~~~~h~~d~~	~~~~i~~e~~	~~0~~	~~0~~
e	~~j~~f	k	0	0
f	l	~~m~~e	0	0
~~g~~	~~~~n~~f~~	~~~~o~~g~~	~~0~~	~~0~~
~~h~~	~~h~~	~~i~~	~~0~~	~~0~~
~~i~~	~~j~~	~~k~~	~~0~~	~~0~~
~~j~~	~~l~~	~~~~m~~e~~	~~0~~	~~0~~
k	~~n~~f	~~o~~~~g~~c	1	0
l	~~h~~~~d~~b	~~i~~e	0	1
~~m~~	~~j~~	~~k~~	~~0~~	~~0~~
~~n~~	~~l~~	~~~~m~~e~~	~~0~~	~~0~~
~~o~~	~~n~~	~~o~~	~~0~~	~~0~~

(*d*)

(*Cont.*)

Table 7.16 (*Cont.*) (*e*) Final state table

Present state	Next state		Output (z)	
	Input (x)		Input (x)	
	0	1	0	1
$*a$	b	c	0	0
b	b	e	0	0
c	f	c	0	0
e	f	k	0	0
f	l	e	0	0
k	f	c	1	0
l	b	e	0	1

(*e*)

7.5 THE STATE ASSIGNMENT

Reversing the analysis procedure of clocked synchronous sequential networks described in Sec. 7.2, the next step in the synthesis procedure is to construct the transition table. In forming the transition table, a binary-code representation for the states of the state table is selected. This is referred to as the *state-assignment* problem.

In clocked synchronous sequential networks, the flip-flops that comprise the memory of the network are only allowed to undergo a single state change for each clock period. Because of this controlled behavior, the assignment of binary codes to the states can be made arbitrarily as long as each state is assigned a unique code. However, different state assignments result in realizations of different costs. This being the case, it seems natural to seek a state assignment that minimizes the cost of the network realization.

If there are s states to be coded, i.e., there are s rows in the state table, then the minimum number of binary digits p needed to code each of these states is the smallest integer greater than or equal to the base-2 logarithm of s. This follows directly from the fact that p binary digits can be used to code 2^p states. Although the use of the minimum number of binary digits in the state assignment guarantees the minimal number of flip-flops in the realization, it does not guarantee the minimal-cost realization. That is, increasing the number of flip-flops, by using more than the minimum number of binary digits to code the states, may result in a decrease of the number of gates in the realization to the extent of achieving a net-cost reduction.

Even under the assumption of using the minimum number of binary digits to code the states, the state assignment problem is not necessarily a simple one. That is, there is no simple procedure to determine the binary code to assign to each state for optimizing network cost. In general, there are $2^p!/(2^p-s)!$ ways of assigning a unique binary code of p binary digits to the s rows of a state table. For example, for a six-row state table in which three binary digits are used to code each state, there

Table 7.17 Illustrations of state assignments. (*a*) State table. (*b*) Transition table for state assignment in binary order. (*c*) Transition table for state assignment based on guidelines

Present state	Next state		Output (z)	
	Input (x)		Input (x)	
	0	1	0	1
*A	A	B	0	0
B	B	C	0	0
C	D	E	0	0
D	F	G	1	0
E	C	B	0	1
F	D	H	1	0
G	B	C	0	1
H	F	G	0	0

(*a*)

Present state ($Q_1Q_2Q_3$)	Next state ($Q_1^+Q_2^+Q_3^+$)		Output (z)	
	Input (x)		Input (x)	
	0	1	0	1
*$A \rightarrow 000$	000	001	0	0
$B \rightarrow 001$	001	010	0	0
$C \rightarrow 010$	011	100	0	0
$D \rightarrow 011$	101	110	1	0
$E \rightarrow 100$	010	001	0	1
$F \rightarrow 101$	011	111	1	0
$G \rightarrow 110$	001	010	0	1
$H \rightarrow 111$	101	110	0	0

(*b*)

Present state ($Q_1Q_2Q_3$)	Next state ($Q_1^+Q_2^+Q_3^+$)		Output (z)	
	Input (x)		Input (x)	
	0	1	0	1
*$A \rightarrow 000$	000	001	0	0
$B \rightarrow 001$	001	011	0	0
$C \rightarrow 011$	110	100	0	0
$D \rightarrow 110$	111	101	1	0
$E \rightarrow 100$	011	001	0	1
$F \rightarrow 111$	110	010	1	0
$G \rightarrow 101$	001	011	0	1
$H \rightarrow 010$	111	101	0	0

(*c*)

are 20,160 different state assignments. Thus, complete enumeration of all possible state assignments is totally prohibitive as an approach for determining the minimal-cost implementation.

How does one then select a state assignment? Occasionally, the nature of the problem might suggest a good choice. For example, in a Moore network state table, if the outputs for each state are distinct, as in the case of counters, then a good choice is to select the state assignment to be the same as the required outputs. In this way, the outputs of the flip-flops themselves become the outputs of the sequential network and no additional output logic is required. However, in most instances, the logic designer must rely on his own judgment when making a state assignment selection. Many guidelines to help achieve this task, involving various degrees of complexity, have been proposed. Examples of such guidelines are presented a little later in this section.

Since the state assignment can be selected arbitrarily, the simplest approach to the state assignment problem is to use the first s binary integers as the binary-code representation of the s states. For now let us use this approach. Table 7.17*a* gives a state table, and Table 7.17*b* is its transition table with such an assignment. The transition table is obtained by simply replacing all occurrences of state A with the binary code 000, all occurrences of state B with 001, all occurrences of state C with 010, etc. With three bits being used for the state assignment, they are denoted by the three state variables Q_1, Q_2, and Q_3.

The transition table of Table 7.17*b* is really a truth table for the combinational logic functions Q_1^+, Q_2^+, Q_3^+, and z in terms of the state variables Q_1, Q_2, Q_3, and input variable x. Thus, it is possible to obtain minimal Boolean expressions to describe each of these functions. To do this, the Karnaugh maps of Fig. 7.22 are constructed. It is a simple matter to transfer the information from the transition table to the Karnaugh maps. For example, the first-row, first-column entries in the next-state and output sections of the transition table correspond to $Q_1Q_2Q_3x = 0000$ in which it is seen that $Q_1^+Q_2^+Q_3^+ = 000$ and $z = 0$. But $Q_1Q_2Q_3x = 0000$ also corresponds to the upper left cell of each Karnaugh map in Fig. 7.22. Thus, the functional value 0 is entered in this cell of each map. In a similar manner, the first-row, second-column entries in the next-state and output sections of the transition table correspond to $Q_1Q_2Q_3x = 0001$ in which it is seen that $Q_1^+Q_2^+Q_3^+ = 001$ and $z = 0$. Since $Q_1Q_2Q_3x = 0001$ corresponds to the second-left cell in the top row of each map, the Q_1^+, Q_2^+, and z map entries are 0's and the Q_3^+ map entry is 1. Once the maps are constructed, it is a simple matter to obtain the minimal next-state and output expressions. In this case, the minimal sum-of-products expressions are

$$Q_1^+ = Q_2Q_3 + \overline{Q}_1Q_2x + Q_1Q_3x$$

$$Q_2^+ = Q_3x + Q_1Q_2x + Q_1\overline{Q}_2\overline{x} + \overline{Q}_1Q_2\overline{Q}_3\overline{x}$$

$$Q_3^+ = Q_3\overline{x} + Q_2\overline{x} + \overline{Q}_2\overline{Q}_3x + Q_1\overline{Q}_2x$$

$$z = Q_1\overline{Q}_3x + \overline{Q}_1Q_2Q_3\overline{x} + Q_1\overline{Q}_2Q_3\overline{x}$$

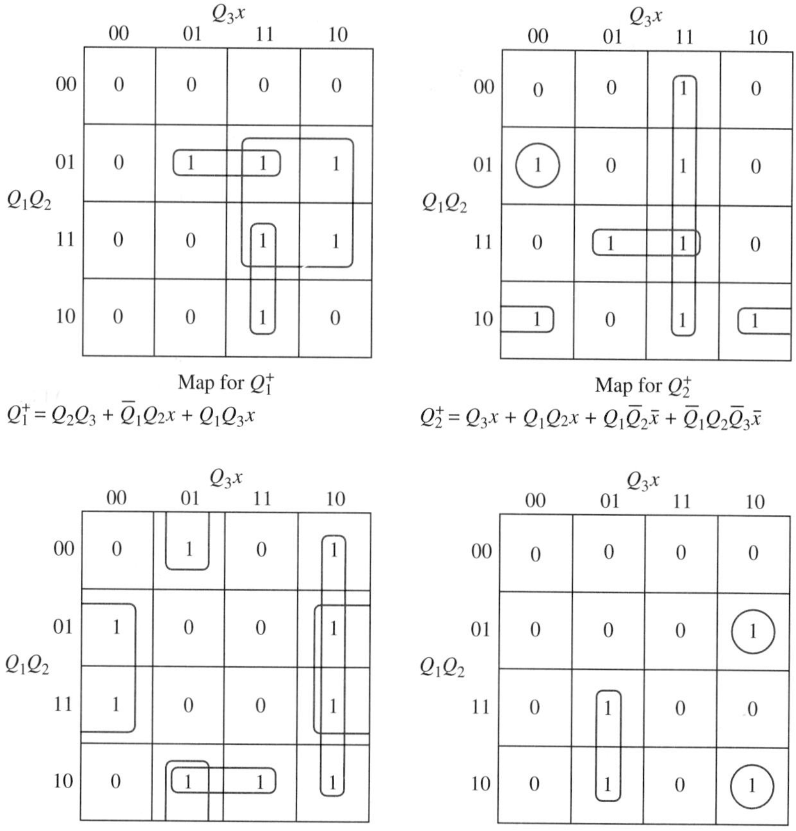

Map for Q_1^+

$Q_1^+ = Q_2Q_3 + \bar{Q}_1Q_2x + Q_1Q_3x$

Map for Q_2^+

$Q_2^+ = Q_3x + Q_1Q_2x + Q_1\bar{Q}_2\bar{x} + \bar{Q}_1Q_2\bar{Q}_3\bar{x}$

Map for Q_3^+

$Q_3^+ = Q_3\bar{x} + Q_2\bar{x} + \bar{Q}_2\bar{Q}_3x + Q_1\bar{Q}_2x$

Map for z

$z = Q_1\bar{Q}_3x + \bar{Q}_1Q_2Q_3\bar{x} + Q_1\bar{Q}_2Q_3\bar{x}$

Figure 7.22 Next-state and output Karnaugh maps for the transition table of Table 7.17*b*.

7.5.1 Some Simple Guidelines for Obtaining State Assignments

Although arbitrary state assignments can be made, simple guidelines have been proposed in an effort to obtain cost-effective state assignments. Only three such guidelines are given here. These three guidelines should suffice to illustrate the general nature of the type of guidelines that have been proposed. However, it is important to understand that the effectiveness of these types of guidelines is subject to some question. In some cases they result in low-cost realizations, but not in other cases. Unfortunately, unless all possible state assignments are tried, the effectiveness of the guidelines is unknown.

Define two states as being *adjacent* if their binary codes differ in exactly one bit. Similarly, two input combinations are considered adjacent if they differ in exactly one bit. The following rules suggest which states should be made adjacent in an attempt to obtain simple Boolean expressions for the next-state and output functions.

> Rule I: Two or more present states that have the same next state for a given input combination should be made adjacent.
>
> Rule II: For any present state and two adjacent input combinations, the two next states should be made adjacent.
>
> Rule III: Two or more present states that produce the same output symbol, i.e., 0 or 1, for a given input combination should be made adjacent. This rule need only be applied to one of the output symbols.

Let us consider the rationale behind the above guidelines. Assume a transition table has n input variables and p state variables. Then, $(n + p)$-variable Karnaugh maps are needed to obtain the minimal expressions for the p next-state functions. For some n-bit input combination and two states that differ in exactly one bit in their p-bit binary codes, the corresponding two $(n + p)$-tuples must also differ in exactly one bit. Each of these $(n + p)$-tuples locates a single cell in an $(n + p)$-variable Karnaugh map. Furthermore, these two cells are physically adjacent due to the structure of Karnaugh maps. If the entries for these two adjacent cells are identical, i.e., both 0 or both 1, in each of the p maps for the next-state functions, then these two cells may be used to form a subcube when writing the expressions from the maps. By extending the above argument, if a power-of-2 number of states are assigned binary codes that correspond to a $2^a \times 2^b$ rectangle on the p next-state maps, then the power-of-2 number of cells result in a subcube when writing the minimal next-state expressions. This is the reasoning behind Rule I. That is, Rule I attempts to provide for subcubes on all the Karnaugh maps for the next-state functions by causing identical entries to appear in adjacent cells.

Now consider Rule II. If two n-bit input combinations differ in exactly one bit, that is, are adjacent, and if they are associated with the same p-bit present state, then they must correspond to two physically adjacent cells in the p next-state Karnaugh maps. Furthermore, if the two next-states themselves are adjacent for the above present state and adjacent inputs, then entries for the corresponding adjacent cells in $p - 1$ of the Karnaugh maps are the same and only in one map do they differ. Hence, subcubes occur in $p - 1$ of the maps. Thus, Rule II also encodes the states so as to provide for the grouping of cells. However, this rule is not as powerful as Rule I since it causes one less subcube to exist in the p next-state maps.

Finally, Rule III does to the output maps what Rule I does to the next-state maps. However, if there are fewer output functions than next-state functions, then the effectiveness of Rule III is diminished.

To illustrate the application of the above rules, again consider the state table shown in Table 7.17*a*. It is noted that state B is the next state for both present states B and G when the input is $x = 0$. Rule I suggests that states B and G should have adjacent codes. Similarly, for the same input, states C and F should be coded as adjacent states since their next states are both state D, and states D and H should be coded as adjacent states since their next states are both state F. Referring to the column for $x = 1$, it is concluded that the pairs of states (A,E), (B,G), and (D,H) should each be coded as adjacent states. To summarize, Rule I proposes the following adjacency conditions should be attempted:

Rule I: $(B,G)(2\times)$, (C,F), $(D,H)(2\times)$, (A,E)

The $(2\times)$ following the pairs (B,G) and (D,H) indicates that the recommended adjacency conditions appear twice and should be given higher priority than those that appear only once. Next consider Rule II. Since $x = 0$ and $x = 1$ are adjacent input combinations, the next-state pair for each present state should be made adjacent according to Rule II. Thus, Rule II recommends the following state adjacencies:

Rule II: (A,B), $(B,C)(3\times)$, (D,E), $(F,G)(2\times)$, (D,H)

Finally, in an attempt to group the 1 entries in the output map, Rule III proposes the following pairs of states should be adjacent:

Rule III: (D,F), (E,G)

Now that the recommended adjacency conditions are established, a state assignment that satisfies these adjacency conditions can be attempted. As an aid for this purpose, a *state-assignment map* is constructed. This map is a Karnaugh map for the state variables in which each cell of the map denotes a combination of the binary digits that can be assigned to a state of the sequential network. A state-assignment map for Table 7.17*a* under the assumption that 3 bits are to be used to code the states is shown in Fig. 7.23. Two cells that are physically adjacent on the map can now be used to define an assignment for two adjacent states recommended by the above rules. Frequently the initial state is coded so as to facilitate the initialization of the network. By having it coded as $00 \cdots 0$, a reset signal can be applied to the asynchronous clear terminals of the flip-flops to force them into their 0-states. Thus, if state A is arbitrarily assigned the code 000, then A is entered in the upper left cell of the state-assignment map. Since state E should be adjacent to state A according to Rule I, in Fig. 7.23 it can be placed in the cell immediately to the right of A, the cell below A, or in the upper right cell.* In this case the cell below A is selected. Continuing in this manner, the cells of the map are

Q_1 \ Q_2Q_3	00	01	11	10
0	A	B	C	H
1	E	G	F	D

Figure 7.23 A state-assignment map for the state table of Table 7.17*a*.

*Recall that the left and right edges of a three-variable Karnaugh map are connected.

filled in using the adjacency conditions recommended by Rules I, II, and III. In the map of Fig. 7.23 all the adjacency conditions are satisfied. However, in general, this is not the case, and an attempt should be made to satisfy as many as possible of the adjacency conditions, with Rule I having the highest priority and Rule III the lowest priority.

Using the state assignment illustrated in Fig. 7.23, the transition table for Table 7.17*a* is constructed as shown in Table 7.17*c*. The corresponding Karnaugh maps for the next-state and output functions are given in Fig. 7.24. One possible set of minimal sum-of-products expressions obtainable from the maps is

$$Q_1^+ = \overline{Q}_1 Q_2 + Q_2\overline{Q}_3 + Q_2\overline{x}$$
$$Q_2^+ = Q_2\overline{x} + Q_1\overline{Q}_3\overline{x} + \overline{Q}_2 Q_3 x + Q_1 Q_2 Q_3$$
$$Q_3^+ = Q_2\overline{Q}_3 + \overline{Q}_2 Q_3 + Q_1\overline{Q}_2 + \overline{Q}_3 x$$
$$z = Q_1 Q_2\overline{x} + Q_1\overline{Q}_2 x$$

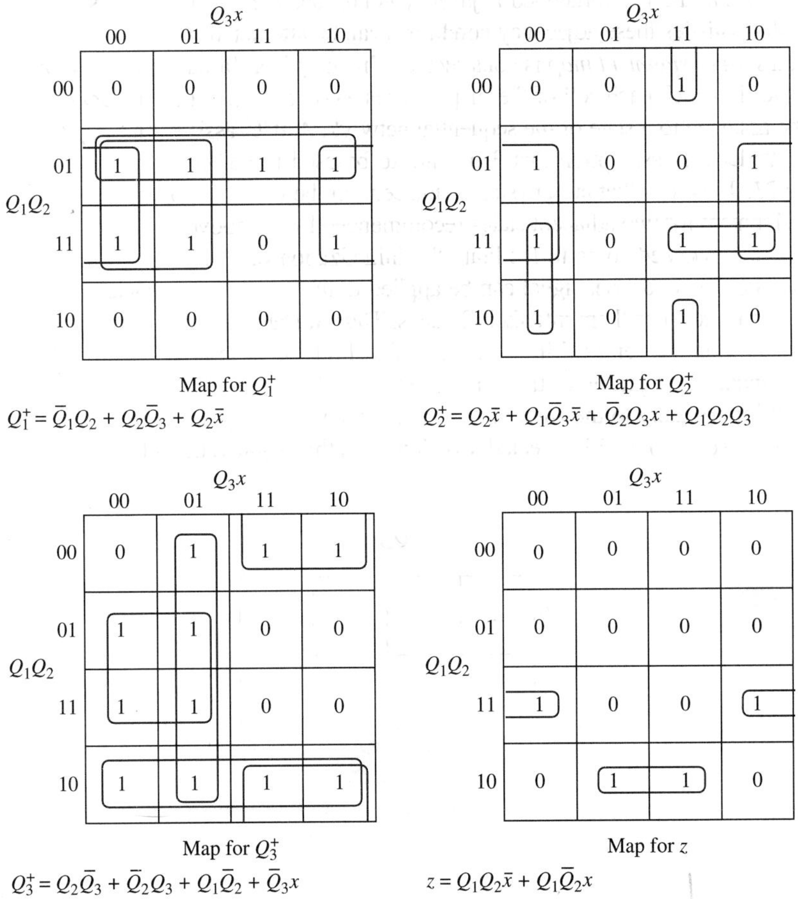

Figure 7.24 Next-state and output Karnaugh maps for the transition table of Table 7.17*c*.

If these expressions are compared against those obtained previously when the states were assigned codes in binary order, then it is seen that simpler expressions resulted.

Again it should be emphasized that the above rules, as well as many others that have been proposed, are only guidelines. Satisfying these rules does not guarantee that a minimal-cost realization results.

7.5.2 Unused States

In the above example, all of the 3-bit combinations were used in the state assignment. With p bits, the number of states s that can be coded is given by

$$2^{p-1} < s \leq 2^p$$

Thus, in general, when coding s states with p bits, some binary combinations are not assigned to any state. In such a case, some of the cells in the Karnaugh maps constructed from a transition table have no entries. The question that then remains is how should the cell entries in these maps be handled. As an answer to this question, two approaches can be proposed.

In the first approach, it is argued that the unused states are not needed for the operation of the sequential network. That is, the network never enters one of these unused states, in which case no next-state needs to be specified. Thus, the corresponding entries in the Karnaugh maps are don't-cares. This is advantageous since don't-care conditions provide greater flexibility when obtaining the minimal expressions for the next-state and output functions.

There is a second argument, however, that can be applied that leads to a different approach in handling the unused states. In this case it is assumed that the network may enter one of the unused states, perhaps, for example, when the network is first turned on, as a result of noise, or as a result of some type of hardware failure. Under such an argument, it may be desirable that the network go to some well-defined state at the end of the clock period, say, for example, the initial state. To do this, the next-state entries for each of the unused states in the transition table should be specified. Consequently, explicit entries, rather than don't-cares, must appear in the Karnaugh maps for the next-state and output functions.*

To illustrate these two approaches of handling unused states, consider the state table shown in Fig. 7.25*a* for a five-state clocked synchronous sequential network. If the first five binary integers are used to code the states and the unused states are allowed to be regarded as don't-cares, then the corresponding transition table becomes that of Fig. 7.25*b*. Three extra rows, with dashed entries, are added to the table to emphasize that no next-state and output entries are being specified for the unused states. Figure 7.25*c* gives the Karnaugh maps for the next-state and

*An example of this philosophy was seen in Sec. 6.9 when designing a self-correcting counter.

output functions as well as the corresponding minimal sum-of-products expressions. Next consider the second approach to handling unused states. Figure 7.25*d* shows the transition table for the state table of Fig. 7.25*a* that results under the assumption that the unused states, if they should occur, are to return the network to initial state *A*. Again the states are assigned codes in binary order. The three unused states now have explicit next-state and output entries. The Karnaugh maps and the minimal-sum equations for the next-state and output functions for the transition table of Fig. 7.25*d* are given in Fig. 7.25*e*. As should be expected, the expressions are not as simple under this second approach due to the absence of don't-cares in the maps.

Present state	Next state		Output (z)	
	Input (x)		Input (x)	
	0	1	0	1
*A	A	B	0	0
B	C	D	1	0
C	A	D	0	1
D	E	A	1	1
E	C	B	0	0

(*a*)

Present state ($Q_1Q_2Q_3$)	Next state ($Q_1^+Q_2^+Q_3^+$)		Output (z)	
	Input (x)		Input (x)	
	0	1	0	1
$A \rightarrow$ 000	000	001	0	0
$B \rightarrow$ 001	010	011	1	0
$C \rightarrow$ 010	000	011	0	1
$D \rightarrow$ 011	100	000	1	1
$E \rightarrow$ 100	010	001	0	0
101	–	–	–	–
110	–	–	–	–
111	–	–	–	–

(*b*)

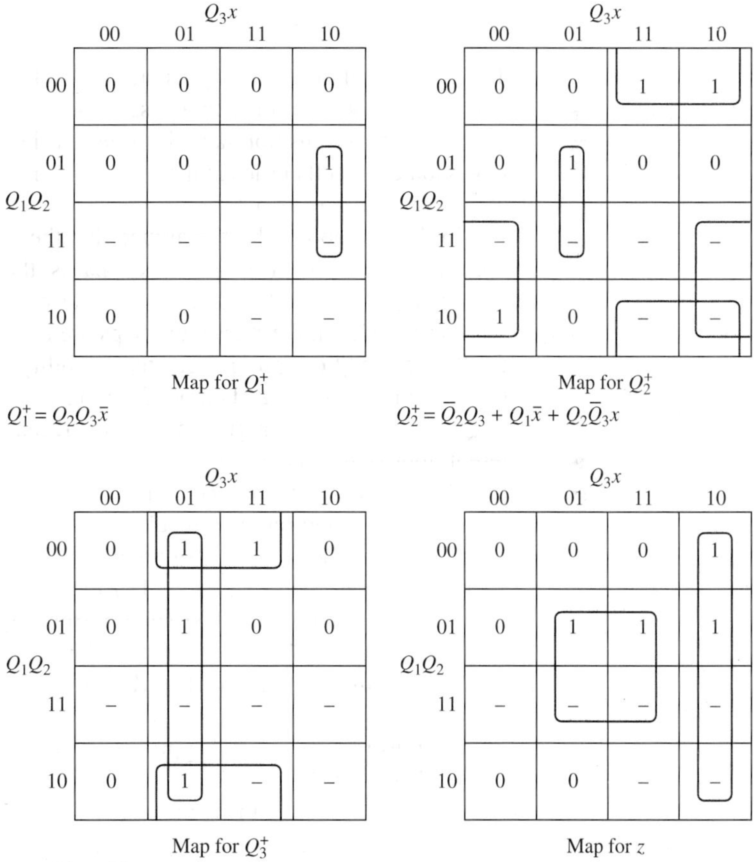

$Q_1^+ = Q_2Q_3\bar{x}$

$Q_2^+ = \bar{Q}_2Q_3 + Q_1\bar{x} + Q_2\bar{Q}_3x$

$Q_3^+ = \bar{Q}_3x + \bar{Q}_2x$

$z = Q_2x + Q_3\bar{x}$

(*c*)

(*Cont.*)

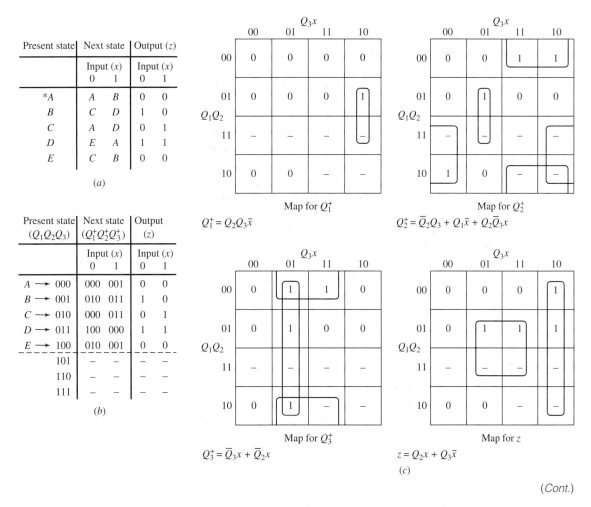

Figure 7.25 Two approaches to handling unused states. (*a*) State table. (*b*) Transition table with don't-cares for unused states. (*c*) Next-state maps, output map, and expressions for table of Fig. 7.25*b*.

Present state ($Q_1Q_2Q_3$)	Next state ($Q_1^+Q_2^+Q_3^+$) Input (x) 0	1	Output (z) Input (x) 0	1
$A \rightarrow$ 000	000	001	0	0
$B \rightarrow$ 001	010	011	1	0
$C \rightarrow$ 010	000	011	0	1
$D \rightarrow$ 011	100	000	1	1
$E \rightarrow$ 100	010	001	0	0
101	000	000	0	0
110	000	000	0	0
111	000	000	0	0

(d)

Map for Q_1^+

Q_1Q_2 \ Q_3x	00	01	11	10
00	0	0	0	0
01	0	0	0	1
11	0	0	0	0
10	0	0	0	0

$Q_1^+ = \overline{Q}_1Q_2Q_3\overline{x}$

Map for Q_2^+

Q_1Q_2 \ Q_3x	00	01	11	10
00	0	0	1	1
01	0	1	0	0
11	0	0	0	0
10	1	0	0	0

$Q_2^+ = \overline{Q}_1\overline{Q}_2Q_3 + \overline{Q}_1Q_2\overline{Q}_3x + Q_1\overline{Q}_2\overline{Q}_3\overline{x}$

Map for Q_3^+

Q_1Q_2 \ Q_3x	00	01	11	10
00	0	1	1	0
01	0	1	0	0
11	0	0	0	0
10	0	1	0	0

$Q_3^+ = \overline{Q}_1\overline{Q}_2x + \overline{Q}_1\overline{Q}_3x + \overline{Q}_2\overline{Q}_3x$

Map for z

Q_1Q_2 \ Q_3x	00	01	11	10
00	0	0	0	1
01	0	1	1	1
11	0	0	0	0
10	0	0	0	0

$z = \overline{Q}_1Q_2x + \overline{Q}_1Q_3\overline{x}$

(e)

Figure 7.25 (*Cont.*) (*d*) Transition table when unused states cause the network to go to state *A*. (*e*) Next-state maps, output map, and expressions for table of Fig. 7.25*d*.

7.6 COMPLETING THE DESIGN OF CLOCKED SYNCHRONOUS SEQUENTIAL NETWORKS

With the determination of a state assignment, a set of state variables is introduced. These variables are the outputs from the flip-flops that comprise the memory portion of the sequential network. Thus, the number of flip-flops in the realization is established. However, one final decision has still to be made before the design of a clocked synchronous sequential network is completed. What type of clocked flip-flops should be used for the memory, i.e., *SR*, *JK*, *D*, or *T?* Depending upon this choice, appropriate excitation signals must be generated by the combinational logic that precedes the input terminals of the flip-flops.

A tabulation of the excitation and output signals in a clocked synchronous sequential network is given by the excitation table. An excitation table is readily constructed from a transition table once the flip-flop type is selected and provides functional descriptions of the combinational logic sections of the sequential network. As was seen in Sec. 7.2, the output sections of both the transition and excitation tables are identical since the output logic portion of the clocked synchronous sequential network is not dependent upon the flip-flop type used in the realization. However, the next-state section of the transition table corresponds to the values of the next-state variables; while the excitation section in the excitation table corresponds to the signal values that must be applied to the flip-flop inputs to achieve the next-state values. How this is done with clocked *JK*, *D*, *T*, and *SR* flip-flops was previously discussed in Chapter 6 and tabulated in Tables 6.5, 6.6, 6.8, and 6.10, respectively. These four application tables for clocked flip-flops are repeated in Table 7.18 for ease of reference.

Assume that clocked *D* flip-flops are to be used in a sequential network realization. For illustrative purposes, again consider the state table of Fig. 7.25*a* and its associated transition table of Fig. 7.25*b*. The corresponding excitation table given in Table 7.19 can now be developed. First of all, as previously mentioned, the output sections of both tables are identical. To see how the entries in the excitation section are obtained, consider the first row, first column of the next-state section of the transition table. In this case, the present state $Q_1Q_2Q_3 = 000$ and input $x = 0$ is to produce the next state $Q_1^+Q_2^+Q_3^+ = 000$. Thus, each of the *D* flip-flops must remain in its 0-state. Referring to the first row of Table 7.18*a*, for $Q_i = 0$ and $Q_i^+ = 0$ it is seen that $D_i = 0$. That is, for a clocked *D* flip-flop to remain in its 0-state, a logic-0 must be applied to its input terminal at the time when the clock signal is to cause the state change. Thus, the entry in the first row, first column in the excitation section of the

Table 7.18 Application tables. (*a*) *D* flip-flop. (*b*) *JK* flip-flop. (*c*) *T* flip-flop. (*d*) *SR* flip-flop

Q	Q^+	D
0	0	0
0	1	1
1	0	0
1	1	1

(*a*)

Q	Q^+	J	K
0	0	0	–
0	1	1	–
1	0	–	1
1	1	–	0

(*b*)

Q	Q^+	T
0	0	0
0	1	1
1	0	1
1	1	0

(*c*)

Q	Q^+	S	R
0	0	0	–
0	1	1	0
1	0	0	1
1	1	–	0

(*d*)

Table 7.19 Excitation table involving D flip-flops corresponding to the transition table of Fig. 7.25b

Present state ($Q_1Q_2Q_3$)	Excitation ($D_1D_2D_3$)		Output (z)	
	Input (x)		Input (x)	
	0	1	0	1
000	000	001	0	0
001	010	011	1	0
010	000	011	0	1
011	100	000	1	1
100	010	001	0	0

excitation table of Table 7.19 is $D_1D_2D_3 = 000$. In a similar manner, for the first row, second column of the next-state section of the transition table in Fig. 7.25b, it is seen for $Q_1Q_2Q_3 = 000$ and $x = 1$, that $Q_1^+Q_2^+Q_3^+ = 001$. In this case, the first two D flip-flops are to remain in their 0-states while the third must change from its 0-state to its 1-state. As indicated by Table 7.18a, this is achieved by having $D_1D_2D_3 = 001$, which is shown as the first-row, second-column entry of the excitation section of Table 7.19. The remaining entries in the excitation section of Table 7.19 are determined in exactly the same manner. Actually, however, as readily seen by Table 7.18a, for clocked D flip-flops $D_i = Q_i^+$. This implies the excitation and transition tables are the same except for the labeling of the excitation and next-state variables. The reader can check that this is indeed the case by comparing Table 7.19 with Fig. 7.25b.

Inasmuch as the transition table is a truth table for the next-state and output functions, the excitation table is a truth table for the excitation and output functions, i.e., the variables associated with the input terminals of the flip-flops as well as the variables associated with the outputs of the network. Thus, the excitation table is used to obtain the excitation and output expressions for the clocked synchronous sequential network. For example, to obtain minimal expressions, Karnaugh maps can be constructed from the excitation table the same way as they were constructed from the transition table. When using D flip-flops, the next-state Karnaugh maps and the D input excitation maps are identical since their transition and excitation tables are the same.

Let us now complete the design, using D flip-flops, of the clocked synchronous sequential network whose state table is given in Fig. 7.25a. Under the assumption that the unused states are to be regarded as don't-cares, the Karnaugh maps of Fig. 7.25c correspond to the excitation and output maps for the excitation table of Table 7.19 where $D_i = Q_i^+$. Thus,

$$D_1 = Q_2Q_3\bar{x} \tag{7.24}$$

$$D_2 = \bar{Q}_2Q_3 + Q_1\bar{x} + Q_2\bar{Q}_3x \tag{7.25}$$

$$D_3 = \bar{Q}_3x + \bar{Q}_2x \tag{7.26}$$

$$z = Q_2x + Q_3\bar{x} \tag{7.27}$$

From these expressions, the logic diagram of Fig. 7.26 is drawn.

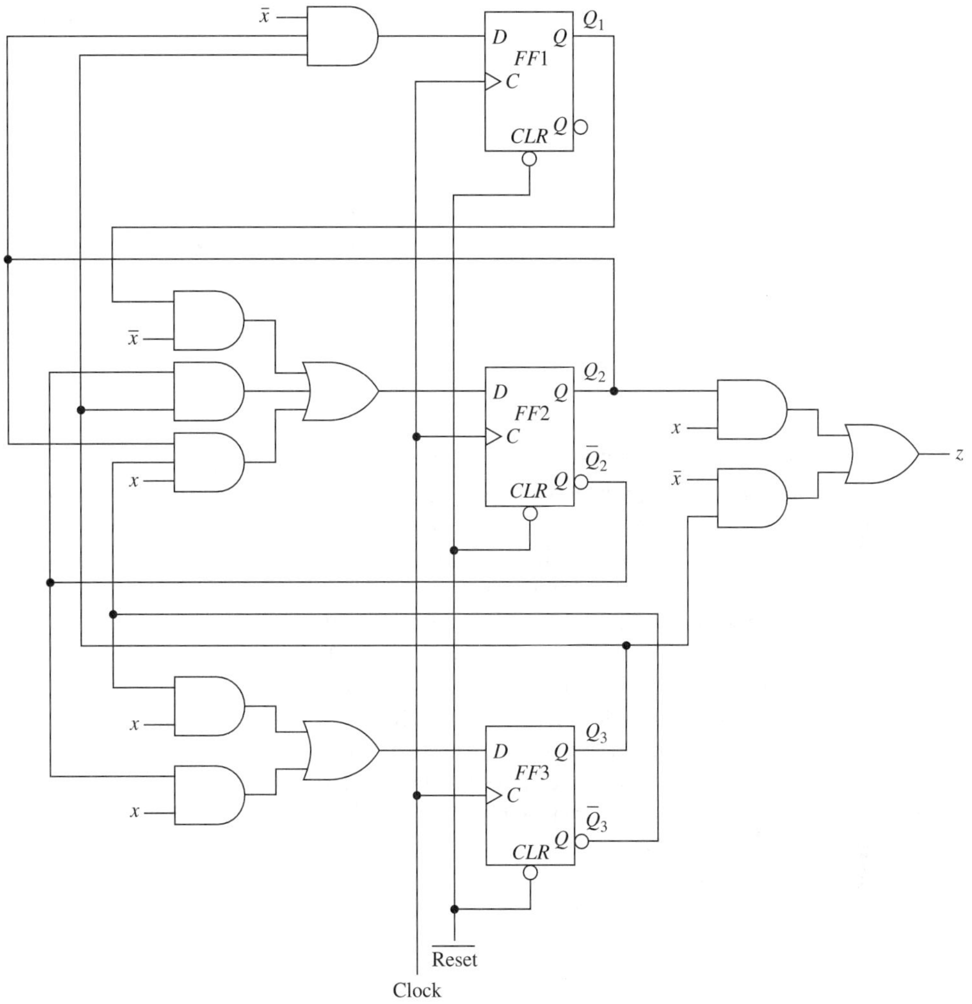

Figure 7.26 Logic diagram for the excitation table of Table 7.19.

In the logic diagram of Fig. 7.26, provision is also made for the initial state. For this particular network, the initial state is state *A*, which is coded as 000. Thus, a reset signal, $\overline{\text{Reset}}$, is applied to the asynchronous clear inputs of the flip-flops to force them into their 0-states whenever $\overline{\text{Reset}} = 0$. This is a typical approach of handling the initialization of synchronous sequential networks.

When *JK*, *SR*, or *T* flip-flops are used in a realization, the excitation and transition tables are different. Consider a realization of the table in Fig. 7.25*b* under the assumption that *JK* flip-flops are to be used and that the unused states are to be regarded as don't-cares. The excitation table is given in Table 7.20. The output section of the excitation table is the same as that of the transition table, since this section of the table is not dependent on the type of flip-flops in the realization. Each entry in the excitation section corresponds to the excitations for the six input terminals of the *JK* flip-flops, J_1, K_1, J_2, K_2, J_3, and K_3. To determine these entries, use is made of Table 7.18*b*, which specifies how the various transitions in the state of a clocked *JK* flip-flop are achieved. For example, for the first row, first column of the next-state section of Fig. 7.25*b*, $Q_1Q_2Q_3 = 000$ and $Q_1^+Q_2^+Q_3^+ = 000$. In this case, all the flip-flops must remain in their 0-states. According to Table 7.18*b*, this is achieved by applying a 0 to the *J* terminal and any logic value, i.e., a don't-care, to the *K* terminal. Thus, the first-row, first-column entry in the excitation section of Table 7.20 is $J_1K_1,J_2K_2,J_3K_3 = 0\text{–},0\text{–},0\text{–}$. Similarly, according to the first row, second column of the table in Fig. 7.25*b*, $Q_1Q_2Q_3 = 000$ and $Q_1^+Q_2^+Q_3^+ = 001$. As before, the flip-flops for Q_1 and Q_2 must remain in their 0-states, which is achieved by applying a 0 to their *J* terminals and selecting any logic value for their *K* terminals. The flip-flop for Q_3, however, must change from its 0-state to its 1-state. According to Table 7.18*b*, this is achieved by applying a 1 to the J_3 terminal and any logic value to the K_3 terminal. Thus, the entry in the first row, second column of the excitation section of Table 7.20 is $J_1K_1,J_2K_2,J_3K_3 = 0\text{–},0\text{–},1\text{–}$. The reader can readily check the remaining entries of Table 7.20.

Using Table 7.20, the Karnaugh maps for the excitations of the six flip-flop inputs and the network output shown in Fig. 7.27 are constructed. The excitations for the unused states are regarded as don't-cares on the maps. If explicit next states are desired for the unused states, then appropriate excitation values must be determined for the unused states. For example, the transition table of Fig. 7.25*d* could be used instead of that of Fig. 7.25*b* to form an excitation table since it was developed under the assumption that state *A* is to be the next state for each of the unused states. In this case, six of the don't-care entries in each map would be replaced by the necessary excitation signals to achieve the desired next state. However, those don't-cares that are a result of the properties of the *JK* flip-flop as indicated in Table 7.18*b* would still appear

Table 7.20 Excitation table involving *JK* flip-flops corresponding to the transition table of Fig. 7.25*b*

Present state ($Q_1Q_2Q_3$)	Excitation (J_1K_1,J_2K_2,J_3K_3)		Output (z)	
	Input (x)		Input (x)	
	0	1	0	1
000	0–, 0–, 0–	0–, 0–, 1–	0	0
001	0–, 1–, –1	0–, 1–, –0	1	0
010	0–, –1, 0–	0–, –0, 1–	0	1
011	1–, –1, –1	0–, –1, –1	1	1
100	–1, 1–, 0–	–1, 0–, 1–	0	0

Q_1Q_2 \ Q_3x	00	01	11	10
00	0	0	0	0
01	0	0	0	1
11	–	–	–	–
10	–	–	–	–

Map for J_1

$J_1 = Q_2Q_3\bar{x}$

Q_1Q_2 \ Q_3x	00	01	11	10
00	–	–	–	–
01	–	–	–	–
11	–	–	–	–
10	1	1	–	–

Map for K_1

$K_1 = 1$

Q_1Q_2 \ Q_3x	00	01	11	10
00	0	0	1	1
01	–	–	–	–
11	–	–	–	–
10	1	0	–	–

Map for J_2

$J_2 = Q_3 + Q_1\bar{x}$

Q_1Q_2 \ Q_3x	00	01	11	10
00	–	–	–	–
01	1	0	1	1
11	–	–	–	–
10	–	–	–	–

Map for K_2

$K_2 = Q_3 + \bar{x}$

Q_1Q_2 \ Q_3x	00	01	11	10
00	0	1	–	–
01	0	1	–	–
11	–	–	–	–
10	0	1	–	–

Map for J_3

$J_3 = x$

Q_1Q_2 \ Q_3x	00	01	11	10
00	–	–	0	1
01	–	–	1	1
11	–	–	–	–
10	–	–	–	–

Map for K_3

$K_3 = Q_2 + \bar{x}$

Q_1Q_2 \ Q_3x	00	01	11	10
00	0	0	0	1
01	0	1	1	1
11	–	–	–	–
10	0	0	–	–

Map for z

$z = Q_2x + Q_3\bar{x}$

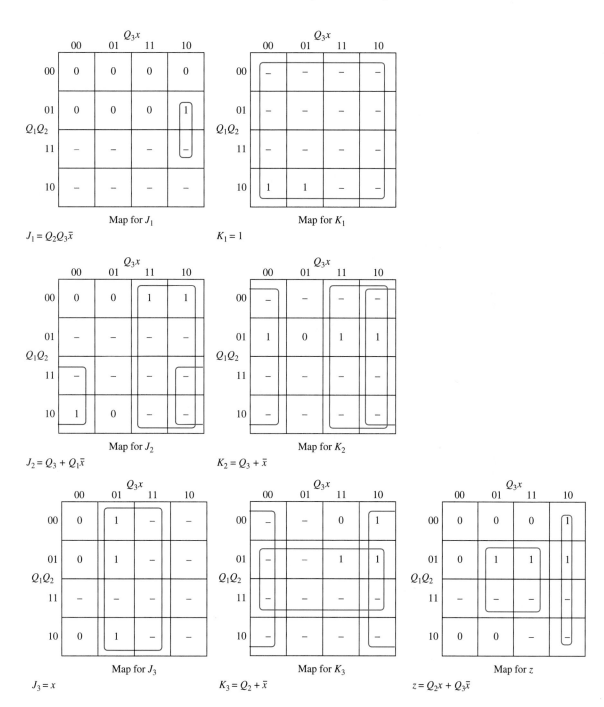

Figure 7.27 Excitation and output maps for the excitation table of Table 7.20.

in the maps. From Fig. 7.27, the excitation and output expressions for a realization are

$$J_1 = Q_2Q_3\bar{x}$$
$$K_1 = 1$$
$$J_2 = Q_3 + Q_1\bar{x}$$
$$K_2 = Q_3 + \bar{x}$$
$$J_3 = x$$
$$K_3 = Q_2 + \bar{x}$$
$$z = Q_2x + Q_3\bar{x}$$

The corresponding logic diagram is shown in Fig. 7.28.

The two realizations just obtained were for Mealy sequential networks. Realizations of Moore sequential networks are obtained by precisely the same proce-

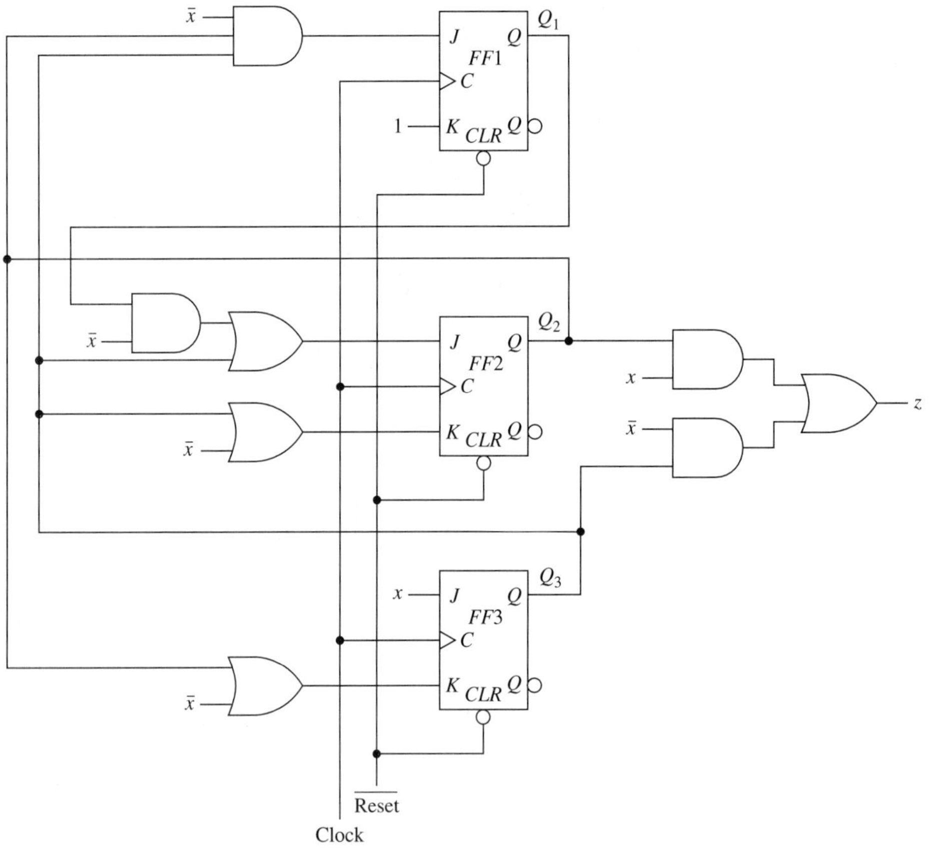

Figure 7.28 Logic diagram for the excitation table of Table 7.20.

Table 7.21 Transition table for the Moore serial binary adder

Present state (Q_1Q_2)	Next state ($Q_1^+Q_2^+$)				Output (z)
	Inputs (xy)				
	00	01	10	11	
$A \rightarrow 00$	00	01	01	11	0
$B \rightarrow 11$	01	11	11	10	0
$C \rightarrow 01$	00	01	01	11	1
$D \rightarrow 10$	01	11	11	10	1

dure. However, unlike those of Mealy sequential networks, the output expressions are only a function of the state variables.

As an illustration of a Moore sequential network realization, consider the state table for the serial binary adder given in Table 7.8. Since there are four states, two binary digits are needed to code the states. The guidelines of Sec. 7.5 suggest the following adjacency conditions should be satisfied:

Rule I: $(A,C)(4\times)$, $(B,D)(4\times)$

Rule II: $(A,C)(4\times)$, $(B,C)(8\times)$, $(B,D)(4\times)$

Rule III: (C,D)

A state assignment that satisfies most of these adjacency conditions is $A = 00$, $B = 11$, $C = 01$, and $D = 10$. This state assignment leads to the transition table given in Table 7.21. This table also serves as the excitation table when D flip-flops are used in a realization. The corresponding Karnaugh maps for the excitation and output functions and their minimal-sum expressions are shown in Fig. 7.29. It should be noted that only a two-variable map is needed for the output expression since the output of the network

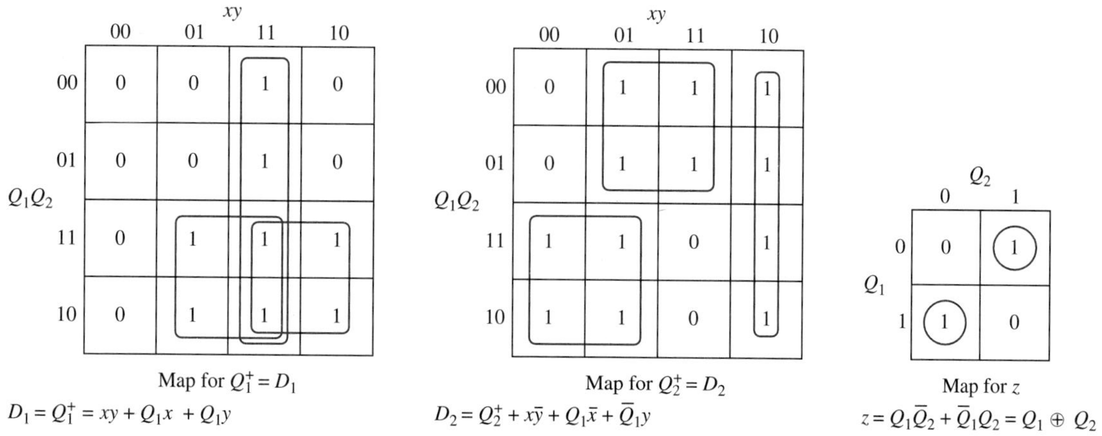

Figure 7.29 Excitation and output maps for the Moore serial binary adder.

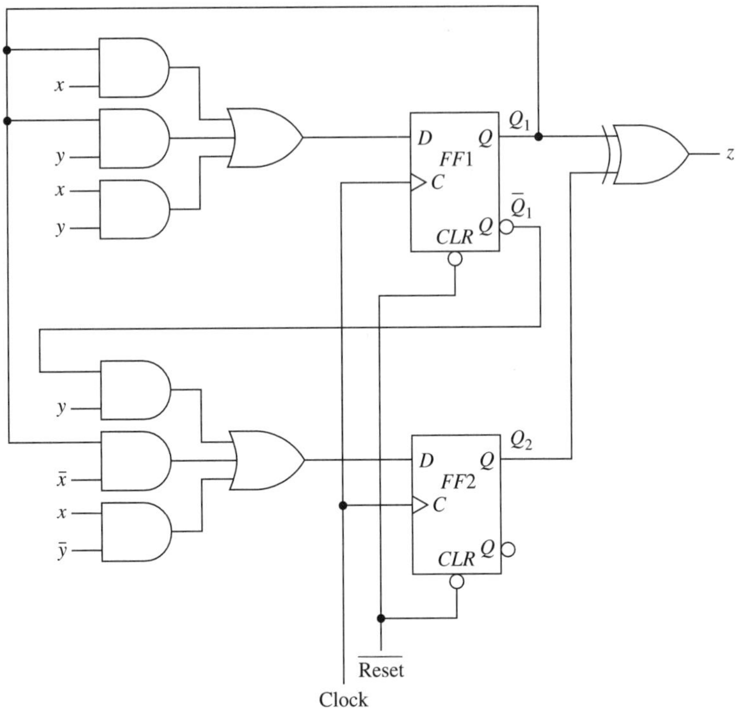

Figure 7.30 Logic diagram for the Moore serial binary adder.

is only a function of Q_1 and Q_2. These equations suggest the logic diagram shown in Fig. 7.30.

7.6.1 Realizations Using Programmable Logic Devices

In the above discussion, it was assumed that individual gates and flip-flops are to be used in a synchronous sequential network realization. An alternate approach to a realization involves the use of programmable logic devices (PLDs) in conjunction with a set of flip-flops. The PLDs provide for the combinational logic needed to generate the outputs and excitations for the synchronous sequential network while the flip-flops form a register to store the state. If clocked D flip-flops are employed, then the basic structure of such a realization for a Mealy sequential network is shown in Fig. 7.31. This figure is simply a rearrangement of the general model of the Mealy sequential network shown in Fig. 7.2 in which a single combinational logic block appears. However, as an alternative, separate PLDs could be employed for the two combinational logic portions of the network. In a similar manner, Moore sequential networks can be realized with PLDs and flip-flops. Flip-flop types other than the D type can also be used for the memory portion of the sequential network. Actually, however, many commercial PLDs are available in which the D flip-flops are already included.

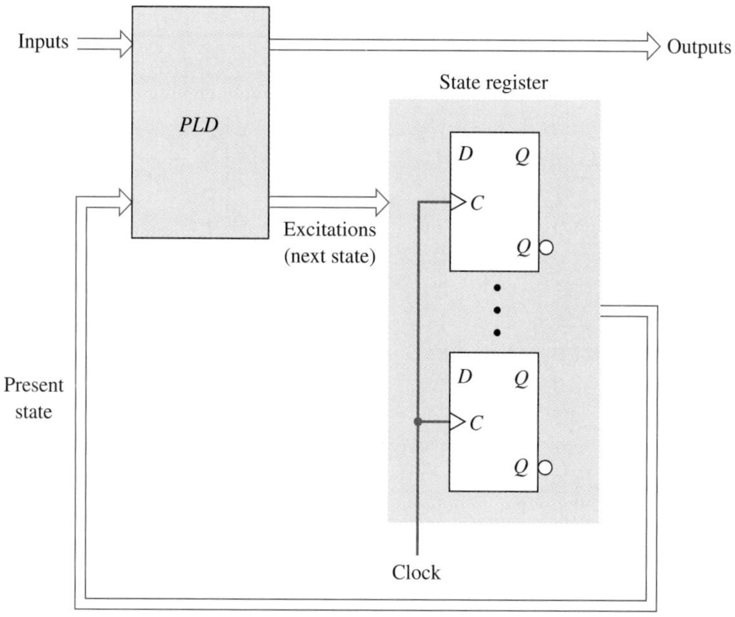

Figure 7.31 General structure of a clocked sequential network realization using a PLD and clocked *D* flip-flops.

For the purpose of the following discussion, it is assumed that the PLDs are purely combinational so that the flip-flops are external to the PLDs. Any of the PLDs discussed in Chapter 5 can be used in the realization of a sequential network; however, only programmable read-only memories (PROMs) and programmable logic arrays (PLAs) are discussed at this time.

As was seen in Sec. 5.8, a PROM consists of a decoder that realizes all the minterms of a fixed number of variables and a programmable or-array that combines the necessary minterms for each of the functions being realized by the PROM. Since all minterms are produced in a PROM, it is a row-by-row realization of the truth table involving several functions. This being the case, no effort needs to be expended to optimize the logic in the combinational network being described by the truth table. Thus, minimal attention needs to be given to the state assignment other than to use the minimal number of flip-flops since one assignment is as good as any other. Furthermore, in a PROM realization of a synchronous sequential network, *D* flip-flops are more practical than *JK* flip-flops since each flip-flop only requires the realization of a single excitation function while two are required for each *JK* flip-flop.

Again consider the state table of Fig. 7.25*a* and the corresponding transition table of Fig. 7.25*b* involving a straight binary assignment and in which the unused states are regarded as don't-cares. The transition table is a truth table for the next-state and output functions, Q_1^+, Q_2^+, Q_3^+, and z, once the additional rows corresponding to the unused states are added as was done in Fig. 7.25*b*. Recalling that for

Table 7.22 Truth table corresponding to the transition table of Fig. 7.25*b*

x	Q_1	Q_2	Q_3	D_1	D_2	D_3	z
0	0	0	0	0	0	0	0
0	0	0	1	0	1	0	1
0	0	1	0	0	0	0	0
0	0	1	1	1	0	0	1
0	1	0	0	0	1	0	0
0	1	0	1	–	–	–	–
0	1	1	0	–	–	–	–
0	1	1	1	–	–	–	–
1	0	0	0	0	0	1	0
1	0	0	1	0	1	1	0
1	0	1	0	0	1	1	1
1	0	1	1	0	0	0	1
1	1	0	0	0	0	1	0
1	1	0	1	–	–	–	–
1	1	1	0	–	–	–	–
1	1	1	1	–	–	–	–

clocked D flip-flops $D^i = Q_i^+$, Table 7.22 is simply the excitation table of Fig. 7.25*b* arranged in the more conventional format of listing all the combinations of the inputs to the PROM, i.e., x, Q_1, Q_2, and Q_3, on the left side of the table and the outputs, i.e., D_1, D_2, D_3, and z, on the right side. Thus, it is seen that a PROM having 4 inputs and 4 outputs is required for the realization of the combinational logic of the sequential network.

Another form of PLD realization of a synchronous sequential network involves PLAs and flip-flops. Again the general structure of Fig. 7.31 applies when clocked D flip-flops are used for the storage of the state. However, the and-array in a PLA

Table 7.23 PLA table for Eqs. (7.24) to (7.27)

Product term	Inputs				Outputs			
	Q_1	Q_2	Q_3	x	D_1	D_2	D_3	z
$Q_2Q_3\overline{x}$	–	1	1	0	1	–	–	–
$\overline{Q}_2Q_3$	–	0	1	–	–	1	–	–
$Q_1\overline{x}$	1	–	–	0	–	1	–	–
$Q_2\overline{Q}_3x$	–	1	0	1	–	1	–	–
$\overline{Q}_3x$	–	–	0	1	–	–	1	–
$\overline{Q}_2x$	–	0	–	1	–	–	1	–
Q_2x	–	1	–	1	–	–	–	1
$Q_3\overline{x}$	–	–	1	0	–	–	–	1

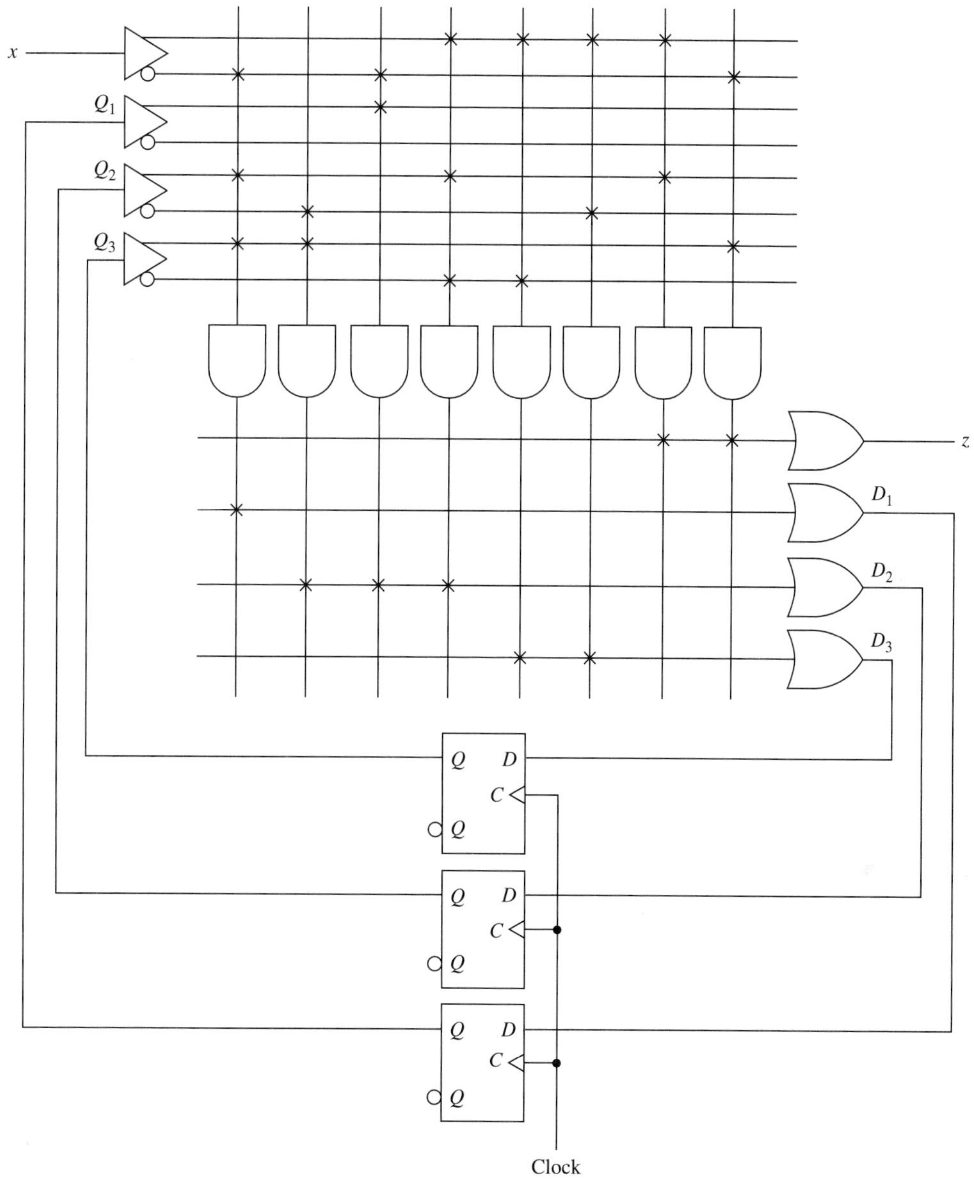

Figure 7.32 A clocked synchronous sequential network realization using a PLA and clocked D flip-flops.

must be programmed to generate all the distinct product terms needed to describe the excitation and output functions. Since different state assignments can result in different algebraic descriptions of the excitation and output functions, selection of a state assignment can affect the size of the PLA that is required for the sequential network.

The minimal-sum excitation expressions for D flip-flops and the output expression for Fig. 7.25*b* were previously written as Eqs. (7.24) to (7.27). These equations can be used to form a PLA table, as was discussed in Sec. 5.9. This table is shown in Table 7.23. In this case, a PLA capable of handling 4 inputs, 8 product terms, and 4 outputs is required for the combinational logic. The realization shown in Fig. 7.32 uses such a PLA along with clocked D flip-flops.

Before closing this discussion on the realizations of synchronous sequential networks, one final point should be mentioned. The minimal expressions obtained in this section were a result of simplifying each of the excitation and output expressions individually. As was pointed out in Chapter 4, when dealing with a set of Boolean expressions, greater simplicity is achieved by sharing terms in the minimal expressions. That was the multiple-output simplification problem discussed in Secs. 4.12 and 4.13. Such an approach is also applicable when dealing with the realizations of synchronous sequential networks.

CHAPTER 7 PROBLEMS

7.1 For the clocked synchronous sequential network shown in Fig. P7.1 construct the excitation table, transition table, state table, and state diagram.

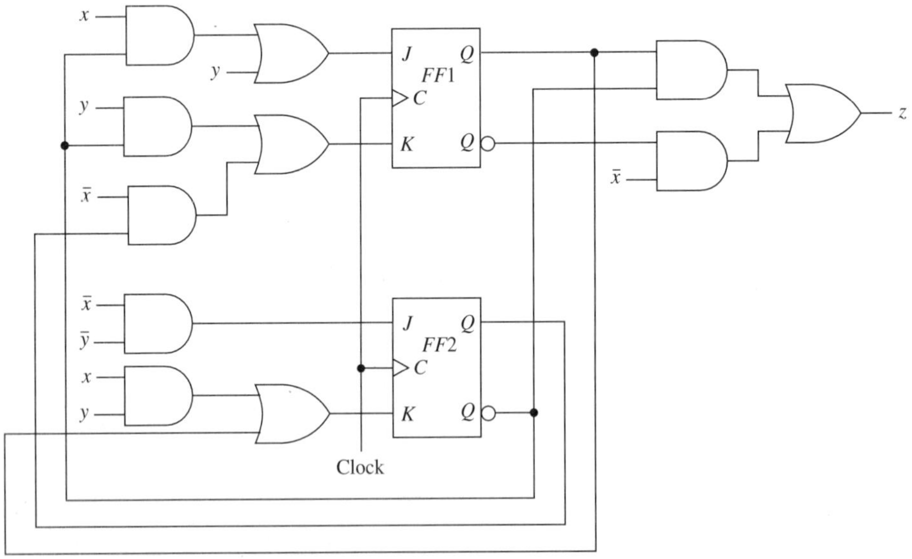

Figure P7.1

7.2 For the clocked synchronous sequential network shown in Fig. P7.2 construct the excitation table, transition table, state table, and state diagram.

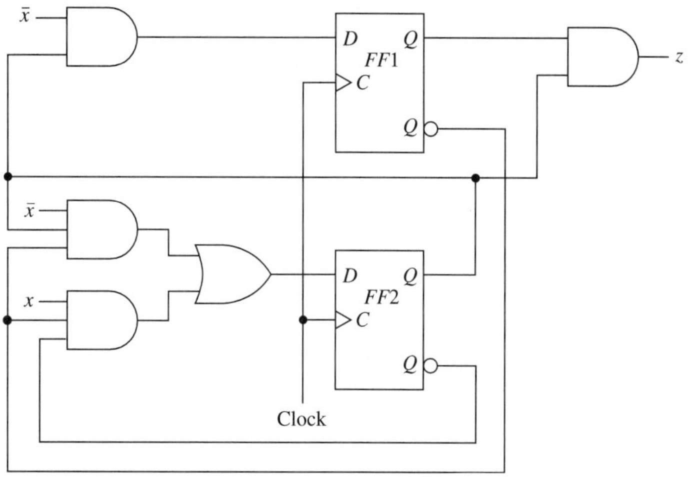

Figure P7.2

7.3 For the clocked synchronous sequential network shown in Fig. P7.3 construct the excitation table, transition table, state table, and state diagram.

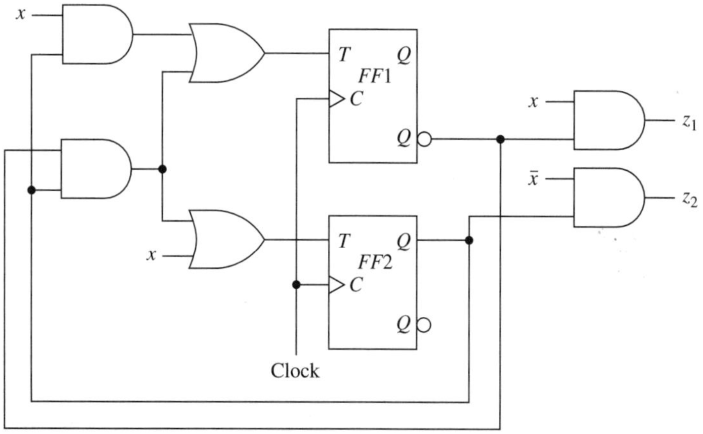

Figure P7.3

7.4 For the clocked synchronous sequential network shown in Fig. P7.4 construct the excitation table, transition table, state table, and state diagram.

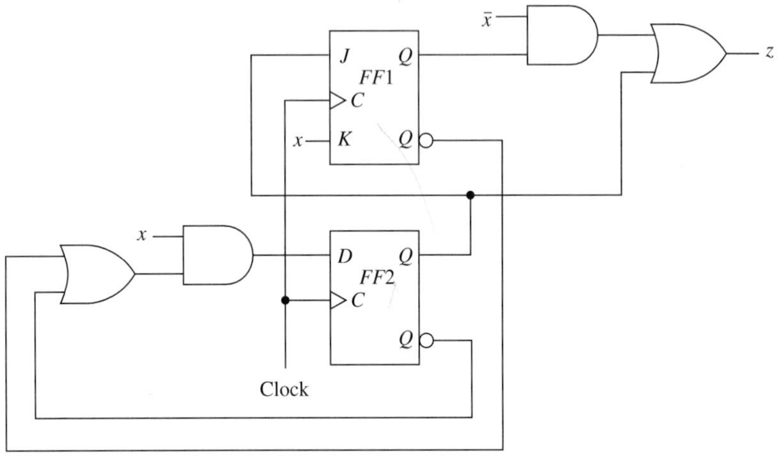

Figure P7.4

7.5 Obtain a minimal state table for a clocked synchronous sequential network having a single input line x, in which the symbols 0 and 1 are applied, and a single output line z. An output of 1 is to be produced coincident with each third multiple of the input symbol 1. At all other times the network is to produce 0 outputs. An example of input/output sequences that satisfy the conditions of the network specifications is

$$x = 0\,1\,1\,0\,1\,0\,1\,1\,1\,1\,0\,0\,0\,1\,1\,1\,0$$
$$z = 0\,0\,0\,0\,1\,0\,0\,0\,1\,0\,0\,0\,0\,0\,1\,0\,0$$

7.6 Obtain a minimal state table for a clocked synchronous sequential network having a single input line x, in which the symbols 0 and 1 are applied, and a single output line z. An output of 1 is to be produced coincident with the first 0 input symbol if it is preceded by exactly one or three 1 input symbols. At all other times the network is to produce 0 outputs. An example of input/output sequences that satisfy the conditions of the network specifications is

$$x = 0\,1\,0\,0\,0\,1\,1\,0\,1\,1\,1\,0\,1\,0\,1\,1\,1\,1\,0\,0$$
$$z = 0\,0\,1\,0\,0\,0\,0\,0\,0\,0\,0\,1\,0\,1\,0\,0\,0\,0\,0\,0$$

7.7 Obtain a minimal state table for a clocked synchronous sequential network having a single input line x, in which the symbols 0 and 1 are applied, and a single output line z. An output of 1 is to be produced for each consecutive 1 input if the group of consecutive 1 inputs is preceded by exactly one 0 input. At all other times the network is to produce 0 outputs. An example of input/output sequences that satisfy the conditions of the network specifications is

$$x = 1\,1\,0\,1\,1\,0\,0\,0\,1\,1\,1\,1\,0\,1\,0\,1\,1\,1$$
$$z = 0\,0\,0\,1\,1\,0\,0\,0\,0\,0\,0\,0\,0\,1\,0\,1\,1\,1$$

7.8 Obtain a minimal state table for a clocked synchronous sequential network having a single input line x, in which the symbols 0 and 1 are applied, and a single output line z. The network is to analyze each sequence of five inputs and produce a 1 output at the time of the fifth input if the sequence is not a valid code group in the 2-out-of-5 code. (See Table 2.8 for the 2-out-of-5 code.) At all other times the network is to produce 0 outputs. An example of input/output sequences that satisfy the conditions of the network specifications is

$$x = 0\,1\,1\,0\,0\,0\,1\,0\,1\,1\,1\,0\,0\,0\,1$$
$$z = 0\,0\,0\,0\,0\,0\,0\,0\,0\,1\,0\,0\,0\,0\,0$$

7.9 Obtain a minimal state table for a clocked synchronous sequential network having a single input line x, in which the binary symbols 0 and 1 are applied, and a single output line z. The network is to analyze each sequence of four binary digits and produce the corresponding 2's-complement of the 4-bit sequence. Assume each 4-bit sequence is occurring with the least significant bit first. An example of input/output sequences that satisfy the conditions of the network specifications is

$$x = 0\,1\,0\,1\,0\,0\,0\,1\,1\,1\,0\,0\,0\,1\,0\,0$$
$$z = 0\,1\,1\,0\,0\,0\,0\,1\,1\,0\,1\,1\,0\,1\,1\,1$$

7.10 In Problem 3.34 an algorithm was given for converting n-bit Gray code groups into their equivalent n-bit binary numbers. (a) Obtain a minimal state table for a clocked synchronous sequential network that regards each 5-bit sequence as a Gray code group, most significant bit first, and produces the corresponding binary number representation. (b) Repeat (a) for converting a 5-bit binary number into its equivalent Gray code group.

7.11 In Sec. 6.7 the serial-in, parallel-out unidirectional shift register was discussed. Obtain a minimal state table describing the behavior of such a register assuming it consists of only the first three stages of Fig. 6.27 and the flip-flops are initially in their 0-states.

7.12 Repeat the final example in Sec. 7.3 by assuming a Mealy network model is to be developed.

7.13 Consider a clocked synchronous sequential network having a single input line x, in which the symbols 0 and 1 are applied, and a single output line z. The network is to analyze the input sequence and determine if all consecutive sequences of 1's that follow a consecutive sequence of 0's have the same parity as that of the preceding consecutive sequence of 0's.

That is, if a consecutive sequence of 0's has an even number of 0's, then the following consecutive sequence of 1's should have an even number of 1's. Similarly, if a consecutive sequence of 0's has an odd number of 0's, then the following consecutive sequence of 1's should have an odd number of 1's. Obtain a minimal state table for a clocked synchronous sequential network that produces an output of 1, coincident with the first 0 input terminating the sequence of 1's, whenever a discrepancy to the above pattern is detected. Outputs of 0 are to be produced at all other times. To handle the initial inputs, use the following rules: (1) If the first input is a 0, then the corresponding output should also be 0. (2) If the first input is a 1, assume the previous sequence of 0's consisted of zero symbols, which can be regarded as an even number of 0's. An example of input/output sequences that satisfy the conditions of the network specifications is

$$x = 0\,0\,0\,1\,1\,0\,0\,0\,0\,1\,1\,0\,1\,0\,1\,1\,1\,0\,1\,1\,0\,0$$
$$z = 0\,0\,0\,0\,0\,1\,0\,0\,0\,0\,0\,0\,0\,0\,0\,0\,0\,0\,0\,0\,1\,0$$

7.14 Obtain a minimal state table for a clocked synchronous sequential network having a single input line x, in which the symbols 0 and 1 are applied, and a single output line z. The network is to produce an output of 1 coincident with each input of 1 if it is immediately preceded by at least three 1's. At all other times the network is to produce 0 outputs. An example of input/output sequences that satisfy the conditions of the network specifications is

$$x = 0\,1\,1\,0\,0\,1\,1\,1\,1\,1\,1\,0\,0\,0\,1\,1\,1\,1\,0\,1$$
$$z = 0\,0\,0\,0\,0\,0\,0\,0\,1\,1\,1\,0\,0\,0\,0\,0\,0\,1\,0\,0$$

7.15 Obtain a minimal state table for a clocked synchronous sequential network having a single input line x, in which the binary symbols 0 and 1 are applied, and a single output line z. The network is to produce an output of 1 whenever the previous three inputs and the current input correspond to the 4-bit binary number equivalents of the decimal numbers 2, 4, 5, 8, or 14 where the current input is considered the least significant bit of the 4-bit binary number. At all other times the network is to produce 0 outputs. For the purpose of determining the first three outputs, assume that no previous inputs are equivalent to 0 binary digits. An example of input/output sequences that satisfy the conditions of the network specifications is

$$x = 0\,1\,0\,1\,0\,0\,1\,0\,0\,0\,1\,0\,1\,1\,1\,0\,1\,0$$
$$z = 0\,0\,1\,1\,0\,1\,0\,1\,1\,1\,0\,1\,1\,0\,0\,1\,0\,0$$

7.16 Repeat Problem 7.15 for the decimal numbers 1, 6, 9, and 14.

7.17 For each of the Mealy network state tables given in Table P7.17, determine a minimal state table.

Table P7.17

Present state	Next state		Output (z)	
	Input (x)		Input (x)	
	0	1	0	1
*A	B	C	1	1
B	D	B	0	0
C	B	A	0	1
D	D	E	0	0
E	F	G	1	1
F	D	F	0	0
G	F	H	0	1
H	F	I	1	1
I	B	E	0	1

(*a*)

Present state	Next state		Output (z)	
	Input (x)		Input (x)	
	0	1	0	1
*A	B	C	0	0
B	C	D	1	0
C	B	E	0	0
D	F	E	0	0
E	G	A	0	0
F	F	H	1	0
G	A	D	1	0
H	D	F	1	1

(*b*)

7.18 For the Moore network state table given in Table P7.18, determine a minimal state table.

Table P7.18

Present state	Next state		Output (z)
	Input (x)		
	0	1	
*A	B	C	1
B	D	E	0
C	A	F	1
D	E	C	0
E	G	H	1
F	B	H	1
G	D	F	0
H	F	E	1

7.19 The state table shown in Table P7.19 is for a clocked synchronous sequential network. Assigning codes in binary order to the states, determine minimal-sum excitation and output expressions for the sequential network assuming the use of (*a*) *D* flip-flops, (*b*) *JK* flip-flops, (*c*) *T* flip-flops, and (*d*) *SR* flip-flops.

Table P7.19

Present state	Next state		Output (z)	
	Input (x)		Input (x)	
	0	1	0	1
A	B	C	0	0
B	A	A	0	1
C	D	A	0	1
D	A	D	0	1

7.20 Repeat Problem 7.19 using a state assignment satisfying as many as possible of the state adjacencies recommended by the rules given in Sec. 7.5. Compare your expressions with those of Problem 7.19.

7.21 The state table shown in Table P7.21 is for a clocked synchronous sequential network. Assigning codes in binary order to the states, determine minimal-sum excitation and output expressions for the sequential network assuming the use of (*a*) *D* flip-flops, (*b*) *JK* flip-flops, (*c*) *T* flip-flops, and (*d*) *SR* flip-flops.

Table P7.21

Present state	Next state		Output (z)
	Input (x)		
	0	1	
A	A	B	1
B	C	A	0
C	A	D	0
D	C	C	1

7.22 The state table shown in Table P7.22 is for a clocked synchronous sequential network. Assigning codes in binary order to the states, determine minimal-sum excitation and output expressions for the sequential network assuming the use of (*a*) *D* flip-flops, (*b*) *JK* flip-flops, (*c*) *T* flip-flops, and (*d*) *SR* flip-flops.

Table P7.22

Present state	Next state		Output (z)	
	Input (x)		Input (x)	
	0	1	0	1
A	B	A	0	0
B	A	C	1	0
C	D	A	0	0
D	D	E	1	0
E	C	D	1	1

7.23 Repeat Problem 7.22 using a state assignment satisfying as many as possible of the state adjacencies recommended by the rules given in Sec. 7.5. Compare your expressions with those in Problem 7.22.

7.24 The state table shown in Table P7.24 is for a clocked synchronous sequential network that is to be realized using *D* flip-flops. (*a*) Assigning codes in binary order to the states, determine minimal-sum excitation and output expressions for the sequential network. (*b*) Using a state assignment satisfying as many as possible of the state adjacencies recommended by the rules given in Sec. 7.5, determine minimal-sum excitation and output expressions for the sequential network.

Table P7.24

Present state	Next state		Output (z)
	Input (x)		
	0	1	
A	*A*	*B*	0
B	*C*	*F*	0
C	*D*	*A*	1
D	*E*	*C*	0
E	*D*	*F*	0
F	*E*	*D*	1

7.25 Repeat Problem 7.24 assuming the use of *JK* flip-flops.

CHAPTER 8

Algorithmic State Machines

The previous chapter was concerned with the classical approach to clocked synchronous sequential network design. In particular, the models of Mealy and Moore served as the basis for the design approach. In this chapter, however, a different approach to clocked synchronous network design is presented which utilizes a flowchart (somewhat analogous to those used in computer programming) as a representation of the desired sequential network behavior. This flowchart approach is capable of readily handling more complex systems than the state diagrams of the previous chapter.

Several concepts previously introduced are used in this chapter. In Chapter 5, realizations of combinational networks involving MSI components and programmable logic devices were studied. It is seen in this chapter that the algorithmic state machine approach is very easily adapted to using these components for the realizations of sequential networks.

Also previously studied were variable-entered Karnaugh maps. These maps provide an effective technique for obtaining near-minimal expressions of a large number of variables. This is precisely what is needed for algebraically describing the realizations of algorithmic state machines. Thus, variable-entered Karnaugh maps are a useful tool in this chapter. ■

8.1 THE ALGORITHMIC STATE MACHINE

An approach to the logic design of a digital system is to partition the system into two entities: a *controller* and a *controlled architecture*, also called the *data processor*. Such a partition is illustrated in Fig. 8.1. The data processor is an architecture that consists of the components needed to provide for the manipulation of data. This includes such things as flip-flops, shift registers, counters, adders/

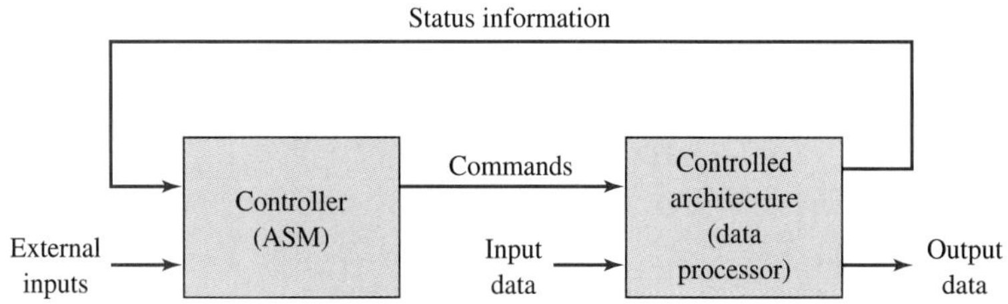

Figure 8.1 Partitioning of a digital system.

subtracters, and comparators, to name just a few. It is the function of the controller to supply a time sequence of commands to the devices of the data processor. Examples of such commands are shift left, shift right, add, subtract, increment, and reset. In addition, the data processor may supply information to the controller about the status of its various devices. For example, the output of a comparator provides an indication of whether its two inputs are equal or which is the larger. Such status information allows for decision making in the controller so that different commands are supplied as warranted by the prevailing conditions. External inputs needed by the overall system to carry out a desired procedure are supplied to the controller; while the input data that are to be manipulated are entered into the data processor. Finally, the results of the data manipulation appear at the output of the data processor.

The above-mentioned controller is designed as a clocked synchronous sequential network having several states, each associated with the production of a set of commands. By sequencing through the various states in some proper order, a series of commands are produced to control the data processor of Fig. 8.1, with the net result of achieving a specified overall system behavior. In general, a well-defined procedure consisting of a finite number of steps to the solution of a problem is called an *algorithm.* Thus, the controller is regarded as a hardware algorithm and, consequently, it is referred to as an *algorithmic state machine*, or, simply, *ASM.*

Although an algorithmic state machine as a controller facilitates the design of larger digital systems incorporating MSI components, an algorithmic state machine can also serve as a stand-alone sequential network model. In this case there is no data processor being controlled and the network being modeled is essentially a classical Mealy network or Moore network. Hence, the algorithmic state machine becomes another approach to clocked synchronous sequential network modeling. Examples of both applications of the algorithmic state machine are given in Sec. 8.3.

Figure 8.2 shows the general model of an algorithmic state machine. The inputs to the machine correspond to the external inputs and status information of Fig. 8.1 and the outputs correspond to command signals. The functions of the various blocks in the model are similar to those already seen in the case of the Mealy and Moore models. In particular, the current state of the machine is given

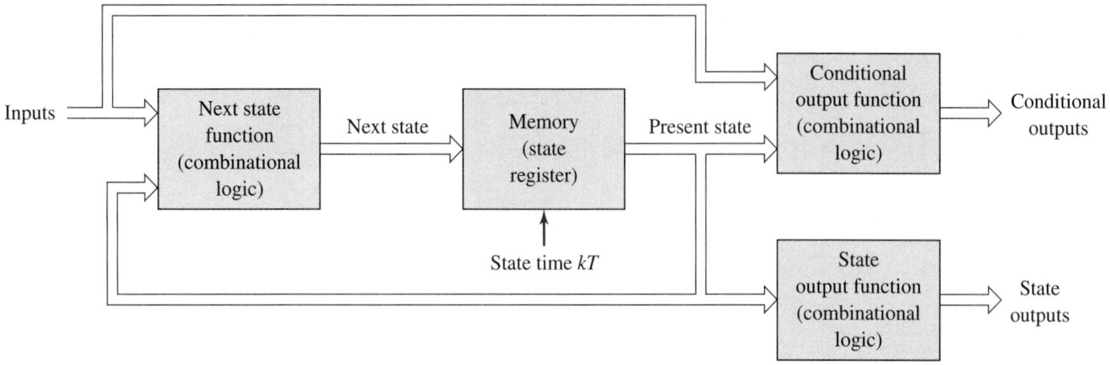

Figure 8.2 Model of an algorithmic state machine.

by the memory block. This block has the capability of storing a sufficient amount of past history so that future behavior of the system is determined. The realization of the memory block is typically a collection of flip-flops referred to as the *state register.* The present state and the current inputs are used to determine the next state of the system. This is denoted by the next-state-function block of Fig. 8.2. Each state lasts for one *state time*, kT, where the next state replaces the present state at the end of a state time. This, in turn, defines the beginning of the next state time.

It was seen in the previous chapter that the Mealy and Moore models of a sequential network differed only in their output functions. In the ASM model, both types of outputs are incorporated. Consequently, two output-function blocks are shown in Fig. 8.2. When the current outputs are a function of the current inputs and the present state, these outputs are referred to as *conditional outputs* since the output values are conditioned upon the inputs. These are the type of output previously associated with the Mealy model of a clocked synchronous sequential network. However, when the outputs of an ASM are only a function of the current state, these outputs are referred to as *state outputs.* Outputs of this type were associated with the Moore model of a clocked synchronous sequential network in the previous chapter.

As indicated above, the algorithmic state machine steps through a series of states, each state lasting for one state time. The timing of an algorithmic state machine is illustrated in Fig. 8.3. A state time is divided into two periods: a *transition period* and a *stable period.* During the transition period, external inputs and status information are applied. Physically, a certain amount of time is needed for the signals to propagate through the logic networks associated with the next-state and output functions. Hence, the next-state and output variables undergo a period of time in which they are changing. All of this occurs during the transition period. Eventually, the variables reach their final, fixed values. Once this occurs, the values are usable by the various devices within the system. The period of time in which the values are usable is the stable period. For meaningful operation of an ASM, the state time must

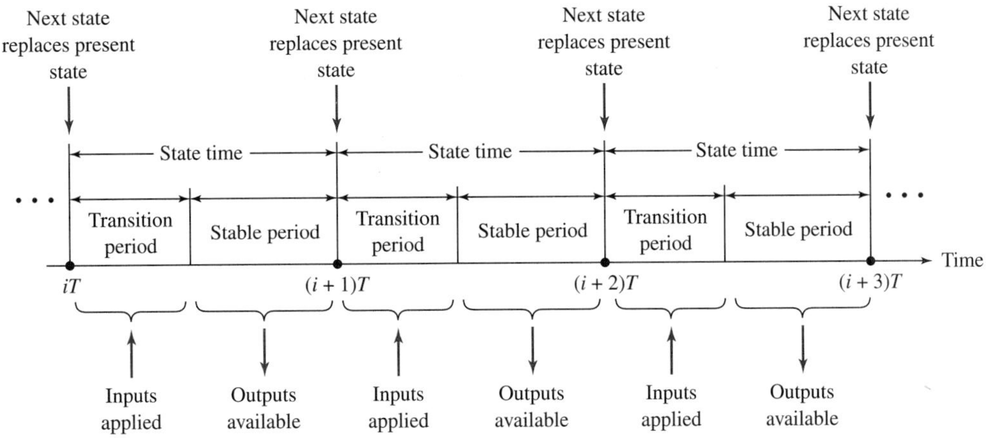

Figure 8.3 Timing of an algorithmic state machine.

be greater than the transition period, i.e., a stable condition must occur during each state time.

To achieve the state times, a periodic signal from a clock is used. Each clock period corresponds to one state time. As mentioned previously, state times are delineated by the present state being replaced by the next state. In other words, upon the completion of each clock period the ASM enters its next state.

If an action is to occur coincident with the synchronizing clock signal, then this occurs at the end of the state time. For example, a shift-right control signal is sent to a shift register in the controlled architecture during the stable period. This signal conditions the shift register so that upon the occurrence of the appropriate triggering edge of the clock, which defines the end of the current state time and the beginning of the next-state time, the actual shift operation occurs. On the other hand, any combinational logic in the controlled architecture is able to respond during the stable period of a state time.

The reader should carefully note the differences between an ASM model and the Mealy/Moore models of the previous chapter. The ASM model involves a more physical interpretation of network operation since the next-state and output functions are defined for the entire stable period of a state time as opposed to the Mealy/Moore models that define sequential network behavior only at the sampling instants. As a consequence, the inputs are assumed fixed during the stable period of the state time. A second difference is that both conditional and state outputs can occur in the same ASM.

8.2 ASM CHARTS

The key to describing the behavior of an algorithmic state machine is a block diagram structure superficially similar to the flowcharts used in software design. These flowcharts are called *ASM charts.* The major difference between these two types of flowcharts lies in their time interpretation. Conventional software flowcharts are used to describe the sequence of events that must occur or tasks that must be performed that lead to a problem solution. Therefore, each boxlike symbol of the conventional software flowchart follows the other in time sequence and the task associated with each boxlike symbol is completed before the task associated with the next boxlike symbol is considered. On the other hand, ASM charts describe a sequence of time intervals. As a consequence, an entire collection of boxlike symbols in an ASM chart corresponds to a *single* time interval, i.e., a state time, and all events occurring within the single time interval are regarded as occurring simultaneously. This seemingly small difference is vital to the understanding and use of ASM charts.

ASM charts consist of three basic components: the *state box*, the *decision box*, and the *conditional output box.* A collection of these components forms an *ASM block* that corresponds to a single state time. As indicated previously, the events within an ASM block occur simultaneously. The overall behavior of an algorithmic state machine is then described by a collection of ASM blocks, denoting a sequence of time intervals. This collection forms the *ASM chart.*

8.2.1 The State Box

The symbol of a state box is shown in Fig. 8.4. A state box represents one state of an ASM. As indicated in the figure, there is a single entry path to a state box and a single exit path from a state box. A name is normally assigned to the box, which appears encircled next to it. This could be a number, letter, or mnemonic. The state code for a state box is also included with the symbol, typically in the upper right corner. The state code is determined when a state assignment is made in much the same way as was done in the previous chapter. Since the state code is not usually known when an ASM chart is initially constructed, it is added at a later time. Finally, the names of the output variables that are *asserted* or *active*, i.e., have a value of logic-1, while the system is residing in the given state are listed as entries within the state box. This is called the *state output list* and pertains to those output variables that are only a function of the state associated with the state box and not of

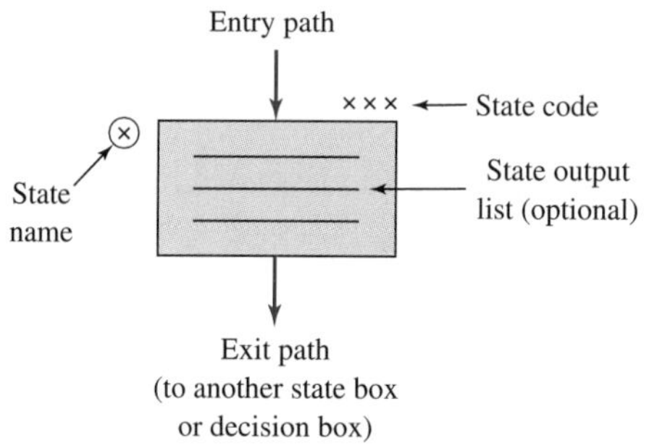

Figure 8.4 The state box.

any inputs. If there are no asserted outputs for a given state, then no entries are placed in the state box.

The state box is the only basic component in an ASM chart that is time-dependent. The system resides in a state box for one full state time. At the end of a state time, the system goes to the state box associated with the next state. In addition, each state output variable appearing in the state box is asserted for the entire stable period of the state time.

The single exit path from a state box can lead to a state box or a decision box. If it leads directly to a state box, then there is an unconditional state transition upon the occurrence of the next clock period. On the other hand, if it leads to a decision box, then interrogation of the system inputs occurs during the current state time and the next state and/or present outputs of the system depend upon the status of these inputs.

8.2.2 The Decision Box

The second basic ASM component is the decision box. Figure 8.5 gives the two alternate forms commonly used. In both cases there is a single entry path. The basic function of a decision box is to provide for next-state alternatives and conditional outputs based on the logic value of a Boolean expression involving the external input variables and the status information variables. The Boolean expression appears as the entry in the decision box. Since the result of the Boolean expression is logic-0 (false) or logic-1 (true), there are two exit paths, one for each of the two possibilities. The exit paths can lead to state boxes, other decision boxes, or conditional output boxes.

There is no time dependence associated with a decision box. Since a decision box always is associated with a state box, its Boolean condition is evaluated during the same state time as that of its associated state box. In this way the decision box is used only to provide alternate paths in an ASM chart.

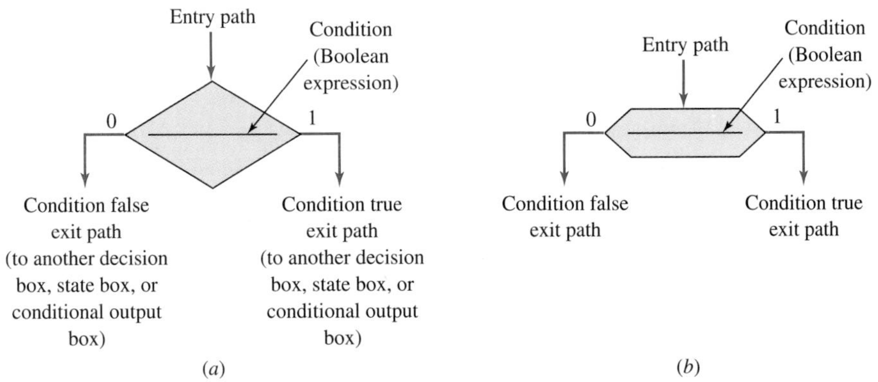

Figure 8.5 The decision box. (*a*) Symbol. (*b*) Alternate symbol.

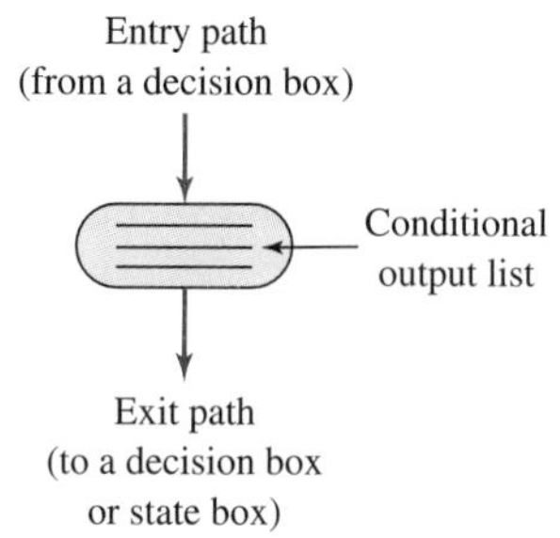

Figure 8.6 The conditional output box.

8.2.3 The Conditional Output Box

The final component of an ASM chart is the conditional output box whose symbol is shown in Fig. 8.6. The conditional output box has a single entry path from a decision box and a single exit path to another decision box or a state box. This box provides a listing, called the *conditional output list*, of output variables that are to have a value of logic-1, i.e., those output variables being asserted. However, the logic-1 value of these output variables must be dependent upon the values of some external input variables or information status variables as well as the present state. Hence, the conditional output box must be preceded by a decision box that specifies the condition for the listed output variables to be asserted, i.e., to have logic-1 values.

As in the case of decision boxes, conditional output boxes have no time dependence associated with them. These boxes are always associated with a state box. However, a decision box must occur in a path between the associated state box and the conditional output box to indicate how the listed output variables are dependent upon the external input variables or status information variables.

8.2.4 ASM Blocks

The basic ASM components are used to construct ASM blocks. An ASM block consists of the interconnection of a single state box along with a collection of decision and conditional output boxes. An ASM block has one entry path, which leads directly to its state box, and one or more exit paths. Each exit path must also lead directly to a state box, possibly itself. The collection of decision and conditional output boxes between the state box and the set of exit paths are all associated with the same state box of the ASM block. A path through an ASM block from its state box to an exit path is called a *link path*. Figure 8.7 shows an example of an ASM block having three decision boxes, two conditional output boxes, and three exit paths. In this case the Boolean conditions associated with the decision boxes are simply single literal Boolean expressions. Also illustrated in the figure are the link paths. In

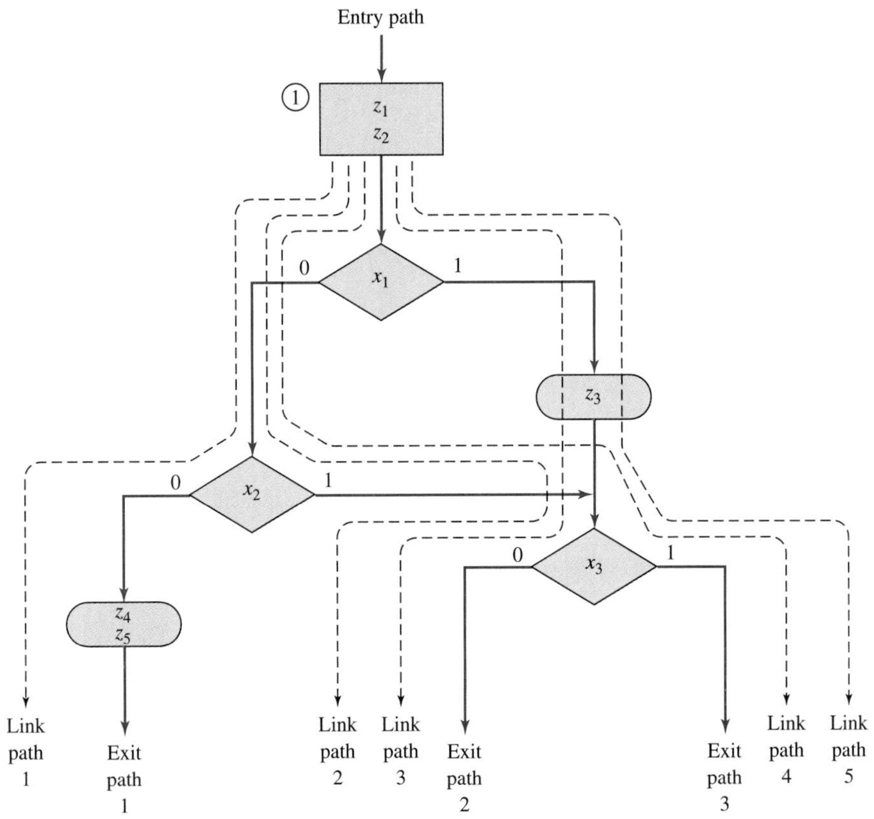

Figure 8.7 Example of an ASM block and its link paths.

this example there are five link paths through the ASM block, which are shown as dashed lines.

An ASM block describes the operation of the system during the state time in which it is in the state associated with the block. In the example of Fig. 8.7, when the system enters the ASM block corresponding to state 1, as indicated by the encircled state name next to the state box, the outputs listed in the state box, z_1 and z_2, are asserted, i.e., $z_1 = z_2 = 1$. The conditions indicated in the decision boxes are evaluated simultaneously to determine which link path (or paths) is to be followed through the ASM block. If a conditional output box is encountered in the selected link path, then the corresponding outputs in the output list also are asserted. Again referring to Fig. 8.7, if $x_1 = x_2 = 0$ during the state time, then the system follows link path 1. In this case, the z_4 and z_5 outputs also are logic-1 since they appear as entries in the conditional output box along the selected link path. On the other hand, the z_3 output is logic-0 since it does not appear as an entry in a selected link path. At the end of the state time, the system exits via exit path 1, entering the ASM block associated with that exit path. Boolean expressions can be

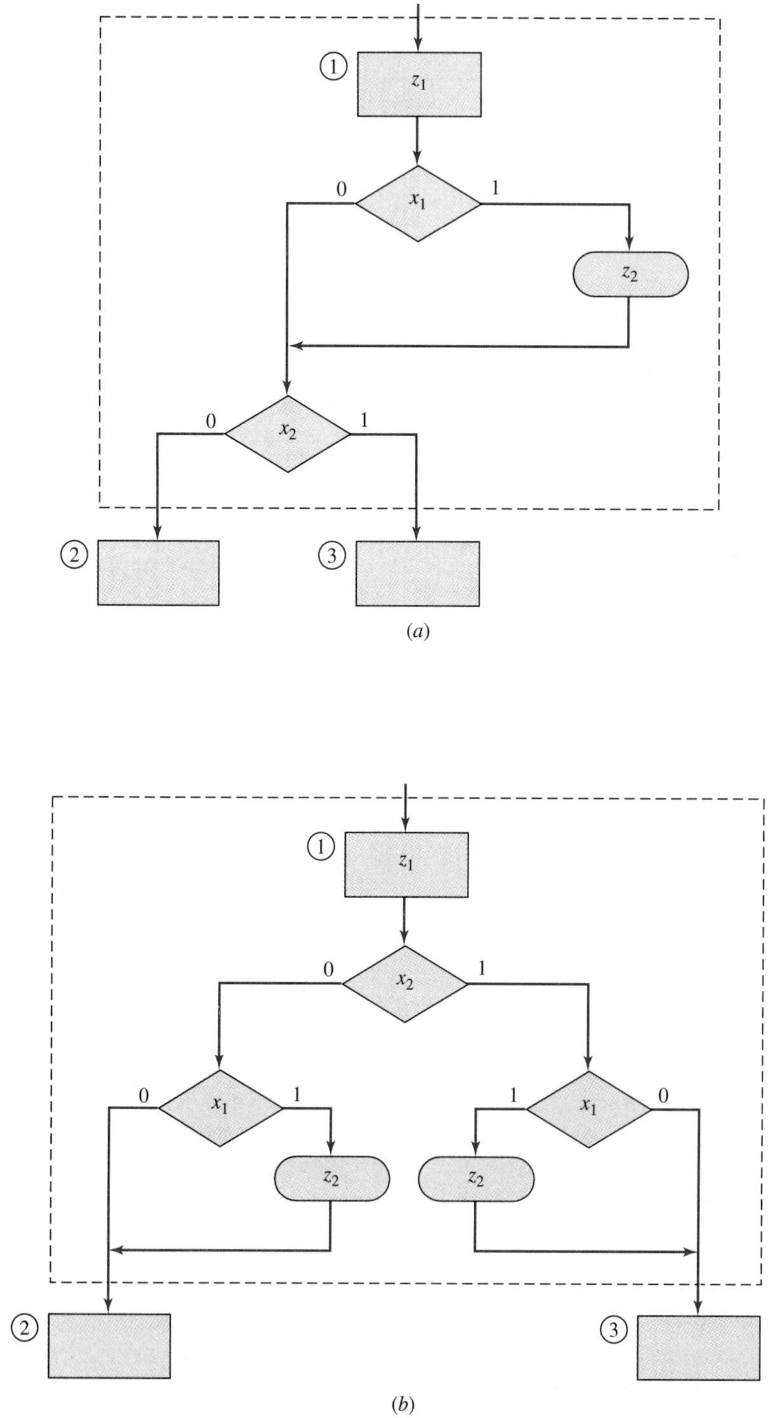

Figure 8.8 Two equivalent ASM blocks.

written for each of the link paths. In this case the corresponding Boolean expressions are

$$
\begin{aligned}
L_1 &= \bar{x}_1\bar{x}_2 \\
L_2 &= \bar{x}_1 x_2 \bar{x}_3 \\
L_3 &= x_1\bar{x}_3 \\
L_4 &= \bar{x}_1 x_2 x_3 \\
L_5 &= x_1 x_3
\end{aligned}
$$

Selected link paths are those that evaluate to logic-1. For this particular example, only one link path is selected for any set of values to the x_1, x_2, and x_3 variables.

Since an entire ASM block corresponds to a single state time and the evaluation of the decision boxes occurs simultaneously, the ordering of the decision boxes and conditional output boxes is immaterial from a time point of view.* Hence any logical arrangement of these boxes that describes the same system behavior becomes an equivalent form of an ASM block. In Fig. 8.8*a* an ASM block is shown enclosed in the dashed lines. The ASM block of Fig. 8.8*b* is equivalent. In both cases, $z_1 = 1$ during the state time since this output is only a function of current state 1. Furthermore, regardless of the value of x_2, $z_2 = 1$ if $x_1 = 1$. Finally, in both cases the next state is 2 when $x_2 = 0$ and the next state is 3 if $x_2 = 1$.

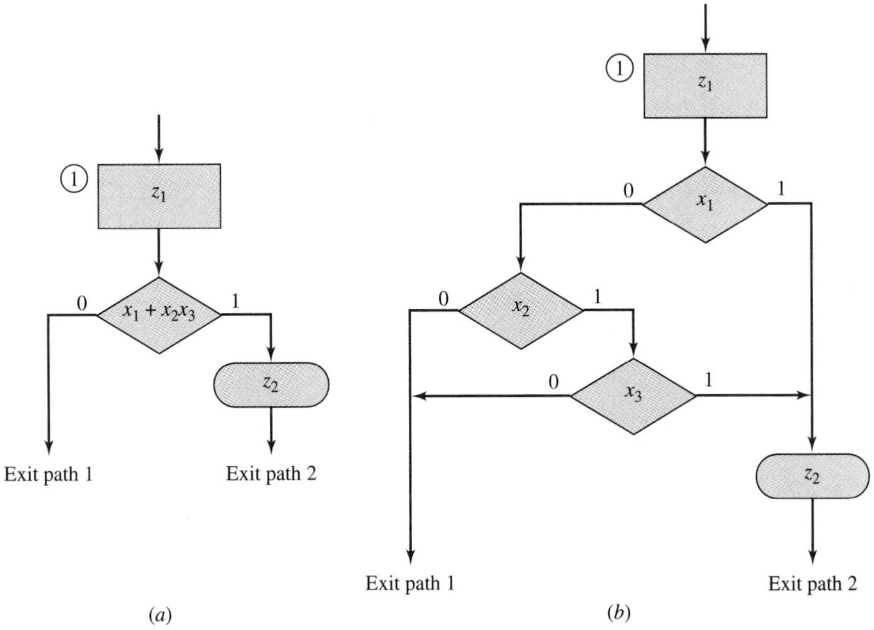

Figure 8.9 Two equivalent ASM blocks. (*a*) Using a single decision box. (*b*) Using several decision boxes.

*The state box must always be the first component in an ASM block.

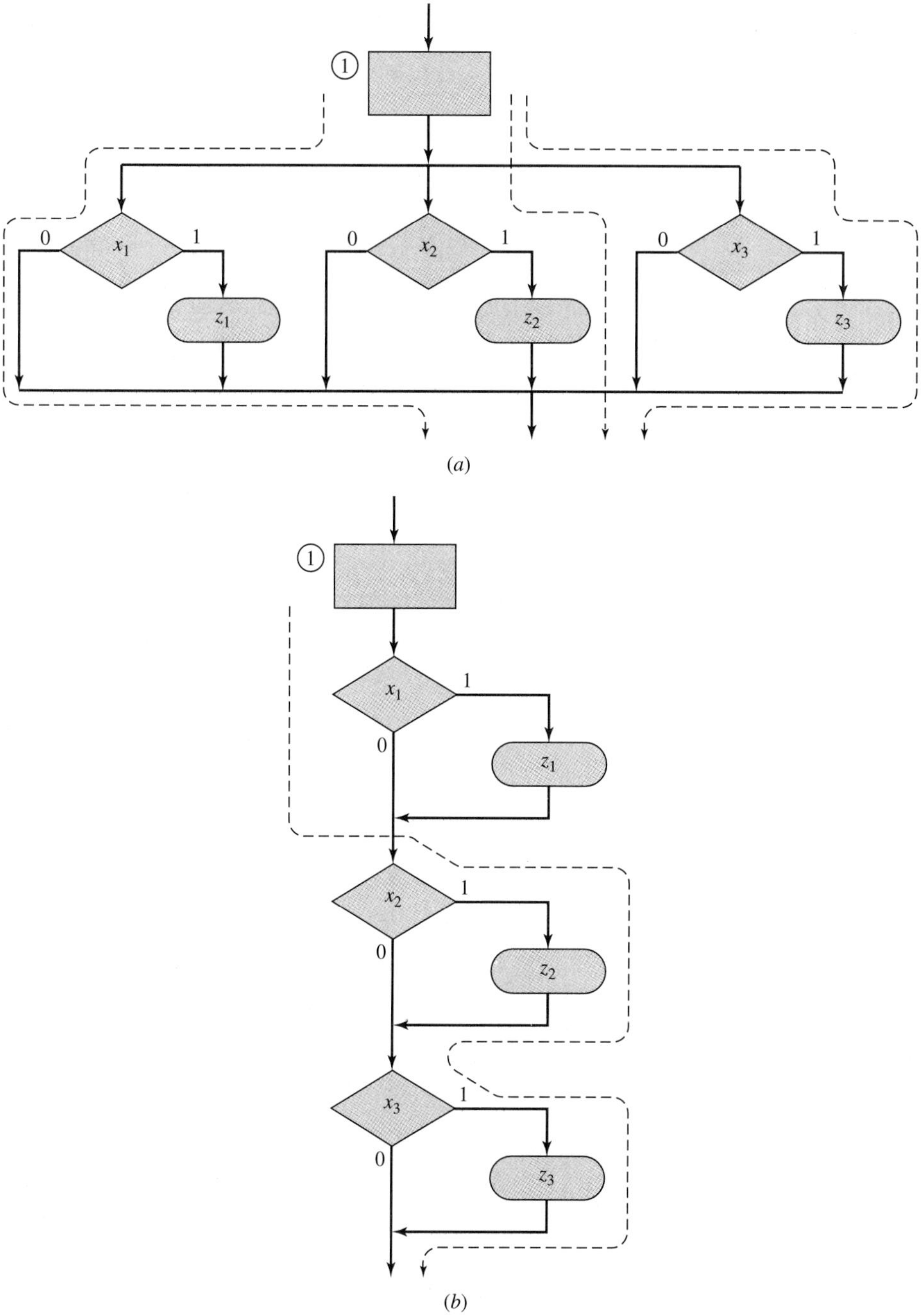

Figure 8.10 Two equivalent ASM blocks. (*a*) Parallel decision boxes. (*b*) Serial decision boxes.

Another example of equivalence between two ASM blocks is shown in Fig. 8.9. In Fig. 8.9*a* the condition associated with the decision box is a Boolean expression consisting of more than a single input variable. The ASM block of Fig. 8.9*b* illustrates the same system behavior using multiple decision boxes in which only one input variable is assigned to a decision box.

In the ASM blocks illustrated thus far, only one link path is selected at any time depending upon the values of the decision-box variables. That this is not necessarily the case is shown in Fig. 8.10. Both ASM blocks are equivalent. In the case of Fig. 8.10*a* the decision boxes are arranged in parallel, with the result that several link paths are selected simultaneously. On the other hand, in Fig. 8.10*b* the decision boxes are arranged in series, with the result that only one link path is selected at any time. As an example showing that the same system behavior is achieved for both of the ASM blocks in the figure, let $x_1 = 0$ and $x_2 = x_3 = 1$. In this case, three link paths are selected in Fig. 8.10*a*, as indicated by the dashed lines, causing $z_2 = z_3 = 1$ since these outputs appear in the selected paths and $z_1 = 0$ since this output does not appear in a selected path. The corresponding selected link path in Fig. 8.10*b* is also shown dashed. This path results in the same output values.

There are two rules that must be observed when constructing ASM blocks. First, for any valid combination of values to the decision-box variables, all simultaneously selected link paths must lead to the same exit path. This constraint is necessary since the selected paths indicate the next state of the system, which must be uniquely determined. Violation of this rule can only occur when more than one path is simultaneously selected. To illustrate this, consider Fig. 8.11. Regardless

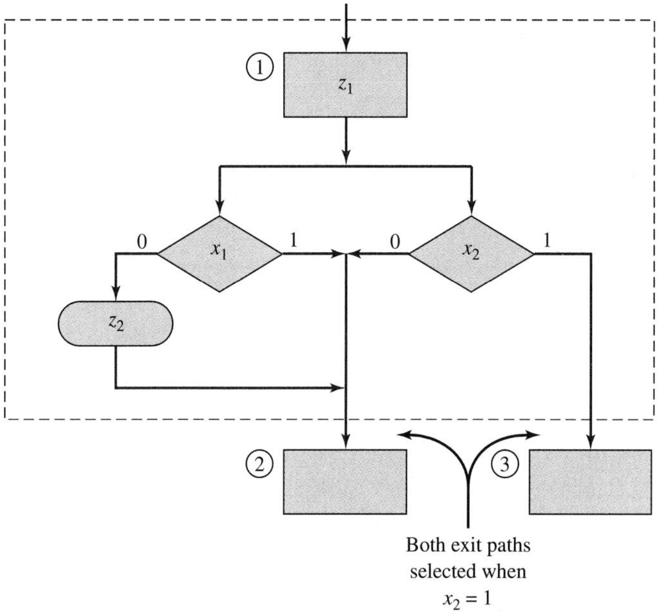

Figure 8.11 Invalid ASM block having nonunique next states.

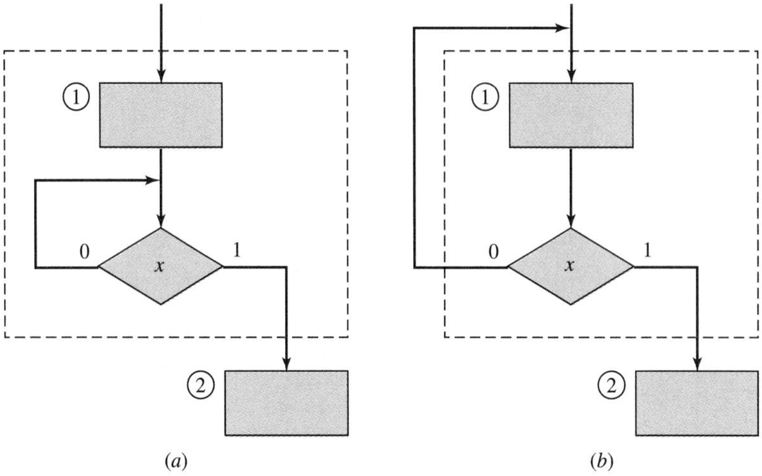

Figure 8.12 Looping. (*a*) Incorrect. (*b*) Correct.

of the value of x_1, when $x_2 = 1$ one selected link path leads to state 2 and another leads to state 3. Thus, the next-state behavior of the system is not uniquely defined. When only one link path is selected at any one time, this problem does not occur.

The second rule that must be observed is that there can be no closed loops that do not contain at least one state box since a state box is the only component that is time-dependent. The ASM block shown in Fig. 8.12*a* is an invalid way of indicating that the system should stay in state 1 as long as $x = 0$. The proper way of expressing this behavior is shown in Fig. 8.12*b*. Here, the feedback loop leaves the ASM block by one of its exit paths and then reenters it via its entry path at the next state time.

8.2.5 ASM Charts

An ASM chart is a collection of ASM blocks interconnected for the purpose of describing the behavior of a clocked synchronous sequential network. A simple example of an ASM chart is given in Fig. 8.13, which describes the behavior of a mod-8 binary counter. There are eight state boxes, each corresponding to one of the states of the counter. The state label appears encircled next to each state box and corresponds to the decimal equivalent of the associated binary count. No decision boxes are needed in this ASM chart since the next state is uniquely determined by the present state. Hence, each ASM block simply consists of a single state box. The output variables of the counter are z_1, z_2, and z_3, which correspond to the three bits of the present count where z_1 is the most-significant-bit value and z_3 is the least-significant-bit value. These output variables appear as entries in the state boxes in accordance to when they are to have the value of 1. Finally, three state variables are

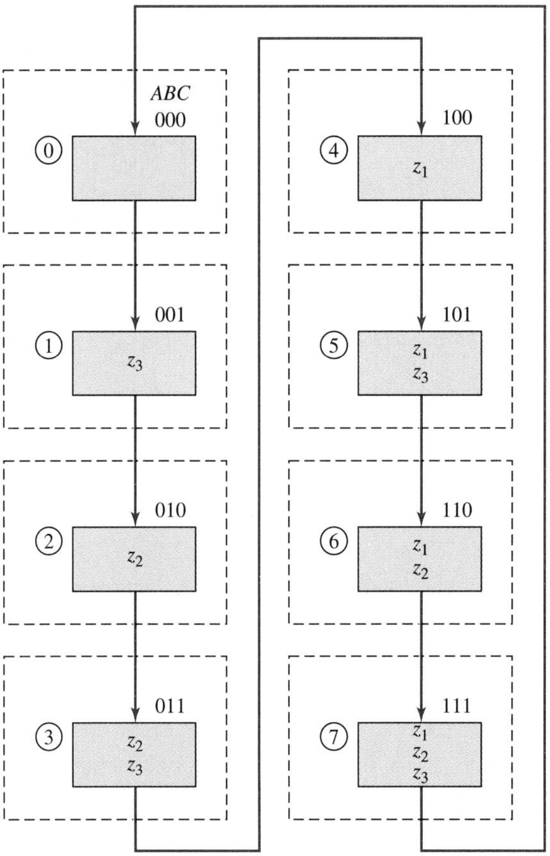

Figure 8.13 ASM chart for a mod-8 binary counter.

needed to code the eight states of the counter. A possible state assignment is shown above and to the right of each state box. The state assignment selected also corresponds to the binary count associated with the state. The letters *A*, *B*, and *C* shown above the state assignment for state 0 are the state variables.

Figure 8.14 illustrates the ASM chart for another mod-8 binary counter. In this case, the counter is to increment or decrement depending upon the value of an input variable *I*. When $I = 0$, the present count is decremented; while when $I = 1$, the present count is incremented. To describe this behavior, each ASM block must consist of a state box followed by a decision box. Within each decision box the input variable *I* appears as an entry to direct the system to the appropriate next state of the counter. The output variables within the state boxes provide for expressing the present binary count as was done in the previous example.

In the next section, additional examples are given of ASM chart construction.

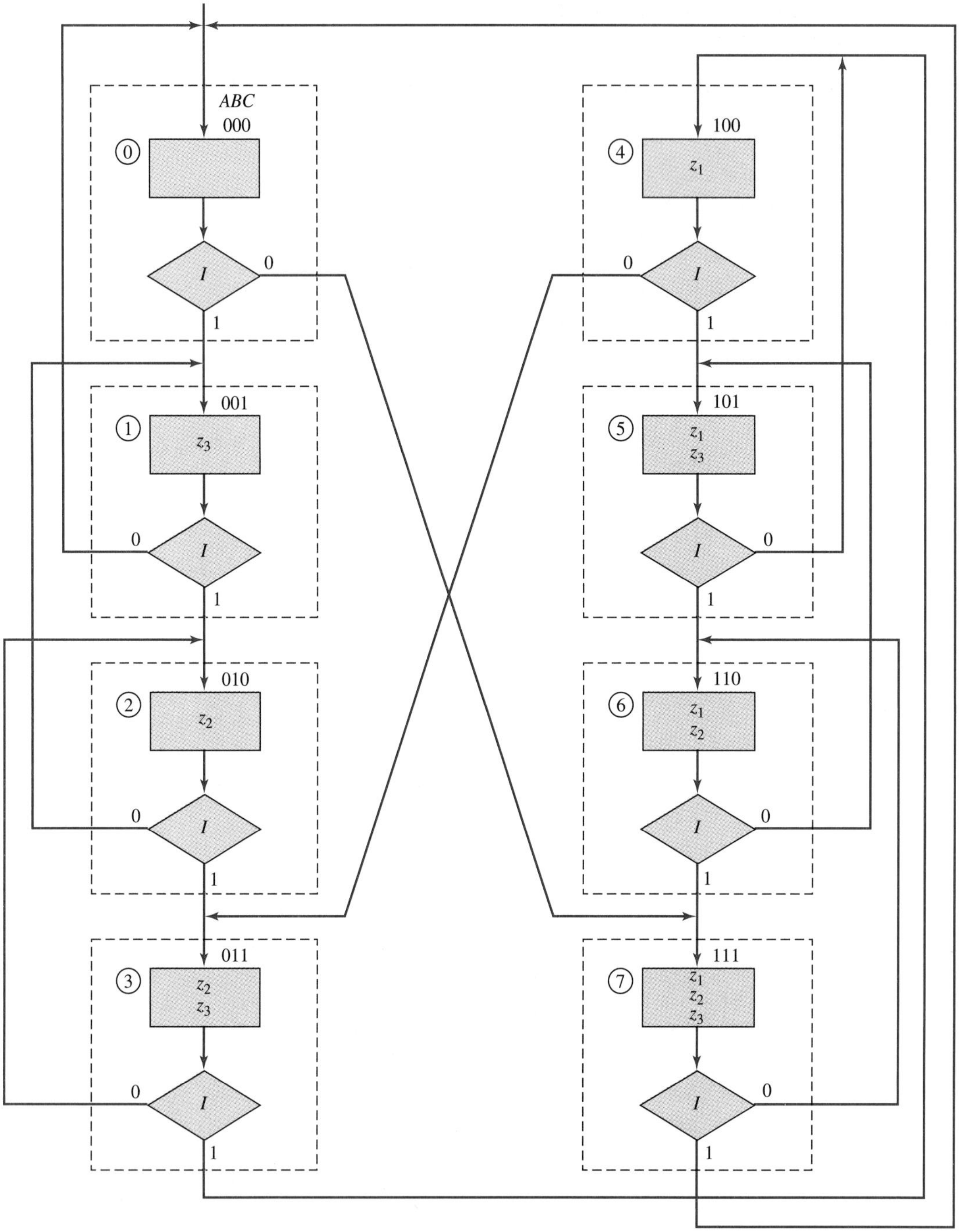

Figure 8.14 ASM chart for a mod-8 binary up-down counter.

8.2.6 Relationship between State Diagrams and ASM Charts

In the previous chapter, Moore and Mealy sequential networks were studied. Both types were modeled with state diagrams. It is a simple matter to convert these state diagrams into ASM charts.

Figure 8.15*a* shows a typical state diagram for a Moore sequential network. Here, outputs are only associated with the states. To construct an equivalent ASM chart for this state diagram, there must be as many state boxes, and correspondingly ASM blocks, in the ASM chart as there are nodes in the state diagram. Figure 8.15*b* shows the corresponding ASM chart. The output variables z_1 and z_2 that have a logic-1 value for a given state are placed as entries in the state boxes since the values

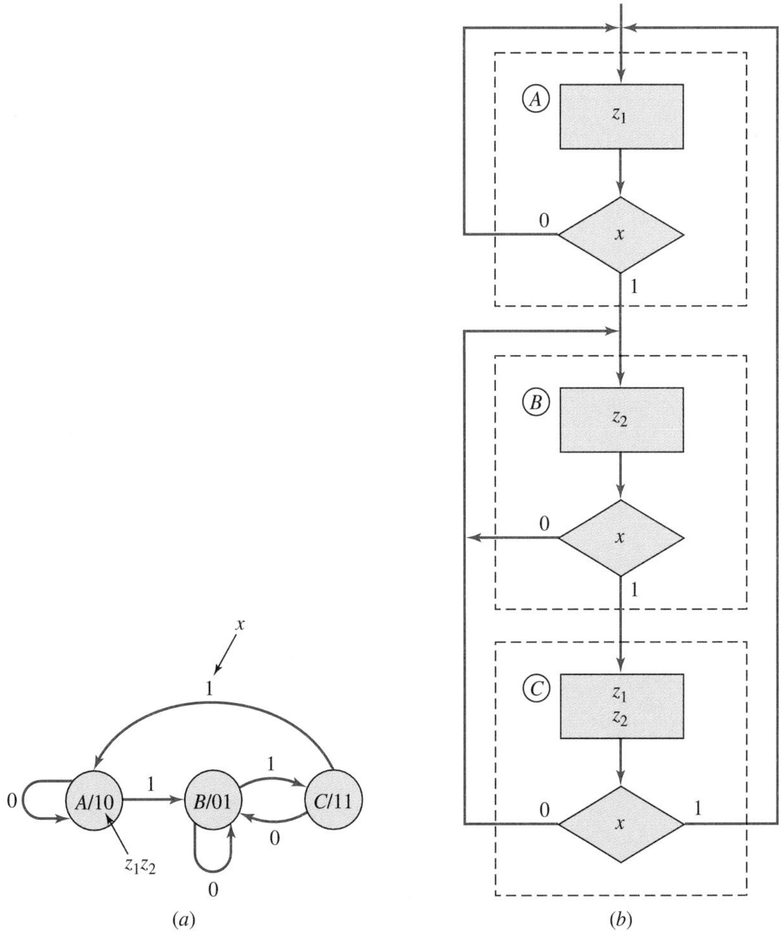

Figure 8.15 Moore sequential network. (*a*) State diagram. (*b*) ASM chart.

of these variables are not a function of the input variable x. The next state of the state diagram depends upon a single input variable x. Hence, a decision box appears in each of the ASM blocks that directs the system control to the appropriate next state based on the value of the input variable.

An example of a Mealy state diagram and its equivalent ASM chart are shown in Fig. 8.16. Again, there are as many state boxes as there are nodes in the state dia-

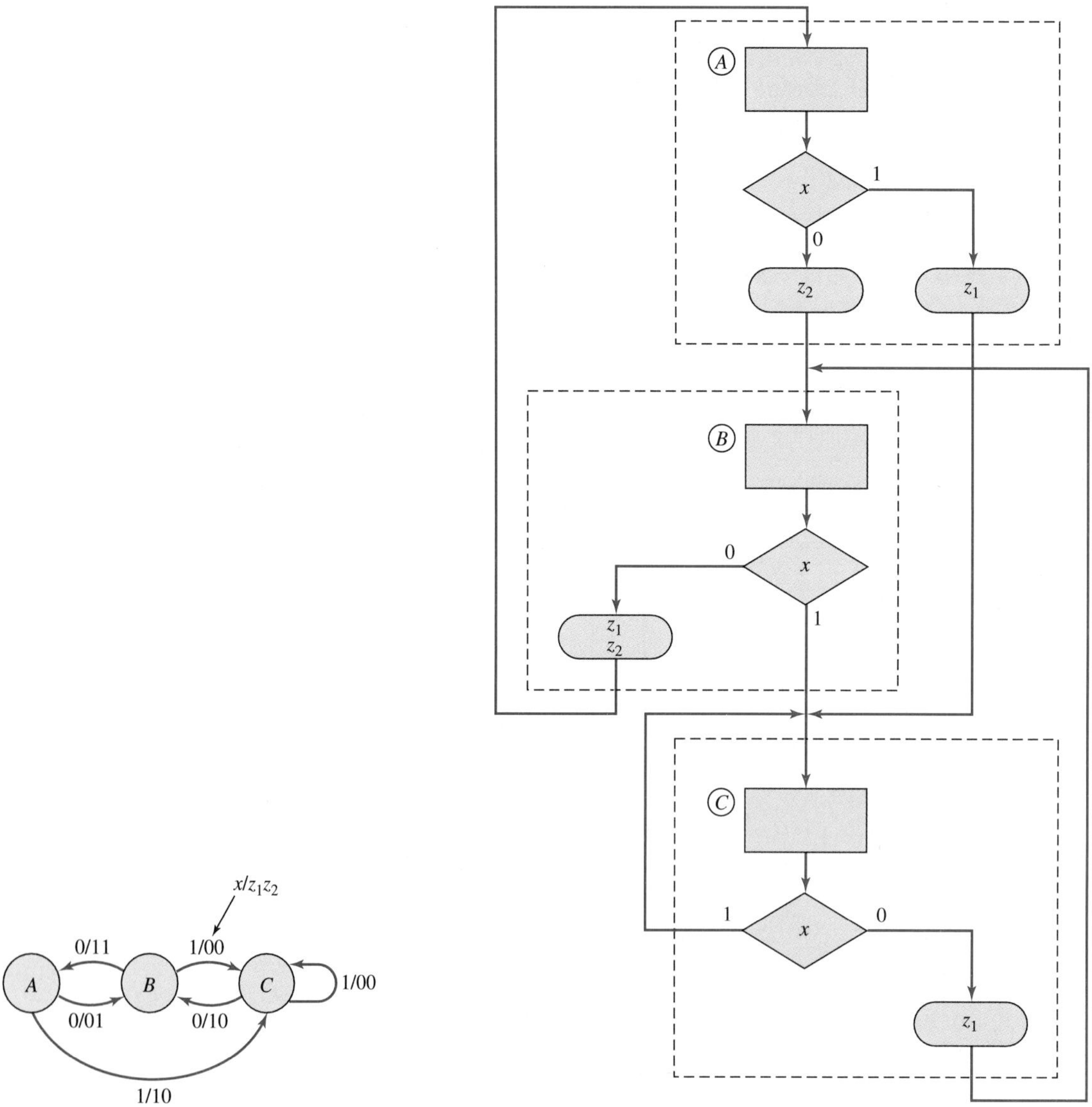

(a) (b)

Figure 8.16 Mealy sequential network. (*a*) State diagram. (*b*) ASM chart.

gram. In this case, no entries appear in the state boxes since the values of the output variables z_1 and z_2 are a function of both the present state and the input variable x. Due to this input dependence, the output variables appear in conditional output boxes following the input variable decision boxes. For example, when in state C, if $x = 0$, then just $z_1 = 1$ and the next state is B. On the other hand, if $x = 1$, then the selected path in the ASM block does not pass through a conditional output box and consequently $z_1 = z_2 = 0$ as required by the state diagram. In this case the system remains in state C.

8.3 TWO EXAMPLES OF SYNCHRONOUS SEQUENTIAL NETWORK DESIGN USING ASM CHARTS

In this section, two examples of ASM chart construction are given. The first involves a sequence recognizer that is modeled as a stand-alone algorithmic state machine, i.e., without a controlled architecture, and illustrates the use of decision boxes containing Boolean expressions having more than a single variable. The second example is a binary multiplier and illustrates an algorithmic state machine as a controller. In this example, the controlled architecture consists of MSI components.

8.3.1 A Sequence Recognizer

Consider the construction of an ASM chart for a synchronous sequential network that is to recognize the input sequence of pairs $x_1x_2 = 01,01,11,00$. That is, an output, z, is to be 1 when $x_1x_2 = 00$ if and only if the three preceding pairs of inputs are $x_1x_2 = 01$, 01, and 11, in that order. The ASM chart is shown in Fig. 8.17. The four dashed boxes in the figure denote the ASM blocks.

State 1 corresponds to the initial state and denotes that the sequence to be recognized has not yet started. The decision box in this ASM block contains the Boolean expression $\overline{x}_1x_2$. This expression evaluates to 1 only if $x_1 = 0$ and $x_2 = 1$. Once this input pair is applied, the system moves to state box 2; otherwise, it remains in state 1 until the condition in the decision box is satisfied.

When the system enters state 2, the first $x_1x_2 = 01$ input pair has already occurred. Again a decision box containing the Boolean expression $\overline{x}_1x_2$ is needed to recognize the second input pair. If the condition is satisfied, then the system moves to state 3. On the other hand, if the condition is not satisfied, then the system returns to state 1 to begin again the recognition of the specified input sequence.

In the ASM block containing state 3, two decision boxes are needed. First, the Boolean expression x_1x_2 is used to determine if the third input pair of the sequence has occurred. If so, the system proceeds to state 4. However, if the expression x_1x_2 evaluates to 0, then it is still necessary to determine if the current input pair is $x_1x_2 = 01$. In such a case, the system returns to state 3 since the last two input pairs have been $x_1x_2 = 01,01$. Only if both decisions evaluate to 0 does the system return to state 1 to begin again the process of recognizing the specified input sequence.

When the system gets to state 4, the input sequence $x_1x_2 = 01,01,11$ has occurred. If at this time the pair of inputs is $x_1x_2 = 00$, as detected by the decision box

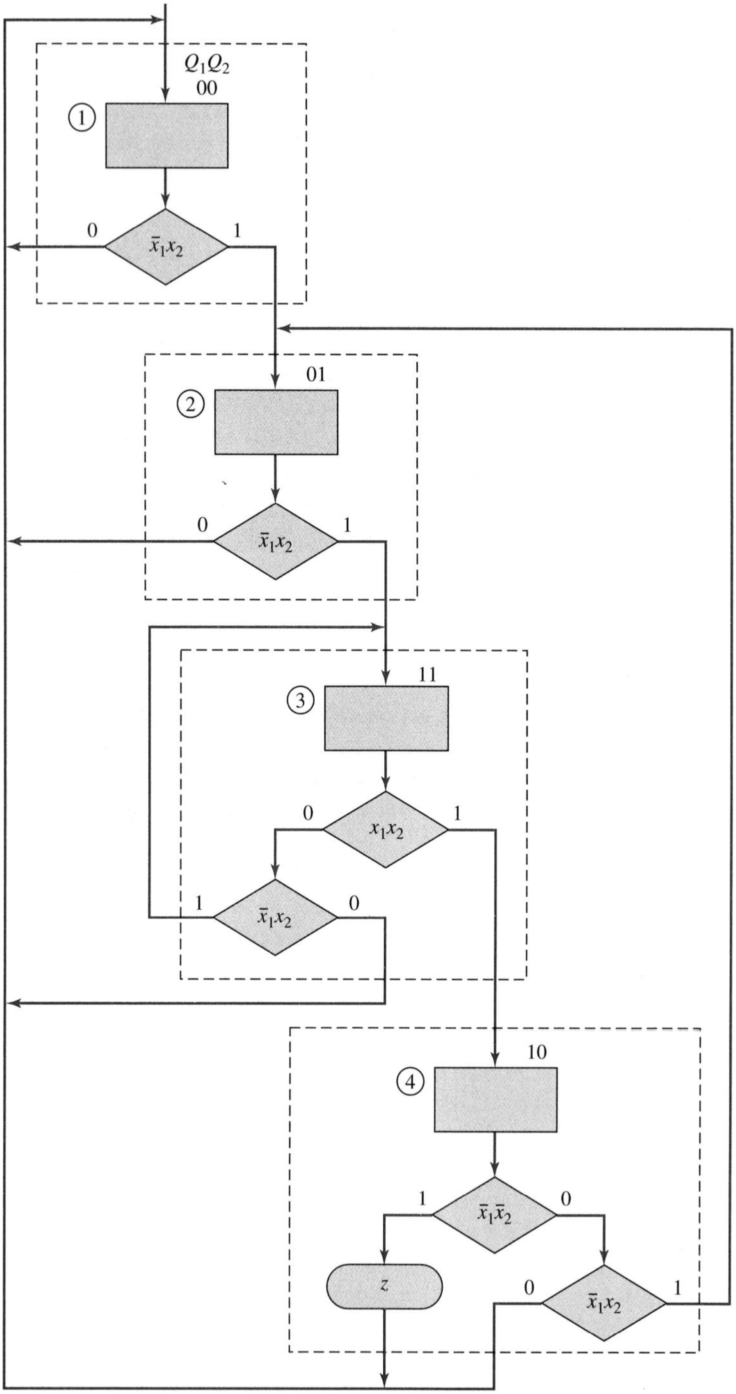

Figure 8.17 ASM chart to recognize the sequence $x_1x_2 = 01,01,11,00$.

containing the Boolean expression $\bar{x}_1\bar{x}_2$, then the output variable z is set to 1, indicating the specified sequence has been recognized, and the system returns to state 1. The output variable z appears in a conditional output box since its assertion is dependent upon the final pair of inputs. However, should the last input pair be $x_1x_2 = 01$, as detected by the decision box containing the Boolean expression $\bar{x}_1x_2$, the system goes to state 2, since this could be the first pair of inputs of a sequence to be recognized. If the test for $x_1x_2 = 01$ should also fail, then the system returns to state 1 and the process of recognizing the indicated sequence is repeated.

A minimum of 2 bits is needed to code the four states of the sequence recognizer. As was discussed in the previous chapter, state assignments are required prior to a realization. A possible state assignment is indicated in the upper right corner of the state boxes where Q_1 and Q_2 are the state variables. A further discussion of state assignments is given in Sec. 8.4.

8.3.2 A Parallel (Unsigned) Binary Multiplier

As a second design example, consider the process of binary multiplication. The pencil-and-paper approach to binary multiplication was previously discussed in Sec. 2.3. At this time an ASM chart for a possible realization of a binary multiplier is developed.

In Fig. 8.18*a*, conventional multiplication of two binary integers is illustrated. Here, an array of partial products is formed as determined by the multiplier digits. This array is then summed to produce the product of the two numbers. It should be noted that, in general, the number of bits in the product of two N-bit integers is $2N$ bits.

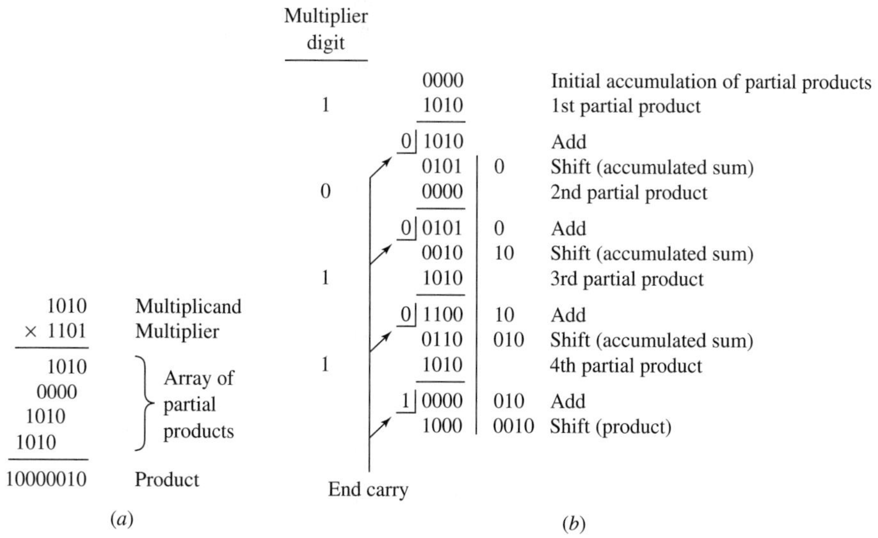

Figure 8.18 Binary multiplication. (*a*) Pencil-and-paper approach. (*b*) Add-shift approach.

An alternate approach to multiplying two binary numbers is shown in Fig. 8.18*b*. Rather than first forming all the partial products and then summing them, in this alternate approach a running sum of the partial products is maintained by adding the multiplicand (if the multiplier digit is 1) or adding zero (if the multiplier digit is 0). The weighting of the multiplier digits, as indicated by the leftwise indentation of the partial products in Fig. 8.18*a*, is replaced by a right shift of the accumulated sum of partial products in Fig. 8.18*b*.

Referring to Fig. 8.18*b*, initially the accumulated sum of partial products is zero since no partial products have yet been formed. The first multiplier digit is then inspected. Since it is 1, the first partial product is the same as the multiplicand. This partial product is then added to the accumulated sum. Recall that when adding two N-bit binary numbers, the sum consists of $N + 1$ bits where the most significant bit of the sum corresponds to the end carry. Finally, the resulting sum in Fig. 8.18*b* is shifted one bit position to the right. This add-shift procedure is repeated for each multiplier digit. As illustrated in Fig. 8.18, the same result is obtained using this variation as the more conventional approach of performing the addition of the array of partial products.

Although the add-shift approach to binary multiplication is not particularly convenient for hand computation, it can provide the basis for a hardware realization of a binary multiplier. In Sec. 8.1, the concept of partitioning a system into a controller and a controlled architecture was introduced where the controller is an algorithmic state machine. In the first example of this section, this partitioning was not necessary, since the entire sequence recognizer was the ASM. In this example, however, a collection of functional elements is incorporated, consisting of registers, a counter along with combinational logic for detecting its content, and a parallel adder that is also combinational logic. These are needed in order to manipulate the data associated with the multiplier. A possible system architecture for a binary multiplier is shown in Fig. 8.19.

As part of the initialization of the system, the two operands are loaded into registers. The multiplier is loaded into register M and the multiplicand is loaded into register B. Register A and flip-flop C, i.e., the carry flip-flop, are set to zero since they correspond to the initial accumulation of partial products. It is assumed that registers A, B, and M are of the same length and equal to the number of bits in each of the two operands. To complete the initialization of the system, a counter is set to the number of bits in each operand, N.

To perform the multiplication, the least significant bit in register M, i.e., M_1, is interrogated and used as the current multiplier bit. Depending upon whether it is 0 or 1, the controller causes zero or the multiplicand, respectively, to be added to, and correspondingly update, the accumulated sum in register A. Since registers A and B each contain N bits, the sum consists of $N + 1$ bits. The most significant bit of the sum is entered into flip-flop C and the remaining N bits of the sum are placed into register A. After the appropriate partial product is added, the contents of flip-flop C, register A, and register M are shifted in unison one bit position to the right with a 0 entering flip-flop C. This results in the next significant multiplier bit appearing in

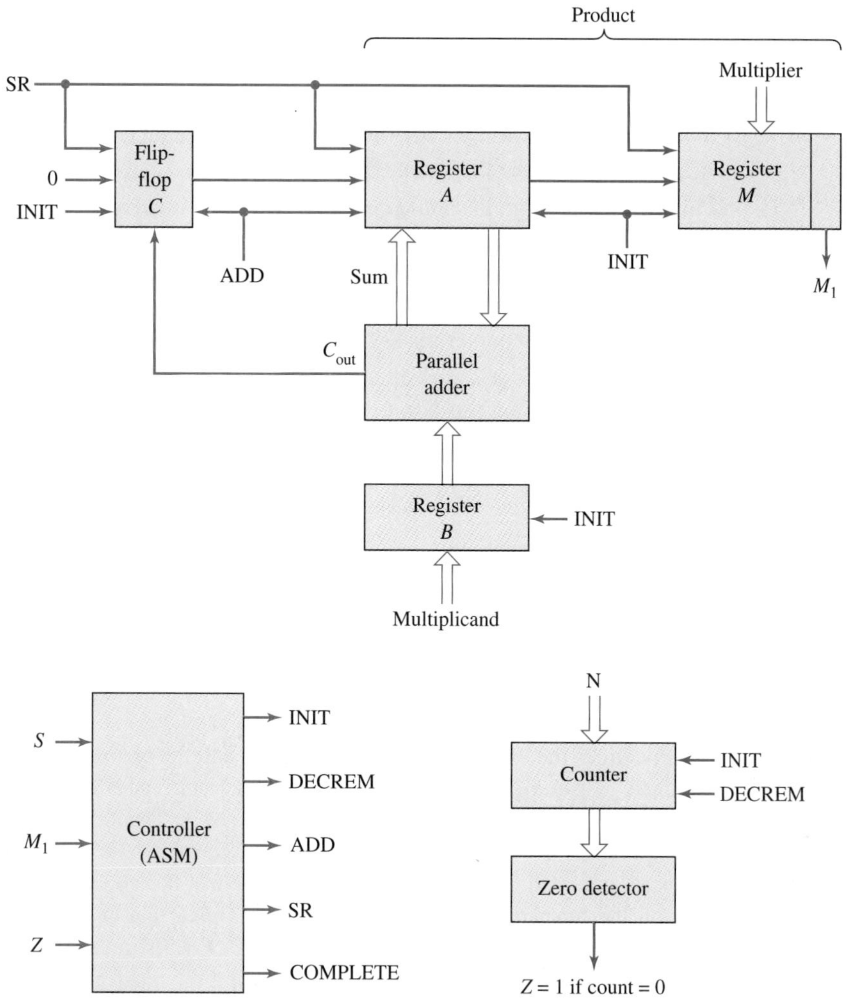

Figure 8.19 Architecture for a binary multiplier.

the least-significant-bit position of register M and is used to determine the next partial product. In addition to the accumulation of the partial products, it is necessary to keep track of the number of shift-right operations so that each multiplier bit is considered. Since the counter initially contains the number of multiplier bits, for each shift-right operation the counter is decremented. When the counter gets to zero, which is indicated by having $Z = 1$, the multiplication process is completed and the $2N$-bit product appears in the A and M registers.

For ease of understanding this example, mnemonics rather than single-lettered variables are used to define the various control signals in the system. However, a mnemonic must be considered as an entity and not as a product of variables. A summary of the signals associated with the controller is as follows:

$S = 1$ indicates the multiplication process is to start.*

M_1 is the multiplier bit appearing at the rightmost end of register M.

$Z = 1$ indicates the content of the counter is zero.

INIT = 1 indicates initialization should be performed. This involves setting flip-flop C and register A to zero, setting the counter to the number of bits in the multiplier, N, and parallel loading the multiplier and multiplicand into registers M and B, respectively.

DECREM = 1 enables the counter for decrementing.

ADD = 1 indicates registers A and B should be added and the resulting $N + 1$ bits entered into register A and flip-flop C.

SR = 1 indicates the contents of flip-flop C, register A, and register M should be shifted as a single entity one bit position to the right while entering a 0 into flip-flop C.

COMPLETE = 1 indicates the multiplication process is completed.

An ASM chart for the controller is shown in Fig. 8.20. State 1 corresponds to an initial state. The system remains in this state until the start signal $S = 1$ occurs. At that time a conditional output INIT = 1 is provided by the controller to carry out the initialization process. The INIT = 1 control signal enables flip-flop C, registers A, B, and M, and the counter so that upon the occurrence of the next triggering time of the clock signal, which defines the end of the current state time and the beginning of the next state time, the C flip-flop and register A are cleared, registers B and M are loaded with the operands, and the counter is set to the value of N. The same triggering time of the clock signal also causes the system to then go to state 2. In state 2, DECREM is asserted and used as an enabling signal to control the counter so that it is decremented on the next triggering time of the clock signal that occurs at the end of the present state time. Also while in state 2, the value of M_1 is interrogated. If $M_1 = 1$ then the content of registers A and B are summed and the result is placed at the inputs to flip-flop C and register A. The flip-flop and register are enabled by the ADD = 1 control signal. On the other hand, if $M_1 = 0$ then the output of the parallel adder is inhibited, effectively causing zero to be added to register A. It should be noted that since the parallel adder consists only of combinational logic, the addition process occurs during the current state time. In either event, when the next triggering time of the clock signal occurs, which defines the end of the current state time, the new accumulated partial sum is entered into flip-flop C and register A as well as the counter being decremented. The system then enters state 3. In state 3 the enabling control signal $SR = 1$ is applied to flip-flop C and registers A and M so that upon the

*It is assumed that the start signal S is synchronized to the master clock. That is, the new value of S occurs at the beginning of a state time. Input signals that are not synchronized to the system clock are said to be asynchronous inputs. Asynchronous inputs are discussed in Sec. 8.7.

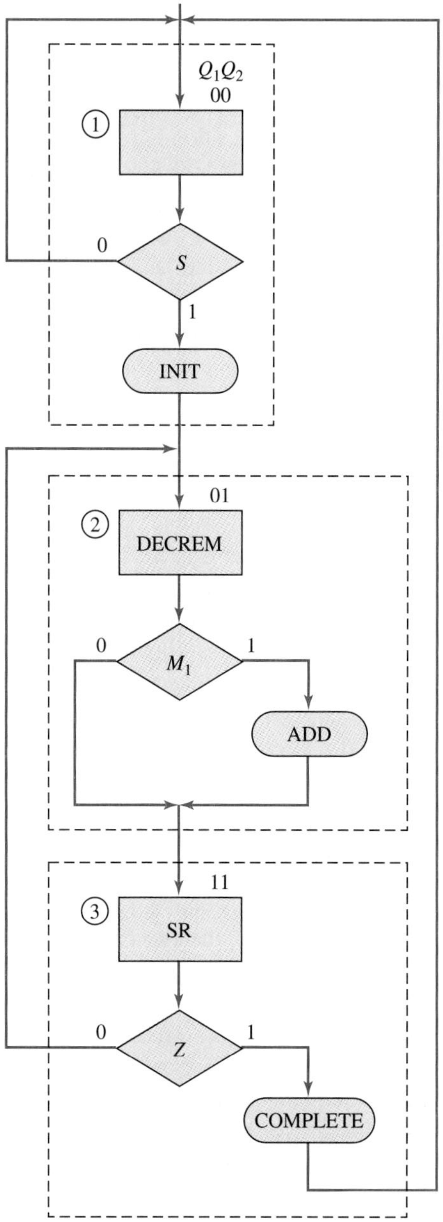

Figure 8.20 ASM chart for a binary multiplier.

next triggering time of the clock signal, which defines the end of the current state time, they are shifted right in unison. Also while in state 3, the controller interrogates the logic value of Z, which is determined by combinational logic to detect if the content of the counter is zero. If $Z = 0$, indicating the content of the counter is not zero, then the add-shift procedure for multiplication is repeated by having the system return to state 2. On the other hand, if $Z = 1$, indicating the content of the counter is zero, then a completion signal, COMPLETE, is asserted and the system returns to state 1 to await another start signal which repeats the entire multiplication process. It should be noted that regardless of the value of Z, the shift-right operation occurs since the enabling control signal $SR = 1$ is associated with the state box.

As in the previous example, a state assignment is included in the ASM chart.

8.4 STATE ASSIGNMENTS

Before obtaining a realization of an ASM chart, it is necessary to code each of its states in terms of binary digits. For a synchronous sequential network having s states, p bits are needed where 2^p is greater than or equal to s. Typically, the smallest value of p that satisfies this restriction is used. This is the state assignment problem that was considered in the previous chapter. As was mentioned at that time, as long as each state has a unique code associated with it, a valid realization for a clocked synchronous sequential network is obtained. However, the complexity of the resulting realization depends upon the state assignment that is selected.

Unfortunately, there are no simple procedures for determining a state assignment that leads to an optimal realization from a cost point of view. Occasionally, the nature of the problem suggests a state assignment as, for example, in the case of counters. However, most of the time it is sufficient to simply determine an assignment that results in a good realization. For this reason some simple rules were introduced in the previous chapter for determining a "good" state assignment. Although those rules can also be used for an ASM, at this time another procedure for a "good" state assignment is given that is based on the concept of the *minimum state locus.*

The premise underlying the minimum state locus state assignment is that the complexity of the realization of a next-state function depends upon the number of state variables that must change value in the transition from one state to the next. Accepting this premise, the complexity of the realization is controllable by minimizing the total number of bit changes associated with all the possible state transitions. The sum of all bit changes for all possible state transitions is known as the *state locus.* Since each state must have a unique binary code, thereby implying each code must differ by at least 1 bit, to achieve the absolute minimal state locus it is necessary to assign the codes so that the transition between two different states having a link path connecting them requires only a single bit change in their state codes. In general, however, it is not possible to obtain an assignment, while also satisfying the constraint of using the minimum number of bits for the state codes, in which all linked-state transitions are associated with a single bit change in their codes. In such a case, the assignment should attempt to minimize the state locus.

To obtain state assignments, it is convenient to use the state-assignment map that was introduced in the previous chapter. A state of a synchronous sequential network is represented by the collective states of a set of flip-flops, i.e., the state register, in which one flip-flop is used for each state variable. Recall that in the state-assignment map, the state variables appear along the axis of the map. In this way, each cell of the state-assignment map corresponds to an assignment to the state variables, or, in other words, a possible code for a state. By entering a state name in a cell, a binary code is assigned to that state.

To illustrate how the minimum state locus concept is applied, consider the ASM chart of Fig. 8.21. At this point, the reader should disregard the indicated state

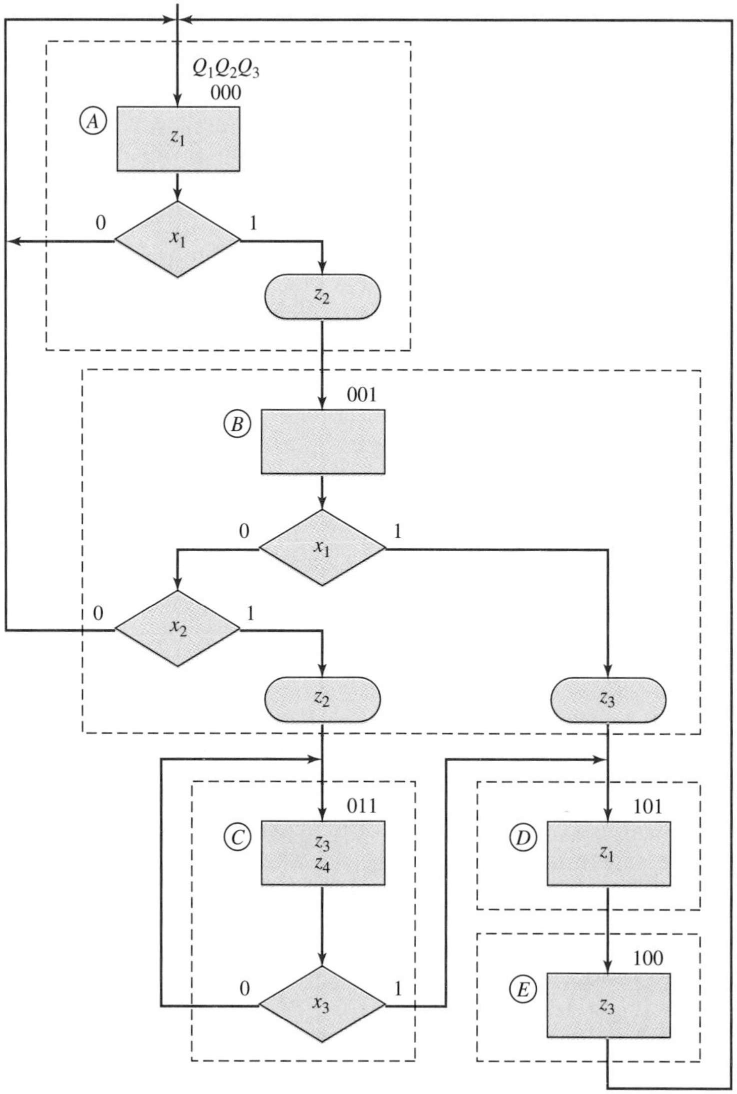

Figure 8.21 An ASM chart.

Q_1 \ Q_2Q_3	00	01	11	10
0	*A*	*B*	*C*	–
1	*E*	*D*	–	–

(*a*)

State transition *A* ⟶	$B = 000$ ⟶	001	1 bit change
State transition *B* ⟶	$A = 001$ ⟶	000	1 bit change
State transition *B* ⟶	$C = 001$ ⟶	011	1 bit change
State transition *B* ⟶	$D = 001$ ⟶	101	1 bit change
State transition *C* ⟶	$D = 011$ ⟶	101	2 bit changes
State transition *D* ⟶	$E = 101$ ⟶	100	1 bit change
State transition *E* ⟶	$A = 100$ ⟶	000	1 bit change
			Total = 8 = state locus

(*b*)

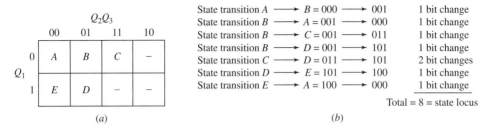

Figure 8.22 A minimum state locus assignment for the ASM chart of Fig. 8.21. (*a*) State-assignment map. (*b*) State locus.

assignment since this is what is being established. To determine a state assignment for an ASM chart using the minimum state locus approach, it is first necessary to consider the link paths. Those link paths that link a state with itself are ignored since no state variables need to change value. In Fig. 8.21 link paths exists between the following pairs of states: *A*→*B*, *B*→*A*, *B*→*C*, *B*→*D*, *C*→*D*, *D*→*E*, and *E*→*A*. Since there are five states in the ASM chart, a minimum of 3 bits are needed to uniquely code each state. Using this number of bits, a state assignment is attempted such that the code for each pair of states that are linked differs in exactly 1 bit. To do this, it is necessary to assign the states to the cells of the state-assignment map such that two linked states appear in adjacent cells. The state-assignment map of Fig. 8.22*a* shows a possible state assignment for Fig. 8.21. In this state assignment all the adjacencies are satisfied with the exception of the transition from state *C* to state *D*. In this example it is not possible to achieve all of the desired adjacencies. Note that three binary combinations are not used for the state assignment since only five of the eight combinations are needed to code the states. This state assignment is also shown above the state boxes in the ASM chart of Fig. 8.21. As indicated in Fig. 8.22*b*, the state locus for this example is eight. Since no smaller state locus is possible, under the constraint of using a minimal number of bits to code each state, this is a minimum state locus assignment.

8.5 ASM TABLES

Although the ASM chart is convenient to describe the behavior of a sequential network, to proceed to the implementation it is frequently desirable to use a tabular representation. In a straightforward manner, ASM charts are converted into tabular form. Several variations are possible that are referred to as the *ASM transition table*, the *assigned ASM transition table*, and the *ASM excitation table.*

8.5.1 ASM Transition Tables

To see how an ASM transition table is constructed, again consider the ASM chart of Fig. 8.21. The corresponding ASM transition table is given in Table 8.1*a*. The transition table consists of five sections that are labeled *link path*, *present state*, *inputs*,

Table 8.1 ASM tables for Fig. 8.21. (*a*) ASM transition table. (*b*) Assigned ASM transition table

Link path	Present state	Inputs x_1	x_2	x_3	Next state	Outputs z_1	z_2	z_3	z_4
L_1	A	0	–	–	A	1	0	0	0
L_2	A	1	–	–	B	1	1	0	0
L_3	B	0	0	–	A	0	0	0	0
L_4	B	0	1	–	C	0	1	0	0
L_5	B	1	–	–	D	0	0	1	0
L_6	C	–	–	0	C	0	0	1	1
L_7	C	–	–	1	D	0	0	1	1
L_8	D	–	–	–	E	1	0	0	0
L_9	E	–	–	–	A	0	0	1	0

(*a*)

Link path	Present state Sym	Q_1	Q_2	Q_3	Inputs x_1	x_2	x_3	Next state Sym	Q_1^+	Q_2^+	Q_3^+	Outputs z_1	z_2	z_3	z_4
L_1	A	0	0	0	0	–	–	A	0	0	0	1	0	0	0
L_2	A	0	0	0	1	–	–	B	0	0	1	1	1	0	0
L_3	B	0	0	1	0	0	–	A	0	0	0	0	0	0	0
L_4	B	0	0	1	0	1	–	C	0	1	1	0	1	0	0
L_5	B	0	0	1	1	–	–	D	1	0	1	0	0	1	0
L_6	C	0	1	1	–	–	0	C	0	1	1	0	0	1	1
L_7	C	0	1	1	–	–	1	D	1	0	1	0	0	1	1
L_8	D	1	0	1	–	–	–	E	1	0	0	1	0	0	0
L_9	E	1	0	0	–	–	–	A	0	0	0	0	0	1	0

(*b*)

next state, and *outputs*. Within the inputs section, all the input variables to the algorithmic state machine are listed. Similarly, all the output variables of the algorithmic state machine appear as column headings in the outputs section. Each link path in the ASM chart is associated with a row in the ASM transition table. The horizontal dashed lines divide the table according to the ASM blocks.

For the ASM block with state A in Fig. 8.21, there are two link paths. As was indicated in Sec. 8.2, these link paths are described by Boolean expressions giving the conditions for their selection. In this case,

$$\text{State transition } A \rightarrow A, \qquad L_1 = \bar{x}_1$$

$$\text{State transition } A \rightarrow B, \qquad L_2 = x_1$$

These two link paths correspond to the first two rows of Table 8.1*a*. In the first row the state A to state A transition is recorded in the present-state and next-state sections of the transition table. Since this transition occurs when $\bar{x}_1 = 1$ or, equivalently, $x_1 = 0$, a 0 is entered under the x_1 input. Furthermore, since this transition is to occur regardless of the values of x_2 or x_3, dashes appear under the x_2 and x_3 inputs. Next, all the output variables that are asserted with the L_1 link path are assigned the value of 1 in the transition table. Since a link path starts at a state box, 1's are assigned to all output variables appearing in the state box as well as to any output variables in conditional output boxes along the link path. All other outputs are assigned 0 values. For link path L_1 there is a 1 in the z_1 output column of Table 8.1*a*; while 0's appear in the z_2, z_3, and z_4 output columns since z_1 is the only output variable asserted with link path L_1.

The second row of the ASM transition table given in Table 8.1*a* corresponds to the second link path for the ASM chart of Fig. 8.21. In this case there is a transition from state *A* to state *B* when $x_1 = 1$. Thus, *A* and *B* appear as entries in the present-state and next-state columns, respectively, of Table 8.1*a*. In addition, a 1 appears under the x_1 input. Since the selection of this link path is not dependent upon the remaining two input variables, dashes are entered under the x_2 and x_3 inputs. Finally, the unconditional output z_1 and the conditional output z_2 occur along link path L_2. Hence, 1 entries are placed under the z_1 and z_2 outputs in the second row of the ASM transition table. The 0 entries under the z_3 and z_4 outputs indicate that these outputs are logic-0 for this link path.

The ASM block for state *B* has three link paths associated with it:

$$\text{State transition } B \rightarrow A, \quad L_3 = \bar{x}_1\bar{x}_2$$

$$\text{State transition } B \rightarrow C, \quad L_4 = \bar{x}_1 x_2$$

$$\text{State transition } B \rightarrow D, \quad L_5 = x_1$$

For link path L_3 to be selected, it is necessary that $\bar{x}_1\bar{x}_2 = 1$, i.e., this is the selected link path when $x_1 = 0$ and $x_2 = 0$. This is indicated in the third row of Table 8.1*a* by having 0 entries appear in the x_1 and x_2 input columns. Since this path is not a function of x_3, a dash occurs in the x_3 column. In a similar manner, link path L_4 is selected when $\bar{x}_1 x_2 = 1$, which corresponds to $x_1 = 0$ and $x_2 = 1$. Finally, link path L_5 is selected if simply $x_1 = 1$. With respect to the two conditional outputs appearing in the ASM block, the z_2 output variable occurs only in link path L_4 and the z_3 output variable occurs only in link path L_5. Thus corresponding 1 entries are placed in the outputs section of the ASM transition table. Notice that no output variables occur along link path L_3. Hence, 0 entries appear in all the output columns of the L_3 row.

Continuing using a similar analysis, the remaining three ASM blocks of Fig. 8.21 result in the final four rows of the ASM transition table of Table 8.1*a*. It should be noted that state *D* unconditionally leads to state *E*. Hence, dashes appear for each input variable in the L_8 row of the ASM transition table. A similar situation occurs for the ASM block associated with state *E*.

8.5.2 Assigned ASM Transition Tables

Once a state assignment is established, the coding of the states is also included in the transition table. This variation is the *assigned ASM transition table*. For the

ASM chart of Fig. 8.21, the assigned ASM transition table is given in Table 8.1*b*. This table is the same as Table 8.1*a* with the addition that the state variables are included in the present-state and next-state sections along with the symbolic state names. For this example the present-state variables are denoted by Q_1, Q_2, and Q_3; while the next-state variables are denoted by Q_1^+, Q_2^+, and Q_3^+, respectively. The codes for the states were determined in the previous section and were entered above each state box in the ASM chart. The entries in the assigned ASM transition table under the present-state and next-state variables are simply the code assigned to each of the states.

ASM tables for the two examples of Sec. 8.3 are given in Tables 8.2 and 8.3. Table 8.2 is for the binary multiplier whose ASM chart appeared in Fig. 8.20 and Table 8.3 is for the sequence recognizer whose ASM chart appeared in Fig. 8.17. Table 8.2 follows directly from the above discussion on the construction of the ASM transition table and the assigned ASM transition table. Table 8.3, however, requires further explanation.

Referring to Fig. 8.17, two link paths exist for the ASM block containing state 1:

$$\text{State transition } 1 \rightarrow 1, \qquad L_1 = \overline{\bar{x}_1 x_2}$$

$$\text{State transition } 1 \rightarrow 2, \qquad L_2 = \bar{x}_1 x_2$$

Particular attention should be given to link path L_1. The entry in the decision box is the Boolean expression $\bar{x}_1x_2$. The logic-0 exit from the decision box is described by

Table 8.2 ASM tables for Fig. 8.20. (*a*) ASM transition table. (*b*) Assigned ASM transition table

Link path	Present state	Inputs S	M_1	Z	Next state	Outputs INIT	DECREM	ADD	SR	COMPLETE
L_1	1	0	–	–	1	0	0	0	0	0
L_2	1	1	–	–	2	1	0	0	0	0
L_3	2	–	0	–	3	0	1	0	0	0
L_4	2	–	1	–	3	0	1	1	0	0
L_5	3	–	–	0	2	0	0	0	1	0
L_6	3	–	–	1	1	0	0	0	1	1

(*a*)

Link path	Present state Sym	Q_1	Q_2	Inputs S	M_1	Z	Next state Sym	Q_1^+	Q_2^+	Outputs INIT	DECREM	ADD	SR	COMPLETE
L_1	1	0	0	0	–	–	1	0	0	0	0	0	0	0
L_2	1	0	0	1	–	–	2	0	1	1	0	0	0	0
L_3	2	0	1	–	0	–	3	1	1	0	1	0	0	0
L_4	2	0	1	–	1	–	3	1	1	0	1	1	0	0
L_5	3	1	1	–	–	0	2	0	1	0	0	0	1	0
L_6	3	1	1	–	–	1	1	0	0	0	0	0	1	1

(*b*)

Table 8.3 ASM tables for Fig. 8.17. (*a*) ASM transition table. (*b*) Assigned ASM transition table

Link path	Present state	Inputs x_1	Inputs x_2	Next state	Output z
L_1	1	1	–	1	0
	1	–	0	1	0
L_2	1	0	1	2	0
L_3	2	1	–	1	0
	2	–	0	1	0
L_4	2	0	1	3	0
L_5	3	0	1	3	0
L_6	3	–	0	1	0
L_7	3	1	1	4	0
L_8	4	1	–	1	0
L_9	4	0	1	2	0
L_{10}	4	0	0	1	1

(*a*)

Link path	Present state Sym	Q_1	Q_2	Inputs x_1	x_2	Next state Sym	Q_1^+	Q_2^+	Output z
L_1	1	0	0	1	–	1	0	0	0
	1	0	0	–	0	1	0	0	0
L_2	1	0	0	0	1	2	0	1	0
L_3	2	0	1	1	–	1	0	0	0
	2	0	1	–	0	1	0	0	0
L_4	2	0	1	0	1	3	1	1	0
L_5	3	1	1	0	1	3	1	1	0
L_6	3	1	1	–	0	1	0	0	0
L_7	3	1	1	1	1	4	1	0	0
L_8	4	1	0	1	–	1	0	0	0
L_9	4	1	0	0	1	2	0	1	0
L_{10}	4	1	0	0	0	1	0	0	1

(*b*)

the complement of the Boolean-expression entry since this exit is to occur when $\bar{x}_1x_2 = 0$. Hence, $L_1 = \overline{\bar{x}_1x_2} = x_1 + \bar{x}_2$. As indicated by this equation, there are two ways in which this path is selected; in particular, when $x_1 = 1$ or when $\bar{x}_2 = 1$. Since there are two possibilities, two rows appear in the ASM transition table for this link path. The first row corresponds to the situation when $x_1 = 1$ and the second to the situation when $x_2 = 0$, i.e., when $\bar{x}_2 = 1$. For the selection of the second link path, L_2, it is necessary that $\bar{x}_1x_2 = 1$. This is achieved when $x_1 = 0$ and $x_2 = 1$, which only requires one row in the ASM transition table.

As a final illustration, consider the ASM block containing state 3 in Fig. 8.17. Three link paths occur in this block; namely,

State transition 3→3, $L_5 = \overline{(x_1x_2)}\,(\bar{x}_1x_2) = \bar{x}_1x_2$

State transition 3→1, $L_6 = \overline{(x_1x_2)}\,\overline{(\bar{x}_1x_2)} = \bar{x}_2$

State transition 3→4, $L_7 = x_1x_2$

Each of these link paths corresponds to a single row in the ASM transition table since the reduced expressions consist of a single term. The remaining rows of Table 8.3 are obtained using similar reasoning.

8.5.3 Algebraic Representation of Assigned Transition Tables

Using the ASM chart once the state assignment is made or the assigned ASM transition table, it is a simple matter to obtain Boolean expressions for the output and next-state functions of an algorithmic state machine. These expressions are a function of the present-state and input variables. To illustrate how this is done, again consider the assigned ASM transition table of Table 8.1*b*. Since there are three next-state variables and four output variables, a total of seven expressions can be written. The assigned ASM transition table is actually a truth table for these seven functions. Thus, for each row in which an output or next-state variable has the logic value of 1, a product term is written in which a present-state or input variable is uncomplemented if its value is 1 in that row and complemented if its value is 0. If a dash appears, then no variable is written. For example, the Q_1^+ next-state variable is 1 for rows corresponding to link paths L_5, L_7, and L_8. Since these link paths occur in the ASM blocks for states B, C, and D, respectively, Q_1^+ is described by the Boolean expression

$$\begin{aligned} Q_1^+ &= BL_5 + CL_7 + DL_8 \\ &= \bar{Q}_1\bar{Q}_2Q_3x_1 + \bar{Q}_1Q_2Q_3x_3 + Q_1\bar{Q}_2Q_3 \end{aligned} \tag{8.1}$$

In a similar manner, the remaining equations for the algebraic description of the assigned ASM transition table of Table 8.1*b* are written as follows:

$$Q_2^+ = \bar{Q}_1\bar{Q}_2Q_3\bar{x}_1x_2 + \bar{Q}_1Q_2Q_3\bar{x}_3 \tag{8.2}$$

$$Q_3^+ = \bar{Q}_1\bar{Q}_2\bar{Q}_3x_1 + \bar{Q}_1\bar{Q}_2Q_3\bar{x}_1x_2 + \bar{Q}_1\bar{Q}_2Q_3x_1 + \bar{Q}_1Q_2Q_3\bar{x}_3 + \bar{Q}_1Q_2Q_3x_3 \tag{8.3}$$

$$z_1 = \bar{Q}_1\bar{Q}_2\bar{Q}_3\bar{x}_1 + \bar{Q}_1\bar{Q}_2\bar{Q}_3x_1 + Q_1\bar{Q}_2Q_3 \tag{8.4}$$

$$z_2 = \bar{Q}_1\bar{Q}_2\bar{Q}_3x_1 + \bar{Q}_1\bar{Q}_2Q_3\bar{x}_1x_2 \tag{8.5}$$

$$z_3 = \bar{Q}_1\bar{Q}_2Q_3x_1 + \bar{Q}_1Q_2Q_3\bar{x}_3 + \bar{Q}_1Q_2Q_3x_3 + Q_1\bar{Q}_2\bar{Q}_3 \tag{8.6}$$

$$z_4 = \bar{Q}_1Q_2Q_3\bar{x}_3 + \bar{Q}_1Q_2Q_3x_3 \tag{8.7}$$

The above Boolean expressions can be simplified if desired. To perform simplification, it is important to realize that these are really incomplete Boolean functions since not all the binary combinations of values to the state variables were used in the state assignment. In this case, all possible combinations of values of the input variables when $Q_1Q_2Q_3 = 010$, 110, and 111 correspond to don't-care conditions. The six-variable Karnaugh map for obtaining the minimal sum-of-products expression for Q_1^+ is shown in Fig. 8.23. In this map, the three rows of dashes correspond to the eight combinations of values of the three input variables, as indicated by the labels along the top of the map, for the three unused state codes, as indicated by the labels along the side of the map. Similar maps are constructed for the remaining functions. The set of simplified sum-of-products expressions for Table 8.1*b* is:

$$Q_1^+ = \overline{Q}_2Q_3x_1 + Q_2x_3 + Q_1Q_3 \tag{8.8}$$

$$Q_2^+ = \overline{Q}_1\overline{Q}_2Q_3\overline{x}_1x_2 + Q_2\overline{x}_3 \tag{8.9}$$

$$Q_3^+ = \overline{Q}_1x_1 + \overline{Q}_1Q_3x_2 + Q_2 \tag{8.10}$$

$$z_1 = \overline{Q}_1\overline{Q}_3 + Q_1Q_3 \tag{8.11}$$

$$z_2 = \overline{Q}_1Q_3x_1 + \overline{Q}_1\overline{Q}_2Q_3\overline{x}_1x_2 \tag{8.12}$$

$$z_3 = \overline{Q}_1Q_3x_1 + Q_2 + Q_1\overline{Q}_3 \tag{8.13}$$

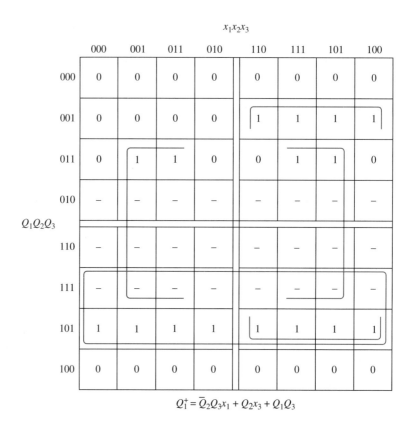

$$z_4 = Q_2 \tag{8.14}$$

$Q_1Q_2Q_3$ \ $x_1x_2x_3$	000	001	011	010	110	111	101	100
000	0	0	0	0	0	0	0	0
001	0	0	0	0	1	1	1	1
011	0	1	1	0	0	1	1	0
010	–	–	–	–	–	–	–	–
110	–	–	–	–	–	–	–	–
111	–	–	–	–	–	–	–	–
101	1	1	1	1	1	1	1	1
100	0	0	0	0	0	0	0	0

$Q_1^+ = \overline{Q}_2Q_3x_1 + Q_2x_3 + Q_1Q_3$

Figure 8.23 Karnaugh map for simplifying the Q_1^+ function of Table 8.1*b*.

It is also possible to obtain the above set of unsimplified Boolean expressions (8.1) to (8.7) directly from the ASM chart. In general, for a next-state variable equation, a product term is needed for each link path that leads to a state in which the given next-state variable has the value 1. In writing the expression, it is necessary to include the algebraic description of the state associated with the link path as well as that of the input conditions along the link path. For the case of an output expression, a product term is needed for each link path that traverses a conditional output box containing the specified output variable. Again the algebraic description of the state associated with the link path is included in the product term. When an output variable appears in a state box, it is only necessary to use the algebraic description of the state in the expression for the output variable. If this procedure is applied to the ASM chart of Fig. 8.21, then Eqs. (8.1) to (8.7) derived previously are again obtained.

8.5.4 ASM Excitation Tables

As was indicated in Sec. 8.1, the present state of an ASM is stored in a register consisting of a collection of clocked flip-flops, i.e., the state register. In Chapter 6 a large variety of clocked flip-flops were introduced for hardware realizations of synchronous sequential logic networks. The assigned ASM transition table only indicates the values of the present-state and next-state variables. These correspond to the present and next values of the flip-flop outputs. However, depending upon the type of clocked flip-flop used, different excitation signals are needed at the flip-flop inputs to achieve these outputs. When the assigned ASM transition table is appended to include the excitations required for the selected clocked flip-flops in the state register of an ASM, it is called an *ASM excitation table.*

Table 8.4 summarizes the rules that were developed in Chapter 6 for achieving the four possible state transitions with clocked D, JK, T, and SR flip-flops. To form an ASM excitation table, it is first necessary to select the type of clocked flip-flops to appear in the state register. Once this is done, the values of the excitation signals for the flip-flops are determined, using the results of Table 8.4, to provide for the state transitions indicated in the assigned ASM transition table. Table 8.5 shows the ASM excitation table for Table 8.1b under the assumption that clocked JK flip-flops are used for the state register. The signals needed at the flip-flop inputs appear in the six columns of the excitations section. To illustrate how the entries are determined,

Table 8.4 State transition excitation signals for clocked D, JK, T, and SR flip-flops

Q	Q^+	D	J	K	T	S	R
0	0	0	0	–	0	0	–
0	1	1	1	–	1	1	0
1	0	0	–	1	1	0	1
1	1	1	–	0	0	–	0

Table 8.5 ASM excitation table for Table 8.1*b*

Link path	Present state				Inputs			Next state				Excitations						Outputs			
	Sym	Q_1	Q_2	Q_3	x_1	x_2	x_3	Sym	Q_1^+	Q_2^+	Q_3^+	J_1	K_1	J_2	K_2	J_3	K_3	z_1	z_2	z_3	z_4
L_1	*A*	0	0	0	0	–	–	*A*	0	0	0	0	–	0	–	0	–	1	0	0	0
L_2	*A*	0	0	0	1	–	–	*B*	0	0	1	0	–	0	–	1	–	1	1	0	0
L_3	*B*	0	0	1	0	0	–	*A*	0	0	0	0	–	0	–	–	1	0	0	0	0
L_4	*B*	0	0	1	0	1	–	*C*	0	1	1	0	–	1	–	–	0	0	1	0	0
L_5	*B*	0	0	1	1	–	–	*D*	1	0	1	1	–	0	–	–	0	0	0	1	0
L_6	*C*	0	1	1	–	–	0	*C*	0	1	1	0	–	–	0	–	0	0	0	1	1
L_7	*C*	0	1	1	–	–	1	*D*	1	0	1	1	–	–	1	–	0	0	0	1	1
L_8	*D*	1	0	1	–	–	–	*E*	1	0	0	–	0	0	–	–	1	1	0	0	0
L_9	*E*	1	0	0	–	–	–	*A*	0	0	0	–	1	0	–	0	–	0	0	1	0

in the L_5 row it is seen that $Q_1Q_2Q_3 = 001$ and $Q_1^+Q_2^+Q_3^+ = 101$. Since flip-flop Q_1 must change from its 0-state to its 1-state, $J_1 = 1$ and $K_1 = -$ according to Table 8.4. Similarly, since $Q_2 = 0$ and $Q_2^+ = 0$, from Table 8.4 it follows that $J_2 = 0$ and $K_2 = -$; and since $Q_3 = 1$ and $Q_3^+ = 1$, it follows that $J_3 = -$ and $K_3 = 0$. All the entries in the excitations section of Table 8.5 are similarly obtained.

As shown in Table 8.4, there is a direct correspondence between the excitation signal on the D input of a clocked D flip-flop and the next state of the flip-flop, i.e., $D = Q^+$. Hence, the ASM excitation table when clocked D flip-flops are used for the state register is the same as the assigned ASM transition table where each next state column heading Q_i^+ is regarded as D_i.

8.6 ASM REALIZATIONS

Once the ASM excitation table is formed, the final step in ASM design is to obtain a realization. In this section, several different realizations for the ASM chart of Fig. 8.21 are presented. In particular, realizations are obtained involving discrete gates, multiplexers, PLAs, and PROMs.

8.6.1 Realizations Using Discrete Gates

An approach to obtaining a discrete-gate realization of an ASM is to first derive the minimal expressions for the excitation and output functions that describe the implementation. The ASM excitation table is really a truth table listing the excitation and output functions in terms of the input and present-state variables. Thus, using any minimization technique, a set of minimal expressions for the excitations and outputs is readily obtained. Once the expressions are written, the logic diagram for the implementation immediately follows.

Consider this approach for the ASM chart of Fig. 8.21. Furthermore, assume that clocked D flip-flops are used for the state register. Recalling that the next-state function Q_i^+ is the same as the clocked D flip-flop excitation function D_i, i.e., $D_i = Q_i^+$, the transition table of Table 8.1*b* becomes an excitation table when the column headings Q_1^+, Q_2^+, and Q_3^+ are relabeled as D_1, D_2, and D_3, respectively. Once this is done, the three excitation expressions $D_i(x_1,x_2,x_3,Q_1,Q_2,Q_3)$, for $i = 1,2,3$, are readily obtained by regarding the resulting excitation table as a truth table. Actually, the unsimplified and minimal-sum forms of these expressions were already given in Sec. 8.5 as Eqs. (8.1) to (8.3) and Eqs. (8.8) to (8.10), respectively. In the same manner, expressions for the four output functions $z_i(x_1,x_2,x_3,Q_1,Q_2,Q_3)$, for $i = 1, \ldots, 4$, are obtained. These also were given in Sec. 8.5 in unsimplified form as Eqs. (8.4) to (8.7) and in minimal-sum form as Eqs. (8.11) to (8.14). Using the minimal-sum expressions, the logic diagram for the realization of the ASM chart of Fig. 8.21 with clocked D flip-flops is shown in Fig. 8.24.

Alternatively, if the state register of the ASM of Fig. 8.21 is to consist of clocked JK flip-flops, then the six columns in the excitations section of Table 8.5 are used to obtain the excitation equations of the JK flip-flop inputs. With a total of six input and present-state variables, the minimal expressions can be determined

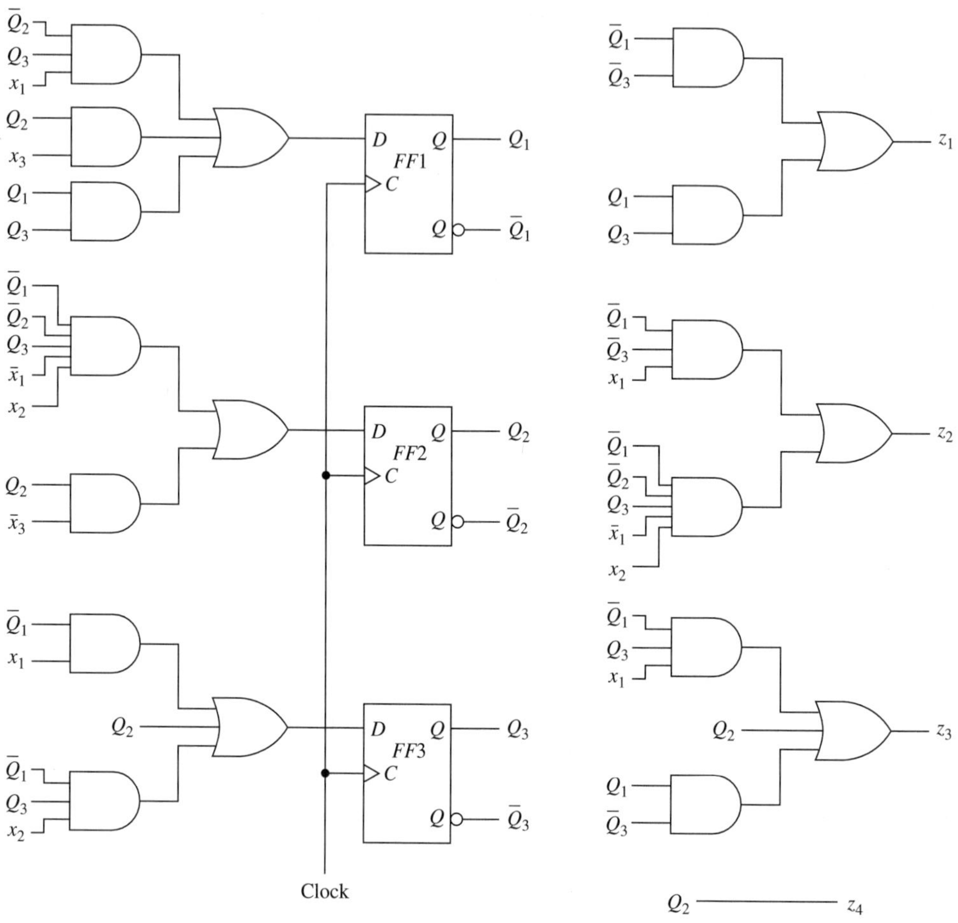

Figure 8.24 Discrete-gate realization with clocked *D* flip-flops for the ASM chart of Fig. 8.21.

using six-variable Karnaugh maps. In constructing the Karnaugh maps, don't-care entries occur for the three state combinations $Q_1Q_2Q_3 = 010$, 110, and 111, which were not used in the state-assignment process, as well as for those cases in which dashes appear in the excitations section of the ASM excitation table.

Unfortunately, Karnaugh maps involving a large number of variables are difficult to use. Typically in ASM design problems, there are many input variables in which only a small subset of them appear in each ASM block. In addition, every block is a function of a fixed set of variables, namely, the state variables. This is precisely a situation when variable-entered Karnaugh maps, which were discussed in Sec. 4.14, are very effective, even though they may not necessarily lead to minimal expressions. In such a case, it is desirable to have the fixed variables serve as the map variables, i.e., those appearing as labels along the map axes, and the infrequently occurring input variables serve as the map-entered variables. As a result, the variable-entered Karnaugh maps needed for representing the excitation and output functions are relatively small for an ASM having a fairly large number of states. For example, a six-variable map can handle an ASM with $2^6 = 64$ states.

When the state variables of a variable-entered Karnaugh map are the map variables, the structure of the map is the same as the state-assignment map that was used when the state assignment was established. Each cell of the variable-entered map corresponds to a single block of the ASM chart. When the ASM tables were constructed in the previous section, the tables were subdivided by dashed lines in accordance with the ASM blocks. Thus, each such group of rows in a table is associated with a single cell of a variable-entered map.

To illustrate the use of variable-entered Karnaugh maps, again consider the ASM chart of Fig. 8.21 under the assumption that the state register of the ASM is to consist of clocked *D* flip-flops. As already mentioned, the assigned ASM transition table of Table 8.1*b* can be used as the ASM excitation table where each next-state variable Q_i^+ is regarded as the D_i excitation variable. The resulting variable-entered maps for the excitation and output functions are shown in Fig. 8.25. Since there are three state variables, Q_1, Q_2, and Q_3, three-variable maps are needed. In the figure, the state-assignment map is also included for reference purposes. The entries in the state-assignment map indicate the state associated with the corresponding cell.

To determine the entries in the excitation and output variable-entered maps for each state of the ASM, it is necessary to algebraically express the excitations and outputs as a function of just the input variables. Thus, the entry within a cell of the excitation and output maps is the sum of the link path expressions for an ASM block, in terms of the input variables for the associated state, in which the excitation and output variables are 1, respectively. For example, state *A* in Fig. 8.25 is associated with the upper left cell of the state-assignment map and correspondingly to the upper left cells of the seven variable-entered maps. Furthermore, the first two rows of Table 8.1*b* correspond to the ASM block for state *A*. In these two rows $Q_1^+ = Q_2^+ = 0$. Since Q_1^+ and Q_2^+ are never 1 for state *A*, the entries in the upper left cells of the Q_1^+ and Q_2^+ maps are 0's. In the Q_3^+ column of the first two rows of Table 8.1*b*, it is seen that $Q_3^+ = 1$ only when $x_1 = 1$. This is described algebraically as $Q_3^+ = x_1$ and, correspondingly, x_1 is entered in the upper left cell of the Q_3^+ map. Looking at the output columns in the first two rows of Table 8.1*b*, it is seen that z_1 is asserted, i.e., $z_1 = 1$, when $x_1 = 0$ and also when $x_1 = 1$. Thus, $z_1 = \bar{x}_1 + x_1$, which simplifies to $\bar{x}_1 + x_1 = 1$. The single 1 entry in the z_2 column is described algebraically as $z_2 = x_1$. Finally, the 0 entries in the first two rows of the z_3 and z_4 columns imply that $z_3 = 0$ and $z_4 = 0$ during state *A*. These four results, 1, x_1, 0, and 0, are now entered in the upper left cells of the output maps for z_1, z_2, z_3, and z_4, respectively.

The entries in the $Q_1Q_2Q_3 = 001$ cells of the excitation and output maps correspond to the ASM block for state *B*. To determine the entries in the excitation

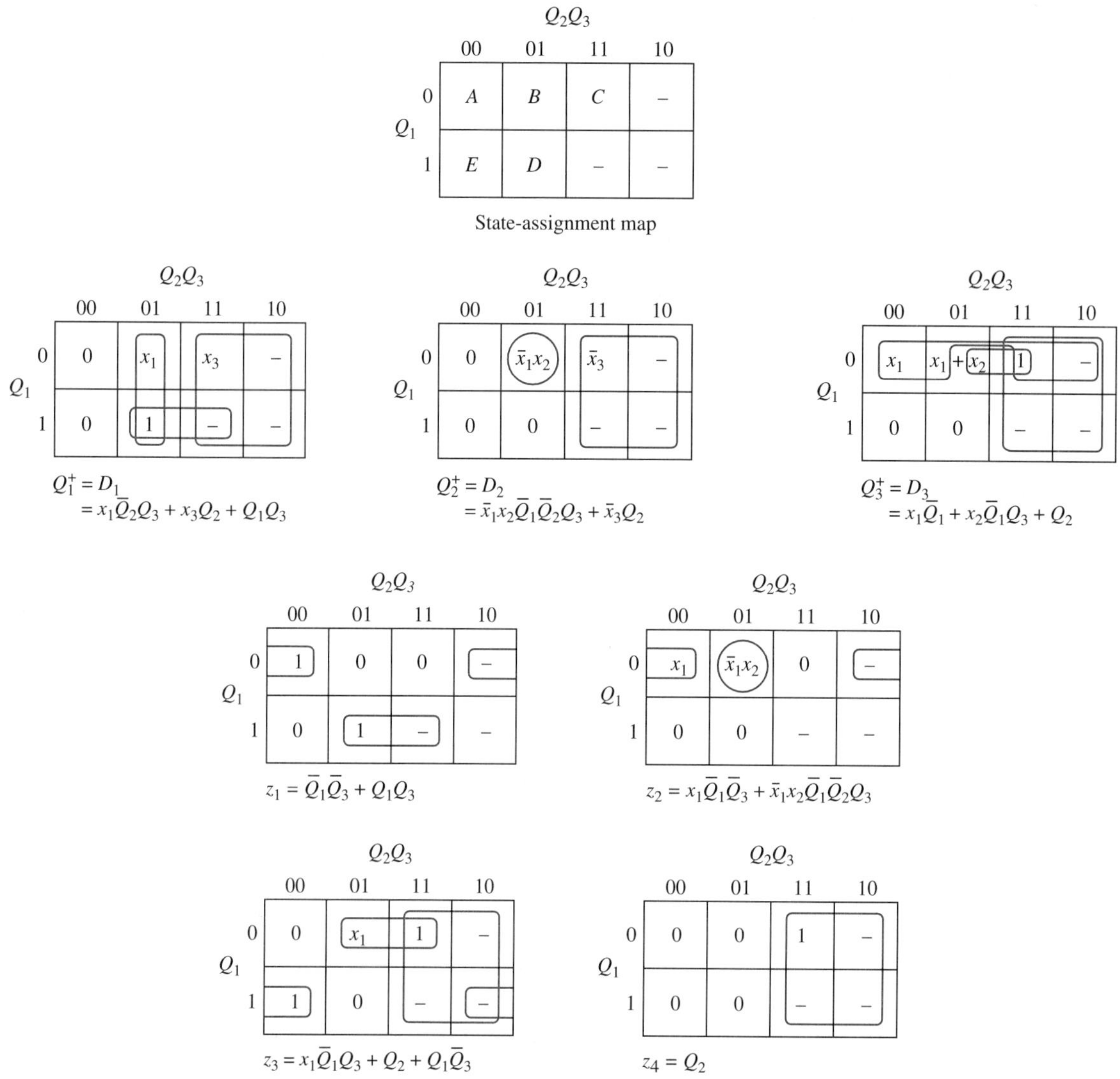

Figure 8.25 Using variable-entered Karnaugh maps to obtain a discrete-gate realization with clocked D flip-flops for the ASM chart of Fig. 8.21.

and output maps for this state, rows L_3, L_4, and L_5 of Table 8.1b are used. The conditions under which the excitation and output variables have the value 1 for state B must be algebraically described in terms of the input variables. These are given as

$$Q_1^+ = x_1, \qquad Q_2^+ = \bar{x}_1x_2, \qquad Q_3^+ = \bar{x}_1x_2 + x_1 = x_1 + x_2$$

$$z_1 = 0, \qquad z_2 = \bar{x}_1x_2, \qquad z_3 = x_1, \qquad z_4 = 0$$

The above results are now entered in the $Q_1Q_2Q_3 = 001$ cells of Fig. 8.25. Considering next the ASM block for state C, rows L_6 and L_7 of Table 8.1b are analyzed. These two rows lead to the results:

$$Q_1^+ = x_3, \qquad Q_2^+ = \bar{x}_3, \qquad Q_3^+ = \bar{x}_3 + x_3 = 1$$

$$z_1 = 0, \qquad z_2 = 0, \qquad z_3 = \bar{x}_3 + x_3 = 1, \qquad z_4 = \bar{x}_3 + x_3 = 1$$

Again the expressions serve as the entries for the seven variable-entered maps. In this case the entries are for the $Q_1Q_2Q_3 = 011$ cells.

For the last two ASM blocks of Table 8.1b, none of the excitation and output variables are a function of the input variables since dashes appear in the L_8 and L_9 rows of the inputs section. In such cases, the variable-map entries simply correspond to the constant values assigned to the next-state and output variables. Thus, for state D:

$$Q_1^+ = 1, \qquad Q_2^+ = 0, \qquad Q_3^+ = 0$$

$$z_1 = 1, \qquad z_2 = 0, \qquad z_3 = 0, \qquad z_4 = 0$$

These values serve as the entries for the $Q_1Q_2Q_3 = 101$ cells of Fig. 8.25. Similarly, for state E, the entries in the $Q_1Q_2Q_3 = 100$ cells are

$$Q_1^+ = 0, \qquad Q_2^+ = 0, \qquad Q_3^+ = 0$$

$$z_1 = 0, \qquad z_2 = 0, \qquad z_3 = 1, \qquad z_4 = 0$$

Finally, the three remaining cells in each map have don't-care entries since they correspond to values of the state variables that were not used in the state assignment.

Having obtained the variable-entered Karnaugh maps, simplified Boolean expressions for the excitation and output variables are readily obtained using the procedure presented in Sec. 4.14. For the current example, the appropriate map groupings are also indicated in Fig. 8.25. The resulting expressions are precisely the minimal sum-of-products expressions previously given in Sec. 8.5 as Eqs. (8.8) to (8.14) for the ASM chart of Fig. 8.21. The logic diagram is shown in Fig. 8.24.

As a second example involving variable-entered Karnaugh maps, consider the ASM excitation table for Fig. 8.21 in which clocked JK flip-flops are used for the state register of the realization. The appropriate excitation table was previously obtained as Table 8.5. Using this table, the variable-entered Karnaugh maps for the six excitation expressions, J_1, K_1, J_2, K_2, J_3, and K_3, are shown in Fig. 8.26. The entries in these maps are obtained by applying the same reasoning as was used in the above example involving clocked D flip-flops. That is, algebraic expressions describing the excitations corresponding to each state, i.e., ASM block, are entered in the cells of the maps. In this case, when an excitation variable has a don't-care value for an ASM block as indicated by a dash, the corresponding entry in the map is also a don't-care. The entries in the maps of Fig. 8.26 are grouped in accordance with the procedure of Sec. 4.14. The resulting excitation expressions are given in the figure. As can be checked by using six-variable Karnaugh maps, these are the minimal sum-of-products expressions. In Fig. 8.26 the maps for the output functions are not

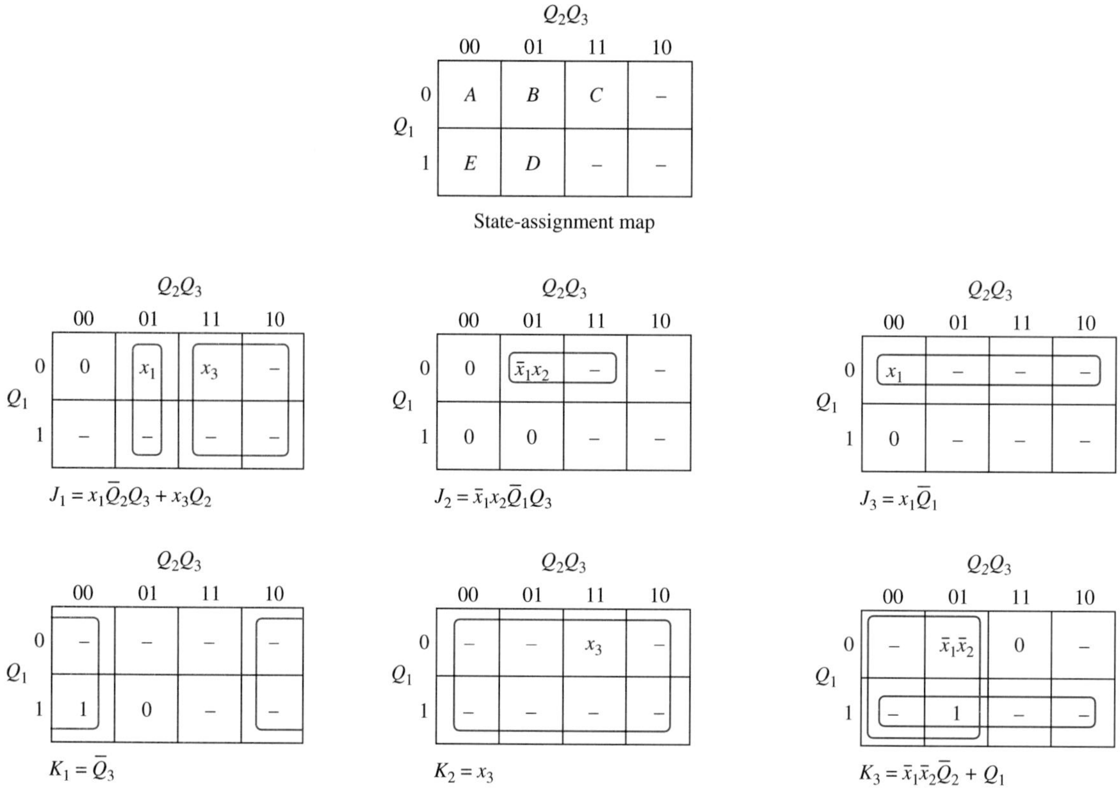

Figure 8.26 Using variable-entered Karnaugh maps to obtain a discrete-gate realization with clocked *JK* flip-flops for the ASM chart of Fig. 8.21.

included since they are identical to those of Fig. 8.25. Again, once the excitation and output expressions are obtained, it is a simple matter to draw the logic diagram for the realization.

8.6.2 Realizations Using Multiplexers

ASM models lend themselves very naturally to realizations involving MSI components and programmable logic devices. These realizations frequently are not based on minimal expressions. In general, as a logic system gets more complex, realizations based on simplified expressions become of less interest and emphasis goes to realizations that are straightforward. Such realizations are normally easier to modify and maintain after the initial design.

Although there are many approaches for obtaining multiplexer realizations of ASMs, the approach presented here is one of the easiest to apply. This approach is again based on the partitioning of the ASM variables into two sets, the state variables and the input variables, as was done when variable-entered maps were used in determining a discrete-gate realization.

One multiplexer is assigned to each excitation and output function. The relationship between the partitioning of the ASM variables and the multiplexer inputs for each excitation and output function is shown in Fig. 8.27. If the state variables are placed on the select lines of the set of multiplexers, then for each state combination the information lines that are selected must correspond to a single ASM block. Recall that the basic behavior of a multiplexer is to connect a single information line to its output line as determined by the signal values on its select lines. Since the signals on the select lines have the effect of selecting a single ASM block, this, in turn, implies that the multiplexer outputs must correspond to the horizontal partitions previously made on the ASM excitation table. Thus, the realization of each partition must appear at the information lines of the multiplexers. These partitions are describable as algebraic expressions in terms of the ASM input variables. Obtaining such algebraic descriptions of the individual partitions of an ASM excitation table is precisely what was done previously when the variable-entered Karnaugh maps were developed for a discrete-gate realization. That is, the cell entries in the maps are the algebraic descriptions needed at the multiplexer information lines. If these algebraic expressions involve only a single variable or a Boolean constant, then they become the actual inputs to the information lines. However, if these algebraic expressions involve more than a single variable, then logic networks must precede the inputs to the information lines. Such logic networks are designed with either discrete gates or additional multiplexers.

To illustrate this approach for an ASM realization with multiplexers, again consider the ASM chart of Fig. 8.21. The variable-entered Karnaugh maps for this ASM chart under the assumption that clocked D flip-flops are used for the state register were previously constructed and are shown in Fig. 8.25. Since there are seven functions to be realized having three state variables, seven 2^3-to-1 multiplexers are

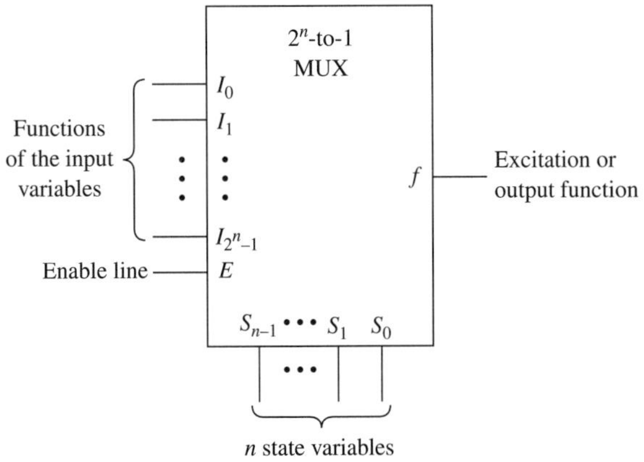

Figure 8.27 Assignment of inputs to a multiplexer for each excitation and output function.

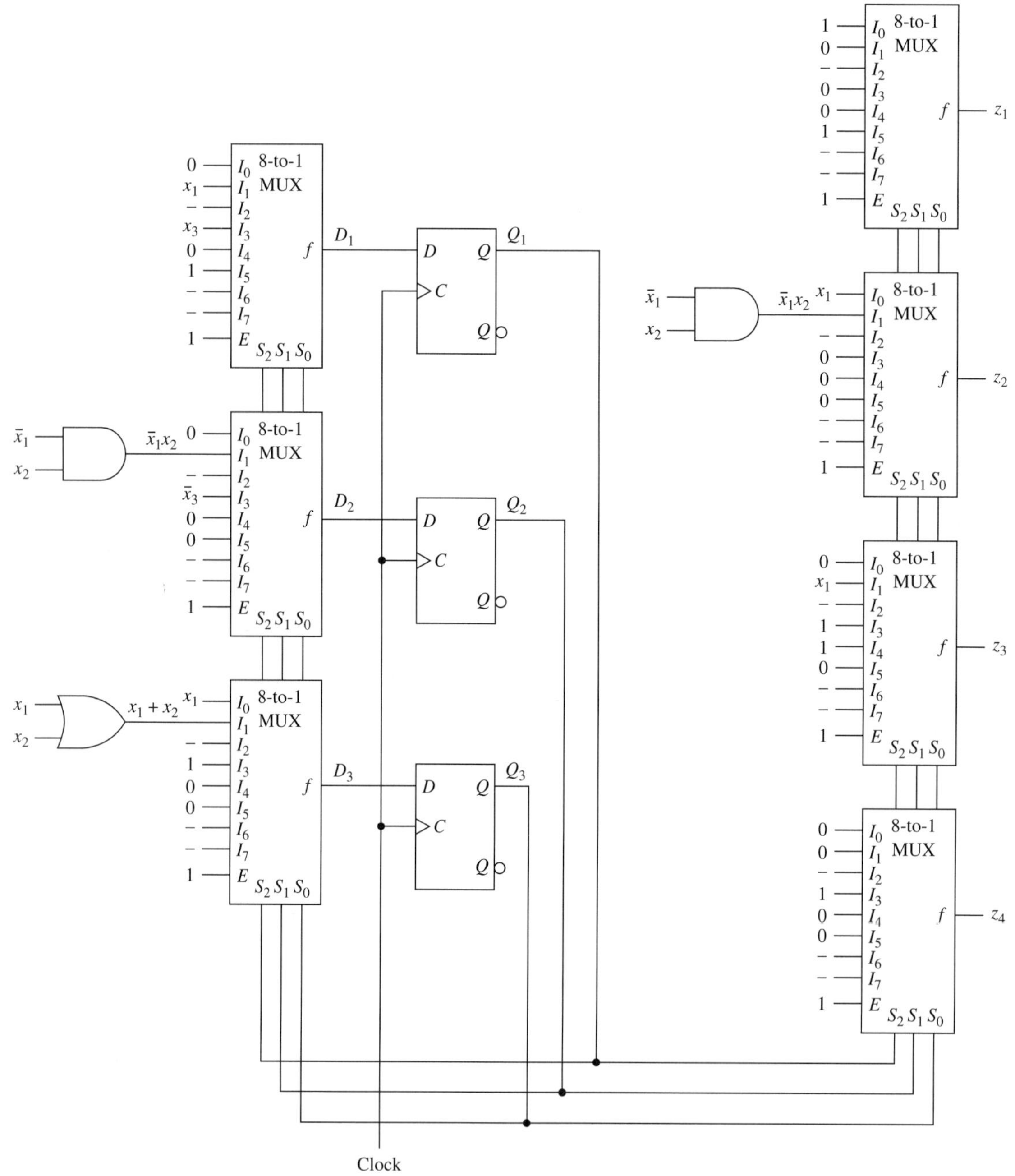

Figure 8.28 Multiplexer realization with clocked D flip-flops for the ASM chart of Fig. 8.21.

needed. The resulting realization is shown in Fig. 8.28. In Fig. 8.21, Q_1 is the most-significant-state variable and Q_3 is the least-significant-state variable. As a result, the three state variables Q_1, Q_2, and Q_3, which are the outputs of the state register, are the inputs to the S_2, S_1, and S_0 select lines, respectively, to each of the multiplexers. Three of the multiplexers are used to generate the excitation functions and four are used for the output functions. The inputs to the information lines of these multiplexers are determined by the cell entries of the corresponding variable-entered Karnaugh maps. Referring to Figs. 8.25 and 8.28, the contents of the $Q_1Q_2Q_3 =$ 000, 001, 011, 100, and 101 cells become the inputs to the I_0, I_1, I_3, I_4, and I_5 information lines, respectively. For example, consider the state $Q_1Q_2Q_3 = 000$ which corresponds to the upper left cell of each map. The entries in these cells are 0, 0, x_1, 1, x_1, 0, and 0 for the Q_1^+, Q_2^+, Q_3^+, z_1, z_2, z_3, and z_4 maps, respectively. Therefore, these serve as the inputs to the I_0 lines of the corresponding seven multiplexers. As a second example, the entries in the $Q_1Q_2Q_3 = 001$ cells of the Q_1^+, Q_2^+, Q_3^+, z_1, z_2, z_3, and z_4 maps of Fig. 8.25 are x_1, $\overline{x}_1x_2$, $x_1 + x_2$, 0, $\overline{x}_1x_2$, x_1, and 0, respectively. Four of these terms are applied directly to the I_1 information lines since they are either a Boolean constant or a single Boolean variable. For those terms that are a function of more than a single variable, the necessary expressions are realized by discrete gates in Fig. 8.28. Alternatively, additional multiplexers can be used to realize these input expressions.

The reader should carefully note that the variable-entered Karnaugh maps in the above example are used only to determine the inputs to the multiplexers and not to obtain simplified expressions. Hence, it is not necessary to formally construct the variable-entered Karnaugh maps. Rather, by applying the reasoning used previously to the various partitions of the ASM excitation table, the algebraic descriptions that lead to the cell entries are tabulated. Then these results are used to determine the inputs to the appropriate information lines.

8.6.3 Realizations Using PLAs

An ASM model is easily realized with PLAs since there is a direct correspondence between an ASM excitation table and a PLA table. The general structure of such a realization is shown in Fig. 8.29. The present state of the ASM is again given by the content of a state register as was done in the previous realizations. As well as the content of the state register, the inputs to the ASM are also the inputs to the PLA. The PLA outputs are the ASM excitation and output signals. The excitation signals are sent to the state register so that the appropriate next state is obtained upon the occurrence of the triggering time of the system clock signal. Thus, the PLA transforms the system inputs and present-state values into the excitation and output values. This is precisely the information that appears in the ASM excitation table.

Each row of the ASM excitation table indicates a present-state and input combination along with the desired excitation and output signals for that present-state and input combination. A row of the table is realized by a single and-gate in the and-array of the PLA. The and-gate has a logic-1 output when the present-state and input combination of the row occurs. A connection is provided in the or-array

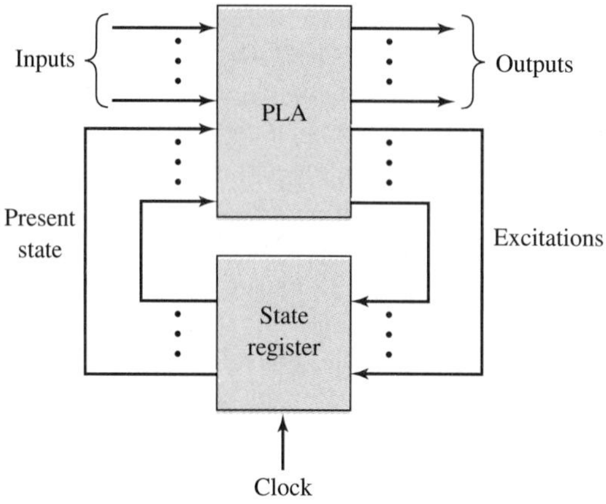

Figure 8.29 Structure of a PLA realization for an ASM.

for any output or excitation variable that is logic-1 for this row. Repeating this procedure for each of the rows in the ASM excitation table results in a PLA realization of the ASM. It should be noted that this approach to an ASM realization requires no maps or algebraic simplifications.

The PLA realization for the ASM chart of Fig. 8.21 is shown in Fig. 8.30 when clocked D flip-flops are used for the state register. Table 8.1b serves as the ASM excitation table for this realization since $D_i = Q_i^+$. Each row, i.e., present state and link path, corresponds to a column in the figure.* The set of crosses in a single column of the and-array generates the and-term associated with the present state and link path specifications of the row. For example, the first row of present state and inputs in Table 8.1b is algebraically described by $\overline{Q}_1\overline{Q}_2\overline{Q}_3\overline{x}_1$. Hence, crosses appear in the corresponding rows for the L_1 column of Fig. 8.30. Crosses are also placed in the same column of the or-array in the PLA if an output or excitation variable is logic-1 for the given row. Again for row L_1, only z_1 has an output of logic-1. Hence a cross appears in the L_1 column, z_1 row of Fig. 8.30. It should be noted that since column L_3 is never needed to produce a logic-1 on an output or excitation line, it really is not needed in the realization. However, it is shown in Fig. 8.30 for completeness.

In Sec. 5.9 the PLA table was introduced as a way of specifying the connections in a PLA. Using the notation for a PLA table presented at that time, the PLA table for the above example is given in Table 8.6. It can be seen that there is a very close similarity between the ASM excitation table and the PLA table.

As an alternate approach to a PLA realization, a set of simplified excitation and output expressions for an ASM is used. Thus, in the above example, rather than using Table 8.1b, an alternate PLA realization can be based upon the simplified expressions that were previously obtained in Fig. 8.25.

*For simplicity, the columns in the figure are labeled by just their link paths.

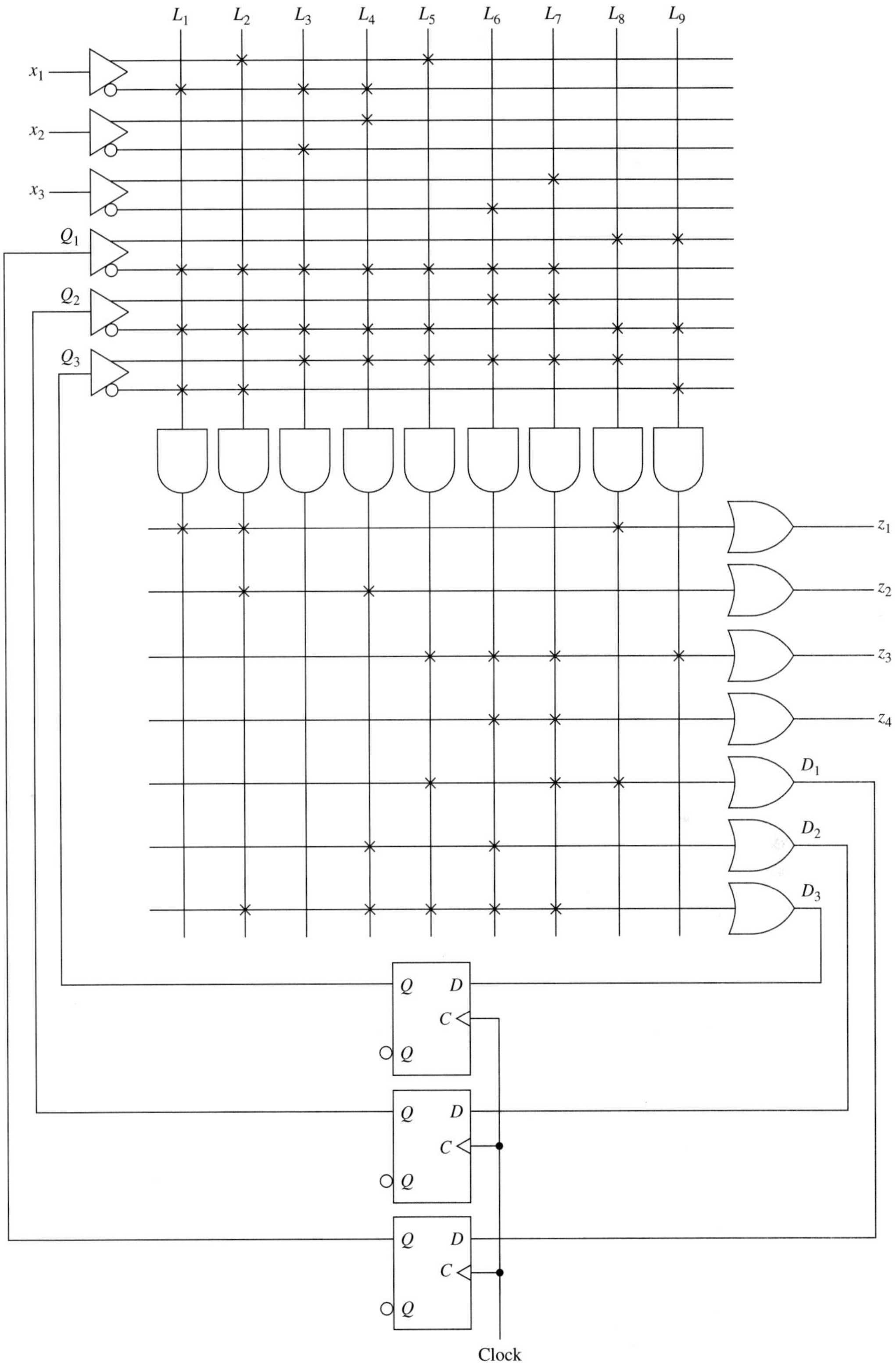

Figure 8.30 PLA realization with clocked *D* flip-flops for the ASM chart of Fig. 8.21.

Table 8.6 PLA table for the realization of Fig. 8.30

Product term	Inputs						Outputs						
	Q_1	Q_2	Q_3	x_1	x_2	x_3	D_1	D_2	D_3	z_1	z_2	z_3	z_4
$\bar{Q}_1\bar{Q}_2\bar{Q}_3\bar{x}_1$	0	0	0	0	–	–	–	–	–	1	–	–	–
$\bar{Q}_1\bar{Q}_2\bar{Q}_3x_1$	0	0	0	1	–	–	–	–	1	1	1	–	–
$\bar{Q}_1\bar{Q}_2Q_3\bar{x}_1\bar{x}_2$	0	0	1	0	0	–	–	–	–	–	–	–	–
$\bar{Q}_1\bar{Q}_2Q_3\bar{x}_1x_2$	0	0	1	0	1	–	–	1	1	–	1	–	–
$\bar{Q}_1\bar{Q}_2Q_3x_1$	0	0	1	1	–	–	1	–	1	–	–	1	–
$\bar{Q}_1Q_2Q_3\bar{x}_3$	0	1	1	–	–	0	–	1	1	–	–	1	1
$\bar{Q}_1Q_2Q_3x_3$	0	1	1	–	–	1	1	–	1	–	–	1	1
$Q_1\bar{Q}_2Q_3$	1	0	1	–	–	–	1	–	–	1	–	–	–
$Q_1\bar{Q}_2\bar{Q}_3$	1	0	0	–	–	–	–	–	–	–	–	1	–
						T/C	T	T	T	T	T	T	T

8.6.4 Realizations Using PROMs

An operational interpretation of a PLA is that its inputs are associated with an address and the outputs are associated with the content of an address. For example, in Fig. 8.30, a particular set of values for x_1, x_2, x_3, Q_1, Q_2, and Q_3 causes a single and-gate to be selected, i.e., to have a logic-1 output. This set of values is regarded as the address of the and-gate. The logic-1 output of this and-gate appears as an input to all the or-gates to which it is connected. These or-gate outputs, in turn, are also logic-1; while those or-gates that are not connected have logic-0 outputs. Hence, the collective set of binary values appearing on the z_1, z_2, z_3, z_4, D_1, D_2, and D_3 lines is regarded as the word stored at the address associated with the corresponding and-gate.

Since the and-array of a PLA is programmable, not all of the state and input variables appear at each and-gate. PROMs, on the other hand, have a complete decoder in their nonprogrammable and-array. Only the outputs are programmable. Thus, it is necessary to expand an ASM excitation table before it can serve as the basis for a PROM realization of an ASM. To do this, any row in an ASM excitation table that has at least one dash in the inputs section must be replaced by a set of rows in which all combinations of values are assigned to the dashes. The outputs remain the same for each of the rows in the set. For example, the first row of Table 8.1*b* is

$Q_1\ Q_2\ Q_3\ x_1\ x_2\ x_3$	$Q_1^+\ Q_2^+\ Q_3^+\ z_1\ z_2\ z_3\ z_4$
0 0 0 0 – –	0 0 0 1 0 0 0

Because of the two dashes in the x_2 and x_3 columns, this row must be expanded into four rows:

$Q_1\ Q_2\ Q_3\ x_1\ x_2\ x_3$	$Q_1^+\ Q_2^+\ Q_3^+\ z_1\ z_2\ z_3\ z_4$
0 0 0 0 0 0	0 0 0 1 0 0 0
0 0 0 0 0 1	0 0 0 1 0 0 0
0 0 0 0 1 0	0 0 0 1 0 0 0
0 0 0 0 1 1	0 0 0 1 0 0 0

It is also necessary to include rows for those combinations of values of the state variables that were not used in the state assignment. The outputs for these rows are regarded as don't-cares. The resulting expanded form of the ASM excitation table now consists of 2^n rows where n is the total number of state and input variables. From the expanded form of the ASM excitation table, the output and excitation functions are readily programmed into a PROM as described in Sec. 5.8.

8.7 ASYNCHRONOUS INPUTS

At the beginning of this chapter on algorithmic state machines, some very definite assumptions were made with regard to timing. In Sec. 8.1 the state time was divided into two periods: the transition period and the stable period. It was assumed that the inputs to the ASM change during the transition period and the new values of the inputs appear fixed during the stable period. Furthermore, it is assumed that the stable period was of sufficient duration so that generated signals are usable.

There are occasions, however, when the timing of the inputs is not controllable. For example, if the source of an input signal is a keyboard, then the signal can occur anytime during the state time. Signals whose time of occurrence is not controllable are said to be *asynchronous.* Another situation in which asynchronous inputs can occur is when they come from another synchronous digital system that has an unrelated clock. Asynchronous inputs in an ASM are frequently identified by appending an asterisk (*) to their labels.

To illustrate the effects of asynchronous inputs, consider the fragment of an ASM chart shown in Fig. 8.31*a*. Assume the system is in state 1, X^* is an asynchronous input, and its current value is logic-0. As was discussed in Chapter 6, flip-flops usually have a setup time associated with them. That is, some time duration is needed in which the excitation signals remain stable before the triggering time of the clock signal in order to guarantee the flip-flops respond appropriately. If the excitation signals change during the setup time, then the responses of the flip-flops are unpredictable. Now consider Fig. 8.31*a*. The system is to remain in state 1, which is coded as $Q_1Q_2 = 00$, as long as X^* is logic-0. However, when X^* becomes logic-1, the system is to go to state 2, which is coded as $Q_1Q_2 = 11$, at the end of the state-1 time. Note that both flip-flops must change state. Now if the input X^* should change from logic-0 to logic-1 late in the state time, then it is possible the excitation signals for the next state may not be stable for the entire setup times of the flip-flops. As a consequence, it is possible that one of the flip-flops may change its state, while the other may not change its state. In such a case, the system goes to either state 3 or state 4, both of which result in incorrect behavior of the ASM. This problem of the next state of a digital system being dependent upon the exact timing of the flip-flop changes is referred to as a *transition race.*

Figure 8.31*b* illustrates a second problem that can occur as a result of asynchronous inputs. In this case, the state assignment is such as to avoid the transition race problem, since only one state variable must change value between

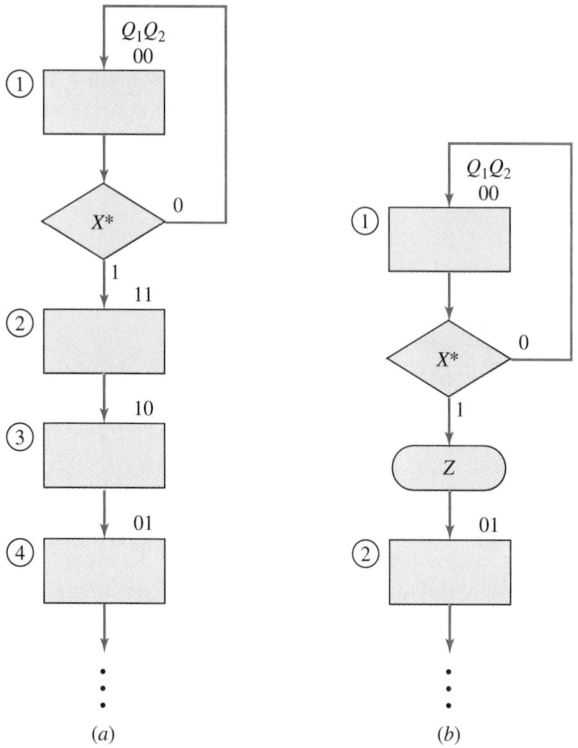

Figure 8.31 Fragments of ASM charts illustrating problems associated with asynchronous inputs. (*a*) Transition race. (*b*) Output race.

states 1 and 2. However, the conditional output box indicates that $Z = 0$ when $X^* = 0$ and that $Z = 1$ when $X^* = 1$. Again assume that X^* changes from logic-0 to logic-1 late during the state-1 time. This means that Z is logic-1 for only a short duration before the occurrence of the triggering time of the clock signal. If the output Z is serving as an input to some other device, e.g., a flip-flop, then it is possible that the short duration in which $Z = 1$ is insufficient for the driven device to recognize the new value of Z and respond properly. This problem is referred to as an *output race.*

The existence of asynchronous inputs are a potential source of problems in a realization. The transition race can be solved by selecting a state assignment that avoids having more than one flip-flop change state between any two linked state boxes. The output race problem can only be avoided by not having both a conditional output box and a decision box with an asynchronous input occur in the same link path.

The best approach to solving the transition and output race problems is to actually eliminate the occurrence of an asynchronous input in the ASM chart.

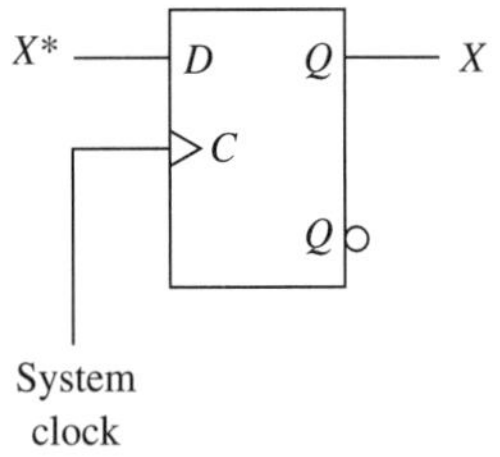

Figure 8.32 Using a clocked *D* flip-flop to synchronize an asynchronous input.

Figure 8.32 illustrates one method in which this is achieved. The asynchronous input X^* is applied to the D input of a clocked D flip-flop. The signal at the clock input is the system clock. The net effect is to synchronize the X^* input to the system clock. The Q output of the flip-flop is now used as the X input to the ASM. Since the output of the flip-flop changes synchronously with the system clock, no transition or output races occur in the ASM as a consequence of the asynchronous input.

Unfortunately, the possibility of the synchronizing flip-flop becoming metastable can still occur. No simple corrective procedure exists for this problem.

CHAPTER 8 PROBLEMS

8.1 Construct as ASM block for state S_1 that has two input variables, x_1 and x_2, and one output variable, z. The output z is asserted if $x_1 = 1$ and $x_2 = 0$. The block exits to state S_2 unless $x_1 = x_2 = 1$, in which case the block exits to state S_3.

8.2 Construct an ASM block for state S_1 that has two input variables, x_1 and x_2, and two output variables, z_1 and z_2. The output z_1 is always asserted and the output z_2 is asserted only if $x_1 = 1$. If $x_1 = 0$, then the system is to remain in state S_1. Otherwise, if $x_2 = 0$, then the block exits to state S_2, and if $x_2 = 1$, then the block exits to state S_3.

8.3. Construct an ASM block for state S_1 that has three input variables, x_1, x_2, and x_3, and three output variables, z_1, z_2, and z_3. The output z_1 is always asserted, the output z_2 is asserted whenever $x_1 = 0$, and the output z_3 is asserted if $x_1 = 1$ and $x_2 = x_3$. The system is to remain in state S_1 whenever z_2 or z_3 is asserted. However, if $x_1 = 1$ and $x_2 \neq x_3$, then the block exits to state S_2.

8.4 Construct an ASM chart for a counter that can have 4, 6, or 8 states. The type of counter, i.e., its modulus, is determined by checking two input variables, x_1 and x_2, only when the counter is in its first state and should remain in this state as long as $x_1 = x_2 = 0$. The counter should act as a mod-4 counter when $x_1 = 1$ and $x_2 = 0$ during its first state, it should act as a mod-6 counter when $x_1 = 0$ and $x_2 = 1$, and it should act as a mod-8 counter when $x_1 = 1$ and $x_2 = 1$. A single output, z, is asserted only during the last state of the counting sequence.

8.5 Construct an ASM chart for a counter having a single input variable G. When $G = 0$, the counter is to behave as a mod-8 binary counter; while when $G = 1$, it is to behave as a mod-8 Gray-code counter. (See Sec. 2.10 for the Gray code.) Let the states of the counter be designated by 0, 1, . . . , 7. During each state, an output is produced denoting the current count and the input variable G is interrogated. When $G = 0$, the next count should be the corresponding next count in binary; and when $G = 1$, the next count should be the corresponding next count in Gray code. Let z_1, z_2, and z_3 denote the output variables where z_1 corresponds to the most significant bit of the count and z_3 the least significant bit.

8.6 Construct an ASM chart for a counter having 8 states whose states are designated by 0, 1, . . . , 7. The output during each state corresponds to either the binary equivalent of the state number or the Gray-code equivalent of the state number. (See Sec. 2.10 for the Gray code.) The binary representation of the state number is produced when $G = 0$, while the Gray-code representation of the state number is produced when $G = 1$. Let z_1, z_2, and z_3 denote the output variables where z_1 corresponds to the most significant bit of the count and z_3 the least significant bit.

8.7 Convert the Moore state diagram of Fig. P8.7 into an equivalent ASM chart. Check only one variable in each decision box. Minimize the number of decision boxes in each ASM block.

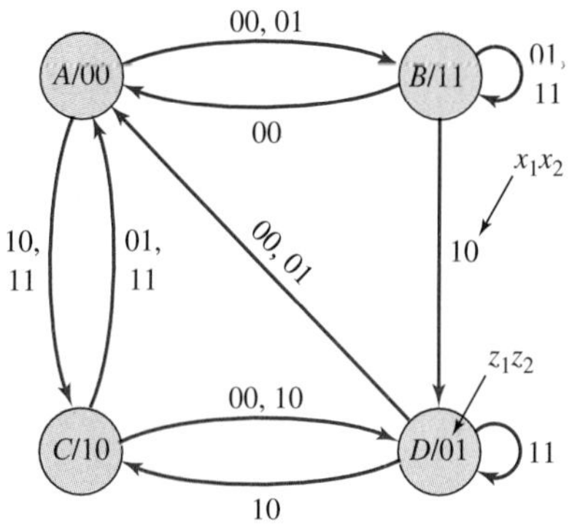

Figure P8.7

8.8 Convert the Mealy state diagram of Fig. P8.8 into an equivalent ASM chart. Check only one variable in each decision box. Minimize the number of decision boxes in each ASM box.

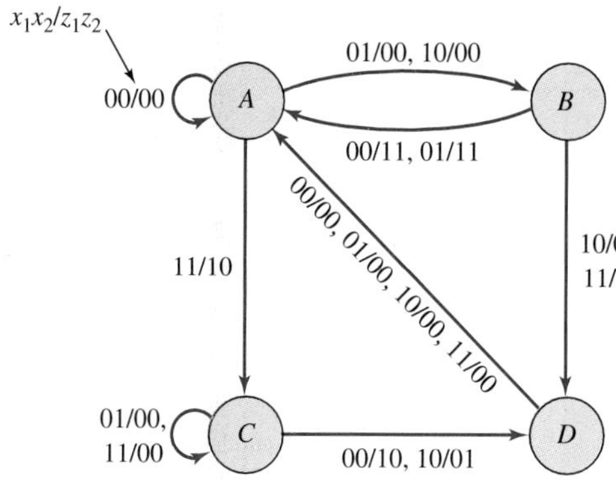

Figure P8.8

8.9 Construct an ASM chart for a sequence recognizer having a single input variable x and a single output variable z. The output variable is asserted if and only if the three input bits following two consecutive input 1's consist of exactly one 1. Once the consecutive pair of 1's is detected, the network must analyze the next 3 bits to determine if exactly one of them is a 1. The output $z = 1$ should be coincident with the third input bit of the 3-bit sequence. Upon completing the analysis of the 3 bits following the pair of 1 inputs, the network is to reset itself and wait for another pair of 1's and then exactly one 1 in the following sequence of 3 bits.

8.10 In Sec. 8.3 the ASM chart for a multiplier was developed based on the controlled architecture shown in Fig. 8.19. Assuming the two operands are each 4 bits in length, the controlled architecture is to be realized using a set of basic devices. Three 4-bit universal shift registers, as discussed in Sec. 6.7 and illustrated in Fig. 6.29, are to be used for registers A, B, and M. The register operation and symbol are shown in Fig. P8.10*a*. The function table and symbol for a 4-bit up/down counter are given in Fig. 8.10*b*. This device is similar to the one discussed in Sec. 6.8 and illustrated in Fig. 6.34 except that it can operate as either an up or down counter depending upon the additional enabling input Up/Dn. (Also see Problem 6.27*b*.) Figure P8.10*c* gives the symbol for a 4-bit parallel binary adder in which the operands are applied to inputs A_3, A_2, A_1, A_0 and B_3, B_2, B_1, B_0, where A_0 and B_0 denote the least significant bits, CO is the carry-out terminal from the adder, and CI is the carry-in terminal. The carry flip-flop in the architecture of Fig. 8.19 is to be a positive edge-triggered D flip-flop. Draw the logic diagram for the controlled architecture of the multiplier using these devices along with any necessary gates. Show the connections and signals at all terminals except for the multiplier and multiplicand inputs, which are available via a parallel transfer during initialization.

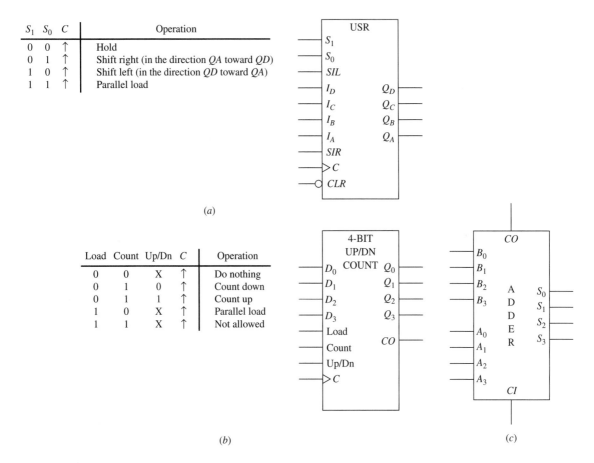

S_1	S_0	C	Operation
0	0	↑	Hold
0	1	↑	Shift right (in the direction QA toward QD)
1	0	↑	Shift left (in the direction QD toward QA)
1	1	↑	Parallel load

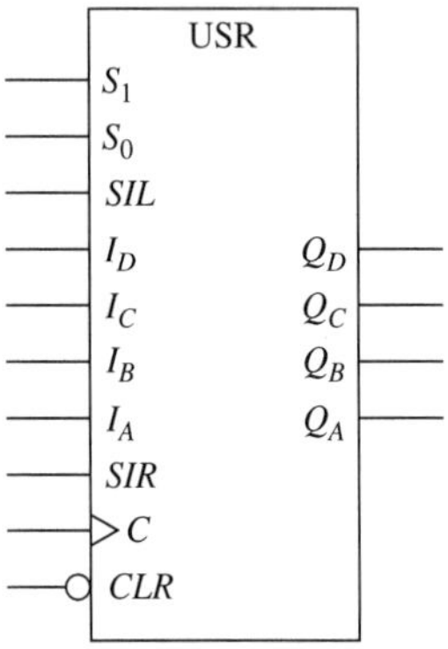

(*a*)

Load	Count	Up/Dn	C	Operation
0	0	X	↑	Do nothing
0	1	0	↑	Count down
0	1	1	↑	Count up
1	0	X	↑	Parallel load
1	1	X	↑	Not allowed

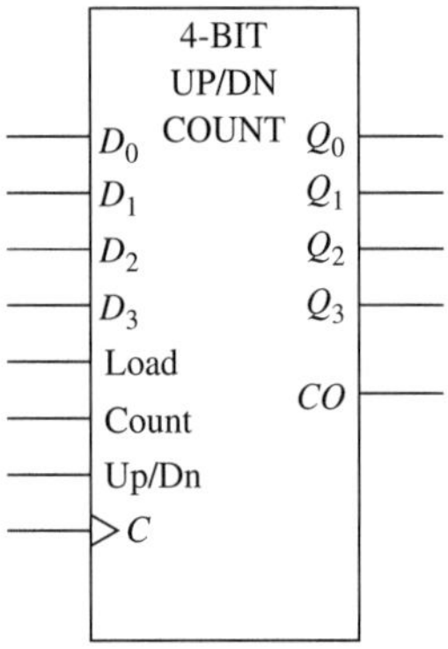

(*b*)

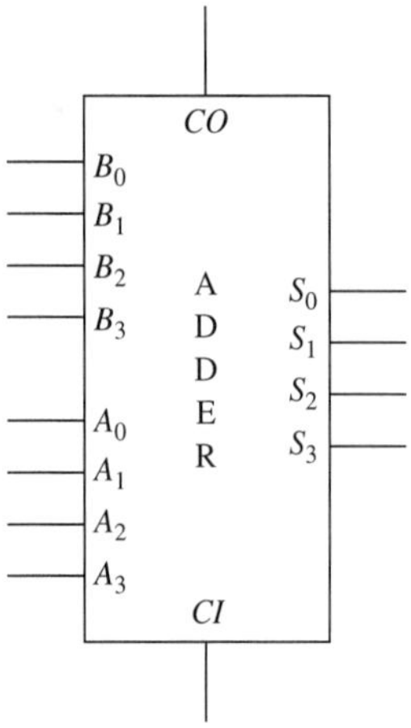

(*c*)

Figure P8.10

8.11 A very simple approach to multiplication involves repeatedly adding the multiplicand the number of times indicated by the multiplier. For example, in decimal $6 \times 3 = 6 + 6 + 6 = 18$. Figure P8.11 shows an architecture to achieve binary multiplication using this procedure. It consists of a counter, a parallel adder, and two registers. Register *A* stores the product and, hence, its length is twice the length of register *B*, which stores the multiplicand. When a start signal S, which is synchronized with the clock, is set to 1, an INIT = 1 signal is produced by the controller. When INIT = 1, register A is cleared, the multiplier is loaded into the counter, and the multiplicand is loaded into register B. The multiplicand is then added to register A, as a result of an ADD = 1 control signal, and the counter is decremented, as a result of a DECREM = 1 control signal, until the multiplication is completed, which occurs when the counter gets to zero. The controller then asserts the completion signal COMPLETE for one state time, after which it returns to the start state and waits for a new start signal. Construct an ASM chart for the controller.

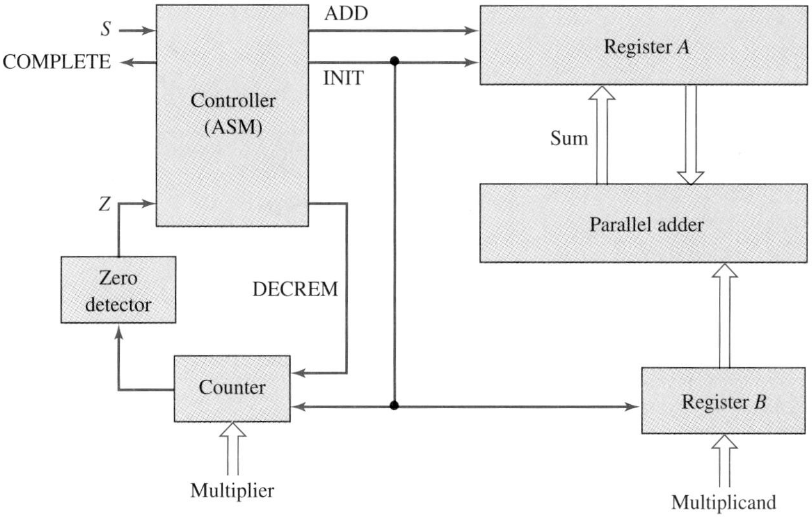

Figure P8.11

8.12 Consider the design of an ultra-slow multiplier which uses three counters to multiply a 4-bit multiplicand by a 4-bit multiplier to obtain an 8-bit product. The function table for the counters is given in Table P8.12. This ultra-slow multiplier uses the principles that multiplication is repeated addition and that addition is repeated incrementation. Counter A receives the multiplicand each time its load signal is asserted and Counter B receives the multiplier each time its load signal is asserted. Both of these counters are 4-bit down-counters. Counter C is an 8-bit up-counter that has the product upon completion of the multiplication process. When a start signal is received, the multiplicand is loaded into Counter A, the multiplier is loaded into Counter B, and Counter C is cleared. To proceed with the multiplication, the controller continuously decrements Counter *A* and increments Counter *C* until Counter *A* reaches zero. Counter *B* is then decremented, indicating the addition of the multiplicand to the running product that is stored in Counter *C*. Counter *A* is then reloaded with the multiplicand and the above process is repeated until Counter *B* reaches zero. At that time, the multiplication process is complete and Counter *C* contains the product. A complete signal is generated at the end of the multiplication process and the system returns to its start state to await another start signal.

a. Draw an appropriate architecture and define a set of necessary control signals.
b. Construct an ASM chart for the controller.

Table P8.12

CLR	LD	CNT	CLK	Operation
L	L	L	↑	Do nothing
L	L	H	↑	Count (up or down depending on type)
L	H	L	↑	Parallel load
L	H	H	↑	Not allowed
H	×	×	↑	Clear counter
×	×	×	↓	Do nothing

8.13 One method of performing unsigned binary division is by the *comparison method*, which strongly resembles the paper-and-pencil method as applied to fractional numbers, i.e., the two operands and the results must all be fractional. An example of these two methods using two 3-bit numbers is shown in Fig. P8.13*a* and *b*. The comparison method involves repeated comparisons/subtractions and shift operations. Initially, the divisor and dividend are compared. If the divisor is less than or equal to the dividend, then division is not performed since the result of the division is not fractional; otherwise, the division process commences. The quotient bits are generated by comparing a working dividend against the divisor. If the working dividend is greater than or equal to the divisor, then the divisor is subtracted from the working dividend and the corresponding quotient bit is 1. On the other hand, if the working dividend is less than the divisor, then the working dividend is left unchanged and the corresponding quotient bit is 0. In pencil-and-paper division, the divisor is compared against a new working dividend after the divisor is shifted right by one bit position. In a realization of this procedure, the new working dividend is achieved by shifting it left by one bit position before the next comparison. The

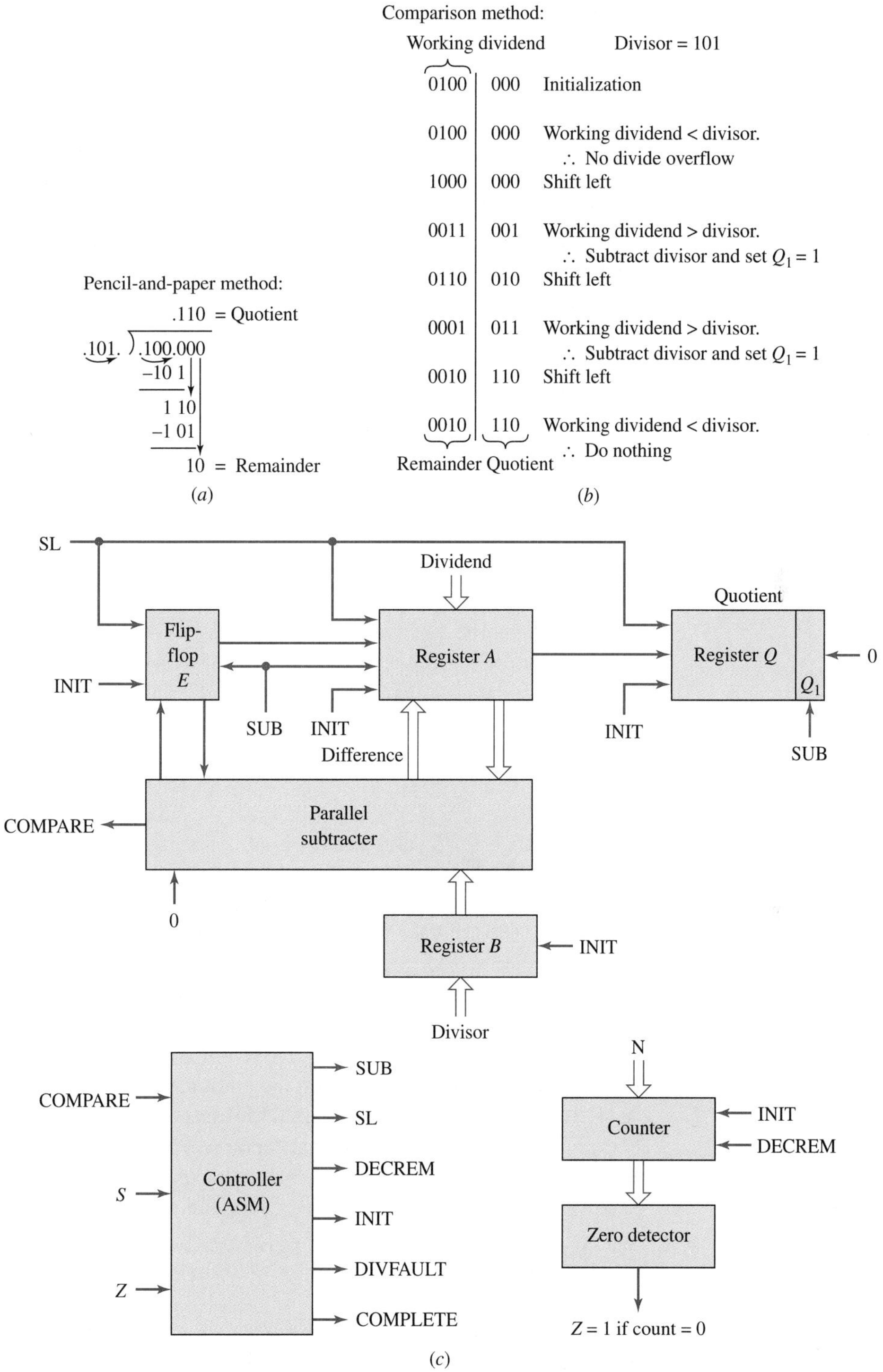
Comparison method:
Working dividend
Divisor = 101
0100 000 Initialization
0100 000 Working dividend < divisor.
∴ No divide overflow
1000 000 Shift left
0011 001 Working dividend > divisor.
∴ Subtract divisor and set Q1 = 1
0110 010 Shift left
0001 011 Working dividend > divisor.
∴ Subtract divisor and set Q1 = 1
0010 110 Shift left
0010 110 Working dividend < divisor.
∴ Do nothing
Remainder Quotient
(b)
Pencil-and-paper method:
.110 = Quotient
.101.).100.000
−10 1
1 10
−1 01
10 = Remainder
(a)
SL
Dividend
Quotient
Flip-flop E
Register A
Register Q
Q1
0
INIT
SUB
INIT
Difference
INIT
SUB
COMPARE
Parallel subtracter
0
Register B
INIT
Divisor
COMPARE
S
Z
Controller (ASM)
SUB
SL
DECREM
INIT
DIVFAULT
COMPLETE
N
Counter
INIT
DECREM
Zero detector
Z = 1 if count = 0
(c)

Figure P8.13

comparisons/subtractions and shift operations are continued until an appropriate number of quotient bits are obtained.

A proposed architecture for the divider is shown in Fig. P8.13*c*. Operation begins upon the occurrence of a start signal ($S = 1$). Next, as the result of an initialization signal (INIT = 1), the dividend is loaded into register A, the divisor is loaded into register B, the counter is loaded with the number of bits in the divisor, extension flip-flop E is cleared, and register Q is cleared. The length of registers A, B, and Q is the same as the number of bits in each of the two operands. The extension flip-flop E is needed during the shift operations so that the most significant bit of register A is not lost. The working dividend consists of flip-flop E and register A. Comparisons between the working dividend and the divisor are done using a parallel subtracter in which an additional 0 is assumed as a most-significant-bit input of the divisor so that the working dividend and the divisor have the same number of bits. When COMPARE = 1, the working dividend is greater than or equal to the divisor; otherwise, COMPARE = 0. After the initialization, the working dividend and divisor are compared to see if the division of two fractional quantities results in a fractional quantity. A divide fault signal (DIVFAULT = 1) is asserted if division should not proceed and the system returns to its starting state to await another start signal. If there is no divide fault, the division process begins by flip-flop E, register A, and register Q shifting left 1 bit as a result of the control signal $SL = 1$. In addition, a 0 is shifted into the least-significant-bit position of register Q (i.e., Q_1). The divisor is then subtracted from the working dividend. If the subtraction is nonnegative (COMPARE = 1), a subtraction signal is asserted by the controller (SUB = 1). This causes a quotient bit of 1 to replace the content of the least-significant-bit position of register Q and the difference to replace the contents of flip-flop E and register A (i.e., the working dividend). Otherwise, the working dividend and Q_1 are left unchanged. The shift-left and compare operations are then repeated. As each quotient bit is determined, the counter is decremented (DECREM = 1) until a content of zero is detected ($Z = 1$). When the division process is complete, the quotient appears in register Q and the undivided remainder appears in register A. A COMPLETE = 1 signal from the controller indicates the termination of the division process, upon which the system returns to its starting state to await another start signal. Construct an ASM chart for the controller involving the above procedure and architecture.

8.14 An algorithm for obtaining the 2's-complement of an unsigned binary number was presented in Chapter 2. In particular, working from right to left, retain all least significant 0's and the first 1, after which each of the remaining higher significant digits is complemented. Figure P8.14 shows an architecture, along with a summary of the control signals, for a 2's-complementer based on this algorithm consisting of an 8-bit shift register and a mod-8 binary counter. When a start signal (S) is set to 1, the register is parallel loaded with an 8-bit binary number and the counter is reset to 0. The 2's-complementing algorithm is then carried out. The least significant bit of the register is interrogated and the appropriate bit of the complemented number is determined and entered into the high end of the shift register upon a shift-right command. The process is continued until the 2's-complement of the original number appears in the shift register. Upon each shift, the counter is incremented to provide an indication of when the process is complete. After forming the 2's-complement, the system returns to its initial state to await another start signal. Construct an ASM chart for the controller.

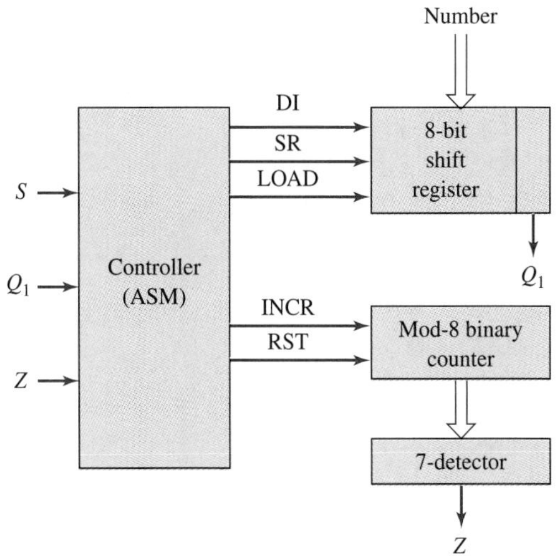

Summary of control signals:
- $S = 1$: Start signal (assumed synchronized to the clock)
- Load = 1: Parallel load the shift register
- RST = 1: Reset the counter
- Q_1: Least significant bit of the shift register
- SR = 1: Shift register right
- INCR = 1: Increment counter
- DI: Data bit to be entered in most-significant-bit position of shift register
- $Z = 1$: The count is 7

Figure P8.14

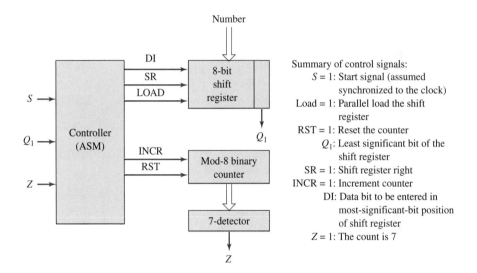

8.15 Draw a diagram for the architecture of a digital system that counts the number of 1's in a binary word and construct an ASM chart for the controller. The system is to consist of a shift register, a counter, and combinational logic to determine when the process is complete. Upon the occurrence of a start signal, the word is loaded in parallel into the shift register and the counter is cleared. The most significant bit is interrogated to determine its value, the counter is incremented if the value of the bit is 1, and the word is shifted in preparation to interrogate the next bit. Upon each shift, a 0 is entered as the least significant bit of the register. Combinational logic is used to detect if at any time all the bits of the shift register are 0's. If so, the total number of 1's has been counted, a completion signal is asserted, and the system returns to its initial state to await another start signal. Clearly list the control signals for the system.

8.16 Construct the assigned ASM transition table for the ASM chart shown in Fig. P8.16.

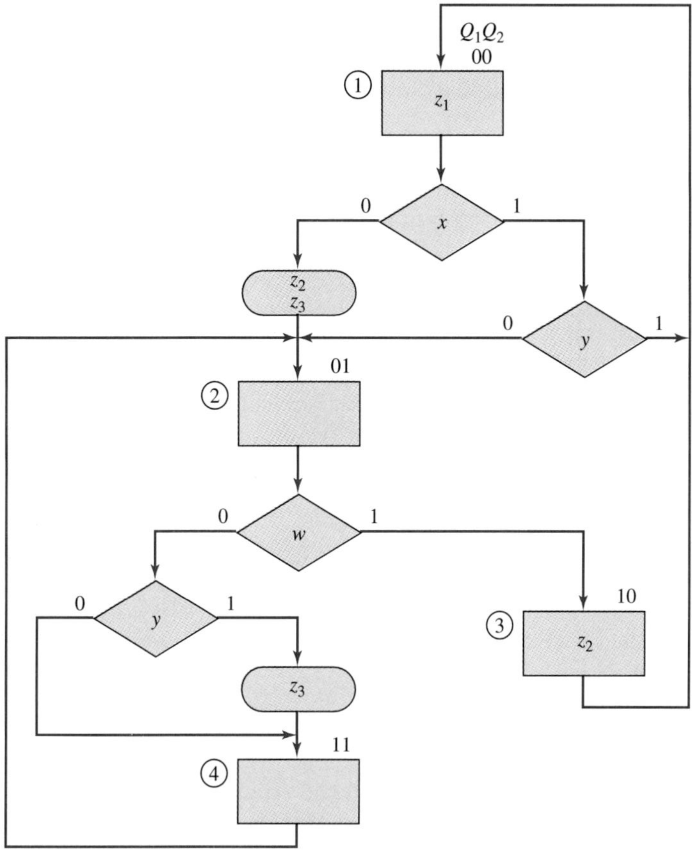

Figure P8.16

8.17 Construct the assigned ASM transition table for the ASM chart shown in Fig. P8.17.

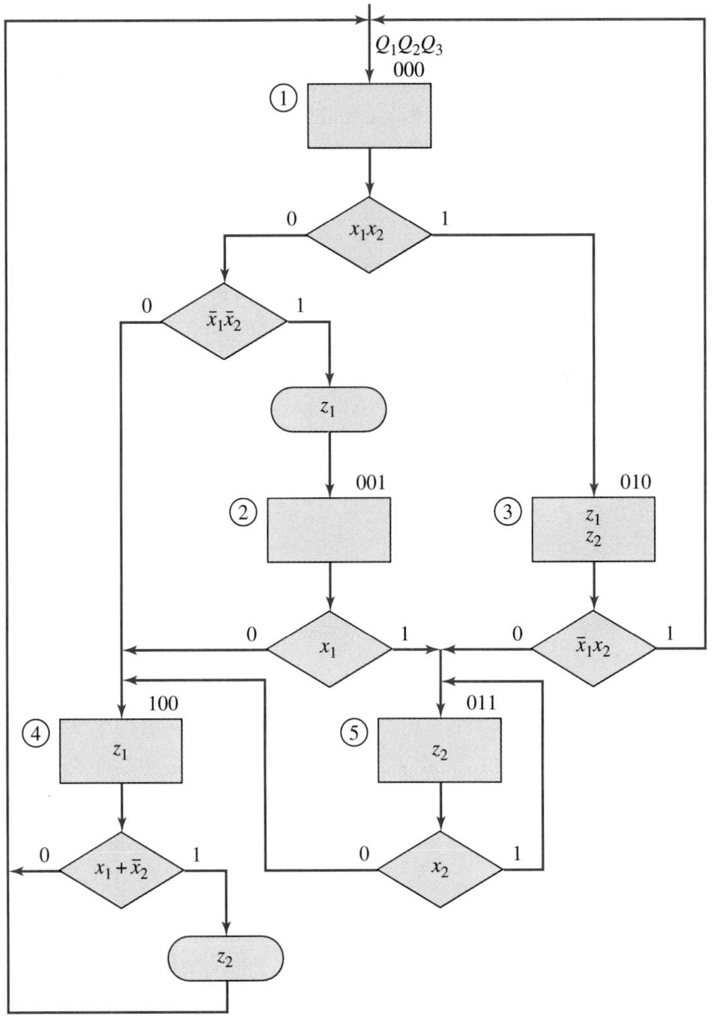

Figure P8.17

8.18 Complete the design of the binary multiplier of Sec. 8.3 having the assigned ASM transition table of Table 8.2*b*. Assume clocked *D* flip-flops are used for the state register.

a. Determine the minimal-sum excitation and output expressions for a discrete-gate realization.

b. Obtain a realization with multiplexers.

c. Construct a PLA table corresponding to a PLA realization.

8.19 Complete the design of the binary multiplier of Sec. 8.3 having the assigned ASM transition table of Table 8.2*b*. Assume clocked *JK* flip-flops are used for the state register.

a. Determine the minimal-sum excitation and output expressions for a discrete-gate realization.

b. Construct a PLA table corresponding to a PLA realization.

8.20 Consider the ASM chart of Fig. 8.17 and corresponding assigned ASM transition table of Table 8.3*b* for the sequence recognizer described in Sec. 8.3. Assume clocked *D* flip-flops are used for the state register.

a. Determine the minimal-sum excitation and output expressions for a discrete-gate realization.

b. Construct a PLA table corresponding to a PLA realization.

8.21 Repeat Problem 8.20 under the assumption that clocked *JK* flip-flops are used for the state register.

8.22 Construct the PLA table based upon simplified *D* flip-flop excitation and simplified output expressions for a PLA realization of the ASM chart given in Fig. 8.21.

CHAPTER 9

Asynchronous Sequential Networks

In Chapter 7, two general types of sequential networks were defined: synchronous and asynchronous. The more commonly occurring are the synchronous sequential networks that were the concern of the previous two chapters. At this time, asynchronous sequential networks are studied.

A general model of a sequential network was shown in Fig. 7.1. It was seen that a sequential network possesses a memory so that its response is dependent upon the time sequence of inputs. Internal states of the network serve to preserve information about the past history of inputs. To control the network behavior, a timing signal was introduced in Chapter 7. This allowed the state changes to be synchronized to a clock signal and that any input changes to be effective only at well-defined instants of time, say, at the triggering edge of the clock signal. These well-defined instants of time are regarded as *sample times.* The input changes may occur any time between the sample times as long as at the sample times the inputs to the flip-flops are at a steady value and any necessary setup time constraints of the flip-flops are satisfied.

By removing this synchronization control, the class of asynchronous sequential networks results. In this case, the input changes themselves are allowed to affect state and output changes in the network. Thus, these networks are capable of high-speed performance since it is no longer necessary to wait for the sample times to occur before the network responds to the input changes. Since asynchronous sequential networks no longer have a synchronizing clock, the memory portion of asynchronous sequential networks consists of unclocked flip-flops or time-delay devices. A time-delay device provides memory by the fact that it takes a finite amount of time for a signal to propagate through it and, correspondingly, serves to store information for that time duration.

It should be expected that the synthesis of asynchronous sequential networks is much more difficult than the synthesis of clocked synchronous sequential networks. In synchronous sequential networks, the sample times have the effect of only connecting the feedback paths for a very short duration. On the other hand, the feedback paths are continuously monitored in asynchronous sequential networks. Thus, after an input change that results in a change in the internal state, this internal-state change can, in turn, initiate another internal-state change, etc. As is seen in this chapter, such timing occurrences are of vital importance when designing asynchronous sequential networks. ■

9.1 STRUCTURE AND OPERATION OF ASYNCHRONOUS SEQUENTIAL NETWORKS

Relative to the general sequential network model of Fig. 7.1, the difference between synchronous sequential networks and asynchronous sequential networks is the memory block. For synchronous sequential networks this block consists of clocked flip-flops and a synchronizing clock signal; while for asynchronous sequential networks it consists of time-delay devices or unclocked flip-flops.

The general structure of an asynchronous sequential network with time-delay devices is shown in Fig. 9.1. This structure has associated with it n input variables, $x_1, x_2, \ldots, x_n$, and m output variables, $z_1, z_2, \ldots, z_m$. The values of the n-tuples $(x_1, x_2, \ldots, x_n)$ are called the *input states*; and the values of the m-tuples $(z_1, z_2, \ldots, z_m)$ are called the *output states* or simply *outputs*. The outputs of the time-delay devices are denoted by the p Boolean variables $y_1, y_2, \ldots, y_p$ that are used to define the in-

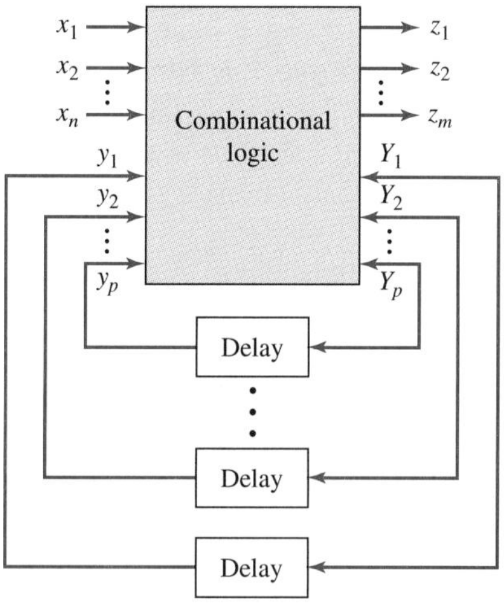

Figure 9.1 General structure of an asynchronous sequential network with time-delay devices.

ternal states, i.e., the memory, of the sequential network and are called the *present-state variables.* The values of the p-tuples $(y_1, y_2, \ldots, y_p)$ are called the *present states.* The inputs to the time-delay devices are denoted by the p Boolean variables $Y_1, Y_2, \ldots, Y_p$ and are called the *next-state variables.* The values of the p-tuples $(Y_1, Y_2, \ldots, Y_p)$ are called the *next states.* Finally, the values of the $(n + p)$-tuples $(x_1, x_2, \ldots, x_n, y_1, y_2, \ldots, y_p)$ are called the *total input states.* It should be noted that there is a distinction between the lowercase y_i variable and the uppercase Y_i variable.

In many realizations of asynchronous sequential networks, the time-delay devices do not explicitly appear. Rather, their effect is a consequence of the actual propagation delays inherent in the gates that comprise the combinational logic. Thus, typically asynchronous sequential networks appear as simply the interconnection of gate elements with one or more feedback loops. However, from a modeling point of view, it is convenient and instructional to show these distributed time delays as lumped time-delay devices.

Figure 9.2 shows the general structure of an asynchronous sequential network when flip-flops are used. This structure is the same as that of clocked synchronous sequential networks except unclocked flip-flops are employed. In this case, the present-state variable y_i corresponds to the flip-flop output Q_i. The excitations are the signals to the flip-flop input terminals, e.g., S_i and R_i when SR flip-flops are used for the memory. These excitations, along with the flip-flop characteristics, determine the next state of the memory devices and, correspondingly, the network.

Important to the operation of an asynchronous sequential network is the concept of *network stability.* An asynchronous sequential network is *stable* for a given

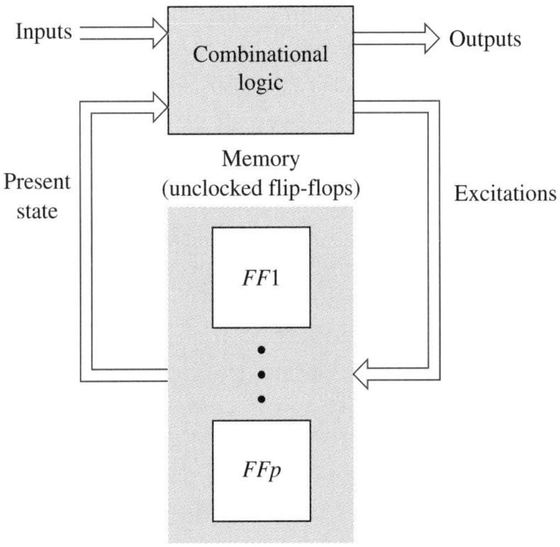

Figure 9.2 General structure of an asynchronous sequential network with unclocked flip-flops.

input state if the next state is the same as the present state; while it is *unstable* for a given input state if the next state and present state are not the same. In terms of the structure of Fig. 9.1, the network is stable for a given input state if $y_i = Y_i$ for each $i = 1,2, \ldots, p$ and unstable if $y_i \neq Y_i$ for at least one $i = 1, 2, \ldots, p$. As long as the network is unstable and the input state is not changed, then after a time delay the next-state signals appear as present-state signals. This implies that, in general, a succession of internal states can occur while the input state is held fixed.

Two assumptions are frequently made regarding the operation of asynchronous sequential networks. First, it is assumed that the input states are never changed unless the network is stable. Thus, the interval between successive input changes must be sufficient for the network to complete its responses to the previous input state and reach a stable state. When this assumption is satisfied, the asynchronous sequential network is said to be operating in *fundamental mode.* The second commonly made assumption is that only one input variable is allowed to change at a time. In this way, two successive input states differ in only the change of one bit in their n-tuples. Unless stated otherwise, both of these constraints are assumed in the remainder of this chapter.

In describing the terminal behavior of an asynchronous sequential network, use is made of tabular representations. These tabular representations are similar to those for Mealy synchronous sequential networks. They are two-dimensional arrays in which the input states serve as the column headings and the present states as the row labels. In this way, a total input state corresponds to a location in the table. The interpretations of these tables, on the other hand, are different from that for synchronous sequential networks.

A typical tabular representation for an asynchronous sequential network is shown in Table 9.1. Such a representation is extremely useful in understanding fundamental-mode operation. For example, let X_a and X_b denote two input-state n-tuples and Z_α, Z_β, Z_γ, and Z_δ various m-tuples for output states. Assume that the asynchronous sequential network is stable for present state s_i and input state X_a. Thus, an operating point is considered as being situated at the X_a-column, s_i-row in the table. It is common practice to encircle all next-state entries that are stable. These are readily detected by noting if the entry in the next-state subtable is the same as the present state as given by the row designator. If the input is now changed to X_b, then according to Table 9.1 the next state is s_j. Changing the input corresponds to a horizontal transition of the operating point in the next-state subtable. After a time duration as determined by the time-delay devices or the inherent delays of the gates in the combinational logic, the present state becomes s_j. This is indicated by a vertical transition of the operating point in the table since the input is being held fixed at X_b. It is now noted in this example that when the present state is s_j and the input state is still X_b, the next state is s_k. Since this is not a stable condition, after another time duration the present state becomes s_k, which is indicated by another vertical transition of the operating point in the table. In this case, the next state of the network is the same as its present state. Thus, the network becomes stable; i.e., no further internal state changes occur. Furthermore, the network remains stable indefinitely unless the input state is

Table 9.1 Illustration of fundamental-mode operation

Present state	Next state					Output				
	Input state					Input state				
	…	X_a	…	X_b	…	…	X_a	…	X_b	…
⋮		⋮		⋮			⋮		⋮	
s_i	…	(s_i)	…	s_j	…	…	Z_α	…	Z_β†	…
⋮		⋮		⋮			⋮		⋮	
s_j	…		…	s_k	…	…		…	Z_γ†	…
⋮		⋮		⋮			⋮		⋮	
s_k	…		…	(s_k)	…	…		…	Z_δ	…
⋮		⋮		⋮			⋮		⋮	

† The output states occurring at these times are usually restricted to Z_α or Z_δ.

changed again. In this example there were two vertical transitions of the operating point before the network became stable. In general, the number of transitions depends upon the actual network design. The reader should carefully note that this is unlike the internal behavior of a clocked synchronous sequential network where the effect of the clock signal is to ensure that multiple state changes do not occur.

The outputs of the asynchronous sequential network that occur during these transitions are determined by referring to the output subtable. An operating point is also considered moving about the output subtable in coincidence with the operating point moving about the next-state subtable. For this example, the output, originally Z_α, becomes Z_β when the input state is changed. It then becomes Z_γ and finally Z_δ as a result of the internal-state changes. As is seen at a later point in this chapter, the outputs Z_β and Z_γ are usually restricted to those of Z_α or Z_δ.

The concept of an unstable condition is the key factor in the operation of asynchronous sequential networks. When an input state is changed, the next stable state that is reached reflects the updated past history of inputs. In general, more than one stable internal state can exist for any input state. Each of these internal states corresponds to a different past sequence of input states. Also, different output states can be associated with each of these stable internal states. The use of operating points moving about a table is a convenient way of describing the effects of input changes upon the network behavior and is used frequently in this chapter.

9.2 ANALYSIS OF ASYNCHRONOUS SEQUENTIAL NETWORKS

The analysis of asynchronous sequential networks proceeds in much the same way as that of clocked synchronous sequential networks. From a logic diagram, Boolean expressions are written and then transferred into tabular form. Different types of tables, i.e., the *excitation table*, *transition table*, *state table*, and *flow table*, are constructed that reflect different degrees of information about the internal state of the network. All of these tables enable the determination of an output sequence for a given input sequence and initial state. The excitation table, transition table, and state table are constructed in the same way as for clocked synchronous sequential networks. However, one new type of table, i.e., the flow table, is introduced as the last tabular form during the analysis procedure.

The analysis of asynchronous sequential networks is presented using two running examples. They are shown in Figs. 9.3 and 9.4 and are subsequently referred to as Examples 9.1 and 9.2, respectively. It is assumed both networks operate in fundamental mode and that only one input variable is allowed to change at a time.

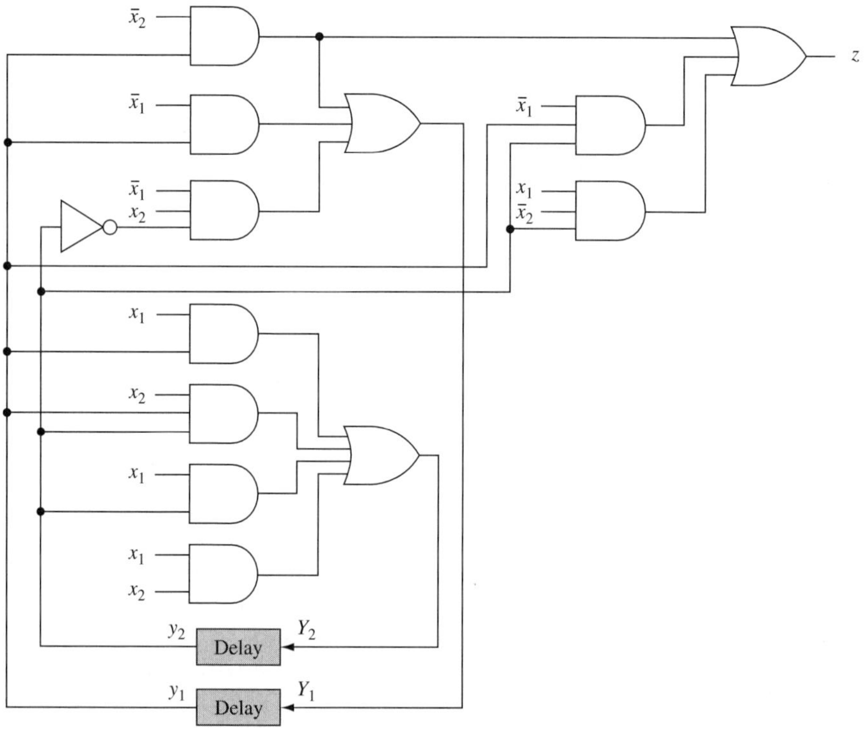

Figure 9.3 Logic diagram for Example 9.1.

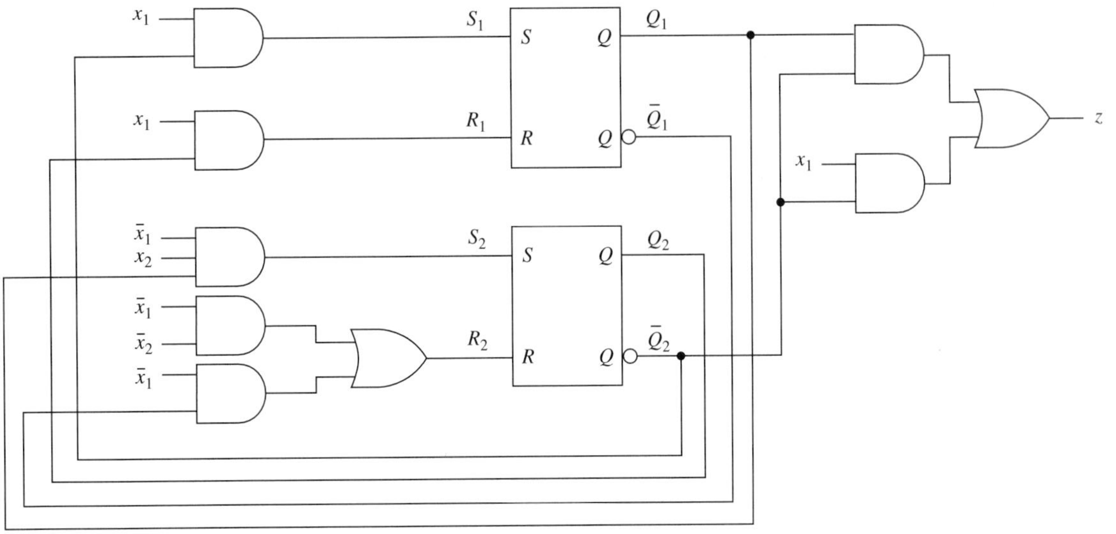

Figure 9.4 Logic diagram for Example 9.2.

For example, if the present input state is $x_1x_2 = 00$, then the next input state is either $x_1x_2 = 01$ or $x_1x_2 = 10$ but cannot be $x_1x_2 = 11$. However, all four combinations of values for the input variables are network input states since the input state $x_1x_2 = 11$ can be applied after either $x_1x_2 = 01$ or $x_1x_2 = 10$ is applied.

To analyze an asynchronous sequential network it is first necessary to define the state variables. This is a simple task if time-delay devices or unclocked flip-flops are used in the feedback loops. In particular, if time-delay devices occur in the feedback loops, then the two ends of a time-delay device are labeled with the present-state and next-state variables y_i and Y_i as previously indicated in Fig. 9.1. Collectively, these define the present state and next state of the network. If unclocked flip-flops appear, then the state variables are readily defined by the flip-flop outputs.

Frequently, however, neither time-delay devices nor unclocked flip-flops occur in an asynchronous sequential network realization. Rather, the existence of the feedback loops alone provides for the memory capability of the network, since the time delays needed for network operation are assumed to be distributed in the logic network itself. In this case, to begin the analysis procedure it is first necessary to select a sufficient number of points in the network so that, if broken, no feedback loops exist. If the feedback loops are determined in this manner, then effort should be made to select a minimum number of such points. Although the determination of a minimum number of points is not necessary to perform asynchronous sequential network analysis, the fewer the number of such points selected the more the analysis procedure is simplified, since fewer state variables need to be defined. Once this is done, time-delay devices are assumed to exist at these points in order to define present-state and next-state variables at the two ends. As indicated previously, these assumed time-delay devices correspond to the lumping of the distributed delays occurring in the gate components in each loop.

Example 9.1, i.e., Fig. 9.3, consists of a gate network with feedback loops. The time-delay devices are shown grayed to symbolize that they do not appear physically in the realization but are a consequence of the distributed gate delays. Since there are only two feedback loops in the network, the present-state variables y_1 and y_2 are defined at the outputs of the implicit time-delay devices and the next-state variables Y_1 and Y_2 at the inputs.

Figure 9.4 shows the logic diagram of Example 9.2. In this diagram, two *SR* latches appear. The outputs of the latches are used to define the present state of the network. In this case, Q_1 and Q_2, rather than Y_1 and Y_2, are selected as the state variables to be consistent with the way state variables were defined for synchronous sequential networks.

9.2.1 The Excitation Table

Once the state variables are defined, the next step in the analysis of asynchronous sequential networks is to determine the excitations that, in turn, determine the next state of the network. These excitations correspond to the inputs at the implicit or explicit time-delay devices or the unclocked flip-flops. The signals at these points are denoted by a set of excitation variables. For time-delay devices, the excitation variables are the same as the next-state variables, i.e., Y_i. In the case of unclocked flip-flops, the excitation variables are assigned to the input terminals of the flip-flops. Next, each output of the asynchronous sequential network is assigned an output variable. Once the assignment of excitation and output variables is completed, algebraic expressions for the excitations and outputs in terms of the input and present-state variables can be written to describe the network behavior.

From the algebraic expressions for the network, it is a simple matter to obtain a corresponding truth table. As was done for synchronous sequential networks, the truth table appears as a two-dimensional array. This is known as the *excitation table* and it is constructed the same way as was done for synchronous sequential networks. In particular, the excitation table consists of three sections; the first, or present-state section, lists all possible combinations of values of the present-state variables and serves as the row designators for the other two sections. The second and third sections of the excitation table, referred to as the excitation and output sections, each consist of a column for each input state of the network. In this way, each location in the excitation and output sections corresponds to a total input state. The excitation equations are readily evaluated for each total input state and the values placed as entries in the excitation section. Similarly, the entries in the output section are determined by evaluating the output expressions for each total input state.

Again consider Example 9.1 (Fig. 9.3). The excitation variables are the two next-state variables Y_1 and Y_2. These excitations are described by the expressions

$$Y_1 = \bar{x}_2 y_1 + \bar{x}_1 y_1 + \bar{x}_1 x_2 \bar{y}_2$$
$$Y_2 = x_1 y_1 + x_2 y_1 y_2 + x_1 y_2 + x_1 x_2$$

Table 9.2 Excitation/transition table for Example 9.1

Present state (y_1y_2)	Excitation/Next state (Y_1Y_2)				Output (z)			
	Input state (x_1x_2)				Input state (x_1x_2)			
	00	01	10	11	00	01	10	11
00	00	10	00	01	0	0	0	0
01	00	00	01	01	0	0	1	0
10	10	10	11	01	1	0	1	0
11	10	11	11	01	1	1	1	0

Next, the expression for the output of the network is determined as

$$z = \bar{x}_2y_1 + \bar{x}_1y_1y_2 + x_1\bar{x}_2y_2$$

These three expressions completely describe the network. From these expressions, the excitation table of Table 9.2 is constructed by evaluating the expressions for each total input state, i.e., present-state/input-state combination.

For Example 9.2 (Fig. 9.4), excitation variables are assigned to the four input terminals of the flip-flops, i.e., S_1, R_1, S_2, and R_2. Once this is done, the corresponding excitation expressions are easily written as

$$S_1 = x_1\overline{Q}_2$$
$$R_1 = x_1Q_2$$
$$S_2 = \bar{x}_1x_2Q_1$$
$$R_2 = \bar{x}_1\bar{x}_2 + \bar{x}_1\overline{Q}_1$$

The evaluation of these four expressions for each total input state forms the excitation section of Table 9.3. Finally, the single output expression is

$$z = Q_1\overline{Q}_2 + x_1\overline{Q}_2$$

Its evaluation for each total input state appears as the output section of Table 9.3.

Table 9.3 Excitation table for Example 9.2

Present state (Q_1Q_2)	Excitation (S_1R_1,S_2R_2)				Output (z)			
	Input state (x_1x_2)				Input state (x_1x_2)			
	00	01	10	11	00	01	10	11
00	00,01	00,01	10,00	10,00	0	0	1	1
01	00,01	00,01	01,00	01,00	0	0	0	0
10	00,01	00,10	10,00	10,00	1	1	1	1
11	00,01	00,10	01,00	01,00	0	0	0	0

9.2.2 The Transition Table

The excitation table describes the behavior of an asynchronous sequential network in terms of the excitation signals in the memory portion of the network. On the other hand, the *transition table* is used to describe the network behavior based on the general model of Fig. 9.1 in which the internal signals are simply the present state and next state. As was done in Chapter 7, to obtain this tabular description requires consideration of the characteristics of the memory devices in the network.

The transition table consists of three sections: the present-state section, the next-state section, and the output section. The column labels of the transition table are identical to those of the excitation table. The entries in the present-state section are a listing of all the combinations of values of the present-state variables and the entries in the output section are the values of the output variables $z_1, z_2, \ldots, z_m$ for each of the total input states. Hence, the present-state and output sections of the transition table are identical with the corresponding sections of the excitation table. However, the entries in the next-state section are the values of the next-state variables $Y_1, Y_2, \ldots, Y_p$ for each of the total input states.

For those asynchronous sequential networks in which memory is achieved by simple feedback loops or time-delay devices, the excitation equations are also the next-state equations. Hence, for these networks the transition table is identical with the excitation table since the entries in the excitation section are exactly the next states of the sequential network for each total input state. Thus, the transition table for Example 9.1 is the same as Table 9.2.

For asynchronous sequential networks that incorporate memory devices other than time-delay devices, it is necessary to consider the characteristics of the memory devices in order to establish the next-state section of the transition table. This can be done using either the characteristic equations of the memory devices given in Fig. 6.25*b* or the flip-flop next-state tables given in Table 6.2. These equations and tables are still valid even though they were originally developed for clocked flip-flops since they describe the effect of the information input values, i.e., the excitations, and the present states of the flip-flops on the next states of the flip-flops.

Each entry in the excitation section of the excitation table corresponds to the input signals to the memory devices as indicated by the column label and the present state of the memory devices as indicated by the entry in the present-state section. From this information and the previously established characteristics of the memory devices given in Table 6.2, the next states of the memory devices are readily determined and entered in the next-state section of the transition table. Alternately, the excitation equations themselves can be substituted into the flip-flop characteristic equations of Fig. 6.25*b* to obtain algebraic expressions for the next-state variables. The next-state section of the transition table is then constructed by evaluating these equations for each total input state.

The above two approaches to constructing the next-state section of the transition table are precisely the same as those used in Sec. 7.2 for clocked synchronous sequential networks. As an illustration of the first approach, consider the total input state $(x_1x_2,Q_1Q_2) = (11,00)$ in Table 9.3. In this case, the excitation is $(S_1R_1,S_2R_2) = (10,00)$

and the present state is 0 for each flip-flop, i.e., $Q_1Q_2 = 00$. The $S_1R_1 = 10$ part of the excitation indicates that a logic-1 is applied only to the set terminal of the first flip-flop. Thus, its next state, Q_1^+, is 1. The $S_2R_2 = 00$ part of the excitation implies that a logic-0 is applied to both input terminals of the second flip-flop. Since the present state of the second flip-flop is 0, according to Table 6.2, its next state also is 0, i.e., $Q_2^+ = 0$. Hence the next-state entry in the transition table for the total input state $(x_1x_2,Q_1Q_2) = (11,00)$ is $Q_1^+Q_2^+ = 10$. The transition table for Example 9.2 is shown in Table 9.4.

In the previous section it was stated that an asynchronous sequential network is stable if the next state and present state of the network are the same. By referring to the transition table, stable conditions are easily identified. When the entry in the next-state section of the transition table is the same as the row label, i.e., present state, in which it appears, then the condition for network stability is satisfied. Referring to Tables 9.2 and 9.4 for Examples 9.1 and 9.2, the stable conditions are indicated by the circled next-state entries.

As explained in Sec. 9.1, the operation of an asynchronous sequential network can be described by means of the motion of operating points in a tabular representation. Consider the effects of the application of an input sequence to the transition table of Table 9.2. The following internal-state behavior is illustrated in the table by the directed arrows in the next-state section. Assume the initial total input state to the network in Example 9.1 is $(x_1x_2,y_1y_2) = (10,00)$. This total input state corresponds to a stable condition with an operating point in the first row, third column of the next-state section of the transition table. If the input state is now changed to $x_1x_2 = 11$, then the network behaves in accordance with the operating point moving from the first row, third column to the first row, fourth column of the table. Table 9.2 indicates that an unstable condition now exists within the network, in particular, $y_1y_2 = 00$ while $Y_1Y_2 = 01$. After a time delay, as determined by the response times of the gates, the present state $y_1y_2 = 01$ results. This internal change in the network corresponds to a vertical transition of the operating point in the next-state section of Table 9.2 to the second row, fourth column, which corresponds to a stable condition. As long as the input state remains unchanged, the asynchronous sequential network remains in this stable state. However, assume the input state is next changed to $x_1x_2 = 01$. The operating point now moves horizontally to the second column. An unstable network condition again is seen to exist since $y_1y_2 = 01$ while $Y_1Y_2 = 00$.

Table 9.4 Transition table for Example 9.2

Present state (Q_1Q_2)	Next state ($Q_1^+Q_2^+$)				Output (z)			
	Input state (x_1x_2)				Input state (x_1x_2)			
	00	01	10	11	00	01	10	11
00	(00)	(00)	10	10	0	0	1	1
01	00	00	(01)	(01)	0	0	0	0
10	(10)	11	(10)	(10)	1	1	1	1
11	10	(11)	01	01	0	0	0	0

After an appropriate delay time, the operating point moves vertically to the first row. This is also an unstable network condition since $y_1y_2 = 00$ and $Y_1Y_2 = 10$. Consequently, after another time delay, the operating point moves vertically to the third row, at which time the network becomes stable. From the definition of fundamental-mode operation, only after the network becomes stable can a new input state be applied. Now assume the input state $x_1x_2 = 01$ is next changed to $x_1x_2 = 00$. This causes the operating point to move horizontally to the first column. It should be noted that the network does not become unstable and, hence, no internal state changes occur.

The above discussion was concerned with the internal operation of a fundamental-mode asynchronous sequential network. To determine the outputs of the network, another operating point is considered moving about the output section of the transition table coincident with the operating point in the next-state section. For the input sequence just described, the output of the network is 0 until the total input state $(x_1x_2,y_1y_2) = (00,10)$ is reached. At that time the output changes to a 1.

9.2.3 The State Table

To determine the output terminal behavior of an asynchronous sequential network, knowledge of the movement of the operating points is sufficient. For this reason, alphanumeric symbols can be used to denote the various states, rather than the actual binary codes, of the network. When these newly defined symbols are used to replace the various binary codes for the states in the transition table, the transition table becomes the *state table.* This is completely analogous to what was done previously for synchronous sequential networks.

Tables 9.5 and 9.6 are the state tables for Examples 9.1 and 9.2. These tables are obtained directly from Tables 9.2 and 9.4, respectively, in which the binary-coded state 00 is replaced by A, 01 by B, etc.

In the state table, the exact values of the signals associated with the internal states of the sequential network are no longer known. However, it is still possible to discuss the operation of the network by means of the operating-point concept, as was done with the transition table. That is, the sequence of symbolic next states and output states that results upon the application of an input sequence to some known initial state can be obtained from the state table.

Table 9.5 State table for Example 9.1

Present state	Next state				Output (z)			
	Input state (x_1x_2)				Input state (x_1x_2)			
	00	01	10	11	00	01	10	11
$00 \to A$	(A)	C	(A)	B	0	0	0	0
$01 \to B$	A	A	(B)	(B)	0	0	1	0
$10 \to C$	(C)	(C)	D	B	1	0	1	0
$11 \to D$	C	(D)	(D)	B	1	1	1	0

Table 9.6 State table for Example 9.2

Present state	Next state				Output (z)			
	Input state (x_1x_2)				Input state (x_1x_2)			
	00	01	10	11	00	01	10	11
$00 \rightarrow A$	Ⓐ	Ⓐ	C	C	0	0	1	1
$01 \rightarrow B$	A	A	Ⓑ	Ⓑ	0	0	0	0
$10 \rightarrow C$	Ⓒ	D	Ⓒ	Ⓒ	1	1	1	1
$11 \rightarrow D$	C	Ⓓ	B	B	0	0	0	0

9.2.4 The Flow Table

In the state tables for asynchronous sequential networks, the operating point in the next-state section may undergo multiple internal-state transitions. For example, if the operating point is at the second row, fourth column of the next-state section of Table 9.5, and if the input state is changed to $x_1x_2 = 01$, then it is seen that the operating point makes two vertical transitions before a stable network condition is reached. These multiple-state transitions are the result of the state-assignment problem in asynchronous sequential networks.

For the purpose of discussing the operation of an asynchronous sequential network, it frequently is not necessary to know all the internal changes that are involved since for fundamental-mode operation input state changes are not permitted unless the network is stable. Thus, it may only be of interest to know the final stable state that the network eventually enters after becoming unstable. In such cases, the entries in the state table representing intermediate unstable states are replaced by the state that is ultimately reached.

Also, at times in studying asynchronous sequential network behavior, the outputs during the unstable conditions may be of little concern. That is, only the outputs associated with stable conditions are of interest. This implies that certain entries in the output section of the state table can be ignored.

Finally, certain input states may be prohibited from following another input state in accordance with the specifications of the operation of the sequential network. For example, as was mentioned in Sec. 9.1, a common assumption in asynchronous sequential networks is that only one input variable can change at a time. In the establishment of the various tables thus far, input restrictions have not been considered. The effects of such input restrictions are easily incorporated into the body of the tables by introducing a symbol to indicate that a transition leading to that point is impossible.

When a state table is modified according to the above discussion, it is called a *flow table*. Thus, the flow table consists of three sections: the present state, the next state, and the output sections. A flow table still describes the overall network behavior; however, some of the details of the operation are no longer shown. To construct a flow table from a state table for a fundamental-mode asynchronous sequential network having input constraints, each noncircled next-state

Table 9.7 Flow table for Example 9.1

Present state	Next state				Output (z)			
	Input state (x_1x_2)				Input state (x_1x_2)			
	00	01	10	11	00	01	10	11
A	Ⓐ	*C*	Ⓐ	*B*	0	–	0	–
B	*A*	*C*	Ⓑ	Ⓑ	–	–	1	0
C	Ⓒ	Ⓒ	*D*	*B*	1	0	–	–
D	*C*	Ⓓ	Ⓓ	*B*	–	1	1	–

entry, i.e., the unstable states, is replaced by the symbol for the stable state that the network eventually enters. Furthermore, any rows having no circled entries are deleted since these rows have influence only during multiple transitions, and hence the operating points in the table no longer enter such rows. In the output section, outputs are specified only for those total input states corresponding to stable conditions. All other output entries are replaced by dashes. Finally, entries within the state table that cannot be entered because of input restrictions are also replaced by dashes.

To illustrate the construction of a flow table, consider the state table for Example 9.1 shown in Table 9.5. The resulting flow table is given in Table 9.7. In this case, unstable state *A* in the second row, second column of the next-state section of Table 9.5 becomes unstable state *C* in Table 9.7, since after two internal-state transitions the operating point originally in the second row, second column enters stable state Ⓒ. Furthermore, this is the only unstable state that must be replaced since it is the only unstable state that leads to another unstable state. Next, the output states are specified in Table 9.7 only for those total input states that have stable internal states associated with them. The output states associated with the unstable states are replaced by dashes. Finally, although it was initially assumed for Example 9.1 that only single input variable changes occur, this does not cause any additional dashes to be entered in the flow table. That this is true will become evident when the flow table for Example 9.2 is next discussed.

For Example 9.2, the flow table shown in Table 9.8 is constructed from Table 9.6. In this example all unstable states lead directly to stable states. Thus,

Table 9.8 Flow table for Example 9.2

Present state	Next state				Output (z)			
	Input state (x_1x_2)				Input state (x_1x_2)			
	00	01	10	11	00	01	10	11
A	Ⓐ	Ⓐ	*C*	*C*	0	0	–	–
B	*A*	*A*	Ⓑ	Ⓑ	–	–	0	0
C	Ⓒ	*D*	Ⓒ	Ⓒ	1	–	1	1
D	*C*	Ⓓ	–	*B*	–	0	–	–

no changes to the unstable states are necessary. Next, entries that should be replaced by dashes are determined. In addition to dashes for the outputs associated with unstable conditions, a dash also appears in the next-state section of the flow table. This dash is a consequence of the input restriction that only one input variable may change value at any time. Hence, once the operating point is at stable state Ⓓ, the input state cannot be changed from $x_1x_2 = 01$ to $x_1x_2 = 10$ and, correspondingly, a dash is placed in the fourth row, third column of the next-state section of the flow table. On the other hand, for example, it is not permissible to replace the C in the first row, third column by a dash since even though the operating point cannot move from the second column to the third column in that row, it can move from the first column, a stable point, to the third column. Thus, the table must specify the ultimate network action for the total input state associated with the first row, third column. By similar reasoning, no additional dashes result in the next-state section of the flow table of Table 9.8 as a consequence of the input restriction.

9.2.5 The Flow Diagram

Inasmuch as state diagrams can be constructed for state tables of clocked synchronous sequential networks, flow diagrams can also be constructed for flow tables of asynchronous sequential networks operating in fundamental mode. Each row of the flow table is represented by a node in the flow diagram. Since, by construction, there is at least one stable state in each row of the flow table, each stable state has a directed branch looping on its own node in the flow diagram. This branch is labeled with the input states associated with the stable state along with the corresponding outputs. The remaining directed branches, denoting the transitions between states, are labeled with just the input states that affect the transitions. The flow diagrams for Tables 9.7 and 9.8 are shown in Figs. 9.5 and 9.6, respectively.

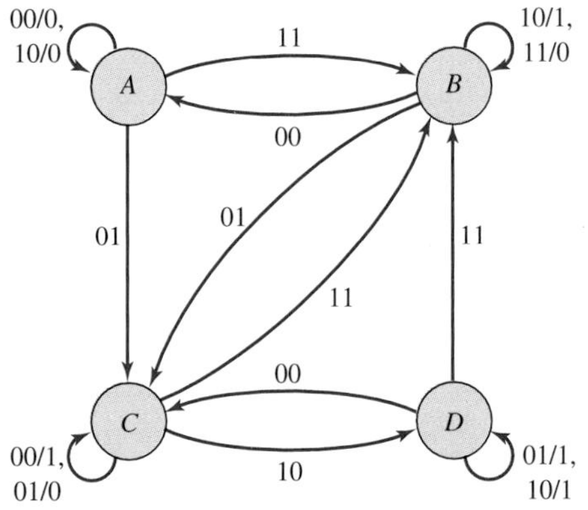

Figure 9.5 Flow diagram for Table 9.7.

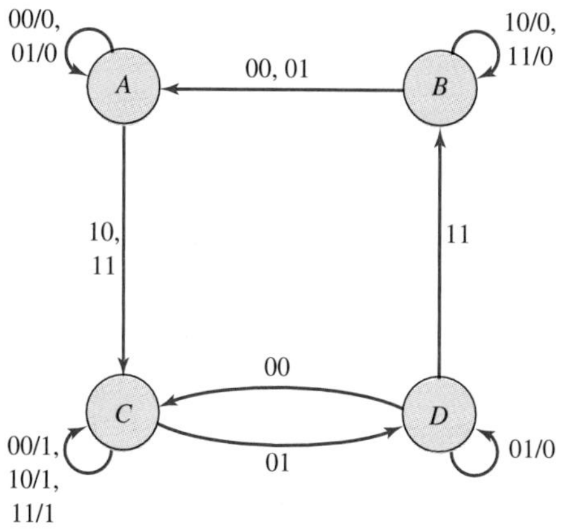

Figure 9.6 Flow diagram for Table 9.8.

9.3 RACES IN ASYNCHRONOUS SEQUENTIAL NETWORKS

With the exception of the total input state $(x_1x_2,y_1y_2) = (11,10)$ in the transition table for Example 9.1, i.e., Table 9.2, for each entry in the next-state section the codes for the present and next states never differ by more than one binary digit. Special attention must be given to the unstable internal states when this is not the case. If two or more next-state variables must change value in response to an input state change, then a *race condition* is said to exist. This occurs in Table 9.2 for the total input state $(x_1x_2,y_1y_2) = (11,10)$. As another example, Table 9.9 gives just the next-state section of a transition table. In this table there are two race conditions, which are indicated with asterisks.

Because of the possibly unequal propagation delays in the feedback loops of asynchronous sequential networks, race conditions can have varying effects. In general, the switching times of the gates or flip-flops within a network are not all exactly the same; some gates or flip-flops may switch before others. The net result is that when two or more next-state variables must change value, one may change before the other in an unpredictable manner.

To illustrate the significance of races, again consider Table 9.9. Assume the total input state is $(x_1x_2,y_1y_2) = (01,00)$. As indicated in the table, the network is stable. Now let the input state be changed to $x_1x_2 = 00$. The next state according to the table should be $Y_1Y_2 = 11$. This implies that both state variables must change value from 0 to 1. If the propagation delays for both feedback loops are identical, then this is indeed the case and the operating point moves to the last row of the $x_1x_2 = 00$ column as desired. However, if the feedback loop propagation delays cause the first state variable to change value before the second state variable, then the new resulting present state becomes $y_1y_2 = 10$ and the operating point moves to the third row.

Table 9.9 Illustrations of race conditions

Present state (y_1y_2)	Next state (Y_1Y_2)			
	Input state (x_1x_2)			
	00	01	10	11
00	11*	(00)	01	11*
01	11	11	11	(01)
10	11	(10)	00	11
11	(11)	10	10	(11)

At this time the network is still unstable according to Table 9.9 with $y_1y_2 = 10$ and $Y_1Y_2 = 11$. After an additional time delay, the operating point moves to the last row in the $x_1x_2 = 00$ column and a stable condition results. On the other hand, if initially the second state variable changes value before the first state variable, then the operating point moves to the second row and then to the fourth row. Thus, it is seen that depending upon the physical properties of the asynchronous sequential network, the operating point initially can move to three different rows upon entering the unstable state having a race condition. To indicate the consequences of the race condition in Table 9.9, three dashed directed lines are shown leaving the unstable state in the first row, first column to signify the three possible transitions that can occur. In this particular example the same stable state results regardless of the outcome of the race condition. If each of the possibilities of a race eventually leads to the same stable state, then the race is said to be *noncritical.* This is precisely what is illustrated in the $x_1x_2 = 00$ column of Table 9.9.

Again consider Table 9.9 and the total input state $(x_1x_2,y_1y_2) = (01,00)$. If the input state is now changed to $x_1x_2 = 11$, then the operating point moves to the fourth column, first row in which a race condition exists. Since two state variables must change value, three possible situations, depending upon the network propagation delays, must be considered. If both state variables change value simultaneously, then the operating point moves to the fourth row, which is a stable condition; while if the first state variable changes value first, then the operating point moves to the third row and finally to the fourth row. In either event the same stable state is reached. On the other hand, however, if the second state variable is the first to change value, then the operating point moves to the second row and the network becomes stable. Thus, depending upon the physical properties of the asynchronous sequential network, different stable states may result. When the alternate possibilities of a race condition lead to different stable states, the race is said to be *critical.* Certainly this is an undesirable situation, since each of these stable states signifies different past histories of inputs. With a critical race, asynchronous sequential network behavior becomes probabilistic and not deterministic as required for normal operation.

To ensure desirable network operation, critical races must be avoided. However, noncritical races are permissible. When the synthesis of asynchronous sequential networks is discussed later in this chapter, critical races are avoided by an appropriate state assignment. Such a state assignment may provide for multiple internal-state transitions. For example, in Table 9.9, if the input state is changed to $x_1x_2 = 01$ when in the total input state $(x_1x_2,y_1y_2) = (11,01)$, then after two internal-state transitions, each only requiring a single internal state variable to change value at a time, the network enters the stable state ⑩. If instead the next-state entry $Y_1Y_2 = 10$ were to appear for the total input state $(x_1x_2,y_1y_2) = (01,01)$, then a critical race would exist and the desired final stable state may not be reached. Thus, multiple internal-state transitions are used to control the internal behavior of the network. When a network undergoes a unique sequence of unstable internal states, then it is said to have a *cycle.*

There is another undesirable condition, involving a cycle, that must be avoided in fundamental-mode asynchronous sequential networks. This is illustrated in the $x_1x_2 = 10$ column of Table 9.9. As can be seen, no stable state is ever reached if the operating point enters this column. Such a closed sequence of unstable states must be avoided since, by definition of fundamental-mode operation, no further input changes are permitted as a result of the network never becoming stable.

9.4 THE PRIMITIVE FLOW TABLE

Up to this point, attention has been on the analysis of asynchronous sequential networks. The main reason for this study was to establish a set of models, i.e., tables, for describing network behavior. At this time the synthesis of asynchronous sequential networks begins. This involves the establishment of the same set of tables discussed in Sec. 9.2 except in the reverse order. Much of the following material is simply a variation of the synthesis procedure for clocked synchronous sequential networks. To illustrate the synthesis of asynchronous sequential networks, two running examples, referred to as Examples 9.3 and 9.4, are used.

The synthesis of asynchronous sequential networks begins with the construction of a flow table. This is an unambiguous description of the desired terminal behavior of the system to be designed that is formed by interpreting a set of specifications. As was seen in Sec. 7.3 for synchronous sequential networks, there are two general approaches to the establishment of an initial model. The states, i.e., information that must be preserved by the system, can be determined a priori or they can be defined as the model itself is being constructed.

For asynchronous sequential networks that are to operate in fundamental mode, it is most convenient to start with a special form of the flow table. This special form is called a *primitive flow table.* A primitive flow table is similar to the flow table introduced in Sec. 9.2 with the exception that it is restricted to having exactly one stable state in each row of the next-state section. In general, after the primitive flow table is constructed, the number of rows can be reduced by a systematic process. The reduced primitive flow table with more than a single stable state in each row of the next-state section will then have the form that was discussed in Sec. 9.2.

9.4.1 The Primitive Flow Table for Example 9.3

Consider now the first running example.

EXAMPLE 9.3

Design a fundamental-mode asynchronous sequential network meeting the following requirements:

1. There are two inputs x_1 and x_2 and a single output z.
2. The inputs x_1 and x_2 never change simultaneously.
3. The output is always to be 0 when $x_1 = 0$, independent of the value of x_2.
4. The output is to become 1 if x_2 changes while $x_1 = 1$ and is to remain 1 until x_1 becomes 0 again.

From the above specifications it is now necessary to establish a primitive flow table that can serve as an unambiguous model of the network behavior. This can be done by determining at least one entry in the flow table that can serve as a starting point. Then, from these initial flow-table entries, additional entries, and correspondingly rows, are introduced as needed to retain past-input information. This process of making entries and adding rows is continued until the table is completely filled in and further expansion of the table is unnecessary.

From the requirements stated above, it is seen that a possible input state to the network is $x_1x_2 = 00$. Since the network is to operate in fundamental mode, this implies that there must be a stable state in the $x_1x_2 = 00$ column of the next-state section of the primitive flow table. Thus, in Table 9.10*a* the entry *A* is placed in the present-state section of the flow table and the circled entry Ⓐ in the first column of the next-state section. Furthermore, since $x_1 = 0$, the output z must be 0 for stable state Ⓐ according to the third requirement of the specifications. Thus, a 0 is entered in the first column of the output section in Table 9.10*a*.

Having established one stable state in the flow table, further entries are determined by assuming that the network is in operation and allowing the inputs to change. That is, further entries are obtained by considering the motion of operating points within the flow table. According to the second requirement, only one input variable is allowed to change value at a time. This implies that the input state $x_1x_2 = 11$ cannot follow the input state $x_1x_2 = 00$. Thus, a dash (–) is placed in the first row, fourth column of the next-state section of Table 9.10*b* to indicate this situation. On the other hand, the input state $x_1x_2 = 01$ can be applied when the network is in stable state Ⓐ. If this input state occurs, then the network must become unstable, since only one stable state is permitted in each row of a primitive flow table, and eventually reach another stable state, say Ⓑ. In terms of the operating point in the next-state section, there is first a horizontal transition and then a vertical transition. Thus, a second row must be added to the table for present state *B*. In the next-state section of the flow table an uncircled entry *B* is placed in the first row, second column and a circled entry

Table 9.10 Obtaining the primitive flow table for Example 9.3

Present state	Next state				Output (z)			
	Input state (x_1x_2)				Input state (x_1x_2)			
	00	01	10	11	00	01	10	11
A	(*A*)				0			

(*a*)

Present state	Next state				Output (z)			
	Input state (x_1x_2)				Input state (x_1x_2)			
	00	01	10	11	00	01	10	11
A	(*A*)	*B*	*C*	–	0	–	–	–
B		(*B*)			–	0	–	–
C			(*C*)		–	–	0	–

(*b*)

Present state	Next state				Output (z)			
	Input state (x_1x_2)				Input state (x_1x_2)			
	00	01	10	11	00	01	10	11
A	(*A*)	*B*	*C*	–	0	–	–	–
B	*A*	(*B*)	–	*D*	–	0	–	–
C			(*C*)		–	–	0	–
D				(*D*)	–	–	–	0

(*c*)

Present state	Next state				Output (z)			
	Input state (x_1x_2)				Input state (x_1x_2)			
	00	01	10	11	00	01	10	11
A	(*A*)	*B*	*C*	–	0	–	–	–
B	*A*	(*B*)	–	*D*	–	0	–	–
C	*A*	–	(*C*)	*E*	–	–	0	–
D				(*D*)	–	–	–	0
E				(*E*)	–	–	–	1

(*d*)

Present state	Next state				Output (z)			
	Input state (x_1x_2)				Input state (x_1x_2)			
	00	01	10	11	00	01	10	11
A	(*A*)	*B*	*C*	–	0	–	–	–
B	*A*	(*B*)	–	*D*	–	0	–	–
C	*A*	–	(*C*)	*E*	–	–	0	–
D	–	*B*	*F*	(*D*)	–	–	–	0
E				(*E*)	–	–	–	1
F			(*F*)		–	–	1	–

(*e*)

(*Cont.*)

Table 9.10 *(Cont.)*

Present state	Next state				Output (z)			
	Input state (x_1x_2)				Input state (x_1x_2)			
	00	01	10	11	00	01	10	11
A	Ⓐ	B	C	–	0	–	–	–
B	A	Ⓑ	–	D	–	0	–	–
C	A	–	Ⓒ	E	–	–	0	–
D	–	B	F	Ⓓ	–	–	–	0
E	–	B	F	Ⓔ	–	–	–	1
F	A	–	Ⓕ	E	–	–	1	–

(f)

Ⓑ is placed in the second row, second column to provide for the internal change that occurs when the input state is changed from $x_1x_2 = 00$ to $x_1x_2 = 01$. These entries are also shown in Table 9.10*b*. Furthermore, since $x_1 = 0$, the output associated with stable state Ⓑ must again be 0 according to the third requirement. By similar reasoning, another row for state C is needed when the input state is changed from $x_1x_2 = 00$ to $x_1x_2 = 10$. An uncircled C entry is placed in the first row, third column and the entry Ⓒ in the third row, third column of the next-state section. The output again is 0 when the network is in stable state Ⓒ since from the network specifications the value of x_2 must change while x_1 is held at the value of 1 before the output can be 1. Finally, since this is a flow table, dashes appear for each output state that is not associated with a stable state. At this point the primitive flow table appears as shown in Table 9.10*b*.

Having determined all the entries in the first row of the primitive flow table, attention is turned to the second row. Assume that the network is in stable state Ⓑ. If the input state is changed to $x_1x_2 = 00$, the network must first become unstable and then reach a stable state. Since stable state Ⓐ already exists in the first column of the next-state section, the possibility of the network returning to this stable state should be considered. From the network specifications, it is only necessary that a stable state with a 0 output be entered since $x_1 = 0$. Hence, proper network operation is achieved if the network returns to stable state Ⓐ and an uncircled A entry is placed in the second row, first column of the next-state section. On the other hand, if the network is again assumed to be in stable state Ⓑ, then changing the input state to $x_1x_2 = 11$ requires that a stable state must appear in the fourth column of the next-state section of the flow table. Thus, an internal change to a stable state Ⓓ is needed. The output for stable state Ⓓ is 0 since x_2 did not change but remained at the value $x_2 = 1$. Finally, a dash is entered in the second row, third column of the next-state section since both input variables cannot change simultaneously. Again, outputs are only specified for the stable states. At this point the primitive flow table appears as in Table 9.10*c*.

Now consider the entry Ⓒ. If the input state changes to $x_1x_2 = 11$, then a stable state must be reached in the fourth column of the next-state section of the primitive flow table. This cannot be state Ⓓ since the fourth requirement of Example 9.3

states that the output is to become 1 when x_2 changes while $x_1 = 1$. Thus, a stable state with a 1 output in the fourth column is needed in the primitive flow table. This necessitates a fifth row for present state E to be added to the table. The entry E is now placed in the third row, fourth column and the entry Ⓔ in the fifth row, fourth column of the next-state section of Table 9.10*d*. The corresponding 1 output for stable state Ⓔ is entered in the output section of the primitive flow table. Also, an A is entered in the third row, first column by reasoning similar to that for the second row, first column and a dashed entry in the third row, second column as the result of the second network requirement. The primitive flow table now appears as shown in Table 9.10*d*.

If the network is operating in stable state Ⓓ and the input state is changed to $x_1x_2 = 10$, then the value of x_2 changes while $x_1 = 1$. Hence, according to the fourth network specification, a stable state with a 1 output must be reached in the third column of the next-state section of the primitive flow table. Since the only stable state in the third column thus far has a 0 output, another row is added to the table for a stable state Ⓕ along with its 1 output. On the other hand, if the input state is changed to $x_1x_2 = 01$ while in stable state Ⓓ, then the operation of the network can return to stable state Ⓑ to satisfy the third network specification. Finally, the input state $x_1x_2 = 00$ can never occur when the network is in stable state Ⓓ since this requires the inputs x_1 and x_2 to change simultaneously. At this point the primitive flow table has the form of Table 9.10*e*.

The remaining entries in the last two rows of Table 9.10*e* are determined by reasoning similar to the above. The completed primitive flow table for Example 9.3 is shown in Table 9.10*f*.

9.4.2 The Primitive Flow Table for Example 9.4

For the second running example of asynchronous sequential network synthesis, an input sequence recognizer is designed.

EXAMPLE 9.4

Design a fundamental-mode asynchronous sequential network meeting the following requirements:

1. There are two inputs x_1 and x_2 and a single output z.
2. The inputs x_1 and x_2 never change or are 1 simultaneously.
3. An output of $z = 1$ is to occur only during the input state $x_1x_2 = 01$ and then if and only if the input state $x_1x_2 = 01$ is preceded by the input sequence $x_1x_2 = 01,00,10,00,10,00$.

As in the previous example, a starting stable state must be established. Since this is an input sequence recognizer, a good starting point is the first state of the sequence. Thus, a stable state Ⓐ is entered in the next-state section of the primitive flow table under the input state $x_1x_2 = 01$ to signify the first input state of the sequence is applied. Furthermore, if it is assumed that no other input states have been applied, then the output must be 0 since it has not been preceded by the sequence to be recognized.

A logical way to now proceed is to introduce the necessary states that lead to an output of 1, indicating the recognition of the specified sequence. This is shown in Table 9.11*a*. Since this is a primitive flow table, only one stable state can appear in each row. Thus, from stable state Ⓐ, an input state of $x_1x_2 = 00$ causes the network to enter stable state Ⓑ on the next row of the flow table. This state signifies that the input sequence $x_1x_2 = 01,00$ has been applied. Next an input state of $x_1x_2 = 10$ results in the network entering stable state Ⓒ. The next input state in the sequence leading to an output of $z = 1$ is $x_1x_2 = 00$. The network must not return to stable state Ⓑ since this would imply that the input state $x_1x_2 = 10$ in the sequence to be recognized has not yet occurred. Hence, a new stable state, Ⓓ, is needed to signify that the applied sequence thus far is $x_1x_2 = 01,00,10,00$. By a similar argument, stable states Ⓔ and Ⓕ are introduced in Table 9.11*a*. Since none of the stable states that have been introduced signifies that the completed desired input sequence has been applied, 0 outputs are associated with each of the stable states. Now assume that the network is in stable state Ⓕ and the input state $x_1x_2 = 01$ is applied. The network must enter a stable state in the second column of the next-state section of the flow table. Furthermore, the output must be 1 at this time since the third requirement given in the specifications of Example 9.4 is satisfied. Thus, stable state Ⓖ is introduced with an associated 1 output.

To complete the primitive flow table for Example 9.4, it is necessary to fill in the missing entries as well as possibly introduce additional states. First, recall that for this asynchronous network only one input variable is allowed to change value at a time. This implies that some of the next-state entries should be dashes. Second, the second statement in the network specifications also states that x_1 and x_2 are never 1 simultaneously. This input restriction implies that only dashes can appear in the fourth column of the next-state section of the primitive flow table. Upon entering the necessary dashes, Table 9.11*b* results.

To Table 9.11*b*, unstable states *A* are entered in the second and fourth rows of the second column of the next-state section of the primitive flow table since the sequence to be recognized is broken by the input state $x_1x_2 = 01$ and, hence, the recognition process must be restarted. An unstable state *B* is entered in the seventh row, first column since the input state for the stable state in that row can serve both as the first $x_1x_2 = 01$ input of a new sequence as well as the last input of the recognized sequence. Finally, two additional stable states, Ⓗ and Ⓘ, must be added to handle the situation that the input state $x_1x_2 = 10$ has occurred more than twice between the two occurrences of the input state $x_1x_2 = 01$, which defines the beginning and end of the input sequence to be recognized. The resulting table is shown in Table 9.11*c*.

To complete the construction of the primitive flow table for Example 9.4, it is only necessary to make the final entries in the last row of Table 9.11*c*. Table 9.11*d* is the completed primitive flow table. In the last row an unstable state *A* indicates

Table 9.11 Obtaining the primitive flow table for Example 9.4

Present state	Next state				Output (z)			
	Input state (x_1x_2)				Input state (x_1x_2)			
	00	01	10	11	00	01	10	11
A	*B*	(*A*)			–	0	–	–
B	(*B*)		*C*		0	–	–	–
C	*D*		(*C*)		–	–	0	–
D	(*D*)		*E*		0	–	–	–
E	*F*		(*E*)		–	–	0	–
F	(*F*)	*G*			0	–	–	–
G		(*G*)			–	1	–	–

(*a*)

Present state	Next state				Output (z)			
	Input state (x_1x_2)				Input state (x_1x_2)			
	00	01	10	11	00	01	10	11
A	*B*	(*A*)	–	–	–	0	–	–
B	(*B*)		*C*	–	0	–	–	–
C	*D*	–	(*C*)	–	–	–	0	–
D	(*D*)		*E*	–	0	–	–	–
E	*F*	–	(*E*)	–	–	–	0	–
F	(*F*)	*G*		–	0	–	–	–
G		(*G*)	–	–	–	1	–	–

(*b*)

Present state	Next state				Output (z)			
	Input state (x_1x_2)				Input state (x_1x_2)			
	00	01	10	11	00	01	10	11
A	*B*	(*A*)	–	–	–	0	–	–
B	(*B*)	*A*	*C*	–	0	–	–	–
C	*D*	–	(*C*)	–	–	–	0	–
D	(*D*)	*A*	*E*	–	0	–	–	–
E	*F*	–	(*E*)	–	–	–	0	–
F	(*F*)	*G*	*H*	–	0	–	–	–
G	*B*	(*G*)	–	–	–	1	–	–
H	*I*	–	(*H*)	–	–	–	0	–
I	(*I*)				0	–	–	–

(*c*)

(*Cont.*)

Table 9.11 *(Cont.)*

Present state	Next state				Output (*z*)			
	Input state (x_1x_2)				Input state (x_1x_2)			
	00	01	10	11	00	01	10	11
A	*B*	(*A*)	–	–	–	0	–	–
B	(*B*)	*A*	*C*	–	0	–	–	–
C	*D*	–	(*C*)	–	–	–	0	–
D	(*D*)	*A*	*E*	–	0	–	–	–
E	*F*	–	(*E*)	–	–	–	0	–
F	(*F*)	*G*	*H*	–	0	–	–	–
G	*B*	(*G*)	–	–	–	1	–	–
H	*I*	–	(*H*)	–	–	–	0	–
I	(*I*)	*A*	*H*	–	0	–	–	–

(*d*)

the first input state of the sequence to be recognized is applied and an unstable state *H* provides for the network to wait for the beginning of the specified input sequence that is to be recognized.

9.5 REDUCTION OF INPUT-RESTRICTED FLOW TABLES

The primitive flow table for an asynchronous sequential network is characterized by having only one total stable state in each row of its next-state section. This is done to facilitate the establishment of a model from the network specifications. However, from the study on the analysis of asynchronous sequential networks, it is known that flow tables obtained from realizations do not necessarily have such a constraint. Furthermore, when states are defined during the formation of a primitive flow table, as was discussed in the previous section, it is conceivable that more states are introduced than necessary in much the same way as was seen when state tables were constructed for clocked synchronous sequential networks. In either event, the primitive flow table has, in general, more rows, i.e., states, than some other flow table that can also adequately serve as the model for the network specifications.

In anticipation of constructing a state table, each row in the flow table must be coded with a set of binary symbols. Since the minimum number of binary digits needed to denote the internal state of a sequential network is the smallest integer greater than or equal to the base-2 logarithm of the number of internal states, it is of interest to determine a minimal-row flow table from the class of flow tables that can model the sequential network being designed. This is known as the *flow table reduction problem.*

The reduction procedure for primitive flow tables is very similar to that for synchronous sequential networks that was presented in Sec. 7.4. However, at that time it was assumed that the state table was completely specified, i.e., no dashes appeared. Flow tables having dashed entries are said to be *incompletely specified.* As was seen in the previous section, primitive flow tables for fundamental-mode asynchronous networks normally do contain dashes. A special type of incompletely specified flow table is the *input-restricted flow table.* An input-restricted flow table for asynchronous sequential networks is a flow table in which (1) all dash entries in the next-state section result only from restrictions of the type "Input state I_i can never immediately follow input state I_j" and (2) the output is specified in the output section if and only if it is associated with a stable total input state. As a consequence, the dashes always align in those rows of the primitive flow table having stable states for the same input state. Primitive flow tables for asynchronous sequential networks in which only one input variable is allowed to change at a time fall into the class of input-restricted flow tables. For example, Table 9.10*f* was subject to the set of restrictions "Input state $x_1x_2 = 00$ can never immediately follow input state $x_1x_2 = 11$, input state $x_1x_2 = 01$ can never immediately follow input state $x_1x_2 = 10$, input state $x_1x_2 = 10$ can never immediately follow input state $x_1x_2 = 01$, and input state $x_1x_2 = 11$ can never immediately follow input state $x_1x_2 = 00$." In addition, certain input constraints, such as inputs x_i and x_j are never 1 simultaneously, also fall under the first condition of input-restricted flow tables. Thus, the two design examples introduced in Sec. 9.4 are modeled by input-restricted flow tables.

In this section a reduction procedure for input-restricted flow tables is presented.* In the next section, a general reduction procedure that is applicable to both input-restricted and non-input-restricted flow tables is discussed. Two present states are said to be *compatible* if for each input state their output states are the same whenever both are specified and their next-states are also compatible whenever they are both specified. Under this concept of state compatibility, the dashed entries in a flow table are allowed to take on different values depending upon the pair of states whose compatibility is being established.

The reduction procedure for input-restricted flow tables is a four-step process. First, compatible pairs of states are established. Next, larger groupings of compatible states are determined, called *maximal compatibles.* From the set of maximal compatibles, a minimal collection of compatible groupings is selected such that every state appears in at least one grouping of the collection. Finally, the reduced flow table is formed. Algorithms are presented and illustrated for each of the steps. However, proofs of the validity of the algorithms are beyond the scope of this book.

9.5.1 Determination of Compatible Pairs of States

The first step of the flow table reduction procedure is to determine which pairs of rows of a flow table can be replaced by a single row in a reduced flow table, i.e., to establish the compatible pairs of states. This is done by the construction and pro-

---

*The reduction procedure is also valid for all completely specified flow tables since the input restriction condition is satisfied vacuously.

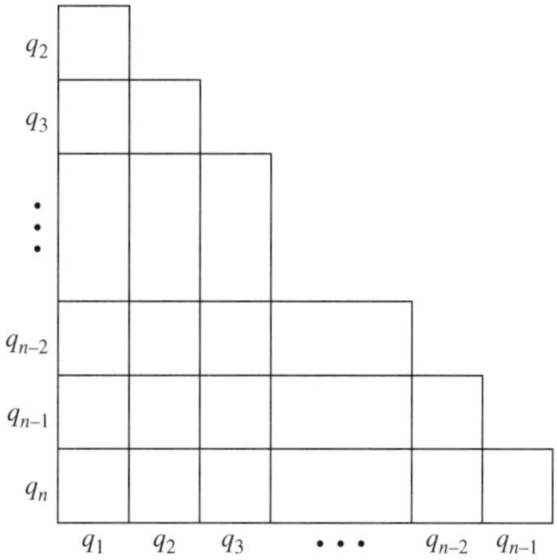

Figure 9.7 The structure of an implication table.

cessing of an implication table in a similar manner as was previously discussed in Sec. 7.4. The process is:

1. Let $q_1, q_2, \ldots, q_n$ be the states of a primitive flow table. Construct an implication table, as shown in Fig. 9.7, so that there is one cell in the implication table for each pair of distinct states. [No cell is needed for the (q_k,q_k) pair since a state is always compatible to itself. Also, since the pairs of states are not ordered, the pair (q_i,q_j) is the same as the pair (q_j,q_i).]
2. Call the cell that corresponds to the pair of present states q_i and q_j the (q_i,q_j)-cell. Place a $\times$ in the (q_i,q_j)-cell if the output states for these present states are contradictory for some input state, that is, if for at least one input state the output states are both specified but not identical.* If there are no contradictory output states for the present states q_i and q_j of the flow table, then enter in the (q_i,q_j)-cell the pair of next-state entries for each input state. Duplications are not entered. For convenience, any next-state pair for the (q_i,q_j)-cell that is (q_i,q_j), (q_j,q_i), or (q_k,q_k) need not be entered since they do not correspond to constraints that must be satisfied when the table is processed. Furthermore, the ordering of the states in each pair is not significant. Hence, in the remainder of the algorithm, the pairs (q_i,q_j) and (q_j,q_i) are not distinguished and are simply referred to as the pair (q_i,q_j). Any next-state pair that consists of a dash and some other state (or another dash) is not entered. Finally, if neither a $\times$ nor pairs of states are entered in the cell, then a check mark is inserted. A check mark denotes that the pair of states (q_i,q_j) are compatible since their outputs are not contradictory and there are no next-state constraints.

---

*It should be noted that a dash is being regarded as a don't-care entry.

3. All state pair entries in the implication table are now inspected by the following process: If the state pair (q_a,q_b) is an entry in the (q_i,q_j)-cell and if the (q_a,q_b)-cell contains a $\times$, then a $\times$ is placed in the (q_i,q_j)-cell. If a $\times$ is placed in the (q_i,q_j)-cell, then any additional entries in the (q_i,q_j)-cell are ignored, and a state pair in another cell, not previously inspected, is selected. On the other hand, if the above procedure does not result in a $\times$ being placed in the (q_i,q_j)-cell and if additional state pairs appear in the (q_i,q_j)-cell that have not been inspected, then the process is repeated on one of these other state pairs.
4. Repeat Step 3 until it is possible to make an entire pass of the implication table using the above inspection procedure without any additional $\times$'s being entered. The process then terminates. If the (q_i,q_j)-cell has no $\times$ at this time, then the states q_i and q_j are compatible.

To illustrate the above algorithm, consider the primitive flow table shown in Table 9.12. This is an input-restricted flow table, as can be seen by the alignment of the dashes. For example, all the dashes align in rows *A*, *D*, and *F* which have stable states for the input state $x_1x_2 = 00$. A similar observation can be made for each of the other input states and their stable states. The first two steps of the above algorithm involve the construction of the implication table and result in the table shown in Fig. 9.8*a*. The remaining two steps involve the processing of the implication table. For example, the entry (*A*,*F*) appears in the (*A*,*C*)-cell. Since a $\times$ appears in the (*A*,*F*)-cell, a $\times$ is now inserted in the (*A*,*C*)-cell. When the above processing procedure is completed, the implication table appears as shown in Fig. 9.8*b*.

Since the third and fourth steps in the above procedure for processing the implication table are identical to those given in Sec. 7.4, the variation given at that time can be used instead. In such a case, Steps 3 and 4 are replaced by the following:

3. The implication table is now processed. If an entry in the (q_i,q_j)-cell is a $\times$, then a $\times$ is placed in every cell that has (q_i,q_j) or (q_j,q_i) as an entry. Once a $\times$

Table 9.12 An input-restricted primitive flow table

Present state	Next state				Output (z)			
	Input state (x_1x_2)				Input state (x_1x_2)			
	00	01	10	11	00	01	10	11
A	(*A*)	*B*	*C*	–	0	–	–	–
B	*D*	(*B*)	–	*E*	–	0	–	–
C	*F*	–	(*C*)	*G*	–	–	1	–
D	(*D*)	*H*	*C*	–	0	–	–	–
E	–	*H*	*I*	(*E*)	–	–	–	1
F	(*F*)	*B*	*I*	–	1	–	–	–
G	–	*H*	*C*	(*G*)	–	–	–	0
H	*A*	(*H*)	–	*E*	–	0	–	–
I	*A*	–	(*I*)	*E*	–	–	1	–

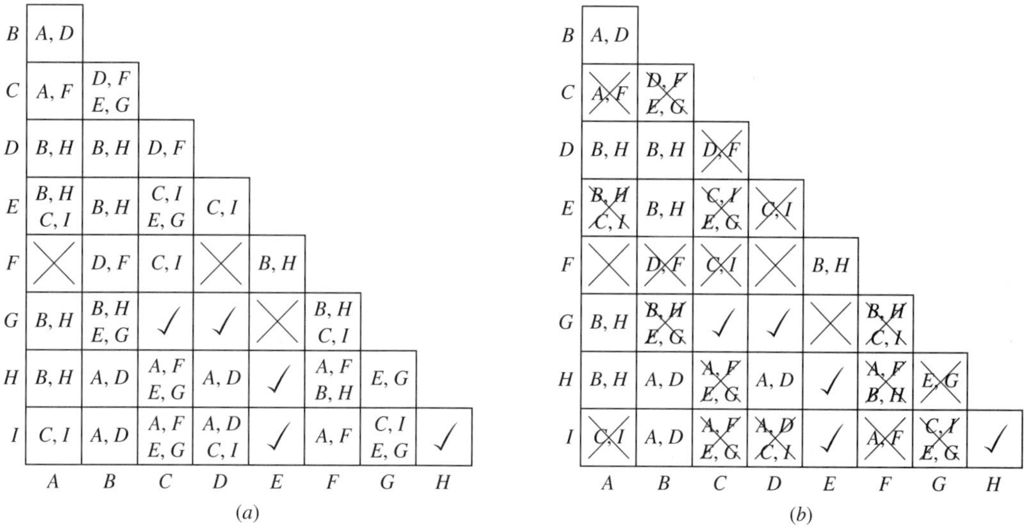

Figure 9.8 Implication table for Table 9.12. (*a*) At the end of the construction phase. (*b*) At the end of the processing phase.

is placed in a cell, all other entries in that cell are ignored in all further steps. Also, a second × is placed in the (q_i,q_j)-cell.

4. Repeat Step 3 until all ×'ed cells have two ×'s. The process then terminates. If the (q_i,q_j)-cell has no ×'s at this time, then the states q_i and q_j are compatible.

The only effect the above variation has on the implication tables of Fig. 9.8 is that two ×'s would occur at the end of the process in those cells of Fig. 9.8*b* that show only a single ×.

9.5.2 Determination of Maximal Compatibles

Once the implication table is processed, it is desirable to determine which set of rows of the flow table can be replaced by a single row of another flow table that can also describe the asynchronous sequential network. This grouping of states is carried out by the following procedure:

1. Starting with the rightmost column of the processed implication table and working toward the left, move to the first column that has a cell that does not contain a ×. Write down all pairs of compatible states for this column as indicated by the axis labels of the cells not containing a ×. This forms the initial *list of compatible classes.*
2. Move to the next column to the left, say column *i*, which contains one or more non-× cells. To all the sets in the list of compatible classes in which state *i* is compatible with all members of a set as evidenced by non-× cells in column *i*, add state *i* to those sets. For all sets in which state *i* is not compatible with all

members of a set in the list of compatible classes but is compatible with a subset of the states, add a new set to the list of compatible classes consisting of state i and the corresponding subset of states. Next, add to the list of compatible classes any compatible pairs of states involving state i that are not a subset of any other set already on the list. Finally, eliminate any set in the list of compatible classes that is a subset of another set in the list.

3. Repeat Step 2 until all columns are examined. Then, add to the list as sets consisting of single states any state that does not appear in at least one of the other sets in the list. The list of compatible classes that results is called the *maximal compatible sets.*

To illustrate the above algorithm, again consider the implication table of Fig. 9.8*b*. Table 9.13 summarizes the list of compatible classes as the columns of the processed implication table are considered. The first column not containing ×'s is column H. Since there is only one cell without ×'s in this column, the initial list of compatible classes consists of the single set $\{H,I\}$. According to Step 2 of the above algorithm, column E is next analyzed since it is the next column to the left having at least one non-× cell. Since state E is compatible with all the states in the set $\{H,I\}$, as indicated by no crosses in the (E,H)- and (E,I)-cells, the set $\{H,I\}$ is replaced by the set $\{E,H,I\}$. Furthermore, the compatible pair $\{E,F\}$ is added to the list of compatible classes since it is not a subset of any of the sets already on the list. The list of compatible classes at this point consists of the two sets $\{E,H,I\}$ and $\{E,F\}$. The next column that is analyzed is column D. Since states D and H are a compatible pair and state H is also contained in the set $\{E,H,I\}$, the set $\{D,H\}$ is added to the list. Also, the set $\{D,G\}$ is added to the list of compatible classes since it is not a subset of any of the sets already on the list. As a result of analyzing column D, the list of compatible classes becomes $\{E,H,I\}$, $\{D,H\}$, $\{E,F\}$, and $\{D,G\}$. Continuing on to column C, it is observed that state C is compatible with state G. Since state G is included in the set $\{D,G\}$, the set $\{C,G\}$ is now added to the list. The list of compatible classes

Table 9.13 Determining the maximal compatible sets for the implication table in Fig. 9.8*b*

Column	List of compatible classes
H	$\{H,I\}$
G	$\{H,I\}$
F	$\{H,I\}$
E	$\{E,H,I\}$, $\{E,F\}$
D	$\{E,H,I\}$, $\{D,H\}$, $\{E,F\}$, $\{D,G\}$
C	$\{E,H,I\}$, $\{D,H\}$, $\{E,F\}$, $\{D,G\}$ $\{C,G\}$
B*	$\{B,E,H,I\}$, $\{B,D,H\}$, $\{E,F\}$, ~~$\{B,E\}$~~, $\{D,G\}$, ~~$\{B,D\}$~~, $\{C,G\}$
A*	$\{B,E,H,I\}$, ~~$\{A,B,H\}$~~, $\{A,B,D,H\}$, $\{E,F\}$, $\{A,D,G\}$, $\{C,G\}$, ~~$\{A,G\}$~~

List of maximal compatible sets:

$\{B,E,H,I\}$, $\{A,B,D,H\}$, $\{E,F\}$, $\{A,D,G\}$, $\{C,G\}$

*Note: Sets deleted as a consequence of Step 2 are shown slashed.

now consists of the five sets $\{E,H,I\}$, $\{D,H\}$, $\{E,F\}$, $\{D,G\}$, and $\{C,G\}$. When column B is analyzed, the sets $\{E,H,I\}$ and $\{D,H\}$ are replaced by sets $\{B,E,H,I\}$ and $\{B,D,H\}$ since state B is compatible with all the states in each of these sets, i.e., states D, E, H, and I. Since states B and E are compatible and state E is a member of the set $\{E,F\}$, the set $\{B,E\}$ is added to the list of compatible classes. Similarly, since states B and D are compatible and state D is a member of the set $\{D,G\}$, the set $\{B,D\}$ is added to the list. However, it is then noted that $\{B,E\} \subseteq \{B,E,H,I\}$ and $\{B,D\} \subseteq \{B,D,H\}$. Thus, the sets $\{B,E\}$ and $\{B,D\}$ are deleted as a consequence of the last statement in Step 2 of the algorithm. The list of compatible classes now becomes $\{B,E,H,I\}$, $\{B,D,H\}$, $\{E,F\}$, $\{D,G\}$, and $\{C,G\}$. Finally, column A is considered. Since state A is compatible with states B and H that appear in the set $\{B,E,H,I\}$, the set $\{A,B,H\}$ is added to the list. Furthermore, state A is compatible with all the states in the sets $\{B,D,H\}$ and $\{D,G\}$, resulting in these sets being replaced by $\{A,B,D,H\}$ and $\{A,D,G\}$. Also state A is compatible with state G in the set $\{C,G\}$, causing the set $\{A,G\}$ to be added to the list. After deleting the two subsets in the list, the five sets of states $\{B,E,H,I\}$, $\{A,B,D,H\}$, $\{E,F\}$, $\{A,D,G\}$, and $\{C,G\}$ remain in the list of compatible classes. These are the maximal compatible sets. It should be noted that no single state sets are added to the list of compatible classes, as mentioned in Step 3 of the algorithm, since every state already appears in at least one set in the list.

9.5.3 Determination of Minimal Collections of Maximal Compatible Sets

In general, not the entire collection of maximal compatible sets is necessary to form the reduced flow table. For the special case of input-restricted flow tables, it is sufficient to select a minimum number of sets such that every state appears in at least one of the selected sets. This selection process can be carried out by inspection. Alternatively, the selection can be achieved by use of a table similar to the prime-implicant table of Chapter 4. To do this, a table is constructed such that all the internal states appear along the abscissa and all the maximal compatible sets appear along the ordinate. A $\times$ is entered in the table at those locations where the set associated with a row contains the state associated with a column. For example, Table 9.14 shows such a table for the maximal compatible sets previously obtained.

Table 9.14 Prime-implicant table concept applied to flow table reduction

		Internal states								
		A	B	C	D	E	F	G	H	I
Maximal compatible sets	$*\{B,E,H,I\}$		$\times$			$\times$			$\times$	$\otimes$
	$\{A,B,D,H\}$	$\times$	$\times$		$\times$				$\times$	
	$*\{E,F\}$					$\times$	$\otimes$			
	$\{A,D,G\}$	$\times$			$\times$			$\times$		
	$*\{C,G\}$			$\otimes$				$\times$		

The problem now is to select a minimum number of rows, i.e., maximal compatible sets, such that each column has at least one × in the selected set of rows. This should be reminiscent of the covering problem associated with prime-implicant tables. Therefore, once the table is constructed, the selection of a minimal set of rows is carried out by using the prime-implicant table reduction concepts of Sec. 4.10. In Table 9.14 it is seen that the sets $\{B,E,H,I\}$, $\{E,F\}$, and $\{C,G\}$ must be selected in order that states C, F, and I appear in at least one set as evident by the circled ×'s. The only states remaining to be covered after this initial selection are states A and D. These states appear in the sets $\{A,B,D,H\}$ and $\{A,D,G\}$. Since both states appear in each of these sets, only one of the two sets needs to be selected. Therefore, one minimal collection of maximal compatible sets, such that all states are included in at least one set, is $\{A,B,D,H\}$, $\{B,E,H,I\}$, $\{E,F\}$, and $\{C,G\}$. Another minimal collection of maximal compatible sets consists of $\{A,D,G\}$, $\{B,E,H,I\}$, $\{E,F\}$, and $\{C,G\}$.

9.5.4 Constructing the Minimal-Row Flow Table

The final step of the flow table reduction procedure is to construct a minimal-row flow table. This can be done using the following algorithm:*

1. Let the original primitive flow table be called Q and the minimal-row flow table to be constructed be called P. Let the minimal collection of maximal compatible sets obtained above be denoted by $C_1, C_2, \ldots, C_s$. Finally, let the input states for flow tables P and Q be denoted by $I_1, I_2, \ldots, I_m$.
2. Assign a state p_i to each of the sets C_i, for $i = 1, 2, \ldots, s$. The present-state section of the minimal-row flow table P consists of states $p_1, p_2, \ldots, p_s$.
3. The entry for row p_i, column I_k in the next-state section of flow table P is left unspecified; i.e., a dash is entered, if the next-state entries in column I_k of flow table Q are unspecified for all members of C_i. Otherwise, the next states for C_i and input I_k are a subset of at least one of the sets $C_1, C_2, \ldots, C_s$. If it is a subset of C_i, then let the entry in row p_i, column I_k of the next-state section of flow table P be $\textcircled{p_i}$; otherwise, choose any one such set, say C_j, and let the entry in row p_i, column I_k of the next-state section of flow table P be p_j.
4. For each stable total input state of flow table P, the entry for row p_i, column I_k in the output section of flow table P is the same as any specified output in column I_k for members of C_i of flow table Q.† For all total input states that are unstable in flow table P, the output state is left unspecified, i.e., a dash is entered.

Again consider Table 9.12. Arbitrarily selecting the minimal collection of maximal compatible sets $\{A,D,G\}$, $\{B,E,H,I\}$, $\{E,F\}$, and $\{C,G\}$, the minimal-row flow table of Table 9.15 results. In this table, state α is used to represent the set of states $\{A,D,G\}$, state β the set $\{B,E,H,I\}$, state γ the set $\{E,F\}$, and state δ the set $\{C,G\}$.

*For an incompletely specified flow table, the reduced flow table is not necessarily unique. This algorithm is one procedure for constructing a reduced flow table.

†It can be proved that contradictory specified outputs never occur.

Table 9.15 A minimal-row flow table corresponding to Table 9.12

Present state	Next state				Output (z)			
	Input state (x_1x_2)				Input state (x_1x_2)			
	00	01	10	11	00	01	10	11
$\{A,D,G\}$: α	(α)	β	δ	(α)	0	–	–	0
$\{B,E,H,I\}$: β	α	(β)	(β)	(β)	–	0	1	1
$\{E,F\}$: γ	(γ)	β	β	(γ)	1	–	–	1
$\{C,G\}$: δ	γ	β	(δ)	(δ)	–	–	1	0

From Table 9.12 it is seen that for the input state $x_1x_2 = 00$ and the set of present states $\{A,D,G\}$, the set of specified next states is $\{A,D\}$. Since $\{A,D\} \subseteq \{A,D,G\}$ and α is the state associated with the set $\{A,D,G\}$, the next-state entry in the α row and $x_1x_2 = 00$ column of Table 9.15 is (α). Similarly, the set of next states for the input state $x_1x_2 = 01$ and the set of states $\{A,D,G\}$ is $\{B,H\}$, by Table 9.12. Since $\{B,H\} \subseteq \{B,E,H,I\}$, and since $\{B,E,H,I\}$ is associated with the state β, the next-state entry in the α row and $x_1x_2 = 01$ column of Table 9.15 is state β. As a final example of determining the next-state entry, consider the set $\{A,D,G\}$ and the input state $x_1x_2 = 11$. The set of next states according to Table 9.12 is $\{G\}$. $\{G\}$ is a subset of both $\{A,D,G\}$ and $\{C,G\}$. The fact that it is a subset of $\{A,D,G\}$ implies that the next-state entry for the α row and $x_1x_2 = 11$ column should be (α). All the remaining next-state entries of Table 9.15 are obtained by a similar process.

To complete the output section of the reduced flow table, it is necessary to consider the stable total input states. For example, the output state for state A and input state $x_1x_2 = 00$ according to Table 9.12 is $z = 0$. The same output occurs for state D under the input state $x_1x_2 = 00$. Finally, the output is not specified for state G and the input state $x_1x_2 = 00$. Since the output state is specified for at least one of the states in the set $\{A,D,G\}$ under the input state $x_1x_2 = 00$, the output state in the α row and $x_1x_2 = 00$ column is $z = 0$. This process is carried out until all the entries of the output section of Table 9.15 for the stable total input states are determined. Dashes are entered for the output states of the unstable total input states.

The flow table reduction procedure can now be applied to the two running design examples, i.e., Examples 9.3 and 9.4. Minimal-row flow tables for these examples are given in Tables 9.16 and 9.17, respectively.

Table 9.16 Minimal-row flow table for Example 9.3

Present state	Next state				Output (z)			
	Input state (x_1x_2)				Input state (x_1x_2)			
	00	01	10	11	00	01	10	11
$\{A,C\}$: α	(α)	β	(α)	γ	0	–	0	–
$\{B,D\}$: β	α	(β)	γ	(β)	–	0	–	0
$\{E,F\}$: γ	α	β	(γ)	(γ)	–	–	1	1

Table 9.17 Minimal-row flow table for Example 9.4

Present state	Next state				Output (z)			
	Input state (x_1x_2)				Input state (x_1x_2)			
	00	01	10	11	00	01	10	11
$\{B\}: \alpha$	β	–	$\textcircled{\alpha}$	–	–	–	0	–
$\{C\}: \beta$	$\textcircled{\beta}$	χ	γ	–	0	–	–	–
$\{D\}: \gamma$	δ	–	$\textcircled{\gamma}$	–	–	–	0	–
$\{E\}: \delta$	$\textcircled{\delta}$	λ	ρ	–	0	–	–	–
$\{F\}: \lambda$	χ	$\textcircled{\lambda}$	–	–	–	1	–	–
$\{H,I\}: \rho$	$\textcircled{\rho}$	χ	$\textcircled{\rho}$	–	0	–	0	–
$\{A,G\}: \chi$	$\textcircled{\chi}$	$\textcircled{\chi}$	α	–	0	0	–	–

9.6 A GENERAL PROCEDURE TO FLOW TABLE REDUCTION

It is possible to generalize the procedure of the previous section to handle any primitive flow table that does not satisfy the input restriction concept. Unfortunately, algorithmic techniques to achieve the necessary selection are complicated and beyond the scope of this text. However, a simpler, two-phase procedure is introduced in this section that is applicable to all primitive flow tables whether or not they satisfy the input restriction constraints. Although the procedure provides for flow table reduction, it does not ensure obtaining a minimal-row flow table in the case of non-input-restricted flow tables. In this two-phase procedure a constraint is made in which dashed entries in a flow table are restricted to single values.* The first phase is to combine rows having their stable states in the same column, thereby reducing the number of stable states for each input state. Then, rows having their stable states in different columns are merged into a single row. The procedure is illustrated for both non-input-restricted and input-restricted flow tables.

9.6.1 Reducing the Number of Stable States

For a non-input-restricted primitive flow table there are at least two stable states for the same input state in which all their dashes do not align. Table 9.18 is an example of a non-input-restricted primitive flow table. In this table it is seen that the dashes do not align in the next-state section for stable states $\textcircled{B}$ and $\textcircled{H}$ when $x_1x_2 = 01$ and for stable states $\textcircled{C}$ and $\textcircled{I}$ when $x_1x_2 = 10$.

In the first phase for reducing the number of rows in a non-input-restricted primitive flow table, an attempt is made to determine if two stable states for the same input state can be combined into a single stable state, i.e., to determine if they are equivalent. To do this, an implication table is again constructed. However, in

*However, even with this constraint the two-phase procedure enables an input-restricted flow table to be reduced to a minimal number of rows.

Table 9.18 A non-input-restricted primitive flow table

Present state	Next state				Output (z)			
	Input state (x_1x_2)				Input state (x_1x_2)			
	00	01	10	11	00	01	10	11
A	Ⓐ	B	C	–	0	–	–	–
B	–	Ⓑ	–	D	–	1	–	–
C	E	–	Ⓒ	F	–	–	0	–
D	–	G	C	Ⓓ	–	–	–	0
E	Ⓔ	H	I	–	0	–	–	–
F	–	B	C	Ⓕ	–	–	–	0
G	–	Ⓖ	–	F	–	1	–	–
H	A	Ⓗ	–	–	–	0	–	–
I	A	–	Ⓘ	–	–	–	0	–

this phase, the dashes are not considered as don't-care entries. Thus, the second step for the construction and processing of an implication table introduced in the previous section is modified as follows:

2. Call the cell that corresponds to the pair of present states q_i and q_j the (q_i,q_j)-cell. Place a $\times$ in the (q_i,q_j)-cell if any of the following conditions occur:
   a. Ⓠ$_i$ and Ⓠ$_j$ are not in the same column.
   b. Ⓠ$_i$ and Ⓠ$_j$ are in the same column but their outputs are contradictory.
   c. Ⓠ$_i$ and Ⓠ$_j$ are in the same column but all the dashes in the q_i and q_j rows do not align.

   If a $\times$ is not entered in the (q_i,q_j)-cell as a result of any of the above three conditions, then the pairs of specified unstable next states are entered, except for duplications and pairs consisting of the same state. Finally, if neither a $\times$ nor pairs of next states are entered in the cell, then a check mark is inserted.

Because of condition a above, $\times$'s are immediately entered into all cells corresponding to a pair of stable states not in the same column of the next-state section of the flow table. This significantly limits the number of cells that have to be considered for other entries. Upon completing the construction of the implication table, it is then processed in exactly the same manner as given by Steps 3 and 4 in the previous section.

As an illustration of the construction and processing of an implication table for a non-input-restricted primitive flow table, again consider Table 9.18. The implication table shown in Fig. 9.9a is the result of applying the above step. It should be noted that a $\times$ is placed in the (A,B)-cell since stable states Ⓐ and Ⓑ occur for different input states, i.e., condition a above, a $\times$ is placed in the (B,H)-cell and (G,H)-cell since the dashes do not align, i.e., condition c above, as well as the outputs are contradictory, i.e., condition b above, and a $\times$ is placed in the (C,I)-cell since the dashes do not align, i.e., condition c above. In the (A,E)-cell the unstable pairs of next states B,H and C,I are entered. Finally, only single pairs of unstable next states

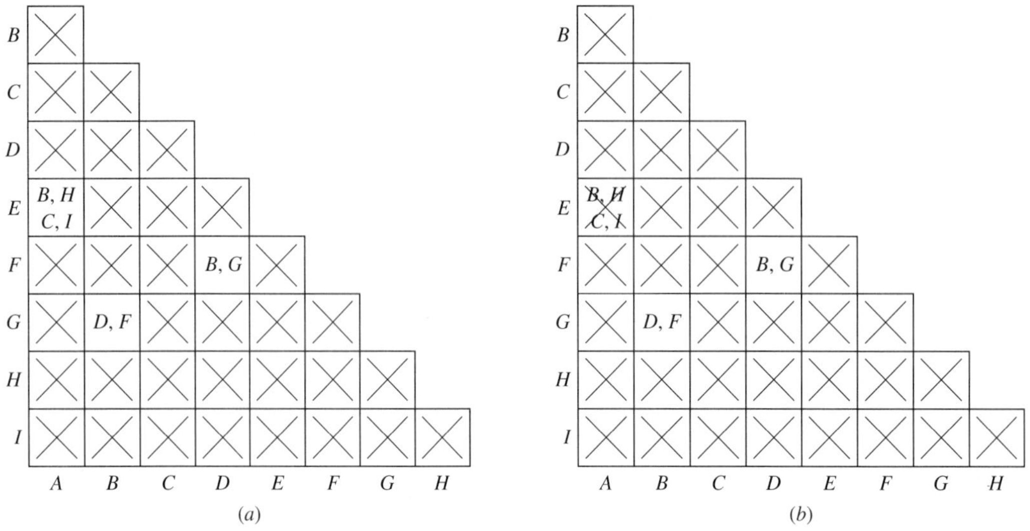

Figure 9.9 Implication table for Table 9.18. (*a*) At the end of the construction phase. (*b*) At the end of the processing phase.

are entered in the (*B,G*)-cell and (*D,F*)-cell. The implication table is next processed using either of the two procedures given in the previous section. After processing, the implication table appears as shown in Fig. 9.9*b*.

Once the equivalent pairs of stable states are established, the reduction of the non-input-restricted primitive flow table proceeds in exactly the same manner as described in the previous section. First the maximal compatible sets are obtained and then the first-phase reduced primitive flow table is constructed. In this case, the maximal compatible sets are always disjoint and the entire collection of maximal compatible sets must be used to form the first-phase reduced primitive flow table. Each maximal compatible set corresponds to a single state in the first-phase reduced primitive flow table.

For the implication table of Fig. 9.9*b*, the maximal compatible sets are $\{A\}$, $\{B,G\}$, $\{C\}$, $\{D,F\}$, $\{E\}$, $\{H\}$, and $\{I\}$. Thus, stable states Ⓑ and Ⓖ are combined into a single state, as well as stable states Ⓓ and Ⓕ. This is simply achieved by deleting rows *G* and *F* from Table 9.18 and replacing all occurrences of *G* and *F* by *B* and *D*, respectively. Once this is done, the non-input-restricted flow table becomes as shown in Table 9.19*a*.

9.6.2 Merging the Rows of a Primitive Flow Table

Having reduced the number of stable states in the primitive flow table for the same input state, the second phase of the reduction procedure attempts to merge rows when the stable states occur for different input states. For example, in Table 9.19*a*, by letting the dash in the first row, fourth column of the next-state section be *D*, the dash in the second row, first column be *A*, and the dash in the second row, third col-

Table 9.19 Reducing the non-input-restricted primitive flow table of Table 9.18. (*a*) After the removal of compatible stable states. (*b*) After the merging of rows. (*c*) Reduced flow table

Present state	Next state				Output (z)			
	Input state (x_1x_2)				Input state (x_1x_2)			
	00	01	10	11	00	01	10	11
A	Ⓐ	B	C	–	0	–	–	–
B	–	Ⓑ	–	D	–	1	–	–
C	E	–	Ⓒ	D	–	–	0	–
D	–	B	C	Ⓓ	–	–	–	0
E	Ⓔ	H	I	–	0	–	–	–
H	A	Ⓗ	–	–	–	0	–	–
I	A	–	Ⓘ	–	–	–	0	–

(*a*)

Present state	Next state				Output (z)			
	Input state (x_1x_2)				Input state (x_1x_2)			
	00	01	10	11	00	01	10	11
$\{A,B,D\}$	Ⓐ	Ⓑ	C	Ⓓ	0	1	–	0
$\{C\}$	E	–	Ⓒ	D	–	–	0	–
$\{E\}$	Ⓔ	H	I	–	0	–	–	–
$\{H,I\}$	A	Ⓗ	Ⓘ	–	–	0	0	–

(*b*)

Present state	Next state				Output (z)			
	Input state (x_1x_2)				Input state (x_1x_2)			
	00	01	10	11	00	01	10	11
$\{A,B,D\}: \alpha$	(α)	(α)	β	(α)	0	1	–	0
$\{C\}: \beta$	γ	–	(β)	α	–	–	0	–
$\{E\}: \gamma$	(γ)	δ	δ	–	0	–	–	–
$\{H,I\}: \delta$	α	(δ)	(δ)	–	–	0	0	–

(*c*)

umn be C, the first and second rows become identical and, corresponding, can be collapsed into a single row. In this case we have

	00	01	10	11	00	01	10	11
$\{A,B\}$	Ⓐ	Ⓑ	C	D	0	1	–	–

The net result is the reduction in the total number of rows in the flow table. By similar reasoning, rows B and C of Table 9.19*a* can be merged by an appropriate, but different, assignment to the dashes. Since in this procedure only one assignment is allowed to each dash, row *B* can be merged with either row *A* or *C*, but not both. Furthermore, it would be useful if an assignment is found that allows more than two rows to be merged. Thus, it is natural to seek the most effective assignment to the dashes, subject to the constraint that at most one assignment is allowed for each dash, so as to optimize the number of row mergers.

As an aid to this optimization problem, a *merger diagram* is constructed. A merger diagram consists of one node for each row of a primitive flow table after having performed the first-phase reduction. The label for the node is the present state for the row. A line is drawn between two nodes if and only if their corresponding rows can be merged. That is, two rows can be merged if their next-state entries, when both specified, are the same. To illustrate the construction of a merger diagram, again consider Table 9.19*a*. Since there are no next-state conflicts in any column in the first and second rows, a line is drawn in the merger diagram between nodes *A* and *B*. By similar reasoning, a line is drawn between nodes *A* and *D*. Then, the second row of next-state entries of Table 9.19*a* is compared with all the rows below it. This results in lines being drawn between nodes *B* and *C*, between nodes *B* and *D*, and between nodes *B* and *I* in the merger diagram. After all the possible row pairs have been considered, the merger diagram shown in Fig. 9.10 results.

It is next desirable to attempt mergers involving more than two rows. In general, a set of rows of a primitive flow table can be merged into a single row if all pairs of corresponding nodes are connected in the merger diagram. For example, referring to Fig. 9.10, since rows *A* and *B* can be merged, rows *B* and *D* can be merged, and rows *A* and *D* can be merged, it is possible to merge all three rows into a single row. On the other hand, row *C* cannot be included in the merger since rows *A* and *C* cannot be merged. By interpreting the merger diagram, an effective set of mergers is obtained that, in turn, results in a reduced flow table. To do this, it is necessary to form a collection of sets of row mergers so that every state is a member of a set and the sets are disjoint. For Table 9.19*a* and its merger diagram of Fig. 9.10, rows *A*, *B*, and *D* are merged into a single row and rows *H* and *I* are merged into a single row. This leaves rows *C* and *E* unmerged. The resulting collection of mergers

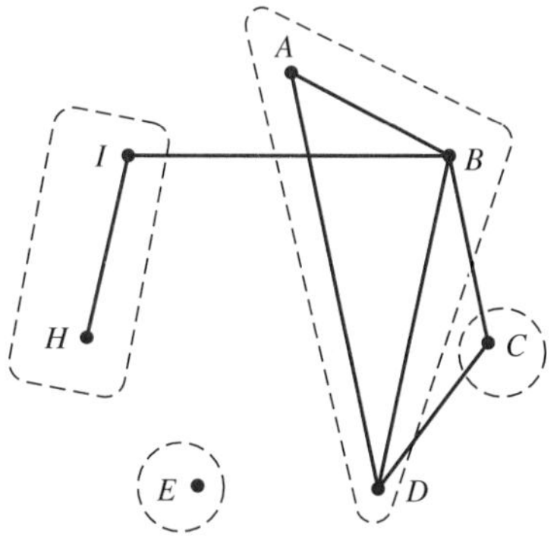

Figure 9.10 Merger diagram for Table 9.19*a*.

for the reduced flow table then becomes $\{A,B,D\}$, $\{H,I\}$, $\{C\}$, and $\{E\}$. This collection of mergers suggests the reduced flow table of Table 9.19*b*. It should be noted in this example that an alternative collection of mergers for a reduced flow table is $\{B,C,D\}$, $\{H,I\}$, $\{A\}$, and $\{E\}$.

To complete the construction of the reduced flow table, each of the sets given in the present-state section of Table 9.19*b* is denoted by a single symbol, e.g., the set $\{A,B,D\}$ by α, the set $\{C\}$ by β, the set $\{E\}$ by γ, and the set $\{H,I\}$ by δ. Then, each of the states in the next-state section is replaced by the set symbol in which it is a member. The final reduced version of Table 9.18 then appears as shown in Table 9.19*c*.

9.6.3 The General Procedure Applied to Input-Restricted Primitive Flow Tables

The above two-phase procedure is also applicable to input-restricted primitive flow tables. For this special case, the procedure always results in a minimal-row flow table, although not necessarily identical to the one produced using the procedure of Sec. 9.5. As an example of applying the two-phase procedure of this section, again consider Table 9.12.

In the first phase of the procedure, equivalent stable states are determined using the implication table. It should be noted that for input-restricted primitive flow tables, condition *c* for inserting crosses in the implication table never occurs. In addition, because of condition *a*, the implication table constructed in this first phase is not the same as the implication table constructed using the procedure of Sec. 9.5. For Table 9.12 and the implication table construction procedure introduced in this section, the resulting implication table is shown in Fig. 9.11*a*. The processed implication table is

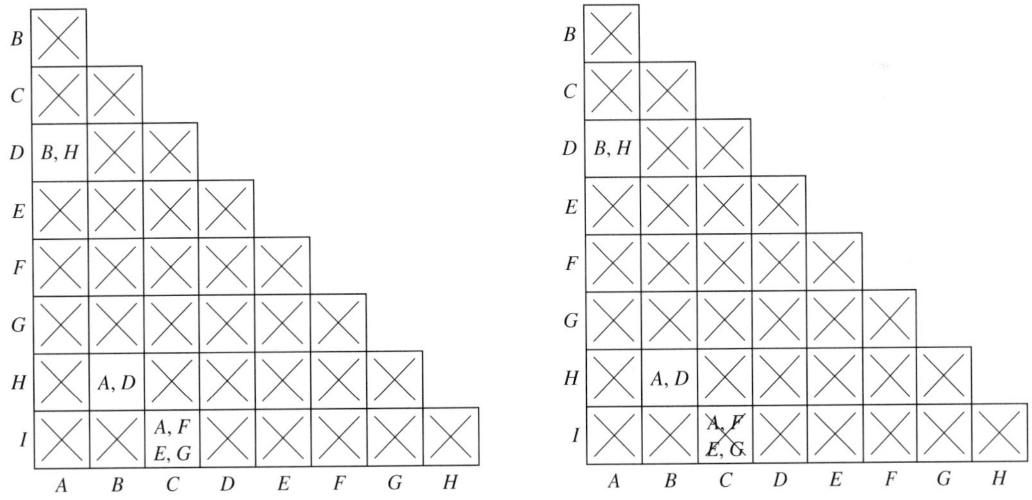

(*a*) (*b*)

Figure 9.11 Implication table for Table 9.12 using the construction procedure of Sec. 9.6. (*a*) At the end of the construction phase. (*b*) At the end of the processing phase.

given in Fig. 9.11*b*. The set of maximal compatible classes is next obtained for the processed implication table. In this case it is simply $\{A,D\}$, $\{B,H\}$, $\{C\}$, $\{E\}$, $\{F\}$, $\{G\}$, $\{H\}$, and $\{I\}$. As a consequence of the equivalency of A and D, row D is eliminated from Table 9.12 and all occurrences of D are replaced by A. Similarly, row H is eliminated from Table 9.12 and all occurrences of H are replaced by B. The resulting first-phase reduced flow table is given in Table 9.20*a*.

In the second phase of the procedure, row merging is performed. The merger diagram corresponding to Table 9.20*a* is given in Fig. 9.12. From the merger dia-

Table 9.20 Reducing the non-input-restricted primitive flow table of Table 9.12. (*a*) After the removal of compatible stable states. (*b*) After the merging of rows. (*c*) Reduced flow table

Present state	Next state				Output (z)			
	Input state (x_1x_2)				Input state (x_1x_2)			
	00	01	10	11	00	01	10	11
A	$\textcircled{A}$	B	C	–	0	–	–	–
B	A	$\textcircled{B}$	–	E	–	0	–	–
C	F	–	$\textcircled{C}$	G	–	–	1	–
E	–	B	I	$\textcircled{E}$	–	–	–	1
F	$\textcircled{F}$	B	I	–	1	–	–	–
G	–	B	C	$\textcircled{G}$	–	–	–	0
I	A	–	$\textcircled{I}$	E	–	–	1	–

(*a*)

Present state	Next state				Output (z)			
	Input state (x_1x_2)				Input state (x_1x_2)			
	00	01	10	11	00	01	10	11
$\{A,G\}$	$\textcircled{A}$	B	C	$\textcircled{G}$	0	–	–	0
$\{B,E,I\}$	A	$\textcircled{B}$	$\textcircled{I}$	$\textcircled{E}$	–	0	1	1
$\{C\}$	F	–	$\textcircled{C}$	G	–	–	1	–
$\{F\}$	$\textcircled{F}$	B	I	–	1	–	–	–

(*b*)

Present state	Next state				Output (z)			
	Input state (x_1x_2)				Input state (x_1x_2)			
	00	01	10	11	00	01	10	11
$\{A,G\}$: α	$\textcircled{\alpha}$	β	γ	$\textcircled{\alpha}$	0	–	–	0
$\{B,E,I\}$: β	α	$\textcircled{\beta}$	$\textcircled{\beta}$	$\textcircled{\beta}$	–	0	1	1
$\{C\}$: γ	δ	–	$\textcircled{\gamma}$	α	–	–	1	–
$\{F\}$: δ	$\textcircled{\delta}$	β	β	–	1	–	–	–

(*c*)

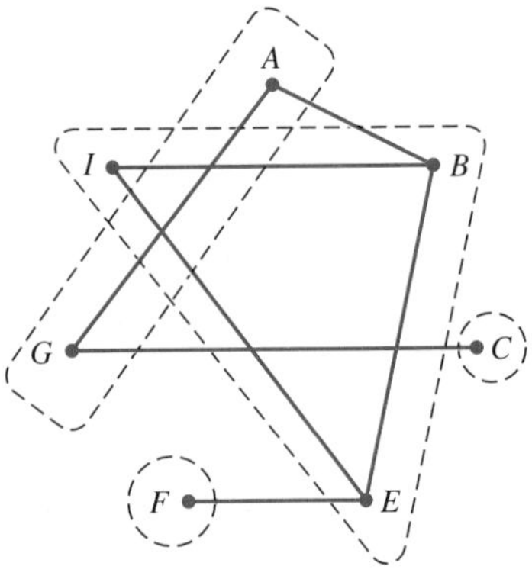

Figure 9.12 Merger diagram for Table 9.20*a*.

gram, it is concluded that two four-row reduced flow tables are possible. In one case, as illustrated by the dashed sections in Fig. 9.12, the merged rows consist of the four sets $\{A,G\}$, $\{B,E,I\}$, $\{C\}$, and $\{F\}$ which is shown in Table 9.20*b*. The second possible set of row mergers leads to the four sets $\{A\}$, $\{B,E,I\}$, $\{C,G\}$, and $\{F\}$. Finally, if the sets in the present-state section of Table 9.20*b* are denoted by single symbols and each of the states in the next-state section is replaced by the set symbol in which it is a member, then the reduced version of Table 9.12 becomes that of Table 9.20*c*.

9.7 THE STATE-ASSIGNMENT PROBLEM AND THE TRANSITION TABLE

If the synthesis procedure is continued in accordance with the reverse of the analysis procedure, then the state table is next formed from the reduced flow table. Then, by assigning a binary code to the states, the transition table is constructed. It is common practice, however, to combine these two steps by working directly with the reduced flow table to establish a suitable assignment of binary codes for the states.

For clocked synchronous sequential networks, no difficulty is encountered in determining a state assignment since any arbitrary state assignment leads to a functional realization. The reason for this simplicity is that only single state changes are possible because of the existence of the synchronizing clock signal. As a consequence, the minimum number of bits is typically used to code the states.

The state-assignment problem for asynchronous sequential networks, however, is appreciably more difficult. In this case arbitrary state assignments do not lead, in general, to workable implementations since the internal time delays may cause a network to become stable in an undesirable state. As was discussed in Sec. 9.3, when only one state variable must change value in the transition between two internal states, the indicated next internal state is entered without difficulty. However, when more than a single state variable must change value in the transition between two states, races occur. These races were classified as noncritical, if the desired stable condition always results, or critical, if it is possible for the network to enter two or more different stable conditions. As an approach in controlling the transition between two states involving more than a single state variable change, a series of transitions, i.e., a cycle, is used. Thus, in general, for proper operation of asynchronous sequential networks the state assignment must be such as to avoid critical races but allow noncritical races and cycles.

It is seen in this section that it is not always possible to use the minimum number of state variables for a state assignment and still prevent the occurrence of critical races. However, by increasing the number of state variables, a state assignment that ensures proper operation is always possible.

9.7.1 The Transition Table for Example 9.3

Since it is necessary to avoid critical races, one approach in establishing a state assignment is to provide for each unstable state to go directly to a stable state as a single transition. In terms of the state assignment, this means that the two internal states that are involved in this transition must differ in exactly one binary digit in their codes. As in the case of synchronous sequential networks, two states are said to be *adjacent* if their binary codes differ in exactly one bit. Thus, in such an approach to the state-assignment problem, it is necessary to determine which states should be adjacent and then attempt to assign a code that satisfies these adjacencies. As an aid toward this objective, an *adjacency diagram* is constructed. An adjacency diagram consists of a node for each state. A line connects two nodes if the states associated with these nodes are to be adjacent.

Consider the reduced flow table for Example 9.3, i.e., Table 9.16. For the input state $x_1x_2 = 10$ it is necessary that internal states β and γ be adjacent if there is to be a single transition from the unstable state in the β row to the stable state in the γ row. Similarly, for the input state $x_1x_2 = 11$, it is necessary to have states α and γ be adjacent to provide for the transition from the first to the third row of the table. Figure 9.13*a* shows the adjacency diagram for Table 9.16. The above adjacency requirements are indicated by the two solid connecting lines between the three nodes.

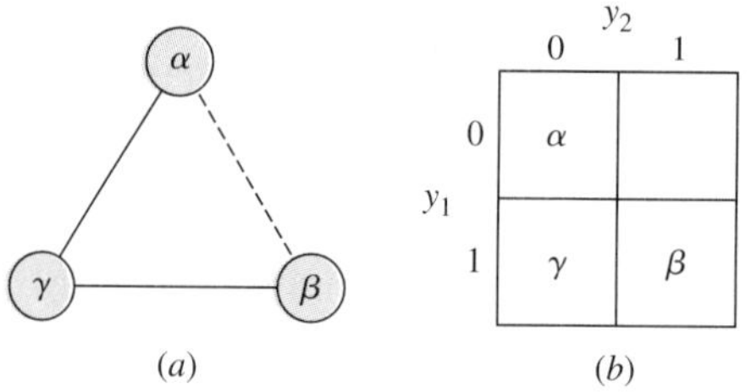

Figure 9.13 Example 9.3.
(*a*) Adjacency diagram.
(*b*) State-assignment map.

For input states $x_1x_2 = 00$ and $x_1x_2 = 01$, a slightly different analysis is necessary. Consider the $x_1x_2 = 00$ column. One possibility is to have the states α and β, as well as α and γ, adjacent. This allows single transitions between the first and second rows, as well as between the first and third rows. However, in Fig. 9.13*a* a solid line already connects the nodes for states α and γ. Rather than have a solid connecting line between the nodes for states α and β, a dotted line is shown to imply that there is an alternative way of achieving the necessary transition if states α and β cannot be made adjacent. This alternative is to have a cycle from the β row to the γ row and then to the α row. Thus, it really is not necessary to have states α and β adjacent since state assignments involving cycles are permissible. Finally, when the $x_1x_2 = 01$ column of Table 9.16 is analyzed, again it is concluded that it is not necessary to have states α and β adjacent, but that a cycle could be set up.

Having obtained the adjacency diagram for Table 9.16, it is next necessary to attempt to establish a state assignment with the desired adjacencies. Since there are three states to be coded in Table 9.16, a minimum of two binary digits is necessary to code each state. Correspondingly, two state variables are needed. To help establish a code for these states, a *state-assignment map*, as was introduced in Sec. 7.5, is constructed. A state-assignment map for Table 9.16 is shown in Fig. 9.13*b*. This map is a Karnaugh map for the state variables. Each cell of the map denotes a combination of the binary digits that can be assigned to a state of the sequential network. Two cells that are physically adjacent on the map suggest an assignment for two internal states that need to be adjacent. For example, let state α be arbitrarily assigned the code $y_1y_2 = 00$; thus, α is entered in the upper left cell of the state-assignment map. Since state γ is to be adjacent to state α, as indicated in the adjacency diagram, it can be placed in either the lower left cell or the upper right cell of the map. Assume it is placed in the lower left cell, thereby assigning it the code $y_1y_2 = 10$. Next, since state β is to be adjacent to state γ, it must be placed in the lower right cell and assigned the code $y_1y_2 = 11$. At this point, the adjacencies indicated by solid lines in the adjacency diagram are satisfied. It is now seen from the state-assignment map that it is not possible to have state α and state β adjacent. However, when a transition is required between the α and β rows, the option of a cycle can be used. As was pointed out earlier, one possible cycle can use the γ row. Another, however, can use the row associated with the assignment $y_1y_2 = 01$ since this internal state can exist in a network realization but was not used to code any of the three internal states given in the flow table. In either case, a state assignment is achieved involving the minimum number of state variables. In summary, Fig. 9.13*b* suggests the following state assignment:

State α — 00

State β — 11

State γ — 10

Now that a state assignment is established, a transition table is constructed. A transition table for the above assignment is shown in Table 9.21*a*. In constructing the next-state section, each stable state is replaced by the appropriate code for that

Table 9.21 Four transition tables for Example 9.3

Present state (y_1y_2)	Next state (Y_1Y_2) Input state (x_1x_2) 00	01	10	11	Output (z) Input state (x_1x_2) 00	01	10	11
α: 00	(00)	10	(00)	10	0	0	0	1
β: 11	10	(11)	10	(11)	0	0	1	0
γ: 10	00	11	(10)	(10)	0	0	1	1
01	–	–	–	–	–	–	–	–

(*a*)

Present state (y_1y_2)	Next state (Y_1Y_2) Input state (x_1x_2) 00	01	10	11	Output (z) Input state (x_1x_2) 00	01	10	11
α: 00	(00)	01	(00)	10	0	0	0	–
β: 11	01	(11)	10	(11)	0	0	–	0
γ: 10	00	11	(10)	(10)	0	0	1	1
01	00	11	–	–	0	0	–	–

(*b*)

Present state (y_1y_2)	Next state (Y_1Y_2) Input state (x_1x_2) 00	01	10	11	Output (z) Input state (x_1x_2) 00	01	10	11
α: 00	(00)	11*	(00)	10	0	0	0	–
β: 11	00*	(11)	10	(11)	0	0	–	0
γ: 10	00	11	(10)	(10)	0	0	1	1
01	00	11	–	–	0	0	–	–

(*c*)

Present state (y_1y_2)	Next state (Y_1Y_2) Input state (x_1x_2) 00	01	10	11	Output (z) Input state (x_1x_2) 00	01	10	11
α: 00	(00)	10	(00)	10	0	0	0	–
β: 11	10	(11)	10	(11)	0	0	–	0
γ: 10	00	11	(10)	(10)	0	0	1	1
01	–	–	–	–	–	–	–	–

(*d*)

state. The unstable states are replaced by the codes of the next states that are to result. For example, in the third and fourth columns of Table 9.16, the unstable states are replaced by their respective stable-state codes since the stable condition is achievable by a single transition as a consequence of the satisfied adjacencies of the state assignment. However, in the first and second columns, cycles are introduced in Table 9.21*a*. To create the cycles, each unstable entry is replaced by the next state, i.e., row designator, that is to result. To clarify the transitions that can occur, the transitions from each unstable state are indicated by arrows.

Two other transition tables for Example 9.3 are shown in Table 9.21*b* and *c*. In Table 9.21*b* the unassigned state $y_1y_2 = 01$ is used for the cycles in the first two columns. In Table 9.21*c* a different approach is used. Since there is only a single stable state in each of the first two columns of Table 9.16, noncritical races may be set up in these columns. The noncritical races are indicated by asterisks in Table 9.21*c*. Since the $y_1y_2 = 01$ row of the transition table is reachable under the assumption of a race, unstable next-state entries must be included in the first two columns of that row to completely specify the possible outcomes of the race.

To complete the transition table for Example 9.3, the output section still needs to be considered. In Table 9.16 it is seen that certain outputs are already specified. It is the outputs for the unstable total input states that remain to be determined. The outputs normally are assigned so that they change at most once during the entire time in which the network is unstable. This is done so as to avoid momentary false outputs. Thus, if the outputs are the same for the initial and final stable total input states, then the same outputs must be assigned to all the unstable total input states involved in the transitions. For example, if for some stable total input state the output is 0, and if after the new input state is applied the resulting stable total input state also has an output of 0, then all the unstable states that might be encountered during the time between the two stable conditions must also have an output of 0. This situation appears in Table 9.21*a* for the total input state $(x_1x_2,y_1y_2) = (01,00)$ since this unstable total state is reachable from the total input state $(x_1x_2,y_1y_2) = (00,00)$ having an output of 0 and eventually reaching the total input state $(x_1x_2,y_1y_2) = (01,11)$ which also has an output of 0. In addition, the output of 0 must be assigned to the total input state $(x_1x_2,y_1y_2) = (01,10)$ since it also occurs during an unstable period of the network as the result of a cycle. A general approach for assigning outputs that always satisfies the requirement of not having more than a single change in the outputs of the network is to assign the same outputs to an unstable total input state as the outputs associated with the stable state that is ultimately entered. This approach is used in completing the output section of Table 9.21*a*.

Although the above procedure for assigning outputs to the unstable total input states always can be carried out successfully, it is more conservative than necessary. For example, consider the total input state $(x_1x_2,y_1y_2) = (11,11)$ in Table 9.21*a*. If the input state is changed to $x_1x_2 = 10$, then the unstable total input state $(x_1x_2,y_1y_2) = (10,11)$ occurs for a short period of time, and the stable condition $(x_1x_2,y_1y_2) = (10,10)$ is reached. Furthermore, this unstable total input state can occur only after the total input state $(x_1x_2,y_1y_2) = (11,11)$, as is seen from

Table 9.21*a* and by recalling that x_1 and x_2 never change simultaneously in this example. With the initial stable condition having the output $z = 0$ and the final stable condition having the output $z = 1$, the output associated with the unstable total input state $(x_1x_2,y_1y_2) = (10,11)$ can be left unspecified without violating the condition that no more than a single change in the output is permissible. To see this, if the output for the unstable total input state is assumed to be 0, then the output remains 0 during the unstable total input state and then changes to 1 when the stable total input state is reached. On the other hand, if the output for the unstable total input state is assumed to be 1, then the output changes as soon as the unstable total input state is reached and remains unchanged when the stable total input state is reached. In either event, the output only changes once and no momentary false outputs occur. By a similar argument, the output for the total input state $(x_1x_2,y_1y_2) = (11,00)$ can also be left unspecified without violating the single output change constraint. This less conservative alternative approach was used to complete the output section of the transition table shown in Table 9.21*d*. As is seen in the next section, don't-care entries in the transition table provide greater flexibility in obtaining minimal expressions for a network realization.

The don't-care output entries mentioned above are also used in completing the output sections of Table 9.21*b* and *c*. For the latter two transition tables, two additional output entries are left unspecified since they are associated with total input states that can never occur. In all other cases, the single output change constraint determines the outputs for the unstable total input states.

9.7.2 The Transition Table for Example 9.4

The reduced flow table for the second running design example, i.e., Example 9.4, is shown in Table 9.17. The adjacency diagram given in Fig. 9.14*a* is constructed from this flow table in a similar manner as for the previous example. Since seven states must be coded, at least three state variables are needed. In attempting to establish a state assignment with three state variables, all the desired adjacencies are satisfied using the state-assignment map shown in Fig. 9.14*b* except for states β and χ. This adjacency is desirable for the input state $x_1x_2 = 01$. However, since it is possible to have state β ad-

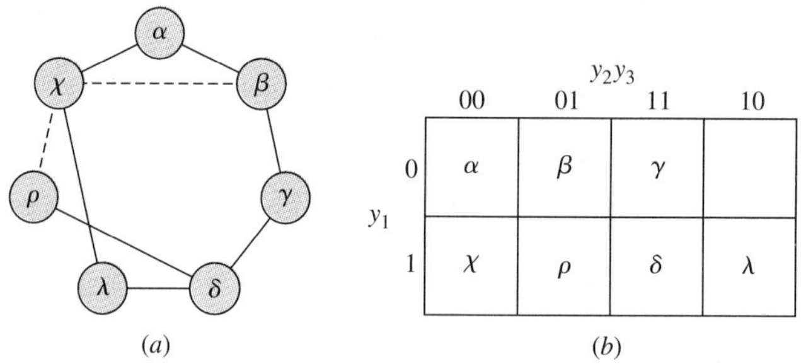

Figure 9.14 Example 9.4. (*a*) Adjacency diagram. (*b*) State-assignment map.

Table 9.22 Transition table for Example 9.4

Present state ($y_1y_2y_3$)	Next state ($Y_1Y_2Y_3$) Input state (x_1x_2)				Output (z) Input state (x_1x_2)			
	00	01	10	11	00	01	10	11
α: 000	001	–	000	–	0	–	0	–
β: 001	001	101	011	–	0	0	0	–
γ: 011	111	–	011	–	0	–	0	–
δ: 111	111	110	101	–	0	–*	0	–
λ: 110	100	110	–	–	–*	1	–	–
ρ: 101	101	100	101	–	0	0	0	–
χ: 100	100	100	000	–	0	0	0	–
010	–	–	–	–	–	–	–	–

jacent to state ρ, the transition from row β to row χ in the $x_1x_2 = 01$ column of Table 9.17 can be achieved by a cycle using row ρ. Thus, it is possible to code Table 9.17 with the minimum number of state variables. The state assignment is given by

State α — 000
State β — 001
State γ — 011
State δ — 111
State λ — 110
State ρ — 101
State χ — 100

If the above state assignment is now applied to Table 9.17, then the transition table given in Table 9.22 results. For clarity, the transitions between internal states are indicated with arrows. The output section of Table 9.22 is constructed under the assumption that the outputs can change at most once while the network is unstable. Even with this restriction, the outputs indicated by asterisks can be left unspecified.

9.7.3 The Need for Additional State Variables

Both of the examples considered thus far were coded with the minimum number of state variables. In general, however, this is not possible, so additional state variables are necessary in order to establish a state assignment that does not introduce critical races. To illustrate this, consider a fundamental-mode asynchronous sequential network having the reduced flow table of Fig. 9.15*a* in which the two inputs never change simultaneously. The corresponding adjacency diagram is given in Fig. 9.15*b*. As can be seen from the adjacency diagram, each state must be adjacent to the other three states. It is not possible to code this flow table with two state variables and have it be free from critical races. However, it is possible to code this table with three state variables to provide a total of eight internal states. Table 9.23 shows a coded version of the flow table of Fig. 9.15*a*. Here a third state variable provides for additional rows in the transition table so that cycles may be used to control the transitions between the states. The transitions are indicated by arrows for clarity.

Using the availability of extra states, as the result of the flow table not having a power-of-2 number of states or by the use of additional state variables, to set up cycles in a transition table is known as a *shared-row* state assignment. These approaches have been illustrated in Tables 9.21*b* and 9.23. Another state-assignment approach that is used involves assigning more than one binary code to each state. This is referred to as a *multiple-row* state assignment. Such a state assignment also requires more than the minimum number of state variables.

In a multiple-row state assignment, each state of the flow table is first replaced by a set of equivalent states and then the states are coded so that at most a single state variable must change value for a transition between two states. A state-assignment map that can be applied to any four-state flow table is given in Fig. 9.16.* In this case, state *a* of a four-state flow table is replaced by equivalent states a_1 and a_2 in some new *expanded* flow table. Similarly, equivalent state pairs are used to replace states *b*, *c*, and *d*. It should be noted in the state-assignment

Present state	Next state				Output (z)			
	Input state (x_1x_2)				Input state (x_1x_2)			
	00	01	10	11	00	01	10	11
A	(A)	(A)	D	D	0	0	–	–
B	(B)	A	(B)	C	1	–	0	–
C	A	(C)	B	(C)	–	1	–	0
D	B	C	(D)	(D)	–	–	1	1

(*a*)

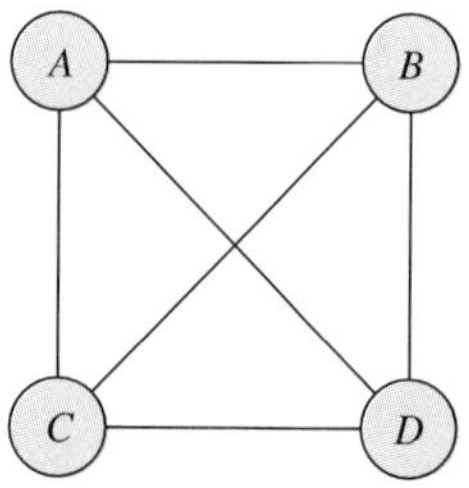

(*b*)

Figure 9.15 A reduced flow table and its adjacency diagram.

*The lowercase letters in the figure correspond to generic states and are assigned to the states of a four-state flow table in any order.

Table 9.23 A coded version of Fig. 9.15*a*

Present state ($y_1y_2y_3$)	Next state ($Y_1Y_2Y_3$)				Output (z)			
	Input state (x_1x_2)				Input state (x_1x_2)			
	00	**01**	**10**	**11**	**00**	**01**	**10**	**11**
A: 000	000	000	010	010	0	0	–	–
B: 001	001	000	001	101	1	–	0	0
C: 100	000	100	101	100	–	1	0	0
D: 010	011	110	010	010	1	1	1	1
011	001	–	–	–	1	–	–	–
101	–	–	001	100	–	–	0	0
111	–	–	–	–	–	–	–	–
110	–	100	–	–	–	1	–	–

map that one of each of the pair of equivalent states is adjacent to one of each of the other pair of equivalent states. For example, state a_1 is adjacent to b_1, c_1, and d_2. In this way, each state in the original four-state flow table can go to one of the equivalent states with only a single state variable change. It should be noted that the two binary codes for the two equivalent states are complementary. General state assignments, such as the one suggested by Fig. 9.16, that can be applied to any flow table are called *universal state assignments.*

To illustrate the use of the universal state assignment suggested by Fig. 9.16, again consider the flow table of Fig. 9.15*a*. This four-state flow table is expanded

y_1 \ y_2y_3	00	01	11	10
0	a_1	b_1	d_1	c_1
1	d_2	c_2	a_2	b_2

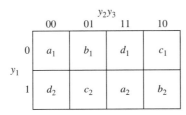

Figure 9.16 State-assignment map for any four-state flow table.

Table 9.24 Applying the universal state assignment of Fig. 9.16 to Fig. 9.15*a*. (*a*) Expanded flow table. (*b*) Transition table

Present state	Next state				Output (z)			
	Input state (x_1x_2)				Input state (x_1x_2)			
	00	01	10	11	00	01	10	11
A_1	(A_1)	(A_1)	D_2	D_2	0	0	–	–
A_2	(A_2)	(A_2)	D_1	D_1	0	0	–	–
B_1	(B_1)	A_1	(B_1)	C_2	1	–	0	–
B_2	(B_2)	A_2	(B_2)	C_1	1	–	0	–
C_1	A_1	(C_1)	B_2	(C_1)	–	1	–	0
C_2	A_2	(C_2)	B_1	(C_2)	–	1	–	0
D_1	B_1	C_1	(D_1)	(D_1)	–	–	1	1
D_2	B_2	C_2	(D_2)	(D_2)	–	–	1	1

(*a*)

Present state ($y_1y_2y_3$)	Next state ($Y_1Y_2Y_3$)				Output (z)			
	Input state (x_1x_2)				Input state (x_1x_2)			
	00	01	10	11	00	01	10	11
A_1: 000	(000)	(000)	100	100	0	0	–	–
A_2: 111	(111)	(111)	011	011	0	0	–	–
B_1: 001	(001)	000	(001)	101	1	–	0	0
B_2: 110	(110)	111	(110)	010	1	–	0	0
C_1: 010	000	(010)	110	(010)	–	1	0	0
C_2: 101	111	(101)	001	(101)	–	1	0	0
D_1: 011	001	010	(011)	(011)	1	1	1	1
D_2: 100	110	101	(100)	(100)	1	1	1	1

(*b*)

into the equivalent flow table shown in Table 9.24*a*. Since state designators are arbitrary in Fig. 9.16, the lowercase letters are assigned to the corresponding uppercase letters in Fig. 9.15*a*. First, each row of Fig. 9.15*a* is replaced by two rows in Table 9.24*a*. For example, row A is replaced by rows A_1 and A_2, row B by rows B_1 and B_2, etc. The letter entries are the same in both rows of the pair that, in turn, are the same as those in the original flow table. In the first row of the pair, the stable states have a 1 subscript; while in the second row of the pair, the stable states have a 2 subscript. Since state A is stable in columns $x_1x_2 = 00$ and $x_1x_2 = 01$ of Fig. 9.15*a*, state A_1 is stable in the first row of the expanded flow table in columns $x_1x_2 = 00$ and $x_1x_2 = 01$ and state A_2 is stable in the second row of these columns.

To determine the subscripts for the unstable states, reference is made to the state-assignment map in Fig. 9.16. The unstable next state in the expanded flow table for a particular row must be adjacent to the stable present state of that row. For example, according to the map, state a_1 is adjacent to state d_2; while state a_2 is adjacent to state d_1. Therefore, the two unstable entries in Table 9.24*a* for row A_1 are D_2; while the two unstable entries in row A_2 are D_1. Also, since A_1 and A_2 are equivalent states, the output entries for the stable states in both rows A_1 and A_2 of Table 9.24*a* are the same as those for row A of Fig. 9.15*a*. In a similar manner, the subscripts for each of the other unstable state entries in Table 9.24*a* are determined as well as the output entries for the stable states. With this procedure, the transition from any state in the original flow table goes to an equivalent state in the expanded flow table while producing the same outputs during the stable states.

From the expanded flow table in Table 9.24*a*, the transition table of Table 9.24*b* immediately follows by applying the universal state assignment suggested by the state-assignment map of Fig. 9.16. The output entries in the transition table for the unstable states are again determined so that an output changes at most once when the network is unstable.

9.7.4 A Systematic State-Assignment Procedure

Before concluding this discussion on the state-assignment problem, one simple systematic state-assignment procedure is explained and illustrated. This is known as the *one-hot method.* If a flow table has p rows, then this procedure requires that p state variables be used. Each of the rows of the flow table is coded by a p-tuple containing exactly one 1. The binary code for row i is given by the p-tuple in which only the ith element is a 1, i.e., $y_1y_2 \cdots y_i \cdots y_p = 00 \cdots 1 \cdots 0$.

To construct the transition table, each stable next-state entry has the same code as its row designator. The code for an unstable next-state entry is determined as follows. Assume there is an unstable next-state entry in row i, column k, and a transition is desired to row j in the same column. Then, the code for the unstable next-state entry in row i, column k is the p-tuple in which just the ith and jth elements are 1; that is, the next-state entry is

$$Y_1Y_2 \cdots Y_i \cdots Y_j \cdots Y_p = 00 \cdots 1 \cdots 1 \cdots 0$$

A row is next added to the transition table with this row designator, i.e., $y_1y_2 \cdots y_i \cdots y_j \cdots y_p = 00 \cdots 1 \cdots 1 \cdots 0$. The next-state entry for this new row and column k is then the p-tuple for the jth row; that is,

$$Y_1Y_2 \cdots Y_i \cdots Y_j \cdots Y_p = 00 \cdots 0 \cdots 1 \cdots 0$$

If this procedure is applied to each unstable next-state entry, then a transition table is obtained in which exactly two transitions occur when it is necessary to go from row i to row j.

Applying the above procedure to the flow table shown in Fig. 9.15*a* results in the transition table of Table 9.25. Arrows are included in Table 9.25 to show how the two transitions occur when the flow table specifies a transition from row i to row j. To avoid having the output change more than once during the transitions, the outputs for the unstable entries are assigned the value of the stable state that is entered.

Needless to say, the establishment of a state assignment for an asynchronous sequential network is rather challenging. Several approaches have been suggested in this section. With so many state-assignment variations possible, several alternative transition tables can result. It is seen in the next section that the final realization is dependent upon the transition table obtained.

Table 9.25 A coded version of Fig. 9.15*a* using the one-hot method

Present state ($y_1y_2y_3y_4$)	Next state ($Y_1Y_2Y_3Y_4$)				Output (z)			
	Input state (x_1x_2)				Input state (x_1x_2)			
	00	**01**	**10**	**11**	**00**	**01**	**10**	**11**
A: 1000	1000	1000	1001	1001	0	0	1	1
B: 0100	0100	1100	0100	0110	1	0	0	0
C: 0010	1010	0010	0110	0010	0	1	0	0
D: 0001	0101	0011	0001	0001	1	1	1	1
1010	1000	–	–	–	0	–	–	–
0101	0100	–	–	–	1	–	–	–
1100	–	1000	–	–	–	0	–	–
0011	–	0010	–	–	–	1	–	–
1001	–	–	0001	0001	–	–	1	1
0110	–	–	0100	0010	–	–	0	0

9.8 COMPLETING THE ASYNCHRONOUS SEQUENTIAL NETWORK DESIGN

Once the state assignment is made and the transition table formed, the final step of the design procedure is to establish the excitation table from which the Boolean expressions for the implementation are obtained. Asynchronous sequential networks most frequently are implemented using simple feedback loops, occasionally with delay elements in the feedback paths. This basic structure was previously illustrated in Fig. 9.1. Alternately, unclocked flip-flops may be used in network realizations as shown in Fig. 9.2. Both types of realizations are now studied.

From the analysis discussion in Sec. 9.2, it is known that when an asynchronous sequential network is constructed with simple feedback loops, the excitation table and the transition table are identical. Thus, to complete the design of an asynchronous sequential network with simple feedback loops, the transition table can be used to construct Karnaugh maps for obtaining the excitation and output expressions. The excitation table (or, equivalently, the transition table in this case) is completely analogous to a truth table. The present-state and input variables are the independent variables and appear along the axes of the Karnaugh maps. The next-state and output variables are the dependent variables, and hence a map is constructed for each of them. The entries in the maps are readily transferred from the excitation table.

Again consider running design Example 9.3. The transition table that is used for the implementation is Table 9.21*d*. Under the assumption that the implementation is to be achieved with just feedback loops, Karnaugh maps are constructed for each of the next-state variables, Y_1 and Y_2, and the output variable, z. Figure 9.17 shows the Karnaugh maps. From these maps the following minimal-sum expressions are obtained:

$$Y_1 = x_2 + y_2 + x_1y_1$$
$$Y_2 = x_2y_2 + \bar{x}_1x_2y_1$$
$$z = x_1y_1\bar{y}_2$$

The above equations suggest the network that is shown in Fig. 9.18. The delay elements are shown grayed in the figure since they usually do not appear physically in the implementation but rather are the result of the internal delays of the gates, which are normally sufficient to assure proper network operation.

If unclocked flip-flops are to be incorporated into the asynchronous sequential network, then the excitation and transition tables are no longer identical. In this case, the excitation table must account for the characteristics of the flip-flops used in the implementation. The only unclocked flip-flops discussed in Chapter 6 were the *SR* latch, consisting of two cross-coupled nor-gates, and the $\overline{S}\,\overline{R}$ latch, consisting of two cross-coupled nand-gates. The relationship indicating the necessary excitation signals on the inputs of a clocked *SR* flip-flop to achieve the various state changes was previously given in Table 6.10. This table is still valid

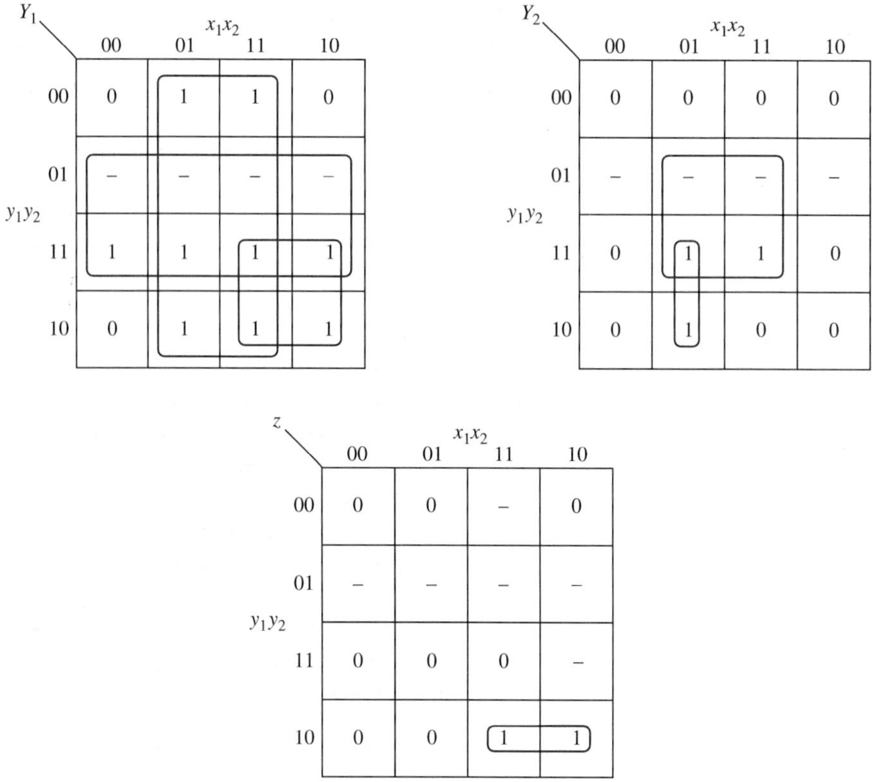

Figure 9.17 Karnaugh maps for the excitation and output expressions for a gate implementation of Example 9.3.

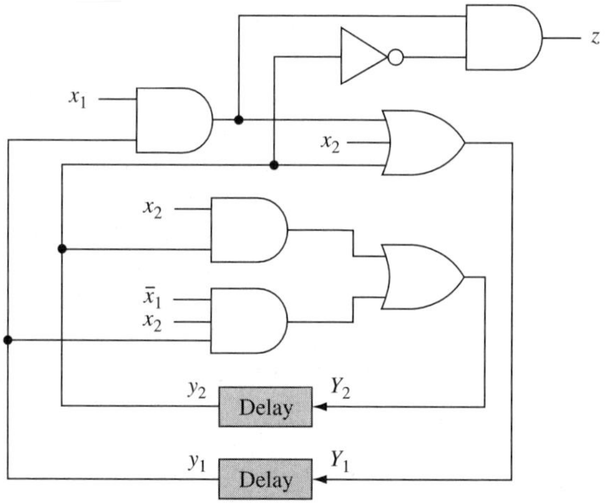

Figure 9.18 Implementation of Example 9.3 with feedback loops.

Table 9.26 Excitation properties of the SR latch and $\overline{S}\overline{R}$ latch

		SR latch		$\overline{S}\overline{R}$ latch	
Q	Q^+	S	R	$\overline{S}$	$\overline{R}$
0	0	0	–	1	–
0	1	1	0	0	1
1	0	0	1	1	0
1	1	–	0	–	1

for the *SR* latch and is repeated in Table 9.26. Table 9.26 also shows how the various state changes are achieved by the excitation signals on the input terminals of the $\overline{S}\overline{R}$ latch.

Knowing the excitation properties of the latches, the excitation table for an asynchronous sequential network is obtained from its transition table in exactly the same way as done previously for synchronous sequential networks. Then, Karnaugh maps can be drawn and used to obtain the necessary excitation and output expressions for the implementation.

To illustrate the use of *SR* latches in the design of an asynchronous sequential network, again consider Example 9.3 and the transition table shown in Table 9.21*d*. Since there are two internal-state variables, two *SR* latches appear in the implementation. The excitation table for this example is given in Table 9.27. To be consistent with the notation in Secs. 9.1 and 9.2, the present-state variables which appear at the outputs of the flip-flops are indicated as Q_1 and Q_2 in the excitation table, rather than y_1 and y_2. The entries in Table 9.27 are determined by specifying the flip-flop excitations needed for the indicated state transitions in the transition table. For example, according to Table 9.21*d*, for input state $x_1x_2 = 00$ and present state $y_1y_2 = Q_1Q_2 = 00$, the next state is $Y_1Y_2 = Q_1^+Q_2^+ = 00$. Thus, both flip-flops must remain in their 0-states. Referring to Table 9.26, in order to keep an *SR* flip-flop in its 0-state, the necessary excitations are $S = 0$ and $R = –$. Hence, the upper left entry in the excitation section of Table 9.27 is $(S_1R_1,S_2R_2) = (0–,0–)$. The other entries in Table 9.27 are obtained in a similar manner. The Karnaugh maps shown in Fig. 9.19 are next constructed by regarding the excitation table as a truth table

Table 9.27 Excitation table for implementation of Example 9.3 with *SR* latches

Present state (Q_1Q_2)	Excitation (S_1R_1,S_2R_2)				Output (z)			
	Input state (x_1x_2)				Input state (x_1x_2)			
	00	01	10	11	00	01	10	11
00	0–,0–	10,0–	0–,0–	10,0–	0	0	0	–
11	–0,01	–0,–0	–0,01	–0,–0	0	0	–	0
10	01,0–	–0,10	–0,0–	–0,0–	0	0	1	1
01	–	–	–	–	–	–	–	–

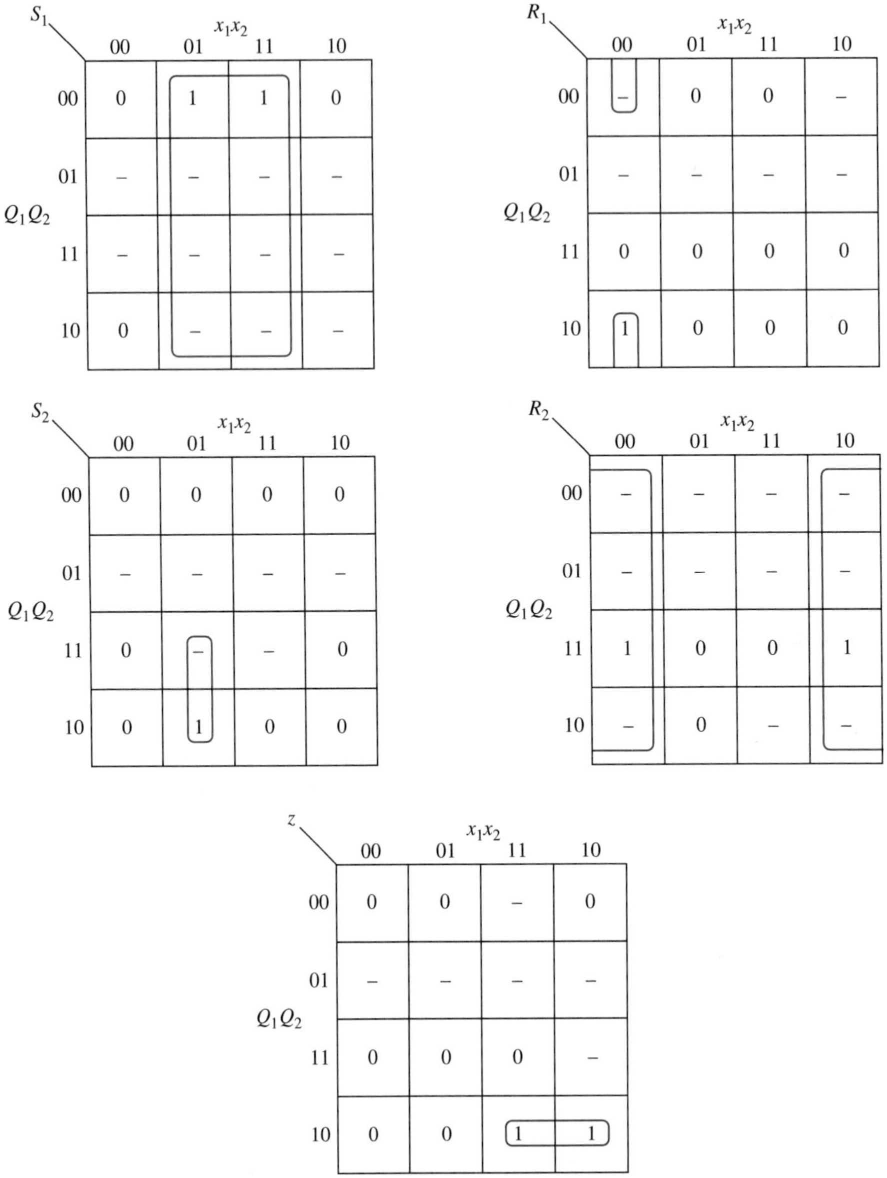

Figure 9.19 Karnaugh maps for the excitation and output expressions for an implementation of Example 9.3 with *SR* latches.

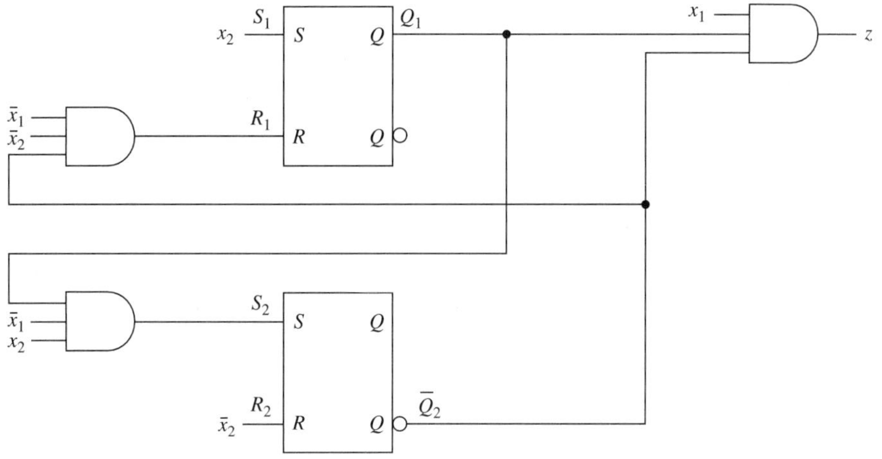

Figure 9.20 Implementation of Example 9.3 incorporating *SR* latches.

and transferring the functional values of the excitation and output variables onto them. From these maps the following minimal-sum expressions result:

$$S_1 = x_2$$
$$R_1 = \bar{x}_1\bar{x}_2\bar{Q}_2$$
$$S_2 = \bar{x}_1x_2Q_1$$
$$R_2 = \bar{x}_2$$
$$z = x_1Q_1\bar{Q}_2$$

These expressions suggest the implementation shown in Fig. 9.20.

Although minimal-sum expressions were used in the above implementations, in general, additional terms are needed in the expressions for a workable realization. This problem is further explored in the next section.

9.9 STATIC AND DYNAMIC HAZARDS IN COMBINATIONAL NETWORKS

The use of Boolean algebra as a mathematical model for logic networks, thus far, has been to describe the steady-state behavior of a network. However, transient effects in a logic network can result in the occurrence of momentary output signals, i.e., *false outputs* or *glitches*, while the components are changing states.* These transient false outputs are the result of the finite propagation delay times of the

*Other causes of false outputs were discussed previously in Secs. 7.2 and 9.7.

components along different paths within the network. Although they are normally of short duration, they are at times undesirable and even have serious effects on the overall operation of a logic network. This is particularly the case in asynchronous sequential networks.

A *hazard* is the potential or actual malfunction of a logic network during the transition between two input states as the result of a single variable change, where a *malfunction* is any deviation from the intended response. From the definition of a hazard it is seen that an actual malfunction does not necessarily have to occur in order for the hazard to be present but, rather, only a potential malfunction. Thus, the detection of hazards does not require a knowledge of the actual physical characteristics of the network devices but can be done using the algebraic representation of a network. Of course, the seriousness of a hazard is dependent upon its actual occurrence, the duration of the momentary output signals, and the components or systems that receive the momentary output signals. In this section, two types of hazards occurring in combinational networks, their detection, and elimination are studied. A third type of hazard is discussed in Sec. 9.10.

9.9.1 Static Hazards

A *static hazard* in a logic network is a transient change of an output value that is supposed to remain fixed during the transition between two input states differing in the value of one variable. When the output is to remain at the value 0 and a momentary 1 output is possible during the transition between the two input states, then the hazard is called a *static 0-hazard.* If the two input states both produce a 1 output in the steady state and a momentary 0 output is possible during the transition between the two input states, then the hazard is called a *static 1-hazard.* The two types of static hazards are shown in Fig. 9.21.

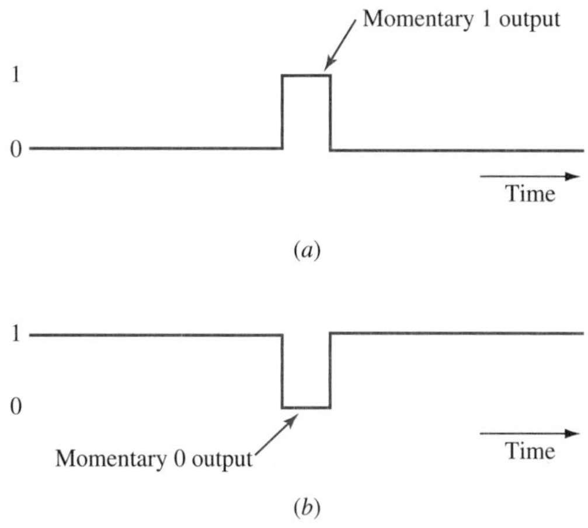

Figure 9.21 Static hazards. (*a*) Static 0-hazard. (*b*) Static 1-hazard.

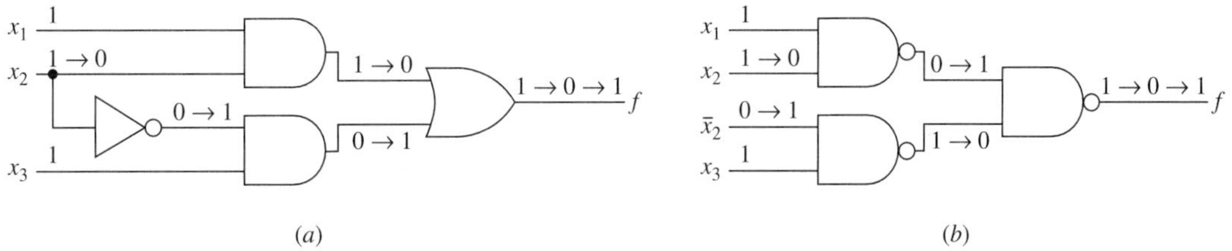

Figure 9.22 Illustrations of static 1-hazards. (*a*) Not-and-or network. (*b*) Nand-nand network.

To illustrate a static 1-hazard, consider the gate network of Fig. 9.22*a*. Assume the input state $x_1x_2x_3 = 111$ is initially applied to the network. Then the upper and-gate has a 1 output, and the lower and-gate has a 0 output. If the input state is next changed to $x_1x_2x_3 = 101$, i.e., just the value of x_2 changes, then the output of the upper and-gate becomes 0, and the output of the lower and-gate becomes 1. For both input states, the output of the network is 1. However, if there is an appreciable propagation delay associated with the not-gate, then the output of the upper and-gate becomes 0 before the output of the lower and-gate becomes 1. This results in a period of time in which neither input terminal to the or-gate is a 1 and, consequently, the output f is 0 for that period of time. Thus, a static 1-hazard exists during the transition between the input states $x_1x_2x_3 = 111$ and $x_1x_2x_3 = 101$.

Now consider the network of Fig. 9.23*a* and again assume that the not-gate has an appreciably greater propagation delay time than the other gates. In this case there is a static 0-hazard in the transition between the input states $x_1x_2x_3 = 000$ and $x_1x_2x_3 = 010$ since it is possible for a logic-1 signal to appear at both input terminals of the and-gate for a short duration.

In order to emphasize a static hazard, it was assumed in the above examples that only the not-gate had an appreciable propagation delay. Certainly, in any physical realization, each gate has a finite propagation delay resulting in delays being distributed throughout the network. Depending upon the values of the delays, momentary output signals may or may not actually occur. Thus, even two-level logic networks can have static hazards. For example, the two-level networks of Figs. 9.22*b* and 9.23*b* are also subject to static hazards when x_2 changes

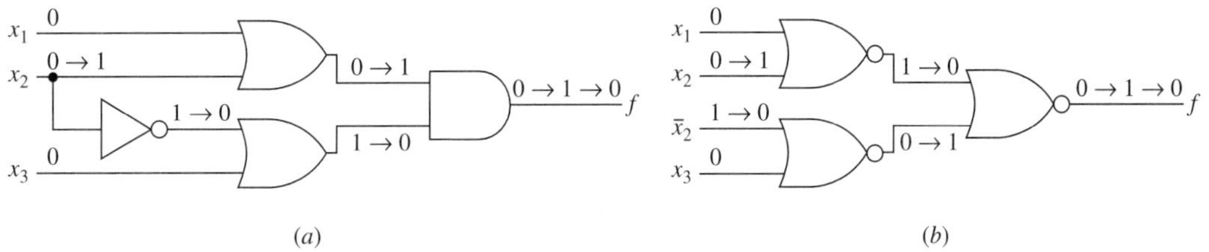

Figure 9.23 Illustrations of static 0-hazards. (*a*) Not-or-and network. (*b*) Nor-nor network.

if the propagation delay time through the lower gate on the first level is greater than the propagation delay time of the upper gate on that level.

In the above examples it should be noted that in each case the static hazard involved a path change in which the two paths both result in the same output. The static hazard is the consequence of no path that "holds" the output at 0, in the case of a static 0-hazard, or 1, in the case of a static 1-hazard, when there is a transition between two input states producing the same output. This observation leads to both the detection and elimination of static hazards.

How serious static hazards are in a combinational network depends upon the devices or systems that receive the momentary transient signals. For example, in a combinational network that is used as an input to a display, these possible momentary transient signals are probably not significant. In synchronous sequential networks, the outputs of the combinational logic normally feed into clocked flip-flops. However, in a properly designed synchronous sequential network these signals are not clocked into the flip-flops until they have reached their steady-state values. Consequently, the transient effects are ignored.

In the case of asynchronous sequential networks, on the other hand, the existence of hazards in the combinational logic can cause the networks to malfunction. To see this, consider the network shown in Fig. 9.24*a*. This network is the same as that of Fig. 9.22*a* in which the f output is connected to the x_3 input. The network of Fig. 9.24*a* can be regarded as the next-state portion of an asynchronous sequential network. The corresponding excitation table for Y is given in Fig. 9.24*b* in which the stable states are shown circled. From the excitation table it is seen that the total input state $(x_1x_2,y) = (11,1)$ corresponds to a stable condition. If the x_2 input is changed to 0, then the operating point simply moves horizontally to another stable total input state $(x_1x_2,y) = (10,1)$. However, since the combinational logic of the asynchronous sequential network is the same as Fig. 9.22*a*, it is subject to a static 1-hazard when x_2 changes. If it is now assumed that a momentary 0 output from the or-gate enters the lower and-gate before the output of the not-gate changes from 0 to 1, then the output of this and-gate remains at 0 after the change has propagated through the not-gate. The net result is that the network becomes stable with the total input state $(x_1x_2,y) = (10,0)$. Clearly, the network is not in the intended

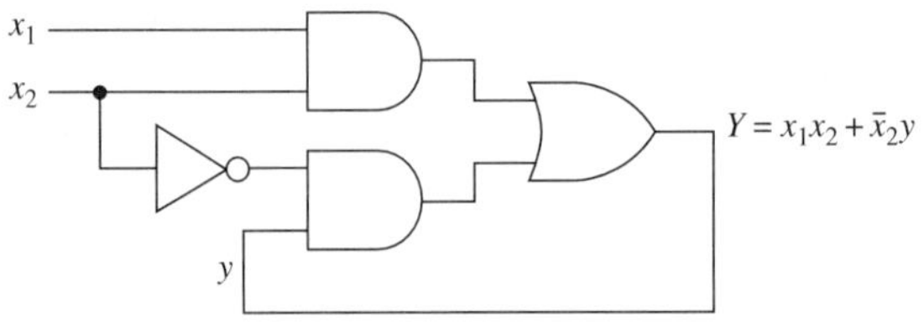

(*a*)

Present state (y)	Next state (Y) Input state (x_1x_2) 00	01	10	11
0	(0)	(0)	(0)	1
1	(1)	0	(1)	(1)

(*b*)

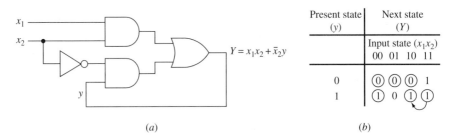

Figure 9.24 Effects of static hazards on the behavior of an asynchronous sequential network. (*a*) Logic diagram. (*b*) Excitation table.

stable state. Thus, the existence of the static 1-hazard has caused the network to malfunction.

9.9.2 Detecting Static Hazards

Static hazards can be detected with the aid of Boolean algebraic expressions in which a variable and its complement are treated as different, i.e., nonrelated, variables. This is necessary since under transient conditions a variable and its complement can momentarily have the same logic value as was seen, for example, by the not-gate in Fig. 9.22*a*, where both its input and output were 0 for a short period of time owing to its propagation delay.

To detect static hazards, the Boolean expression for the network is first written in a form that is in one-to-one correspondence with the network. Using the distributive and DeMorgan's laws, the expression is then manipulated into its sum-of-products form, i.e., as a disjunctive normal formula, for the detection of static 1-hazards and into its product-of-sums form, i.e., as a conjunctive normal formula, for the detection of static 0-hazards. All the theorems of Boolean algebra can be used for the manipulation *except* for $X\overline{X} = 0$, $X + \overline{X} = 1$, and any theorems whose validity is dependent upon these two expressions, e.g., $X + \overline{X}Y = X + Y$ and $X(\overline{X} + Y) = XY$.* These exceptions are due to the constraint that a variable and its complement must be regarded as different variables in transient analysis. The absorption laws, however, should be applied, i.e., $X + XY = X$ and $X(X + Y) = X$, so that no subsuming terms are in the final expressions. The resulting normal formulas are referred to as the *transient normal formulas.* The product terms in the transient disjunctive normal formula are called *1-terms* and the sum terms in the transient conjunctive normal formula are called *0-terms.*

Consider first the transient disjunctive normal formula. Each 1-term corresponds to a path through the network that provides a 1 output. Furthermore, each of the 1-terms not containing a pair of complementary literals also corresponds to a single subcube on a Karnaugh map. A property of Karnaugh maps is that two assignments of the independent variables that differ in the value of exactly one element appear as two adjacent cells within a map. Thus, if two adjacent 1-cells on the map occur within a subcube for a single 1-term, then the output of the network must have the value 1 during the transition between the corresponding input states since only one path is involved. On the other hand, if there are two adjacent 1-cells on the map that do not occur within a subcube of a single 1-term, then there must be a path change for the 1 output of the network upon the occurrence of a change in the value of a single variable. The two paths involved correspond to the two different 1-term subcubes. In the process of switching from one path to the other, a momentary 0 output signal can occur if the original term producing a 1 output changes to 0 before the term originally producing a 0 output changes to 1. That is, a static 1-hazard exists. Thus, by plotting all the 1-terms not containing a complementary pair of literals in a transient disjunctive normal formula, all

*Another example is the consensus theorem. See Problem 3.1(*e*).

the static 1-hazards are readily detected by noting if each pair of adjacent 1-cells is contained in some single subcube.

For Fig. 9.22*a*, the transient disjunctive normal formula is immediately found to be

$$f_{tr} = x_1x_2 + \bar{x}_2x_3$$

A similar result is also obtained from Fig. 9.22*b*; in particular,

$$\begin{aligned} f_{tr} &= \overline{\overline{(x_1x_2)}\ \overline{(\bar{x}_2x_3)}} \\ &= \overline{\overline{(x_1x_2)}} + \overline{\overline{(\bar{x}_2x_3)}} \\ &= x_1x_2 + \bar{x}_2x_3 \end{aligned}$$

If the two 1-terms x_1x_2 and $\bar{x}_2x_3$ are plotted on a Karnaugh map, then the subcubes of 1-cells shown in Fig. 9.25*a* result. Since there are two adjacent 1-cells that are not contained in a common subcube, the map implies that a static 1-hazard exists in the transition between $x_1x_2x_3 = 101$ and $x_1x_2x_3 = 111$. This is exactly what was previously noted when this network was analyzed earlier. In addition, from inspection of the Karnaugh map it is now known that this is the only static 1-hazard for this network.

Similarly, the 0-terms of the transient conjunctive normal formula of a network can be used to detect static 0-hazards. A 0-term has the value 0 only when each of its literals has the value 0. Hence, each 0-term corresponds to a set of input states that causes the output of a combinational logic network to be 0. Static 0-hazards are detected by mapping all the 0-terms that do not contain a pair of complementary literals and noting if there are any two adjacent 0-cells not contained in some single 0-term subcube.

Again consider Fig. 9.22*a*. The transient conjunctive normal formula is obtained as follows:

$$\begin{aligned} f_{tr} &= x_1x_2 + \bar{x}_2x_3 \\ &= (x_1 + \bar{x}_2x_3)(x_2 + \bar{x}_2x_3) \\ &= (x_1 + \bar{x}_2)(x_1 + x_3)(x_2 + \bar{x}_2)(x_2 + x_3) \end{aligned}$$

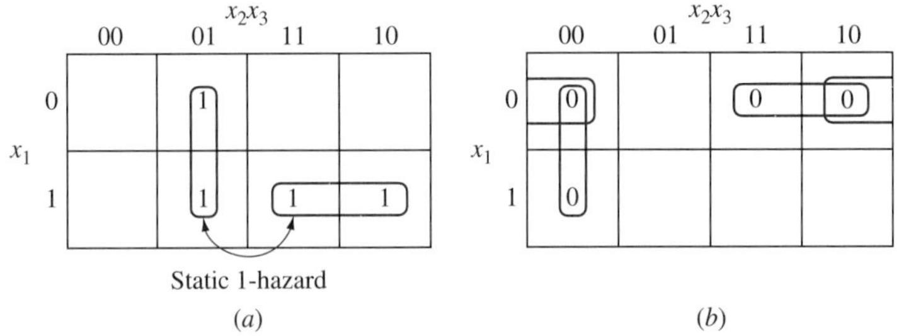

Figure 9.25 Karnaugh maps for detecting static hazards in the networks of Fig. 9.22. (*a*) 1-term subcubes. (*b*) 0-term subcubes.

When the three 0-terms not containing complementary literals, i.e., $(x_1 + \bar{x}_2)$, $(x_1 + x_3)$, and $(x_2 + x_3)$, are plotted on a Karnaugh map, the subcubes of 0-cells shown in Fig. 9.25*b* result. It is seen that this network has no static 0-hazards since each pair of adjacent 0-cells is contained within some single subcube.

Now consider the combinational logic network of Fig. 9.23*a*. The transient disjunctive normal formula is

$$f_{tr} = (x_1 + x_2)(\bar{x}_2 + x_3)$$
$$= x_1\bar{x}_2 + x_1x_3 + x_2\bar{x}_2 + x_2x_3$$

and the transient conjunctive normal formula is simply

$$f_{tr} = (x_1 + x_2)(\bar{x}_2 + x_3)$$

Identical transient expressions are also obtained from Fig. 9.23*b*. The 1-terms $x_1\bar{x}_2$, x_1x_3, and x_2x_3 are plotted on the Karnaugh map shown in Fig. 9.26*a* and the 0-terms $(x_1 + x_2)$ and $(\bar{x}_2 + x_3)$ are plotted on the Karnaugh map shown in Fig. 9.26*b*. From these maps it is seen that the network has no static 1-hazards and that a static 0-hazard exists in the transition between the input states $x_1x_2x_3 = 000$ and $x_1x_2x_3 = 010$.

Since the 1-terms and 0-terms of the transient normal formulas are used to detect static hazards, the need that subsuming terms be deleted should be clear. The fewer the number of literals in a term, the larger the number of cells in a subcube on a map. If any subsuming term is also entered in the map, then it appears as a subcube within some larger subcube. Correspondingly, such subcubes are not relevant for the determination of static hazards.

Although 0-terms are used to detect static 0-hazards, there is an observation that can be made about the nonexistence of static 0-hazards and 1-terms. If no 1-term in the transient disjunctive normal formula contains a variable and its complement, then there are no conditions in which the transient disjunctive normal formula has the value 1 when some variable is changing value. Thus, the network must not have a static 0-hazard. As a result, no static 0-hazards can occur in a two-level realization based on a disjunctive normal formula unless there are

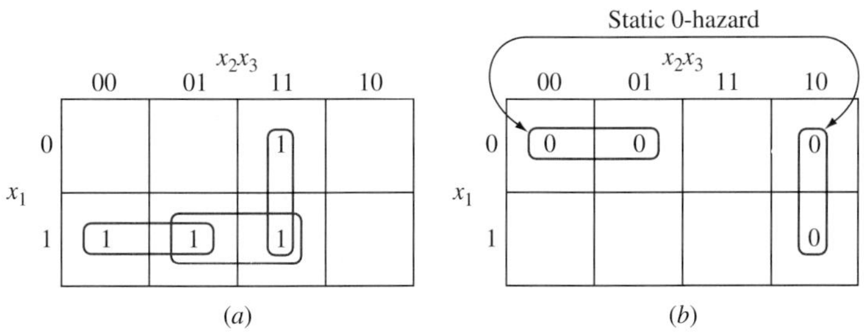

Figure 9.26 Karnaugh maps for detecting static hazards in the networks of Fig. 9.23. (*a*) 1-term subcubes. (*b*) 0-term subcubes.

gates having a pair of complementary literals as their inputs. Obviously, the inclusion of such gates in a realization makes no sense. On the other hand, the presence of 1-terms in the transient disjunctive normal formula with a pair of complementary literals does *not* imply that the network has static 0-hazards. The existence of 1-terms with complementary literals is only a necessary, but not sufficient, condition for a static 0-hazard to exist.

Similar remarks can be made about 0-terms in the transient conjunctive normal formula. In this case, a network has no static 1-hazards if there are no 0-terms containing a pair of complementary literals.

9.9.3 Eliminating Static Hazards

The above discussion on the detection of static hazards also suggests a method for their elimination. Additional logic is used to provide the holding action that is needed to eliminate the static hazards. This additional logic is determined by ensuring that any two adjacent cells on a Karnaugh map with the same logic-value entry are included in a common subcube.

Again consider Fig. 9.22*a*. This network has a static 1-hazard as indicated in the Karnaugh map of Fig. 9.25*a*. The network can now be modified so that it is free of the static 1-hazard by introducing a subcube containing the two 1-cells that indicate the hazard, i.e., the subcube corresponding to the product term x_1x_3. The inclusion of a gate in the realization corresponding to this product term provides a constant 1-output holding path for the two input states $x_1x_2x_3 = 101$ and $x_1x_2x_3 = 111$. The disjunctive normal formula for an implementation free of static 1-hazards thus becomes

$$f(x_1,x_2,x_3) = x_1x_2 + \bar{x}_2x_3 + x_1x_3$$

Figure 9.27*a* shows the modified realization of Fig. 9.22*a* in which the static 1-hazard is eliminated. Furthermore, this network is free of static 0-hazards since the above expression is also its transient disjunctive normal formula and there are no 1-terms containing a pair of complementary literals.

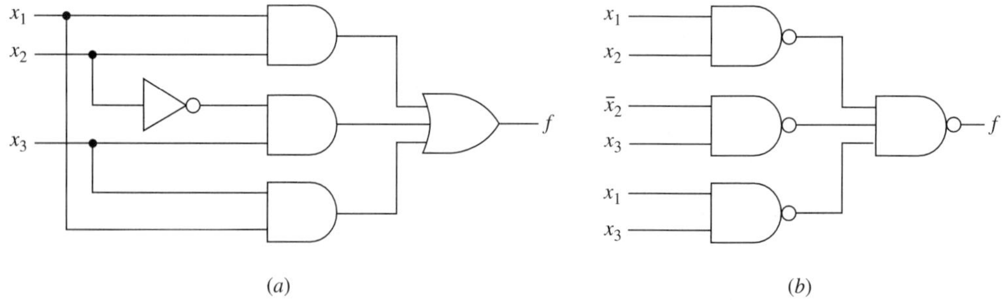

Figure 9.27 Elimination of the static 1-hazard from the networks of Fig. 9.22.

It is interesting to consider the factored forms of the above equation. These are the expressions

$$f(x_1,x_2,x_3) = x_1x_2 + x_3(x_1 + \bar{x}_2)$$

and

$$f(x_1,x_2,x_3) = \bar{x}_2x_3 + x_1(x_2 + x_3)$$

The realizations based on these expressions are also free of both static 0-hazards and static 1-hazards since application of the distributive law to an expression does not cause static hazards to be introduced in a realization. Similarly, static hazards are not introduced into a realization as a consequence of the use of DeMorgan's laws. Thus, the nand-gate realization of Fig. 9.27*b* is free of static hazards.

The network of Fig. 9.23*a* can now be modified so as to eliminate the static 0-hazard. As is evident from Fig. 9.26*b*, this can be done by the inclusion of the sum term $x_1 + x_3$ in the algebraic expression for the realization. The resulting expression is

$$f(x_1,x_2,x_3) = (x_1 + x_2)(\bar{x}_2 + x_3)(x_1 + x_3)$$

The network obtained from this expression is shown in Fig. 9.28*a*. This network is now free of both static 0-hazards and static 1-hazards.

Some modifications are also possible to the above equation and it will still describe realizations that are free of both types of static hazards. In particular, the distributive and DeMorgan's laws may be applied. Thus, the nor-gate realization of Fig. 9.28*b* as well as realizations based on the expressions

$$f(x_1,x_2,x_3) = (x_1 + x_2)(x_3 + x_1\bar{x}_2)$$

and

$$f(x_1,x_2,x_3) = (\bar{x}_2 + x_3)(x_1 + x_2x_3)$$

have this property.

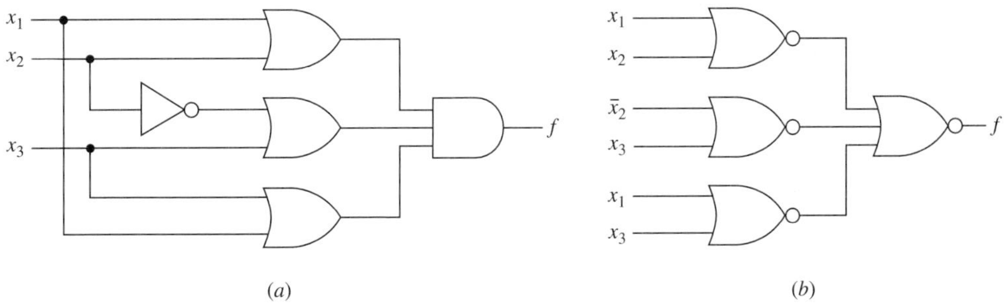

Figure 9.28 Elimination of the static 0-hazard from the networks of Fig. 9.23.

9.9.4 Dynamic Hazards

There is another type of hazard associated with combinational networks, called a *dynamic hazard*, that is responsible for false outputs. These hazards occur when the output of a network is to change between its two logic states, but a momentary false output signal occurs during the transient behavior. Figure 9.29 illustrates dynamic hazards. Formally, a dynamic hazard is defined as a transient change occurring three or more times at an output terminal of a logic network when the output is supposed to change only once during a transition between two input states differing in the value of one variable.

To illustrate a dynamic hazard, consider the gate network shown in Fig. 9.30. The reader can readily check that this network is free from both static 0-hazards and static 1-hazards. Now consider the input states $x_1x_2x_3 = 000$ and $x_1x_2x_3 = 100$. For the first input state, the steady-state output is 0; while for the second input state, the steady-state output is 1. To facilitate the discussion of the transient behavior of this network, assume there are no propagation delays through gates *G*3 and *G*5 and that the propagation delays of the other three gates are such that *G*1 can switch faster than *G*2 and that *G*2 can switch faster than *G*4. When x_1 changes from 0 to 1, the change propagates through gate *G*1 before gate *G*2 with the net effect that the inputs to gate *G*3 are simultaneously 1 and, correspondingly, the network output changes from 0 to 1. Then, when the x_1 change propagates through gate *G*2, the lower input to gate *G*3 becomes 0 and the network output changes back to 0. Finally, when the $x_1 = 1$ signal propagates through gate *G*4, the lower input to gate *G*5 becomes 1 and the network output again changes to 1. It is therefore seen that during the change of the x_1 variable from 0 to 1, the network output appears as shown in Fig. 9.29*a*. In this case, the output undergoes the sequence $0 \rightarrow 1 \rightarrow 0 \rightarrow 1$, which results in three changes when it should have undergone only a single change.

Dynamic hazards are more difficult to detect than static hazards. Since they are capable of producing false outputs, their severity depends upon the devices or systems that may receive them. As indicated previously, false outputs in the combinational logic of asynchronous sequential networks can cause malfunctions. However, combinational logic networks that are designed to be free of static hazards can also be free of dynamic hazards.

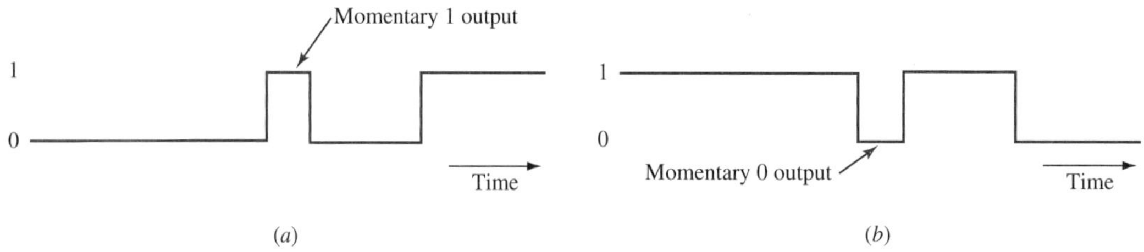

Figure 9.29 Dynamic hazards.

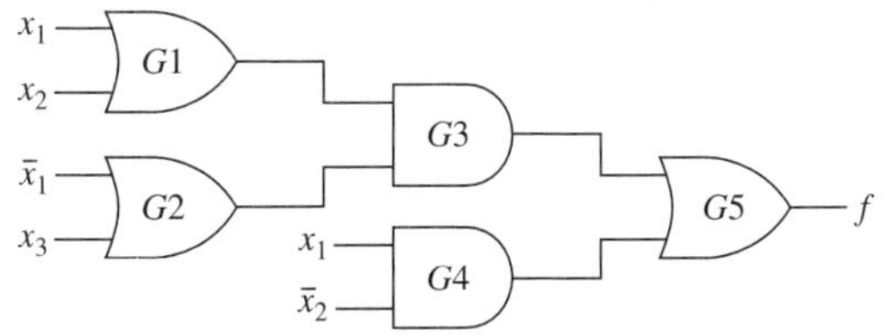

Figure 9.30 An illustration of a dynamic hazard in a gate network.

9.9.5 Hazard-Free Combinational Logic Networks

It can be proved that if a combinational logic network is implemented directly from a disjunctive normal formula (having no product terms containing a variable and its complement) in which additional terms are included so that there are no static 1-hazards, then the network is free from static 0-hazards and dynamic hazards. In a similar manner, if a combinational logic network is implemented directly from a conjunctive normal formula (having no sum terms containing a variable and its complement) in which additional terms are included so that there are no static 0-hazards, then the network is free from static 1-hazards and dynamic hazards. Combinational networks that are free from static and dynamic hazards are said to be *hazard-free.* Thus, direct realizations of disjunctive normal formulas obtained from Karnaugh maps are hazard-free by the inclusion of product terms in which all pairs of adjacent 1-cells appear in a common subcube. Similarly, direct realizations of conjunctive normal formulas obtained from Karnaugh maps are hazard-free if additional sum terms are included in which all pairs of adjacent 0-cells appear in a common subcube. As a result, the networks of Figs. 9.27*a* and 9.28*a* are hazard-free.

Some modifications are permissible to the above hazard-free normal formulas without introducing hazards in the corresponding realization. In particular, the distributive laws and DeMorgan's laws may be applied. Therefore, if these normal formulas are used as the starting point to obtain nand-gate or nor-gate realizations as was previously discussed in Sec. 3.9, then the resulting realizations are also hazard-free. Consequently, the networks of Figs. 9.27*b* and 9.28*b* are hazard-free. Additional levels of logic may also be introduced if they are simply the consequence of the distributive and DeMorgan's laws being applied.

By referring to Fig. 9.17, it can now be concluded that the feedback realization shown in Fig. 9.18 for running Example 9.3 is hazard-free.

9.9.6 Hazards in Asynchronous Networks Involving Latches

It has been pointed out that momentary false signals in asynchronous sequential networks can result in improper operation. For this reason, the combinational logic portion of an asynchronous sequential network should be hazard-free. However, when unclocked flip-flops are incorporated in an asynchronous sequential network, it is possible to relax some of the constraints imposed by a hazard-free realization. To see this, consider first the *SR* latch consisting of two cross-coupled nor-gates. A momentary 1 signal on either the *S* or *R* inputs can cause it to set or reset, respectively. However, a momentary 0 signal on either of these inputs has no effect on the flip-flop state. Therefore, the combinational logic that precedes the input terminals of an *SR* latch does not have to be free of static 1-hazards but must be free of static 0-hazards. This implies that a network realized from a minimal disjunctive normal formula, i.e., a minimal-sum expression, can be used for the combinational logic and that additional terms to eliminate the static 1-hazards are not necessary. Furthermore, two-level networks are always free of dynamic hazards as long as no gate has both a variable and its complement as inputs. As indicated previously, the minimal expressions can also be modified using the distributive laws and DeMorgan's laws without introducing hazards in the realizations.

Similar remarks apply to asynchronous sequential networks that utilize $\overline{S}\,\overline{R}$ latches corresponding to cross-coupled nand-gates. In this case only momentary 0 signals must be avoided. This can be achieved when the logic realization preceding the input terminals of the $\overline{S}\,\overline{R}$ latches is based on the minimal conjunctive normal formulas, i.e., minimal-product expressions.

Figure 9.31*a* shows the general structure for an acceptable realization of each state variable of an asynchronous sequential network when minimal-sum excitation expressions and an *SR* latch (shown as cross-coupled nor-gates) are used. If nor-gates with multiple inputs are available, then it is possible to combine the or-gates in the combinational logic portion of the network and the nor-gates of the latch to form the structure shown in Fig. 9.31*b*. That these two networks are equivalent immediately follows since

$$Q = \overline{[(R_1 + \cdots + R_n) + \overline{Q}]} = \overline{(R_1 + \cdots + R_n + \overline{Q})}$$

and

$$\overline{Q} = \overline{[(S_1 + \cdots + S_m) + Q]} = \overline{(S_1 + \cdots + S_m + Q)}$$

As another variation for an acceptable realization of an asynchronous sequential network, assume minimal-sum set and reset excitation expressions are obtained

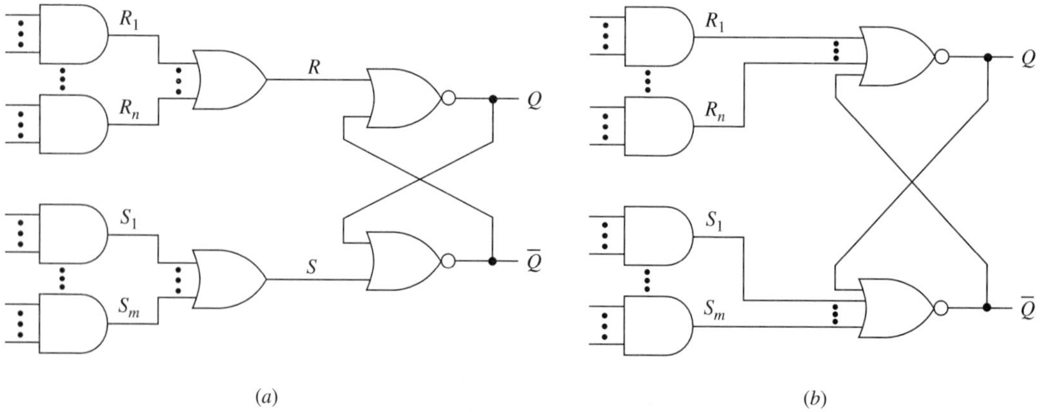

Figure 9.31 *SR* latch realizations of asynchronous networks.

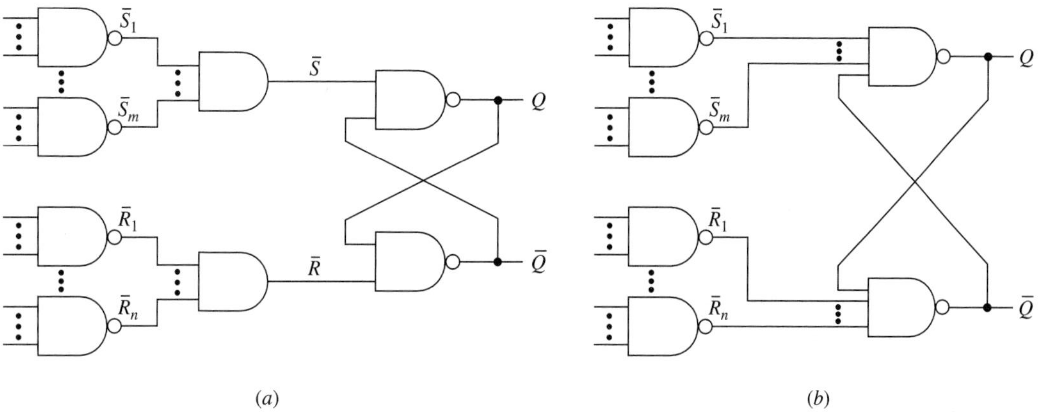

Figure 9.32 $\overline{S}\overline{R}$ latch realizations of asynchronous networks.

in which no term consists of complementary literals and, correspondingly, describe a network free of static 0-hazards. For each state variable the expressions are

$$S = S_1 + \cdots + S_m$$

and

$$R = R_1 + \cdots + R_n$$

Since DeMorgan's law can be applied to expressions without introducing hazards in a realization, the set and reset expressions can be rewritten as

$$\overline{S} = \overline{S}_1 \cdots \overline{S}_m$$

and

$$\overline{R} = \overline{R}_1 \cdots \overline{R}_n$$

These expressions suggest the realization given in Fig. 9.32*a* involving an $\overline{S}\overline{R}$ latch that is shown as cross-coupled nand-gates. By combining the and-gates of the combinational logic portion of the network and the cross-coupled nand-gates, the general structure shown in Fig. 9.32*b* results. Since the networks for S and R are free of static 0-hazards but not necessarily free of static 1-hazards, the complementary networks for $\overline{S}$ and $\overline{R}$ are free of static 1-hazards but not necessarily free of static 0-hazards. Thus, momentary 1-signals may still be present at the $\overline{S}$ and $\overline{R}$ terminals of Fig. 9.32*a*. However, recall that momentary 1 signals to an $\overline{S}\overline{R}$ latch have no effect on the state of the latch.

The duals of each of the networks shown in Figs. 9.31 and 9.32 can also be constructed. Such networks would correspond to acceptable realizations of asynchronous sequential networks based on minimal-product excitation expressions and involving latches.

9.10 ESSENTIAL HAZARDS

Even after avoiding critical races and eliminating static and dynamic hazards, a fundamental-mode asynchronous sequential network may still malfunction. These networks are also subject to still another type of hazard, called the *essential hazard.*

This hazard is the result of the effects of a single input variable change reaching one feedback path before another feedback path. In particular, as a result of a single input variable change, a state variable may also change. It is possible that the effect of this state variable change will propagate through the logic network and initiate the change of another state variable before the original input variable change has had time to propagate through the entire network. That is, some gates may sense the change in the feedback signal, as a result of the input variable change, before sensing the input variable change itself. In such a case, the asynchronous sequential network may become stable in a state other than the one intended. The existence of an essential hazard is embedded in the logical behavior of the asynchronous network and can be detected directly from its flow table. Essential hazards can always be eliminated in a realization by the insertion of sufficient delays in the feedback paths.

9.10.1 Example of an Essential Hazard

For simplicity, a contrived example is used to illustrate an essential hazard. Consider the flow table and transition table shown in Fig. 9.33*a* and *b* for an asynchronous sequential network operating in fundamental mode.* Only the present-state and next-state sections are shown since the output sections are not relevant in the following discussion. A realization that is free of critical races as well as static and dynamic hazards is given in Fig. 9.33*c*. Assume the delay element shown grayed in the lower feedback path does not exist. If the total input state is $(x, y_1 y_2) = (0,00)$, then the network is stable. Ideally, if the input x is changed from 0 to 1, then the output of the lower or-gate changes to 1 and remains at this value

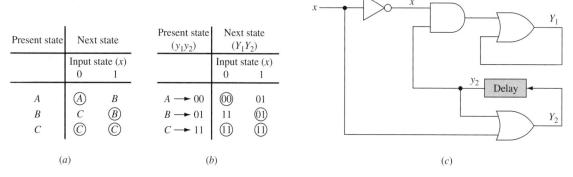

Present state	Next state	
	Input state (x)	
	0	1
A	(A)	B
B	C	(B)
C	(C)	(C)

(*a*)

Present state ($y_1 y_2$)	Next state ($Y_1 Y_2$)	
	Input state (x)	
	0	1
A → 00	(00)	01
B → 01	11	(01)
C → 11	(11)	(11)

(*b*)

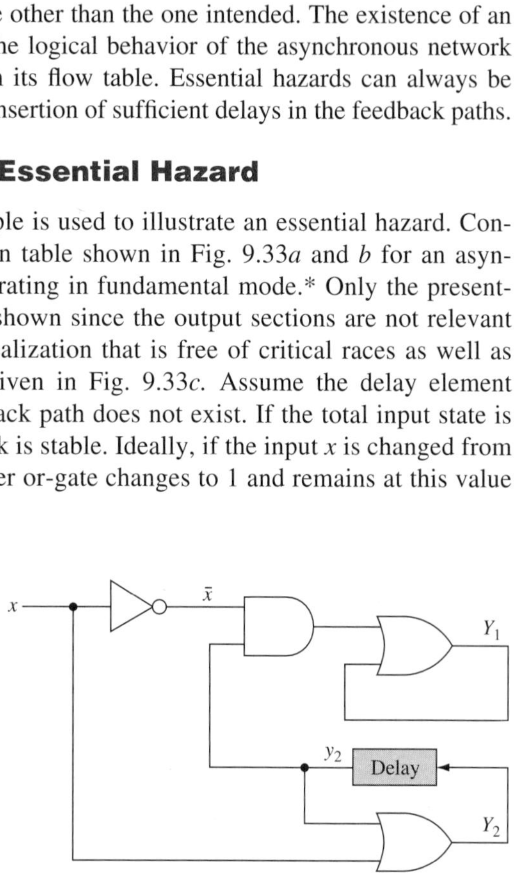

(*c*)

Figure 9.33 Illustrating the effects of an essential hazard. (*a*) Flow table. (*b*) Transition table. (*c*) Logic diagram.

*Although the reader may feel that this flow table may not correspond to a practical asynchronous sequential network, the behavior indicated in this flow table may be embedded in larger flow tables and is the cause of the essential hazard. This is elaborated upon later in this section.

because of the feedback path around the gate. The network then becomes stable under the total input state $(x,y_1y_2) = (1,01)$. This corresponds to stable state Ⓑ in Fig. 9.33*a*.

Now assume that an appreciable propagation delay time is associated with the single not-gate of Fig. 9.33*c*, and that again the stable total input state initially is $(x,y_1y_2) = (0,00)$. When the x input is changed from 0 to 1, y_2 becomes equal to 1 as indicated previously. However, if the change in the x input is delayed through the not-gate so that the $\bar{x}$ input to the and-gate is still 1, then when y_2 becomes 1 (recall it has been assumed that the delay element is not present) there is a 1 output from the and-gate. As a result, the output from the upper or-gate changes from 0 to 1. Furthermore, it remains at this value because of the feedback path around the upper or-gate. When the change in the x signal finally propagates through the not-gate and the and-gate, the output from the and-gate becomes 0. This has no effect on the upper or-gate since its output is locked at 1. The network is now stable under the total input state $(x,y_1y_2) = (1,11)$. This corresponds to stable state Ⓒ in the $x = 1$ column of Fig. 9.33*a*. In view of the delay in the not-gate, the network has not operated as intended since it has become stable in the third row, second column of Fig. 9.33*a* instead of the second row, second column. If sufficient delay is inserted in the feedback loop around the lower or-gate as indicated, then this undesirable behavior is prevented.

The above operation is also describable in terms of an operating point moving about the flow and transition tables shown in Fig. 9.33*a* and *b*. With the operating point at Ⓐ, changing the x input from 0 to 1 should result in the operating point moving to Ⓑ after the value of y_2 changes. However, if the change in x is not reflected to Y_1 before the y_2 change has occurred, then insofar as Y_1 is concerned the operating point has moved straight down to the second row, first column of the flow and transition tables. Since this corresponds to an unstable condition, the value of y_1 changes, and the operating point moves to the third row, first column. As soon as the change in x is reflected to Y_1, the operating point moves to the third row, second column, and a stable condition is maintained.

9.10.2 Detection of Essential Hazards

There are six basic patterns that can appear in the next-state sections of fundamental-mode flow tables under the assumption of a single input-variable change. These patterns are shown in Table 9.28. The two columns L and R denote two input states that differ in the value of one input variable. Certainly, these columns do not necessarily have to appear physically next to each other when the patterns are contained in an actual flow table. The row labels appearing in the basic patterns correspond to those rows that may be involved with the motion of an operating point under the change in the value of a single input variable. In all six cases, assume that the operating point is initially at stable state Ⓐ in the L column. In Table 9.28*a*, when the value of an input variable is changed, there are no changes in the values of the state variables since a stable state appears in the R column for the same row as the initial state. Hence, no essential hazards can occur. In Table 9.28*b* and *c*, upon the change

Table 9.28 Basic flow table patterns for fundamental-mode operation involving a single input-variable change

	L	R
A	Ⓐ	Ⓐ

(*a*)

	L	R
A	Ⓐ	B
B	Ⓑ	Ⓑ

(*b*)

	L	R
A	Ⓐ	B
B	A	Ⓑ

(*c*)

	L	R
A	Ⓐ	B
B	C	Ⓑ
C	Ⓒ	B

(*d*)

	L	R
A	Ⓐ	B
B	C	Ⓑ
C	Ⓒ	Ⓒ

(*e*)

	L	R
A	Ⓐ	B
B	C	Ⓑ
C	Ⓒ	D
D	–	Ⓓ

(*f*)

of the value of the input variable, the operating point moves to the second row. However, independently of whether it is in the first or second column, because of propagation delays, the network eventually becomes stable in the second row, second column. Again these patterns illustrate the nonexistence of essential hazards. Table 9.28*d* also illustrates the nonexistence of an essential hazard. If the operating point gets to the third row in the first column as a result of the propagation delays, then when the input change is finally detected, the operating point moves to the third row, second column, and eventually to stable state Ⓑ in the second row. Table 9.28*e* and *f* illustrates essential hazards. The first of these is the same as Fig. 9.33*a*, which already has been discussed. In Table 9.28*f*,* if the operating point gets to the third row, first column, and the input change is finally detected, then the operating point moves to the third row, second column, and then to the fourth row, second column. Hence, stability may be reached at Ⓓ rather than at Ⓑ as intended.

Formally, an essential hazard is defined in terms of a flow table. The definition actually involves a test for its detection. An essential hazard for a fundamental-mode flow table (and, hence, for a fundamental-mode asynchronous sequential network) corresponds to a stable total input state Ⓢ and a change in the value of a single input variable x, such that with the flow table initially in state Ⓢ, three

*The dash in Table 9.28*f* denotes any entry.

consecutive changes in x result in a state other than the one arrived at after the first change in x.

The present-state and next-state sections of the minimal-row flow table for running Example 9.4 (Table 9.17) are reproduced in Table 9.29*a*. By application of the above definition, it is seen that state $\textcircled{\alpha}$ upon the input change of x_1 corresponds to an essential hazard. In particular, if an operating point is initially in state $\textcircled{\alpha}$ of Table 9.29*a*, then after the first change in x_1 the operating point goes to stable state $\textcircled{\beta}$. Letting the x_1 variable change again, the operating point goes to stable state $\textcircled{\gamma}$. Finally, changing the x_1 variable for a third time, the operating point goes to stable state $\textcircled{\delta}$. Since the stable states reached after the first and third change in x_1 are different, state $\textcircled{\alpha}$ upon the change of the input variable x_1 corresponds to an essential hazard. This is an example of the pattern of Table 9.28*f* embedded in some larger flow table. All the essential hazards appearing in Table 9.29*a* are tabulated in Table 9.29*b*.

As was illustrated for the network shown in Fig. 9.33*c*, the insertion of delay elements can prevent a malfunction due to essential hazards. If an essential hazard exists, then the change in the state variable involved must be delayed long enough to allow the change of the input variable to reach all the network elements that it affects.

Table 9.29 Essential hazards in Example 9.4. (*a*) Portion of Table 9.17. (*b*) Tabulation of essential hazards

Present state	**Next state**			
	Input state (x_1x_2)			
	00	**01**	**10**	**11**
α	β	–	$\textcircled{\alpha}$	–
β	$\textcircled{\beta}$	χ	γ	–
γ	δ	–	$\textcircled{\gamma}$	–
δ	$\textcircled{\delta}$	λ	ρ	–
λ	χ	$\textcircled{\lambda}$	–	–
ρ	$\textcircled{\rho}$	χ	$\textcircled{\rho}$	–
χ	$\textcircled{\chi}$	$\textcircled{\chi}$	α	–

(*a*)

Initial internal state	**Initial input state (x_1x_2)**	**Changing variable**
α	10	x_1
β	00	x_1
γ	10	x_1
δ	00	x_2
χ	00	x_1

(*b*)

Although the above discussion of essential hazards involved asynchronous sequential networks with simple feedback loops, essential hazards can also be present in realizations involving latches since they are inherent in the logical behavior of the network. Again, the elimination of the essential hazards can be achieved by the addition of delays in the feedback paths for the present-state variables.

In conclusion, asynchronous sequential networks are subject to malfunction from several sources. To achieve a design that functions properly, three constraints must be satisfied:

1. A state assignment must be selected which is free of critical races.
2. Additional logic should be incorporated to make the combinational logic hazard-free.
3. Delays may need to be included in feedback paths to eliminate essential hazards.

CHAPTER 9 PROBLEMS

9.1 Analyze the asynchronous sequential network shown in Fig. P9.1 by forming the excitation/transition table, state table, flow table, and flow diagram. The network operates in fundamental mode with the restriction that only one input variable can change at a time.

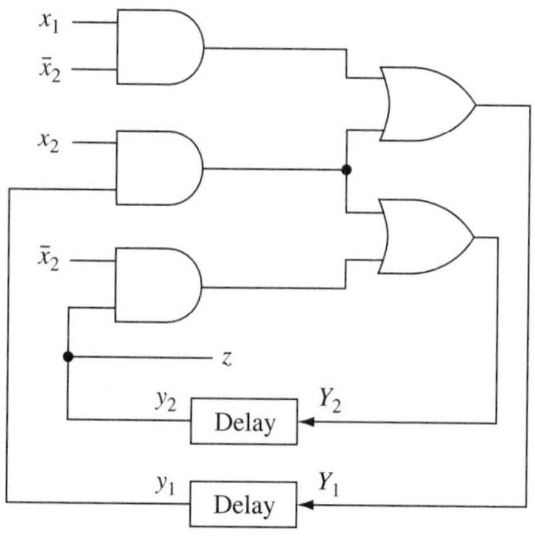

Figure P9.1

9.2 Analyze the asynchronous sequential network shown in Fig. P9.2 by forming the excitation/transition table, state table, flow table, and flow diagram. The network operates in fundamental mode with the restriction that only one input variable can change at a time.

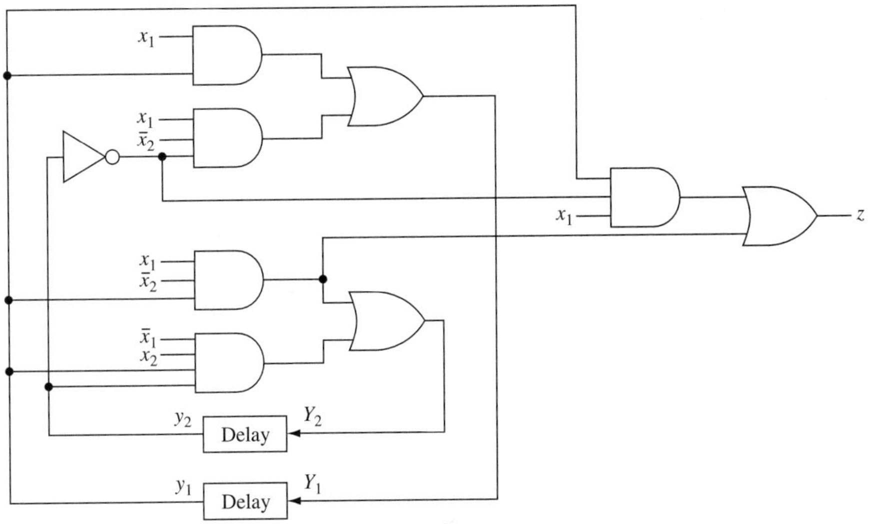

Figure P9.2

9.3 Analyze the asynchronous sequential network shown in Fig. P9.3 by forming the excitation table, transition table, state table, flow table, and flow diagram. The network operates in fundamental mode with the restriction that only one input variable can change at a time.

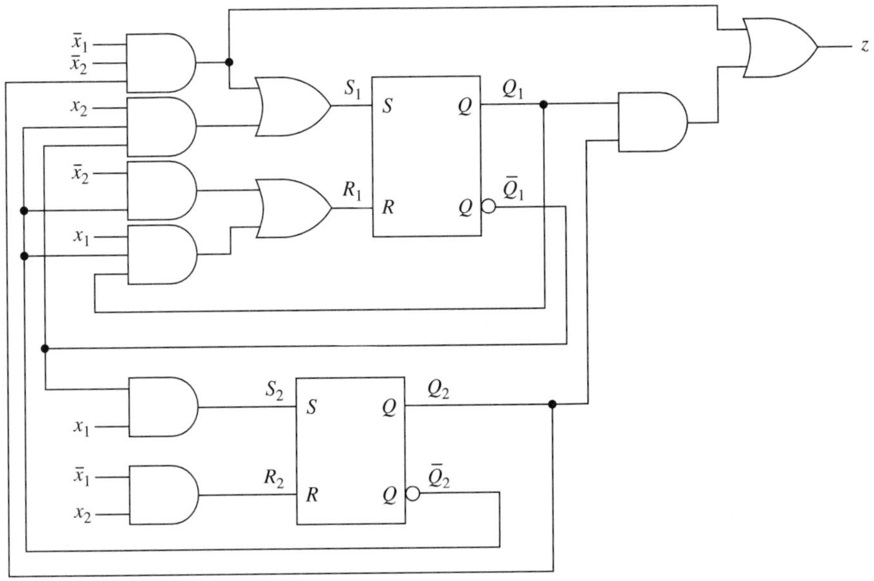

Figure P9.3

9.4 Obtain a primitive flow table and a minimal-row flow table for a fundamental-mode asynchronous sequential network meeting the following requirements:

a. There are two inputs x_1 and x_2 and a single output z.
b. The inputs x_1 and x_2 never change simultaneously.
c. The output is to be 1 only when the values of x_1 and x_2 are both the same and x_2 was the variable that changed value causing x_1 and x_2 to become the same.

9.5 Obtain a primitive flow table and a minimal-row flow table for a fundamental-mode asynchronous sequential network meeting the following requirements:

a. There are two inputs x_1 and x_2 and a single output z.
b. The inputs x_1 and x_2 never change simultaneously.
c. The output is to be the same as x_1 if $x_2 = 1$. However, if $x_2 = 0$, the output is to remain fixed at its last value before x_2 became 0.

9.6 Obtain a primitive flow table and a minimal-row flow table for a fundamental-mode asynchronous sequential network meeting the following requirements:

a. There are two inputs x_1 and x_2 and a single output z.
b. The inputs x_1 and x_2 never change simultaneously.
c. The output is to be 1 every other time the input state is $x_1x_2 = 10$; otherwise, the output is to be 0.

9.7 Obtain a primitive flow table and a minimal-row flow table for a fundamental-mode asynchronous sequential network meeting the following requirements:

a. There are two inputs x_1 and x_2 and a single output z.
b. The inputs x_1 and x_2 never change simultaneously.
c. The output is to be 1 if x_1 was the last input variable to change value. On the other hand, the output is to be 0 if x_2 was the last input variable to change value.

9.8 Obtain a primitive flow table and a minimal-row flow table for a fundamental-mode asynchronous sequential network meeting the following requirements:

a. There are two inputs x_1 and x_2 and two outputs z_1 and z_2.
b. The inputs x_1 and x_2 never change simultaneously.
c. The output is to be a binary number that indicates the number of times x_1 or x_2 has changed value up to three changes. On the fourth change of either x_1 or x_2, the output is to reset to the binary number 00, and the network is to renew its counting. Assume the network starts with input state $x_1x_2 = 00$ having the output $z_1z_2 = 00$.

9.9 Obtain a primitive flow table and a minimal-row flow table for a fundamental-mode asynchronous sequential network meeting the following requirements:

a. There are two inputs x_1 and x_2 and a single output z.

b. An input variable is said to "cycle" if it initially has the value 0, changes to 1, and then returns to 0.

c. The inputs x_1 and x_2 never change or are 1 simultaneously. Therefore, no x_1 cycle overlaps or coincides with an x_2 cycle.

d. The network is to "remember" how many more times x_1 has cycled than x_2. That is, each cycle of the x_1 variable is to cause the network to increase its count by 1, and each cycle of the x_2 variable is to cause the network to decrease its count by 1. However, the network is not to remember above the count of 3. Thus, once the count of 3 is reached, it is to remember this number until the x_2 variable cycles, thereby decreasing the remembered count to 2. Similarly, once the count of zero is reached, it remains at zero until the x_1 variable cycles, thereby increasing the remembered count to 1.

e. An output of 1 is to occur coincident with $x_2 = 1$ if the count remembered by the network is greater than zero.

9.10 In Sec. 6.2, the problem of contact bounce was discussed. Obtain a primitive flow table and a minimal-row flow table for the fundamental-mode asynchronous contact debouncer network shown in Fig. P9.10. The output is to be $z_1z_2 = 10$ when the switch is in position *A* and is to remain at $z_1z_2 = 10$ until the center contact first reaches position *B*. When the switch is in position *B*, the output is to be $z_1z_2 = 01$ and remain at $z_1z_2 = 01$ until the center contact first reaches position *A*. Assume that while the center contact bounces, it does not return to its initial position; i.e., the switch is either open or in its new desired position.

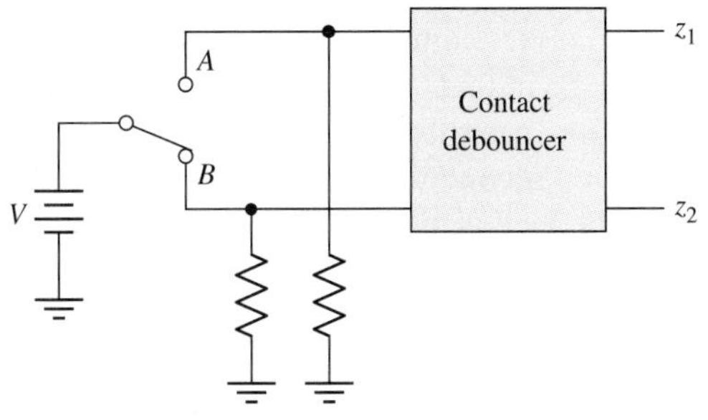

Figure P9.10

9.11 Figure P9.11 shows a circular disk, in which one-half is opaque and the other half is transparent, connected to the shaft of a motor. Two light beams and photocells are separated by 90°. When a light beam shines through the transparent material and strikes a photocell, there is an output signal from the photocell. When a light beam is stopped by the opaque material, there is no output signal from the photocell. For the case shown in Fig. P9.11, the signals entering the logic network are $x_1 = 1$ and $x_2 = 0$. Obtain a primitive flow table and a minimal-row flow table for the fundamental-mode asynchronous sequential logic network in which $z = 1$ when the motor shaft is rotating clockwise and $z = 0$ when the motor shaft is rotating counterclockwise. When the direction of rotation is changed, the output signal should change as soon as possible, i.e., within one-quarter of a revolution.

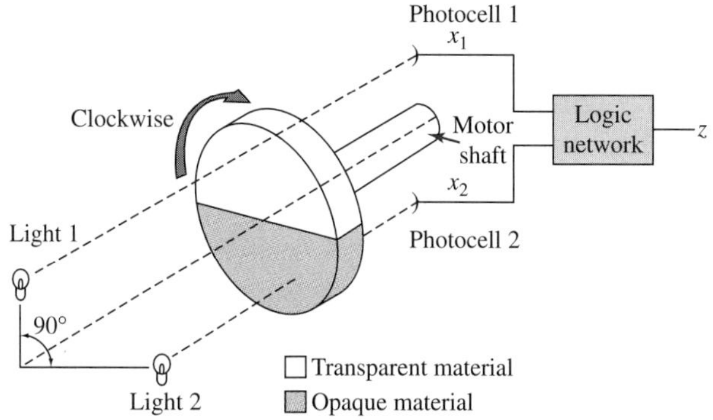

Figure P9.11

9.12 Obtain a primitive flow table and a minimal-row flow table for a fundamental-mode asynchronous sequential network that operates a combination lock. The network is controlled by two keys, K_1 and K_2, each having two positions. Let $K_i = 0$ denote the first position and $K_i = 1$ denote the second position. A single output $z = 1$ is used to open the lock when the correct combination is applied. To open the lock, both keys must initially be in their first positions. Then key K_2 must be placed in its second position, returned to its first position, and then placed in its second position for a second time. Finally, upon placing key K_1 in its second position, the lock is to open. After the lock has been opened, placing either key in its first position allows it to be locked again ($z = 0$). If a mistake is made in working the combination for the lock, then the combination may be started again only after both keys are placed in their first positions. Assume the position of only one key is changed at a time.

9.13 Obtain a primitive flow table and a minimal-row flow table for a fundamental-mode asynchronous sequential network that behaves like a delay line. In particular, the network is to have two inputs x_1 and x_2 and two outputs z_1 and z_2. The outputs at any time are to be the same as the last previous input state. Assume that the inputs x_1 and x_2 never change simultaneously.

9.14 Figure P9.14 shows a test-track setup for measuring the elapsed time of a single run of a car. On the first lap of the track, upon breaking the first light beam, a reset signal is applied to the timer. The signal remains until the car just passes the first photocell, at which time no signals are applied to the timer. On the second lap of the track, upon breaking the first light beam, the timer is actuated and remains actuated until the second light beam is broken. Obtain a primitive flow table and a reduced flow table for the fundamental-mode asynchronous sequential logic network.

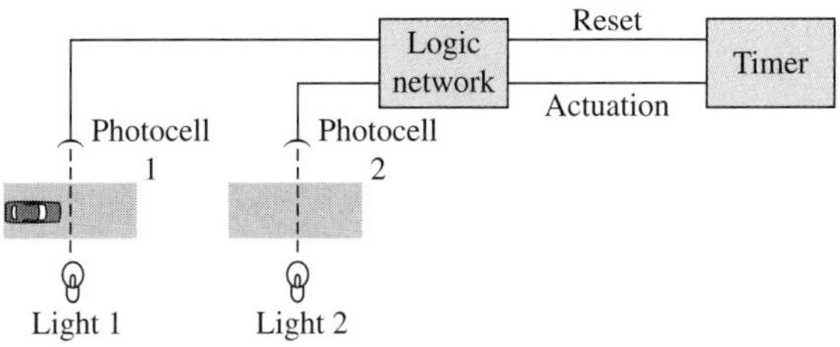

Figure P9.14

9.15 The primitive flow table shown in Table P9.15 is for a fundamental-mode asynchronous sequential network. (*a*) Determine its minimal-row version using the procedure given in Sec. 9.5. (*b*) Determine its minimal-row version using the procedure given in Sec. 9.6.

Table P9.15

Present state	Next state				Output (z)			
	Input state (x_1x_2) 00	01	10	11	Input state (x_1x_2) 00	01	10	11
A	(A)	B	E	–	0	–	–	–
B	A	(B)	–	H	–	1	–	–
C	G	–	(C)	I	–	–	0	–
D	(D)	F	C	–	1	–	–	–
E	A	–	(E)	I	–	–	0	–
F	D	(F)	–	H	–	1	–	–
G	(G)	B	C	–	0	–	–	–
H	–	F	C	(H)	–	–	–	0
I	–	B	E	(I)	–	–	–	0

9.16 For Table 9.12, it was seen in Sec. 9.5 that another minimal collection of compatible sets consisted of $\{A,B,D,H\}$, $\{B,E,H,I\}$, $\{E,F\}$, and $\{C,G\}$. Using this collection, determine the minimal-row flow table.

9.17 Each of the reduced flow tables shown in Table P9.17 is for a fundamental-mode asynchronous sequential network. For each table, determine a state assignment involving a minimum number of variables that allows a realization free of critical races. Then, construct the corresponding transition table. Assign outputs where necessary such that there is at most a single output change during the time the network is unstable. In all cases it is assumed that the inputs x_1 and x_2 never change simultaneously. Finally, obtain the minimal-sum expressions for realizations using just feedback loops and realizations using *SR* latches.

Table P9.17

Present state	Next state				Output (z)			
	Input state (x_1x_2)				Input state (x_1x_2)			
	00	01	10	11	00	01	10	11
A	(*A*)	(*A*)	*D*	(*A*)	0	0	–	0
B	(*B*)	*A*	*C*	–	1	–	–	–
C	*B*	(*C*)	(*C*)	(*C*)	–	1	1	1
D	*A*	–	(*D*)	*C*	–	–	0	–

(*a*)

Present state	Next state				Output (z)			
	Input state (x_1x_2)				Input state (x_1x_2)			
	00	01	10	11	00	01	10	11
A	(*A*)	(*A*)	*B*	*D*	0	0	–	–
B	(*B*)	*D*	(*B*)	*D*	1	–	1	–
C	*A*	*A*	(*C*)	(*C*)	–	–	0	0
D	*A*	(*D*)	*C*	(*D*)	–	1	–	1

(*b*)

Present state	Next state				Output (z)			
	Input state (x_1x_2)				Input state (x_1x_2)			
	00	01	10	11	00	01	10	11
A	(*A*)	*B*	*C*	(*A*)	0	–	–	0
B	(*B*)	(*B*)	*D*	*C*	1	0	–	–
C	*B*	(*C*)	(*C*)	(*C*)	–	1	0	1
D	*A*	–	(*D*)	*C*	–	–	1	–

(*c*)

9.18 The reduced flow table shown in Table P9.18 is for a fundamental-mode asynchronous sequential network. Determine a state assignment involving a minimum number of variables that allows a realization free of critical races. Construct the corresponding transition table. Assign outputs where necessary such that there is at most a single output change during the time the network is unstable. Assume that the inputs x_1 and x_2 never change or are 1 simultaneously.

Table P9.18

Present state	Next state				Output (z)			
	Input state (x_1x_2)				Input state (x_1x_2)			
	00	01	10	11	00	01	10	11
A	(*A*)	*B*	(*A*)	–	0	–	0	–
B	*C*	(*B*)	(*B*)	–	–	0	1	–
C	(*C*)	*D*	*G*	–	0	–	–	–
D	*E*	(*D*)	(*D*)	–	–	0	1	–
E	(*E*)	*F*	*B*	–	0	–	–	–
F	(*F*)	(*F*)	*D*	–	0	0	–	–
G	*A*	–	(*G*)	–	–	–	1	–

9.19 The reduced flow table shown in Table P9.19 is for a fundamental-mode asynchronous sequential network. Using the universal multiple-row state assignment given in Fig. 9.16, construct the corresponding expanded flow table and transition table. Assign outputs where necessary such that there is at most a single output change during the time the network is unstable. Assume that the inputs x_1 and x_2 never change simultaneously.

Table P9.19

Present state	Next state				Output (z)			
	Input state (x_1x_2)				Input state (x_1x_2)			
	00	01	10	11	00	01	10	11
A	(*A*)	*B*	(*A*)	*D*	1	–	0	–
B	*D*	(*B*)	(*B*)	*C*	–	0	1	–
C	*A*	(*C*)	(*C*)	(*C*)	–	1	1	0
D	(*D*)	*C*	*A*	(*D*)	0	–	–	1

9.20 Figure P9.20 gives a universal shared-row state assignment involving four state variables that can be used for any flow table having from five to eight states. In this figure, the eight states are designated by the letters *a* to *h*. Since four state variables are involved, eight of the cells in the given state-assignment map are blank and are used in the transition between two lettered states. That is, it is possible to go between any two lettered cells via a series of single variable changes using the blank cells without going through any third lettered cell. Apply this state assignment to the flow table of Table P9.18 and obtain the corresponding transition table. So that no output changes more than once during the transitions, assign the outputs for the unstable entries to the value of the stable state that is entered.

y_1y_2 \ y_3y_4	00	01	11	10
00	a	b		
01			c	d
11	e	f		
10			g	h

Figure P9.20

9.21 In Table 9.25, the outputs for total input states $(x_1x_2,y_1y_2y_3y_4) = (00,0010)$ and $(x_1x_2,y_1y_2y_3y_4) = (00,1010)$ were assigned as 0's to avoid momentary false outputs. Can unspecified output assignments be made to either of these two total input states while still avoiding momentary false outputs?

9.22 The reduced flow table shown in Table P9.19 is for a fundamental-mode asynchronous sequential network. Using the one-hot method, construct the corresponding transition table. So that no output changes more than once during the transitions, assign the outputs for the unstable entries to the value of the stable state that is entered.

9.23 The internal design of a clocked flip-flop can be regarded as an asynchronous sequential network. Figure P9.23 gives the symbol for a negative edge-triggered T flip-flop. When $T = 1$ and C changes from 1 to 0, i.e., the negative edge, the state of the flip-flop changes. Under all other input conditions, the output does not change. Assuming T and C do not change

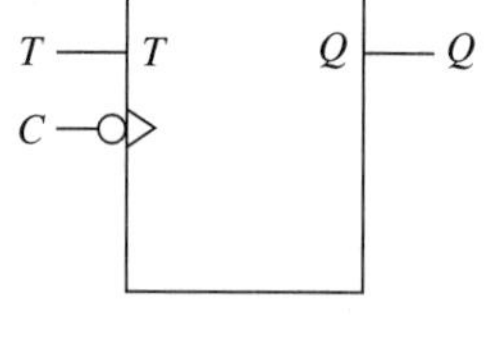

Figure P9.23

simultaneously, design the flip-flop with inputs T and C and output Q by first forming a primitive flow table, reducing it, and making an appropriate state assignment free of critical races. Then, obtain the minimal-sum expressions for a realization using just feedback loops and a realization using SR latches.

9.24 For the logic diagram of Fig. 9.24, assume the propagation delay through each gate is the same and that the network is in the total input state $(x_1x_2,y) = (11,1)$. Sketch the timing waveforms of x_2 and the outputs of the four gates when the x_2 input is changed to 0. Comment on the network behavior.

9.25 For each of the gate networks shown in Fig. P9.25, determine all the static 1-hazards and static 0-hazards. Redesign each network to be hazard-free and having the same output gate as in the figure.

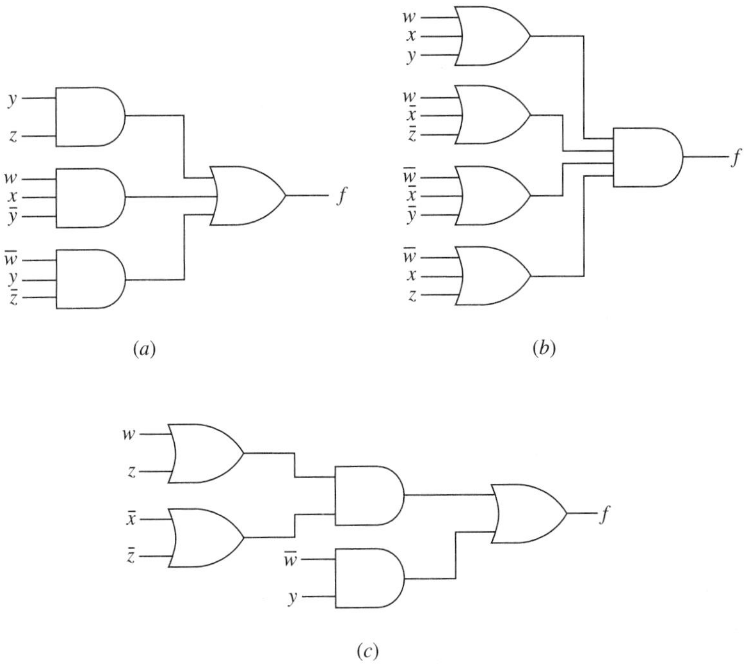

Figure P9.25

9.26 For the gate network of Fig. 9.30, determine the transient disjunctive and conjunctive normal formulas and show that the network is free of static hazards.

9.27 Modify each of the designs obtained in Problem 9.17 with just feedback loops so as to avoid static hazards.

9.28 Using the transition table for Example 9.4 given in Table 9.22, complete the design with simple feedback loops by obtaining the minimal-sum expressions for the realization. Include any terms needed to avoid static hazards.

9.29 For each of the flow tables shown in Table P9.29, assume that the value of only one input variable can change at a time. List all the essential hazards by stating the initial internal states, the initial input states, and the changing variables.

Table P9.29

Present state	Next state			
	Input state (x_1x_2)			
	00	01	10	11
A	(A)	B	B	–
B	A	(B)	(B)	C
C	–	D	B	(C)
D	A	(D)	B	(D)

(*a*)

Present state	Next state			
	Input state (x_1x_2)			
	00	01	10	11
A	(A)	(A)	C	B
B	C	(B)	C	(B)
C	(C)	A	(C)	D
D	A	A	(D)	(D)

(*b*)

APPENDIX A

Digital Circuits

In Chapter 3, logic gates were introduced to perform the Boolean operations in a combinational logic network. At that time attention was directed to the interconnections of the logic gates as opposed to the circuit details of the gates themselves. Actually there are many different circuit designs for the logic gates. These designs are dependent upon the components and circuit technology used.

There are several ways of measuring the quality of digital circuits. Section 3.10 included discussions of propagation delays, fan-out, noise margin, and power dissipation. Propagation delays are the finite times it takes for circuits to respond to changes at their inputs. To achieve high operating speeds, low propagation delay times are desirable. As is seen in this appendix, the number of gates connected to a gate output, i.e., the fan-out, is also a limiting factor in overall system performance. Induced noise from the environment in which a circuit operates can cause circuits to respond incorrectly. The immunity of a circuit to induced noise is measured by the noise margin. Finally, power is consumed during circuit operation. Circuit designs requiring low power are constantly being sought since they have less heat dissipation and allow for smaller systems.

Depending upon the circuit components and technology used, different tradeoffs are achieved between propagation delays, fan-out, noise margins, and power dissipation. A class of digital circuits having a common circuit technology and general structure is called a *logic family*. This appendix emphasizes three logic families: *transistor-transistor logic* (TTL), *emitter-coupled logic* (ECL), and *complementary metal-oxide semiconductor logic* (CMOS logic). Within each logic family, several circuit variations exist. These are referred to as its *logic series*. The circuits within the series have, in addition to a specific circuit technology and structure, some common distinctive characteristics. For example, within the TTL logic family there are several logic series, such as 54/74 standard TTL, Schottky TTL, advanced Schottky TTL, low-power Schottky TTL, and advanced low-power Schottky TTL. Determining an appropriate logic family and series for a given application is dependent upon what operating requirements must be met by the system.

It is not the intention of this appendix to delve into the details of circuit design, but rather to provide a general understanding of some logic families, their properties, and their operation. In order to do this, it is assumed that the reader has a knowledge of Ohm's law, Kirchhoff's current and voltage laws, and how to analyze linear circuits. The logic families to be studied utilize semiconductor diodes, bipolar junction transistors, and field-effect transistors as their primary components. For the purpose of the analysis of the different gate circuits, a set of simple models are introduced for these components. These models provide a first-order approximation of the component behavior that is adequate for the purpose of explaining the general operation of the digital circuits.

Since the digital circuits to be discussed are to perform logic functions, the input and output signals of the circuits are at one of two values so that a logic-1 is assigned to one signal value and a logic-0 to the other. As was discussed in Chapter 3, a logic value is actually assigned to a range of signal values. However, for simplicity in discussion, a nominal value of the signal is used as its true value.

Finally, in the course of studying digital circuits, there are many occasions to refer to the voltages at various points within a circuit. Unless indicated otherwise, e.g., by double subscripts or arrows, it is assumed the voltage at a point is stated with respect to ground. ■

A.1 THE *pn* JUNCTION SEMICONDUCTOR DIODE

Certain materials have a conductivity, i.e., capability of conducting current, between that of insulators and conductors. These materials are called (intrinsic) *semiconductors*. The two most common semiconductor materials are silicon and germanium. Within these materials there are two mechanisms for the conduction of current—*holes*, which are positive charge carriers, and *electrons*, which are negative charge carriers. If impurities are added to the (intrinsic) semiconductor material, called *dopants*, then the balance between the number of holes and electrons can be changed and controlled. The result is a material having an increased conductivity. Depending upon the type of impurity, the doped semiconductor material is known as *p-type*, when positive charge carriers predominate, or *n-type*, when negative charge carriers predominate.

A.1.1 Semiconductor Diode Behavior

The semiconductor diode is a two-terminal device fabricated so that there is an abrupt transition between regions of *p*-type semiconductor material and *n*-type semiconductor material. The *p*-type material forms the *anode* of the diode; while the *n*-type forms its *cathode*. The free charge carriers near the junction in each region are now capable of crossing the junction. Since the *p*-type material has free positive charge carriers, when they move to the *n* side of the boundary a net positive charge occurs at that side of the boundary. Similarly, when free negative charge carriers in the *n*-type material move to the *p* side, they cause a net negative charge to occur there. The result of this motion is an electrostatic potential being built across the *pn* junction with the *n* side positive with respect to the *p* side. An equilibrium condition in which no further net charge accumulates in each region eventually results since the polarity of the electrostatic potential is such as to oppose the flow of positive charge carriers from the *p* side to the *n* side and the flow of negative charge carriers from the *n* side to the *p* side. If current is to flow through the diode, then external energy must be supplied to overcome the effect of the electrostatic potential across the junction.

Now assume an external voltage source is placed across the diode such that the anode is made positive with respect to the cathode. In this case, the diode is said to be *forward biased.** For external voltages less than the opposing electrostatic potential of the *pn* junction, little current flows. However, for external voltages greater than the electrostatic potential of the *pn* junction, the polarity of the external voltage source is such as to overcome the effect of the opposing electrostatic potential. The holes and electrons are now able to readily cross the *pn* junction in opposite directions, resulting in a large current flowing through the device. This condition is referred to as the *conducting state*, or *on state*, of the diode. The voltage at which current starts to flow readily is referred to as the *threshold voltage* of the diode.

On the other hand, if an external voltage source is placed across the diode such that the anode is made negative with respect to the cathode, then the diode is said to be *reverse biased*. In this case the polarity of the external voltage source is such as to enhance the electrostatic potential of the junction and thereby further inhibit the flow of charge carriers. Thus, essentially no current flows through the diode. This condition is referred to as the *cutoff state*, or *off state*, of the diode.

Although the above discussion is an oversimplified analysis of the behavior of a *pn* junction and the semiconductor diode, some general conclusions can still be made. A diode acts as a switch to current since it offers a low resistance to the flow of current when it is forward biased, thus allowing current to flow easily, and offers a high resistance to current when it is reverse biased. Furthermore, because of the electrostatic potential of the junction, the diode must be forward biased by some amount corresponding to the threshold voltage before it readily conducts. Figure A.1 shows a physical representation of a diode and its symbol. The current-voltage (*I-V*) characteristic curve of a typical semiconductor diode is shown in Fig. A.2.

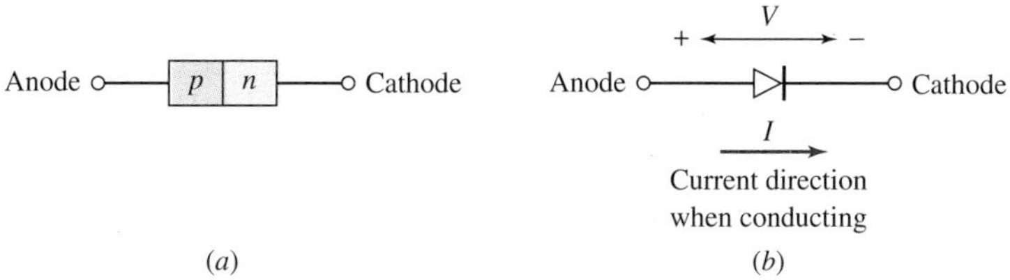

Figure A.1 The *pn* junction semiconductor diode. (*a*) Physical representation. (*b*) Symbol.

*It is helpful to note that forward bias corresponds to a relatively positive voltage on the *p*-type material and a relatively negative voltage on the *n*-type material.

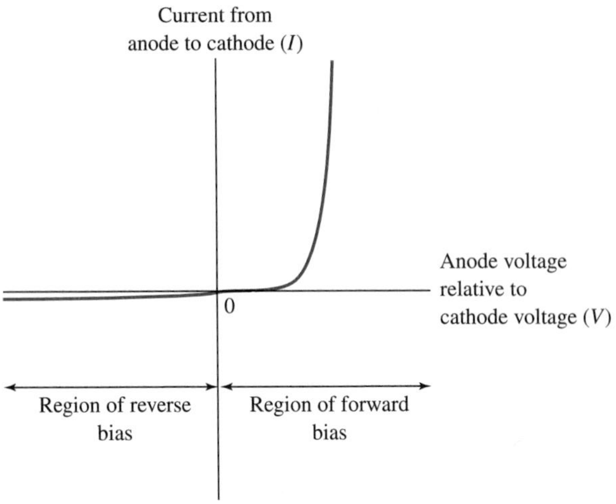

Figure A.2 *I-V* characteristic curve of a *pn* junction semiconductor diode.

A.1.2 Semiconductor Diode Models

The characteristic curve of Fig. A.2 shows the fact that a diode readily conducts current in only one direction. The slight negative current that flows when it is reverse biased is called the *reverse saturation current*. Furthermore, appreciable forward current starts to flow at some (ill-defined) forward-biased threshold voltage. Once conducting, the magnitude of the forward current is strongly determined by external circuit resistances. In the case of silicon semiconductor material, the threshold voltage is on the order of 0.65 V and the fully on voltage drop across the diode is about 0.75 V. An analytical expression that describes the behavior of a theoretical diode is

$$I = I_s\,(e^{qV/nkT} - 1)$$

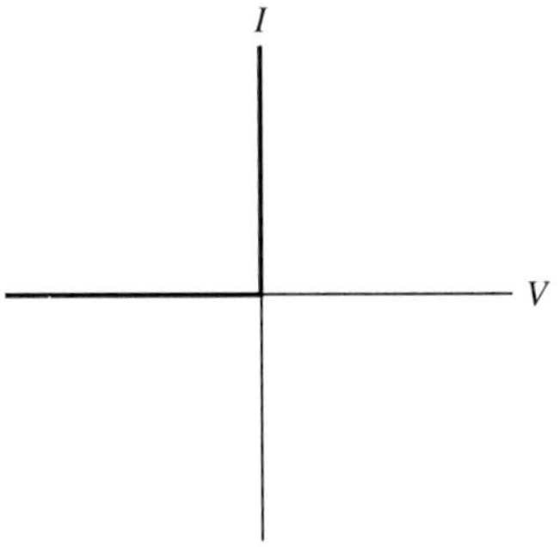

Figure A.3 *I-V* characteristic curve of the ideal diode.

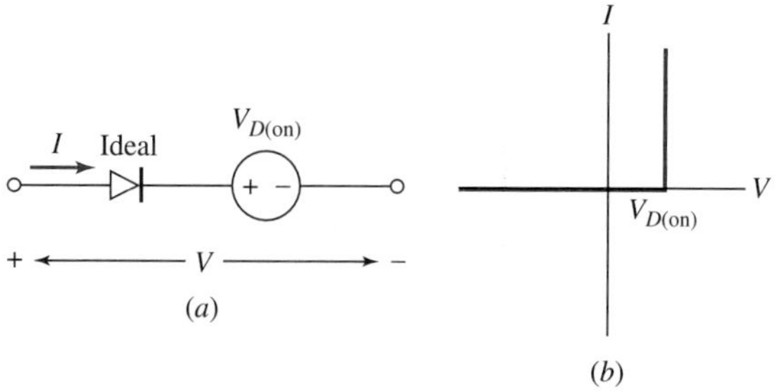

Figure A.4 A diode model. (*a*) Circuit equivalent. (*b*) *I-V* characteristic curve.

where I is the current through the diode, I_s is the reverse saturation current, V is the drop across the diode, q is the charge of an electron (1.602×10^{-19} C), n is a constant depending on the material and the physical structure of the diode, k is Boltzmann's constant (1.38×10^{-23} J/K), and T is the absolute temperature (in degrees Kelvin). The theoretical diode equation very closely fits the actual diode characteristic curve.

For the analysis of digital circuits it is convenient to use a piecewise-linear model of the diode characteristic curve. An *ideal diode* is one whose *I-V* characteristic is as shown in Fig. A.3. It acts as a perfect current switch since it only allows current to flow through it when it is forward biased. Furthermore, there is no voltage drop across an ideal diode when it is conducting. Thus, it appears as a closed, or short, circuit when forward biased and as an open circuit when reverse biased.

Although the ideal diode can serve as a model of an actual diode, a better model is shown in Fig. A.4. Here a voltage source is placed in series with the ideal diode. This model considers the effect of the drop across the diode when it is conducting, $V_{D(\text{on})}$, and emphasizes the necessity of an applied voltage greater than the threshold voltage of the *pn* junction to allow current to flow. Thus, for applied voltages less than $V_{D(\text{on})}$, zero current is assumed to flow; while the drop across the diode is constant for any value of forward current. The value of the forward current is determined by resistances and voltage sources external to the diode. Unless otherwise stated, this model for the semiconductor diode with $V_{D(\text{on})}$ equal to 0.7 V is used in future discussions.

A.2 DIODE LOGIC

From the study of Boolean algebra and logic design, it was seen that and-gates and or-gates are fundamental logic elements. At this time it is shown how diodes are used to construct these gates. Although the logic circuits discussed later in this appendix are far superior to the simple circuits of this section, the study of diode logic provides for a preliminary understanding of digital circuits upon which to build.

A.2.1 The Diode And-Gate

Consider the circuit of Fig. A.5*a*. Assume that a supply voltage V_+ is applied to the resistor of this circuit, and that the inputs are restricted to the voltages V_0 and V_1 where $V_+ > V_1 > V_0$.* When each input has V_0 volts applied, both diodes are forward biased as a result of the supply voltage V_+. If it is assumed that the diodes are ideal, then they conduct and have no voltage drops across them. The result is that the circuit output, x_0, must also be V_0 volts. Actually, the voltage at the output is $V_0 + V_{D(\text{on})}$ volts, but for simplicity of discussion the ideal diode assumption is used in this section.†

Next assume one of the inputs, say, x_1, is at V_0 volts and the other, x_2, is at V_1 volts. In this case, diode D_1 is forward biased and hence conducts, causing the output to become V_0 volts. Diode D_2, on the other hand, is reverse biased, thereby in the cutoff state, since its anode is at V_0 volts as a consequence of diode D_1 conducting and its cathode is at the assumed input of V_1 volts. Finally, if both diodes have V_1 volts applied, then again they both conduct since, with $V_+ > V_1$, the diodes are forward biased. Figure A.5*b* summarizes the output of the circuit for all the possible input voltage combinations.

Since the input and output voltages of the circuit can only be V_0 and V_1, it is possible to assign logic-0 to one of these voltages and logic-1 to the other. When the relatively more positive voltage is assigned a logic-1 and the relatively more negative voltage is assigned a logic-0, it is said that *positive logic* is being used. Thus, if V_0 in Fig. A.5*b* is replaced by the logic symbol 0 and V_1 by the logic symbol 1, then the table of Fig. A.5*c* results. It is seen that this is precisely the definition of the and-operation that was introduced in Chapter 3; i.e., $x_0 = x_1x_2$. Hence, the circuit of Fig. A.5*a* is a physical realization of the and-operation and is consequently called

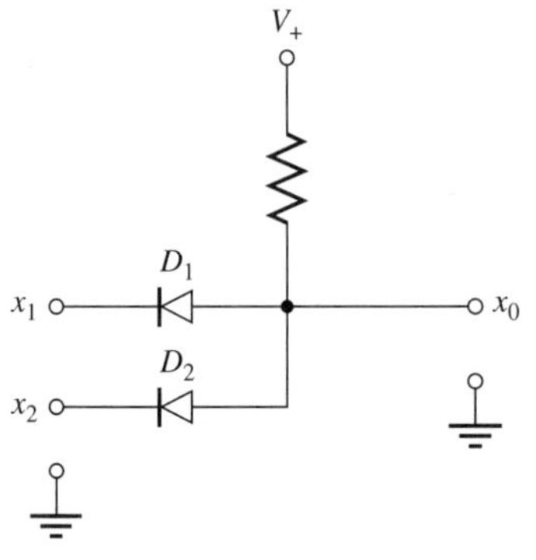

(*a*)

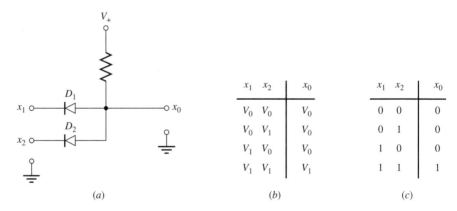

x_1	x_2	x_0
V_0	V_0	V_0
V_0	V_1	V_0
V_1	V_0	V_0
V_1	V_1	V_1

(*b*)

x_1	x_2	x_0
0	0	0
0	1	0
1	0	0
1	1	1

(*c*)

Figure A.5 Two-input diode and-gate and its terminal characteristics where $V_+ > V_1 > V_0$. (*a*) Circuit. (*b*) Voltage characteristic assuming ideal diodes. (*c*) Logic characteristic.

*By convention, these voltages are stated with repect to ground.

†The ideal-diode assumption is justifiable if $V_0 >> V_{D(\text{on})}$.

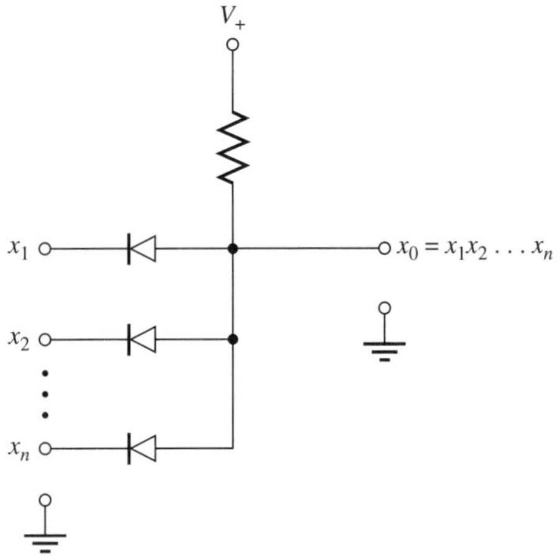

Figure A.6 General diode and-gate.

an *and-gate*. Occasionally, this gate is referred to as a *positive and-gate* to emphasize the use of the positive-logic assignment.

If additional diodes are added to the circuit of Fig. A.5*a*, then the circuit shown in Fig. A.6 results. In this circuit, the output voltage is V_1 only when all the input voltages are at V_1; otherwise, the output voltage is V_0. Hence, this is an n-input and-gate. Again, the output voltages are a few tenths of a volt above those specified since ideal diodes are being assumed.

A.2.2 The Diode Or-Gate

Reversing the diodes of Fig. A.5*a* and applying a supply voltage V_- to the resistor results in the circuit shown in Fig. A.7*a*. As before, let the inputs to this circuit be restricted to the two voltages V_0 and V_1 and assume $V_- < V_0 < V_1$. Furthermore, for

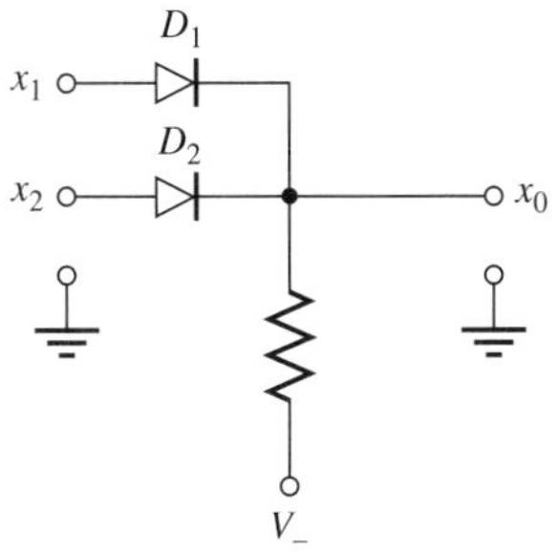

(*a*)

x_1	x_2	x_0
V_0	V_0	V_0
V_0	V_1	V_1
V_1	V_0	V_1
V_1	V_1	V_1

(*b*)

x_1	x_2	x_0
0	0	0
0	1	1
1	0	1
1	1	1

(*c*)

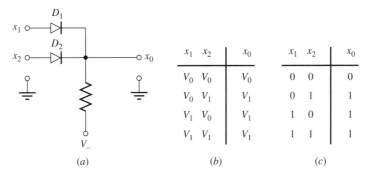

Figure A.7 Two-input diode or-gate and its terminal characteristics where $V_- < V_0 < V_1$. (*a*) Circuit. (*b*) Voltage characteristic assuming ideal diodes. (*c*) Logic characteristic.

simplicity, also assume the diodes are ideal. If both inputs have the same voltage applied, say, V_0 volts, then both diodes are forward biased, as a result of the supply voltage V_-, causing the output x_0 to become V_0 volts. Actually, the output is $V_0 - V_{D(\text{on})}$ volts if the ideal diode assumption is removed. Similarly, if both inputs have the voltage V_1 applied, then again both diodes conduct. This causes the output to be V_1 volts. Now consider the situation in which the x_1 input is V_0 volts and the x_2 input is V_1 volts. Since diode D_2 is forward biased, it conducts, clamping the output to V_1 volts. This, in turn, causes diode D_1 to become reverse biased since its anode is at V_0 volts and its cathode is at V_1 volts. Finally, in the case of the x_1 input being V_1 volts and the x_2 input being V_0 volts, diode D_1 conducts and clamps the output to V_1 volts; while diode D_2 is in its cutoff state. These results are summarized in Fig. A.7*b*.

Again using the concept of positive logic, the V_0 entries in Fig. A.7*b* can be replaced by the logic symbol 0 and the V_1 entries by the logic symbol 1. This results in the table of Fig. A.7*c*. It is seen that this is the definition of the or-operation, i.e., $x_0 = x_1 + x_2$. Hence, this circuit is called an *or-gate* or, when emphasizing the positive-logic assignment, a *positive or-gate*.

As in the case of the and-gate, additional diodes can be added to the circuit of Fig. A.7*a* to form the realization of an *n*-input diode or-gate. This is shown in Fig. A.8. The gate of Fig. A.8 has an output of V_0 volts only if all its inputs are V_0 volts; otherwise, the output is V_1 volts. If the ideal diode assumption is removed, then the output voltages are $V_{D(\text{on})}$ volts below those specified.

A.2.3 Negative Logic

The concept of positive logic was used in determining the logic behavior of the diode gates. Alternately, the relatively positive voltage can be associated with logic-0; while the relatively negative voltage is associated with logic-1. This is referred to as *negative logic*. Under this assignment, the positive and-gate of Fig. A.5*a* becomes a negative or-gate, and the positive or-gate of Fig. A.7*a* becomes a negative and-gate. Unless stated otherwise, the positive-logic convention is always assumed in this appendix.

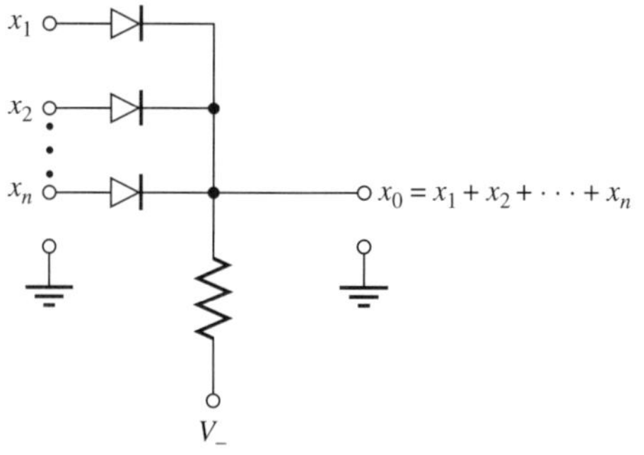

Figure A.8 General diode or-gate.

A.3 THE BIPOLAR JUNCTION TRANSISTOR

The basic bipolar junction transistor is a three-terminal semiconductor device. The terminals are called the *base*, *emitter*, and *collector*. There are two types of bipolar junction transistors—the *npn* and the *pnp*. Both types are fabricated from a single crystal of pure silicon or germanium semiconductor material in which suitable impurities are added to form the three regions. In the case of the *npn* bipolar junction transistor, a very thin layer of *p*-type semiconductor material is sandwiched between two layers of *n*-type material. The *p*-type material forms the base of the transistor, while the two layers of *n*-type material are used for the collector and emitter. On the other hand, a *pnp* bipolar junction transistor has *n*-type semiconductor material for the base sandwiched between two layers of *p*-type material, one layer for the collector and the other for the emitter. Figure A.9 shows the symbols and physical representations for both types of transistors. The arrow at the emitter of the symbol denotes the direction of forward, or easy, conventional current flow. As emphasized by the physical representations for the transistors, it should be noted that a transistor consists of two *pn* junctions. The bipolar transistor circuits in this appendix only utilize *npn* transistors.*

Figure A.10 gives the positive directions of conventional current flow for an *npn* transistor where I_C, I_B, and I_E are the collector, base, and emitter currents, respectively. The directions of positive potential drops are also shown in Fig. A.10. That is, the voltage V_{BE} is considered positive when the potential at the base terminal is more positive than the potential at the emitter terminal, the voltage V_{CE} is positive when the potential at the collector is more positive than the potential at the emitter, and the voltage V_{BC} is positive when the potential at the base is more positive than the potential at the collector. It should be noted that the use of double subscripts emphasizes a potential drop between two transistor terminals as opposed to a voltage with respect to ground. Also, the subscripts indicate the assumed polarity for a positive voltage drop. Thus, if V_{BC} is positive, then V_{CB} must be negative.

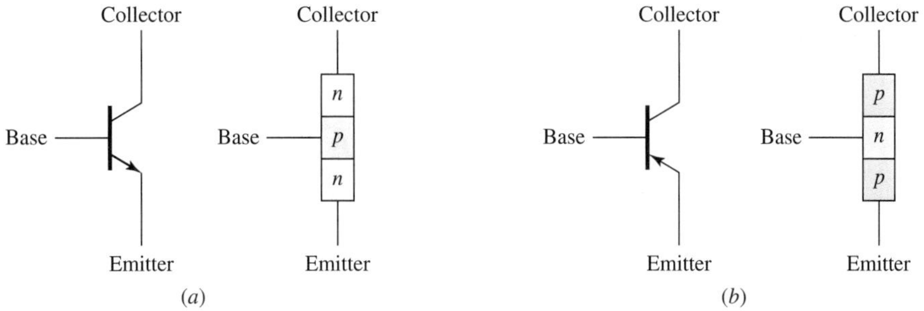

Figure A.9 Bipolar junction transistor symbols and physical representations. (*a*) *npn* transistor. (*b*) *pnp* transistor.

*Essentially, the operation of *pnp* transistors is the same as that of *npn* transistors except for the directions of current flow and the polarities of the voltages, which are reversed.

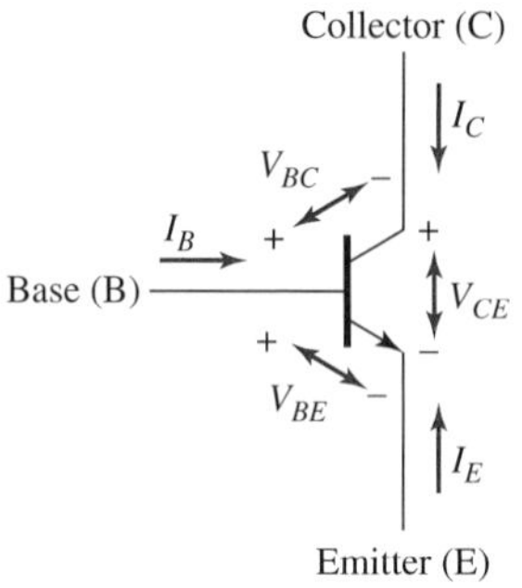

Figure A.10 Positive reference directions in an *npn* transistor.

As in the case of the *pn* junction diode, when discussing transistor operation it is necessary to consider the potentials across the junctions formed by the *p*-type and *n*-type materials, i.e., V_{BC} and V_{BE}. A junction is said to be *forward biased* if the voltage at the *p*-type material terminal is more positive than the voltage at the *n*-type material terminal. On the other hand, a junction is said to be *reverse biased* when the voltage at the *n*-type material terminal is more positive than the voltage at the *p*-type material terminal. For example, in an *npn* transistor, when V_{BE} is positive the base-emitter junction is forward biased and when V_{BE} is negative the base-emitter junction is reverse biased.

A.3.1 Simplified dc Transistor Operation

The internal operation of a bipolar transistor is a very complex process in which both electrons and holes serve as charge carriers (and hence the qualifying word bipolar is used*). At this time a very simplified explanation of transistor behavior is given in order to justify the device models of this section. This presentation does not pretend to substitute for the study of physical electronics.

For this cursory analysis, two behavioral effects are considered. First, it is noted that a bipolar transistor has two *pn* junctions. The forward and reverse biasing of these junctions produces effects similar to those of semiconductor diodes. There is, however, a second effect that occurs in transistors—the charge carrier transfer effect.

The charge carrier transfer effect is illustrated in Fig. A.11 for an *npn* transistor. Assume the base-emitter junction of the transistor is forward biased and the base-collector junction is reverse biased. Since the base-emitter junction is forward biased, the free electrons in the emitter region readily enter the base region, while the free holes in the base region cross the junction into the emitter region. During

---

*In Sec. A.9 another type of transistor, the field-effect transistor, which has only a single type of charge carrier, is studied.

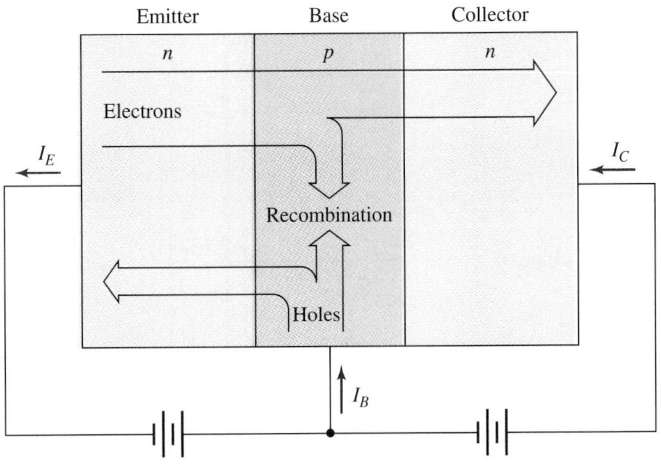

Figure A.11 The charge carrier transfer effect for normal operation of an *npn* transistor.

the fabrication of the transistor, the base region is more lightly doped with impurities than the emitter region. The result is that the electrons predominate and constitute most of the flow of emitter current.* Some of the electrons that enter the base region recombine with the holes. However, the base region is intentionally fabricated to be very narrow. Thus, most of the electron charge carriers from the emitter region make their way to the base-collector junction. With the voltage source across the base-collector junction such that the collector is positive with respect to the base, the free electrons in the base region are swept across the base-collector junction. The result is that the majority of the free electrons from the emitter region are transferred into the collector region. It turns out that the net collector current is a fixed fraction of net emitter current. This proportionality factor is α_F and is in the order of 0.98.

Although both the collector and emitter regions of an *npn* bipolar transistor consist of *n*-type material, from a behavioral point of view the transistor is not symmetrical owing to different degrees of doping in these regions. If the base-collector junction is forward biased and the base-emitter junction reverse biased, then there is a charge carrier transfer effect in which the emitter current is related to the collector current by a proportionality factor α_R. However, because of the behavioral nonsymmetry of the transistor, the factor α_R is considerably less than unity.

The *pn* junction and charge carrier effects can now be incorporated into a single circuit model for an *npn* transistor. Such a circuit model is shown in Fig. A.12, which is known as the *Ebers-Moll model*. The two diodes represent the two *pn* junctions and the two ideal current generators represent the charge carrier transfer effects. I_{DE} and I_{DC} correspond to the currents across the base-emitter and base-collector

*Conventional current is in the opposite direction to electron flow.

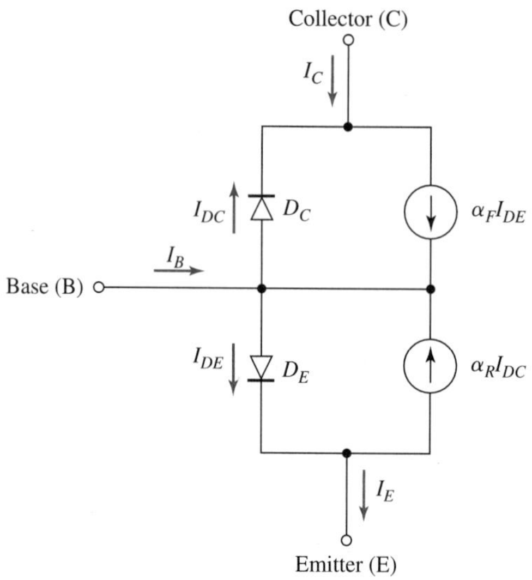

Figure A.12 A circuit model for an *npn* transistor.

junctions due to the junction biases, respectively, as governed by the theoretical diode equation $I = I_S(e^{qV/nkT} - 1)$.

Depending upon the polarity of the biases across each of the transistor junctions, i.e., forward or reverse, four operating modes (or regions) are defined. The four operating modes are

1. *Normal active mode*: the base-emitter junction is forward biased and the base-collector junction is reverse biased.
2. *Inverted* (or *reverse*) *active mode*: the base-emitter junction is reverse biased and the base-collector junction is forward biased.
3. *Cutoff mode*: the base-emitter junction is reverse biased and the base-collector junction is reverse biased.
4. *Saturation mode*: the base-emitter junction is forward biased and the base-collector junction is forward biased.

A piecewise linear model is developed in this section for each of these modes to simplify circuit analysis.

A.3.2 Normal Active Mode

In the normal active operating mode, the base-emitter junction is forward biased and the base-collector junction is reverse biased. Diode D_C in Fig. A.12 represents the base-collector junction. Since negligible current flows through a diode when it is reverse biased, it can be assumed that $I_{DC} = 0$ and that the diode behaves as an open circuit. Consequently, the current generator $\alpha_R I_{DC}$ must also be zero. The net effect of the $I_{DC} = 0$ assumption permits the removal of the base-collector diode D_C and the current generator $\alpha_R I_{DC}$ from the circuit model of Fig. A.12. In addition, the piecewise linear model previously given in Fig. A.4*a* can replace the base-emitter diode D_E. Figure A.13*a* shows the resulting circuit model for the normal active mode of a transistor where $V_{BE(\text{on})}$ is the drop across the base-emitter junction when its diode is conducting.

From Fig. A.13*a* it is seen that

$$I_C = \alpha_F I_{DE} \tag{A.1}$$

and

$$I_B = I_{DE} - \alpha_F I_{DE} = (1 - \alpha_F) I_{DE} \tag{A.2}$$

Solving for I_{DE} in Eq. (A.2) and substituting it into Eq. (A.1) gives

$$I_C = \frac{\alpha_F}{1 - \alpha_F} I_B$$

$$= \beta_F I_B$$

where

$$\beta_F = \frac{\alpha_F}{1 - \alpha_F}$$

β_F is called the *(forward) beta* or *dc current gain* of the transistor. A typical value for β_F is 50. Since $I_C = \alpha_F I_{DE} = \beta_F I_B$, the current generator of Fig. A.13*a* which is a function of α_F and I_{DE} can be replaced by a current generator that is a function

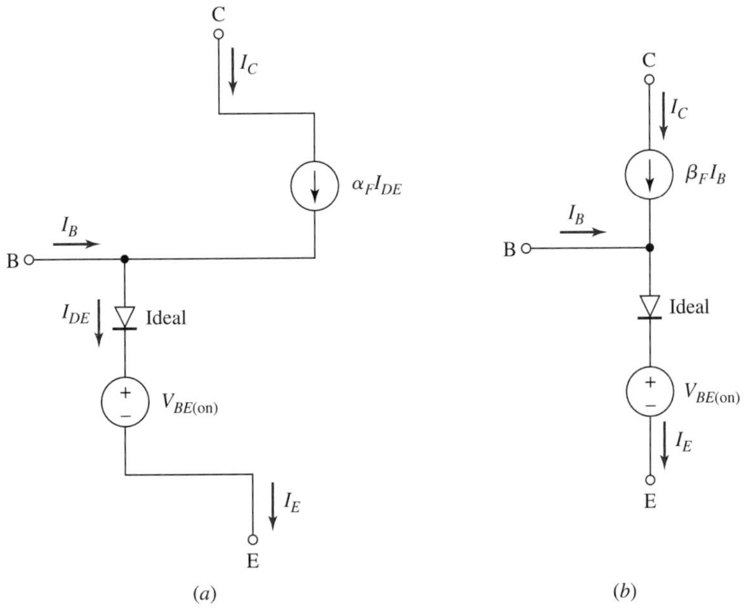

Figure A.13 Circuit models for the normal active mode when $I_{DC} = 0$.

of the base current I_B and the β_F of the transistor. This circuit model is shown in Fig. A.13*b*.

For convenience in future discussions, a slightly modified form of the circuit model of Fig. A.13*b* is desirable. First, in order for base current to flow, the base-emitter junction must be sufficiently forward biased so as to overcome the junction drop $V_{BE(\text{on})}$. In this situation, the ideal diode acts as a short circuit and can be replaced by a wire in the circuit model. Second, an ideal current generator can support any voltage necessary to maintain a constant current flow. Thus, the bottom terminal of the current generator in Fig. A.13*b* can be moved to the bottom terminal of the voltage generator. These two modifications yield the circuit model of Fig. A.14. This is the model that is used in future discussions for the normal active mode when $V_{BC} < 0$ and the base-emitter junction is sufficiently forward biased so that $I_B > 0$. It should be noted for both Figs. A.13*b* and A.14, $I_E = (1 + \beta_F)I_B$. Unless otherwise indicated, $V_{BE(\text{on})}$ is taken as 0.7 V.

It is in the normal active mode that a transistor is operated as a current amplifier. Here, a small change in the base current controls a large change in the collector current.

A.3.3 Inverted Active Mode

When the base-emitter junction of a bipolar transistor is reverse biased and the base-collector junction is forward biased, the transistor is operating in the inverted active mode. This is the same as the normal active operating mode with the roles of the collector and emitter being reversed. By treating I_{DE} as zero in Fig. A.12, the cir-

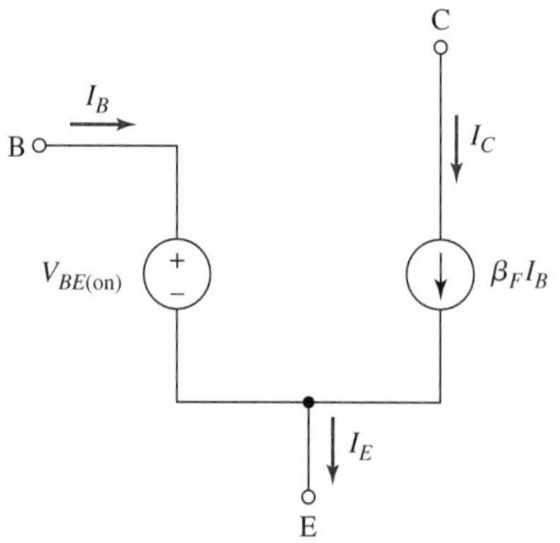

Figure A.14 Circuit model for the normal active mode when $V_{BC} < 0$ and the base-emitter junction is sufficiently forward biased so that $I_B > 0$.

cuit model shown in Fig. A.15*a* is obtained for this mode. Furthermore, using a similar analysis to that of the normal active mode it follows that

$$-I_E = \frac{\alpha_R}{1-\alpha_R} I_B$$
$$= \beta_R I_B$$

where

$$\beta_R = \frac{\alpha_R}{1-\alpha_R}$$

Thus, the circuit model shown in Fig. A.15*b* can be drawn. With α_R being much less than unity, β_R, the *reverse dc current gain*, also is much less than unity.

A variation to the circuit model of Fig. A.15*b* is given in Fig. A.16 in which it is assumed that the base-collector junction is sufficiently forward biased so that $I_B > 0$. This assumption allows the ideal diode to be replaced by a short circuit and the upper terminal of the current generator to be moved to the collector terminal of the model. In future discussions, a value of 0.5 V is used for $V_{BC(\text{on})}$.

A.3.4 Cutoff Mode

The third mode of transistor operation is the cutoff mode. In this case both the base-collector junction of the transistor and the base-emitter junction are reverse biased. Since both diodes of Fig. A.12 are reverse biased, the only currents flowing in these

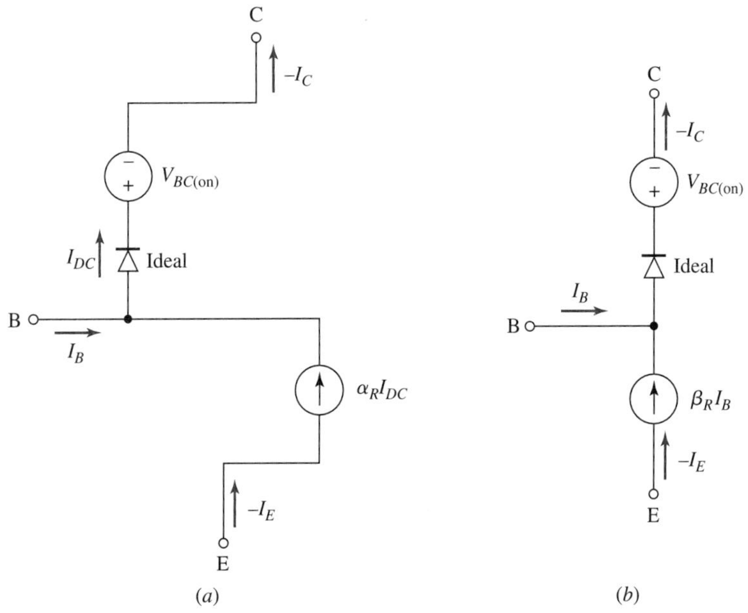

Figure A.15 Circuit models for the inverted active mode when $I_{DE} = 0$.

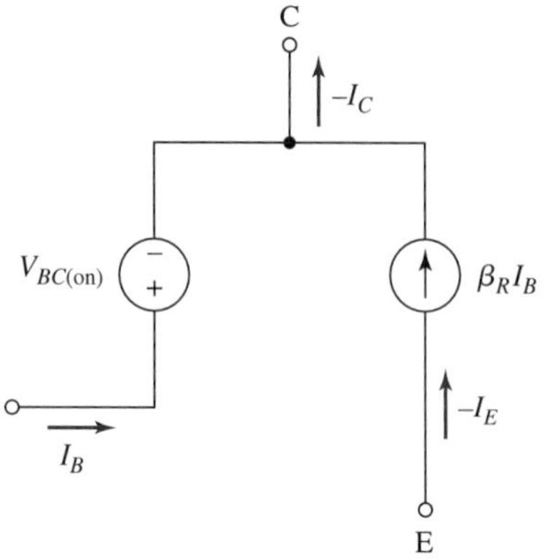

Figure A.16 Circuit model for the inverted active mode when $V_{BE} < 0$ and the base-collector junction is sufficiently forward biased so that $I_B > 0$.

diodes are the small reverse saturation currents. However, using the diode model previously developed, the currents I_{DC} and I_{DE} are approximated as zero. The net effect of this assumption is that the diodes and current generators of Fig. A.12 can each be replaced by open circuits. Therefore, a simplified circuit model for the cutoff mode is also an open circuit at the site of the transistor as illustrated in Fig. A.17, with the result that $I_B = I_C = I_E = 0$.

In this appendix there are many occasions in which the base-collector junction of the transistor is reverse biased, but its base-emitter junction is just slightly forward biased, i.e., with $0 < V_{BE} < V_{BE(\text{on})}$. In this situation the diode model of Fig. A.4 still allows the assumption that I_{DC} and I_{DE} are zero. Thus, when $V_{BC} < 0$ and $0 < V_{BE} < V_{BE(\text{on})}$, the transistor is regarded as being in the cutoff mode.

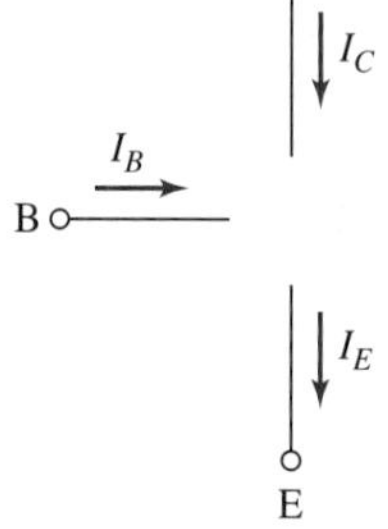

Figure A.17 A circuit model for the cutoff mode.

A.3.5 Saturation Mode

The final operating mode of the transistor is the saturation mode. Here, both the base-emitter and base-collector junctions are forward biased. Using the diode circuit model given in Fig. A.4*a* and the circuit model of an *npn* transistor given in Fig. A.12, the circuit model of Fig. A.18 results. If it is assumed that both junctions are sufficiently forward biased so that both I_{DC} and I_{DE} are greater than zero, then

$$I_C = \alpha_F I_{DE} - I_{DC} \tag{A.3}$$

and

$$I_E = I_{DE} - \alpha_R I_{DC}$$

Summing the terminal currents of the transistor, it follows that

$$I_B = I_E - I_C = (1 - \alpha_F)\, I_{DE} + (1 - \alpha_R)\, I_{DC} \tag{A.4}$$

Since α_F and α_R are both positive and less than unity, I_B is nonzero and positive. Furthermore, multiplying Eq. (A.4) by $\alpha_F/(1 - \alpha_F)$, i.e., β_F, and comparing it to Eq. (A.3), it is seen that in saturation $\beta_F I_B > I_C$. The actual values of I_B and I_C (as well as I_E since $I_B = I_E - I_C$) depend upon the circuitry external to the transistor. Furthermore, under the assumption that both I_{DC} and I_{DE} are greater than zero, it follows that the ideal diodes must be short circuits and hence $V_{CE(\text{on})} = V_{BE(\text{on})} - V_{BC(\text{on})}$ must be constant.

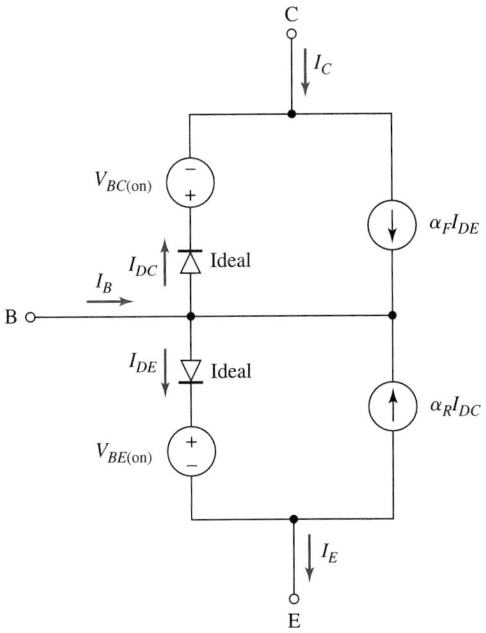

Figure A.18 *npn* transistor model using the diode approximation.

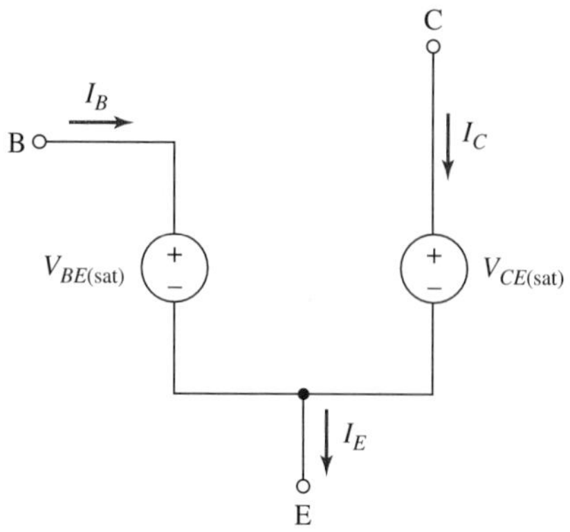

Figure A.19 A circuit model for the saturation mode when the condition $\beta_F I_B > I_C$ is satisfied.

A simplified circuit model for the saturation mode of an *npn* transistor, under the above assumptions, is given in Fig. A.19. In this figure, $V_{BE(sat)}$ is used instead of $V_{BE(on)}$ to emphasize that the model refers to the saturation mode as well as to conform to the fact that in reality $V_{BE(sat)}$ is slightly larger than $V_{BE(on)}$.* In actuality, the voltage drop across each junction is not the same. This accounts for the voltage source $V_{CE(sat)}$ in the figure. A typical value of $V_{CE(sat)}$ for an *npn* transistor is 0.2 V. Unless otherwise stated, the values of $V_{CE(sat)} = 0.2$ V and $V_{BE(sat)} = 0.7$ V are used in all future discussions when applying the circuit model of Fig. A.19. In addition, by Kirchhoff's voltage law, it follows that $V_{BC(sat)} = 0.5$ V.

Since the piecewise linear diode model is being used, special mention is necessary for the case when the base-emitter junction is sufficiently forward biased so that it is readily conducting but the base-collector junction is only slightly forward biased, i.e., $0 < V_{BC} < V_{BC(on)}$. In this situation, the circuit model for the transistor shown in Fig. A.18 does not reduce to that of Fig. A.19 but rather becomes that for the normal active mode since in this case $I_{DC} = 0$. Thus, from the point of view of circuit modeling, the saturation of a transistor is regarded as occurring only when both junctions are sufficiently forward biased so that each junction is represented by a voltage source (with the consequence that the collector-emitter voltage of the transistor is modeled by a voltage source) and the inequality $\beta_F I_B > I_C$ holds.

A.3.6 Silicon *npn* Transistor Characteristics

As in the case of diodes, characteristic curves are used to describe the terminal behavior of transistors. Typical collector and base characteristic curves for a silicon *npn* transistor are given in Fig. A.20. The collector characteristic curves in Fig. A.20*a*

*The reader should keep in mind that the *I-V* characteristic of a *pn* junction is exponential and hence the drop across the base-emitter junction is different from when current conduction first starts and when the transistor is in saturation.

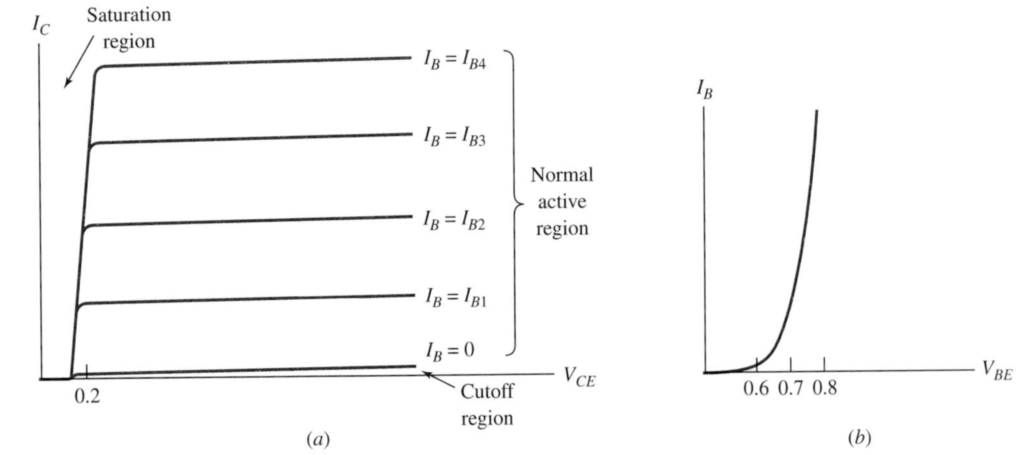

Figure A.20 Silicon *npn* transistor characteristic curves. (*a*) Collector characteristic curves where $0 < I_{B1} < I_{B2} < I_{B3} < I_{B4}$. (*b*) Base characteristic curve.

show how I_C and V_{CE} are related for various values of constant base current. It should be noted in Fig. A.20*b* that the base characteristic curve is essentially the same as that of a *pn* junction diode.

It is interesting to obtain the corresponding set of "characteristic curves" that are produced by the various circuit models that have been developed in this section. This is done in Fig. A.21. As can be seen, the characteristics generated by the various circuit models do serve as a good first-order approximation of transistor terminal behavior.

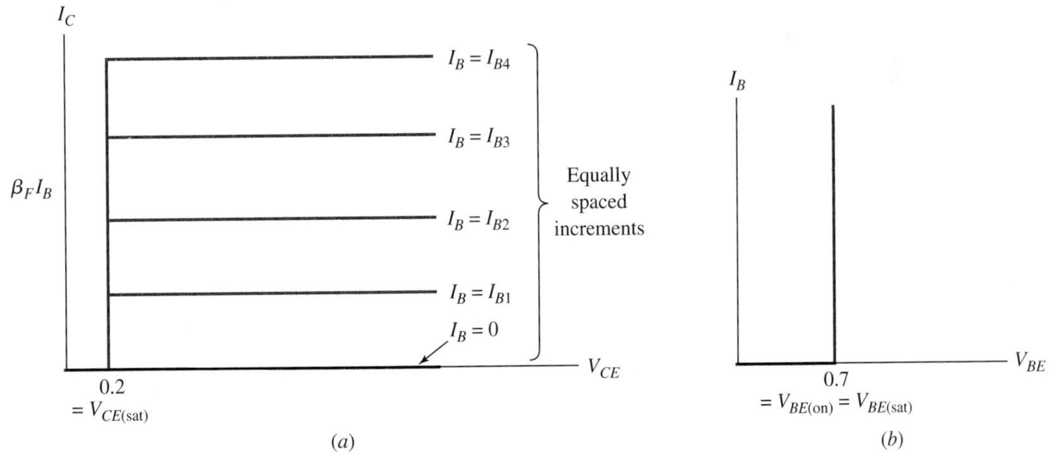

Figure A.21 Piecewise linear approximation of the silicon *npn* transistor characteristic curves. (*a*) Collector characteristic curves where $0 < I_{B1} < I_{B2} < I_{B3} < I_{B4}$. (*b*) Base characteristic curve.

A.3.7 Summary

At this time it is perhaps wise to reiterate the key points of this section. A circuit model of an *npn* transistor was given in Fig. A.12. Four modes (or regions) of transistor operation were then defined. To facilitate circuit calculations in the remainder of this appendix, a set of simplified circuit models were developed for the various operating modes. However, since a piecewise linear approximation was used for the diodes in the circuit model, the various operating regions become dependent on the two specific voltages $V_{BE(on)}$ and $V_{BC(on)}$ rather than the base-emitter and base-collector junctions, V_{BE} and V_{BC}, simply being forward or reverse biased. In particular, a transistor is regarded as being in the normal active mode when $V_{BE} \geq V_{BE(on)}$ and $V_{BC} < V_{BC(on)}$. A circuit model of a transistor in the normal active mode is given in Fig. A.14. This is the linear operation of a transistor which is characterized by the relationship $I_C = \beta_F I_B$. The inverted active mode occurs when $V_{BE} < V_{BE(on)}$ and $V_{BC} \geq V_{BC(on)}$. In this case the transistor is modeled by the circuit shown in Fig. A.16. When $V_{BE} < V_{BE(on)}$ and $V_{BC} < V_{BC(on)}$, the transistor is in cutoff and the simple open-circuit model of Fig. A.17 applies. Finally, a transistor is in saturation when $V_{BE} \geq V_{BE(on)}$ and $V_{BC} \geq V_{BC(on)}$. Figure A.19 gives the corresponding circuit model of the transistor. The circuit components external to the saturated transistor determine the base and collector currents in this mode and the inequality $\beta_F I_B > I_C$ is used to test for the saturation condition. Unless otherwise stated, in the circuit models $V_{BE(on)} = V_{BE(sat)} = 0.7$ V, $V_{BC(on)} = V_{BC(sat)} = 0.5$ V, and $V_{CE(sat)} = 0.2$ V.

A.4 THE TRANSISTOR INVERTER

The first basic transistor circuit to be studied is the inverter circuit shown in Fig. A.22. The output of the circuit is taken across the collector-emitter terminals of the transistor. It is assumed that no additional circuitry is connected to the output so that all

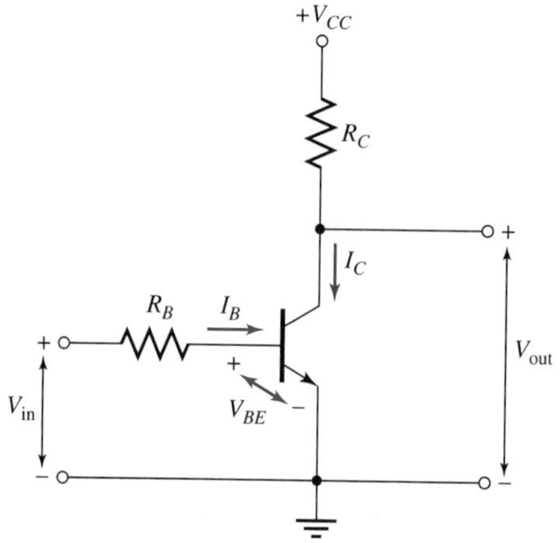

Figure A.22 The basic transistor inverter circuit.

the current at the collector terminal, I_C, is also flowing through resistor R_C. In such a case, the circuit is referred to as being *unloaded*.

Assume that V_{CC} is positive and sufficiently large so that the base-collector junction of the transistor is reverse biased for some range of values of V_{in}. Let us now determine the output voltage V_{out} as a function of V_{in} as V_{in} varies from 0 to V_{CC} volts. A plot of V_{out} versus V_{in} is referred to as the *transfer characteristic* of the circuit.

For the range $0 \leq V_{in} < V_{BE(on)}$, the base-emitter junction of the transistor is insufficiently forward biased to cause the base-emitter junction diode to conduct. Since V_{CC} is positive and large, the base-collector junction is reverse biased. The net result is that $I_B = 0$ and the transistor is in its cutoff mode. With the transistor in cutoff, $I_C = 0$. Furthermore, since the circuit is unloaded and no current is flowing through resistor R_C, $V_{out} = V_{CC}$ volts in the range $0 \leq V_{in} < V_{BE(on)}$ as shown in the transfer characteristic of Fig. A.23.

When $V_{in} = V_{BE(on)}$, the base-emitter junction diode is just sufficiently forward biased to enable conduction. Assuming $V_{CC} > V_{BE(on)}$, the base-collector junction of the transistor is reverse biased and the transistor enters its normal active mode. The transition from cutoff to the normal active mode is referred to as the *edge of cutoff* (abbreviated EOC).

With the transistor now in its normal active mode, its behavior is modeled by the circuit of Fig. A.14. This results in the equivalent circuit of the transistor inverter shown in Fig. A.24. As V_{in} increases, the voltage across the base-emitter junction remains at $V_{BE(on)}$ while the base current is given by

$$I_B = \frac{V_{in} - V_{BE(on)}}{R_B}$$

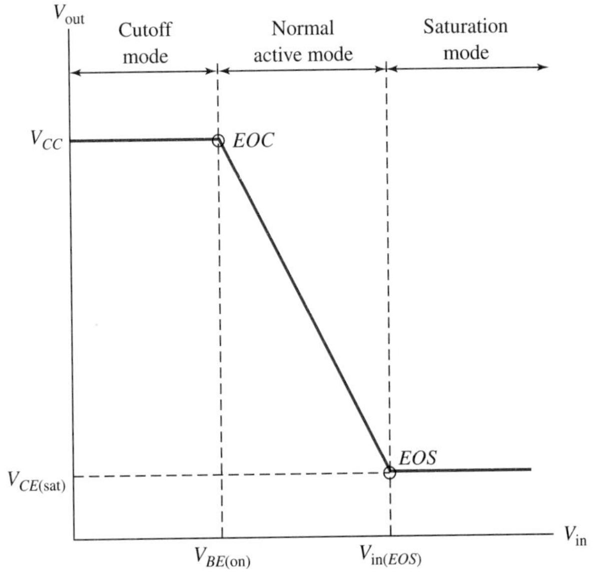

Figure A.23 Transfer characteristic of the unloaded transistor inverter circuit.

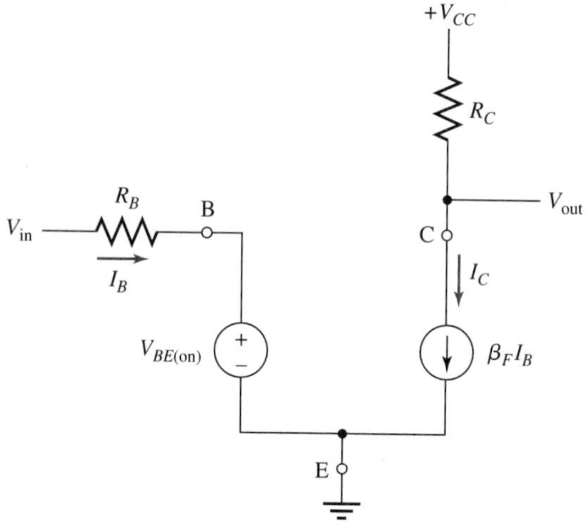

Figure A.24 The transistor inverter equivalent circuit in the normal active mode.

Furthermore, collector current, I_C, flows and is computed as

$$\begin{aligned} I_C &= \beta_F I_B \\ &= \beta_F \frac{[V_{\text{in}} - V_{BE(\text{on})}]}{R_B} \end{aligned}$$

Since the transistor inverter is unloaded, the collector current also flows through the resistor R_C. It immediately follows that in the normal active mode

$$\begin{aligned} V_{\text{out}} &= V_{CC} - I_C R_C \\ &= V_{CC} - \frac{\beta_F [V_{\text{in}} - V_{BE(\text{on})}] R_C}{R_B} \end{aligned}$$

Thus, V_{out} decreases linearly as V_{in} increases as shown in the transfer characteristic of Fig. A.23.

Since the output voltage decreases as the input voltage increases, eventually the voltage across the transistor becomes $V_{CE(\text{sat})}$. At this point the transistor enters its saturation mode. The transition between the normal active mode and the saturation mode is referred to as the *edge of saturation* (abbreviated EOS). Once the transistor becomes saturated, according to the transistor circuit model of Fig. A.19, the voltage drop between its collector and emitter remains constant at $V_{CE(\text{sat})}$ even if V_{in} is increased. In this case, the transistor collector current becomes constant at its maximum value

$$I_{C(\text{EOS})} = \frac{V_{CC} - V_{CE(\text{sat})}}{R_C} \tag{A.5}$$

Of course, as V_{in} increases while the transistor is saturated, the base current I_B increases further. The net result is that $\beta_F I_B > I_{C(\text{EOS})}$ during saturation.

In Fig. A.23 the input voltage at the edge of saturation is indicated by $V_{\text{in(EOS)}}$. This input voltage can readily be calculated. Equation (A.5) gives the collector current at the edge of saturation. At this point the linear relationship between the base and collector currents must also still hold; i.e., $\beta_F I_{B(\text{EOS})} = I_{C(\text{EOS})}$. Therefore,

$$\begin{aligned} I_{B(\text{EOS})} &= \frac{I_{C(\text{EOS})}}{\beta_F} \\ &= \frac{V_{CC} - V_{CE(\text{sat})}}{\beta_F R_C} \end{aligned} \tag{A.6}$$

Referring to the input portion of the circuit in Fig. A.22 and using Eq. (A.6), at the edge of saturation

$$\begin{aligned} V_{\text{in(EOS)}} &= I_{B(\text{EOS})} R_B + V_{BE(\text{on})} \\ &= \frac{[V_{CC} - V_{CE(\text{sat})}]R_B}{\beta_F R_C} + V_{BE(\text{on})} \end{aligned}$$

Since it has been assumed that V_{CC} is sufficiently large so as to allow the transistor to enter all three of its operating modes as V_{in} increases, it is necessary that $V_{CC} > V_{\text{in(EOS)}}$.

From the transfer characteristic of Fig. A.23, it is a simple matter to establish that the transistor circuit of Fig. A.22 serves as a realization of a Boolean not-gate. To see this, assume the input is restricted to the two values $V_{CE(\text{sat})} = 0.2$ V and V_{CC}. Since $V_{BE(\text{on})} = 0.7$ V and $V_{CE(\text{sat})} < V_{BE(\text{on})}$, when $V_{\text{in}} = V_{CE(\text{sat})}$ the transistor is in cutoff and $V_{\text{out}} = V_{CC}$. Also, when $V_{\text{in}} = V_{CC}$ the transistor is in saturation and $V_{\text{out}} = V_{CE(\text{sat})}$. If logic-0 is now assigned to $V_{CE(\text{sat})}$ and logic-1 to V_{CC}, then the logic behavior of the transistor inverter circuit becomes that of the Boolean not-gate.

Digital circuits whose output transistor is normally in cutoff and saturation for the two logic conditions are referred to as *saturating logic*.

A.4.1 Loading Effects

In the above discussion, the transistor inverter was unloaded. Typically the output of a digital circuit is connected to the inputs of additional digital circuits. Figure A.25 illustrates the connection of additional inverters as loads to a single inverter circuit. For generality, it is assumed that there are N loads, each identical to the driving inverter circuit.

When V_{in} of the driving gate is high, transistor Q_{Drive} is forced into saturation and its output becomes $V_{CE(\text{sat})}$. This is the voltage at point F in Fig. A.25. Under the assumption that $V_{CE(\text{sat})} = 0.2$ V and $V_{BE(\text{on})} = 0.7$ V, it immediately follows that all of the load transistors are insufficiently forward biased, and, consequently, all of them are in their cutoff modes. Since no current can flow into the base terminals of

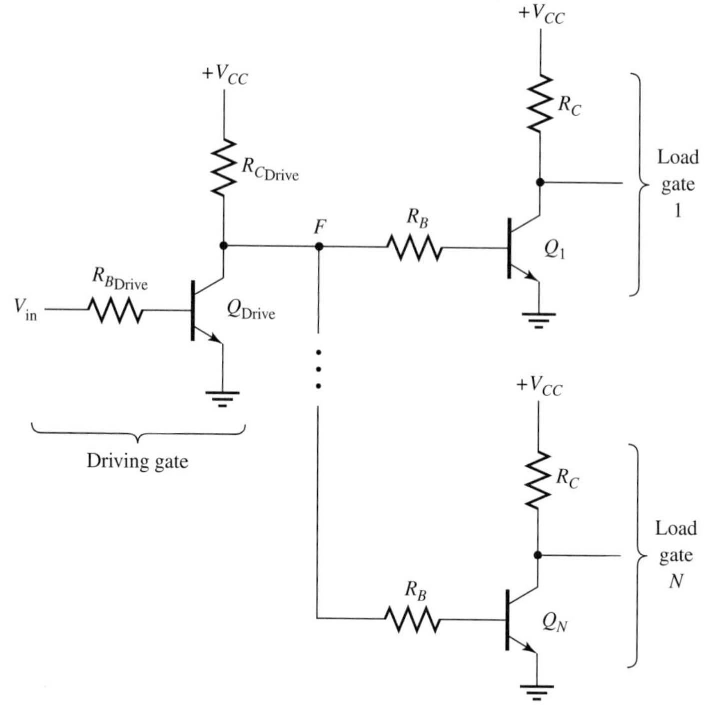

Figure A.25 A loaded transistor inverter.

the load transistors, all the current through $R_{C_{\text{Drive}}}$ flows into the collector of transistor Q_{Drive}. This current is given by Eq. (A.5) and the output voltage of the driving gate, i.e., at point F, is $V_{CE(\text{sat})} = 0.2$ V. Thus, it is seen that the load gates have no effect upon the driving gate when V_{in} is high.

Now consider the case when V_{in} is low, i.e., $V_{\text{in}} < V_{BE(\text{on})}$. Transistor Q_{Drive} is in its cutoff mode and causes its output, point F, to become high. For proper operation the voltage at point F should be sufficiently high so as to ensure that all the load transistors, Q_1 to Q_N, saturate. Looking into the loads from point F, the driving gate sees the base-emitter junctions of the load transistors, which appear as *pn* junction diodes, along with the input resistors R_B. Since these diodes are turned on under the assumption that the load transistors are saturated, they are regarded as voltage sources of value $V_{BE(\text{sat})}$ in accordance with the circuit model of Fig. A.19. The resulting equivalent circuit of the loaded transistor inverter when V_{in} is low is shown in Fig. A.26*a*. The loads effectively consist of the parallel connection of N identical resistors R_B and voltage sources $V_{BE(\text{sat})}$. The parallel connection of N identical voltage sources is equivalent to a single source of the same value and the parallel connection of N equal resistors R_B is equivalent to a single resistor of value R_B/N. Thus, the circuit of Fig. A.26*a* reduces to that of Fig. A.26*b*. It is now a simple matter to determine the voltage at point F. From the figure it follows that

$$V_F = V_{CC} - I_{\text{Drive}} R_{C_{\text{Drive}}}$$

and

$$I_{\text{Drive}} = \frac{V_{CC} - V_{BE(\text{sat})}}{R_{C_{\text{Drive}}} + \dfrac{R_B}{N}}$$

Substituting the expression for I_{Drive} into the expression for V_F,

$$V_F = V_{CC} - \frac{[V_{CC} - V_{BE(\text{sat})}]\, R_{C_{\text{Drive}}}}{R_{C_{\text{Drive}}} + \dfrac{R_B}{N}} \tag{A.7}$$

Equation (A.7) shows the effect of the loads upon the driving gate. In particular, as N increases, V_F decreases. In order to saturate the load transistors the voltage V_F must be at least equal to $V_{\text{in(EOS)}}$. Thus, there is an upper limit to the allowable value of N for proper operation.

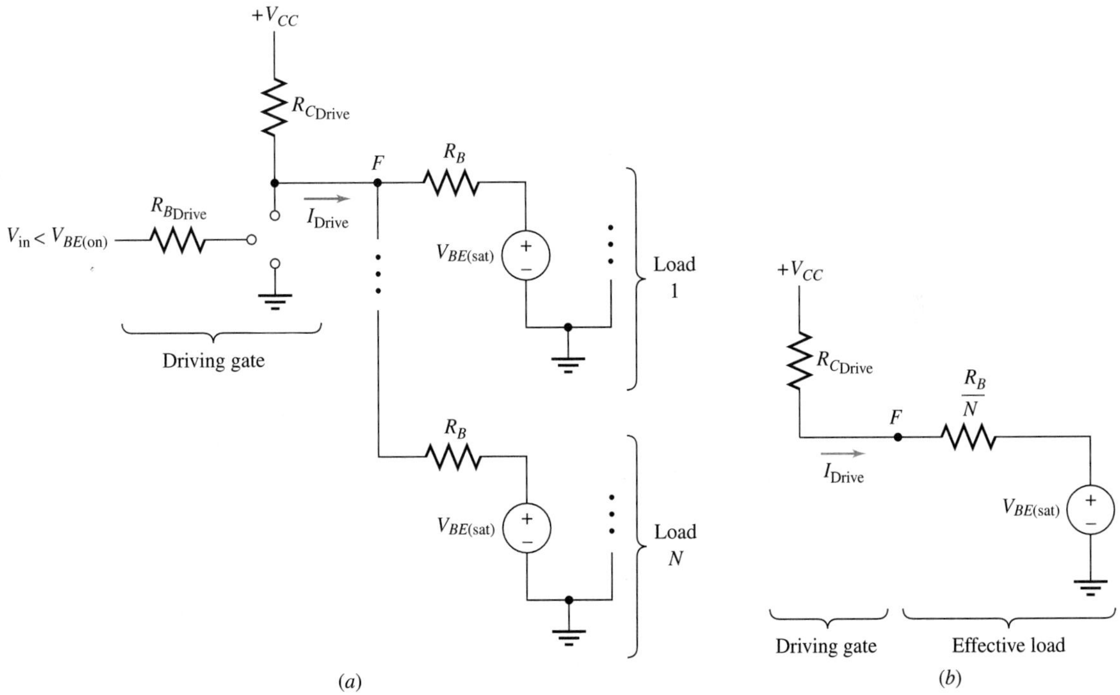

Figure A.26 A loaded transistor inverter when its input is low. (*a*) Equivalent circuit illustrating the effective load to the driving gate. (*b*) Alternate equivalent circuit.

A.5 GATE PERFORMANCE CONSIDERATIONS

There are several factors that go into the decision of selecting the logic gates suitable for a given application. Among these are the immunity to induced noise, temperature range of the operating environment, gate switching speed requirements between the logic-0 and logic-1 states to achieve a given overall operating speed of the system, loading effects upon the gates, and power supply requirements. For this reason, several different logic families, as well as a variety of circuit variations within a given logic family, are made available. In Sec. 3.10, several gate performance properties were introduced. At this time, these properties are reviewed in preparation for establishing the advantages and disadvantages of the various logic families studied in this appendix.

A.5.1 Noise Margins

In the previous section, the transfer characteristic of an unloaded inverter circuit was obtained. When dealing with saturating logic, one observation that can be made from the transfer characteristic is that over the range of input voltages that result in cutoff, the output is constant. Similarly, over the range of input voltages that result in saturation, again the output is constant. The implication of these observations is that *ranges* of input voltages can be assigned to a logic value and that input voltage variations within these ranges do not affect the logic behavior of the gate. Thus, in

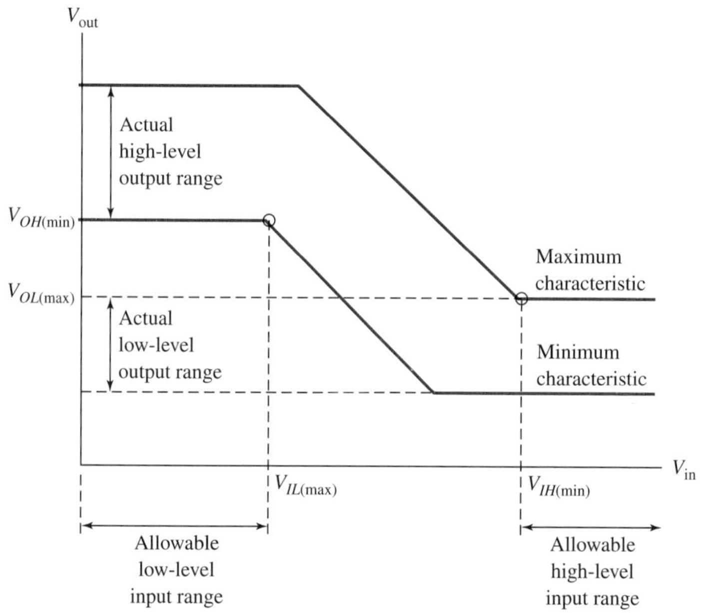

Figure A.27 Minimum and maximum transfer characterisitics of a digital circuit.

positive logic, any voltage within the range assigned to logic-0 is regarded as a *low input*; while any voltage within the range assigned to logic-1 is regarded as a *high input*. This result of a range of voltages corresponding to a single logic value is one reason for the high overall reliability normally attributed to digital circuits.

The actual transfer characteristic of a gate is dependent upon several factors. For one thing, the output voltage of a gate can depend on loading effects, as was seen in the previous section. Furthermore, transistor characteristics (and other circuit component behavior) are subject to variations in manufacturing as well as dependent upon the temperature of operation. Finally, the voltages from the power supplies used in circuits are also subject to some variations, which, in turn, affect the signal values in the circuit. Thus, assuming ranges of permissible loads, temperature, and power supply variations, the transfer characteristic of a gate lies between some manufacturer-specified minimum and maximum characteristics as shown in Fig. A.27.

The two circled breakpoints in the figure on the minimum and maximum characteristics are of notable interest. In particular, the manufacturer guarantees that any input voltage less than $V_{IL(\max)}$ is recognized by the gate as corresponding to a low-voltage (logic-0) input. On the other hand, any input voltage greater than $V_{IH(\min)}$ is recognized by the gate as corresponding to a high-voltage (logic-1) input. Furthermore, the manufacturer guarantees that the low-voltage (logic-0) output of the gate does not exceed $V_{OL(\max)}$, and that the high-voltage (logic-1) output of the gate does exceed $V_{OH(\min)}$. Of course, this assumes that any manufacturer-specified loading, temperature, and power supply constraints are adhered to.

The input and output voltages associated with the two breakpoints of Fig. A.27 provide a measure of the gate's immunity to induced noise. Figure A.28, which is the same as Fig. 3.21*b*, plots the four voltages on a straight line. The difference

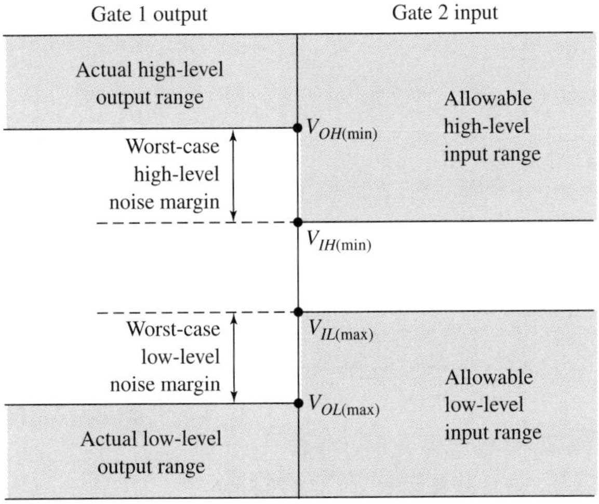

Figure A.28 Noise margins.

between $V_{IL(\max)}$ and $V_{OL(\max)}$ provides a measure of the amount of induced noise that can be added to the input of a gate and still have it regard the input as logic-0. Similarly, the difference between $V_{OH(\min)}$ and $V_{IH(\min)}$ provides a measure of the amount of induced noise that can be subtracted from the input of a gate and still have it regard the input as logic-1. These two figures of merit are called the *worst-case low-level noise margin* and the *worst-case high-level noise margin*, respectively. Of course, since for any particular gate, its characteristic curve lies between the minimum and maximum characteristics specified by the manufacturer, the actual noise margins for the gate are better than those indicated.

A.5.2 Fan-Out

It was seen in the previous section that when loads are connected to the output of a digital circuit, the output signal levels are affected. This is a consequence of the fact that there is a current flow between gates and hence a power consumption. For reliable operation the amount of this current is limited. The number of circuits (measured in terms of similar gates in the same logic series) connected to the output of a digital gate as loads is called the *fan-out* of the gate. The maximum number of such loads that can exist without impairing the normal operation of a gate is referred to as the gate's *fan-out capability*.

A.5.3 Speed of Operation and Propagation Delay Times

Digital signal changes cannot occur instantaneously. This implies that there is a limitation to a gate's overall speed of operation. Figure A.29 shows an inverter circuit with input and output waveforms. The input waveform is assumed to be ideal for

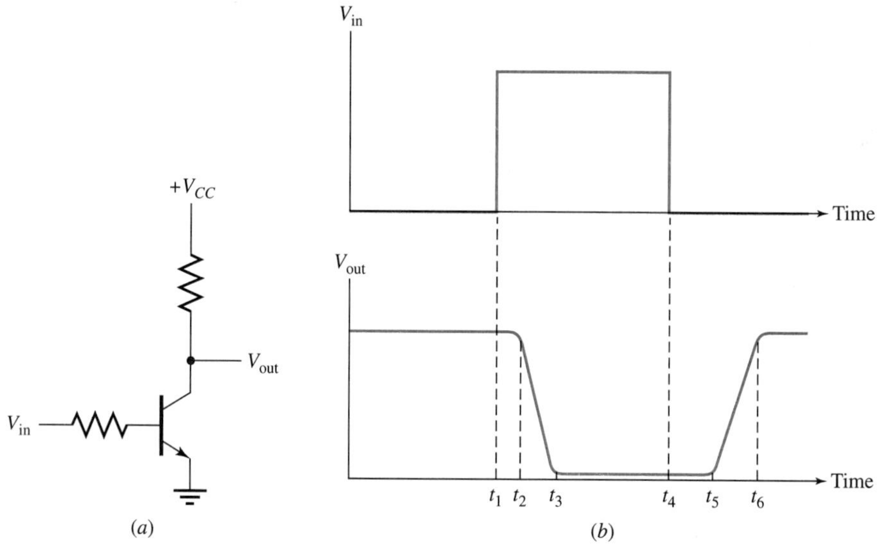

Figure A.29 Switching times. (*a*) Inverter circuit. (*b*) Input and output waveforms.

emphasis. Furthermore, it is assumed that the transistor operates between cutoff and saturation.

At time t_1 the input is changed with the intention of causing the transistor to go from cutoff into saturation. However, it is not until time t_2 that the output effectively starts to change. This time delay is attributed to the capacitive effect between the base and emitter of the transistor as well as the time needed for the charge carriers to move. The actual switching occurs between times t_2 and t_3, which is strongly dependent upon the capacitance between the collector and ground. Normally, the 10 and 90 percent points of the final value of the signal are used to measure t_2 and t_3. Similar behavior occurs at time t_4 when the transistor is intended to go from saturation into cutoff. Again there is a time delay, $t_5 - t_4$, before the output starts to respond. As noted above, this delay is partially due to the base-emitter capacitance. In addition, under the assumption that the transistor is saturated, a significant part of this delay is due to the large number of charge carriers in the base region of the transistor that must be removed before switching can occur. For this reason the time difference $t_5 - t_4$ is typically greater than that of $t_3 - t_2$. This storage effect is an inherent problem associated with saturating logic and has resulted in the development of other logic circuits not subject to this problem. Finally, the actual output change occurs between times t_5 and t_6, which is related to the capacitance appearing between the collector of the transistor and ground. As gates are connected in series, these delay times are cumulative, and thus affect the overall operating speed of a digital system.

Input and output waveforms are frequently drawn as shown in Fig. A.30 when finite rise and fall times are to be indicated. As already mentioned, the output of a gate does not respond instantaneously to the change at its input. This is known as

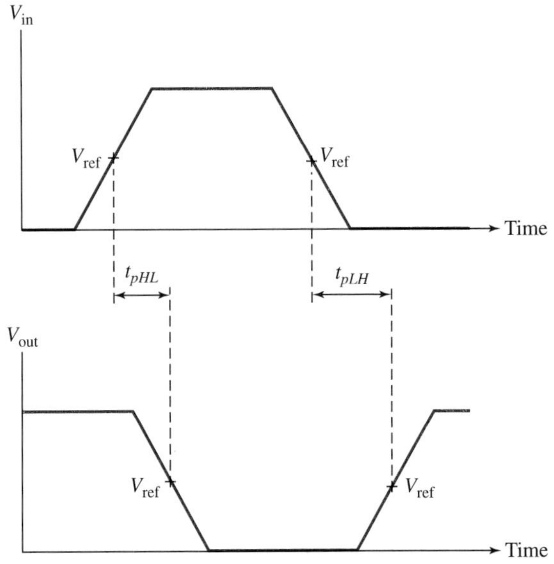

Figure A.30 Propagation delay times.

the *propagation delay time*, which differs depending upon whether the output transition is going from cutoff to saturation or from saturation to cutoff. Measurement of the propagation delays is done using some reference point, V_{ref}, during the rise and fall times, say the 50 percent point as indicated in the figure. t_{pHL} is defined as the propagation delay time for the output to change from its high level to its low level as a consequence of an input change; while t_{pLH} is defined as the propagation delay time for the output to change from its low level to its high level as a consequence of an input change.

A.5.4 Power Dissipation

Power dissipation is of major concern in the design of a digital system. Efforts are constantly being made so as to minimize power dissipation, which is divided into two components—*static power dissipation* and *dynamic power dissipation.* Static power dissipation occurs as a consequence of the flow of currents while the circuit is in its steady state. Dynamic power dissipation, on the other hand, occurs as the result of current flow due to changes of the input signals to the circuit. All currents must be provided by the power supply. Thus, the greater the power requirements of a digital system, the greater the need for a larger power supply. Unfortunately, the faster a circuit operates, the greater its power requirements. For this reason a figure of merit of a circuit is its *delay-power product*, which is the product of the propagation delay time and the power dissipation of the gate.

A.6 DIODE-TRANSISTOR LOGIC (DTL)

Diode-transistor logic (DTL) was the forerunner to the popular *transistor-transistor logic* (TTL). Although DTL is no longer in use, an understanding of DTL aids in the understanding of TTL. For this reason, this section studies the operation of the basic DTL gate.

As shown in Fig. A.31*a*, the basic DTL nand-gate consists of three sections—an input diode and-gate, a coupling circuit, and an output inverter. To understand the general operation of the gate, first assume that at least one input, x_1 or x_2, is low at 0.2 V and any inputs that are high are at 5 V. Also, assume no loads are connected to the output of the DTL gate. Since the corresponding diode for each low input is forward biased due to the power supply voltage V_{CC}, the voltage at point P is $V_{\text{in}} + V_{D(\text{on})} = 0.2 + 0.7 = 0.9$ V. Current flows from V_{CC}, through R_1, and through each forward-biased input diode. Furthermore, with the voltage at point P being 0.9 V, diodes D_1 and D_2 are insufficiently forward biased to turn them on since a minimum of two diode drops, or 1.4 V, is required before current can flow through them. Hence, no current flows through D_1 and D_2 and, correspondingly, no current flows into the base of Q_1. The net result is that transistor Q_1 is in cutoff, no current flows through R_2, and the voltage at point f is $V_{CC} = 5$ V. This situation corresponds to the first three rows of Fig. A.31*b*, where L is used to denote a low voltage of 0.2 V and H is used to denote a high voltage of 5 V.

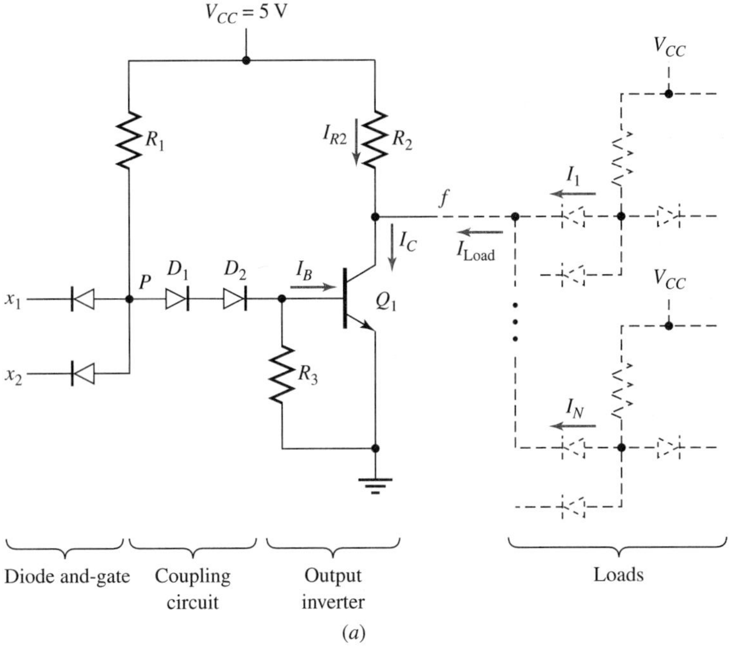

V_{x1}	V_{x2}	V_f
L	L	H
L	H	H
H	L	H
H	H	L

(*b*)

x_1	x_2	f
0	0	1
0	1	1
1	0	1
1	1	0

(*c*)

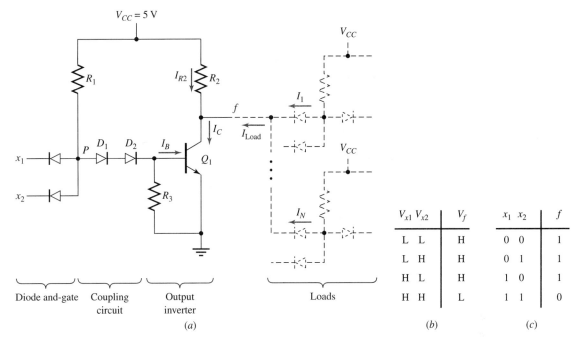

Figure A.31 A two-input DTL nand-gate. (*a*) Circuit diagram. (*b*) Voltage table. (*c*) Truth table.

In actuality, as was indicated in Sec. A.5, input and output signals are not restricted to single exact values but rather are associated with ranges of values. Thus, L and H on the input side of the voltage table of Fig. A.31*b* really denote signal values in the allowable low-level input range, i.e., L $\leq V_{IL(\max)}$, and high-level input range, i.e., H $\geq V_{IH(\min)}$, respectively. Correspondingly, on the output side of the voltage table, L $\leq V_{OL(\max)}$ and H $\geq V_{OH(\min)}$. For simplicity in presentation, single exact values are used to illustrate circuit operation.

Consider now the case when both input voltages in Fig. A.31*a* are high at 5 V. As the inputs go from their low to high values, the voltage at point P starts to rise. When the voltage at point P gets to 1.4 V, diodes D_1 and D_2 start to conduct current through R_3 to ground. However, it is not until the voltage at point P is sufficiently high to overcome the base-emitter junction voltage of transistor Q_1 that base current flows and the transistor starts to conduct collector current. The circuit is designed so that transistor Q_1 operates in saturation when on. At this time, the voltage at point P is equal to $V_{D1(\text{on})} + V_{D2(\text{on})} + V_{BE(\text{sat})} = 0.7 + 0.7 + 0.7 = 2.1$ V. Furthermore, with the voltage at point P clamped at 2.1 V and the two inputs at 5 V, the two input diodes are reverse biased and no current flows through them. Hence, the flow of current is from V_{CC}, through R_1 , and through the two coupling diodes. Although some current flows through R_3, most of the current flows into the base of transistor Q_1 to guarantee saturation. With transistor Q_1 saturated, the voltage at the output of the gate, point f, is $V_{CE(\text{sat})} = 0.2$ V. This corresponds to the last line in Fig. A.31*b*.

Under the assumption of positive logic, a low voltage in Fig. A.31*b* is replaced by logic-0 and a high voltage is replaced by logic-1. This results in the truth table shown in Fig. A.31*c*. From this table it immediately follows that $f = \overline{x_1x_2}$, which is the definition of the nand operation. By using additional input diodes, a nand-gate for more than two input variables is constructed.

Resistor R_3 in Fig. A.31*a* is used to improve the speed performance of the gate. When transistor Q_1 is in saturation, it is necessary to remove the minority charge carriers from the base region of the transistor before it can go into cutoff. As a result of removing these charge carriers, current flows away from the base terminal. Resistor R_3 provides a path to ground for this current. If resistor R_3 were not present, then it would be necessary to remove the charge carriers by a flow of current through diodes D_1 and D_2 in the reverse direction. Since current does not flow readily in that direction, the switching time of transistor Q_1 would be relatively high. Thus, the smaller the value of R_3, the faster the output transistor can switch. There is a limit, however, to how small the value of R_3 can be made. When transistor Q_1 is in saturation, current is diverted from the base to resistor R_3. It is seen shortly that the fan-out capability of the gate is dependent upon the base current. Hence, by decreasing R_3, the fan-out capability of the gate is also decreased.

A.6.1 Loading Effects

In Sec. A.4 the effects of transistors as loads to a transistor inverter circuit were shown. The allowable number of loads was limited by the amount of current the driving transistor was capable of supplying to the loads. For DTL gates, the fan-out of a gate is limited by the amount of current the output transistor stage is capable of sinking, since it must accept current from the input diodes of the load gates.

Again refer to Fig. A.31*a*. However, now assume the DTL gate has N identical DTL gates connected to its output as loads. These loads are the dotted portion of the figure. First consider the case when the output of the driving gate, point f, is high at 5 V. This occurs when transistor Q_1 is in cutoff. The input diodes of the loads connected to f are reverse biased and, hence, the currents $I_1, \ldots, I_N$ are 0 and no current flows between the driving and load gates.* Thus, there is no significant loading effect upon the driving gate.

Now consider the situation when the output of the driving gate, point f, is low. In this case, transistor Q_1 for proper operation is in saturation and the voltage at point f is $V_{CE(\text{sat})} = 0.2$ V. The load diodes connected to point f are forward biased and a net current of $I_{\text{Load}} = I_1 + \cdots + I_N$ flows from the load network toward the driving gate. This current, along with the current component I_{R2}, flows into the collector of transistor Q_1. Transistor Q_1 stays in saturation as long as $\beta_F I_B > I_C = I_{R2} + I_{\text{Load}}$. Thus, for a given β_F and I_B, there is a limit in the number of permissible loads that allows transistor Q_1 to remain in saturation.

*Reverse leakage currents are being ignored in accordance with the diode model.

A.6.2 Modified DTL

From the above discussion it follows that the fan-out capability of a DTL gate is increased by increasing the base current to the output transistor. A modified form of DTL that does this is shown in Fig. A.32. Comparing Figs. A.31*a* and A.32, the only difference is in the coupling circuit. In Fig. A.32, the effective series connection of two coupling diodes still exists since the base-emitter junction of transistor Q_1 serves as one of the coupling diodes. In addition, the circuit is designed so that transistor Q_1 operates in its normal active mode and serves as a current amplifier.

When the inputs to the gate are both high at 5 V, transistors Q_1 and Q_2 are turned on. The voltage at point P is clamped at $V_{BE1(\text{on})} + V_{D(\text{on})} + V_{BE2(\text{sat})} = 0.7 + 0.7 + 0.7 = 2.1$ V and, consequently, the input diodes are reverse biased. There is a current component through resistor R_2. Owing to the direction of this current component, the base-collector junction of transistor Q_1 is reverse biased and, hence, transistor Q_1 is in its normal active mode. According to the circuit model of Fig. A.14, it follows that the emitter current of transistor Q_1 is $(1 + \beta_F)I_{B1}$. This amplified current is now available to the output transistor stage of the DTL gate. As a consequence, with a larger amount of current available at the base of transistor Q_2, more loads can be connected to the output of the modified DTL gate and still have transistor Q_2 remain in saturation.

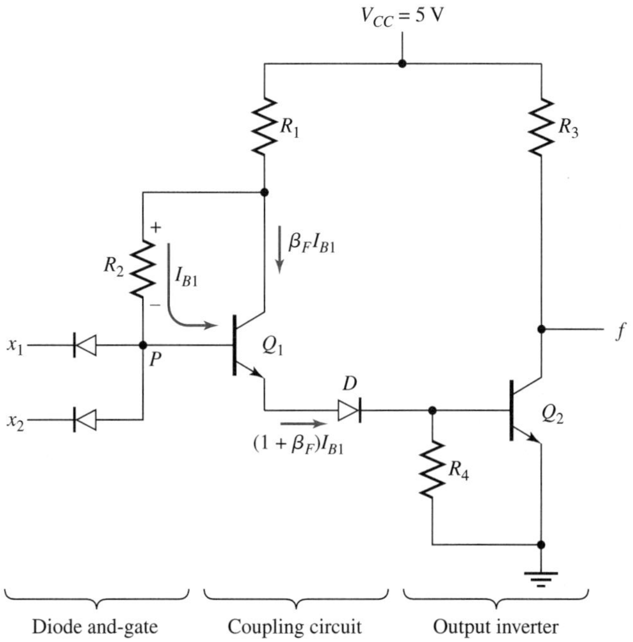

Figure A.32 A two-input modified DTL nand-gate.

A.7 TRANSISTOR-TRANSISTOR LOGIC (TTL)

A basic two-input *transistor-transistor logic* (TTL) nand-gate is shown in Fig. A.33. This gate is essentially a modification of the DTL nand-gate given previously in Fig. A.31. Comparing these two figures, the first difference that is noted is the use of a multiemitter *npn* transistor as the input stage in place of the diode and-gate. Each emitter consists of *n*-type semiconductor material having a common junction with the *p*-type base material. Hence, the multiemitter junctions can be regarded as a collection of *pn* junction diodes whose anodes are connected together. From a steady-state point of view, this configuration with resistor R_1 essentially forms a diode and-gate. In addition, the two coupling diodes D_1 and D_2 of Fig. A.31 are replaced by the base-collector junction of transistor Q_1 and the base-emitter junction of transistor Q_2, respectively. The final stage, consisting of a transistor inverter, is the same in both figures. Thus, it should be expected that the logic behavior of the gate in Fig. A.33 is a nand-gate just like that of Fig. A.31.

To appreciate the advantages of TTL over DTL, a more detailed analysis of the TTL nand-gate is necessary. For this analysis, the circuit models and approximations previously introduced in Sec. A.3 are used. In particular, it is assumed that $V_{BE(on)} = V_{BE(sat)} = 0.7$ V, $V_{BC(on)} = V_{BC(sat)} = 0.5$ V, and $V_{CE(sat)} = 0.2$ V. The details of the analysis are illustrated in Fig. A.34. First assume both inputs are high at 5 V as indicated in Fig. A.34*a*. This causes the base-collector junction of transistor Q_1 and the base-emitter junctions of transistors Q_2 and Q_3 to be forward biased. The

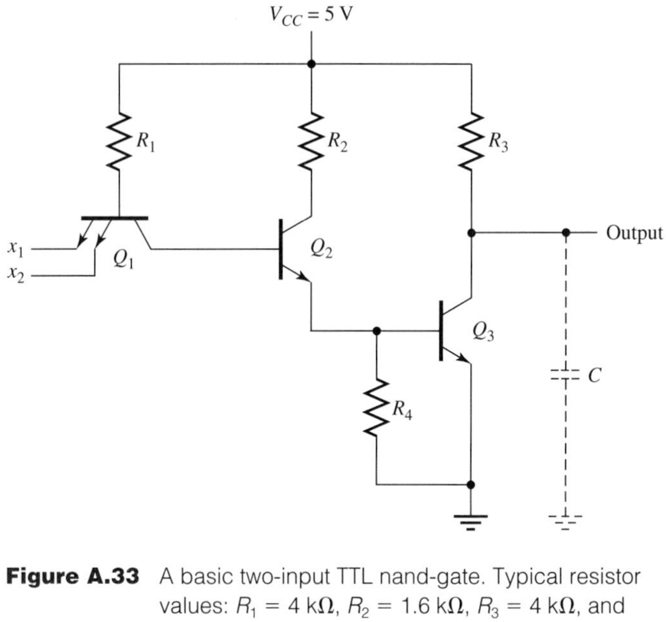

Figure A.33 A basic two-input TTL nand-gate. Typical resistor values: $R_1 = 4\ \text{k}\Omega$, $R_2 = 1.6\ \text{k}\Omega$, $R_3 = 4\ \text{k}\Omega$, and $R_4 = 1\ \text{k}\Omega$.

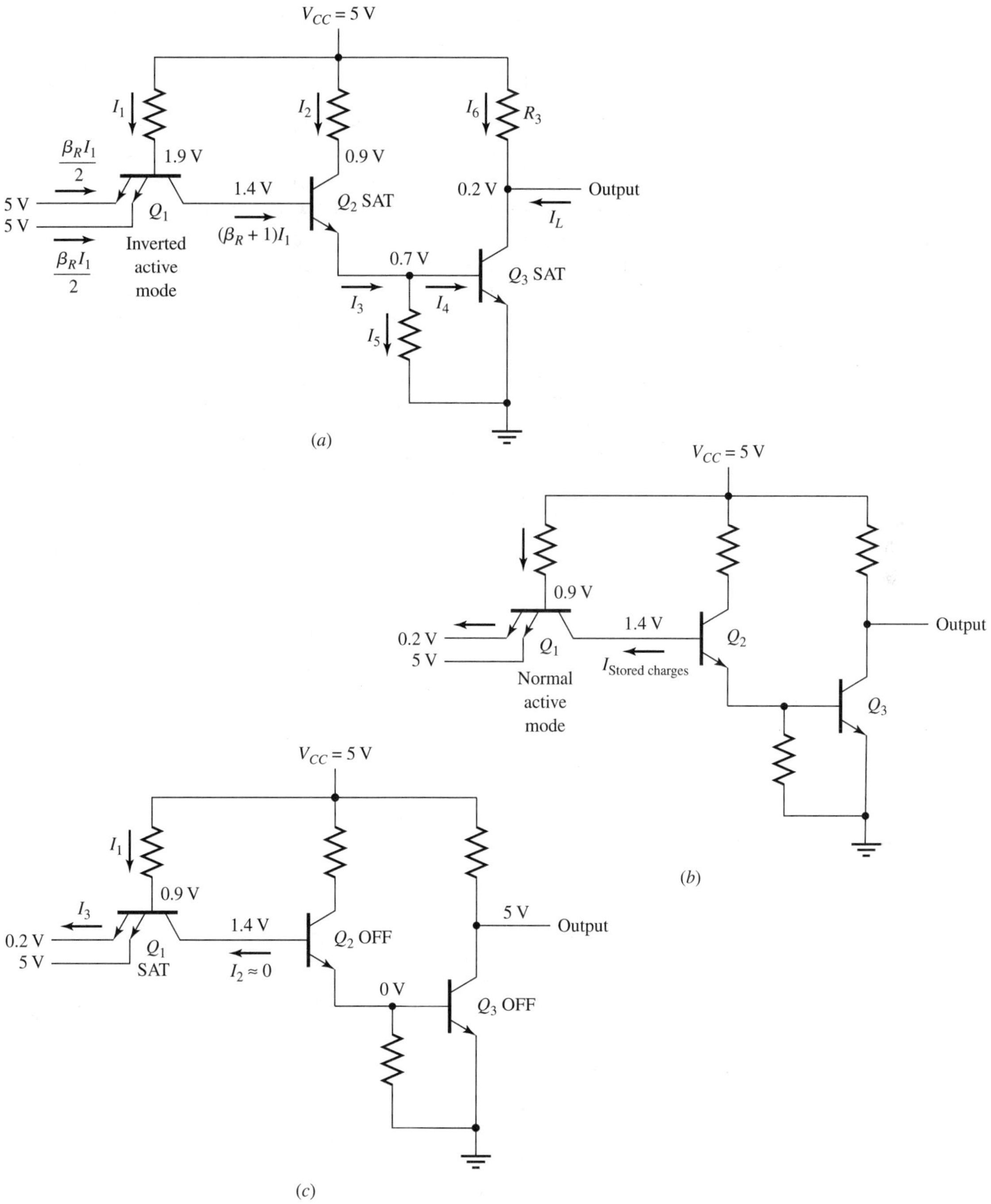

Figure A.34 Analysis of a two-input TTL nand-gate. (*a*) Circuit conditions when all inputs are high. (*b*) Circuit conditions immediately following an input change. (*c*) Circuit conditions after transient effects.

circuit is designed so that transistors Q_2 and Q_3 saturate, causing the output of the gate to become $V_{CE3(\text{sat})} = 0.2$ V, which corresponds to the low-level logic value. Since transistors Q_2 and Q_3 are saturated, the voltage at the base of Q_3 is $V_{BE3(\text{sat})} =$ 0.7 V and the voltage at the base of Q_2 is $V_{BE3(\text{sat})} + V_{BE2(\text{sat})} = 0.7 + 0.7 = 1.4$ V. Finally, since the base-collector junction of transistor Q_1 is forward biased, the voltage at its base becomes $V_{BE3(\text{sat})} + V_{BE2(\text{sat})} + V_{BC1(\text{on})} = 0.7 + 0.7 + 0.5 = 1.9$ V. Since all the inputs are at 5 V, it is seen that the input base-emitter junctions are reversed biased. As a consequence of the base-emitter junctions of Q_1 being reverse biased and its base-collector junction being forward biased, transistor Q_1 is operating in its inverted active mode. As indicated in Fig. A.34*a*, a small current is flowing into the emitter terminals in accordance with the transistor circuit model of Fig. A.16.

Next consider the situation when at least one input is low at 0.2 V. This is illustrated in Fig. A.34*c*.* The corresponding base-emitter junction of transistor Q_1 is forward biased, clamping the base of transistor Q_1 to $V_{\text{in}} + V_{BE1(\text{sat})} = 0.2 + 0.7 =$ 0.9 V. This allows for the flow of base current I_1. The voltage on the base of transistor Q_1 is insufficient to support the base-collector junction drop of transistor Q_1 and the base-emitter junction drops of transistors Q_2 and Q_3. Hence, transistors Q_2 and Q_3 are in cutoff and the output voltage is 5 V. Furthermore, since transistor Q_2 is in cutoff, its base current, I_2, is approximately zero. Thus, $\beta_{F1}I_1 > I_2 = 0$, which implies that transistor Q_1 is in saturation and that $I_1 = I_3$.

The above analysis illustrated in Fig. A.34*a* and *c* corresponds to steady-state conditions of the TTL nand-gate. In this analysis, the base-collector junction of transistor Q_1 was regarded as simply a *pn*-junction diode. However, in the process of switching transistor Q_1 from its inverted active mode to its saturation mode when at least one input goes low, there is also a transistor action effect that results in a reduction of the gate's propagation delay time. To see this, again consider Fig. A.34. Since transistor Q_1 in Fig. A.34*a* is not saturated, it is capable of switching quite rapidly. Furthermore, transistors Q_2 and Q_3 cannot come out of saturation until the stored charges are removed from their bases. Thus, when at least one input goes low to 0.2 V, the base of transistor Q_1 quickly goes to 0.9 V since the corresponding *pn* junction becomes forward biased, while its collector remains at 1.4 V. This is illustrated in Fig. A.34*b*. It can now be seen that at the time of switching, the base-collector junction of transistor Q_1 is reverse biased by $1.4 - 0.9 = 0.5$ V and the base-emitter junction is forward biased. This causes transistor Q_1 to enter its normal active mode, which permits a large collector current to flow. This collector current corresponds to the removal of the stored charges of transistors Q_2 and Q_3. It is not until these stored charges are removed that transistor Q_1 enters saturation. The net effect is the quick removal of the stored charges and, correspondingly, rapid switching of transistors Q_2 and Q_3 from saturation to cutoff. As a result of this transistor action, TTL is much faster than DTL.

---

*The transient situation illustrated ion Fig. A.34*b* is discussed shortly.

A.7.1 Wired Logic

With some logic gates, it is possible to connect their outputs together so as to achieve logic behavior at the connection. This is known as *wired logic*.

Consider two TTL nand-gates of the type shown in Fig. A.33. If the outputs are connected together, then the wired output appears at the collectors of the parallel connection of the two output transistors. This is illustrated in Fig. A.35*a*. The wired output is high if both output transistors are in cutoff. If at least one output transistor is in saturation, then the wired output is at the relatively low voltage $V_{CE3(\text{sat})} = 0.2$ V. Thus, the voltage at the wired connection is high if and only if the outputs of both of the individual gates are high. Under the assumption of positive logic, it now follows that effectively an and-operation is achieved at the wired connection. The overall effect is shown in Fig. A.35*b*. The and-gate is implicit by the wired connection and is referred to as a wired and-gate. If the two TTL gates correspond to the functions $\overline{x_1x_2}$ and $\overline{x_3x_4}$, then the overall function $\overline{(x_1x_2)}\,\overline{(x_3x_4)} = \overline{x_1x_2 + x_3x_4}$ is obtained as a consequence of connecting together the two gate outputs.

It should also be noted that resistors R_3 from the two gates in Fig. A.35*a* are also placed in parallel when the gate outputs are connected. This results in an effective resistance of $R_3/2$ and, correspondingly, increases the power dissipation of the gate whose output transistor Q_3 is in saturation. For this reason, TTL gates without resistor R_3, as shown in Fig. A.36, are available commercially specifically for applications in which the wired-and capability is desirable. This is known as

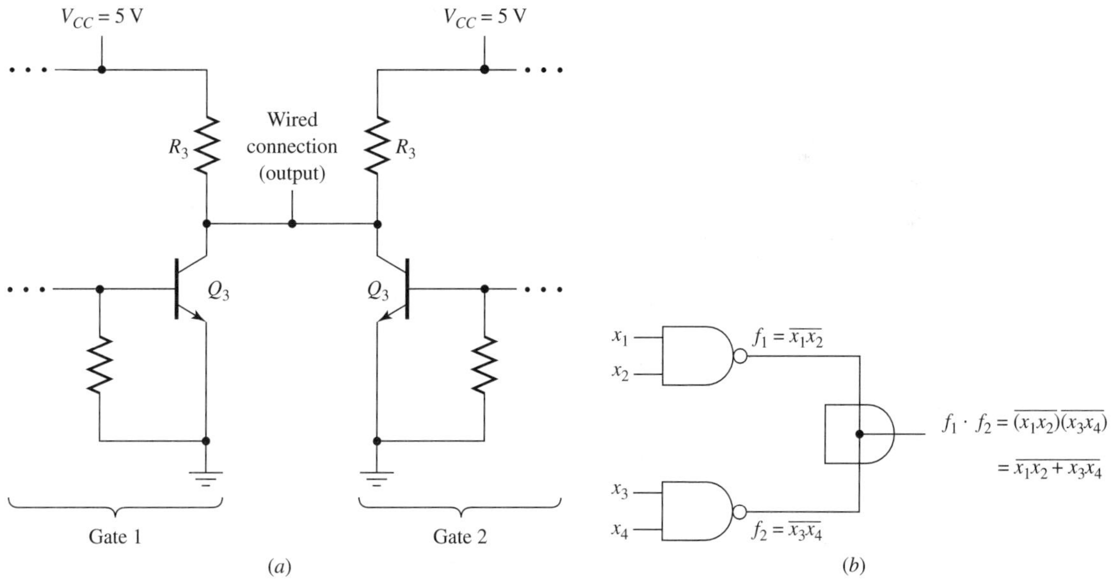

Figure A.35 Wired logic. (*a*) Connecting the outputs of two nand-gates of the type shown in Fig. A.33. (*b*) Logical effect of wired connection.

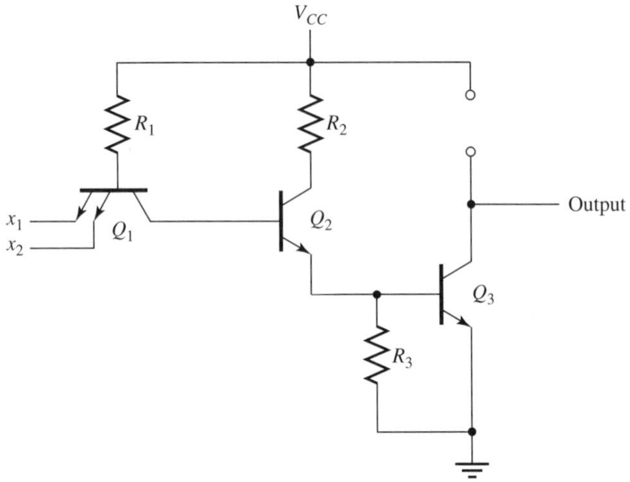

Figure A.36 A two-input open-collector TTL nand-gate.

open-collector TTL. Of course, after the outputs of open-collector TTL gates are connected together in a network, a single collector resistor, referred to as a *passive pull-up resistor*, must be added externally.

A.7.2 TTL with Totem-Pole Output

The speed of operation of a logic gate is also dependent upon the parasitic output capacitance. This capacitance appears as the dotted capacitor, C, in Fig. A.33 and is associated with the wiring capacitance, the input diode capacitance of the load gates, and the collector-emitter capacitance of transistor Q_3. The rate at which this parasitic capacitor is charged and discharged affects the switching time of the driving gate.

The discharging of capacitor C occurs when the output of the gate goes from its high value to its low value, or, correspondingly, when Q_3 goes from cutoff to saturation. The discharge path is through Q_3 with a time constant of $R_{Q3(\text{on})}C$ where $R_{Q3(\text{on})}$ is the small conducting resistance of transistor Q_3 and is in the order of 20 Ω. On the other hand, capacitor C must be charged when the output of the gate goes from its low value to its high value. In this case, the charging path is through resistor R_3 and the associated time constant is R_3C. A typical value of R_3 is 4 kΩ.

By reducing the value of R_3, the output low-to-high switching time of the gate is decreased. However, a low value of R_3 increases the power consumption of the circuit when the output is low. To see this, as indicated in Fig. A.34*a*, there is a current component through R_3 when transistor Q_3 is in saturation. The power dissipation in R_3 is given by $(V_{CC} - V_{CE3(\text{sat})})^2/R_3$. Thus, as R_3 is decreased, the power dissipation is increased. It can now be concluded that it is desirable to have R_3 be as small as possible while the output is switching from its low to high value in order to have a small RC time constant, and have R_3 be as large as possible when the gate is in its steady state with a low output in order to have low power dissipation. One way this is achieved is by the use of an *active pull-up circuit* known as a *totem-pole output*. A two-input TTL nand-gate with a totem-pole output is shown in Fig. A.37.

An analysis of the TTL nand-gate with a totem-pole output is given in Fig. A.38. First consider the case in which both inputs are high as indicated in Fig. A.38*a*. As shown shortly, the value of a high input is approximately 3.6 V. In this situation, transistors Q_2 and Q_3 are forced into saturation and transistor Q_1 is in the inverted active mode in a similar manner as the basic TTL nand-gate analyzed previously in Fig. A.34. Since transistor Q_2 is in saturation, the voltage at its collector is $V_{CE2(\text{sat})} + V_{BE3(\text{sat})} = 0.2 + 0.7 = 0.9$ V. This is also the voltage at the base of transistor Q_4. Furthermore, since transistor Q_3 is in saturation, the voltage at the cathode of diode D_1 is $V_{CE3(\text{sat})} = 0.2$ V. With a voltage difference of $0.9 - 0.2 = 0.7$ V between the base of transistor Q_4 and the output, there is insufficient force to support the base-emitter drop of transistor Q_4 and the diode drop of D_1 to allow current to flow through these two elements. Thus, transistor Q_4 and diode D_1 are in cutoff. With transistor Q_4 in cutoff, no current flows through the low-valued resistor R_3. As a result, the objective of having no power dissipation in this section of the circuit has now been achieved when the output of the gate is low. However, transistor Q_3 is still sinking current due to the loads.

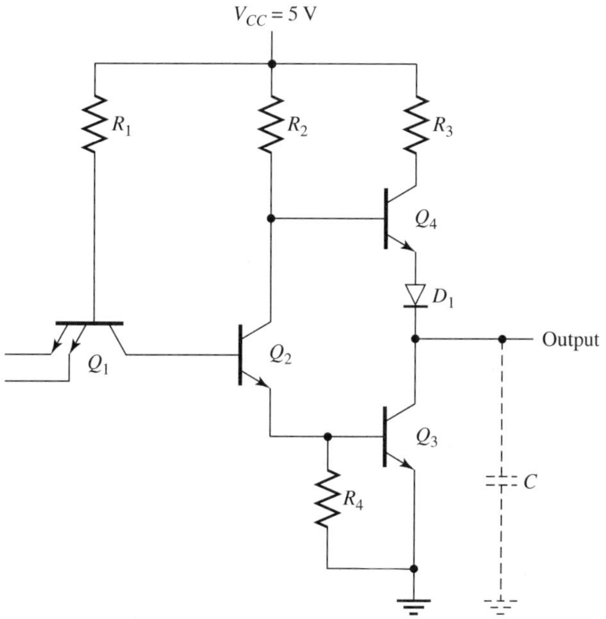

Figure A.37 A two-input TTL nand-gate with totem-pole output. Typical resistor values: $R_1 = 4$ kΩ, $R_2 = 1.6$ kΩ, $R_3 = 130$ Ω, and $R_4 = 1$ kΩ.

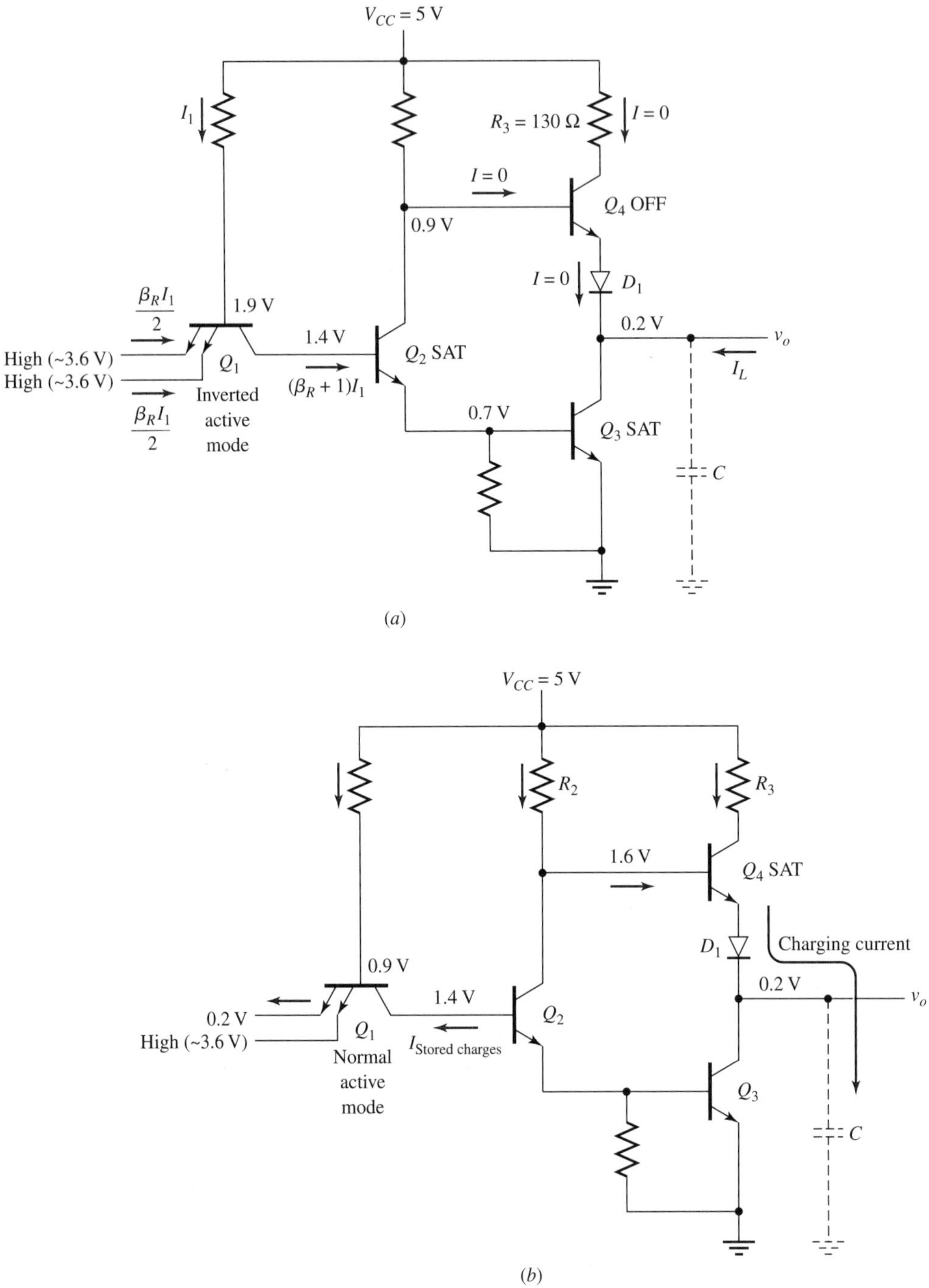

Figure A.38 Analysis of a two-input TTL nand-gate with a totem-pole output. (*a*) Circuit conditions when all inputs are high. (*b*) Circuit conditions immediately following an input change.

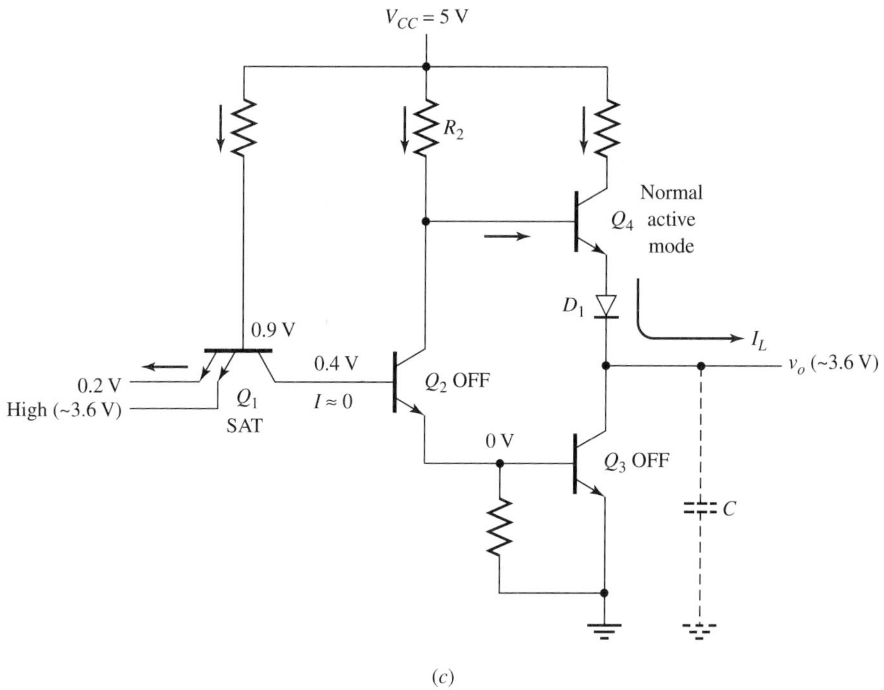

Figure A.38 (*c*) Circuit conditions after transient effects.

Now assume there is a change in one of the gate inputs to a low value, i.e., 0.2 V. This is shown in Fig. A.38*b*. As explained previously, transistors Q_2 and Q_3 are quickly turned off. However, since the voltage across the parasitic capacitance cannot change instantaneously, the collector of transistor Q_3 must remain momentarily at 0.2 V. Owing to the supply voltage V_{CC} and resistor R_2, diode D_1 conducts and transistor Q_4 enters saturation. The voltage at the base of transistor Q_4 is $V_{BE4(\text{sat})} + V_{D1(\text{on})} + v_o = 0.7 + 0.7 + 0.2 = 1.6$ V. The collective resistance of resistor R_3, the saturation collector-emitter resistance of transistor Q_4, and the on resistance of diode D_1 is in the order of 150 Ω. This collective resistance along with the parasitic capacitance C is the RC time constant that determines the charging rate of the parasitic capacitance. This collective resistance is much less than that of resistor R_3 in Fig. A.33. The net effect is that the output quickly changes from its low value to its high value.

As the parasitic load capacitor charges, the base and collector currents of transistor Q_4 decrease, causing the transistor to enter its normal active mode as indicated in Fig. A.38c. In the steady state, the load current, I_L, is the very small current governed by the β_R of the load gates. As can be seen from the figure, the output voltage of the gate is given by $v_o \approx V_{CC} - V_{BE4(\text{on})} - V_{D1(\text{on})} = 5 - 0.7 - 0.7 = 3.6$ V if the small drop across resistor R_2 is neglected. This is the high output voltage of the TTL nand-gate with a totem-pole output.

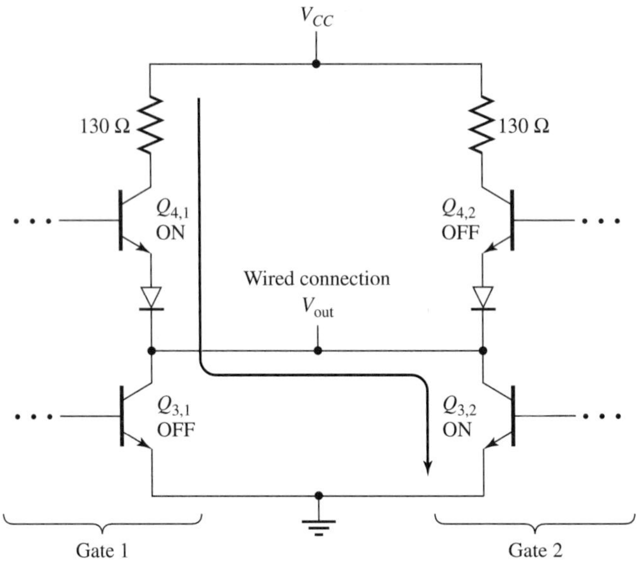

Figure A.39 Wired-logic effects of TTL gates with totem-pole outputs.

A disadvantage of the totem-pole output is that it does not permit wired logic. To see this, note that in the steady state, one transistor in the totem pole is in cutoff while the other is in either saturation or its normal active mode depending upon whether it is the upper or lower transistor. Figure A.39 shows the output stages of two TTL gates in which the output terminals are wired together. Assume the inputs to these gates are such that transistor $Q_{3,1}$ is off and transistor $Q_{4,2}$ is off. For proper operation, transistor $Q_{4,1}$ should be in its normal active mode and transistor $Q_{3,2}$ should be in saturation. It is seen from the figure that in such a situation there is a low-impedance path from the power supply V_{CC} through the 130-Ω resistor of gate 1 and the on transistors $Q_{4,1}$ and $Q_{3,2}$ to ground. This path draws a large current. With such a large collector current in transistor $Q_{3,2}$, this transistor comes out of saturation, causing it to enter its normal active mode. The net consequence is that the output voltage rises to some value above $V_{OL(\max)}$, the maximum allowable voltage for logic-0. Hence, any gates connected to V_{out} do not receive a valid input signal.

A.7.3 Three-State Output TTL

There are many variations to the basic TTL circuits that have been discussed thus far. As was shown above, wired logic is not permissible with the TTL nand-gate of Fig. A.37 having the totem-pole output. However, for the special situation in which several TTL gate outputs are tied together to a common bus with the constraint that only one of these gates is to control the signals on the bus, there is a special form of TTL gate that is used which retains the advantages of the totem-pole output. This variation is illustrated in Fig. A.40 and is called TTL with *three-state output*. To the

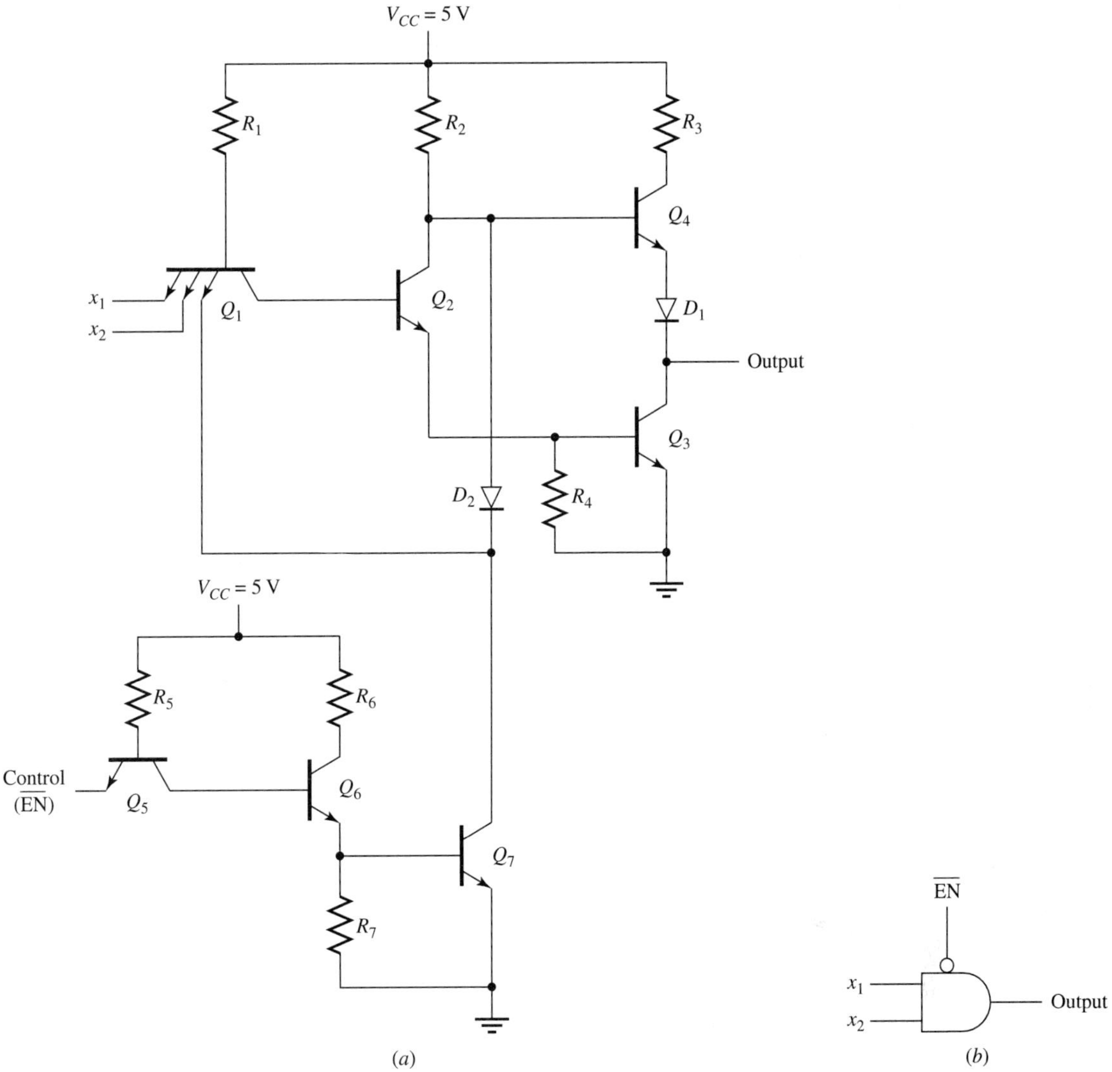

Figure A.40 TTL nand-gate with three-state output. (*a*) Circuit diagram. (*b*) Logic symbol.

gate of Fig. A.37 there is now added a controlling circuit consisting of transistors Q_5, Q_6, and Q_7, resistors R_5, R_6, and R_7, and diode D_2. In essence, a single-input open-collector TTL gate having a control input $\overline{EN}$ is added to the TTL gate with the totem-pole output.

To understand how this circuit works, first consider the case when the control input $\overline{EN}$ is at logic-0, i.e., at 0.2 V. This causes transistor Q_5 to go into saturation and to turn off transistors Q_6 and Q_7. With transistor Q_7 behaving as an open circuit, there are no conduction paths from the V_{CC} supply voltage through either diode D_2 or the emitter of transistor Q_1 connected to the collector of transistor Q_7. The net result is that the additional circuitry, i.e., the open-collector TTL gate portion of Fig. A.40*a*, has no effect upon the operation of the basic TTL nand-gate portion. In this case, the output of the TTL nand-gate with three-state output is dependent solely upon the inputs x_1 and x_2 as discussed previously for the TTL nand-gate with totem-pole output. That is, the output of the gate is a high or low voltage value depending upon the applied inputs.

Now assume the control input $\overline{EN}$ in Fig. A.40*a* is at logic-1, say, 5 V. As in the case of open-collector TTL, transistor Q_5 goes into the inverted-active mode and base current flows into transistors Q_6 and Q_7. This permits collector current to flow in transistor Q_7. In particular, a conduction path is established from V_{CC} through resistor R_2 and diode D_2 into the collector of transistor Q_7. By circuit design, transistor Q_7 saturates, causing the voltage at the base of transistor Q_4 to become $V_{CE7(\text{sat})} + V_{D2(\text{on})} = 0.2 + 0.7 = 0.9$ V. This, in turn, causes transistor Q_4 to enter cutoff since this is an insufficient force to drive current through the base-emitter junction of transistor Q_4 and diode D_1. In addition, a second conduction path exists from V_{CC} through resistor R_1 and the emitter of transistor Q_1 connected to the collector of transistor Q_7. As a consequence, the voltage at the base of transistor Q_1 becomes $V_{CE7(\text{sat})} + V_{BE1(\text{sat})} = 0.2 + 0.7 = 0.9$ V. In such a case, transistors Q_2 and Q_3 are forced into cutoff, again due to an insufficient driving force. Thus, when the control input $\overline{EN}$ of Fig. A.40*a* is at logic-1, both transistors Q_3 and Q_4 of the totem pole are forced into cutoff, with the net effect that the output of the gate appears as an open circuit or, equivalently, a high impedance. This high-impedance condition is regarded as the third state of this TTL gate.

In summary, there are three states associated with the output of the gate shown in Fig. A.40*a*. When the control input $\overline{EN}$ is logic-0, the output is at logic-0 if the inputs x_1 and x_2 are both at logic-1. In this case, transistor Q_3 is in saturation and transistor Q_4 is in cutoff. Also when the control input $\overline{EN}$ is logic-0, the output is at logic-1 if at least one input x_1 or x_2 is at logic-0. Here, transistor Q_3 is in cutoff and transistor Q_4 is in its saturation mode. Finally, when the control input $\overline{EN}$ is at logic-1, both transistors Q_3 and Q_4 are in cutoff independent of the inputs x_1 and x_2. This is the third or high-impedance state of the output. A logic symbol for a three-state nand-gate is shown in Fig. A.40*b*.

The outputs of several three-state TTL gates can be wired together if at most only one of the control inputs is allowed to be at logic-0 at any time. In such a case, the corresponding gate controls the logic output of the wired connection, while all the remaining gates are in their high-impedance state. If two or more gates should have their control inputs at logic-0 simultaneously, then the problems discussed previously of wired logic with totem-pole output gates occur and improper operation results.

A.7.4 Schottky TTL

Another TTL variation involves the use of Schottky transistors. Two of the factors that determine the operating speed of a logic gate are the charging and discharging of the load capacitances and the storage delay time in taking a transistor out of saturation.* The use of the totem-pole output aided the charging and discharging of the load capacitances. The use of Schottky transistors improves the speed performance by keeping the transistors from deep saturation, thereby reducing the storage delay effect.

In Sec. A.1 the *pn*-junction diode was described. A diode can also be fabricated by forming a metal to *n*-type semiconductor junction. The metal forms the anode and the *n*-type semiconductor forms the cathode of the diode. These are called *Schottky diodes*. Such diodes are capable of faster switching since they involve only the flow of majority carriers, i.e., electrons. The consequence of this is that there is no storage of minority carriers in the *pn*-junction region that would otherwise have to be removed before the diode is turned off. The *I-V* characteristic curve of the Schottky diode is similar to that of Fig. A.2 except the drop across the diode is approximately 0.4 V when conducting. The symbol for the Schottky diode is shown in Fig. A.41*a*. When a Schottky diode is placed between the base and collector of an *npn* bipolar transistor as shown in Fig. A.41*b*, the resulting configuration is referred to as a *Schottky transistor*. The symbol for a Schottky transistor is given in Fig. A.41*c*.

Again consider the TTL nand-gate of Fig. A.37 with the totem-pole output. Under steady-state conditions, transistors Q_1, Q_2, and Q_3 are in saturation depending upon the applied inputs. To take the transistors out of saturation it is first necessary to remove charges that are stored in the base regions. In the case of transistor Q_2, the transistor action of Q_1 is used to remove the stored charges. However, in general, if a transistor is prevented from going into saturation when on, then the transistor can switch much more rapidly since fewer stored charges must be removed. In the case of Schottky TTL gates, transistors Q_1, Q_2, and Q_3 of Fig. A.37 are replaced by Schottky transistors to achieve the desirable effect of avoiding saturation.

To understand how saturation is avoided, consider the circuit configuration of Fig. A.41*b*. Normally, when a transistor is in saturation, the collector-emitter drop is

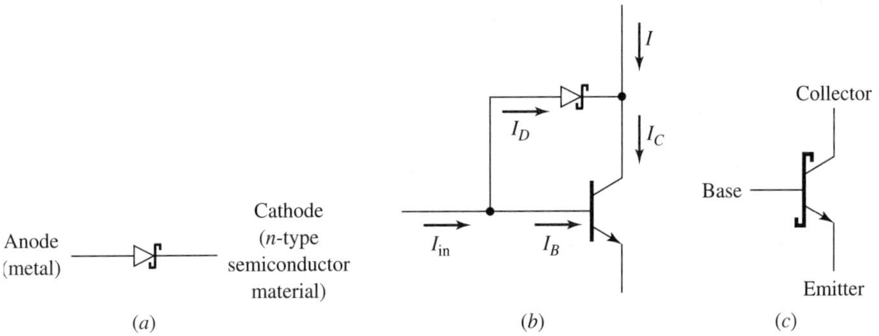

Figure A.41 (*a*) Symbol of the Schottky diode. (*b*) Circuit configuration of the Schottky transistor. (*c*) Symbol of the Schottky transistor.

*The storage delay effect was discussed in Sec. A.5.

0.2 V. In addition, the base-emitter drop of an on transistor is 0.7 V. By placing the Schottky diode between the base and collector of the transistor, the collector-emitter voltage of the transistor is prevented from going below 0.3 V and, hence, the transistor is kept from saturating. What happens is that when the collector-emitter voltage reaches 0.3 V as a consequence of a large input current I_{in}, the Schottky diode starts to conduct, which, in turn, prevents the collector voltage from going any lower, i.e., $V_{CE} = V_{BE(\text{on})} - V_{D(\text{on})} = 0.7 - 0.4 = 0.3$ V. A current I_D is diverted through the conducting Schottky diode so that $\beta_F I_B = I_C$ where I_C is the total current that the transistor must sink, i.e., $I_C = I_D + I$. For different values of current I as a consequence of, say, a different number of loads, the diverting current I_D adjusts accordingly.

A.7.5 Concluding Remarks

In this section, two basic forms of TTL, i.e., open-collector and totem-pole output, were discussed in detail. These are referred to as standard TTL. Two variations, i.e., three-state output TTL and Schottky TTL, were also introduced. Over the years, several other variations or series of TTL have been developed for achieving better gate performance. Although Schottky TTL provides greater speed than standard TTL, this was achieved by increasing the power dissipation of the gate. By using larger resistor values, there resulted low-power Schottky (LS) TTL. In time, additional circuit modifications were incorporated with the intent of reducing the power dissipation and increasing the operating speed. This has led to advanced-Schottky (AS) TTL and advanced-low-power-Schottky (ALS) TTL gates.

A.8 EMITTER-COUPLED LOGIC (ECL)

In the previous section it was noted that to improve the switching speed, i.e., to reduce the propagation delay time, of a logic gate, transistors are prevented from becoming saturated. At this time, the final bipolar logic family, *emitter-coupled logic* (ECL), also referred to as *current-mode logic* (CML), is studied. This logic family has the highest speed of operation, which is achieved by operating the transistors in the normal active mode. Although emitter-coupled logic, in general, is fast, the power consumption is high and the voltage swing between logic-0 and logic-1 is small, with the consequence that the noise margin is low.

The basic ECL gate shown in Fig. A.42*a* is studied in this section. It should be noted that both or and nor outputs are provided from this circuit. Hence, it is referred to as an or/nor-gate. The logic symbol for an or/nor-gate is given in Fig. A.42*b*. The ECL gate consists of three basic sections: the current switch or differential amplifier, the emitter-follower level restorers, and the reference supply. Since the objective here is to understand the gate's basic principle of operation, the analysis is greatly simplified through the use of approximations. Furthermore, rather than viewing the entire circuit at once, the approach that will be taken is to build it up by considering each of the three sections in turn.

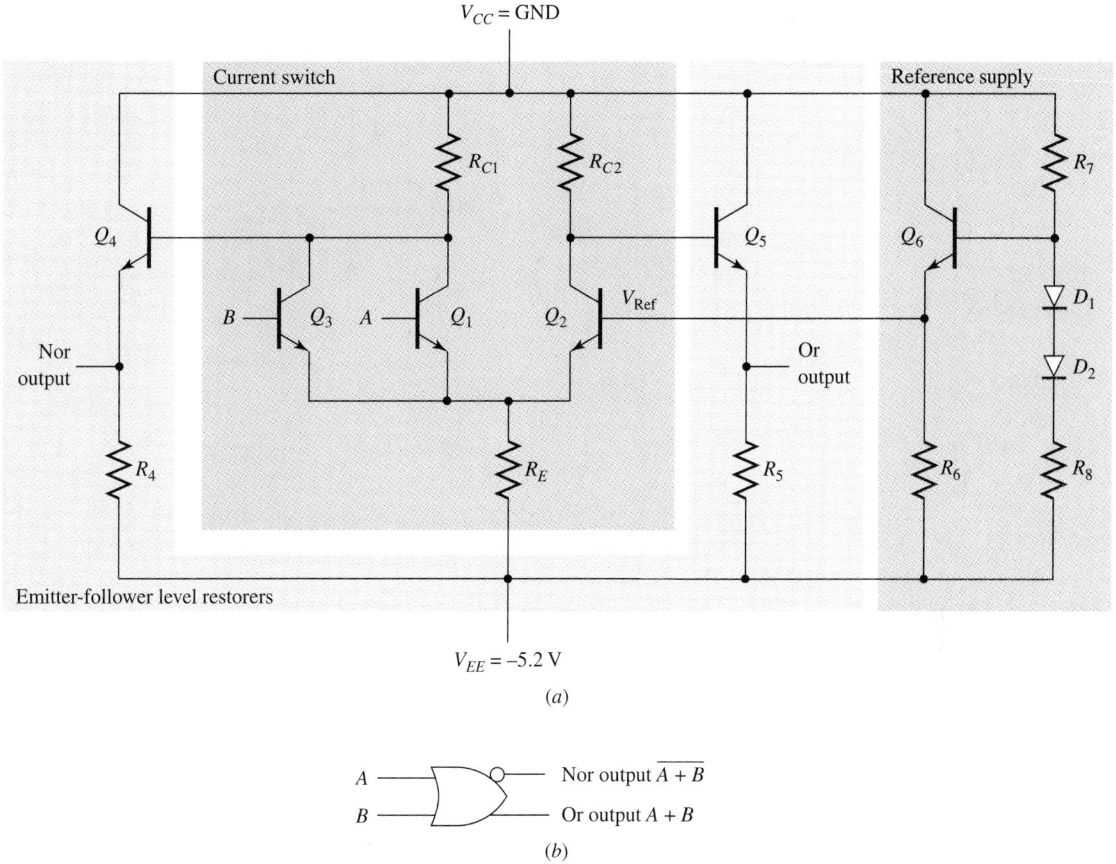

Figure A.42 A two-input ECL or/nor-gate. (*a*) Circuit diagram. Typical resistor values: $R_{C1} = 290\ \Omega$, $R_{C2} = 300\ \Omega$, $R_E = 1.18\ \text{k}\Omega$, and $R_4 = R_5 = 1.5\ \text{k}\Omega$, $R_6 = 2\ \text{k}\Omega$, $R_7 = 300\ \text{k}\Omega$, and $R_8 = 2.3\ \text{k}\Omega$. (*b*) Logic symbol.

A.8.1 The Current Switch

A one-input current switch is shown in Fig. A.43*a*. The single input is applied to the base of transistor Q_1; while a reference voltage, V_{Ref}, is applied to the base of transistor Q_2. Assume the input voltage at terminal *A* is -1.6 V and $V_{\text{Ref}} = -1.15$ V. The voltage difference between the base of transistor Q_2 and the supply voltage V_{EE} is sufficiently positive so as to forward bias the base-emitter junction of transistor Q_2. As a result, the voltage at point *X* becomes $V_{\text{Ref}} - V_{BE2(\text{on})} = -1.15 - 0.7 = -1.85$ V. Consequently, the base-emitter junction of transistor Q_1 is reversed biased by $V_A - V_X = -1.6 + 1.85 = 0.25$ V, causing it to be in cutoff. Thus, no current flows through transistor Q_1, while current flows through transistor Q_2. Since there is no collector current for transistor Q_1, there is no current through resistor R_{C1}. Hence, the voltage at the collector of transistor Q_1 is ground as indicated in Fig. A.43*a*.

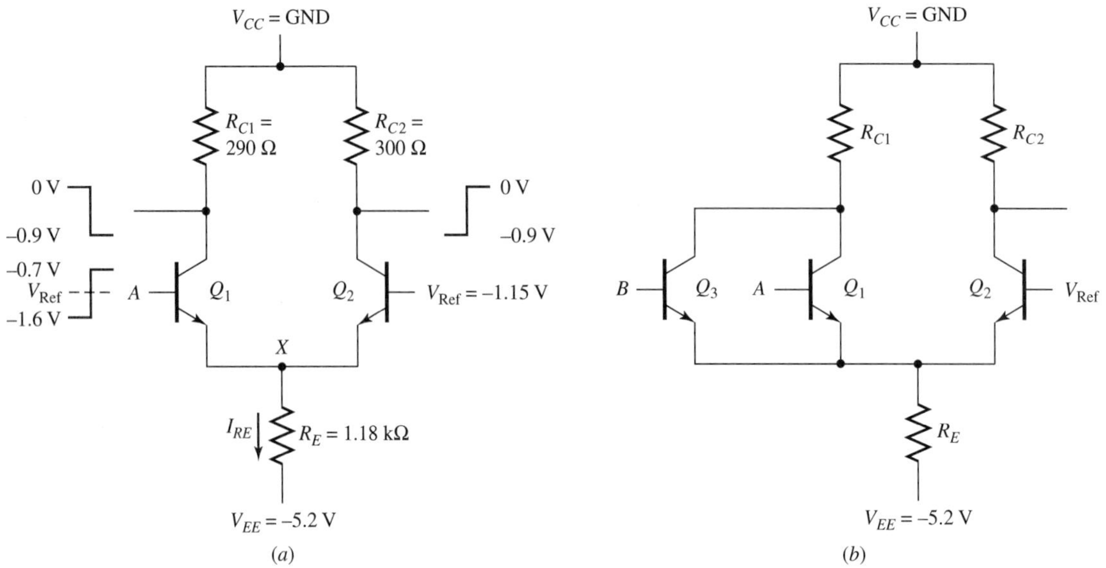

Figure A.43 The current switch. (*a*) One-input switch. (*b*) Two-input switch.

Let us now further consider the current flow through transistor Q_2. As a result of the voltage at point X being -1.85 V and the bias supply V_{EE} being -5.2 V, the current I_{RE} is $(V_X - V_{EE})/R_E = (-1.85 + 5.2)/1.18 = 2.84$ mA. If it is assumed that transistor Q_2 is operating in its normal active mode, then, for transistor Q_2, $I_C = \beta_F I_B$ and $I_E = (\beta_F + 1)I_B$. Under the assumption that $\beta_F >> 1$ for transistor Q_2, then $I_C \approx I_E$. Using this approximation of the Q_2 collector current, the collector voltage of transistor Q_2 is $V_{CC} - I_C R_{C2} = 0 - 2.84 \times 0.3 = -0.9$ V as indicated in Fig. A.43*a*. It should be noted that in this situation the base-collector junction of transistor Q_2 is reversed biased, which justifies the assumption that this transistor is operating in its normal active mode.

A similar analysis of the current switch can be performed when input A to the base of transistor Q_1 is raised to -0.7 V. In this case, transistor Q_1 operates in its normal active mode, while transistor Q_2 is in cutoff. To see this, with $V_A = -0.7$ V, then $V_X = V_A - V_{BE1(\text{on})} = -0.7 - 0.7 = -1.4$ V. This causes the base-emitter junction of transistor Q_2 to be forward biased by $V_{\text{Ref}} - V_X = -1.15 + 1.4 = 0.25$ V. However, this forward bias is insufficient to turn on transistor Q_2 since it is less than the required base-emitter drop of 0.7 V. The current I_{RE}, which is the same as the emitter current of transistor Q_1, is $(V_X - V_{EE})/R_E = (-1.4 + 5.2)/1.18 = 3.22$ mA. The collector current of transistor Q_1 can be approximated by its emitter current since the β_F of the transistor is very large. Hence, the collector voltage of transistor Q_1 is approximately $V_{CC} - I_{RE}R_E = 0 - 3.22 \times 0.29 = -0.9$ V. It should be observed that with a collector voltage of -0.9 V, the base-collector junction of transistor Q_1 is forward biased by 0.2 V. However, since this is less than the needed base-collector diode drop for conduction, this insufficient forward bias results in the transistor operating in its normal active mode. Finally, with transistor Q_2 in cutoff, no current flows through resistor R_{C2}, with the result that the collector voltage of transistor Q_2 is ground. The collector voltages for both transistors when $V_A = -0.7$ V are indicated in Fig. A.43*a*.

In summary, the circuit of Fig. A.43*a* provides for the switching of current between transistors Q_1 and Q_2 depending upon whether or not the input voltage at the base of transistor Q_1 is above or below the reference voltage at the base of transistor Q_2. In addition, these transistors operate in either their normal active mode or in cutoff. Finally, it should be noted that the output voltage at the collector of transistor Q_2 is in phase with the input base voltage of transistor Q_1, while the output voltage at the collector of transistor Q_1 is out of phase with the input voltage.

Additional inputs can now be added to the current switch of Fig. A.43*a*. A two-input current switch, shown in Fig. A.43*b*, is constructed by placing transistor Q_3, with input B at its base, in parallel with transistor Q_1. If V_A and V_B are both relatively low, i.e., -1.6 V, then transistor Q_2 conducts and both transistors Q_1 and Q_3 are in cutoff. The collectors of transistors Q_1 and Q_3 become a relatively high voltage, i.e., 0 V, since no current flows in the left side of the circuit. The collector of transistor Q_2 is a relatively low voltage, i.e., -0.9 V, since a voltage drop occurs across resistor R_{C2} because of the flow of current in the right side of the circuit. On the other hand, if at least one input V_A or V_B is relatively high, i.e., -0.7 V, then the corresponding transistor(s) are turned on and transistor Q_2 is in cutoff. In this case, the voltage at the collectors of transistors Q_1 and Q_3 is relatively low, i.e., -0.9 V, since there is a voltage drop across resistor R_{C1} due to the flow of current in the left side of the circuit; while the collector of transistor Q_2 is relatively high, i.e., 0 V, since no current flows in the right side of the circuit. This result is summarized in Table A.1.* As shown by the table, under the assumption of positive logic, i.e., a relatively low voltage denotes a logic-0 and a relatively high voltage denotes a logic-1, the voltage at the collectors of transistors Q_1 and Q_3 corresponds to the nor-function and the voltage at the collector of transistor Q_2 corresponds to the or-function.

Table A.1 Input/output behavior of the two-input current switch of Fig. A.43*b*

V_A	V_B	$V_{\text{Collector } Q1/Q3}$	$V_{\text{Collector } Q2}$
L	L	H	L
L	H	L	H
H	L	L	H
H	H	L	H

*The fact that the relatively high and low voltage values at the input and output terminals are different is addressed shortly. At this point only their relative values are pertinent.

A.8.2 The Emitter-Follower Level Restorers

As indicated in Fig. A.43*a*, the inputs to the current switch are −0.7 V and −1.6 V, while the outputs from the current switch are 0 V and −0.9 V. Since the output voltages are different from those of the input voltages, the output signals from a current switch cannot serve as input signals to another current switch. To correct this situation, emitter-follower output stages are added at the current switch outputs as shown in Fig. A.44. One emitter-follower output stage consists of transistor Q_4 and resistor R_4 and the other output stage consists of transistor Q_5 and resistor R_5. The outputs from the entire circuit are now taken at the emitters of the emitter-follower output stages.

Considering the path from V_{CC} to V_{EE} consisting of resistor R_{C1}, the base-emitter junction of transistor Q_4, and resistor R_4, it is seen that the base-emitter junction of transistor Q_4 is forward biased. That transistor Q_4 operates in its normal active mode follows from the fact that current flow through resistor R_{C1} causes the base-collector junction of the transistor to become reverse biased. If it is assumed that the base current of transistor Q_4 is very small, and hence the IR_{C1} drop due to the base current is negligible, then it follows that the voltage at the emitter of transistor Q_4 is one *pn* junction drop, i.e., 0.7 V, below its base. Thus, the output of the gate at the emitter of transistor Q_4 varies between −1.6 V and −0.7 V when the voltage at its base varies between −0.9 V and 0 V. This results in output voltages that are compatible with those assumed as inputs to the current switch. In a similar manner, the emitter-follower circuit consisting of transistor Q_5 and resistor R_5 provides for the appropriate level shift of the voltages at the collector of transistor Q_2.

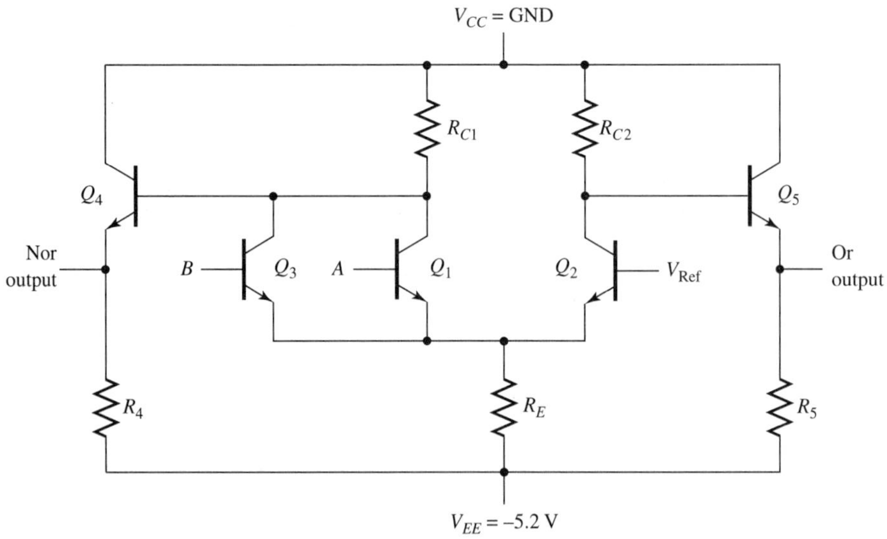

Figure A.44 The two-input current switch with emitter-follower level restorers.

A.8.3 The Reference Supply

The ECL or/nor-gate requires a reference supply voltage V_{Ref}. This is normally done by adding the circuit shown in Fig. A.45 to that of Fig. A.44. Transistor Q_6 operates in its normal active mode since the voltage at its base is sufficiently more positive than V_{EE} so as to cause its base-emitter junction to be forward biased, and its base-collector junction to be reverse biased as a consequence of the current flowing through resistor R_7. If it is assumed that the base current of transistor Q_6 is small so that it can be ignored, then the current flowing through resistor R_7 is the same as the current flowing through diodes D_1 and D_2 and resistor R_8. This current is given by

$$I = \frac{V_{CC} - V_{D1(\text{on})} - V_{D2(\text{on})} - V_{EE}}{R_7 + R_8} = \frac{0 - 0.7 - 0.7 + 5.2}{0.3 + 2.3} = 1.46 \text{ mA}$$

Thus, the voltage at the base of transistor Q_6 is $V_{CC} - IR_7 = 0 - 1.46 \times 0.3 = -0.44$ V and the voltage at the emitter of transistor Q_6 is one *pn* junction drop below its base, or -1.14 V. This is a close approximation to the -1.15 V that was assumed in Fig. A.43*a*.

A.8.4 Wired Logic

Wired logic is possible with ECL gates. Figure A.46 shows the outputs of the emitter followers from two ECL gates tied together. In this case the output voltage at the wired connection becomes that of the more positive of the individual gate output voltages. If this were not the case, then one of the base-emitter junctions of an emitter follower would be greater than a single base-emitter junction drop. Thus, the net effect is that of a wired-or.

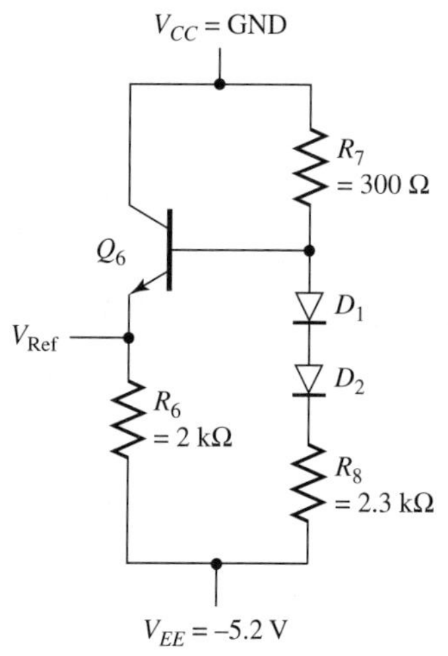

Figure A.45 The ECL gate reference supply.

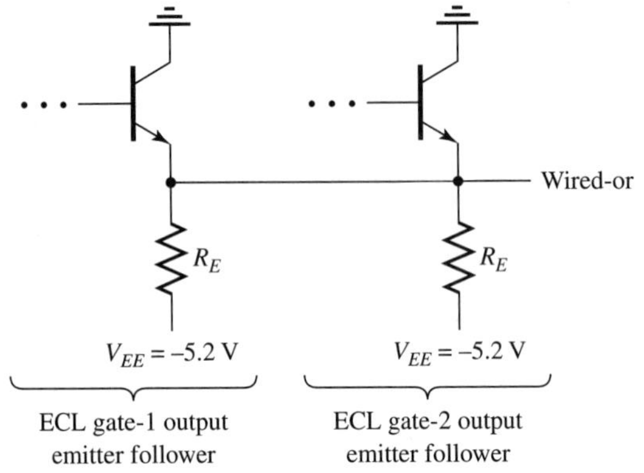

Figure A.46 Wired-or connection of two ECL gates.

Although conceptually the wired-or operation is achieved by the connection of Fig. A.46, this is not a practical arrangement since the two R_E resistors become connected in parallel. Thus, modified forms of ECL are fabricated that alleviate this problem. An open-emitter configuration is achieved by having the R_E resistors appear at the input terminals of the current switch rather than at the output terminals of the emitter followers. Such a configuration is shown in Fig. A.47.

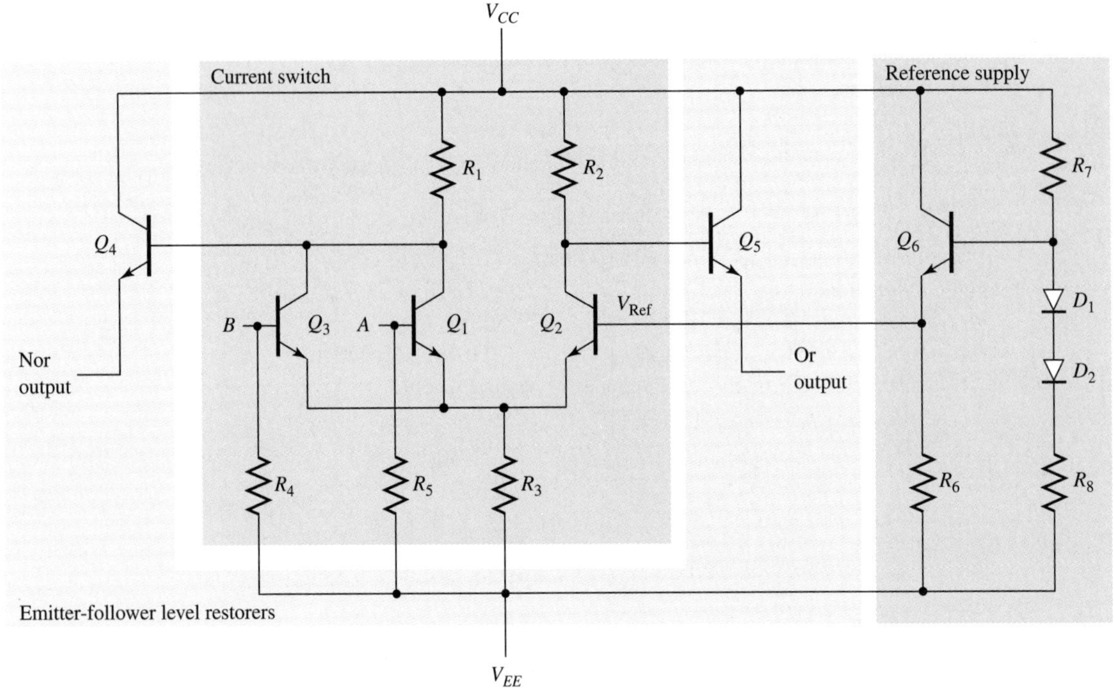

Figure A.47 A two-input ECL or/nor-gate with open-emitter outputs. Typical resistor values: $R_1 = 220\ \Omega$, $R_2 = 245\ \Omega$, $R_3 = 779\ \Omega$, $R_4 = R_5 = 50\ \text{k}\Omega$, $R_6 = 6.1\ \text{k}\Omega$, $R_7 = 907\ \Omega$, and $R_8 = 4.98\ \text{k}\Omega$.

A.9 THE MOS FIELD-EFFECT TRANSISTOR

At this time another semiconductor device—the *field-effect transistor* (abbreviated FET)—is introduced. Unlike the bipolar semiconductor transistor in which two different types of charge carriers flow through semiconductor material, in the FET there is only one type of charge carrier, either electrons or holes, flowing through semiconductor material. Hence, field-effect transistors are also referred to as *unipolar transistors*. The field-effect transistor derives its name from the fact that an electric field is used to create the necessary conduction path.

There are two basic types of field-effect transistors—MOSFETs (or *metal-oxide-semiconductor field-effect transistors*) and JFETs (or *junction field-effect transistors*). For logic purposes, MOSFETs are normally used. JFETs, on the other hand, are more commonly used for linear or analog circuits. In this appendix, only the operation and applications of MOSFETs are discussed.

MOSFETs have several desirable properties that have attributed to their use in very-large-scale integrated circuits such as microprocessors and memory arrays. In general, they are smaller and simpler to fabricate than bipolar transistors. In addition, by making an appropriate connection, an FET is used to realize a high-value resistor. Finally, due to their high input resistance, FET digital circuits draw very little input current and, hence, have low power dissipation. On the other hand, normally FET digital circuits tend to be slower in switching than bipolar transistor digital circuits.

A.9.1 Operation of the *n*-Channel, Enhancement-Type MOSFET

The metal-oxide-semiconductor FET derives its name from the three layers that make up its structure, namely, a layer of metal, oxide, and semiconductor. Four variations of the MOSFET are fabricated. These are known as the *n*-channel, enhancement-type MOSFET; the *p*-channel, enhancement-type MOSFET; the *n*-channel, depletion-type MOSFET; and the *p*-channel, depletion-type MOSFET. At this time the operation of the *n*-channel, enhancement-type MOSFET is discussed. Later, comments on the other three variations are made.

The structure of the *n*-channel, enhancement-type MOSFET is illustrated in Fig. A.48*a*. A *p*-type silicon semiconductor material, called a *substrate*, is doped with *n*-type impurities. These two *n*-type regions form the *source* and *drain* of the MOSFET. The silicon wafer is next coated with an oxide layer (usually silicon dioxide), except for openings leading to the source and drain, which serves as an insulating layer. Finally, metal is laid in the openings leading to the source and drain as well as over the oxide layer between the source and drain. The metal between the source and drain is known as the *gate*, since a voltage applied to this point serves to control the flow of current in the MOSFET.

Now assume the substrate is connected to the source and voltages are applied to the gate and drain, as shown in Fig. A.48*b*, where it is initially assumed that $V_{GS} = 0$ and V_{DS} is small. As shown in the figure, this results in two back-to-back *pn* junctions between the source and the drain. The source-substrate *pn* junction is zero-biased and the drain-substrate *pn* junction is reverse-biased. As a result, no current

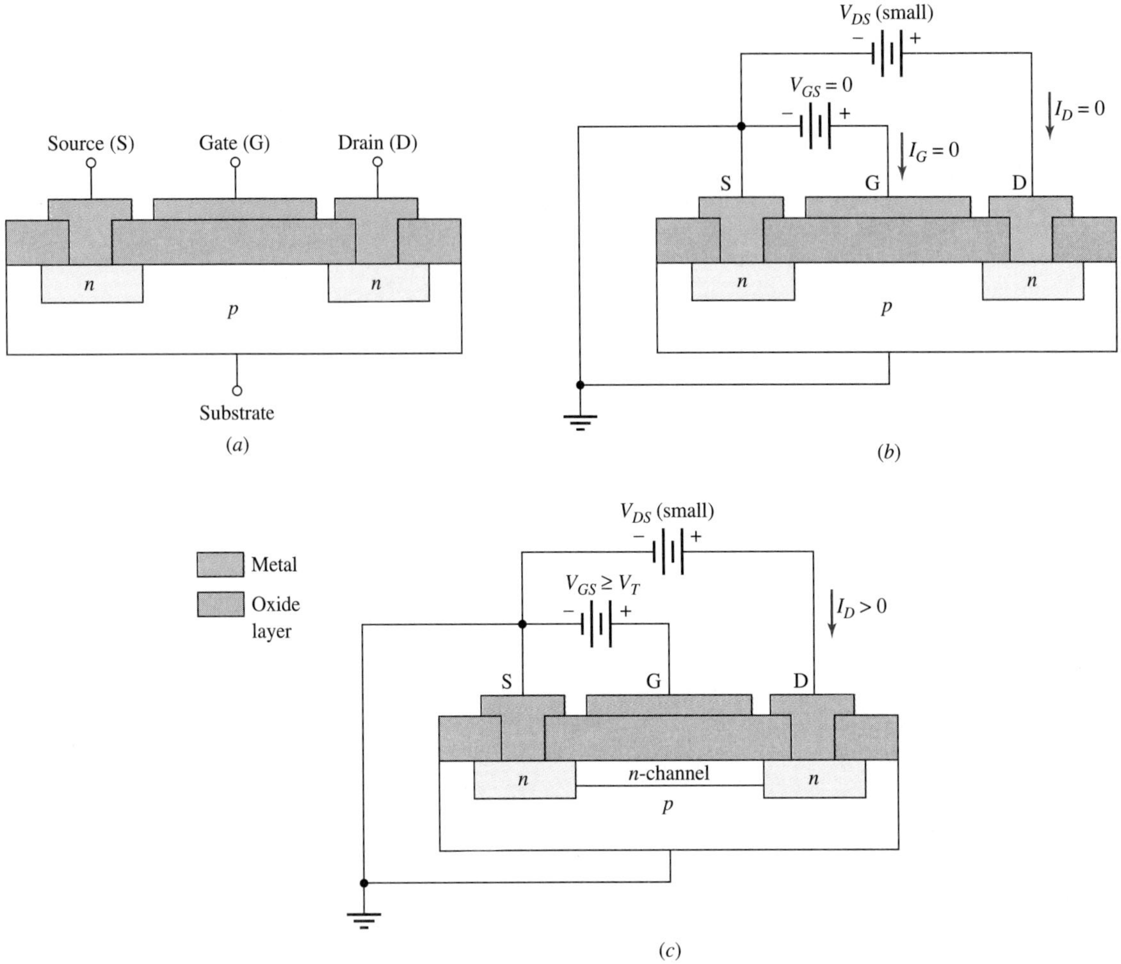

Figure A.48 The *n*-channel, enhancement-type MOSFET. (*a*) Basic structure. (*b*) The off state. (c) Formation of an *n*-channel.

flows between the source and drain terminals* and the transistor is said to be *off*. Furthermore, with the gate terminal insulated from the substrate by the oxide layer, in essence a parallel-plate capacitor is formed and no dc current flows at the gate.

If V_{GS} is now increased, then an electric field is created between the gate and source. The polarity of this electric field causes positive charges (holes) to be repelled from the area under the gate terminal and negative charges (electrons) to be brought to the surface of the substrate between the source and drain. Eventually at some gate voltage, called the *threshold voltage* V_T,† a sufficient concentration of electrons results between the source and the drain, called an *n-channel*, which

*The effect of any leakage currents is ignored in this presentation.

†Typically, $1\text{ V} < V_T < 4\text{ V}$.

causes the material under the gate terminal to become that of n-type as shown in Fig. A.48c. The n-channel now ties the source to the drain and provides a path for electron conduction. The "thickness" of this channel is controlled by the voltage V_{GS} applied to the gate. With a positive potential V_{DS} applied between the drain and source, as indicated in Fig. A.48c, electrons are free to move from the source through the channel to the drain. This results in a drain current flow I_D and the transistor is said to be *on*. The amount of the current flow is dependent upon both V_{GS} and V_{DS}.

Let us now consider the effects of V_{DS} and V_{GS} once the channel is formed. Referring to Fig. A.48c, as V_{GS} is increased above the threshold value, the channel widens, which causes the channel resistance to decrease. Furthermore, since $V_{GS} = V_{GD} + V_{DS}$, if V_{DS} is small, then $V_{GS} \approx V_{GD}$. This implies that the voltage difference between the gate and every point of the silicon surface underneath the gate is constant and hence the channel has a uniform width. This gives rise to the set of straight-line characteristics shown in Fig. A.49a.

Next consider the effect of keeping V_{GS} constant and increasing the value of V_{DS}. Assume the channel has been formed with the voltage $V_{GS} = V_T + V$. The channel width at the source end is simply a function of V_{GS}. Thus, even though V_{DS} increases, the channel width at the source end remains constant. However, with $V_{DS} = V_{DG} + V_{GS}$, the channel width at the drain end starts to decrease as shown in Fig. A.50a since V_{GD} is decreasing (i.e., V_{DG} is increasing). That is, the field effect on the points of the silicon surface beneath the gate and between the gate and the drain is decreasing. This narrowing of the channel at the drain end causes the channel resistance to increase, giving rise to a nonlinear I_D-V_{DS} characteristic. The process continues until the channel width becomes zero at the drain end as illustrated in Fig. A.50b. This condition is referred to as *pinch off*.

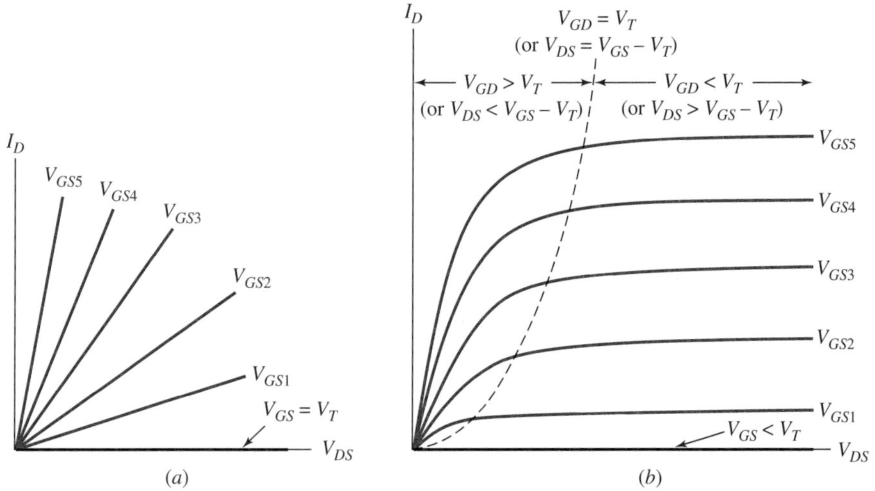

Figure A.49 The I_D-V_{DS} characteristics of an n-channel, enhancement-type MOSFET where $V_T < V_{GS1} < V_{GS2} < V_{GS3} < V_{GS4} < V_{GS5}$. ($a$) Small values of V_{DS}. (b) Large values of V_{DS}.

Since a voltage of V_T is needed to create a channel, there is no channel at the drain end when $V_{GD} \leq V_T$. Furthermore, with $V_{DS} = V_{DG} + V_{GS}$, $V_{GS} = V_T + V$, and $V_{GD} = V_T$, it follows that pinch off occurs when $V_{DS} = V$ (or, equivalently, $V_{DS} = V_{GS} - V_T$). The behavior of the MOSFET prior to pinch off is illustrated by the characteristic curves appearing to the left of the dashed curve in Fig. A.49*b*.

Once pinch off occurs, the drain current is no longer significantly dependent upon V_{DS}. Hence, for $V_{GD} < V_T$ (or, equivalently, $V_{DS} > V$) the I_D-V_{DS} characteristics become as shown to the right of the dashed curve in Fig. A.49*b*. In this region of the characteristics, the pinched-off end of the channel occurs before the drain region as shown in Fig. A.50*c*. However, drain current continues to flow since electrons are injected from the pinched-off end of the *n*-channel into the depleted region and drift to the drain terminal.

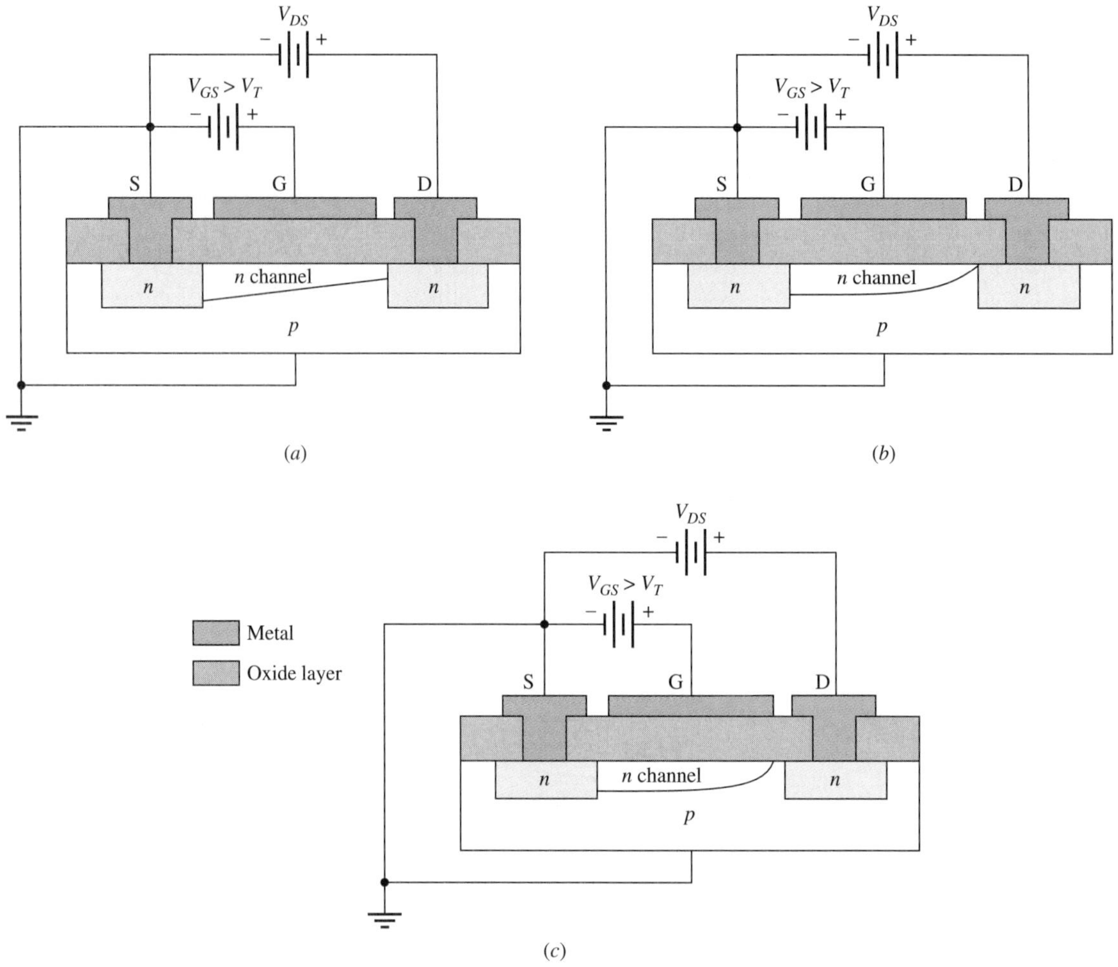

Figure A.50 The effect of increasing V_{DS} on a created *n*-channel. (*a*) *n*-channel before pinch off. (*b*) *n*-channel at pinch off.(*c*) *n*-channel after pinch off.

A.9.2 The *n*-Channel, Depletion-Type MOSFET

In the operation of the above MOSFET, it was necessary to apply at least some threshold voltage to the gate in order to create (or enhance) a conducting channel. A second type of MOSFET structure, known as the *n*-channel, depletion-type MOSFET, is shown in Fig. A.51*a*. Here a lightly doped *n*-channel is placed between two heavily doped *n*-regions that form the source and drain. In this device, when $V_{GS} = 0$, a conduction path between the source and drain already exists and the transistor is on. By applying a negative voltage to the gate, as illustrated in Fig. A.51*b*, the created electric field between the gate and source has the effect of depleting the charges in the channel. Thus, as the negative gate voltage increases, the depletion

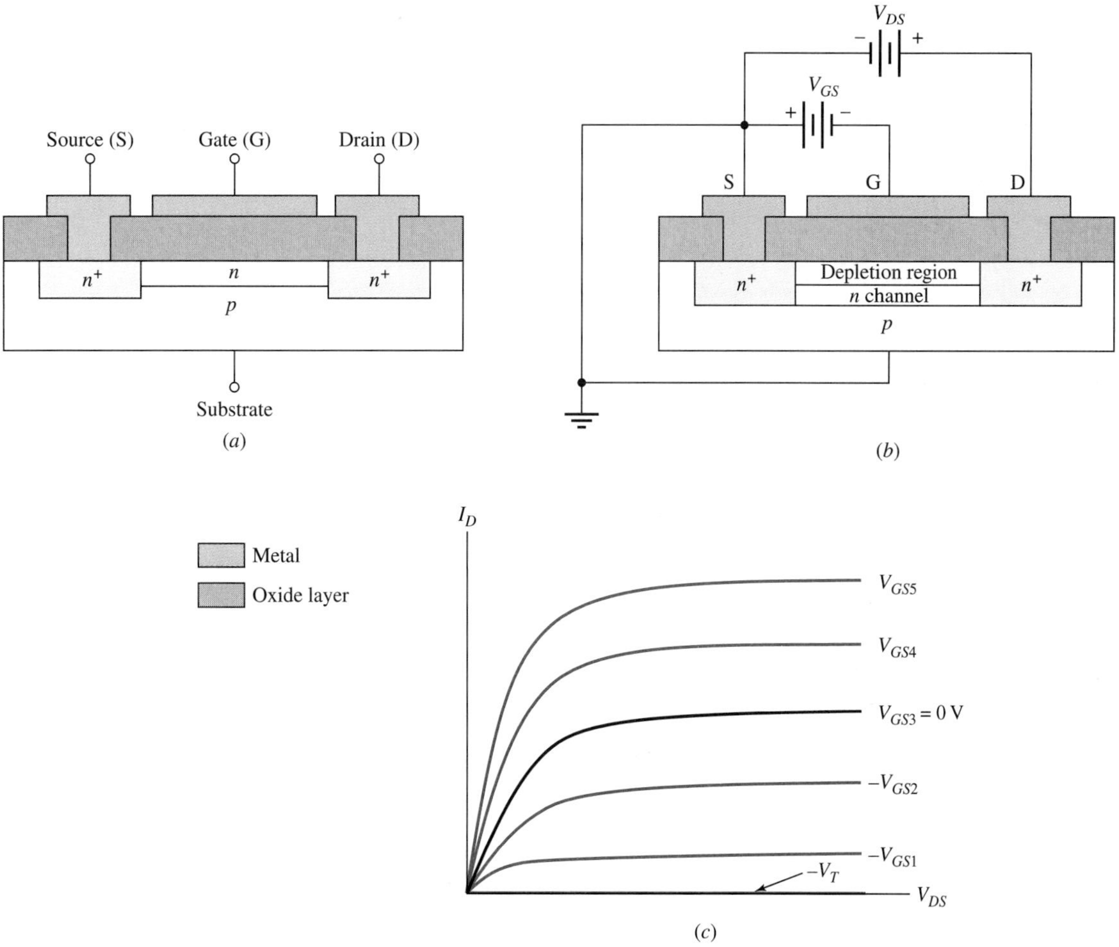

Figure A.51 The *n*-channel, depletion-type MOSFET. (*a*) Basic structure. (*b*) Effect of $-V_T < V_{GS} < 0$. (*c*) I_D-V_{DS} characteristics where $-V_T < -V_{GS1} < -V_{GS2} < 0 < V_{GS4} < V_{GS5}$.

region also continues to increase. At some negative threshold voltage, $-V_T$, the drain and source terminals become disconnected and the transistor is cut off. Typical I_D-V_{DS} characteristics for an *n*-channel, depletion-type MOSFET are shown in Fig. A.51*c*.

A.9.3 The *p*-Channel MOSFETs

As in the case with the bipolar transistor, it is possible to interchange the *n* and *p* dopings of the semiconductor material to create the *p*-channel, enhancement-type MOSFET and the *p*-channel, depletion-type MOSFET. For these MOSFETs the current carriers in the channel are holes (positive charges). The operation and characteristics of these devices are similar to that of the corresponding *n*-channel MOSFET in which all current and voltage polarities are reversed. In this case the threshold voltage for the enhancement-type MOSFET is negative and the threshold voltage for the depletion-type MOSFET is positive.

A.9.4 Circuit Symbols

The circuit symbols for the four types of MOSFETs introduced are shown in Fig. A.52. In these symbols, the space between the gate terminal and the three other terminals represents the insulating oxide layer. The vertical line connecting the drain, sub-

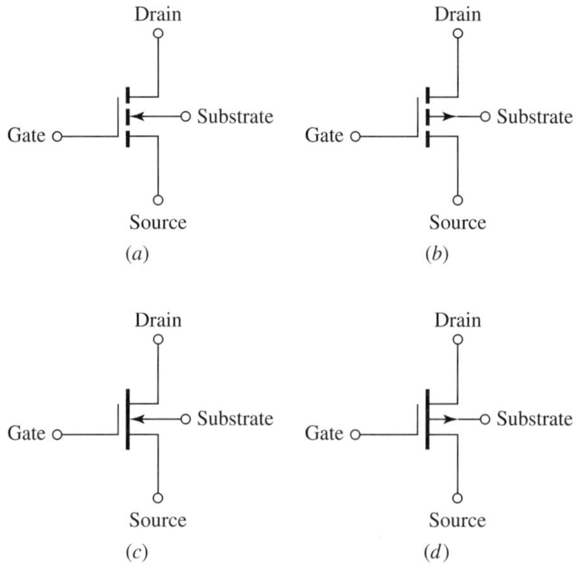

Figure A.52 MOSFET symbols. (*a*) *n*-channel, enhancement-type MOSFET. (*b*) *p*-channel, enhancement-type MOSFET. (*c*) *n*-channel, depletion-type MOSFET. (*d*) *p*-channel, depletion-type MOSFET.

strate, and source terminals denotes the channel. In the case of the depletion-type MOSFETs this line is shown unbroken since the channel is initially present. For the enhancement-type MOSFETs, the vertical line denoting the channel appears broken to emphasize that the channel must be created. The arrow on the substrate line points in the direction from the p-type to n-type regions of the substrate-to-channel pn junction. Thus, it points toward the channel in the case of the n-channel devices and away from the channel in the case of the p-channel devices. Finally, by convention, the horizontal line of the gate terminal is frequently drawn closer to the source terminal than to the drain terminal.

A.9.5 The MOSFET as a Resistor

It was mentioned at the beginning of this section that one of the advantages of MOSFETs is their ability to be used as two-terminal resistors. Because of their small size these resistors are very efficient "spacewise" in very-large-scale integrated circuits.

To construct a resistor with the n-channel, enhancement-type MOSFET, the drain and gate terminals are connected together as shown in Fig. A.53a. With this connection $V_{DS} = V_{GS}$. Thus, the terminal behavior of the nonlinear resistor, between the drain and source terminals, is obtained by plotting the locus of points on the I_D-V_{DS} characteristics for which $V_{DS} = V_{GS}$ where $V_{DS} = V_T$ when $I_D = 0$. This is shown in Fig. A.53b as the dashed curve. The reciprocal of the slope of this characteristic corresponds to the resistive value of the MOSFET resistor.

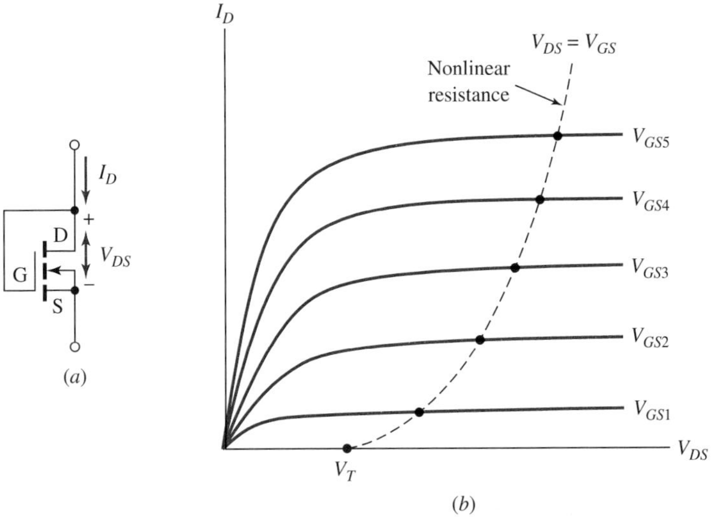

Figure A.53 An enhancement-type MOSFET resistor. (a) Device connection. (b) Resistor characteristic as the locus of points on the MOSFET I_D-V_{DS} characteristic curves where $V_T < V_{GS1} < V_{GS2} < V_{GS3} < V_{GS4} < V_{GS5}$.

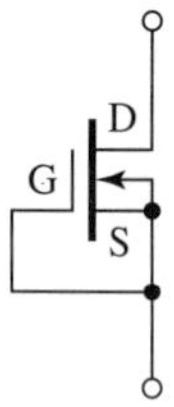

Figure A.54 A depletion-type MOSFET resistor.

Another possible implementation of a MOSFET resistor is to use an n-channel, depletion-type MOSFET. Since the channel already exists when $V_{GS} = 0$, the realization simply involves tying the gate and source terminals together as shown in Fig. A.54. In this case the terminal behavior of the nonlinear resistor is the $V_{GS} = 0$ curve on the I_D-V_{DS} characteristics of the MOSFET, which is shown heavy in Fig. A.51c.

An analytical expression describing the I_D-V_{DS} characteristics of a MOSFET is a function of both the channel width and length. The slope of the resistor characteristic realized by the MOSFET connection is also a function of these two dimensions. In particular, the resistance is directly proportional to the channel length and inversely proportional to the channel width. During the fabrication process, by controlling these two dimensions, it is possible to achieve different values of resistors on the same IC chip.

A.9.6 Concluding Remarks

In ending this section on MOS field-effect transistors, some final remarks are in order. Since the gate terminal is insulated from the substrate by the oxide layer, a parallel-plate capacitor is created. For this reason there is essentially no current flow at the gate terminal in the static condition. Thus, unlike bipolar transistors, these devices offer a high input impedance. However, during transient conditions there is a gate current as the gate capacitance is charged and discharged.

As in the case of bipolar transistors, when the MOSFET is off, the drain-source resistance is extremely high. On the other hand, a conducting MOSFET in which the channel has not been pinched off is in its low-resistance state. However, this drain-source resistance is significantly greater than the collector-emitter resistance of a saturated bipolar transistor. For this reason the resistance cannot, in general, be ignored.

Up to this point, the substrate has always been connected to the source terminal so as to reverse bias the drain-substrate pn junction and zero bias the source-substrate pn junction. In integrated circuits, however, the substrate is common to many MOSFETs. Hence, in order to obtain the reverse bias condition, it is necessary to connect the substrate to the most negative voltage when n-channel MOSFETs are used and to the most positive voltage when p-channel MOSFETs are used. In this case, a reverse bias (as opposed to a zero bias) results between the source and substrate. The net effect of this, in general, is that as the reverse bias between the source and substrate increases, the magnitude of the threshold voltage needed to create a channel also increases. In future discussions, however, this effect is ignored.

As should have been evident from the discussion on the operation of MOSFETs, the names "source" and "drain" are derived from the fact that normally the charge carriers flow from the source to the drain. However, owing to the symmetrical construction of the MOSFET it is possible to use it as a bilateral device.

Finally, since the gate and substrate form a capacitor, a static charge can accumulate between these terminals. If this charge results in a sufficiently high voltage, say, about 100 V, then breakdown can occur, causing the oxide layer to be damaged. For this reason, care must be taken in handling MOSFETs so as to avoid permanent damage to them.

A.10 NMOS AND PMOS LOGIC

When logic networks are designed using n-channel MOSFETs, they are referred to as *NMOS* networks. Similarly, networks involving p-channel devices are called *PMOS* networks. In this section it is shown how NMOS and PMOS logic gates are constructed. However, unlike the bipolar gates studied previously, these simple gates are not available as standard packages in SSI and MSI form. Rather, NMOS and PMOS logic networks are intended for large-scale integration and, as such, are used for the fabrication of complex logic networks on a single chip.

A.10.1 The NMOS Inverter (Not-Gate)

One possible fabrication of an NMOS inverter is shown in Fig. A.55a. Here an n-channel, enhancement-type MOSFET Q_2 is used as the load resistor of the circuit. Since the gate of transistor Q_2 is connected to the supply voltage $+V_{DD} > V_{T2}$

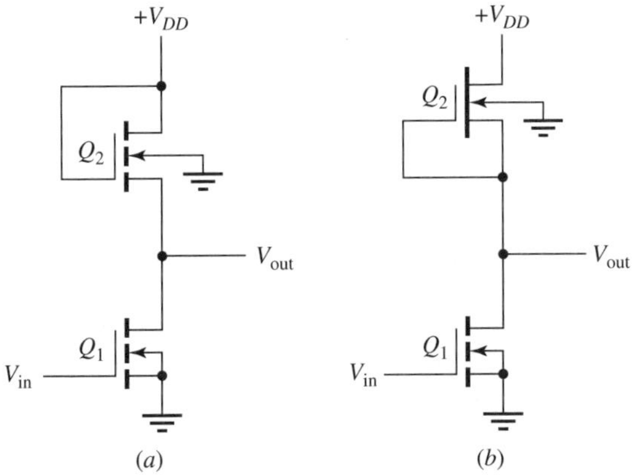

Figure A.55 NMOS inverters. (a) An n-channel, enhancement-type MOSFET used as a load resistor. (b) An n-channel, depletion-type MOSFET used as a load resistor.

where V_{T2} is the threshold voltage of transistor Q_2, transistor Q_2 is always on. In general, it is necessary that the on resistance of transistor Q_2 be much greater than the on resistance of transistor Q_1. This becomes evident in the course of analyzing the various MOS-type gates. Hence, as was indicated in the previous section, the channel length and width of transistors Q_1 and Q_2 are fabricated to achieve this property.

Now assume the input V_{in} is less than the threshold voltage V_{T1} of transistor Q_1, i.e., logic-0. Then transistor Q_1 is off and transistor Q_2 is on. If no current is being drawn at the output terminal, then the drop across transistor Q_2 is V_{T2}* and the output voltage is $V_{DD} - V_{T2}$, which, by design, is in the relatively high voltage range corresponding to logic-1. On the other hand, if V_{in} is greater than V_{T1}, say, $V_{DD} - V_{T2}$, i.e., logic-1, then both transistors Q_1 and Q_2 are on, creating a path for current flow. Under the assumption that the on resistance of transistor Q_1 is much less than that of transistor Q_2, the output voltage is close to ground, which is in the low voltage range corresponding to logic-0. Hence, the circuit of Fig. A.55*a* has the logic behavior of a not-gate.

As an alternative, the NMOS inverter is fabricated using a depletion-type MOSFET load resistor as shown in Fig. A.55*b*. Although this circuit is more complex to fabricate owing to the two different types of MOSFETs appearing on the same chip, an improvement in circuit performance is possible. Recall from the previous section that the depletion-type MOSFET load resistor characteristic is simply the $V_{GS} = 0$ curve on the I_D-V_{DS} characteristics. Since this curve passes through the origin, as shown in Fig. A.51*c*, it follows that the drop across the MOSFET load resistor is zero when it conducts no current. Hence, for the inverter circuit shown in Fig. A.55*b*, when transistor Q_1 is off, the output voltage is V_{DD} as opposed to $V_{DD} - V_{T2}$ for the case of Fig. A.55*a*.

A.10.2 NMOS Nor-Gate

A two-input NMOS nor-gate is shown in Fig. A.56*a*. It consists of a MOSFET load resistor in series with the parallel connection of two *n*-channel, enhancement-type MOSFETs. If the two inputs *A* and *B* are less than the threshold voltages of their corresponding MOSFETs, i.e., logic-0, then channels are not created in either of the lower transistors and the output approaches the supply voltage V_{DD}, i.e., logic-1. Now if the input to at least one of the lower transistors is greater than its threshold voltage, i.e., logic-1, then the corresponding transistor turns on. Provided that the resistance of the upper load transistor is much greater than that of the lower transistor that is on, the output approaches ground, i.e., logic-0.

The above behavior is summarized in Fig. A.56*b*, where a low voltage, L, corresponds to logic-0 and a high voltage, H, corresponds to a logic-1. From the discussion on Boolean algebra, this table describes the nor function, i.e., $f = \overline{A}\,\overline{B} = \overline{A+B}$.

---

*As is seen from the resistor characteristic in Fig. A.53*b*, $V_{DS2} = V_{T2}$ when $I_{D2} = 0$.

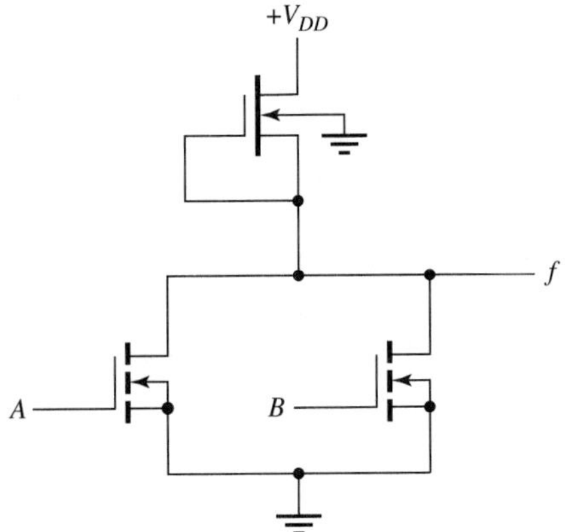

(a)

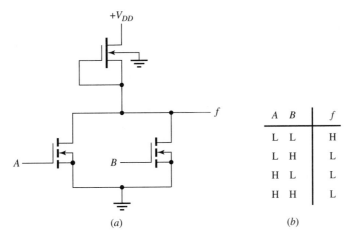

A	B	f
L	L	H
L	H	L
H	L	L
H	H	L

(b)

Figure A.56 NMOS nor-gate. (*a*) Circuit diagram. (*b*) Voltage table.

A.10.3 NMOS Nand-Gate

Figure A.57*a* shows a two-input NMOS nand-gate. In this case a MOSFET load resistor is placed in series with the serial connection of two *n*-channel, enhancement-type MOSFETs. If at least one input voltage is less than the threshold voltage needed to create a channel, i.e., logic-0, then the corresponding MOSFET is off, causing the output to approach V_{DD}, i.e., logic-1. Only when both inputs are greater than the threshold voltage values of the MOSFETs are the *n*-channels formed. If the

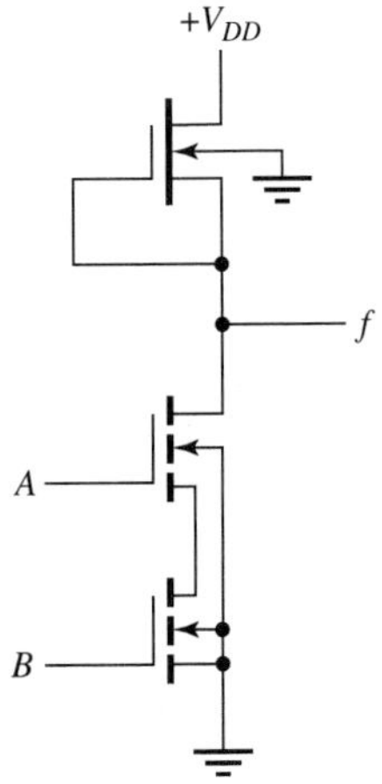

(a)

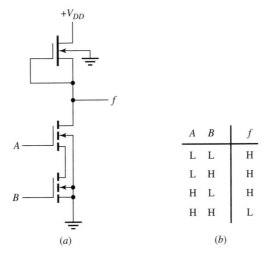

A	B	f
L	L	H
L	H	H
H	L	H
H	H	L

(b)

Figure A.57 NMOS nand-gate. (*a*) Circuit diagram. (*b*) Voltage table.

on resistance of these two lower transistors is much less than the MOSFET load resistor, then the output is close to ground potential, i.e., logic-0. This behavior is summarized in Fig. A.57*b* and corresponds to the Boolean expression $f = \overline{AB}$, which is the nand function.

A.10.4 PMOS Logic

For *p*-channel, enhancement-type MOSFETs a negative voltage is needed at the gate terminal to form a channel. Figure A.58 shows a PMOS inverter, nand-gate, and nor-gate. Applying the positive logic convention to these circuits, logic-0 is approximately $-V_{DD} < -V_T$, which is the low-voltage signal value; while logic-1 is approximately ground, which is the high-voltage signal value.

A.10.5 Performance

The above nor-gates and nand-gates were constructed with only two input terminals. By introducing additional input transistors, gates having a larger number of inputs are obtained. These additional transistors are placed in parallel in the case of the NMOS nor-gate (or PMOS nand-gate) and in series in the case of the NMOS nand-gate (or PMOS nor-gate). Since resistance in series is additive, it is necessary to control the on resistance of the input transistors during fabrication to ensure that the total series resistance is much less than that of the MOSFET load resistor. In this way a relative low output voltage, i.e., logic-0, less than the threshold voltage of the gates being driven, is obtained. This limits the number of possible inputs in the case of the NMOS nand-gate (or PMOS nor-gate).

The fan-out for the above gates is limited by speed requirements. The input to a MOS gate is at the gate terminal, which appears as a capacitive load to a driving

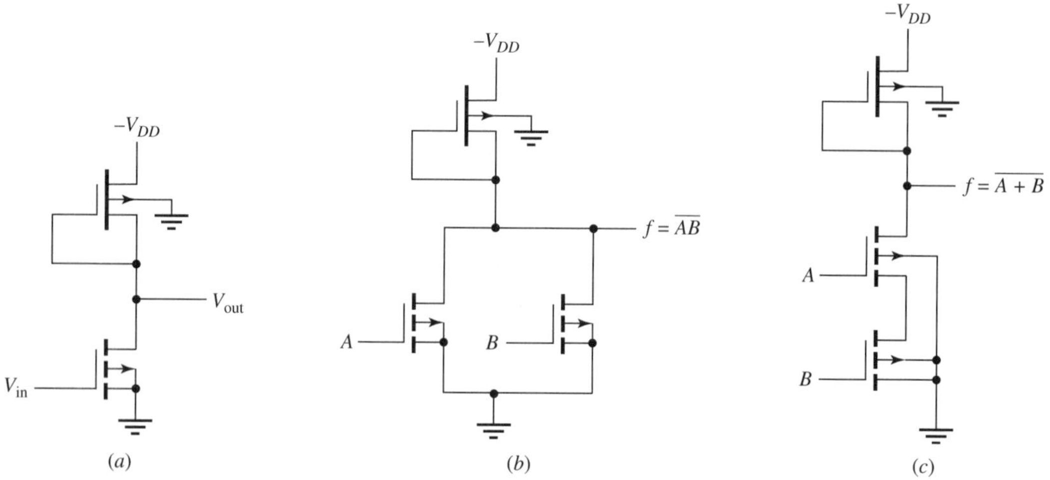

Figure A.58 PMOS logic gates. (*a*) Not-gate. (*b*) Nand-gate. (*c*) Nor-gate.

MOS gate. Since capacitance is additive when in parallel, adding MOS gate loads to a driving gate increases the load capacitance that must be charged and discharged. In the case of NMOS gates, the discharge path, when the output must go from a relatively high to a low voltage, is through the relatively low on resistance of the series or parallel connection of input transistors. This is illustrated in Fig. A.59*a*, where the MOSFET load resistor is indicated by R_L. Here the discharge time constant is $R_{on}C$ where R_{on} is the effective on resistance of the transistor configuration having logic inputs. On the other hand, the charging path, when the output must go from a relatively low to a high voltage, is through the MOSFET load resistor. This is illustrated in Fig. A.59*b*. The charging time constant is R_LC, where R_L is the on resistance of the MOSFET load resistor. Since the value of R_L is necessarily relatively high to separate the logic-0 and logic-1 signal values, i.e., $R_L >> R_{on}$, discharging of the capacitive load is faster than charging. In both cases, increasing the fan-out increases the value of C and correspondingly the propagation delay times. Similar remarks can also be made about PMOS logic.

In the NMOS circuits of this section, when the output is low, there is a conduction path from the power supply, through the MOSFET load resistor, and the series/parallel connection of transistors to ground. Consequently, power is consumed under this static condition, i.e., when the inputs are not changing. This occurs for one of the four possible input combinations in the case of the two-input NMOS nand-gate and for three of the four possible input combinations in the case of the two-input NMOS nor-gate. However, when the output is high, little static power is dissipated since essentially no dc current is drawn.

PMOS circuits also have the property that there is static power dissipation for only one of the two output states. This occurs when the output is high, i.e., the output is at ground potential.

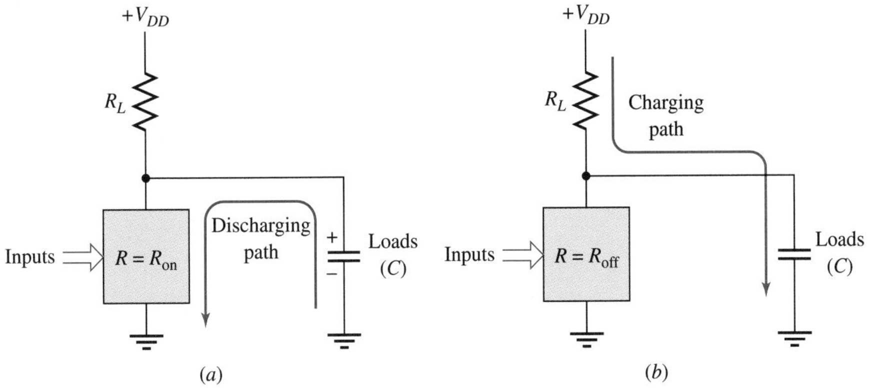

Figure A.59 Fan-out limitation of NMOS gates. (*a*) Output switching from a relatively high to low voltage. (*b*) Output switching from a relatively low to high voltage.

A.11 CMOS LOGIC

The final logic family to be studied is the *complementary MOS*, or, CMOS, logic family. This logic family utilizes both *n*-channel and *p*-channel, enhancement-type MOSFETs within the same circuit. Unlike NMOS and PMOS circuits, CMOS digital circuits are available as standard small-scale and medium-scale integrated packages for use in logic design. In addition, CMOS circuits are also used for very-large-scale integrated digital circuits such as memories and microprocessors.

As is seen in this section, CMOS circuits offer several improvements over NMOS and PMOS circuits. In particular, the relatively high MOSFET load resistor is eliminated, which results in faster switching speeds. Second, the static dc power dissipation is significantly decreased.

A.11.1 The CMOS Inverter (Not-Gate)

As was the case with the NMOS and PMOS logic families, the inverter is the basic circuit around which the CMOS logic family is developed. The basic CMOS inverter is shown in Fig. A.60. It consists of a *p*-channel, enhancement-type MOSFET, Q_p, in series with an *n*-channel, enhancement-type MOSFET, Q_n, in which their drain terminals are connected together as well as their gate terminals. The input to the circuit is the common gate terminal and the output is the common drain terminal.

To understand the operation of the inverter, assume V_{in} is ground, i.e., logic-0. In this case the gate-to-source potential of transistor Q_n is zero, which is insufficient to create the *n*-channel needed for conduction, with the consequence that transistor Q_n is off. On the other hand, the gate-to-source potential of transistor Q_p is $-V_{DD}$. Such a large negative potential on the gate terminal of transistor Q_p relative to its source terminal causes the *p*-channel to be formed, which, in turn, results in transistor Q_p being turned on. Since transistors Q_n and Q_p are in series, the same drain-source current, which is very small, must flow through both of them. Hence, with

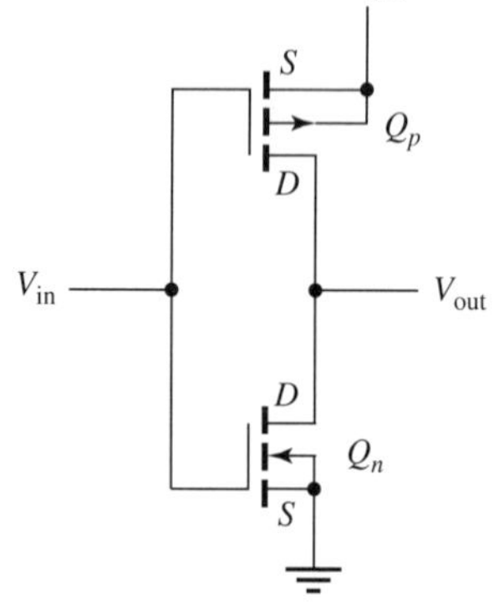

Figure A.60 CMOS inverter.

transistor Q_n appearing as a very high resistance and transistor Q_p as a relatively low resistance, the voltage drop across transistor Q_p is very small and the output is approximately $+V_{DD}$, or logic-1.

Now consider the case when the input to the CMOS inverter is $+V_{DD}$, i.e., logic-1. Here, the gate-to-source potential of transistor Q_p is zero; while the gate-to-source potential of transistor Q_n is $+V_{DD}$. This results in no channel being formed in transistor Q_p; while a channel is formed in transistor Q_n. Thus, transistor Q_p is off and appears as a very high resistance; while transistor Q_n is on and appears as a relatively low resistance. Again with transistors Q_p and Q_n being in series, negligible current can flow between the supply $+V_{DD}$ and ground and the output becomes approximately ground potential, i.e., logic-0. From a logic point of view, the circuit of Fig. A.60 has the behavior of an inverter or not-gate.

A.11.2 CMOS Nor-Gate

To construct a CMOS nor-gate, the gate terminals of both a p-channel, enhancement-type MOSFET and an n-channel, enhancement-type MOSFET are used for each input. The p-channel transistors are connected in series; while the n-channel transistors are connected in parallel. The output is taken at the connection between the serial and parallel configurations. Figure A.61 shows the structure of a two-input nor-gate.

In operation, if at least one of the inputs is at $+V_{DD}$, i.e., logic-1, then the associated p-channel transistor is turned off since a channel is not created. This causes the series connection of p-channel transistors to act as a very high resistance. Simultaneously, the associated n-channel transistor is turned on since a channel is created. This causes the parallel connection of n-channel transistors to act as a relatively low

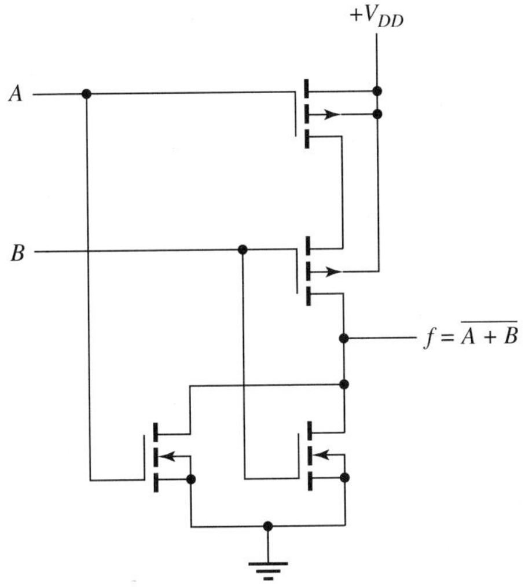

Figure A.61 A two-input, CMOS nor-gate.

resistance and, consequently, the output is connected to ground, i.e., logic-0. Only when all of the inputs are at ground, i.e., logic-0, are all of the *n*-channel transistors in the parallel connection turned off and appear as a very high resistance; while simultaneously causing all of the *p*-channel transistors in the series connection to be turned on and appear as a relatively low resistance. The result in this case is that the output approaches $+V_{DD}$, i.e., logic-1. This is the behavior of a nor-gate.

A.11.3 CMOS Nand-Gate

As in the case of the CMOS nor-gate, each input of a CMOS nand-gate requires the use of an *n*-channel, enhancement-type MOSFET and a *p*-channel, enhancement-type MOSFET. However, the serial and parallel configurations of MOSFETs are now reversed. That is, the *p*-channel transistors are connected in parallel, while the *n*-channel transistors are connected in series. A two-input, CMOS nand-gate is illustrated in Fig. A.62.

For the CMOS nand-gate, if at least one input is at ground, i.e., logic-0, then the associated *n*-channel transistor is turned off since a channel is not created, and the associated *p*-channel transistor is turned on since a channel is created. This causes the series connection of *n*-channel transistors to appear as a very large resistance, while the parallel connection of *p*-channel transistors appears as a relatively low resistance. The net effect is that the output approaches $+V_{DD}$, i.e., logic-1. Only when all of the inputs are at $+V_{DD}$, i.e., logic-1, do all of the *p*-channel transistors get turned off and all of the *n*-channel transistors get turned on. With the parallel connection of *p*-channel transistors now appearing as the very large resistance and the series connection of *n*-channel transistors appearing as a relatively low resistance, the output approaches ground, i.e., logic-0. This is the logic behavior of a nand-gate.

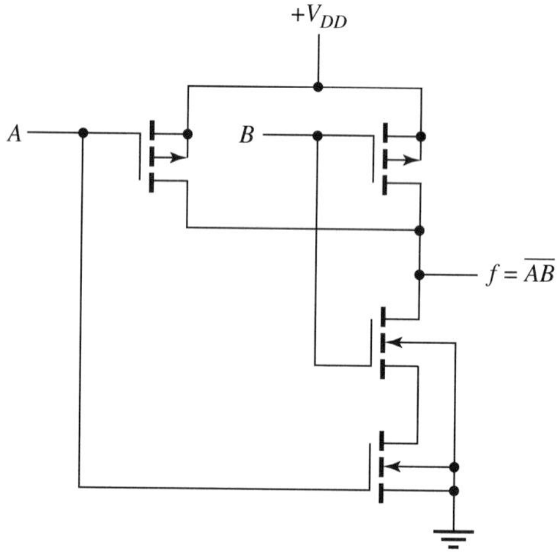

Figure A.62 A two-input, CMOS nand-gate.

A.11.4 Performance

The reader should note that for the three circuits described in this section, very little dc current flows within them while in either of their logic states since either the upper half or the lower half of the circuit, which form a series connection, appears as a very high resistance. Thus, the static power dissipation in each case is extremely small. There is, however, dynamic power dissipation when the circuit output changes state. Furthermore, with little dc current flowing, the two logic levels are very close to $+V_{DD}$ and ground, which implies that good noise margins are attainable.

In general, the output of a CMOS logic circuit is connected to the gate terminals of MOSFETs of another CMOS logic circuit. This load appears capacitive to the driving circuit as in the case of NMOS and PMOS circuits. However, depending upon the logic state of the driving circuit, either the upper half or the lower half appears as a relatively low resistance for charging or discharging the capacitive load. Thus, unlike the NMOS and PMOS circuits of the previous section, rapid switching is possible independent of the current state of the circuit.

APPENDIX A PROBLEMS

A.1 Consider the diode circuit shown in Fig. PA.1 using ideal diodes, i.e., $V_{\text{Diode(on)}} = 0$ V.

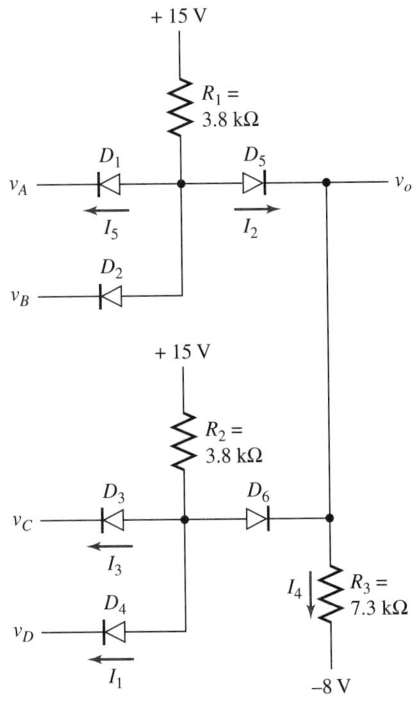

Figure PA.1

a. If $v_A = v_C = 6$ V and $v_B = v_D = -2$ V, which diodes are conducting and which are not conducting? Determine the voltage v_o and the current I_1.

b. If $v_A = v_B = 6$ V and $v_C = v_D = -2$ V, which diodes are conducting and which are not conducting? Determine the voltage v_o and the currents I_2 and I_3.

c. If $v_A = v_B = v_C = v_D = -2$ V, which diodes are conducting and which are not conducting? Determine the voltage v_o and the current I_4.

d. If $v_A = v_B = v_C = v_D = 6$ V, which diodes are conducting and which are not conducting? Determine the voltage v_o and the current I_5.

A.2 Consider the diode circuit shown in Fig. PA.2 where $V_{\text{Diode(on)}} = 0.7$ V.

a. If $v_A = v_B = 5$ V and $v_C = v_D = 10$ V, which diodes are conducting and which are not conducting? Determine the voltage v_o and the current I_1.

b. If $v_A = v_C = v_D = 5$ V and $v_B = 10$ V, which diodes are conducting and which are not conducting? Determine the voltage v_o and the current I_2.

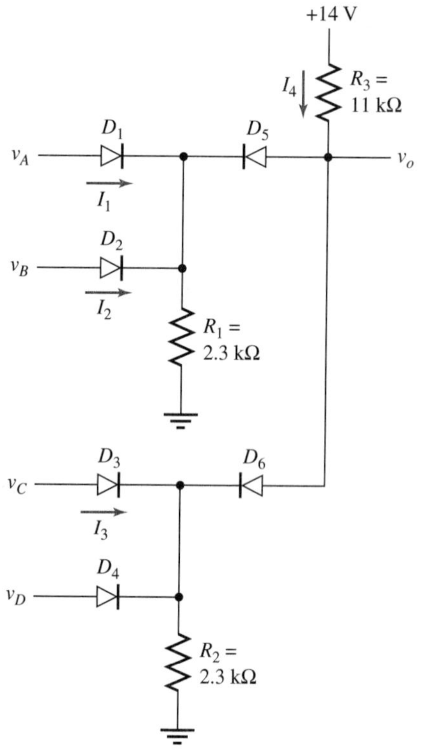

Figure PA.2

c. If $v_A = v_B = v_C = 10$ V and $v_D = 5$ V, which diodes are conducting and which are not conducting? Determine the voltage v_o and the current I_3.

d. If $v_A = v_B = 10$ V and $v_C = v_D = 5$ V, which diodes are conducting and which are not conducting? Determine the voltage v_o and the current I_4.

A.3 Assume the transistor inverter circuit shown in Fig. PA.3 is connected to five identical transistor inverter circuits (as was shown in Fig. A.25). Plot the transfer characteristic by calculating the edge-of-cutoff and edge-of-saturation breakpoints. Determine the high-level and low-level noise margins of the loaded circuit.

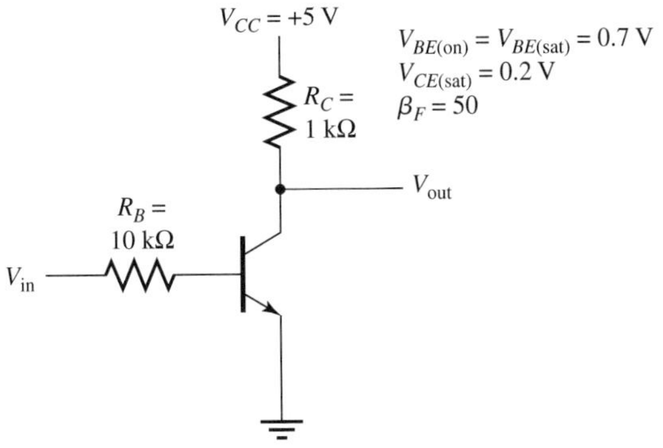

Figure PA.3

A.4 Assume the transistor inverter circuit shown in Fig. A.22 is connected to N other identical transistor inverter circuits as its loads as was shown in Fig. A.25.

a. Show that the maximum value of N (i.e., the fan-out) which allows the load transistors to operate in cutoff and saturation is

$$N \le \left[\frac{\beta_F(V_{CC} - V_{BE(sat)})}{V_{CC} - V_{CE(sat)}}\right] - \left[\frac{R_B}{R_C}\right]$$

b. What is the maximum fan-out of the loaded transistor inverter circuit given in Problem A.3?

A.5 The relationship developed in Problem A.4 is an upper limit on the fan-out of a loaded transistor inverter circuit. The value of N made no provision for a noise margin. A lower fan-out is obtained when a noise margin for the load gates is considered. Assume a high-level noise margin of 0.5 V is desired for the transistor inverter circuit of Fig. PA.3 when connected to identical transistor inverter circuits as was shown in Fig. A.25. Determine the maximum fan-out of the circuit. (Hint: This is equivalent to determining the maximum fan-out when the voltage at point F in Fig. A.25 is increased from the minimum allowable input high voltage by the desired high-level noise margin.)

A.6 To ensure proper operation of saturated logic, the transistors are forced into deep saturation. This is achieved by overdriving the bases of the load transistors. The base overdrive factor k is defined as

$$k = \frac{I_B}{I_{B(\text{EOS})}}$$

where I_B is the actual base current used to saturate the transistor and $I_{B(\text{EOS})}$ is the base current that brings it to the edge of saturation. Assume the transistor inverter circuit shown in Fig. PA.3 is connected to 10 identical transistor inverter circuits. Determine the base overdrive factor of each load transistor.

A.7 Consider the loaded DTL gate shown in Fig. A.31 where $R_1 = 4\ \text{k}\Omega$, $R_2 = 2\ \text{k}\Omega$, $R_3 = 5\ \text{k}\Omega$, and $\beta_F = 20$ for the transistor. Assume the load gates are identical to the driving gate. Perform the following calculations when all the inputs to the driving gate are high at 5 V. Let $V_{D(\text{on})} = V_{BE(\text{on})} = V_{BE(\text{sat})} = 0.7$ V and $V_{CE(\text{sat})} = 0.2$ V.

a. Determine the base current I_B.

b. Determine the maximum collector current that Q_1 can sink and still remain in saturation.

c. Determine the maximum current supplied by each load gate.

d. Determine the current I_{R2} through resistor R_2.

e. Determine the maximum fan-out of the gate.

A.8 Consider the DTL gate shown in Fig. A.32 where $R_1 = 1.6\ \text{k}\Omega$, $R_2 = 2.2\ \text{k}\Omega$, $R_3 = 2\ \text{k}\Omega$, $R_4 = 5\ \text{k}\Omega$, and $\beta_F = 20$ for each transistor. Assume the gate is loaded with identical DTL gates. Perform the following calculations when all the inputs to the driving gate are high at 5 V. Let $V_{\text{Diode(on)}} = 0.7$ V, $V_{BE(\text{on})} = V_{BE(\text{sat})} = 0.7$ V, and $V_{CE(\text{sat})} = 0.2$ V.

a. Determine the base current of transistor Q_1.

b. Determine the base current of transistor Q_2.

c. Determine the maximum collector current that Q_2 can sink and still remain in saturation.

d. Determine the maximum current supplied by each load gate.

e. Determine the current through resistor R_3.

f. Determine the maximum fan-out of the gate.

A.9 Consider the basic TTL nand-gate shown in Fig. A.33, having the typical resistor values given in the caption, in which all its inputs are at 5 V. Let $V_{BE(\text{sat})} = V_{BE(\text{on})} = 0.7$ V, $V_{BC(\text{sat})} = V_{BC(\text{on})} = 0.5$ V, $V_{CE(\text{sat})} = 0.2$ V, $\beta_R = 0.1$ for transistor Q_1, and $\beta_F = 20$ for each transistor.

a. Determine the minimum value of β_F needed for transistor Q_2 to ensure that it saturates.

b. Determine the maximum current that can be supplied by the loads and still ensure that transistor Q_3 saturates.

c. Determine the maximum fan-out of the gate if it is loaded with identical gates.

A.10 Analyze the TTL gate shown in Fig. PA.10 when $v_A = v_B = 0.2$ V.

a. Determine I_{B1}, I_{C1}, $I_{E1(A)}$, $I_{E1(B)}$, I_{B2}, I_{C2}, I_{E2}, I_{B3}, I_{C3}, and I_{E3}.

b. Assume Q_4 is in the normal active mode and loads are connected to the gate. Determine the maximum allowable value of I_L, i.e., the value of I_L that brings Q_4 to the edge of saturation.

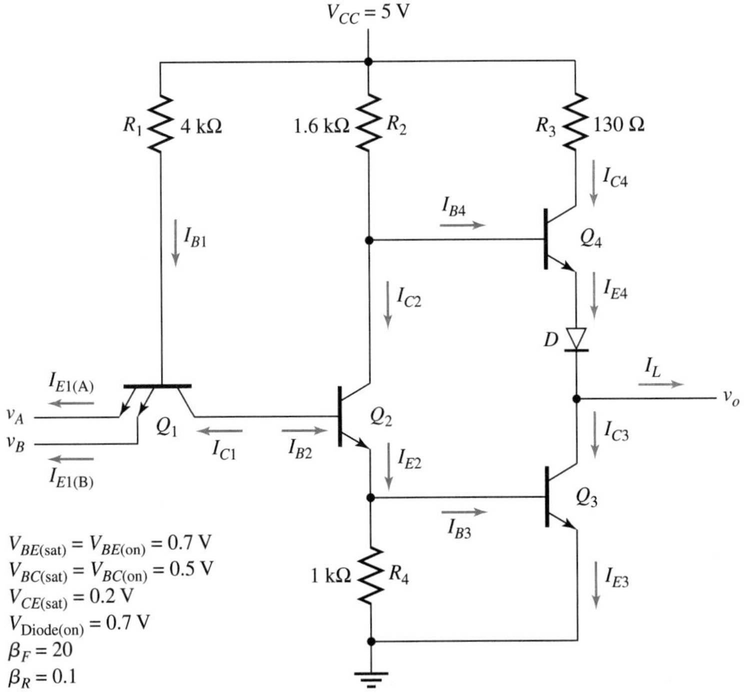

$V_{BE(sat)} = V_{BE(on)} = 0.7$ V
$V_{BC(sat)} = V_{BC(on)} = 0.5$ V
$V_{CE(sat)} = 0.2$ V
$V_{Diode(on)} = 0.7$ V
$\beta_F = 20$
$\beta_R = 0.1$

Figure PA.10

A.11 Analyze the TTL gate shown in Fig. PA.10 when $v_A = v_B = 3.6$ V. Assume Q_2 and Q_3 are in saturation when on.

a. Determine I_{B1}, I_{C1}, $I_{E1(A)}$, $I_{E1(B)}$, I_{B2}, I_{C2}, I_{E2}, I_{B3}, I_{B4}, I_{C4}, and I_{E4}.

b. Assuming loads are connected to the gate, determine the maximum allowable value of I_L, i.e., the value of I_L that brings Q_3 to the edge of saturation.

A.12 Consider the ECL or/nor-gate of Fig. A.47, having the typical resistor values given in the caption, in which $V_{CC} = 0$ V and $V_{EE} = -5.2$ V. Assume $V_{\text{Ref}} = -1.32$ V and the two logic signals are -1.75 V and -0.75 V. Let $V_{BE(\text{on})} = 0.75$ V.

a. Determine I_{R3} and the voltages at the collectors of transistors Q_1 and Q_2 of the current switch when both gate inputs are -1.75 V. Assume the emitter and collector currents are the same for the transistors in the current switch.

b. Determine I_{R3} and the voltages at the collectors of transistors Q_1 and Q_2 of the current switch when at least one gate input is -0.75 V. Assume the emitter and collector currents are the same for the transistors in the current switch.

c. Assuming load resistors are connected to the outputs of the gate, show that the gate outputs are compatible with the assumed inputs.

A.13 a. In Sec. A.10 n-channel MOSFETs were only placed in series and parallel to realize the nand and nor logic functions. In general, n-channel MOSFETs can be arranged in a series/parallel configuration, e.g., as shown in Fig. PA.13. Determine the voltage table for this NMOS circuit having inputs V_{DD} and ground. Assuming positive logic, obtain a minterm canonical expression describing the circuit.

b. From a positive logic point of view, the series connection of n-channel MOSFETs results in the overall complementation of the and-ing of the input logic variables. Similarly, the parallel connection of n-channel MOSFETs results in the overall complementation of the or-ing of the input logic variables. In general, a series/parallel configuration of n-channel MOSFETs results in the overall complementation of the and-ing or or-ing of the input logic variables

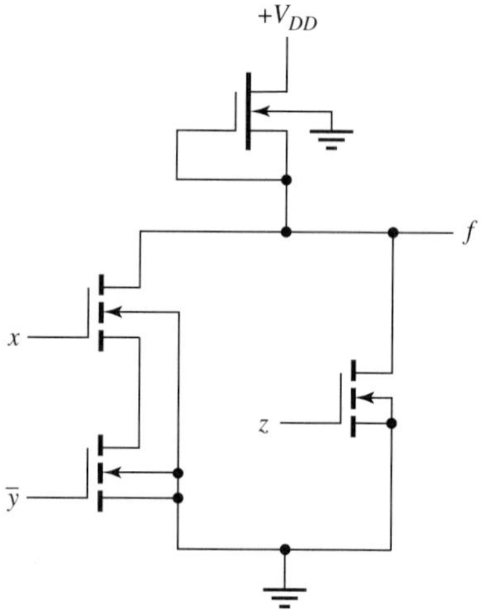

Figure PA.13

as determined by whether the MOSFETs are in series or parallel, respectively. Write a Boolean expression for the circuit of Fig. PA.13. Verify that the expression agrees with the canonical expression obtained in part (*a*).

c. Draw the circuit diagram for an NMOS circuit that realizes the Boolean expression $f(x,y,z) = \overline{x}\overline{y} + xz$.

A.14 a. In Sec. A.10 *p*-channel MOSFETs were only placed in series and parallel to realize the nor and nand logic functions. In general, *p*-channel MOSFETs can be arranged in a series/parallel configuration, e.g., as shown in Fig. PA.14. Determine the voltage table for this PMOS circuit having inputs $-V_{DD}$ and ground. Assuming positive logic, obtain a minterm canonical expression describing the circuit.

b. From a positive logic point of view, the parallel connection of *p*-channel MOSFETs results in the overall complementation of the and-ing of the input logic variables. Similarly, the series connection of *p*-channel MOSFETs results in the overall complementation of the or-ing of the input logic variables. In general, a series/parallel configuration of *p*-channel MOSFETs results in the overall complementation of the or-ing or and-ing of the input logic variables as determined by whether the MOSFETs are in series or parallel, respectively. Write a Boolean expression for the circuit of Fig. PA.14. Verify that the expression agrees with the canonical expression obtained in part (*a*).

c. Draw the circuit diagram for a PMOS circuit that realizes the Boolean expression $f(x,y,z) = \overline{x}\,(y + \overline{z})$.

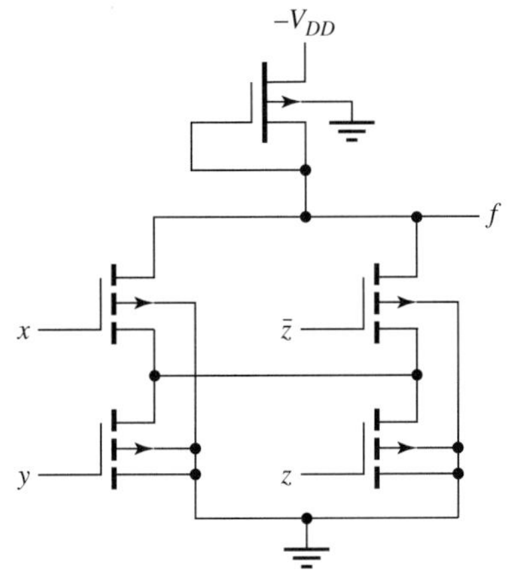

Figure PA.14

A.15. a. In Sec. A.11 it was seen that a CMOS circuit consists of NMOS and PMOS subcircuits in series. As was studied in Problems A.13 and A.14, NMOS and PMOS circuits can be series/parallel configurations of

MOSFETs. Determine the voltage table for the CMOS circuit of Fig. PA.15 having inputs V_{DD} and ground. Assuming positive logic, obtain a minterm canonical expression describing the circuit.

b. From a positive logic point of view, the same relationships between circuit logic behavior and component configurations discussed in Problems A.13 and A.14 also hold for the NMOS and PMOS subcircuits of a CMOS circuit. Therefore, by observing the configuration of MOSFETs in either the NMOS or PMOS subcircuits, a Boolean expression describing a CMOS circuit can be directly written. Write a Boolean expression for the CMOS circuit of Fig. PA.15 and verify that the expression agrees with the canonical expression obtained in part (*a*).

c. Draw the circuit diagram for a CMOS circuit that realizes the Boolean expression $f(w,x,y,z) = \overline{[(w + x)\, y + \overline{y}\,\overline{z}]}$. Be sure the NMOS and PMOS subcircuits are realizing the same logic expression.

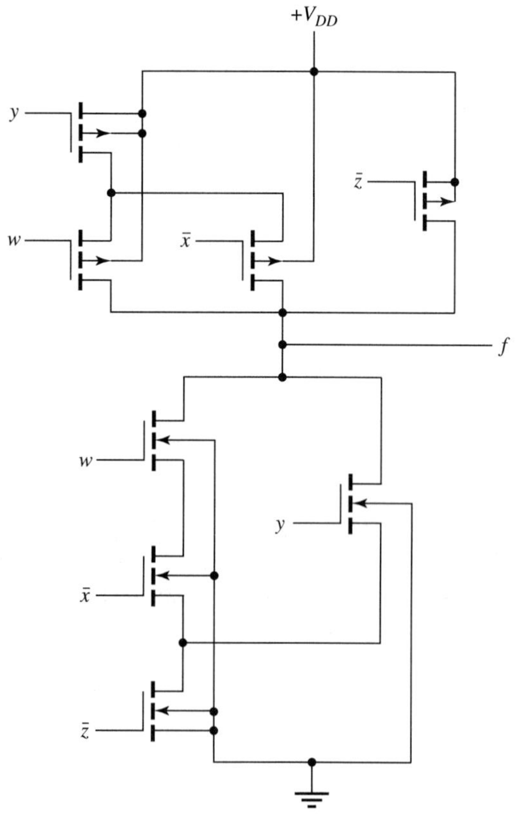

Figure PA.15

APPENDIX B

Tutorials

B.1 A GENTLE INTRODUCTION TO ALTERA MAX+PLUS II 10.1 STUDENT EDITION

Dr. Travis E. Doom
Department of Computer Science and Engineering
Wright State University

Implementing simple circuits with ICs on a prototyping breadboard and debugging such circuits with an oscilloscope and a multimeter is an invaluable educational experience. Complex circuits, however, are typically designed, tested, and debugged on a sophisticated simulator before an attempt is made to implement the device in hardware. An important objective for any course in digital design is to familiarize students with the simulation tools that are used to design, prototype, test, and debug digital systems. The advantages of using simulators in an academic setting are the same as those motivating their use in industry settings; simulators allow the designer to focus on the *design* of the system instead of spending valuable time tracking down misplaced wire connections, shorts, malfunctioning ICs, and faulty power supplies.

Altera MAX+plus II is one of the leading simulation packages used in the digital design industry. The student edition of MAX+plus II is available on the CD-ROM included in this textbook. MAX+plus II is designed principally as an industry tool, hence it supports an overwhelming array of features that are not relevant to students just beginning their studies of digital design. This tutorial covers the most important features of MAX+plus II—those features necessary to design and test the combinational and sequential circuits of the complexity commonly found in an introductory digital design laboratory.

B.1.1 Conventions Used in This Tutorial

This tutorial assumes that the reader is comfortable with the Microsoft Windows operating system. Therefore, no attempt is made to provide detailed information regarding how to create directory folders, select menu options, bring windows into focus, and other application details common to all Windows applications. If you are not comfortable using Microsoft Windows then you should attempt to become so before continuing this tutorial.

Many functions of MAX+plus II can be invoked in multiple ways: menu options, menu shortcuts, shortcut icons, and keyboard shortcuts for most common functions. This tutorial uniformly focuses on the menu and shortcut-menu (the menu that appears when you hold down the right mouse button) options for using this tool. With practice, you may find that you prefer other methods to invoke tool options and functionality but uniform use of the menu provides a simple starting point. To simplify the description of selecting menu options, we use → symbol to indicate a submenu. Thus, the instruction File → New indicates that one should select the top level File menu option and then select the New option from the File menu. Similarly, the instruction Rclick → Copy indicates the use of the shortcut menu, in this case to Right click (and hold) to bring up the shortcut menu, then to select the Copy option.

B.1.2 Installing Altera MAX+Plus II 10.1 Student Edition

The complete instructions for installing a student edition of MAX+plus II can be found in the Readme.txt file on the CD-ROM. Included here is a brief overview of the process. If you have access to laboratory computers that have MAX+plus II preinstalled you need not reinstall the software.

Step 1. Install the software from the CD-ROM. Note that the version of Altera MAX+plus II available on the CD-ROM requires a PC running Windows 95 (or a more current Microsoft operating system) and at least 80 MB of free hard drive space. To install the software, explore the CD-ROM drive and launch the application mp2_101se.exe.

Step 2. Obtain a student software license. Many of the features of MAX+plus II are disabled unless you obtain a license. Student licenses are free, but they do not come with the CD-ROM. To obtain the license necessary to use the full student edition software, visit http://www.altera.com/maxplus2-student. Under "Free Licenses" select "MAX+plus II Software for Students and Universities." Select the appropriate software package (MAX+plus II 10.1) and select Continue. You will be asked to provide the 8-hex digit volume serial number for the hard drive of the machine you wish to license. In Windows, select Run from the Start menu and type *command* in the textbox to open a DOS command shell, then type *dir /p*. The volume serial number should be displayed at the top of the listing. Type *exit* to end the command shell. Enter the hard drive serial number and complete the web-form in full. After you submit the web-form, Altera will e-mail your license information to the specified address (this usually takes only a few minutes).

Step 3. Install the license. Altera will send you a lengthy e-mail containing the complete (and overly complex) instructions to install the free student license. In brief, you need to (1) create a file named license.dat using your favorite text editor anywhere on your system (C:\max2work\license.dat is a fine choice). Then you must (2) copy the lines in the e-mail that start with the word "FEATURE" as well as the lines that follow them into the license.dat and save the file. Figure B.1 shows the contents of an example license.dat. Finally, (3) start MAX+plus II and use the Options → License Setup menu to specify the location of your license file.

B.1.3. The Basics

To demonstrate design entry in MAX+plus II we implement a simple 1-bit comparator with enable. This simple combinational circuit has three inputs (A, B, and EN) and a single output (EQ). The output (EQ) is asserted if, and only if, the device is enabled (EN=1) and input A is equal to input B.

B.1.4 Creating a New Project

First, locate (or create) a directory in which you wish to store your files. In a classroom laboratory, you may ask your instructor to specify which directory you should use. If necessary, use the Windows Explorer to create a new directory to store your work. Throughout this tutorial, the directory C:\max2work is used to store project files.

Launch MAX+plus II from the Windows Start menu. Starting MAX+plus II opens the MAX+plus II *Manager.* The first step in creating a new project in the

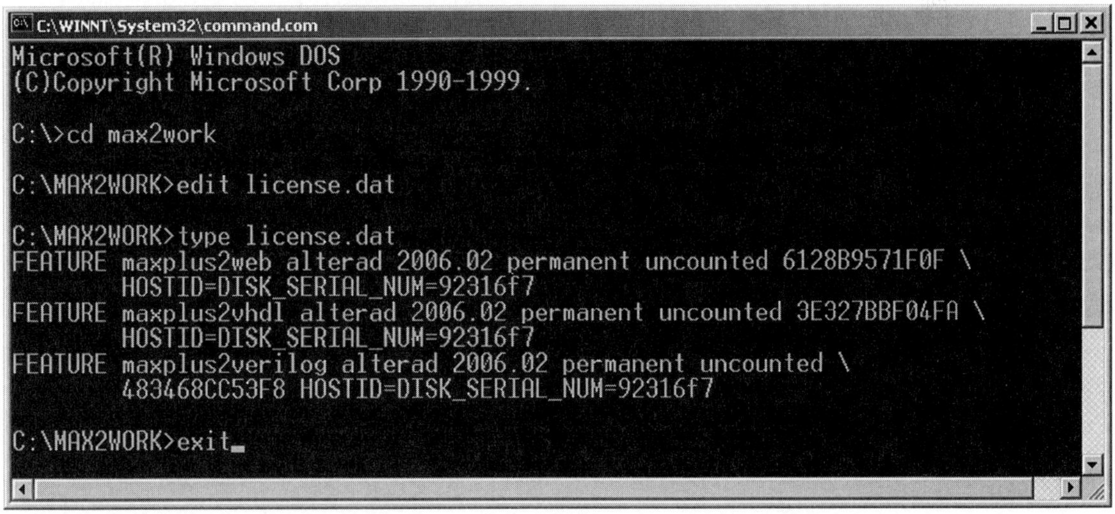

Figure B.1 An example of a license.dat file. Contact http://www.altera.com/maxplus2-student to receive the free license for your computer.

Manager is to give the project a storage location and name. Select File → Project → Name to provide a directory location and name for your project. Name this tutorial circuit *example1*.

B.1.5 Creating a New Schematic

To implement a combinational circuit by drawing a schematic, we must launch the Graphic Editor application within the MAX+plus II Manager. Start the Graphic Editor by using the menu MAX+plus II → Graphic Editor. Give the schematic a name using File → Save As. Save this schematic as *example1*.

B.1.6 Importing Schematic Symbols

Symbols are added to the schematic by importing circuit elements from standard or user-defined libraries. First, we import the symbols representing the inputs and outputs of the device. Position your mouse in the Graphic Editor window and hold down the right mouse button to bring down the shortcut menu, then select Enter

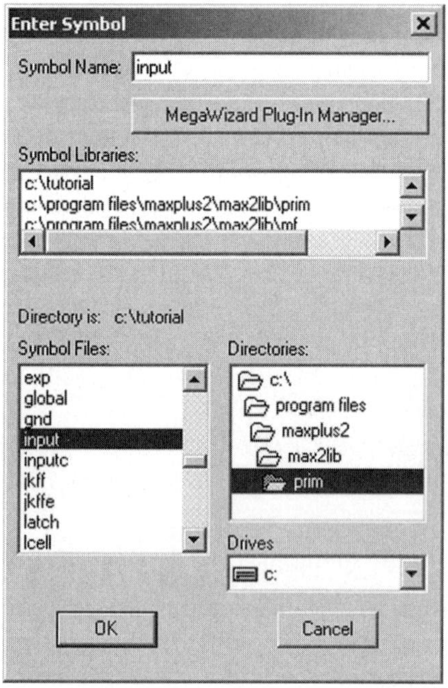

Figure B.2 The Enter Symbol pop-up menu. Double-click on the line in the Symbol Libraries box ending in "prim" to get the listing shown in the Symbol Files box.

Symbol to open the Enter Symbol pop-up menu (see Figure B.2). In the box labeled Symbol Libraries select the "prim" (primitives) library with a double click. A list of circuit elements available in the prim library will be displayed in the Symbol Files box. Use the scroll bar to find the "input" primitive and select it, then click OK. An input symbol should appear in the Graphic Editor window.

The 1-bit comparator has three inputs, so we need to enter three "input" primitives. You can either repeat this process to import two more input primitives or use Rclick → Copy and Rclick → Paste or CNTL+drag to duplicate the existing input element.

Once a symbol has been entered into the editor, it can be modified by dragging it to a specific location or by using the shortcut menu to name, rotate, or otherwise customize the device. Drag all three inputs on the left-hand side of the schematic and name them A, B, and EN by selecting each one and using Rclick→ Edit Pin Name.

Use Rclick→ Enter Symbol to import an XNOR gate and place it appropriately. You can simplify finding a particular symbol in the Symbols Files box by selecting the list (click on any device in the box) and then by typing the first few characters in the name of the device that you wish to import.

B.1.7 Drawing and Removing Wires

If you position your mouse over the *pinstubs* at the ends of the symbols you should notice your mouse pointer change from an arrow to a crosshair. Clicking on a pinstub and dragging your mouse creates a wire segment. Dragging your mouse to another pinstub connects the two devices with a wire (also referred to as a *net* or *node*). You can delete a segment of wire by selecting it (it should turn red) and using the Rclick → Delete shortcut menu or the delete key. You can also create wires by selecting the wire drawing tool (use F3 or select the wire tool from the buttons on the left-hand side of the window). The wire tool allows you to lay out your wires with more precision. When finished with the wire tool you must return to the selection tool by using the Esc key or the selection tool arrow from the buttons on the left-hand side of the window.

Connect the A and B inputs to the XNOR gate. Import a two-input AND gate (AND2) and an output pin and wire the 1-bit comparator with enable as shown in Figure B.3.

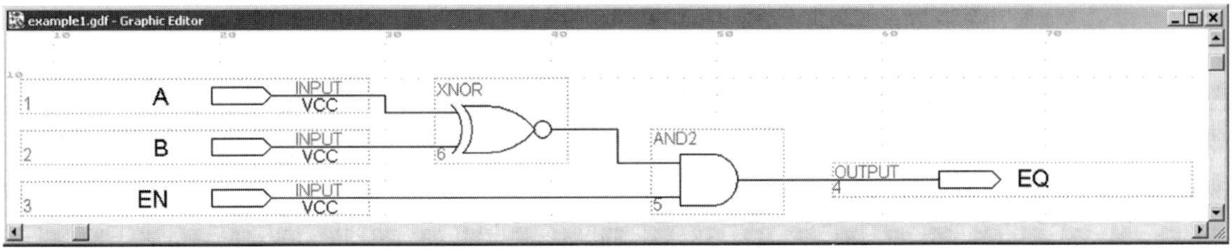

Figure B.3 *Example1.* Schematic of a 1-bit comparator. Build this device as *example1.*

B.1.8 Compiling the Schematic

When a computer program is written in a high-level language (such as C++) it must be compiled into an executable before it can be run. If there is a syntax error in the program, then the compiler will identify the error and try to help the programmer correct it. Likewise, schematics in MAX+plus II must be compiled before their behavior can be simulated. Should there be an obvious implementation error (such as an output that is unused or an input that is not connected), then the compiler will produce a warning or error message to help the designer debug the schematic.

Circuits are complied by using File → Project → Save & Compile or MAX+plus II → Complier and then clicking Start. You must recompile your project every time you make changes to it. Compile your *example1* schematic now.

B.1.9 Using the Messages Window to Debug Compiler Errors

As you enter symbols into your schematic, you should notice a small number in the bottom left-hand corner of the dotted box that surrounds each symbol. This number is the symbol's device ID and is used by the compiler to identify an error in the same way that the compiler for a programming language identifies an error by line number. If an error is found during compilation, the compiler identifies the problem and attempts to help you resolve it by opening the Messages window (Figure B.4). Each line of text in the Messages window corresponds to a message, warning, or error. Errors are identified by using the Device ID and node label that is incorrectly used.

In your *example1* circuit, delete the wire connecting the input EN and the AND2 gate, then save and compile the device. You will get an error message similar to that shown in Figure B.4. Note that the error message shows that the device ID :5 (the AND2 gate in the implementation of the 1-bit comparator shown in Figure B.3) and the specific input of that device which is in error (in this case IN2, the second input).

If you have multiple implementation errors, then you may have multiple messages in the Messages. Click the "Message" button to cycle through the error mes-

Figure B.4 The Messages window.

sages. Click "Help on Message" to get more information on the specific error that is currently highlighted. Click "Locate" to change your window focus to the exact location of the error in the schematic.

B.1.10 Simulating the Device

Once a device has been successfully compiled, its functionality may be observed, tested, and debugged by simulating its behavior. MAX+plus II is not a real-time simulation tool. Therefore, input timing waveforms must be specified before running the simulation.

Use MAX+plus II → Waveform Editor to open the waveform editor. Inputs to the device being simulated must be added as probe points to the editor. A list of all available probe points is created during compilation and saved as a Simulator Netlist File (SNF) file. In the Waveform Editor window use Rclick → Enter Nodes from SNF and click the List button in the pop-up menu. Select the nodes you wish to use as input or output probe points by using the => button or by double-clicking the node names in the list. For *example1* select all three inputs (A, B, EQ) and the output (EQ) as shown in Figure B.5.

Waveforms must be defined to specify the values of the inputs during the simulation run. These waveforms are sometimes referred to as *test vectors.* The values of each input at a specific period of time are controlled by selecting portions of the input waveform and setting them to appropriate values. A portion of a waveform

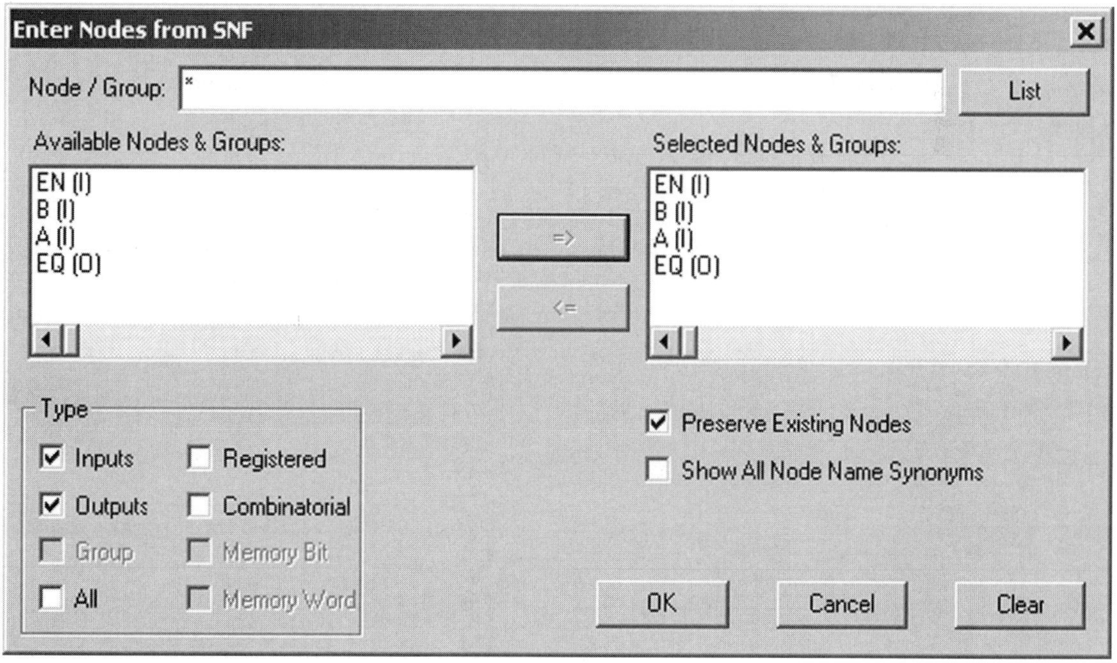

Figure B.5 Selecting input and output probe points for timing waveforms.

is selected by left-clicking and dragging the mouse over it. The minimum portion of the waveform that can be selected is changed by using Option → Grid Size. The value for the selected portion of the waveform can then be specified using Rclick → Overwrite. The total length of the simulation can be specified using File → End Time. The waveforms are saved by using use File → Save to save the simulation test vectors as a *.scf file.

For *example1,* set the Grid Size to 10 ns, set the End Time to 80 ns and construct the input waveforms shown in Figure B.6. Save the waveform as example1.scf.

After you have defined the behavior of the circuit's inputs over time, the simulator can be used to determine the behavior of the device's outputs. Use MAX+plus II → Simulator to start the simulator. Edit the Start / Finish times (if desired) and click Start to execute the simulation. Click Open SCF to bring up the Waveform Editor and view the results of the simulation. Verify that the output EQ behaves as expected.

B.1.11 Techniques to Help Manage Complexity

Simple devices can be created in a single schematic using the techniques just discussed. More complex devices, however, require more sophisticated techniques to design and simulate. Complex designs are not generally implemented on a single schematic. Instead, the problem is generally decomposed into several smaller problems of lesser complexity. Each of these devices is designed, implemented, and tested separately, then they are interconnected to solve the original problem. This section of the tutorial introduces several techniques for dealing with such complexity.

B.1.12 Creating User-Defined Symbols

The schematic for any user-created device can be used to generate a new symbol for use in future designs. A symbol for a device is created by using File→ Create Default Symbol. The default symbol can be labeled, rotated, or otherwise customized by using File → Edit Symbol. Once created, a symbol for a device can be used in the schematics of more complex devices. Create a symbol for *example1* and verify that it matches the symbol shown in Figure B.7. Use File → Save As to save the symbol as example1.sym.

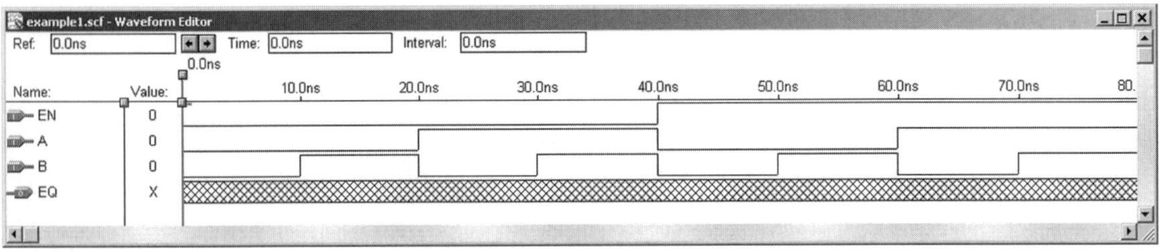

Figure B.6 An input waveform to test the 1-bit comparator.

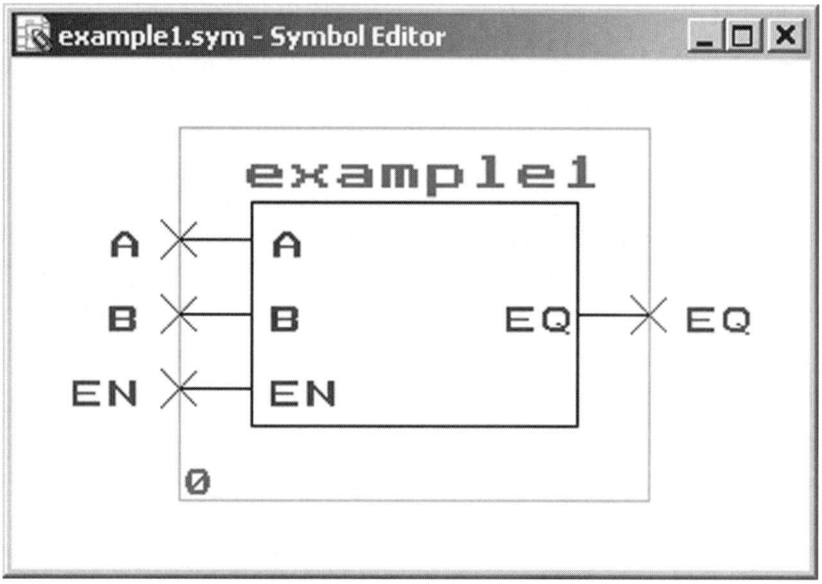

Figure B.7 The default symbol created for the 1-bit comparator *example1.*

B.1.13 Using Logical Connections

A wire (net/node) can be given a label by selecting the wire and using Rclick → Edit Node/Bus Name. Any two nodes with the same label are considered connected to the same wire and thus connected "logically," even if a wire is not physically drawn between the two points in the schematic. This ability to create logical connections allows complex schematics to be drawn without cluttering the schematic with wires. Become familiar with the use of logical connections by implementing, compiling, and simulating the device shown in Figure B.8.

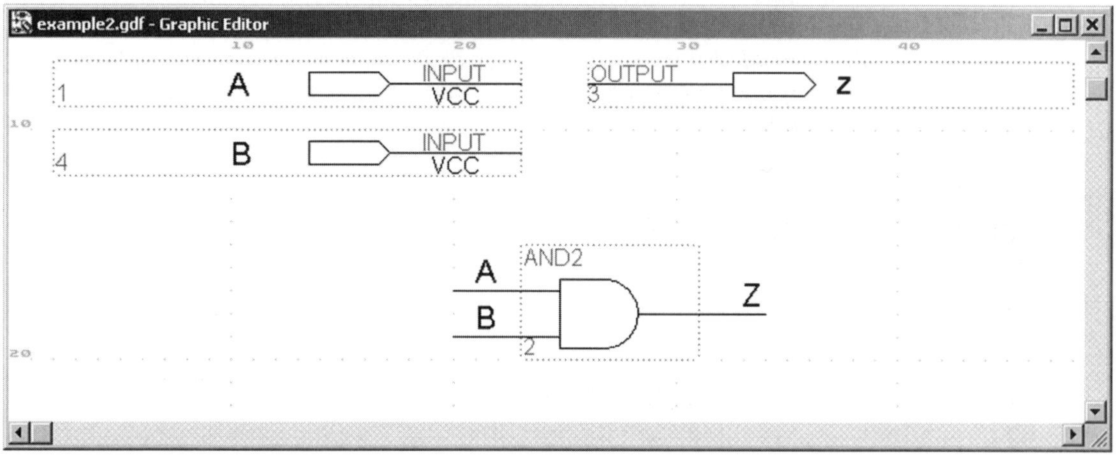

Figure B.8 *Example2.* This schematic demonstrates the use of logical connections.

B.1.14 Using Buses

A wire is a node that propagates a single-bit signal value. A node that propagates a multibit signal value is called a *bus*. Buses are used to reduce complexity by grouping together large numbers of related signal values into a single input or output of a device.

To create a bus, select an existing node, use Rclick → Line Style, and select the thick line symbol (second from the top). To indicate the number of signals contained in the bus, you must give the bus a name with the suffix [m..n] where m is the name of the MSB of the bus and n is the name of the LSB of the bus. For example, a bus named x[1..0] is a 2-bit bus composed of signals x[1] and x[0]. The values from a bus can be *ripped* into smaller buses (or single signal wires) by creating nodes and naming them appropriately. For example, the LSB of a bus named x[1..0] can be ripped from the bus by creating a wire with the name x[0]. Signals can be merged to create a new bus in the same fashion. Note: The merged or ripped nodes need not be physically connected to the bus—a logical connection is sufficient. Become familiar with buses by implementing, compiling, and simulating the circuit shown in Figure B.9.

B.1.15 Simulating a Device of Moderate Complexity

We now use the 1-bit comparator implemented previously to implement a slightly more complex device—a 4-bit iterative comparator. Use File → New and select Graphic Editor File to start a new schematic. Use Rclick → Enter Symbol to create four copies of our 1-bit comparitor and use buses and logical connections to create the schematic shown in Figure B.10. Use File → Save As to name the schematic example4.gdf and compile the schematic using File → Project → Save & Compile. If you are asked if you would like to change the project before compiling, click Yes.

Now that we have drawn the schematic for the device, we must create input waveforms for the simulation. Even though this device has nine inputs (EN, A3, A2, A1, A0, B3, B2, B1, B0), creating the input waveforms will not be significantly complex because we grouped the A and B inputs into two 4-bit buses. Open the Waveform Editor by selecting MAX+plus II → Waveform Editor. In the Waveform Editor window, Rclick → Enter Nodes from SNF and click List to see a list of

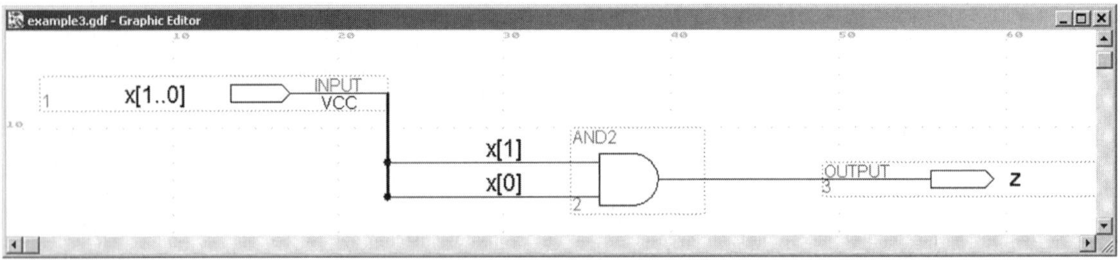

Figure B.9 *Example3.* A 2-bit AND gate with a 2-bit input bus.

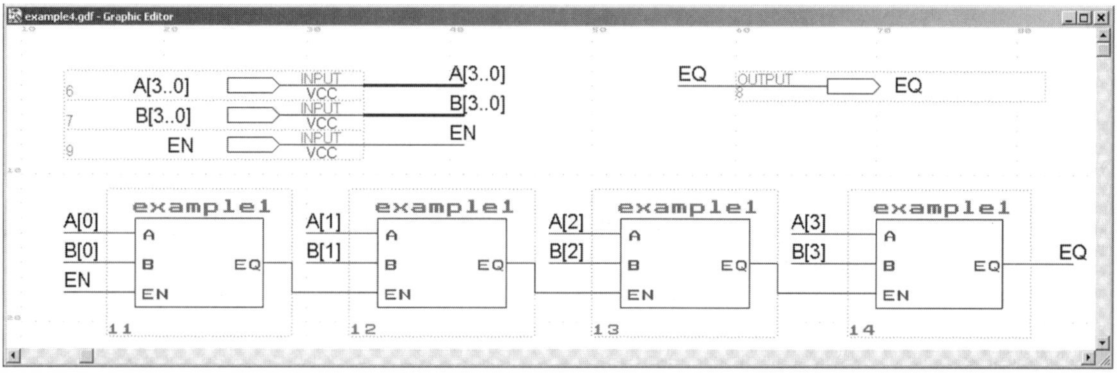

Figure B.10 *Example4.* An iterative 4-bit comparator with enable.

the schematic I/O pins. Note that the signal values for the bus inputs are available in both their grouped and ungrouped forms. For this simulation, we want to use the bused inputs, so select inputs A[3..0], B[3..0], EN, and the output EQ as shown in Figure B.11.

Reorder the nodes, if necessary, so that EN is at the top of the waveform window, followed by A[3..0], B[3..0], and lastly EQ. The nodes can be reordered by

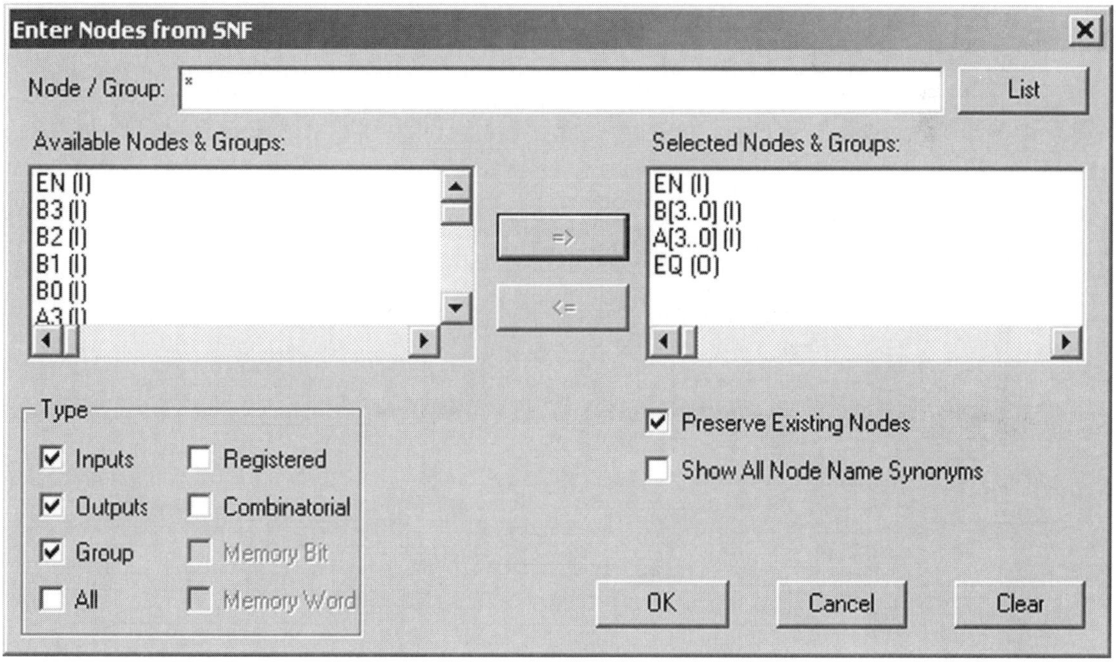

Figure B.11 Selecting bus inputs from the Simulator Netlist File.

dragging the input and output symbols to the left of the node name to its new position in the list order. Use Options → Grid Size to set the selectable waveform resolution to 20 ns. Now select waveform A[3..0] from 0 ns to 20 ns. Set the multibit value for A during this period of time by using Rclick → Overwrite → Group Value and entering the appropriate value in hexadecimal notation.

To simplify the process of testing complex circuits, the Waveform Editor provides a mechanism for autoincrementing inputs values over a selected range. Select the A[3..0] waveform from 0 ns to 300 ns. Use Rclick → Overwrite → Count Value to set the input waveform. For the A input, use a starting value of 0, an increment of 1, a multiplier of 3, and count in binary. Using this technique, create the waveform for input B shown in Figure B.12. Enable the device by setting EN high, set the simulation time to 300 ns using File → End Time, and save the waveform. Start the simulator using MAX+plus II → Simulator and observe the results of the simulation.

This device has nine inputs (EN, A3, A2, A1, A0, B3, B2, B1, B0) and so a full test of the device would require considering 512 (2^9) different input assignments. For devices of even moderate complexity full testing may not be feasible. In general, designers attempt to create input waveforms that test a significant enough portion of the device's intended functionality to provide high confidence in the device's correctness. Designing small sets of test vectors that provide high confidence that the circuit performs correctly is a skill that takes significant practice.

B.1.16 Increasing Your Mastery

MAX+plus II is an incredibly sophisticated design tool. This tutorial has exposed you to only a very small fraction of the functionality this tool provides. Armed with this knowledge, however, you can quickly increase your ability with this tool and tackle increasingly difficult design problems. In addition to simple combinational devices, the primitives library contains symbols for the common sequential primitives used in introductory sequential circuit design, including the positive-edge triggered D flip-flop (dff), JK flip-flop (jkff), SR flip-flop (srff), and T flip-flop (tff). Furthermore, the mf library contains symbols for most "standard" SSI, MSI, and

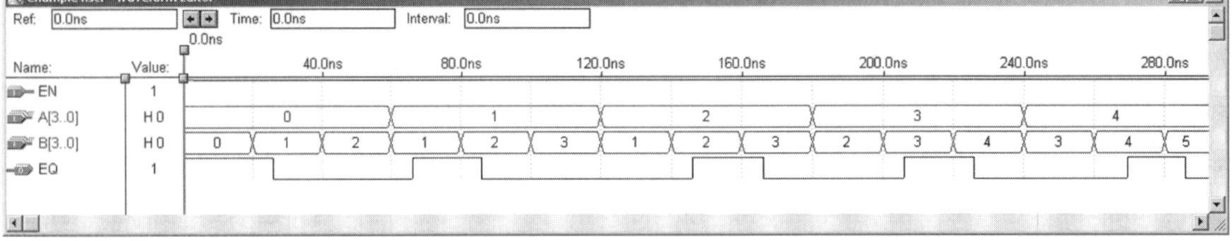

Figure B.12 Timing waveforms for the 4-bit comparator.

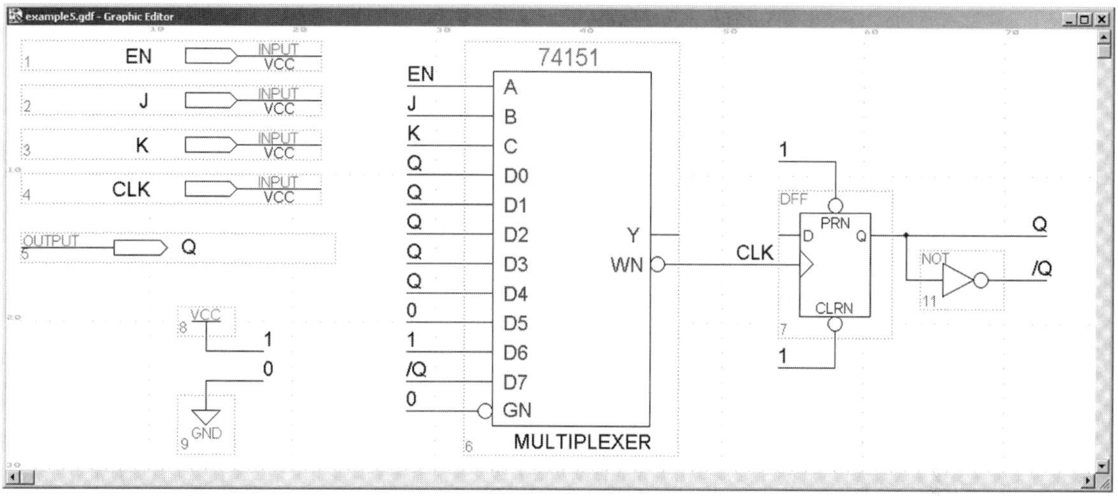

Figure B.13 *Example5.* A JK flip-flop with Enable.

LSI digital devices, including the devices of the 74XX family. You can access the mf library by using Rclick → Enter Symbol and then double-clicking on the file that ends in *mf* instead of *prim.*

Increase your MAX+plus II skills by creating the simple sequential device shown in Figure B.13. This device implements a JK flip-flop with Enable using a 74151 multiplexor and a positive-edge D flip-flop. Implement the device, create input waveforms, and simulate the circuit to verify and debug its behavior.

B.1.17 MAX+plus II Help

After completing this tutorial, you should be familiar with the basics of MAX+plus II and ready to use this tool to create devices of your own design. As the complexity of your designs increase, you will run into situations not covered by this brief tutorial. MAX+plus II has an immense help database to aid you in mastering any new concepts and techniques. MAX+plus II help can be invoked by using Help → Search. Use Help → "How to use MAX+plus II help" now to get started.

B.1.18 Conclusion

Many students find Altera MAX+plus II to be an immense and daunting software package. After completing this tutorial, however, you are well prepared to design, implement, and test devices of the complexity generally encountered in introductory digital design courses. More important, with practice (and significant use of the Help files), you will find that your ability to use MAX+plus II to implement devices of greater complexity will grow quickly.

B.2 A GENTLE INTRODUCTION TO LOGICWORKS™4

A. J. Thomas Jr.
Department of Computer Science
Tennessee State University

B.2.1 Introduction

This tutorial assumes the reader has access to a computer on which LogicWorks™4 is installed. Instructions for installing LogicWorks are provided with its program package. There are versions of the LogicWorks software for both the IBM PC-compatible and Macintosh™ platforms. For this tutorial, a PC running a Microsoft operating system (Windows™ 3.1 or above), and the LogicWorks software, version 4.0 or above, is assumed. The reader is referred to the LogicWorks user manual for further system requirements.

This tutorial does not describe how to use the operating system provided on the computer. It is assumed the reader already knows how to perform such actions as running programs, operating a mouse, minimizing and maximizing windows, and the like. A reader who is not familiar with these operations must learn them before proceeding.

B.2.2 What Is LogicWorks?

LogicWorks is editing and simulation software for the design and simulation of the operation of digital and analog circuits. Features include circuit construction/connection, circuit simulation at continuously variable speed, many built-in devices, and a device editor that allows modifying existing device behavior and creation of new devices.

B.2.3 Starting LogicWorks

To start the LogicWorks program double-click on its icon (Figure B.14). Once LogicWorks has started, its opening screen will appear; it looks like Figure B.15.

LogicWorks' opening screen has five windows: (1) The Circuit Window, (2) The Timing Diagram Window, (3) The Drawing Toolbar Window, (4) The Simulator Control Window, and (5) The Parts Window. Any of these windows can be moved, resized, or closed by the usual means, to suit your needs. These windows are presented further in the following section.

Figure B.14 LogicWorks icon.

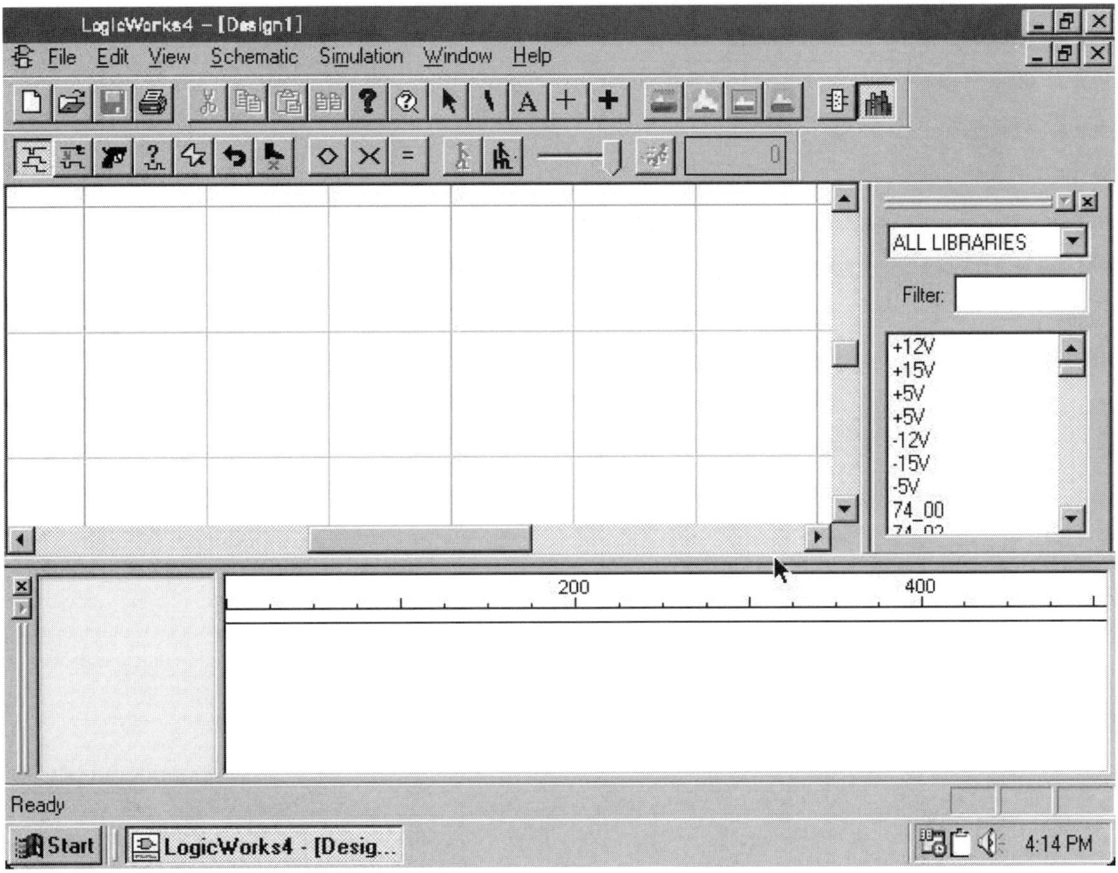

Figure B.15 LogicWorks opening screen.

B.2.4 LogicWorks' Five Windows

1. **Circuit window.** This is LogicWorks' main window, where circuits are constructed and displayed. The left side of the title bar of the circuit window shows the name of the circuit file displayed in that window. Multiple circuit windows can be open simultaneously; however, only one window at a time can be the "current" window. The current window is the topmost one. Any other windows will be partially or fully hidden by the current window. Any other window can be made current by clicking anywhere in that window. The circuit window has faint gridlines for perfectly aligning circuits and circuit devices when needed.
2. **Timing window** The timing window is an optional window, used primarily for circuits with continuously changing inputs like a clock. It displays a timing diagram waveform of signals in the circuit (Figure B.16). The timing window is independent of the circuit window, in that it can be closed without closing the circuit window.

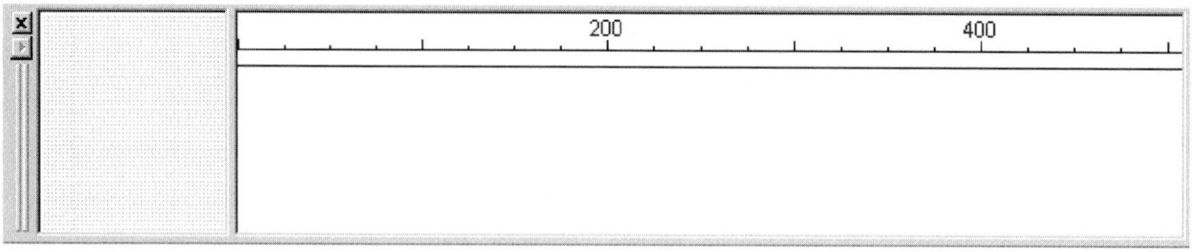

Figure B.16 The timing window.

3. **Drawing Toolbar window.** The Drawing Toolbar window, and the Simulator Control window that follows, appear in LogicWorks opening screen as fixed button bars near the top of the screen. However both can be detached as floating windows. The Drawing Toolbar is a button bar (Figure B.17) above the Simulator Control button bar. Both are always on top of any circuit window, whether as button bars or detached as floating windows. The Drawing Toolbar contains 21 buttons. Some of these buttons change the cursor to the icon showing on the button in the Drawing Toolbar. The Drawing Toolbar buttons in Figure B.17, left to right, are (1) New circuit/text/symbol; (2) Open file; (3) Save file; (4) Print; (5) Cut; (6) Copy; (7) Paste; (8) Duplicate; (9) Get info, used to get statistics on a circuit; (10) Signal probe, used to view and change signal logic values in a circuit; (11) the pointer arrow (looks like the standard Windows cursor), used for selecting or dragging objects; (12) Zap (delete), the lightning bolt cursor, used to delete objects from the circuit window; (13) Text (**A**), used to type text in the circuit window; (14) Draw Signal button (+), used to create a new signal line or extend an existing signal; (15) Draw bus button (**+**), used to create a new bus line or extend an existing bus; (16) Zoom out; (17) Zoom in; (18) Fit to window; (19) Normal size; (20) PROM/RAM/PLA Wizard; (21) Parts Palette, used to add/remove the parts palette to/from the LogicWorks screen.
4. **The Simulator Control Toolbar.** The Simulator Control Toolbar gives control over the simulation speed of a running circuit. The toolbar also has buttons that control zoom in, out, and reset of the timing window (Figure B.18). The Simulator Control toolbar contains 15 buttons. The Simulator Control buttons, left to right in Figure B.18, are (1) Show/hide timing; (2) Add signals to timing; (3) Triggers; (4) Simulation parameters; (5) Stick/unstick signals; (6) Reset simulator; (7) Clear Unknowns; (8) Zoom in; (9) Zoom out; (10) Normal size; (11) Single step; (12) Stop simulator; (13) Simulator speed slider; (14) Run simulator; (15) Simulation time, not a button but a display of simulation time.
5. **Parts window.** The Parts window appears in the LogicWorks opening screen as a fixed window on the upper right side; however, it can be moved and resized. The Parts window contains a library of all of LogicWorks built-in devices and circuits (Figure B.19). The Parts window displays the devices in one library at a time. The library currently being displayed is shown in the library box at the top. If the display is ALL LIBRARIES, as in Figure B.19, then all devices in all libraries are available in the parts list. Clicking the down arrow yields a drop-down list of all Parts libraries. The devices

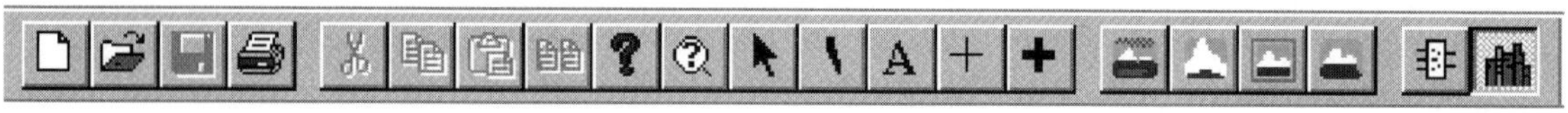

Figure B.17 The Drawing Toolbar window.

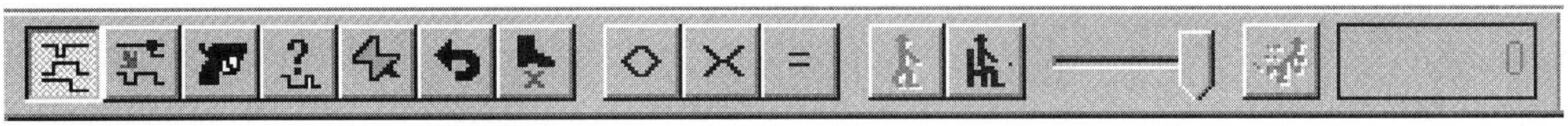

Figure B.18 Simulator Control Toolbar.

in a library are shown in the scrollable list below the drop-down list. Any one of these devices can be selected for placement in the circuit window by double-clicking on the device. The LogicWorks cursor at this point changes to a flickering image of the LogicWorks symbol for the selected device, and the device can be placed at the desired location in the circuit window by clicking at that location. The middle text box, labeled Filter:, is a string-matching box that allows you to type characters of a device name, and the list below it displays only devices matching the string typed.

B.2.5 LogicWorks Built-in Devices

LogicWorks built-in devices are organized into categorical libraries, shown one at a time at the top the Parts window. Each library contains multiple devices, shown for a given library in the list at the bottom of the Parts window. Table B.1 shows the built-in device libraries in the order they appear in the Parts window and a general description of some of the devices in them.

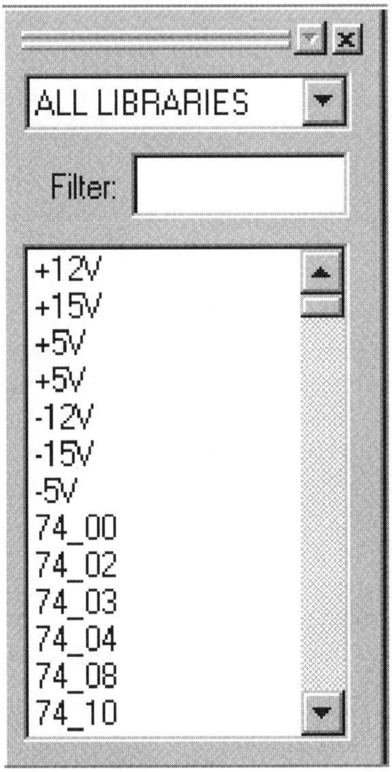

Figure B.19 Parts window.

Table B.1 Built-in devices libraries

Library Name	Description
7400devs.clf	7400-series types, 7400–74393.b
connect.clf	Voltage and connection symbols
discrete.clf	Analog devices
demolib.clf	I/O devices, etc.
Makepid.clf	Miscellaneous gates (some duplicates) and combinational circuits
Pseudo.clf	Various ground, voltage, page, and port connectors
Spice.clf	Miscellaneous devices compatible with SPICE
Simulation Gates.clf	Main digital gates: AND—2, 3, 4, 5, 8 inputs; various number of input inversion bubbles NAND—2, 3, 4, 5, 8, 16 inputs; various number of input inversion bubbles NOR—2, 3, 4, 5, 8 inputs NOT OR—2, 3, 4, 5, 8 inputs; various number of input inversion bubbles XNOR—2, 4, 8 inputs XOR—2, 4, 8 inputs
Simulation IO.clf	Main I/O devices
Simulation Logic.clf	Main combinational and sequential circuit ICs

B.2.6 Placing a Device in the Circuit Window

If the Parts palette is not already on screen, it can be turned on by clicking on Part Palette in the View main menu command. Then click the down arrow at the top of the Parts Palette. This gives a drop-down list of all the device libraries. Click on the device library desired. The devices in the selected library appear in the list at the bottom of the Parts Palette. If more devices are listed than will show in the list at one time, the list becomes scrollable. Scroll the list to get the desired device to show, or browse the list. Once your device is showing in the list, double-click its name. Move the cursor over the circuit window. The cursor will then be a flickering image of the device you selected. Place the device anywhere in the circuit window you desire. Click once, and the device is placed at that location in the circuit window. You may place as many copies of the same device as you wish by clicking the locations. When you finish placing your devices, you can reset the cursor back to the arrow cursor by clicking the arrow button on the Drawing Toolbar.

B.2.7 Moving a Device in the Circuit Window

For this and the next section, the circuit paths that form the connections between devices are called *wires,* since that is the actual hardware they simulate.

Once a circuit is constructed you can move any device in it by clicking on the device, holding down the mouse button, and dragging the device to any desired new location within the circuit window. Any wires attached to the device will be adjusted continuously to maintain all preexisting connections to the device. This applies if the device is moved along a path "in line" with the wires. If the device is moved along some path perpendicular to the wires, then the wire(s) may bend at 90° angle(s) or lay one on top of another. See the next section for adjusting wires, should their appearance be undesirable after moving a device.

B.2.8 Drawing Circuit Connections ("Connecting Wires")

To draw circuit connections between devices, place the very tip of the arrow cursor on the very end of a device lead. Every device has a built-in lead wire already attached to it. Click, hold down, and drag. When you hit the right spot, you will see a gray line behind the arrow cursor. While still holding down the mouse button, drag until the very tip of the arrow is on the very tip of the lead of the device you want to connect to. Moving just a little into the lead will not hurt, to make sure you have made the connection. Release the mouse button and the connection is made. For each drawn wire you get one 90° bend in the wire. If you want more, release and reclick the mouse button without moving the mouse. You get one additional 90° bend in the wire for every time you do this. Making connections in LogicWorks takes some practice and patience. To test whether you have made the connections desired, click anywhere on the wire. Every wire and every lead of every device connected to that wire highlights yellow. LogicWorks normal, deselected, color of wires is red.

Whenever three or more wires intersect, an intersection dot appears. This is a standard circuit schematic symbol to indicate an electrical junction of three or more wires.

To move a wire, click anywhere along a straight segment of the wire, hold down, and drag. By repeating this, you can change the configuration of wires in a whole circuit.

B.2.9 Concluding Remarks

This tutorial introduced the basic use of the LogicWorks software. It shows how to start LogicWorks, introduces the five screen windows/toolbars, lists all device categories, and shows such basic operations as placing and moving a device and drawing circuit connections.

B.2.10 REFERENCES

1. Brown, S. and Z. Vranesic, *Fundamentals of Digital Logic With VHDL Design*, New York: McGraw-Hill, 2000.
2. Capilano Computing Systems, Ltd., *LogicWorks 4: Interactive Circuit Design Software for Windows and Macintosh*, Menlo Park, CA: Addison-Wesley, 1999.

BIBLIOGRAPHY

Armstrong, D. B., "A Programmed Algorithm for Assigning Internal Codes to Sequential Machines," *IRE Trans. Electron. Computers,* vol. EC-11, no. 4, pp. 466–472, August 1962.

Bartee, T. C., "Computer Design of Multiple-Output Logical Networks," *IRE Trans. Electron. Computers,* vol. EC-10, no. 1, pp. 21–30, March 1961.

Blakeslee, T. R., *Digital Design with Standard MSI & LSI,* 2d Edition, New York: John Wiley, 1979.

Boole, G., *An Investigation of the Laws of Thought,* London: Macmillan, 1854, reprinted, New York: Dover, 1973.

Cadden, W. J., "Equivalent Sequential Circuits," *IRE Trans. Circuit Theory,* vol CT-6, no. 1, pp. 30–34, March 1959.

Caldwell, S. H., *Switching Circuits and Logical Design,* New York: John Wiley, 1958.

Chu, Y., *Digital Computer Design Fundamentals,* New York: McGraw-Hill, 1962.

Clare, C. R., *Designing Logic Systems Using State Machines,* New York: McGraw-Hill, 1973.

Colclaser, R. A., D. A. Neamen, and C. F. Hawkins, *Electronic Circuit Analysis,* New York: John Wiley, 1984.

Fletcher, W. I., *An Engineering Approach to Digital Design,* Englewood Cliffs, NJ: Prentice-Hall, 1980.

Givone, D. D., *Introduction to Switching Circuit Theory,* New York: McGraw-Hill, 1970.

Givone, D. D., and R. P. Roesser, *Microprocessors/Microcomputers: An Introduction,* New York: McGraw-Hill, 1980.

Green, D., *Modern Logic Design,* Workingham, England: Addison-Wesley, 1986.

Grinich, V. H., and H. G. Jackson, *Introduction to Integrated Circuits,* New York: McGraw-Hill, 1975.

Hamming, R. W., "Error Detecting and Error Correcting Codes," *Bell Syst. Tech. J.,* vol. XXVI, no. 2, pp. 147–160, April 1950.

Hayes, J. P., *Introduction to Digital Logic Design,* Reading, MA: Addison-Wesley, 1993.

Hill, F. J., and G. R. Peterson, *Introduction to Switching Theory & Logical Design,* 3d Edition, New York: John Wiley, 1981.

Huffman, D. A., "The Synthesis of Sequential Switching Circuits," *J. Franklin Inst.,* vol. 257, no. 3, pp. 161–190, March 1954; no. 4, pp. 275–303, April 1954.

Huffman, D. A., "The Design and Use of Hazard-Free Switching Networks," *J. Ass. Computing Machinery,* vol. 4, no. 1, pp. 47–62, January 1957.

Huntington, E. V., "Sets of Independent Postulates for the Algebra of Logic," *Trans. Amer. Math. Soc.,* vol. 5, pp. 288–309, July 1904.

Karnaugh, M., "The Map Method for Synthesis of Combinational Logic Circuits," *Trans. AIEE, Pt. I, Communications and Electronics,* vol. 72, pp. 593–599, November 1953.

Katz, R. H., *Contemporary Logic Design,* Redwood City, CA: Benjamin/Cummings, 1994.

Kohavi, Z., *Switching and Finite Automata Theory,* 2d Edition, New York: McGraw-Hill, 1978.

MacSorley, O. L., "High-Speed Arithmetic in Binary Computers," *Proc. IRE,* vol. 49, no. 1, pp. 67–91, January 1961.

Mano, M. M., *Digital Design,* 2d Edition, Englewood Cliffs, NJ: Prentice-Hall, 1991.

McCluskey, E. J., Jr., "Minimization of Boolean Functions," *Bell Syst. Tech. J.,* vol. 35, no. 6, pp. 1417–1444, November 1956.

McCluskey, E. J., Jr., "Minimum-State Sequential Circuits for a Restricted Class of Incompletely Specified Flow Tables," *Bell Syst. Tech. J.,* vol. 41, no. 6, pp.1759–1768, November 1962.

McCluskey, E. J., Jr., "Transients in Combinational Logic Circuits," in R. H. Wilcox and W. C. Mann (eds.), *Redundancy Techniques for Computing Systems,* pp. 9–46, Washington, DC: Spartan Books, 1962.

McCluskey, E. J., Jr., "Fundamental Mode and Pulse Mode Sequential Circuits," *Proc. IFIP Congress 1962, Int. Conf. Information Processing,* Munich, August 27–September 1, 1962, pp. 725–730, C. M. Popplewell (ed.), Amsterdam: North Holland, 1963.

McCluskey, E. J., *Introduction to the Theory of Switching Circuits,* New York: McGraw-Hill, 1965.

McCluskey, E. J., *Logic Design Principles,* Englewood Cliffs, NJ: Prentice-Hall, 1986.

McCluskey, E. J., Jr., and H. Schorr, "Essential Multiple-Output Prime Implicants," *Proc. Symp. Mathematical Theory of Automata,* Microwave Research Institute Symposia Series, vol. XII, pp. 437–457, Brooklyn, NY: Polytechnic Press of the Polytechnic Institute of Brooklyn, April 1962.

Mealy, G. H., "A Method for Synthesizing Sequential Circuits," *Bell Syst. Tech. J.,* vol. 34, no. 5, pp. 1045–1079, September 1955.

Millman, J., *Microelectronics: Digital and Analog Circuits and Systems,* New York: McGraw-Hill, 1979.

Moore, E. F., "Gedanken-Experiments on Sequential Machines," in C. E. Shannon and J. McCarthy (eds.), *Automata Studies,* Princeton, NJ: Princeton University Press, pp. 129–153, 1956.

Paull, M. C., and S. H. Unger, "Minimizing the Number of States in Incompletely Specified Sequential Switching Functions," *IRE Trans. Electron. Computers,* vol. EC-8, no. 3, pp. 356–367, September 1959.

Petrick, S. R., "A Direct Determination of the Irredundant Forms of a Boolean Function from the Set of Prime Implicants," *Air Force Cambridge Res. Center, Tech. Rept. 56–110,* Bedford, MA, April 1956.

Prosser, F. P., and D. E. Winkel, *The Art of Digital Design,* 2d Edition, Englewood Cliffs, NJ: Prentice-Hall, 1987.

Pyne, I. B., and E. J. McCluskey, "An Essay on Prime Implicant Tables," *J. Soc. Ind. Appl. Math.,* vol. 9, no. 4, pp. 604–631, December 1961.

Quine, W. V., "The Problem of Simplifying Truth Functions," *Amer. Math. Monthly,* vol. 59, no. 8, pp. 521–531, October 1952.

Richards, R. K., *Arithmetic Operations in Digital Computers,* Princeton, NJ: D. Van Nostrand, 1955.

Roth, C. H., Jr., *Fundamentals of Logic Design,* 4th Edition, St. Paul, MN: West, 1992.

Sandige, R. S., *Modern Digital Design,* New York: McGraw-Hill, 1990.

Shannon, C. E., "A Symbolic Analysis of Relay and Switching Circuits," *Trans. AIEE,* vol. 57, pp. 713–723, 1938.

Shannon, C. E., "The Synthesis of Two-Terminal Switching Circuits," *Bell Syst. Tech. J.,* vol. 28, no. 1, pp. 59–98, January 1949.

Shiva, S. G., *Introduction to Logic Design,* Glenview, IL: Scott, Foresman, 1988.

Texas Instruments Engineering Staff, *The TTL Data Book,* Dallas: Texas Instruments, 1988.

Tinder, R. F., *Digital Engineering Design: A Modern Approach,* Englewood Cliffs, NJ: Prentice-Hall, 1991.

Unger, S. H., "A Study of Asynchronous Logical Feedback Networks," *M.I.T. Res. Lab. Electron. Tech. Rept. 320,* April 26, 1957.

Unger, S. H., "Hazards and Delays in Asynchronous Sequential Switching Circuits," *IRE Trans. Circuit Theory,* vol. CT-6, no. 1, pp. 12–25, March 1959.

Unger, S. H., "Flow Table Simplification—Some Useful Aids," *IEEE Trans. Electron. Computers,* vol. EC-14, no. 3, pp. 472–475, June 1965.

Unger, S. H., *Asynchronous Sequential Switching Circuits,* New York: Wiley-Interscience, 1969.

Unger, S. H., *The Essence of Logic Circuits,* Englewood Cliffs, NJ: Prentice-Hall, 1989.

Veitch, E. W., "A Chart Method for Simplifying Truth Functions," *Proc. Ass. Computing Machinery,* Pittsburgh, PA, pp. 127–133, May 2, 3, 1952.

Wakerly, J. F., *Digital Design: Principles & Practices,* 3d Edition, Upper Saddle River, NJ: Prentice-Hall, 2000.

Ware, W. H., *Digital Computer Technology and Design, Volume I,* New York: John Wiley, 1963.

Weeg, G. P., "Uniqueness of Weighted Code Representations," *IRE Trans. Electron. Computers,* vol. EC-9, no. 4, pp. 487–489, December 1960.

White, G. S., "Coded Decimal Number Systems for Digital Computers," *Proc. IRE,* vol. 41, no. 10, pp. 1450–1452, October 1953.

Whitesitt, J. E., *Boolean Algebra and Its Applications,* Reading, MA: Addison-Wesley, 1961.

Wiatrowski, C. A., and C. H. House, *Logic Circuits and Microcomputer Systems,* New York: McGraw-Hill, 1980.

INDEX

A

G

H

I

J

K

R

S

W

X

Z